THE BIG BEND

RONNIE C. TYLER

THE BIG BEND

A HISTORY OF THE LAST TEXAS FRONTIER

Office of Publications
National Park Service   U.S. Department of the Interior   Washington, D.C.
1975

About This Book

The Big Bend, an account of human society in one of the most rugged and remote parts of this country, is the collaborative work of the National Park Service, U.S. Department of the Interior, and the Amon Carter Museum of Western Art, Fort Worth. Prepared as a reference companion to an exhibition on the Big Bend presented by the Amon Carter with subsequent showings at a number of other Texas museums in 1975-76, the volume is intended to supply a needed interpretive narrative for the exhibition, to introduce park visitors to the human record in the Big Bend country, and to fill a considerable gap in available professional studies on the Big Bend. This publication can be purchased from the Superintendent of Documents, Government Printing Office, Washington, DC 20402.

Library of Congress Cataloging in Publication Data

Tyler, Ronnie C.
    The Big Bend.
      1. Big Bend region, Tex. – History.   2. Big Bend
National Park—History.   I. Title.
F392.B54T9   917.64'93'03   74–23533

Foreword

Big Bend National Park is a place of special interest for the Amon Carter Museum of Western Art, for the park, like the museum, can be regarded as an offspring of the late Amon G. Carter.

Amon Carter was among the first Texans to recognize the wild beauty of the Big Bend, and the opportunity it offered to preserve intact important remnants of the last Texas frontier. Ron Tyler, Curator of History at the Amon Carter, discovered this dual aspect of the Big Bend for himself as he was exploring the history of the Mexican border.

His study is in the best traditions of Western history. His narrative combines an understanding of the region's physical setting with a clear description of its exploration and settlement, a story which had been virtually lost in recent decades. Not a guide book, it will nevertheless conduct you through 400 years of Big Bend history. A multitude of illustrations show us the park as it was seen by early settlers, the U.S. Cavalry, brigands, Apaches, Comanches, wax smugglers, and wetbacks. W. D. Smithers' photographs are some of the first views of the Big Bend; those by Bank Langmore are among the latest and best. Together, photos and text bring us a new vision of the Mexican boundary and the startling world of the Big Bend. This happy collaboration with Park Service specialists has now given us this volume and an exhibition that will do much to stimulate historical interest in a little known region.

Mitchell A. Wilder
Director, Amon Carter Museum of Western Art

Acknowledgments

Many people have assisted in the research and preparation of both the book and the accompanying exhibition: Dr. Ross A. Maxwell, former superintendent of Big Bend National Park and professor of geology at the University of Texas at Austin; Mr. and Mrs. Hart Greenwood of Alamito; W. D. Smithers of El Paso; Dr. Calhoun Harris Monroe and Floride Harris of El Paso; and W. P. Cameron of Mineral Wells consented to be interviewed. Mrs. Lee Bennett of Marfa, Dr. Clifford B. Casey of Alpine, and Frank Temple of Lubbock shared their material and research. Joe Coltharp, Curator of Photography for the Humanities Research Center at the University of Texas (Austin), Dr. Chester V. Kielman, Librarian-Archivist at the Barker Texas History Center, University of Texas (Austin); Roy Sylvan Dunn, Curator of the Southwest Collection at Texas Tech University, Lubbock; Carol Crowfoot, Curator of Photography at the Texas State Library, Austin; Elmer O. Parker and his staff, Old Military Records Division, National Archives and Records Service, Washington, D.C.; Joan Cobb and her staff in the Photography Division, National Archives; Irvil P. Schultz, librarian, U.S. Geological Survey, Denver, and Dr. Ignacio Rubio Mañe, Director, Archivo General de la Nación, México, D.F., helped me with their respective collections; Peggy Ponton of Big Bend National Park helped prepare the historical sites appendix.

I received many helpful suggestions from Dr. Sandra L. Myres, University of Texas (Arlington); Dr. Dorman Winfrey, Director, Texas State Library; Dr. Donald Everett, Trinity University, San Antonio; Peter Koch, Alpine; Prof. Miram A. Lowrance, Sul Ross State University; Steve Schuster, El Centro College, Dallas; Jane Pattie, Fort Worth; David Clary, National Park Service, Omaha; Leonard Sanders, Jr., *Fort Worth Star-Telegram;* and from my wife Paula.

Nancy G. Wynne, librarian, and Margaret McLean, former newspaper archivist of the Amon Carter Museum, helped collect materials throughout the project. Faythe Taylor typed the manuscript many times, and Karen Dewees prepared the index.

R. T.
Fort Worth, Texas, April, 1975

Contents

1/World of the Big Bend

Although hard bread and unsalted venison did not make a holiday feast, Texas Ranger Capt. Charles L. Nevill probably enjoyed his meal as he pondered his good fortune. He was, after all, alive – a remarkable blessing, considering his recent adventures. A few days earlier, when he and four of his best rangers had set out to accompany a State land survey on a float down a section of the Rio Grande known as the Big Bend, they had thought a good deal about the dangers of traveling through an uncharted terrain. Yet such considerations had not adequately prepared them for the river's unsympathetic fury.

Nevill, his four rangers, and surveyors John T. Gano, Edward L. Gage, and E. M. Powell – "the greenest set of boatmen that ever started down any river" – had set out from Presidio del Norte on December 19, 1881, intending to navigate a previously unexplored section of the Rio Grande. Nevill was aware that other expeditions had attempted to float these canyons but had been stopped by natural obstacles – or fear. He saw more clearly the difficulties ahead when he damaged his own boat the first day, and his fears increased when his party entered the mountains. The banks rose higher around them, and the current swept them along toward the first big rapids. The men cautiously steered their boats around threatening boulders, and with the dangers temporarily behind them were able to proceed. "Everything went lovely," Nevill wrote. "The boys learned 'to boat' very fast."

But soon carelessness, deceptive currents, and whirlpools combined to teach the overconfident crew a lesson. They slammed into a rock, scattering men, supplies, and over 300 rounds of ammunition across the water. "I was carried down the river like I was shot out of a gun," Nevill recalled. "I had on my big boots, coat, pistol and belts, and of course as soon as I struck an eddy I sank. When I came up, I caught on a rock and by standing up my head and shoulders would be out of the water."

The rumors about the treacherous canyons and rapids of the Rio Grande were true. The captain no doubt swore at his carelessness as he perched precariously on the rock, clutching his

The mighty gorge of Santa Elena Canyon, an obstacle to early explorers, is one of the most dramatic spectacles in the Southwest.

1

favorite pipe between his teeth. While gesturing to a companion about to swim into the current, Nevill lost his balance and slipped off the rock. "I went under . . . [and] was so played I thought I would never make it out." Having "no further use for a fine pipe, . . . I spit it out."

Nevill finally pulled himself ashore and took stock. He, Gano, and a ranger had almost drowned. Besides his field glass, he lost nearly all the ammunition and most of the food. Christmas dinner consisted of fresh venison without salt. Neither coffee nor sugar survived the mishap. Nevill was sick for several days, but resumed the trip on January 2, only to face Santa Elena Canyon, the "one with a bad reputation – one that no outfit ever ventured to tackle before," he wrote. Recalling that the boundary survey team of 1852 had scouted the canyon, then sent an empty boat through but that "no two planks came out together," Nevill and his party decided that not everyone should risk a canyon that local Mexicans described as "utterly impassable." Two boatmen, in fact, deserted before reaching the canyon. Nevill took two men who could not swim and rode up on the Mesa de Anguila to watch the surveyors' progress. "I was so high above them, when they would hallow at me I could not distinguish a word said, and they could not hear me at all," he reported. The boatmen halted at the rock slide on January 4 and lost a day and a half portaging around it. Everyone finally reached the mouth on January 9.[1]

The Nevill-Gano expedition was the first documented float through Santa Elena, but Nevill's brief published report did not attract attention. What was even then acknowledged to be one of the least known and most beautiful sections of the State remained unknown. While Clarence King, John Wesley Powell, and Ferdinand V. Hayden were describing the majestic beauty of the Sierra Nevadas, the Grand Canyon, and Yellowstone National Park, Texans grew curious about the vast "Great Bend." The Mexican Boundary Survey team had wrecked its boats in Mariscal Canyon in 1852. Western artist George Catlin floated down the Rio Grande in 1855 but apparently left no journals or pictures. By 1883 curiosity had so overcome the editor of the *El Paso Daily Herald* that he appealed to other newspapers to contribute to an expedition to explore the Big Bend. Its "sublime and majestic scenery" would soon be available to the Nation from detailed reports he would publish, he predicted. "Texas is about to eclipse anything that has heretofore been produced within the limits of North America." [2]

An expedition similar to the one the editor had visualized was organized in 1899 when Robert T. Hill of the U.S. Geological Survey floated from Presidio to Langtry. Intrigued by rumors of ghosts in the Chisos Mountains, bandits lurking along the river, and 7,000-foot gorges, Hill and his small party left Presidio in October. Three weeks later they pulled themselves from the sandy Rio Grande with geographical and geological data for Hill's study and the first photographs of the region. Although Hill believed they were in constant danger, the trip in reality was little more than a pleasant float through one of the most scenic areas of the Southwest. "We . . . navigated and mapped three hundred and fifty miles of a portion of one of America's greatest rivers which hitherto had been considered impassable," Hill boasted. Traveling through the "longest and least known . . . and . . . least accessible" canyons in the country, Hill "escaped dangers which had over-

Texas Ranger Charles L. Nevill (left).
Dr. Robert T. Hill (above, second from left)
with his party shortly after leaving the
Rio Grande near Langtry, Texas, in 1899.

Hill's camp at Leon Rock, near Fort Davis.

whelmed those who had attempted the cañons before: and our little party dispersed contented with its success." [3]

Though Hill found no 7,000-foot deep canyons, his survey culminated years of desire and several attempts to navigate the Big Bend canyons. Hill's successful trip disproved rumors of cutthroat bandits lurking behind each cliff and corrected the fanciful tales of tricks that nature played on unsuspecting intruders. [4]

Many dangers Hill encountered were simply the products of a desert climate and an unbelievably rugged landscape. Even today the most impressive feature of the Big Bend is its vastness. Lodged squarely in the crook where the Rio Grande encounters the southern tip of the Rocky Mountains and turns abruptly from a leisurely southeastern course to the northeast – hence the name Big Bend that Lt. William H. C. Whiting applied in 1849 – the country remains in its "original chaotic state." Including the territory from Candelaria or Ruidoso on the Rio Grande 50 miles eastward to Marfa, then paralleling the Southern Pacific Railroad tracks for over 100 miles through Alpine, Marathon, Sanderson, and Dryden on the north, the Big Bend has always been an out-of-the-way place visited only by the adventurous or patient.

The cultural area encompassed in the term "Big Bend" is often larger. It includes Fort Davis, 20 miles beyond Alpine, where soldiers and Texas Rangers who patrolled the three-quarters of a million acres that now make up the National Park were stationed. Present-day Van Horn, 55 miles northwest of Fort Davis, is usually included in the region, and some think of the Big Bend and the Trans-Pecos as being practically synonymous. Writers have always considered the Big Bend in broad terms. Folklorist J. Frank Dobie researched the Trans-Pecos for several of his stories of lost Spanish treasures, wild mustangs, and cowboys. It is also the scene of untold stories that would rival Dobie's best and the legends of Pecos Bill himself. To Lt. William Echols, viewing this terrain from the back of a camel in 1860, the Bend was a "picture of barrenness and desolation," a place fit to be called the last frontier in Texas. Nor did 40 years ameliorate its ruggedness, for surveyor O. W. Williams found it so impassable in 1901 that he had to make many of his measurements by triangulation rather than by chain.[5]

Although the region is geologically complex, the Indians had a simple explanation for the unusual landscape. When the Great Creator had completed the earth and placed the stars in the sky, the fish in the sea, and the birds in the air, He had a massive heap of stony rubble left over. He hurled it into the Trans-Pecos where it landed in a pile and became known as the Big Bend. Ross A. Maxwell, a geologist and former superintendent of the national park, has offered a more scientific explanation, which relies on standard geological theories. Fossil shells, sedimentary rocks, and other evidence indicate that the Big Bend once lay under a shallow sea. As the continent heaved and shifted, various parts of the land were exposed to the air, permitting the growth of swamp vegetation and providing habitat for many animals now long extinct.

Over 100 million years ago a general shift in the continent produced the Rocky Mountains and the Sierra Madres, which extend from Canada to Mexico. The Chisos Mountains jut out of the Big Bend desert between the two, a mass of twisted and crumpled

THE BIG BEND REGION

MILES   0   31   62
KILOMETERS 0   50   100

Temple Canyon, photographed by Hill in 1899.

rock but not as high as either major range. Further shifting created Terlingua Fault, an elongated block of the earth's crust that broke and tilted upward. Thousands of years later the Rio Grande, aided by the drainage patterns of the fault itself, patiently carved Santa Elena Canyon.

The remains of this process not only explain the existence of a complex region, but also provide some of the Big Bend's most interesting features. Dinosaur bones, evidence of marshes, two skulls of a crocodile-like monster, and other examples have been found. The popular flagstone rocks of the Boquillas Formation are the remains of lime mud deposited during the early Upper Cretaceous period 130 million years ago. Other animal remains familiar only to professional paleontologists are thought to have been native to the Big Bend.

The ruggedness of the land is matched by the harsh climate. The sun scorches down most of the year, and only vegetation adapted to heat and drought flourishes. Big Bend residents endure dry summers, broken only by 15 to 17 inches of rainfall annually from dark clouds apparently snagged on the peaks of the towering Chisos. The surrounding lowlands are less fortunate, receiving only 10 to 12 inches each year. Simply put, the Big Bend is a desert,

**Maverick Mountain, at the northwest entrance
to the national park, in an evening rainstorm.**

Photograph by Bank Langmore

occupying the northern part of what once was the vast Chihuahuan Desert that covered two-thirds of the present Mexican state of Chihuahua, one-half of the state of Coahuila, and a large portion of western Texas. The Rio Grande, which has cut canyons through the heart of the mountains, seems at times to have its very existence threatened by this ferocious desert.

The Spaniards had a name for such an area: *despoblado,* or uninhabited land. The Big Bend is the mouth of the *despoblado,* which, on the map, appears as a funnel-shaped area bounded on the east by the road from Saltillo to San Juan Bautista, near Eagle Pass, Texas; on the west by the road from Chihuahua City to El Paso; and on the south by Parras and Torreón. It forms the northern boundary of this desolate yet impressive region. The Spaniards so feared the hostility of both Indians and the land that they traveled from El Paso to San Juan Bautista by circling southward through the frontier settlements of Mapimí, Laguna de la Leche, Cuatro Ciénegas, and Monclova, then swinging northward along one of the well-traveled routes. Only the Rio Grande penetrates the *despoblado,* although several other rivers play around it. Battered and worn smooth by wind-whipped sand, its features show the marks of a perpetual struggle—wind, rain, and sun matched against the land. Even the vegetation marks off and defends its living space. "Each plant in this land is a porcupine," wrote a 19th-century traveler. "It is nature armed to the teeth." [7]

The most recognizable feature of the Big Bend begins near Lajitas where the Rio Grande meanders through the foothills of the Mesa de Anguila and the Sierra Ponce. Santa Elena Canyon is shallow and open for the first 11 miles, with the river gathering momentum as it approaches the mesa. Steep cliffs and narrow passages mark the beginning of the deepest portion of the gorge. In the swifter current, boatmen are less sure, the margin for error considerably reduced. The canyon walls reach 1,500 feet, virtually imprisoning every creature that enters. Hill and his crew watched in sympathy as a covey of quail attempted to fly high enough to escape the rocky confines, only to fail and settle exhausted on one of the pinnacles. [8]

Santa Elena, which probably received its name from Louis

Ramírez who founded the nearby Mexican settlement of the same name, has always offered a challenge to those who would navigate the Rio Grande. About 6 miles from the mouth of the canyon is a rock slide that has troubled all canyon explorers. Arthur C. V. Schott, the draftsman with the Boundary Survey team, unimaginatively sketched the "falls" in 1852. The Nevill party took a day and a half to portage their boats over the rocks, and Hill called the spot Camp Misery. Trapping down the Rio Grande in the first decade of this century, T. M. Meler hesitated before entering the canyon. Just as the party almost decided not to risk the unknown dangers of the chasm, they spotted a message carved on the face of a large rock by Hill and the Geological Survey expedition of a few years before. "So we sed if uthers could go thro we could do it too," Meler reported. Their confidence was shaken, however, when just a mile inside the canyon they came face to face with the rock slide—20-foot boulders piled 200 to 300 feet high, with water pouring through. But Meler and his party carried their boats over and continued. "It was some haird job but wee wer haird trappers," he explained.[9]

Another well-known feature of the canyon, located just a mile below the rock slide on the Mexican side, is Smuggler's Cave, a dark opening about halfway up the wall, reportedly a hideout for cattle rustlers and outlaws. Smoke discoloration on the ceiling and tobacco and sardine cans on the ground seem to indicate a more recent resident than an Indian or a 19th-century bandit. Hill was particularly impressed with rumors of badmen on the loose in the Big Bend. He called that portion of the river below Lajitas Murderer's Canyon.[10]

The mouth of the canyon is the most spectacular sight. Flowing placidly from the 1,500-foot precipice, the river idles over a vast, fertile floodplain, as Terlingua Creek, the tributary in the Big Bend most likely to contain water, joins it at the base of the fault. The mouth of the canyon was the most often seen part of what is today the national park, even during the 18th and 19th centuries, when it was variously called the "wall" of San Damasio, the "Great Cañon San Carlos," and the "Grand Puerta." The lowlands at the mouth of the canyon were a beautiful sight to Meler and his friends, because "it taken us most of 4 days to git thrown that hole." The Geological Survey party "lingered long in contemplation of this most remarkable feature."[11]

Today the trip can be made in a day if the water is high enough. Usually it is a pleasant 2-day float, made enjoyable by the feeling that grips the traveler when night descends and the canyon

**The mouth of Santa Elena Canyon, photographed
by Ansel Adams in 1949.**

is lighted only by moonlight reflecting off the walls and the water. Then, if not before, one is convinced of the grandeur of nature and the insignificance of a solitary man. It is only one of many places in the Big Bend where a traveler can be alone with his thoughts for a long period. Shielded from mechanical interruptions–and even radio waves – the interior of Santa Elena Canyon is an expressive reminder of what Hill and his 19th-century comrades were among the first to see.

Farther down river is Mariscal Canyon, the least accessible of the national park's three major canyons. Isolated at the southernmost tip of the Big Bend, Mariscal probably received its name from a local *jefe*, Albino Villa Alfelias, a well-known Indian fighter. The Spanish word *mariscal* can mean either marshal or blacksmith. Perhaps it also connoted an important person, or chief, such as Alfelias. Because of its proximity to the old Spanish presidio of San Vicente, Mariscal has also been known as Little San Vicente Canyon.

Carved from rugged Mariscal Mountain, the canyon contains some of the most spectacular scenery on the river. Sheer walls reach 1,600 feet. The horizon is squeezed into ribbons of light that separate the cliffs, illuminating the river as it forces its way over rock slides and boulders worn smooth. While it has no rock slide to equal the one in Santa Elena, Mariscal can be difficult to navigate if the river is high. The 1852 Boundary Survey team wrecked their boat, probably in Mariscal, and were forced to continue the journey on foot.[12] Mariscal is perhaps the most often traveled of the three major canyons, easily floated in less than a day, even when the water is low. It was inhabited until recently by a man who wanted to get away from civilization. He lived in a shallow cave on the Mexican side of the river, and dubbed his camp Dropp Knife, Mexico. A short distance upriver is the Big Bend's best known candelilla wax camp, where the candelilla plant is boiled and pure wax was recovered. It stands on the Mexican side of the river, and can be visited by almost everyone who floats through the canyon. Floaters must paddle furiously to complete the trip through Mariscal Canyon, because the winds at the canyon exit blow upriver with force.

Boquillas, the longest of the Rio Grande canyons, is carved from the massive limestone peaks of the Sierra del Carmen range. Boquillas' walls are more open than Mariscal's and reach as high as 1,500 feet. Some have suggested that the gorge is named Boquillas (a slang form of "little mouths" in Spanish) because of the canyon's narrow mouth. Perhaps it got the name from the hundreds of small erosions in the Sierra del Carmen range, which resembled little mouths. The Spanish word itself translates as the opening to a pant's leg or the mouth of an irrigation canal, either of which could be construed to be related to the mouth of a canyon. The high peak near its entrance is Schott Tower, named for Arthur Schott.

Boquillas is possibly the least known of the canyons historically. Both the American and Mexican boundary survey teams marched around it rather than risk its unknown dangers in 1851 and 1852. Col. Emilio Langberg of the Mexican team cited its length and the "many opportunities its land gives for enemy ambushes" as his reason for circling the canyon. Although Captain Nevill's party might have floated through it in 1882, they left no record that they did. The first documented passage through Boquillas was Hill's expedition of 1899, which discovered that Boquillas is probably the calmest of the three major canyons. Adventurers frequently raft or canoe through the canyon today, making a leisurely trip of 2 or 3 days. There are no rapids or dangerous spots in the canyon, and the small Mexican village at the mouth makes it one of the most frequented spots in the national park.[13]

In the midst of the Big Bend desert stands the Chisos Mountains, a legendary refuge of ghosts and spirits. They reminded Colonel Langberg of "distant figures like castles and turrets whose heights can be seen from afar; one never loses sight of this beautiful range through nearly all the expedition." Although Chisos was the name of a tribe of Indians, the term has now been inextricably associated with ghosts, an association first mentioned in print by Hill in 1901. But the old storyteller Natividad Lujan once told Judge O. W. Williams of Fort Stockton a spellbinding tale about the Apache chieftain Alsate that might explain the association of ghosts with the mountains. The warrior was betrayed to Mexican officials at San Carlos by Leonecio Castillo. The tribe was then marched off into slavery in southern Mexico, and Alsate was executed. It was soon whispered among the residents of the Big Bend that Alsate's ghost roamed his old hunting grounds. When Castillo, the informer, left the country, the ghost disappeared. Believing that the danger had passed, Castillo returned. So did the ghost.

One version of the story describes a confrontation between

Castillo and the ghost of Alsate. Castillo had stopped for the night in a cave in the Chisos when he recalled betraying the chief. Thinking of Alsate's oath of revenge, Castillo laughed out loud, then glanced up to see Alsate's face carved in the features of the mountain across the valley. He quickly turned away, seeking to blot out the vision, but he heard Alsate's soul crying out for revenge. Castillo disappeared from the Big Bend. Although the tale varies from storyteller to storyteller, the rock formation named for Alsate is easily seen in Green Gulch in the Chisos, about a mile east of the basin road junction.[14]

Others have claimed that the term "ghosts" is associated more directly with events that happen in the mountains themselves. Some have reported that the play of moonlight creates a "spooky" effect on the gray vegetation of the mountainsides. One hunter claims to have seen an entire valley illuminated as if in daylight, while Ross A. Maxwell has described a "luminous pulsating light" dancing over the mountain peaks or on the roads. Several newspapers have carried stories of strange "Marfa lights," with the usual explanation of ghosts of long-departed Indians and lost gold mines that glow at night. But Maxwell offers a more reasonable explanation: perhaps the lights are reflections of moonlight produced by tiny mineral grains or the phosphorescent glow given off by rotten wood.

Of course, there are those who insist that the mountains themselves might have been shrouded in mist—and therefore appeared "ghostly"—when seen by the Spaniards. Still, the mystery of the Chisos and the ghosts remains. "Nowhere have I found such a wildly weird country," wrote an 1896 visitor to the Chisos. "The very silence is oppressive. A man grows watchful for his own safety and becomes awe-struck by nature in her lofty moods." [15]

One of the most magnificent sights in the Big Bend is the view from the South Rim of the Chisos. Half a day's journey from the Basin, the South Rim can be reached on foot or horseback. After passing by Boot Rock, Boot Canyon, and Boot Springs, one can see on a clear day Santa Elena Canyon some 20 miles to the southwest and Schott Tower another 25 miles to the east. The visitor who watches majestic vultures soar off the rim cannot help but understand the feelings of Texas Ranger Captain E. E. Townsend as he looked out over the Big Bend from the nearby Burro Mesa:

> It was a vision of such magnitude as to stir the sluggish soul of a Gila Monster. It was so awe-inspiring that it did deeply touch the soul of a hardened human bloodhound. . . . I resolved that upon the arrival of my ship I would buy the whole Chisos Mountains as a . . . playground for myself and friends

15

High on the south rim of the Chisos.

Terlingua ●

118

Rio

Grande

Mesa de Anguila

Terlingua
Abaja ●   ● Coyote

Santa
Elena
Canyon

Castolon ●

MEXICO

BIG BEND NATIONAL PARK

0	MILES	5	10
0	KILOMETERS	8	16

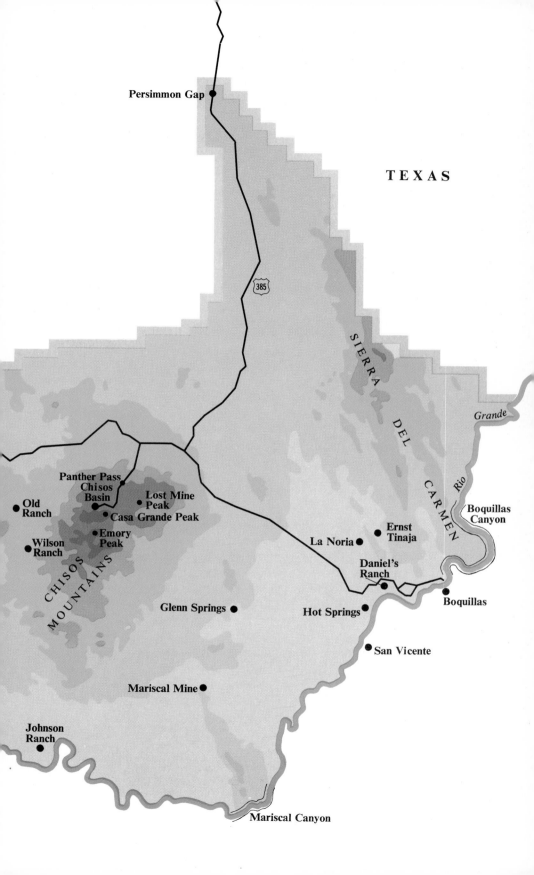

Persimmon Gap

TEXAS

385

SIERRA DEL CARMEN

Rio Grande

Panther Pass
Chisos
Basin

Lost Mine
Peak

Casa Grande Peak

Old
Ranch

Emory
Peak

Wilson
Ranch

CHISOS MOUNTAINS

La Noria

Ernst
Tinaja

Boquillas
Canyon

Daniel's
Ranch

Boquillas

Glenn Springs

Hot Springs

San Vicente

Mariscal Mine

Johnson
Ranch

Mariscal Canyon

and that when no longer wanted, I would give it to the State. . . .[16]

The pinnacle of Emory Peak, 7,800 feet high and often enveloped by clouds, is accessible to hardy climbers over a 1-mile side trail. If anything, the vista from here is even more majestic. Only from high above the surrounding desert is the mountainous nature of the Big Bend fully apparent. The Basin lies 2,400 feet below. The massive peaks of the Sierra del Carmen, reaching miles into Mexico, where they are called the Fronteriza Range, break the view to the east, while Mariscal Mountain is visible to the southeast, and Terlingua Fault dominates the southwestern vista.

The Chisos are alpine heights in the midst of a desert. In a sense, they form a biological island. Plants and animals that once flourished throughout the region when it was wetter and cooler are now isolated in the mountains, trapped in the mild heights because they cannot survive in the desert. Completely contained within the national park, the Chisos reach almost 8,000 feet above sea level. They are located in the center of a trough formed by the Mesa de Anguila on the southwest and the Sierra del Carmen-Santiago Mountain range on the northeast.[17]

Passing Green Gulch, the highway continues through Panther Pass and into the Basin, a depression from 1,500 to 2,000 feet deep. The Basin is surrounded by the tallest peaks in the Chisos. To the southeast is Casa Grande (7,500 feet), or Big House, a sheer cliff that reflects a prism of colors in the evening sun. The highest peak in the cluster is Emory Peak (7,835 feet), named for William H. Emory, the chief surveyor of the U.S. Boundary Survey team of 1852. Between Casa Grande and Emory Peak is Toll Mountain, named for Roger W. Toll, a former superintendent of Yellowstone National Park, who was instrumental in establishing Big Bend National Park. Ward Mountain is named after Johnny Ward, a cowboy on the G4 Ranch. Carter Peak, the small mountain near the Window, or the "pour-off," as the only drainage outlet in the Basin is called, was named for Amon G. Carter, a Fort Worth newspaper publisher who lent his influence and enthusiasm to the drive to establish the park. Across the Window from Carter Peak is Vernon Bailey Peak, named after a pioneer field naturalist of the 1920's. Finally, Pulliam Peak is named for Bill Pulliam, who had a ranch at its foot for years.[18]

The view from the Chisos Basin includes other well-known features that have legends associated with them. Not far from Alsate's Face, in Green Gulch, is Lost Mine Peak. Supposedly the Spaniards stationed at Presidio San Vicente worked a mine in the mountains. An old trail leading from the presidio up Juniper Canyon encourages those who would believe the story—and has misled literally hundreds of treasure hunters—but the trail does not lead up the peak. At least, if it did, the way has now been lost. The mouth of the mine could be found, according to the legend, only by standing at the door of the old presidio on Easter morning and marking the spot where the first rays of the sun strike the Chisos. There is no record that a mine ever existed in this part of the Chisos, but if there were one, Maxwell has discredited this method of finding it. The sun's rays strike the mountains at slightly different angles each year, because Easter does not fall on the same day each year. Anyway, if the sky is clear, sunlight will strike Emory Peak first because it is the highest point in the mountains. Near Lost Mine Peak is the Watchman's House. According to the same legend, the ghost of an Indian slave, left there by the Spaniards to guard the mine, lives in a small cave on the slopes of the peak.[19]

The Chisos Basin has long been the most hospitable region. For years it was the home or hideout of Indians and badmen. Later the Civilian Conservation Corps established a camp there, followed by the headquarters of the national park. When the park's headquarters was moved to Panther Junction, the cabins, restaurant, and motel facilities for the park remained in the Basin, surely one of the most beautiful spots in the Big Bend.

The terrain and climate combine to render the Big Bend formidable to anyone traveling across it without reliable transportation. The terrain is rough, unpredictable, and hazardous. The desert is unyielding – unless one knows the secrets of extracting food and water from cacti – and unforgiving of the slightest error in judgment or conduct. The history of the Big Bend, therefore, is the story of man's efforts to overcome the natural obstacles that work in concert to defeat him. Before roads were built into the Big Bend only one race successfully lived there – the Indians.

2/Spanish Explorers

For the peaceful, sedentary Puebloan tribes who lived at the confluence of the Rio Grande and the Río Conchos and the nomadic, aggressive Comanches and Apaches who rode from their winter abodes north of the Rio Grande to raid and plunder the frontier villages each summer, the *despoblado* was home. Its well-concealed, infrequent water holes that dried up periodically, its mapless mountains and gorges, and its haunting emptiness protected them from the slow, ill-equipped Spanish soldiers who clumsily pursued them along the northern frontier.

To the Spaniards the Big Bend was only an obstacle to their domination of other parts of the frontier. Their advance into the Bend was a slow, calculated effort required to defend their frontier settlements and to establish a direct line of communications along the frontier. Curious about the mysterious *despoblado,* the Spaniards knew no more than the 19th-century French traveler who summed up contemporary knowledge of the region all too well when he observed that "there is no vegetation other than brambles, no view other than the immense sandy plains . . . . Words cannot convey the strangeness and supreme melancholy of the landscape." [1]

The Search for Gold

The first Spanish expeditions, however, did not enter the Big Bend for either defensive reasons or out of curiosity, but for gold. The first expeditions into the Big Bend were little more than blind efforts to discover another Mexico. The Spanish quest for New World treasures met unqualified success when Hernando Cortez conquered the advanced Aztec civilization in 1521, securing wealth and thousands of Indian slaves. Montezuma's fantastic empire renewed the Spaniards' belief in such legends as the seven wealthy cities of Cibola (supposedly established by seven renegade Portuguese bishops), Queen Califia and her Amazon woman empire, and the Gran Quivira.

The Spaniards quickly established a governmental system in Mexico to control the Indians, and devoted much of their energy to exploration and treasure-hunting. The king appointed a viceroy

Indian pictographs, such as these at Hot Springs, are common in the Big Bend.

for Mexico City, who was the chief officer of the crown in the New World. He handled all civil matters, and granted commissions to adventurers and would-be explorers to search other areas for advanced civilizations or wealth. All exploration in the empire was carefully regulated by the viceroy, with the crown receiving a stipulated percentage of any discoveries. The Spanish empire was probably the most disciplined one in the New World. Its procedures were carefully thought out by the king and his council, and disobedient subjects were quickly punished.

In the decades following the conquest, Spanish adventurers fanned out along the Gulf of Mexico coast in search of another rich native kingdom, an undertaking that led to the first contact with the Big Bend. In February 1528 Pánfilo de Narváez led an expedition to Florida in search of treasure, only to suffer hostile Indian attacks and abandonment by the ships that were supposed to pick them up. The survivors constructed small boats with the intention of sailing along the coast to Mexico, following the course charted by Alonso Álvarez de Piñeda a few years before. In November 1528 the ragged survivors landed on the coast of Texas, probably on Galveston Island. They called it the Isle of Misfortune.

The first Spaniard to reach the Big Bend may have been Alvar Núñez Cabeza de Vaca, the leader of the small party. After spending 7 years with the Indians – first as a captive, then as an honored medicine man – he escaped and headed westward, hoping to find a Spanish settlement. He may have crossed the present national park, though more probably he passed north of the Chisos Mountains, perhaps nearer the Guadalupe Mountains on the Texas-New Mexico border. He eventually encountered a Spanish slave-hunting party and returned to Mexico City, where he told of the Indian civilizations to the north.[2]

Although the Spaniards finally concluded they were not interested in the Big Bend itself, it took them several expeditions and more than a century to reach the decision. The viceroy sent a small exploratory expedition northward to find out whether a more ambitious foray would be useful. Then in 1540 a major expedition under Francisco Vázquez de Coronado set out for the same country. Coronado was the first white man to see the Hopi and Zuñi villages of Arizona and the Pueblos of New Mexico; some of his men discovered the Grand Canyon of the Colorado River. But the Southwest was not another Mexico, and the Spaniards turned their attention elsewhere.[3]

Los Entrados

What probably was the first Spanish penetration of the Big Bend came years later as a result of the natural expansion of the frontier northward. Mining settlements had been founded, and Spaniards thrust their expeditions into unknown territory to enslave the hapless Indians. Thus they reached the Río Conchos and followed it to La Junta de los Ríos, at the confluence of the Rio Grande and the Río Conchos. They were too late to see the pre-basketmaker culture that lived at La Junta – Indians who probably combined a mixture of traits from their own hunting and gathering culture with others acquired from the Pueblos who lived up the Rio Grande – but they did encounter Indians they called the Jumanos.[4]

The first Spanish contact with the Jumanos might have been Cabeza de Vaca and his ragged party, for the Indians later reported that they vaguely remembered seeing four bearded men. The first documented contact with the Jumanos of La Junta came in 1581. One of the Indian slaves captured in 1579 told of large settlements to the north, populated by natives who raised cotton for clothing and had plenty of food.

Inspired by the prospect of converts, Fray Agustín Rodríguez, a Franciscan lay brother stationed in the mining village of San Bartolomé, received permission in 1581 from the viceroy to make the *entrada*. Fray Francisco López and Fray Juan de Santa María accompanied Rodríguez. The military commander of the party was Francisco Sánchez, known more widely as "El Chamuscado" (or, "the singed one," probably because of his red hair), who was interested only in finding riches. Following the slavers' path down the Río Conchos, the Rodríguez party encountered the Jumanos at La Junta. "The . . . people . . . are very handsome, very spirited, very active and more intelligent than the people previously met," recorded Hernán Gallegos, a member of the Chamuscado party. "They are of large stature. Their faces, arms and bodies are striped with pleasing lines. These people are cleaner and more modest than . . . [the others they had met.] They go about naked . . . [and] wear their hair in the shape of skull-caps."[5]

The Jumanos were an established civilization. In fact, the Indians were probably the fringe settlements of the Pueblos, who had migrated down the Rio Grande as far as La Junta between 1200 and 1400. By the time Rodríguez visited them, their farming culture extended up the Conchos a few miles. Because the Jumano culture probably had peaked and begun to decline before the Spaniards encountered it, there is much confusing information concerning its origin and civilization.[6]

Two distinct groups of Indians were called Jumanos by the Spaniards: the puebloan culture at La Junta, and a tribe of nomadic hunters in the Chisos and Davis Mountains. Since they both belonged to the Uto-Aztecan language group, some authorities speculate that they were at one time part of the same group that dispersed because of a food shortage. The Chisos Indians the Spaniards encountered in the area of the national park probably were forced to turn to hunting, but even less is known about them.[7]

After moving down the Rio Grande to La Junta (a climate change probably allowed them to cultivate more of the desert), the Jumanos then encountered difficulty. A severe drought may have disrupted their culture. The Indians Cabeza de Vaca saw were in such desperate condition that they ate their seeds instead of planting them. By the 15th century the Jumanos Rodríguez visited had dispersed their communities, probably because the land would not support large concentrations of people. The shifting, unsettled conditions continued for the Jumanos, because the Spaniards and unfriendly Indians from the north combined with the climate to drive them from their homes.[8]

After visiting the Jumanos, Rodríguez and Chamuscado turned northwestward, traveling to the upper reaches of the Rio Grande in New Mexico. Finding no riches, Chamuscado was soon ready to return to Mexico. The friars remained to minister to the Indians, although they would no longer be protected by their soldiers. Although the expedition failed to discover new wealth, Rodríguez and Chamuscado opened the route by which other parties would enter New Mexico. For years Spaniards traveling this route were the only foreigners to enter the Big Bend.[9]

Rodríguez's expedition led directly to the next *entrada*. Antonio de Espejo, a wealthy rancher in the Querétaro and Celaya districts, used the alleged threat to the friars' safety as an excuse to organize another expedition in 1582, hoping, of course, to explore further and find the fabled cities. After the Franciscan priests in

Santa Bárbara pleaded that they be allowed to go along because they had not heard from their brethren, even the viceroy agreed that such a task should be undertaken. Espejo and his companions traveled the path of Rodríguez and López. They talked with the Indians at La Junta, including some who claimed to have vague memories of Cabeza de Vaca and his friends. There they learned that Rodríguez and López were dead, but continued on to New Mexico since the real purpose of the expedition was to explore the new land.[10]

They searched New Mexico extensively without finding any mineral riches, finally reaching the Pecos River. Marching down that stream to the vicinity of present-day Toyah Lake, near the city of Pecos, they met some Jumano Indians who told them of a more direct route. The Jumanos pointed out that the expedition would save time by marching overland to La Junta and offered to guide them. Espejo thus became the second Spaniard to pass through the Big Bend. He did not find it as inhospitable as later explorers, describing the "many watering places in creeks and marshes on the way," and receiving "fish of many kinds, prickly pears and other fruits . . . buffalo hides and tanned deerskins" from the Jumanos. His good fortune probably can be credited to his Indian guides.[11]

In addition to the licensed expeditions of Rodríguez and Espejo, Gaspar Castaño de Sosa illegally passed through the Big Bend in 1589. The ambitious Gaspar, lieutenant-governor of Nuevo León, led a colonizing party northwestward from Monclova, hoping to settle in the productive lands in the north. Perhaps the party entered the Big Bend region near the present Rio Grande Village, as some authorities claim. More likely it crossed near the Pecos River and paralleled it, following closely the route that Espejo had traveled to New Mexico. The Spaniards' presence was documented in Indian pictographs in the southeastern corner of the Trans-Pecos. Although the fringes of the Big Bend had been penetrated, it still had not been explored.[12]

The Church Returns

The Indians themselves were responsible for the next expedition. Priests had visited La Junta in the past only because the Río Conchos provided a good route to New Mexico. After the Spaniards shifted the Chihuahua City-Santa Fé road westward to El Paso, La Junta was isolated. It was soon deserted. A Jumano chief, Juan de Sabeata, surprised the Spaniards when he visited El Paso in 1684 and requested that the friars come back. His request was granted by the governor, and Capt. Juan Domínguez de Mendoza organized an expedition.[13]

The venture was commercial as well as religious, like so many Spanish endeavors. In addition to helping Jumanos, the Spaniards still hoped to find the fabled cities of the north. Mendoza was instructed to travel as far as the Nueces River, where he was to search for pearls and riches.[14]

The captain provided one of the first detailed reports on the Big Bend. Leading his men down the Rio Grande, he met Fray Nicholás López and Fray Juan Zavaleta, who had come down the Conchos. The combined party journeyed northeastward across the Big Bend country, passing through much of the same land that Espejo had visited over a century before. Mendoza went down the river as far as Alamito Creek, then turned northeastward, passing by San Esteban and Antelope Spring. Continuing through Paisano Pass, the party marched to the southeast of Músquiz Canyon through Leoncito Draw to the spring, which Mendoza named San Pedro de Alcantara. A few days later he christened present-day Fort Stockton (Comanche Springs in the 19th century) San Juan del Río. Mendoza, in fact, named most of his campsites in the Big Bend, although none of them has retained the designation. He went as far as present-day Menard County before turning back in May 1684. Fathers Acevedo and Zavaleta remained at La Junta to minister to the needs of the Jumanos, while Mendoza and Father López returned to Mexico to present their memorials to the viceroy and urge that La Junta be granted a mission. All hope of the La Junta mission vanished, however, when a French expedition under command of La Salle landed on the Texas coast in January 1685, threatening Spanish control in that region, and forcing the Spaniards to recall their frontier forces. It was not until 1715 that Franciscans were able to reestablish missions at La Junta.[15]

Defense

The changing relationship with the Indians of the *despoblado* soon required the Spaniards to turn their attention from religious and financial interests to defense. The first Spanish contacts with the Indians were of a cautious but friendly nature. Coronado encountered some hostility but probably as much curiosity in New Mexico and Arizona. The Indians of La Junta had welcomed the Spaniards. "Standing on top of their houses they showed great mer-

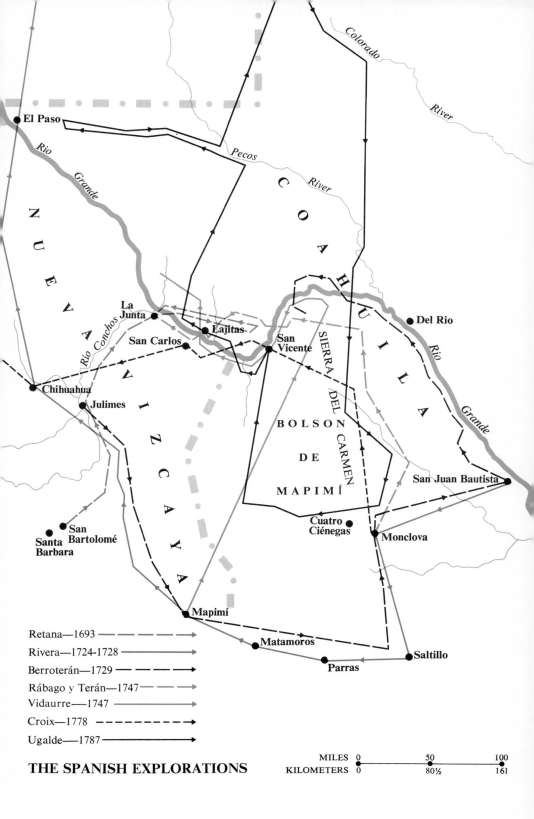

THE SPANISH EXPLORATIONS

Retana—1693
Rivera—1724-1728
Berroterán—1729
Rábago y Terán—1747
Vidaurre—1747
Croix—1778
Ugalde—1787

MILES 0   50   100
KILOMETERS 0   80½   161

riment on seeing us," Gallegos recalled. Juan de Oñate, colonizer of New Mexico, later noted that, "We were not disturbed by them, although we were in their land, nor did any Indian become impertinent." The French seem to have proved that Europeans could trade and coexist with the natives.[16]

But the Spaniards provoked hostility, and the Indians' attitude changed drastically. First, the Spaniards seized Big Bend Indians and sold them as slaves to mine operators in Mexico. Then, the Spaniards severely punished the Indians who resisted, as if to show the natives the power of the Europeans. When a group of Apaches raided Gaspar Castaño de Sosa's camp near the Pecos River, killing one friendly Indian and driving off some stock, the Spaniards pursued, killing several Apaches and capturing four. One was hanged, the other three kept for interpreters. Although the Spaniards were no doubt convinced that harsh measures were necessary, such reactions precluded any possibility of peaceful coexistence.[17]

The Indians quickly struck back. For months after the incident they raided Spanish settlements across the northern frontier with impunity, then retreated into the *despoblado* where the Spaniards could not follow. The Apaches and their neighbors, nomadic hunters and excellent warriors, proved immune to the methods that had humbled the more civilized natives of central Mexico and the upper Rio Grande. In addition to the cunning of the Indians, the Spaniards had to deal with the problems of the *despoblado* itself. The Big Bend thus assumed a negative importance to the Spaniards. There would be no reward for sacrifice in its conquest; survival depended on it.

Realizing that the Chisos Indians in the Big Bend were some of the more ardent troublemakers, Gov. Gabriel del Castillo of Nueva Vizcaya dispatched Juan Fernández de Retana to La Junta to rout them from their stronghold in 1693. An able military man, Retana closed in on the Chisos in an area south of the Rio Grande, where they had recently been involved in a struggle with another tribe and had lost their horses. He trapped them on Peñol de Santa Marta. After several assaults on the height, he convinced them to surrender. Most of the Chisos returned peacefully to La

Junta, where they had lived for years, and asked that the Spaniards again send missionaries to them. A few months later Retana conducted another foray into the Rio Grande country. Marching from La Junta toward the junction of the Pecos and the Rio Grande, apparently without crossing the Rio Grande, he encountered another hostile band of nomads and defeated them. He would have pursued them until they were dispersed, but he elected to return because the waterholes in the *despoblado* were dry.[18]

Retana's raids seemed only to aggravate the Indians. Their attacks continued. In central Mexico the Spaniards had confronted a people who controlled the area; once the dominant tribe was conquered, the land belonged to the Spaniards. On the frontier, however, one or two successes did not assure control. Victory meant only that one or two bands were now scattered. The Indians could easily regroup and raid again. When a tribe such as the Chisos was finally beaten and pacified, another tribe migrated from the north to take its place. The Indians were a continuous threat, requiring constant vigilance. The Europeans at this point must have shared the impression that the Indians soon were to have: that there was no end to the wave upon wave of enemies entering their land.[19]

Apaches in the Big Bend

The Indians who migrated southward to fill the void left when the Chisos turned to more peaceful ways were the Mescalero Apaches. Pressed from their traditional hunting grounds by the Comanches and Utes, the Apaches moved first into New Mexico, then into Texas and Mexico, raiding Spanish settlements. There are many bands of Apaches and often the same band was called different names, adding to the confusion. The Mescalero Apaches (from mescal eater) established *rancherías* in New Mexico, where they raised crops in spring and summer and roamed from southern New Mexico to northern Mexico, including the Big Bend. They historically were the most warlike of the Apaches. Their small, isolated settlements made ideal targets for the far-ranging, aggressive Comanches, who rode into village after village, pillaging, killing, and driving the Apaches even farther south. The continual pressure from the north forced the Apaches into conflict with the less-feared Spaniards, who could not penetrate the *despoblado* with the same ease.[20]

Although they led a meager existence, the Mescaleros solved the mystery of living in the Big Bend. They seldom, if ever, established permanent residences there, but did locate *rancherías* in the mountains, which they occupied seasonally. They knew how to live as they crossed the *despoblado,* which the Spaniards and later the

Americans could only do by carrying provisions with them. They knew through experience where the *tinajas,* or temporary water-holes, were located and when they would have water in them. They knew the edible plants. And they knew they could not stay long in one place without exhausting the land's scanty fare. So they traveled light and moved quickly from place to place, continually eluding their pursuers merely by fleeing into the *despoblado.* They were the only people who learned to live in harmony with the raw forces of nature in the Big Bend.

A New Policy Toward the Indians

Defeats and wasteful expeditions soon forced the Spaniards to reevaluate their frontier policy in the light of the realities of the Big Bend. The terrain ruled out a large expedition to end the Indian threat, because the Indians were much more accustomed to the desert than were the Spaniards. There was serious doubt, in fact, that an isolated Spanish force could defeat them in a pitched battle in the *despoblado.*

The presidio plan recommended in 1667 by Gov. Antonio de Oca Sarmiento of Nueva Vizcaya, therefore, received serious consideration. One of the first suggestions as to how to overcome the raiders, the presidio plan recognized that a few, widely spread Spanish troops were no match for the Indians in such a vast land. The shrewd Oca suggested to the viceroy that a line of "watchtowers" be established at vulnerable points. The watchtowers, or presidios, would be staffed with 10 soldiers and four friendly Indians each and would be spaced evenly across the frontier so they could support each other. Oca was thus the first to formulate the plan that ultimately became the backbone of the Spanish, and later the Mexican, defense of the northern frontier. "If the plan is not adopted our total desolation is daily anticipated," he concluded.[21]

Don José Francisco Marín, an agent of the viceroy, refined the plan. After viewing the disarray of the Spanish forces on the frontier, he concluded that the nomad's advantage would be difficult to overcome unless the Spanish troops took the offensive rather than waiting for the Indians to ride out of the *despoblado* and attack another defenseless village. Francisco Marín further suggested that the governor of the northern provinces be a military

The ruins of the San Vicente Chapel, which was
constructed as part of a presidio-mission by the
Spanish in 1774.

man, and that European colonization along the frontier be encouraged. Revealing the Spaniard's ignorance of the canyons and rapids of the Rio Grande, he suggested that it would be an easy matter for the colonists to reach sites along the river, because they
could simply be transported from the gulf in boats.[22] Most of
Francisco Marín's proposals were accepted, but his colonization
scheme was rejected. It would be decades before the Big Bend felt
the impact of the presidial system.

By the time Pedro de Rivera, an influential viceregal ap-
pointee, conducted an investigation of the frontier in 1728, the situation had changed. The Apaches were under increasing pressure
from the best warriors on the plains, the Comanches, who had migrated southward in bands searching for hunting grounds not disputed by more powerful tribes. A simple people who lived off
roots, insects, jack rabbits, and other wild creatures and plants, the
Comanches became supreme warriors – and predators – with the
acquisition of the horse. Not only were the Comanches and
Apaches at war with each other; both preyed on the isolated settlements along New Spain's northern frontier.[23]

Rivera therefore resolved to follow Oca's plan and advised
that the presidios along the southern rim of the *despoblado* be
moved northward and located along the Rio Grande to establish a

31

line that the raiders supposedly could not penetrate. Several residents of the area recommended to Rivera that to be successful a presidio had to be located in the *despoblado* itself, preferably at La Junta de Los Ríos. Some authorities also recommended La Junta, but Rivera disagreed. He believed that a site southeast of the junction would be more advantageous. The viceroy ordered Capt. José de Berroterán of the presidio of Conchos to take 70 men, march into the *despoblado,* and find the best location for the presidio.[24]

Captain Berroterán, a cautious officer, planned his expedition carefully. Following José Antonio de Ecay Múzquiz's recommendation that the easiest route into the region was along the Rio Grande, he gathered his force at Conchos in January 1729, and circled eastward around the *despoblado* – via the frontier villages of Mapimí, Laguna de la Leche, Cuatro Ciénegas, and Monclova–to San Juan Bautista. Although their instructions called for them to divide into two groups to scout for hostile Indians as well as search for a site for the presidio, Berroterán and his council decided that they should remain together because the country was completely unknown.

Berroterán apprehensively left San Juan Bautista on March 28. Gone less than a week, he received a message from the governor of Coahuila reporting Indian raids in the Parras and Saltillo areas and requesting that he relinquish part of his force for defense of the towns. Proceeding cautiously, Berroterán feared for the success of his mission and again decided to hold his force together. His officers warned that the Indian scouts were moving too slowly, but were not sure if it was from ignorance of the land or an intentional effort to hamper the expedition. "Thus I remained in a state of confusion," reported Berroterán, "awaiting the return of the scouts, hoping that one of them might be able to extricate me from this labyrinth."

As Berroterán marched into the vicinity of present-day Langtry, he noticed that the river banks got steeper. He crossed to the left bank of the Rio Grande and followed it closely for 5 more days. They camped near present-day Dryden and held a council. Supplies were low, they had found no site that they could recommend for a presidio, and they feared that they would be lost in the desert. The council voted to discontinue the expedition. Berroterán ordered the soldiers from Monclova and San Juan Bautista to return by the outward route, while he and his troops elected to bypass La Junta and travel across the *despoblado* to the Río Conchos. Although they marched 2 days without water and had to abandon several horses and mules, they reached their presidio safely.[25]

Berroterán had been the first to cross the *despoblado,* but his mission was a failure. He had explored much new territory, yet had found neither hostile Indians nor a site for the presidio. Rivera denounced him for faintheartedness. The captain had been hesitant from the first, he claimed. "He knew nothing of the country he was to traverse, but seemed to know beforehand what was going to happen," Rivera wrote Gov. Ignacio Francisco de Barrutia of Nueva Vizcaya. Of course, "the officers and men knew nothing of the land ahead, for it is a fact that for all discovery one presupposes a lack of knowledge of the places ahead." Rivera insisted that the job should have been simple. Although he admitted that "its banks offer some difficult places," he claimed that all Berroterán had to do was follow the Rio Grande.[26]

The governor of Coahuila, meanwhile, was still interested in establishing a presidio along his northern frontier to fend off hostile raids by the Apaches. After a survey of the frontier in 1734, Gov. Blas de la Garza Falcón had asked the viceroy to permit establishment of a post at a site to be determined, then reconnoitered the banks of the Rio Grande in search of a location the following year. It was a difficult march. Reaching the Río San Diego, he learned that the terrain ahead did not improve and that his advance party had found traces of Apaches nearby. Low temperatures, snow, and dry waterholes killed several horses in January 1736. Somewhere near present-day Randale, Garza Falcón decided to turn back. Berroterán had gone farther. Garza Falcón did recommend a site for the presidio about 30 miles south of present-day Del Rio, and construction was completed in 1738. [27]

If Berroterán and Garza Falcón proved anything by their expeditions, it was that La Junta could not be approached from the southeast via the river. Several years of speculation regarding the nature and course of the river in the *despoblado* were ended, but the unfortunate answer was that the Spaniards could expect no relief from the agonies of the desert. It continued to shelter the Indians from retribution for decades.

In his report Berroterán claimed that the Apaches raided the frontier with impunity because there were no presidios between

33

San Juan Bautista and El Paso. He reported to the viceroy that after the Indians entered "this unpopulated, long and wide gulf," they controlled the eastern border of Nueva Vizcaya and western Coahuila and could "easily destroy and annihilate" the two provinces. He argued that the area could not be inhabited by settlers because the "gulf or pocket" – the *despoblado* – contained "steep places, dry places, few waterholes, and great distances." He recommended that the presidios of San Bartolomé and Conchos be moved to the Rio Grande frontier, where they possibly would slow the Indians who came "like waves of the sea—when one ends, another follows." Although Berroterán technically failed in his mission to find a location for the presidio, his experience on the frontier gave credence to his recommendations, and his opinion was still valued by the officials in Mexico City.[28]

Having found no better plan, the viceroy and his advisors took up Berroterán's suggestions 18 years later. The viceroy agreed that the presidios should be placed along the Rio Grande and dispatched three expeditions to explore northern Coahuila and Chihuahua for good sites. He sent Capt. Joseph de Ydoiaga from San Bartolomé to La Junta; Capt. Fermín Vidaurre was to seek another route. The new governor of Coahuila, Pedro de Rábago y Terán led the most difficult expedition, which would attempt to cross the *despoblado* from Coahuila to La Junta.[29]

Boquillas is the longest and calmest of the three major canyons of the Rio Grande.

Rábago left Monclova in November 1747 with 20 soldiers and 10 Indians. At Sacramento he picked up 45 more soldiers. He marched to the Río Escondido, then to Arroyo de la Babia. Following the Arroyo, he found an old Indian trail into the mountains. He passed the Mesa de los Fresnos (about 100 miles from present-day Santa Rosa), then marched into the Sierra del Carmen. The terrain was rough, with little water and several abandoned Indian camps. On December 2 the expedition reached the Rio Grande upriver from Rio Grande Village. "Its banks were explored and no passing area was found on account of its currents coming so close to the mountain ranges," wrote Rábago. "The rocks make a high wall along the upper and lower part: In spite of this, I ordered all of the train to pass from the other bank . . . and we camped . . . ," thus becoming the first Spanish expedition to enter what is today Big Bend National Park. This new ford, located probably below Mariscal Canyon, Rábago named Santa Rita.[30]

Rábago was not satisfied with his campground. The "sandy land, some hillocks and little grass" were inadequate to support his expedition. He sent 17 soldiers and a corporal upriver in search of rich grassland for the horses, then ordered his Indian auxiliaries to scout the mountains, probably the Chisos to the north or northwest for a pass.

After celebrating Mass on December 3, Rábago walked a short distance from camp to inspect the "banks and hilly areas" near the river, where he found "several veins" of ore. After speculating about "good mineral sources" in the Big Bend, he investigated the fertile strip that parallels the Rio Grande, concluding that there was not enough of the lowland to support farming in the immediate area. The region, in addition, was "so boxed in between mountain and mountain" that Rábago thought it impassable. The Indian scouts returned, reporting that several old Apache campgrounds were located in the Chisos Mountains.

Rábago had hoped to follow the river northwestward, but canyons and steep banks forced him to find another route. After learning of a better camping place upriver. Rábago marched in a northwesterly direction, stopping for the night without water in his haste to find the site. On December 5 he found one of the hot springs along the Rio Grande. This place he named Santa Bárbara. At another abandoned Apache camp he found three horses that the Indians had left behind in their hasty retreat. Encountering unusually cold weather for the Big Bend, Rábago continued his march northwestward to an area where squash plants grew up

35

to the water's edge. He named it El Real de las Calabasas.

Rábago marched on, with the Chisos Mountains on his right and the Terlingua Fault, which he named the "wall" of San Damasio, on his left. He saw the jagged bluffs of the Chisos, the twin peaks that the Anglo-Americans later named Mule Ears, and on December 11 probably became the first European to see steep-walled Santa Elena Canyon, which he found too forbidding to explore. The party marched along Terlingua Creek, which they named El Arroyo, then turned westward to the Rio Grande again, probably near the modern village of Lajitas. On December 18 Rábago sighted Nuestra Señora de Guadalupe, one of the pueblos of La Junta. The Rábago expedition was the first to march across the *despoblado* and reach La Junta.[31]

Rábago remained there for several days, visiting with the mission fathers and inquiring about the conditions of the surrounding country. He spent a few days exploring the Rio Grande on either side of La Junta, then followed the Conchos upriver for a few miles. On December 29 he directed his party eastward on the return journey. They followed Indian trails to the vicinity of present-day Terlingua. Wanting to return via a different route, they circled northward around the Chisos Mountains to San Vicente. Deciding not to follow the river back to San Juan Bautista because his scouts had sighted the sheer walls of Boquillas Canyon, Rábago crossed to the right bank and divided his force. One group he directed to return to Sacramento by the path they had followed enroute, while his force attempted to find a new route to Monclova.

The other two expeditions explored better known territory. Captain Ydoiaga marched down the Río Conchos to La Junta, in the neighborhood of what its today the village of Shafter. Captain Vidaurre saw what is now the national park, but only after Rábago had already been there. Vidaurre left the Presidio of Mapimí in November 1747, following a northeasterly course until he reached the Rio Grande near present-day Del Rio. He found tracks left by Rábago's party as he marched toward La Junta.[32]

The *despoblado* was no easier to penetrate physically because of Rábago's marches, but he had crossed the breadth of the region to La Junta and had mapped new routes from both Sacramento and Monclova. The land was as harsh as ever for the unknowing, but with trails and waterholes marked, the Spaniards could now apply pressure to their enemy even in the *despoblado*.

As a result of his reconnaissance, Rábago agreed that a presidio should be located at La Junta. On his visit to Indian *rancherías* in the La Junta area he had found horses that belonged to settlers in Saltillo, Sacramento, Monclova, and Nuevo León, including some stolen from members of his expedition. Even among peaceful Indians, Rábago had found two Indian women captives from missions near San Juan Bautista. Both they and the horses had been captured by the Apaches on their wide-ranging forays and traded to the natives at La Junta. He believed that a presidio at La Junta would help decrease the number of raids. Seeing the Rio Grande as the first line of defense for the Spanish frontier, the captain also recommended that the presidio of Santa Rosa be moved closer to the river.

Never known for their hasty decisions, the Spanish officials in Mexico City requested more information. Rubín de Celís was sent in 1750 to explore the territory between El Paso and La Junta. But increased Indian raids on the Nueva Vizcaya frontier finally convinced the authorities that a La Junta presidio was necessary. Work on Nuestra Señora de Belén, or Presidio del Norte, was completed in July 1760.[33]

If the Spaniards thought that a lone presidio at La Junta would stop the incursions of the Apaches, they were mistaken. Frontier settlers could have told them of the ineffectiveness of a few troops scattered among the mountains and canyons of the Big Bend. Pushed southward by their mortal enemies, the Comanches, the Apaches continued their plundering, seemingly immune to all the official acts of the Spanish bureaucracy.

Reforms Reach the Frontier

Charles III, the new Bourbon monarch who came to the throne of Spain in 1759, is known as the reforming king. He seized power in Madrid amid great domestic difficulties and declining prestige abroad. Strict mercantile policies had led to widespread smuggling; centralized authority in the viceregal capital of Mexico City had led to neglect of the frontier. The poorly protected frontier, in fact, was one of the most vexing colonial problems. Charles decreed reorganization of the colonial administration and opened numerous colonial ports to international trade. The impact of his reforms finally reached the frontier when a trusted officer, the Marquis de Rubí, made an inspection trip covering some 7,500 miles along the entire frontier of New Spain in 1767. While Rubí was on his way to inspect the La Junta presidio, he learned that the governor of Coahuila had ordered the post evacuated and relocated at Julimes, several days journey up the Río Conchos. Rubí turned and headed for El Paso, bypassing the Big Bend because there were no settlements to be inspected. After his reconnaissance, however, he agreed with Berroterán and Rábago that the Rio Grande was a natural defense line. If the Spaniards could stop the Apaches before they entered the *despoblado,* the settlements of Nueva Vizcaya and Coahuila would be safe. He advised that the northern presidios near the *despoblado* be moved to the Rio Grande. The presidio at Julimes was to be returned to La Junta.[34]

Two important results came out of Rubí's inspection. First, Rubí's engineer and lieutenant produced one of the first maps that shows the Big Bend. Nicholás de Lafora and Joseph Urrútia, Ensign of the Regiment of America, were both with Rubí as he bypassed the Big Bend. From their own observations and by gleaning information from other maps and travel descriptions, Lafora and Urrútia mapped the entire frontier. Their map shows the Big Bend trapped between a somewhat unrealistic nook of the Rio Grande and the Pecos River, which erroneously curves abruptly to the northwest on the map. The presidios of Julimes, Cerro Gordo, and San Sabá (all of which would soon receive new names in the coming reorganization of the frontier defenses) are shown adjacent to the Rio Grande on the right bank, but somewhat out of position. Cerro Gordo is located at what would be more nearly the southernmost tip of the Bend, rather than in the location of present-day San Carlos. San Sabá appears downriver from what probably is the Pecos—much too far east for the actual site, which is present-day San Vicente. These inaccuracies would probably have been cleared away if Lafora and Urrútia had visited the sites while on their tour. The Big Bend itself is correctly shown as mountainous and occupied by Mescalero Apaches. Despite these difficulties, the Lafora-Urrútia map is a significant document for two reasons: the Big Bend is shown to be an important part of the Spanish frontier defenses, and the map is a technical achievement for Spanish mapmakers in 1771.

One of the first maps of the Southwest to
identify the Big Bend region, the 1771 Lafora
map showed Mescalero Apaches living there.

39

40 **Spanish Explorers**

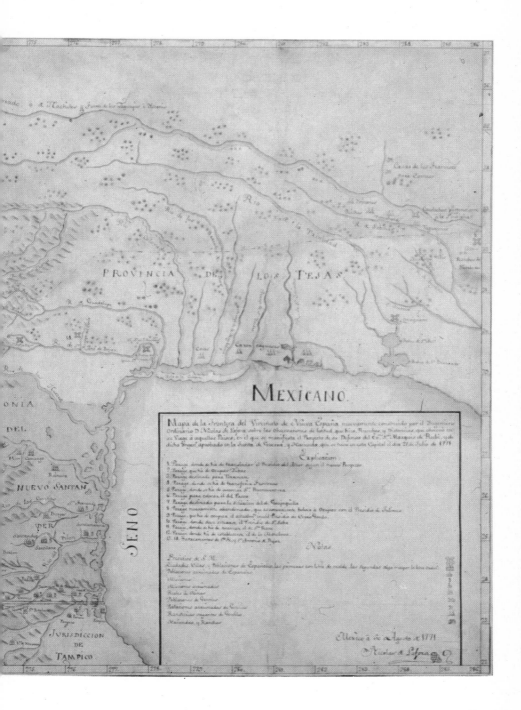

41

The second result of the Rubí expedition was that the king issued the New Regulations of 1772, which embodied, among other things, Rubí's plan to relocate the presidios along the Rio Grande frontier. Viceroy Antonio María Bucareli appointed one of his favorites, Hugo Oconor, to carry out Rubí's recommendations.[35]

As a part of his frontier reorganization, Oconor made a thorough tour of the Big Bend. Before leaving on his inspection, he studied the diaries of Berroterán and Rábago. Then he headed for the frontier to supervise the moving of the presidios. Leaving from San Fernando de Austria in April 1773, he camped several miles upriver from San Juan Bautista, searching for a new site for the presidio of Monclova. He finally decided on the Río San Rodrigo. Leaving men there to build that presidio, Oconor moved upriver to the Arroyo de Agua Verde, about 20 miles south of Del Rio. There he ordered the presidio of Santa Rosa established. With the assistance of Lipan guides, Oconor rode into the Big Bend, probably following Rábago's route, where he located a site for the presidio of San Vicente. He positioned the fort near the Rio Grande, next to a well-known Indian ford. He ordered the presidio of San Sabá moved from the Río San Sabá in present-day Menard County, where it was exposed to attack and useless to a frontier defense line, to San Vicente. To cover the 100 miles of desert between Agua Verde and San Vicente, Oconor proposed that another presidio be established at La Babia, south of the Rio Grande and almost directly between Santa Rosa and San Sabá. The Big Bend country could not be left unprotected, he argued, because it was the main trail for Indians raiding the frontier settlements farther south.

Oconor then moved upriver to the Arroyo de San Carlos. He ordered the presidio of Cerro Gordo relocated to a small mesa about 15 miles south of the Rio Grande, believing that the new Presidio de San Carlos would benefit from the nearby water, farming land, wood, stone, and other resources. Oconor finally reached La Junta, which had been abandoned in 1751, because of the uncooperative attitudes of various frontier officials. He was dismayed to find only the ruins of the old presidio. Indians had burned the buildings, leaving only the parched adobe structure.

Oconor marched up the Río Conchos to investigate the presidio at Julimes, ordering it moved back to La Junta. He continued his tour of the frontier, relocating presidios as he went. He returned in 1774 to check construction and found that San Carlos was almost finished, but that San Vicente was behind schedule.[36]

Oconor's plan, however, was destined to fail. As a result of his journey, San Vicente and San Carlos were established in the Big Bend country south of the Rio Grande. But the plan was based on theory and on a similar project – the Roman military colonies – that had been successfully carried out, but under significantly different circumstances. Oconor had not considered the realities in the Big Bend in making his plans. A line of posts that proved convincing on a map in bureaucratic discussions simply did not provide the promised impenetrable wall or even offer adequate protection for nearby settlers. Despite an aggressive campaign carried out under Oconor's instructions against the Indians of the Big Bend, another investigation soon proved that the frontier could not be guarded by widely separated posts or so few troops.[37]

Las Provincias Internas

In 1776 the northern provinces of New Spain were reorganized. According to the reforms instituted by Charles III, the entire frontier was included in one administrative unit called the Provincias Internas. Charles named Teodoro de Croix, one of his ablest military men, commander general of the provinces. Croix arrived in Mexico City in December and remained there almost a year studying the reports of frontier governors and captains. He found a dismal scene, and decided that Oconor's reorganization was a mistake. The governor of Coahuila reported that the number of raids had actually increased since construction of the new presidios. José Rubio, an experienced frontiersman, described soldiers and presidios in such miserable shape that it was difficult to tell which was a worse problem, the Indians or the soldiers. The troops' weapons were old and ineffectual, the officers were poorly prepared and corrupt, discipline was lax. Communication was slow, the soldiers' pay lagged behind schedule, and the officers extracted a percentage when it did arrive.[38]

Croix hoped to implement an aggressive policy. He immediately requested an additional 2,000 troops for the frontier, then left on an inspection trip along with his chaplain, Father Juan Agustín de Morfi, who kept a detailed diary of the trip and later wrote a history of Texas. While circling the *despoblado,* Morfi noticed the situation was so desperate that many farmers had sentry boxes in their cornfields where they could hide in case of a sudden

Indian attack. Croix and Morfi visited the Big Bend presidios of San Carlos and San Vicente in early 1778. After several conferences, Croix decided that the Rio Grande was ineffective as a defense line. Moving the presidios to the river left the settlements unprotected.[39]

Several suggestions came out of Croix's talks. The frontiersmen urged the commander general to mount a 3,000-man campaign against the Apaches. The conferees suggested that detachments from Nueva Vizcaya be instructed to march into the *despoblado,* rout the Apaches, then turn northward to the presidios of San Carlos and San Vicente and meet troops from Coahuila, who, meantime, would have swept through the Sierra del Pino, and along the Río de San Pedro, the Ojos de las Nuezes, and the Agua Amargosa. Croix's officers also hoped to turn the Indians against each other by signing treaties with one faction or the other, thereby renewing old tribal hostilities, but they did not place as much confidence in this suggestion as in the offensive campaigns. Finally, Croix urged that the presidios again be relocated nearer the people.[40]

Croix's plans for a massive campaign against the Indians were doomed, however, when Spain entered the war against England in 1779. With all his military might sequestered for the European conflict, the king ordered Croix to employ peaceful means to overcome his enemies in New Spain. The commander general was, nevertheless, allowed to modify the frontier defenses to suit his scheme. He was convinced that placement of San Carlos and San Vicente on the Rio Grande was an error that created an artificial frontier. There was little support for either fort, communications were poor, and they were isolated, even though they had been intended to guard two important fords. Croix suggested that the garrisons be moved, but that the physical plants of the two presidios be kept to serve as bases against the Indians. Only La Junta would remain in the Big Bend area. Croix wanted to defend what he considered to be the real frontier, the area of the northernmost villages along the edge of the *despoblado,* not a false frontier created by bureaucratic decree.[41]

A More Aggressive Policy

Still, the Spaniards were not helpless. Juan de Ugalde, the governor of Coahuila, undertook a series of campaigns designed to break up the Apache concentrations in the Big Bend. The soldiers had ventured cautiously into the Bolson de Mapimí, in the heart of the *despoblado,* in 1779. A second campaign in 1780 took them to San Fernando de Austria, then to Monclova Vieja, and finally to Agua Verde. In 1781 Ugalde got as far as the Arroyo de la Babia and the deserted presidio of San Vicente before turning back. He found that the Indians had burned the presidio, destroying the roof and the main gate; it would provide little protection in a campaign. Ugalde made a third expedition into the *despoblado* in the spring of 1782, capturing or killing 50 Indians and regaining some 400 head of stock. A fourth expedition, terminating in early 1783, led him into the Big Bend country and completed his sweep of the entire Bolson region.[42]

After the close of the American Revolution and the Spanish committment of troops to Europe, the Spanish bureaucracy allowed hostilities to resume along the frontier. Ugalde's most extensive campaigns came in 1787. He set out in the snow of winter and reached San Vicente in March. After learning that the Indians were camped in the Chisos Mountains, he crossed the Rio Grande into the Big Bend National Park area and attacked the Mescalero band under chief Zapata Tuerto.

When Ugalde marched to San Carlos, he received a warning from the captain at La Junta that he was now in Nueva Vizcaya, beyond his range of authority. Ugalde angrily responded that he was in hot pursuit of Indians who had attacked his domain, but then realized that the Mescaleros who lived in this region were friendly to the Spaniards who occupied La Junta and had, in fact, signed treaties with them. It was the usual procedure for the Indians: they were friendly to the soldiers who guarded the region where they lived, and raided only in other areas.

Although Capt. Juan Bautista Elguézabal of La Junta insisted that the redmen were at peace with the Spaniards and tried to stop Ugalde, the Coahuila governor continued his assault. He raided a small *ranchería* near the Bofecillos Mountains, killing one and capturing six Indians. He turned northward, hoping to find another camp, but the Indians had been warned and had fled toward the Pecos. After further reconnaissances, Ugalde returned to Santa Rosa in August, where he met Picax-ande Ins-tinsle, the pressured Llanero leader, and concluded a treaty. Ugalde had risked a campaign into the *despoblado* and a jurisdictional conflict with his

45

46

Working from maps like this, Spaniards logically
concluded that the Rio Grande was navigable.
No topographic features are shown on this
"La Paz" map, which was probably made by
a cartographer who never visited the New World.

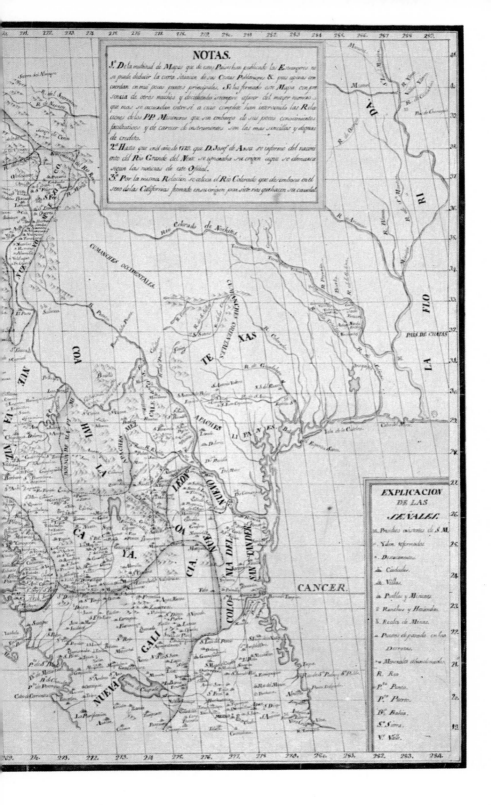

NOTAS.

1ª. De la multitud de Mapas que de estos Paises han publicado los Estrangeros no se puede deducir la cierta situacion de sus Costas Poblaciones &. pues apenas convienen en muy pocos puntos principales. Se ha formado este Mapa con presencia de otros muchos y decidiendo siempre á favor del mayor numero que mas se acuerdan entre sí: a cuio complète han intervenido las Relaciones de los PP. Misioneros que sin embargo de sus pocos conocimientos facultativos y de carecer de instrumentos son las mas sencillas y dignas de credito.

2ª. Hasta que en el año de 1770. que D. Josef de Anza se informo del nacimiento del Rio Grande del Norte se ignoraba su origen aqui se demarca segun las noticias de este Oficial.

3ª. Por la misma Relacion se coloca el Rio Colorado que desemboca en el seno de las Californias formado en su origen por siete rios que hacen su caudal.

EXPLICACION
DE LAS
SEÑALES.

a. Presidios existentes de S. M.

Ydem. reformados

Descubrimientos

Ciudades.

Villas.

Pueblos y Misiones.

Ranchos y Haciendas.

Reales de Minas.

Puestos de parada en los Derroteros.

Minerales abandonados.

R. Rio

P.ta Punta.

P.to Puerto.

B.a Bahia.

S.a Sierra.

V. Villa.

neighbor to the west, but he had achieved the desired end: peace in his domain. The viceroy approved.[43]

About 1783 an unknown Spanish mapmaker, confessedly using maps of foreign cartographers as well as travel accounts by various explorers, attempted to set down in graphic form all that the Spaniards then knew of the Big Bend. The general outline is fairly accurate. The bend in the river is recognizable, with the southernmost dip coming in Mariscal Canyon. San Carlos and San Vicente are correctly located south of the river, while the Chisos Indians are shown to be in control of the domain to the north. The Chisos Mountains are correctly positioned, and what appears to be the Basin, where the motel and cabin facilities are located today, is labeled "Basilio," which in today's usage translates as Basilian (a monk), but might have been somehow related to "basin" or "cloister" in the language of the 18th century. Dedicated to the "principe de la Paz"–hence the name "La Paz" map–the chart is probably the most accurate contemporary Spanish map of the Big Bend, even though it is the work of a cartographer who most likely never visited America.[44]

Judging from the La Paz map, the Spaniards probably knew more about the Indians than the Big Bend itself. To keep the Apaches at peace, the Spaniards had to protect them, for the warlike Comanches continued to press southward. The officials at La Junta guarded one Apache party during a buffalo hunt, and Ugalde offered protection to a group of Mescaleros who ventured into buffalo territory in late 1787. The Comanches attacked, but were repulsed by the Spaniards. The system apparently was working.[45]

During the last quarter century of Spanish rule in New Spain, the Indians were virtually at peace with the Spaniards on the frontier. Gov. Juan Bautista de Anza of New Mexico and Gov. Domingo Cabello of Texas concluded a treaty with the Comanches which called for the Comanches to aid the Spaniards in defeating the Apaches still at war. The increasing number of soldiers and location of the presidios made the raiding more difficult. Rubí's inspection along with Oconor's recommendations and Croix's visits had increased the efficiency, discipline, and training of the troops.

Oconor, Croix, and Ugalde had carried out campaigns designed to disperse the concentration of Indians throughout the *despoblado,* and Ugalde continued his forays, staying out as long as 7 months in 1789.[46]

In addition to putting military pressure on the Indians, the Spaniards also held out several inducements to peace. A friendly attitude by the commanders of the presidios made the Indians realize that the Spaniards could make their life easier. Reviving a program that had been used for over a century to help the Pueblos, the Spaniards offered the Indians food for their first year of peace and farm equipment and seed in subsequent years. The Spaniards also took advantage of the Apaches' fear of the marauding Comanches. When Viceroy Revilla Gigedo outlined a realistic program for peace in 1791 – the Spaniards would protect the Indians if they lived in peace – the Indians were quick to accept.[47]

Thus, a century of conflict came to an end. The Spaniards withdrew from the Big Bend. Their initial exploratory efforts had been failures. When it became evident that the Indians were difficult converts and that the Big Bend was not another Mexico, with gold and silver stored by the roomful, the Spaniards turned their attention elsewhere. They entered the Big Bend only because it was in the way; for years the route to New Mexico led down the Río Conchos to the Rio Grande and up that river to Santa Fe. The Big Bend finally captured the Spaniards' attention because of the nomadic and hostile Indians who hid there. It then became necessary to find a route through the *despoblado,* to locate presidios there, and finally to conduct raids of several months' duration in the heart of the present-day national park. The Spaniards were never interested in the Big Bend for any reason other than peace; it was an obstacle to overcome in establishing a secure frontier. But their peace did not last. The hostile Comanches continued their southward migration, soon presenting an even more serious threat that the Spaniards would not be around to answer.

3/The Chihuahua Trail

"Jack" Hays was an unusual man: respected captain of a Texas Ranger company during the Mexican War, good shot, eloquent commander, and shrewd military man, yet kind, respectful, and resourceful. For all that, he often bemused those who met him for the first time, for he was less than 5 feet tall, weighed about 150 pounds, and had a smooth, whiskerless face. A disciplined man in modest clothes, John Coffee Hays had an impenetrable countenance. His firm jaw foretold determination, and his piercing eyes betrayed nothing. "The fame of Colonel Hays rested on a substantial basis," explained one who had followed him. "It was acquired by hard fighting, by suffering privations, and by the exhibition of the high qualities adorning a citizen and soldier." [1] It was "Jack" Hays who, in 1848, led an expedition of adventurous, naive Texans into the Big Bend.

Hays' trip was not the result of a foolhardy plan. Dr. Henry Connelly, an American living in the city of Chihuahua and later Territorial Governor of New Mexico, had gathered between $200,000 and $300,000 in specie and gold bullion and organized a wagon train for such a trip in 1839. He hoped to initiate trade between Chihuahua and New Orleans, which he believed to be a more lucrative market than either Santa Fe or Independence, Mo. Leaving the Mexican city on April 3, the doctor crossed the Rio Grande at Presidio del Norte, a small village surrounding the site of La Junta de los Rios, and headed through the Big Bend along a route similar to the one Mendoza had charted over a century and a half before. Bouncing across the Texas plains, through the Cross Timbers to Fort Towson, and down the Red River and the Mississippi, he reached New Orleans a few months later with no unusual difficulties. [2]

New Orleans, unfortunately, was depleted of many goods that the merchants could have easily sold in Chihuahua, but after several weeks they obtained calicoes, prints, unbleached cottons, cloths, silks, and other items. The return trip was equally uneventful, except for a minor accident that cost them about $30,000 worth of goods when the steamboat towing them up the Red River

Sunset from the south rim of the Chisos.

51

Photograph by Bank Langmore

hit a snag. The 80-wagon train cut such a swath across the Texas prairies that their trail remained visible for several years. They left an even more graphic sign of their presence when they could not find their route through the dense Cross Timbers and were forced to hack a new trail.[3]

In West Texas the traders encountered Comanches, but passed them without a fight. Finding the Pecos too deep to ford, they resorted to an "expedient characteristic of the Prairies," according to Josiah Gregg, a veteran Santa Fe trader. They emptied several barrels, tied them to the bottom of each wagon, and floated it across the river. When they reached Presidio del Norte they found that the governor with whom they had reached agreement before leaving had died. Because he had no investment in the project, the new governor was not as friendly to their endeavors and threatened to charge the full tariff. Forty-five days were required to negotiate a compromise. The caravan finally entered Chihuahua on August 27, 1840. "The delays and accumulated expenses of this expedition caused it to result so disastrously," claimed Gregg in 1844, "that no other enterprise of the kind has since been undertaken."[4]

Hays knew that the caravan had not ended satisfactorily for the investors, but it had stirred interest in a wagon route through the Big Bend. While in New Orleans, Connelly had assured the Louisianians that if their government would encourage the commerce, "the whole trade of Chihuahua, and as far west as the Pacific ocean," would be theirs. Some reporters waxed enthusiastic, claimed that Chihuahua contained the "richest gold mines in all Mexico" and that bullion would find its way to New Orleans even though the Mexican government prohibited its exportation. The distant *Western Star* of Lebanon, Ohio, believed that Americans should come to know Chihuahua better. Texans held even stronger convictions because a change in the trade pattern obviously would divert commerce to San Antonio, Houston, or Corpus Christi. The editor of the Houston *Morning Star* endorsed efforts to establish a permanent post on the Red River for the Chihuahua trade, hoping, of course, that Houston might be able to divert some of the trade because of its favorable location near the Gulf of Mexico.[5] Con-

Henry Connelly   Capt. "Jack" Hays

nelly's expedition had proved that the trip could be made, and that the trade could be profitable under favorable conditions.

Others hesitated, however, wondering if Connelly had not been extremely fortunate in safely crossing a virtually unexplored region known to be populated with hostile Indians. Few travelers had entered the Big Bend since the Spaniards had recalled their soldiers in the face of the on-rushing Comanches. Yet Connelly's caravan encountered only routine difficulties. The Indian threat combined with the poor return on investment and the Mexican War proved sufficient to dampen for a few years whatever enthusiasm there might have been in a Chihuahua Trail.

Interest rekindled in 1847 when Maj. John Polk Campbell and 39 Mexican War veterans left Chihuahua headed for Fort Towson via Presidio del Norte. Traveling over a route that the editor of the *Western Star* claimed was superior to the Santa Fe Trail, Campbell and his party safely reached their destination several weeks later, having sighted no hostile Indians. Three other Mexican War veterans in Chihuahua, Ben Leaton, John W. Spencer, and John D. Burgess, thought the route had a good future and decided to establish a mercantile business at Presidio. After buying property in the village in 1848, they left for the United States to purchase sale goods. Upon their return they learned that the land on the left bank now belonged to the United States as a result of the Treaty of Guadalupe Hidalgo, which ended the Mexican War. They obtained land from several Mexicans on the American side and moved their operations across the river. Leaton constructed a fortification to protect his property (today a historic site). Theirs was the first American settlement in the Big Bend.[6]

53

The Hays-Highsmith Expedition

By this time "Jack" Hays had decided to lead his own party into the Big Bend. He found merchants and newspapermen throughout the State excited about the expedition; among those who signed up for the trek was Samuel Maverick, a prominent citizen of San Antonio, who was given the task of keeping a journal of the trip. The expedition was widely publicized in the State's newspapers. Expectations ran high. On August 27 the party left San Antonio and headed for El Paso. At the Llano River they joined Capt. Samuel Highsmith and his Texas Rangers, who were to protect them from Indian attack.[7]

Oblivious of the dangers, the 35 adventurers set out on September 4 up the Llano. They crossed Comanche Creek and James Creek, then proceeded to the Nueces River. At Las Moras Creek, a tributary of the Rio Grande, they met some friendly Indians who advised them to pursue a more westerly course. As they paralleled the Rio Grande, crossing creek after creek, Hays finally realized that the inaccurate map he carried was worthless. He eventually arrived at the river the Indians called "Puerco," which had steep banks and such a crooked course (Hays crossed it eight times within a mile) that he renamed it Devil's River. The march continued uneventfully into the Big Bend.

There the trouble began. Food ran short. Men turned to eating their mules, prickly pears, and whatever else they could find. The expedition's physician, a Doctor Wahm, strangely refused to eat. Two nights later he went insane, perhaps from eating some of the many alkaline plants that grow in the Big Bend, and fled into the hills. Sam Maverick noted in his journal that the men killed and ate a panther on October 2 and began eating bear grass on the 7th. Passing near Boquillas Canyon in the Sierra del Carmen, the party crossed to the Mexican side of the river near San Vicente, hoping to find food. The mountains were even more rugged on the right bank. By the time they stumbled onto the village of San Carlos, the site of the abandoned Spanish presidio, Hays and his campanions had been without food for 12 days.[8]

Rumors of their hardships quickly filtered back to San Antonio. Several adventurers had left the city a few days after Hays, and near Devil's River they overtook the expedition. After traveling with them for a few days, however, the disheartened late-starters returned to San Antonio. They reported that Hays was out of provisions, traveling over rugged ground and already killing his horses for food. Because the party was gone so long, many suspected a disaster. The editor of the *Corpus Christi Star,* who had hoped that the Chihuahua Trail would one day reach as far as his city, conceded that the expedition had encountered "more difficulties than had been anticipated." [9]

But the Hays party had endured the worst of the Big Bend. They refreshed themselves with bread and milk in San Carlos, then continued the journey to Presidio del Norte. While at Presidio, the Texans provisioned themselves at Ben Leaton's ranch. They purchased mules and food from Leaton and remained there about 10 days, recovering from their near-fatal march across the Big Bend.[10]

El Paso, their original goal, lay 150 miles farther west, but the men physically could not continue. The leaders decided to give up. They voted to return to San Antonio by a more northerly route, passing by Horsehead Crossing and Live Oak Creek. This route was not so treacherous as their outbound path, and they did not suffer as much from either heat or lack of water. But they did encounter Indians who stole six horses, which they recovered a few days later. On December 12 a battered force trudged into San Antonio, having traveled some 1,303 miles by their own calculation.[11]

Hays gave reports of his trip to the citizens of San Antonio who had sponsored it and to the Federal Government, which was interested in establishing a fort in the Big Bend. His route west was treacherous, he said. "The whole of this part of the country, from the mouth of Devil's River up the Rio Grande, as far as San Carlos, a town 40 miles south of Presidio del Norte, is one constant succession of high broken mountains, destitute of timber and water." Returning by a more northerly course, he found a better trail and more water. Had his guide been competent or the map accurate, he might have had no problem on the way out, but the guide was "entirely ignorant of this part of the country"–few people besides Indians knew anything substantial of the Big Bend in 1848–and the map was sketchy. His mistakes led Hays and his party into avoidable hardships. After dismissing the guide, Hays took charge of the party and led it to San Carlos by his own reckoning.

Hays characteristically minimized the Indian attack and recommended the northern route as the safe, easier one. By avoiding the lower portion of the Big Bend, the wagon trains would be able to pass over "beautiful and level country," he said. The only obstacle would be the Pecos River, which could easily be forded except during seasonal crests.[12]

Travelers in the Big Bend

The discovery of gold in California drew others to the Big Bend. By 1849 literally thousands of gold seekers were traveling to California; many observers expected the Forty-Niners to find a route across Texas. "Reference to the map indicated that an overland route to the new El Dorado would . . . pass . . . not very far from Austin," wrote John S. Ford, a doctor and former Texas Ranger recently returned from Mexico. Austin citizens decided to send Ford on an exploratory trip to see whether a good road could be found between Austin and El Paso. Since the U.S. Army was also looking for a western route, Ford joined Maj. Robert S. Neighbors, Texas Indian Agent, for the jaunt. They left in March, tracing a route north of the Big Bend, by Brady's Creek, Horse-

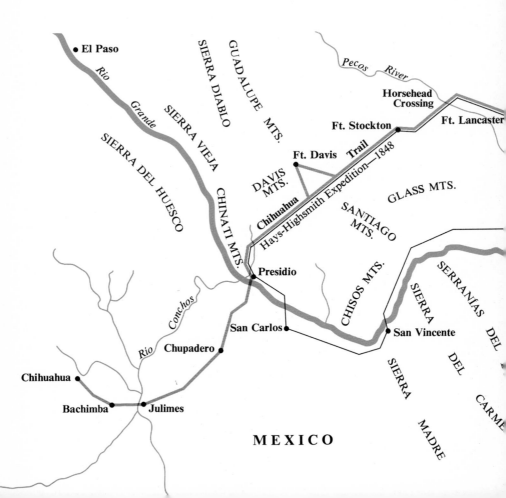

head Crossing, then west to the headwaters of the Concho River. After reaching Brady's Creek, they swung southward through Fort Mason, Fredericksburg, and San Antonio.[13]

Immigrants obviously needed an up-to-date map. So in the fall of 1848 Jacob de Cordova rushed into print with a map drawn by Robert Creuzbaur, the head draftsman of the State land office. Few details are shown for the Big Bend, but a caravan route from the Arkansas River in 1840 is depicted. If Creuzbaur intended to show Connelly's route, he probably placed it several miles too far north. For months de Cordova's map was the only one listed for sale in the advertisements of the *New York Tribune*. Using information gleaned from expeditions by Capt. John C. Frémont, Lt. Philip St. George Cooke, Lt. William H. Emory, Dr. Adolph Wislizenus, from Hays, Neighbors, and Ford following the war, and from the records of the State land office, Creuzbaur prepared his own guide book to aid the hundreds of Forty-Niners who were passing through Texas on their way to California. Entitled *Route*

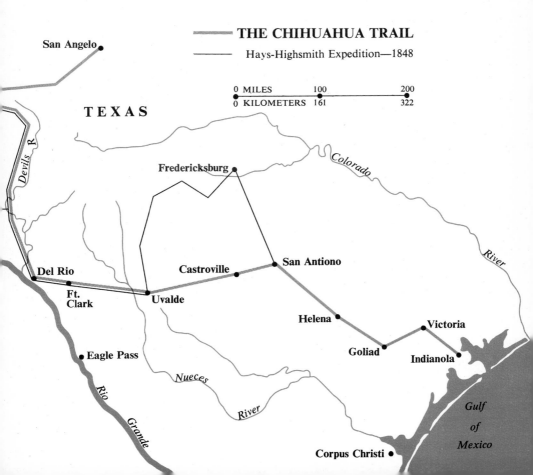

THE CHIHUAHUA TRAIL

Hays-Highsmith Expedition—1848

0 MILES 100 200
0 KILOMETERS 161 322

TEXAS

San Angelo

Devils R.

Colorado

Fredericksburg

Del Rio
Castroville   San Antiono
Ft. Clark   Uvalde

Eagle Pass   Helena   Victoria

Goliad   Indianola

Nueces

River

Rio Grande

River

Gulf of Mexico

Corpus Christi

From the Gulf of Mexico and the Lower Mississippi Valley to California and the Pacific Ocean, the Creuzbaur work had a sizable national audience. On it Creuzbaur specifically drew Connelly's trail, indicating that the doctor passed closer to what is today the national park than he really did. Still, there is almost no information on the Big Bend itself, for little was known in 1849. Interest in the western route was so great that the *Texas State Gazette* also published the route of another Forty-Niner for all other "western adventurers" who were interested in where the waterholes and passes were throughout West Texas.[14]

Hays and his fellow travelers had crossed the most difficult part of the Big Bend. Their success encouraged others. Traders and Forty-Niners launched out across the plains. George W. B. Evans and a party from Ohio tried a different route. Instead of heading west from San Antonio, they journeyed through Eagle Pass and San Fernando. Hiring a Mexican guide, they then turned westward toward San Carlos, roughly along the path that Rábago had traveled a century before. It was a difficult journey through a bleak country at least as rough as the trails on the American side of the Rio Grande. "Kind reader, this is work, labor that requires the strength and exertion of every muscle of the body, and nature almost sinks under these repeated trials and privations," Evans noted in his journal. "Our limbs are sore and stiffened by this continued labor, and God only knows when we will find ourselves again upon the plains below." For an 80-mile stretch the party found no waterhole. One member of the group was lost in the desert. Evans also mistrusted the guide. Threatened by Apaches and Comanches every step of the way, he feared that the guide probably had agreed to lead the party into an ambush in return for part of the booty. The *despoblado* was so barren that they marched to within 10 miles of San Carlos without realizing it. Searching for words to "convey a perfect idea of this almost forsaken town," Evans pointed out that there were houses of "dried mud" and "upright poles plastered with mud." "There are no streets, but everything of or concerning this town is arranged in admirable confusion." The Forty-Niners continued the journey to Presidio del

Norte and Chihuahua, having crossed one of the most rugged parts of the *despoblado*.[15]

Corpus Christi merchants, in a favorable position on the Gulf of Mexico to make their city a shipping center, showed interest in the Chihuahua trade. The editor of the *Corpus Christi Star* argued with newspapermen in Houston as to which city was better located for the trade. The editor of the *Star* printed stories about the Hays expedition and was anxious to get the formal report. In September 1848 he announced plans of H. L. Kinney and other Corpus merchants to sponsor a wagon train to "open the road for permanent trade with Chihuahua." The expedition would be as "large as possible," he declared, and an "invitation is held out to all who may wish to join it." Kinney also hoped to obtain the U.S. mail contract for western Texas.[16]

While the train organized, the editor raved about the possibilities of trade over the western road. He glorified Lts. Francis T. Bryan's and Nathaniel Michler's trailblazing in early 1849. He printed letters from travelers claiming a good road existed from Corpus to Presidio del Norte. And his publicity campaign was successful. The editor of the *New Orleans Picayune* was convinced that the Hays route would divert trade from Santa Fe to Texas. "A glance at the map shows that San Antonio is the nearest from the United States to Chihuahua," he concluded, and "a trail or plank road" from San Antonio to the coast would rapidly bring the trade to New Orleans.[17]

The long train was finally ready for departure from Corpus Christi on July 17, 1849. For over a week, carts gathered in the city, and teamsters drove their wagons through the streets, a few leaving each day for the rendezvous point. Gen. William L. Cazneau, a prominent businessman, led such other well-known residents as Col. Jacob Snively in an effort to establish trading posts at Presidio del Norte and El Paso del Norte. Bearing perhaps $90,000 worth of goods for Chihuahua, the 100-man party headed westward toward Leona Creek. When they reached the Big Bend, Indians "hovered about" the 50 wagons so threateningly that the teamsters finally fired upon them. Whatever happened to the train — we have no evidence of its fate — the next trace of Cazneau has him founding a trading post at Eagle Pass the following year to foster his plans for Mexican trade.[18]

Cazneau was not the only speculator in the Chihuahua trade. In May 1849, Capt. W. W. Thompson left Fredericksburg with a party headed for El Paso. Employing Joe Robinson, the Delaware Indian who had been with Hays, the Thompson party traveled the

59

**Robert Creuzbaur's map was in great demand by
the argonauts en route to the California gold fields.
He was among the first to suggest a route
through the unknown Big Bend country.**

AUTHORITES

1. Fremont's Map of 1848.

2. Emory's Map of 1847.

3. Wislizenus's Map of 1847.

4. The Records of the Genl. Land-
   Office of the State of Texas.
   And others.

northern route, anticipating few hardships. Robert Hunter, a member of the expedition, expressed their shock at the country in a letter to his wife. "We have travelled two hundred and forty miles without seeing any timber and at two different times we drove two days and nights without water over mountains and ravines on the route that Jack Hays said he found water so plenty, and if he had been in sight he would not have lived one minute. Our mules suffered immensely, but the men done very well as we had gourds and kegs." [19]

A Houston editor predicted a "snug little fortune" for the Bayou City merchant who left the city with his goods and declared that he would "not unload them till his wagon arrived at the public square" in El Paso. Persons who made the trip with Neighbors in 1850 reported that common products such as tobacco, domestics, and coffee were selling at seven or eight times their price in Houston. Although the Houston merchant intended to continue on to California to hunt for gold, the editor predicted that "we should not be surprised to hear that this adventurer should conclude to forego his journey to California and return to Houston for another stock of goods for the Chihuahua market. . . ." Such was the optimism that awaited the trade. [20]

An expedition under a Major Sprague was organized in San Antonio to start in April 1850 for El Paso. The caravan consisted of 200 Mexican carts and two companies of mounted troops. A local editor reported that other Alamo City merchants had departed for New Orleans and New York to purchase trade goods. Newspapers quickly reported journeys across the Trans-Pecos, emphasizing the ever-decreasing amount of time required to make the journey and the fact that difficulties were minor. One Robert Hays made the trek in just 31 days, and two merchants named Durand and Holliday made it in less than 20 days, according to the editor of the *San Antonio Ledger*. [21]

But merchants were more interested in the trip made by Maj. W. S. Henry, of the 3d Infantry Regiment in the summer of 1850, because he carried many goods and wagons. Departing El Paso on August 26, Henry, along with 18 persons, three wagons with mules, and one ambulance, arrived in San Antonio on September 13, causing the *Western Texan* to think it was the "quickest trip ever made with wagons." The *San Antonio Texan* noted the visit of 30 or 40 emigrants who passed through the city en route to the gold fields of California, as well as Charles Wiggins' wagon train that left San Antonio in the spring of 1850 for El Paso and the Chihuahua trade. The editor also reported that several other merchants were loading their goods at Indianola and Lavaca in preparation for the trip to Chihuahua. An encouraging account of the route and conditions came from a traveler who made the journey from Fredericksburg. "I had as pleasant a trip as could be expected," he reported. Following such successful journeys, the editor of the *Western Texan* declared the search for a route to El Paso and Chihuahua over. "It is now reduced to a 'fixed fact' that the best, safest, and shortest route . . . is through Texas, by way of San Antonio."[22]

Conflict with the Indians

Although newspapermen boosted the route for the good it would do their cities, they all realized the primary difficulty with the western route–the Indians. Many Argonauts had made the trip through the Big Bend without a fight, but the Comanches and Apaches were becoming increasingly inhospitable. A "reliable gentleman" who traveled through northern Mexico in 1849 reported that there was "scarcely a ranch throughout all those states that has not been sacked by the Indians." Durand and Holliday, on their return trip from El Paso, found the road to be "much infested" by them. The "insolent and hostile disposition manifested by these savages" forced the pair to confine their traveling to night. A party of travelers arrived in La Grange from Presidio del Norte to report that the Apaches were "almost daily committing depredations . . . plundering the inhabitants and driving off their stock." The country was in "miserable condition" according to James T. Peacock, a member of the expedition. Indians constantly crossed the Rio Grande into Mexico, where they robbed and killed the inhabitants "with impunity," then returned to Texas. Another party was stopped by Mescalero Apaches, probably led by Chief Gomez, who demanded cattle but refused to specify how many, preferring to leave that to the discretion (or fear) of the owners. Considered the terror of Chihuahua and West Texas, Gomez and his warriors claimed the Davis Mountains and the Big Bend as their domain and challenged anyone who entered. Other parties were raided, travelers wounded, and cattle stolen.[23]

The Comanches and Apaches were protecting their last

stronghold: the *despoblado*. Applying to the newcomers what had been an enormously successful formula in Mexico, they had ruled supreme in the Trans-Pecos ever since the departure of the Spaniards, when Mexico won its independence in 1821. Weakened by internal difficulties, Mexico had never been able to establish any measure of control over the Big Bend, then lost the region entirely in 1836 when Texas won its independence. Nor could the Texans exert any influence beyond the Pecos River. For years the Big Bend was left to the Indians, who rode from their homes in present-day New Mexico, Oklahoma, and West Texas through the Big Bend into Mexico, where they killed and plundered the settlements along the northern border in what has become recognized as one of the most sustained devastations of the advancing frontier. Then they returned, leaving a path of destruction and prairie fires as they eluded their pursuers, much as their ancestors had done in the previous century. The struggle for supremacy began when the newcomers seeking trade with El Paso and Chihuahua, gold in California, or settlement in the Big Bend itself infringed on what the Indians had kept to themselves for decades.

Apaches and Comanches occupied the Big Bend more or less by default. Buffeted and forced from more fertile lands to the north, they had moved into the void known as the *despoblado* and adjusted their life styles. The meager existence they gleaned from the sparse plants and fleet animals of the Big Bend soon convinced them that they could live better by stealing from the frontier villages and frequent wagon trains that ventured through the region, a logical conclusion for a people that had been driven from their original homelands and continually pressured by the advancing Anglo-Americans, who took the land for their own sustenance.

The Indians were difficult to defeat, for they alone knew how to exist in the Big Bend. The Sol family of the Comanches, for example, lived for years in West Texas and Mexico, ravaging Mexicans to earn their living. Led by Arriba el Sol, the matriarch of the clan, they made their permanent home somewhere along the Colorado River of Texas, but roamed for much of the year in the Big Bend and northern Mexico. Arriba el Sol had two grandsons, Bajo el Sol and Mague, who were talented leaders and

A Lipan warrior encountered by the U.S. Boundary Survey. From a lithograph in Emory's *Report*.

excellent warriors. Because Comanche warriors were free to choose their own leaders, the Sols had a large following.[24]

The Great Comanche War Trail

The Sols entered Mexico over the Comanche War Trail, which crossed the Trans-Pecos from the northeast, then split into two forks when it reached the Big Bend. One fork crossed the Rio Grande near present-day Lajitas, then continued into Mexico via San Carlos and the Río Conchos valley. The main trail crossed the Rio Grande at the Chisos ford, between Santa Elena and Mariscal Canyons, then continued by the Laguna de Jaco into the eastern portion of the *despoblado*. So distinctive was this trail that explor-

65

Muchos Toros, a sub-chief in Bajo el Sol's band.

ers never failed to mention it if they saw it. A mile wide in places, it was littered with the skeletons of livestock driven from Mexico. Colonel Langberg reported that it was "wider than any 'royal road,' " and "so well beaten that it appears that suitable engineers had constructed it." The land was rutted and in some spots vegetation was burned off, graphically revealing the extent to which the Comanches had subdued the heretofore untamed Big Bend country.*

The Sols spent most of each summer camping in abandoned mining districts, around waterholes, and at times near springs known to the Mexicans. While their horses and animals grazed on

---

* Today the great trail is almost invisible, even to the trained eye. A research team from the University of Texas found that erosion and vegetation have changed the complexion of the thoroughfare and made it almost impossible to distinguish the trail from the surrounding desert.

The Chihuahua Trail

the best grass the *despoblado* could produce, the warriors participated in several camp games: horse racing and a form of ball playing probably similar to lacrosse. Because they were not disturbed in the *despoblado,* the Sols could establish fairly peaceful camps and disperse small raiding parties in all directions.

The warriors prepared for a raid by gathering at Bajo el Sol's tepee and dancing to rhythms beaten out with sticks. Then the warriors met in council with the elders to ensure a successful mission. The warriors spent the night at the edge of the camp, and the next day began their march, riding all of each day until they reached their destination. The raiding parties were sometimes quite large; often they were as small as half-a-dozen warriors. They raided any tempting target along the route. When they reached their destination, they spent the night nearby and attacked the following day. They took everything they could: livestock, blankets, church ornaments, harness gear, housewares, and captives.

They herded their booty back through the Big Bend via the Chisos ford to avoid coming too close to Presidio del Norte. Once again in Texas, they traded the livestock, sold the other goods, and ransomed the captives. In return they received rifles, bullets, swords, tobacco, whiskey, and other goods from the American traders, and iron for arrow tips and spear points from the Mexicans at San Carlos, which often made them better armed than the Mexican army. Col. Emilio Langberg, Inspector of the Military Colonies of Chihuahua, complained to Maj. Jefferson Van Horne that Ben Leaton had been supplying the Apaches and Comanches with lead, powder, arms, and "other articles of ammunition." Chihuahua Governor Ángel Trias charged Leaton with "a thousand abuses, and of so hurtful a nature, that he keeps an open treaty with the Apache Indians . . . ." [25]

The Sols managed by shrewd diplomacy to prevent the Mexicans from organizing a unified effort to exterminate them. When the Mexican government declared a "war of extermination" on the Indians of the north, the Sols responded by making treaties with the local governments, agreeing that they would not raid in that particular area and would help fight the Apaches. This not only left the Sols free to raid in other areas of Mexico, but it also gave them protection in the region where they concluded the treaty. Other Indians performed similar feats with the United States and Mexico, reaching an agreement with one country while continuing to raid in the other. Indian Agent Robert S. Neighbors feared that was the arrangement some Northern Comanches had with Chihuahua in 1854. The United States had difficulty making treaties with the

Indians of the Big Bend, on the other hand, because contact was sporadic. The Indians were not only hostile, they were also elusive. When Agent J. A. Rogers dispatched an interpreter to arrange contact with the Mescaleros, for example, he found only a few near Presidio del Norte, because a drought had driven them from the Big Bend.[26]

The Southwestern Scalp Hunters

The Mexican government tried several measures to stop the Sols and their allies. The military was seemingly useless because

James Kirker, also called "Santiago," whose name usually struck fear in the hearts of Mexicans and Indians alike.

68

William A. "Bigfoot" Wallace delivered the mail and fought Indians in the Big Bend.

the officers did not know either the ways of Indian warfare or the *despoblado*. Individual ranches, even the large ones, were virtually helpless against the hit and run raids of the Sols. For their own defense citizens constructed featureless houses of thick adobe. There were no windows or chimneys. "Many are built like forts, and may be considered as such," concluded George Evans, who viewed them in 1846. Ben Leaton copied the pattern for his ranchhouse near Presidio, which still stands, as did Milton Faver at his La Ciénega Ranch. In desperation, the local governments in Chihuahua and Durango offered bounties on scalps of unfriendly Indians, sometimes as much as $200 for each scalp, with additional money for the hair of a leader like Bajo el Sol. Dozens of Americans went south during the 1830s and after the Mexican War to take advantage of the opportunity. Some, who had intended to go to California and search for gold instead, soon found that scalp hunting was like "discovering a mine." Joel Glanton and James Kirker became near celebrities on the border because of their prowess in gathering scalps. Adventurers, ex-Texas Rangers, former U.S. soldiers, and villains joined them in the "vile industry." They were not always too careful about whose scalp they collected, because it was difficult to distinguish among Anglo, Mexican, or Indian once the lock had shriveled and dried, but the Mexican officials might have felt their cause had been served anyway. Samuel E. Chamberlain, famous for his paintings of the Mexican War and himself a scalp hunter for a short time, noted that Gen. José Urrea encouraged the bounty hunters, but held them in such low esteem that he "seemed equally pleased when Ranger or Indian went under."[27]

When merchants and explorers crossed the Big Bend, therefore, they entered the domain of the Apaches and Comanches. As the trade along the trail increased, incidents of harassment by Indians became more frequent. South of San Antonio the Indians seemed to have "entire possession" of the road. By 1852 every arrival of the mail train brought tales of new depredations: Apaches riding down on teamsters en route from Fort Fillmore, N. Mex., to Leona Station (Fort Inge), Texas; Indians attacking the mail train itself. William A. ("Bigfoot") Wallace was in charge of the mail train when his party was attacked on the afternoon of September 9, 1852. While they were camped near the Painted Caves of the Pecos River, more than 30 redmen charged into their midst. "We raised our rifles to fire on them," Bigfoot later recalled. "The Indians . . . fell back, circling around us [and] took possession of the top of Big Bluff, directly over our camp, and then the *fandango* began . . . ." The fight lasted but a short time, and there were only a few casualties. Rather than risk death in another frontal assault, the Indians waited until the whites broke camp. Bigfoot had anticipated their move, however, and retreated. "I could not by any means pass the Indians with the mail on mule back," he claimed after he had returned to San Antonio. But, still hoping to fulfill the mailman's creed, Wallace took on reinforcements – bringing his total force to nine – and headed for El Paso again. "If we cannot clear the road," he promised, "we shall fight it out with them." Any survivors would make their way to El Paso for the return mail.[28]

Each wagon train had to be prepared for an Indian attack. August Santleben, who freighted on the Chihuahua Trail for several years, recalled that the teamsters in his train realized that they were watched throughout the trip. They always left two men to guard the mules, even during meals. If possible, teamsters stood watch from a prominent peak, so they could view the entire area around the camp. At night, four men stood guard and were relieved every 2 hours. While in transit the freighters always stood ready to circle their wagons to provide a makeshift fort for protection against the expected attack. Unless the teamsters were overpowered by superior numbers, said Santleben, this tactic usually worked. There was no delay in resuming the trip after the Indians retreated, for all but two teams remained hitched during the engagement.[29]

Barren Country

Indian attacks were not the only hardship confronting travelers. The country was deserted; where there were once continuous orchards, gardens, haciendas, and "happy peons, shepherds and goatherds" between El Paso and Presidio, according to a correspondent who signed himself Melnotte, now there was only a "collection of squalid mud huts. All is desolation and ruins" because of the raids. Scarcity of water and grass often forced the teamsters to travel from waterhole to waterhole. This procedure frequently slowed Santleben's progress, for sometimes he made only 30 miles a day, when he could have pushed on perhaps twice that distance in better country. D. A. Tucker wrote that he and the 72 men in his party remained "on the hinges of starvation" during more than half their trip from East Texas to California. Colonel Langberg of the Mexican Boundary Survey team discovered discarded wagons and graves of American travelers between Santa Rosa and San Carlos.[30]

The same factors that had defeated the Spaniards withstood the American assault. Harsh terrain was rendered even more inhospitable by the severity of the Big Bend weather. In the fall water and grass became scarce. Capt. William Smith described the immense "suffering and loss" among the pioneers headed for El Paso in August 1854. The Fairchild and McClure expedition lost 200 head of cattle for lack of water. Dunlap's party lost 700 cattle while passing through the Big Bend. Smith reported that the path

71

was "literally strewn with their carcases [*sic*]." Terrain caused a particular problem because the freight wagons were built for level ground. The wagon bed was 24 feet long, but only 4½ feet wide. High loads usually made the vehicle top-heavy. Santleben pointed out that this made the wagons sway from side to side, putting the weight first on one set of wheels and then the other. The load was easier to pull, but when the teamsters encountered the rougher roads in the Big Bend, the wagons frequently turned over. So the teamsters used ropes to hold them upright while they passed through the roughest parts of the country. Sometimes a dozen men were needed on the ropes to keep a load from spilling. Santleben recalled that the route between San Antonio and El Paso was a "constant drag." [31]

Nor was there any law enforcement in the towns along the route. Tucker reported that everyone had survived the "difficulties and privations" along the road, except for Walter Beard, who had been stabbed by B. B. Lee, another member of the expedition in El Paso. James Poole, who passed through El Paso, decried the "lynch law" that prevailed in the town. [32]

Diplomacy

At Presidio the traders had to go through Mexican customs, which could be an ordeal. Since there were no firm customs laws, according to George L. Macmanus, the American consul in Chihuahua, the traders had to negotiate with the customs officer when they arrived at Presidio. When James P. Hickman arrived in Chihuahua in 1858, he was presented with a bill for the same tax he had paid in Presidio. When he refused to pay, his wagons were confiscated and the matter was taken to court. There a stalemate occurred. The justice of the peace, realizing that Hickman was being cheated, refused to rule against Hickman because he was right. But the justice also refused to rule against the government for fear that he himself would be punished. "The govor. is winking at the whole transaction," concluded Macmanus, "thus Mr. Hickman is swindled out of his money." The matter was resolved, of course, by Hickman paying the tax, but Macmanus asked the American government to protest the decision, claiming that "we are in constant dread of some new imposition . . . ." [33]

Because of the Chihuahua Trail, the Big Bend was on the verge of becoming an important trade route. The Hays expedition had attracted publicity throughout Texas and Louisiana. The Ford-Neighbors party found what probably was a better route to El Paso, and Forty-Niners, traders, and settlers began their move into the Big Bend. Yet if this upstart trail were to rival the established Santa Fe Trail, several things had to be accomplished. It had to be made safe from Indians, and it had to be further surveyed and physically improved. In 1850 the power to accomplish these goals rested with the Army and the Topographical Engineers.

4/ The Topographical Engineers

The great Chihuahua Desert, capped by the Chisos Mountains and penetrated only by the Rio Grande and its tributaries, must have played through Lt. Col. Joseph E. Johnston's mind as he prepared the official report on his reconnaissance of the Big Bend in 1850. While searching for a wagon road through the Big Bend, he had crossed tiny streams and creeks that bore the names of mighty rivers and often lived up to their names during the rainy season. After studying Indian trails in Wild Rose Pass and Persimmon Gap, he had learned from the Mexicans south of the Rio Grande that devastating raids were a common occurrence and had to be accepted as a fact of life.

Johnston's immediate tasks were to explore the river and the Big Bend for a site for an army post. He probably noted, as he drew one of the first accurate maps of the region, that there were almost no permanent settlements or place names in the Big Bend, and he might have suspected that the Topographical Engineers would play a great role in opening up the country to settlers. He clearly made the most of a difficult situation, for there were few benefits attached to the job of chief Topographical Engineer in Texas when he was appointed to the post in 1848.[1]

Johnston first arrived in the Big Bend about the time merchants became interested in West Texas. The United States had acquired the vast Southwest in the Mexican War of 1846-48. Many people believed that this area could not be absorbed into the Union because it was so large and removed from the settled portion of the country. Col. John J. Abert, commander of the Topographical Engineers, believed the situation was so desperate that first priority should be assigned to completing a road into the new territory. The "integrity of the Union" was at stake, he said. Part of the proposed route that would extend from San Antonio, Tex., to San Diego, Calif., had been charted by Lt. William H. Emory, who had explored from Santa Fe to the Gila River as a member of Col. Stephen W. Kearny's "Army of the West" in 1846, but the 500-mile stretch from San Antonio to El Paso del Norte was an un-

The Rio Grande between Presidio and the western boundary of the park.

75

Photograph by Bank Langmore

known highway of horrors to most merchants.[2]

Secretary of War William L. Marcy had already directed the engineers to find a better road between San Antonio and Santa Fe, and by 1849 they were hard at work. With the knowledge gleaned by the Hays-Highsmith expedition, Lts. William H. C. Whiting and William F. Smith had set out for El Paso to find a route that would serve both military and commercial purposes. Contending with hostile Apaches and lack of water, Whiting and Smith did improve upon the Hays-Highsmith route to the extent that their trail was used for the first mail run between San Antonio and El Paso in 1850, but they did not fully satisfy the requirements of the army. "Unless some easy, cheap, and rapid means of communicating with these distant provinces be accomplished," said Abert, "there is danger, great danger, that they will not constitute parts of our Union." [3]

The experience of Hays, Ford, and Whiting showed that the job would be strenuous. Assuming that the Indians could eventually be suppressed, Lt. William F. Smith, who knew the Big Bend first-hand, predicted that the foremost obstacle in their path would be the inhospitable terrain. "When the nature of the country is seen by those who may hereafter pass over the road," he remarked, "it may excite surprise; but it will not be that so practicable a route has been found, but rather that any was found at all." [4]

But in 1849 the Indians had not been conquered. The Mexicans were never able to pacify the frontier, even as successfully as Spain had. The Mexican War brought people into the Big Bend, and a process of reclamation began. Johnston and his men were among the first Americans to deal with the Indians of the Big Bend.

Exploration of the Rio Grande

Johnston divided up the exploration of the Big Bend. He first assigned men to explore further the routes that had already been mapped: Hays-Highsmith, Ford-Neighbors, and Whiting-Smith. Lt. Francis T. Bryan was dispatched to explore the Ford-Neighbors route, while he and Lt. Smith took the southern route. The harsh country forced Johnston to look for other routes as well. Although he was unaware of the thwarted Spanish dreams of navigating the Rio Grande, he probably knew of Gen. Thomas J. Green's claim in

1844 that "a steamboat can leave Pittsburg, and go to within three hundred miles of the navigable waters of the Gulf of California," presumably via the Rio Grande and the Río Conchos. Johnston hoped that the Rio Grande might be navigable and strongly urged that the engineers devote their time to its exploration between Eagle Pass and the confluence of the Rio Grande and the Pecos. He pointed out that by using the river the army could shorten the distance that goods had to be hauled overland. He also wanted to open the river to steamboat traffic, a much more economical means of transportation than wagons. Secretary of War C. M. Conrad's hope also soared as he informed the President that navigation of the Rio Grande would save the army both time and money. [5]

Acting on instructions from Abert, the engineers momentarily directed their efforts toward a thorough exploration of the river. They were probably influenced by the enthusiasm of Maj. W. W. Chapman, who reported Capt. John Love's trip up the Rio Grande in 1850. Chapman claimed that Love had navigated upriver as far as Presidio, a distance of approximately 1,000 miles. The land trip to El Paso could have been shortened by several hundred miles if Chapman's report had been true, but it did not take the engineers long to disprove it. Johnston instructed Lts. Martin L. Smith and Nathaniel Michler to begin at Ringgold Barracks, on the lower Rio Grande in Starr County, and proceed upriver. Lts. William F. Smith and Francis T. Bryan journeyed to El Paso, where they put in the water and floated as far downriver as they could. Smith and Michler explored the river to a point some 80 miles above the confluence of the Rio Grande and the Pecos, where they ran out of provisions and had to turn back. Even at that, one of their men said he had been with Love and insisted that the Smith-Michler party had gone further upriver than Love had. And their observations differed sharply from Love's, raising serious doubts as to the accuracy of Chapman's report. Although Smith recommended that some improvements be made on the river and felt that it could be navigated as far as Isletas, or Kingsbury's Falls, he certainly was not as optimistic as Love or Chapman. [6]

Lieutenants Smith and Bryan, coming downriver from El Paso to Presidio, suffered problems from the beginning. Finding the Rio Grande up several feet from normal and running swiftly, they immediately lost two provision boats, and required almost 2 weeks to travel 20 miles. After numerous other difficulties, they reached Presidio, where they concluded that the survey could not be conducted any farther because of the canyons. They had not yet seen Santa Elena, Mariscal, or Boquillas. [7]

**Joseph E. Johnston's 1850 map was one of the
first accurate studies of the Big Bend.**

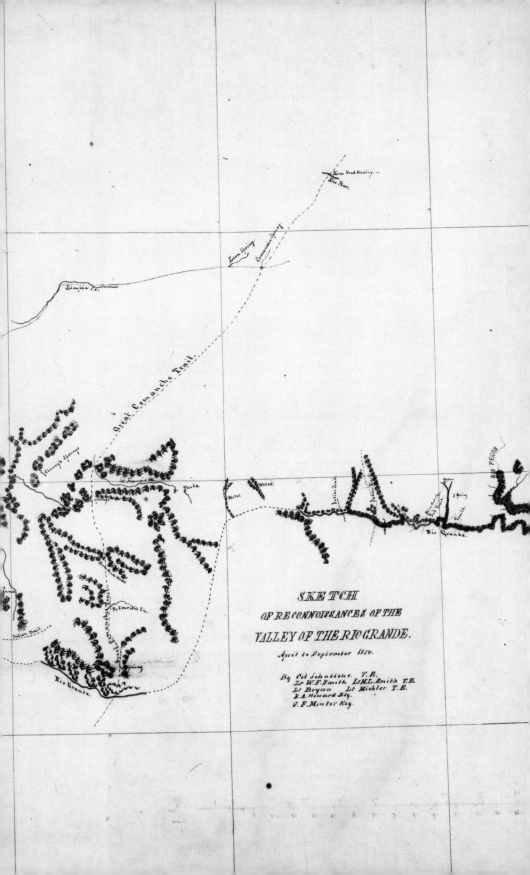

Horse Head Crossing.
Rio Pecos.

Iron Spring
Commanche Spring

Limpia Cr.

Great Comanche Trail.

Cherry's Spring

St. Francisco Cr.

Fanks.

Water
Water

RIO PECOS

Spring

Rio Grande.

Rio Grande.

Indian Trail

Ft. Franklin Cr.

Rio Grande.

SKETCH
OF RECONNOISSANCES OF THE
VALLEY OF THE RIO GRANDE.

April to September 1850.

By Col Johnstone. T.E.
Lt W.F. Smith Lt M.L. Smith T.E.
Lt Bryan   Lt Michler T.E.
R.A. Howard Esq.
J.F. Minter Esq.

Johnston's men had tried. They had groped about the fringes of the Big Bend, but could not penetrate its heart. Johnston had ordered them to explore the Rio Grande, but saw them defeated by rapids, canyons, and a lack of supplies. "Strong armed parties" were forced to accompany the engineers throughout their trek because of the threat of Indian attack. As he drew the map that was to accompany his official report, Johnston had to admit that there was still much he did not know about the Big Bend. Confidently reporting that "the country in question is uninhabited, except the neighborhood of Presidio del Norte," he was forced to leave out important information: lengthy portions of the Rio Grande remained unmapped, key geographical and geological features were omitted, and only portions of the many Indian trails that crisscrossed the Big Bend were included. Just as in the Spanish era the fringes had been probed, but the Big Bend itself remained a mystery. Its exploration was left to yet another team.[8]

The Green-Chandler Expedition

The expedition that finally explored the Big Bend was a part of the joint boundary survey, required by Article V of the Treaty of Guadalupe Hidalgo. The treaty provided for two commissions, made up of representatives of both the United States and Mexico, to conduct a survey of the new border. John B. Weller was appointed the first U.S. Commissioner, while Gen. Pedro García Condé was named the Mexican commissioner. After establishing the westernmost boundary below San Diego, the commissioners moved to El Paso del Norte, where they met to locate the initial boundary point on the Rio Grande. On May 4, 1850, Whig President Zachery Taylor replaced Democrat Weller with a Whig, John Russell Bartlett, a prominent bibliophile and amateur ethnologist from Providence, R.I. Bartlett landed on the Texas coast and proceeded to El Paso where he began his work. The engineers worked westward first, then returned to El Paso. There Chief Surveyor William H. Emory discovered that Bartlett had not yet returned from the

William H. C. Whiting was the first man to use the term Big Bend in print.

80

John Russell Bartlett   **William H. Emory**

west and made plans immediately to complete the survey down the
Rio Grande. By the summer of 1852, the survey had reached the
Trans-Pecos.[9]

By then the surveyors were laboring under considerable hardship. Commissioner Bartlett's continued absence had fomented
ill-will in the camp, leading one man to remark "that he came out
here only to write a book." (Bartlett did, of course, write one of
the classics of Western travel literature, his *Personal Narrative*.)
"We as yet have not heard what part of the world he inhabits,"
continued the grumbler. Bartlett's spending added to the hardship,
for the survey team was bankrupt. Some believed that he had already drawn on the next year's appropriation. Others, who were
used to having their government drafts rejected by the merchants,
were relieved when they arrived at Presidio del Norte, "a new field
for credit – they have not found us out yet." The Indians further
complicated the surveyors' job. They "are now becoming worse,
they come now and take mules from under ones nose with no fear.
I expect some night to hear the rascals in the house," commented
G. Clinton Gardner, Clerk to the Chief Astronomer and Head of
the Scientific Corps. If the engineers had known of Col. Emilio
Langberg's troubles the previous year, they could have better prepared for their task. There was not even an open path, reported
the colonel. They had "to pass the artillery by hand in various
places because of the rugged terrain." To complicate their task,
"the sun was beating down with all its force, and the camp gave
few hopes for pasture for the horses, as two years of drought had
nearly destroyed all the forage."[10]

81

Emory, nevertheless, decided that the river between Presidio and the mouth of the Pecos had to be surveyed. Short of able scientists and military men, he first selected his clerk, Gardner, for the task. Elated at the opportunity to receive the "credit of having carried a survey over an unknown country," Gardner hoped that the man most fitted for the task, Marine Tyler Wickham Chandler, would not arrive in camp in time. "My only hopes are that he will refuse it as rather a rough place for such a nice personage as himself," Gardner confided to a sister. The ambitious young man's chances faded, however, when Chandler returned to camp from a trip east and proved "desirous of taking charge." [11]

On August 8 Emory ordered Chandler to commence the survey at Presidio del Norte and proceed downriver to the mouth of the Pecos, or until he met another party coming upriver. Chandler was well qualified for the task. Born in 1819, he received his A.B. and M.A. degrees from the University of Pennsylvania. He worked as city engineer and surveyor for Philadelphia before joining the boundary commission, and gathered natural history collections for the Smithsonian Institution while in the Southwest. Aside from his personal enthusiasm, Chandler was also temperamentally qualified for his work. "You will find Mr. Chandler to be a bag of gass if you give him a chance to explode," Gardner wrote his father. "He can tell you more tales about the commission than I know you will believe, yet a great number of them I expect you will find to be so." [12]

Chandler was ordered to note islands or points where the boundary might be in doubt, because the treaty specified the border as the deepest channel of the river. Warning him that the "peculiar topographic features" of the Big Bend might force him to "deviate from the prescribed methods of operating," Emory gave Chandler a map made by Langberg. Though it was vague, the map indicated the forbidding landscape ahead and was far better than anything the Americans had. Because Chandler had the most difficult assignment of the survey, Emory gave him Lt. Duff C. Green and a 35-man escort for protection. [13]

The man who would make geological drawings and sketches for Chandler was Arthur C. V. Schott, a naturalist, engineer, and physician. A young man with little experience, he was hardly in the same class as the other artists on the survey: Seth Eastman, Henry C. Pratt, Harrison Eastman, and Bartlett, a good watercolorist in his own right. Since none of Schott's original drawings survived— we have only a few technical sketches—it's difficult to evaluate his work. He apparently served the scientific ends of the mission well enough, and must be judged as an artist by the engravings that appear in Emory's published report.

As the survey began, Lieutenant Green collected more men and supplies. "There is nothing to be had of any description of food between here and Fort Duncan," Emory had advised. Therefore Green traveled to El Paso, where he met Bartlett, who demanded that the lieutenant escort him to Eagle Pass. But Green refused and returned to Presidio, anxious to begin the survey before too much of the new food supply was gone. He expected the survey to take 100 days, even though Emory thought it could be done in 60 if the work was "prosecuted diligently."

Because Green was concerned that his refusal to escort Bartlett might endanger his career, he later pointed out in his report that his orders were to let nothing interfere with the survey. He felt justified in returning to Presidio and Chandler's party. He hoped that there were enough soldiers at Fort Fillmore to escort Bartlett, and he defended his decision by saying that the commissioner could have gathered an escort elsewhere if he had really tried. "Mr. Bartlett was very particular in his inquiries about the routes to Chihuahua, and it is my firm conviction that when I left him he made up his mind to go through Mexico, so he very readily seized the opportunity offered him by the Mexicans. . . ." Green neglected to say that Emory had promised him a promotion if he successfully completed the survey.[15]

The Bofecillos Mountains

Green and Chandler faced another problem as they started out: the rugged Bofecillos Mountains, which in Schott's sketches appear almost impenetrable. The valley around Fort Leaton, near Presidio, was most pleasant, said Chandler. But in the mountains the valley became only a small path, and rocks and tree branches impeded travel. Green had to take his escort to the Mexican side, leaving his wagons behind, to continue the march. When Green crossed, the river was three times its normal height. Before Chandler could follow him, the river had risen even higher, causing a 5-day delay in the march. In the first 3 miles on the Mexican side, most of Green's 80 mules became dispersed. Of the five left, only two still had their loads. Rounding up the others, he found that they

83

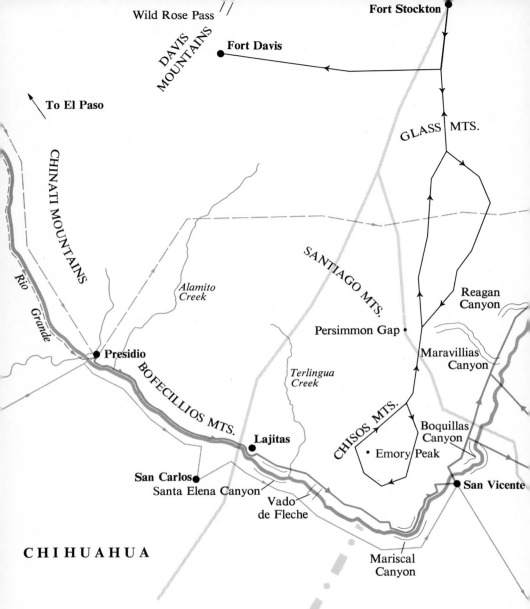

Wild Rose Pass

DAVIS MOUNTAINS

Fort Davis

Fort Stockton

To El Paso

GLASS MTS.

CHINATI MOUNTAINS

Rio Grande

Alamito Creek

SANTIAGO MTS.

Persimmon Gap

Reagan Canyon

Maravillias Canyon

Presidio

BOFECILLIOS MTS.

Terlingua Creek

CHISOS MTS.

Lajitas

Emory Peak

Boquillas Canyon

San Carlos
Santa Elena Canyon

Vado de Fleche

San Vicente

CHIHUAHUA

Mariscal Canyon

SURVEYS OF THE ENGINEERS

Johnston—1849

Smith-Michler—1850

Langberg, Mexican Survey—1851

Chandler-Green—1852

Smith-Bryan—1850

Michler—1853

Camel Corps—1859

Comanche Trail

TEXAS

Pecos

River

Rio Grande

To San Antonio

SERRANÍAS

DEL

BURRO

SIERRA

DEL

CARMEN

COAHUILA

Duff C. Green

Eagle Pass

● San Fernando

0	MILES	25
0	KILOMETERS	40

● Santa Rosa

had lost all their coffee. "Knowing the necessity of contentment to perfect discipline," he commented, "I purchased some coffee for seventy five cents per pound." [16]

Although imposing, the Bofecillos Mountains were less treacherous than those farther downriver. It was "utterly impossible" for Green to take his mule train along the river bank, and because he was to survey the border as closely as possible, Chandler had to separate from Green and the escort party and float down the river in boats. Green, meanwhile, took the pack train and traveled as best he could along the Mexican side. Besides the rough terrain, he faced the "continual disengagement of mules from their loads." But Chandler was in worse condition on the river. He had lost his boats and supplies in one of the recurring "dangerous and long rapids" at the mouth of the canyon. Thereafter he found traveling on foot easier, and soon reached Comanche Crossing where he established his camp. Green located the camp, probably near the present village of Lajitas, as Chandler was "eating his last piece of pork . . . entirely destitute of kitchen furniture." Chandler decided to wait at Comanche Crossing until more supplies could be obtained from Presidio.[17]

Comanche Crossing, or Pass, as Chandler called it, had long been a famous ford where many of the Indians crossed the river with their booty from raids conducted in Mexico. Chandler observed "broad, well-beaten trails" leading to the Rio Grande from both sides. The country near the crossing was barren, but vegetation paralleled the river. "Sterile plains" stretched northwestward, with only the "rocky barriers" of the Solitario range in the north to break the monotony. While waiting for the supplies from Presidio, Chandler and Green met the famous Comanche Chief Mano, who was traveling with his band of Indians from the headwaters of Red River to Durango, Mexico. When the Comanches first approached, the Americans were, of course, cautious. Because he was in Mexico and anxious to avoid an international incident, Green sent a Mexican helper to confer with the chief and arrayed his troops across the river from the Indians. Mano claimed that he had been at peace with the Americans for more than a year and that he only wanted to cross into Mexico. He and Green entered into a "treaty," exchanged gifts – he gave Green a horse, Green gave him

**This woodcut, reproduced from Emory's _Report_,
shows the entrance to Bofecillos Canyon.**

a beef that could not travel – and made as good a show of force as
each dared. Mano then crossed the river headed toward the village
of San Carlos. Only after he arrived at Fort Duncan did Green
learn that Mano had attacked and killed four travelers on the San
Antonio road and was headed to Mexico with his loot.

Santa Elena Canyon

Immediately downriver from the pass the Rio Grande winds
through the San Carlos Mountains and into what Green called
the Great Cañon San Carlos, probably Santa Elena Canyon.
When the party came to the entrance to the canyon, Chandler
stayed on the river. Schott paused to sketch the view for later publication, while Green was forced to try to find a more hospitable
route for his mules. The following day they met at the entrance of
the canyon and Chandler told Green the results of a reconnaissance by one of his assistants. On September 29 Thomas Thompson had gone into the canyon as far as he could. About 100 yards
past the entrance Thompson discovered what are today called the
"mirror-twins," a pair of canyons leading off both to the left and
the right. They forced him to make a long detour and eventually
prevented him from getting to the river. Before he returned, however, he observed a "perpendicular fall," probably a reference to
the now famous rock slide that provides excitement for the float

87

trips through Santa Elena. "One of the men with me is a boatman belonging to the survey," reported Thompson, "and he expressed the opinion that it would be impossible for the boat to pass this fall in safety." [19]

Using Thompson's information, Chandler decided to make as good a survey as possible without going through the canyon. Climbing onto the Mesa de Anguila, he saw the river hundreds of feet below him. "Dashing with a roaring sound over the rocks, the stream, when it reached the canyon, suddenly becomes noiseless, and is diminished to a sixth of its former width," he observed. "It enters the side of this vast mountain, which seems cut to its very base to afford a passage to the waters." Chandler saw numerous bends in the canyon, causing the swift current to crash against the vertical walls and rendering the river unfit for navigation. "The rapids and falls which occur in quick succession, make the descent in boats entirely impracticable," he concluded. Schott sketched the "falls of the Rio Bravo" from his vantage point atop the mesa. [20]

Chandler, too, saw the famous "rapids of the Rio Grande." "From the cañon wall the river may be seen far below," he wrote, "at a distance so great as to reduce it in appearance to a mere thread; and from this height the roar of the rapids and falls is scarcely perceptible." He estimated the fall in the river to be 12 feet during the course of the rapids, but he was so far away that it was little more than an educated guess. After viewing the mouth of

After viewing the "falls" from the top of the Mesa de Anguila (right), the Boundary Survey team decided not to try to float through Santa Elena Canyon.

Santa Elena Canyon, one of the most impressive sights in the Big Bend, Chandler reported that the river "is hemmed in" by the mesa for 10 miles, then "leaves it with the same abruptness that marks its entrance." [21]

Green soon discovered what he considered to be the best location for the fort that Johnston wanted to build. When Chandler had seen enough of the canyon, Green employed a Mexican, probably from nearby San Carlos, to guide them around Santa Elena on the Mexican side of the river. But they were forced to return to American soil to continue the survey because the river cuts through Terlingua Fault and emerges into flat land at the mouth of Santa Elena, leaving all the rough territory on the Mexican side. Two days' march from the mouth of the canyon, Green and the party camped at what he called "Vado de Fleche," or Ford of the Arrows, probably in the vicinity of present-day Castolon. Here "the country is more open, the valleys broader, and . . . susceptible of cultivation," wrote Chandler. "In the whole course of the Rio Grande," concluded Green, "I never saw a place so definitely marked for a miltary post as the valley near this ford." There were several reasons for his recommendation. The ford was the main Indian crossing, it was within two days' march of the only other ford of any consequence, Comanche Crossing, and a road could be constructed to join the San Antonio-El Paso road, more than 100 miles to the north. Cotton, timber, and good bottom land were immediately available. [22]

It was also at this point that the survey team had an excellent view of Mount Emory, or Emory Peak as it is called today. "Whenever the spectator was elevated sufficiently to see beyond the valley of the river," wrote Chandler,

> two prominent peaks were always presented to his view: one of these marks a summit in the range of the Mexican Sierra Carmel [sic]; and the other, from its peculiar shape and great height, was long and anxiously watched during the progress of our survey. From many places on the line it was taken as a point on which to direct the instruments; and, though the face of the country might change during our progress down the river, still, unmistakable and unchangeable, far above the surrounding mountains, this peak reared its well known head. The windings of the river, and the progess of our survey, led us gradually nearer to this point of interest, and it was found to be a part of a cluster, rather than range, of mountains on the American side, known as "Los Chisos." For this . . . we have proposed the name of Mount Emory. [23]

89

From that point Schott sketched several views of the Chisos, one trying to give an impression of the beauty and grandeur of the area, others to show the geologically diverse character of the mountains.

Mariscal Canyon

As the survey party reached Mariscal Canyon, where the river slices through Mariscal Mountain, the terrain grew rougher. Chandler stuck to the river and his surveying while Green took the remainder of Chandler's party and the pack train and headed for smoother ground. With the boaters, Chandler soon came on another "series of falls or sharp rapids far down in the abyss" where the "roaring of the waters announced a more than usual disturbance." They lost one of their boats. "It was impossible to carry the line nearer the bed of the river than the summits of the adjoining hills," Chandler determined. Two days were required to get out of the canyon, a trip which normally takes only 6 to 8 hours today. "Through these mountains the river forces its way, forming a cañon that equals the San Carlos in many places both in ruggedness and grandeur," he reported. Reaching San Vicente, the site of the abandoned presidio, Chandler left a survey flag and a note for the Mexican surveyor, Col. José Salazar Ylarregui, who had agreed to connect the point with his survey. A typical Spanish corral-type fortress, the presidio seemed ensconced in the last small clearing before the imposing Sierra del Carmen stops the eye. While at the presidio in 1851, Colonel Langberg noted that he could see the "half circle" of the river as it began its sweep northeastward to form the bend. He observed that the chapel was still standing, and that Comanches and Mescaleros had used the presidio patio after it had been deserted by the Mexican army. Standing on the American side of the river, Schott recorded Presidio San Vicente and the surrounding terrain. His is the only known view, although some ruins remain today.[24]

Boquillas Canyon and the Sierra del Carmen

Chandler had anticipated that the country beyond San Vicente would be smooth and less hazardous. That, unfortunately, was not the case. It proved to be just as "rough and broken" as that he had just covered. Green experienced "great trouble" in find-

The ruins of presidio San Vicente, on the Mexican
side of the Rio Grande, can be seen in the right
center of this woodcut from Emory's *Report*.

ing trails and water for his men and animals. As they progressed,
they found their route barred by deep arroyos that almost proved
insurmountable. They passed the Canyon of Sierra del Carmen,
probably what is called Boquillas Canyon today, another of those
"rocky dungeons" that imprisons the Rio Grande. Although the
traveling was rough, Chandler could still appreciate the virgin
beauty of the desert that he crossed. "No description can give an
idea of the grandeur of the scenery through these mountains,"
he reported. "There is no verdure to soften the bare and rugged
view; no overhanging trees or green bushes to vary the scene from
one of perfect desolation. Rocks are here piled one above another,
over which it was with the greatest labor that we would work
our way." [25]

The mules rapidly exhausted themselves on the long detours
necessary to move only a few miles downriver. Trying to find a
better route, Green crossed over to the Mexican side again, but
discovered that the "character of the country" there was just as de-
pressing. He located an arroyo which he hoped to be able to follow

91

Capt. Arthur T. Lee was one of the few artists
to paint the Rio Grande canyons during the
1850s. This view is probably near present-day
Lajitas, the entrance to Santa Elena Canyon.

to its source, where he then hoped he could find another farther east and follow it back to the river, thus avoiding the worst mountains along the banks of the river. But after marching miles from the river, he found no arroyo to lead him back. He sent out scouts with orders to find a way back to the river, but their search was in vain. Late on October 23 he saw a "fine new beaten trail" leading in exactly the opposite direction. Feeling anxious about Chandler and his party and knowing that they were without rations or bedding, Green ordered two men to follow the trail and if possible reach the river. They took bread and meat, in the event they found Chandler. The next day Green sent two more scouts out searching for Chandler, ordering them to stay close to the river. "Each hour my anxiety increased," he later reported, "for I saw most reasonable grounds to suppose that this party of gentlemen would be subjected to the awful pang of hunger and perhaps be so reduced in strength as when found to be unable to come into camp." [26]

Chandler surely was in trouble. Along with his boat he had lost all the extra clothing and provisions. His men had been reduced to existing on the barest rations and their "scanty wardrobes scarcely afforded enough covering for decency." "The sharp rocks of the mountains had cut the shoes from their feet, and blood, in many instances, marked their progress through the day's work." The same illusion that frustrates and defeats doomed men in the desert plagued Chandler's men. "Beyond the Sierra Carmel [sic], the river seemed to pass through an almost interminable succession of mountains," he said. "Cañon succeeded cañon; the valleys, which alone had afforded some slight chances for rest and refreshment had become so narrow and devoid of vegetation that it was quite a task to find grass sufficient for the mules." Finally, he crossed over to the Mexican side, hoping to find a passable route. Astonishingly, Chandler's party continued its survey work through all the rigorous march. With only this "slight interruption," he reported with much understatement, "the line of survey was carried on . . . ." [27]

Green, meanwhile, continued his march to the river, hoping to cross Chandler's path. About 11 p.m. on October 29 Chandler and his assistant, E. A. Phillips, found Green's trail and stumbled into his camp. They had marched in one day what had required two for the mules, reported Green. "Mr. Phillips and I walked . . . more than forty miles without water except once finding a little in a rock and for more than forty hours we were destitute for food," Chandler revealed. Two gentlemen had met in the desert. "After the usual salutation on such occasion," said Green, "I asked Mr. Chandler if he, from his knowledge of the position of his party, could think of anything I could do to relieve them." Chandler replied that there was nothing more to be done, that the men had been cared for as well as possible. The scientist in Chandler probably caused him to minimize the drama and danger of the situation, and this report is not so graphic as Green's because Chandler chose to omit "any but an incidental allusion to the difficulties of the survey." [28]

Maravillas Canyon

As the reunited party approached Maravillas Canyon, or Cupola Mountain in what is today the Black Gap Wildlife Management Area, they were in desperate condition, having lost boats, mules, and supplies. Again Schott's sketch gives some impression of the hopelessness that the explorers must have felt as they beheld the endless mountains before them. The river seemed to be so small as to be inconsequential, lost in the never-ending folds of earth that stretched as far as one could see. Temple and Reagan Canyons were monuments to the fact that the expedition would be unable to continue. The country was so rugged that Schott, unable to see all of it himself, had to depend upon the "primitive" sketches that Charles Abbott had made on his float trip through some of the canyons in order to map the region. Schott, in fact, left the party and returned to Fort Duncan by way of the San Pedro River and San Felipe Creek, rather than stay on the river. Green and Chandler sent out scouts to examine the routes back to the river. On November 3 Green informed Chandler that he felt they should discontinue the survey. The main problems were the character of the land they were approaching and the shortness of provisions. The following day Dr. C. C. Parry, a member of Chandler's party, referred to the "unexpected difficulty" of the country in also recommending that the survey cease. In addition to low rations and badly damaged boats, Parry mentioned the "destitute condition of the employees of the Commission . . . many of them are already nearly barefoot all poorly prepared for the prompt and efficient performance of their several duties over a country so rough and beset with thorns as this[.] I am therefore fully of your opinion that the work cannot be safely prosecuted further . . . ." Chandler himself admitted that some of his men had gone without food for 78 hours.[29]

Survey Suspended

With these reports in hand, Chandler then notified Emory that he had suspended the survey, having covered only 40 miles. "I have with great difficulty and exertion brought the line to the entrance of the cañon near this camp and after careful reconnoisances made both by myself and Lieutenant Green, I believe that the country in advance is impracticable to be surveyed with the means now at my disposal – my boats are unfit to transport the provisions necessary for the surveying party for more than one day . . . ." He would have had to depend upon the mule train for supplies, he said, and Green could find no accessible route to the river. After a brief conference, Green and Chandler started out for Fort Duncan via the safest route, through Santa Rosa, Coahuila, guided by a Mexican who knew the region. Not all the men stayed with the main party; some went by boat, preferring to risk "their lives in the remains of the best boat to walking with the train during the necessarily long marches that are before us, suffering as they are from want of shoes and other clothing," he wrote at the time. Chandler then, perhaps unwittingly, indicated the apprehension with which he undertook the march across northern Mexico: "I . . . expect (God willing) to report to you in person with my

Chandler and Green broke off surveying in Boquillas Canyon, almost out of supplies and with their boats wrecked, and headed across Mexico to Fort Duncan, near Eagle Pass, Texas.

notes in about eighteen days." [30] (Apparently the men in the boat arrived safely at Eagle Pass, presumably becoming the first men to float through the Hot Springs, Burro, and Upper and Lower Madison rapids of the lower canyons, because Chandler's letter reached Emory.)

Chandler and Green knew that the desperate party faced more than just desert country and a shortage of food. They also faced the very real threat of Indian attack. Writing from his camp on the San Felipe River, Schott, now surveying another part of the river, reported that about 25 armed and well-mounted Lipan Apache Indians had followed them for 3 days, and they were constantly afraid of being attacked. On his way to Chihuahua, meanwhile, Commissioner Bartlett, who had taken what he thought was a safer route, suffered the only full-scale attack in the area. One man was killed and several mules stolen. As they neared Santa Rosa, Chandler and Green were stopped by several Negroes, exslave members of the Seminole Chief Wild Cat's band who had fled to Mexico. Soon the party was confronted by Wild Cat himself, who threatened Green with a supposed 50 men concealed in the brush and who demanded to know why Americans had come into his country. After a short conference, in which Green claimed that he had three times as many men as Wild Cat, the chief withdrew and allowed the party to pass unharmed. The remainder of the march from Santa Rosa to Fort Duncan proved uneventful, and the party arrived on November 24. [31]

Michler Survey

The following spring Emory dispatched Lt. Nathaniel Michler to complete the survey from the point near Reagan Canyon to the mouth of the Pecos River, approximately the point at which Smith and Michler had stopped in 1850. Michler organized his party in San Antonio, including disassembled boats which he thought he might have to use, and rode west over the San Antonino-El Paso road. At Pecos Springs he turned south, hoping to strike the Rio Grande at the point where the survey was to begin. The road was rough, but Michler was equal to the task. The first 50 miles, from the Pecos to King's Springs, the course was nearly due west, enabling him to avoid the numberless "impassable arroyos" that cut abrupt swaths toward the river. His men scouted toward the Chisos Mountains, but found the country "cut up by immense chasms, closed in by steep cliffs, unseen until standing upon the very edge of their fearful depths." In the distance Michler saw the awesome Sierra del Carmen range, the primary obstacle that had blocked the progress of Chandler and Green's party. "The nearer we approached the river," he continued, "the more rough the country became; deep ravines and gullies constantly impeded the progress of the wagons, and the whole surface was covered with sharp angular stones and a growth of underbrush armed with thorns." [32]

About 10 miles from the river, the terrain became so difficult that the wagons had to be eased down the steep slopes by ropes. But Michler successfully located the initial point of the survey, the spot at which Chandler had suspended operations, and went to work. He found the same hostile conditions that had defeated Chandler, yet with fresh crewmen Michler pushed on. "It was impossible to approach the river from the first twenty miles of the survey," he reported, because it was "very tortuous." Michler thus bypassed Temple and Reagan Canyons, the names assigned to the canyons by Hill in 1899. Then he came to Irwin and Nichol Canyons, with their "banks . . . composed of high perpendicular masses of solid rock, resembling more the work of art than of nature." Rather than boat through the canyons, Michler first elected to work from horseback and wagons, but noted that they frequently had to make 25- or 30-mile detours to get around the arroyos that cut up the desert floor. South of present-day Dryden he located another fork of the Indian crossing and included a sketch of it with his report.

There the team was forced to use the boats. They unpacked them, only to find that the sun had warped the freshly cut, uncured lumber. After assembling the crooked planks and sending the wagons to Eagle Pass with the remainder of the party, Michler put the boats in the water. "Upon trial, we found the boats, which were our only resource, would float – the only thing that could be said in their favor," he dryly noted. With worried troops manning the oars, they set out in two skiffs and a flatboat. He probably was nearing Langtry Canyon.

He had entered the river at a "short break" in the canyon where the water rushed through "rocky banks" a dozen feet high. As the party drifted further into the canyon the wall grew higher, causing Michler to believe it "incredible that the bed of the stream could have been formed through ledges of solid rock." He described the narrow bed of the river that was "hemmed in by continuous and perfect walls of natural masonry" from 50 to 300 feet high. As the river narrowed, appearing "extremely contracted," the walls of the canyon appeared "stupendous" as they rose "perpendicularly" out of the water.

Immediately upon entering the most spectacular part of the canyon. Michler realized they were in danger. The boats were too small for the rough current and were viciously slammed against the walls. The first day out the crew floated through a canyon so narrow that the oarsmen could touch the walls with the tips of their oars. The river was only about 25 feet wide at that point. As they started through the pass they saw an "immense bowlder" dividing the main channel, leaving only a "narrow chute" for the boats. A rapids blocked the entire course of the river for several hundred feet, with the "whole mass of water" rushing through, "foaming and tumbling in a furious manner." Although the two skiffs made it safely through the narrow channel, the flatboat was not so lucky. "Totally unmanageable" said Michler, it ran "square against the rocky walls, splintering and tearing away her entire front." The crew was "knocked flat on their backs and the boat-hooks left firmly imbedded in the crevices of the rocks." As the boat started sinking, two Mexican crew members, both expert swimmers, jumped into the water, seized the lines, and pulled the boat to a sand bar, saving men and provisions. Michler and crew repaired the wreckage and continued their remarkable journey the following day.

As they passed canyon after canyon, they found the current so swift and the falls and bends so frequent that it was impossible to stop and take readings for the survey. Artist Schott sketched one of the canyons below Boquillas, perhaps Reagan or Nichol Canyon. The mountains there are not so imposing, but they still torture the river and imprison anyone who dares enter. "The only practicable way of making the survey through the cañon," reported Michler, "was by allowing the boats to drop down the channel, taking the direction of the courses and timing the passage from bend to bend; when opportunity offered, the speed of each boat was ascertained by distance accurately measured on land. . . ." The survey had covered approximately 125 miles when the team arrived at the mouth of the Pecos, which Michler described as being "a rolling mass of red mud, the water tasting like a mixture of every saline ingredient. . . ." (The water of the Rio Grande is also extremely high in mercury content because of the quicksilver deposits in the Big Bend.) They continued downriver to Fort Duncan, where they met the other members of the party. Michler and party had floated down one of the wildest rivers on the continent.

When Michler covered the distance from the Maravillas Canyon area to the mouth of the Pecos, the entire length of the Rio Grande that comprised the international boundary had been carefully surveyed by the Topographical Engineers. Smith and Michler reported on the portion from Ringgold Barracks to several miles past the mouth of the Pecos; Michler from the Pecos to below Boquillas Canyon; Chandler from Boquillas to Presidio del Norte; and Smith from Presidio del Norte to El Paso. Other excursions, such as that of Captain Love, had also covered parts of the river.

Even before all the reports were in, Colonel Abert knew that it was not likely that steamboats could navigate past the point they already served. He did ask M. L. Smith whether he had accurately calculated his estimate for improving the river as far as the Isletas, but finally concluded that there were too many disadvantages. The river itself, first of all, was simply too shallow and contained too many obstacles for a steamboat of any size. Improvements would have been costly if, indeed, they had been feasible. Then, should Abert have decided to improve the river, the question would have had to come before an international arbitration board with Mexico, for Article VII of the Treaty of Guadalupe Hidalgo stipulated that neither country should "construct work . . . not even for the purpose of favouring new methods of navigation" without the consent of the other Nation. Congressman D. L. Seymour of New York, a member of the House Committee on Commerce, asked the Corps of Engineers about possible improvements, but his efforts got no further than committee discussions. The hope that the Rio Grande might ultimately be found navigable died slowly, for it would have made travel through one of the most remote sections of the country less expensive and less dangerous.[33]

The chief means of transportation for years to come obviously would be the wagon road built by the Topographical Engineers. It had taken several explorations of optional routes and hard work once the path had been selected, but the engineers were confident that they had chosen the road that best took advantage of the existing waterholes and grasslands.

The first step to replace the old wagon road west were taken when Andrew P. Gray surveyed West Texas for the Texas Western Railroad Company in 1854. A former member of the Topographical Engineers, Gray organized his party of 19 men in San Antonio and on January 1, 1854, set out for Fort Chadbourne. The trip across the Llano Estacado (the Staked Plains) and the northern part of the Trans-Pecos was accomplished with relative ease. The proposed railroad route, of course, did not enter the Big Bend region of the Trans-Pecos because it was too rugged.[34]

Fort Davis

To protect this western road the army established Fort Davis in 1854. Several sites were considered. All the engineers and surveyors who had trekked through the Big Bend had offered recommendations as to where the fort should be constructed. Green had opted for either of two points near the Comanche Trail: near present-day Lajitas or between Santa Elena and Mariscal Canyons. Bvt. Maj. Gen. George M. Brooke agreed with him. "There should be strong Garrisons in the Great Bend opposite San Carlos, which is the key to the country called on Disturnell's map 'Bolson de Mapimi.' Indians passing at this place go to Chihuahua, Monclova, Parras and Durango – laying the whole country to waste," concluded the general. Brooke also believed a post should be located

Arthur T. Lee's watercolors are probably the best record of Fort Davis's early years.

opposite Presidio del Norte. Another site under consideration, and the eventual location of the fort, was Painted Comanche Camp. The actual location of the fort was determined by Bvt. Maj. Gen. Persifor F. Smith, who visited the Trans-Pecos himself in September and October of 1854 to investigate the potential sites. Painted Comanche Camp offered more wood, water, and grass. It was strategically located, commanding the western road, yet was within

Not all the West Texas Indians were hostile. These Indians probably traded with the soldiers at Fort Davis, where Capt. Arthur T. Lee made this painting.

striking distance of the Comanche Trail. The post was named for Secretary of War Jefferson Davis.[35] Now preserved and partially reconstructed, the fort is a National Historic Site.

One of the officers stationed there in 1855 was Zenas R. Bliss, a youthful graduate of the U.S. Military Academy who had already tasted frontier service at Fort Duncan. After making the 17-day stage trip from San Antonio to Fort Davis, Bliss realized that Indians seemed to attack about half the stages. One of Bliss' friends was a good-humored captain named Arthur T. Lee, an artist with a good eye and considerable talent. Lee left a remarkable record of the fort during the mid-1850s, including several of the Indians who frequented it. After living at the post for several months, both Bliss and Lee realized that they were in danger of

103

being attacked by Indians if they ventured so much as a couple of miles from the post. The army clearly had a difficult task ahead.[36]

The Camel Experiment

Because of its harsh terrain and climate, the Big Bend was the scene of an unusual experiment in desert transportation in 1859 and 1860. Secretary of War Jefferson Davis authorized the importation of camels for use on the western frontier in 1855. This was not the first time the army had contemplated using camels in the West. Twenty years before, Maj. George H. Crosman, who was then serving in Florida, had recommended their use. Maj. Henry C. Wayne took up Crosman's idea in 1848 and recommended that the War Department bring camels in from the Middle East. Wayne also contacted then-Senator Jefferson Davis of Mississippi, who became interested in the idea. In 1854, while serving as Secretary of War, Davis teamed up with Senator James Shields of Illinois to persuade Congress to vote money for the project. A bill providing $30,000 for the importation of camels passed Congress in 1855. The first load of 34 camels landed at Indianola on May 14, 1856. The second shipment of 44 arrived on February 10, 1857.

Major Wayne took the camels to San Antonio, where he set up camp at Val Verde, or Camp Verde, as it became known, a few miles outside the city. The first experiments with the camels were immediate successes. Many San Antonio citizens, thoroughly familiar with oxen and mules on the Chihuahua Trail, doubted the merit of camels in West Texas. Seeking to quiet their skepticism, Wayne gave a demonstration for an impromptu crowd gathered around the plaza. He ordered a camel to kneel, then had two bales of hay tied onto him. Realizing that each bale weighed over 300 pounds, the crowd feared the camel could not get up. Then, emphasizing his point, Wayne tied two more bales on the animal, a total of more than 1,200 pounds. The camel rose without difficulty and walked off, carrying the load. The Texans were so convinced that one of the "poets of Texas" composed some lines to commemorate the occasion, said Wayne.[37]

When President James Buchanan took office in 1857, John B. Floyd replaced Davis as Secretary of War, but the experiments with camels went on. Floyd ordered the wagon road from Fort Defiance, New Mexico, to the Colorado River surveyed with camels. Lt. Edward F. Beale, a veteran of the Mexican War and Superintendent of Indian Affairs in California and Nevada, was chosen to head the Camel Corps. He reached Fort Davis in the summer of 1857 and soon left with his camels for the assignment in the West.[38]

Camels in the Big Bend

Using camels Beale left behind, 2d Lt. William H. Echols of the Topographical Engineers and Lt. Edward L. Hartz conducted experiments in the Big Bend in 1859. In that year Maj. Gen. David M. Twiggs, commander of the Department of Texas, wanted a thorough reconnaissance of the country to locate supply routes for the far-flung posts in the Trans-Pecos. Twenty-four camels, loaded with between 300 and 500 pounds of equipment and supplies, were marched westward to the Pecos, then on to Fort Davis.[39]

Lieutenant Echols departed for the Big Bend on July 11. He varied the burdens of the animals, but they each carried an average of 400 pounds. The march continued uneventfully until they reached Nine Point Draw, or Dog Canyon. While trying to weave their way through the intricate passages, several camels fell down with their loads, and had it not been for the Indian trails Echols could hardly have gotten his party through the canyon. "A rougher, more rocky, more mountainous, and rugged country, can scarcely be imagined," wrote Hartz. After leaving the canyon, the soldiers probably followed Dog Canyon out onto the prairie, which was covered with luscious grass only recently watered by one of the cloudbursts typical of the Big Bend. Echols found water in several places, but correctly guessed that it was not permanent. He let the camels drink their fill, expressing surprise when their capacity proved to be nearer 15 or 20 gallons than the 20 or 30 pints the Secretary of War had led him to expect.

On July 16 Echols found the Comanche Trail and camped near a small spring, perhaps near present-day McKinney Springs. The Rio Grande was still 27 miles away, over a "most laborious and exhausting march." Echols bypassed Roy's Peak, Rice's Canyon, and the watershed of Tornillo Creek on the way to the river. He also discovered one of the characteristics of the Big Bend country: the infrequent but torrential rains which cause flash floods and erode the chalky, dry soil. "Our trail crossed, in the course of the day, no less than fifty-seven arroyos, some of them from fifty to seventy feet in depth, with plane banks inclining frequently as much as forty-five degrees," Hartz reported. At the Rio Grande, the soldiers had to abandon a horse and a mule that had become exhausted by the heat and distance.

On July 18 the train moved down the river, finding grass and water opposite the old Presidio San Vicente. As they headed farther downriver, however, the terrain grew rougher. On the 19th Echols decided that they had accomplished their mission and could return. The same hostile ground that had forced Chandler and Green to discontinue their survey now caused Echols to turn northward. Marching between the Comanche Trail and Tornillo Creek, Hartz described their relief at finding more grass and water, thus ending the mystery of how the Indians could so easily penetrate the *despoblado* while the Spaniards entered only cautiously. The Indians knew the country and the favors it offered. But even the Indians, used to seeing the pack trains of the army or Chihuahua traders silhouetted against the horizon, probably were now surprised by the awkward forms of the camels, seemingly "perched in mid-air" as they traversed the foothills of the Sierra del Carmen.

The party camped near Roy's Peak after a march of 21 miles. Another horse had to be abandoned since there was no water at the camp. The next day Echols found the trail he had followed en route to the Rio Grande. Hoping to return by another route, he headed eastward away from his trail, probably marching southeast of Dagger Mountain. This detour presented new problems. First, they encountered a dense growth of soapweed, whose slender, short blades tipped with tough thorns about an inch long could lame the camels. But the camels knew how to walk through them, putting their feet alongside the plant, then crushing them over to avoid the thorns. The growth was so dense, however, that progress was slow. Second, the terrain grew rougher as the party attempted to descend the cliffs of a small canyon. Several of the camels fell, narrowly escaping injury. After clearing the canyon, Echols turned northward, located his trail again, and followed it back to Camp Stockton.

After the force reached Camp Stockton, Hartz attempted to summarize the camels' performance. They had climbed hills and mountains of the "most difficult nature," crossed streams and prairies made almost impassable by deep arroyos, ravines, and maguey, gone nearly 5 days without water, and eaten much less

An unknown artist, probably a soldier, painted this small watercolor of camels crossing a West Texas stream on the way to Big Bend.

food than a horse or a mule. Covering between 20 and 34 miles a day, they had marched through the "most difficult country in northwestern Texas," reported Hartz, who had his directions slightly askew. Nor did they appear to suffer physically. What Hartz said about the camels also reveals the true nature of the Big Bend. The army had sought a rough country in which to try the camels, and they had found it in the Big Bend.

Echols had another opportunity to take the camels to the Big Bend the following year. General Twiggs still hoped to build another fort in the region, and he also wanted a good road constructed between that post and Fort Davis. Leaving Fort Davis on July 14, Echols marched down the Fort Davis-Presidio del Norte road, searching for a favorable site near the San Carlos Crossing, because it would have easy access to the road. He found the road "magnificent," but might have guessed that the expedition would have trouble when one of his men tested the water at nearby San Esteban and found it undrinkable. The men were also hampered by the "old song of 'the falling of packs,' " because the camel drivers had not yet learned how to secure the loads.[40]

As he pushed farther into the desert, Echols, by now a veteran Big Bend explorer, wryly observed that, "I cheerfully concur with all who regard this region as impassable." He found no suitable site for a fort at the San Carlos Crossing. He headed downriver, circling around the Mesa de Anguila, toward Comanche Crossing, which Green and Johnston regarded as the best possible location for a fort. Marching down the Lates Laguna, probably Terlingua Creek, he beheld a "wonderful curiosity," a "place where the stream runs through a mountain precipice, about 1,500 feet high." The guide had directed the party to Santa Elena Canyon, one of the first tourist attractions in the Big Bend, which Echols called "The Grand Puerta." A few miles farther downriver Echols located the crossing, which he, too, agreed was a good site for a fort.

On July 27 Echols headed back to Fort Davis by a different route. After striking Terlingua Creek, he turned due north, probably marching into the Terlingua area. He believed that a road could be built through that area easily enough until he encountered a mountain, perhaps Wildhorse Mountain. After climbing the

Camels made several trips across the Southwest, but the experiment was discontinued when the Civil War began.

mountain to survey the area, he concluded that much work would have to be done to make the road usable. As he started down the mountain, he saw a pool of water some 1,000 feet below. Because they could not reach it, he named it "Inaccessible Tank." The next morning Echols rode into the canyon, hoping to find a way through. He found that the canyon got deeper, but was able to lead his party safely through. As the terrain worsened, Echols realized that he would not be able to locate the road and headed back to the trail. He had found a fairly good road – but there was an obstacle, "the precipitous side of a mountain, rugged, rocky, and several hundred feet high" that could not be overcome. Because of injury to the camels and mules, the party could go no further. They had to discontinue the reconnaissance without finding a satisfactory route. After 3 days without water, they finally found some on August 1. Echols passed by what was rapidly becoming a well-known landmark to the Topographical Engineers – Camel's Hump, a small mountain in the prairie between Adobe Walls Mountain and Red Bluff. Today a curiosity, it is marveled at by travelers who have little idea that camels once roamed the Big Bend.

A combination of circumstances insured that camels would not be used on a large scale in West Texas. There was, of course, the cultural bias toward the "Missouri mule" that the camel could not overcome. But the Civil War ended the experimentation before pragmatic teamsters and surveyors could render their decision. When the Union army vacated Fort Davis, several camels were simply turned loose. Some of them ventured into Mexico, where they turned up in circuses years after the trial in the desert had been forgotten. A few fell into the hands of promoters, who tried unsuccessfully to wring a living from them. The experiment was not resumed after the Civil War, because the railroad became the dominant mode of overland transportation for the country.

Further exploration in the Big Bend, as well as the construction of the fort that General Twiggs had wanted, was also cut short by the Civil War. The Engineers had, however, made several important contributions in the Trans-Pecos. First, they had opened the country to travel both by the military and by merchants and travelers. Second, they had charted routes across West Texas that rendered defense of the region easier. Indian strongholds were penetrated; pursuit was surer. Third, the line of communication that Colonel Abert had wanted was established, although it would not prevent the disruption of the Union. Finally, the Engineers gave many enduring place names to the Big Bend, such as Emory Peak and Camel's Hump.

5/Settling the Big Bend

From the settled portions of Texas, the trails pointed westward toward the Big Bend country, and during the last half of the 19th century emigrants slowly made their way through the Trans-Pecos to California or some other El Dorado. Many travelers elected to settle in Fort Davis, Marfa, or Alpine, or on isolated ranches farther south after seeing the Big Bend only one time. Word of mouth advertising brought others to live there, to improve their health, to start over, or just to settle in a "new" country. It is a "fantastic country, like no other I've ever seen," said one traveler after his first glimpse of the Big Bend. Another was impressed with the "cool, bracing and invigorating" air after spending his first few nights in Marfa. But newcomers, more accustomed to the "human proportions" of the eastern or midwestern landscapes, were more taken with physical features of the land. "I was raised in a country where trees of a fair size were not uncommon, and where the prevailing and general hue was green or yellow in spring, summer and fall, and white in winter," recalled Judge O. W. Williams of Fort Stockton. "The everlasting neuter grays and browns of this arid country, not relieved by any trees, have for many years been monotonous to me. Yet, this dry, drab country charms one in its own way," he admitted. "The air is generally clear, the sunsets gorgeous, and the general scope of view large." [1]

The Chihuahua Trail

Many emigrants saw the Big Bend for the first time as they traveled along the Chihuahua Trail. Moving over paths blazed by Hays, Ford, and Johnston, the traders increased as the exchange grew more profitable after the Civil War. "The commerce is entirely inland and mostly in the hands of foreigners," reported Charles Moye, from his vantage point as U.S. Consul in Chihuahua, "particularly the wholesale establishments." Several families earned a livelihood from it, although few became wealthy. In San Antonio John Monier, a Frenchman, was the first merchant to send mule trains to Mexico via the Big Bend, followed quickly by John Gargin and August Santleben. Mexican companies like Rocke Garady and David and Daniel Sada of Monterrey, Nuevo León, and the González brothers of Saltillo, Coahuila, offered

The ruins of Mariscal Mine, near Terlingua.

111

Photograph by Bank Langmore

goods for sale in Chihuahua. The goods moved in wagons drawn by mules or oxen across the "great deserts" between Chihuahua and the dispersal points – San Antonio and Independence, Mo. The trade across Texas had an advantage, because transportation cost only 10 cents silver per pound, reported Moye, while the cost on the Missouri route was 12 cents per pound.[2]

Fairly well-defined by the 1870's, the Chihuahua Trail began on the Gulf Coast in Powderhorn Bayou. Indianola was the principal port. The ponderous wagons reminded Thomas Ruckman, a resident of Helena, Texas, of a "great cloud of smoke" when he saw them "winding and worming" their way through the town northwestward. They passed along the Guadalupe River, through Victoria and Goliad. After Helena, the wagons jolted to a ford on Cibolo Creek, then to the San Antonio River, which they followed into the Alamo City. There the poet Sidney Lanier saw the "long train of enormous, blue-bodied covered wagons," which "lumbered" through the city, spending as little time as possible in San Antonio before setting out on the long road to Chihuahua.[3]

From San Antonio the route ran due west through Castroville and Uvalde to Fort Clark, 150 miles to the west, the real "jumping off place." Thirty-five miles farther west the trail hit the Rio Grande, turned northward and paralleled Devil's River almost to its source. There the wagons cut westward again, to Fort Lancaster. As they entered the Big Bend they gradually turned southwestward to Fort Stockton and Fort Davis and picked up the route to Presidio that John D. Burgess had charted when he supplied beef to the soldiers at Fort Davis. Passing by the present location of Marfa, the merchants could see Cathedral Rock looming several hundred feet in the air to the southeast. The Chinati Mountains and Elephant Rock broke the monotony of the desert en route to the small border village of Presidio. Many travelers purchased supplies from Ben Leaton, whose fortified adobe structure still overlooks fertile fields of cotton and corn along the Rio Grande.[4]

Forty miles south of the border the wagons entered the worst part of the Chihuahuan Desert. Terrain that had successfully defied the Spaniards and early Anglo-Americans only gradually yielded to the commercial thrusts of entrepreneurs. There were no wells between Rancho de la Mula and Chupadero, and it was 150 miles to

August Santleben's stageline, shown here in 1866 in San Antonio, made one trip a month to either Monterrey or Chihuahua.

Julimes, the site of the old Spanish presidio on the Río Conchos. The worst was over at Julimes. They then swung westward to Bachimba, then northwestward to Chihuahua. The arduous trip paid off handsomely for wary merchants who negotiated successfully with their Mexican counterparts.[5]

The Chihuahua trade with San Antonio and other Texas cities was well established by 1851 and continued, except during the Civil War, until the Southern Pacific and the Texas & Pacific railroads completed their tracks across West Texas in 1882. The Chihuahua Trail was significant for several reasons. First, it diverted some of the lucrative trade from Santa Fe and El Paso to San Antonio, giving merchants along the route a saving in transportation costs and helping San Antonio become the chief distribution center for goods throughout the Southwest. Second, it helped open the Big Bend and led many persons to settle permanently in the region. The trail provided a livelihood for persons in the Big Bend who would have had difficulty living there without the trade.[6]

The economic assets of the Big Bend – virgin grasslands, minerals, fertile river valleys – remained untapped. Only after the Topographical Engineers had opened the country to exploration were they generally rumored, but for all practical purposes these resources remained inaccessible until the U.S. Army tamed the Indians and the railroad made transportation easier. Texans thus longed for completion of the railroad across the Trans-Pecos. They had been encouraged by Andrew Gray's Texas Western Railroad survey in 1854 and by the predictions of those who visited the proposed route. One traveler who crossed the prairies in 1868 noted that it would not be difficult to find a route. A few years later the editor of the *Austin Statesman* pointed out that the railroad

113

would soon open the State's last unknown region. He correctly forecast that it would stimulate ranching and mining and concluded that the Big Bend would then be one of the best sections of the State to settle in. He envisioned a "plain covered with farms and villages and cities" throughout West Texas, a land that at one time had been the home of the wild Comanches and Apaches.[7]

Conquest of the Indians

The Big Bend was still the home of Indians in 1867. Even Fort Davis had been left to the mercy of the Mescaleros. After the army withdrew from the fort in 1861, the Confederates lacked adequate forces to maintain it. When Union troops arrived from California a year later, they found it deserted, some of the buildings burned, others wrecked. Relations with the Trans-Pecos Indians were so bad in 1867 that Gov. J. W. Throckmorton of Texas asked the army to escort a trial judge to El Paso. "Unless the military authorities can furnish him an escort it will be impossible for him to make the journey in time," Throckmorton pointed out. Three children and one woman were reported captured by the Indians in January and February 1871.

It was not until 2 years after the Civil War that Federal troops reoccupied Fort Davis. After Capt. Edward S. Meyer reopened the old military road, the new commander, Lt. Col. Wesley Merritt, tackled his threefold job of reconstructing the fort, reclaiming most of the Big Bend from the Indians, and controlling his newly-assigned Negro troops.[8]

Merritt built the quarters from stone, as originally planned. Defeating the Indians proved more difficult. Although the all-Negro regiments of the 9th and 10th Cavalry and the 24th and 25th Infantry quickly proved their worth against the Apaches, solving his third problem, they often could not find the quarry. The area the "buffalo soldiers" had to patrol made their job difficult. "These posts are so distant from each other that marauding parties of Indians can easily pass between them without being discovered," claimed Maj. Gen. David M. Twiggs in 1857, "and, if discovered, it is very difficult to overtake them; indeed, there is not one case in fifty where a command can come up with them." A year later General Twiggs again called attention to the problem of space. "Fort

Davis is one hundred and eighty miles from Fort Lancaster . . . it is between these points [that] most of the depredations on this road are committed."

Knowledge of the land gave the Indians an advantage in the Big Bend. After robbing several sheep camps and killing two herders, a party of Comanches, including a captured white man named Clinton L. Smith, "pulled for the breaks of the Rio Grande, somewhere in the Big Bend country. . . . We sure had to ride to out-run our pursuers," Smith recalled, but they were safe after they reached the river.

The military pressure initially proved effective. In September 1871 the principal bands of the Mescalero Apaches came to Fort Stanton, New Mex., and agreed to a peace that lasted only 4 years. By 1876 depredations were increasing and civilian authorities again demanded action. While Apaches elsewhere in the Southwest had settled on their reservations, Chief Gomez kept his warriors in the Big Bend busy.[9]

The Indians did not attack wagon trains and ranches simply because they were warlike. They were desperate for food. With both white men and Indians hunting wild game, the supply thinned, leaving redmen without any adequate source of food. In the past they had been able to raid into Mexico almost at will, but the United States had agreed in the Treaty of Guadalupe Hidalgo to stop the international raids, denying them another source of supplies. Most of the Mescaleros were unsatisfied with the reservations on which they were placed. After studying the Indian situation in 1854, Capt. Randolph B. Marcy and Agent Neighbors concluded that "the Mescalero . . .will not willingly remove from their old planting grounds between the 'Presidio del Norte' and the 'Horsehead Crossing' of the Pecos where they have planted corn for several years." Marcy and Neighbors recommended that they be given the lands which they already lived on in the interest of a "speedy, peaceable, and permanent settlement." But the Apaches were not given lands in Texas because the State kept all its public lands when it joined the Union. Texas Indian policy was later characterized by the great photographer of Indians, Edward S. Curtis, as " 'Go elsewhere or be exterminated.' " Indians were a Federal problem as far as the State's officials were concerned, and they would have to be given Federal land. Many Indians were, therefore, placed on land in New Mexico that they considered inferior to what they had surrendered.[10]

Upset at this disregard for their rights, the Apaches grew discontented. The small groups scattered across the Big Bend raided

115

Men and officers of Troop D, 3d Cavalry, at Fort Davis about 1880.

Victorio led the last resistance of the Apaches to the U.S. Cavalry in the Big Bend.

116   **Settling the Big Bend**

isolated areas. In August 1878, Victorio, a chief who had ridden with the great Mangas Coloradas, led 80 of his people from their New Mexico reservation into the Sacramento Mountains and became a rallying symbol for all the discontented Indians in West Texas. Most white men thought that the Indian menace would eventually pass away, as surely as the whites would one day own all the land. But before this could occur, Texans had to deal with the reality of hostile Indians.[11]

While increasing numbers of travelers were becoming impressed with the beauty and uniqueness of the country, the Indian threat grew more serious. A correspondent for the *San Antonio Daily Express* wondered at the "scene of legends both of war and of love" that must have taken place within the "frowning heights and narrow passes . . . sylvan retreats and ferny grottos" of Wild Rose Pass, but facts jolted him back to the reality of 1877. "However this may be, there is nothing romantic in the unpleasant fact that the red man still lingers here, and avails himself of every chance to steal and murder. The canyon has always been dangerous ground, and up to this time the Apaches commit frequent depredations in the vicinity." Scattered raids were reported throughout the Big Bend by Victorio's warriors filtering southward from the San Carlos reservation. "The country is inhabited, and furnishes a favorite haunt for thieving and marauding bands of Indians." Another reporter noted that a party of 15 Indians had stolen more than 200 horses and mules from an area ranch in January 1879. "The country from . . . [Del Rio] to El Paso has not been a safe one by any means," another traveler concluded. The editors of the *Daily Express* feared their city might lose some of the Chihuahua trade because of the depredations. "What is the remedy?" pleaded the writer. "The present system of military protection is totally inefficient. With the utmost zeal on the part of the officers and men, who are stationed at such great distances apart, it is frequently impossible to catch the Indians, who plan their devilment with great cunning and elude pursuits by means of their superior knowledge of the country." There is good evidence, too, that many soldiers feared Victorio and did not want to catch him. Capt. George A. Purrington encountered Victorio on the Rio Grande in 1880, but left his commander powerless to "explain satisfactorily why he did not follow and attack." [12]

By June 1879, Victorio had proved to be an able, aggressive match for the cavalry. After leaving the reservation, he had headed for the Big Bend, where he was joined by Chief Caballero and another party of Mescaleros. Some have speculated that Caballero had volunteered to go out and try to convince Victorio to surrender. If this is true, he failed, for his warriors joined the rebel chief. Raiding on both sides of the Rio Grande, Victorio attracted the attention of the warriors who had remained on the reservation, and many slipped off to join him. From 80, his band soon had increased to between 200 and 300.[13]

Victorio would not be easily defeated. In contrast to past failures at cooperation, the United States and Mexico agreed to band together. Col. Joaquín Terrazas of Chihuahua coordinated his forces with those of the United States, permitting American forces to cross into his State in pursuit of the Apaches. The Americans, meanwhile, adopted a different approach. After years of futile effort, Brig. Gen. Edward O. C. Ord created the District of Pecos and appointed Col. Benjamin H. Grierson to pacify the Indians. Grierson established subposts to watch the principal waterholes and trails. His soldiers patrolled the entire Big Bend, gathering much information that aided them in their pursuit. Grierson himself toured the country and sent detailed reports to headquarters.[14]

Hearing that Victorio had emerged from the mountains of northern Mexico, Grierson took to the field with a small escort. He learned that the chief was headed in his direction. Grierson, another officer, six men, and Grierson's teenage son, Robert, fortified the Tinaja de las Palmas, near Quitman on the Rio Grande. Hearing that the Apaches were camped only 10 miles away, Grierson sent for reinforcements and got 14 additional men. The Apaches rode into the ambush on the morning of July 30, 1880. Trapped, they turned to flee, but were cut off by Lt. Leighton Finley and 10 cavalrymen. When Capt. Nicholas Nolan arrived from Quitman with reinforcements, Victorio retreated and scattered his warriors in Mexico.

Grierson knew that Victorio was not defeated. In early August the chief crossed into Texas en route to New Mexico and again encountered one of Grierson's patrols. Believing that the chief would have to visit Rattlesnake Springs, Grierson fortified that waterhole and waited. The Apaches attacked the troopers there, but found them too well dug in. Hoping to distract the soldiers, Victorio then turned on a passing supply train, but Grierson's men

Col. Benjamin H. Grierson chased
Victorio into Mexico.

Col. William H. Shafter followed Grierson as
commander and continued the Army's
"pacification" program.

attacked his rear as he closed in on the wagons. Victorio was again
forced to retreat into Mexico. Grierson had not captured the chief,
but he had prevented him from returning to the New Mexico reservation, which probably would have been a source for new
warriors.[15]

Peace finally came to West Texas when Victorio was killed in
a skirmish with Mexican troopers at Tres Castillos in northern
Chihuahua. Colonel Terrazas with a force of volunteers and Tara-
humari Indian scouts engaged the Apaches in October 1880.
When the battle was over, Terrazas, who had never seen the chief,
learned from two Mexican captives that Victorio was among the
dead. By the time Col. William Shafter arrived at Fort Davis for
his second tour of duty in March 1881, the Indians had been quieted. There were still occasional raiding parties of desperate Indians that swooped down from their hideouts in the mountains, stealing a few cattle or horses, but none of Victorio's band remained.
"There were some roving bands of the different tribes that found a
refuge in the mountain fastness of the Rio Grande where game and
fish were abundant and where a vast country two or three hundred
miles in length on either side of the river was totally uninhabited,"
wrote Capt. W. J. Maltby of the Texas Rangers, but as settlement   119

increased and game decreased, even they joined their countrymen on the reservation. Colonel Shafter had little problem driving the tired and hungry natives out of the Big Bend and forcing them onto reservations.[16]

Coming of the Railroad

The following year two railroads linked the Big Bend region with the rest of Texas. The task was difficult, for bridges had to be built over almost 200 rivers and arroyos, and water tanks had to be placed at 20-mile intervals. Over 300 construction workers and 100 trackmen were employed on the job by the Texas & Pacific Railroad by the fall of 1881. Seventeen cars of iron and 40 cars of ties were used each day. Crews strung telegraph wires along the track as it was completed, and a contractor followed the company with more than 180 beeves for food. When H. N. Dimick, from Uvalde, visited one of the construction camps in April 1882, he reported that the company had 3,000 Chinese at work on the tracks. They lived in a "town of tents covering an area as large as the town of Uvalde," he reported. Marveling at the cluster, he noted that a "regular store" on one of the railroad cars provided the workers with anything they wanted. A combination of the Southern Pacific and the Galveston, Harrisburg and San Antonio, a part of the Texas and Pacific, extended service to what became Alpine in 1882, with the Southern Pacific building from the west and the GH & SA working from the east. They drove the last stake just west of the Pecos River on January 12, 1882. "The huge Chihuahua wagon will be a thing of the past, traditional and somewhat doubtful," exulted the Fort Davis correspondent for the *San Antonio Daily Express,* but the future was less certain. "We are no longer the frontier, for we will have fallen into the embrace of the iron monster and will possibly perish beneath its wheels." [17]

The twin obstacles of Indians and poor transportation had now been removed. For the first time many prospective settlers realized that the Big Bend was more than inhospitable desert. Soon ranchers and miners, health seekers and opportunists, began combing the Big Bend in search of unclaimed grassland or undiscovered minerals. Enough were successful to encourage others to try.[18]

Ranching in the Big Bend

The ranchers were the first to come. The foundation for the cattle industry was laid early. Formal ranching did not begin until after the Mexican War, but cattle had roamed the Big Bend for centuries. The frequent Spanish expeditions to New Mexico brought cattle with them to supply food and milk for the travelers. The Indians brought back cattle after their raids in northern Mexico. One of the main cattle raising areas of Spanish Texas was the Rio Grande Valley, where cattle roamed free as far upriver as the Nueces.[19] Some probably wandered even farther, perhaps reaching the Big Bend. Herds also were brought to the Spanish presidios of San Vicente and San Carlos. Stray cattle undoubtedly became the nucleus of the wild bands that roamed the country. Thus cattle were in the Big Bend long before men moved in to organize one of the best ranching areas in the State.

There were several reasons why the industry itself did not develop more rapidly. Although the Spaniards ranched in both New Mexico and Texas, rugged country and the hostile Indians excluded them from the Big Bend. There were other difficulties. The Big Bend was a disputed land until the United States defeated Mexico in 1848. In addition, it was too far from centers of commerce to make ranching profitable. Most settlers came only after the railroad arrived in 1882.[20]

The Big Bend was ideally suited for ranching. This "natural cow country" is rich in grama grasses, shrubs, trees, and edible cacti for hungry cattle. The soil is good; the rainfall limited but timely. Water is scarce, but plentiful enough in the springs and creeks for ranching. James B. Gillett, a former Texas Ranger who became foreman of the G4 Ranch, found Terlingua Creek to be a "bold running stream, studded with cottonwood timber and . . . alive with beaver," even as late as 1885. Much of the land in the Big Bend is above 3,000 feet in elevation and is thus free from the 100 degrees plus temperatures of the desert in summer. The winters are rarely harsh.[21]

The First Ranchers

The first ranchers to settle in the Big Bend were fiercely self-reliant. Ben Leaton, John Spencer, and John Burgess felt that ranching would be profitable, but marauding Indians did not allow them to realize a profit. Cattle were brought into the area after Fort Davis was established in 1854. Spencer, probably the first important rancher in the area, and a handful of competitors were lured into supplying beef to the fort garrison. He had tried to raise horses on his ranch near Presidio, but there was no nearby market,

121

and the Indians preyed on them. Knowing that the redmen wanted horses more than cattle, and that the soldiers needed the beef, he decided to change to cattle ranching in the mid-1850s. He negotiated a contract with Col. Washington Seawell, commander at the fort, and bought a herd of Mexican cattle to move to his ranch.[22]

The first large-scale cattleman in the Big Bend was Milton Faver, a former freighter on the Santa Fe Trail. Little is known about Faver, and much of that seems contradictory. An Englishman, or perhaps a Frenchman, he reportedly spoke Spanish, French, and German besides English. He was frequently referred to as baronial in appearance, and liked tailor-made suits, rare meat, good wine, and peach brandy. Faver told Zenas Bliss, who was stationed at Fort Davis, that he was a Virginian who had come west because of consumption. Others said that he left Missouri because he thought a man he had shot had died. He described to Bliss his trip across the plains to Santa Fe, his wanderings in Mexico, his eventual settling in the Big Bend. Although Faver lost much of his land late in life, he never seemed to lose his discipline and confidence.

In 1857 he operated a general merchandising store in Presidio, but soon turned to the livestock business. After he took up ranching, it was evident he had a talent for it. Moving away from the security of Fort Davis in 1856, he located his fortress-like headquarters on Cibolo Creek near the Chinati Mountains, 30 miles north of Presidio. To combat the hostility of the Indians and

Milton Faver was one of the first ranchers in the Big Bend.

122

of nature, Faver built his residence with thick adobe walls and heavy gates. Gunports were spaced evenly across the walls, and a small cannon, obtained from Fort Davis, guarded the area. The house is still occupied today, making it one of the oldest ranches in the Big Bend. Faver soon established several more ranches, including one stocked with sheep. He traded with the Indians, endured several of their attempts to wipe him out,* and prospered. Faver's herd eventually grew from the original 300 head to an estimated 10,000 to 20,000. When Bliss visited him in the 1880s, he was a wealthy man.[23]

Other Ranchers

While Spencer and Faver built the large herds, smaller ranchers located near Fort Davis to supply the needs of the soldiers. When Bliss arrived at the fort in 1855, Daniel Murphy, whose herd was located near the post, was the beef contractor. He later established a ranch in Toyah Valley in the Davis Mountains. Five miles down Limpia Canyon, Diedrick Dutchover raised sheep unsuccessfully because the Indians raided so often he could not make money. Bliss warned that no one was safe more than 2 miles from the post. In April 1877, two of Murphy's men were killed within a few hundred yards of another ranch as they gathered wood. Dutchover finally sold the remainder of his flock to the soldiers. E. P. Webster lived at the fort, preferring to take no unnecessary risks. He ran his cattle on the nearby range under army protection. Another early rancher who sought army contracts was Manuel Músquiz, a recent immigrant from Mexico who established his ranch south of the fort, in what is today Músquiz Canyon. Although he was frequently harassed by the Indians, he refused to leave the substantial home that he had built there for his family.[24]

After the Civil War, would-be ranchers moved rapidly into the Big Bend. Dutchover returned for another try, while Sam Miller, the civilian butcher at the fort, also decided to get a "beef contract" with the army. He soon had over 300 oxen and beef cattle pastured nearby. Colonel Grierson and Sgt. Charles Mulhern built herds while they were in the military at Fort Davis, then remained after their discharge. "Uncle John" Davis established his ranch not far from Faver's in 1870. Probably impressed by the fortress that Faver had constructed, Davis built a similar one on the

---

* Residents of the Big Bend still tell of an Indian who tried to sneak under the tin roof of the fortress during an attack. One of the defenders spotted the intruder and pinned him between the roof and the adobe wall with his saber.

The courthouse and jail in Marfa in 1882.

Frontier Towns

Although there were several settlements in the Big Bend before 1882, most of the larger towns grew up after the Southern Pacific Railroad crossed the Trans-Pecos. Marfa and Alpine both trace their beginning from the railroad. Today they are thriving centers for the Big Bend ranching country.

The depot in Alpine.

**By the turn of the century Marfa was
a flourishing cattle town.**

**Alpine grew quickly. This street scene
indicates its affluence about 1900.**

**One of Alpine's grocery stores
about 1921.**

banks of Alamito Creek. He quickly developed a large herd of cattle and horses and was competing successfully with Faver and the others for the available market. Bliss commented in his reminiscences that fresh meat on the hoof was always available while he was at Fort Davis.[25]

George Crosson, a freighter who had traveled the Chihuahua Trail in the 1860s, became one of the better known ranchers in the area. Realizing that the railroad would soon come through the region, bringing with it a new form of prosperity, Crosson decided to establish a sheep ranch near Fort Davis. His operation was highly successful. A correspondent for the *San Antonio Daily Express* who visited the ranch in 1877 found Crosson's flocks in good condition, yielding a high quality wool. "His success has been satisfactory, notwithstanding attacks and depredations that would have discouraged a less energetic and determined man," the correspondent noted. Just before the traveler arrived, in fact, Crosson, his herders, and several soldiers fought off a party of Indians who were driving off his horses and mules. Crosson had 10,000 sheep in his pastures when H. N. Dimick, of Uvalde, visited his ranch in 1882. A later traveler pronounced him "one of the most successful sheepmen in the state . . . ."[26]

Another knowledgeable sheepman was Lawrence Haley, whose ranch Dimick also visited. After touring the land, the newcomer concluded that "Mr. Haley and Mr. Crosson have got the key to this country. They have the best range and the most water that I have found since I left home . . . ." Dimick was so impressed, in fact, that he leased an extensive parcel of land himself. Destined to become one of the largest landholders in the Big Bend, John A. Pool, Sr., arrived from Missouri in 1885. He bought Faver's Ciénega Ranch and eventually owned land from Marfa to the Rio Grande.[27]

One of the most beautiful spots in the Big Bend went to Lucas C. Brite, a young cowboy who reached Capote Mountain with his herd in October 1885. "Had one stood on the Capote Mountain and viewed the surroundings," Brite later recalled, "he would most likely have been impressed with the thought that the country was just as God had made it, not a trace of man was visible. Not a house in sight; no fences, no windmills, no water places, not even a road and no livestock of the domestic order." With his 140 cattle Brite built a large ranch and a fortune that allowed him to become a philanthropist in his old age.[28]

Another famous ranchman in the Big Bend was Richard M. Gano, former Civil War general and preacher. John, his son, moved to the Big Bend, where he served as deputy surveyor for Presidio County, which at that time included all of what would become Big Bend National Park. Gano was able to accumulate one of the largest ranches in the Big Bend. John, his brother, and a partner, E. L. Gage, even established a land office in Dallas. They organized the Estado Land and Cattle Company to handle their far-flung ranching activities in the Big Bend. The Ganos owned over 55,000 acres of land in the southern part of what is today Brewster County, in Block G4 of the survey. G4 became the name of the ranch.[29]

James B. Gillett, the ranch manager, recalled that the "Ganos had it all to themselves." In 1885 they shipped 2,000 head of cattle from Dallas and Denton counties in north Texas to their ranch. From Uvalde County they drove another 2,000 head overland to the Big Bend. Meanwhile, they had purchased another 2,000 and shipped them by rail to Marathon. By late summer they had 6,000 head of cattle grazing on their rich G4 pasture land. Initially the company prospered, increasing until the herd was estimated at almost 30,000 by 1891. But drought and other problems combined to decrease that number considerably. By the time the company was disbanded in 1895, only 15,000 head could be rounded up. Even at that the G4 did not suffer as much as the neighbors during the severe droughts of the mid-1880s. Most of the small cattlemen in the northern Big Bend lost heavily, but "not a head of G4 cattle died for the want of grass or water," claimed Gillett. Presumably, they died of natural causes, were rustled, lost or sold.[30]

Although the decline of such vast empires discouraged some smaller ranchers, others continued to settle in the Big Bend. Perhaps they were inspired by the example of W. L. "Uncle Billy" Kingston. Newly married, he set out for the West with 107 cattle, his wagon and team, and $4.70 in cash. At some point west of the Pecos River, he saw some cowboys dressing a calf that looked so good he inquired where it had been raised. Told that the calf had been nourished in the Big Bend, "Uncle Billy" forsook his plan of settling in Arizona and turned southward to the Big Bend. He soon agreed to buy 160 acres and leased another 2,500. Before he

**Stopping for supper during an 1895 trail drive.
These Big Bend cowhands are on their way to a
railhead in Kansas.**

died "Uncle Billy" had a 40,000–acre ranch. Others from all
parts of the State followed him. Some of the settlers were former
Texas Rangers who had guarded the railroad surveying team as it
inched westward, or who were stationed at Fort Davis as part of
the famous Frontier Battalion. There were novices like Capt. A. E.
Shepherd, who traded his interest in a fleet of Great Lakes freighters for the Iron Mountain Ranch, near Marathon. G. W. Evans
moved to the Big Bend because the country around Lampasas,
Tex., was getting too crowded. His brother-in-law, John Z. Means,
joined him in the move. "There were some cattle rustlers in the
country," said Mrs. Evans, "but things were fairly peaceful."[31]

The Big Bend was soon settled. John Beckwith brought 100
Herefords to his ranch on Maravillas Creek in 1878. H. L. Koker-
not and his uncle purchased extensive holdings in 1883. The fol-
lowing year Capt. Pat Dolan brought graded cattle to his range in
Limpia Canyon, and W. B. Hancock drove cattle from Uvalde to
Alpine. In 1885 W. T. Henderson settled at the mouth of the

These cowboys are doctoring a yearling infected with the screw worm during a 1935 roundup.

creek, and Jim Wilson located some 30 miles upstream. Big Benders owned more than 60,000 head of cattle in 1886, the year of the first big roundup.

Trail Drives

The ranchers faced many problems, some heightened because of the isolation or harshness of the country. The first documented trail drive in the Big Bend occurred in 1864, the result of the debilitating effects of the Civil War. Conditions favored the growth of the ranching industry in 1860; there was a steady influx of settlers, the mail route was frequently used, and Fort Davis remained as a deterrent to Indians who threatened to steal the herds. But when the war broke out, the troops were removed, several leading citizens left to join forces with the Confederacy, and the passenger and freight traffic along the Chihuahua Trail diminished considerably. Because the State's resources went toward the Confederate war effort, residents of the area turned to Mexico for markets and supplies. Thousands of cattle were trailed through the Big Bend during the 1860s. W. A. Peril organized a herd and drove it from Fort McKavett country, near the old San Sabá presidio and mission in present-day Menard County, over the Chihuahua Trail to

129

Starting the roundup, 1889.

Mexico, and in 1868 Capt. D. M. Poer took 1,200 head from Fort Concho to the Terrazas hacienda in Chihuahua. W. O. Burnam and several neighbors in Burnet County organized a herd to take to Mexico in 1868. They reported no trouble from Indians, but said that Mexican rustlers stole some of their longhorns.[32]

Will Tom Carpenter was an experienced cowhand by the time he reached the Big Bend in the early 1890s. A veteran of long trail drives through Fort Worth, he moved to a ranch south of Alpine and operated it for the Hereford Cattle Company. "It was an incorporated company, a bunch of Boston Guys," Carpenter later wrote, "it wasn't a big Ranch, only about 3,000 head of cattle." During Christmas week 1892, Carpenter began driving 1,760 head of cattle into the teeth of a norther. "It was trying to storm and do Everything Else but something nice," he recalled. "The fog would be so thick of nights that we couldn't see the cattle, and they would just walk off from 7 or 8 men on gard. We lost the herd 3 different nights before we got off with them . . . it was right in their Range and they wanted to get away and did," he explained. The situation improved slightly when it snowed and the sky cleared, leaving two and one-half inches of snow on the ground. When they reached the Pecos River, Carpenter had difficulty getting the cattle to enter the water, although they could walk across on firm river-bottom. "Those cattle had been raised in those mountains south of Alpine," said Carpenter, "the biggest water they had ever seen was a spring, only when a big rain happened along, which wasn't very often. So they was afraid of so much water." After coaxing them across the river, Carpenter and his crew herded the cattle on to their destination with little problem, but cold weather cost them several cattle.[33]

Rustlers

There were other hazards as well. Rustlers were common because of the many unbranded longhorns roaming the region. Even those with brands often had such simple marks that they could be easily altered. The Mexican border was close and enticing. Nobody was immune. Even the Texas Rangers themselves were once victimized by a daring gang of rustlers near Fort Davis in January 1882. While the Rangers were occupied elsewhere, Dave Rudabaugh, an escapee from the Las Vegas, N. Mex. jail, stole their horses. After securing other horses from the fort, the Rangers followed the bandits' trail, but by then it was cold, and they got away.[34]

A gang that specialized in stealing herds from settlers who had not yet located their land conducted several thefts near the Davis Mountains in 1885. They were captured by local cattlemen working with Texas Rangers, and more than 300 head of cattle were recovered.

The stereotype of the Big Bend bandit soon became the Mexican rustler who dashed across the river to gather in some longhorns, then retreated to safety across the Mexican border. But it did not always work. After losing 1,200 head of cattle from their ranches along Maravillas Creek in 1893, the cattlemen pursued the Mexicans across the river and recovered their cattle. The Big Bend ranchers were probably more troubled by Americans, or at least residents of Texas. Ranger Capt. Charles Nevill pursued Tom Blue and two Mexicans to Presidio del Norte in December 1881 because they were suspected of stealing several mules at Carrizo Springs. Still, rustling was one of the problems that caused Milton Faver to quit ranching.[35]

The Big Bend ranchers began to record their brands in 1875, indicating that the cattle industry had become so widespread that identification was necessary and that cattle rustling was a problem. Diedrick Dutchover and John Davis recorded their brands in 1877; George Crosson followed in 1878.[36]

Stampedes

Perhaps even more hazardous than rustlers were the occasional stampedes that took a heavy toll in stock and, sometimes, cowboys. According to the old-timers, most of the stampedes took place near the Pecos River, where the grass and water were so salty that the cattle became tense and irritable. In addition, the region was swamped with kangaroo rats that frequently set off stampedes by spooking or irritating the cattle. Probably the most famous Big Bend stampede took place at Robber's Roost in 1896. "I saw a sight I never expected to see again," recalled Arthur Mitchell. "Mountains of meat – gory from torn flesh. Grotesque shapes with broken necks, broken horns; here and there a slight movement indicating that somewhere below were a few not yet smothered." It happened during the annual roundup on the Mitchell ranch. The cowboys had corralled 1,500 head of cattle near the rim of Robber's Roost. Something, probably a coyote or panther, set off the herd. The cowboys realized instantly that they had a stampede on their hands. "Snatching whatever was handy – a slicker, a saddle blanket, or better still a flaming torch from the camp fire," remembered F. A. Mitchell, "they leaped into the corral brandishing their assorted weapons in the face of the maddened herd." But they were too late. Literally hundreds of cattle plunged over the cliff. The cowboys worked through the night to save those they could reach, but it was not until morning that they realized the hopelessness of their task. "It was an appalling sight," continued Mitchell. "By a miracle no human body had been added to this gruesome mound." [37]

Tom Granger, a trail hand with Norman and Morgan of Presidio County, recalled the most peculiar stampede of his life. As a 16-year-old boy, he was helping drive a herd to Amarillo in March 1890 in an electrical storm. "The cattle were milling and hard to hold," he remembered, "then electricity got to playing over their backs, and running along their horns like lights." Granger confessed that he was frightened as the thunder and lightning cracked and the cattle charged – but so were the more seasoned hands. A stampede was not to be taken lightly.[38]

Drought

The drought of 1885 left most Big Bend cattlemen desperate. The pastures suffered, waterholes dried up, and the pools and streams that still held water were badly overcrowded by thirsty cattle. Then a bad winter caused the stock to scatter. The drought of 1886 proved equally harsh. The cattle were moved from poor ranges to good pasture wherever possible. But still they died. Nineteen were left dead on one campsite. Uneasily noting that they needed to take action, the cattlemen began talking of a general roundup. Finally, they set aside 2 weeks in August for it. Two groups of cowboys swept through the Bend, saving most of the cattle.[39]

But some ranchers could not go on. One of the most notable failures was Frank Collinson, an Englishman who immigrated to Texas in 1872 at age 16. After learning the trade at the Circle Dot Ranch in Medina County, Collinson came to the Big Bend in 1882. "At the time it was a veritable 'no man's land,' " he recalled, "and few people had ventured into its deep, rugged, and almost impassable canyons." At first Collinson thought the Big Bend would have been poor ranch country, but he soon changed his mind. By 1888 he had convinced the Coggin brothers (Samuel and M. J.) and Henry Ford, a Brownwood banker, to invest in a ranch in the Glass Mountains, near Marathon. But the droughts continued, and the cattle market fell sharply. By 1891 the Big Bend had received no measurable rainfall for 3 years. Collinson drilled wells, but did not find sufficient water. "Over half the cattle from San Antonio to the Rio Grande are dead," he informed his partners in 1892. The following year was no better. "The Pecos is nearly dry and is so strong of alkali that it take[s] the skin of[f] the tongues of any animals that try to drink," he wrote Samuel Coggin. By June 1894, Collinson had been whipped. He had found by hard experience that the sod was poor and the water scarce. "I faced such problems half my life and concluded that the Big Bend is another Pharaoh's Dream," he later wrote; "a few good years are followed by more lean years, which eat up all that the good years have made, and then some."[40]

Barbed Wire Empire

The open-range days in the Big Bend were numbered. The roundups and other cattle industry procedures worked only so long as the range was available to everyone. The coming of many small ranchers to the Big Bend led to widespread fencing. There might have been some fencing as early as 1885, but W. F. Mitchell did not close in his pastures near Robber's Roost until 1888. Pat Coleman and W. W. Bogel renewed the trend in 1893, when they enclosed their pasture. By 1895 Humphris and Company had fenced a 16-section range. The last stronghold of the open range was gone by 1900.

When fences closed the range, they changed the nature of the cattle business. Fences made possible the improvement of herds, thus numbering the days of the wild Texas longhorns, which could no longer compete successfully in the eastern markets with the better breeds from other ranges. By 1876 W. S. Ikard, a central Texas rancher, had already imported Herefords. The Northwestern Texas Cattleman's Association, meeting in Dallas in 1883, adopted resolutions urging the improvement of Texas cattle. John Beckwith, George W. Evans, Jim and Beau McCutcheon, Pat Dolan, and Jim Hilder had brought better stock into the Big Bend in the 1880s, but most ranchers had not yet fenced their lands and could not participate in the herd improvements. By the 1890s most of the area cattlemen were raising the quality of their herds with Shorthorns, Durhams, and Herefords. The *Marfa New Era* proudly boasted of a steer raised on the J. B. Irving ranch at Alpine in 1911. It was "said to be a many record breaker, weighing on the hoof 1740 pounds . . . ." [41]

Folklore in the Big Bend

One of the great legacies of the cattle industry is the folklore it has provided for the Big Bend. One of the most intriguing legends concerns the MURDER calf. The incident that inspired the story occurred during the general roundup of January 1891. Henry H. Powe, a rancher, disputed with Fine Gilliland, a cowboy working for one of the big ranches, the ownership of an unbranded calf. After a heated argument, both men drew their pistols and Gilliland shot Powe to death, then fled. He was later tracked down by the Texas Rangers in the Glass Mountains and shot. The cowboys who saw Gilliland kill Powe commemorated the occasion by branding the disputed calf with the word MURDER and turning him loose. There the legend takes over. Although there is evidence that the yearling was taken to Montana in the drive, some contend that it stayed in Texas, wandering through the Big Bend, shying away from other cattle, an outcast. Others insist that it turned prematurely gray, that the hair on the brand turned red, and even that the brand grew with the calf until the word MURDER practically covered his side. Thus marked, the steer supposedly wandered throughout the Big Bend looking for the man who made him a grim reminder of a violent event.[42]

Mining

The Big Bend was more than good ranching country; it was also rich in mineral resources. Spaniards and Americans alike searched the region for gold and silver. The Spaniards stationed at Presidio San Vicente reportedly had a mine in the Chisos Mountains that could not be worked because the expense of getting the metal out cost more than it produced. Other Spaniards were supposed to have buried treasure in the mountains, while legends tell of silver supposedly hidden at several sites. The tales of buried treasure and gold and silver mines later led many prospectors on futile searches, and still lure hundreds of treasure-hunters into the Big Bend each year with their hunches and electronic metal detec-

Ore wagons load up at the Shafter mine in the 1890s before heading for Marfa, 45 miles away.

A firewood train arriving in Terlingua, 1934.

tors. While the Big Bend has produced no lost Spanish treasures --
and it is not likely to -- it has yielded some silver ore and great
quantities of quicksilver.[43]

Silver mining lasted only a short time. Ore was discovered in
the Chinati Mountains, near Milton Faver's ranch. John W. Spencer mined there on a small scale in the 1860s, taking what he could
to Mexico in burro carts to be smelted. Professor Wilhelm H. Stee-
ruwitz, a well-known geologist who visited the region in 1878, reported the presence of gold and silver, but it was not until 1882
that Spencer found evidence of enough silver to enlarge his operations. A vein in the Chinatis seemed to have a high ore content,
according to Fort Davis assayers. Gathering capital from California, where entrepreneurs were more willing to invest in mining,
Spencer formed the Presidio Mining Company, with W. S. Noyes
of San Francisco as president and Lt. John Bullis and Gen. William R. Shafter of Fort Davis holding interests.[44]

Because of the deserted nature of the country around the
Chinatis, everything had to be brought in by wagon. The machinery was transported to Paisano Pass on the Southern Pacific Railroad and hauled to the mine site by wagon. Humphris and Company of Marfa supplied 4,000 cords of wood annually, because
timber was scarce in the Chinatis. The company even cut lumber in northern Mexico, ignoring the international complications, in
order to get wood for the furnace. [45]

Marfa could have been the market for the silver miners. Four
years after Spencer began working his claim, the *Marfa New Era*

found the prospects "most encouraging" for both the miners and the city. "It will not be long before Marfa will be shipping more silver bullion than any point in the southwestern silver district," wrote the editor. He even predicted that when the riches of the Chinatis became well known, easterners would be anxious to invest in the venture. That would mean "prosperity and wealth for Marfa," he concluded. What wealth there was, however, went through the town of Shafter, which was established to accommodate the miners.[46]

If not large, the Chinati silver mines at least proved profitable. The Shafter mine changed hands in 1910, and the new owners announced their intention of introducing a new cyanide process. Oil replaced wood as fuel, keeping wagons busy hauling oil from Marfa. In 1913 the 50-ton mill was replaced with a 300-ton mill, and the refining process was improved by replacing quicksilver with cyanide, permitting 600 tons of ore to be treated in 24 hours. The miners encountered veins as rich as $500 per ton and others as poor as $8 per ton. Nevertheless, they made money. They tunneled through the Chinati Mountains, running shafts in every direction until they had more than 100 miles of tunnels that finally yielded over $20,000,000 in silver. At times the mines employed as many as 300 men and built Shafter, a company town between Marfa and Presidio consisting of a club house, a hospital, a boarding house, and family houses. The partially abandoned town stands today as a physical reminder of the strike. When the silver ran out, mining ceased as quickly as it had begun.[47]

There were hints of coal in the Big Bend. In 1886 a prospector named McKenzie found some coal seams northwest of Marfa, near Eagle Springs. Although he was not overwhelmed by the production, he found the yield "highly satisfactory" and still had capital to invest in cattle. O. W. Williams noticed a vein of poor quality coal in the Chisos Mountains while surveying in 1902. Coal was mined in the 1930s near Terlingua to provide fuel for the quicksilver furnaces after the companies began to run short of wood, but production was never impressive.[48]

In what might have been a unique discovery, W. A. Robbins and S. H. Eaton announced in 1909 that they had discovered the kind of lime rock in the Solitario Mountains that made good lithographic stones. The finest lithographic stones were imported from a Bavarian quarry discovered by the man who perfected the lithographic technique, Alois Senefelder. Robbins and Eaton felt that they had found a stone good enough to be commercially valuable, but little came of this discovery.[49]

Some of the more interesting artifacts in the Big Bend — remains of old wooden towers and pieces of cable and ore buckets — owe their existence to the Corte Madera Mine in Mexico near Boquillas. The editor of the *Alpine Avalanche* reported in February 1910 that 250 tons of lead and zinc ore were to be transported across the river on a 6-mile-long cable, then shipped to the Southern Pacific station at Marathon in cars pulled by traction engines. The cable tramway was an ingenious device to avoid hauling the ore over rough terrain and floating it across the river. The tramway's 90 ore buckets and 15 water buckets could carry 7½ tons of ore an hour. The mines, offices, and living quarters were in Mexico; the terminal was in Ernst Valley, on the American side. Today the ruins of the tramway can still be seen by hiking along the Ore Terminal Trail.[50]

Quicksilver

Although reports of quicksilver in the Big Bend had circulated for years, no one had ever taken them seriously. The Indians had used cinnabar for their war paint and for the red pigments in paintings that can still be seen in scattered shelters of the Big Bend. In 1847 Dr. Ferdinand Römer, a German scientist visting Texas, traded an Indian a leather lasso for a small quantity of quicksilver, or mercury. Both Texans and Mexicans heard reports before 1850 of the quicksilver, but no serious explorations were undertaken until 1884 when Juan Acosta reportedly showed a specimen to Ignatz Kleinman, who operated a general store in Presidio, Texas. Kleinman took up a claim near what became known as California Hill and went to work. He failed to find sufficient quantities to make the mine profitable, but did interest a California company in taking over the search. They abandoned the attempt after finding little ore, although they were on top of one of the richest fields in the country. The site of their operations became known as California Hill when one of the miners carved that inscription on a rock.[51]

Quicksilver mines quickly dotted the landscape around Terlingua. Mining began there in 1894 when George W. Manless and Charles Allen investigated the rumors of rich quicksilver deposits in the region. They found the deposits about 90 miles south of Alpine, at that time little more than a station on the Southern Pacific Railroad. The Marfa and Mariposa Mining Company, named after the town and Mariposa County, California, where a huge quicksilver mine was located, was the first to profitably extract quicksilver from the Big Bend. Organized in 1896, the company took up a claim near present-day Terlingua, where the California company had failed, and extracted over 9,000 flasks of mercury (3 quarts, or 76 pounds per flask) by 1903. The gross sale for the company in 1901 and 1902 was more than $350,000. After the "easy" ore had been mined, however, the company disbanded.

At its height the Marfa and Mariposa Company employed 1,000 to 1,500 persons. The four or five white families lived in stone houses belonging to the company, but the Mexicans lived in tents or crude stone huts. The laborers were paid with a punch-out check redeemable anytime at the company store or in cash at the end of the month. Although the store stocked only the barest necessities, it did a good business. Sugar, corn, beans, and flour were brought in by the carload. Work clothing, a few bolts of calico, blue denim, and shirting also were stocked. The store's revenue was usually $100,000 to $150,000 annually. A popular saying in Terlingua, reported C. A. Hawley, the company bookkeeper, was that the mine was a silver mine, but the store was a gold mine.

The ore proved to be rich but the mines were almost inaccessible. The wagon road from Marfa, about 100 miles to the northwest, was at best a difficult route. Six miles from the mine it became impossible for wagons. The supplies had to be loaded on pack mules for the trip across dry and badly eroded paths. Everything except fuel (the plentiful mesquite trees) had to be hauled in. Several Mexicans made a little money hauling goods to Terlingua and quicksilver to Marfa with their Studebaker wagons. Strong enough to carry 3 to 4 tons, the wagons required 10 days for a round trip to Marfa. There was little profit in the freighting, for the Mexicans charged only a half-cent a pound and the only thing they could carry out was quicksilver.[52]

The first miners employed only primitive methods and used shafts no deeper than 200 feet. After the ore was brought to the surface it was loaded into a small car and transported to an aerial tramway. The car was then hand-pushed back to the mine, while the ore was transported over the tramway to the ore crusher, half a mile away. From the crusher, walnut-sized chunks of ore were taken to the smelter.

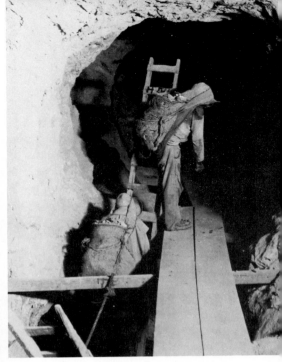

Mexican miners loaded up to 80 pounds of ore on their backs before heading for the surface.

Waldron Mine

Quicksilver mining in the Big Bend boomed in World War I, and slowly played out afterwards. One of the latecomers was the Waldron Mining Company, which began operation in 1916. Production ended before World War II. Few documents of the company have survived, and there is little record of its activities other than a remarkable series of photographs made during the mine's early years.

The entrance to the main shaft.

A tram car carried the cinnabar ore to the crusher, which reduced it to walnut-sized lumps.

Inside the extracting furnace, a hot fire vaporized the mercury in the crushed ore.

Condensers liquified the mercury, which was collected in reservoirs and bottled in standard 76-pound flasks.

The brick furnace measured about 20 feet square and 40 feet high. Two or three weeks of continuous heating was required for the furnace to reach 360 degrees, the temperature at which quicksilver vaporizes from ore. The fumes went out the top of the furnace through a series of 8 or 10 slightly smaller condensers, connected by a pipe. A partition alternately extended from the ceiling of the condenser almost to the floor, then from the floor almost to the ceiling, forcing the smoke from the furnace to describe an upside-down arch in passing through each condenser. The quicksilver gathered in the condensers and ran into buckets. A smoke stack 30 to 40 feet high attached to the last condenser carried off the rest of the vapor and smoke.[53]

Work in the mines was difficult. The miners worked 10 hours a day, most of the labor underground and all of it manual. The ore was loosened by pick and hammer and gathered up by shovel. The work was also dangerous. In February 1908 a blast killed one man and seriously injured another at the Shafter mine. Even the candles used to light the shafts proved dangerous, for they often gave off too little light for the men to avoid open shafts and other hazards. "Miner's consumption," caused by the polluted air, killed several workers every year.

There was no hospital but the company employed a doctor who cared for all the employees. Although the treatment ostensibly was free, the Mexican laborers had one day's wages per month withheld for the medical fund, but white men only $1. The men worked 7 days a week for $1 to $1.50 per day. Sometimes an exceptional worker would be paid as much as $2 per day. Yet C. A. Hawley, the bookkeeper for Marfa and Mariposa Company, got $100 a month plus free rent and goods from the company store at cost.[54]

Several other companies competed with the Marfa and Mariposa Company. Howard E. Perry, a Chicago businessman, organized the Chisos Mining Company in 1902. By 1905 the Terlingua Mining Company, Colquitt-Tigner Mining Company, Texas Almaden Mining Company, Big Bend Cinnabar Mining Company, and Excelsior Mining Company were all in operation in and around Terlingua. When O. W. Williams saw Terlingua in early 1902 he

The water was free at the Chisos Mine, but everyone had to come to the tank to get it. The house commanding the view of Terlingua belonged to Howard E. Perry, the mine owner.

noted that considerable improvement had been made in the last 2 years. The companies employed probably 300 men to haul wood, water, and ore, and work the furnaces. The freight teams kept the road dusty as they brought in supplies and hauled quicksilver to the railhead at Marfa. Texas soon was the number two quicksilver-producing State in the Nation.[55]

Perry's Chisos Mining Company lasted longer and produced more than any other. Perry bought his land in the Big Bend in 1887 and turned down several offers to sell it at a slight profit before he decided to investigate. He found that his land contained quicksilver and set out to mine it. After opening the mine in 1902, he returned to Chicago to direct his affairs there, leaving the mine in control of a succession of managers.

Perry made several changes in his operation. At first using the crude methods of the Marfa and Mariposa Mining Company, he improved his equipment, enabling his men to dig deeper and extract more ore. James Lafarelle reported in 1910 that the depth had already reached 520 feet and that they were planning to go to 1,000 feet in the new shafts.[56]

The quicksilver industry received a good boost when James Norman took some Terlingua ore to the Saint Louis World's Fair in 1904. The specimens were so good that several companies filed claims in the region, but most were never more than small-time or non-producing companies. Capitalized at $500,000 when it opened, for example, the Terlingua Mining Company installed a 45-ton furnace, but fell on hard times and was worth only $35,025 when it closed in 1903.[57]

143

Perry's success drew other prospectors to the Big Bend. They quickly learned that the secret of his success was that his tract was the richest in the region. The quicksilver ore was limited to a relatively small area near Terlingua. Within an area about 14 miles long by 4 miles wide, 30 or more mines were dug, but most of the 150,000 or so flasks of mercury produced came from about 6 mines. The Chisos Company produced more than two-thirds of that total. The Marfa and Mariposa Company produced between 20,000 and 30,000 flasks, leaving all the other companies with a total of less than 30,000 flasks.[58]

Today Terlingua is one of the best known ghost towns in the Southwest and a monument to the lively industry that once flourished in the Big Bend. The site of the World Champion Chili Cookoff, a highly promoted and colorful celebration dedicated to boosterism and local chauvinism, it has also been designated a historic site by the State. The deserted general store, post office, movie house, jailhouse, and church suggest the activities that Terlinguans participated in each week during the heyday of the village. But the nearby cemetery is a reminder that life in the mines was hard, for most of the gravestones tell of those who died young. Dominating the entire perspective is Perry's abandoned house. Located on a hill overlooking the village, this sturdy, two-story building is symbolic of what has happened in Terlingua. From the front porch one can see the deserted mine shafts that brought hundreds of workers to the Big Bend early in the century, and in the distance Santa Elena Canyon and the Chisos Mountains, the impressive landscape which attracts visitors today.

Mariscal Mine

The discovery at Terlingua sent prospectors searching throughout the Big Bend for quicksilver ore. The site that became known as Mariscal Mine was discovered in 1900 by Martin Solís in Mariscal Mountain, just a few miles north of the river. It was not effectively mined until a store owner from Boquillas, D. E. Lindsey, filed a claim on Solís' site and began operation of what he called the Lindsey Mine. His profits were cut considerably because he transported ore via pack mules to the Chisos Mining Company for refining. He finally sold out to T. P. Barry and Isaac Singer, who, in turn, sold out to W. K. Ellis in 1916. Ellis installed his own refining plant and between July 1917 and May 1919 shipped 894 flasks of mercury. When the price of quicksilver dropped after World War I, Ellis sold his holdings to the Mariscal Mining Company, a New York corporation that worked the mines until 1927 when it finally declared bankruptcy. The mine was sold at a sheriff's auction in 1936. William D. Burcham, the company's president, tried to open it again during World War II, but produced only 97 flasks of mercury and soon closed it. Today the mine and old buildings are one of the more interesting remains in the southern part of the national park.[59]

Other Settlers

Settlers came to the Big Bend for various reasons. Max A. Ernst immigrated from Germany to Texas in 1873 at age 16. He lived in Alpine a few years before moving to La Noria, on Tornillo Creek. In 1898 he leased a section of land containing a waterhole called the Big Tinaja. He established a small store by the same name, and later became justice of the peace, coroner, law enforcer, marriage bureau, notary public, and postmaster of Boquillas, Tex. For a time Kit Williams of Louisiana acted as postmaster, because Ernst could not legally hold the jobs of mail carrier and postmaster simultaneously, though he would relinquish neither. Jesse Deemer, later a storekeeper in Boquillas, was a German mining operator working in northern Mexico when he first arrived in the Big Bend. Cipriano Hernández, a native of Camargo, Chihuahua, and an employee in the Shafter mines, moved to a plot of land near Santa Elena Canyon in 1903. He ran a small supply store in a community called Santa Helena, Tex., until 1914 when the name was changed to Castolon. Today the small village of Santa Elena, Chihuahua, is located across the river from Castolon.[60]

Several persons moved to the Big Bend for their health. Milton Faver might have been the first one, arriving in the early 1850s to alleviate a severe case of tuberculosis. After the railroad linked the Trans-Pecos with the rest of Texas, the word spread quickly. J. R. Landrum, who later managed Ernst's store and post office, suffered from chronic bad health and hoped that the dry climate of West Texas would help him. So did J. O. Langford, a malaria sufferer who took up a claim at Hot Springs on the Rio Grande in 1909. A skinny, wan man with thin lips, deep-set eyes, and a pleasing personality, Langford decided to make a health resort out of the hot springs. He received plenty of publicity from the Marfa and Alpine editors, who published accounts of those who had been cured as a result of the treatment and his plans for the

A candelilla wax maker and his family, in front
of their home at Glenn Springs in 1917.
They lived in this shack until they could build
themselves an adobe home.

Burros at Bullis Gap, loaded with candelilla
wax plants gathered in the mountains, 1913.

C. D. Wood's wax plant in full operation, 1917.

resort. There were even suggestions that a second resort be built at another set of hot springs near Castolon on the Mexican side of the river. T. J. Miller, who operated a small store at San Vicente, came to the Big Bend hoping that his wife's health would improve.

By the late 1890s there were enough people scattered throughout the Big Bend that two second-class roads were opened, one from Marathon to Boquillas, the other from Alpine to Terlingua. When a man named Pitts drove his 4-cylinder Acme over the hills from Marfa to Presidio in 1908, he received excited attention from the townspeople along the route and praise from the editor of the *New Era*. At Shafter the school children were dismissed from class and followed the car through the dusty streets. "Actual running time to Presidio, counting out stops, 70 miles in 3 hours 53 minutes," declared the editor. "Chauffeur Pitts states the roads out of Marfa are as good as any in the state. . . ."[61]

Guayule

As the new age of chemistry dawned, scientists found uses for Big Bend plants. "Guayule, the rubber plant, formerly despised and useless, has produced a few hundred million dollars worth of rubber in Mexico and Texas," reported the editor of the *Alpine Avalanche* in 1911. "It has brought riches to those who took advantage of the opportunity when they were asked to invest in the guayule rubber enterprises." Several factories were established along the railroad, but the industry did not last long. The guayule was soon exhausted, and Big Benders turned to other ways of earning a living.[62]

Wax Making

The candelilla plant provided the raw material; unemployed Mexicans supplied the muscle; white men usually provided the capital. In 1911 Oscar Pacius, a director of the Continental Wax Company of Little Rock, Ark., visited Marfa and Alpine and announced his intention of establishing 10 wax factories in the Big Bend. The company already had four producing factories in Mexico, he explained. Pacius declared that his company expected to be able to make about $600 per ton of wax. By the time he reached Alpine in the fall of 1911 the name of his company had been changed to the Rio Grande Wax Company, but the enthusiasm had not diminished. Another important producer was C. D. Wood, who established factories at McKinney and Glenn Springs in 1911.[63]

Wax making is still a major industry in the Big Bend on both sides of the border. In Mexico the government monopolizes production, assigning quotas to producers and guaranteeing them a

147

certain income each year. In the United States a small number of firms buy most of the independently produced wax. Because the Mexican wax makers have no market for their product after they fill the government quota, some observers claim that smuggling wax into the United States is common. Although candelilla wax has been in demand since 1911, the process by which the pure wax is secured has changed little. The plant, which grows wild in the Big Bend, is heated in a mixture of water and sulfuric acid. When the wax loosens from the plant, it floats to the top of the vat, and is scooped off and put into barrels to harden. It is used in candles, phonograph records, insulation of electrical wires, leather and wood polishes, as an agent in the manufacture of celluloid, and as a waterproofing. Early in the century it was an important sealing wax. Today most of the wax goes to the chewing gum industry. Ruins of old wax-rendering operations can be found throughout the park, and wax factories still operate outside the park.

Fur Traders

A common frontier livelihood that might not be expected in the Big Bend was fur-trapping along the Rio Grande. T. M. Meler floated down the river trapping beavers at the turn of the century. Perhaps the best known trapper in the Big Bend was James Mc-Mahon, who escorted Hill through the canyons in 1899. He lived well into this century, trading furs for goods at Johnson's Trading Post, in the southern part of what is now the national park.

Elmo Johnson buying furs at his trading post in the Big Bend, 1929. He enjoyed a good reputation among trappers for his fair prices.

The trappers brought the furs of fox, coyote, wildcat, and skunk into the border trading posts. Often they skinned goats to supplement their income. Many pelts were captured in the mountains along fur trails that stretched sometimes 100 miles through the wilderness. As barter, Elmo Johnson offered wood, other kinds of fur, chino grass, ropes, and various finished items or food. Regular fur traders, in fact, made up his best customers.[64]

The Unwritten Code

By the turn of the century the Big Bend was fairly well settled. Small villages had grown up near waterholes – Tornillo Creek, La Noria, Glenn Springs, and Robber's Roost – and along the Rio Grande. A number of farms flourished in the Lajitas-Castolon area. Ranching, mining, wax making, merchandising, law enforcement, and the military provided a living for the early settlers. Society began to organize into various groups. Livestock associations, promoting pure-bred cattle, exerted strong influences. Rev. William B. Bloys, the "Cowboy Preacher," held annual camp meetings in Skillman's Grove. Soon Bloys Camp Meeting was an event that not many Big Benders missed. Disciples of Christ, Baptists, Methodists, and Presbyterians attended the affair.[65]

The early settlers gradually evolved a code of unwritten laws that governed their community. Probably the most obvious one was the frontier's raw, aggressive brand of equality. A white man was accepted at face value. No questions were asked about the years before he came to the Big Bend; no information was usually volunteered. Texas had much the same reputation during its youthful years when "GTT" meant "Gone to Texas," usually for a bad reason. In the Big Bend it was accepted that a man might be using an assumed name. Thus there are several stories about Milton Faver's background, including the possibility that he was a murderer and that he had been jilted by his Mexican girlfriend. C. A. Hawley was hardly surprised when a neighbor calling himself Tom White came into the post office at Terlingua and claimed a pension check addressed to John M. Southard. He cashed the check with no questions asked when White explained that he was Southard and had changed his name when he moved to the Big Bend. Perhaps the point is better made by the cowboy who, when conversation around the campfire lagged, challenged his companions to create a little excitement by telling their real names.[66]

The fact that white men were accepted as they were emphasizes a second unwritten law of the Big Bend: dark-skinned men were not accepted at all. Racial prejudice in various forms was evident to the newcomer. Hawley, a mid-westerner unaccus-

**This family, living near Polvo in 1916, built their
adobe house between boulders.**

tomed to the racial segregation of the South and Southwest, was
surprised to discover that the Mexican stage driver rode with the
whites but did not eat with them. Working for the Terlingua mining companies, he also learned that Mexicans were employed for
menial jobs and manual labor, but not for the management positions. "In this state," a Brewster County lawyer explained, "we
have one set of laws for white people and one for Mexicans, all in
the same words and in the same book." Prejudice tainted every relationship between white and brown, even to the point that Hawley, as manager of the company store, intimidated a poverty-
stricken Mexican woman into buying her groceries at more
infrequent intervals and in larger quantities because he had grown
tired of selling her a small amount each day. Only later did he
learn that she bought meagerly because she usually did not have
enough money to buy in larger measures. When a ranch or store
was robbed, the authorities immediately assumed that Mexicans
were to blame. Pilares, Chihuahua, was attacked without warning
in both 1917 and 1918 by Americans seeking revenge for raids on
Texas ranches. Several residents were killed, including the mayor of
nearby Candelaria. The amazing explanation, accepted without
qualm by the Anglo-Americans, was that "anyone living in that
particular area, and those who were familiar with it, were aware
that no innocent Mexicans lived in Candelaria and Pilares, Mex-

Nick Merfelder at his Fort Davis home, 1896.
He was the post's musician, barber, photographer,
and justice of the peace.

ico." An army lieutenant searching for bandits in northern Mexico revealed a similar attitude. Flying over the Río Conchos, he saw four mounted horsemen. "I shot a few rounds at them from about 1,000 feet altitude (too high to hit them), to see if they would return the fire. Since they dashed into the high brush without responding, I concluded they were not bandits, but Mexican cowboys. The only way to tell a bandit from a cowboy was to use such a test."[67]

The prejudice extended to Negroes, but had less opportunity for expression because there were few blacks in the Big Bend. The editor of the *Alpine Avalanche* opposed further Negro immigration into Alpine in 1909. Under the headline, "Not Wanted in Alpine," he editorialized that they would disrupt the community. He also suggested a few months later that those already in the city would have to behave in an exemplary manner or be run off. At that, Alpine was hardly different from any other Texas city of the day.[68]

A third unwritten code, which lasted well into the 20th century, required everyone to arm and defend himself. A peaceful

This baptism took place a few miles from Marathon, during the early 1900s.

Frontier Life

Although life on the Big Bend frontier was more strenuous than in settled parts of the West, residents found time to be social, often by taking a Sunday ride in the surrey, attending a friend's wedding, or visiting the local saloon.

152

This Marathon saloon, shown in 1910, kept a pet bear so customers would buy it a beer.

A Shafter family, photographed in the 1890s,
in their two-seater carriage.

Mexicans gambling in Polvo, Texas.

A wedding in 1898 at Boquillas, Mexico.

153

man who disdained liquor and "gun-totin," Hawley abhorred such practices. But he had little influence. As justice of the peace, he frequently asked men charged with violation of the law why they carried weapons. Their invariable response was that no one would respect them if they went unarmed. They apparently feared the social pressure more than the consequences.

The result of disputes involving a deliberate or insulting wrong usually was a gunfight. Hawley remembered hearing the calm pronouncement of final judgment several times: "Well, somebody has got to be killed." This unwritten rule was responsible for the death of Roselle Pulliam, a Big Bend rancher who crossed paths with Jim Gillespie, a well-known cowboy. After purchasing hundreds of cattle in Mexico, Gillespie brought them into Texas, probably without paying all the duty required by law. He cut the fences as he crossed Pulliam's ranch, and Pulliam sought revenge by reporting the approximate number of cattle Gillespie had brought in to the Customs officers. The officials impounded the herd, waiting for the question to be settled. Gillespie's consequent grudge against Pulliam could be settled only by a gunfight. Pulliam moved to New Mexico to avoid the confrontation, but the episode ended tragically when he returned to Alpine to visit his father and Gillespie killed him. It would have been virtually impossible to have secured a conviction, said Hawley, because the murderer had followed the unwritten laws of the country. In this instance, the jury never had the chance because Gillespie himself was killed before his case came to trial.[69]

Law Enforcement

The arrival of the railroad spurred the growth of several towns in the Big Bend: Marfa, Alpine, Marathon. As the unruly element moved in with progress, so did the few individuals who became lawmen. The Texas Rangers patrolled the region throughout the last quarter of the 19th century. Their famous Frontier Battalion did everything from chasing Indians and bandits to accompanying surveyors down the Rio Grande. After retiring from the Rangers, Capt. Charles L. Nevill remained in the Big Bend, first as sheriff of Presidio County, then as a rancher. An even better known lawman who settled in the Big Bend was James Gillett, who retired from the Rangers to become marshall in El Paso. After Nevill and Gillett bought a small ranch in the Big Bend together, it was not difficult for Nevill to convince Gillett that he had been a lawman long enough. He left his marshall's post to become foreman of the G4 Ranch, which was owned by the Ganos and was near enough to his own ranch that he could also care for it. Another popular Ranger who spent a few years in the Big Bend with Nevill was Jeff Milton, who left the service in 1883 and went on to serve with distinction in the U. S. Customs Service.

D. E. Lindsey, the man who filed the claim on Mariscal Mine, first came to the Big Bend as a mounted inspector for the U.S. Customs Service. But the man who perhaps best symbolizes law enforcement in the Big Bend is Thomas Creed Taylor, who was stationed at Pena Colorado, near Marathon, shortly after the turn of the century. He quit the Rangers in 1904 and ranched until 1918, when he joined the Customs Service. In 1942 he was elected sheriff of Presidio County, and held that office for 4 years.[70]

The man who later became known as the "father of the Big Bend National Park" also initially came as a law enforcement officer. Born in Colorado County, Tex., in 1871, Everett Ewing Townsend joined the Texas Rangers at age 19, but resigned after only 18 months with the Frontier Battalion. Moving to Presidio, he joined the U. S. Customs Service and became familiar with the Big Bend while fulfilling his job of scouting along the borders for smugglers. The enthusiasm he gained for the Big Bend while employed by Customs was the foundation of the Big Bend National Park.[71]

Americans came to the Big Bend in three phases. First, the traders and explorers passed through, finding the region neither hospitable nor available, for the Indians controlled it. Then, the U.S. Army and its associates moved into the Fort Davis area. Only vital occupations such as beef contracting could flourish. Not until the Big Bend had been pacified did the third phase – miners, farmers, ranchers, merchants, health seekers, and settlers – begin. Another barrier was isolation. As the Big Bend was drawn into Texas commerce through the Chihuahua traders and later through the railroad, more people settled there – and with them an unsavory element of frontier society.

6 / Bandits Along the Border

The same conditions that rendered the Big Bend difficult to explore and even harder to homestead attracted dozens of bandits around the turn of the century. The sparse settlement, isolation, and rugged terrain seemed at times to constitute an environment more favorable to the lawbreaker than to the settler. The arroyos, canyons, caves, and mountains had first found use as campsites for Indians and explorers. Now they served as hideouts, for "the backwash from the frontiers of Texas was already lapping along the west banks of the Pecos," noted historian J. Evetts Haley. The natural features of the Big Bend proved to be more than just a hideout. Indians and bandits transformed the canyons and mountain chains into fortresses. "Few Americans realize the impregnability and isolation of this frontier," claimed Robert T. Hill, after a first-hand look in 1899.[1]

While many crimes were the result of stained honor or passion, others were the result of considerable contemplation. Hardened criminals hid in the natural shelters of the region. One of Billy the Kid's companions from New Mexico, Jesse Evans, rustled cattle there and hid out in Fort Stockton. He and his gang pulled a robbery in Fort Davis, then headed for the border. They had hoped to cross the river in the Presidio area, but found out that they were likely to be arrested by the Mexican *Rurales* and turned around. A Texas Ranger party encountered them about 15 miles north of Presidio. In the ensuing gunbattle one Ranger and one bandit were killed. The others were arrested.[2]

After trailing a bandit gang into Mexico, U.S. authorities and vigilante bands often forgot about due process of the law and the rights of their victims. Only the military were authorized to cross the Rio Grande in pursuit of bandits, and then only in special cases, but seldom were the laws obeyed. Rancher Jim P. Wilson and his party followed a band that reportedly had murdered a family, stolen some horses, and crossed the river. Upon his return Wilson explained the battle with the usual evasive yet revelatory explanation so highly esteemed on the frontier: "When we overtook

A rocky perch on the south rim of the Chisos.

157

Photograph by Bank Langmore

them, it just naturally scared them to death, so we rounded up our horses and come on back."[3]

After the Southern Pacific Railroad established rail service from San Antonio to El Paso, the more daring bandits turned to the relatively easy job of robbing trains along lonely stretches of track. In October 1891 the Texas Rangers captured five members of a gang that had held up a train in the vicinity of Samuels station near Langtry. A shootout occurred as the Rangers closed in on the desperadoes. When the leader was shot and wounded, he "took out a book and pencil, wrote his will, bequeathing all his property to his brother, took out his pistol and blew out his brains." The other bandits were taken to El Paso for trial.[4]

There were, of course, the routine incidents that law enforcement officers had to contend with. Texas Ranger Sgt. J. T. Gillespie of the Frontier Battalion reported to Capt. Neal Coldwell on January 10, 1882, that an Indian squaw had been "brutally murdered" only 2 days before at Fort Davis. He suspected a black soldier of the murder. The baker at the post, John Schueller, was killed in February 1882. As usual, a Mexican was suspected of the murder. When the railroad crews drew near the fort, barroom brawls became commonplace. Mexicans, gamblers, and railroaders participated in a fatal fight in Kelsey's Saloon in September 1881 in which John Jones, foreman of nearby Rooney's ranch, was killed. The citizens understandably asked for more protection. The region "is a favorable resort of the murderers and desperadoes driven from other sections of the state," claimed the citizens of Pecos County as they requested more Rangers for their county.[5]

Robert T. Hill obviously had heard many of these stories as he began his trip through the canyons of the Big Bend. The storekeeper at Polvo, just upriver from Bofecillos Canyon, showed Hill's party the "splotches of blood" where the previous merchant had been robbed and murdered the year before. Old-timers counseled that the Big Bend was infested with thieves and murderers who disliked any intruders and felled their prey by shooting into sleeping camps at night. Two members of Hill's party refused out of "sheer fright" to go any further. The others proceeded with caution. Whenever possible they hid their camp in bushes and kept loaded rifles handy. E. E. Townsend, himself a former sheriff of

Camp King in the 1890s. Nevill's Texas Ranger
battalion patrolled the frontier from this outpost
12 miles north of Alpine.

Brewster County, believed that Hill had exaggerated, but conceded
some danger. "Away from the railway," concluded Hill, "the Big
Bend – sometimes called the Bloody Bend – is known as a 'hard
country,' that is, one in which . . . civilization finds it difficult to
gain a foothold." [6]

The Mexican Revolution and the Big Bend

The most serious difficulties with bandits developed after the
Mexican Revolution erupted in 1911. By 1910 there were at least
20 large ranches in a 250-square-mile area of the Big Bend vulnerable to attack. Only a few cavalrymen, Texas Rangers, and
mounted customs officers patrolled the region. They worked together closely, but the task would have been impossible even for
twice as many defenders, for the territory was extensive, the hiding
places numerous, and access too easy. Gen. Frederick Funston reported in 1916 that the Big Bend Military District alone was 500
miles long and that "practically all" the mobile army in the United
States was stationed along the international boundary. Still, it was
impossible to patrol the entire area. [7]

The revolution that exploded in Mexico in 1911 was the
product of decades of economic poverty and political suppression.
Several of the initial conflicts occurred along the U.S.-Mexico border largely because the insurrectionists either had sought exile in
the U.S. or had come to recruit Mexicans living in the United

159

States. The Mexican government suspected that the revolutionaries were enlisting men in the Big Bend, particularly in Presidio and Boquillas, Texas. The Mexican Embassy in Washington requested that the United States take action to assure that the bands would be broken up before they crossed the river into Mexico. Starving guerrilla bands roamed northern Mexico, causing fear that they might plunder the defenseless ranches in the Big Bend.

As the revolutionary forces of Pancho Villa, the most effective revolutionary on the border, attacked Ojinaga, formerly Presidio del Norte, residents of the Big Bend tensed. Refugees deluged the small railroad town of Marfa, 60 miles north of Ojinaga, only to be shipped to El Paso camps. After being defeated at Ojinaga, an estimated 125 revolutionaries took refuge in San Antonio, a village across the Rio Grande from Candelaria. Such a combustible situation led one New York newspaper to report erroneously in 1911 that Terlingua had been devastated by Mexican desperadoes and many people slain.[8]

As the revolutionaries regrouped in the Big Bend, a brave Associated Press reporter, E. S. O'Riley, ventured down the river to El Polvo in search of a "scoop." He encountered two Mexicans who offered to take him to meet José La Cruz Sánchez, a prominent

After the Mexican revolutionaries attacked Ojinaga in 1911, refugees fled to Marfa and settled into camps.

guerilla leader and a well-known ranchman in Chihuahua. O'Riley went with the Mexicans and waited in a nearby vacant house for Sánchez to appear. Overhearing that his hosts were government *Rurales* who did not want him to write any stories about the insurrectionists, O'Riley announced he was leaving. The men realized their pretense had failed; now he would have to be killed. Jerking out their pistols, they ordered O'Riley to go with them to Ojinaga, saying that he would never again see Sánchez. Thinking fast and recklessly, the correspondent hit the man nearest him and drew his weapon. "The first shot dropped an assailant before he could fire. Each of the others got in a shot at close range, but by a miracle, went wild, and before a second round could be fired, O'Riley's deadly aim had done its work. One he was compelled to shoot the second time." The reporter then rode back to the American side of the river and filed his remarkable story.

As incidents occurred up and down the Rio Grande, official crossings at established border checkpoints became more difficult. Customs inspectors, Texas Rangers, and soldiers prevented anyone bearing arms or carrying ammunition from entering the United States. The Mexican commander at Ojinaga likewise limited entry, provoking a complaint from Congressman William R. Smith, whose district included Presidio.[10]

A raid did occur in June 1911 at nearby San Antonio, Chihuahua, on a ranch owned by Lamar Davis, an American. Inez Salazar and a band of 30 revolutionists surrounded the ranch house and demanded provisions, guns and ammunition, horses and saddles. Francisco and Dario Sánchez, the ranch managers, were able to contact the government commander at Presidio, who sent a party to chase the raiders away, but not before they escaped with rifles, saddles, horses, mules, 70 bushels of wheat, and some ammunition. Families in San Antonio fled to the American side of the river to escape harm. Ranchers were terrified, since the bandits could just as easily cross the river. The commander of the Southern Department at Fort Sam Houston pointed to the raid on the Davis ranch as the excuse to keep the few troops already in the Big Bend there, rather than withdraw them, as some military men were pressuring him to do.[11]

The following year a government officer scattered a band of 25 bandits just across the river from Candelaria. He then left a dozen of his troops at San Antonio to help the Americans under Capt. Frank A. Barton pacify the area. The captain interpreted the incident as proving that the Mexican government could now control its side of the border.[12]

Continual disturbances soon proved him wrong. The commander at Fort Sam Houston reported in March 1912 that there was concern all along the border, although no official had yet requested troops. J. O. Langford, who operated a bath concession at Hot Springs, realized his family was in danger when he heard that the bandits and revolutionists were moving freely across northern Mexico. Residents vacated San Vicente, Mexico, the village that had grown up near the old presidio. Langford advised all his customers to gather at his house, which could be transformed into a fort. When he learned the bandits had plundered Boquillas and San Vicente, Mexico, he concluded that he was in imminent danger. Langford and Jesse Deemer of Boquillas rode to Marathon and requested that troops be stationed near the river. Lt. James L. Collins and 25 men were dispatched to La Noria, where they rode along the river.[13]

Troops Leave the Big Bend

Early in 1913, however, the troops were withdrawn. Lieutenant Collins sent a message to Langford that they were returning to Marathon and that he should move his family to a safer location. "That word shook me up," recalled the resort owner. "I realized that Collins would not have risked court martial for revealing army secrets if he had not felt that our danger here was immediate and great." Langford gathered up his family and what belongings he could carry and left Hot Springs to the mercy of the bandits.[14]

The raiders were not long in coming. With his brothers, José and Manuel, Chico Cano had been terrorizing the Big Bend for several years. They were suspected of killing an officer in January 1913, when U.S. Customs Inspectors Joe Sitters and J. S. Howard and cattle association inspector J. W. Harwick arrested a Mexican for smuggling and horse stealing. Headed toward jail, they were ambushed. Sitters and Howard were wounded, Howard fatally. "They were not Carranzistas, they were not Villistas, they were not anything," claimed E. W. Nevill of the Canos. "Whoever is in charge on the border . . . they are with." The following month a band of robbers crossed the Rio Grande and raided the Lee Hancock ranch, 14 miles northeast of Alpine. They escaped with guns, saddles, ammunition, and five good horses. They also raided the Lawrence Haley ranch, taking saddles, bridles, and several other items. A posse was organized by Sheriff J. Allen Walton, but the bandits escaped. "The lower part of Brewster County is a desolate and broken mountain country," reported the *Alpine Avalanche,* "and . . . it would be a hard matter to locate anyone familiar with that section who was trying to avoid detection. As the Mexicans are known to be bad men and are armed to the teeth, there has been much uneasiness felt about those who are pursuing them. . . ."[15]

Such incidents provoked citizen demands that the soldiers be returned to the Big Bend. J. R. Landrum, postmaster at Boquillas, appealed to Texas Senator Morris Sheppard for help, pointing out that Boquillas was 100 miles from the railroad, was "scarcely settled," and provided an inviting target for raiders. The situation had been calm until the troops withdrew, he wrote, but now the citizens were apprehensive. He asked Senator Sheppard to use his influence with the War Department to return the troops. The *Alpine Avalanche* also called attention to the necessity of troops being assigned to the border. Texas Governor Oscar B. Colquitt wired President William H. Taft that troops were still needed along the border, then authorized Sheriff Walton to deputize as many men as he felt necessary to "properly safe-guard the interests of the citizens." But the commander of the Southern Department, worried about the need for troops in other areas, replied that conditions were quiet enough in the Big Bend and that no troops were necessary.[16]

Despite the commander's allegation, bandits plundered the Big Bend with regularity from 1915 to 1918. Small bands would gather just across the Rio Grande, determine their target, and dash across the river. In May 1915, Capt. G. C. Barnhart of the 15th Cavalry reported a murder on the American side of the river by some Villa men. They crossed the river and killed Pablo Jiménez by shooting and beating him. "I have a piece of his skull," wrote Barnhart.[17]

Hoping to obtain some aid for the Big Bend, Texas Governor James Ferguson asked President Woodrow Wilson in 1915 to station troops at Boquillas and opposite Pilares. Secretary of War Lindley M. Garrison replied after consulting General Funston, commander of the Southern Department, that the situation there was "one . . . very near to justifying martial law." But he recommended no action. To Governor Ferguson's renewed requests, Funston finally answered that he had sent some patrols into the Big Bend and could do no more. Believing that many of the bandits were citizens of Texas, Funston insisted that the problem was partially civil and should be handled by the Texas Rangers or the local sheriff. He convinced Garrison of his logic, and the Secretary advised the President that nothing more should be done. "The distance from Brownsville to El Paso . . . is over twelve hundred miles, following the windings of the river," he wrote, "and part of it is about as inaccessible and difficult a country as can be imagined, so that it will not in any circumstances be possible to station troops throughout that entire stretch . . . ." [18]

The unrest and periodic border raids continued. Four bandits attempted to wreck a train east of Alpine in March 1916, but were captured by alert soldiers before they could inflict any damage. Most people felt that the raids were the work of members of Pancho Villa's band. A significant force in the Mexican Revolution until he was defeated at the battle of Celaya and driven into the desert of northern Chihuahua, Villa had turned to guerrilla warfare and depended on aid from the United States to survive. But in 1916 President Wilson discontinued all aid to Villa, hoping to bring an end to the revolution and enable President Venustiano Carranza to restore order to Mexico. In retaliation for the decision – and to obtain food and supplies for his ragged troops – Villa raided Columbus, N. Mex., on March 9, 1916, hoping to involve the United States in the conflict and thereby embarrass President Carranza. Many felt that the attack on Columbus was a signal to Villa's men along the border that they could now raid isolated U.S. settlements with impunity. But Villa cannot be blamed for all the raids because his troops could not possibly have reached as many points as were attacked. Most likely bandit gangs took the opportunity to line their own pockets, giving the blame – or credit – to Villa. [19]

Many politicians as well as residents were provoked by the disturbances and demanded action. Senator Marcus A. Smith of Arizona pressed for a full-scale invasion of Mexico. "It strikes me it would be a very splendid idea to give the Mexicans an object lesson of our strength," he wrote Secretary of War Newton D. Baker. "It will cost money, but it will be worth the price," The President, of course, did send Gen. John J. Pershing into Mexico to chastize Villa for the raid at Columbus, but the Big Bend itself remained unprotected. [20]

Capt. C. D. Wood

After the raid on Glenn Springs, two troops of
the 6th Cavalry arrived and set up camp.

Raids on Glenn Springs and Boquillas

The worst raids in the Big Bend occurred on the night of
May 5, 1916, when a party of approximately 80 bandits, probably
including several Texas Mexicans, crossed the river near San Vicente and raided Glenn Springs and Boquillas. Located on a rise in
the foothills of the Chisos Mountains, Glenn Springs was the home
of C. D. Wood and W. K. Ellis, partners in a wax factory employing about 50 Mexicans. The village was protected by a sergeant
and recently arrived troopers of the 14th Cavalry. Wood and Ellis
had established a small general store to serve the needs of the
workers and their families, and this apparently was the main target
of the bandits.[21]

Boquillas was an even smaller community. Situated directly
across the river from the Mexican village by the same name, it was
the terminal for the aerial tramway that transported silver ore
from the nearby mines in Mexico. Jesse Deemer's small store there
attracted the bandits.

The bandits split into two groups as they crossed the river
and proceeded unnoticed to their targets. Seventy-five headed toward Glenn Springs, and the remainder turned toward Deemer's
store. For a force of this size, the few troops deployed at Glenn

165

Several soldiers fought the bandits from this adobe cook house at Glenn Springs.

Springs were wholly inadequate. The first group rode into Glenn Springs a few minutes before midnight, surprising the sleeping village. Firing into every dwelling, the raiders soon had Sgt. Charles E. Smyth and six soldiers surrounded inside a barricaded adobe hut. Using Springfields and Colts, the troopers fought bravely and held the bandits off until one tossed a torch onto the thatched roof, turning it into an inferno. When they abandoned the house, three were shot, but the sergeant and three others escaped into the night. Two other troopers escaped by remaining inside their tent.

The bandits then turned to C. G. Compton's house. One broke down the door; another fired into the structure, killing 7-year-old Tommy, alone in the house. Compton had taken Tommy's younger sister to the hut of one of the Mexican families for safety and had failed to return for Tommy before the bandits closed in. Tommy's brother, Robert, a deaf-mute, somehow wandered through the village unharmed as the fighting raged.

Other members of the band looted the general store. Everything that could be packed was taken, except the sauerkraut, which they apparently believed to be spoiled. Larger bundles, such as the heavy bags of flour and corn were left behind because they would slow the return to Mexico.

Wood, a veteran of the Philippine campaign, was unable to offer any aid to the hapless residents of Glenn Springs. Asleep in his home 2 miles from the village, he was awakened by the sound of shots. He first thought that the Mexicans were celebrating *Cinco de Mayo,* the holiday recalling Mexico's defeat of the French at

Puebla in 1862. When he realized that they weren't, he quickly dressed and aroused his neighbor, Oscar de Montel, another army veteran. Carrying rifles, they hurried through the night to the village, toward the flames and sound of shooting. Before they got there, the firing stopped and the flames died. Wood and Montel continued on in darkness. "We stumbled through whipping brush and annoying cactus," said Wood. Two hours passed before they reached the village.

"Quién vive?" (literally, "who lives?"), shouted the bandits' picket as the pair approached. It was a challenge. The response, common during the Revolution, should have been "Viva Villa" ("Villa lives"), but Montel either was confused or did not know the password.

"Quién es?" ("Who is it?), he answered – wrongly. Montel had revealed himself as an outsider. Bullets whistled by the pair as the sentinel began firing in the direction of the voice. The pair hid in the hills until daybreak when the bandits left with their wounded, the loot, and nine cavalry horses. Wood found the body of only one bandit, although there was evidence that several others had been wounded. Ellis escaped harm and drove to Marathon the next day to report the incident.[22]

Near daybreak the other party struck Boquillas. Realizing that they were outmanned, Deemer and his Negro clerk, Monroe Payne, offered no resistance. Indeed, they gave the bandits all their money, allowed them to select the merchandise they wanted from the shelves, and helped them pack it. In no hurry because they knew they were safe in such an isolated place, the raiders worked methodically until 10 a.m. when they were joined by several of the group that had devastated Glenn Springs. The force then took

Jesse Deemer

Monroe Payne

167

Deemer and Payne captive and crossed the river. Deemer probably would have been killed immediately had not several bandits urged that he be spared because of his many kindnesses to Mexican families around Boquillas.[23]

As the raiders passed through Boquillas, Mexico, they split up. One group paused at the American-managed silver mine to rob the company store and take the mine payroll. They also took six more prisoners, including Dr. Homer Powers, the mine physician, and the superintendent, a man named Halter. By this time so loaded with booty that they could hardly carry it, the bandits confiscated a truck belonging to the mining company. Lt. Col. Natividad Álvarez piled the loot onto the truck and ordered Powers and the three mine officials to get in. The other group, with Deemer and Payne, rode ahead.

The truck driver now took advantage of the Mexicans' ignorance of trucks. He drove as slowly as possible, allowing the mounted horsemen to get several miles ahead. Then he stalled the motor, complaining that it had overheated. As the motor "cooled off," the driver and the other Americans plotted their escape. They pretended that the truck was stuck and tried to push it. Unable to free it, they suggested that if the guards would push, they could get it started. The Mexicans complied. The driver, meanwhile, had slipped the gears into reverse and, when the bandits pushed, he released the clutch, knocking them to the ground. The Americans quickly gathered up the weapons and captured the bandits. The prisoners were taken to Boquillas and delivered to the Brewster County sheriff. They were later sentenced to life in prison for the raids.[24]

Coming so soon after Villa's Columbus raid, the Boquillas and Glenn Springs attacks were serious international matters. Pershing's foray into Mexico after Villa increased tension between the governments of Mexico and the United States. President Carranza then demanded the withdrawal of American forces from Mexico before concluding agreements on other pressing matters. Generals Hugh Scott, Army Chief of Staff, and Funston of the United States and Alvaro Obregón of Mexico met in El Paso to negotiate Pershing's withdrawal. At that point the bandits crossed

Natividad Álvarez, one of the raiders.

into the Big Bend and pillaged the two villages, whereupon the two governments took hard positions. Carranza denounced the raids, claiming that they were the work of lawless elements residing on the American side of the border, and Scott and Funston concluded that the Big Bend was practically defenseless and predicted that such raids would continue. The attacks on Glenn Springs and Boquillas threatened to completely disrupt the negotiations, but General Scott, believing that the Mexicans were powerless to stop such incursions, indicated that the United States would not walk out of the meetings.[25]

Langhorne's Pursuit

Although Mexico was upset because Pershing and his troops were in Chihuahua, Scott saw no alternative to sending more troops if the bandits were going to be punished and Deemer and Payne rescued. Troops A and B of the 8th Cavalry under Maj. George T. Langhorne were assigned the task. A handsome, "dapper" officer, well-liked by his men, Langhorne was a decisive, courageous leader. A good horseman, the major led his men in drills as well as in combat. On the way from Fort Bliss, El Paso, to Marathon, Langhorne and his men paused at Boquillas, Tex., to secure information, then headed into the desert, complete with reporters, photographers, and a motion picture crew. The journalists rode in two Ford sedans, loaded with grain for the horses. Langhorne brought along his chauffeur-driven Cadillac touring car, also loaded with grain. They knew they were entering some of the most difficult terrain the Southwest had to offer. "The country isn't bad," said one of the cameramen. "It's just worse. Worse the moment you set foot from the train, and then, after that, just worser and worser." Langhorne's

169

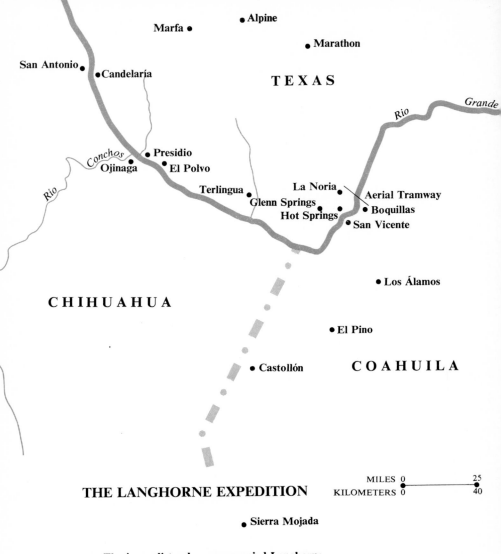

Alpine
Marfa •
• Marathon

San Antonio •
•Candelaría

T E X A S

Rio Grande

Conchos
• Presidio
Ojinaga • El Polvo

Rio

Terlingua •
La Noria •
Aerial Tramway
Glenn Springs •
• Boquillas
Hot Springs •
San Vicente

C H I H U A H U A

• Los Álamos

• El Pino

• Castollón
C O A H U I L A

THE LANGHORNE EXPEDITION

MILES 0   25
KILOMETERS 0   40

• Sierra Mojada

The journalists who accompanied Langhorne
and their Mexican guards.

Col. George T. Langhorne was more successful but received less publicity than Gen. John Pershing in leading an American force into Mexico in pursuit of bandits in 1916.

instructions called for him to go to Glenn Springs and track down and attack the bandits, if necessary following them into Mexico. On May 11 he crossed the border.[26]

The bandits, meanwhile, had split up. One group crossed the river at San Vicente and rode to El Pino and Sierra Mojada; the other band forded the river near Deemer's store. They had a 3-day headstart in familiar country.

As Langhorne began the pursuit in earnest, he received word from Deemer that he and Payne were being held at El Pino, that they were being well cared for, and that the bandits would trade them for Colonel Álvarez and the other prisoners taken by the truck driver and his companions. Believing that the bandits did not yet know he was in Mexico and that they were only 15 miles ahead in the cars, Langhorne decided to take two dozen of his best marksmen and move ahead in the cars. The cavalry was to follow as quickly as possible. Langhorne was not the first to underestimate the rugged Big Bend landscape. After making only 9 miles in 2 hours, he decided to halt and wait for the cavalry. They made camp, slept fitfully, and spent the next day at a well called Aguaita, awaiting nightfall to begin the forced march.[27]

A few hours later Langhorne and his men surrounded El Pino. They advanced cautiously, creeping to within 400 yards of the village before attacking. But the bandits were gone. Learning of the soldiers' approach the previous night, they scattered. Deemer and Payne, left in custody of the village *jefe,* were now "liberated" by the army.[28]

According to one reporter, Deemer had a fine perspective on events. His first question upon meeting the troops reportedly was, "How is the Verdun battle doing?," indicating to the reporter that

Deemer knew that far more turned on the European battle than upon his capture. Deemer again drew the reporter's admiration when he turned down Major Langhorne's invitation to dine because of a previous engagement – dinner with some Mexican friends in one of El Pino's tumbled-down *jacales*.[29]

The troops had hardly settled in the temporary quarters when word came that some of the bandits had been seen in the nearby village of Rosita, about 15 miles down the road. Major Langhorne faced a difficult decision. He was already more than 100 miles deep into Mexican territory, and he knew that Carranza's forces might soon be gathering to meet him. The captives were free, so the only reason to continue the pursuit was to punish the raiders and possibly recover the loot. Langhorne felt that the Mexicans should be punished, and he could not deny the enthusiasm of his men. "I dropped my coffee, borrowed a rifle and two bandoleers of ammunition from the soldier nearest me," recalled Lieutenant Cramer, and "we started after them." [30]

But the search was unfruitful. With a dozen men in the Cadillac and Fords, the soldiers approached Rosita. Four or five bandits dashed from a house into the brush in view of the troops. The soldiers unsuccessfully pursued them on foot, for the cars could not penetrate the thicket. Another bandit mounted a horse and rode off down the road. Returning to the Cadillac, several troops set out after him, their weapons blazing. He, too, escaped. "The last we saw of them the big car was bounding over the ditches and bushes like a steeplechaser, to the tune of a merry cannonading," said Cramer. The other soldiers continued to Rosita, where they learned that the bandits had been warned again and had fled.[31]

Major Langhorne now established a temporary camp at El Pino. While he waited for the rest of his force, he sent out scouting parties to search for the bandits. Lieutenant Cramer was given command of eight men and told to return to El Pino by a circuitous route that would allow him to search for a band of raiders reportedly staying at Castillón Ranch. When Cramer protested that the country did not offer anything in the way of food or water – a problem that hundreds before him had faced – and requested permission to pack rations, Langhorne refused, saying that it would be a "valuable experience" for Cramer, allowing him to "exercise . . . great ingenuity."[32]

Telling his sergeant to secretly purchase what food he could from the soldiers and residents of Rosita, Cramer set out for Castillón. Approaching cautiously, he surprised about a dozen armed men, apparently ready to travel, at the Santa Anita well. He correctly guessed that they were part of the bandit gang but his logic — "the *pacífico* always wears a big straw sombrero" — was not the soundest. Deploying his men along a crest overlooking the well, Cramer ordered them to fire about an hour after sunset. When the soldiers opened up, one bandit fell. The soldiers rushed over the hill and down toward the windmill. Two other bandits now fell wounded. At the foot of the hill an old man held up his hands and pleaded that he was a *pacífico,* captured a few days before and now forced to accompany the bandits. His hand had been shattered from a bullet wound. Cramer left him under guard and pursued the others.[33]

The bandits were soon lost in the darkness. Cramer returned to the windmill to survey the victory. In their fright the Mexicans had abandoned a wagon, 17 horses and mules, nine rifles, two swords, and several saddles, bridles, and packs. They apparently had escaped with nothing more than their hand guns and the clothes they wore. But not everything had gone well. For safekeeping the guards had put the old man in the well. It made an ideal prison, but his wound bled so profusely that it spoiled the water. As badly as they wanted rest, the weary troops had to continue their march in hope of finding drinkable water.

Before reaching camp, they had quite a scare. The Mexican government had demanded that Langhorne withdraw his troops or face attack, and U.S. intelligence had picked up several rumors to the effect that an elite force of Yaqui Indians from the Secretary of War's personal guard was being sent to deal with the intruders. The Americans were tense. As Cramer and his men rode slowly toward Cerro Blanco with their booty, one of the troopers spotted a cloud of dust behind them "My heart sank," remembered the lieutenant, "as I was not in any shape to fight, with my men nearly dead with fatigue, and all the plunder to hamper us. I saw visions of being attacked by a bunch of bandits or by Carranza troops, and the spoiling of my success, and the losing of my loot, just as I was about to get into camp with it." Cramer ordered his men to set up an ambush, but found that there was not time. The men simply lay down in the road and prepared to fight the 15 men advancing on them.[34]

173

Just before they opened fire, one of Cramer's men shouted that the approaching troops were Americans. He saw in the dim light of dawn that all the horses were black and of similar size and that the men were uniformed. The party turned out to be a detachment from Troop A that had seen Cramer's troops, their scraggly looks, and their plunder and had concluded that they were the bandits. Cramer's sharp-eyed trooper prevented a disaster.[35]

The excursion into Mexico was a success. Deemer and Payne were freed, most of the supplies taken from both Glenn Springs and Boquillas recaptured, and several bandits killed and wounded, five captured, and the others dispersed. Langhorne's report convinced Col. Frederick W. Sibley that the mission had been completed, and General Funston recalled the force. Langhorne's men had been in Mexico 16 days, had traveled more than 550 miles, and had suffered no casualties. Although the Carranza government was upset at the incursion the foray was in many ways more successful than Pershing's more widely publicized pursuit of Villa.[36]

Occupation of the Big Bend

After the Glenn Springs and Boquillas raids, Generals Scott and Funston sent a joint telegram to President Wilson asking that the National Guard be called out against border bandits. Acting according to a long-range plan intended to intimidate Mexico by placing guardsmen at strategic points along the border, the President issued the order on May 9 calling up the Texas, New Mexico, and Arizona National Guards. Because of the threat of conflict with Carranza's forces in Mexico, and because the National Guard was the only reserve the United States had, President Wilson called all guardsmen into active duty a few months later. By midnight, July 4, troops from 14 States had taken up positions along the Mexican border. By the end of the month over 100,000 men had been sent to four major assembly areas, three in Texas and one in Arizona.[37]

General Scott then continued his discussions with Obregón from a strengthened hand. Pershing's army was still in Chihuahua, and the National Guard lined the border, anxious for action. "I told him that if he wanted to lose his country, the surest way to do it would be to attack Pershing," Scott later wrote. Under these cir-

Troop B, 1st Cavalry of the Texas National Guard on their way to Ruidosa in 1916.

cumstances, Scott and Obregón concluded their talks, reaching a lengthy agreement that stipulated that Pershing would pull back but be allowed to remain in Mexico. Although President Carranza repudiated the agreement, Scott concluded that it "made little difference . . . since everything went on as if agreed upon by all."

One of the companies sent to the Big Bend was Company I, 4th Texas Infantry. After several months in Marathon, the company was transferred south to Stillwell's Crossing and La Noria, both on the Rio Grande. Their specific duty was to guard the region against further incursions by Mexican raiders. One member of the company, Lt. William P. Cameron of Mineral Wells, Texas, reported that the area was quiet while they were there. Cameron had his camera to prove it: troops on guard, troops at mess, troops cleaning up, troops at leisure. But no troops in battle. They spent most of their time stringing telephone wire through the Sierra del Carmen and Boquillas Canyon to Boquillas, Texas, thus eliminating one of the greatest problems in the Big Bend – slow communication.[38]

Another national guardsman who left a personal view of police duty in the Big Bend was Jodie P. Harris, also from Mineral Wells. A cartoonist, Harris drew caricatures and lettered a four-page weekly newspaper called *The Big Bend, a Paper with a Muzzle: Without a Mission.* The paper was printed by the *Fort Worth*

175

These soldiers replaced their hot tents with cooler
mud houses that provided protection from the
wind and helped settle the choking dust.

WE HAVE CAPTURED THE
BIG BEND COUNTRY AND
HAVE DECLARED IT A NATIONAL
PARK

MEXICO

BIG BEND
U.S.

SAND   SAND

"SEPTEMBER MORN"
SEP 26-16 ON THE BORDER   J.DIE

MEXICO

800 FT.
MOUNTAIN

FORT

PA.
CAMP

TRENCHES

5TH
CAVALRY

GLENN SPRINGS
LOCATED 3 MILES
No. of RIO GRANDE
RAIDED MAYS 1916
TWO SOLDIERS AND
ONE WHITE BOY LOST
THBR LIVES

THE ONLY
RESIDENT

WHERE THE SOLDIERS
WBRB KILLED

NOW GUARDED BY
250 SOLDIERS
THE SMALL WAX
PLANT IS THE
ONLY INDUSTRY

POST OFFICE & STORE

FORT

ALY-6-1916

WHAT ARE THEY
GUARDING?

WAX PLANT

According to this Jodie Harris cartoon, the
troops found little to protect at Glenn Springs.

One of Harris' characters declared that the Big
Bend was good for nothing but a national park.

Star-Telegram and included in its Sunday editions. His postcards were mailed home to Mineral Wells to be displayed in the local drug store. Perhaps his most persistent complaint was that the National Guard was in the Big Bend for no reason and that they were kept there for even less cause. Several of his cartoons pictured unhappy privates engaged in makeshift jobs, officers dreaming up busy-work for the troops, and awe-struck soldiers looking at Big Bend scenery. But most of his criticisms seemed to be routine, for all the men knew of the raids at Glenn Springs and Boquillas.

The soldiers in the Big Bend undoubtedly felt that their presence was unnecessary, but that did not stop them from appreciating the beauty and uniqueness of the land. Some of Harris' cartoon cards called attention to landmarks of the Big Bend. He joined what had already become a widespread park movement by drawing two soldiers admiring the scenery and agreeing that the region should be made a park. Another humorously made its point by showing soldiers trying to move a wagon mired in sand up to its axle. The soldiers are suggesting, tongue in cheek, that the Bend is good for nothing but a national park. Harris also promoted the idea of a park in his newspaper. When the bill to create such a park finally reached Congress, guardsmen from several States who had served there in 1916 supported it.[39]

Major Langhorne's punitive action and the presence of the National Guard kept bandits from crossing into the Big Bend for over a year, but conditions in Mexico improved only slowly and in Europe they worsened considerably. In late 1916 Company I was called from the Big Bend and the following year sent to Europe. Although they were replaced with other guardsmen, the country was not patrolled as closely as before, and by 1917 the bandits were back.

Brite Ranch Raid

Many Texans were shocked on Christmas Day 1917 to learn that raiders had crossed the border and attacked the L. C. Brite Ranch. About sunup that day approximately 45 bandits rode into the ranch, located a few miles west of Marfa, and routed it. The bandits were able to surprise the ranchers, because they usually had the help of an informer, often a ranch employee, who advised when the ranch would be deserted. Because of the ruthless daring — and because it happened on Christmas Day — news of the attack was carried in newspapers across the country. The Big Bend was in the news again.[40]

The bandits had carefully planned the raid. They probably chose Christmas Day because they knew few people would be at the ranch. Indeed, the Brites were at their home in Marfa when the bandits rode up. Only T. T. Van Neill, the ranch foreman, and his family were there. Before the attack began, the bandits cut the telephone lines leading to the ranch.

Van Neill's father was up making coffee. As he sat sipping the brew in the dawn light, he saw the bandits ride into the ranch complex and disperse. He ran into his son's room, grabbed a rifle, and shot the man who appeared to be the leader. The bandits then returned the fire. The pair held the bandits off from the house, but were unable to get any help.

The raiders took two ranch hands prisoner. They sent one in to tell Neill and his father that the other would be killed if they did not surrender. Mrs. Neill dissuaded Van and his father from fighting to the last and encouraged them to give the bandits the key to the store, hoping that they would then go away. The bandits looted the store, then rounded up the best horses on the ranch. Meanwhile, they had captured Mickey Welch, the postman, and two passengers in the mail stage, who were killed, probably because they recognized some of the gang.

Mickey Welch's mail stage.

Rev. H. M. Bandy.

After the 1917 raid, L. C. Brite built this adobe fort, but it was never needed.

Several hours later, as the raiders continued their leisurely looting, the Rev. H. M. Bandy and his family arrived at the ranch for Christmas lunch with the Neills. The bandits agreed to allow Bandy and his passengers to go to the Neill house. All recognized the danger they were in, although they did not know at that time that Welch and his passengers had been murdered. Bandy knelt and led everyone in prayer, then asked for a rifle to help defend the house.

Help soon arrived and everyone in the house was rescued. The bandits did not know that James L. Cobb, a neighbor, had heard the shots and had driven to the ranch to investigate. He saw the Mexicans looting the ranch, then drove to the nearest telephone and called the sheriff. John A. Pool, Sr., also reached the ranch after the raid. Soon a large posse gathered in automobiles to pursue the bandits. In fact, they almost caught them at Brite's Ranch. Volunteers arrived as the bandits were headed down Candelaria Rim, only 8 miles away. The robbers were slowed considerably by all their loot. The posse followed and might have wounded some of them, but they could not follow the trail down the rim in cars. Although the body of one of the bandits was dressed in a Carranzista uniform, the Neills attributed the raid to Chico Cano and his gang.

Capt. Jerry Gray's company of Texas Rangers at Marfa, 1918. They replaced the company dismissed after the Pilares raid.

The next day a larger party gathered to pursue the raiders. By December 27 the Americans had surrounded Pilares, Mexico, where they suspected the bandits lived. A shoot-out occurred and many people were killed. Estimates vary from 8 to 50. They recovered much of the loot taken at the Brite Ranch, but some innocent people undoubtedly were killed. The Texas Adjutant General investigated the matter and concluded that although the Americans had handled the problem in an unorthodox manner, justice had been served. The governor disagreed and dismissed Capt. J. M. Fox and his entire company of Texas Rangers as a result. Some contended that Fox's dismissal was a political move. He was clearly in violation of the law, however, in following the unwritten code of the Big Bend.[41]

Nevill Ranch Raid

Although the Pilares attack was intended to impress upon the Mexicans the fact that any raids would be punished, the forays did not stop. The last large-scale raid in the Big Bend occurred 3 months later on the Ed Nevill Ranch. Nevill and John Wyatt had leased a ranch about 6 miles down the Rio Grande in Presidio County. The ranch had no telephone; the nearest neighbor was 12 miles away.

On March 25, 1918, the army captain at Van Horn received a report from one of his informers across the border that some bandits were planning a raid on the nearby Bell Ranch. A patrol dispatched to the area found no bandits. On hearing the report in Van Horn, Ed Nevill left for his ranch. He arrived after an 8-hour ride to find the ranch peaceful. Thinking that there was no danger, he and his son were sitting in the front room discussing the next day's chores when some horsemen rode up. Thinking they were the troopers returning from the Bell Ranch, Nevill was not alarmed. But when he saw they were Mexican bandits, he reached for his rifle and started shooting. They exchanged fire with the raiders, then ran for a ditch about 250 yards from the house. Ed Nevill made it, although he had his rifle shot from his hands and his hat knocked off. His son was fatally wounded in the head just four steps out of the house. The bandits also murdered the wife of one of the Mexican ranch hands and made off with the horses, ranch

Chico Cano (center), the tough Mexican bandit, and his pursuer, Capt. Leonard F. Matlack (right).

supplies, clothes, and bedding. Chico Cano again was credited with the raid.

Langhorne, who had been promoted and named commander of the Big Bend district, received word of the attack at midnight. He immediately ordered Troop G at a nearby ranch to proceed to Nevill's. They arrived at 3:30 a.m. Troop A was sent by rail to Valentine, where they disembarked, rode to the Rio Grande, and joined Troop G. The bandits had crossed near Pilares, and the soldiers followed.

Rather than wait for the troops to surround their camp, the bandits set up an ambush. A vicious battle followed. Some reports claimed that 32 bandits and one American were killed. The soldiers continued the fighting in Pilares, destroying several houses. Again they found some of the stolen loot in the village, adding to its reputation as an outlaw hangout.

The raid on the Nevill Ranch was the big raid in the Big Bend. There were several smaller ones, but as the situation in Mexico began to stabilize and the surveillance in Texas increased, the raids decreased. After the National Guard was recalled from the Big Bend, Langhorne's 8th Cavalry squadron was stationed at Marfa and given instructions to patrol the Rio Grande country.

Several planes were lost in the Big Bend while searching for bandits.

Believing that the temporary posts should be bolstered, the government leased land from Howard E. Perry and Wayne R. Cartledge in 1919 to build Camp Santa Helena near what is today Castolon. The post was never constructed as originally planned, for a large force was no longer necessary. The final plans called for one officers' quarters, two barracks, one kitchen mess, one lavatory, two quarters for non-coms, two stables, one blacksmith shop-guardhouse combination, one hay shed, and a grain barn, but only one barracks, a lavatory, a barn, a corral and stables, and one building each for officers and noncommissioned officers was built. The camp was ready for occupation in early 1920.[42]

When Pancho Villa's men attacked Ciudad Juárez for the third time in June 1919, the American government ordered the Army Air Service to begin regular patrols along the river. Surveillance in the Big Bend was the responsibility of two military districts: the Big Bend District, which stretched from Comstock to Sanderson to Boquillas, and the El Paso District, which included Boquillas to Presidio to Marfa. The "Big Chickens," as the horse soldiers called the flimsy DeHavillands, were supposed to find out where Villa had gone. They were also to spot any bands and move in close to determine what they were doing and which direction they were headed. Any bandit movements were to be reported to the troops on the ground. Although the pilots were not supposed to cross the Rio Grande, they often did, particularly if they were looking for something. As the raids in the Big Bend decreased, the ranchers grew appreciative of the "River Pilots." [43]

This esteem was proven in August 1919, when two flyers, Lt. H. G. Peterson and P. H. Davis, went down near Boyame, Chihuahua. Flying upriver from Lajitas, Peterson and Davis mistook the Río Conchos for the Rio Grande and unwittingly headed into Mexico. Four connecting-rod bearings burned out, forcing them to land in rough terrain. Still thinking they were over the United States, the airmen made certain that they landed on the northern side of the river. Coming down in pasture covered with mesquites, paloverde, and greasewood, they broke the landing gear and wrecked the plane. (The DeHavillands, often called a "flaming coffin" by the pilots, had an unretractable axle connecting the two front landing wheels; rough terrain or brush would break the axle and sometimes flip the plane over.) Believing they were in Texas, the lieutenants headed downriver, expecting to find Candelaria and the army post there.[44]

Peterson and Davis were captured by Chico Cano's gang, led by Jesús Rentería, variously called "Corklet," "Gancho" (or hook, because he had an artificial arm and steel hook), or "Mocho" (maimed). Rentería was well known in the Big Bend as one of Cano's most vicious murderers. During the raid on the Brite ranch he reportedly had sat on Mickey Welch's body while an accom-

The ransom money for the captured lieutenants leaves the Marfa National Bank.

183

plice held his hair and slit the man's throat with a pen knife. Rentería was assisted in the capture by "Slim" Olívas and Delores Navarrette.

The lieutenants were allowed to send out messages saying that they were being held for ransom, but that they were well treated and in good health. A messenger delivered Rentería's demand for a $15,000 ransom to Dawkins Kilpatrick, a storekeeper and a rancher at Candelaria on August 17. Send $15,000 in cash by midnight, August 18, or the flyers would be killed, he wrote. When word of the airmen's capture reached a group of Big Bend ranchers attending Bloys Camp Meeting, near Marfa, the money was raised in less than 10 minutes. Grateful for the aid they had received from the "River Pilots," the ranchers authorized the Marfa National Bank to deliver the money to Capt. Leonard F. Matlack at Candelaria.

Negotiating with Rentería by notes delivered by Tomás Sánchez, Matlack arranged for ransoming the prisoners one at a time. Peterson was brought safely to the American side. When Matlack returned for Davis, he overheard the bandits planning to kill them after the money was delivered. Acting quickly, he drew his pistol on the bandits and ordered Davis to get on the horse behind him. Matlack returned to the Rio Grande by a different route and avoided a suspected ambush.

Captain Matlack performed bravely. He brought the airmen back to the American side safely, and he saved $6,500 of the rancher's money ($1,000 was given to Sánchez for his assistance). Colonel Langhorne declared that the officer deserved a decoration.

As soon as the officers were safe, Colonel Langhorne ordered troops into Mexico to chase Rentería and his men. The "River Pilots" served as their "eyes," flying low over the harsh terrain, searching for any suspects. Messages were then dropped to the cavalry, indicating the direction the suspects were headed. The results were immediate. Sergeant William H. Nealing's patrol encountered three Mexicans who immediately surrendered. Although they were not members of Rentería's band, they were wanted by U.S. authorities. They were turned over to the civilian scouts, who took them off into a canyon and shot them. (An officer was later court mar-

**The pilots communicated with troops on the
ground by dropping messages.**

tialed for the action.) Lts. F. S. Estill and R. H. Cooper spotted
Rentería's gang on the afternoon of the first day. Flying low over
the canyons and mountains, they suddenly realized that three
horsemen below were firing at them with rifles. Turning the craft
toward the trio (the Marlin machine guns were aimed by pointing
the plane at the target), pilot Estill began firing. As they flew by,
Cooper fired more rounds with the Lewis machine gun mounted on
the rear cockpit. They reported that both Rentería and his white
horse were killed. (Of course, stories still circulate in the Big Bend
that Rentería survived the attack and now lives in one of the border towns.)

Langhorne recalled the troops and proclaimed success. Rentería was reported killed. Four other bandits were killed by the
civilian scouts. Almost half of the ransom money was saved. The
bandits, who at one time had reigned supreme in the Big Bend,
were no match for the DeHavillands. The Big Bend was on the
verge of peace after a decade of turmoil.

The Big Bend figured in another pilot search in 1921. Lt. Alexander Pearson, a crack pilot in the 12th Aero Border Patrol
Squadron, attempted to fly from the Pacific to the Atlantic across
the southern United States with only two service stops. The crankshaft broke, forcing him down near Columbus, N. Mex. After re-
pairs, he flew into Fort Bliss at El Paso on February 8, 1921. He
left Fort Bliss the next day, intending to land in San Antonio or
Houston. But he encountered a fierce norther in the Big Bend and
was blown far off course. Somewhere over the mountains the bearings of his crankshaft froze up, forcing him to land in rough terrain. Like Peterson and Davis, he thought he was in the United

185

**The 1st Cavalry Division, from Fort Bliss, Texas,
arrives in Marfa in 1929 for maneuvers.**

States when he was really in Mexico. He walked along the Rio Grande, hoping to find a ranch or a village. Two Mexican horsemen aided him, and he met J. E. Murrah, foreman of the Rutledge ranch, who loaned him a horse for the ride into Sanderson. "A good meal and bed was all I wanted that night, as I was pretty well exhausted," he told reporters. "The worst thing about this is that I lose my chance to try the transcontinenal record." Pearson's plane was finally repaired and flown out of the valley where he had landed – "Las Vegas de los Ladrones" (the Lowlands of the Thieves) – on the Mexican side of the river east of Boquillas.[45]

By 1921 the Big Bend had quieted down to a point where the army could discontinue aerial patrols. The circumstances that spawned the raids were unique. Mexico had undergone tremendous revolution and social upheaval. Settlement in the Big Bend was so sparse that defense was practically impossible. Several wealthy ranches, two large mines, and numerous wax factories were within easy striking distance of the Rio Grande. J. O. Langford operated his resort at Hot Springs, Jesse Deemer his store at Boquillas, and Brite his ranch in the Capote Mountains. Most of them evacuated their homes at one time or another during the chaotic years. One who stayed was Dawkins Kilpatrick, who mounted a machine gun on the roof of his store in Candelaria. Army occupation, increased settlement, and stability in Mexico combined to bring peace. Soon fur trappers hunted their prey in the Rio Grande and Río Conchos canyons, farmers moved into the Castolon area to raise cotton, and ranchers returned to their herds.

The Big Bend's reputation for violence died hard, but by the turn of the century civilization had overtaken the region. While outlaws, cattle rustlers, and smugglers did not disappear, their feats became less colorful and less publicized. Some of the most fanciful material about the blood-thirsty thieves and bandits was written by Hill after his seemingly uneventful trip down the Rio Grande in 1899. But even former Texas Ranger E. E. Townsend had to admit 30 years later that Hill had exaggerated the lawlessness of the Big Bend. With the end of the Mexican revolutionary era, a peace that had existed with a few sensational interruptions was reestablished, and the dream of the early-day National Guardsmen – that the Big Bend be made a national park – grew into a reality.

7/The National Park

Quiet spoken and somewhat timid, Everett Ewing Townsend was nevertheless a man of deeds. Coming to the Big Bend young, he had seen firsthand its spellbinding mountains and canyons. He had ridden through the cacti and riverbottom on horseback as a customs inspector for the United States government and searched its valleys and deserts as a Texas Ranger. As sheriff of Brewster County the Big Bend was his paradise; as a member of the Texas legislature it became a personal cause. Throughout the struggle to establish a national park in West Texas, Townsend made contacts, wrote letters, and lobbied with the influential. He was a cowboy who had spent most of his life in the nearest thing to the frontier in West Texas, rather than a forceful man or a diplomat. He wanted to preserve what was left of the Texas wilderness for others, and by the time he was through, the Big Bend was a national park, and he was its "father." [1]

When Texas deeded 707,894 acres of the Big Bend country to the Federal Government in 1944, it was the fruit of many years of dreaming and working by scores of people. Townsend was, perhaps, the first to think of the region as a park. But the soldiers who came in 1916 helped spread the notion. Col. Frederick W. Sibley and Col. George T. Langhorne, who had spent several years riding through the rough country, recounted the splendor of the region. The early visitors were impressed with grandeur that local residents took for granted, and returned home carrying news of the Chisos, Santa Elena Canyon, and the great variety of bird life. So when the proposal for a Big Bend National Park surfaced in 1935, there was ready made national support for the idea.

One of Jodie Harris' illustrated postcards to the "folks back home" pictured a conversation between Major Coulter of the 10th Pennsylvania and Capt. E. A. Davis of Company I, 4th Texas. "The Big Bend is a wonderful country – moulded by nature for a park" says Coulter. "Sure!" answers Davis. "It's Great! When we get back home let's start a move to make it a *National Park*." Shown on a cliff overlooking the camp, the two men seem to be sharing what Harris terms a "new Big Bend." Picked up by the

"The Window" (sometimes called "The Pour Off")
in the Chisos Basin.

Photograph by Bank Langmore

Fort Worth Star-Telegram, the picture was spread across the State.[2]

The Big Bend found new friends in the 1920s. Victor Schoffelmayer, agricultural editor for the *Dallas Morning News* and president of the Texas Geographic Society, first visited the proposed park with Dr. W. D. Hunter's entomological expedition in 1920. His writing popularized the region as, in Robert Hill's phrase, the "Garden of Gods." In 1923 Max Bentley, a freelance journalist, sat talking with a friend beside the placid waters of the Rio Grande. "Some day this will become a great national park," the acquaintance ventured. Bentley listened with curiosity as the man recounted the wonders of the Big Bend: the scenic attractions, the interesting geological and biological examples, the Chisos Mountains, the Rio Grande itself. Impressed, he returned to Alpine and wrote the first news article promoting the idea for a Big Bend National Park.[3]

Texas Canyons State Park

Still nothing was done to transform the idea into reality until 1931 when a newly-elected state legislator, R. M. Wagstaff from Abilene, became interested in the Big Bend. Wagstaff had seen the December 1930 issue of *Nature Magazine,* in which J. Frank Dobie, a folklorist and writer on the faculty at the University of Texas, had summarized the "distinctive charms" of Texas and lamented the fact that none of the millions of acres of Texas' public land had been set aside for a park. The scenery and international character of the Big Bend particularly intrigued him. During the second session of the 42nd legislature, Wagstaff began to investigate whether the State owned any land in the Big Bend that might be set aside for a park. As a lawyer, he was familiar with the laws regarding the State's public lands, so he called upon Land Commissioner J. H. Walker, feeling that there was real potential for a park in West Texas. Wagstaff and Walker discovered that the State did own thousands of acres in the Big Bend, and they also found out that several other tracts had been sold but had been forfeited within the last few months because of non-payment of interest. Walker could have proceeded with forfeiture of the land at that moment, but the policy of the General Land Office required that the owners be notified that the interest was overdue and that

Although the soldiers were glad to leave the Big Bend, they recognized the uniqueness of the country and suggested it should be a national park.

Everett E. Townsend, "father" of Big Bend National Park.

they be given an opportunity to pay. He suggested that Wagstaff defer filing his bill for a State park until the next session of the legislature, when the owners' options would have expired and they would know precisely how much land the State owned.

Wagstaff was ready for action when the next session of the legislature convened in January 1933. Checking with the land office, he found that none of the owners had paid the interest and that many more acres were now legally in the hands of the State. Since he was from Taylor County, a long way from the Big Bend, Wagstaff contacted Townsend, then the representative from the 87th District including Brewster County, and B. Frank Haag of Midland, the 88th District, for support for the bill. By then Wagstaff had found Hill's 1901 article on the canyons of the Rio Grande and had been transported by the scientist's descriptions and pictures. Thrusting the story before Townsend, he asked, "Is this article true? Do you have all of this wonderful scenery out in your district?" Although Townsend felt that much of Hill's writing about the bandits of the Big Bend was exaggerated, he readily confirmed that Big Bend contained all the scenes Wagstaff referred to, and more. "But 99 percent of the people of our own state don't know of its existence," he lamented.[4]

191

Wagstaff pursued the idea. "Don't you have a lot of unsold public school land along the canyons?" "Doubtless there is," answered Townsend. "It's not worth a damn for any commercial purpose, so why should people bother to own it?" Townsend was correct, but most of the river bottom, mountain, and scenic land was privately owned.

Wagstaff spurred Townsend into action. Not wanting to begin without consulting his constituents, Townsend first wrote to several, then returned to Alpine to talk with them. Assured of their cooperation, he came to Austin with a portfolio of excellent pictures of Santa Elena, Mariscal, and Boquillas canyons, the Chisos Mountains, and other scenic points in the Big Bend. Many of the pictures used to publicize the region were either taken by or gathered by a photographer who had first come to the Big Bend as a mule teamster in 1916, W. D. Smithers of Alpine.

Supported by Townsend and Haag, Wagstaff introduced a bill setting aside fifteen sections of land for a park. Given its first reading on Texas Independence Day, March 2, 1933, the bill called for an appropriation of $5,000 to be paid the public school fund for the land. The bill was referred to the appropriations committee, where Townsend, with his encyclopedic knowledge of the Big Bend, a no-nonsense attitude, and a portfolio of pictures, proved to be an excellent lobbyist. J. Frank Dobie, who had first caught Wagstaff's attention with his article, also testified effectively on behalf of the measure. The committee reported favorably on the bill, giving the three West Texas legislators what they considered a major victory during the economy-minded 1930s. Although the bill was introduced late in the session, they maneuvered to get it before the legislature before adjournment. On May 19, Speaker Coke Stevenson laid the bill before the House. It was amended to reserve all the minerals for the public school fund, to correct some descriptions of the land, and to lower the appropriation from $5,000 to $1,250. Still feeling that they had a good bill, the sponsors accepted the amendments, and Wagstaff moved that the law requiring the bill to be read a third time on another day be suspended. His motion carried, and the bill was passed 90 to 27.[5]

The measure was then sent to the Senate where Ken Regan of

Pecos was its sponsor. Although time was short, Senator Regan maneuvered the bill through without delay. The appropriation was further lowered to $1,000, but the Senate approved it 26 to 3 on May 24. The following day it went back to the House for concurrence. The House concurred by a large majority, 109 to 3. Enrolled, signed by the Speaker, and sent to the Secretary of State, the bill was signed by Gov. Miriam A. ("Ma") Ferguson on May 27. Since the law contained a clause making it effective immediately, Texas Canyons State Park was established upon the governor's signature.[6]

But the lawmakers were not through. When the legislature met in special session in September 1933, Governor Ferguson allowed two bills increasing the size of the park to be introduced. Townsend sponsored a measure transferring all lands that had been forfeited because of non-payment of taxes south of latitude 29° 25′ in Brewster and Presidio counties to the State for the park. Wagstaff introduced a bill to change the name of the park to Big Bend State Park and withdraw from sale all public school lands in Brewster County south of 29° 25′. Both bills were referred to the Committee on Public Lands and Buildings, where they were reported favorably. Townsend's bill came up first, so Wagstaff attached his as an amendment, and both bills passed as a single measure on October 4. The Senate added minor amendments, and 8 days later, on the last day of the session, the House concurred. Governor Ferguson signed the bill on October 27. An estimated 150,000 acres were added to the park.[7]

Big Bend National Park

Townsend was still not satisfied. He immediately began urging Congressman R. Ewing Thomason to introduce legislation creating a national park in the Big Bend. When Thomason was in Alpine, Townsend invited him to visit the park site. When the congressman refused, saying he did not have time, Townsend began to apply pressure. "Well, Ewing," Townsend reportedly said, "you're going to [visit the park] if I have to threaten you with your constituency or a six-shooter." The phone calls, telegrams, and letters of park supporters made Thomason aware of the significance of the project. "Tell that Ewing Townsend I'll come see the park if he'll call off his dogs." pleaded the congressman. Thomason visited the Big Bend in November 1933 and was so impressed with what he saw that he immediately began to work on a bill to establish a national park. Townsend continued to support the park concept every chance he got. "I am so full of it that I have got to unload on someone, and just at present you

**Amon Carter Peak, the "Window," and Vernon
Bailey Peak were first photographed by Hill in
1899 and named by Park Service officials
decades later.**

are the only available victim and will have to suffer the consequences," he wrote Col. Robert H. Lewis of Fort Sam Houston.
Judge R. B. Slight had similarly talked with Senator Tom Connally
during one of the senator's brief visits to Alpine.[8]

Before the legislation could be passed, much work had to be
done. It fell primarily to Townsend to prepare for the distinguished
visitors who must visit the Big Bend before any action could be
taken on a national park. The park promoters hoped for a Civilian
Conservation Corps camp for the Big Bend to do the necessary development work, but several applications had proved unsuccessful
because there was no adequate water supply. One good source at
Government Spring was unavailable because the owners wanted
more than the Alpine Chamber of Commerce could afford to pay.
On three occasions the chamber failed to get other sites approved.

Townsend's suggestion enabled the organization to succeed on
the fourth try. Some of the best land in the hoped-for park was in
the Chisos Mountains basin, where Townsend's nephew, Ira Hec-

The Civilian Conservation Corps built roads and blazed trails for the first visitors to the planned national park.

tor, owned a large plot of land. Thinking that water was available there, Townsend convinced Hector to deed the land to the county. Residents from Alpine and Marathon contributed money for the well. Townsend took the digging crew into the basin, while James Casner, president of the Chamber of Commerce, requested that the county commissioners build a road into the basin. By the time the crew began digging at a site suggested by Dr. C. L. Baker, head of the geology department of Texas A. & M. College, time was running out on the fourth CCC camp application.

The men were at work by 9 a.m. April 16, 1934. Mrs. Townsend cooked lunch and her husband carried it to the men so no time would be lost. By 2:45 p.m. they drew out the first bucket of water. The following day they rigged a gasoline pump to keep the water out of the well so they could dig deeper. Because water had to be found immediately, Townsend called the well *Agua Pronto*. A road grader soon cut a path into the basin, and the government approved the location for the CCC camp.[9]

Teams of specialists quickly visited the region. The National Park Service filed a report on the Big Bend in January 1935, pointing out the advantage of the area as a national park. Members of the CCC camp constructed barracks in the basin as headquarters for the operations and built roads and cleared trails in preparation for opening the park.[10]

195

Texas Senators Connally and Morris Sheppard and Representative Thomason introduced identical bills in Congress on March 1, 1935, calling for the establishment of the Big Bend National Park when Texas deeded adequate land to the Federal Government. The bill passed, and President Franklin D. Roosevelt signed it into law. Allowing for private donation of as much as 1,500,000 acres, the legislation was only an enabling act with no appropriation or enforcement provision. The actual acquisition of the land was left to the State of Texas. Newspapers across the state carried the news. "Sweeping vistas . . . will greet visitors to Texas' first national park in the Big Bend," a reporter for the *Fort Worth Star-Telegram* noted.[11]

Dream of an International Park

National Park Service officials, meanwhile, were at work on a more ambitious project. When Senator Sheppard presented the idea of a Big Bend park to President Roosevelt in February 1935, he suggested that it should really become an international park. The President liked the idea, and Secretary of the Interior Harold Ickes set about to make it a reality. Assistant Director Conrad L. Wirth of the National Park Service and several colleagues met with a Mexican commission in Alpine in August 1935 to discuss the prospects. The group made a pack trip into the mountains, climbed to the South Rim, and viewed the magnificent Sierra del Carmen on the Mexican side of the river, Elephant Tusk Mountain to the south, and Santa Elena Canyon 20 miles to the west. Following Wirth's report — which predicted that the international park would "be one of the greatest recreational and educational ventures ever undertaken by the National Park Service" — meetings were held in El Paso in October and November. As a result, a temporary joint park commission was established.[12]

The idea won new friends in 1936. Secretary of State Cordell Hull set up a formal commission to meet with the Mexican commission to plan the park, forest reserves, and wildlife refuge, not only for a Big Bend but for other prospective international parks. In February, the joint commission again met in Alpine to inspect the proposed Mexican park area. Entering through the small village of Boquillas, the commission spent several days in the

The Sierra del Carmen is even wilder and more impressive on the Mexican side of the border.

Sierra del Carmen, the Fronteriza range, and in nearby villages. They returned through San Carlos, visiting Castolon, Tex., as they emerged from Mexico. (This conference was marked by tragedy, when Roger W. Toll, the superintendent of Yellowstone National Park, and George Wright of the Park Service's wildlife research division, were killed in a car wreck. Toll Mountain, adjacent to Casa Grande, and George Wright Peak, both in the Chisos, are named for the officials.) Another meeting was held in El Paso in November, and boundaries for the proposed park were agreed upon: the western point was downriver from Lajitas, the eastern point just above Stillwell Crossing. Markers were set at these points.[13]

Creating a National Park

Meanwhile, the Park Service had sent a group of scientists into the Big Bend to explore its features and locate possible wildlife refuges. One of them was a young geologist who had recently received his Ph.D. from Northwestern University. Dr. Ross A. Maxwell had never been west of San Antonio, but the job in the Big Bend was a good one during the Depression. "I did not know what I was getting into," Maxwell later recalled. "When I

197

went out to Big Bend and took a look at it I was ready to throw in the sponge. I stayed at the CCC camp because there was nowhere else to stay." Former Texas Governor Pat Neff, chairman of the State Parks Board, visited the Big Bend in June 1936. "The Big Bend is the last Texas frontier," he wired the *Waco Tribune Herald*. Working diligently at their tasks, the boys of the CCC camp, said Neff, possessed the "atmosphere of an academy of science . . . ." The preliminary work was done, and the national park moved closer to reality.[14]

Enthusiasm for the Big Bend park climaxed in 1937. With so much publicity directed toward an international park, the State legislature moved to fulfull the terms of the Federal act. The lawmakers authorized an expenditure of $750,000 to purchase privately held land for the national park. As news of the action was carried in newspapers throughout the State, Walter Prescott Webb, well-known historian and member of the faculty of the University of Texas, embarked upon a trip through Santa Elena Canyon, hoping to call attention to the splendors of the Big Bend. As author of the famous *Texas Rangers,* Webb was familiar with the trouble Capt. Charles L. Nevill had in attempting the same trip in 1881. He was also advised by Hill, who had made the trip in 1899 and who now, in 1937, was a special writer for the *Dallas Morning News*. The party took several precautions. Guided by experienced river men, the expedition would be tracked by Coast Guard planes. They also had special, flat-bottom boats made of steel, instead of the clumsy wooden crafts that Hill was forced to use. "Four men in two steel rowboats required 30 hours to travel the 15 miles of treacherous rapids in the boulder-choked Rio Grande," announced the *Houston Chronicle* upon completion of the trip. In the tradition of other river men, Webb carved his name and the date of his float on a prominent rock in the canyon.[15]

Webb's trip also had another purpose. He had been commissioned by the Park Service to prepare a historical handbook that would serve as a visitor's introduction to the Big Bend. He rapidly acquainted himself with the existing historical material, and then he contacted several old friends in the region to begin preparation for the trip. In addition to the publicity expected as a result of the float, Webb wanted to get to know the Big Bend personally so he could write more knowledgeably. He also contacted several large newspapers across the state and made arrangements to sell them feature stories on his trip.[16]

Webb, along with thousands of other Texans, undoubtedly was shocked when Gov. James V. Allred vetoed the measure on grounds that no money had been appropriated for the land and that the general fund could not stand the strain. Both West Texans and the Park Service were upset. "Was very sorry indeed to read that Governor Allred vetoed the Big Bend Park Bill," wrote Thomas V. Skaggs, who guided Webb through the canyon. "To me our young governor is a funny edition. If and when he visits west of the Pecos again I think the residents out there may greet him with the welcome the Comanches greeted the buffalo, in season." On December 15, 1937, the Park Service abandoned the CCC camp, and Maxwell left; there was no place else to stay. "The whole Big Bend park idea seemed dead," he recalled. The citizens of Brewster County had taken the project about as far as they could.[17]

Texas Big Bend Park Association

But the Big Bend was too good an idea to die. When the *Fort Worth Star-Telegram* carried a vigorous editorial favoring the national park, the resourceful supporters of the idea saw another opportunity. The newspaper had suggested that instead of the State

These floaters reached the rock slide in Santa Elena Canyon just a few days after Walter P. Webb completed his trip through the canyon.

A Marfa school exercise on Liberty Loan Day, during World War I.

On the Eve of the National Park

Shortly after the turn of the century, Big Bend residents found life a bit kinder. Mining brought in many new families, and the automobiles and the railroad ended the oppressive isolation. Social functions that were impossible earlier now became commonplace.

200

A Baptist encampment at Paisano, 1921.

**Mexicans cross the Rio Grande near Lajitas
with a load of stove wood and chinograss, 1916.**

A get-together at the Mariposa Mine Store, 1917.

Early sightseers at Jordan's Gap, near Marfa.

appropriating the money for the land acquisition, a million people should contribute $1 each. Herbert Maier, the Park Service's regional director, endorsed the proposal in a letter to managing editor James R. Record of the *Star-Telegram*. Maier's plea was supported by James E. Casner of Alpine and Dr. H. W. Morelock, president of Sul Ross State College, who met with Record. The result was the establishment of the Texas Big Bend Park Association, an organization of influential citizens across the State, with the goal of raising money to buy the land.[18]

The Executive Committee of the association met in May 1938 in Austin to discuss ways of raising the money. Amon G. Carter, publisher of the *Star-Telegram*, was elected chairman, and, in a politically wise move, Governor Allred was named honorary president. The committee viewed movies of the Big Bend and adopted guidelines for raising funds and putting out information. The members of the committee themselves pledged $12,500 and expected to raise another $12,500 in other cities. They hoped to raise money from popular subscription, wealthy persons and foundations, and legislative appropriation. The Depression, international difficulties, and finally World War II seriously impaired these plans, however, and the committee soon directed its efforts primarily toward securing an adequate legislative appropriation.[19]

Although the main thrust of the committee was to secure State funds, other possibilities were not overlooked. A. F. Robinson, an Alpine resident, donated 320 acres for the park. The public was invited to join the association. Chairman Carter hoped for 30,000 memberships at $1 each, and before the campaign was launched 53 persons had paid the token dues. The *Star-Telegram* successfully urged its readers to contribute to a general fund that would be turned over to the association for purchase of the needed land. In September 1942, when the newspaper closed out its effort, $8,346.88 had been raised from 659 persons, with donations ranging from 5 cents to $100.[20]

By mid-1941 the committee's efforts were bearing fruit. An executive headquarters had been established in Fort Worth. The State Parks Board had determined that the land necessary for the establishment of the park would cost almost $1,400,000, so the committee set its goal as a $1,500,000 appropriation from the legislature. Newspapers across the State announced support of the measure. Dr. Morelock had been given permission by his Board of Regents to spend as much time as necessary on the development of the park. He traveled more than 25,000 miles across the State in its support. H. R. Smith and J. E. Mowinkle, Texas oilmen, covered the expenses of a color movie about the Big Bend for service clubs, school groups, and anyone else who was interested. Carter himself took a great interest in the park and spent both time and money in its support. He issued statements to the press, gave interviews on radio station WBAP of Fort Worth, and continued to chair the meetings of the executive committee. Gov. W. Lee O'Daniel signed the bill appropriating $1,500,000 for the purchase of the land in July 1941.[21]

Land Acquisition

Then the first real difficulty with the Big Bend project arose. Under authority of the State act, the State Parks Board established the Big Bend Land Department to appraise and purchase the land. Eugene Thompson was named administrator of the department and chief appraiser and Townsend associate administrator. More than 3,000 persons owned land in the Big Bend, but only 55 of them lived there. The department's task was complicated by having to locate other owners throughout the world and because not everyone wanted to sell. It was eased somewhat by the fact that over half the land needed was owned by only 20 people.[22]

Some delay resulted when Rep. A. H. King of Throckmorton, Tex., filed an injunction to prohibit the State from spending the $1,500,000, but the State Supreme Court rejected the suit. Another possible conflict concerned mineral rights. When the legislature passed the original appropriations bill in 1937, it reserved mineral rights for the permanent school fund because the representatives feared the loss of a large amount of revenue. The 1941 appropriation also had the reserve attached, but Townsend fought hard to get it removed, for he knew that such a clause would be unacceptable to the National Park Service. [23]

When Gov. Coke Stevenson ceremonially presented the park to M. R. Tillotson, regional director of the Park Service on September 5, 1943, he again called attention to the proposal for an international park, which had lain dormant during the war years and the frenzy of land acquistion. The only thing that had happened since the boundary had been marked in 1937 was that both the United States and Mexican commissions had been reconstituted. As chairman of the U.S. commission, Tillotson visited Mexico City

A sheepherder's place, below North Peak in the
Chisos. Hill photographed this scene in 1899.

The National Park

in June 1942 to discuss the matter with the new members of the Mexican board. Little more was achieved than an expression of interest and a promise to study the matter.[24]

In February 1944 Governor Stevenson delivered the deed to Amon G. Carter, president of the Texas Big Bend Park Association, for formal presentation to President Roosevelt. Carter formally gave the document to the President in a ceremony on July 6, 1944. Six days later the National Park Service announced that the Big Bend Park was officially open. Secretary of the Interior Ickes had already approved Ross A. Maxwell's appointment as superintendent, a logical choice since the soft-spoken geologist had conducted one of the initial park service studies of the area. In taking charge of the park, Maxwell noted that it included "scientific phenomena and scenic beauty mingled with historic incidents along the Texas-Mexico frontier that give it a charm and color that is not known in any other park." Interpretation in the park has tended to emphasize the uniqueness of its biological characteristics. It contains desert, shrubland, woodland, and grassland. Scientists soon realized that it also contained a remarkable number of bird species, making it a paradise for bird watchers.[25]

The New Park

Maxwell faced several problems. The most significant one was the presence of ranchers whom the Park Service had given permission to remain on the land until January 15, 1945. There were about 50 active ranchers in the park, running about 25,000 head of cattle, 20,000 to 30,000 head of sheep and goats, and 1,000 to 2,000 head of horses. The land was badly overgrazed. Nor could the people and stock be moved easily. Since 1944 was a very dry year, thousands of cattle would have died if the ranchers had been forced to move their livestock by that winter. Strays roamed through the park for more than 5 years.

Whatever maintenance and construction Maxwell did in the park was accomplished under wartime conditions. There was no food service, no grocery store, and tires and gas were rationed. Maxwell had a dump truck, a pickup, and a passenger car to conduct the business of the park. There were only five employees on the staff, including the superintendent, so "everybody was a ditch digger or a truckdriver."

Maxwell saw few visitors during the first years of operation, but he prepared basic facilities in case someone got stranded. He put some surplus army cots in the old CCC cottages for emergencies. The first visitors to the park usually fell into two categories: those in love with the area, and those who had not known what to expect and did not want to spend time there once they found out. Maxwell encountered a couple from Austin who had come to enjoy the solitude of the Big Bend. They had been warned to bring along food, but had not brought enough. They had a couple of cans of soup, some sausage, and other bland items. After 2 days Maxwell decided he had better check on them. He found them completely out of food but unwilling to leave. Since they had eaten nothing for 24 hours, he took them to his cottage and fed them beans and coffee. Another couple stayed a shorter time. When they drove into the basin, Maxwell started walking toward the car to see if he could be of assistance. "The man had gotten out of the car and taken two or three deep breaths of that sweet air, and was looking around just sort of awed by Casa Grande," Maxwell recalled. "The wife did not even get out of the car. She just shouted his name and told him to get back in the car and 'get me out of this place.' " [26]

When the time came for dedicating the national park, officials again brought up the idea of an international park. The dedication had been postponed by both World War II and the Korean War. In May 1954, Dr. Bryan Wildenthal, Morelock's successor as president of Sul Ross State College, wrote Carter about plans for the dedication. Meantime, Park Service officials and local Big Bend residents had been active, hoping to arouse interest in the international park in the neighboring Mexican states of Coahuila and Chihuahua. M. L. Tillotson had spoken over a Chihuahua City radio station. Former President Morelock of Sul Ross had contacted many individuals. Wildenthal thought that the occasion of the dedication would be the ideal time to renew discussion of the international project.

But the idea had not suffered from lack of attention over the years. President Franklin Roosevelt had written Mexican President Manuel Avila Camacho in October 1944 that he hoped that the project could be reviewed after the war. Avila Camacho responded in kind and ordered the Mexican park department to conduct studies in the region. After Roosevelt's death, President Harry S. Truman pursued the idea. In 1947 an International Park Commission was established. Apparently the main Mexican objection to the

**Big Bend residents built their homes of whatever
they could find. This is the home of a *curandero-
avisador* and his family. As a *curandero*,
this Mexican shaman "healed" the sick, using herbs
from "nature's pharmacy." As an *avisador*,
he gave warnings and advice to his patients.**

park was that they did not have as much government-owned land as
Texas did. Most of the land on the river was owned by miners,
ranchers, and lumbermen who were loath to sell. The Mexican Federal Government did not want to act without the cooperation, or at
least the consent, of the local States. Thus action on what the Mexican had planned to call *Parque Nacional de la Gran Comba* was
postponed indefinitely.[27]

The Big Bend National Park was dedicated on November 21,
1955. Secretary of the Interior Douglas McKay delivered the main
address. Gov. Allan Shivers of Texas and Gov. Jesús Lozoya of
Chihuahua were present. Two men who contributed so much to
the drive for a national park had died before the dedication took
place: Everett E. Townsend and Amon G. Carter.[28]

The Secretary spent much of his time talking about Mission
66, a ten-year program to develop roads, bridges, trails, and other
facilities that would make the national parks more accessible to the

The Chisos Mountains, wild, vast, and trackless,
are a fitting symbol of the Big Bend.

Photograph by Bank Langmore

Amon G. Carter, President of the Texas Big Bend Park Association, presents the deed to Big Bend National Park to President Franklin D. Roosevelt.

public. Practically all the development in the Big Bend – the Panther Junction park headquarters, the tourist facilities in the Chisos Basin, the store and camping grounds at Rio Grande Village – took place during those 10 years.

This phase ended when Mrs. Lyndon B. Johnson visited the park in April 1966. Traveling with Secretary of the Interior Stewart Udall and Mrs. Udall, National Park Service Director George Hartzog, Jr., 70 members of the White House staff, the Washington press corps, and dozens of other reporters, photographers, and film crews, the First Lady brought in one of the largest entourages ever seen in the Big Bend.[29]

The numerous travel writers realized the uniqueness of the land. It was a wonderland for biologists and geologists; they called attention to the international aspects of its history, and they noted its overwhelming vastness. At least twice, for the U.S. Army's experiment with camels during 1859 and 1860 and for astronaut training in 1964, the Big Bend has been used for its harsh terrain and unforgiving climate.

The Big Bend, of course, has easily survived the successive waves of human occupation. The timeless face of the land emphasizes that fact. The Big Bend protected the Indians against the encroachment of the Spaniards and the Anglo-Americans. It gradually yielded to exploration, but the hostile environment helped insure the survival of one of the country's most fascinating regions. Relics of the historical drama are preserved at Fort Davis National Historic Site, Guadalupe Mountains National Park, Chamizal National Memorial at El Paso, and Fort Leaton State Park near Presidio, as well as Big Bend National Park.

The Big Bend is now a source of inspiration for artists, writers, photographers, scientists, and vacationers. The Chisos Mountains continue to shelter an isolated alpine environment; the desert nourishes hundreds of different species of cacti; and the Rio Grande erodes away a few more inches of limestone canyon every year. Today the sights that only a few 19th-century travelers saw after heroic efforts are available to nearly everyone. Hiking and horse trails lead up into the Chisos along the South Rim or Lost Mine trails. Most visitors drive across the desert in air-conditioned comfort to see the fossil bone exhibit, Dagger Flat, Mariscal Mine, or Wilson's Ranch. And float trips through Santa Elena, Mariscal, and Boquillas Canyons are almost a daily occurrence. E. E. Townsend's lament that most people in the State were unaware of the Big Bend is no longer true. It finally is recognized as one of the great wonders of the Southwest.

Historic Sites
of the Big Bend

Although some Big Bend place names recall the days of the Spaniards and Indians, most are of more recent origin, reflecting the Anglo-American society that settled the region as well as the pragmatic and common character of the settlers. The hopes and dreams of people, as well as their philosophy and vision, can often be seen in the names they apply to their surroundings. The dominant human thread running through the history of the Big Bend is that survival requires hard work. Practicality and directness are virtues in such circumstances, as the many obvious names signify.

In such country little was done if it did not have to be. Thus many landmarks went without names until 1903 when surveyor Arthur A. Stiles conducted a study of the region. He consulted the local citizens before applying the place names to his map. M. A. Ernst, storekeeper and justice of the peace in Boquillas, convened a jury for the purpose of considering and approving place names. Each member had a topographical feature named for him, but as Stiles reported, "there were barely enough people living in the country to furnish names for all the places." So they resorted to friends and relatives. Many of the more exotic sounding Spanish and Indian names were consequently forgotten. (In fairness to Ernst's jury, it must be pointed out that frequently the previously awarded names were unknown to them and have only been turned up by recent research.[1])

Most geographical features have obvious names. Mule Ears Peak is perhaps the best example. Located in the southwestern reaches of the Chisos, near Trap Mountain, these durable peaks were probably named by teamsters who were coaxing their mule teams through the Big Bend. Cow Heaven Mountain has a more obscure origin. Located northwest of Mariscal Mountain, this formation reportedly got its name when a local rancher observed that the land was so barren that a cow "would have to go to Heaven" if stranded on it, because there was no grass. Casa Grande, Santa Elena, Terlingua Creek, Burro Mesa, Mariscal, Boquillas, and numerous other points illustrate the Spanish-Mexican influence. Other names, such as Maverick Mountain, Cow Heaven, and Dogie

Mountain, testify to the importance of the ranching industry.[2]

It took little imagination to apply the names of common reptiles and animals, plants or legends to prominent landmarks—Panther Peak and Spring, Rattlesnake Mountain, Alamo, Willow, and Cottonwood Creeks, Ash and Oak Springs, Chisos Mountains. The presence of the National Park Service is evident in such names as Vernon Bailey Peak, Roger Toll Peak, George Wright Peak, and Carter Peak. Early pioneers are honored by such names as Nevill Springs, Stillwell Mountain, and Roy's Peak.

The land is still being named. During a recent study of the park, the Geological Survey searched for historic names for prominent landmarks, but applied their own creations when no historic names could be found. Such minute naming of features is only possible, or necessary, after the development of exact mapping techniques and aerial photography, and large numbers of visitors want to know what each hill or border is called and why.

The following guide lists only the most important extant historical sites. Most of them can be reached by car, but some require travel over primitive roads or strenuous hikes. Additional interpretative material is available at park headquarters on the better known sites. Sites marked with an asterisk * are located on primitive roads, where conditions change with the weather. A park ranger should be consulted before traveling in the back country.

Guide to Sites

Big Bend National Park

Barker Lodge   Today a research station associated with Sul Ross State University. Once a National Park Service ranger station. Located northwest of Boquillas Canyon on the spur road.

The Basin of the Chisos Mountains   Site of the Civilian Conservation Corps camp in 1934 that prepared the way for the national park. Now lodging facilities and a restaurant are located there.

Comanche Trail   A historical marker at Persimmon Gap commemorates the hectic past of the great Comanche War Trail. Beyond the gap the trail divided into several paths. One path crossed the Rio Grande near Lajitas, today a small community with a general store and a post office. Often a mile wide and lined with the bones of horses and cattle in the 19th century, the trail was the route Comanches took to and from Mexico during the raids of the "Comanche Moon," which one historian called the most sustained and devastating assault by one civilization on another.

*Coyote   Abandoned Mexican farm village, comprising some 10 adobe and stone ruins, clustered on the west bank of Alamo Creek at point where it flows from the terraces onto the Rio Grande floodplain. Mexican cemetery across the creek bed on an eminence overlooking the village. Located along the road from Castolon to Santa Elena Canyon.

Emory Peak   One of the highest peaks in Texas and the highest point in the Chisos Mountains at 7,835 feet. Named after Maj. William H. Emory, head of the Boundary Survey team that explored the Rio Grande in 1852. Although the engineers never climbed the peak, they used it as a point of reference throughout their survey. A hiking trail leads from the Basin to the top.

G-4 Ranch   In 1880 the G-4 Ranch covered 55,000 acres of open range in Southern Brewster County (Survey Block G-4). This ranching operation consisted of 6,000 head of cattle, controlled by 10 cowboys and a foreman. The cowboys worked out of three camps; one at Aqua Frio, 18 miles north of Terlingua Creek near Santa Elena Canyon, and a main camp west of Chisos at Oak Spring.

*Glenn Springs Located 9 miles down the unimproved Glenn Springs Road from the junction on the Panther Junction–Rio Grande Village paved road. The site of one of the earliest wax camps in the Park, Glenn Springs was also an army station and a small settlement. It is best known for the bandit raid that occurred in 1916. The rifle pits can still be seen lining the crest of the low ridge that overlooks the settlement site, along with the remains of a water system that brought water into the settlement and wax works. A large ranch house was located here; the holding pen, corral, and dipping chute are still visible.

*Johnson's Ranch Located about 16 miles east of Castolon on the unimproved river road. Johnson's Ranch was a successful ranch, a border trading post, a wayside stop for travelers, and a landing area for flyers during the border troubles in 1919. After Elmo Johnson purchased the ranch in 1928, the landing field was developed and officially opened by the U.S. Army on July 6, 1929. Its purpose was to train young aviators and to serve as a lookout station and check point on the International Boundary. Johnson occupied the ranch until the Park Service purchased the land.

*La Noria Located a few miles up the unimproved Old Ore Road from the junction on the Panther Junction-Rio Grande Village road. The name is Spanish for "The Well." When the region was farmed, La Noria became a small village known for the post office which operated there and as a stopover point for travelers. It was formally called Old Boquillas when the first map of the area was published; changed its name to La Noria when the village moved to its present site on the Rio Grande. There are few visible remains today.

*Luna Residence About midway on the unimproved road between Maverick and Santa Elena Canyon. One of the most photographic ruins in the park, the *jacal* of Gilberto Luna illustrates the struggle of man versus the elements in the Big Bend. Luna himself lived to the age of 109.

*Mariscal Mine   Located south of Glenn Springs on the un-improved river road, the main processing plant, building, pay-master's office, superintendent's house, employee's residences, com-pany store, barracks and brick kiln still remain. Although the view from the mine is magnificent, the area is dotted with open mine shafts and extreme caution must be used in viewing the site.

Old Ranch   The remains of the adobe ranch house built by Sam Nail in 1916 stand south of the Santa Elena junction on the park road to Castolon. His windmill and water tank continue to provide a watering place for birds and wildlife. Recommended as a pleasant picnic area.

Persimmon Gap   The point at which the Great Comanche Trail penetrated the Santiago Mountains. Now the north entrance to the Park. A Historical Site Marker on Tex. 385 from Marathon points out the spot where the trail crossed the mountains.

Wilson Ranch   On Camino Buena Vista road (or Castolon road), about 11 miles south of the main park road junction. Homer Wilson, a relative late-comer to the Big Bend, built a profitable ranch that is probably the best preserved one in the National Park. Here all the functions of a ranch can be seen. The bunkhouse, ranch house, cistern, corral and stubbing post, dipping chute, and chicken coop and pens remain as mute testimony to the activity that once enlivened the ranch. A trail leads from the overlook to the ranch.

Castolon – Santa Elena Canyon Area

Castolon   Named after a settler called Castulo, the village was first a subpost of the border patrol (1910-14), then the site of an army post during the border troubles with Mexico. The moun-tain identified with Castolon is Cerro Castellan – from the Spanish word meaning castle. Located just above the river on the Castolon road, the village is a popular visitor stop. Farming, commerce, border troubles, and local dwellings–the four major historical themes of the Big Bend National Park–are all represented here.

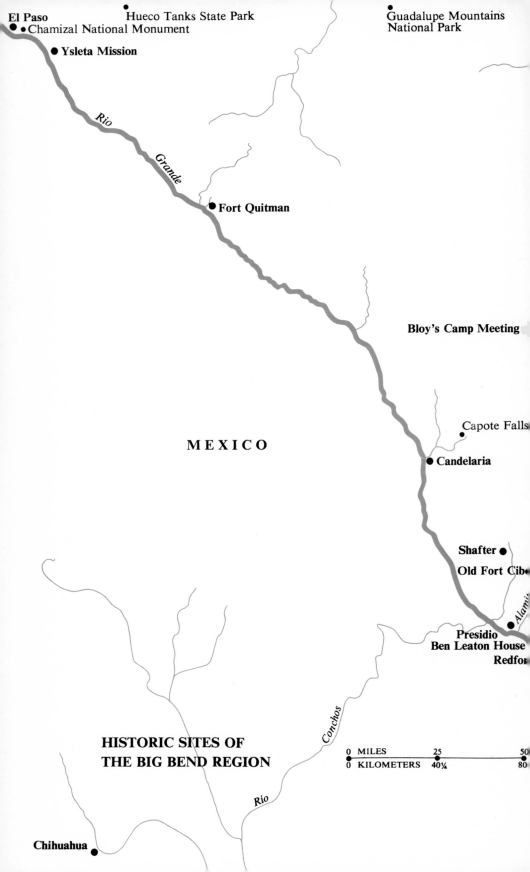

El Paso

Hueco Tanks State Park

Guadalupe Mountains
National Park

Chamizal National Monument

Ysleta Mission

Rio

Grande

Fort Quitman

Bloy's Camp Meeting

Capote Falls

MEXICO

Candelaria

Shafter

Old Fort Cib

Alami

Presidio
Ben Leaton House
Redfo

Conchos

HISTORIC SITES OF
THE BIG BEND REGION

| 0 | MILES | | 25 | | 50 |
| 0 | KILOMETERS | 40¼ | | 80 |

Rio

Chihuahua

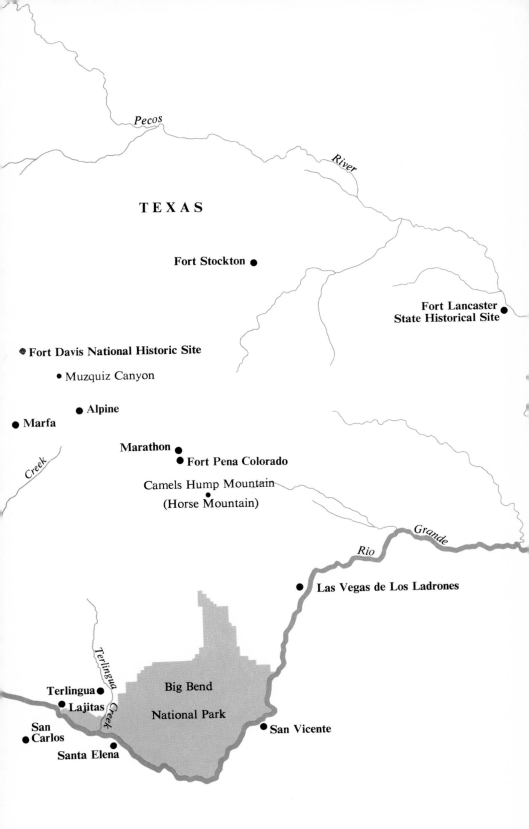

Pecos

River

TEXAS

Fort Stockton ●

Fort Lancaster
State Historical Site ●

● **Fort Davis National Historic Site**

● Muzquiz Canyon

● **Alpine**

● **Marfa**

Marathon ●
● **Fort Pena Colorado**

Camels Hump Mountain
(Horse Mountain) ●

Creek

Rio Grande

● **Las Vegas de Los Ladrones**

Terlingua Creek

Terlingua ●
● **Lajitas**

Big Bend

National Park

San
● **Carlos**

● **San Vicente**

Santa Elena

Dorgan Farm House Of exceptional architectural interest, this house stands just above the river road between Castolon and Santa Elena Canyon. It commands an outstanding view of the Chisos Mountains, the Rio Grande floodplain and the Sierra del Carmen as they stretch into Mexico. The huge stone fireplace in the central room is constructed from large slabs of petrified wood. Four huge ceiling beams (only two remain) radiated from a center point to the four corners.

Old Castolon The Old Castolon Store, located here, is probably one of the oldest buildings in the National Park. It was a border trading post from the days when Castolon was first settled. Founded by Cipriano Hernández about 1900.

Santa Elena Canyon At the end of the Castolon road. The most spectacular of the major canyons of the Big Bend, Santa Elena was one of the last to be floated and documented. The Boundary Survey of 1852 bypassed it, believing that their fragile boats would be wrecked. The first documented trip through the canyon was by surveyor John T. Gano in 1882. U.S. Geological Survey member Dr. Robert T. Hill took the first photographs of the interior of the canyon in 1899.

Sublett Farm House Near the Dorgan residence above the river road between Castolon and Santa Elena Canyon. The Rio Grande floodplain was a fertile area for cultivation of cotton, corn, and other crops. The Sublett Farm House is an adobe structure, of which only the main walls still stand.

*Terlingua Abaja The name in Spanish means "Lower Terlingua." Many ruins remain to suggest the activity that once thrived in this old Mexican village, located several miles north of the unimproved road between Santa Elena Canyon and Maverick. Settled earlier than the mining village of Terlingua, Terlingua Abaja still has its old adobe chapel and cemetery.

Daniel's Farm House   Located in the west picnic grounds area at Rio Grande Village. Original owner was J. M. Graham. The Daniel's Farm Complex dates from about 1920 and illustrates the cotton farming that flourished in the Rio Grande Valley around Boquillas. It was named for John R. Daniels, who owned it when the park was established. Of interest architecturally, the structure is of adobe with a viga and cane ceiling, adobe roof, and flagstone floor.

*Hot Springs   Located on the Rio Grande on the two-mile unimproved spur road off the Panther Junction-Rio Grande Village road. Once developed as a health resort and trading post, this is the site of J. O. Langford's original store, motel, and residence. Several hot springs that flow into the Rio Grande near the confluence of Tornillo Creek gave the site its name, and provided a living for Langford and his family for several years. A few small springs still flow but the major hot springs used by Langford have since been silted in by flooding from the Rio Grande. Indian pictographs, kitchen middens, and mortar holes at the foot of the cliffs near the springs testify to occupation by nomadic Indian tribes.

Ore Tramway Line   Visible just off the Boquillas Canyon spur road, the tramway line and terminal were used near the turn of the century to transport ore from the Del Carmen silver and lead mine in Mexico, across the Rio Grande, to the terminal on the American side. The mine was closed about 1906.

Senator Berkeley Cottage   Located by the river near the group campground at Rio Grande Village. This cottage belonged to State Senator Benjamin F. Berkeley of Alpine, who used it as a vacation residence. He called it Ojos de Boquillas. Today it is a NPS employee residence.

*Ernst Tinaja   *Tinaja* is Spanish for a large, earthen storage jar. In the center of the Ernst Canyon, one mile off the Old Ore Road, is a huge natural cistern in the limestone cliffs. It is known as the Ernst Tinaja and is waterfilled the year round.   221

The Big Bend Region

Alpine   The County Seat of Brewster County is located at the junction of Tex. 67 and 118. The community began as a section of the Southern Pacific Railroad and was first called Burgess Springs, then Osborne. To obtain water rights from a local rancher the railroad changed the name to Murphyville. In 1888, when it became the county seat, local citizens changed its name to Alpine. It is still an important rail head for the local ranchers.

Bloys Camp Meeting   Began in 1890, the Bloys Camp Meeting is still celebrated at Skillman's Grove (named for Henry Skillman) in the Davis Mountains, west of Fort Davis on Tex. 166.

Camel Hump (or Horse Mountain)   Located on Tex. 385 between Marathon and Big Bend National Park, about 8 miles south of Marathon, the mountain got its name from the camels that traipsed through the Big Bend before the Civil War. Lts. Edward L. Hartz and William Echols supplied the name in 1859. Also known as Horse Mountain.

Capote Falls   Located on private property off Texas 67 in the Cienega Mountains, the Capote Falls, 175 feet, are the highest falls in Texas. *Capote* is Spanish for Cape.

Chamizal National Monument   This monument, located on Cordova Island in the Rio Grande River south of El Paso, commemorates the peaceful settlement of a 99-year boundary dispute between Texas and Mexico. The Chamizal Treaty was signed in 1963.

Fort Davis National Historic Site   Established along the San Antonio to El Paso road in 1854, Fort Davis was meant as a way-station and protective stronghold for troops and travelers in the sparsely settled territory. The post was abandoned in 1891 when there was no longer a need for army protection. Located on Tex. 17 at the north end of the town of Fort Davis.

Fort Lancaster State Historical Site   This Federal military outpost was established in 1855 along the old military road from San Antonio to El Paso. It was finally abandoned in 1868, after the frontier had bypassed it. Located 33 miles west of Ozona on U.S. 290.

Fort Pena Colorado   Four miles southwest of Marathon in Brewster County, the ruins of this old fort and surrounding grounds are maintained as a county park with picnic and recreational facilities. The fort was established in 1880 to protect the Chihuahua Trail from marauding Mescalero Apaches. It was abandoned in 1893.

Fort Quitman   The remains of the fort are located on the Rio Grande off Tex. 192 near the community of Fort Quitman. The military installation was established in 1858 and abandoned in 1877.

Fort Stockton   The stone and adobe ruins of this fort remain north of the business district of the town of Fort Stockton on Tex. 290 in Pecos County. Located at Comanche Springs, the fort was built in 1859 to protect the San Antonio–San Diego Mail Route. After the Civil War it was garrisoned by Negro troops. It was abandoned in 1886.

Guadalupe Mountains National Park   Located in Hudspeth and Culbertson Counties, this is the newest national park in Texas. It is noted for its wild, rugged landscape, Permian limestone fossils, and Signal Peak of 8,751 feet, the highest in Texas. A campsite and information center are located off Tex. 62 near Pine Springs Canyon.

Hueco Tanks State Park   The 738-acre park is located 32 miles northeast of El Paso off Tex. 62. There is the site of the last Indian battle in El Paso County and the large, natural limestone cisterns for which the park is named. The area was long used by Indians as a campsite and their drawings and pictographs cover the surrounding caves and cliffs. The cisterns were also used by wagon trains heading for California and by the Butterfield stagecoaches.

Lajitas   Located in southeastern Brewster County on Tex. 170 is Lajitas, which derives its name from the little flat rocks

223

of the Boquillas formation. *Lajitas* means flags stones. The village is located at the San Carlos ford of the Rio Grande on the Old Comanche Trail.

Ben Leaton House A State park located a few miles downriver from Presidio enroute to Lajitas. Formerly called Fortin de San Jose. Ben Leaton acquired title in 1846. Overlooking the floodplain of the Rio Grande, it is a formidable structure and served its owner well through several Indian attacks. Leaton was one of the earliest merchants and ranchers in the Big Bend country. Recently restored by the Texas State Park Service.

Marathon Probably the site of an Indian culture, settled by white men only after the Civil War. A military subpost was established there in 1879, and the town began in 1882 when the Texas & New Orleans Railroads arrived. Located on Tex. 90 and 385, it is one of the main entrances to Big Bend National Park.

Marfa Established in 1881 as a water stop on the Texas & New Orleans Railroads, Marfa was named by the wife of the railroad president after the heroine of a Russian novel. Located on Tex. 90 and 67.

HISTORIC SITES OF BIG BEND NATIONAL PARK

0 MILES 5 10
0 KILOMETERS 8 16

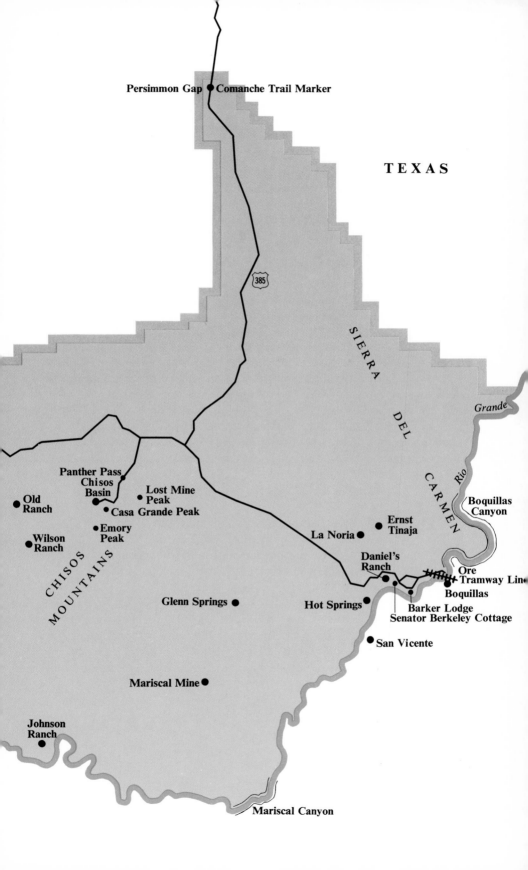

Old Fort Cibolo   A private fort located off Tex. 67 near Shafter. Milton Faver built three fortresses in the Big Bend. Remains are located near Big Springs Cibolo, which supplied water for the fort.

Presidio   Located on the Rio Grande on Tex. 67, Presidio is immediately opposite Ojinaga, Mexico, and is an important point of entry to and from Mexico. Originally an outpost of Mexico, called El Presidio del Norte (the fort of the north), the area was awarded to the U.S. in 1848 by the treaty of Guadalupe Hidalgo.

Redford   Located south of Presidio on Tex. 170, Redford is a small farming community on the Rio Grande. The settlement was originally Mexican and called Polvo, which means dust. It is the site of a fort and a customs station.

San Vicente and San Carlos   Sites of Spanish presidios located on the Mexican side of the Rio Grande. San Vicente is located on a small mesa about 3 miles from the San Vicente crossing on the river. Only fragments of the chapel walls remain. Established in 1774, San Carlos is located on the other side of the Sierra Ponce range in Mexico about 15 miles south of Lajitas or about 10 miles southwest of Castolon. Inaccessible except by 4-wheel drive vehicle or backpacking, San Vicente can be seen by binoculars from the top of a hill at the crossing. Both places are mentioned in many legends, and villages exist nearby.

Shafter   Between the Chinati and Cienega Mountains on Tex. 67, lies Shafter, a mining ghost town. From 1880 to 1940 it was a center for silver mining activities in Presidio County. Abandoned mines, machinery and buildings remain. Shafter is located 20 miles north of Presidio.

Terlingua   Located on Tex. 170 a few miles west of Study Butte outside the west entrance of Big Bend National Park. Today the site of the World Champion Chili Cookoff, the village of Terlingua, during its heyday, was the site of numerous quicksilver mines. The most important was the Chisos Mining Company, responsible for most of the remains that are visible today; the general store, the movie house, the jail house, the chapel, and the two-story house belonging to the mine owner, Howard Perry.

Ysleta Mission   Located 8 miles southeast of El Paso on Tex. 80, lies Ysleta, the oldest permanent settlement in Texas. The community was founded in 1680. The missions, San Antonio de las Tiguas (also called Nuestra Señora del Carmen) and San Miguel del Socorro, were built there in 1682. Both missions have suffered the effects of flood, fire, and time, but their ruins remain.

Bibliographical Essay

There is only a limited amount of information on various aspects of Big Bend National Park for the visitor who wants to know more about it. Former Big Bend Chief Naturalist Roland H. Wauer produced three handbooks that prove useful for driving, hiking, camping, or floating: *Guide to the Backcountry Roads and the River* (Big Bend National Park, Texas, 1970); *Hiker's Guide to the Developed Trails and Primitive Routes* (Big Bend National Park, Texas, 1971); and *Road Guide to the Paved and Improved Dirt Roads* (Big Bend National Park, Texas, 1970). Wauer has also written the best study on birds of the park, *Birds of Big Bend National Park and Vicinity* (Austin and London, 1973). For the botanist, Barton H. Warnock of Sul Ross State University has compiled *Wildflowers of Big Bend Country, Texas* (Alpine, 1970).

To historians the most important material for study of the Big Bend are the manuscript collections in various depositories across the country. The archives of the University of Texas at Austin contains several collections that relate to the Big Bend. General information can be found there in the Big Bend Scrapbook and the Brewster County Scrapbook. Over the years staff members have clipped various newspapers and magazines for material primarily related to the establishment of the national park. Several unpublished manuscripts relating to communities in the region are also in the files, including a typescript of probably the most useful Spanish document on the Big Bend, the diary of Pedro de Rábago y Terán's expedition. The original is in the Archivo General de la Nación, Mexico City. Although most of the information relating to the Texas Rangers is in the Adjutant General's Records of the Archives, Texas State Library, Austin, some material is located in the Adjutant General's Office (Texas) Records Transcripts, of the University of Texas Archives.

Another important source is the National Archives and Records Service, Washington, D.C. Material on the Topographical Engineers' explorations and the army's pacification in the Big Bend, such as letters sent and received by the Topographical Engineers, are also available on National Archives microfilm publications. Information on the bandit raids and subsequent army action can be found in Record Group 94, Office of the Adjutant General Documents File, National Archives. These records include documents from Big Bend residents complaining of conditions, letters from government officials regarding their action, and, finally, Maj. George Langhorne's official report of his "little punitive expedition" into Mexico.

At least five other collections contain important information on the Big Bend. A copy of the fascinating diary kept by Mexican Col. Emilio Langberg on a trip from San Carlos to Old Monclova in 1851 is in the Western Americana Collection at Yale University. Langberg's comments supplement the journals of Americans who traveled through the Big Bend in the 1850s, and provide one of the few Mexican sources for the period. The Western Americana Collection also houses the papers of William H. Emory, who replaced Bartlett as the U.S. Commissioner for the Boundary Survey. Other material on the Boundary Survey is found in the DeGolyer Foundation Library, Southern Methodist University, Dallas, Texas. The George Clinton Gardner Papers provide another opinion on the Green-Chandler exploration of the Big Bend in 1852. The personal papers of Col. Benjamin H. Grierson are located at the Newberry Library in Chicago. Grierson was a significant figure in the conquest of the Indians around the Fort Davis and Big Bend region, conducting several campaigns against Victorio. The personal papers of Walter P. Webb, a consulting historian for the Park Service during the 1930s when the proposed Big Bend National Park was under study, were recently given to the Texas State Library. Another person instrumental in the establishment of the park was Amon G. Carter of Fort Worth. President of the Texas Big Bend Park Association, Carter encouraged others around the State to support the park idea and contribute their money. His papers are available in the files of the Amon G. Carter Foundation, Fort Worth.

Although much historical material is available on the Big Bend country, little is general enough to be of interest to the layman. There are several surveys that might fill that void. Though it was published years ago, Carlysle G. Raht, *The Romance of Davis Mountains and Big Bend Country* (El Paso, 1919), has been the best history of the region for decades. Drawing on published information, personal knowledge of the region, and interviews with residents, Raht provided an easily readable account of the area. The book is out of date, however, for much research has been conducted and much has happened in the Big Bend since it was published.

Several other surveys are also available: Virginia Madison, *The Big Bend Country of Texas* (2d ed. rev. New York, 1968), emphasizes popular tales, folklore, and many incidents that are included because of their flavor or color rather than their authenticity; Ross A. Maxwell, *The Big Bend of the Rio Grande: A Guide to the Rocks, Landscape, Geologic History, and Settlers of the Area of the Big Bend National Park* (Austin, 1968), is more reliable, emphasizing the prehistory and geology of the region; and Clifford B. Casey, *Mirages, Mysteries and Reality, Brewster County, Texas: The Big Bend of the Rio Grande* (Hereford, Texas, 1972), exclusively a history of Brewster County, mostly in the 20th century. The book was issued in such limited numbers that it is no longer available for purchase at most bookstores.

Many of the curious and interesting place names of the Big Bend are discussed in Virginia Madison and Hallie Stillwell, *How Come It's Called That? Place Names in the Big Bend Country* (New York, 1968), but the book must be used with care because of conflicting accounts of how several of the place names originated. Madison and Stillwell seemed to have depended heavily upon oral tradition in many instances.

One of the best sources on the 19th–century history of Presidio County, which at one time included all present-day Brewster County, is John E. Gregg, "The History of Presidio County" (M.A. thesis, University of Texas, Austin, 1933). A resident of the county, Gregg spent years in his research and interviewing. His work was also published in the centennial edition of *Voice of the Mexican Border* (1936).

Very little is available to the layman on the Spanish period in the Big Bend, although there is a great deal of material on the Spaniards in the Southwest, some of which relates to the Big Bend. Perhaps the most useful is Robert S. Weddle, *San Juan Bautista, Gateway to Spanish Texas* (Austin, 1968), which includes a comprehensive account of the Spanish expeditions into the Big Bend that left from San Juan Bautista. A more thorough treatment of the region is found in several chapters of Carlos E. Castañeda, *Our Catholic Heritage in Texas, 1519–1936* (7 vols., Austin, 1936–1950), but the set has long been out of print and is usually available only in specialized libraries. Still more scarce is Victor J. Smith's account of "Early Spanish Exploration in the Big Bend of Texas," *West Texas Historical and Scientific Society Publications*, II (1928).

Almost all of the 16th–century Spanish expeditions that crossed into the Big Bend have received extensive attention from scholars, including translation of their official journals or diaries. Cleve Hallenbeck, *Álvar Núñez Cabeza de Vaca: The Journey and Route of the First European to Cross the Continent of North America, 1534–1536* (Glendale, 1940), contends that Cabeza de Vaca went through the Big Bend, while Carl O. Sauer, *Sixteenth Century North America: The Land and the People as Seen by the Europeans* (Berkeley, Los Angeles, and London, 1971), concludes that he journeyed north of the Big Bend. Later Spanish expedition journals can be found in Herbert E. Bolton, *Spanish Exploration in the Southwest, 1542–1706* (New York, 1967 reprint) and in books published by the Quivira Society: George P. Hammond and Agapito Rey (eds.), *Expedition Into New Mexico Made by Antonio de Espejo, 1582–1583, as Revealed in the Journal of Diego Pérez de Luxán, a Member of the Party* (Los Angeles, 1929); Lawrence Kinnaird (ed.), *The Frontiers of New Spain: Nicholas de LaFora's Description, 1766–1768* (Berkeley, 1958). Rex E. Gerald, *Spanish Presidios of the Late Eighteenth Century in Northern New Spain* (Santa Fe, 1968), has written about the two presidios established in the Big Bend, San Carlos and San Vicente.

Information on the contact between Spaniards and Indians can be found in Alfred B. Thomas, *Teodoro de Croix and the Northern Frontier of New Spain, 1776–1783* (Norman, 1941), Max L. Moorhead, *The Apache Frontier: Jacob Ugarte and Spanish-Indian Relations in Northern New Spain, 1769–1791* (Norman, 1968), and in two articles by Al B. Nelson: "Campaigning in the Big Bend of the Rio Grande, 1787," *Southwestern Historical Quarterly*, XXXIX (Oct., 1935), and "Juan de Ugalde and Picax-ande Ins-tinsle, 1787–1788," *Southwestern Historical Quarterly*, XLIII (Apr., 1940). Among the unpublished sources, James M. Daniel, "The Advance of the Spanish Frontier and the Despoblado" (Ph.D. dissertation, University of Texas, Austin, 1955) is probably the most helpful.

Almost no material is available on the Mexican period in the Big Bend, largely because the territory was practically isolated and left to the Indians until the end of the Mexican War when the United States took possession of it. Anglo-American expeditions soon penetrated the unknown region, led by John Coffee Hays in 1848. Perhaps the most obtainable source on the Hays expedition is James K. Greer, *Colonel Jack Hays, Texas Frontier Leader and California Land Builder* (New York, 1952), which contains a good account of the journey, and Rena Maverick Green (ed.), *Samuel Maverick, Texan: 1803–1870* (San Antonio, 1952), which includes Maverick's diary of the expedition.

The first military expedition into the Big Bend – and the report in which the term "big bend" first appeared in print – was led by Lt. William H. C. Whiting, whose diary is published in Ralph P. Bieber (ed.), *Exploring Southwestern Trails, 1846–1854* (Glendale, 1938), but others were quick to follow. The most easily available account of the Topographical Engineers in the Big Bend is Ronnie C. Tyler (ed.), "Exploring the Rio Grande: Lt. Duff C. Green's Report of 1852," *Arizona and the West,* X (Spring, 1968). It contains the diary that Green, the military commander who accompanied the civilian surveyor through the heart of the Big Bend, submitted after he reached Fort Duncan. The surveyor was M. T. W. Chandler, whose report is printed in a scarce set compiled by William H. Emory, the Chief Surveyor and later Commissioner of the Boundary Survey team, *Report on the United States and Mexican Boundary Survey. . . .* (2 vols.; Washington: Government Printing Office, 1857–1859).

After gold was discovered in California, many men crossed through the Big Bend region en route to the goldfields. Numerous diaries and accounts have been published; among the best are George P. Hammond and Edward H. Howes (eds.), *Overland to California on the Southwestern Trail, 1849: Diary of Robert Eccleston* (Berkeley, 1950); George W. B. Evans, *Mexican Gold Trail: The Journal of a Forty-Niner,* ed. by Glenn S. Dumke (San Marino, 1945), and Robert W. Stephens (ed.), *A Texan in the Gold Rush: The Letters of Robert Hunter, 1849–1851* (Bryan, Texas, 1972).

Trails were soon established through the Big Bend. One of the first pathfinders was the team of Neighbors and Ford, whose story is told in W. Turrentine Jackson, *Wagon Roads West: A Study of Federal Road Surveys and Construction in the Trans-Mississippi West, 1846–1869* (Berkeley, 1952), John S. Ford, *Rip Ford's Texas,* ed. by Stephen B. Oates (Austin, 1963), and Kenneth F. Neighbours, "The Expedition of Major Robert S. Neighbors to El Paso in 1849," *Southwestern Historical Quarterly,*

LVIII (July, 1954). The best account of the later teamsters who used the Chihuahua Trail is August Santleben, *A Texas Pioneer: Early Staging and Overland Freighting Days on the Frontiers of Texas and Mexico,* ed. by I. D. Affleck (New York, 1910).

The trail that has attracted the most curiosity, both from those who pioneered in the Big Bend and those who read about it, is the Great Comanche War Trail, which led from West Texas into the Big Bend, then forked before entering Mexico. One of the first studies of it is J. Evetts Haley, "The Great Comanche War Trail," *Panhandle-Plains Historical Review,* XXIII (1950). But the Topographical Engineers mentioned it as a possible location for a fort (Tyler, ed., "Green's Report," and Chandler in Emory, *Report of the Mexican Boundary*), and Judge O. W. Williams recorded the stories that Natividad Luján recalled about it in S. D. Myres (ed.), *Pioneer Surveyor, Frontier Lawyer: The Personal Narrative of O. W. Williams, 1877–1902* (El Paso, 1966). Ralph A. Smith's research on Indian raids into Mexico has led him into detailed study of the trail: "The Comanche Bridge Between Oklahoma and Mexico, 1843–1844," *Chronicles of Oklahoma,* XXXIX (Spring, 1961), and "The Comanche Sun Over Mexico," *West Texas Historical Association Year Book,* LXVI (1970). An archaeological expedition from the University of Texas studied the trail several years ago, but decided that they really did not have enough experience with century-old trails to reach any conclusions. A report on their research is published in T. N. Campbell and William T. Field, "Identification of Comanche Raiding Trails in Trans-Pecos Texas," *West Texas Historical Association Year Book,* XLIV (Oct., 1968).

The Anglo-Americans quickly found that they would have to wrest the territory from the Indians, who had inhabited it for centuries. The Spaniards initially had little difficulty, for they found only the remnants of Puebloan civilizations that were declining by the 16th century. The Mexicans and Anglo-Americans found different Indians in the Big Bend, however, because the more warlike tribes from the plains moved southward during the 19th century. The best information on the Indians themselves remains W. W. Newcomb, *The Indians of Texas: From Prehistoric to Modern Times* (Austin, 1961), but Dorman H. Winfrey and James M.

Day (eds.), *The Indian Papers of Texas and the Southwest, 1825–1916* (5 vols., Austin, 1966), contains a wealth of information. Probably the best material on the Indians of the mid-19th century in the Big Bend and northern Mexico is found in a series of articles published in various journals by Ralph A. Smith, who has spent years searching Mexican as well as United States archives and newspapers for elusive details of unremembered conflicts. The tremendous amount of information he has assembled is revealed in the series of articles in the bibliography. "The Comanche Sun Over Mexico" is perhaps his most penetrating article on the Indians of the Big Bend.

Conquest of the Indians and establishment of United States military control over the Big Bend is told by Barry Scobee, *Fort Davis, Texas, 1583–1960* (El Paso, 1963); Robert M. Utley, *Fort Davis National Historic Site, Texas* (Washington, 1965); William H. Leckie, *The Buffalo Soldiers: A Narrative of the Negro Cavalry in the West* (Norman, 1967); in two articles by Frank M. Temple: "Colonel B. H. Grierson's Victorio Campaign," *West Texas Historical Association Year Book*, XXV (Oct., 1959), and "Colonel B. H. Grierson's Administration of the District of the Pecos," *West Texas Historical Association Year Book*, XXXVIII (Oct., 1962); and Dan L. Thrapp, *Victorio and the Mimbres Apaches* (Norman, 1974).

Accounts of early cattlemen and ranchers can be found in several sources. Many early residents reminisced in the pages of *Voice of the Mexican Border*, a magazine published for several years during the 1930s. Clifford B. Casey, in his report for the National Park Service, *Soldiers, Ranchers and Miners in the Big Bend* (Washington, 1969), included much material on early ranchers and residents of the region. Additional information is included in Casey's *Mirages, Mysteries, and Reality*. Noel L. Keith has recorded the story of *The Brites of Capote* (Fort Worth, 1961), who became benefactors of Texas Christian University to the extent that Brite Divinity School is named for the family. Mrs. O. L. Shipman also wrote of early ranchers in *Taming the Big Bend: A History of the Extreme Western Portion of Texas from Fort Clark to El Paso* (Marfa, 1926). Lewis Nordyke has included accounts of many Big Bend ranchers in his *Great Roundup: The Story of Texas and Southwestern Cowmen* (New York, 1955). A good summary of ranching in the Big Bend is Robert M. Utley, "The Range Cattle Industry in the Big Bend of Texas," *Southwestern Historical Quarterly, LXIX* (April, 1966).

Some ranchers and cowmen chose to tell their own story, such

235

as Will Tom Carpenter, *Lucky 7: A Cowman's Autobiography,* ed. by Elton Miles (Austin, 1957), and Frank Collinson, *Life in the Saddle,* ed. and arr. by Mary W. Clarke (Norman, 1963).

Settlement in the Big Bend is recounted by several who home-steaded land, such as J. O. Langford with Fred Gipson, *Big Bend, A Homesteader's Story* (Austin, 1952), who operated the Hot Springs Bath, and C. A. Hawley, "Life Along the Border," *West Texas Historical and Scientific Society Publications,* XX (1964), who worked for one of the mining companies in Terlingua. The best storyteller of the Big Bend was Judge O. W. Williams of Fort Stockton, whose tales are recorded in Myres (ed.), *Pioneer Surveyor, Frontier Lawyer.* Judge Williams not only wrote his own accounts of the country, but also set down the folklore of significant informants like Luján, an old Mexican who seemed to know all the stories of the Big Bend.

Mining played a large part in development of the region, but little literature has been produced on it. A good study of one company is James M. Day, "The Chisos Quicksilver Bonanza in the Big Bend of Texas," *Southwestern Historical Quarterly,* LXIV (Apr., 1961). Perhaps the most comprehensive is Kathryn B. Walker, "Quicksilver Mining in the Terlingua Area," (M.A. thesis, Sul Ross State College, 1960). But the best account of mining operations and life is C. A. Hawley's, for he lived in Terlingua and worked for the mines for years. His reminiscences in "Life Along the Border" provide an intimate view of mining and the life it created. Casey also has researched the history of mining in the Big Bend and presented it in *Soldiers, Ranchers, and Miners.*

One incident that changed the history of the Big Bend was the coming of the railroad in 1882. The Chihuahua Trail ceased to be so important; isolation was no longer such a major factor. Only one work treats the subject of railroads in Texas, S. G. Reed, *A History of the Texas Railroads and of Transportation Conditions Under Spain and Mexico and the Republic and The State* (Houston, 1941). *From Ox-Teams to Eagles: A History of the Texas and Pacific Railways* (Dallas, n.d.) adds little to the story that Reed tells.

Many colorful characters lived in the Big Bend during its development. One of the best known was E. E. Townsend, who became known as the father of the national park. His biography has been written by Lewis H. Saxton and Clifford B. Casey, "The Life of Everett Ewing Townsend," *West Texas Historical and Scientific Society Publications,* XVII. J. Evetts Haley covers the few years that Jeff Milton spent in the Big Bend in *Jeff Milton, a Good Man with a Gun* (Norman, 1948). Leavitt Corning, Jr., treats Ben Leaton and Milton Faver as thoroughly as possible in *Baronial Forts of the Big Bend* (San Antonio, 1967). Much must go unsaid about these two formidable characters, however, for so little is known about them. James B. Gillett has written his own story in *Six Years With the Texas Rangers, 1875 to 1881* (New Haven, 1925). Much public mention was given the "badmen" of the Big Bend when Robert T. Hill published his account of a float from Presidio to Langtry in "Running the Cañons of the Rio Grande," *Century Illustrated Monthly Magazine,* LXI (Nov., 1900-Apr., 1901). A later account of Hill's expedition is Ronnie C. Tyler, "Robert T. Hill and the Big Bend," *The American West,* X (Sept. 1973).

Material on the bandit era in the Big Bend is plentiful. Some of it contains exaggerations, but two of the best accounts are Clarence C. Clendennen, *Blood on the Border: The United States Army and the Mexican Irregulars* (London, 1969), a work by a scholar who was a member of Pershing's punitive expedition, and Herbert M. Mason, *The Great Pursuit* (New York, 1970). Supplementary sources written by men who went with Major Langhorne into Mexico are James Hopper, "A Little Mexican Expedition," *Collier's,* LVII (July 15, 1916), and Stuart W. Cramer, Jr., "The Punitive Expedition from Boquillas" *U.S. Cavalry Journal,* XXVIII (Oct., 1916). Walter P. Webb, *The Texas Rangers: A Century of Frontier Defense* (Boston, 1935) also contains some material on the Rangers and bandits

Other first-hand accounts of the military participation in the Big Bend are Stacy C. Hinkle, *Wings Over the Border: The Army Air Service Armed Patrol of the United States-Mexico Border, 1919–1921* (El Paso, 1970), and *Wings and Saddles: The Air and Cavalry Punitive Expedition of 1919* (El Paso, 1967). C. D. Wood, owner of the wax factory that was raided at Glenn Springs, told his own story in "The Glenn Springs Raid," *West Texas Historical and Scientific Society Publications,* XIX (1963), and W. D. Smithers, a photographer and journalist who came to the Big Bend in 1916, wrote an account of the bandit raids in *Pancho Villa's Last Hangout – On Both Sides of the Rio Grande in the Big Bend Country* (Alpine, n.d.).

The best surveys of the establishment of the Big Bend National Park are R. M. Wagstaff, "Beginnings of the Big Bend Park," *West Texas Historical Association Year Book,* XLIV (Oct., 1968), Clifford B. Casey, "The Big Bend National Park," *West Texas Historical and Scientific Society Publications,* XIII (1948), and Madison, *Big Bend,* ch. 16. Former Superintendent of the park, L. A. Garrison, wrote "A History of the Proposed Big Bend International Park," which was distributed over a limited area in mimeograph form, but was never published.

I. Primary

A. Manuscripts

- Adjutant General's Office (Texas) Records Transcripts. Archives, University of Texas, Austin.
- Adjutant General's Records. Archives, Texas State Library, Austin.
- "Annual Report for the Fiscal Year 1916 of Major Frederick Funston, U.S. Army, Commanding Southern Department," in Records of the Adjutant General's Office. Record Group 94, National Archives, microfilm publication.
- Big Bend Scrapbook. Archives, University of Texas.
- Bliss, Zenas R. "Reminiscences of Zenas R. Bliss Major General United States Army." Copy in Archives, University of Texas.
- Brewster County Scrapbook. Archives, University of Texas.
- Carter, Amon G., Foundation Files. Fort Worth, Texas.
- Despatches from United States Consuls in Chihuahua, 1826-1906. Roll 1, vol. 1, Aug. 18, 1826–Dec. 31, 1869. National Archives microfilm.
- Emory, William H., Papers. Western Americana Collection, Yale University, New Haven, Conn.
- Gardner, George Clinton, Papers. De Golyer Foundation Library, Southern Methodist University, Dallas, Texas.
- Grierson, Benjamin H., Collection. Newberry Library, Chicago.
- Langberg, Emilio. "Itinerario de la Espedición de San Carlos, Chih. á Monclova Viejo." Copy in Guajardo Collection in Western Americana Collection, Yale University.
- Letters Received by the Topographical Bureau of the War Department, 1824–1865. Microcopy 506, roll 36, I-J, September 1838–December 1854. National Archives.
- Letters Sent by the Topographical Bureau of the War

Department and by Successor Division in the Office of the Chief of Engineers. Vol. II, Oct. 16, 1848–Sept. 15, 1849; microcopy No. 66, Roll 13, National Archives.
- Office of the Adjutant General Document File. Record Group 94, National Archives.
- Rábago y Terán, Pedro de. "Diario de la Campaña executado por el Governador de Coahuila." Typescript in Archives, University of Texas Library.
- Webb, Walter P., Papers. Archives, Texas State Library.

B. Interviews
- W. P. Cameron, Mineral Wells, Texas, July 2, 1970.
- Mr. and Mrs. Hart M. Greenwood, Ciénega Ranch, May 8, 1973.
- Dr. Ross A. Maxwell, Austin, April 6, 1973.
- Dr. Calhoun Harris Monroe, El Paso, November 9, 1971.

C. Maps
- Derotero Topográfico de la espedición que desde San Carlos hasta Piedras Negras II Regreso por la Laguna de Laco a Chihuahua hiso el inspector inter. Colonias Militares de ese estado Coronel Don E. Langberg en el año 1851. Colección de Mapas del Estado de Chihuahua, Sociedad Mexicana de Geográfica y Estadística, México.
- "Map of Southern Part of Presidio County," by John T. Gano. Texas State Land Office, Austin.

D. Government Documents
- "Echols Diary," in *Report of the Secretary of War,* 36th Cong., 2d Sess., Sen. Ex. Doc. No. 1.
- Emory, William H. *Notes of a Military Reconnaissance From Fort Leavenworth, in Missouri, to San Diego, in California.* . . . 30th Cong., 1st Sess., Sen. Ex. Doc. No. 41.
- —————————. *Report on the United States and Mexican Boundary Survey.* . . . Washington, 1857–1859. 2 vols.
- Miller, Hunter. Ed. *Treaties and Other International Acts of the United States of America.* Washington, 1937. 8 vols.
- "Reports of Reconnaissances, etc.," in *Report of the Secretary of War.* . . . 31st Cong., 1st Sess., Sen. Ex. Doc. No. 64.
- *Report of the Secretary of War,* 32nd Cong., 1st Sess., Sen. Ex. Doc. No. 1.
- *Report of the Secretary of War,* 36th Cong., 1st Sess., Sen. Ex. Doc. No. 2.
- *Report of the Secretary of War,* 31st Cong., 1st Sess., Sen. Ex. Doc. No. 32.

E. Newspapers
- *Alpine Avalanche.* 1907, 1909, 1911, 1913, 1916, 1951.
- *Arkansas State Gazette.* Little Rock. 1839.
- *Austin Daily Statesman.* 1882.
- *Austin Dispatch.* 1937.

- *Big Spring Herald.* 1941.
- *Corpus Christi Star.* 1848.
- *Daily National Intelligencer.* Washington, D.C. 1848.
- *The Daily Picayune.* New Orleans. 1849–50.
- *Dallas Morning News.* 1937–38, 1941, 1944.
- *Democratic Telegraph and Texas Register.* Houston. 1848.
- *El Paso Daily Times.* 1883, 1886, 1899.
- *Fort Worth Star-Telegram.* 1935, 1942–43, 1955, 1958.
- *Galveston Civilian.* 1871.
- *Houston Chronicle.* 1938.
- *Leslie's Illustrated.* New York City. 1855, 1858.
- *The Morning Star.* Houston. 1841.
- *The New Era.* Marfa. 1908–11.
- *New York Herald.* 1849.
- *Rocky Mountain News.* Denver. 1936.
- *San Angelo Standard-Times.* 1941–42.
- *San Antonio Daily Express.* 1877, 1879–82, 1938.
- *San Antonio Herald.* 1857.
- *San Antonio Ledger.* 1852.
- *San Antonio Light.* 1942.
- *San Saba Weekly News.* 1891.
- *The South-Western American.* Austin. 1851.
- *The Statesman.* Austin. 1881.
- *The Texas Monument.* La Grange. 1851.
- *The Texas Republican.* Marshall. 1849, 1850.
- *Texas State Gazette.* Austin. 1849–51.
- *Victoria Advocate.* 1878.
- *Waco Tribune-Herald.* 1936.
- *The Western Star.* Lebanon, Ohio. 1840.
- *Western Texan.* San Antonio. 1850–52.

F. Books
- Bailey, L. R. Ed. *The A. B. Gray Report.* Los Angeles, 1973.
- Bartlett, John R. *Personal Narrative of Explorations and Incidents in Texas, New Mexico, Sonora and Chihuahua.* New York, 1852. 2 vols.
- Bolton, Herbert E. Ed. *Athanase de Mézières and the Louisiana-Texas Frontier,* 1768–1780. Cleveland, 1914. 2 vols.
- ——————. Ed. *Spanish Exploration in the Southwest, 1542–1706.* New York, 1967 reprint.
- Brinckerhoff, Sidney B., and Faulk, Odie B., Eds. *Lancers for the King: A Study of the Frontier Military System of*

*Northern New Spain, with a Translation of the Royal
Regulations of 1772.* Phoenix, 1965.
- Carpenter, Will Tom. *Lucky 7: A Cowman's Autobiography.* Ed.
by Elton Miles. Austin, 1957.
- Chamberlain, Samuel E. *My Confession.* Ed. by Roger
Butterfield. New York, 1956.
- Collinson, Frank. *Life in the Saddle.* Ed. and Arr. by Mary
Whatley Clarke. Norman, 1963.
- Connelley, William E. Ed. *Doniphan's Expedition and the
Conquest of New Mexico and California.* Kansas City, 1907.
- Evans, George W. B. *Mexican Gold Trail: The Journal of a
Forty-Niner.* Ed. by Glenn S. Dumke. San Marino, 1945.
- Ford, John S. *Rip Ford's Texas.* Ed. by Stephen B. Oates.
Austin, 1963.
- Fulcher, Walter. *The Way I Heard It: Tales of the Big Bend.*
Ed. by Elton Miles. Austin, 1959.
- Gillett, James B. *Six Years With the Texas Rangers, 1875 to
1881.* New Haven, 1925.
- González Flores, Enrique, and Almada, Francisco R., Eds.
*Informe de Hugo de O'Conor sobre el estado de las
Provincias Internas del Norte, 1771–76.* México, 1952.
- Green, Rena Maverick. Ed. *Samuel Maverick, Texan:
1803–1870.* San Antonio, 1952.
- Gregg, Josiah. *Commerce on the Prairies: or the Journal of a
Santa Fe Trader.* New York, 1844. 2 vols.
- Hackett, Charles Wilson. Ed. *Historical Documents Relating
to New Mexico, Nueva Vizcaya, and Approaches Thereto.*
Washington, 1923–1937. 3 vols.
- Hammond, George P., and Howes, Edward H. Eds. *Overland
to California on the Southwestern Trail, 1849: Diary of
Robert Eccleston.* Berkeley, 1950.
- —————————, and Rey, Agapito. Eds. *Expedition Into
New Mexico Made by Antonio de Espejo, 1582–1583, as
Revealed in the Journal of Diego Pérez de Luxán, a
Member of the Party.* Los Angeles, 1929.
- Harris, Benjamin B. *The Gila Trail: The Texas Argonauts and
the California Gold Rush.* Ed. by Richard H. Dillon.
Norman, 1960.
- Hodge, Frederick W. Ed. *Spanish Explorers in the Southern
United States.* New York, 1907.
- Hunter, J. Marvin. *The Boy Captives, Being the True Story of
the Experiences and Hardships of Clinton L. Smith and
Jeff D. Smith.* Bandera, Texas, 1927.
- Kendall, George W. *Narrative of the Texan Santa Fe
Expedition, Comprising a Description of a Tour Through
Texas.* New York, 1844. 2 vols.
- Kinnaird, Lawrence. Ed. *The Frontiers of New Spain:
Nicholas de LaFora's Description, 1766–1768.* Berkeley, 1957.
- Langford, J. O., with Gipson, Fred. *Big Bend, A Homesteader's
Story.* Austin, 1952.

- Leclercq, Jules. *Voyage au Mexique de New-York à Vera-Cruz en suivant les routes de terre.* Paris, 1885.
- Lesley, Lewis B. Ed. *Uncle Sam's Camels: The Journal of May Humphreys Stacey Supplemented by the Report of Edward Fitzgerald Beale, 1857–1858.* Cambridge, 1929.
- Maltby, W. J. *Captain Jeff, or Frontier Life in Texas with the Texas Rangers.* Colorado, Texas, 1906.
- Morfi, Fray Juan Agustín de. *Diario y derrotero (1777–1781).* Ed. by Eugenio del Hoyo and Malcolm D. McLean. Monterrey, 1967.
- Myres, S. D. Ed. *Pioneer Surveyor, Frontier Lawyer: The Personal Narrative of O. W. Williams, 1877–1902.* El Paso, 1966.
- Porras Muñoz, Guillermo. Ed. *Diario y derrotero de lo caminado, visto y obcervado en el discurso de la vista general de precidios, situados en las Provincias Ynternas de Nueva España, que de orden de su magestad executó D. Pedro de Rivera, Brigadier de los Reales Exercitos.* México, 1945.
- Römer, Ferdinand. *Texas, With Particular Reference to German Immigration and the Physical Appearance of the Country.* Trans. by Oswald Mueller. San Antonio, 1935.
- Ross, Marvin C. Ed. *George Catlin: Episodes From Life Among the Indians and Last Rambles.* Norman, 1959.
- Santleben, August. *A Texas Pioneer: Early Staging and Overland Freighting Days on the Frontiers of Texas and Mexico.* Ed. by I. D. Affleck. New York, 1910.
- Scott, Hugh L., *Some Memoirs of a Soldier.* New York and London, 1928.
- Simmons, Marc. Trans. and Ed. *Border Comanches: Seven Spanish Colonial Documents, 1785–1819.* Santa Fe, 1967.
- Stephens, Robert W. Ed. *A Texan in the Gold Rush: The Letters of Robert Hunter, 1849–1851.* Bryan, Texas, 1972.
- Thomas, Alfred B. Trans. and Ed. *After Coronado: Spanish Exploration Northeast of New Mexico, 1696–1727.* Norman, 1935.
- —————————. *Teodoro de Croix and the Northern Frontier of New Spain, 1776–1783.* Norman, 1941.
- Winfrey, Dorman H., and Day, James M. Eds. *The Indian Papers of Texas and the Southwest, 1825–1916.* Austin, 1966. 5 vols.

G. Articles
- Coldwell, Capt. Neal, to Gen. John B. Jones, Fort Davis, July 10, 1880, in *Voice of the Mexican Border,* I (Dec., 1933).

• Cramer, Stuart W. "The Punitive Expedition from Boquillas," *U.S. Cavalry Journal,* XXVIII (Oct., 1916).

• Crimmins, M. L. Ed. "Two Thousand Miles by Boat in the Rio Grande in 1850," *West Texas Historical and Scientific Society Publications,* V, 1933.

• Day, D. T. "Quicksilver in 1894," *U.S. Geological Survey, 16th Annual Report,* Pt. 3.

• Duke, Escal F. Ed. "A Description of the Route from San Antonio to El Paso by Captain Edward S. Meyer," *West Texas Historical Association Year Book,* XLIX (1973).

• Gillett, J. B. "The Old G4 Ranch," *Voice of the Mexican Border,* I (Oct., 1933).

• Haley, J. Evetts. Ed. "A Log of the Texas-California Cattle Trail, 1854," *Southwestern Historical Quarterly,* XXXV (Jan., 1932) and (Apr., 1932), XXXVI (July, 1932).

• Hammond, George P., and Rey, Agapito. Eds. "The Rodríguez Expedition to New Mexico, 1581–1582," *New Mexico Historical Review,* II (July, 1927).

• Hawley, C. A. "Life Along the Border," *West Texas Historical and Scientific Society Publications,* XX, 1964.

• Hill, Robert T. "Running the Cañons of the Rio Grande," *Century Illustrated Monthly Magazine,* LXI (Nov., 1900–Apr., 1901).

• Hopper, James. "A Little Mexican Expedition," *Collier's, the National Weekly,* LVII (July 15, 1916).

• Mecham, J. Lloyd. "The Second Spanish Expedition to New Mexico: An Account of the Chamuscado-Rodríguez Entrada of 1581–1582," *New Mexico Historical Review,* I (July, 1926).

• Meler, T. M., to Roy L. Swift, Cordell, Oklahoma, Aug. 3, 1939, in *American White Water,* XI (Spring, 1966).

• Mitchell, F. A. "The Stampede at Robber's Roost," *Voice of the Mexican Border,* I (Oct., 1933).

• Moore, Mary Lu, and Breene, Delmar L. Trans. and Eds. "The Interior Provinces of New Spain: The Report of Hugo O'Conor, January 30, 1776," *Arizona and the West,* XIII (Autumn, 1971).

• Peril, W. A. "From Texas to the Oregon Line," in J. Marvin Hunter. Ed. *The Trail Drivers of Texas.* 2nd ed. rev. Nashville, 1925.

• Reindrop, Reginald C. Trans. "The Founding of Missions at La Junta de los Rios," *Supplementary Studies of the Texas Catholic Historical Society,* I (Apr., 1938).

• Sanderlin, Walter S. "A Cattle Drive from Texas to California: The Diary of M. H. Erskine, 1854," *Southwestern Historical Quarterly,* LXVII (Jan., 1964).

• Shrode, Maria H. "Overland by Ox-Train in 1870; From Sulphur Springs, Texas, to San Diego, California," *Quarterly of the Historical Society of Southern California,* XXVI (Mar., 1944).

• Simpich, Frederick. "Down the Rio Grande," *National Geographic Magazine,* LXXVI (Oct., 1939).

- Tharp, B. C., and Kielman, Chester V. Eds. "Mary S. Young's Journal of Botanical Explorations in Trans-Pecos Texas, August-September, 1914," *Southwestern Historical Quarterly,* LXV (Jan. and Apr., 1962).
- Townsend, E. E. "Rangers and Indians in the Big Bend Region," *West Texas Historical and Scientific Society Publications,* Bulletin No. 56, 1935.
- Tyler, Ronnie C. Ed. "Exploring the Rio Grande: Lt. Duff C. Green's Report of 1852," *Arizona and the West,* X (Spring, 1968).
- "Up the Trail in 1890 – Experiences of Drive Told by Tom Granger, Ft. Davis," *Alpine Avalanche* (Anniversary Edition), Sept. 14, 1951.
- Wagstaff, R. M. "Beginnings of the Big Bend Park," *West Texas Historical Association Year Book,* LXIV (Oct., 1968).
- Westerlund, Peter. "Reminiscences of a Trip to Pike's Peak and Down the Rio Grande in the Year 1859, at the Time of the Pikes Peak Gold Craze," *Swedish American Historical Society Yearbook,* II (1908).
- Whiting, William H. C. "Journal of William Henry Chase Whiting, 1849," in Ralph P. Bieber. Ed. *Exploring Southwestern Trails, 1846–1854: Philip St. George Cooke, William Henry Chase Whiting, Francois Xavier Aubry.* Glendale, 1938.
- Wood, C. D. "The Glenn Springs Raid," *West Texas Historical and Scientific Society Publications* XIX, (1963).

II.   Secondary

A. Books

- Adams, Ramon F. *A Fitting Death for Billy the Kid.* Norman, 1960.
- Bannon, John F. *The Spanish Borderlands Frontier, 1513-1821.* New York, 1970.
- Bender, Averam B. *The March of Empire: Frontier Defense in the Southwest, 1848–1860.* Lawrence, 1952.
- Bobb, Bernard E. *The Viceregency of Antonio María Bucareli in New Spain, 1771–1779.* Austin, 1962.
- Bolton, Herbert E. *Coronado on the Turquois Trail: Knight of Pueblos and Plains.* Albuquerque, 1949.
- Braddy, Haldeen. *Pancho Villa at Columbus: The Raid of 1916.* El Paso, 1965.
- Brown, William E., and Wauer, Roland H. *Historic Resources Management Plan, Big Bend National Park.* Washington, 1968.

- Casey, Clifford B. *Mirages, Mysteries and Reality, Brewster County, Texas: The Big Bend of the Rio Grande.* Hereford, Texas, 1972.
- ————. *Soldiers, Ranchers and Miners in the Big Bend.* Washington, 1969.
- Castañeda, Carlos E. *Our Catholic Heritage in Texas, 1519–1936,* Austin, 1936. 7 vols.
- Clendennen, Clarence C. *Blood on the Border: The United States Army and the Mexican Irregulars.* London, 1969.
- Corning, Leavitt, Jr., *Baronial Forts of the Big Bend.* San Antonio, 1967.
- *Corpus Christi: 100 Years.* Corpus Christi, 1952.
- Dobie, J. Frank. *The Longhorns.* Boston, 1941.
- Douglas, William O. *Farewell to Texas: A Vanishing Wilderness.* New York, 1967.
- Faulk, Odie B. *Too Far North–Too Far South.* Los Angeles, 1967.
- Foreman, Grant. *Advancing the Frontier, 1830-1860.* Norman, 1933.
- Fowler, Harlan D. *Camels to California: A Chapter in Western Transportation.* Stanford, 1950.
- *From Ox-Teams to Eagles: A History of the Texas and Pacific Railways.* Dallas, n.d.
- Fuentes Mares, José. *Y México se refugio en el desierto: Luis Terrazas, historia y destino.* México, 1954.
- Geiser, Samuel W. *Men of Science in Texas, 1820–1880.* Dallas, 1959.
- Gerald, Rex E. *Spanish Presidios of the Late Eighteenth Century in Northern New Spain.* Santa Fe, 1968.
- Goetzmann, William H. *Army Exploration in the American West, 1803–1863.* New Haven, 1959.
- ————. *Exploration and Empire: The Explorer and the Scientist in the Winning of the American West.* New York, 1967.
- Greer, James K. *Colonel Jack Hays, Texas Frontier Leader and California Land Builder.* New York, 1952.
- Haley, J. Evetts. *Fort Concho and the Texas Frontier.* San Angelo, 1952.
- ————. *Jeff Milton, a Good Man with a Gun.* Norman, 1948.
- Hallenbeck, Cleve. *Álvar Núñez Cabeza de Vaca: The Journey and Route of the First European to Cross the Continent of North America, 1534–1536.* Glendale, 1940.
- Hine, Robert V. *Bartlett's West: Drawing the Mexican Boundary.* New Haven, 1968.
- Hinkle, Stacy C. *Wings and Saddles: The Air and Cavalry Punitive Expedition of 1919.* El Paso, 1967.
- ————. *Wings Over the Border: The Army Air Service Armed Patrol of the United States-Mexico Border, 1919–1921.* El Paso, 1970.

245

- Horgan, Paul. *Great River: The Rio Grande in North American History*. New York, 1954. 2 vols.
- Jackson, W. Turrentine. *Wagon Roads West: A Study of Federal Road Surveys and Construction in the Trans-Mississippi West, 1846–1869*. Berkeley, 1952.
- Jones, Billy M. *Health Seekers in the Southwest, 1817-1900*. Norman, 1967.
- Keith, Noel L. *The Brites of Capote*. Fort Worth, 1961.
- Leckie, William H. *The Buffalo Soldiers: A Narrative of the Negro Cavalry in the West*. Norman, 1967.
- Levy, Benjamin. *Hot Springs, Big Bend National Park: Historic Structures Report, Part 1, Historical Data*. Washington, 1968.
- Madison, Virginia. *The Big Bend Country of Texas*. Rev. Ed. New York, 1968.
- ——————, and Stillwell, Hallie. *How Come It's Called That? Place Names in the Big Bend Country*. Albuquerque, 1958.
- Martin, George C. *Archaeological Exploration of the Shumla Caves*. San Antonio, 1933.
- Mason, Herbert M. *The Great Pursuit*. New York, 1970.
- Maxwell, Ross A. *The Big Bend of the Rio Grande: A Guide to the Rocks, Landscape, Geologic History, and Settlers of the Area of the Big Bend National Park*. Austin, 1968.
- Merk, Frederick. *Slavery and the Annexation of Texas*. New York, 1972.
- Miles, Elton. "Old Fort Leaton: A Saga of the Big Bend," in Wilson M. Hudson. Ed. *Hunters & Healers: Folklore Tales & Topics*. Austin, 1971.
- Moorhead, Max L. *The Apache Frontier: Jacobo Ugarte and Spanish-Indian Relations in Northern New Spain, 1769–1791*. Norman, 1968.
- Myres, Sandra L. *The Ranch in Spanish Texas*. El Paso, 1969.
- Newcomb, W. W. *The Indians of Texas, From Prehistoric to Modern Times*. Austin, 1961.
- Nordyke, Lewis. *Great Roundup: The Story of Texas and Southwestern Cowmen*. New York, 1955.
- Ogle, Ralph H. *Federal Control of the Western Apaches, 1848–1886*. Albuquerque, 1940.
- Pennsylvania University, Committee of the Society of Alumni, *Biographical Catalogue of the Matriculates of the College. . . . 1749–1893*. Philadelphia, 1894.
- Raht, Carlysle G. *The Romance of Davis Mountains, and Big Bend Country*. El Paso, 1919.
- Reed, S. G. *A History of the Texas Railroads and of*

Transportation Conditions Under Spain and Mexico and the Republic and The State. Houston, 1941.

- *Report of the Big Bend Area, Texas.* U.S. Department of the Interior, National Park Service, State Park E C W, Dist. III, Jan., 1935.

- Richardson, Rupert N. *The Comanche Barrier to South Plains Settlement: A Century and a Half of Savage Resistance to the Advancing White Frontier.* Glendale, 1933.

- Sauer, Carl O. *Sixteenth Century North America: The Land and the People as Seen by the Europeans.* Berkeley, 1971.

- Scobee, Barry. *Fort Davis, Texas, 1583–1960.* Fort Davis, Texas, 1963.

- ————. *The Steer Branded Murder: The True and Authentic Account of a Frontier Tragedy.* Houston, 1952.

- Shipman, Mrs. O. L. *Taming the Big Bend: A History of the Extreme Western Portion of Texas From Fort Clark to El Paso.* Marfa, 1926.

- Sonnichsen, C. L. *I'll Die Before I'll Run: The Story of the Great Feuds of Texas.* New York, 1951.

- ————. *The Mescalero Apaches.* Norman, 1958.

- Thrapp, Dan L. *Victorio and the Mimbres Apaches.* Norman, 1974.

- Utley, Robert M. *Fort Davis National Historic Site, Texas.* Washington, 1965.

- Wauer, Roland H. *Birds of Big Bend National Park and Vicinity.* Austin, 1973.

- ————. *Guide to the Backcountry Roads and the River.* Big Bend National Park, Texas, 1970.

- ————. *Hiker's Guide to the Developed Trails and Primitive Routes.* Big Bend National Park, Texas, n.d.

- ————. *Road Guide to the Paved and Improved Dirt Roads.* Big Bend National Park, Texas, 1970.

- Webb, Walter P. *The Texas Rangers: A Century of Frontier Defense.* Boston, 1935.

- Webb, Walter P. and Carroll, H. Bailey. Eds. *The Handbook of Texas.* Austin, 1952. 2 vols.

- Weddle, Robert S. *San Juan Bautista, Gateway to Spanish Texas.* Austin, 1968.

- Wheat, Carl I. *Mapping the Transmississippi West, 1840-1861.* San Francisco, 1957–1963. 5 vols.

- Wirth, Conrad L. *Boundary Line Report: Big Bend National Park Project, Texas.* Washington, 1935.

- Wormington, H. M. *Prehistoric Indians of the Southwest.* Denver, 1964.

B. Articles

- Bender, A. B. "Opening Routes Across West Texas, 1848–1850," *Southwestern Historical Quarterly,* XXXVII (Oct., 1933).
- Bolton, Herbert E. "The Jumano Indians in Texas, 1650–1771," *Quarterly of the Texas State Historical Association,* XV (July, 1911).

- Campbell, T. N. and Field, William T. "Identification of Comanche Raiding Trails in Trans-Pecos Texas," *West Texas Historical Association Year Book,* XLIV (Oct., 1968).
- Casey, Clifford B. "The Big Bend National Park," *West Texas Historical and Scientific Society Publications,* XIII, 1948.
- —————. "The Trans-Pecos in Texas History," *West Texas Historical and Scientific Society Publications,* V, 1933.
- Christiansen, Paige W. "Hugo O'Conor's Inspection of Nueva Vizcaya and Coahuila, 1773," *Louisiana Studies,* II (Fall, 1963).
- Clifton, Minnie D. "A History of the Bloys Camp Meeting," *West Texas Historical and Scientific Society Publications,* XII, (1947).
- Connelley, Harry. "Big Bend National Park Project Reality at Last," *West Texas Today* (Sept., 1941).
- Coopwood, Bethel. "The Route of Cabeza de Vaca," *Quarterly of the Texas State Historical Association,* III (Oct., 1899), (Jan. and Apr., 1900).
- Davis, T. C. "The Cross-In Ranch: History and Development of a Pioneer Ranch," *Voice of the Mexican Border,* I (Oct., 1933).
- Day, James M. "The Chisos Quicksilver Bonanza in the Big Bend of Texas," *Southwestern Historical Quarterly,* LXIV (Apr., 1961).
- Dobie, J. Frank. "The Texan Part of Texas," *Nature Magazine,* XVI (Dec., 1930).
- Faulk, Odie B., and Brinckerhoff, Sidney B. "Soldiering at the End of the World," *The American West,* II (Summer, 1966).
- Foree, Kenneth, Jr. "Our New Park on the Rio Grande," *The Saturday Evening Post* (Dec. 2, 1944).
- Gregg, John E. "History of Presidio County," *Voice of the Mexican Border* (Centennial Edition), 1936.
- Haley, J. Evetts. "The Great Comanche War Trail," *Panhandle-Plains Historical Review,* XXIII (1950).
- Hill, Robert T. "The Cinnabar Deposits of the Big Bend Province of Texas," *Engineering and Mining Journal,* LXXIV (Sept. 6, 1902).
- —————. "The Great Chisos Rift Along the Canyons of the Rio Grande," *American Association, Proceedings,* LXIX (1900).
- Johnson, J. Harlan. "A History of Mercury Mining in the Terlingua District of Texas," *The Mines Magazine* (Sept., 1946).
- Kelley, Charles, Jr., "Factors Involved in the Abandonment of Certain Peripheral Southwestern Settlements," *American Anthropologist,* LIV (July-Sept., 1952).
- —————. "The Historic Indian Pueblos of La Junta de los Rios," *New Mexico Historical Review,* XXVI (Oct., 1952); (Jan., 1953).

• ————————. "Juan Sabeata and Diffusion in Aboriginal Texas," *American Anthropologist,* LVII (Oct., 1955).

• ————————. "The Route of Antonio de Espejo Down the Pecos River and Across the Texas Trans-Pecos Region of 1583: Its Relation to West Texas Archeology," *West Texas Historical and Scientific Society Publications,* VII, (1937).

• Lammons, Bishop F. "Operation Camel: An Experiment in Animal Transportation in Texas, 1857–1860," *Southwestern Historical Quarterly* LXI, (July, 1957).

• Martin, Mabelle E. "California Emigrant Roads Through Texas," *Southwestern Historical Quarterly,* XXVIII (Apr., 1925).

• Mecham, J. Lloyd. "Antonio de Espejo and His Journey to New Mexico," *Southwestern Historical Quarterly,* XXX (Oct., 1926).

• Mellard, Rudolph. "Early West Texas Cattle and Horse Brands," *Voice of the Mexican Border,* I (Feb.-March, 1934).

• Miles, Elton. "Chisos Ghosts," in Mody C. Boatright, Wilson M. Hudson, and Allen Maxwell. Eds. *Madstones and Twisters.* Dallas, 1958.

• Neighbours, Kenneth F. "The Expedition of Major Robert S. Neighbors to El Paso in 1849," *Southwestern Historical Quarterly,* LVIII (July, 1954).

• Nelson, Al B. "Campaign in the Big Bend of the Rio Grande, 1787," *Southwestern Historical Quarterly,* XXXIX (Oct., 1935).

• ————————. "Juan de Ugalde and Picax-ande Ins-tinsle, 1787–1788," *Southwestern Historical Quarterly,* XLIII (Apr., 1940).

• Park, Joseph R. "Spanish Indian Policy in Northern Mexico, 1765–1810," *Arizona and the West,* IV (Winter, 1962).

• Ponton, Brownie, and McFarland, Bates F. "Alvar Núñez Cabeza de Vaca: A Preliminary Report of His Wanderings in Texas," *Quarterly of the Texas State Historical Association,* I (Jan., 1898).

• Reeve, Frank D. "The Apache Indians in Texas," *Southwestern Historical Quarterly,* L (Oct., 1946).

• Saxton, Lewis H. and Casey, Clifford B. "The Life of Everett Ewing Townsend," *West Texas Historical and Scientific Society Publications,* XVII.

• Schick, Robert. "Wagons to Chihuahua," *The American West,* III (Summer, 1966).

• Schoffelmayer, Victor H. "The Big Bend Area of Texas: A Geographic Wonderland," *Texas Geographic Magazine,* I (May, 1937).

• Schulman, Edmund. "Dendrochronology in Big Bend National Park, Texas," *Tree-Ruling Bulletin,* XVIII (Oct., 1951–Jan., 1952).

• Scobee, Barry. "The First General Cattle Round-Up of the Davis Mountains-Big Bend District," *West Texas Historical and Scientific Society Publications,* III (1930).

• Shipman, Jack. "The Lone Red Murder Yearling of West Texas," *Voice of the Mexican Border,* I (Feb.–March, 1934).

• Skaggs, Jimmy M. "A Study in Business Failures: Frank Collinson in the Big Bend," *Panhandle-Plains Historical Review,* XLIII, 1970.

- Smith, Ralph A. "Apache Plunder Trails Southward, 1831–1840," *New Mexico Historical Review*, XXXVII (Jan., 1962).
- ———.. "The Comanche Bridge Between Oklahoma and Mexico, 1843–1844." *Chronicles of Oklahoma*, XXXIX (Spring, 1961).
- ———. "The Comanche Invasion of Mexico in the Fall of 1845," *West Texas Historical Association Year Book*, XXV (Oct., 1959).
- ———. "The Comanche Sun Over Mexico," *West Texas Historical Association Year Book*, LXVI (1970).
- ———. " 'Long' Webster and 'The Vile Industry of Selling Scalps,' " *West Texas Historical Association Year Book*, XXXVII (Oct., 1961).
- ———. "Mexican and Anglo-Saxon Traffic in Scalps, Slaves, and Livestock, 1835–1841," *West Texas Historical Association Year Book*, XXXVI (Oct., 1960).
- ———. "Poor Mexico, So Far From God and So Close to the *Tejanos*," *West Texas Historical Association Year Book*, XLIV (1968).
- ———. "The Scalp Hunters in the Borderlands, 1835–1850," *Arizona and the West*, VI (Spring, 1964).
- Smith, Victor J. "Early Spanish Exploration in the Big Bend of Texas," *West Texas Historical and Scientific Society Publications*, II, 1928.
- Smithers, W. D. "Bandit Raids in the Big Bend Country," in *Pancho Villa's Last Hangout — On Both Sides of the Rio Grande in the Big Bend Country*. Alpine, n.d.
- ———. "Nature's Pharmacy and the Curanderos" and "The Border Trading Posts," *West Texas Historical and Scientific Society Publications*, XVIII, 1961.
- Temple, Frank F. "Colonel B. H. Grierson's Victorio Campaign," *West Texas Historical Association Year Book*, XXV (Oct., 1959).
- ———. "Colonel B. H. Grierson's Administration of the District of the Pecos," *West Texas Historical Association Year Book*, XXXVIII (Oct., 1962).
- ———. "Colonel Grierson in the Southwest," *Panhandle-Plains Historical Review*, XXX (1957).
- Tyler, Ronnie C. "Robert T. Hill and the Big Bend," *The American West*, X (Sept., 1973).
- Utley, Robert M. "Pecos Bill on the Texas Frontier," *The American West*, VI (Jan., 1969).
- ———. "The Range Cattle Industry in the Big Bend of Texas," *Southwestern Historical Quarterly*, LXIX (Apr., 1966).

- Vigness, David M. "Don Hugo O'Conor and New Spain's Northeastern Frontier, 1764–1776," *Journal of the West,* VI (Jan., 1957).
- Webb, Walter P. "The Big Bend of Texas," *Panhandle-Plains Historical Review,* X (1937).
- Wright, Mrs. Joel E. "Early Settling of the Big Bend," *West Texas Historical and Scientific Society Publications,* XIX, 1963.

C. Unpublished Typescripts
- Garrison, L. A. "A History of the Proposed Big Bend International Park," Mimeographed article in the files of the Amon G. Carter Foundation, Fort Worth.
- Raborg, William A. "The Villa Raid on Glenn Springs," Typescript in Sul Ross State University Library, Alpine, Texas.

D. Unpublished Theses
- Daniel, James M. "The Advance of the Spanish Frontier and the Despoblado." Unpublished Ph.D. Dissertation, University of Texas, 1955.
- Gregg, John E. "The History of Presidio County." M. A. Thesis, University of Texas, 1933.
- Hitchcock, Totsy N. "Representative Individuals and Families of the Lower Big Bend Region, 1895–1925." Unpublished M. A. Thesis, Sul Ross State College, 1960.
- Lammons, Bishop F. "Operation Camel: An Experiment in Animal Transportation in the Southwest, 1857–1860." Unpublished M. A. Thesis, Trinity University, 1955.
- Starnes, Gary B. "Juan de Ugalde (1729-1816) and the Provincias Internas of Coahuila and Texas." Unpublished Ph.D. Dissertation, Texas Christian University, 1971.
- Walker, Kathryn B. "Quicksilver Mining in the Terlingua Area." Unpublished M. A. Thesis, Sul Ross State College, 1960.

Notes

The complete entry for all citations can be found in the bibliography.

Chapter 1

1   Nevill to Z. L. Nevill, in the *Austin Daily Statesman,* Feb. 25, 1882; Nevill to Adj. Gen. W. H. King, Camp Manske Cañon, Feb. 4, 1882, copy in Adjutant General's Office (Texas) Records . . . Transcripts.

2   Goetzmann, *Exploration and Empire: The Explorer and the Scientist in the Winning of the American West,* 430-66, 489-576; Goetzmann, *Army Exploration in the American West, 1803-1868,* 185-86; Ross (ed.), *George Catlin: Episodes From Life Among the Indians and Last Rambles,* 174-75; Townsend, "Rangers and Indians in the Big Bend Region," *West Texas Historical and Scientific Society Publications,* Bulletin No. 56 (1935), 43-46; quotation in *El Paso Daily Times,* June 18, 1883.

3   *El Paso Daily Times,* Oct. 31, 1899; Hill, "Running the Cañons of the Rio Grande," *Century Illustrated Monthly Magazine,* LXI (Nov., 1900-Apr., 1901), 371-87.

4   The Mexican Boundary Survey team had estimated the depth of the canyons at much more realistic figures in 1852, but the report was of limited distribution and virtually unknown to laymen. *El Paso Daily Times,* July 13, 1899; Hill, "Running the Cañons of the Rio Grande," *ibid.,* 371-87.

5   Lieutenant Whiting made reference to the Big Bend in his journal on March 12, 1849. See "Journal of William Henry Chase Whiting, 1849," in Bieber (ed.), *Exploring Southwestern Trails, 1846-1854: Philip St. George Cooke, William Henry Chase Whiting, Francois Xavier Aubry,* 265. Quotations in Echols' Diary, in *Report of the Secretary of War,* 36th Cong., 2d Sess., Sen. Ex. Doc. No. 1, 41. See also letter from O. W. Williams, Fort Stockton, Texas, Feb. 23, 1901, in Myres (ed.), *Pioneer Surveyor, Frontier Lawyer: The Personal Narrative of O. W. Williams, 1877-1902,* 222; Casey, *Mirages, Mysteries and Reality, Brewster County, Texas: The Big Bend of the Rio Grande,* 1-4; and Fulcher, *The Way I Heard It: Tales of the Big Bend,* ed. by Elton Miles, xix.

6   Maxwell, *The Big Bend of the Rio Grande: A Guide to the Rocks, Landscape, Geologic History, and Settlers of the Area of Big Bend National Park,* 1.

7   Daniel, "The Advance of the Spanish Frontier and the Despoblado," 1-11; quotation in Jules Leclercq, *Voyage au Mexique de New-York à Vera-Cruz en suivant les routes de terre,* 15.

8   Hill, "Running the Cañons," 380.

9   Madison and Stillwell, *How Come It's Called That? Place Names in the Big Bend Country,* 53; Emory, *Report on the United States and Mexican Boundary Survey. . . .,* I, Pt. 2, p. 55; Nevill to Z. L. Nevill, in the *Austin Daily Statesman,* Feb. 25, 1882; Hill, "Running the Cañons," 379; quotation in Meler to Roy L. Swift, Cordell, Oklahoma, August 3, 1939, in *American White Water,* XI (Spring, 1966), 32.

10   Hill, "Running the Cañons," 378; Maxwell, *The Big Bend,* 87-91.

11   Pedro de Rábago y Terán, "Diario de la Campaña executado por el Governador de Coahuila." See also Tyler (ed.), "Exploring the Rio Grande: Lt. Duff C. Green's Report of 1852," *Arizona and the West,* X (Spring, 1968), 55; Echols' Diary, 47; Meler to Swift, Cordell, Oklahoma, Aug. 3, 1939; Hill, "Running the Cañons," 381.

12   Madison and Stillwell, *How Come It's Called That?,* 51; Hill, "Running the Cañons," 382; Maxwell, *The Big Bend,* 52-53; Tyler (ed.), "Green's Report," 54.

13   Nevill to Adj. Gen. W. H. King, Camp Manske Canyon, Feb. 4, 1882, copy in Adjutant General's Office (Texas), Records Transcripts; Emilio Langberg, "Itinerario de la Espedición de San Carlos, Chih. à Monclova Viejo," 12.

14   Hackett (ed.), *Historical Documents Relating to New Mexico, Nueva Vizcaya, and Approaches Thereto,* II, 221, 331; Miles, "Chisos Ghosts," in Boatright, Hudson, and Maxwell (eds.), *Madstones and Twisters,* 116-17; Myres (ed.), *Pioneer Surveyor,* 257-64.

15   Miles, "Chisos Ghosts," 107-08; quotation in Maxwell, *The Big Bend,* 79.

16   Madison and Stillwell, *How Come It's Called That?,* 38; Madison, *The Big Bend Country of Texas,* 230.

17   Maxwell, *The Big Bend,* 79.

18   Madison and Stillwell, *How Come It's Called That?,* 29-33, 59.

19   Maxwell, *The Big Bend,* 51, 72.

Chapter 2

1   Leclercq, *Voyage au Mexique,* 33.

2   The most recent consideration of Cabeza de Vaca's route is Sauer, *Sixteenth Century North America: The Land and the People as Seen by the Europeans,* 117-22. See also Ponton and McFarland, "Alvar Núñez Cabeza de Vaca: A Preliminary Report of His Wanderings in Texas," *Quarterly of the Texas State*

Historical Association, I (Jan., 1898), 166-86; Coopwood, "The Route of Cabeza de Vaca," *Quarterly of the Texas State Historical Association,* III (Oct., 1899), 108-40, (Jan.,1900), 177-208, (Apr., 1900), 229-64; and Hallenbeck, *Álvar Núñez Cabeza de Vaca: The Journey and Route of the First European to Cross the Continent of North America, 1534-1536,* 155.

3 Bolton, *Coronado on the Turquois Trail: Knight of Pueblos and Plains,* 23-39, 49-200.

4 For a discussion of the early Spanish *entradas* into the Big Bend, see Castañeda, *Our Catholic Heritage in Texas, 1519-1936,* Vol. I: *The Mission Era: The Finding of Texas, 1519-1693,* 157-94. See also Martin, *Archaeological Exploration of the Shumla Caves;* Bolton, "The Jumano Indians in Texas, 1650-1771," *Quarterly of the Texas State Historical Association,* XV (July, 1911), 68.

5 Bolton (ed.), *Spanish Exploration in the Southwest, 1542-1706,* 137; Mecham, "The Second Spanish Expedition to New Mexico: An Account of the Chamuscado-Rodríguez Entrada of 1581-1582," *New Mexico Historical Review,* I (July, 1926), 266; quotation in Hammond and Rey (trans. and ed.), "The Rodríguez Expedition to New Mexico, 1581-1582," *New Mexico Historical Review,* II (July, 1927), 252.

6 Newcomb, *The Indians of Texas, From Prehistoric to Modern Times,* 230; Wormington, *Prehistoric Indians of the Southwest,* 112-13.

7 Newcomb, *Indians of Texas,* 226-28; Frederic J. Dockstader to Virginia Madison, July 24, 1957, quoted in Madison and Stillwell, *How Come It's Called That?,* 29-30.

8 Hodge (ed.), *Spanish Explorers in the Southern United States,* 103-04; Kelley, "The Historic Indian Pueblos of La Junta de los Rios," *New Mexico Historical Review,* XXVI (Oct., 1952), 257-95, and (Jan., 1953), 20-51; Kelley, "Factors Involved in the Abandonment of Certain Peripheral Southwestern Settlements," *American Anthropologist,* LIV (July-Sept., 1952), 363.

9 Mecham, "Chamuscado-Rodríguez Entrada," 267-70; see also Hammond and Rey (trans. and ed.), "Rodríguez Expedition to New Mexico," 334-62.

10 Mecham, "Antonio de Espejo and His Journey to New Mexico," *Southwestern Historical Quarterly,* XXX (Oct., 1926), 118; Bolton (ed.), *Spanish Exploration,* 161-95; Hammond and Rey (eds.), *Expedition Into New Mexico Made by Antonio de Espejo, 1582-1583, As Revealed in the Journal of Diego Pérez de Luxán, a Member of the Party,* 45-128; Kelley, "The Route of Antonio de Espejo Down the Pecos River and Across the Texas Trans-Pecos Region of 1583; Its Relation to West Texas Archeology," *West Texas Historical and Scientific Society Publications,* VII (1937), 7-25.

11 Bolton (ed.), *Spanish Exploration,* 190; Kelley, "Route of Espejo," 9.

12 Bolton (ed.), *Spanish Exploration,* 200-01.

13 Kelley, "Juan Sabeata and Diffusion in Aboriginal Texas," *American Anthropologist,* LVII (Oct., 1955), 984.

14 Bolton (ed.), *Spanish Exploration*, 314-15.

15 *Ibid.*, 320-43; see also Smith, "Early Spanish Exploration in the Big Bend of Texas," *West Texas Historical and Scientific Society Publications*, II (1928), 59-68; Reindrop (trans.), "The Founding of Missions at La Junta de los Rios," *Supplementary Studies of the Texas Catholic Historical Society*, I (Apr., 1938), 5-28; Castañeda, *Our Catholic Heritage in Texas, 1519-1936:* Vol. III; *The Mission Era: The Missions at Work, 1731-1761*, 197-99.

16 Hammond and Rey (eds.), "The Rodríguez Expedition to New Mexico, 1581-1582," *New Mexico Historical Review*, II (July, 1927), 256; Letter of Oñate, in Bolton (ed.), *Spanish Exploration*, 253.

17 Sonnichsen, *The Mescalero Apaches*, 33.

18 Bannon, *The Spanish Borderlands Frontier, 1813-1821*, 30; *Autos* made by Gen. Juan de Retana, July 19 to July 30, 1693, and "Declaration of Captain Juan de Retana, September 5, 1693," in Hackett (ed.), *Historical Documents*, II, 329-35, 343-49.

19 Daniel, "Advance of the Spanish Frontier," 115-16.

20 Thomas, *After Coronado: Spanish Exploration Northeast of New Mexico, 1696-1727*, 23-24; Newcomb, *Indians of Texas*, 107-09.

21 "Report of Governor Antonio de Oca Sarmiento to the señor viceroy El Parral, March 12, 1667," in Hackett (ed.), *Historical Documents*, II, 91.

22 Daniel, "Advance of the Spanish Frontier," 107-09.

23 Newcomb, *Indians of Texas*, 156-67.

24 Porras Muñoz (ed.), *Diario y derrotero de lo caminado, visto y obcervado en el discurso de la vista general de precidios, situados en las Provincias Ynternas de Nueva España, que de orden de su magestad executó D. Pedro de Rivera, Brigadier de los Reales Exercitos.*

25 Quotations in Weddle, *San Juan Bautista, Gateway to Spanish Texas*, 196-204; see also Castañeda, *Our Catholic Heritage in Texas, 1519-1936*, Vol. II: *The Mission Era: The Winning of Texas, 1693-1731*, 336-46. Colonel Langberg experienced difficulty traveling over the same land years later. See Langberg, "Itinerario de La Espedición."

26 Quoted in Daniel, "Advance of the Spanish Frontier," 170-71.

27 Weddle, *San Juan Bautista*, 206-10. See also Castañeda, *Missions at Work*, 203-07.

28 Quoted in Daniel, "Advance of the Spanish Frontier," 186-87.

29 Weddle, *San Juan Bautista*, 228-29; Daniel, "Advance of the Spanish Frontier," 187, 196-97.

30   All the material on Rábago y Terán's journey is taken from
Rábago y Terán, "Diario de la Campaña," with consideration of the
judgments made by Daniel, Weddle, and Castañeda, *Missions at Work,*
211-19, regarding location sites mentioned in the journal. See also
Kelley, "The Historic Indian Pueblos of La Junta," *New Mexico
Historical Review,* XXVI (Oct., 1952), 272-73, 294, (Jan., 1953),
31, 38, 40, 46.

31   Quotations in Rábago y Terán, "Diario de la Campaña," 157-60,
163.

32   Daniel, "Advance of the Spanish Frontier," 186-97;
Castañeda, *Missions at Work,* 220-23.

33   Daniel, "Advance of the Spanish Frontier," 203.

34   Kinnaird (ed.), *The Frontier of New Spain: Nicholas de
LaFora's Description, 1766-1768,* 12.

35   Brinckerhoff and Faulk (eds.), *Lancers for the King: A
Study of the Frontier Military System of Northern New Spain,
with a Translation of the Royal Regulations of 1772;* Bobb, *The
Viceregency of Antonio María Bucareli in New Spain, 1771-1779,*
131.

36   Flores and Almada (eds.), *Informe de Hugo de O'Conor
sobre el estado de las Provincias Internas del Norte, 1771-76,* and
Moore and Breene, "The Interior Provinces of New Spain: The Report
of Hugo O'Conor, January 30, 1776," *Arizona and the West,*
XIII (Autumn, 1971), 265-82. See also Christiansen, "Hugo
O'Conor's Inspection of Nueva Vizcaya and Coahuila, 1773,"
Louisiana Studies, II (Fall, 1963), 164-67; and Vigness,
"Don Hugo Oconor and New Spain's Northeastern Frontier,
1764-1776," *Journal of the West,* VI (Jan., 1967), 27-40.

37   Gerald, *Spanish Presidios of the Late Eighteenth Century in
Northern New Spain,* 12-13, 37-40; Moore and Breene, "Report
of O'Conor," 269.

38   Thomas, *Teodoro de Croix, and the Northern Frontier of New
Spain, 1776-1783,* 22-24; Faulk and Brinckerhoff, "Soldiering
at the End of the World," *The American West,* III (Summer, 1966),
28-37.

39   Thomas, *Teodoro de Croix,* 25, 45-58; Morfi, *Diario y
derrotero (1777-1781),* 125, 129.

40   Bolton (ed.), *Athanase de Mézières and the Louisiana-Texas
Frontier, 1768-1780,* II, 158; Thomas, *Teodoro de Croix,* 38.

41   Thomas, *Teodoro de Croix,* 43-51; Moorhead, *The Apache
Frontier: Jacobo Ugarte and Spanish-Indian Relations in Northern
New Spain, 1769-1791,* 120-23.

42   Daniel, "Advance of the Spanish Frontier," 263-67; Starnes,
"Juan de Ugalde (1729-1816) and the Provincias Internas of Coahuila
and Texas," 44, 57.

43   Nelson, "Campaigning in the Big Bend of the Rio Grande,
1787," *Southwestern Historical Quarterly,* XXXIX (Oct., 1935),
200-27; Nelson, "Juan de Ugalde and Picax-ande Ins-tinsle,
1787-1788," *Southwestern Historical Quarterly,* XLIII (Apr., 1940),
438-64.

44 Wheat, *Mapping the Transmississippi West, 1540-1861,* I, 121-23.

45 Moorhead, *The Apache Frontier,* 221-36.

46 *Ibid.,* 143-69; Starnes, "Juan de Ugalde," 96; Marc Simmons (trans. and ed.), *Border Comanches: Seven Spanish Colonial Documents, 1785-1819,* 14-15, 21-22.

47 Park, "Spanish Indian Policy in Northern Mexico, 1765-1810," *Arizona and the West,* IV (Winter, 1962), 340-41.

Chapter 3

1 Ford, *Rip Ford's Texas,* 68-69, quotation on 107.

2 Gregg, *Commerce on the Prairies: or the Journal of a Santa Fe Trader,* I, 162-65; *The Louisianian,* July 26, 1839, quoted in the *Arkansas State Gazette* (Little Rock), Sept. 4, 1839; Foreman, *Advancing the Frontier, 1830-1860,* 164; Connelley (ed.), *Doniphan's Expedition and the Conquest of New Mexico and California,* 277-82.

3 *Arkansas State Gazette,* Sept. 4, Oct. 9, 1839; Kendall, *Narrative of the Texan Santa Fe Expedition, Comprising a Description of a Tour Through Texas,* II, 120.

4 Gregg, *Commerce on the Prairies,* I, 162-64.

5 Quotations in the *Arkansas State Gazette,* Sept. 4, 1839; *The Western Star* (Lebanon, Ohio), Dec. 11, 1840; *The Morning Star* (Houston), Mar. 27, 1841.

6 Connelley (ed.), *Doniphan's Expedition and the Conquest of New Mexico and California,* 451-52; Gregg, "The History of Presidio County," 45.

7 Greer, *Colonel Jack Hays, Texas Frontier Leader and California Land Builder,* 217-18.

8 Wahm was cared for by some friendly Indians until he made his way back to civilization about a year later. Hays' Report, in the *Democratic Telegraph and Texas Register* (Houston), Dec. 28, 1848; Greer, *Jack Hays,* 391, n. 14; Green (ed.), *Samuel Maverick, Texan: 1803-1870,* 223, 336.

9 *Corpus Christi Star,* Dec. 5, 1848.

10 Hays' Report; Gregg, "History of Presidio County," 45.

11 Hays to William L. Marcy, San Antonio, Dec. 13, 1848, in *Senate Executive Documents,* No. 32, 31st Cong., 1st Sess., 32-33; Greer, *Jack Hays,* 224-25.

12 Hays' Report; Hays to Marcy, San Antonio, Dec. 13, 1848.

13 Ford, *Rip Ford's Texas,* 113-29; Jackson, *Wagon Roads West: A Study of Federal Road Surveys and Construction*

in the Trans-Mississippi West, 1846-1869, 37-39; Neighbours,
"The Expedition of Major Robert S. Neighbors to El Paso in 1849,"
Southwestern Historical Quarterly, LVIII (July, 1954), 36-59.

14   Wheat, *Mapping the Transmississippi West,* III, 64, 68,
274; *Texas State Gazette* (Austin), Nov. 3, 10, 1849, Apr. 27, 1850.

15   Evans, *Mexican Gold Trail: The Journal of a Forty-Niner,*
xv, 60, 76-77.

16   *Democratic Telegraph and Texas Register,* Dec. 28, 1848;
Corpus Christi Star, Sept. 19, Dec. 23, 30, 1848; *Texas State Gazette,*
Dec. 1, 1849.

17   *Corpus Christi Star,* Mar. 17, 24, 31, 1849; *Texas State Gazette,*
Nov. 16, 1850.

18   *Corpus Christi Star,* July 21, 1849; *The Daily Picayune*
(New Orleans), Aug. 21, 1849; *Corpus Christi: 100 Years,*
57; quotation is in *The Daily Picayune,* Aug. 31, 1849. See also
Webb and Carroll (eds.), *The Handbook of Texas,* I, 532.

19   *Texas State Gazette,* Aug. 25, 1849; Hunter to his wife,
Presidio del Norte, June 2, 1849, in Stephens (ed.), *A Texan
in the Gold Rush: The Letters of Robert Hunter 1849-1851,*
13-14.

20   *The Texas Republican* (Marshall), July 13, 1849.

21   *The Texas Republican,* Mar. 28, 1850; *Texas State Gazette,*
Nov. 24, 1849; *The Daily Picayune,* Nov. 13, 1850.

22   Quotation in *Western Texan* (San Antonio), Sept. 10, 1850;
San Antonio Texan, quoted in the *Texas State Gazette,* May 4, 1850;
quote in *Texas State Gazette,* Sept, 20, 1851; quotation in *Western
Texan,* Oct. 2, 1851.

23   Quotation in *Texas State Gazette,* Nov. 24, 1849; quotation
in *The Daily Picayune,* Nov. 13, 1850; quotation in *The Texas
Monument* (La Grange), Feb. 25, 1851; *Galveston Weekly News,*
Aug. 1, 1854; Smith, "Poor Mexico, So Far From God and So
Close to the *Tejanos," West Texas Historical Association Year Book,*
XLIV (Oct., 1968), 78; Hammond and Howes (eds.), *Overland
to California on the Southwestern Trail, 1849: Diary of Robert
Eccleston,* 138.

24   Emory, *Report,* I, 86-89.

25   See Campbell and Field, "Identification of Comanche Raiding
Trails in Trans-Pecos Texas," *West Texas Historical Association
Year Book,* XLIV (Oct., 1968), 128-44. O. W. Williams himself
saw the trail. Myres (ed.), *Pioneer Surveyor,* 278-81. Maj. J.
Van Horne to Maj. George Deas, Post opposite El Paso, N.M.,
Nov. 8, 1849, plus enclosures (Langberg to Van Horne, El Paso, Oct.
23, 1849, and Trias to Langberg, Chihuahua, Oct. 10, 1849), in
Winfrey and Day. *The Indian Papers of Texas and the Southwest,
1825-1916,* V, 50-53; Langberg, "Itinerario de la Espedición," 7.

26   For material on the Sol family, see Smith, "The Comanche
Sun Over Mexico," *West Texas Historical Association Year Book,*
LXVI (1970), 25-62. For material on the Comanche Trail, see
Smith, "The Comanche Bridge Between Oklahoma and Mexico,
1843-1844," *Chronicles of Oklahoma,* XXXIX (Spring, 1961), 54-69;

and "Apache Plunder Trails Southward, 1831-1840," *New Mexico Historical Review,* XXXVII (Jan., 1962), 20-42. See also Rogers to Peter H. Bell, San Antonio, Sept. 3, 1851, in Winfrey and Day (eds.), *Indian Papers of Texas,* III, 141; and Neighbors to Elisha M. Pease, San Antonio, Apr. 10, 1854, in V, 171.

27 Quotations are in Fuentes Mares, *Y México se refugio en el desierto: Luis Terrazas, historia y destino,* 144, and Chamberlain, *My Confession,* 270. For material on the raids and on the scalp hunters, see articles by Smith: "Mexican and Anglo-Saxon Traffic in Scalps, Slaves, and Livestock, 1835-1841," *West Texas Historical Association Year Book,* XXXVI (Oct., 1960), 89-115; " 'Long' Webster and 'The Vile Industry of Selling Scalps,' " *West Texas Historical Association Year Book,* XXXVII (Oct., 1961), 99-120; "The Scalp Hunters in the Borderlands, 1835-1850," *Arizona and the West,* VI (Spring, 1964), 5-22; and "Poor Mexico, So Far From God and So Close to the *Tejanos,*" *West Texas Historical Association Year Book,* XLIV (Oct., 1968), 78-105. See also Evans, *Mexican Gold Trail,* 84-85.

28 *San Antonio Ledger,* Sept. 2, 1852; *The Texas Republican,* Mar. 28, 1850, Oct. 16, 1852, quoting the *San Antonio Ledger.*

29 Santleben, *A Texas Pioneer: Early Staging and Overland Freighting Days on the Frontiers of Texas and Mexico,* 115, 117, 119.

30 *Ibid.,* 114. *Western Texan,* Sept. 30, Oct. 28, 1852; *The Texas Republican,* Jan. 10, 1850, Apr. 8, 22, 1854, quoting the *Galveston News* and the *Western Texan;* Langberg, "Itinerario de la Espedición," 14.

31 Quotation in *Galveston Weekly News,* Aug. 1, 1854; Santleben, *A Texas Pioneer,* 111.

32 *The Texas Republican,* Jan. 10, 1850; *San Antonio Ledger,* quoted in *The South-Western American* (Austin), June 11, 1851. Miles weaves some even more fantastic tales in "Old Fort Leaton: A Saga of the Big Bend," in Hudson (ed.), *Hunters & Healers: Folklore Tales & Topics,* 88-89.

33 Macmanus to Secretary of State Lewis Cass, Chihuahua, Jan. 28, 1859, in Despatches from United States Consuls in Chihuahua, 1826-1906.

Chapter 4

1 For a summary of Johnston's life, see Webb and Carroll (eds.), *Handbook of Texas,* I, 920.

2 Quotation in Abert to Stephen Markoe, Washington, May 18,

1849, in Letters Sent by the Topographical Bureau of the War Department and by Successor Division in the Office of the Chief of Engineers. See also Emory, *Notes of a Military Reconnaissance From Fort Leavenworth, in Missouri, to San Diego, in California. . . .*, Sen. Ex. Doc. 41, 30th Cong., 1st Sess. El Paso del Norte is present-day Ciudad Juárez. El Paso, Texas, was not founded until 1850 when it was called Franklin. It took the name El Paso when Ciudad Juárez changed its name.

3 Quotation in Abert to Markoe, Washington, May 18, 1849, in Letters Sent. See also Bieber (ed.), *Exploring Southwestern Trails*, 34-35; Raht, *The Romance of Davis Mountains and Big Bend Country*, 127. Someone on the expedition wrote long letters to the *New York Herald* reporting their progress and difficulties. See July 13, 1849.

4 "Reports of Reconnaissances, etc.," *in Report of the Secretary of War. . . .*, 31st Cong., 1st Sess., Sen. Ex. Doc. 64, 49.

5 *Ibid.*, 27; *Report of the Secretary of War*, 32d Cong., 1st Sess., Sen. Ex. Doc. 1, 112; Green quoted in Merk, *Slavery and the Annexation of Texas*, 162.

6 Crimmins (ed.), "Two Thousand Miles by Boat in the Rio Grande in 1850," *West Texas Historical and Scientific Society Publications*, V (1933), 44-45. See also Horgan, *Great River: The Rio Grande in North American History*, II, 808-09; Johnston to W. F. Smith, San Antonio, April 9, 1850, Johnston to Abert, San Antonio, January 7, 1851, Johnston to Abert, San Antonio, September 11, 1850, and Smith to Johnston, San Antonio, January 6, 1851, in Letters Received by the Topographical Bureau of the War Department, 1824-1865.

7 W. F. Smith to Johnston, San Antonio, October 26, 1850, and Johnston to Abert, San Antonio, January 7, 1851, in Letters Received.

8 Quotations are in Johnston to Abert, Sept. 11, 1850, and Johnston to "General," Jan. 6, 1851, in *ibid.*

9 Goetzmann, *Army Explorations in the American West*, ch. 5; Faulk, *Too Far North – Too Far South*, ch. 6.

10 Gardner to Sarah, El Paso, Nov. 27, 1851, Gardner to father, Camp opposite Presidio del Norte, July 10, 1852, and Gardner to father, Frontera near El Paso, Mar. 27, 1852, all in George Clinton Gardner Papers; Langberg, "Itinerario de la Espedición," 4.

11 Gardner to Alida, Camp on the Rio Grande above Presidio del Norte, July 29, 1852, in Gardner Papers.

12 Duff C. Green to Emory, Camp opposite Presidio del Norte, Aug. 30, 1852, Emory to Bartlett, on road near first crossing of San Pedro River, Sept. 18, 1852, in William H. Emory Papers; Geiser, *Men of Science in Texas, 1820-1880;* Pennsylvania University, Committee of the Society of Alumni, *Biographical Catalogue of the Matriculates of the College. . . .* 1749-1893, 107; Gardner to father, Frontera near El Paso, Feb. 6, 1852, in Gardner Papers. Chandler later served as a meteorological observer for the Smithsonian Institution at the Falls of the Saint Croix, Wisconsin, and finally died in Brazil in 1868 while in the service of the Brazilian government.

13 Emory to Chandler, Presidio del Norte, August 8, 1852, and Emory to Green, Presidio del Norte, August 30, 1852, in Emory Papers. See Langberg's map, "Derotero Topográfico de la espedición que desde San Carlos hasta Piedras Negras II regreso por la Laguna de Laco a Chihuahua hiso el inspector inter. Colonias Militares de ese estado Coronel Don E. Langberg en el año 1851," in the Colección de Mapas del Estado de Chihuahua.

14 The best work on the artists of the survey is Hine, *Bartlett's West: Drawing the Mexican Boundary.* See also Tyler (ed.), "Green's Report," 51; Emory to Charles Radziminski, Camp opposite Presidio del Norte, August 28, 1852, and Emory to Green, Camp opposite Presidio del Norte, August 30, 1852, in Emory Papers.

15 Tyler (ed.), "Green's Report," 52; Lt. Dixon S. Miles to Emory, Fort Fillmore, August 13, 1852, and Emory to Green, Camp opposite Presidio del Norte, Aug. 30, 1852, in Emory Papers; *San Antonio Ledger,* Sept. 2, 23, 1852; Bartlett, *Personal Narrative of Explorations and Incidents in Texas, New Mexico, Sonora and Chihuahua,* II, 396-97.

16 Chandler, "San Vicente to Presidio del Norte," in Emory, *Report,* I, 80, quotation in Tyler (ed.), "Green's Report," 54.

17 Chandler, "San Vicente," 81; quotation in Tyler (ed.), "Green's Report," 54.

18 For information on the Indian trail and crossing, see Haley, *Fort Concho and the Texas Frontier,* ch. 1; Smith, "Comanche Bridge Between Oklahoma and Mexico," 54-56; "The Comanche Invasion of Mexico in the Fall of 1845," *West Texas Historical Association Year Book,* XXV (Oct., 1959), 4-5. See also Chandler, "San Vicente," 81; Tyler (ed.), "Green's Report," 54-55.

19 Thompson to Chandler, Camp near San Carlos, October 1, 1852, in Emory Papers; Wauer, *Guide to the Backcountry Roads and the River,* 27.

20 Chandler, "San Vicente," 82.

21 *Ibid.;* Tyler (ed.), "Green's Report," 55-56.

22 Tyler (ed.), "Green's Report," 56; Chandler, "San Vicente," 83.

23 Chandler, "San Vicente," 83.

24 *Ibid.,* 83-84; Emory to Chandler, Presidio del Norte, Aug. 8, 1852, in Emory Papers; Langberg, "Itinerario de la Espedición," 9.

25 Chandler, "San Vicente," 84; Tyler (ed.), "Green's Report," 56.

26 Tyler (ed.), "Green's Report," 57.

27 Chandler, "San Vicente," 84-85.

28 Quotations in Chandler to Emory, Camp on Rio Grande, Nov. 4, 1852, in Emory Papers; quotes in Tyler (ed.), "Green's Report," 57-58; Chandler, "San Vicente," 85.

29 Green to Chandler, Camp on Rio Grande, Nov. 3, 1852, Schott to Emory, Fort Duncan, n. d., Parry to Chandler, Camp on Rio Grande, Nov. 4, 1852, all in Emory Papers.

30 Chandler to Emory, Camp on Rio Grande, Nov. 4, 1852, in Emory Papers; Tyler (ed.), "Green's Report," 58.

31 Schott to Emory, Camp on Rio San Felipe, Oct. 1, 1852, Charles Radziminski to Emory, Saltillo, Dec. 10, 1852, in Emory Papers; Tyler (ed.), "Green's Report," 59-60.

32 The description of Michler's survey comes entirely from his report, in Emory, *Report*, I, 74-79.

33 Miller (ed.), *Treaties and Other International Acts of the United States of America*, V, 217; Abert to Seymour, Washington, Mar. 2, 1852, in Letters Sent.

34 Bailey (ed.), *The A. B. Gray Report.*

35 Scobee, *Fort Davis, Texas 1583-1960*, 5-8; Utley, *Fort Davis National Historic Site, Texas*, 5-7; Brooke to Gen. Winfield Scott, San Antonio, May 28, 1850, in Winfrey and Day (eds.), *Indian Papers of Texas*, III, 120.

36 Bliss, "Reminiscences of Zenas R. Bliss Major General United States Army," I, 153, 175. See also Webb and Carroll (eds.), *Handbook of Texas*, I, 175.

37 Lesley (ed.), *Uncle Sam's Camels: The Journal of May Humphreys Stacey Supplemented by the Report of Edward Fitzgerald Beale (1857-1858)*, 4-12. See also the *San Antonio Herald*. Jan. 31, 1857; Fowler, *Camels to California: A Chapter in Western Transportation*, 32-45.

38 Lesley (ed.), *Uncle Sam's Camels*, 6-7, 13; Jackson, *Wagon Roads West*, 245-46, 249.

39 Lesley (ed.), *Uncle Sam's Camels*, 45-46; Diary of Lieutenant Hartz in *Report of the Secretary of War*, 36th Cong., 1st. Sess., Sen. Ex. Doc. No. 2, 422-41. The account of the 1859 expedition is taken entirely from Hartz.

40 The account of the 1860 expedition is taken from Echols' journal, 33-50.

Chapter 5

1 Langford, *Big Bend, A Homesteader's Story*, 4; Hawley, "Life Along the Border," *West Texas Historical and Scientific Society Publications*, XX (1964); Myres, *Pioneer Surveyor*, 238.

2 Utley, *Fort Davis*, 113; Schick, "Wagons to Chihuahua," *The American West*, III (Summer, 1966), 74; quotation in Moye to Sec. of State William H. Seward, Chihuahua, June 3, 1867, in Chihuahua Consular Despatches.

3 Schick, "Wagons to Chihuahua," 76.

4 *Ibid.*, 77-78.

5 *Ibid.*, 77-79, 87-88.

6 Moorhead, *Chihuahua Trail*, 198-99.

7 *Galveston Civilian*, April 9, 1871; quotation in *The Statesman* (Austin), Dec. 2, 1881; Thrapp, *Victorio and the Mimbres Apaches*, 218-19.

8 Information on the Indian campaigns is taken from Scobee, *Fort Davis*, 37-145; Utley, *Fort Davis*, 17-47; Utley, "Pecos Bill on the Texas Frontier," *The American West*, VI (Jan., 1969), 4-13, 61-62; and Leckie, *The Buffalo Soldiers: A Narrative of the Negro Cavalry in the West*, chs. 4, 6, 8. See also Winfrey and Day (eds.), *Indian Papers of Texas*, IV, 215, 330; Duke (ed.), "A Description of the Route from San Antonio to El Paso by Captain Edward S. Meyer," *West Texas Historical Association Year Book*, XLIX (1973), 139.

9 Sonnichsen, *Mescalero Apaches*, 71-72, 158; Winfrey and Day (eds.), *Indian Papers of Texas*, IV, 387, 394, 398; Twiggs to Col. L. Thomas, San Antonio, June 16, 1857, and Aug. 24, 1858, in V, 204, 260-61; Hunter, *The Boy Captives, Being the True Story of the Experiences and Hardships of Clinton L. Smith and Jeff D. Smith*, 146; Ogle, *Federal Control of the Western Apaches, 1848-1886*, in *Publications in History*, IX (July, 1940), 183.

10 See Marcy and Neighbors to Gov. Bell, Fort Belknap, Sept. 30, 1854, in Winfrey and Day (eds.), *Indian Papers of Texas*, III, 190; quotation in Newcomb, *Indians of Texas*, 333.

11 Richardson, *The Comanche Barrier to South Plains Settlement: A Century and a Half of Savage Resistance to the Advancing White Frontier*, 172-77, 375-76; Sonnichsen, *Mescalero Apaches*, 58, 60-61, 161.

12 Quotations in *San Antonio Daily Express*, June 15, 26, 1877. See also July 4, 1879, Dec. 1, 1880. Col. Edward Hatch quoted in Sonnichsen, *Mescalero Apaches*, 185, n. 1.

13 Sonnichsen, *Mescalero Apaches*, 164-72; Thrapp, *Victorio*, 220-67.

14 See, for example, the reports of 1879 (manuscripts in the Grierson Collection, Newberry Library, Chicago). I am indebted to Frank M. Temple, of Lubbock, Texas, for use of transcripts of the Grierson material that he made while completing his study of the colonel. See Temple, "Colonel B. H. Grierson's Victorio Campaign," *West Texas Historical Association Year Book*, XXV (Oct., 1959), 99-111; "Colonel B. H. Grierson's Administration of the District of the Pecos," *West Texas Historical Association Year Book*, XXXVIII (Oct., 1962), 85-96; Thrapp, *Victorio*, 284.

15 Sonnichsen, *Mescalero Apaches,* 173-84; Thrapp, *Victorio,* 286-88.

16 Sonnichsen, *Mescalero Apaches,* 188; Rister, *The Southwestern Frontier, 1865-1881,* 203-17; Maltby, *Captain Jeff, or Frontier Life in Texas with the Texas Rangers,* 95; *San Antonio Daily Express,* Sept. 15, 1881; Jan. 29, 1882; Thrapp, *Victorio,* 293-307.

17 *San Antonio Daily Express,* Aug. 11, 1881.

18 *Daily Statesman* (Austin), Oct. 25, 1881; *San Antonio Daily Express,* Sept. 17, 1881, May 4, 1882. See also Reed, *A History of the Texas Railroads and of Transportation Conditions Under Spain and Mexico and the Republic and The State,* 191, 197; *From Ox-Teams to Eagles: A History of the Texas and Pacific Railways,* 29-30; Casey, *Mirages, Mysteries and Reality,* 22.

19 Myres, *The Ranch in Spanish Texas, 1691-1800,* 18.

20 Casey, *Soldiers, Ranchers and Miners in the Big Bend,* 142.

21 *Ibid.,* 146, 148; Utley, "The Range Cattle Industry in the Big Bend of Texas," *Southwestern Historical Quarterly,* LXIX (Apr., 1966), 421; quotation in Gillett, "The Old G4 Ranch," *Voice of the Mexican Border,* I (Oct., 1933), 82.

22 Casey, "The Trans-Pecos in Texas History," *West Texas Historical and Scientific Society Publications,* V (1933), 12.

23 Corning, *Baronial Forts of the Big Bend,* 44, 53-55; Bliss, "Reminiscenses," I, 263-64; Gregg, "History of Presidio County," *Voice of the Mexican Border,* 23, 41; interview with Mr. and Mrs. Hart M. Greenwood, Ciénaga Ranch, May 8, 1973.

24 Gregg, "History of Presidio County," *Voice of the Mexican Border,* 22; Bliss, "Reminiscences," I, 175, 260; *San Antonio Daily Express,* June 15, 1877, 2; Scobee, *Fort Davis,* 23-24, 41-43.

25 Utley, "Range Cattle Industry," 427; Bliss, "Reminiscences," I, 171.

26 *San Antonio Daily Express,* June 15, 1877, May 4, 1882, June 23, 1882; Davis, "The Cross-In Ranch: History and Development of a Pioneer Ranch," *Voice of the Mexican Border,* I (Oct., 1933), 76-77.

27 *San Antonio Daily Express,* May 4, 1882, June 23, 1882; interview with Mr. and Mrs. Hart M. Greenwood.

28 Keith, *The Brites of Capote,* 3-6.

29 Casey, *Soldiers, Ranchers and Miners,* 150-51. See also "Map of Southern Part of Presidio County" by John T. Gano in Texas State Land Office, Austin.

30 Gillett, "The Old G4 Ranch," 82-83. See also Gillett, *Six Years With The Texas Rangers, 1875 to 1881,* 238-39.

31 Shipman, *Taming the Big Bend: A History of the Extreme Western Portion of Texas From Fort Clark to El Paso,* 115-19; Nordyke, *Great Roundup: The Story of Texas and Southwestern Cowmen,* 83, quotations on 84, 202-03.

32 Peril "From Texas to the Oregon Line," in Hunter (ed.), *The Trail Drivers of Texas,* 411-12; Utley, "Range Cattle Industry," 426.

33 Carpenter, *Lucky 7: A Cowman's Autobiography,* 111-16.

34 *Daily Statesman,* Feb. 12, 1882. For further information on Rudabaugh see Adams, *A Fitting Death for Billy the Kid,* 31-32, 127, 157, 160, 186, 197, 216-17, 296.

35 Utley, "Range Cattle Industry," 436; Raht, *Romance of Davis Mountains and Big Bend Country,* 377; Gregg, "History of Presidio County," *Voice of the Mexican Border,* 41; Nevill to Capt. Neal Coldwell, Camp Manske Cañon, Dec. 12, 1881, in Adjutant General's Records.

36 Utley, "Range Cattle Industry," 428; Mellard, "Early West Texas Cattle and Horse Brands," *Voice of the Mexican Border,* I (Feb.-Mar., 1934), 289-90.

37 Madison, *Big Bend Country,* 139-42; Mitchell, "The Stampede at Robber's Roost," *Voice of the Mexican Border,* I (Oct., 1933), 90.

38 "Up the Trail in 1890 – Experiences of Drive Told by Tom Granger, Ft. Davis," *Alpine Avalanche,* Sept. 14, 1951, 22.

39 Wright, "Early Settling of the Big Bend," *West Texas Historical and Scientific Society Publications,* XIX (1963), 61; *El Paso Daily Times,* May 27, 1886; Scobee, "The First General Cattle Round-Up of the Davis Mountains-Big Bend District," *West Texas Historical and Scientific Society Publications,* III (1930), 45-47.

40 Quotations in both Collinson, *Life in the Saddle,* 207, 214, and Skaggs, "A Study in Business Failure: Frank Collinson in the Big Bend," *Panhandle-Plains Historical Review,* XLIII (1970), 12, 14, 16.

41 Utley, "Range Cattle Industry," 439-40; *The New Era* (Marfa), Jan. 7, 1911.

42 Dobie, *The Longhorns,* 61-64; Scobee, *The Steer Branded Murder: The True and Authentic Account of a Frontier Tragedy;* Shipman, "The Lone Red Murder Yearling of West Texas," *Voice of the Mexican Border,* I (Feb.-Mar., 1934), 271-73.

43 Hitchcock, "Representative Individuals and Families of the Lower Big Bend Region, 1895-1925," 4-5.

44 *Victoria Advocate,* Sept. 28, 1878.

45 Madison, *Big Bend Country,* 169-70.

46 *El Paso Daily Times,* May 30, 1886.

47 Madison, *Big Bend Country,* 169-71; *The New Era,* June 18, 1910.

48 *El Paso Daily Times,* May 30, 1886; Maxwell, *The Big Bend,* 117; Myres (ed.), *Pioneer Surveyor,* 233-34.

49 *The New Era,* Aug, 14, 1909.

50   Wauer, *Backcountry Roads and the River,* 11-12; Wauer, *Hiker's Guide to the Developed Trails and Primitive Routes,* 22, 24.

51   Römer, *Texas, With Particular Reference to German Immigration and the Physical Appearance of the Country,* 268; Johnson, "A History of Mercury Mining in the Terlingua District of Texas," *The Mines Magazine* (Sept., 1946), 390; Walker, "Quicksilver Mining in the Terlingua Area," 22-23.

52   Day, "Quicksilver in 1894," *U.S. Geological Survey, 16th Annual Report,* Pt. 3, 601; Hawley, "Life Along the Border," 19.

53   Hawley, "Life Along the Border," 43-45; Walker, "Quicksilver Mining in the Terlingua Area," 28, 42.

54   Hawley, "Life Along the Border," 15, 17, 20, 51; *The New Era,* Feb. 15, 1908.

55   Day, "The Chisos Quicksilver Bonanza in the Big Bend of Texas," *Southwestern Historical Quarterly,* LXIV (Apr., 1961), 429; Walker, "Quicksilver Mining in the Terlingua Area," 37; Myres (ed.), *Pioneer Surveyor,* 227-29 .

56   Day, "Chisos Quicksilver Bonanza," 433-34; *Alpine Avalanche,* Mar. 31, 1910.

57   Walker, "Quicksilver Mining in the Terlingua Area,", 45.

58   Casey, *Soldiers, Ranchers and Miners,* 217-19.

59   *Ibid.,* 228-31; Wauer, *Guide to the Backcountry Roads,* 17.

60   *Alpine Avalanche,* Apr. 5, 1907; Casey, *Mirages, Mysteries and Reality,* 106-07.

61   *The New Era,* Mar. 7, 1908, Apr. 3, May 22, 1909, Nov. 19, 1910; *Alpine Avalanche,* Oct. 14, 1909; Casey, *Mirages, Mysteries and Reality,* 121; Jones, *Health Seekers in the Southwest, 1817-1900,* 103-04.

62   *Alpine Avalanche,* Nov. 2, 1911.

63   *The New Era,* Apr. 29, 1911; *Alpine Avalanche,* Oct. 26, 1911, Nov. 2, 1911.

64   Smithers, "Nature's Pharmacy and the Curanderos" and "The Border Trading Posts," *West Texas Historical and Scientific Society Publications,* XVIII, 42, 45, 49.

65   Clifton, "A History of the Bloys Camp Meeting," *West Texas Historical and Scientific Society Publications,* XII (1947).

66   Hawley, "Life Along the Border," 47; Sonnichsen, *I'll Die Before I'll Run: The Story of the Great Feuds of Texas,* 86.

67   Hawley, "Life Along the Border," 9, 12, 15, 52; quotation in Smithers, "Bandit Raids in the Big Bend Country," in *Pancho Villa's Last Hangout — On Both Sides of the Rio Grande in the Big Bend Country,* 79; *The New Era,* July 18, 1908, 1; quotation in Hinkle, *Wings and Saddles: The Air and Cavalry Punitive Expedition of 1919,* 32-33.

68   *Alpine Avalanche,* Oct. 21, Dec. 2, 1909.

69   Hawley, "Life Along the Border," 82-85.

70   Hitchcock, "Families of the Lower Big Bend," 13-14, 22, 54-55; Haley, *Jeff Milton, a Good Man with a Gun,* 66-92.

71   Saxton and Casey, "The Life of Everett Ewing Townsend,"
West Texas Historical and Scientific Society Publications,
XVII, 37-40.

Chapter 6

1   Hill, "Running the Cañons," 372; Haley, *Jeff Milton,* 58.
2   Capt. Neal Coldwell to Gen. John B. Jones, Fort Davis,
July 10, 1880, in *Voice of the Mexican Border,* I (Dec., 1933),
174-76; Adams, *Billy the Kid,* 4, 80, 88, 133, 240.
3   Madison, *Big Bend Country,* 47-48.
4   *San Saba Weekly News,* Oct. 30, 1891.
5   Gillespie to Coldwell, Fort Davis, Jan, 10, 1882, in Adjutant
General's Records; *San Antonio Daily Express,* quotation in Aug.
9, 1879, Aug. 11, 1881, Feb. 25, 1882, issues.
6   Hill, "Running the Cañons," 371, 376; Saxton and Casey,
"Everett Ewing Townsend," 53-54.
7   "Annual Report for the Fiscal Year 1916 of Major Frederick
Funston, U.S. Army, Commanding Southern Department," in Records
of the Adjutant General's Office, 1, 42; Hawley, "Life Along
the Border," 74-75.
8   Second Asst. Sec. of State Alvey A. Adee to Sec. of War
Jacob Dickinson, Washington, Nov. 19, 1910, in Office of the
Adjutant General Documents File, 1716354, Box 6314, Doc. No.
1716354; *The New Era,* Jan. 28, 1911; Hawley, "Life Along the
Border," 74.
9   *The New Era,* Feb. 4, 1911.
10   *Ibid.,* Feb. 11, 1911.
11   Statement of Francisco and Dario Sánchez, in Office of the
Adjutant General Documents File, 1716354, Box 6316, Doc. No.
1716354/A-784.
12   Captain Barton to Adjutant General, Department of Texas,
Candelaria, June 8, 1911, in Office of the Adjutant General
Documents File, 1716354, Box 6316, Doc No. A-771.
13   Duncan to Adjutant General, San Antonio, March 9, 1912,
in Office of the Adjutant General Documents File, 1716354, Box
6807, Doc. No. 1875135/A-143; Langford, *Big Bend,* 140-44.
14   Langford, *Big Bend,* 150-51.
15   Sitters and several companions later arrested Cano and two
of his men for the murder of Howard. Another ambuscade resulted in
his freedom, but that apparently was not enough for Cano. Three
years later he and several others rode by Sitters' camp, purposely
leaving a trail. At daybreak when the officers took up the trail, Cano

and his gang staged another ambush, killing Sitters and a companion. See *Alpine Avalanche*, Feb. 20, 1913; Smithers, "Bandit Raids," 65, 67; Webb, *The Texas Rangers: A Century of Frontier Defense,* 498.

16   Landrum to Sheppard, Boquillas, Texas, March 4, 1913, and Brig. Gen. Tasker H. Bliss to Adj. Gen. George Andrews, Fort Sam Houston, Mar. 24, 1913, in Office of the Adjutant General Documents File, 2008188, Box 7128, Doc. No. 2019224; *Alpine Avalanche*, Feb. 20, 27, 1913.

17   Barnhardt to Commanding General Southern Department, Marfa, May 22, 1915, in Office of the Adjutant General Documents File 2212358, Box 7644, Doc. No. 2292205.

18   Wilson to Garrison, Cornish, N.H., July 12, 1915, Garrison to Wilson, Washington, July 22, 1915, Doc. No. 2264551-E; Ferguson to Funston, Austin, June 25, 1915, and Funston to Ferguson, Fort Sam Houston, July 1, 1915, Doc. No. 2264551-D; quotation in Garrison to Wilson, Washington, Mar. 2, 1915, Bliss to Chief of Staff, Washington, June 22, 1915, and Garrison to Wilson, Washington, June 22, 1915, Doc. No. 2264551-C; all in Office of the Adjutant General Documents File 2212358, Box 7644.

19   In fact, several historians contend that Villa was not involved in the Columbus raid, that it was carried out by bandits, or perhaps by some of his men, who were delighted that he got the blame. Braddy, *Pancho Villa at Columbus: The Raid of 1916,* 1, 15-16, convincingly argues that Villa was there. See also "Annual Report of Major General Funston," 19; Clendennen, *Blood on the Border: The United States Army and the Mexican Irregulars,* chs. 9 and 10.

20   Smith to Baker, Washington, Mar. 23, 1916, in Office of the Adjutant General Documents File, 2377632, Box 8143, Doc. No. 2383978.

21   For accounts of the Glenn Springs and Boquillas raids, see *Alpine Avalanche,* May 11, 1916; Wood, "The Glenn Springs Raid," *West Texas Historical and Scientific Society Publications,* XIX (1963), 65-71; Raht, *Romance of Davis Mountains and Big Bend,* 350-58; Maxwell, *The Big Bend,* 61-67; Mason, *The Great Pursuit,* ch. 10; Smithers, "Bandit Raids," 71-74.

22   Barnum to Adjutant General, Fort Sam Houston, May 7, 1916, in Office of the Adjutant General Documents File, 2398805, Box 8132, Doc. No. 1361.

23   Smithers, "Bandit Raids," 72.

24   *Ibid.*; Maxwell, *The Big Bend,* 67.

25   Copy of Carranza to Eliseo Arrandondo, México, May 8, 1916, Doc. No. 2399537; Scott and Funston to Secretary of War, El Paso, May 7 and 8, 1916, Docs. No. 13 and 16, all in Office of the Adjutant General Documents File, 2398805, Box 8132.

26   James Hopper, "A Little Mexican Expedition," *Collier's, the National Weekly,* LVII (July 15, 1916), 6; Langhorne to Col. F. W. Sibley, Deemer's Store, May 22, 1916, in Office of the Adjutant General Documents File, 2398805, Box 8132, Doc. No. 2398805-V; Mason, *Great Pursuit,* 186.

27 Langhorne to Sibley, Deemer's Store, May 22, 1916; Cramer, "The Punitive Expedition from Boquillas," *U.S. Cavalry Journal,* XXVIII (Oct., 1916), 211-12.

28 Hopper, "Little Mexican Expedition," 22; Langhorne to Sibley, Deemer's Store, May 22, 1916; Cramer, "Punitive Expedition from Boquillas," 213; the *Alpine Avalanche,* May 18, 1916.

29 Hopper, "Little Mexican Expedition," 22.

30 Langhorne to Sibley, Deemer's Store, May 22, 1916; quotation in Cramer, "Punitive Expedition from Boquillas," 213.

31 Cramer, "Punitive Expedition from Boquillas," 214.

32 *Ibid.,* 217-18.

33 *Ibid.,* 219-20.

34 *Ibid.,* 223; Funston to Adjutant General, Fort Sam Houston, May 20, 1916, in Office of the Adjutant General Documents File 2398805, Box 8132.

35 Cramer, "Punitive Expedition from Boquillas," 223-24.

36 Smithers, "Bandit Raids," 74; Raborg, "The Villa Raid on Glenn Springs."

37 Clendennen, *Blood on the Border,* 287, 289-90.

38 Scott, *Some Memoirs of a Soldier,* 527-28.

39 Interview with W. P. Cameron, Mineral Wells, July 2, 1970.

40 Interview with Dr. Calhoun H. Monroe, El Paso, Nov. 9, 1971.

41 Smithers, "Bandit Raids," 67, 69, 71.

42 *Ibid.,* 74-79; Webb, *The Texas Rangers,* 499-504.

43 Casey, *Soldiers, Ranchers and Miners,* 47-51, 57-58; interview with Mr. and Mrs. Hart M. Greenwood.

44 Hinkle, *Wings Over the Border: The Army Air Service Armed Patrol of the United States-Mexico Border, 1919-1921,* 10-12.

45 Hinkle, *Wings and Saddles,* 8-10, 12-22, 24, 28-38, 55-65, contains a thorough account of the ransom of the flyers.

Chapter 7

1 Interview with Ross A. Maxwell, Austin, April 6, 1973; Saxton and Casey, "Everett Ewing Townsend," v.

2 August 12, 1916 is the date on the postcard pictured in a *Fort Worth Star-Telegram* story, Apr. 5, 1958, Sec. 5, 16.

3 Schoffelmayer, "The Big Bend Area of Texas: A Geographic Wonderland," *Texas Geographic Magazine,* I (May, 1937), 1; *Dallas Morning News,* Oct. 12, 19, 23, 1937; Connelly, "Big Bend National Park Project Reality at Last," *West Texas Today* (Sept., 1941).

4 Dobie, "The Texan Part of Texas," *Nature Magazine,* XVI (Dec., 1930), 343-46, 393, 395; Wagstaff, "Beginnings of the Big Bend Park," *West Texas Historical Association Year Book,* XLIV (Oct., 1968), 3-4, 6.

5 Wagstaff, "Beginnings of the Big Bend Park," 7, 9, 11.

6 *Ibid.,* 11-12.

7 *Ibid.,* 12, 14.

8 Foree, "Our New Park on the Rio Grande," *The Saturday Evening Post,* Dec. 2, 1944, 106; Madison, *The Big Bend,* 231-32; Townsend to Lewis, Nov. 25, 1933, copy in Brewster County Scrapbook.

9 Interview with Maxwell; Madison, *The Big Bend,* 233-34.

10 *Report on the Big Bend Area, Texas.* U.S. Department of the Interior, National Park Service, January 1935.

11 Casey, *Soldiers, Ranchers and Miners,* 188; *Fort Worth Star-Telegram,* June 24, 1935.

12 Garrison, "A History of the Proposed Big Bend International Park"; *Fort Worth Star-Telegram,* June 24, 1935.

13 *Rocky Mountain News* (Denver), Feb. 26, 1936.

14 Interview with Maxwell; *Waco Tribune Herald,* June 28, 1936.

15 *Austin Dispatch,* Apr. 19, 1937; *Dallas Morning News,* May 11, 1937; *Houston Chronicle,* Art Gravure Section, Feb. 27, 1938.

16 Because of the uncertainty of establishing the park and because the Park Service insisted that the project be completed immediately, Webb never finished the history of the Big Bend that he had proposed. Instead, he submitted an account of his trip through Santa Elena Canyon that remains unpublished. See Webb to Herbert Maier, Feb. 3, 1938, and "Materials Prepared as a Basis for a Guide to Points of Interest in the Proposed Big Bend National Park," in the Walter P. Webb Papers.

17 Skaggs to Webb, McCamey, Texas, June 10, 1937, in Webb Papers; interview with Maxwell.

18 Maier to Record, Oklahoma City, July 13, 1937, in Carter Foundation files; Madison, *The Big Bend,* 235.

19 Minutes of the Meeting of the Executive Board Texas Big Bend Park Association, and Mayes to Morelock to Carter, May 9, Alpine, in Carter Foundation files.

20 Audit of the TBBPA in Carter Foundation files; *Fort Worth Star-Telegram,* Sept. 13, 1942, Sec. 1, 5; *Dallas Morning News,* Sept. 15, 1939.

21 Memo from Harry Connelly to Carter, Fort Worth, Dec. 6, 1941, and radio script, Feb. 16, 1941, in Carter Foundation files; *San Antonio Express,* July 19, 1938, Mar. 5, 1941; *San Angelo Standard-Times,* Apr. 11, 1941; Madison, *The Big Bend,* 236; Saxton and Casey, "Everett Ewing Townsend," 61; *Big Spring Herald,* Mar. 5, 1941.

22 Interview with Mr. and Mrs. Hart M. Greenwood.

23 *Dallas Morning News,* Aug. 9, 16, 1941. Casey, *Soldiers, Ranchers and Miners,* 189, 250-51; Madison, *Big Bend,* 237-38; *San Antonio Light,* Mar. 1, 1942; *San Angelo Standard-Times,* Feb. 27, 1942.

24   *Fort Worth Star-Telegram,* Sept. 6, 1943; Garrison, "Big Bend International Park."

25   Madison, *Big Bend,* 239-40; *Dallas Morning News,* June 7, 1944, Sec. 1, 2; Wauer, *Birds of Big Bend National Park and Vicinity.*

26   Interview with Maxwell.

27   Garrison, "Big Bend International Park." *Fort Worth Star-Telegram,* Nov. 21, 1955, 1. Madison, *Big Bend,* 251-52. Another excellent summary of the establishment of the national park is Casey, "The Big Bend National Park," *West Texas Historical and Scientific Society Publications,* XIII (1948), 26-42.

Historic Sites

1   Madison and Stillwell, *How Come It's Called That?,* 5-7.

2   *Ibid.,* 4, 6-7, 51, 57-58, 74; Maxwell, *The Big Bend,* 4, 83.

Index

277

Francisco Marín, José, 30–31
Fredericksburg, Tex., 57, 59, 63
Frémont, John C., 57
Fronteriza Range, 18, 197
Frontier Battalion (Texas Rangers),
    128, 154, 155, 158
Funston, Frederick, 159, 163–64,
    168–69, 174
Fur trappers and traders in Big Bend,
    148–49

G
G4 Ranch, 18, 121, 126, 155
Gage, Edward L., 1, 127
Gallegos, Hernán, 23, 28
Galveston, Harrisburg and San
    Antonio Railroad, 120
Gano, John T., 1–2, 127, 155
Gano, Richard M., 127
Garady, Rocke, 111
Gardner, G. Clinton, 81, 82
Gargin, John, 111
Garrison, Lindley M., 163, 164
Garza Falcón, Blas de la, 33
Geological formation of Big Bend, 5,
    7
George Wright Peak, 197
Gigedo, Revilla, 49
Gila River, 75
Gillespie, J. T., 158
Gillespie, Jim, 154
Gillett, James B., 121, 126, 154–55
Gilliland, Fine, 134
Glanton, Joe, 70
Glass Mountains, 133, 134
Glenn Springs, Tex., 147, 149, 171,
    176, 177
Glenn Springs Raid, 165–69
Gold mining, 135, 136
Goliad, Tex., 112
Gomez, 63, 115
Government Spring, 194
Granger, Tom, 132–33
Gray, Andrew P., 101, 113
Gray, Jerry, 179
Green, Duff C., 83–87, 89–91,
    94–97, 101, 106, 108
Green Gulch, 15, 18, 19
Green, Thomas J., 76
Gregg, Josiah, 52
Grierson, Benjamin H., 118–19, 123

Grierson, Robert, 118
Guadalupe Mountains, 22
Guadalupe River, 112
Guayule, 147

H
Haag, B. Frank, 191, 192
Haley, J. Evetts, 157
Haley, Lawrence, 126, 162
Halter, ——, 168
Hancock, Lee, 162
Hancock, W. B., 128
Harris, Jodie P., 175, 176, 177, 189,
    191
Hartz, Edward L., 105–07
Hartzog, George, Jr., 210
Harwick, J. W., 162
Hawley, C. A., 139, 142, 149, 150, 154
Hays-Highsmith expedition, 54–56,
    58, 59, 73, 76
Hays, John Coffee ("Jack"), 51, 53,
    54–56, 57, 58, 59, 111
Hays, Robert, 62
Hector, Ira, 194–95
Helena, Tex., 112
Henderson, W. T., 128
Henry, W. S., 62–63
Hereford Cattle Company, 130
Hernández, Cipriano, 145
Hickman, James P., 72
Highsmith, Samuel, 54–56, 58
Hilder, Jim, 134
Hill, Robert T., 3–4, 7, 10, 11, 13,
    14, 98, 148, 157, 158, 159, 187,
    190, 191, 194, 198, 204
Holliday, ——, 62, 63
Horsehead Crossing, 55, 56–57, 115
Hot Springs, Tex., 20, 145, 147, 162,
    187
Hot Springs rapids, 97
Houston Chronicle, 198
Houston, Tex., 52, 59, 62
Howard, J. S., 162
Hull, Cordell, 196
Humphris and Company, 134, 136
Hunter, Robert, 62
Hunter, Dr. W. D., 190

I
Ickes, Harold, 196, 205
Ikard, W. S., 134

279

Picture Credits

The National Park Service and the Amon Carter Museum gratefully acknowledge the generosity of Mr. Bank Langmore, Dallas, Texas, in contributing his splendid photographs of the Big Bend region to both the exhibition and this book. Many other individuals and institutions contributed illustrations, as listed below, and thanks is due them also.

- Alabama Department of Archives and History: p. 85.
- Ansel Adams: p. 12.
- American Antiquarian Society: pp. 46–47.
- Amon Carter Museum of Western Art: pp. 107, 153 (middle), 182, 210.
- Arizona Historical Society: p. 81 (Bartlett).
- Clifford Casey, Alpine, Tex.: pp. 31, 169, 170.
- From William E. Connelley, *Doniphan's Expedition . . .* (1907), p. 277: p. 53.
- Emory's *Report*: pp. 65, 66, 87, 88, 91, 96.
- El Paso Public Library: p. 3 (Nevill).
- *Fort Worth Star Telegram*, April 5, 1958: p. 191 (left).
- Mr. and Mrs. Hart Greenwood, Marfa, Texas: p. 130.
- Junior Historians, Marfa, Texas: pp. 122, 125, 140, 160, 200 (top).
- Bank Langmore: pp. ii–iii, xii, 8–9, 16, 50, 74, 110, 156, 188, 208–09.
- Library of Congress: pp. 78 (Johnston), 80 (Whiting), 81 (Emory), 119 (Shafter).
- Ministerio del Ejército, Madrid, Spain: pp. 39–41.
- Missouri Historical Society: p. 68.
- National Archives: pp. 78–79, 116 (Victorio), 119 (Grierson), 176 (top), 183.
- Western History Collections, University of Oklahoma Library: pp. 53 (Hays), 69.
- University of Rochester: pp. 101, 102–03.
- Rochester Historical Society: pp. 92–93.
- Sul Ross State University Library, Alpine, Texas: pp. 159, 176 (bottom two).
- Texas State Library, Austin, Texas: pp. 60–61, 197.
- Ronnie C. Tyler: p. 20.
- Barker Texas History Collection, University of Texas, Austin: p. 124.
- Hunter Collection, Humanities Research Center, University of Texas, Austin: p. 113.
- W. D. Smithers Collection, Humanities Research Center, University of Texas, Austin: pp. 34, 116, 125 (middle and bottom), 128, 129, 135, 140 (right), 141, 143, 146, 148, 150, 151, 152, 153 (top and bottom), 165, 166, 167, 171, 175, 178, 179, 181, 185, 186, 191 (Townsend), 195, 199, 200, 201, 207.
- U.S. Geological Survey, Denver: pp. 3, 4, 7, 136, 194, 204.
- Wells Fargo Bank, History Room, San Francisco: p. 108.

As the Nation's principal conservation agency, the Department of the Interior has responsibility for most of our nationally owned public lands and natural resources. This includes fostering the wisest use of our land and water resources, protecting our fish and wildlife, preserving the environmental and cultural values of our national parks and historical places, and providing for the enjoyment of life through outdoor recreation. The Department assesses our energy and mineral resources and works to assure that their development is in the best interests of all our people. The Department also has a major responsibility for American Indian reservation communities and for people who live in Island Territories under U.S. administration.

☆ U.S. GOVERNMENT PRINTING OFFICE : 1975 O − 596−615

For sale by the Superintendent of Documents, U.S. Government Printing Office
Washington, D.C. 20402
Stock Number 024–005–00579–0
Catalog Number I 29.2:B 48/3

CORPS (en général) (voir aussi : les parties correspondantes...)

Les cheveux

Le cuir chevelu

La tête

Les yeux

Les oreilles

Le nez

Les lèvres

Les dents

Le cou

La gorge

Les épaules

Les bras

Les coudes

Les doigts

    le pouce

    l'index

    le majeur

    l'annulaire

    l'auriculaire

Le cœur

Le sang

Les seins

Les poumons

L'estomac

Le dos

Les articulations

La peau

Les os

L'utérus

Les intestins

Les jambes

Les genoux

Les chevilles

Les pieds

Les orteils

ANNEXE II 333, 334, 335

Liste des principaux malaises et maladies et de leur signification probable abrégée.

Abcès

Accident

Acné

Acouphène

Alcoolisme

Allergies

Alzheïmer

Amputation

Angoisse

Anorexie

Appendicite

Arthrite

Articulations

Autisme

Basse pression

Boulimie

Brûlure, brûlement, fièvre

Burnout

Cancer

Cellulite

Cholestérol

Cigarette

Cœur

Constipation

Crampe

Démangeaisons, irritations

Dépression

Diabète

Diarrhée

Douleur

Eczéma

Empoisonnement

Enflure (œdème)

Engourdissement, insensibilité

Entorse

Étouffement, essoufflement

Étourdissement, perte de connaissance, coma

Fatigue

Gangrène

Gaz

Grippe

Haute pression

Hypoglycémie

Incontinence

Infarctus

Infections

Insomnie

Leucémie

Malaise

Mononucléose
....

Nausée
....

Nerf sciatique
....

Paralysie
....

Peau
....

Poids (excès de...)
....

Poumons
....

Raideur (articulation)
....

Rhumatisme
....

Ronflement
....

Saignements
....

Sclérose en plaque
....

Scoliose
....

Sida
....

Tics
....

Torticolis
....

Tumeur, kyste
....

Zona
....

ITE (maladies en...)

Toutes les maladies en « **ite** » sont habituellement reliées à de la colère ou de la frustration puisqu'elles sont reliées à des inflammations.

ABASIE

Bien que mes muscles et tout mon mécanisme de marche ne me causent pas de malaise, je ne peux que marcher partiellement ou en suis incapable. C'est mon système de commande situé au cervelet qui peut être affecté, soit par une lésion, un trouble vasculaire ou une tumeur. Cela provient parfois d'une grande peur en rapport avec mes pensées, qui a eu pour effet de **me figer sur place**. Cette peur ou culpabilité est liée au fait d'avancer dans la vie. Il serait bon que je trouve la cause de cette insécurité ou de cette culpabilité et que je développe plus de confiance en moi. Je peux commencer à me visualiser en train de marcher de plus en plus aisément, en même temps que j'amplifie mon sentiment de confiance en moi. Je prends aussi conscience que la vie m'apporte les outils nécessaires « à mon avancement ».

ABCÈS ou EMPYÈME (en général)

Un **abcès** est un type d'infection caractérisée par la formation et l'accumulation de pus aux dépens des tissus normalement constitués. Il produit habituellement une saillie (une bosse) et je le retrouve seulement sur le tissu corporel ou sur un organe. L'**abcès** indique que je manifeste une réponse à la **colère** ou à une blessure émotionnelle, à un sentiment **d'irritation**, de **confrontation**, de **vengeance**, **d'incapacité ou d'échec** (le pus est relié aux fluides de mon corps et à mes émotions). C'est souvent **un excès d'irritation ou de mécontentement que je n'arrive pas à exprimer par rapport à moi, à une personne ou une situation.** Des pensées malsaines, qui peuvent aller jusqu'à la vengeance et qui « fermentent » vont produire l'infection et le pus. Cette frustration retenue peut se présenter afin de faire **aboutir** une situation, c'est-à-dire **crever l'abcès**. Elle peut produire chez moi un bouleversement mental (comme un gonflement) entraînant le vide et l'épuisement. Ce type d'infection **(abcès)** est uniquement une manifestation (ou une création) du mental, de mes pensées. Il est grand temps que je passe à autre chose, que je change d'attitude, si je veux améliorer mon sort... et mon corps, avant qu'une infection plus généralisée ne se manifeste. De plus, l'**abcès** correspond à un profond **chagrin**, voire même à du **désespoir intérieur** qui vont engendrer un sentiment profond d'impuissance ou d'échec. Le vide et l'épuisement peuvent s'ensuivre. Il apparaît à la **source** du chagrin, c'est-à-dire que l'émotion vécue est associée à la fonction et à la partie du corps où l'**abcès** se manifeste. Par exemple, s'il se situe sur ma **jambe**, il est relié aux résistances et aux conflits, qui m'indique que je dois orienter ma vie dans certaines directions. S'il se situe au niveau de mes **yeux,** il s'agit d'une difficulté à voir qui je suis, ce que je suis, où je vais et ce qui s'en vient pour moi. Au niveau de mes **pieds**, j'ai des difficultés, des questionnements ou des peurs reliés à l'avenir ou à sa conception. À mes **oreilles**, c'est quelque chose que j'entends. À mes **hanches**, j'ai de la difficulté à m'élancer dans la vie et ainsi de suite. Tout ceci

est relié à **l'habileté de me tenir debout**, à exprimer mon indépendance et ma liberté. J'accepte ↓♥ au niveau du cœur de faire aboutir mes peurs, mes insécurités, mes craintes, et mon **abcès** aboutira lui aussi. **L'abcès superficiel** qui est accessible à la vue ou au toucher correspond à une **rage** concernant des situations de ma vie qui peuvent être « facilement identifiables ». Il possède également une correspondance avec la partie du corps affectée telle que le cou, le dos, les doigts, etc. **L'abcès profond** peut se retrouver à l'intérieur de mon corps et correspond à une **déception** par rapport à des sentiments plus profonds de mon être. Selon sa position, un **abcès** peut avoir des conséquences graves. Par exemple, s'il est logé au niveau du cerveau, il est lié à mon individualité et à l'idée que je me fais de moi-même ; au niveau des poumons, lié à la vie ; des reins, lié aux peurs ; au foie, lié à la critique. Je peux trouver pourquoi cette **colère ponctuelle** arrive dans ma vie en allant voir la signification correspondante à la partie concernée. Je peux ainsi mettre plus d'amour et de compréhension par rapport à la situation qui m'a amené à vivre cette colère. **L'abcès en bouton de chemise** désigne un ou plusieurs **abcès superficiels** qui sont reliés à un autre **abcès** profond ou à des tissus plus profonds. Il est donc invisible à l'œil nu. Ainsi, mon corps me dit que ma **colère** affecte maintenant ma vie extérieure et intérieure. C'est comme si « cette **irritation** me transperçait le corps » et m'exprimait le besoin pressant de guérir ces blessures par l'amour. **L'abcès chaud** entraîne habituellement une réaction inflammatoire et peut se former rapidement. Le fait que l'**abcès** s'entoure fréquemment d'une membrane indique bien que cela provient d'une pensée non bénéfique qui provoque de la colère. **L'abcès froid** ne présente pas de réaction inflammatoire et sa progression est plutôt lente. Il peut être dû à des champignons ou au bacille de Koch. Ce type d'**abcès** indique que ma colère se manifeste sous forme de **déception** ou de **résignation** face à une situation. J'accepte ↓♥ les nouvelles pensées d'amour et je reste ouvert au niveau du cœur à mon entourage, plutôt que de fixer mon attention sur mes anciennes blessures, sur mon passé ou sur certaines formes de vengeance. En prenant conscience de ce processus d'acceptation ↓♥, l'**abcès** est alors sujet à disparaître pour toujours.

ABCÈS ANAL (voir : ANUS — ABCÈS ANAL)

ABCÈS DE LA DENT (voir : DENT [abcès de la...])

ABCÈS DU CERVEAU (voir : CERVEAU [abcès du...])

ABCÈS DU FOIE (voir : FOIE [abcès du...])

ABDOMEN (voir : VENTRE)

ACCIDENT

L'**accident** est très souvent synonyme de **culpabilité**. Il est relié à mes **culpabilités**, à ma manière de penser et à mon fonctionnement dans la société. Il dénote aussi une certaine **réaction envers l'autorité**, même à plusieurs aspects de la violence. Il peut arriver que j'aie de la difficulté à m'affirmer face à cette autorité, à parler de mes besoins, de mes points de vue, etc. **Je me « fais alors violence » à moi-même.** L'**accident** indique un besoin direct et immédiat de passer à l'action. Le besoin inconscient de changement est tellement grand que la pensée utilise une situation extrême, voire dramatique pour me faire prendre conscience que je dois probablement changer la direction que j'emprunte actuellement. **C'est une forme d'autopunition consciente ou inconsciente.** La partie du corps blessée durant l'**accident** est habituellement déjà malade ou affaiblie, que ce soit par une maladie, un malaise, une coupure, une brûlure ou toute prédisposition aux accidents. L'**accident** me permet d'observer cette faiblesse en la faisant remonter à la surface. L'**accident** est aussi mon incapacité à me voir et à m'accepter ↓♥ tel que je suis. **Puisque je suis responsable à 100 % de mes actes et de ma vie entière, je peux m'expliquer davantage pourquoi je me suis attiré telle forme d'accident.** Attiré, dites-vous ? Oui, car tout ceci vient de mes pensées les plus profondes, de mes « patterns » ou schémas de pensée d'enfance. Il est fort possible que je m'attire des punitions <u>si, aujourd'hui, j'ai l'impression</u> de faire quelque chose et de **ne pas être correct**. Exactement comme dans mon enfance ; j'étais puni quand je **n'étais pas correct**. C'est enregistré dans mon mental et il est temps de changer mon attitude. Le côté « moral » de l'être humain l'amène à se punir s'il se sent coupable, d'où la douleur, les afflictions et les **accidents**. Il est essentiel de savoir que je peux me sentir coupable dans une situation quelconque **si et seulement si** je sais que je fais du mal à autrui. <u>**Dans toutes les autres situations, je suis responsable mais non coupable.**</u> Je dois me souvenir que je suis ma propre autorité (dans le sens d'individu). J'ai besoin de prendre ma place dans l'univers. Je dois cesser de me faire violence. Comme je l'ai écrit plus tôt, l'**accident** est rattaché à la **culpabilité** et celle-ci à la **peur** par rapport à une situation. La peur de ne pas être correct est souvent perçue sous l'aspect de la culpabilité plutôt que sous celui de la responsabilité. L'**accident** m'oblige souvent à cesser ou à ralentir mes activités. Une certaine période de questionnement s'ensuit. En restant ouvert et objectif par rapport à moi-même, je découvrirai rapidement la ou les raisons de cet **accident**. Ai-je perdu le contrôle d'une situation ? Est-il temps pour moi de changer d'orientation, de direction ? Ai-je de la difficulté à écouter mes signes intérieurs ou mon intuition, si bien que je m'attire un signe **radical** sur le plan physique ? Ai-je observé comment l'**accident** s'est produit ? Quel était mon état avant et

après ? Il est très important de revoir les conditions entourant l'**accident** ; j'analyse les mots utilisés et je prends conscience qu'ils mettent en évidence ce que je vis au moment de l'**accident**. J'observe tous les signes et les symboles de cette situation (**accident**) et j'écoute ma voix intérieure pour trouver une solution qui m'évitera probablement d'aggraver tout ceci. La **prédisposition aux accidents** est un état qui survient durant une relation conflictuelle avec la réalité, l'incapacité d'être pleinement présent et conscient de l'univers tel qu'il se présente à moi. C'est comme si je voulais être ailleurs. Je suis déconnecté de ce qui arrive autour de moi, peut-être parce que je trouve ma réalité inacceptable ou difficile à vivre. J'ai besoin d'être plus **branché** sur moi-même pour découvrir ma sécurité et ma confiance intérieures.

ACCIDENT CÉRÉBRO-VASCULAIRE (A.C.V.)
(voir : CERVEAU — ACCIDENT CÉRÉBRO-VASCULAIRE [A.C.V.])

ACCOUCHEMENT (en général)
(voir aussi : GROSSESSE / [maux de...] / [... prolongée])

L'**accouchement** est peut-être l'une des expériences de transition les plus traumatisantes qui soit pour l'enfant qui naît. C'est un phénomène naturel ; moi, en tant que femme, je délivre l'enfant que je porte. Les douleurs de l'**accouchement** peuvent être reliées à plusieurs peurs, surtout celles de souffrir et d'accoucher, à la douleur accumulée par rapport à mon **propre enfant intérieur**. Les malaises ou les souffrances peuvent aussi provenir du fait que l'enfant qui va naître me rappellera constamment la réalité et la responsabilité que je peux avoir par rapport à mon enfant intérieur. Je peux nourrir des inquiétudes face à **cette partie de moi composée de ma chair et mon sang** dont je prends la responsabilité. Dans cette situation, comme dans bien d'autres, l'**accouchement** amène plusieurs croyances plus ou moins fondées, par exemple celle qu'il faut souffrir pour accoucher (comme pour être belle !). Ce qui n'est pas nécessairement vrai, surtout sur les plans de conscience supérieurs. Les douleurs peuvent plutôt ramener en moi, surtout inconsciemment, **le souvenir douloureux d'avoir passé du monde de lumière à celui plus limitatif de la matière dans un corps physique**. Plusieurs autres questions peuvent aussi surgir : Qu'est-ce qui m'attend après la naissance de cet enfant ? Est-ce que je serai autant désirable pour mon conjoint ? Suis-je une bonne mère ? Mon enfant a-t-il tout ce dont il a besoin ? Se peut-il que je ne désire pas **accoucher** parce que je suis dans un état bienheureux, aimée et cajolée davantage par mon conjoint. Quoi qu'il en soit, **accoucher** est une expérience formidable. Elle permet de montrer réellement mon habileté à faire face aux moments de transition et de changements futurs. Je fais confiance, en sachant que j'ai toute la force et l'énergie nécessaires pour mettre mon enfant au monde et m'en occuper adéquatement.

ACCOUCHEMENT — AVORTEMENT, FAUSSE-COUCHE

L'**avortement,** ou **fausse-couche, est** un arrêt de la grossesse avant le 180ᵉ jour (6,5 mois environ) de gestation. En général, on parlera d'**avortement** dans le cas d'interruption volontaire de la grossesse (I.V.G.). Lorsque l'**avortement** sera spontané, c'est-à-dire quand il s'agit de la perte non provoquée du fœtus, on parlera alors de **fausse-couche.** Lorsque je fais une **fausse-couche,** je me questionne à savoir qui désirait un enfant, moi ou mon conjoint ? Inconsciemment, j'ai peur que l'enfant à naître change ma vie de couple, mon travail, mes habitudes. Je crains de ne pas posséder les qualités nécessaires pour devenir une bonne mère et cela peut remonter à des moments vécus dans ma propre enfance. Il se peut aussi que l'âme qui devait s'incarner ait changé d'idée. Il faut donc que je reste ouverte au niveau du cœur et que je mette les énergies en branle pour régler cette situation « immature » ; autrement, les grossesses futures risquent d'être complexes et incomplètes. Amour, responsabilité et respect mutuel des conjoints (s'il y a lieu) sont les sentiments essentiels qui doivent être manifestés si je veux que mon enfant arrive **à terme.**

ACCOUCHEMENT PRÉMATURÉ

Un **accouchement prématuré** est celui qui a lieu entre la vingt-neuvième et la trente-huitième semaine de l'absence des règles. Lorsque ceci arrive, il se peut que je ne me sente pas suffisamment **mûre** pour rendre cet enfant à terme et que je souhaite, d'une manière non consciente, me débarrasser de lui avant qu'il soit à terme. Je peux vouloir « rejeter » inconsciemment cet enfant, comme moi-même je peux me sentir rejetée parfois. L'angoisse, même inconsciente, d'avoir à assumer une responsabilité à laquelle je ne suis pas prête, ou le fait que je ne me sente pas prête, peut me faire « désirer ardemment **accoucher** le plus tôt possible » afin de faire cesser cette angoisse de l'attente. De toute façon, que je veuille faire cesser cette angoisse ou que je renie cet enfant, cet état de conscience est généralement nié. Je m'imagine le scénario, moi, une femme qui renierait consciemment mon enfant ? C'est possible, mais cette situation se transforme la plupart du temps en rejet inconscient de cette merveilleuse expérience. Quoi qu'il en soit, j'accepte ↓♥ que tout est arrivé pour le mieux, pour moi et pour l'enfant à naître.

ACHILLE (tendon d'...) (voir : TENDON D'ACHILLE)

ACIDOSE (voir aussi : GOUTTE, RHUMATISME)

L'acide est souvent relié à ce qui ronge le métal et à ce qui est amer (« aigreur psychique »). Ainsi, l'**acidose** indique que j'ai **refusé d'assimiler** une situation qui s'accumule maintenant à un niveau inconscient, entraînant sur le plan

corporel un grand taux d'acidité dans le sang ou dans le liquide dans lequel baignent les cellules. **Assimiler** signifie résoudre, traiter, régler tout problème, situation ou conflit qui me dérange, que je refuse, qui **empoisonne** mon existence ! Par exemple, je peux me demander quelle est la situation (souvent de nature émotionnelle) qui me ronge intérieurement et qui me rend si **amer face à la vie**. Il est possible que je vive actuellement une situation qui fait remonter en moi de l'insatisfaction concernant les rapports que j'avais avec **ma mère**. Je peux même vivre une insatisfaction semblable avec mes enfants, des amis ou des employés pour lesquels je me sens « **comme une mère** ». L'**acidose métabolique** qui a rapport à mon corps en général reflétera mon côté amer envers la vie en général. L'**acidose respiratoire ou acidose gazeuse** provient du fait que je n'élimine pas suffisamment le gaz carbonique lors de ma respiration. Ainsi, mon côté amer dans la vie a plutôt rapport à mes relations avec mon environnement et les gens qui m'entourent. Dans le cas de l'**acidose lactique**, on retrouve une quantité excessive d'acide lactique dans le sang. Puisque le sang transporte normalement la joie, il s'en trouve que mon côté amer dans la vie et tout ce qui s'y passe m'affectent grandement. C'est pourquoi je peux retrouver cet état si je suis diabétique (qui correspond à de la tristesse profonde), si je vis de l'insuffisance rénale (qui correspond à de grandes peurs face à la vie), si j'ai la leucémie, une forme de cancer du sang (qui correspond au fait que j'ai toujours l'impression d'avoir à me battre dans la vie). Dans le cas extrême, le **rhumatisme** est la conséquence directe et parfois inévitable d'un excès d'acidité qu'est l'**acidose**. J'accepte ↓♥ de voir et de traiter au niveau du cœur les situations de ma vie, même si elles m'irritent et m'agacent. En mettant l'attention sur un processus conscient d'ouverture et d'acceptation ↓♥, je peux éviter de supporter physiquement cette maladie douloureuse (autant que son traitement !). Je résous les situations pour vivre davantage la joie, la libération et la paix intérieure.

ACNÉ (voir : PEAU — ACNÉ)

ACOUPHÈNE (voir : OREILLES — ACOUPHÈNE)

ACRODERMATITE (voir : PEAU — ACRODERMATITE)

ACROKÉRATOSE (voir : PEAU — ACROKÉRATOSE)

ACROMÉGALIE (voir : OS — ACROMÉGALIE)

A.C.V. (voir : CERVEAU — ACCIDENT CÉRÉBRO-VASCULAIRE [A.C.V.])

ADDISON[1] (maladie d'...) (voir aussi : SURRÉNALES [maux de capsules])

La **maladie d'Addison** est caractérisée par une insuffisance des glandes surrénales[2]. **C'est une forme de déception par rapport à moi-même**. C'est un état extrême de sous-alimentation émotionnelle et spirituelle. Avoir cette maladie peut signifier que j'ai vécu beaucoup de soumission dans mon enfance face à l'un ou l'autre de mes parents. J'ai pu me sentir agressé psychiquement, vivre un traumatisme ou une irritation intense où je pouvais sentir ma vie en danger. Cet état m'a amené à vivre une grande insécurité face à l'avenir et à douter grandement de mes capacités. Cette maladie se distingue par une attitude extrêmement défaitiste, une absence de but ou d'intérêt pour moi-même ou pour ce qui m'entoure. Je vis beaucoup d'anxiété et d'antipathie. Il est temps que je prenne ma place, que j'aille de l'avant et que je manifeste l'énergie à élaborer certains buts personnels sans attendre l'approbation et le consentement de mon entourage, peu importe l'importance de ma démarche (mon but). J'essaie de trouver une méthode qui m'aidera à me **connecter** davantage à mon moi intérieur qui possède des ressources illimitées et une estime de soi élevée.

ADÉNITE (voir aussi : GANGLION [... lymphatique], INFLAMMATION)

Lorsque j'ai une inflammation d'un ganglion du système lymphatique, c'est que je vis de l'insécurité reliée à de la peur sur le plan affectif. La partie du corps qui est touchée me donne une indication de l'aspect de ma vie dont il s'agit. Je cherche à connaître la source de ma peine afin de m'aider à prendre conscience de la peur qui m'habite et de développer ma confiance pour dépasser cette émotion.

ADÉNOÏDES (voir : VÉGÉTATIONS ADÉNOÏDES)

ADÉNOME (voir aussi : SEINS [maux aux...])

De façon générale, un **adénome** est une tumeur bénigne qui se retrouve sur une glande. Comme toute tumeur, cela provient d'un choc émotionnel qui s'est densifié sur la partie du corps qui est reliée au choc émotionnel, que ce soit le pancréas, le foie, un sein, un rein, la prostate et même les glandes endocrines. J'accepte ↓♥ les évènements passés, afin de me permettre d'aller de l'avant, en toute confiance.

---

1. **ADDISON (Thomas) :** Médecin anglais qui, en 1855, a décrit la maladie comme une insuffisance surrénalienne lente.
2. **Glandes surrénales :** Glandes endocrines situées sur les reins en forme de pyramide et qui ont pour fonction de produire de l'adrénaline qui régularise le pouls et la pression sanguine principalement. Ce sont ces glandes qui lorsque ma vie ou celle d'un autre est en danger, peuvent me permettre de développer une force surhumaine pour ma survie.

ADÉNOPATHIE (voir aussi : GANGLION [... lymphatique], INFECTIONS, INFLAMMATION, TUMEUR(S))

L'**adénopathie** se caractérise par une augmentation du volume des ganglions lymphatiques et peut provenir d'une inflammation, d'une tumeur ou d'une infection. Puisque les ganglions du système lymphatique agissent comme des petits reins du système lymphatique, cela signifie que je vis un stress ou un choc émotionnel relié à des peurs sur le plan affectif. Je me sens ainsi bloqué, pris sur ce plan-là. La région affectée m'indique plus précisément l'aspect de ma vie qui est touché, que ce soit le thorax, l'abdomen, le cou, l'aisselle, l'aine. J'ai avantage à développer mon autonomie et ma confiance, afin de prendre ma vie en main !

ADHÉRENCE

Si « j'adhère » d'une manière excessive, ou si « je reste accroché » à des idées négatives, malsaines ou inadéquates, à de la rancune, à de la **haine**, à de la colère vis-à-vis de quelqu'un, à de la **culpabilité**, à des rêves illusoires, à une vie trop centrée sur le milieu familial ou sur le foyer (par exemple, la mère couveuse), je risque de manifester des **adhérences** au niveau des viscères[3]. Certaines sont **pathologiques**, c'est-à-dire qu'elles surviennent à la suite d'une inflammation liée à de la **rage** ou à une tumeur quelconque qui provient d'émotions refoulées. Ces **adhérences** sont caractérisées par une forme de soudure de deux organes du corps par un tissu conjonctif. Je décide de laisser aller le passé, les vieilles idées et les pensées négatives qui freinent mon bonheur. Je vis dans le moment présent et je savoure chaque instant de ma vie.

AGITATION (voir aussi : HYPERACTIVITÉ)

L'**agitation** est un état qui va m'atteindre si je suis une personne très nerveuse mais qui réussit quand même à canaliser ses énergies du mieux qu'elle peut ! C'est proche d'un **état d'urgence**, un processus d'extériorisation des émotions, souvent un cri d'alarme pour montrer aux autres comment je me sens intérieurement : pris, méfiant, peureux dans certaines situations, entreprenant mais souvent maladroit et surtout très énervant pour les gens de mon entourage ! Si je suis très **agité** physiquement et intérieurement, je peux vivre une forme de déséquilibre car j'ai de la difficulté à rester « centré » (stable et ancré) sur moi-même : j'utilise donc cet état inconsciemment parce que j'ai besoin d'augmenter ma confiance en moi, de me prouver que je peux réussir, en attirant l'attention : « *Regardez-moi aller !* ». Je reste calme, je communique verbalement mes sentiments et mes besoins et tout sera pour le mieux.

---

3. **Viscères :** Terme général pour désigner chacun des organes contenus à l'intérieur du crâne, de la cage thoracique ou de l'abdomen.

AGORAPHOBIE (voir aussi : ANGOISSE, MORT, PEUR)

L'**agoraphobie** vient des mots grecs **AGORA** (qui signifie *place publique*) et **PHOBUS** *(crainte)*. C'est la panique de la foule et celle aussi d'en avoir peur. Elle est fortement reliée à une peur inconsciente de la mort. Si je suis atteint d'**agoraphobie**, je suis probablement une personne très sensible, réceptive à plusieurs niveaux (surtout psychique[4]) et possédant une imagination très fertile. Je suis très dépendant sur le plan affectif et je n'ai jamais vraiment coupé le(s) lien(s) maternel(s). J'ai de la difficulté à discerner mon vrai moi de ce que je **crée** sur le plan psychique, c'est-à-dire des formes-pensées, ce qui entretient mes angoisses. Je suis semblable à une **éponge** : j'absorbe les émotions d'autrui (surtout les peurs) sans discerner, filtrer ou protéger ce qui m'appartient du reste et j'amplifie autant mes peurs que celles des autres. J'ai donc tendance à me replier sur moi-même, à me sentir responsable de tout, à communiquer très peu sauf avec la personne en qui j'ai **énormément confiance**, avec qui je me sens en **sécurité** ; je m'isole donc par crainte de m'éloigner de cette forme de sécurité. Je peux même penser être atteint de folie et je **dois cesser de croire cela le plus tôt possible**. Il m'est facile de tout « contrôler » à un endroit où je suis en totale sécurité. Cependant, dès que je quitte celui-ci, tout s'effondre ! J'angoisse pour tout, comme si mes peurs m'envahissaient au point où j'ai l'impression de perdre le contrôle ! Dès qu'une expérience me stimule trop fortement (naissance, accident, décès, catastrophe), je risque de m'enfoncer encore dans mes angoisses (les bruits, les gens, etc.), sans jamais trouver de situation durable, d'où l'amplification de l'**agoraphobie**. De plus, mon niveau de critique est élevé parce que je vis beaucoup d'insécurité, je fais peu confiance et je crois que les choses et les situations ne vont pas aussi bien que je le voudrais : donc, **je critique**. L'**agoraphobie** sous-tend parfois un conflit avec ma mère, que je vais constamment critiquer. Je dois changer mon attitude dès maintenant. J'accepte ↓♥ une à une mes peurs, telles qu'elles sont, car je sais qu'elles empoisonnent ma vie, mais elles peuvent aussi me faire avancer ! **J'apprends à m'aimer et à m'accepter** ↓♥, à aimer mon côté maternel et protecteur (mère), à me construire un univers physique et intérieur plein de bonheur, sans critique ni dépendance. J'ai aussi avantage à m'exprimer dans ma communication verbale et ma créativité. Je dois dépasser la crainte de « perdre ma place » et être en harmonie avec moi ! Je reste responsable de mon bonheur, même si j'ai tendance à croire que je détermine à la fois le bonheur et le malheur d'autrui. J'accepte ↓♥ de prendre des risques et d'aller au-devant de mes craintes qui freinent mon pouvoir créatif. Cela m'aidera à maîtriser davantage ma vie et mes pulsions intérieures. Une sexualité équilibrée et active aura l'avantage de me faire décrocher de cette fixation émotionelle liée au plan mental.

---

4. **Psychique :** Au niveau de mes pensées, au niveau mental.

AGRESSIVITÉ (voir aussi : ANGOISSE, ANXIÉTÉ, NERFS [crise de...], NERVOSITÉ, SANG — HYPOGLYCÉMIE)

L'**agressivité** est une quantité d'énergie refoulée qui découle la plupart du temps d'une frustration vécue dans une expérience ou une situation. C'est souvent inconscient et cette frustration peut empoisonner tellement ma vie et mon existence que je prends l'**agressivité** comme moyen d'expression (l'**agressivité** en est un), comme soupape à toute cette pression existant en moi. C'est un moyen de me défendre car je me sens attaqué, non respecté, abusé, tendu, incompris. Je veux que l'on me comprenne ! Il peut m'être difficile de rester ouvert et de laisser couler l'énergie. Il est évident qu'une personne en état d'**agressivité** se coupe temporairement et plus particulièrement de l'énergie spirituelle et de l'ouverture du cœur. C'est un état **inné, instantané** et irréfléchi de défense et de protection. Si je suis agressif, j'ai souvent le **sentiment** d'être le plus fort car je décide d'attaquer le premier. Je me mets dans un état de domination-soumission et je suis **déchiré** face à moi-même. La personne face à moi agit comme un **miroir**. Je projette une partie de moi qu'il me reste à accepter ↓♥ et cela **presse** mon **bouton** !5 Conséquence ? L'excitation s'amplifie, la tension monte et c'est maintenant l'apparition de la contraction musculaire ! Je suis raide et tendu, sur mes gardes, prêt à bondir contre les attaques ! Je suis sur la défensive et je lutte contre mes angoisses. Que faire ? Rester ouvert, travailler sur moi en **premier**, écouter mon intuition et ma voix intérieure qui me protègent et qui guident mes pas.

AIGREURS, BRÛLEMENTS D'ESTOMAC
(voir : ESTOMAC — BRÛLEMENTS D'ESTOMAC)

AIR (mal de l'...) (voir : MAL DE MER)

ALCOOLISME (voir aussi : ALLERGIES [en général], CANCER DE LA LANGUE, CIGARETTE, DÉPENDANCE, DROGUE, SANG — HYPOGLYCÉMIE)

L'abus des boissons alcooliques cause un ensemble de troubles : physiquement, le corps change et se crispe, les capacités et le fonctionnement du cerveau diminuent, les systèmes nerveux et musculaire deviennent **tendus et surtendus**. Semblable à toutes les autres formes de dépendance, l'**alcoolisme** se manifeste principalement au moment où j'ai besoin de **combler un vide affectif ou intérieur profond,** un aspect de moi-même qui « empoisonne » vraiment mon existence ! Je peux boire abusivement pour diverses raisons : **fuir ma réalité**, quelle que soit la situation (conflit ou

---

5. **Presse mon bouton :** Expression qui indique que l'on peut activer un élément déclencheur d'une réaction ou d'une émotion.

autre) parce que cela ne me convient pas ; résister à mes peurs, à l'autorité (surtout paternelle) et aux gens que j'aime car j'ai justement peur de me dévoiler au grand jour, tel que je suis ; me donner le **courage** d'aller de l'avant, de parler, d'affronter les gens (remarquez que, si je suis un peu « feeling »[6], je suis souvent plus ouvert car je suis moins fixé sur mes inhibitions[7]...) ; me donner un sentiment de puissance et de force ; me donner du pouvoir dans une relation affective parce que mon état va sûrement déranger l'autre. Je ne vois plus les situations qui peuvent être dangereuses pour moi. Je vis de la solitude, de l'isolement, de la **culpabilité**, de **l'angoisse intérieure**, de **l'incompréhension** et une certaine **forme d'abandon** (familial ou autre) et j'ai le sentiment d'être une personne **inutile**, **sans valeur**, inapte, inférieure et incapable d'être et d'agir pour moi-même et pour les autres. J'ai alors besoin « d'un p'tit remontant ». Souvent, je veux fuir une situation conflictuelle ou qui me fait mal en « noyant ma peine » ou toute autre émotion avec laquelle j'ai de la difficulté à « dealer »[8]. L'**alcoolisme** peut être relié à une ou à plusieurs situations qui me créent une tension. Lorsque je prends un verre d'alcool, cette tension diminue dans un premier temps et j'enregistre alors la relation qui semble être : tension — alcool — bien-être. Ce qui veut dire que lorsque je vis une tension, je prends un verre d'**alcool** et je me sens mieux. Par la suite, il se peut que je développe un **automatisme** et qu'à chaque fois que je vis une tension, l'information inscrite dans mon cerveau soit de prendre un verre d'alcool pour me sentir mieux. Une des sources de l'**alcoolisme** est la difficulté que j'ai connue, étant enfant, à transiger avec une famille où un de ces membres (et très souvent le père ou la mère) était **alcoolique** : il y a généralement plus de discorde, parfois de la violence physique et psychologique ou de l'abus de toutes sortes. Je peux même vouloir chercher à me dissocier de la famille dans laquelle je suis et qui ne me convient pas. Il y a alors baisse de mon sens moral : les spectacles de discorde fréquents provoquent chez moi une dévaluation des images parentales et la non-intégration des structures éthiques. Dans certaines familles aussi, l'accoutumance à l'alcool est favorisée par l'éducation, les adultes ayant amené l'enfant que j'étais à boire par jeu ou rendant l'absorption habituelle et régulière de boisson comme **normale**. Les troubles névrotiques et les altérations de la personnalité qui en découlent sont des facteurs puissants **d'alcoolisme** chez moi qui suis devenu adulte. Même des carences nutritionnelles peuvent conduire à la recherche d'une complémentarité alimentaire procurée par l'**alcool**. L'**alcoolisme** peut provenir aussi de mon état qui est hypoglycémique, d'autant plus que les molécules d'**alcool** peuvent se transformer rapidement en sucre sanguin (temporairement). C'est ce qui

---

6. **Feeling :** Expression utilisée pour dire qu'une personne commence à être sous l'effet de l'alcool ou un peu ivre.

7. **Inhibitions :** Phénomène d'arrêt, de blocage d'un processus psychologique.

8. « **Dealer** » **:** Anglicisme voulant dire *relever le défi*.

explique que si je suis **alcoolique** mais que j'arrête de consommer, je peux me retrouver à boire une quantité impressionnante de café, source de stimulant par la **caféine**, et de sucre, de pâtisserie ou de dessert (source de sucre). Parfois, je vais aussi fumer considérablement puisque la cigarette m'apporte la source de stimulant (augmentation du rythme cardiaque) dont j'ai besoin pour me sentir en forme. Il est important pour moi de découvrir ce qui cause cette tristesse reliée à l'hypoglycémie dans ma vie, puisque je n'ai pas réglé la cause. Une autre cause de l'**alcoolisme** peut être les allergies. Ainsi, je peux être alcoolique seulement au cognac, au gin, au rye ou au scotch, etc. Il semble que seulement cette sorte de boisson en particulier peut me satisfaire. Il est alors probable que je sois allergique à l'un ou l'autre des ingrédients qui ont servi à fabriquer cette boisson particulière, que ce soit dans un cas le blé, l'orge, le seigle, etc. Je peux alors me demander à quoi ou à qui suis-je allergique. L'**alcoolisme** peut aussi provenir d'une personne ou d'une situation que je n'ai pas acceptée ↓♥ lorsque j'étais jeune. Si j'ai été victime d'attouchements sexuels indésirables, ou dont je me sens coupable, venant d'une personne **alcoolique** lorsque j'étais jeune, il se peut qu'en pensant à cette situation, cela me porte à boire. Si je n'ai pas accepté ↓♥ la colère de mon père alcoolique, il se peut très bien que, par un phénomène d'association, je fasse des colères **comme mon père** et que je devienne **alcoolique**. Ainsi, je peux boire pour oublier mes soucis, mon passé et l'avenir mais surtout le **présent**. Je fuis sans cesse et je me crée un univers illusoire et fantaisiste, une forme d'exaltation artificielle pour fuir le monde physique et ainsi dissocier une réalité souvent difficile d'un rêve continuellement insatisfait. Je perds alors contact, pour un certain temps, avec mes sentiments de solitude, d'incompréhension, d'impuissance, de ne pas être comme les autres, de rejet de moi-même. Je peux abandonner mes responsabilités et j'en suis « délivré » pour un moment. Cette situation ne fait qu'empirer à mesure que je manifeste une dépendance à l'**alcool** (ou aux drogues) car je deviens de plus en plus insatisfait de mon existence. Je veux me séparer de la réalité en m'en allant dans un monde d'illusion mais, quand je « dégrise », la réalité m'apparaît encore plus difficile à vivre et alors survient la dépression. Je n'ai pas toute ma **tête**, surtout lorsque je deviens dépendant, du même type de dépendance affective que **j'aurais peut-être voulu avoir** et que j'ai l'impression que **mon père ou ma mère** ne m'ont jamais donnée. Être aimé sans condition... Il est temps de mettre l'attention sur mes belles qualités physiques et spirituelles, même si le passé a été douloureux pour moi et que, d'une certaine façon, ma bouteille a souvent été mon **meilleur ami**. À partir de maintenant, j'accepte ↓♥ de régler ma vie, de commencer à aimer mes qualités et ce que je suis. Je suis maintenant sur la voie de la réussite. Je serai à même de me respecter davantage et de trouver plus facilement la solution à mes problèmes (expériences) au lieu d'être dans un état temporaire ou presque permanent de fuite et de désespoir.

ALEXIE CONGÉNITALE (aveuglement des mots)
(voir : YEUX — ALEXIE CONGÉNITALE)

ALLERGIE(S) (en général) (voir aussi : ALCOOLISME, ASTHME)

L'**allergie** est l'état d'un sujet qui, par contact antérieur avec un antigène approprié, a acquis la propriété de réagir lors d'une agression seconde par le même antigène d'une manière différente, souvent plus violente et incontrôlable. Une **allergie** est une réponse suractivée du système immunitaire à un antigène extérieur. La substance allergène n'entraîne pas de réaction chez la plupart des gens mais est identifiée à moi comme dangereuse par le système immunitaire. Cette réponse, résultant d'une cause intérieure, est souvent le moyen par lequel le corps m'indique que je vis un état d'agressivité et d'hostilité par rapport à une personne ou à une situation quelconque, en fonction de l'interprétation par le mental de ce que je vis de si spécial. Les **allergies** (incluant la fièvre des foins) sont semblables à l'asthme mais la réaction se situe davantage au niveau des yeux, du nez et de la gorge, plutôt que dans les poumons et sur la poitrine. À quoi suis-je **allergique** ? Qu'est-ce qui me suractive tant ? Qu'est-ce qui cause réellement l'irritation et la forte réponse émotionnelle de mon corps (reniflement, écoulement des yeux, envie de pleurer) ? Ce sont toutes des réponses du **système émotionnel**, la libération d'émotions supprimées par une réaction de mon corps. Celui-ci réagit à quelque chose, une sorte de symbole mental, parce qu'il essaie de rejeter, d'occulter[9] ou d'ignorer ce qui le dérange. Je rejette donc une partie de moi qui m'agresse. C'est le moyen que j'utilise pour exprimer mes émotions, pour **faire sortir le méchant** ! Rien ne peut arrêter cette réaction de refus pour l'instant et cela n'est pas rationnel, parce que cela fait partie du domaine de l'instinct et de l'inconscient. C'est comme s'il y avait quelque chose qui n'a pas affaire là, un **ennemi** qui dérange mes barrières de protection. Cet ennemi prend ce **pouvoir**, mon pouvoir d'être et de faire, et cela m'impressionne. Je suis **impressionné** par le pouvoir des autres au détriment du mien. Je me sens menacé par une certaine peur inconsciente que je refuse de vivre. Les **allergies** tendent donc à indiquer un **profond niveau d'intolérance**, peut-être la peur d'avoir à participer pleinement à la vie, à me libérer de toutes béquilles émotives qui me supportent et qui me permettraient de vivre l'autosuffisance. J'ai peut-être de la difficulté à discerner, à choisir, à prendre la place qui me revient. La caractéristique propre à la personne **allergique** est souvent l'impression de ne pas être **assez correct** ! Je veux attirer et avoir l'attention, la sympathie et le support d'autrui. Est-ce que j'utilise l'**allergie** pour avoir de l'amour ? C'est possible. En tout cas, une chose est sûre: j'ai une **allergie** parce que je refuse une partie de moi-même et mon combat inconscient est grand. **C'est ma résistance, ma façon de dire non**. J'ai le pouvoir de décider ce qui est convenable pour moi dans mon propre univers.

---

9. **Occulter :** Effacer de ma mémoire consciente ou de ma sensibilité.

13

Les individus peuvent être **allergiques** à toutes sortes de choses : aliments, objets, formes, odeurs. Tout ce qui, de près ou de loin, implique les cinq sens (particulièrement l'odorat qui est le sens le plus puissant du point de vue de la mémoire). Mon mental enregistre une foule d'impressions **bonnes ou mauvaises** pour moi. Il est fort possible que si je suis **allergique** à quelque chose, c'est que mon mental l'a associé à un certain souvenir **bon ou mauvais** et que mon instinct le refoule en ce moment. L'**allergie** apparaît souvent à la suite d'un événement où je me suis senti **séparé** d'une chose, d'un animal, d'une personne. Lorsque je revis une situation qui me rappelle cet événement triste et déchirant pour moi, j'aurai cette **allergie** car, quelque part, mon corps (mes sens) se souvient de tout et tout est enregistré dans mes cellules. Si la situation vécue s'accompagne d'une grande angoisse, ce sont mes sinus qui seront touchés (**rhume des foins**, éternuements). Si la peur prédomine, mon **allergie** s'exprimera plus par la toux (difficulté à respirer) et si c'est plutôt la séparation elle-même que j'ai vécue difficilement, les réactions allergènes se retrouveront plus du côté de la peau (eczéma, urticaire, dermite etc.). L'**allergie** à un aliment (par exemple : le sucre et l'alcool chez l'alcoolique) est reliée à une expérience où, étant placé dans une situation où j'ai dû dire **non** à ce que j'aimais peut-être le plus, la fustration s'en suit et j'y deviens **allergique**. C'est souvent une peur du nouveau et de l'aventure, un manque de confiance face à la vie. Je me sens maintenant obligé de me priver de cette sorte de joie, en pensant que la vie est quelque chose d'ordinaire, sans défi. Qu'est-ce que je veux éviter d'affronter ? Qu'est-ce qui me fait tant réagir ? Qui m'effraie tant intérieurement ? Y a-t-il quelque chose dont je me méfie au point de l'éloigner de moi ? Il semble que, dans certains cas, mon mental fasse une association de certaines situations avec des substances par le biais des homonymes. Ainsi, si j'ai dû laisser mon travail (mon boulot) que j'aimais pour me consacrer à la vie religieuse, je suis devenu **allergique** au bouleau (l'arbre). Quelques années plus tard, ayant accepté ↓♥ et intégré ce changement, l'**allergie** a disparu. Voici un autre exemple : un bébé nouveau-né est **allergique** aux pêches (le fruit). Pourquoi ? Parce que sa mère impatiente et sur le point d'accoucher, quelques mois auparavant, avait dit à son conjoint : « *Dépêche-toi, on va être en retard à l'hôpital !* » Ici, le mot « dépêche », est l'homonyme de « **des pêches** ». Ainsi, à la base de l'**allergie,** il y a toujours une émotion d'irritabilité ou de frustration associée à un produit ou à une situation pour ce qu'il représente pour me rappeler ce malaise à intégrer ou à conscientiser. En commençant à accepter ↓♥ au niveau du cœur ma vie et mes peurs, le processus d'intégration s'enclenchera et les **allergies** qui compliquent mon existence retourneront dans l'univers. J'ai besoin de paix intérieure et surtout d'amour. Je reste ouvert et tout sera pour le mieux.

ALLERGIE AUX ANTIBIOTIQUES

L'**antibiotique**[10] (anti = *contre*/bio = *vie*) est un corps (d'origine bactérienne ou autre) spécialisé dans la lutte contre les microbes. Mais les microbes représentent eux aussi la vie. Il y a donc contradiction. Comme le rôle de l'antibiotique est de « tuer » une certaine forme de vie en moi, pourquoi donc serais-je **allergique aux antibiotiques** ? Probablement parce que je refuse certaines formes de vie, certaines situations **vivantes** de mon existence (expériences diverses et plus ou moins agréables). J'ai une prise de conscience à faire et c'est d'accepter ↓♥ ces expériences car, même si elles peuvent être difficiles pour moi, j'ai une leçon à tirer de celles-ci. Je fais confiance à mon potentiel créatif.

ALLERGIE AUX ANIMAUX (en général)

Les **animaux** possèdent un instinct et une sexualité innés et chaque animal représente une facette de l'amour. Donc, une **allergie à un animal**, en général, correspond à de la **résistance** par rapport à l'aspect instinctif ou sexuel que l'animal représente pour moi. J'accepte ↓♥ tous les aspects de la sexualité. J'accepte ↓♥ aussi mes désirs, tant conscients qu'inconscients, car ils font partie intégrante de mon être.

ALLERGIE AUX CHATS

Le **chat** est un animal beaucoup plus sensible à ce qui est **invisible** que la majorité des personnes. Il se peut qu'une **allergie aux chats** soit davantage en rapport avec l'aspect de ma personnalité qui peut « sentir » des choses (côté ou aspect féminin), sans pour autant que j'aie des preuves concrètes de ceci. Je peux donc vivre de l'intolérance car je n'ai pas de preuve (sur le plan rationnel). Il est donc clair que le **chat (ou la chatte)** symbolise le **côté sexuel féminin**[11], et toutes les qualités féminines telles que douceur, charme et tendresse. J'ai donc à accepter ↓♥ un de ces aspects que je refuse probablement, soit de recevoir ou de manifester.

NOTE : Cette **sensibilité féline** s'explique par le fait que la morphologie du chat possède un système nerveux situé surtout en périphérie du corps, contrairement à l'être humain dont le système nerveux est davantage à l'intérieur du corps. Cette morphologie particulière rend le chat plus **sensible** aux vibrations ou aux énergies particulières des personnes et des endroits ou, si l'on veut, de ce qu'une personne ou un endroit **dégage**.

---

10. **Antibiotique :** C'est à Sir Alexander Flemming, ce médecin et bactériologiste britannique(Darve 1881 - Londres 1955) que l'on doit la découverte, en 1928, de la pénicilline qui ne pourra être extraite qu'en 1939 et essayée sur les humains en 1941, ce qui a ouvert l'ère des antibiotiques.

11. **Féminin :** Voir : FÉMININ (principe...)

ALLERGIE AUX CHEVAUX

Le **cheval** est associé à **l'aspect instinctif de la sexualité**. Comme l'instinct est relié davantage au premier chakra (ou coccyx)[12], la peur peut se traduire par celle « d'avoir de bas instincts sexuels », et se manifeste par une **allergie** à cet animal fort et fougueux. Il se peut que je trouve que la sexualité n'est pas assez spirituelle pour moi-même, si je sens au fond de moi le désir de vivre ces expériences pour m'aider à amener davantage la spiritualité dans la matière. Je m'ouvre donc à de nouvelles expériences qui vont m'aider à me connaître davantage et à m'épanouir.

ALLERGIE AUX CHIENS

On dit que le **chien** est le « *meilleur ami de l'homme* » (de l'être humain), alors je peux me demander, lorsque je vis ce type d'**allergie**, quelle personne ou quelle situation par rapport à l'amitié fait monter de la colère en moi. Si je suis **allergique aux chiens**, je peux même vivre de l'agressivité et même une certaine violence vis-à-vis de la sexualité que je relie à l'amitié. Il se peut que je vive un malaise, ne sachant pas très bien définir pour moi la place que prennent la sexualité, l'amitié et l'amour. Ce malaise fait monter de la colère en moi, qui se manifeste sous forme d'**allergie**. Je délimite les paramètres de l'amitié, je la définis afin d'éclaircir certaines situations de ma vie qui se trouvent peut-être pour le moment dans une zone grise. Je me respecte dans mes besoins et dans mes choix.

ALLERGIE — FIÈVRE DES FOINS (RHUME)

Cette **allergie** est fondamentalement à la base d'une réaction au pollen, grain végétal formant l'**élément masculin** de la fleur. Cet élément masculin véhicule le symbole de la reproduction et de la fertilisation. Cette **allergie** affecte habituellement les yeux, le nez et les sinus. L'**allergie** est à la base d'une **résistance** à une situation dans ma vie, d'un souvenir passé. Il est donc possible que **je résiste** souvent inconsciemment **à une forme de la sexualité ou à certains aspects de celle-ci**, surtout si ce que je sens par rapport à la sexualité ne « sent pas bon ». Il est certain que je peux **m'attirer** une allergie pour plusieurs raisons mais une chose est sûre : j'étouffe ou je me sens étouffé par une situation. Je me révolte, quelque chose ne me convient pas du tout mais je le fais quand même pour faire plaisir et j'étouffe. Je change d'idée sous l'influence de quelqu'un, je suis prêt à n'importe quoi, et j'étouffe. Je peux me sentir **étouffé** dans les choses à dire ou à faire, surtout que j'ai de la difficulté à prendre ma place et à dire non. J'ai tendance à vivre aussi beaucoup de culpabilité. Je manipule pour avoir ce que je veux... Vous voyez

---

12. **Premier chakra :** Le premier chakra est l'un des sept principaux centres d'énergie dans le corps et il est situé au niveau du coccyx, à la base de la colonne vertébrale.

la programmation ? Elle peut être autant mentale (manière de pleurer) que « saisonnière », car la période estivale est idéale pour la manifestation de cette allergie, surtout si j'ai besoin d'une excuse pour en faire moins durant cette belle période de l'année ! Certaines personnes ont la **fièvre des foins** pendant des périodes allant jusqu'à sept ans ! Il est temps que je change cela immédiatement ou du moins que j'en prenne conscience. Je prends conscience que le **rhume des foins** peut devenir un moyen qui me permet d'éviter certaines situations, car je ne serais pas capable de toute façon de refuser de faire une tâche ou d'aller à un endroit en particulier. Donc, maintenant, j'ai une bonne raison ! En prenant mon espace vital, ma « bulle » de lumière[13], je suis en mesure de m'ouvrir aux autres sous mon vrai jour, sans artifices. La première manifestation du **rhume des foins** peut avoir été inconsciemment reliée à un événement marquant et où j'ai probablement vécu de fortes émotions. Lorsque la même période de l'année revient, je me souviens ou, plutôt, mon corps se souvient et c'est le **rhume des foins** qui apparaît. Il est donc important que je prenne conscience de cet événement pour que je puisse briser le « pattern » de la maladie : je n'aurai plus besoin d'elle à l'avenir car j'ai fait la prise de conscience que je devais faire. Le **rhume des foins** n'était qu'un signe pour m'aider à arrêter et à trouver la cause profonde de mon malaise. Je vais me sentir plus libre, plus maître de ma vie. J'accepte ↓♥ ce qui est bon pour moi-même, même si cela implique une certaine forme de sexualité nouvelle et inconnue. Je sais que tout est possible, dans l'amour et l'harmonie.

ALLERGIE AUX FRAISES

L'**allergie aux fraises** est associée à de la frustration qui met en contradiction le sentiment d'amour et de plaisir, ce dernier étant un besoin fondamental pour moi, aussi bien que la nourriture ou le sommeil. Cette **allergie** peut provenir d'un événement que j'ai vécu ou justement que je n'ai pas vécu par rapport à une personne ou à une situation. Un sentiment de haine et de frustration allié à de la culpabilité peut faire naître en moi cette **allergie**. Le plaisir fait tellement partie de ma vie, en tant qu'être humain, que les fortes crises d'**allergie aux fraises** peuvent provoquer une incapacité à respirer, pouvant amener la mort. Les poumons représentent la vie et je mets ainsi en évidence, par ma crise, un besoin fondamental dans ma vie qui n'a pas été comblé. Il est important que je prenne conscience de mes besoins fondamentaux en sachant que lorsque je prends de la nourriture, c'est de l'amour que j'ai pour moi ; lorsque je prends du sommeil, c'est de l'amour que j'ai pour moi; lorsque j'ai du plaisir, c'est aussi de l'amour que j'ai pour moi. L'**allergie aux fraises** peut provenir aussi d'un sentiment que j'ai pu

---

13. **Ma « bulle » de lumière :** Je peux m'imaginer et me visualiser dans une bulle de lumière, ce qui augmente ma protection face à mon environnement et me donne davantage confiance.

ressentir à l'endroit d'une personne ou qu'une personne a éprouvé à mon égard. Par exemple j'ai pu me dire : « *J'y aime pas la fraise, celui-là* », voulant signifier qu'il a un visage que je n'aime pas ou, comme on dit : « un visage qui ne me revient pas ». Je dois accepter ↓♥ que chacun d'entre nous a son individualité avec ses qualités et ses peurs, et qu'en chaque être, il y a cette étincelle qui brille.

ALLERGIE À L'HUILE ou AU BEURRE D'ARACHIDE

Lorsque je prends de l'**huile d'arachide** ou du **beurre d'arachide,** cela active en moi la mémoire d'un événement où lorsque étant jeune, j'en ai particulièrement « arraché ». J'ai alors pu avoir l'impression que l'on me faisait faire des travaux sans que je me sente suffisamment rémunéré (en argent, en affection, etc.). Cela me mettait intérieurement en colère de travailler « pour des peanuts[14] ». En essayant de trouver l'événement ou les situations où j'ai pu vivre un tel sentiment, je pourrai modifier ma mémoire émotive et régulariser la situation. Je prends conscience de tous les aspects de ma vie où je me sens aidé et où la vie est pour moi relativement facile, et j'amplifie ce sentiment de bien-être pour m'aider à équilibrer les sentiments de difficulté que j'ai pu enregistrer dans mon enfance.

ALLERGIE AU LAIT ou AUX PRODUITS LAITIERS

Le lait représente le **contact** avec la mère dès les premiers instants de mon arrivée en ce monde. C'est un aliment complet qui me permet d'avoir tous les nutriments dont j'ai besoin pour ma croissance dans les premières semaines de ma vie. Puisque originellement j'obtiens ce lait avec le **contact** avec ma mère, cette nourriture est en plus significative de **l'amour que je reçois de ma mère.** Alors, si dans mon entourage, il y a une personne que j'ai identifiée, soit ma mère ou une autre personne « qui joue le rôle de ma mère » et que je vis de la frustration par rapport à elle dans le rôle que je lui ai prêté, cela peut expliquer pourquoi je fais **une allergie au lait.** Je vis de la frustration par rapport à la forme d'attention et même de critique que cette personne me porte, ce qui rend désagréable le « contact » que je peux avoir avec elle. Si cette **allergie** se développe à la naissance, je dois vérifier quelles sont les peurs ou les frustrations que pouvait vivre ma mère lorsqu'elle me portait, faisant miennes ses peurs ou ses frustrations qui m'ont amené à vivre cette **allergie.** Cette attention que l'on me porte pourrait me faire dire : « *Pour qui elle se prend ? Se prend-elle pour ma mère ?* » Il est important pour moi de mettre de l'amour dans la situation et d'harmoniser mes sentiments par rapport à ce lien privilégié et fondamental pour la survie de l'espèce et qui est enregistré en moi, celui du lien d'une mère et de son enfant.

---

14. **Peanuts :** Au Québec, on utilise souvent le mot anglais « peanuts » pour **arachides**. « Travailler pour des peanuts » signifie : « Travailler pour presque rien ».

ALLERGIE AUX PIQÛRES DE GUÊPES ou D'ABEILLES

J'ai certainement l'impression d'être constamment **harcelé** ou **critiqué** par mon entourage immédiat. Ainsi, cela agit sur moi comme si « on me piquait » constamment. Lorsque je me fais réellement piquer physiquement, cela fait se déclencher la haine que j'ai accumulée en moi dans toutes ces situations où je me sentais attaqué. J'apprends à prendre la place qui me revient et j'examine les moyens à prendre pour que la critique diminue dans mon entourage et que je puisse me détacher davantage de ce que les autres peuvent penser de moi.

ALLERGIE AUX PLUMES

Suis-je devenu **allergique** à une situation ou à une personne qui me donne l'impression d'être **cloué au sol** et de ne pouvoir **m'envoler** pour me sentir plus libre et heureux ? Il est alors très probable que je vive de la colère reliée au fait que j'éprouve intérieurement le sentiment de me **sentir pris** entre une situation quelconque et la **liberté que je recherche** pour être plus heureux.

ALLERGIE AUX POISSONS ou AUX FRUITS DE MER

Je connais l'expression « être **poisson** » qui veut dire que je suis une personne qui « se fait avoir » facilement. Ainsi, mon **allergie** traduit bien mon sentiment de **frustration** face à une ou à plusieurs situations où **je me suis trouvé naïf**. Je dois prendre ma place et prendre conscience que la vie est une suite d'expériences pour apprendre. Plus j'augmenterai ma confiance en moi et mon sens des responsabilités, plus ce sentiment s'estompera et fera disparaître cette **allergie**.

ALLERGIE AU POLLEN (voir : ALLERGIE — FIÈVRE DES FOINS)

ALLERGIE À LA POUSSIÈRE

Comme la **poussière** est reliée à la **saleté** et à **l'impureté**, si je suis **allergique à la poussière**, je vis de l'insécurité face à des aspects de ma vie que je peux croire être « sales et impurs » et il est fort probable que cette peur se manifeste dans ma sexualité. Si je suis **allergique à la poussière**, il se peut que j'aie grandement à m'occuper de l'estime de moi. Aussi, l'expression utilisée dans la religion : « *Tu es poussière et tu retourneras en poussière* » traduit bien le sentiment d'inutilité que je peux vivre ou sentir dans certaines situations. L'expression « *Tout s'envole en poussière* » permet aussi de traduire le sentiment d'inutilité qui peut m'habiter face à ce que j'ai entrepris ou à ce que j'entreprends, que ce soit sur le plan psychologique, affectif (émotionnel) ou matériel. Même si je n'ai pas de symptôme physique lié à une **allergie à la**

poussière, il se peut que je sois une personne « maniaque de la propreté ». Ici, je veux dire de façon excessive. Je peux alors regarder quelle partie de moi peut trouver ma sexualité sale ou me demander si j'ai peur que ce soit sale. J'apprends à me valoriser et à valoriser tout ce que je fais.

ALZHEIMER[15] (maladie d'...) (voir aussi : AMNÉSIE)

Cette maladie amène une dégénérescence des cellules du cerveau qui se traduit par une perte progressive des facultés intellectuelles conduisant à un état démentiel (la folie). Cette maladie des temps modernes, caractérisée principalement par le désir inconscient de terminer sa vie, d'en finir une fois pour toutes, de quitter ce monde ou de **fuir ma réalité,** est due à l'incapacité chronique d'accepter ↓♥, de faire face ou de « *dealer* »[16] avec cette même réalité, avec les situations de la vie car j'ai peur et j'ai mal. Je me rends ainsi insensible à mon entourage et à mes émotions intérieures. « Je m'engourdis », « je m'étourdis » et la vie me semble ainsi plus facile. L'**Alzheimer** se rapporte à une certaine forme de démence. Cette manifestation amène principalement la dégradation de ma mémoire, la confusion mentale et l'incapacité à m'exprimer clairement, la violence, certaines formes d'inconscience de l'environnement, même un comportement d'innocence se rapprochant de celui de l'enfant. **Le désespoir, l'irritabilité, le mal de vivre** m'amènent à me replier sur moi-même et à vivre « dans ma bulle ». Je me laisse « mourir à petit feu ». Cette maladie m'indique que j'ai le mal de vivre, que je fuis une situation qui me fait peur, m'irrite ou me blesse. C'est une situation grave à première vue dont je peux rester inconscient longtemps. On me voit comme une personne « normale » et équilibrée mais on constate que je me replie sur moi-même par désespoir, colère ou frustration, ce qui me rend insensible au monde qui m'entoure. Je refuse de sentir ce qui se passe autour de moi et en moi ; je préfère me laisser aller. Je peux avoir beaucoup de difficulté à laisser aller mes vieilles idées tellement il y en a dans ma mémoire ! Et comme mon attention est beaucoup plus centrée sur le passé que sur l'**instant présent**, la mémoire à court terme devient complètement déficiente et s'**atrophie**, n'apportant rien de nouveau ni de créatif. Conséquence : la mémoire s'**use** de vieilles choses au lieu de générer des idées neuves et fraîches. Du point de vue médical, les facteurs émotionnels et mentaux ainsi que leurs correspondances corporelles (liquides, sang, tissus et os) sont impliqués dans la manifestation de cette maladie. Lorsque le sang est supprimé de certaines régions du cerveau, une sorte de traumatisme mental en résulte. Ce sont des réactions très violentes au niveau cérébral. C'est une sorte de retrait du flot sanguin cérébral de ces régions. Il peut y avoir une peur extrême de toutes les facettes de la vieillesse ou de l'aube de la mort, ce qui entraîne un retour inconscient vers un

---

15. **ALZHEIMER (Alois) :** Neuropathologiste allemand qui décrivit en 1906 des   altérations du cerveau sur une personne atteinte de démence (folie).

16. **« Dealer » :** Anglicisme voulant dire *relever le défi*.

comportement d'enfant et l'occultation[17] du présent, du passé et de l'avenir pour les ignorer. Mon corps, attaqué par la dégénérescence des cellules du cerveau, me prépare inconsciemment à cette période où je devrai « partir[18] ». Cela se traduit par un comportement enfantin où je me permets de vivre et de « réaliser » tous mes fantasmes et toutes mes fantaisies. L'amour et le soutien sont nécessaires dans une telle expérience. Je vis le moment présent et j'accepte ↓♥ de laisser aller le passé en commençant à m'occuper de moi !

AMÉNORRHÉE (absence des règles)
(voir : MENSTRUATIONS — AMÉNORRHÉE)

AMNÉSIE (voir aussi : MÉMOIRE [... défaillante])

L'**amnésie** est la perte de ma mémoire, partielle ou totale, autant des informations déjà acquises dans le passé que celles présentes. L'**amnésie** est comparable à la maladie d'Alzheimer sous plusieurs aspects. La personne **amnésique** souffre terriblement du moment présent dans sa vie actuelle. Mon **désir de fuir** et de « partir » est tellement grand (peu importe la situation vécue) que je me replie sur moi par **douleur, colère, incapacité** ou **désespoir** et je m'enferme en devenant insensible à presque tout. Je m'évade, je m'engourdis ou je me rends insensible à une personne ou à une situation. Je refuse de vivre les situations et les expériences de tous les jours, peu importe leur intensité. La douleur intérieure est proportionnelle à la gravité de l'**amnésie**, qu'elle soit partielle (occultation[19] mentale partielle d'images très douloureuses de l'enfance) ou totale (tentative inconsciente d'avoir une nouvelle vie et un nouveau désir de vivre car je ne peux plus vivre avec cette **première** vie !). La honte et la culpabilité peuvent se manifester, quelle que soit la raison. Je tente d'ignorer plusieurs choses, dont ma famille et plusieurs situations difficiles. Je suis plus ou moins séparé de la réalité présente. Le processus d'acceptation ↓♥ et d'intégration est très important car le phénomène d'**occultation** de certaines expériences par le mental peut me jouer des tours dans des expériences futures. Il est possible que je vive certaines d'entre elles sans savoir ni comprendre pourquoi elles m'arrivent ! C'est une prise de conscience quotidienne par rapport à qui je suis et à ce qu'il me reste à régler dans ma vie pour reprendre contact avec mon vrai **moi supérieur**.

AMPHÉTAMINE (consommation d'...) (voir : DROGUE)

---

17. **Occultation :** Le fait d'effacer de sa mémoire consciente ou de sa sensibilité.
18. **Partir :** Employé ici de préférence au terme « mourir ».
19. **Occultation :** Le fait d'effacer quelque chose de sa mémoire consciente ou de sa sensibilité.

AMPOULES (voir : PEAU — AMPOULES)

AMPUTATION (voir aussi : AUTOMUTILATION)

L'**amputation** totale ou partielle d'un membre, qu'elle soit pratiquée pour des raisons accidentelles ou médicales (gangrène, tumeur), est très souvent reliée à une **grande culpabilité** face à un aspect de ma vie. Si on **ampute** mon pied gauche, c'est comme si ma peur ou ma culpabilité est telle que je

préfère « mourir » à la direction à prendre ou à celle que j'ai prise dans ma vie affective ; la jambe droite concerne ma peur ou ma culpabilité devant mes responsabilités, etc. Si je vis une **amputation**, il est important de me rappeler que mon corps, énergétiquement, n'est pas amputé, afin de rester ouvert à l'aspect métaphysique que représente la partie amputée. Ainsi, si j'ai eu la jambe droite **amputée,** je peux mettre l'amour, la compréhension et l'intégration pour la prise de conscience que j'ai à faire pour aller plus rapidement de l'avant dans mes responsabilités **comme si j'avais toujours ma jambe**. Je fais disparaître toute culpabilité, en sachant que je fais toujours pour le mieux.

AMYGDALES — AMYGDALITE (voir aussi : GORGE, INFECTION)

Les **amygdales,** qui signifient « amandes », font partie du système immunitaire et de la lymphe (liquide nettoyant du corps humain) et sont définies comme des filtres qui contrôlent tout ce qui circule au niveau de la gorge (qui correspond à la créativité, à la communication). Lorsqu'elles sont enflammées, j'ai de la **difficulté à avaler** et je risque d'étouffer. Je refoule ainsi mes émotions et « j'étouffe » ma créativité. Il y a une situation qui m'étouffe à travers laquelle je refoule mes sentiments de **colère** et de **frustration**. Une **amygdalite (ite = colère)** se manifeste généralement lorsque ma réalité que j'avale amène une **intense irritation** au point où mes filtres (**les amygdales**) ne peuvent tout prendre et deviennent rouges de colère par rapport à ce qui arrive, à la révolte intérieure que je vis. Ce peut être la peur de ne pas pouvoir atteindre un but visé ou de ne pas être capable de réaliser quelque chose d'important pour moi, faute de temps ou d'opportunité. J'ai l'impression que je suis sur le point d'obtenir quelque chose qui m'est cher (un travail, un conjoint, une auto, etc.) mais je crains qu'elle m'échappe et que je doive m'en passer, ou que je ne puisse en jouir qu'en partie ou pas pleinement, ce que je trouve « dur à avaler ». Un conflit intérieur très intense est « étouffé » et non exprimé. C'est un blocage, la fermeture de cette voie de communication. Ai-je l'impression qu'il y a une situation que « j'avale de travers » ? Je vis de la rébellion face une personne proche de moi (famille, école, travail) voire même de la révolte. Si je suis un enfant, j'ai souvent des **amygdalites** car je ne suis pas encore suffisamment conscient de ce qui arrive ou je n'ai pas le contrôle des événements. Je vis de la **frustration** liée à ce que

je dois « avaler » dans la vie. Si je veux régler l'**amygdalite**, j'accepte ↓♥ les choses telles qu'elles sont autour de moi, je prends le temps d'analyser les situations qui dérangent ma vie avec calme et sérénité. Il est possible et facile d'enseigner cette attitude aux enfants qui sont prêts à cela. Notons que **l'ablation des amygdales** signifie l'acceptation ↓♥ d'avaler la réalité sans qu'elle soit filtrée ou censurée (protégée) au préalable. C'est une absence de protection. Je dois traiter cette situation d'une façon différente qui serait plus harmonieuse pour moi.

ANDROPAUSE (voir aussi : PROSTATE / [en général] / [maux de...])

L'**andropause,** propre à l'homme, correspond à la ménopause chez la femme, même si cela ne correspond pas à un changement hormonal équivalent. Toutes les insécurités reliées à la vieillesse, aux capacités sexuelles, aux sentiments d'inutilité et de faiblesse se manifestent intérieurement et physiquement par des malaises aux organes génitaux (surtout la prostate) et à un ou plusieurs aspects du concept masculin. En tant qu'homme, je dois prendre ma place dans l'univers en harmonie avec chaque aspect de ma personne, le côté féminin autant que le côté masculin.

ANÉMIE (voir : SANG — ANÉMIE)

ANGINE (en général) (voir aussi : GORGE [maux de...])

L'**angine** est caractérisée par un resserrement au niveau de la gorge, dû à une inflammation aiguë du pharynx. Il y a quelque chose qui ne « passe pas », une émotion bloquée qui m'empêche de dire à mon entourage mes véritables besoins. J'ai le sentiment qu'en serrant la gorge (chakra ou centre d'énergie de la créativité et de **l'expression**), je ne peux exprimer ce que je vis et ce que je ressens face aux autres et je continue à mettre inutilement l'attention sur cette croyance. Je dois trouver ce qui m'a amené à penser à cela. Je peux habituellement trouver une réponse dans les dernières **48 heures** précédant le malaise. Serait-ce une légère irritation (conduit enflammé) ou une petite frustration **que je n'avale pas** et qui subsistera jusqu'à ce que je change mon attitude et mes pensées ? « Pas question d'avaler cette histoire » même si cela « me met le feu à la gorge ». Ce peut aussi être des pensées noires et négatives par rapport à quelqu'un ou à une situation. Y a-t-il quelque chose que je veux absolument « attraper » ; comme, par exemple, un nouvel emploi, un résultat scolaire exceptionnel qui m'éviterait une situation où j'aurais à me justifier, à m'expliquer ou à rendre des comptes ? Peu importe la raison, il est temps de rester ouvert et de réouvrir ce canal même si **ma vive sensibilité a été blessée**. Mes besoins fondamentaux doivent être satisfaits et j'y ai droit comme tout le monde. Je reste ouvert à mes besoins et centré sur mon être intérieur si je veux éviter ce genre d'**angine** au niveau de la gorge.

ANGINE DE POITRINE ou ANGOR (voir aussi : CŒUR)

Angine vient du mot latin ANGENE qui signifie **serrer**. C'est un malaise très vif associé à la région principale du cœur (centre énergétique de l'amour). Ce manque temporaire d'oxygène au niveau des muscles entourant le cœur apporte toutes les conséquences que je connais : insuffisance du débit sanguin dans cette région, intervention chirurgicale, pontage, etc. Le cœur représente souvent le moteur ou **l'engin** de mon système. Lorsque je donne trop d'amour (avec une attitude d'attachement), il se peut que le cœur se fatigue de toutes ces préoccupations et qu'il n'éprouve plus suffisamment de joie[20] dans ces situations (d'où le débit sanguin diminué). Si je suis en situation d'**angine**, je prends possiblement la vie et les choses que je fais et que j'aime **beaucoup trop à cœur**. Mes inquiétudes (autant que mes joies) sont amplifiées exagérément : je m'irrite et je me blesse facilement, je vis de l'insatisfaction, de la tristesse ou de l'irritation par rapport à une situation qui, somme toute, **n'est pas si grave que cela**. Il se peut que je reçoive un premier signal d'alarme de mon corps à la suite de ces états d'être : spasmes ou douleur perçant le cœur. Ce dernier lance un S.O.S afin que je prenne conscience des sentiments qui m'habitent et du fait que je suis en quelque sorte en train de me détruire par mes pensées disharmonieuses, mettant en péril mon harmonie intérieure, et me donnant « mauvaise conscience ». De grandes joies peuvent aussi amener des crises d'**angine** car, à ce moment, le centre d'énergie de l'amour (le cœur) s'ouvre davantage et peut activer la mémoire de grandes peines qui sont présentes et ainsi provoquer une crise d'**angine**. Je fais peut-être beaucoup par obligation et non avec joie et plaisir. Ainsi, la joie arrête de circuler. C'est comme si je mettais l'attention sur les autres (leur bonheur et leurs malaises) plutôt que sur mon bien-être à moi en premier. Mon ego est tellement présent et **actif** qu'il est séparé de la totalité de l'être, ce qui entraîne un **blocage sur le plan émotionnel**. C'est une augmentation inconsciente de l'estime de soi en plaçant presque exclusivement l'attention sur autrui. C'est le principe judéo-chrétien du don par le sacrifice : **Donner aux autres ! Je deviens vulnérable et la peur de m'ouvrir à ceux que j'aime se manifeste**. « Plus rien ne m'atteint mais les douleurs commencent ! » Spasmes, points au cœur, extrémités froides (mains et pieds). Mon corps m'avertit sérieusement que quelque chose cloche (cet avertissement est généralement plus reconnaissable sur le plan métaphysique-psychique que physique). Je peux vouloir inconsciemment quitter la « vie terrestre » parce que j'ai l'impression d'être étouffé par les soucis et que je ne sais pas comment m'en sortir, mais le temps n'est pas nécessairement venu ! Qu'est-ce que je crains, au fond ? La vie est un échange continuel. Je donne autant que je reçois, comme la contraction et la dilatation des vaisseaux sanguins, sinon je vis un déséquilibre et mon attention doit revenir à cet équilibre nécessaire à une vie

---

20. **Joie :** Puisque le sang est relié à la joie, une diminution du débit sanguin exprime justement cette diminution de la joie reliée à l'amour.

saine. C'est un processus fondamental dans l'existence humaine car je suis un être divin qui doit s'exprimer dans cet équilibre. Ma prise de conscience est celle-ci : Je cesse de prendre la vie au sérieux et je reste ouvert ! C'est facile car je n'ai pas envie de mourir mais j'ai **envie de vivre**, de m'ouvrir à l'amour et de cesser toute lutte de pouvoir. Je mets mon attention sur les beaux côtés de la vie. J'apprends à m'aimer tel que je suis : mon énergie vitale pourra ainsi reprendre vie. Ce sont les premiers pas vers un rétablissement sérieux de cette maladie. Un dernier point à signaler : surveiller toutes les expressions reliées au cœur : « un cœur de pierre, un cœur dur, il n'a pas de cœur, c'est un sans cœur » etc. Chaque expression est l'indication qu'il se passe quelque chose qui mérite mon attention...

ANGIOME PLAN (voir : TACHES DE VIN)

ANGOISSE (voir aussi : ANXIÉTÉ, CLAUSTROPHOBIE)

L'**angoisse** est caractérisée par un état de désarroi psychique où j'ai le sentiment d'être **limité** et **restreint dans mon espace** et surtout **étouffé** dans mes désirs. Je sens mon espace limité par des frontières qui, en réalité, **n'existent pas**. « Je suis pris » ou « je me sens pris au piège ». Je suis d'accord avec le fait que les gens envahissent mon espace psychique et ceci se manifeste chez moi par une sorte de **resserrement** intérieur. Je laisse donc de côté mes besoins personnels pour plaire en premier aux autres, pour attirer l'amour dont j'ai besoin (même s'il y a d'autres façons de faire). Le resserrement m'amène généralement à amplifier mes émotions et mon émotivité générale au détriment d'un équilibre adéquat. Puisque je vis dans le brouillard, la confiance en moi sera ébranlée, le désespoir et même le goût de ne plus lutter vont prendre place. Quelle peut être la situation où je me suis senti resserré étant jeune si bien que je reproduis encore fidèlement ce « pattern »[21] aujourd'hui ? (à noter qu'**angoisse** et claustrophobie sont synonymes par le mot **resserrement**.) C'est naturel pour mon corps de combler mes besoins **psychiques** fondamentaux : le besoin d'air pour vivre et respirer, l'espace entre moi et les autres personnes, la liberté de décider et de discerner ce qui est bon pour moi. Si, à partir de maintenant, je réponds à mes attentes face à la vie **en premier**, il y a de fortes chances pour que je laisse celles des autres à leur place : comme cela, je suis plus certain d'être en accord avec eux ! Et sans violer leur espace[22], parce que je dois me souvenir que si je me sens étouffé, c'est parce que j'étouffe consciemment ou non les gens autour de moi. L'**angoisse** apparaît aussi comme une attente inquiète et oppressante, appréhension de « quelque chose » qui pourrait advenir, dans une tension

---

21. **Pattern :** Schéma de pensée qui fait se répéter des événements dans ma vie.
22. **Espace :** Signifie ici laisser aux autres la liberté de pensée ou d'action et les respecter .

diffuse effrayante et souvent sans nom. Elle peut être liée à une menace concrète **angoissante** (telle que mort, catastrophe personnelle, sanction). Il s'agit davantage d'une peur souvent liée à rien d'immédiatement perceptible ou exprimable. C'est pourquoi les sources profondes de l'**angoisse** sont à retrouver souvent chez l'enfant que j'ai été et sont souvent reliées à la peur de l'abandon, de perdre l'amour d'un être cher et à la souffrance. Quand je me retrouve dans une situation semblable, l'**angoisse** refait surface. Chaque fois qu'une de ces peurs ressurgit ou qu'une situation, soit imaginaire ou réaliste, est vécue, cela est perçu par mon inconscient comme un signal d'alarme : où un danger est présent, l'**angoisse** réapparaît encore plus fort. Lorsque je suis enfant, l'**angoisse** se manifeste souvent par la peur de l'obscurité et une tendance à vivre une vie solitaire. À partir de maintenant, j'use de discernement, de courage et de confiance dans la vie pour me respecter et laisser aller les autres sans regrets dans leur espace et je bannis de ma vie tout remord. Je vais ainsi voir « plus clair » et avancer dans la vie avec beaucoup plus de lucidité.

ANGOR (voir : ANGINE DE POITRINE)

ANKYLOSE (état d'...) (voir aussi : ARTICULATIONS [en général], PARALYSIE [en général])

État d'engourdissement caractérisé par la disparition généralement **temporaire** des mouvements d'une ou de plusieurs de mes articulations. L'**ankylose** est partielle mais peut être totale si je décide de devenir complètement inactif ; c'est le premier pas vers la paralysie, autant physiquement qu'en pensée. Je dois prendre conscience de la responsabilité à prendre si je décide de rester là, à ne rien faire, à ne pas vouloir sentir ni bouger. Qu'est-ce que je crains ? Est-ce l'inconnu, ce qui m'attend, quelque chose de nouveau pour moi qui me dérange ? Est-ce quelque chose que je n'ai pas du tout envie de faire ? Je peux aller voir la partie du corps impliquée afin de me donner des informations additionnelles sur la source de mon **ankylose**. Par exemple, si c'est dans le bras, suis-je dans un état où je refuse les nouvelles expériences de vie ? Ai-je le sentiment d'être mutilé ? S'il s'agit d'une épaule, est-ce que je trouve la vie lourde ; qu'une personne ou qu'une situation est « tout un fardeau » ? Est-ce que la solitude ou la nécessité de faire face à l'inconnu congestionne mes pensées ? S'il s'agit d'un pied, quelle est la direction que je ne veux pas prendre et face à laquelle je « m'engourdis » ? Si c'est mon corps en entier, je m'engourdis face à quelque chose ou à quelqu'un : il s'agit d'une forme de fuite. Je suis conscient que **j'accumule** de l'énergie dans cette partie du corps et qu'inconsciemment, **j'angoisse**. Il est temps pour moi d'aller de l'avant ! À partir de maintenant, je suis conscient de mes fautes (ou plutôt de mes responsabilités) et de mes expériences de vie et je les reconnais. J'accepte ↓♥ de reprendre le mouvement laissé temporairement et je

mobilise de nouveau mes pensées en restant ouvert. Je manifeste un esprit davantage créateur.

ANNULAIRE (voir : DOIGT — ANNULAIRE)

ANOREXIE (voir aussi : APPÉTIT [perte d'...], BOULIMIE, POIDS [excès de...])

L'**anorexie** est caractérisée par un **rejet** complet de la vie. C'est le dégoût total pour tout ce qui est vivant en moi et qui peut entrer dans mon corps **laid** pour l'alimenter. Ce sentiment peut même se transformer en haine. Il existe plusieurs symboles de vie : l'eau, la nourriture, l'aspect maternel (mère), l'amour, le côté féminin. C'est le désir ardent et inconscient d'échapper à la vie, de se détester et de **se rejeter** car je vis la peur extrême de m'ouvrir à la merveilleuse vie autour de moi. Je vis du **découragement** à un point tel que je me demande ce qui pourrait m'aider. J'ai le désir inconscient de « disparaître » pour déranger le moins possible mon entourage. Je me rejette donc en permanence. L'**anorexie** et l'obésité viennent d'un sentiment profond inassouvi d'amour et d'affection, même si les deux maladies prennent physiquement des chemins complètement divergents. Plusieurs troubles de l'alimentation reposent sur la **relation mère-enfant** dans laquelle il existe ou il a existé un conflit. En plus, il s'agit très souvent d'une **contrariété quant à mon territoire** que j'ai l'impression de ne pas avoir, de perdre ou qu'on ne respecte pas. Ce territoire peut être constitué autant de mes possessions physiques (vêtements, jouets, auto, maison, etc.) que de mes possessions non physiques (mes droits, mes acquis, mes besoins, etc.) ou des personnes qui m'entourent (mon père, ma mère, mes amis, mon mari, etc.). Je vis une contrariété qui est récente par rapport à quelqu'un ou à quelque chose que **je ne peux pas éviter** et que je ne digère pas. Bien que l'**anorexie** se retrouve le plus souvent à l'adolescence, celle-ci existe aussi chez le bébé et chez le jeune enfant. Si je me mets à la place du bébé, je me rends compte que le refus de manger peut découler d'un contact troublé entre ma mère et moi : ce peut être la privation du sein maternel et de la chaude ambiance physique qui devraient accompagner la tétée, la façon artificielle de nourrir, dosée et trop rigide dans son application, la sur ou la sous-alimentation imposée par respect pour une courbe de poids idéal avec mépris de certains rythmes alimentaires individuels changeants. Je peux réagir à cela par un refus progressif de me nourrir, des vomissements, la perte de poids, des troubles du sommeil, des caprices alimentaires, etc. Il est important que moi, comme mère, je respecte les goûts, les rythmes propres à l'enfant et que je cesse de vouloir être la mère parfaite et surprotectrice. Si je suis un enfant un peu plus vieux et que je manifeste l'**anorexie,** elle est habituellement plus atténuée et se caractérise par un « petit appétit », étant un petit mangeur qui déteste la corvée des repas, ayant des caprices alimentaires avec refus obstiné de certains aliments, achevant rarement ma portion, vomissant fréquemment et mastiquant sans fin la même bouchée. À cet âge, la table et ses impératifs sociaux jouent un rôle important, car les repas sont une réunion familiale sous l'autorité parentale où

des réactions ou des conflits peuvent survenir. L'**anorexie** est fondamentalement mon besoin de combler un vide intérieur de **nourriture affective. J'ai besoin de l'amour et de l'acceptation↓♥ inconditionnelle de ma mère intérieure. L'anorexie**, contrairement à l'obésité, est la tentative de faire mourir de faim mon vide intérieur pour le rendre tellement petit qu'il disparaîtra et qu'il ne demandera plus rien du tout. C'est l'une des raisons pour lesquelles je continue à me voir gros (fixation mentale sur la grosseur) même si je suis mince et svelte. Autrement dit, je continue à voir mes besoins affectifs et émotionnels très grands et je me sens dépassé par eux. L'**anorexie** peut également se rapporter à un sentiment d'être grondé par la vie et par **ma mère**, symbole maternel qui me pousse quand même vers le désir d'indépendance et d'individualité. C'est la raison pourquoi je rejette la nourriture **en même temps que ma mère**, parce que j'ai toujours eu l'impression de sentir uniquement son puissant contrôle maternel dans ma jeunesse. Je vis donc le sentiment d'être hors de mon propre contrôle par rapport aux événements et je tente d'une manière exagérée de reprendre ce contrôle. « Je n'aime pas la manière qu'a ma mère de m'aimer et je la déteste pour cela. » « Je veux rester une jeune fille ou un jeune garçon car je veux me rapprocher le plus possible d'une forme de "pureté" physique et intérieure. » (C'est durant la puberté que se manifeste généralement l'**anorexie**.) C'est une recherche absolue de jeunesse. En tant que jeune fille ou jeune garçon, je refuse les stades sexuels reliés à mon âge, si bien que toute tentative d'intimité sexuelle, de découverte et d'abandon vers un éventuel partenaire (absence de maturité) sont quasi inutiles. Si je vis tout cela d'une manière profonde, c'est fréquemment relié à un profond traumatisme sexuel passé, à un abus ou à une insécurité affective. Cette expérience a amené le désespoir à prendre place dans mon corps physique et « j'ai fermé la porte » à mes désirs physiques, spirituels et émotionnels. Accepter↓♥ graduellement ma féminité ou mon côté intuitif et émotif chez le garçon est essentiellement la première chose à faire pour régler mon état **anorexique**. J'utilise la manière que je veux, mais je dois le faire ! J'accepte↓♥ une certaine intimité sexuelle, féminine et même maternelle (car j'ai à apprendre à aimer ma mère !). J'apprends à aimer mon corps et à aimer les autres ! J'y vais lentement, car c'est une situation délicate où je dois m'ouvrir à l'amour et à la beauté de l'univers. Je demande de l'aide, si nécessaire. Et surtout, je reste ouvert à ce que la vie me réserve ! Acceptation↓♥ et amour inconditionnels seront grandement appréciés. Je fais des activités (sportives ou autres), si possible. Voici une parenthèse intéressante. En tant que personne **anorexique**, je peux avoir l'impression de me retrouver intérieurement comme prise dans des « anneaux » (anneau-rexique), comme si j'étais à l'intérieur de plusieurs « houla-houp » qui m'isolent du reste du monde tout en intensifiant mon sentiment de limitation face à la vie. Je reste ouvert à tout autre signe de ce genre. Je me visualise en train de me libérer de ces anneaux en leur disant « *MERCI* » pour la prise de conscience qu'ils m'ont aidé à faire tout en sachant que maintenant, ils ne sont plus nécessaires. Je visualise aussi cette image : à chaque inspiration, plus de lumière entre en moi afin de remplir mon sentiment de vide intérieur.

ANTHRAX (voir : PEAU — ANTHRAX)

ANURIE (voir : REINS — ANURIE)

ANUS

L'**anus** est l'orifice du rectum, l'endroit par où je laisse aller ce dont je n'ai plus besoin. Les problèmes ici sont reliés au fait de « retenir et de laisser aller » ; c'est pourquoi si je suis un enfant et que je constipe ou que je salis ma couche, c'est souvent pour me venger de parents que je considère comme autoritaires, manipulateurs ou abusifs. C'est l'endroit de décharge des principales toxines du corps humain. L'**anus** se situe au niveau du bassin, proche du coccyx et du premier chakra ou centre d'énergie, le siège entre le soi et l'univers qui m'entoure. Il est relié à la base énergétique du corps. Certaines peurs intérieures, le stress et les émotions s'évacuent par cet orifice. Je peux vérifier les situations suivantes : « Qu'est-ce que je tente d'ignorer au point de le retenir ? Jusqu'où puis-je me laisser aller ? Suis-je capable de relaxer et de laisser la vie me guider ? Suis-je prêt à vivre de nouvelles sensations face à la vie ? » J'apprends à me faire confiance, tout en laissant aller ce dont je n'ai plus besoin et en le remplaçant par de nouvelles idées, des attitudes positives et de nouveaux projets !

ANUS — ABCÈS ANAL (voir aussi : ABCÈS [en général])

L'**abcès** est un amas de pus, de **frustrations** et d'**irritabilité** lié à une **situation que je ne veux pas lâcher ou laisser aller** (anus). Souvent, même si je me retiens, cela m'échappe malgré moi. Cet **abcès** sortira ou se manifestera de toute façon. Il est possible que je sois en colère contre moi-même car je ne veux pas « évacuer », céder devant certaines fixations mentales qui nuisent à ma vie présente. Je peux même être rempli de vengeance par rapport à une situation passée ou à quelqu'un à qui je refuse de pardonner. Ce malaise me dit que je dois faire confiance à la vie et à ce qu'il y a de beau autour de moi. Je me fie à quelqu'un ou à quelque chose et, surtout, je pardonne aux gens qui m'entourent. Je m'abandonne et je fais confiance à la vie.

ANUS — DÉMANGEAISON ANALE (voir aussi : PEAU — DÉMANGEAISONS)

Les **démangeaisons** sont reliées à des remords et à de la culpabilité par rapport à mon passé. Quelque chose m'irrite ou me chatouille et je me sens coupable dans ce que j'ai à retenir ou à laisser aller. C'est dans mon intérêt d'écouter mon corps et d'atteindre la satisfaction en tout car la culpabilité ne fait que freiner mon évolution, sans véritables bénéfices.

ANUS — DOULEURS ANALES (Recto-colite)

Les **douleurs anales** (appelées recto-colites) sont reliées à la **culpabilité**. Je me fais mal car je ne me crois pas assez efficace pour réaliser mes désirs. C'est une forme d'autopunition, une irritation, l'envie de me condamner d'une manière qui manifeste une blessure intérieure, ma sensibilité déchirée à la suite d'un événement passé que je n'ai pas encore accepté ↓♥. Je vis une détresse profonde qui peut amener la perte sanguine et même, dans certains cas, l'hémorragie. Je peux accepter ↓♥ de devenir plus responsable de mes désirs, arrêter de me dévaloriser dans ce que je suis et cesser de m'empêcher de vivre et de me punir inutilement. Je pourrais cesser d'être incommodé en ayant le « derrière en feu », et repartir à neuf en acceptant ↓♥ davantage mes expériences passées, présentes et à venir et ainsi foncer davantage dans la vie.

ANUS — FISSURES ANALES

Les **fissures anales** sont de légères fentes entraînant le saignement au niveau de l'**anus**, ce qui signifie une certaine **perte de joie** de vivre reliée à une situation que je dois changer. Si je vis de la tristesse qui peut me « **fendre le cul** », je vérifie ce qui entraîne cette tristesse et j'accepte ↓♥ les changements dans ma vie. Surtout, **je cesse d'attendre après les autres pour changer**. J'élimine ma frustration, ma colère face à une personne ou à un événement « qui me fend le derrière » ou face auquel je peux me sentir « assis entre deux chaises ».

ANUS — FISTULES ANALES (voir aussi : FISTULES)

Une **fistule anale** trouve son origine dans une situation que je vis et où j'expérimente de la **colère** par rapport à ce que je veux retenir et que je n'arrive pas à garder en moi. C'est comme si je voulais garder de vieux déchets du passé (vieilles formes-pensées, émotions, désirs) mais je n'y arrive pas. Je peux même entretenir des sentiments de vengeance par rapport à quelqu'un ou à quelque chose. La manifestation est la **fistule**, sorte de canal communiquant anormalement entre un viscère et la peau. Je n'arrive pas à me décider entre le physique et le spirituel, entre les désirs et le détachement (au sens large). Je reste ouvert au niveau du cœur et j'accepte ↓♥ avec volonté de vider complètement ces « poubelles » d'idées noires, malsaines et vengeresses **ici et maintenant**.

ANXIÉTÉ (voir aussi : ANGOISSE, NERFS [crise de ...], NERVOSITÉ, SANG — HYPOGLYCÉMIE])

L'**anxiété** est une certaine **peur de l'inconnu** qui peut se rapprocher de l'état d'angoisse. Elle se manifeste par certains symptômes : maux de tête, chaleurs, crampes, palpitations nerveuses, grandes transpirations, tensions, augmentation du débit de la voix, sanglots et même insomnies. Si je suis

anxieux, je peux vivre le « frisson de l'angoisse » : ce frissonnement vient du froid et me rappelle que j'ai peur. C'est une maladie qui me sert la gorge, qui me fait perdre la maîtrise de moi-même et le contrôle des événements de ma vie, m'empêchant d'user de **bon sens** et de discernement. Je peux aussi ressentir soit un déséquilibre, soit une déconnexion entre le monde physique sur lequel je peux avoir un certain contrôle et mes perceptions par rapport au monde immatériel pour lesquelles je n'ai pas toujours d'explications ou de compréhension rationnelle. Je n'ai plus le contrôle : le « ciel peut me tomber sur la tête » à tout moment ! Je peux être **anxieux** dans n'importe quelle situation : *JE DEVIENS CE SUR QUOI JE PORTE MON ATTENTION.* Si mon attention est constamment centrée sur la peur de ceci ou de cela, il est certain que je vivrai de l'**anxiété** qui peut être reliée de près ou de loin à ce qui se rapproche de la peur de la **mort** ou à ce qui pourrait me la rappeler. La mort, les choses que j'ignore ou que je ne vois pas, mais qui peuvent exister, font monter en moi cette peur. Alors, même si je crains l'inconnu et que je **nie inconsciemment la vie et son processus**, je place maintenant mon attention sur ceci : j'ai confiance qu'il m'arrive le mieux, pour moi, à l'instant présent et dans l'avenir. Les symptômes disparaîtront, ainsi que la peur de mourir.

APATHIE (voir aussi : SANG — ANÉMIE / HYPOGLYCÉMIE / MONONUCLÉOSE)

L'**apathie** est une forme d'insensibilité ou de nonchalance. J'abandonne face à la vie, je deviens indifférent et je n'ai aucune motivation à changer quoi que ce soit. L'**apathie** peut survenir à la suite d'un choc, d'un traumatisme ou de toute autre situation négative qui m'enlève toute ma joie de vivre ou ma raison d'être en ce monde. Je peux vouloir **partir** d'une situation en la fuyant par manque de motivation ou de joie ou par peur d'être déçu. Je résiste et je refuse de voir et de sentir ce qui se passe à l'intérieur de moi et autour de moi, m'amenant à un certain taux d'insensibilité afin de me protéger. L'**apathie** peut aussi être reliée à la honte profonde et à la culpabilité. Je tente ainsi de devenir insensible à mon être intérieur. J'accepte ↓♥ de m'ouvrir à la vie et à de nouvelles expériences agréables que je maintiens afin de trouver un nouveau but à ma vie. J'y mets l'attitude voulue.

APHONIE ou EXTINCTION DE VOIX

La voix est l'expression de soi, la créativité. Une trop grande émotion (détresse, inquiétude) peut m'amener à ne plus savoir quoi dire ou quelle direction prendre ni comment interpréter cette direction par rapport à l'émotion vécue. Il se peut que cette forte émotion ait été vécue sur le plan sexuel et se répercute plus directement sur la gorge ou sur les cordes vocales car, d'une certaine façon, mon deuxième centre d'énergie (sexuel) est relié plus directement à la gorge, mon cinquième centre d'énergie. De toute façon, ma sensibilité (hyperémotivité) en a pris un coup et je n'arrive plus à dire quoi que

ce soit ! J'en ai le souffle coupé ! Si je disperse trop mes énergies, notamment à la suite d'un choc émotionnel, un « vide » intérieur va se créer en raison de mon désarroi intérieur et les sons vont être « engouffrés » par ce vide. C'est donc important pour moi de reprendre contact avec le *souffle de ma communication intérieure*. Il est même possible que cette expérience me protège parce que je suis dans un état où je ne dois plus parler, où je ne peux plus dire de secrets. Est-ce que j'utilise d'une manière saine ma voix et mes cordes vocales ? Dois-je rester silencieux pendant un certain temps ? On dit parfois : la parole est d'argent et le silence est d'or... J'apprends à exprimer mes émotions, ma créativité et mes idées de la façon où je me sens le mieux, dans le respect de mes capacités.

APHTE (voir : BOUCHE — APHTE)

APOPLEXIE (voir : CERVEAU — APOPLEXIE)

APPENDICITE (voir aussi : ANNEXE III)

L'**appendicite** est définie comme l'inflammation du CÆCUM (du latin « Aveugle ») situé à la base du gros intestin. Cette maladie provient d'une **colère reliée à une tension ou à une situation aiguë** que je n'arrive pas à régler et qui me fait « bouillir » intérieurement. Il s'agit le plus souvent d'une situation sur le plan affectif qui vient déséquilibrer ma sensibilité et mes émotions. Ma peur peut avoir suscité cet événement car j'entretenais des pensées noires et je me faisais du souci, ce qui l'a fait se manifester. Je me sens comme dans un « cul-de-sac » (c'est la forme de l'**appendice**) parce que j'ai le sentiment d'être opprimé, ce qui déclenche en moi **peur, insécurité, lassitude, abandon**. Le plus souvent, cette contrariété est en rapport avec un ou des membres de la famille ou en lien avec les principes et les idées rattachés à la famille. Ce peut être une situation qui a rapport à l'argent, et particulièrement à l'argent de poche. Ce peut être aussi quelque chose ou quelqu'un que je voudrais voir « s'ajouter » ou « s'incorporer » à ma vie mais une circonstance l'en empêche. Par exemple, je veux peut-être que mon conjoint vienne vivre chez-moi mais il ou elle ne veut pas ou je n'ai pas suffisamment de place pour l'héberger etc. Il y a une « obstruction » au courant de vie et je refoule une multitude d'émotions. Cela peut même aller jusqu'à la peur de vivre. Je n'arrive plus à filtrer efficacement les nouvelles réalités pour m'en protéger. Je ne vois pas d'autre issue à ma vie. J'ai besoin de parler de ce que je vis, j'ai besoin de « vider mon sac » car j'ai de la difficulté à digérer ce qui se passe, je trouve cela très moche et désappointant. Les symptômes habituels sont la chaleur, la rougeur, reliée à l'inflammation, et la douleur, reliée à la tension. J'éprouve une très **vive souffrance** lorsque l'**appendicite** se transforme en **péritonite** (éclatement de l'**appendice**). Je laisse la vie prendre son cours et j'accepte ↓♥ les situations de mon existence comme ce qu'il y a de

mieux pour moi. Je reste ouvert au niveau du cœur et je laisse tomber mes protections (barrières) doucement et harmonieusement.

APPÉTIT (excès d'...) (voir aussi : BOULIMIE, SANG — HYPOGLYCÉMIE)

La nourriture représente la vie et est également reliée au **plaisir**, à une certaine **joie de vivre**. La nourriture comble donc mon (mes) besoin(s) physique(s) et émotionnel(s) et un excès peut vouloir dire que je veux compenser pour avoir plus de vie en moi, ayant besoin **de combler un vide intérieur**. C'est une insatisfaction intérieure profonde face à l'amour et une **faim d'amour** (comme la « soif d'amour »), un besoin de diminuer une tension ou simplement de m'occuper pour ne pas avoir besoin de réfléchir à mon sujet. J'évite de regarder à l'intérieur de moi et je trouve dans la nourriture ce sentiment de liberté et de satisfaction à combler tous mes désirs, quelle que soit la quantité absorbée. C'est peut-être le cas lorsque je suis en état d'hypoglycémie qui est relié à un manque de joie dans ma vie, ou à un désir excessif pour le sucré (relié à l'amour) qui montre un besoin évident de tendresse et d'affection. Chez les enfants, il est facile de reconnaître leurs besoins affectifs carencés :[23] ils manifestent aisément le goût pour tout ce qui est sucré. Que je sois un adulte ou un enfant, c'est toujours mon cœur d'enfant qui est blessé et je dois donner davantage d'amour à mes enfants ou en recevoir pour combler mes besoins. Je dois rester ouvert à cette belle énergie d'amour pour trouver un équilibre, une véritable communication, une reconnaissance du moi, un échange entre ce que je suis et ce dont j'ai besoin. L'appétit s'équilibre du même coup lorsque je suis mieux comblé émotionnellement.

APPÉTIT (perte d'...) (voir aussi : ANOREXIE)

Comme la nourriture est reliée à la vie, une perte d'appétit peut être attribuée à de la **culpabilité** (je ne mérite pas de vivre, j'ai peur, je me protège) ou à une perte de joie, de motivation face à une personne ou à une situation. Je refuse d'aller de l'avant, d'avoir des impressions nouvelles et des expériences excitantes qui me rendent encore plus joyeux. Je refuse d'absorber, de digérer, de **manger le nouveau** qui se présente à moi dans la vie parce que cela ne me convient pas. En restant ouvert au niveau du cœur à l'aventure et à la vie, j'augmente ma propre estime de moi et je peux accepter ↓♥ les « nouvelles impressions » (nouveaux goûts) et faire un pas de plus. L'équilibre de l'appétit reviendra. *Comme « l'appétit vient en mangeant », la VIE vient avec la VIE !*

APPRÉHENSION

L'**appréhension** est reliée à un **doute**, à une crainte par rapport à une situation ou à une personne face à laquelle je sens du « danger ». Intérieurement, je vis de l'incompréhension par rapport à ce qui m'arrive. Mon

---

23. **Carencés :** En manque.

33

mental commence à fabuler sur toutes sortes d'idées et je risque d'être décentré. Je place mon attention sur mon être intérieur à partir de maintenant et j'accepte ↓♥ au niveau du cœur les expériences de la vie, tout en me protégeant.

ARTÈRES (voir : SANG — ARTÈRES)

ARTÉRIOSCLÉROSE ou ATHÉROSCLÉROSE
(voir aussi : SANG / ARTÈRES / CIRCULATION SANGUINE)

L'**athérosclérose** est une maladie dégénérative qui provient de la formation de dépôts lipidiques (sortes de gras) sur les parois des artères. L'**artériosclérose** est aussi une maladie dégénérative qui provient de la destruction des fibres musculaires et élastiques qui la forment. L'une ou l'autre des maladies se manifeste par un durcissement des artères et des artérioles, impliquant surtout un épuisement et une perte d'élasticité au niveau de la paroi de celles-ci, une capacité plus faible de dilatation et de circulation du sang, une augmentation des dépôts graisseux, donc moins d'amour exprimé au niveau du cœur. Cet état progressif se manifeste si je suis **endurci**, si je suis ou si je deviens **inflexible** ou **tendu** en ce qui a trait à la communication et à mes pensées. C'est la manifestation d'une **résistance très forte** et d'une **étroitesse d'esprit** physique et intérieure. L'expression et la réception d'amour deviennent limitées et restreintes. J'ai des idées fixes et impitoyables, je suis souvent intransigeant, rigide, et sans compassion ; j'ai aussi tendance à ne voir que le côté sombre ou négatif de la vie. Je peux refouler inconsciemment mes émotions et dire non à l'amour car je crains de m'exprimer. Où et quand ai-je déjà vécu une expérience traumatisante qui me fait même détester une partie de moi-même au point de la renier et où me suis-je senti rejeté ? Cette maladie est donc probablement reliée à une blessure amoureuse ou à la non-reconnaissance de cet amour dans ma vie. À quoi bon voir ce qui est excellent pour moi ? Pourquoi exprimer mes sentiments ? Mon corps m'indique qu'il y a un changement à faire par rapport à mon comportement face à la vie. En acceptant ↓♥ d'avoir une attitude plus ouverte, tolérante et douce par rapport à moi-même et aux expériences que je vis, tout le processus d'union avec le moi intérieur et l'univers se manifeste davantage. Je fais montre de joie, de sérénité et de flexibilité envers ceux et celles qui m'entourent et je m'abandonne à la véritable expression de l'amour. Les gens de mon entourage sentiront ce changement. J'ai aussi à développer plus de créativité (artère = art-terre) sur le plan physique et avec la matière. La vie prend soin de moi.

ARTHRITE (en général)
(voir aussi : ARTICULATIONS [en général], INFLAMMATION)

L'**arthrite** est définie comme l'inflammation d'une articulation. Elle peut affecter chacune des parties du système locomoteur humain : les os, les

ligaments, les tendons ou les muscles. Elle se caractérise par de l'inflammation, de la raideur musculaire et de la douleur qui **correspondent,** au plan métaphysique, à de la **fermeture,** de la **critique,** du **chagrin,** de la **tristesse** ou de la **colère.** Symboliquement parlant, la grâce et la liberté de mouvement sont les principales qualités liées à l'articulation. Quand celle-ci devient inflexible ou qu'elle se durcit, l'**arthrite** est associée à une certaine forme de **rigidité** de mes pensées (des pensées cristallisées), de mes attitudes ou de mes comportements, si bien que toutes les émotions profondes que je devrais exprimer normalement le sont par la manifestation physique de cette maladie. Ainsi, l'**arthrite** survient si je suis trop **inflexible, trop exigeant, têtu, intolérant, très moraliste, critiqueur, restreint ou trop orgueilleux** par rapport à moi-même, aux autres ou aux situations de mon existence. Un sentiment d'impuissance accompagne habituellement la souffrance qui me freine. Je vis le sentiment particulier d'être **mal aimé,** de ne pas être aimé et apprécié **à ma juste valeur,** ce qui amène chez moi beaucoup de **déception** et **d'amertume** face à la vie et de la mauvaise humeur. Je manifeste alors un esprit exagérément rationnel. Je critique souvent sur tout ou rien parce que j'ai peur de la vie et que j'éprouve souvent une forme **d'insécurité chronique.** Je me sens **exploité** ; je fais des actions et pose des gestes plus pour faire plaisir aux autres que par volonté réelle et intérêt, si bien que je dis « oui » par devoir alors qu'en vérité, c'est non. J'ai peut-être vécu un traumatisme d'enfance et je refoule maintenant mes émotions, sans admettre ce qui s'est passé (occultation) car « j'ai beaucoup souffert dans une telle expérience et je me permets (inconsciemment) de blâmer et de me plaindre pour que les autres puissent comprendre jusqu'à quel point j'ai eu mal ». Cette manifestation se rapporte au complexe du **sacrifice de soi.** L'**arthrite** peut provenir aussi de la façon dont je me traite ou je **traite** les autres par rapport à la critique. L'**arthrite** occasionne aussi une sorte d'action **rétrograde** ; j'ai l'impression d'être ramené vers l'arrière sur le plan énergétique, comme si on m'indiquait de faire autre chose d'autre dans une direction différente, plutôt que d'aller vers l'avant. Puisque ma peur, ma faible estime de moi et ma rigidité font en sorte que de profondes émotions se créent par rapport au pourquoi, au comment ou à la direction de mes mouvements dans la vie, je peux avoir le sentiment d'être contraint, restreint, immobilisé ou renfermé. J'éprouverai alors une inhabileté à fléchir (mon attitude), à être mentalement flexible ou capable d'abdiquer. L'**articulation arthritique** m'indique ce que je vis et me donne plus d'informations. Au niveau des **mains** (doigts), la question est : Est-ce que je fais vraiment ce que je désire et ce que je veux faire ? Est-ce que j'ai une bonne « prise de main » sur mes propres affaires ? Y a-t-il des gens à qui je n'ai plus le goût de « donner la main » ? Ma liberté et ma spontanéité à « manier » ce qui se passe dans mon univers sont limitées par ma rigidité et ma dureté. Aux **coudes** : « Est-ce que je suis inflexible aux changements de directions à prendre dans ma vie ? Est-ce que je permets aux autres d'être libres et d'exprimer leur plein potentiel ? Aux **genoux** : Devant qui ou quoi ai-je l'impression de devoir

me mettre à genoux et devant qui ou quoi je ne veux pas plier ? À partir de maintenant, je vérifie mes véritables intentions par rapport à l'amour. Je dois changer ma façon de penser et adopter une nouvelle attitude face aux situations de ma vie. En restant ouvert à l'amour qui est omniprésent (partout) et en l'exprimant de façon plus honnête, libre et spontanée, mon cœur sera rayonnant et je respecterai les autres autant que moi-même. Amitié, compréhension et pardon sont maintenant disponibles pour moi.

ARTHRITE — ARTHROSE (voir aussi : ARTICULATIONS, OS)

L'**arthrose** est la manifestation intensifiée de l'arthrite. C'est une maladie d'usure articulaire des os d'origine mécanique et non inflammatoire comme l'**arthrite**, une aggravation profonde de la structure osseuse, localisée ou habituellement généralisée à l'ensemble du corps. Cependant, ce sont davantage les articulations soumises à d'importantes contraintes mécaniques qui sont concernées telles que celles de la colonne vertébrale (vertèbres cervicales [du cou], vertèbres lombaires [bas du dos]), des hanches, de la main, des genoux, des chevilles. La douleur qu'elle occasionne est d'origine « mécanique » et non inflammatoire et apparaît habituellement après un effort soutenu et disparaît au repos (cette maladie porte aussi le nom de rhumatisme d'usure). Lorsque je souffre d'**arthrose**, c'est comme si j'amplifiais davantage mes attitudes, mes « patterns » et mes pensées rigides. Cette maladie est reliée à un **durcissement mental**, à une absence de « chaleur » dans mes pensées (le froid et l'humidité accélèrent l'apparition de l'**arthrose**), souvent par rapport à l'autorité. C'est la motivation exagérée à accomplir une action sans chercher le repos ou l'équilibre (je me rends jusqu'au bout de mes limites sans m'arrêter à savoir si je m'en demande trop), une **impression de subir** une personne ou une situation maintenant devenue intolérable, ou une forte réaction refoulée par rapport à une forme quelconque d'**autorité**. Je suis très intransigeant et rigide envers moi-même. Mon corps me parle et j'ai présentement intérêt à l'écouter ! Je peux intégrer cette maladie en commençant à accepter ↓♥ **consciemment** que je vis de la colère et que mes pensées sont rigides. L'énergie qui s'écoule à travers moi est fluide, harmonieuse, en **mouvement**. En restant ouvert au niveau du cœur à cette énergie et en reconnaissant que j'ai quelque chose à changer, je peux renverser le processus et améliorer ma santé ! Je deviens plus flexible et j'accepte ↓♥ les autres tels qu'ils sont, sans vouloir les changer. La flexibilité au niveau de mon corps physique réapparaîtra alors.

ARTHRITE DES DOIGTS (voir : DOIGTS — ARTHRITIQUES)

ARTHRITE GOUTTEUSE (voir : GOUTTE)

ARTHRITE — POLYARTHRITE

La **polyarthrite** est une inflammation portant simultanément sur plusieurs articulations. Cette maladie vient m'indiquer une difficulté à accomplir des gestes que j'étais capable d'exécuter autrefois avec beaucoup de dextérité. Maintenant, j'ai l'impression d'être plus maladroit ou gauche. Je me dévalorise donc par rapport à cette activité où j'excellais et j'ai l'impression de perdre de la dextérité, de la force ou de la précision. Cette maladie se retrouve par exemple chez la couturière qui, après quelques années, à l'impression d'être plus lente, moins habile. Les sportifs sont souvent atteints de **polyarthrite**, à cause principalement du sentiment de dévalorisation qu'ils peuvent vivre parce qu'ils ne performent pas à 100 % ou que leurs performances ont diminué. J'apprends à m'accepter ↓♥ avec mes forces et mes faiblesses. Même si j'ai l'impression d'être moins bon ou moins efficace, je regarde toute l'expérience que j'ai acquise au fil des années. Je reconnais qu'elle est un atout précieux qui fait de moi une personne exceptionnelle. La **polyarthrite** peut se produire aussi si je suis compulsif, très **obstiné** ou moralisateur. J'ai tendance à me sacrifier pour les autres, ce qui résulte souvent d'une agression refoulée ; mais jusqu'à quel point j'agis avec amour, en me respectant ? La rigidité tant physique qu'intérieure s'aggrave à cause de cette obstination profonde à ne pas vouloir changer.

ARTHRITE RHUMATISMALE (voir aussi : RHUMATISME)

L'**arthrite rhumatismale** est actuellement considérée comme l'affection articulaire la plus grave. Elle est habituellement généralisée à l'ensemble du corps plutôt qu'à une seule articulation. Le système immunitaire est si malade qu'il commence à s'autodétruire, s'attaquant au tissu conjonctif des articulations (collagène), si bien que le risque d'une infirmité généralisée avec de la douleur et du gonflement articulaire est à craindre. C'est carrément une attaque de mon propre moi, tellement les fortes émotions de **rancune** et de **douleur n'arrivent pas à s'exprimer**. L'**arthrite rhumatoïde** est reliée à un **profond mépris de soi**, à une **haine** ou à une **rage refoulée depuis longtemps**, à une **critique de soi** si intense que cela affecte l'énergie la plus fondamentale de mon existence. J'ai vécu des expériences où je me suis senti très **honteux** ou **coupable**. C'est la manifestation d'une **critique** beaucoup plus importante **face à l'autorité** ou à tout ce qui représente l'autorité pour moi : individu, gouvernement, etc. **Je refuse de me plier à cette autorité**, peu importe les conséquences ! C'est comme si je « ruminais » constamment l'autorité en la critiquant. Ma mobilité devient limitée et je n'arrive pas à m'exprimer librement (dans le cas notamment de certaines directions à prendre et que j'ai à communiquer avec mon entourage d'une manière fluide et gracieuse), car mes articulations sont trop douloureuses. Mon corps devient rigide, comme mes attitudes. Je n'arrive pas à exprimer mes fortes émotions et j'ai l'impression d'être constamment

opprimé et soumis. J'adopte alors des comportements d'effacement, d'autosacrifice, et je rumine mes émotions sans pouvoir les exprimer. « Je sers de bouc émissaire en me sacrifiant à une cause quelconque » ; « on est toujours sur mon dos ». L'ouverture au niveau du cœur est essentielle si je veux libérer toutes les émotions qui empoisonnent mon existence. À partir de maintenant, je reprends mon plein pouvoir sur ma vie, en commençant par m'aimer et par m'accepter ↓♥ tel que je suis. Je prends la place qui me revient !

ARTHROSE (voir : ARTHRITE — ARTHROSE)

ARTICULATIONS (en général) (voir aussi : ARTHRITE — ARTHROSE)

Une **articulation** est une partie du corps où se réunissent deux ou plusieurs os permettant un mouvement adapté[24] à l'anatomie du corps humain (synonyme : joint, jonction, jointure). L'**articulation** représente la **facilité**, la **mobilité**, l'**adaptabilité** et la **flexibilité**, donnant au mouvement grâce et fluidité. Toutes ces qualités simples sont possibles avec une **articulation** en parfait état. Cependant, elle a aussi ses limites. Comme l'os représente la forme d'énergie la plus « dense », la plus fondamentale de mon existence, les problèmes **articulaires** sont impliqués dans toutes les composantes physiologiques du corps humain (tissu, sang, etc.). Ainsi, un trouble articulaire indique une **résistance**, une certaine raideur dans mes pensées, dans mes actions ou dans l'expression de mes émotions souvent refoulées. Une inflammation survient si j'ai peur d'aller de l'avant : je deviens incapable de bouger, j'ai de la difficulté à changer de direction, je joue le jeu d'être détaché émotionnellement, je n'agis pas avec spontanéité, j'hésite ou je refuse de m'abandonner à la vie et de faire confiance. Lorsque j'ai de la douleur ou de la difficulté à bouger, mon corps exprime que je ne veux pas comprendre (ou accepter ↓♥ de comprendre) quelque chose qui me limite dans l'expression du Soi. Par rapport à ma rigidité à comprendre, en regardant la partie du corps affectée, je peux activer le processus qui consiste **à accepter ↓♥ que j'ai quelque chose à comprendre**. Par exemple, les **poignets**, les **coudes**, les **épaules** ou les **mains** douloureuses indiquent que je dois cesser une action ou un travail quelconque. Je veux me replier sur moi-même (**coudes**) car je suis fatigué ou las de faire ce que je fais ou d'être ce que je suis ; je ne veux plus en être responsable (**épaules**). Les **hanches**, les **genoux** et les **pieds** (membres inférieurs) indiquent que je ne désire plus poursuivre la vie avec les difficultés qu'elle comporte. Je dois me rappeler que l'attention sur un seul et même endroit (c.-à-d. fixer inconsciemment l'énergie ou l'émotion sur une seule **articulation**) peut faire cristalliser cette énergie et immobiliser l'**articulation**. Dans ce cas-ci, le processus d'acceptation ↓♥ au niveau du

---

24. Les os du crâne reliés entre eux sont généralement considérés comme des articulations immobiles.

cœur est essentiel pour intégrer la prise de conscience par rapport à cette maladie et ainsi s'en libérer. Une **jointure** est un endroit où deux os se rencontrent. Un malaise ou une maladie concernant celle-ci dénote une inflexibilité par rapport à moi-même ou envers une personne ou une situation. Je peux trouver face à quel aspect de ma vie j'ai avantage à être plus flexible en regardant quelle partie de mon corps est affectée. Est-ce que ce sont les **jointures** de mes **doigts**, de mes **poignets**, de mes **chevilles**, etc. ?

ARTICULATIONS — ENTORSE

Les **entorses** se retrouvent au niveau de l'une ou l'autre de mes articulations et sont dues à une lésion des ligaments d'une de celles-ci. Les articulations représentent la **flexibilité** et ma capacité de me plier aux différentes situations de ma vie. Le **poignet** et la **cheville** sont l'expression de l'énergie, juste avant qu'elle ne se manifeste dans le physique. L'**entorse** me signale que j'applique les freins. Je **résiste** ou je vis de l'**insécurité** face à la direction que je prends (**cheville**) ou dans ce que je fais (**poignet**) présentement ou ce que je pourrais faire dans une nouvelle situation. Je vis de la culpabilité et je veux me punir parce que je résiste. Je vis une tension mentale qui ne peut plus être tolérée. Dépendamment de mon taux de résistance, de colère, de culpabilité ou de tension mentale, j'aurai une **entorse** bénigne aussi appelée **foulure,** où les ligaments sont simplement distendus, ou une **entorse** grave, où les ligaments sont rompus ou arrachés. Je prends conscience de ce que je faisais et ressentais au moment où c'est arrivé. Je peux me demander : Suis-je sur le point de faire quelque chose auquel il serait préférable de renoncer ? Est-ce que la façon dont je traite une situation me cause une tension ou une angoisse réelle ? Est-ce que je siège sur une base instable et dérangeante mentalement ? J'accepte ↓♥ de prendre le temps de me réorienter ou d'apporter les changements nécessaires pour que je puisse être bien dans ma peau et aller de l'avant librement. J'accepte ↓♥ la présence de cette **entorse** pour m'amener à faire des changements. Si l'acceptation ↓♥ est faite, la guérison va être rapide et complète. Mais si, parce que maintenant je ne peux pas ou peu marcher, je me dévalorise et je me sens inutile et « bon à rien », la guérison sera beaucoup plus longue. C'est pourquoi j'ai avantage à voir cette situation (l'**entorse** et ce qu'elle implique) d'une façon positive et constructive.

ARYTHMIE CARDIAQUE (voir : CŒUR — ARYTHMIE CARDIAQUE)

ASPHYXIE (voir : RESPIRATION — ASPHYXIE)

ASTHÉNIE NERVEUSE (voir aussi : BURNOUT)

L'**asthénie nerveuse** est semblable au « burnout », qui est une forme

d'épuisement énergétique et nerveux. Cependant, elle est différente de la fatigue, qui est un phénomène naturel, puisqu'elle ne provient pas du travail ou d'un effort et qu'elle ne disparaît pas nécessairement avec le repos. La manifestation s'installe à différents niveaux (physique et intérieur), plusieurs états ou sentiments fondamentaux refont surface : peur, tristesse profonde, émotivité amplifiée, remords d'expériences passées et même amertume. Même si l'**asthénie**, qu'elle soit somatique, psychique ou réactionnelle, peut découler de plusieurs causes, je vérifie ce qui m'amène à manifester cet état. Je peux changer cela à la condition de trouver la cause profonde qui m'a amené à « perdre » toute ma belle détermination d'être et de faire et à avoir une attitude passive et de fuite devant l'effort.

ASTHME (appelé aussi « cri silencieux »)
(voir aussi : ALLERGIES, POUMONS [maux aux...], RESPIRATION [maux de...])

L'**asthme** est une affection respiratoire caractérisée par la difficulté à respirer, pouvant même aller jusqu'à la suffocation. Lors d'une crise d'**asthme**, la réaction du système immunitaire face aux substances causant des allergies (allergènes) est tellement forte qu'elle peut entraîner un blocage de la respiration corporelle, des sifflements respiratoires et parfois même la mort. J'ai besoin de prendre la vie en moi (inspiration) et je n'arrive pas à donner (expiration) au point où je commence à paniquer (j'**inspire** facilement mais j'**expire** avec difficulté), si bien que la **respiration**, c'est-à-dire mon habileté à respirer, devient insuffisante et très limitée car je libère un minimum d'air. Est-ce que je m'accroche à certaines personnes ou à certaines choses que je refuse de laisser aller ? Est-ce que je m'étouffe avec de la rage ou de l'agressivité que je refuse de voir au point où cela me « prend à la gorge » ? Est-ce que j'ai peur de manquer de quelque chose, surtout d'amour ? Ainsi, l'**asthme** est fondamentalement relié à l'action d'« étouffer ». Je me sens **pris à la gorge**, je **suffoque**, j'**étouffe** par rapport à un être aimé ou à une situation. **Je me sens limité dans mon espace.** Je peux même vivre de la dispute qui m'amène à la confrontation, à l'affrontement et qui empoisonne ma vie. J'utilise l'**asthme** pour attirer l'amour, l'attention ou une forme de **dépendance affective**. L'**asthme** étant semblable à l'asphyxie et à l'allergie, je peux avoir le sentiment d'être limité et de me **laisser envahir par les autres dans mon espace vital**, d'être facilement impressionné par le pouvoir des autres au détriment du mien, de vouloir faire plaisir, d'accomplir des actions qui ne me conviennent pas, allant même jusqu'à étouffer pour signifier une révolte intérieure reliée à une situation. C'est un excellent moyen de me sentir fort, d'obtenir tout ce que je veux en manipulant autrui... Comme personne, si je ne veux pas voir mes limitations, la confiance en moi sera remplacée subitement par de l'inquiétude et de l'angoisse. Je ne saurai pas comment « dealer » avec mes émotions et je sentirai une grande solitude. J'aurai à apprendre à bien connaître mes forces et mes faiblesses afin d'être en harmonie avec la vie et de me permettre d'apprécier celle-ci. Les autres feront tout pour me sauver ! J'ai l'image d'une personne faible qui exige beaucoup

d'amour sans être prête au don d'Amour, comme un enfant qui crie pour ses besoins sans avoir la maturité de partager et de s'ouvrir suffisamment au don divin. La vie est un **échange mutuel, équilibré et constant entre donner et recevoir.** Tout cela est évidemment relié à une **peur du passé**, à une sorte d'amour étouffant que j'ai interprété comme tel (généralement maternel), à une tristesse de la prime enfance refoulée. C'est aussi une peur remontant à ma première respiration, lors de ma naissance, où je me suis senti étouffé ou apeuré par **ma mère** (inconsciemment) ou par une situation semblable. Ainsi, la respiration symbolise l'indépendance de vie, l'individualité, la capacité de respirer soi-même. Je n'arrive pas à manifester un sentiment d'indépendance, à vivre ma propre vie, je me sens rejeté par l'arrivée de quelqu'un d'autre, j'éprouve des difficultés à me prendre en main et à décrocher de mes attaches parentales (une dépendance répressive, surtout face à la mère ou à la conjointe). **Je ne conçois pas de me séparer de cette merveilleuse image (ma mère) douce et rassurante, de me marier ou de voir mes parents divorcer sans que je sois en réaction !** Je suis en colère « bleue », je suis fou de rage et la crise d'**asthme** s'ensuit. Je vérifie si le malaise revient périodiquement et je change ma programmation mentale. Je prends maintenant ma vie en main, je donne généreusement et tranquillement **sans forcer**. Je reconnais humblement ce que je suis capable de réaliser même si cela semble peu et, surtout, j'accepte ↓♥ de m'ouvrir au niveau du cœur et de travailler avec le processus d'intégration qui correspond à ce dont j'ai vraiment besoin. Tout s'arrangera pour le mieux, je serai satisfait, comblé d'amour, de tendresse et doté d'une respiration normale et équilibrée. J'apprends à m'aimer et à aimer la vie.

ASTHME DU BÉBÉ

L'**asthme du bébé** est encore plus prononcé que l'**asthme commun.** Le nourrisson a tellement peur de la vie et de vivre qu'il manifeste déjà à ce stade le refus d'être ici. Il est bon que je lui parle en pensée ou en parole avec un cœur ouvert pour lui dire combien il est aimé, apprécié et que je veille à lui procurer ce dont il a besoin.

ASTIGMATISME (voir : YEUX — ASTIGMATISME)

ATAXIE[25] DE FRIEDREICH

L'**ataxie de Friedreich** est une maladie du système nerveux caractérisée par des dégénérescenses touchant la mœlle épinière et le cervelet[26]. Elle a généralement pour origine un schème de pensée chez moi, en tant que mère. Ce schème est si puissant que le fœtus que j'ai engendré (l'enfant en gestation)

---

25. **Ataxie :** Signifie l'incoordination des mouvements.
26. **Cervelet :** Est situé à la base du crâne; il est responsable de la coordination des muscles nécessaires à l'équilibre et au mouvement.

le capte et répond à celui-ci sans condition (comme l'amour d'une mère pour son enfant). Je m'attends tellement à avoir un enfant qui répondra à mon ou à mes rêves qu'il finira par sentir une totale impuissance à me combler. Étant cet enfant, j'ai peur de ne pas pouvoir accomplir tout ce que ma mère me demande et de ne pas être à la hauteur de ce pourquoi je me suis programmé. J'ai peur de ne pas avoir le **véhicule physique** (A- « taxi »-e) approprié au bon moment. Il se manifeste alors un blocage en ce qui a trait à mon développement. Quel que soit l'âge de l'enfant, je me dois, en tant que mère, de lui expliquer que j'ai peut-être des idéaux pour lui, mais que c'est parce que je l'aime et que je veux ce qu'il y a de mieux pour lui. Quelles que soient les forces ou les difficultés de mon enfant, je l'aime tel qu'il est et il n'a pas à devenir un « superman ». Si l'enfant est au stade de gestation, je peux lui parler intérieurement parce que, même à cet âge, il comprend tout ce que je lui dis. S'il est un peu plus âgé, je prends le temps de lui parler : il sentira alors tout l'amour que j'ai pour lui et le processus de guérison pourra alors s'enclencher. Rien ne vaut l'amour et le pardon pour rétablir l'harmonie entre deux êtres.

ATHÉROSCLÉROSE (voir : ARTÉRIOSCLÉROSE)

ATTAQUE CARDIAQUE (voir : CŒUR — INFARCTUS [... du myocarde])

AUDITION (maux d'...) (voir : OREILLES — SURDITÉ)

AURICULAIRE (voir : DOIGTS — AURICULAIRE)

AUTISME

L'**autisme** est le refus ultime de faire face à la réalité physique du monde extérieur, ce qui amène une forme de repli sur mon monde intérieur où règnent l'imaginaire et les fantasmes. Je fuis une situation ou mon entourage parce que j'ai trop mal, ou parce que je vois ma sensibilité bafouée. Ma peine, ma tristesse ou mon désespoir sont tellement grands que je me « coupe » du physique tout en continuant à avoir ce même corps physique. Le monde extérieur m'apparaît comme hostile et menaçant. Le fait que moi, en tant que personne **autistique**, je me sois « renfermé » volontairement dans ma « bulle » hermétique implique que je reçoive des milliers d'informations par jour qui sont « emmagasinées » et « stockées » dans mon monde intérieur au lieu d'échanger celles-ci avec d'autres personnes. Je me retrouve dans un trou noir, une route qui me paraît sans issue. J'ai l'impression que les standards que je dois atteindre sont tellement élevés qu'il est plus facile de me retrancher dans un mutisme plutôt que d'avoir à me dépasser constamment et d'avoir à « rendre des comptes » aux autres (parents, professeurs, autorité, patron, etc.). Il est possible de traiter ce genre de cas, mais les guérisons seront beaucoup plus intérieures qu'extérieures, en supposant

qu'elles existent. Quoi qu'il en soit, mon entourage doit être capable de communiquer à partir de l'intérieur (ou du monde intérieur) avec **moi** pour m'amener à me connecter de nouveau ou davantage au monde physique. Ainsi, en me projetant dans mon monde intérieur, on est plus à même de prendre contact avec moi et de mieux reconnaître mes besoins et mes peurs pour que je puisse ensuite manifester la confiance et l'ouverture nécessaires pour reprendre contact avec le monde physique.

AUTOLYSE (voir : SUICIDE)

AUTOMUTILATION (voir aussi : AMPUTATION)

L'**automutilation** est un comportement qui m'amène à m'infliger des blessures ou des lésions. Il se peut que cette attitude puisse provenir d'un état mental déjà perturbé comme chez les psychotiques, les schizophrènes, les enfants déficients. Cependant, cela peut provenir du fait que je vive une grande culpabilité dans ma vie qui peut être associée à une grande irritabilité retournée contre moi, puisque je ne me sens pas digne d'être ce que je suis. Je peux aussi me servir de ces blessures que je m'inflige pour m'attirer de l'attention, que j'identifie à de l'amour. C'est comme si je voulais manifester physiquement ma souffrance intérieure pour pouvoir m'en libérer et mettre à jour mon besoin d'être aimé. Il est certain que, dans de telles situations, j'ai besoin d'aide extérieure. Je commence donc à demander de l'aide intérieure et je regarde dans mon entourage qui pourrait m'aider directement ou indirectement à retrouver l'estime de moi, la joie de vivre que j'ai le droit, moi aussi, de goûter.

AUTORITARISME

La personne qui manifeste de l'**autoritarisme** est fortement en réaction, consciemment ou non, par rapport à l'autorité, quelle qu'en soit la forme. Je crois fermement que c'est là le seul moyen de me faire comprendre et de faire saisir aux autres le « comment ça marche » : « *C'est comme cela que ça fonctionne dans cet univers !* » Malheureusement (surtout pour les gens utilisant ce pouvoir sur une masse d'individus), je manifeste un caractère égocentrique à outrance. La colère se retrouve en toile de fond, surtout quand je sens une résistance face à ce que je demande. Je fais aussi la « sourde oreille » à ce que l'on peut me dire. Comme personne **autoritaire**, je pourrai aussi **grincer des dents** ou avoir des **problèmes de genoux.** « *Il n'est pas question que je plie devant qui que ce soit !* » Rien ne m'arrête, ni situation ni circonstance sauf peut-être **celles qui atteignent directement et profondément mon cœur blessé**. Le besoin d'amour est grand chez moi comme individu et il n'y a que l'ouverture du cœur pour permettre à la lumière d'éclairer ma triste vie. Le pire supplice que je peux subir comme personne **autoritaire** est de me mettre à genoux devant plus grand que moi ; c'est habituellement à ce niveau que se manifestent les malaises d'ordre physique. Si le cœur ne s'ouvre pas, la vie s'en

43

chargera. Le besoin d'amour est grand. Plus j'en serai conscient, plus je serai à même de rechercher les moyens de combler cet amour et de guérir mon cœur blessé.

AVANT-BRAS (voir : BRAS [malaises aux...])

AVEUGLE (voir : YEUX — AVEUGLE)

AVORTEMENT (voir : ACCOUCHEMENT — AVORTEMENT)

BÂILLEMENT

Le **bâillement** est une « maladie d'imitation naturelle » plus ou moins acceptée ↓♥ en société et en raison de ses conventions (je dis naturelle, car à ce jour, il n'y a pas de traitement médical pour soigner celle-ci). Je dis **d'imitation** parce qu'elle se manifeste impulsivement et inconsciemment chez une personne qui en voit une autre faire cette action. C'est le signe d'aller au lit ou de me reposer quand je suis fatigué, épuisé et que j'ai besoin de refaire mes forces. C'est aussi un signe d'insatisfaction alimentaire car il m'arrive de **bâiller** si je n'ai pas suffisamment mangé. Je m'ennuie au point où je l'exprime d'une manière inconsciente, que je sois seul à regarder la télévision ou en compagnie d'une personne qui ne me convient pas ! « Je veux qu'on me laisse tranquille ! » **Bâiller** fait partie de la vie et je l'accepte ↓♥ avec amour et ouverture. Il est important de laisser aller cette expression corporelle contestée par les principes d'éducation d'autrefois !

BALLONNEMENTS
(voir aussi : ESTOMAC / [en général] / [maux d'...], GAZ)

Les **ballonnements** sont dus à un gonflement d'air ou d'eau au niveau de l'estomac et du ventre. Ils sont reliés à une frustration affective, au **sentiment** d'être insatisfait sur le plan affectif. Je dis **sentiment** car c'est une création de mon mental, l'impression cérébrale que mon estomac en veut toujours plus, que je veux encore plus d'attention et d'affection. Je n'arrive pas à voir vraiment ce que la vie me donne de si bien. Je vérifie sincèrement à quel point je suis vraiment comblé affectivement. C'est toujours une question de perception intérieure. Je suis maintenant conscient que la vie me donne exactement ce dont j'ai besoin dans le moment présent. J'accepte ↓♥ d'« être » une personne souriante, de vivre et de voir les beaux côtés de la vie, et de rester ouvert...

BAS DU DOS (voir : DOS — BAS DU DOS)

BASSE PRESSION
(voir : TENSION ARTÉRIELLE — HYPOTENSION [trop basse])

BASSIN (voir aussi : HANCHES [maux de...])

Le **bassin** est la partie osseuse qui réunit et qui sépare en même temps la partie inférieure de la partie supérieure du squelette humain. C'est **l'endroit d'origine** de **tous les mouvements** de déplacement, de locomotion et d'action du corps. Il correspond au fait de **m'élancer dans la vie**. Le **bassin** représente le **pouvoir** sous toutes ses formes. C'est le récipient qui accueille les énergies du pouvoir qui entretiennent l'ego. Si j'ai un **bassin large** ou très large (avec de grosses fesses), je crois inconsciemment que la vie ou les situations de ma vie **limitent** mon pouvoir. Je cherche donc à le reprendre. Je cherche à compenser physiquement en bloquant d'une manière involontaire toutes les énergies à cet endroit (peur, insécurité, colère). Il pourra s'ensuivre un malaise ou un conflit en ce qui a trait à ma sexualité. Il est important que les énergies circulent plus harmonieusement dans mon corps et que je crois sincèrement avoir fait ce qu'il fallait. Même si je veux prendre du pouvoir, je peux prendre conscience et accepter ↓♥ avec le cœur qu'il **n'y a pas de pouvoir** à prendre sauf celui du plan mental. Si je veux libérer toutes ces énergies et retrouver un meilleur équilibre énergétique, je commence à m'aimer tel que je suis, à manifester de la joie, de la confiance et de la foi dans tout ce que je fais. Je vide ce récipient de pouvoir et je laisse circuler la vie. D'autre part, si j'éprouve quelques difficultés au niveau de mon **bassin**, il est possible que je déprécie l'importance de mes besoins fondamentaux comme le logement, la nourriture, la sexualité. J'ai à reconsidérer l'importance que je dois attribuer aux différents aspects de ma vie pour qu'elle soit assise sur des bases solides et saines.

BÉBÉ BLEU (voir : ENFANT BLEU)

BÉGAIEMENT (voir aussi : BOUCHE, GORGE [en général])

Le **bégaiement** est la manifestation d'un trouble d'élocution, une difficulté partielle ou grave à parler, à dire et à m'exprimer clairement (cela va de quelques mots par accident à un trouble régulier). Il est relié à la gorge, au centre de la communication et de l'expression de soi. Il se peut que mon **bégaiement** provienne d'un blocage affectif ou sexuel découlant de mon enfance. Ceci ne veut pas nécessairement dire que j'ai vécu des attouchements, mais j'ai pu enregistrer une peur, consciemment ou non, par rapport à ma sexualité en relation avec une personne ou un événement. C'est une forme **d'insécurité profonde** venant de l'enfance qui est reliée à la peur d'un parent (la mère ou le père). C'est une sorte de **refoulement**, une incapacité à maîtriser adéquatement mes pensées et mes émotions intenses et la tentative échouée de

contrôler l'expression de mon langage qui n'est plus spontané (ce type de désordre peut arriver tôt dans l'enfance lorsque l'enfant a été ridiculisé dans son droit de pleurer : « *Ne pleure pas !* »). Je transforme alors cette émotion en **bégaiement**. J'ai peur d'être « clair », j'hésite, je n'arrive pas à dire clairement ce que je ressens, je refoule et déforme mes paroles par peur du rejet ou par anxiété. *Si je dis clairement ce que je vis, mes parents vont-ils le prendre ? Suis-je assez correct pour eux ? Est-ce que je réponds à leurs attentes ? Me permettent-ils d'être ce que je suis ? Mes paroles dépassent-elles mes pensées ?* Il y a de fortes chances qu'un ou que mes deux parents soient très autoritaires et dominateurs. Je me sens jugé, contrôlé, critiqué et même ridiculisé suffisamment pour que je finisse par croire que mes paroles ne valent rien. Comme enfant, on peut aussi m'avoir empêché de m'exprimer. Je manifeste alors toutes sortes de désordres de comportement, allant de la timidité au repli sur moi. Le premier pas est d'accepter ↓♥ de m'ouvrir au niveau du cœur à mes **pensées**, à mes **paroles,** à mes **actions** et surtout à mes **émotions** et mes **désirs**. Il est important que je prenne le temps et que je respecte la « vitesse d'être » qui est la mienne. Je me respecte tel que je suis, sans jugement ni critique. J'accepte ↓♥ d'exprimer mes idées, mes joies, mes peines et mes peurs. Je peux alors commencer à me faire confiance, à ressentir mes émotions, mes sentiments et à m'ouvrir aux gens que j'aime. Ainsi, je retrouve un calme intérieur qui me permet de m'exprimer avec beaucoup plus d'assurance. J'éviterai ainsi les bafouillages, la bousculade des mots à cause d'un esprit trop actif, ou la retenue de certains mots dont je crains la répercussion.

BESOINS (en général) (voir : DÉPENDANCE)

BILIAIRES (calculs...) (voir : CALCULS BILIAIRES)

BLEUS (voir : PEAU — BLEUS)

BOSSE DE BISON (voir : ÉPAULES VOÛTÉES)

BOSSU (voir : ÉPAULES VOÛTÉES)

BOUCHE (en général) (voir aussi : GENCIVES)

La **bouche** représente l'ouverture à la vie. C'est un organe sensoriel sensible et sélectif. C'est la porte d'entrée de la nourriture, de l'air et de l'eau. C'est à cause d'elle si je peux parler (lèvres, langue, cordes vocales), communiquer et faire sortir mes émotions et mes pensées. C'est une sorte de pont entre mon être intérieur et l'univers autour de moi (la réalité). La **bouche** est donc la manifestation de ma personnalité, de mes appétits, de mes désirs,

de mes attentes et de mes traits de caractère. Elle permet de m'ouvrir à tout ce qui est **nouveau** : sensations, idées et impressions. Ainsi, elle est une voie (« voix ») à double sens et les difficultés que je vis ont fondamentalement un double aspect, intérieur et extérieur.

BOUCHE (malaise de...)
(voir aussi : CANCER DE LA BOUCHE, CHANCRE [en général], HERPÈS [...buccal], MUGUET)

La **bouche** est la porte de l'appareil digestif et des voies respiratoires où j'accepte ↓♥ de prendre tout ce qui est nécessaire à mon existence physique (eau, nourriture, air), émotionnelle et sensorielle (excitations, désirs, goûts, appétits, besoins, etc.). Ainsi, **les malaises à la bouche** sont l'indication que je fais preuve d'une certaine étroitesse d'esprit, que j'ai des idées et des opinions rigides et que j'éprouve de la difficulté à prendre et à **avaler** ce qui est **nouveau** (pensées, idées, sentiments, émotions). Il y a une situation que je ne peux pas « gober » : ce sont souvent des paroles entendues qui m'ont dérangé ou blessé ou des paroles que j'aurais aimé entendre et qui n'ont pas été dites. Je veux donc répliquer ou répondre et je ne le fais pas parce que je me sens inconfortable dans la situation ou que l'occasion ne se présente tout simplement pas. Je reste donc « pris » avec ce que j'ai à dire. Mon corps m'envoie le message que je manifeste peut-être des idées malsaines par l'intermédiaire de ma **bouche**, que j'ai à changer d'attitude par rapport à moi-même et aux autres. L'exemple type est le **chancre ou ulcère buccal** (**herpès**) qui se manifeste habituellement à la suite d'un stress ou d'un traumatisme pendant ou après une période nerveuse intense ou une maladie. Il me montre de quelle manière triste et irritable je prends la réalité quotidienne. Il est possible **que je me sente « poigné »** : que je me sente **pris** dans la situation (bouché), que je rumine une situation désagréable depuis longtemps ou que j'aie vraiment besoin de recouvrer ma complète liberté en disant ce que j'ai à dire, même si cela risque de me déplaire. Je peux aussi « avoir faim » d'amour, d'affection, de connaissance, de spiritualité, de liberté, etc. Si j'ai l'impression que ce dont j'ai besoin n'est pas accessible ou irréaliste, ma bouche affamée réagira à la sensation de manque que je ressens. Je prends ma place en restant ouvert et flexible à ce qui débute pour moi, à ce qui est **nouveau**, pourvu que ce soit en harmonie.

BOUCHE — APTHE

L'**apthe** est une lésion superficielle sur la muqueuse buccale (bouche)[27] caractérisée par une petite protubérance blanche. Elle apparaît parce que je réagis facilement (sensibilité) à mon entourage, aux « vibrations », à l'ambiance d'une situation. Je **souffre silencieusement la bouche fermée**. Elle est aussi le signe que j'**ai des difficultés à prendre racine** et que je n'arrive pas

---

27. L'**apthe** se retrouve parfois sur la muqueuse génitale.

à m'exprimer, à dire ce que je pense ou même à réagir, car je ne crois pas avoir le pouvoir de le faire. Je peux, étant jeune, m'être retrouvé dans une situation où je me suis senti mal à l'aise par rapport à une situation dont j'ai eu connaissance et où j'ai été incapable de réagir ou de m'affirmer. Si je revis une situation semblable aujourd'hui me rappellant, même inconsciemment, cette expérience, des **aphtes** apparaîtront. Mes paroles sont vaines et incomplètes parce que je suis trop nerveux. Je reste muet, sans même penser à me révolter ! Si je vis une injustice, du dégoût ou une insatisfaction cachée (dans la bouche), si j'ai envie de me « vider le cœur », je peux le faire en restant ouvert et en harmonie avec moi-même. Cependant, comme ces protubérances blanches sont très douloureuses, dès que j'ouvre la bouche pour m'exprimer, je les sens et ça me fait mal. Si je veux éviter de les voir revenir d'une façon plus grave, je commence à m'exprimer ouvertement et calmement dès maintenant.

BOUCHE — HALEINE (mauvaise...)
(voir aussi : GENCIVE — GINGIVITE, GORGE [maux de...], NEZ [maux au...])

La **mauvaise haleine** est la conséquence directe de ma difficulté à traiter intérieurement et extérieurement les situations que je vis. Cette difficulté peut provenir du fait que je reste sur mes positions par rapport à certaines idées que je n'exprime pas et qui pourrissent sur place. La difficulté peut provenir aussi du fait que je n'arrive pas à prendre le dessus en période de grand changement dans ma vie et que les idées anciennes stagnent trop longtemps par rapport à la rapidité du changement que je vis. Je vérifie jusqu'à quel point je peux « prendre » les situations de ma vie. Il est important que je communique avec les personnes concernées afin de leur faire part de mes émotions et de mes pensées afin de me « débarrasser » de ma **mauvaise haleine.** Cette dernière est souvent reliée à des pensées de médisance, de haine, de vengeance que j'ai contre moi-même ou contre une autre personne et dont j'ai honte. L'air que j'inspire et qui nourrit mes cellules est chargé de toutes mes pensées, tant positives que négatives. Par quelles pensées qui grugent mon intérieur mon **haleine** est-elle infectée ? Souvent, ces pensées peuvent être inconscientes. Lorsqu'une personne vit cette situation constamment, il serait bon de le lui dire afin qu'elle en prenne conscience, et qu'elle remédie à ce problème qui peut persister déjà depuis un bon moment. Le sachant, elle aura l'occasion d'expérimenter le pardon. Soit le pardon envers elle-même pour avoir entretenu des pensées malsaines, ou celui envers une autre personne pour lui en avoir tant voulu. Il est bon de me souvenir que lorsque l'amour et l'honnêteté seront des ingrédients de base de mes pensées, mon **haleine** redeviendra fraîche. Je me libère des pensées malsaines du passé. Maintenant, je respire la fraîcheur de mes nouvelles pensées positives d'amour, envers moi-même et envers les autres.

BOUCHE — MUGUET (voir : MUGUET)

BOUCHE — PALAIS

Le **palais** est le plafond osseux de la cavité buccale. Celui-ci sera affecté si je croyais avoir reçu ou acquis quelque chose (par exemple un nouvel emploi) mais qu'on me le soutire par la suite. Je vivrai donc une grande frustation et déception car je pensais que cette chose m'appartenait déjà mais on me l'a soutirée. Je dois me demander pourquoi cette situation s'est produite. Est-ce que j'avais trop d'attentes ? Est-ce que je dois mettre des efforts à regagner ce que je croyais avoir perdu ou peut-être en est-il mieux ainsi ? Voilà les questions que je peux me poser afin que l'harmonie revienne et que mon **palais** guérisse.

BOUFFÉES DE CHALEUR (voir : MÉNOPAUSE)

BOULIMIE (voir aussi : ANOREXIE, APPÉTIT [excès d'...], POIDS [excès de...])

La **boulimie** une maladie compulsive, un besoin incontrôlable d'absorber de la nourriture en grande quantité, un déséquilibre nerveux car je suis en **réaction totale** face à la vie. La **boulimie** présente les mêmes causes intérieures que l'obésité et l'anorexie. Je mange avec excès pour me satisfaire complètement ou pour retrouver une forme d'amour et d'affection (la nourriture symbolise la vie, l'amour et les émotions). J'essaie de combler émotionnellement un profond vide intérieur en moi, une haine de moi si grande (dégoût, mépris) que je veux remplir ce vide à tout prix, préférant me laisser dominer par la nourriture (la vie) plutôt que de m'ouvrir à la vie. Je renie une partie de moi-même, une situation et je vis du chagrin ou de la colère car je me sens isolé, séparé ou rejeté. Je rejette mon corps totalement ; je refuse de vivre sur cette terre. J'ai peur de perdre ce que j'ai et je ressens de l'insécurité parce que je suis peut-être différent des autres. Je ne me sens plus capable de « mordre dans la vie ». Je n'ai pas tout ce que je veux ou je **ne maîtrise pas suffisamment** mes désirs et mes émotions. Je recherche constamment le besoin criant de me sentir plus fort que la nourriture, que mes sentiments et mes émotions. Je préfère donc me faire vomir plutôt qu'être en santé, car je me méprise profondément. Je vis généralement une profonde dépression, un désespoir, une angoisse que je cherche à apaiser, une frustration pour laquelle je cherche à compenser, j'ai une image de moi que je veux revaloriser. La **boulimie** est très reliée à la mère (source de vie), au côté maternel et à la création. Suis-je en réaction par rapport à ma mère ? Est-ce que j'ai le sentiment d'avoir été contrôlé et brimé étant jeune, si bien qu'en mangeant ainsi, je veux fuir ma mère, la neutraliser (au sens métaphysique) ou quitter cette planète ? Ai-je de la joie à me comporter de cette façon ? Se peut-il que j'aie vécu l'étape de sevrage quand j'étais bébé comme un **abandon** ? Comme si on « m'arrachait » à ma mère ? Si c'est le cas, j'ai l'impression que je vais « mourir de faim », d'où le besoin de manger de grandes quantités de nourriture pour combler le vide et pour faire diminuer mon stress. Comme **personne boulimique**, je dois rester ouverte à l'amour. La nécessité

d'accepter ↓♥ que j'ai quelque chose à comprendre de cet état dépressif me conduit à l'amour et j'apprends à m'aimer et à m'accepter ↓♥ davantage en tant que canal pour l'énergie divine. Je suis sur terre pour accomplir une mission pour moi, avec ma mère et avec les gens que j'aime. Pourquoi ne pas apprécier la beauté de l'univers ? J'accepte ↓♥ mon corps tel qu'il est, l'ego et ses limites, la nourriture comme don de vie. J'accepte ↓♥ l'amour pour moi-même et pour les autres et je découvre les joies d'être en ce monde. C'est tout.

BOURDONNEMENT D'OREILLES
(voir : OREILLES — BOURDONNEMENT D'OREILLES)

BOURSOUFLURE (voir : ENFLURE)

BOUTONS (..., ... sur tout le corps) (voir : PEAU — BOUTONS)

BOUTONS DE FIÈVRE (voir : FIÈVRE [boutons de...])

BRADYCARDIE (voir : CŒUR — ARYTHMIE CARDIAQUE)

BRAS (en général)

Les **bras** représentent ma **capacité à accueillir les nouvelles expériences de vie**. Je les utilise pour toucher et pour serrer, pour exprimer ma créativité, mon potentiel d'action et mon amour. Je peux entrer en contact avec les gens, m'approcher d'eux et les accueillir dans mon univers. Je leur montre aussi que je les aime avec joie et harmonie. À cause d'eux, je passe à l'action, je fais mon travail ou je m'acquitte de mes obligations. Mes **bras** communiquent et expriment donc mes attitudes et mes sentiments intérieurs. Les **bras** sont très proches du cœur et ils sont reliés à celui-ci. Ainsi, les gens sentent que l'amour et l'énergie émanent de mon cœur lorsque je suis ouvert. Chaque main renferme un centre d'énergie, situé dans la paume, qui représente un des 21 centres d'énergie mineurs (ou chakras). Les deux centres d'énergie des mains sont reliés directement au cœur. Ainsi, mes **bras** permettent d'extensionner mon cœur et d'aller porter de l'amour physiquement et énergétiquement. Par contre, si je croise les **bras** instinctivement, je me protège ou je me ferme à certaines émotions qui ne me conviennent pas.

BRAS (malaises aux...)

Les **malaises aux bras** sont reliés à la difficulté de manifester l'amour dans ce que je fais, dans mon travail ou dans mes actions de tous les jours. C'est un blocage d'énergie, une **retenue** à faire quelque chose pour moi-même ou pour autrui. Je peux alors sentir de la rigidité musculaire, de la douleur ou de la chaleur

(inflammation). Mes **bras** deviennent moins mobiles et plus tendus, mes articulations (épaules, coudes), plus douloureuses. Je sais que le rôle de mes **bras** est dans leur capacité à prendre les nouvelles situations et les nouvelles expériences de ma vie. Je suis peut-être en réaction vis-à-vis une nouvelle situation ; je ne trouve plus mon travail motivant ; je suis frustré ou irrité parce que je ne parviens pas à m'exprimer convenablement, ou parce que j'ai de la difficulté à réaliser un projet. Une situation que je qualifie « d'échec » pourra s'extérioriser par une douleur aux **bras**. Ce sont généralement les **os de mes bras** qui seront affectés lorsque je ne suis plus capable de faire aussi bien qu'auparavant une activité professionnelle ou sportive dans laquelle j'excellais. Je n'arrive pas à prendre les gens que j'aime dans mes **bras** ; je refuse de reconnaître que j'en ai plus qu'assez d'une situation qui est néfaste pour moi (**en avoir plein les bras**). En général, avoir mal aux **bras** signifie que j'en prends trop. C'est peut-être aussi quelque chose que je ne **prends** pas ou que je refuse de prendre. Je n'ai peut-être plus envie de communiquer avec les autres au niveau du cœur, je doute de toutes mes capacités à réaliser quelque chose. Aller de l'avant dans la vie me semble difficile. Les douleurs sont donc une manière inconsciente de montrer que je souffre. J'ai peut-être à « lâcher prise » à « laisser aller », une situation ou une personne que je veux « retenir » à tout prix. Une difficulté avec l'autorité peut se manifester dans le **bras droit**, tandis que ce sera mon **bras gauche** qui sera affecté si je vis un conflit à exprimer mon amour et ma gentillesse. Les hommes ont une tendance naturelle à vouloir surdévelopper les muscles de leurs bras qui sont un symbole de force et de puissance, ce qui dénote leur difficulté et leur résistance à exprimer l'énergie du cœur et le côté douceur. Au contraire, des **bras** plus minces et faibles m'indiquent une timidité dans l'expression de mes émotions et une résistance à laisser couler l'énergie. Je me retiens de plonger dans la vie et d'en profiter au maximum. Mes **bras** correspondent plus à mon expression intérieure. Mes **avant-bras**, eux, sont reliés à l'expression extérieure, le « faire ». « Je retrousse mes manches » et je passe à l'action ! La douceur présente le côté interne de mes avant-bras, manifeste ma sensibilité et je peux avoir des hésitations avant d'exprimer physiquement des choses dans l'Univers. J'ai peut-être à changer mes habitudes ou ma façon de faire et cela m'est tellement difficile, en raison de ma rigidité, que mes **avant-bras** vont aussi se raidir. Une irritation cutanée au niveau du **bras** est reliée à une frustration ou à une irritation dans ce que je fais ou ne fais pas, dans la manière de m'exprimer et dans ce qu'il peut m'arriver à la suite de l'intervention des autres. Je dois manifester plus d'amour dans ce que je fais, m'investir, m'ouvrir avec confiance aux autres, serrer dans mes **bras** avec amour et affection les gens que j'aime (l'image du père qui serre son fils en témoignage d'amour). Je me rappelle que l'action de serrer quelqu'un est souvent thérapeutique. J'estime mes belles qualités de communication, de tendresse et d'ouverture. Je place mon attention sur les activités intéressantes. Je me pratique à voir les bons côtés de toute situation. Je le fais en réalisant que c'est merveilleux, que je suis mieux que je ne le pensais. Je me change les idées car j'en ai besoin.

BRIGHT[28] (maladie de...) (voir aussi : REINS [problèmes rénaux])

La maladie de **Bright** est appelée aussi **néphrite chronique**. C'est un mal, mais non une maladie[29], inflammatoire grave des reins, accompagné d'œdème[30] (gonflement) et d'une insuffisance à éliminer les urines. Habituellement, les reins dégénèrent ou meurent assez rapidement. C'est plus profond que les maladies de rein en général (sclérose). Je souffre, et je vis une **frustration** ou une **déception** si intense par rapport à une situation où j'ai un sentiment de perte, que j'en arrive à considérer ma vie ou ma propre personne **comme un échec total** (les reins sont le siège de la peur). J'ai peur de ne pas être assez correct, assez bien, assez **bright** (intelligent). Une ouverture du cœur est nécessaire si je veux manifester un changement d'attitude pour guérir cet état.

BRONCHES (en général) (voir aussi : POUMONS)

Les **bronches** sont les conduits par lesquels l'air entre dans mes poumons. Ils représentent la vie. Un malaise ou une douleur au niveau de mes **bronches** signifie habituellement que j'ai le mal de vivre, que j'ai moins d'intérêt et de joie dans ma vie. Les **bronches** représentent mon espace vital, mes délimitations, le territoire plus particulièrement lié à mon couple, ma famille et mon milieu de travail. Si j'ai l'impression que je vais perdre mon territoire ou quelqu'un qui s'y rattache, mon insécurité va déclencher un malaise aux **bronches.** Cela m'indique que je dois faire confiance, que, si j'ai bien délimité mon territoire et que je le fais respecter autant que je fais respecter mes droits, personne ne pourra m'« envahir » car l'espace de chacun sera bien délimité et chacun pourra vivre dans le respect et l'harmonie. Je vérifie quelle personne ou quelle situation est associée à cette douleur et ce que je dois faire pour changer cela. J'ai avantage à créer des situations qui sont propices au rire et à la détente.

BRONCHE — BRONCHITE (voir aussi : POUMONS [maux aux...])

La **bronchite** (ite = colère) se caractérise par l'inflammation de la muqueuse des **bronches**, conduits menant l'air de la trachée jusqu'aux poumons. C'est une maladie essentiellement reliée à la respiration et à l'action de prendre la vie et l'air avec désir et goût (inspiration) pour ensuite les rejeter temporairement avec détachement (expiration). L'inflammation signifie que je vis de la **colère**, une **frustration** ou de la **rage** par rapport à des émotions

---

28. **Bright (Richard) :** Médecin anglais (1789-1858) qui fut le premier à étudier la néphrite chronique ou insuffisance rénale.

29. Curieusement, la **néphrite chronique** n'est pas une maladie parce qu'elle est une conséquence d'affections qui atteignent certaines parties des reins.

30. **Œdème :** Rétention anormalement élevée dans les tissus de l'organisme. C'est aussi appelé communément « faire de la rétention d'eau ».

refoulées, des paroles que j'ai besoin d'exprimer et de laisser sortir, une situation étouffante où je me sens brimé, un conflit empreint d'agressivité et de critique (bouleversements dans le milieu familial, disputes, etc.). Si cette situation conflictuelle implique des disputes et des affrontements très intenses, je pourrai même développer un **cancer des bronches**. Il existe un trouble intérieur, une perturbation qui m'empêche de manifester mon être véritable, de faire respecter convenablement mes droits. Je tente de communiquer avec mes proches mais je n'arrive pas à une certaine paix intérieure. La situation familiale est trop difficile. Je ressens alors un certain découragement face à la vie et je cesse de lutter pour continuer mon chemin. J'ai peu de joie de vivre et j'ai une profonde lassitude intérieure. La **toux** indique que je veux me libérer en rejetant quelque chose ou quelqu'un qui me dérange et me met en colère. Si je ne désire pas une **bronchite chronique**, je dois changer ma façon de voir la vie, **mon attitude**. Je suis né dans une famille où chacun des membres vit des expériences semblables aux miennes. Mes parents, mes frères et mes sœurs apprennent comme ils le peuvent eux aussi. Je dois commencer à voir la joie et l'amour en moi et en chaque expérience de ma vie. J'accepte ↓♥ que mon bonheur personnel soit ma responsabilité et je cesse de croire que les autres me rendront heureux. Prendre mes décisions et respirer par mes propres moyens, c'est le premier pas vers mon indépendance !

BRONCHE — BRONCHITE AIGUË
(voir : RESPIRATION — TRACHÉITE)

BRONCHOPNEUMONIE (voir aussi : POUMONS [maux aux...])

La **bronchopneumonie** est une inflammation respiratoire atteignant les bronchioles et les alvéoles pulmonaires. C'est directement relié à la vie, au fait que je me sens diminué et limité par la vie elle-même. Je la sens injuste envers moi et cela m'irrite. Je suis en colère contre la vie. C'est une infection **plus grave** que la simple bronchite ou la **pneumonie** parce que **la douleur intérieure est plus profonde**. J'ai à respirer la vie d'une nouvelle manière et avec une approche différente, pleine d'amour et de joie.

BRÛLEMENTS D'ESTOMAC
(voir : ESTOMAC — BRÛLEMENTS D'ESTOMAC)

BRÛLURES (voir aussi : ACCIDENT, PEAU [en général])

La **brûlure,** par différentes sources physiques (chaleur, froid, etc.), provoque une lésion de la peau. La peau est la limite entre l'intérieur et l'extérieur, la frontière entre mon univers intérieur et le monde autour de moi. Il y a quelque chose qui me **brûle** à l'intérieur : une profonde douleur, des émotions profondes et violentes refoulées (colère, chagrin, désespoir) si bien

que je retourne tout ceci contre moi sous forme de **culpabilité** et **d'autopunition (brûlure)**. Une **brûlure** peut impliquer plusieurs niveaux du corps (la chair, le tissu mou, les liquides du corps, parfois les os). Une **brûlure** « émotive » ou « mentale » se manifeste physiquement d'une manière très forte et agressive. Je vérifie la partie du corps brûlée. Pour les **mains**, c'est probablement parce que je me sens très coupable d'accomplir quelque chose relié à **une situation dans le présent**. Pour les **pieds**, ils concernent l'avenir et la direction prochaine de mes actions. Il se peut que je vive une peur de connaître une nouvelle personne ou une nouvelle situation parce que je **brûle** de connaître cette personne ou cette situation. Je crains peut-être que mes projets s'envolent en fumée. Je peux avoir aussi un **désir brûlant** de me retrouver avec une personne que j'aime. Je peux aussi vérifier le type de **brûlure** : les liquides (eau bouillante, gaz) peuvent être reliés à une **réaction émotionnelle violente** alors qu'une **brûlure** avec une substance plus solide (braise, métaux, etc.) implique davantage une **brûlure** (combustion) sur les plans **mental ou spirituel**. Il existe différents types de **brûlures** que l'on classe en fonction de leur profondeur. Ainsi, tout ce qui a été dit plus haut est valable pour ce qui suit avec plus ou moins d'intensité, selon la « profondeur » de la brûlure. Ainsi, les brûlures au **premier degré** qui touchent la partie superficielle de la peau, comme un coup de soleil, peuvent impliquer de la contrariété dans des situations de ma vie. Celles au **deuxième degré** ont trait davantage à de la peine par rapport à un ou des aspects de ma vie que je juge important. Les brûlures au **troisième degré,** qui affectent la peau dans toute sa profondeur, peuvent attaquer un muscle, un tendon ou un organe. Ces brûlures correspondent à une colère et une agressivité intenses qui percent mes protections naturelles tant physiques que psychiques. On ne peut revenir physiquement en arrière sur les cas de **brûlures** graves. Cependant, toutes les qualités divines (amour, tendresse, respect, etc.) peuvent se manifester pour me permettre d'intégrer l'expérience d'une **brûlure** importante. Au lieu de voir seulement les difficultés et les problèmes de ma vie, j'accepte ↓♥ de voir maintenant l'amour dans chaque situation de ma vie. L'amour est partout et je reste ouvert pour tirer les leçons des expériences que je vis. C'est le processus normal d'intégration au niveau du cœur.

BRUXISME (voir : DENTS [grincement de...])

BUCCAL (herpès...) (voir : HERPÈS [...buccal])

BUERGER (maladie de[31]...) (voir aussi : CIGARETTE, ENGOURDISSEMENT, INFLAMMATION, SANG — CIRCULATION SANGUINE)

---

31. **Maladie de Buerger :** Aussi appelée maladie de Léo Buerger.

La **maladie de Buerger** est une maladie qui implique une obstruction plus ou moins marquée de la circulation dans les bras et les jambes, causée par une inflammation des parois des vaisseaux sanguins. Cette maladie concerne principalement les fumeurs et ce sont souvent les agents irritants dans le sang provenant de la cigarette qui sont la cause de cette inflammation. Mon corps m'indique, par mes engourdissements aux bras et aux jambes, que je cherche à me rendre insensible aux situations de la vie, ce qui est relié aux bras, et à ce qui s'en vient pour moi dans l'avenir, ce qui est relié aux jambes. Il est grand temps de prendre en considération le message que mon corps me donne et d'accepter ↓♥ « de voir plus clair » dans ma vie. En cessant de fumer, je ne m'en porterai que mieux.

BURNETT (syndrome de...) (voir : BUVEURS DE LAIT [syndrome de...])

BURNOUT ou ÉPUISEMENT
(voir aussi : ASTHÉNIE NERVEUSE, DÉPRESSION)

Le **burnout** se manifeste généralement après l'abandon d'une lutte où j'aurais voulu exprimer un certain idéal mais sans succès. Le temps et les énergies consacrés à vouloir réaliser cet idéal sont tellement importants que je m'épuise et me rends malade. C'est un **vide intérieur profond** parce que je refuse une situation dans laquelle je veux voir un changement vrai, concret et durable, que ce soit au travail, dans ma famille ou dans mon couple. Je suis très perfectionniste et dévoué, je veux atteindre mon idéal. C'est peut-être aussi une partie de moi que je n'accepte ↓♥ pas. J'ai le sentiment de me battre contre l'humanité entière car il me semble qu'elle fonctionne en désaccord avec mes attentes et mes convictions profondes. « Pourquoi continuer ? J'abandonne, c'en est trop pour moi. » Les **burnout** sont très fréquents chez les enseignants et les infirmiers, en réaction respective face à leur système de travail. C'est une forme de compulsion car je veux **à tout prix** changer le système avec des approches plus adaptées aux temps modernes. Si j'ai l'impression de vouloir sauver le monde, je dois vérifier mon attitude dès maintenant. Le **burnout** est aussi une maladie de **fuite**. Je peux me demander : Qu'est-ce que je cherche à fuir en travaillant avec excès ? Est-ce que j'ai peur de me retrouver face à moi-même ? Est-ce que j'ai besoin d'une raison pour ne plus être avec un conjoint qui m'est insupportable ? Qu'est-ce que j'essaie de prouver en même temps que je fuis la peur de l'échec ? Les symptômes du **burnout** sont assez clairs : fatigue mentale et physique, énergie vitale à la baisse, pensées incohérentes ! L'épuisement survient, et après, le calme et le repos se manifestent pour que je puisse refaire mes énergies. Il faut surtout cesser de croire que je **dois** plaire à tout le monde ! C'est un rêve et la vraie réalité, c'est de savoir que j'accomplis de mon mieux ce que j'ai à faire en donnant 100 % de moi-même, et je retrouve la sérénité, la paix intérieure et le vrai amour dans l'action.

BURSITE (voir aussi : ARTHRITE, BRAS [malaises aux...]), COUDES, ÉPAULES, INFLAMMATION, TENDON D'ACHILLE)

La **bursite** est l'inflammation ou le gonflement de la bourse au niveau de l'articulation de l'épaule, du coude, de la rotule ou des tendons d'Achille (près du pied). Cette bourse qui ressemble à un petit sac contient un liquide réduisant la friction au niveau des articulations. La bourse procure donc un mouvement fluide, aisé et gracieux. La **bursite** indique une **frustration** ou une **irritation intense**, de la **colère retenue** par rapport à une situation ou à quelqu'un que j'ai vraiment envie de « frapper » dans le cas où les bras sont concernés (épaule ou coude), ou de donner « un coup de pied » dans le cas où les jambes sont concernées (rotule ou tendon d'Achille), tellement je suis enragé ! Mes pensées sont **rigides** et quelque chose ne me convient absolument pas ! J'en ai assez et, au lieu d'exprimer ce que je vis, je retiens mes émotions. Il est possible de trouver la cause du désir de frapper en regardant ce que je peux faire et ne pas faire avec ce bras douloureux. Si j'ai mal au côté gauche, c'est relié au plan affectif. Au côté droit, ce sont les responsabilités et le « rationnel » (par exemple : le travail). J'ai de la douleur même si je me retiens de frapper quelqu'un. Je dois trouver une façon plus adéquate d'exprimer ce que je ressens. Je trouve la cause de ma douleur, je reste ouvert et je change d'attitude en acceptant ↓♥ davantage mes sentiments et mes émotions. Je pourrai les transformer en amour et en harmonie à mon avantage et pour le bien-être d'autrui. La **bursite** est souvent reliée à ce que je vis par rapport à mon travail. Mon corps ne fait que me dire d'adopter une attitude plus positive afin de m'adapter aux nouvelles situations qui se présentent.

BUVEURS DE LAIT (syndrome des...)
(voir aussi : ACIDOSE, APATHIE)

Lorsque mon sang est trop alcalin (en opposition à acide) et que j'ai une insuffisance rénale, j'ai ce qu'on appelle le **syndrome des buveurs de lait** ou **syndrome de Burnett**. Il provient habituellement du fait que je prends du lait de façon excessive et sur une longue période de temps ou que je consomme des médicaments antiacides. Je cherche à combler un vide intérieur provenant de l'amour maternel dont je ne me suis pas senti comblé. L'état de fatigue et d'apathie me rappelle jusqu'à quel point ce besoin était important pour moi. Cela ne veut pas dire que j'ai eu une mère qui ne m'aimait pas, mais que moi, j'avais peut-être un plus grand besoin. Il se peut aussi que ce que je trouve amer dans ma vie, je cherche à le combler par ce qui me rappelle le plus la douceur dans ma vie comme dans mon enfance et qui me rappelle l'amour de ma mère. Je dois commencer dès maintenant à prendre soin de moi-même, comme une mère le ferait. J'accepte ↓♥ les douceurs de la vie en sachant que je suis une personne exceptionnelle qui mérite ce qu'il y a de mieux.

CÆCUM (voir : APPENDICITE)

CALCULS (en général) (voir aussi : CALCULS / BILIAIRES / RÉNAUX)

Le **calcul** est une concrétion pierreuse qui se forme par précipitation de certains composants (calcium, cholestérol) de la bile ou de l'urine. Le **calcul** est l'accumulation (ou si on veut « l'addition ») d'idées fausses, de conceptions erronées de la réalité qui peut être illustrée par l'expression « Faire une erreur de calcul », des émotions et des sentiments refoulés ; une concentration de pensées telle une masse d'énergie qui se solidifie et se cristallise au point de former des pierres très dures dans l'organe où la cause de la maladie se manifeste. Je dois faire confiance à la vie et savoir que je peux « compter » sur mon pouvoir divin qui me permettra de voir les événements avec une plus grande ouverture d'esprit et en toute sécurité.

CALCULS BILIAIRES ou LITHIASE BILIAIRE
(voir aussi : FOIE [maux de...], RATE)

Le **calcul biliaire** est généralement un ou des dépôts de cholestérol ou de chaux. Dans le langage populaire, on dit parfois « avoir des **pierres au foie** ». Il vient de la bile. Ce liquide sécrété par le foie sert à la digestion des aliments. La bile passe par la vésicule biliaire et le **calcul** formé se retrouve dans cette même vésicule (un seul gros ou plusieurs petits). La bile est légèrement amère et visqueuse et manifeste l'**amertume** intérieure, la peine, l'agressivité, l'insensibilité, le ressentiment, la frustration ou le mécontentement que j'ai et que je sens envers moi-même ou envers une ou plusieurs personnes. Les **calculs** représentent une douleur plus profonde que les simples symptômes au niveau de la rate, du foie ou de la vésicule biliaire. C'est de l'énergie cristallisée, des sentiments et des **pensées très dures**, de l'**amertume**, de l'**envie** et même de **la jalousie** solidifiées sous forme de cailloux et qui ont été entretenues et accumulées au fil des années. Les **calculs** peuvent être « cachés » depuis longtemps, mais une émotion soudaine et violente peut les faire surgir « consciemment » avec des douleurs intenses. Souvent, je suis décidé à aller de l'avant, à foncer, à ouvrir des portes mais **quelque chose m'arrête**, me limite ou m'étouffe et mes actions sont souvent exécutées par peur. Je deviens alors frustré de la vie, je manifeste des attitudes « amères » et irritantes vis-à-vis des gens, je n'arrive pas à me décider car je manque de courage et mes forces intérieures sont mal canalisées. Je n'ai pas la maîtrise de moi-même. C'est la raison pour laquelle j'ai des **calculs biliaires**. Qu'est-ce qui influence ma vie ? Suis-je trop orgueilleux ? Même si les **calculs** sont l'expression d'une **vie endurcie**, je dois accepter ↓♥ de me libérer du passé et avoir une attitude et des **pensées plus douces**, une ouverture différente à la vie en laissant aller le passé, les sentiments lointains et les vieilles émotions amères, me permettant ainsi de manifester l'amour véritable. Le processus d'acceptation ↓♥ au niveau du cœur m'aidera à voir plus clair dans ma vie et à mieux découvrir le chemin qui améliorera ma situation.

CALCULS RÉNAUX ou LITHIASE URINAIRE (voir aussi : REINS)

Les **calculs rénaux**, aussi appelés **pierres au rein**, sont reliés au rein, siège de la peur. C'est la formation de pierres ou cristaux venant de quantités abondantes de **sel d'acide urique**, déchet hormonal du rein. L'acide urique représente de vieilles émotions à évacuer. Le **calcul** peut se former dans les différentes parties du système urinaire. C'est une masse d'énergie solidifiée créée à partir des pensées, des peurs, des émotions et des sentiments agressifs éprouvés envers quelqu'un ou une situation. Bien que les **calculs** se forment dans les reins, ils n'y originent pas. Le rein est un filtre d'émotions des déchets du corps. L'abondance des sels d'acide urique indique l'abondance de sentiments agressifs solidifiés car ils ont été longtemps retenus. « Je vis des frustrations et des sentiments agressifs dans mes relations depuis si longtemps que mon attention est uniquement fixée là-dessus. » Une personne équilibrée a les « reins solides », mais différents traits de caractère peuvent causer les **calculs** : je suis très autoritaire, souvent à l'extrême, **dur envers moi-même et les autres**, je décide et je fais mes choix en « réaction », je reste sérieusement accroché au passé, je manque de volonté et de confiance. Les **calculs rénaux** impliquent souvent un tiraillement intérieur entre ma volonté et mes décisions qui amènent un excès d'autoritarisme : me sachant faible et ayant peur, je « mobilise » toutes les forces disponibles à un même endroit pour accomplir certaines tâches, et lorsque la période de stress est passée, cette concentration durcit pour former les **calculs**. Je dois commencer par retrouver une certaine paix intérieure si je veux arrêter d'avoir des **calculs**. Je devrais moins m'attarder à certaines situations conflictuelles et à certains problèmes car, en continuant ainsi, je m'empêche d'aller de l'avant. Je dois les régler définitivement et voir le futur avec calme et souplesse. C'est une question de conscience et d'attitude.

CALLOSITÉS (voir : PEAU — CALLOSITÉS)

CALVITIE (voir : CHEVEUX — CALVITIE)

CANAL CARPIEN (syndrome du...) (voir : CRAMPE DE L'ÉCRIVAIN)

CANCER (en général)

Le **cancer** est l'une des principales maladies du 20e siècle. Des cellules anormales **cancéreuses** se développent et, le système immunitaire ne réagissant pas à la présence de ces cellules, elles prolifèrent donc rapidement. Les êtres humains ont souvent des cellules précancéreuses dans l'organisme mais le système immunitaire, c'est-à-dire le système de défense naturelle de notre corps, les prend en charge avant qu'elles ne deviennent cancéreuses. C'est

parce que ces cellules anormales se développent de façon incontrôlée[32] et incessante qu'elles peuvent nuire au fonctionnement d'un organe ou d'un tissu, pouvant ainsi affecter des parties vitales de l'organisme. Lorsque ces cellules envahissent diverses parties du corps, on parle de **cancer généralisé**[33]. Le **cancer** est lié principalement à des **émotions refoulées**, du **ressentiment profond** et parfois de longue date, par rapport à quelque chose ou une situation qui me perturbe encore aujourd'hui et face à laquelle je **n'ai jamais osé exprimer mes sentiments profonds**. Même si le **cancer** peut se déclarer rapidement à la suite d'un divorce difficile, d'une perte d'emploi, de la perte d'un être cher, etc., il est habituellement le **résultat** de plusieurs années de **conflit intérieur**, de **culpabilité**, de **blessures**, de **peines**, de **rancunes**, de **haine**, de **confusion** et de **tension**. Je vis du **désespoir**, du **rejet de moi**. Ce qui se passe à l'extérieur de moi n'est que le reflet de ce qui se passe à l'intérieur, l'être humain étant représenté par la cellule, et le milieu de vie ou la société par les tissus. Plus souvent qu'autrement, si je suis atteint de **cancer**, je suis une personne aimante, dévouée, pleine d'attention et de bonté pour mon entourage, extrêmement sensible, semant amour et bonheur autour de moi. Pendant tout ce temps, mes émotions personnelles sont refoulées au plus profond de moi. Je me conforte et me leurre en trouvant satisfaction à l'extérieur plutôt qu'à l'intérieur de moi-même puisque j'ai une très **faible estime de moi**. Alors que je m'occupe de tout le monde, **je mets de côté mes besoins personnels**. Puisque la vie ne semble plus rien m'apporter, je capitule et manque d'envie de vivre. À quoi bon lutter ! Si je vis beaucoup d'**émotions fortes, de haine, de culpabilité, de rejet**, je vais être en très forte réaction (comme la cellule) ; je vais même me sentir responsable des problèmes et des souffrances des autres et je voudrai m'**autodétruire**. « J'en veux à la vie », « elle est trop injuste ». Je joue à la « Victime » de la Vie et je deviens bientôt « Victime » du **cancer**. C'est habituellement la « haine » envers quelqu'un ou une situation qui va me « gruger l'intérieur » et qui va amener les cellules à s'auto-détruire. Cette haine est profondément enfouie à l'intérieur de mon être et je n'ai pas souvent conscience qu'elle existe. Elle est enfouie derrière

---

32. Selon les travaux du docteur **Ryke Geerd Hamer,** le cancer est le développement de **cellules spécialisées et organisées** provenant d'un programme spécial émis par le cerveau en réponse à un surstress psychologique.

33. **Cancer généralisé :** Dans le cas de **cancer généralisé**, il est souvent question de métastases, c'est-à-dire de cellules cancéreuses qui proviendraient d'autres cellules cancéreuses ailleurs dans le corps et qui auraient été transportées par le sang ou la lymphe. Il semblerait qu'il existe peu ou pas d'évidence sur cette hypothèse des cellules cancéreuses se transportant d'un endroit à l'autre. Il pourrait s'agir plutôt du fait que **le premier cancer qui provenait d'un conflit** ait amené à se manifester **et à mettre en évidence un autre conflit** qui lui provoque un autre **cancer** et ainsi de suite.

mon masque de « bonne personne ». Mon corps se désagrège lentement car mon âme se désagrège aussi : j'ai besoin de combler mes désirs non satisfaits au lieu de ne faire plaisir qu'aux autres. Je dois m'offrir des joies, des « petites douceurs ». J'ai accumulé ressentiment, conflits intérieurs, culpabilité, l'autorejet par rapport à moi-même parce que j'ai toujours agi en fonction des autres et non pas en fonction de ce que je veux. La patience exemplaire et présente chez moi s'accompagne très souvent d'une faible estime de soi. J'évite de me donner de l'amour et de l'appréciation car je crois que je ne le mérite pas. Ma volonté de vivre devient presque nulle. Je me sens inutile. « À quoi bon vivre ? » C'est ma façon d'en finir avec la vie. Je m'autodétruis et c'est là un **suicide déguisé**. J'ai l'impression d'avoir « raté » ma vie et je vois cette dernière comme un échec. La partie du corps atteinte m'éclaire quant à la nature de mon (mes) problème(s) : cela m'indique par rapport à quels schèmes mentaux ou quelles attitudes je dois adopter afin d'amener la maladie à disparaître. Je dois **reprendre contact avec mon « moi » intérieur** et **m'accepter ↓♥ tel que je suis** avec mes qualités, mes défauts, mes forces et mes faiblesses. J'accepte ↓♥ de laisser tomber de vieilles attitudes et habitudes morales. L'**acceptation** ↓♥ de ma maladie est essentielle pour que je puisse ensuite « lutter ». Si je refuse d'accepter ↓♥ ma maladie, comment puis-je la guérir ? J'**ouvre mon cœur et je prends conscience** de tout ce que la vie peut m'apporter et à quel point j'en fais partie. En recevant un traitement en guérison naturelle, en massage ou toute autre technique avec laquelle je me sens à l'aise, cela aura pour effet une harmonisation qui me permettra d'ouvrir ma conscience à toutes les merveilles de la vie et à la beauté qui m'entourent et qui renforcera ainsi mon système immunitaire.

CANCER DE LA BOUCHE

Le **cancer de la bouche** peut se situer au niveau du plancher de la bouche, des lèvres, de la langue, des gencives ou du palais. Comme la peau est la ligne de démarcation entre l'extérieur et mon intérieur, la bouche, elle, est la porte d'entrée, le vestibule entre ce qui entre (air, nourriture, liquide) et ce qui en sort (air, paroles véhiculant les émotions). Il se peut que je sois une personne de qui on dit « qu'il mange son prochain ». Je peux entretenir des sentiments de destruction envers une ou plusieurs personnes, ce qui me fait dire : lui, je le mangerais ! voulant signifier que je lui veux du tort ou sa mort dans un certain sens. J'ai donc un grand besoin de laisser entrer en moi des sentiments d'amour, et d'en exprimer envers les gens qui m'entourent et moi-même, en me disant des mots d'amour.

CANCER DES BRONCHES (voir : BRONCHES — BRONCHITE)

CANCER DU COL UTÉRIN (voir aussi : UTÉRUS)

Le **col de l'utérus** (comme l'utérus) représente la féminité, la matrice

originelle et le **foyer maternel**. Je refoule probablement certaines émotions concernant mon **foyer**, ma **famille** ou toutes situations reliées à ces deux aspects. Je peux me sentir coupable, rancunier ou haineux mais je n'en parle pas. Le foyer représente souvent un idéal à atteindre, que ce soit en rapport avec mon couple ou ma famille. Je peux vivre de grandes peurs, de l'insécurité ou de la culpabilité à l'idée que ce foyer ne se formera pas comme je le voudrais, ou bien qu'il risque de se dissoudre, ce qui représenterait pour moi un échec. S'ensuivra une dévalorisation par rapport à qui je suis et ce que je suis capable de réaliser. Ai-je peur de revivre dans mon foyer le jugement d'un échec que j'ai pu avoir dans le foyer où j'ai grandi ? Ce type de **cancer** est profondément lié aux principes du foyer nourricier, à mes attitudes et mes comportements par rapport à celui-ci. **J'accepte** ↓♥ de regarder d'un nouvel œil ce foyer qui est le mien !

CANCER DU CÔLON (voir aussi : INTESTIN [maux aux...]/ CONSTIPATION)

Le **côlon** est une partie du gros intestin où je digère les aliments. C'est l'un des types de **cancer** les plus fréquents en Amérique du Nord à cause de la consommation excessive de viande, de grains raffinés, de sucre, etc. Ces aliments sont difficiles à digérer et à assimiler. Cependant, il existe aussi d'autres raisons : la recherche continuelle de satisfactions, de plaisirs et de désirs matériels, additionnés aux différents états physiques, émotionnels et mentaux que je peux vivre chaque jour (atteinte de l'excellence, anxiété, angoisse, etc.) sont les principales causes d'un désordre alimentaire ou digestif. J'ai peu de joie intérieure, je suis plus ou moins satisfait de ma vie telle qu'elle est. Je me sens souillé sur un aspect de moi-même. Je mange et je refoule mes émotions : c'est plus facile et mes besoins sont comblés beaucoup plus rapidement. Je choisis une forme de récompense qui m'est accessible très aisément. Je recherche une certaine satisfaction que je me plais à retrouver dans la nourriture grasse et lourde. Le stress, le mode de vie et l'hérédité sont probablement aussi des facteurs prédisposant à ce type de maladie. Le **cancer du côlon** peut découler de causes semblables à celles de la **constipation** mais avec un facteur émotionnel plus important et profond. Dans le cas de la **constipation**, ce sont les énergies ou émotions plus en surface qui sont en cause alors que dans le cas du **cancer du côlon**, ce sont les énergies et les émotions situées plus en profondeur qui sont en cause. C'est pourquoi mes intestins peuvent fonctionner normalement ou régulièrement et que je peux quand même développer un **cancer du côlon**. Mes intestins font donc ce qu'ils peuvent pour me garder en santé et je me dois de les respecter en préservant leur bon état le plus longtemps possible. Je **m'ouvre davantage** aux joies de la vie et **j'exprime** les émotions qui font partie de ma vie ! Je commence à **pratiquer** différentes formes de **relaxation physique et intérieure** qui m'aideront à prendre le temps de vivre une existence plus équilibrée.

CANCER DE L'ESTOMAC (voir aussi : ESTOMAC [maux d'...])

Si j'ai le **cancer de l'estomac**, je dois prendre conscience du « morceau » ou de la situation que je ne suis pas capable de digérer. Cette situation « qui ne passe pas » , je la vis d'une façon très intense et très forte. « *C'est abominable ce que l'on m'a fait, ce que j'ai dû subir. En plus, je n'ai rien vu venir !* » Cela peut exprimer ce que je vis. Il est important que je prenne conscience du pourquoi de cette situation et quelle leçon j'ai à en tirer afin « de faire passer la tempête » et que le **cancer** se résorbe. Je ne peux qu'être gagnant si je laisse aller ma colère et ma rancune et que je les remplace par l'acceptation ↓♥ et le pardon.

CANCER DU FOIE (voir : FOIE [maux de...])

CANCER DES GANGLIONS (... du système lymphatique)
(voir aussi : ADÉNITE, ADÉNOPATHIE, GANGLION [... lymphatique])

Le système lymphatique se retrouve dans mon corps en parallèle à mon système sanguin. Il transporte un liquide transparent et blanchâtre appelé la lymphe qui sert à nourrir les cellules. Parce que la lymphe contient des protéines et des lymphocytes (globules blancs), elle joue un rôle important dans le processus d'immunité et de défense de l'organisme. Le système lymphatique est relié plus directement à mes émotions, à mon côté affectif. Les **ganglions** sont comme de petits reins du système lymphatique et servent à filtrer la lymphe de ses impuretés, un peu comme les reins pour le système sanguin. Alors, un **cancer des ganglions** m'indique de grandes peurs, de la culpabilité et du désespoir par rapport à mes émotions sur les plans amoureux et sexuel. Même si je vis présentement une vie amoureuse harmonieuse, il se peut que de profondes déceptions refassent surface sous cette forme de **cancer**. Je dois accepter ↓♥ que tout peut prendre sa place à l'intérieur de moi dans l'harmonie et dans l'amour, en travaillant sur mon enfant intérieur blessé.

CANCER DU GRAIN DE BEAUTÉ
(voir : PEAU — MÉLANOME MALIN)

CANCER DE L'INTESTIN (... grêle)
(voir aussi : CANCER DU CÔLON, INTESTINS [maux aux...])

Ce **cancer** se retrouve habituellement au niveau de **l'intestin grêle**. Lorsque je développe cette maladie, je dois me poser la question : Qu'est-ce que je ne suis pas capable de digérer et qui passe « de travers » ? Cela peut être une parole qui m'a été dite et que je trouve méchante ou peut être aussi une action que je trouve injuste et non acceptable. Le morceau est tellement gros à avaler que je ne sais pas si je vais réussir à le digérer. Je peux aussi vivre une très grande peur à savoir si je vais toujours avoir assez de « nourriture dans le

frigo ». J'ai peur de mourir de faim par manque de vivres. Quelle que soit la situation, je développe une attitude plus positive, en sachant que la vie veut ce qu'il y a de mieux pour moi et que j'accepte ↓♥ de vivre dans l'abondance. J'apprends aussi à pardonner aux personnes qui peuvent m'avoir dit ou fait quelque chose que j'ai de la difficulté à digérer. Je prends le temps d'exprimer à cette personne comment je me sens pour ramener l'harmonie dans cette situation. J'élimine la rancune de ma vie et la remplace par la compréhension et l'ouverture d'esprit.

CANCER DE LA LANGUE (voir aussi : ALCOOLISME, CIGARETTE)

Même s'il est admis que le **cancer de la langue** peut être favorisé par le tabagisme ou l'alcoolisme, **il provient d'un profond sentiment de désespoir signifiant que je n'ai plus le goût de vivre.** De plus, ce mal de vivre, il se peut que je ne l'exprime pas et que je refoule ainsi ces émotions à l'intérieur de moi. L'alcoolisme et le tabagisme ne sont que les amplificateurs des sentiments que je vis ; par l'alcoolisme, je fuis mes émotions, par le tabagisme, je fais un écran à ces émotions que je ne veux pas voir. Puisque c'est avec la **langue** que je vais chercher la nourriture afin de pouvoir la mâcher avec mes dents, si j'ai un **cancer de la langue,** je dois me demander si, au sens figuré, j'ai l'impression de ne pas être capable **d'attraper le « morceau de nourriture ».** Je vois ce que je veux attraper comme vital pour moi. Cela peut être un travail, de la nourriture, une nouvelle relation, etc. Je cherche à reprendre le goût de vivre, à augmenter mon estime de soi et j'apprends à exprimer mes émotions. Je découvrirai ainsi tout ce que la vie a de beau à m'offrir. Je passe à l'action et je vais chercher ce dont j'ai besoin car je le mérite !

CANCER DU LARYNX (voir aussi : CIGARETTE, GORGE [maux de...])

Lorsqu'une tumeur maligne s'installe sur les parois du **larynx**, cela signifie que j'éprouve un grand besoin d'exprimer ma peine intérieure. J'aurais besoin de hurler toute ma peine et j'ai peur d'exprimer mon désarroi. Y a-t-il une personne ou une situation qui m'empêche de m'exprimer ? Peut-être que je me dis : *Je suis aussi bien de me la fermer, car cela ne donnerait rien que je parle !* J'ai l'impression qu'on me tombe dessus et je voudrais me mettre en colère mais je n'ose pas. Je ne me sens pas respecté pour ce que je suis. Ainsi, j'ai à apprendre à prendre ma place et à exprimer ce qui est pour moi la vérité. Cela m'aidera à comprendre davantage la place que j'occupe dans mon environnement et dans l'Univers.

CANCER DE L'ŒSOPHAGE (voir : ŒSOPHAGE [l'...])

CANCER DES OS (voir : OS [cancer des...])

CANCER DES OVAIRES (voir : OVAIRES [maux aux...])

CANCER DE LA POITRINE (voir : CANCER DU SEIN)

CANCER DES POUMONS
(voir aussi : CIGARETTE, POUMONS [maux aux...])

Comme les poumons sont reliés directement à ma capacité de vivre, le **cancer des poumons** m'indique **ma peur de mourir.** En effet, il y a une situation dans ma vie qui me ronge par en dedans et me donne l'impression que je meurs. C'est peut-être à la suite d'une séparation ou d'un divorce, de la mort d'un être cher, de la perte d'un emploi qui est très important pour moi. En fait, toute situation qui pour moi représente, consciemment ou inconsciemment, ma raison de vivre. Lorsque ma raison de vivre disparaît ou que j'ai peur qu'elle disparaisse, cela met en évidence que l'autre possibilité qui se présente à moi est d'une certaine façon, la mort. Alors, qu'en est-il de la relation que l'on fait entre les fumeurs et le **cancer des poumons** ? Je peux me demander si c'est la fumée de cigarette qui m'amène le **cancer des poumons** ou si c'est la peur de mourir qui m'amène à fumer des cigarettes et, conséquemment, me fait développer le **cancer des poumons**. Lorsque je fume, je mets un voile sur des émotions qui me dérangent et qui m'empêchent de vivre. Ne solutionnant pas le conflit, celui-ci peut grandir en moi au point de me faire développer un **cancer des poumons.** Alors, j'ai à accepter ↓♥ la vie et à penser qu'à chaque inspiration et expiration, c'est la vie qui circule en moi par l'air que je respire. Je décide que je veux vivre par delà mes peurs et que la vie mérite d'être vécue, que je mérite de vivre.

CANCER DE LA PROSTATE (voir : PROSTATE [maux de...])

CANCER DU SANG (voir : SANG — LEUCÉMIE)

CANCER DU SEIN (voir aussi : SEINS [maux aux...])

Les **seins** représentent la féminité et la maternité. Cette sorte de **cancer** indique généralement certaines attitudes et pensées profondément enracinées depuis la tendre enfance. Depuis les années 60, à certains endroits dans le monde, la femme s'affirme davantage, prend sa place dans la société et veut aller de l'avant. Je peux donc avoir de la difficulté à exprimer mes vrais sentiments, à trouver un équilibre entre mon rôle de mère et de femme accomplie. Ces conflits intérieurs profonds me tourmentent en tant que femme qui cherche le juste équilibre. On a découvert que ce type de **cancer** vient généralement d'un **fort sentiment de culpabilité intérieure** envers soi ou envers un ou plusieurs de ses enfants : « *Pourquoi est-il au monde ? Qu'ai-*

*je fait pour l'avoir ? Suis-je une assez bonne **mère** ou **femme** pour m'en occuper ? »* Toutes ces questions augmentent mon niveau de culpabilité, m'amenant à me rejeter moi-même et augmentant ma peur que les autres me rejettent. Je dois me rappeler que « l'amour pour mon enfant est toujours présent mais que mes pensées sont très puissantes et que je dois être vigilante ». Si je me juge trop sévèrement, toute ma colère et mon rejet seront amplifiés et mes émotions seront « évacuées » au niveau de mes seins, qui deviennent le symbole de mon « échec ». Un **cancer du sein** veut donc m'aider à prendre conscience que je vis une situation conflictuelle, celle-ci pouvant être autant face à moi-même que face à quelqu'un d'autre et étant reliée à un élément faisant partie de mon espace vital, de mon « petit nid ». Il s'agira bien souvent de mes enfants, mes « oisillons », ou de quelqu'un que je considère comme tel (par exemple ma mère malade que je sens démunie, comme « un petit enfant »). Je peux avoir peur que mon « nid » (foyer) se désagrège. Je peux aussi avoir une grande peur ou un grand stress par rapport à la survie d'un ou de mes enfants. Dans un sens plus large, le « nid » peut englober mon conjoint, mon foyer, mes frères et sœurs, particulièrement s'ils vivent sous le même toit. C'est donc face à la famille, ce qui historiquement pourrait être appelé **le clan**, que j'ai l'impression ou que j'ai peur qu'il y ait démantèlement, éclatement. Les hommes autant que les femmes peuvent développer cette sorte de **cancer**, qui est souvent le conflit intérieur masculin à accepter ↓♥ sa propre nature féminine divine. Il arrive que certains hommes manifestent leur côté féminin et maternel presque autant que les femmes. En tant qu'homme, je ne serai jamais une femme mais, énergétiquement, je peux être autant et même plus féminin que celle-ci. C'est pourquoi le **cancer du sein,** chez moi qui est un homme, est associé à l'estime de moi et à ma capacité d'exprimer naturellement mon côté féminin inné. Il peut être relié au fait même d'être un homme et au désir inconscient d'être une femme. C'est un aspect que je devrai équilibrer dans ma vie. Le côté gauche est du domaine affectif et le droit, du rationnel. Le **cancer au sein gauche** désigne donc toutes les difficultés affectives et les émotions refoulées chez moi en tant que femme et j'ai avantage à accepter ↓♥ la **femme** et la **mère** en moi, et les sentiments intérieurs que je vis par rapport à chacun de ces deux rôles. Au **sein droit**, le **cancer** indique la femme **responsable** et ce que l'on attend de moi (ce que je m'attends à faire avec cette femme « extérieure »). À noter que cela aussi s'applique aux hommes, bien que le **cancer du sein** chez les hommes soit plus rare. Pour moi, en tant que femme dans l'univers physique, le volume et la forme de mes **seins** peuvent avoir une certaine importance selon les circonstances. On remarque que si mon côté masculin est dominant (Yang)[34], je peux avoir des **seins** plus petits ou je peux les considérer souvent comme inutiles ou sans valeur. Le corps parle et mes **seins** aussi ; c'est à moi de décider de l'importance

---

34. **Yang :** C'est le nom que l'on donne en médecine chinoise à l'énergie rationnelle ou masculine. L'énergie affective ou féminine est appelée **Yin**.

accordée à ce symbole féminin et sexuel. La recherche d'un équilibre est importante et le corps s'ajustera énergétiquement en conséquence des décisions prises par la femme (ou l'homme) dans l'avenir. **Tout est dans l'attitude, l'amour et l'acceptation ↓♥ de soi**.

CANCER DES TESTICULES

C'est dans les **testicules** que se fait la production des spermatozoïdes essentiels à la reproduction. Si je développe un **cancer des testicules**, je dois vérifier si je vis un sentiment intense dû à la perte d'un enfant, ou quelque chose dans ma vie qui m'était aussi important ou précieux qu'un enfant. Je peux avoir vécu le décès d'un de mes enfants, que ce soit par maladie, dans un accident ou à la suite d'un avortement. Ce peut être aussi, par exemple, un de mes enfants qui est parti « en claquant la porte » et que je n'ai jamais revu. Puisqu'il est sorti de ma vie brusquement, je peux vivre cette situation comme la **perte** d'un être cher, comme s'il était décédé. Un autre exemple peut être aussi lié à moi comme homme d'affaires qui, à cause de mauvais placements financiers, ai perdu l'entreprise « que j'avais mise au monde » et que je considérais comme « mon bébé ». Quelle que soit la situation vécue, je prends conscience des sentiments qui m'habitent ; je les accepte ↓♥ pour m'aider à guérir mes blessures, réapprendre à rire et regarder maintenant vers l'avant au lieu de ressasser le passé.

CANDIDA (voir aussi : INFECTIONS)

Il y a plusieurs sortes de **candida**. La forme la plus fréquente chez l'être humain est le **candida albican**. Même s'il peut se retrouver chez l'homme ou la femme, c'est souvent chez la femme que l'on en entend le plus parler. **Candida** est un mot latin qui signifie **blanche**. C'est une infection vaginale provenant de la prolifération de champignons sous forme de levure. Elle ressemble à de la levure blanche et croûteuse qui se manifeste à la suite d'un désordre de la flore vaginale. Les bactéries du vagin contrôlent normalement le **candida** mais cette fois-ci, la situation change. Cette infection est naturellement reliée à mon **engagement** face à moi-même ou à mon partenaire par rapport à ma sexualité, à des situations, expressions et émotions non exprimées à la suite de certains conflits personnels antérieurs. Je remets en cause mon activité sexuelle et ma sexualité, mon ouverture à partager avec mon partenaire des aspects plus intimes de moi-même. L'infection risque de se produire dans la mesure où, par exemple, j'ai un nouveau partenaire et ma relation est très intime avec lui. Il y a des chances que je m'ouvre davantage à l'amour, au partage et au don. C'est nouveau pour moi et j'ai besoin d'un peu de temps pour traiter cette récente situation, même si le **candida** se manifeste. Le **candida** peut également découler du sentiment d'avoir été **abaissé** ou d'être ou de **se sentir sexuellement abusé** par quelqu'un. C'est une forme de **protection physique et sexuelle** car l'**irritation** m'empêche de faire l'amour. Qu'est-ce qui m'irrite tant ? Je vérifie quel est l'aspect intérieur de ma

sexualité qui est dérangé et je trouve la véritable cause de l'irritation physique et intérieure. J'ai à prendre ma place dans la vie en me respectant. Je dois devenir le **candidat** qui remportera la victoire et qui prendra la première place. Je prends le temps de voir et d'évaluer ce qui se passe et j'accepte ↓♥ l'amour, l'ouverture et la patience intérieures autant que ceux de mon partenaire.

CARDIAQUE (crise...) (voir : CŒUR — INFARCTUS [... du myocarde])

CARIE DENTAIRE (voir : DENTS — CARIE DENTAIRE)

CATARACTE (voir : YEUX — CATARACTE)

CÉCITÉ (voir : YEUX [maux d'...])

CELLULITE

La **cellulite** est caractérisée parfois par l'inflammation du tissu cellulaire cutané ou sous-cutané. La **cellulite** est habituellement de nature féminine (quoique possible chez les hommes) et se manifeste par la rétention d'eau et une augmentation de la distribution irrégulière des toxines et des graisses aux fesses, aux jambes, à l'abdomen, à la nuque, au dos, etc. La **cellulite** est reliée à des anxiétés, à des aspects de moi-même que je retiens, des émotions refoulées, des **regrets** et des **ressentiments** que je garde. C'est relié à l'engagement par rapport à moi-même ou à quelqu'un d'autre. **Je crains de m'engager pleinement** avec la personne que j'aime et je refuse d'aller de l'avant. Cette peur peut avoir sa source dans un événement où j'ai vécu de l'**abandon**. Je refuse de voir une partie de ma jeunesse, car souvent, j'ai été blessé et marqué par certaines expériences **traumatisantes** qui m'agressent encore aujourd'hui et qui freinent ma créativité et mon cœur d'enfant. La **cellulite** se retrouve beaucoup plus chez les femmes que chez les hommes car moi, en tant que femme, je commence très jeune à m'en faire avec mon **apparence**, avec ma **silhouette** que je veux parfaite selon les normes de la société. L'aspect esthétique est excessivement important. Je vérifie quels sont les sentiments qui m'empêchent d'aller de l'avant et j'accepte ↓♥ de les intégrer doucement au quotidien.

CÉPHALÉE (voir : TÊTE [maux de...])

CERNÉS (yeux...) (voir : YEUX — CERNES)

CERVEAU (en général)

C'est la centrale énergétique, l'unité centrale du traitement de toutes les informations de la merveilleuse machine humaine. Le **cerveau** est relié au septième chakra (chakra de la couronne) ou centre d'énergie et à la glande pinéale aussi appelée épiphyse du **cerveau**. Il possède deux hémisphères distincts. L'hémisphère droit, le Yin des Chinois, représente le côté féminin (introverti), la créativité, la globalité, l'intuition, les perceptions et l'art ; c'est l'hémisphère **récepteur**. L'hémisphère gauche, le Yang, est celui qui **donne**, qui « domine », qui est extraverti, agressif, rationnel, logique et qui analyse tout. Chaque hémisphère contrôle la moitié opposée du corps (l'hémisphère droit contrôle le côté gauche, et vice-versa). Le croisement des nerfs cervicaux vers le côté opposé se fait au niveau des yeux, siège du chakra ou centre d'énergie du troisième œil situé à la racine du nez entre les sourcils. Le **cerveau** est l'organe représentant le centre de l'univers, l'identification à toute forme de divinité.

CERVEAU (maux au...)

Les problèmes de mon **cerveau** m'indiquent que j'ai tendance à vouloir **comprendre** avec ma tête et mon côté rationnel toutes les situations que je vis. Je mets de côté mes émotions avec lesquelles j'ai peur d'entrer en contact, essayant de me convaincre qu'elles ne servent à rien ou qu'elles peuvent être plus nuisibles qu'utiles. J'ai acquis une grande rigidité quant à ma façon de penser et je veux absolument avoir raison ! Il est donc difficile pour moi de changer d'opinion et d'admettre que je peux m'être trompé. J'ai donc avantage à mettre de côté mon côté trop « adulte », sérieux et rationnel et à retrouver mon côté « enfant » qui aime rire, avoir du plaisir et qui rayonne par sa naïveté et son désir d'apprendre.

CERVEAU (abcès du...)

Lorsque l'**abcès** atteint mon **cerveau** parce qu'il provient d'une infection de mes sinus ou de mon oreille moyenne ou de toute autre partie du corps, cela indique ma colère face à la prise en charge de ma vie et la peur que j'ai de perdre le contrôle de mon autonomie. J'ai alors à faire confiance dans le pouvoir divin qui m'habite et qui me guide vers des solutions qui m'aident à découvrir mon plein potentiel.

CERVEAU (tumeur au...)

La **tumeur** est une prolifération excessive de cellules anormales au **cerveau**. La **tumeur** est reliée à **des émotions refoulées, des remords profonds, des souffrances du passé**. Au **cerveau**, la **tumeur primitive**[35] qui se développe à partir des cellules du **cerveau** signifie que ma

---

35. Voir la note de bas de page au sujet du **cancer généralisé** dans la section **CANCER (en général)**.

centrale du traitement des informations enregistre encore certaines idées, croyances ou schèmes mentaux **qui n'ont plus leur raison d'être** ! La **tumeur** résulte d'un choc émotionnel et violent relié à une situation ou une personne que j'ai **beaucoup aimée** ou à quelque chose qui m'a fait beaucoup souffrir ou face auquel j'entretiens encore aujourd'hui de la haine, de la rancune, des peurs, de la colère et des frustrations. Si ma **tumeur** se situe sur la partie supérieure du **cerveau**, au milieu ou à l'hyppophyse, c'est souvent que j'ai vécu un choc émotionnel ou j'ai une grande peur par rapport à ma spiritualité, mon intuition, etc. Je suis très **entêté** et je refuse de changer ma façon de voir la vie et de traiter la réalité présente. C'est un conflit mental profond d'être ici en ce moment, d'accepter ↓♥ ma vie et tout ce qui l'accompagne. Je suis **rigide** et **figé** dans mes pensées, je suis confus intérieurement. Je véhicule une énergie mentale qui ne correspond plus à mes besoins les plus profonds et qui est l'opposé de mes désirs divins. Mon corps réagit fortement, et surgit alors une production hors contrôle de certaines cellules du **cerveau**. C'est un état critique et dangereux et je dois changer mon attitude fermée en une ouverture du cœur si je veux arrêter cette **tumeur**. À partir de maintenant, j'accepte ↓♥ de voir la vie d'une manière plus ouverte et flexible. Elle est en constante transformation et évolue toujours vers le mieux. C'est ma confiance personnelle qui me permettra d'atteindre ce but.

CERVEAU — ACCIDENT CÉRÉBRO-VASCULAIRE (A.C.V.)

(voir aussi : INFARCTUS [en général], SANG / [en général] / ARTÈRES / CIRCULATION SANGUINE, TENSION ARTÉRIELLE — HYPERTENSION)

Ce type de malaise est relié à la circulation sanguine et aux vaisseaux sanguins. Il peut se manifester dans plusieurs situations qui sont toutes reliées à l'amour. Ce genre d'**accident** est une réaction très forte, un **non catégorique** à une situation que je refuse de vivre. Je vis une **résistance** ou une **amertume** intérieure reliée à l'amour, au processus de la vie, aux changements et aux événements (incapacité, vieillesse, mort...). La première manifestation de ce type de malaise est la **haute pression** causée par le rétrécissement ou le resserrement de mes **artères** qui expriment l'amour. La pression monte car j'essaie de garder les choses telles qu'elles sont. L'**artère** affectée se situe au niveau du **cerveau**, siège des principes fondamentaux de mon existence. Cette **artère** peut **rétrécir**, se **rupturer** et endommager **gravement** le **tissu cérébral** et l'activité générale du **cerveau**. Une grave attaque (ou un caillot sanguin) peut causer la mort ou la paralysie. J'ai tellement mal intérieurement que je souhaite quitter cet univers ! Mes douleurs intérieures et les émotions dissimulées et refoulées m'empêchent d'exprimer tout mon potentiel d'amour. Toutes mes peurs sont amplifiées (la perte d'un être cher, l'entrée à la maison de retraite, la solitude et l'absence de soutien affectif, loin des gens que j'aime, moins d'attention et de soin, etc.) et ma vie ne vaut plus la peine d'être vécue. Je n'arrive plus à m'adapter aux changements futurs car c'est trop pour moi. L'amour est le principe

fondamental de toute vie. Je vérifie les symptômes possibles d'un tel accident et je suis à l'écoute de ma voix intérieure. Si j'ai besoin d'amour et d'attention, **je le demande** car c'est important pour moi. J'accepte ↓♥ cette situation accidentelle ou l'attaque cardiaque potentielle, car elle m'indique que je dois rester ouvert à l'amour divin et que cet amour divin verra à combler mes besoins. Sous l'effet d'un corps étranger ou d'un caillot dans une artère, ou à cause de l'épaississement de la paroi interne d'une artère, celle-ci peut se boucher, empêchant le sang de nourrir une partie du **cerveau**. Ceci est appelé un **accident cérébro-vasculaire ischémique** ou **infarctus cérébral**. Une peur de perdre mon autonomie associée à un choc émotionnel peut m'amener à vivre cette situation. La partie du **cerveau** affectée ainsi que les fonctions qui s'y rattachent (parole, locomotion, équilibre, etc.) m'indiquent sous quel aspect cette peur se manifeste dans ma vie. Je peux avoir l'impression de prendre les moyens dans ce que je veux vivre. Dans le cas des **accidents cérébro-vasculaires hémorragiques**, c'est une artère qui éclate, ce qui produit un épanchement de sang sur une partie du **cerveau**. Il se peut que je vive une tension tellement grande dans mon milieu familial ou de travail que la tension accumulée se libère par cet éclatement de ma joie de vivre (le sang) qui symbolise toute la peine que je vis dans cette situation. Selon que l'**accident** se produit dans la partie du **cerveau** droit (côté intuitif) ou du côté gauche (côté rationnel), je pourrai identifier davantage le message que mon corps me donne, refaire la paix avec moi-même et me rétablir plus rapidement. Je visualise mon **cerveau** baignant dans un liquide fait de lumière blanche et dorée pour permettre à toutes mes cellules nerveuses de se régénérer ou de répartir le travail d'une nouvelle façon, afin que je puisse retrouver la santé plus rapidement.

CERVEAU — APOPLEXIE (voir aussi : CERVEAU — SYNCOPE, SANG — HÉMORRAGIE)

L'**apoplexie** survient à la suite de la diminution de l'oxygénation au **cerveau** et amène une perte de connaissance de courte durée, complète et brutale. Elle résulte très souvent d'une hémorragie cérébrale. La crise d'**apoplexie** est la manifestation du besoin extrême de **résister à la vie** et aux **changements**, du **rejet** et de la **négation** de plusieurs aspects de ma vie et de mon être. Le véhicule de ma joie de vivre, le sang, n'arrive plus à irriguer convenablement une partie du **cerveau**. Cette partie arrête de fonctionner et la paralysie s'ensuit. Si je résiste à la vie, je suis d'accord d'abandonner et de rester fermé. Je préfère mourir : c'est plus facile et la destruction est mon seul salut. C'est la défaite ! Cette paralysie m'empêche d'exprimer pleinement mon énergie vitale et mon potentiel créatif. Mes activités sont maintenant limitées. Si je veux retrouver la joie qui alimente ma vie, je dois vite m'ouvrir à l'intuition et à l'amour et exprimer davantage ce que je ressens. Je commence surtout à faire de plus en plus confiance à la vie.

CERVEAU (commotion) ou COMMOTION CÉRÉBRALE

La **commotion cérébrale** est l'ébranlement de l'ensemble du **cerveau** lors d'un traumatisme du crâne, aboutissant à un coma provisoire. La **commotion** est une forme de fuite, un moyen brusque et direct de m'arrêter et d'observer franchement ce qui se passe dans ma vie. La **commotion cérébrale** vient me faire réaliser qu'inconsciemment, je m'accroche tellement à mes vieilles idées ou attitudes qu'elles se heurtent aux nouvelles qui veulent prendre place. Je suis amené indirectement à m'arrêter, à faire un examen de ma vie et voir dans quelles directions je veux maintenant me diriger. Je reviens à mes priorités. Aussi, j'ai peut-être la tête « trop pleine d'idées », je m'éparpille trop, j'ai besoin de revenir sur terre. Il y a bousculade et le choc s'ensuit. La **commotion** survient à la suite d'une blessure à la tête ou d'un accident qui « choque » la tête, le **cerveau** et le mental. Mon corps est temporairement « parti » et inconscient. Où suis-je rendu dans ma vie ? Quelle direction vais-je prendre ? Est-ce que mon mental va dans toutes les directions en même temps, sans orientation réelle ? J'ai probablement besoin de revenir sur la terre, dans la réalité, pour régler « dans le réel » et d'une façon plus adéquate les situations que je vis actuellement. Il est possible d'éviter la **commotion** en acceptant ↓♥ de rester très ouvert à ce qui se passe dans ma vie.

CERVEAU — (congestion au...) (voir : CONGESTION)

CERVEAU — ENCÉPHALITE

L'encéphale comprend le **cerveau**, le cervelet et le tronc cérébral. L'encéphale est donc la partie supérieure de mon système nerveux qui contrôle tout mon organisme. L'encéphale représente donc mon individualité à son plus haut niveau. Même si en général la tête représente aussi mon individualité, l'encéphale représente mon individualité intérieure. Lorsqu'il y a affection inflammatoire (au niveau) de l'encéphale, appelée **encéphalite**, cela correspond à de la colère par rapport à qui je suis. Je dis non à la vie pour les changements qu'elle me présente. Je crains de perdre mon individualité, mes acquis dans ce que je suis. J'ai peur de perdre le contrôle de moi-même et de ce qui m'arrive ou de ce qui peut m'arriver. Je me sens limité dans l'expression de moi-même. J'ai à m'ouvrir à de nouvelles facettes de moi-même, à faire confiance à la vie. Je remplace la rigidité par la flexibilité, l'encadrement strict de certaines parties de moi-même par de l'ouverture afin de découvrir de nouvelles facettes de moi-même. Je me donne l'amour et la compréhension dont j'ai besoin et je laisse la paix intérieure s'installer en moi.

CERVEAU — ÉPILEPSIE

L'**épilepsie** est causée par une mauvaise communication entre les cellules du **cerveau**. L'influx nerveux accumulé qui en résulte crée une surcharge et la

formation d'ondes de chocs qui attaquent les autres parties de mon **cerveau**. Les crises d'**épilepsie** peuvent être de différentes intensités. Ainsi, je peux faire partie des personnes qui sont simplement « dans la lune » pendant quelques instants ou faire partie de ceux qui perdent conscience complètement et subissent des convulsions assez fortes pendant cinq à dix minutes. Pour vivre une telle situation, c'est sûrement parce que je crois que la vie ne m'apporte que rejet, violence, colère et désespoir. J'ai l'impression de toujours avoir à combattre. Je me sens persécuté. Je me sens coupable de l'agressivité qui monte en moi et je la refoule. J'en ai assez, cela me demande beaucoup trop d'effort. Je rejette cette vie qui s'acharne à me faire souffrir. Je veux devenir insensible en me repliant sur moi-même. C'est souvent le désespoir ou la colère qui m'y incite. En même temps, je vais me sentir persécuté par la vie, laissant celle-ci véhiculer une certaine violence envers moi. Le rejet de soi est extrême et il en résulte un conflit d'individualité. Lors de la crise d'**épilepsie**, mon corps se raidit pour protester contre ces blessures et les convulsions déferlent, telles de très fortes vagues qui me permettent de laisser sortir ma colère, mon amertume et mon agressivité longtemps réprimées. Je n'ai d'autre choix que de me laisser aller aux sentiments intenses qui m'habitent. Je fuis dans l'inconscient ces situations qui me font tant souffrir, soit parce que j'ai peur, que je suis dérangé ou que je souffre. Le mental n'a, à ce moment, aucun contrôle. L'**épilepsie** avertit ainsi mon entourage de mon grand besoin d'amour et d'attention. La cause profonde de l'**épilepsie** remonte souvent au début de l'enfance et peut même remonter au temps de la grossesse : comme enfant, je me suis hautement culpabilisé ; cela me suit tout au long de ma vie et je vois celle-ci comme un combat de tous les jours. Il peut aussi s'agir d'un abus, sexuel ou autre, ou perçu comme tel, ou d'un rejet antérieur ou vécu dans la tendre enfance comme une **séparation**. Le fait de se sentir séparé de quelqu'un implique une perte de contact sur le plan physique avec celui-ci. La **crise d'épilepsie** peut donc devenir une manière d'obtenir ou de gagner davantage d'attention aussi bien que de renforcer mon sentiment de supériorité. Comme **l'épilepsie** indique une surcharge du **circuit nerveux,** cela démontre que ce avec quoi je dois traiter dans ma vie de tous les jours prend trop de place ; il se produit une situation où je dois choisir. Ce sentiment d'être surchargé peut être le résultat d'événements que j'amplifie (j'exagère) dans mon esprit (mental). Cette exagération peut conduire à l'arrogance en m'amenant à penser que j'en sais plus que quiconque. Il peut aussi exister une tendance à une trop grande abstraction ou encore, une trop grande adhésion aux royaumes psychiques. J'évite ainsi de traiter avec la réalité objective. L'é**pilepsie** peut aussi être la conséquence d'une peur bleue que j'ai (par rapport à la mort, la maladie, peur de perdre quelqu'un, etc.). Une coloration de motricité, comme pour m'empêcher d'avancer, s'ajoute à ma peur (par exemple : si je dois me rendre à des funérailles (mort) et que je ne veux pas y aller). Je prends conscience de ce qui se passe en moi et j'accepte ↓♥ de ne plus concentrer mes efforts sur le négatif seulement et de voir à quel point l'univers m'apporte aussi amour et beauté.

CERVEAU — ÉQUILIBRE (perte d'...) ou ÉTOURDISSEMENTS

Sur le plan physique, l'**équilibre** est maintenu par la répartition de mon poids sur mon corps, ce qui me permet de me mouvoir sans pencher d'un côté ou de l'autre. Les commandes du mouvement, quant à elles, viennent de mon **cerveau** : soit de mon système visuel, de mon système proprioceptif[36], soit de mon système vestibulaire dans mon oreille interne. Lorsque mon **cerveau** se sent **bousculé** et **dépassé** par les situations ou les événements, il est tiraillé dans toutes les directions en même temps et **perd son équilibre**. La **perte d'équilibre ou l'étourdissement** sont souvent associés à l'**hypoglycémie**[37] : je manque de douceur dans ma vie. Cette fuite peut être reliée à une situation ou à un individu dont j'ai l'impression que l'évolution est trop rapide pour moi. Ces vertiges se produisent quand ma réalité devient accablante, car j'ai entretenu de fausses idées qui ont fait surface en conséquence de mes attentes qui n'ont pas été nécessairement satisfaites. Je perds alors mon sentiment d'équilibre et d'harmonie. Bien que **l'étourdissement** puisse provenir de différentes causes d'ordre physique comme l'**hypoglycémie** (manque de sucre dans le sang), l'**hypotension** (basse pression sanguine), un **ralentissement cardiaque**, ce malaise est relié à la **fuite**. En effet, lorsque je me sens tiraillé, consciemment ou non, je cherche à « m'étourdir » pour oublier ce que je vis. Je prends conscience que je vais dans trop de directions à la fois et je m'accorde le temps nécessaire pour reprendre mon **équilibre**. J'accepte ↓♥ de me donner du temps et des douceurs. Je prends le temps de savourer tout ce qui est beau et bon dans ma vie.

CERVEAU — ÉTAT VÉGÉTATIF CHRONIQUE
(voir aussi : CHRONIQUE [maladie...])

Lorsque je suis dans cet état, je n'ai pas d'activité consciente décelable. Je vis dans un état communément appelé « **végétatif** ». Mon **cerveau** est affecté à la suite d'un arrêt circulatoire prolongé ou à cause d'un traumatisme crânien. Comme mon **cerveau** correspond à mon individualisme, je vis de grandes peurs ou de la culpabilité, jusqu'à vouloir inconsciemment fuir la vie. Le fait que je sois encore en vie permet à mes proches d'apprivoiser graduellement mon départ de ce monde et de m'exprimer leur amour tandis que moi, je peux commencer à me préparer dans le calme à quitter ce monde pour des réalités et des plans de conscience supérieurs.

---

36. **Système proprioceptif :** Fait de récepteurs microscopiques me renseignant sur mes articulations, du tonus musculaire et de la position de mes articulations.

37. **Hypoglycémie :** Manque de sucre (glucose) dans le sang.
(voir : SANG — HYPOGLYCÉMIE)

CERVEAU — HÉMIPLÉGIE (voir aussi : CERVEAU / [abcès du...] / ACCIDENT CÉRÉBRO-VASCULAIRE [A.C.V.])

L'**hémiplégie** est une paralysie d'une moitié du corps (gauche ou droite) causée par une lésion du **cerveau**. Elle peut survenir après un grand choc, tant physique qu'émotionnel, comme par exemple le décès d'un être cher, ce qui amènera souvent un état très profond de désespoir et une sensibilité grandement affectée. Une explosion de rage peut aussi en être la cause. Mon corps me dit qu'une partie de moi ne peut plus agir. Est-ce un sentiment d'impuissance face à une situation contrariante ? Le côté qui est affecté m'indique si c'est davantage mon côté affectif (côté gauche) ou mon côté rationnel (côté droit) qui est en cause. Je me donne du temps pour guérir mes blessures, sachant que toute expérience, aussi difficile soit-elle, m'amène à devenir une personne plus forte.

CERVEAU — MÉNINGITE
(voir aussi : INFLAMMATION, SYSTÈME IMMUNITAIRE, TÊTE)

La **méningite** est une infection du liquide cérébral résultant de l'inflammation de la membrane recouvrant le **cerveau** et la mœlle épinière. Elle indique une faiblesse du système immunitaire et une incapacité à s'autoprotéger. La **méningite** me signale une faiblesse et une incapacité à lutter contre des pressions extérieures très fortes, surtout sur le plan intellectuel. C'est souvent parce que j'ai de la difficulté à me protéger. Étant hypersensible, je vis tout plus intensément et je suis affecté plus profondément, même par des choses qui semblent banales pour d'autres. Cette maladie me donne comme message de me préserver des coups venant de l'extérieur et de ne pas me sentir coupable des agissements des autres, tout en me responsabilisant moi-même. Autrement, c'est la **révolte** qui gronde, je suis contrarié et la frayeur s'empare de moi. Comme le **cerveau** régit le corps entier, la **méningite** implique une profonde faiblesse intérieure qui m'attaque au plus profond de mon être. Comme la **méningite** met en péril la centrale de commande de mon corps, le **cerveau**, je dois impérativement décider de vivre et de me prendre en main, de garder la « tête haute » et de faire jaillir en moi cette force intérieure qui me permettra de continuer une vie enrichissante et remplie d'expériences merveilleuses.

CERVEAU — PARALYSIE CÉRÉBRALE

La **paralysie cérébrale** survient souvent dès la naissance et se manifeste par une anomalie au niveau du **cerveau**. Le muscle cérébral est paralysé partiellement ou en entier, selon la nature du traumatisme. Je me demande souvent pourquoi moi, comme enfant, dès la naissance, je souffre déjà de cette **paralysie**. Je peux supposer une trame karmique antérieure[38], un pattern ou

---

38. « **Une trame karmique antérieure** » : Pour ceux qui croient à la réincarnation, cela veut dire que cela peut provenir d'une cause reliée à une vie antérieure.

une expérience « avant la naissance » si violente, un traumatisme mental si intense qu'il entraîne une fermeture complète, un arrêt de tout mouvement vers l'avant, empêchant la progression. C'est un état encore irréversible (je dis « encore » car on ne peut prédire la médecine du futur) et je ne peux être libéré de ceci malgré l'amour inconditionnel et l'attention des gens autour de moi. La guérison est davantage sur le plan spirituel, si elle se manifeste.

CERVEAU — PARKINSON[39] (maladie de...)
(voir aussi : NERFS, TREMBLEMENTS)

La maladie de **Parkinson** est la détérioration des centres nerveux du **cerveau**, particulièrement dans les régions contrôlant les mouvements. Des tremblements apparaissent et affectent habituellement les mains et la tête. Lorsque je tremble, c'est parce que je ressens ou vois un danger qui me guette ou guette quelqu'un que j'aime ; que ce soit la crainte de perdre le contrôle (que je perds de plus en plus !), l'insécurité ou l'impuissance d'aller de l'avant dans la vie. Je peux aussi avoir vécu un traumatisme, un abus ou des difficultés qui ont laissé des traces et face auxquelles je vis les sentiments suivants : peine, frustration, culpabilité, rage, dépression qui m'amènent à l'épuisement, au découragement, et que je veux fuir au lieu d'y faire face et de les régler. Je m'autodétruis lentement, produisant la détérioration de la fonction nerveuse actuelle. Une impuissance au niveau de la motricité de mes membres supérieurs (particulièrement mes bras et mes mains) a sa source très souvent dans une situation que je vis où je voulais repousser une personne, une chose ou un événement ou, au contraire, que je voulais retenir et je me suis senti incapable (soit physiquement ou moralement) de le faire. Si ce sont les membres inférieurs qui sont touchés (mes jambes et mes pieds), c'est avec ceux-ci que j'aurais voulu soit repousser ou ramener à moi la personne, chose ou événement concerné. J'ai le goût de fuir cette situation dans laquelle je me sens dépassé et que je perçois comme étant sans issue. Je dois me reprendre en main et apprendre à contrôler MA vie et non pas celle des autres, en faisant confiance en la Vie, et me dire que je mérite de vivre.

CERVEAU — SYNCOPE

Une **syncope** se diagnostique par la perte de conscience complète, réversible, mais brève. La perte de conscience provient d'un manque d'oxygénation du **cerveau**. Elle peut être la conséquence d'un arrêt cardiaque mais pas nécessairement. Cela peut provenir d'une forme d'asphyxie ou être lié à des vaisseaux sanguins qui se dilatent brutalement à la suite d'un choc émotionnel, laissant peu de sang au **cerveau**, donc peu d'oxygène. C'est l'esprit

---

39. **PARKINSON (James) :** Ce médecin anglais (1755-1824) décrivit la maladie de la *paralysie tremblante* qui porte aujourd'hui son nom.

qui quitte mon corps pour un court instant. C'est comme si je choisissais de me replier sur moi-même et de me couper du monde physique ; je suis en révolte, ne sachant plus comment faire face à une certaine situation. Cet état ne peut être comparé à celui d'un yogi[40] puisque ce dernier est en pleine maîtrise d'une discipline visant à libérer son esprit de toutes contraintes du corps dans l'harmonisation du mouvement, du rythme et du souffle. Je prends conscience de ce qui m'a amené à fuir ainsi mon corps physique, quelle est l'angoisse, le sentiment de panique intérieur qui a produit une telle situation. Je sais qu'en toutes circonstances, je suis guidé et protégé et j'accepte ↓♥ de rester pleinement conscient de la vie qui est en moi.

CERVEAU — TICS

Les **tics**, définis comme étant l'exécution soudaine de mouvements répétitifs et involontaires, démontrent un dérèglement de la tension nerveuse et un déséquilibre au niveau du **cerveau**. Si j'ai un ou des **tics**, il y a de fortes chances que je sois un être très émotif, que je refoule beaucoup d'agressivité et qu'étant jeune, j'aie perçu l'éducation reçue comme rigide et perfectionniste. De cette façon, j'extériorise mon inquiétude et l'amertume que je ressens au fond de moi. Si je suis un garçon, il se peut que j'aie été affecté par des actions que quelqu'un qui représentait l'autorité pour moi a pu me demander de faire. Cela expliquerait pourquoi il y a près de 4 fois plus de garçons que de filles qui ont des **tics**. C'est que les filles, en général, sont plus réceptrices par rapport à l'autorité et donc, moins affectées, toujours en général, par cet aspect. Je peux m'être senti contrarié par rapport à certains mouvements qu'on m'a empêché de faire étant plus jeune (comme par exemple si on m'interdisait de bouger à l'église) et que maintenant mon corps bouge, bien malgré moi, comme par réaction et rébellion face à ce qu'on m'a déjà interdit de faire. Je peux même avoir eu l'impression de « perdre la face » devant quelqu'un. J'ai intérêt à prendre conscience de cet état et à exprimer clairement mes besoins.

CHAGRIN (voir aussi : MÉLANCOLIE)

Le **chagrin** est relié à une forme d'anxiété, une inquiétude ou une tristesse qui se manifeste par des pleurs, des sons de douleurs, de la solitude. Mon cœur est blessé et malade à la suite d'une expérience passée regrettable et douloureuse. Mon **chagrin** peut être long ou ne durer qu'un instant. Je cherche la cause véritable souvent profonde ou inconsciente. Après des années, plusieurs blessures d'enfance peuvent ressurgir ainsi que certaines prises de conscience. Je reste ouvert à ce que je vis et j'identifie rapidement la véritable

---

40. **Yogi :** Se dit d'une personne qui a atteint un certain stade dans son évolution spirituelle. Par la pratique de la méditation, elle peut quitter son corps consciemment pour une durée variable. Certaines personnes peuvent même ralentir ou pratiquement arrêter les battements de leur cœur pour le faire repartir ensuite.

source de mon **chagrin** pour pouvoir le changer. J'accepte ↓♥ ma prise de conscience et je l'intègre. De cette façon, je retrouve ma joie de vivre et j'en ressors « grandi ».

CHALAZION (voir aussi : PAUPIÈRES)

C'est une petite tumeur inflammatoire (nodule rouge, souple) située habituellement sur le bord intérieur de la paupière. Comme la tumeur est généralement reliée au choc émotionnel, elle se produit lorsque je vis une émotion intense par rapport à ce que je vois ou à ce que j'ai vu. Je peux vérifier quelle paupière ou quel œil est affecté : l'œil gauche est du domaine affectif alors que l'œil droit représente le rationnel et les responsabilités. Je reste ouvert à ce que je vois et je suis davantage centré sur moi-même.

CHALEURS (avoir des...) (voir : MÉNOPAUSE)

CHALEUR (coup de...) (voir aussi : FIÈVRE)

Les **coups de chaleur** peuvent survenir à la suite d'une exposition prolongée au soleil, que ce soit à la plage ou lors d'autres sports extérieurs, à la suite d'un chauffage intensif l'hiver ou lorsque je me trouve dans une pièce très petite et mal aérée. Je peux ainsi me retrouver avec une faiblesse musculaire générale, la peau brûlante et sèche, le visage grisâtre et les yeux cernés. Sur le plan métaphysique, la chaleur peut être associée soit à l'amour lorsqu'il s'agit de guérison parce qu'il y a plus d'énergie en circulation, soit à de la colère lorsqu'il s'agit de fièvre ou de brûlure. Ici, le **coup de chaleur** représente de la culpabilité face à l'amour reliée à un sentiment de manque d'estime de soi. J'ai besoin d'aimer et d'être aimé et je n'arrive pas à trouver la façon de le faire, à combler ce vide intérieur qui est en moi et à neutraliser cette insatisfaction. Mon corps tout entier m'indique le besoin urgent de combler cet amour. Je cherche comment augmenter cette estime de soi, ou comment intégrer une situation qui m'a affecté dans l'enfance et qui remonte maintenant à la surface. J'aime la vie et la vie me le rend bien.

CHAMPIGNONS (voir : PIEDS — MYCOSE)

CHAMPIGNONS MAGIQUES (consommation de...)
(voir : DROGUE)

CHANCRE (en général) (voir aussi : ULCÈRE [en général])

Le **chancre** se retrouve à un endroit isolé de la peau ou des muqueuses sous forme d'ulcère. C'est le signe d'une maladie contagieuse à ses débuts et qui est souvent d'origine vénérienne. Je vis de la colère qui a trait à mes

rapports sexuels. L'endroit où le **chancre** apparaît m'indique plus précisément ce que je vis dans cette situation. Ainsi, le **chancre** peut se retrouver sur les parties génitales, sur l'anus, sur le visage, sur les muqueuses de la bouche. Lorsqu'un **chancre** sous forme d'ulcère contenant du pus se retrouve **dans la bouche,** c'est que je m'empêche de dire certaines choses. Je suis mécontent, je désapprouve certaines situations dans ma vie et je n'ose pas en parler. Je retiens certaines paroles, et donc elles **fermentent** et produisent du pus. J'accepte ↓♥ de parler et de m'exprimer **même si** je suis en désaccord avec la vie et les autres. Je dois le faire si je veux rester ouvert à l'énergie active de la parole et de l'expression de soi. Je m'accepte ↓♥ dans ma sexualité et je me donne le droit de découvrir l'amour qui m'aidera à m'épanouir.

CHANCRE — ULCÈRE BUCCAL (HERPÈS)
(voir : BOUCHE [malaise de...])

CHAT DANS LA GORGE (voir : GORGE — CHAT DANS LA GORGE)

CHEVEUX (en général)

Protégeant la partie cutanée de la tête, les **cheveux** symbolisent la force, la liberté, la beauté et la puissance (pensons à Samson dans la Bible). Ils sont reliés directement à la dignité de l'être, à l'essence du pouvoir. Ils me mettent en contact avec l'énergie spirituelle, cosmique et supracosmique. Mes **cheveux** poussent près du septième chakra ou centre d'énergie, le chakra couronne. On les appelle « antennes » parce qu'ils relient le physique au spirituel. L'état des **cheveux** est aussi la représentation de la puissance sexuelle, génitale et reproductive. Plusieurs mythes existent au sujet des **cheveux** (les blondes, les brunes, les chauves...). Il est important de savoir que mes **cheveux** sont l'image du pouvoir que j'ai pour diriger ma propre vie. Qu'est-ce que je veux vraiment dans la vie ? Est-ce que j'ai l'impression que les autres dirigent ma vie ? La force et le courage de prendre les rênes de ma vie augmenteront mon sentiment de liberté et la vigueur de mes **cheveux**. Les **cheveux** reflètent la joie de vivre d'une personne et leur propreté indique l'intérêt qu'ils ont à prendre soin d'eux, à être ici. J'observe les différents états de mes **cheveux** qui correspondent à certains états intérieurs (**cheveux** fendillés, ternes, minces ou cassants, épais, etc.). Je reste ouvert à ce merveilleux pouvoir du ciel que sont mes **cheveux** !

CHEVEUX (maladie des...)

Plusieurs causes peuvent amener l'apparition de **maladies des cheveux**. Un grand choc émotionnel, une réaction excessive d'impuissance face à une situation, un conflit latent ou plusieurs sentiments refoulés tels que le désespoir, les inquiétudes, l'ennui. La nervosité s'installe, l'instabilité

émotionnelle grandit, les forces et les ressources intérieures s'épuisent. Je vis un désordre intérieur. Cette insécurité peut provenir de ma peur de la mort ou du fait que rien n'est permanent, que tout peut changer soudainement et sans avertissement. Je me ferme aux énergies vitales et mes **cheveux** changent d'apparence. Ils tombent, deviennent gras ou secs, blanchissent (**cheveux blancs**), ils perdent leur éclat. Les **pellicules** apparaissent, résultat d'un conflit intérieur par rapport à moi et à mon rôle social. J'ai besoin d'oxygène ! C'est la première chose à faire pour ramener force et vitalité aux **cheveux**. Je prends conscience que j'ai besoin de changer mes pensées et mon attitude face aux situations de la vie. J'accepte ↓♥ de rester ouvert et j'observe ce qui se passe en ce moment, surtout la façon dont je m'y prends pour affronter les différentes situations de ma vie et je cesse de m'**arracher les cheveux** !

CHEVEUX (perte de...) (voir aussi : CHEVEUX — CALVITIE)

Les **cheveux** sont le miroir d'une certaine force intérieure. Je pense à Samson (dans les écritures de l'Ancien Testament) qui perdait sa force les **cheveux** coupés... Les **cheveux** représentent le lien entre le physique et le spirituel, ce qui me relie au cosmos et à l'énergie spirituelle. On les compare souvent à une forme d'antenne avec l'au-delà. Il est dit que l'hérédité est le facteur principal de la **calvitie,** plus fréquente chez le sexe masculin. Cependant, parmi les différents types de **calvitie**, on retrouve le type **chauve-barbu,** lequel est associé à l'individu qui utilise plus ses facultés intellectuelles que ses facultés émotionnelles. **La perte de cheveux** signifie que je me suis éloigné du divin en moi. Je suis une personne axée sur le plan matériel plutôt que spirituel. Il se peut que j'aie beaucoup d'intuition mais je préfère m'en tenir davantage à des aspects plus matériels, plus rationnels. J'essaie le plus possible de tout contrôler car j'ai peur de m'ouvrir et de perdre le contrôle. Je refuse le fonctionnement de base de la vie, prétextant que je peux faire mieux qu'elle. Toute crainte intérieure entraîne l'incapacité d'agir, le désespoir et des tensions qui me prennent au dépourvu. C'est une illusion de croire faire mieux que la vie elle-même. Je n'ai pas à me battre contre la vie car elle est **toujours avec moi** pour m'appuyer et elle m'aidera si je l'écoute et si je reste ouvert. Je n'ai qu'à demander en toute quiétude et la vie me donnera ce que je mérite. C'est le début ; je dois faire confiance à la vie et à mon être intérieur et voir les solutions partout car elles existent ! Le monde est là pour m'aider. Qu'ai-je besoin d'autre ?

CHEVEUX — CALVITIE (voir aussi : CHEVEUX [perte de...])

La **calvitie** est la perte définitive (partielle ou totale) de **cheveux**. Souvent, si je perds mes **cheveux**, je vis une ou plusieurs situations où la **tension est si grande** que je m'en « arrache les **cheveux** ». Plusieurs expériences stressantes ou même traumatisantes peuvent accélérer le processus de la calvitie. Un accouchement qui est source de peur ou d'inquiétude (la

femme peut perdre ses **cheveux**), un choc émotionnel grave, une séparation, beaucoup de tension au travail ou au foyer, le goût de se surpasser sur le plan matériel ou une dévalorisation au plan intellectuel. Lorsque je vis une foule d'inquiétudes et de grandes peurs, je perds le contact avec mon pouvoir intérieur divin. J'accepte ↓♥ de faire confiance à la vie avec l'attitude que tout sera pour le mieux.

CHEVEUX GRIS

Les **cheveux gris** symbolisent la sagesse. Cependant, l'apparition soudaine de **cheveux gris** est reliée au stress, à une situation où j'ai vécu un choc émotionnel intense. Lorsque cela arrive dans la vingtaine, cela représente de grandes inquiétudes (tension ou stress), conscientes ou inconscientes par rapport au fait de se laisser guider spirituellement. Est-ce que je crois avoir besoin de vivre sous pression et que les pressions dans ma vie sont nécessaires pour mon « bien » ? C'est possiblement un pattern relié à la performance dans cette vie-ci. Habituellement, les **cheveux gris** apparaissent avec l'âge et cela signifie une baisse de vigueur et de force vitale. Je révise mes attitudes générales et j'accepte ↓♥ que la vie continue telle qu'elle est, ni plus ni moins et je me libère du fardeau d'être compétitif.

CHEVEUX — PELADE

La **pelade** est une maladie de la peau caractérisée par la **perte de cheveux** en plaques arrondies. Cela peut provenir d'un choc émotionnel, de la colère et d'une renonciation à ma partie spirituelle ou à ce qui me connecte à mes valeurs les plus élevées. J'ai avantage à refaire la paix avec moi-même et à envisager les solutions qui me permettront de mieux vivre en harmonie avec mes buts les plus élevés.

CHEVEUX — TEIGNE
(voir aussi : CHEVEUX [perte de...] / CALVITIE / PELADE)

Les **teignes** sont des champignons parasites et contagieux qui affectent la surface de ma peau, mes poils, mon cuir chevelu et mes ongles. Je me laisse « attaquer », « détruire », déranger par les autres, parce que j'ai peu confiance en moi. Je me sens laid et sale. Je peux avoir l'impression que je perds le contrôle de certaines situations. Ainsi, mon chapeau de chef (mes **cheveux**) en seront affectés. Je peux me sentir très dérangé par les propos des autres et être affecté par l'idée qu'ils ont que « si le chapeau te fait, mets-le donc » ! Je laisse les autres décider pour moi. Mon corps me dit de prendre ma place, de me faire confiance. Moi seul ai du pouvoir sur ma vie.

CHEVILLES (voir aussi : ARTICULATIONS)

La **cheville** est une partie du corps très flexible et mobile. Elle sert à

soutenir le corps et, par sa position physique, elle subit de grandes pressions. C'est une sorte de pont, de lien entre moi et la terre. C'est à cause d'elle si je suis « groundé »[41] au sol, si l'énergie spirituelle voyage du haut vers le bas et vice-versa, si je suis en contact avec la terre-mère. C'est également l'endroit où j'exprime ma capacité d'avancer, de me lever et de rester debout, stable et ancré. La **cheville** exécute les changements de direction et par conséquent, elle représente mes décisions et mes engagements qui se prennent en tenant compte de mes croyances et de mes valeurs. Toute blessure ou douleur aux **chevilles** est reliée à ma capacité de demeurer flexible, tout en changeant de direction. Si j'ai peur de ce qui s'en vient, si je suis inflexible face à une décision à prendre, si je vais trop vite sans réfléchir, si j'ai peur de mes responsabilités présentes ou futures, si j'ai l'impression d'être instable, je risque de freiner l'énergie dans mes **chevilles**. Selon l'intensité du blocage d'énergie et de ma fermeture au courant de vie, il peut en résulter une foulure, une entorse ou une fracture. Je ne peux pas me tenir debout sans mes **chevilles**. J'ai peut-être à « m'appuyer » sur de nouvelles façons de voir les choses, de nouveaux « critères » qui sont plus ouverts et flexibles. Elles prennent soin de moi et de mon être intérieur, elles me supportent dans la vie. Si une **cheville** cède ou se brise, je n'ai plus de base solide, j'ai besoin de changer de direction, je vis un conflit mental. Ma **cheville** ne peut plus me supporter et c'est le corps entier qui cède physiquement. Dans un certain sens, ma vie s'effondre aussi, mais c'est plus l'image qu'il y a quelque chose qui ne va pas qu'un effondrement réel de la personne. Au sujet de l'**entorse**, la **cheville** tordue, c'est l'énergie qui se « tord » dans la **cheville** et ma structure de support est déformée. Il n'y a plus rien de clair et défini. Quand je suis confronté à quelque chose de très profond, un changement **obligatoire** pour mon mieux-être, c'est la **cassure ou la fracture** qui se manifeste. J'ai vraiment à changer de direction. C'est mon honneur, ma sécurité, mon but et ma direction dans la vie qui sont concernés. Peu importe le malaise, la période d'immobilité qui suit permet à mon corps et à mon être intérieur d'intégrer adéquatement l'aspect de ma vie à changer et permet aussi à la merveilleuse transformation qui s'en vient pour moi de prendre place ! J'accepte ↓♥ la vie et tout ce qu'elle dispose sur ma route. Cela m'aidera à embrasser la vie du bon côté !

CHOLÉRA (voir : INTESTINS — DIARRHÉE)

CHOLESTÉROL (voir : SANG — CHOLESTÉROL)

CHRONIQUE (maladie...)

Le mot **chronique** vient de « chronos » qui veut dire « temps ». La

---

41. **Groundé :** Anglicisme signifiant se sentir connecté à la terre ou au monde matériel.

maladie chronique peut prendre des mois ou des années à s'installer. Pour une maladie, le terme **chronique** suggère quelque chose de permanent, d'irréversible et qu'on ne peut à la limite que corriger. Je développe une **maladie chronique** lorsque je refuse d'évoluer par crainte de ce que l'avenir me réserve. Quelle que soit la **maladie chronique** que je me suis attirée, je peux me demander ce que j'avais l'impression de ne pouvoir changer. Sur quel aspect de ma vie ai-je l'impression de me dire : « De toute façon, on ne peut rien y faire, ou on ne peut rien y changer » ? Quels « cadeaux » cette maladie m'apporte-t-elle sous forme d'attention de la part de mon entourage, de la confirmation de ma résignation à changer mon point de vue sur la vie, etc. ? La solution facile pour moi est sans doute de ne rien faire parce qu'il semble qu'il n'y ait rien d'autre à faire que de baisser les bras. Le défi que j'ai à relever est de me prendre en main, d'ouvrir ma conscience à l'idée que tout est possible. Je peux me documenter sur des résultats obtenus par des personnes qui avaient des **maladies chroniques** et se sont guéries. Quelles approches ont-elles utilisées ? Parfois, lorsque les moyens conventionnels n'ont pas donné de résultats, je peux investiguer des thérapies alternatives, énergétiques ou autres, **avec discernement**, pour savoir laquelle pourrait m'aider. En partant avec l'idée que tout est possible, je serai plus à même de trouver des solutions qui, si elles ne me guérissent pas complètement de ma maladie, m'aideront à améliorer ma santé physique, mentale et émotionnelle.

CHUTE DE PRESSION
(voir : TENSION ARTÉRIELLE — HYPOTENSION [trop basse])

CIGARETTE (voir aussi : BUERGER [maladie de...],
CANCER DE LA LANGUE, DÉPENDANCE, POUMONS)

La **cigarette** est reliée aux poumons, symbole de vie, de liberté et d'autonomie, de communication entre moi et l'univers. Elle est considérée comme une forme de protection, un « voile » qui me permet de cacher certaines angoisses profondes. Je crois me protéger par cet écran de fumée qui m'enveloppe et qui m'empêche de voir la vérité. Inconsciemment, la **cigarette** comble aussi des besoins inassouvis de l'enfance : premières tétées, chaleur, amour, affection de la mère. J'allume une **cigarette** sans y penser, c'est une habitude, un geste machinal, une manie devenue tellement importante pour moi. J'ai besoin d'équilibrer en plus ou en moins ma nervosité, mon excitabilité nerveuse. Je veux retrouver « l'apaisement de ma mère », la sécurité de celle-ci. Si je fume, **c'est parce que je fuis** une situation trop désagréable, ma famille, ma vie. Cette fumée rend encore plus nébuleuse mes décisions. La **cigarette** augmente le rythme cardiaque et agit à titre de stimulant. Quelles sont les décisions que je n'arrive pas à prendre et qui me rendent la vie fade ? J'identifie mes vrais besoins. J'accepte ↓♥ de communiquer davantage et d'une manière plus aisée. Si je veux arrêter de

fumer, il serait bon que je trouve la cause émotionnelle à laquelle cette habitude est reliée, ce qui facilitera grandement l'arrêt. Je verrai alors plus clairement ce que je veux vraiment dans la vie et mes besoins seront comblés en harmonie avec mon être véritable.

CINÉPATHIE (voir : MAL DES TRANSPORTS)

CINÉTOSE (voir : MAL DES TRANSPORTS)

CIRCULATION SANGUINE (voir : SANG — CIRCULATION SANGUINE)

CIRRHOSE (...du foie) (voir : FOIE — CIRRHOSE [... du foie])

CLAUDICATION (marche irrégulière)
(voir aussi : SYSTÈME LOCOMOTEUR)

La **claudication** est caractérisée par une irrégularité de la marche. La cause peut être musculaire, neurologique, liée à la paralysie ou à la raideur d'un pied, d'un genou ou d'une hanche. Il est certain que dans ma vie, tout ne « marche » pas comme je le voudrais. Je veux aller de l'avant mais des peurs m'empêchent d'avancer de façon harmonieuse. En identifiant ces peurs, je pourrai remettre plus d'harmonie dans ma vie, ce qui m'aidera à retrouver plus de régularité dans ma marche.

CLAUSTROPHOBIE (voir aussi : ANGOISSE)

Claustrophobie vient du mot latin « claustrale » qui signifie « enfermé ». C'est donc la peur irrationnelle d'être étouffé ou pris dans une situation ou un endroit clos (ascenseur, avion, grotte et tunnel) où je n'ai « aucun contrôle » sur ce qui se passe. Pour cette raison, je souffre de **claustrophobie**, l'angoisse de vivre dans des endroits « fermés », seul ou avec d'autres personnes. Cela peut provenir du moment de ma naissance, lorsque je devais passer par le « tunnel » du col utérin. J'ai pu capter la peur de ma mère à ce moment-là. Aussi, la peur peut provenir du moment où je me trouvais dans cet endroit clos et sécuritaire qu'était l'utérus de ma mère et que les contractions m'ont forcé à quitter, ce qui a fait naître en moi une grande peur de l'inconnu, de ce qui peut se passer. Ainsi, de me retrouver dans un endroit clos peut me rappeler cette grande peur que j'ai enregistrée en moi. J'ai l'impression d'être **prisonnier** et **enfermé** dans une situation où je suis entièrement impuissant. Que dois-je faire ? Je vérifie d'abord si cette peur ne viendrait pas d'une pensée quelconque, d'une fixation mentale dont l'origine remonte aux premières périodes de ma vie. La plupart du temps, cette phobie provient d'une « crainte sexuelle » qui se serait produite durant l'enfance. Cela ne veut pas nécessairement dire que des attouchements

ou des abus sexuels ont eu lieu dans l'enfance mais plutôt que la crainte a été enregistrée dans la mémoire émotionnelle et que je me suis senti pris ou que j'ai eu peur de me sentir pris dans cette situation à caractère sexuel. J'accepte ↓♥ de passer à l'action et de me libérer de celle-ci par le moyen qui me conviendra le mieux. Souvent, une psychothérapie pourra être adéquate pour changer la mémoire émotionnelle et m'amener à vivre avec plus de liberté intérieure.

CLAVICULE (douleur à la..., fracture de la...)
(voir aussi : ÉPAULES, OS — FRACTURE)

La **clavicule** est un os long en forme de « **S** » allongé que je retrouve au niveau de l'épaule et rattaché au sternum, en haut et au centre de la cage thoracique. Comme la **clavicule** est reliée directement à l'épaule, une douleur à la **clavicule** signifie ma colère en regard des responsabilités que l'on me donne et face auxquelles je peux vivre un sentiment de soumission et d'obligation. Le plus souvent, une fracture à la **clavicule** arrive à la suite d'une chute sur l'épaule et indique que je vis une forte pression face à mes responsabilités. L'émotion engendrée peut m'amener à penser que je vais « casser » sous le poids de mes responsabilités. Je regarde les situations avec objectivité et je commence à comprendre que la vie ne peut me donner plus de responsabilités que je ne peux en prendre. Je fais confiance et je m'efforce de trouver des solutions ou un autre point de vue qui m'aidera à mieux prendre la vie.

CLOUS (voir : PEAU — FURONCLES)

COCAÏNE (consommation de...) (voir : DROGUE)

COCCYX (voir : DOS [maux de...] — BAS DU DOS)

CŒUR (en général) (voir aussi : SANG)

Le **cœur** est relié au quatrième chakra ou centre d'énergie. Il représente l'amour (mes émotions, ma capacité d'aimer), la joie, la vitalité et la sécurité. L'énergie du **cœur** irradie dans tout le corps, surtout entre le cou et le plexus solaire. Le **cœur** est une sorte de pompe énergétique qui fait circuler la vie (le sang) à travers le corps tout entier. Cette circulation sanguine distribue l'énergie vitale nécessaire au bonheur, à l'équilibre, à la joie de vivre et à la paix intérieure. Il est donc essentiel que je manifeste l'amour en dirigeant l'énergie du **cœur** vers les plus belles énergies spirituelles disponibles. Plus je mets l'attention sur l'amour, la compassion et le pardon, plus mon **cœur** travaillera dans la joie, la paix et l'allégresse. Mon **cœur** sera affectivement stable et à l'abri de toutes les déceptions. Un **cœur** au rythme doux et harmonieux indique une personne calme intérieurement. Mon rythme cardiaque varie lorsque je suis déséquilibré,

perturbé en amour ou sensible à mes émotions. J'accepte ↓♥ de m'ouvrir à l'amour, je remets tout blâme au soin de l'univers, je cesse de me critiquer au point de me rendre malade et surtout j'accepte ↓♥ de me pardonner. C'est en me pardonnant que je peux accepter ↓♥ davantage l'amour des autres.

CŒUR (mal au...) (voir : NAUSÉES)

CŒUR — ANGINE DE POITRINE ou ANGOR
(voir : ANGINE DE POITRINE)

CŒUR — ARYTHMIE CARDIAQUE

Le **cœur** représente l'amour et des **problèmes de palpitations** sont pour moi comme un signal d'alarme, un appel au secours en ce qui a trait à l'amour. Une peur profonde de perdre ou de ne pas avoir l'amour dont j'ai tant besoin fait en sorte que mes **problèmes de palpitations** sont comme un cri au secours par rapport à l'amour. Dans le cas où les ventricules du **cœur** se contractent de façon anarchique et inefficace, il s'agit alors de **fibrillation ventriculaire**. Cet état peut provenir d'un trouble cardiaque, d'une électrocution, d'un moment de panique dans le cas du fœtus (à la naissance). Si cet état n'est pas réglé rapidement, c'est la mort subite. Cela dénote une décision importante que j'ai à prendre dans ma vie par rapport à l'amour et qui est vitale. Je commence par me donner tout l'amour dont j'ai besoin afin de remplacer mes inquiétudes par plus de sécurité intérieure et je fais confiance à la vie. La **tachycardie** se caractérise par la contraction rythmique irrégulière du **cœur**. Ses battements s'accélèrent à plus de 90 pulsations par minute, et cet état est souvent dû à des émotions fortes. Une situation angoissante, un effort physique ou mental et la peur provoquent un déséquilibre affectant momentanément mon **cœur** qui me lance un S.O.S. La **bradycardie** quant à elle est un ralentissement des battements cardiaques. L'accumulation de peines profondes pourra m'amener ce malaise, comme si mon **cœur** n'en pouvait plus de souffrir et décidait d'arrêter de battre. Dans l'une ou l'autre de ces situations, je prends conscience que l'amour est en jeu. Je respire calmement et profondément, je suis à l'écoute de mon **cœur**.

CŒUR — INFARCTUS (... du myocarde)
(voir aussi : INFARCTUS [en général])

Lorsque j'entends parler de quelqu'un qui a eu un **infarctus**, dans le langage populaire, cela signifie habituellement que la personne a eu un **infarctus du myocarde**. C'est aussi appelé « crise cardiaque » ou « attaque cardiaque ». L'organe le plus fréquemment touché par un **infarctus** est le **cœur**, le centre de l'amour à l'intérieur de moi, le noyau de mes émotions. L'attaque cardiaque est pour le corps une façon désespérée de me montrer que

je vais trop loin, que je mets beaucoup trop d'attention sur les aspects matériels, externes et anodins de ma vie, mon statut social, au lieu de revenir à l'essentiel de ma vie qui est la joie de vivre du **cœur** en famille, d'exprimer l'amour, de s'aimer soi-même, de savourer chaque moment avec intensité. Je tiens tellement à tout ce qui fait partie de mon « territoire » (<u>ma</u> femme, <u>mon</u> travail, <u>mes</u> amis, <u>ma</u> maison, etc.) que si j'ai l'impression d'avoir perdu ou que je suis sur le point de perdre quelque chose ou quelqu'un à l'intérieur de mon territoire, je peux résister à ce qui arrive et je ferai une **crise cardiaque**. Je voudrais « de tout mon **cœur** » rester le chef, le maître à bord. Les attaques cardiaques sont aussi reliées à mes propres sentiments et à ce que je vis par rapport à ceux-ci. Jusqu'où suis-je capable de sentir l'amour et de l'exprimer aux autres ? Jusqu'à quel point suis-je capable de m'aimer et de m'accepter ↓♥ tel que je suis ? Est-ce que je m'oblige à être « quelqu'un d'autre » et à en faire trop pour prouver aux autres ce que je suis et ce que je vaux ? C'est ma colère, ma frustration, mon agressivité qui, trop longtemps refoulées, n'en peuvent plus et qui explosent. La découverte des aspects les plus importants et significatifs de la vie ne se réduit pas à la quantité d'argent gagné ou au succès que j'ai. Autant le **cœur** peut être associé à la compassion et à l'amour, autant il peut être associé à son opposé qui est l'hostilité, la haine et le rejet. L'attaque cardiaque survient souvent dans une période de ma vie où, soit que la compétition est trop forte, soit que je vis une pression financière, combinée à la désaffection grandissante de la famille et des proches aimés. C'est la séparation entre mes sentiments, mon implication, mes relations et l'Univers ainsi que ses rythmes naturels qui atrophient mon **cœur**. Je pense rejeter les autres mais dans le fond, je me rejette moi-même. Il me faut aller avec le courant et prendre le temps d'accepter ↓♥ tout ce que la vie a à me donner et à m'apprendre, afin de retrouver la paix intérieure et de ressentir dans tout mon corps la tendresse, la douceur, l'amour qui m'habitent et qui ne demandent qu'à nourrir mon **cœur** et à le garder en santé.

CŒUR — PÉRICARDITE

La **péricardite** est une infection du **péricarde**, membrane enveloppant le **cœur**. Puisqu'elle sert à protéger le **cœur**, il y aura **péricardite** si je sens que mon **cœur** va être attaqué, autant au sens propre que figuré. Au lieu de manifester de la colère, je reste calme et je demande à être protégé en tout temps, sachant que tout ce qui arrive est pour le mieux.

CŒUR — PROBLÈMES CARDIAQUES

Parce que le **cœur** symbolise l'amour, la paix et la joie de vivre, les **problèmes cardiaques** proviennent souvent d'un manque d'amour, de tristesse, d'émotions enfouies qui refont surface même après plusieurs années. Mon **cœur** est endurci par mes blessures antérieures. Je crois sincèrement que la vie est difficile, stressante et qu'elle est un combat de tous les instants. Je me

sens souvent en position de survie, dans un état où je pense que seul mon effort rapportera quelques dividendes. Je suis inquiet, surexcité, angoissé ou trop fragile pour garder mon équilibre émotionnel. J'étouffe inconsciemment mon enfant intérieur et l'empêche d'exprimer toute cette merveilleuse joie de vivre. Le **cœur** est associé à la glande du thymus ; cette dernière qui est responsable de la production des cellules-T du système immunitaire s'affaiblit et résiste de moins en moins aux invasions si je vis beaucoup de colère, de haine, de frustration ou de rejet de moi-même. Le **cœur** a besoin d'amour et de paix. La vie est faite pour être prise avec l'attitude d'un enfant : ouverture, joie, curiosité et enthousiasme. Même si j'ai des besoins affectifs à combler, j'essaie de rester dans un équilibre harmonieux, avec une ouverture du **cœur** suffisante pour apprécier chaque geste de mon existence. J'accepte ↓♥ de m'aimer davantage, de rester ouvert à l'amour pour moi et les autres. Je m'amuse, je me détends, je prends le temps d'être. J'arrête de me « prendre au sérieux ». Je me sens libre d'aimer sans obligation, sachant que je suis heureux quand même. Il existe plusieurs expressions pour décrire le **cœur** et ses différents états : être « *sans cœur* », « *avoir du cœur* », « *écouter son cœur* ». Si quelqu'un me fait une remarque comme « *tu n'as pas de cœur* », je vérifie ce message que la vie m'envoie. C'est peut-être le signe que j'aurais avantage à changer quelque chose. Est-ce je vis un déséquilibre ? Ai-je des palpitations ? Suis-je perturbé sur le plan émotionnel ? Qu'importe la réponse, je n'attends pas d'être malade pour comprendre et accepter ↓♥ les changements dans ma vie. Je reste éveillé, j'ouvre mon **cœur** à tout ce qui est bénéfique pour moi.

CŒUR — TACHYCARDIE (voir : CŒUR — ARYTHMIE)

CŒUR — THROMBOSE CORONARIENNE

Une thrombose coronarienne est la formation d'un caillot dans une artère coronaire (au niveau du **cœur**). Ce blocage de la circulation du sang peut mener à un infarctus du myocarde. Ce caillot affecte l'organe principal qui représente l'amour, soit le **cœur**. Je me dois de vérifier ce qui dans ma vie m'empêche d'aimer librement. Cela peut être une colère, un ressentiment violent que j'ai pu avoir face à quelqu'un que j'aime. En quoi est-ce que je me sens attaqué dans mon amour-propre ? Ai-je eu une nouvelle qui semblait me déposséder de ma raison de vivre, de ce qui me permettait de manifester mon amour ? Je fais la paix avec moi-même et avec les autres. Pour régler cette situation, je prends conscience des forces d'amour qui m'habitent, je m'abandonne et je découvre que l'Univers m'apporte le soutien dont j'ai besoin.

COLÈRE (voir aussi : ANNEXE III, DOULEUR, FOIE, INFECTIONS)

La **colère** est l'exaltation de l'état affectif et un mode d'extériorisation brutale de celui-ci, se traduisant par une excitation tant physique que verbale, progressivement croissante, allant jusqu'aux cris, bris d'objets, agressivité, tremblements, etc. La **colère** est un cri d'alarme spontané, la manifestation d'une **révolte intérieure**, un violent mécontentement accompagné d'agressivité. Avant deux ans, c'est un simple moyen de réagir ou d'extérioriser un malaise intérieur (froid, faim, etc.), mais par la suite, c'est plus un moyen d'opposition et de réaction aux interdictions, pouvant devenir un moyen de chantage affectif et de domination. Ces émotions qui m'envahissent se manifestent généralement au niveau de mon foie, par l'apparition de toxines qui peuvent engendrer une **crise de foie**. Mes pensées s'affolent, se bousculent, s'amplifient jusqu'à ce que **je ne vois plus clair**. Ma pression monte et je deviens *rouge de colère*. Qu'est-ce qui me dérange à ce point et qui me fait exploser ? Si je suis en **colère**, c'est important de chercher la raison qui provoque cet état. Je peux vivre un sentiment de faiblesse, d'injustice, de frustration, d'incompréhension, d'impuissance, etc., qui peut être exagéré ou grossi par ma grande émotivité et mon impulsivité. Lorsque je l'identifie, je réalise que le conflit se répète inconsciemment et qu'il peut même provenir de situations que je n'ai pas réglées depuis l'enfance, et alors, l'intégration sera plus rapide. J'accepte ↓♥ de m'ouvrir à l'amour que je peux manifester ici et maintenant. Je reste attentif et **vigilant** à tous les signaux indiquant une **colère** éventuelle et je ne m'emporte pas inutilement.

COLIQUE (voir : INTESTINS — COLIQUES)

COLITE (mucosité du côlon) (voir : INTESTINS — COLITE)

CÔLON (cancer du...) (voir : CANCER DU CÔLON)

COLONNE VERTÉBRALE (en général) (voir aussi : DOS)

Selon le classement que l'on fait en Occident, on compte **33 vertèbres** en commençant par le haut, soit :

7 cervicales[42], plutôt minces,
12 dorsales[43], plutôt épaisses,
5 lombaires[44], plus fortes,
5 sacrées[45], soudées formant un triangle vers le bas,
4 coccygiennes, soudées et atrophiées.

La **colonne vertébrale**, tel le pilier d'une construction, représente l'appui, la protection et la résistance. Donc, la **colonne vertébrale me**

soutient et me protège dans toutes les situations de ma vie. **Elle est mon pilier physique et intérieur**. Sans elle, je m'effondre. La **colonne vertébrale** symbolise aussi mon énergie la plus fondamentale et la plus spirituelle. Elle représente ma flexibilité et ma résistance face aux différents événements de ma vie. Les déviations de la **colonne vertébrale** (scoliose, lordose, etc.) sont reliées à la partie profonde de tout mon système énergétique. Lors d'un blocage, des douleurs physiques apparaissent. Des sentiments d'impuissance, un fardeau trop lourd à porter, un besoin affectif ou émotionnel insatisfait, etc., font que je me sens attaqué dans ma solidité et dans ma résistance. J'ai l'impression que c'est moi **le pilier** au sein de ma famille, de mon travail et par rapport à toute situation ou organisation dans laquelle je suis impliqué. Qu'adviendrait-il aux autres si je n'étais pas là ? Est-ce que tout s'effondrerait ? La **colonne vertébrale** est reliée à tous les différents aspects de mon être par le squelette, à travers le système nerveux central et par la distribution sanguine centrale. Chaque pensée, sentiment, situation, réponse et impression est imprimé dans la **colonne vertébrale** aussi bien que dans les parties pertinentes impliquées du corps concernées. Je regarde la région affectée et j'identifie la cause du blocage. Peu importe la raison, j'accepte ↓♥ de rester ouvert à la cause et l'intégration est plus harmonieuse. Je rebâtis la nouvelle personne que je veux être.

COLONNE VERTÉBRALE (déviation de la...) (en général)

Une **déviation de la colonne vertébrale** symbolise principalement une résistance à vivre pleinement ma vie. La façon dont je me tiens dans la vie, ma difficulté à laisser la vie me soutenir et à laisser aller les vieilles idées se manifesteront par une **déviation de la colonne vertébrale** qui se courbera vers le côté, vers l'avant ou vers l'arrière... Je décide de me prendre en main et de me « tenir droit » face à la vie, avec confiance et détermination.

COLONNE VERTÉBRALE (déviation de la...) : BOSSU
(voir : ÉPAULES VOÛTÉES)

---

42. **Cervicale :** Vient du latin *cerveaux* qui veut dire « nuque ».
43. **Dorsale :** Vient du latin *dorsum* qui veut dire « dos ».
44. **Lombaire :** Vient du latin *lumbus* qui veut dire « rein ».
45. **Sacré :** Ce mot fait référence à ce qui est inviolable ou à ce qui nous impose un grand respect. Dans ce cas-ci, il s'agirait de l'endroit d'où partirait l'énergie de la Kundalini, cette énergie spirituelle qui part du bas de la colonne vertébrale et monte jusqu'au sommet de la tête, pour mener à l'illumination.

COLONNE VERTÉBRALE (déviation de la...) : LORDOSE

La **lordose** est une courbure physiologique de la **colonne vertébrale** se creusant vers l'avant. J'ai de la difficulté à me tenir debout parce que j'ai **honte de ce que je suis, je ne m'aime pas**. Je vis souvent de la soumission face à mon père ou à ce qui représente l'autorité pour moi, car je me sous-estime face à lui, je me sens inférieur à lui. Je me sens écrasé par les autres, j'ai très peu confiance en moi et je suis incapable d'exprimer mes idées et mes opinions. Je bouillonne intérieurement et cette colère me ronge. Je dois **apprendre à m'aimer**. J'accepte ↓♥ de **prendre ma place** car chacun a un rôle à jouer dans l'univers. J'apprends à **exprimer mes idées et mes opinions librement** et je me sens mieux avec moi-même.

COLONNE VERTÉBRALE (déviation de la...) : SCOLIOSE

La **scoliose** est une déviation latérale de la **colonne vertébrale**. Lorsque j'en suis atteint, j'ai l'impression de porter sur mes épaules un très lourd fardeau. Comme cela dépasse tout espoir d'accomplissement, je vis de l'impuissance et du désespoir. Mes responsabilités me font peur, je suis indécis dans mon orientation. L'énergie se bloque et la **scoliose** en est la manifestation physique. Cela se présente souvent à l'adolescence : comme je suis à la recherche d'une identité, trop vieux pour être un enfant et trop jeune pour être un adulte, la vie et les responsabilités semblent énormes. J'aurai tendance à me comparer à mes frères, soeurs, cousins et cousines. Puisque j'ai souvent l'impression qu'ils sont meilleurs que moi, je me dévaloriserai et cela s'exprimera par une **scoliose**. La **scoliose** est donc reliée à un **désir de fuir** une situation ou quelqu'un. Je vérifie ce qui se passe dans ma vie et qui m'empêche de me sentir bien. J'**accepte ↓♥ de vivre au présent**, c'est-à-dire un jour à la fois. Je prends conscience d'être à l'école de la vie et de vivre en harmonie avec ce qui m'entoure. Je retrouve la joie et, chaque jour, je réalise que j'ai la force et la capacité de relever le défi !

COLONNE VERTÉBRALE — DISQUE DÉPLACÉ
(voir aussi : DOS [maux de...], LUXATION)

Relié à la **colonne vertébrale** (le support de mon corps), le **disque déplacé** dénote que je ne me sens pas appuyé. Je ne me sens pas à la hauteur, je manque de confiance en moi. Je prends conscience qu'à chaque fois que j'ai cherché une réponse ou un soutien, j'y ai trouvé la confirmation de ce que je savais ou ressentais déjà. **J'accepte ↓♥ d'écouter ma voix intérieure** qui, elle, est toujours là pour m'appuyer et me guider. **J'apprends à me faire confiance** et je découvre toute la force qui est en moi et le bonheur que cela m'apporte de me tenir debout, libre et sans craintes. Je suis **supporté** dans tout ce que j'entreprends.

COL UTÉRIN (cancer du...) (voir : CANCER DU COL UTÉRIN)

COMA (voir aussi : ACCIDENT, CERVEAU — SYNCOPE, ÉVANOUISSEMENT)

Le **coma** survient dans la majorité des cas à la suite d'un **accident**. Il arrive très souvent que, juste avant de me retrouver dans le **coma**, j'aie vu la mort arriver sur moi, comme si « ma dernière heure était venue ». Au lieu d'être conscient à 100 % de ce moment, le **coma** survient juste avant. La « conscience » se débranche. Souvent, lorsque je me réveille à la suite d'un **coma**, ma mémoire a effacé les moments de traumatismes intenses qui ont été vécus. Ce qui produit un accident est une culpabilité reliée à la fuite face à une personne ou une situation. Si j'ai de la difficulté à « dealer » avec cette culpabilité, je me réfugie dans un **coma**. Le **coma** vient du grec « *kôma* » qui signifie « *sommeil profond* ». Cet état est relié au désir intense de **fuir** une personne ou une situation. J'ai tellement **mal** intérieurement que je me replie sur moi car je vis beaucoup de désespoir, de solitude ou de frustration. Je veux me rendre insensible aux difficultés de la vie. Je me protège par ce sommeil profond. Il me rend insensible à ce qui se passe autour de moi. Je préfère vivre cet état d'inconscience totale, jusqu'à ce que ma vie puisse être plus agréable. J'ai une décision à prendre : vivre ou partir. C'est la même décision à prendre dans le cas d'un **coma diabétique** qui est causé par un excès de glucose (sucre sanguin) dans le sang et plus particulièrement au cerveau. Ma tristesse est tellement grande que j'ai envie de fuir ce monde dans lequel je vis. Même si le **coma** peut durer de longues périodes (semaines et années), il est très important pour mes proches de me témoigner de l'amour, de l'affection et de me dire que la décision de partir ou de rester m'appartient. Lorsque je suis dans le **coma**, mon cerveau peut être actif au point que je peux entendre les gens qui parlent ou ressentir leur présence et les impressions qu'ils dégagent même si moi, présentement, je ne peux pas bouger ou m'exprimer. Il arrive que la peur de la mort me retienne ici dans l'inconscience. Il faut donc me rassurer et me dire que je peux partir en toute sécurité si je le désire. Si je peux voir les énergies d'une personne dans le **coma,** je peux remarquer qu'il y a une coupure importante des liens énergétiques, selon la profondeur du **coma**. Il serait donc approprié de faire des traitements énergétiques pour régulariser la situation.

COMÉDONS (voir : PEAU — POINTS NOIRS)

COMMOTION (... DE LA RÉTINE)
(voir : YEUX — COMMOTION DE LA RÉTINE)

COMMOTION CÉRÉBRALE (voir : CERVEAU [commotion])

COMPULSION NERVEUSE

La **compulsion** est un trouble du comportement caractérisé par une envie irrésistible d'accomplir certains actes à laquelle le sujet ne peut résister sans angoisse. Cette compulsion peut se retrouver dans la sexualité, la nourriture, la boisson, les achats, l'excès de propreté, etc. La **compulsion nerveuse** se rapporte à un aspect de ma personnalité que je juge négatif, qui me déplaît au point que je refuse de le voir. Je le refoule au plus profond de moi. Tant et aussi longtemps que je refuse de le voir et de l'accepter ↓♥, la vie m'amène à vivre de plus en plus de situations où j'ai à faire face à cet aspect de ma personnalité. Lorsque je vis de la **compulsion nerveuse**, je regarde ce qui m'a dérangé, j'accepte ↓♥ de lui faire face au lieu de **fuir. J'accepte ↓♥ d'être un humain** avec des forces, des faiblesses, des qualités et des défauts. Je prends conscience que **je suis mon plus sévère juge,** je me pardonne et **j'apprends à m'aimer**. Le fait de m'accepter ↓♥ tel que je suis me permettra de m'épanouir harmonieusement et je n'aurai plus à me défouler par la **compulsion**.

CONGÉNITAL (voir : INFIRMITÉS CONGÉNITALES)

CONGESTION (... AU CERVEAU / ... AU FOIE / ... AU NEZ / ... AUX POUMONS)

La **congestion** est le système de défense du corps mis en place pour répondre à des attaques répétées contre une certaine partie de mon corps. Différentes parties peuvent être congestionnées. **Au foie :** Elle représente la critique refoulée, l'irritation intérieure que j'accumule car je n'arrive pas à l'exprimer verbalement. Je peux vivre du mécontentement, de l'amertume ou de la déception. **Au nez (sinus) :** Quelle est la situation ou la personne que je ne peux pas sentir et qui me met en colère ? **Aux poumons :** Je me sens étouffé par mes relations familiales, que ce soit mes parents, ma conjointe ou mon conjoint, mes enfants, etc. Mes **échanges** familiaux sont-ils aussi harmonieux que je le souhaite ? Est-ce que je me fais trop de souci ? **Au cerveau :** Je me sens dépassé, je ne sais plus comment réagir face à certaines personnes ou situations. Mon cerveau ne fonctionne plus avec autant de clarté et de rapidité qu'avant. Il est conseillé de se tenir loin de la boisson ou des drogues. Peu importe l'endroit du corps atteint, il en résulte de la frustration, de l'irritation et de la rage face aux autres et à moi-même. Je prends le temps de vérifier ce qui me dérange actuellement dans ma vie et j'en assume la responsabilité. J'accepte ↓♥ de prendre la place qui me revient, **ma place**. Je réalise l'importance d'**exprimer ce que je ressens** et je le fais sans attaquer les autres. Puisque j'exprime mes sentiments, je n'accumule ni frustration, ni haine. Lorsque je suis ouvert et réceptif, les autres le sont. Je me sens à nouveau en harmonie avec moi-même et avec ceux qui m'entourent.

CONJONCTIVITE (voir : YEUX — CONJONCTIVITE)

CONSTIPATION (voir : INTESTINS — CONSTIPATION)

CONTUSIONS (voir : PEAU — BLEUS)

COQUELUCHE (voir : MALADIES DE L'ENFANCE)

CORONAIRE (voir : CŒUR — THROMBOSE CORONARIENNE)

CORPS (en général) (voir : ANNEXE I)

CORS AUX PIEDS (voir : PIEDS — DURILLONS)

CÔTÉ DROIT (voir : MASCULIN [principe...])

CÔTÉ GAUCHE (voir : FÉMININ [principe...])

CÔTES

Les **côtes** font partie de la cage thoracique. Elles protègent le cœur et les poumons (organes vitaux) contre les dommages, les blessures extérieures et les agressions. Une **côte** brisée ou fêlée indique donc que ma protection est diminuée et que je suis vulnérable aux pressions extérieures face à l'amour, à mon autonomie et à mon besoin d'espace. Je me sens coincé entre moi-même (mes **côtés** spirituel et émotionnel) et le monde physique dans lequel je vis. Je me sens fragile et ouvert à toutes formes d'attaques. Je peux avoir l'impression que je n'ai pas le contrôle sur ma vie, que je suis sans ressource et exposé au danger. Souvent, si je me casse ou fêle une **côte**, je vis une situation particulière face à un membre de ma famille. J'aurai une indication de la personne concernée selon l'emplacement de la **côte** touchée. Si ce sont les **côtes** basses, il y a probablement un conflit avec un enfant ou un petit-enfant. Une **côte** latérale représente plutôt une situation conflictuelle face à un frère ou une sœur ou un(e) cousin(e) et les **côtes** hautes représentent un parent ou un grand-parent. J'identifie la ou les situations qui me créent tant de pression. J'accepte ↓♥ de regarder l'événement avec simplicité, d'exprimer franchement ce que je ressens tout en étant à l'écoute des autres. Je sais maintenant que la communication est un outil me permettant de me respecter tout en respectant les autres.

COU (en général)

Le **cou** est la partie du corps qui supporte la tête. Ce lien entre le corps et l'esprit est aussi le pont qui permet à la vie de se manifester, il est l'expression vivante, celui qui autorise le mouvement le plus fondamental. Il représente la **flexibilité**, la **souplesse** et la **direction anticipée.** Il est multidirectionnel et il élargit ma vision extérieure de l'univers. Je peux tout voir autour de moi et, grâce à la flexibilité de mon **cou**, je peux regarder une situation sous tous les angles (devant, derrière...). Mon point de vue devient plus objectif. Un **cou** en bonne santé me permet de prendre de meilleures décisions. Tout ce qui donne la vie traverse le **cou** : l'air, l'eau, les aliments, les circulations sanguine et nerveuse. Il unit la tête et le corps et permet la libre expression de soi, la parole vivante (voix) et l'amour. Le **cou** sépare donc l'abstrait du concret, le matériel du spirituel. Il est important de garder mon **cou** en santé car il me permet de voir ce qui m'entoure avec un esprit ouvert, en laissant de côté toute forme d'entêtement et d'étroitesse d'esprit (**cou** raide). Puisque la gorge se situe au niveau du **cou**, si j'ai de la difficulté à avaler mes émotions, si je les « ravale », ceci peut créer une tension au niveau de mon **cou** où se trouve le centre d'énergie de la communication. Le **cou** correspondant à la conception, il représente aussi mon sentiment d'appartenance, mon droit d'être sur cette terre, me donnant ainsi un sentiment de sécurité et de plénitude.

COU — TORTICOLIS
(voir aussi : COLONNE VERTÉBRALE — HAUT DU DOS, NUQUE [... RAIDE])

Le **torticolis** démontre, entre autres, que je vis de l'insécurité. **J'ai des résistances à voir tous les côtés des situations que je vis**. Mes muscles du **cou** se contractent, mon **cou** se raidit et je n'arrive plus à tourner la tête. Mon inflexibilité m'empêche d'apprécier l'aide que l'on souhaite m'apporter et qui aiderait à faire évoluer les choses qui me semblent difficiles. Je préfère garder la tête droite et associer mon mal à un « coup de froid ». J'ai intérêt à prendre conscience que cette froideur a plutôt touché mon cœur, provoquant ainsi un blocage d'énergie. Je peux aussi chercher à **fuir** une situation inconfortable qui me demande de m'affirmer et de prendre position. Il est aussi important que je m'arrête pour constater dans quelle direction je refuse de regarder ou quelle est la chose que je m'entête ou m'obstine à voir, dire ou faire, et qui fait « bien mon affaire » ... Si j'acceptais de m'ouvrir à une nouvelle façon de voir les choses ou à de nouvelles idées, ma vie en serait peut-être grandement améliorée et mon **torticolis** disparaîtrait. Est-ce qu'il se pourrait qu'il y ait une personne, une chose ou une situation que je voudrais et que je ne voudrais pas regarder en même temps à cause de ma timidité, de ma honte ou de mon sens moral qui est très fort ? Si la raideur empêche ma tête de tourner de gauche à droite, je peux me questionner pour savoir à qui ou à quoi je refuse de dire non. Si au contraire j'ai de la difficulté à dire oui avec ma tête, c'est peut-être que je rejette d'emblée de nouvelles idées. Mon corps me dit

d'accepter ↓♥ de voir et d'apprécier l'instant présent et de reconnaître toutes les nouvelles choses qui font partie de ma vie.

COUDES (en général)

Les **coudes** représentent la liberté de mouvement, la flexibilité, la facilité à changer de direction dans les nouvelles situations ou les expériences de vie. C'est l'articulation souple et flexible du bras qui permet la créativité et l'expression gracieuse de mes gestes quotidiens. Une douleur ou de la rigidité au **coude** signifie un manque de flexibilité, la peur de me sentir « pris » ou coincé dans une situation déplaisante. Les **coudes** étant reliés à l'action, je peux être rigide et juger les gens qui ont une façon de faire différente de la mienne et qui peuvent remettre en question mes propres habitudes. Je résiste à une nouvelle direction à prendre en bloquant inconsciemment l'énergie du cœur qui se rend jusqu'à cette articulation. Deux **coudes** en santé permettent de bien serrer quelqu'un dans ses bras. Je peux mettre plus d'énergie à faire tout ce que je veux. Je trouve alors facile d'accepter ↓♥ la vie et ses nombreux changements. Je m'abandonne plus facilement et elle prend soin de moi comme je le mérite. Même si j'ai parfois peur de me laisser aller, je me sens « poussé du **coude** » par une autre personne, je dois « serrer les **coudes** » pour me protéger. Je reste ouvert à l'amour, ce qui m'aide à vivre plus facilement les expériences quotidiennes sans agressivité, avec souplesse et ouverture d'esprit.

COUDES — ÉPICONDYLITE

Plus connue sous le nom de ***tennis elbow*** en médecine sportive, l'**épicondylite** est une inflammation au niveau de l'articulation du **coude**. Mes **coudes** me donnent la flexibilité nécessaire dans les changements de direction. Dans le cas d'une inflammation, je dois prendre conscience du pourquoi ou de ce à quoi j'oppose tant de résistance. Il se peut que je développe de la frustration à la suite d'événements répétitifs qui se présentent dans ma vie et j'ai l'impression que je dois constamment **amortir les coups**. J'accepte ↓♥ ensuite de laisser aller mes vieilles idées et mes vieux patterns pour prendre la meilleure direction pour mon évolution. J'accepte ↓♥ aussi de laisser circuler l'amour dans les événements qui se présentent à moi.

COUP DE CHALEUR (voir : CHALEUR [coup de...])

COUP DE FROID (voir : FROID [coup de...])

COUP DE SOLEIL (voir : INSOLATION)

COUPURE

La **coupure** indique un désordre émotionnel, une profonde douleur mentale qui se manifeste dans le physique. Elle me fait prendre conscience d'une plaie intérieure. C'est un avertissement, un signe que je dois réévaluer la direction dans laquelle je vais. Je veux aller trop vite et faire trop rapidement. C'est le signe d'un conflit intérieur profond. Je pousse mes limites un peu trop loin ! Je regarde l'endroit où je me coupe et l'activité que je faisais à ce moment, ça me permet d'identifier l'aspect à intégrer. Par exemple, une **coupure** aux mains indique peut-être que je me sens coupable d'exprimer ma créativité dans les situations quotidiennes ou que je suis irrité parce que je fais une chose que je n'aime pas ; je me dépêche et je deviens **coupable.** J'accepte ↓♥ ce que j'ai à comprendre, j'assume mes choix et je fais le changement qui s'impose.

COURBATURE

La **courbature** est une sensation d'endolorissement, de fatigue des muscles après un effort inhabituel ou à la phase initiale de certaines infections virales (grippe, hépatite, etc.). La **courbature** se manifeste par un blocage d'énergie au niveau des muscles. Elle est reliée à la douleur ressentie lorsqu'un besoin (affectif ou émotionnel) n'a pas été satisfait. Alors que l'énergie emmagasinée dans mes muscles s'exprime généralement par un mouvement ou un geste, je bloque inconsciemment cette énergie au niveau du muscle. Je suis donc en réaction intérieure (douleur mentale) et je l'exprime physiquement par ces **courbatures**. J'ai besoin de changer mon comportement, de bouger dans la bonne direction sans être en réaction. La **courbature** se situe à différents niveaux et les douleurs osseuses indiquent une douleur intérieure très profonde. J'en suis affecté jusqu'au fond de mon être, de mon espace. J'accepte ↓♥ d'être ce que je suis, de vivre l'instant présent, sachant que la vie comble intérieurement mes besoins les plus fondamentaux.

CRAMPE(S) (en général)

Une **crampe** est la contraction involontaire, douloureuse et passagère d'un muscle ou d'un groupe musculaire. Les **crampes** indiquent une grande tension intérieure (parfois excessive). Je retiens l'énergie divine et l'empêche de circuler en moi car je suis coincé, limité. Certains de mes patterns mentaux ont besoin d'être intégrés davantage. Actuellement, je vis beaucoup de **pression** et de **tension** qui peuvent être accompagnées d'un sentiment d'impuissance face à quelque chose ou à une situation. Je me demande bien quoi faire et quelle est la meilleure solution pour moi. Puisque j'ai peur, je me **cramponne**, je m'accroche à des idées fixes. J'appréhende la vie au point où je bloque radicalement (« verrouille ») l'énergie à un endroit précis. Selon l'endroit de la **crampe**, j'ai un indice de ce que je dois changer : une **crampe au pied**, la direction que je prends ; une **crampe à la jambe**, ma façon

d'avancer dans la vie ; une **crampe à la main**, mes actions et mes entreprises. Je suis conscient des douleurs intérieures qui m'accablent et je réalise que je peux changer ceci. J'accepte ↓♥ de lâcher prise et de rester ouvert à l'énergie divine. Je prends le temps de m'arrêter et de réfléchir. Cet instant d'arrêt me permet de repartir plus lentement et d'une manière différente, d'être mieux dans ma peau.

CRAMPES ABDOMINALES (voir aussi : VENTRE)

L'abdomen est relié au chakra de l'intuition et de la créativité. Ainsi, la **crampe abdominale** indique la peur de suivre mon intuition, mon refus de me laisser aller pleinement à ma créativité, en bloquant l'énergie divine à cet endroit, c'est à dire près ou plus bas que le nombril. Ainsi, j'arrête tout processus me permettant de voir ce qui peut m'aider à avancer normalement. J'ai peur de découvrir l'avenir sans cesse profitable pour moi. J'accepte ↓♥ de m'ouvrir et de faire confiance à la vie. De cette façon, je peux me laisser guider davantage par mon intuition et je peux utiliser ma créativité pour aller dans la direction qui me convient, en harmonie avec ce que je suis.

CRAMPE DE L'ÉCRIVAIN
(voir aussi : DOIGTS [en général], MAINS [en général], POIGNET)

C'est la sensation d'avoir des engourdissements ou des fourmillements dans les doigts, causée par la compression du nerf médian dans le canal carpien, situé dans la zone antérieure du poignet. Je suis habité par une grande **tension intérieure** et lorsque j'écris, j'y mets énormément d'effort. Qui est-ce que je veux **impressionner** ? Qui est-ce que je veux convaincre ? Moi ou les autres ? Je suis **prétentieux** et mes idées de grandeur font de moi une personne **trop ambitieuse**. Il est possible que je porte un masque, cachant ainsi ma personnalité réelle, ce qui me protège contre le jugement des gens. Comme la douleur peut se manifester davantage la nuit ou le matin au réveil, alors que je suis encore connecté aux mondes intérieurs, cette douleur me rappelle les ajustements que je dois faire à l'intérieur de moi pour être plus flexible. À partir de maintenant, je fais les choses naturellement, en prenant le temps d'être vraiment moi-même. Je n'ai rien à prouver à personne. J'accepte ↓♥ de m'aimer tel que je suis, sans artifices et en demeurant totalement libre dans mes attitudes. C'est le premier pas vers une grande réalisation, la Réalisation de soi.

CRAMPES MUSCULAIRES (en général)

La **crampe** d'origine **musculaire** indique que je **retiens** quelque chose que je ne veux pas laisser aller. C'est une grande **tension intérieure** qui s'exprime par un blocage d'énergie au niveau **musculaire**. Le muscle, lui, représente l'énergie, la vie et la force. Ainsi, je « bloque » la vie en ne laissant pas aller ces vieilles pensées qui changent et qui se transforment dans le corps

en évolution. J'ai encore de vieux principes préconçus et je les véhicule dans mes actions de tous les jours. Il est important de vérifier quelle partie du corps est affectée par les **crampes**. J'apprends dès maintenant à me laisser aller au niveau du cœur, à m'ouvrir davantage aux nouvelles possibilités susceptibles de me faire avancer. Je ne peux changer le passé mais je suis conscient des beautés présentes. La méditation et une technique de rebalancement énergétique aident à laisser aller ces tensions superflues et à harmoniser davantage mes corps énergétiques.

CRISE CARDIAQUE (voir : CŒUR — INFARCTUS [... du myocarde])

CRISE DE FOIE (voir : INDIGESTION)

CROHN (maladie de...) (voir : INTESTINS — CROHN [maladie de...])

CROUP (voir : GORGE — LARYNGITE)

CROÛTE DE LAIT (voir : PEAU — ECZÉMA)

CUISSES (en général) (voir aussi : JAMBES / [en général] / [maux aux...])

La **cuisse** est un muscle qui représente le mouvement et la force d'aller de l'avant. Des **cuisses** fortes et puissantes indiquent une personne bien enracinée au sol, ayant de grandes réserves énergétiques utilisables pour son autorité et son **évolution spirituelle**. Ces « réservoirs » naturels indiquent aussi l'état d'esprit. Ainsi, en restant inactif trop longtemps, je risque d'accumuler des réserves inutiles. Cela dénote que j'ai peur de prendre ma place, que je trouve **injuste** plusieurs situations de jeunesse vécues principalement face à mes parents, que je n'ai pas acceptées ↓♥ et face auxquelles je vis beaucoup de **ressentiment**. **Manquer** de quelque chose peut être effrayant pour moi ! Donc, je fais des « réserves ». Je continue à véhiculer dans mes **cuisses** ces pensées **inconscientes** et à transporter tout ce matériel excédentaire. Je vis de la colère, du **ressentiment** et de la frustration parce que j'ai l'impression de travailler sans grand succès. En ayant de grosses **cuisses** bien « dodues » (et très serrées entre les jambes), je bloque inconsciemment l'énergie à cet endroit et ma sexualité risque de changer car l'énergie reste « stagnante » au niveau du bassin. Il peut y avoir un barrage de résistances mentales qui m'empêche de m'exprimer pleinement ou de trouver ma direction. Il est temps de me libérer et de laisser passer cette énergie d'amour qui ne demande qu'à s'exprimer. Je laisse couler cette énergie vers le bas, vers mes **cuisses** et mes jambes qui en ont besoin davantage, ce qui m'aidera à m'enraciner à la terre, à être plus « groundé » et ainsi, amènera un

plus grand équilibre entre mes côtés spirituel et physique. Ceci aidera à faire partir la déprime que je vis. Mon corps s'équilibre et je me débarrasse de la rancune accumulée dans ma jeunesse. Même si, parfois, j'ai l'impression d'être fermé, je regarde mes biens matériels et je les accepte ↓♥ pour ce qu'ils sont dans ce monde, c'est-à-dire des serviteurs de l'univers.

CUISSES (maux de...) (voir : JAMBES — PARTIE SUPÉRIEURE)

CULPABILITÉ (voir : ACCIDENT)

CUSHING[46] (syndrome de...)
(voir aussi : SURRÉNALES [maux de capsules])

Conséquence d'une surproduction d'une hormone des glandes surrénales, le **syndrome de Cushing** se manifeste par un désordre mental et physique, un déséquilibre qui amène le sentiment d'**être envahi** par les autres, du fait que j'ai perdu graduellement tout contact avec mon propre pouvoir. Un sentiment d'impuissance est vécu. Ainsi, par réaction, je tends à vouloir écraser consciemment ou non les gens autour de moi. Lorsque ces glandes fonctionnent de façon anormale, je vois apparaître une série de symptômes connus sous l'appellation de **syndrome de Cushing**. Je me rends compte que certaines parties du corps se transforment : le visage, le cou, le tronc et je constate aussi que les membres inférieurs maigrissent. Je vis un débalancement physique et mental. Je me sens impuissant, je n'ai plus conscience du pouvoir qui m'habite. Je suis en état de survie et il est important pour moi que je reprenne davantage contact avec la réalité en posant des gestes qui m'aideront. J'utilise ce pouvoir pour améliorer ma qualité de vie. J'apprends à me faire confiance, j'accepte ↓♥ de prendre ma place et de vivre en fonction de ce que je ressens et de ce que je suis.

CUTICULES (voir : DOIGTS — CUTICULES)

CYPHOSE (voir : COLONNE VERTÉBRALE [déviation de la...], DOS [maux de...])

CYSTITE (voir : VESSIE — CYSTITE)

DALTONIEN (voir : YEUX — DALTONISME [non perception des couleurs])

---

46. **Cushing (Harvey William) :** Neurochirurgien américain qui, en 1832, a décrit certains troubles liés aux glandes surrénales.

DÉMANGEAISONS (voir : PEAU — DÉMANGEAISONS)

DÉMANGEAISONS À L'ANUS
(voir : ANUS — DÉMANGEAISON ANALE)

DÉMANGEAISONS VAGINALES (voir aussi : VAGIN [en général])

Les **démangeaisons vaginales** sont reliées à la sexualité et au principe féminin. Si cela me démange, c'est qu'en ce qui a trait à mes relations sexuelles, quelque chose me contrarie, mon partenaire m'impatiente. Comme je le ferais dans le cas de **démangeaisons** ordinaires, je me demande ce qui m'irrite, me dérange et m'agace. Lorsque les **démangeaisons** apparaissent, je trouve la cause et j'apprends à communiquer, à dialoguer à cœur ouvert afin d'exprimer ce que je ressens.

DENTS (en général)

Les **dents** symbolisent les **décisions**, la solide porte d'entrée qui me permet de mordre à « pleines **dents** » dans la vie ! Réalité intérieure et extérieure passent par mes **dents** qui sont l'un des moyens pour m'exprimer entièrement dans cet univers. La **dent** est un des organes annexes très durs qui représente l'énergie fondamentale de mon être. La capacité intérieure d'accueillir les nouvelles idées, l'amour et la nourriture intérieure se manifeste par des **dents** saines et dures. Les **dents** sont, en partie, le miroir de l'être. Lorsque la nourriture passe à travers ma bouche, cette dernière transmet aussi des sentiments qui peuvent affecter mes **dents** à plus ou moins long terme. Ainsi, des **dents** altérées (par exemple : cariées) indiquent une faible **affirmation de soi**, une réalité inacceptable pour moi et la **peur de prendre ma place** dans l'univers avec les responsabilités que cela implique. Même si j'ai de la difficulté à prendre certaines décisions bénéfiques pour moi, je dois rester ouvert aux moyens disponibles me permettant de dépasser les situations les plus délicates. Les **dents** représentent aussi ma volonté à aller de l'avant, à bien faire les choses, ma capacité à donner vie à mes pensées et à mes émotions. Un conflit profond, de la culpabilité reliée à une situation émotionnelle véhiculée en paroles, ou tout autre dérangement intérieur peuvent se manifester par une réaction aux **dents** et même aux gencives. Je peux donc « serrer les **dents** » pour me défendre d'une agression extérieure dans une situation qui me fait fortement réagir. Je ferme la porte, en résistant à ce qui veut entrer en moi ou, au contraire, à ce qui a besoin de sortir de moi. Les **incisives** (les dents d'en avant) se rapportent au fait d'avoir à « trancher » face à un choix, c'est-à-dire oui ou non, faire ou ne pas faire telle action, etc. Les **canines** sont davantage liées au fait de pouvoir exercer une certaine autorité sur les décisions que j'ai à prendre. Elles peuvent être affectées lorsque je me sens « déchiré » face à une décision à prendre. Les **prémolaires**

m'indiquent mon degré d'accord par rapport à mes décisions. Quant aux **molaires**, elles représentent mon degré de contentement face aux décisions qui ont été prises ou qu'il me reste à prendre. Ce sera l'**émail de la dent** qui sera atteint lorsque j'ai l'impression que je n'ai pas le droit de « mordre » dans une situation et la **dentine** sera affectée lorsque je pense ne pas pouvoir être capable de « mordre » dans une situation, doutant de moi-même, de mes capacités. J'accepte ↓♥ de rester ouvert à l'amour, sans avoir peur de perdre la gratitude des autres. Je m'aime tel que je suis, avec toutes mes qualités. Je dois prendre soin de mes **dents**, elles « habillent » ma personnalité. Les **dents** n'ont pas de masque ! Je reste moi-même, sans me juger et en demeurant ouvert aux critiques extérieures. Je transforme mes pensées en amour véritable et mes **dents** restent en santé !

DENTS (maux de...)

Les **problèmes dentaires** sont reliés aux **décisions**, particulièrement lorsque j'ai mal aux dents. Je **reporte la prise de décisions** parce que les conséquences de ces choix m'effraient, m'insécurisent. C'est associé à la responsabilité personnelle, à ma capacité de prendre des décisions, sans avoir peur de ce qui va arriver plus tard. Si j'ai une **rage de dents**, il se peut fort bien que la **rage** se soit emparée de moi parce que je m'en veux de ne pas pouvoir communiquer ce que je veux. J'ai le goût de « montrer les dents » pour prendre ma place et montrer que j'existe. Je veux qu'on m'écoute, qu'on me respecte. Je prends conscience qu'en communiquant mes besoins et mes désirs, les **rages de dents** n'auront plus raison d'être. Lorsqu'il s'agit de **tartre sur les dents**, c'est une forme d'**agression intérieure**, une réaction qui n'a pas été réglée et qui refait surface. Cela peut m'amener à durcir mes positions face aux décisions que j'ai à prendre ou que j'ai prises. Mes comportements peuvent changer. Sachant qu'il n'est pas bénéfique pour moi d'être à la merci de mon imagination, je développe plutôt le côté créatif des circonstances. J'essaie de trouver un moyen de structurer davantage ma pensée et mes idées ; ainsi, il me sera plus facile de prendre de judicieuses initiatives liées à ce que je vis actuellement. J'accepte ↓♥ d'être conscient de ce qui se passe dans ma vie, de comprendre l'essence de la détermination qui gère mon univers. Je vérifie le côté affecté par les **problèmes dentaires** et j'apporte la solution qui convient. S'il est en haut, je pense à l'intuition et à l'instinct tandis qu'en bas, c'est davantage une décision du domaine rationnel et logique, quelque chose de voulu physiquement.

DENT (abcès de la...)

Puisque cet **abcès** se retrouve dans les tissus qui enveloppent la racine dentaire, cela démontre ma colère par rapport à une décision à prendre. Comme l'infection est située dans la cavité centrale de la **dent**, cela indique la contrariété que je vis par rapport à une décision qui me ronge par en dedans

(de-dent). Il est alors temps que je prenne la décision avec le plus d'amour et d'harmonie possible en tenant compte des valeurs les plus élevées qui gouvernent ma vie, dans le respect de moi-même et des autres.

DENTS (carie dentaire)

La **carie dentaire** est la manifestation d'une **douleur intérieure** extrême. **Quelque chose me ronge** jusqu'au plus profond de mon être. Je n'arrive pas à exprimer ce mal qui me ronge et l'inflammation fait son apparition. La **dent** commence à ramollir et c'est souvent douloureux, en raison de la sensibilité nerveuse présente au niveau de la **dent**. La structure de la **dent** est la plus rigide du corps humain. La **carie dentaire** concerne l'aspect « mental ». Est-ce de la **haine** ou de la **rancune** vis-à-vis de quelqu'un ? Il se peut que « je montre les **dents** » quand je me sens attaqué. Quelle est la véritable cause de ma douleur ? La raison première augmentera mes chances de renverser ce processus de destruction. Je peux aussi avoir vécu une situation où j'avais le goût de « mordre » quelqu'un en situation d'autodéfense et que je ne l'ai pas fait car « un enfant bien éduqué ne fait pas ce genre de choses ». J'avais souvent des **caries** étant enfant, car j'ai une « **dent**» contre une personne. Il se peut aussi que je vive un conflit familial où j'assume difficilement ce que je reçois de mon entourage et que je doive filtrer ce conflit avec mes **dents** par le processus de mastication. Car mes **dents** me permettent de filtrer et de discriminer ce qui entre à l'intérieur de mon corps et, par le fait même, dans mon Univers en général. Je cesse de chercher la cause physique (alimentation, sucre, etc.). Je laisse plutôt évoluer mes pensées et je change ma manière de voir les situations de ma vie. Je prends la vie avec « un grain de sel » et je permettrai ainsi à mes « **dents de sagesse** » de se développer et de se fortifier. Ce sera beaucoup plus profitable pour moi !

DENTS — DENTIERS ou FAUSSES DENTS

Le **dentier** me donne l'illusion d'une forte vitalité. En effet, semblable aux vraies **dents**, il donne l'impression d'être vrai, d'être sincère comme de vraies **dents** ! Rien n'est plus faux ! Puisque je veux une réponse claire, je vais au fond des choses. Suis-je capable de vivre mes expériences avec courage et sincérité, comme avec mes vraies **dents** ? Suis-je déterminé à être ce que je suis vraiment, à m'affirmer, à « croquer » dans la vie ? Je cesse de vivre en fonction des autres. J'accepte ↓♥ d'être moi-même et, en m'affirmant, je trouve la satisfaction et le bonheur.

DENTS (grincement de...)
(voir aussi : AUTORITARISME, MÂCHOIRES [maux de...])

Les **dents** représentent les décisions et une certaine forme d'agressivité. Le **grincement de dents** est donc une **colère inconsciente** qui remonte à la surface, une **rage refoulée** qui s'exprime souvent la nuit. Je suis très nerveux

intérieurement, je me retiens de dire ou de faire certaines choses. Comme je n'arrive pas à prendre des décisions claires et précises, le **grincement de dents** est **l'expression physique de ma tristesse et de mon agressivité réprimée**. Comme une porte mal graissée, le **grincement de dents** m'indique ma peur à m'ouvrir pour prendre des décisions et le bruit exprime une forme de gémissement intérieur. J'accepte ↓♥ de prendre conscience de cet état sans le refouler et de l'exprimer comme je le vis présentement. J'accepte ↓♥ ma sensibilité et les émotions qui font surface et je réalise que mes incertitudes m'amènent à vivre beaucoup plus de tension intérieure que le fait de prendre les initiatives qui s'imposent. Lorsque je prends une décision, je me libère et je me sens plus épanoui.

DENT DE SAGESSE INCLUSE

La sagesse est une grande qualité. J'ai le bonheur de la manifester dans cette vie-ci. Elle me permet de m'ouvrir à l'univers et me procure des **bases solides** dans tout ce que j'entreprends. Ainsi, une **dent de sagesse** qui refuse de sortir, de « prendre sa place », signifie que sur le plan mental, je refuse encore de prendre tout l'espace qui me revient. Je dois le faire consciemment pour développer toutes les qualités divines essentielles à mon évolution. J'accepte ↓♥ de laisser la nature suivre son cours et d'ouvrir ma conscience pour grandir et voir les changements en moi ! Ils me rapporteront !

DÉPENDANCE (voir aussi : ALCOOLISME, CIGARETTE, DROGUE)

Une **dépendance** est reliée à un profond **vide intérieur**, à une tentative extérieure de vouloir combler principalement un manque d'amour de soi ou un manque affectif rattaché à l'un de mes parents. Par la **dépendance** (alcool, drogue, nourriture, cigarette, sport, sexe), je veux combler ce vide, ce désespoir et cette tristesse. Ma vie est dénuée de sens, elle ne satisfait pas mes désirs les plus profonds. Je vis de la révolte face au monde extérieur et j'ai de la difficulté à préserver mon ego. Je n'arrive pas à m'aimer tel que je suis et cette incapacité temporaire se manifeste par de la colère et de la rancœur face à l'univers. La **dépendance** est donc une sorte de **substitut** qui m'aide à vivre temporairement dans un monde sans problème. Alors que l'alcool m'amène une certaine extase et de l'engourdissement par rapport à ce que je vis, les drogues « non prescrites » (cocaïne, haschich, héroïne, LSD, PCP, marijuana, etc.) me dirigent vers de nouvelles sensations avec le désir d'atteindre des sommets inconnus de conscience. Toute **dépendance** entraîne donc des réactions du corps humain plus ou moins connues. Ces formes d'abus sont fondamentalement négatives et divers types de peurs incontrôlées (névroses) peuvent surgir si la **dépendance** est forte (par exemple : drogues). Enfin, une **dépendance** peut se manifester à travers une certaine tendance (par exemple : sexuelle) qui est difficilement maîtrisable. Le premier pas important à faire est de prendre conscience de ma situation. Cela demande beaucoup

d'amour et de courage pour affronter et pour briser cet esclavage qui dérange ma vie. J'accepte ↓♥ d'être ouvert à l'inconnu, à la voie qui me mènera vers mes objectifs de Réalisation de soi. L'amour inconditionnel est le début de ma guérison. Je demande aux autres, je cherche, je vérifie, je fais les premiers pas. Je recherche quelle méthode de guérison naturelle peut m'aider à me centrer, à m'harmoniser et à augmenter mes forces intérieures afin de me permettre d'intégrer avec amour les différents manques vécus durant ma jeunesse. Les responsabilités ne m'effraient plus et je reprends contact avec l'être divin que je suis.

DÉPÔTS DE CALCIUM

Le **calcium** est un minéral correspondant à l'énergie la plus « rigide » du corps humain, c'est-à-dire l'os. Le **calcium** est donc relié à mon énergie mentale, à la structure mentale de mon être. Le **dépôt** se forme lorsque l'énergie se fixe et se « cristallise » (semblable aux pierres du foie) à un endroit donné apportant douleur et inflammation. Pourquoi en est-il ainsi ? Parce que les **dépôts de calcium** proviennent généralement des pensées immuables, du **manque de souplesse par rapport à l'autorité** que je refuse d'accepter ↓♥. Je considère que de me plier à cette exigence supplémentaire dans ma vie m'empêche d'être totalement libre. Une façon de changer ces **dépôts de calcium** en amour est de pratiquer l'ouverture d'esprit et de mettre l'accent sur la communication. J'accepte ↓♥ qu'en étant ouvert aux autres, je subis moins l'autorité et que je vis beaucoup plus un partage. Ainsi, je demeure autonome, libre et j'acquiers la sagesse !

DÉPRESSION (voir aussi : NEURASTHÉNIE)

La **dépression** implique une **profonde tristesse intérieure**, une accumulation d'émotions refoulées provoquant un conflit entre le corps et l'esprit. Cette maladie est reliée à un événement marquant de ma vie. La **dépression** se traduit par de la **dévalorisation** et de la **culpabilité** qui me rongent de l'intérieur. Si je suis **dépressif**, je me sens misérable, moins que rien. Je vis dans le passé constamment et j'ai de la difficulté à en sortir. Le présent et l'avenir n'existent pas. Il est important d'effectuer un changement maintenant dans ma façon de voir les choses parce que ce n'est plus comme avant. La **dépression** est souvent une étape décisive dans ma vie (par exemple : l'adolescence) parce qu'elle m'oblige à me remettre en question. Je veux avoir une vie différente à tout prix. Je suis bouleversé entre mes idéaux (mes rêves) et le réel (ce qui se passe), entre ce que je suis et ce que je veux être. C'est un débalancement intérieur (peut-être chimique ou hormonal) et mon individualité est méconnaissable. Je me sens limité dans mon espace et je perds doucement le goût de vivre, l'essence de mon existence. Je me sens inutile. En d'autres termes, la **dépression** a sa source dans une situation que je vis face à mon territoire, c'est-à-dire ce qui appartient à mon espace vital, que ce soient

des personnes (mes parents, mes enfants, mes amis, etc.), des animaux (mon chien, mes poissons, etc.), ou des choses (mon travail, ma maison, mes meubles, etc.). Le conflit que je vis peut être lié à un élément de mon territoire que j'ai peur de **perdre** ; à une **dispute** qui a lieu sur mon territoire et qui me dérange (par exemple : les disputes entre frères et sœurs). Voici des expressions qui montrent comment je peux me sentir : « *Tu m'étouffes !* » ; « *Tu me pompes l'air !* » ; « *Fais de l'air !* » Parfois aussi, j'éprouve de la difficulté à délimiter ou à marquer mon espace, mon territoire. Qu'est-ce qui m'appartient en exclusivité et qu'est-ce qui appartient aux autres ? Les **personnes dépressives** sont souvent très perméables à leur entourage. Je ressens tout ce qui se passe autour de moi et ceci décuple ma sensibilité, d'où un sentiment de limitation et l'impression d'être envahi par mon entourage. Ainsi, j'abandonne parce que je trouve la charge trop lourde. Je n'ai plus le **goût de vivre** et je me sens **coupable** d'être ce que je suis. Je peux même avoir tendance à l'autodestruction. Je peux aussi avoir « besoin d'attention » pour m'aider à me valoriser ; la **dépression** devient à ce moment un moyen inconscient pour « manipuler » mon entourage. Le rire ne fait plus partie de ma vie. Peu importe la raison, je vérifie dès maintenant la ou les causes sous-jacentes à mon état **dépressif**. Ai-je vécu de la pression étant jeune ? Quels sont les événements marquants vécus dans mon enfance qui font paraître ma vie si insignifiante ? Est-ce la perte d'un être aimé, ma raison de vivre ou la direction de ma vie que je n'arrive plus à voir ? Fuir la réalité et mes responsabilités ne sert à rien (par exemple : suicide) même si cela semble être le chemin le plus facile. Il est important de constater les responsabilités de ma vie car il me faudra plus que des antidépresseurs pour faire disparaître la **dépression** : je dois aller à la source. À partir de maintenant, je réalise que je suis un être unique. J'ai des valeurs intérieures exceptionnelles. Je peux reprendre la maîtrise de moi et de ma vie. J'ai le choix de « lâcher » ou de « lutter ». J'ai tout ce qu'il faut pour changer ma destinée. En me responsabilisant, j'acquiers plus de liberté et mes efforts sont récompensés.

DERMATITE (voir : PEAU — DERMATITE)

DIABÈTE (voir : SANG — DIABÈTE)

DIAPHRAGME

Le **diaphragme** est la grande paroi musculaire qui sépare la partie supérieure (poumons et cœur) de la partie inférieure (foie, estomac, intestins, etc.) de mon être. Elle représente la respiration, **la capacité de m'abandonner** complètement en respirant profondément. J'ai besoin d'être « relaxe » pour pouvoir bien respirer à la vie. Le **diaphragme** est efficace lorsque je m'abandonne à la vie. Si certaines tensions apparaissent, c'est parce que je **retiens**, je **refoule** ou je **bloque** des énergies libératrices qui sont

bénéfiques pour moi. Je peux vivre certaines situations qui m'empêchent d'exprimer librement mes sentiments et mes pensées les plus profonds. Peut-être que mon mode de vie m'empêche d'être réellement ce que je suis, ce qui m'amène à respirer d'une manière superficielle et limitée. Le **diaphragme** est relié à la période des premiers mouvements du fœtus, où je découvre que quelque chose d'autre existe à part moi. Donc, devenu adulte, cette région se bloque quand les échanges entre mon monde intérieur et mon monde extérieur sont conflictuels, par exemple si je <u>fais</u> beaucoup de choses qui sont vides et superficielles, sans profondeur. Je dois prendre conscience que la vie m'apporte beaucoup de bien. Qu'à partir de maintenant, je n'ai pas à me retenir inutilement, je fais confiance et je peux me laisser aller davantage à la vie. Le **diaphragme** est un muscle d'une grande importance qui, lorsque je respire pleinement, me permet d'entrer en contact avec mon moi intérieur et de rejoindre l'énergie de l'univers. Dès à présent, je vois ma vie d'une manière toute différente. J'exprime librement, ici et maintenant, mes pensées, mes sentiments, mes émotions profondes...

DIARRHÉE (voir : INTESTINS — DIARRHÉE])

DIGESTION (maux de...) (voir : INDIGESTION)

DIPHTÉRIE (voir aussi : GORGE, LARYNX)

La **diphtérie** se caractérise par la formation de membranes au larynx et au pharynx (gorge), provoquant de l'enflure. J'ai de la difficulté à avaler. Puisque la gorge me permet de parler, de communiquer et d'échanger, cela m'indique que je me **retiens** lors d'échanges avec les autres. Je n'arrive pas à exprimer ce que je ressens, je **ravale** mes émotions et mes besoins. J'ai **peur du rejet** et je **présume** de la réaction des autres. Je réalise qu'il est essentiel que je fasse connaître mes besoins et mes sentiments plutôt que de les étouffer. Je dois changer. J'ai à m'accepter ↓♥ tel que je suis et apprendre à m'aimer. Si je m'aime et si je me respecte, les autres m'aimeront et me respecteront en retour.

DISLOCATION (voir : OS — DISLOCATION)

DISQUE DÉPLACÉ
(voir : COLONNE VERTÉBRALE — DISQUE DÉPLACÉ)

DIVERTICULITE (voir : INTESTINS — DIVERTICULITE)

DOIGTS (en général)

Les **doigts** sont le prolongement de mes mains et l'outil servant à la manifestation de mes actions dans ma vie de tous les jours. Ils représentent l'action dans **le moment présent, les détails du quotidien.** Par le toucher, je peux aimer, caresser, gronder, construire et créer. Mes **doigts** sont la manifestation concrète de mes pensées, de mes sentiments. Une blessure au **doigt** m'indique que j'essaie peut-être d'en faire trop, que je vais trop loin ou trop vite. Je porte mon attention sur trop de choses en même temps et mes énergies sont dispersées. Je me préoccupe trop des choses à faire. Peu importe la nature de la blessure (coupure, écorchure, verrue, etc.), je m'en fais avec mes actions présentes. Habituellement, le niveau de la blessure et le genre de tissu impliqué (la peau ou les os) sont importants. Par exemple, une coupure jusqu'à l'os indique une blessure plus profonde qu'une simple éraflure. Je vérifie le(s) **doigt**(s) impliqué(s) et la réponse à mes questions sera plus claire. À partir de maintenant, je prends le temps de faire une chose à la fois car j'accepte ↓♥ ma dimension humaine et je **coupe** mon impatience qui me pousse à avancer trop rapidement.

DOIGTS — POUCE

Le **pouce** est relié à la **pression**, celle que je me place sur les épaules autant que celle que j'exige des autres ! C'est un **doigt** puissant qui symbolise la force, mon besoin de pouvoir et qui sert à pousser, à juger, à presser ainsi qu'à apprécier les actions des autres (**pouce** en haut ou en bas) autant que mes propres interventions. Lorsque je montre le **pouce** vers le haut en tenant la main fermée, je donne mon approbation ; le **pouce** vers le bas, mon désaccord ou mon rejet. Le **pouce** est relié à mon **intellect,** à mes échanges interpersonnels et à ma sensibilité. Le **pouce** détermine donc le genre de contacts que j'ai avec les autres et moi-même. Puisqu'un enfant suce son **pouce** dans les situations où il se sent insécure, le **pouce** représente donc la sécurité et la protection. Toutes les blessures au **pouce** sont reliées à un trop plein d'effort mental, une accumulation excessive d'idées et de **soucis** et une tendance à être défaitiste. Est-ce que mes échanges avec les autres sont sains ? Est-ce que je **pousse** trop les autres ou est-ce que je me sens **poussé** par une vie trépidante ? Le **pouce** symbolise aussi la vie et la survivance, l'envie de vivre sa vie et non de mourir (si je garde mon **pouce** à l'intérieur d'une main fermée, je suis une personne introvertie qui a peut-être envie de mourir ou qui sent le besoin de se replier sur soi pour se protéger du monde extérieur). À partir de maintenant, je fais tout pour être en paix avec moi-même. J'observe les signes reliés à mon **pouce** et je reste vigilant lorsque quelque chose m'arrive. Je laisse monter la tristesse qui m'habite. J'accepte ↓♥ la vie et les situations sans faire trop de drame car je sais que l'univers prend soin de moi !

DOIGTS — INDEX

L'**index** représente l'**ego** sous tous ces aspects : **autorité, orgueil, suffisance...** Dans mes comportements non verbaux, lorsque j'active mon **index** en le pointant souvent, cela indique un **rejet d'autorité**, qu'elle soit parentale ou autre. J'essaie d'exprimer l'autorité de façon « réactive », c'est-à-dire en réaction avec les différentes formes d'autorité présentes. Ma peur de l'autorité peut même me causer des troubles de digestion. J'ai peur d'être pris au piège, de ne pas être reconnu à ma juste valeur. J'ai peur de l'autorité et je n'accepte ↓♥ pas qu'elle soit présente dans ma vie. Je veux faire valoir mon point à tout prix ! Lorsque j'utilise mon **index** pour imposer mes idées d'une manière assez autoritaire, c'est ma façon d'affirmer mon « pouvoir personnel ». Je prends conscience que souvent, ce sont mes peurs qui me font agir de la sorte. J'ai une grande sensibilité émotionnelle et j'ai besoin de me sentir en sécurité dans la vie. Je réalise qu'avoir raison pour un tout ou un rien n'est pas ce qui compte. Je conserve mes énergies pour les choses importantes. Est-ce l'autorité qui me dérange vraiment ? Il s'agit peut-être d'un sentiment d'impuissance ou d'insécurité remontant à mon enfance face à l'autorité parentale. À partir de maintenant, j'accepte ↓♥ les formes d'autorité qui me dérangent en sachant qu'elles sont là pour me faire évoluer positivement.

DOIGTS — MAJEUR

Le **majeur**, le **doigt** le plus long de la main, **représente la créativité, la sexualité et la colère.** Bref, il symbolise beaucoup de choses et je dois (**doigt** !) lui porter une attention toute particulière. Une blessure à ce **doigt** signifie que ma vie sexuelle ne va pas comme je le souhaite ou que je m'incline trop facilement devant le destin. Je vis du chagrin ou une tension lié à de l'insatisfaction, et la colère s'installe doucement. Cette réaction m'empêche de réaliser mes désirs secrets. Mon côté créatif est restreint par un manque de confiance. Dès à présent, j'identifie quel est l'aspect de ma sexualité ou de ma créativité qui est en cause. J'accepte ↓♥ d'exprimer mes besoins plutôt que de laisser la colère monter. Je réalise que seules mes peurs (l'orgueil) m'empêchent de m'exprimer.

DOIGTS — ANNULAIRE

Annulaire, du mot « anneau », est le **symbole de l'union** et représente mes liens affectifs. Toute blessure à ce **doigt** provient d'un **chagrin** ou d'une difficulté dans mes relations affectives : cela peut être face à mon mari, ma femme, mes enfants et, dans certains cas, même face à mes parents. Cette blessure est la manifestation extérieure d'une blessure intérieure dont je n'ai probablement parlé à personne. Il m'est difficile de faire l'**union** avec moi-même, de vivre avec ce chagrin intérieur qui m'accable. J'ai peut-être tendance à exagérer la situation. Qu'est-ce qui me dérange ? J'accepte ↓♥ de me détacher pour mieux voir la situation. Qu'est-ce qui m'empêche de m'exprimer ? Est-ce que je

présume de la réaction de l'autre ? J'apprends à vérifier et je réalise qu'entre **présumer** et **savoir**, il y a une très grande différence. Vérifier me permet d'avoir des relations beaucoup plus harmonieuses et m'apprend aussi à dialoguer.

DOIGTS — AURICULAIRE (petit doigt)

L'**auriculaire** est directement relié au **cœur**. Il représente la **famille** ainsi que tous les aspects familiaux de ma vie, particulièrement l'amour et l'harmonie familiale. Lorsque je m'inflige une blessure à ce **doigt**, cela indique que je vis des émotions par rapport à ma famille que j'aurais avantage à extérioriser, un manque d'harmonie à l'intérieur de mon couple ou un simple manque d'amour de soi. Un dommage quelconque au **petit doigt** (écorchure, brûlure, etc.) dénote assurément une trop grande émotivité. J'ai sûrement la fâcheuse habitude de m'en faire avec des riens et mon émotivité prend le dessus. Je deviens prétentieux et cela me déséquilibre et m'empêche de comprendre les gens et les événements de ma vie. J'accepte ↓♥ de regarder les événements et les situations avec la simplicité d'un enfant. En les dédramatisant et en faisant montre d'ouverture d'esprit, j'apprends à m'affirmer et à communiquer. Je vais de l'avant beaucoup plus allègrement. J'ai besoin de beaucoup plus de calme intérieur. Au lieu de jouer un rôle et de vivre dans un monde où les apparences priment sur « l'être », j'ai avantage à revenir aux choses simples et à être moi-même.

DOIGTS ARTHRITIQUES

L'arthrite symbolise **la critique**, l'autopunition, la réprobation, un manque profond d'amour. Ainsi, les **doigts** (c'est-à-dire les détails du quotidien) **arthritiques** indiquent donc le sentiment d'être mal aimé et d'être victime des événements dans ma vie de tous les jours. Je remets le pouvoir aux autres. J'accepte ↓♥ de m'aimer et de me pardonner car, si je ne m'aime pas, comment les autres peuvent-ils m'aimer ?

DOIGTS — CUTICULES

La **cuticule** est une couche très mince de peau, une sorte de pellicule qui se forme à la base de l'ongle. Plus la **cuticule** est épaisse et pousse rapidement, plus j'ai tendance à être dur envers moi. **Je me critique** constamment pour des futilités parce que je suis perfectionniste. J'accepte ↓♥ de voir que je suis un être humain en évolution et que je fais toujours mon possible. Je cesse de me juger aussi sévèrement et je m'accepte ↓♥ tel que je suis afin de pouvoir continuer à avancer harmonieusement.

DOIGTS DE PIEDS (voir : ORTEILS)

DOS (en général)

Le **dos** représente le **soutien et le support de la vie**. C'est l'endroit qui me protège si je me sens impuissant face à une personne ou une situation (**tourne le dos**), en cas de besoin. Si mon fardeau est trop lourd, si je manque de support ou si je ne me sens pas assez supporté (affectif, monétaire, etc.), mon **dos** réagira en conséquence et certaines douleurs (courbatures) peuvent faire leur apparition. Je peux avoir le **dos large** et être capable d'en prendre ou bien m'incliner humblement, me courber par respect ou acceptation ↓♥. Peu importe la raison, un **mal de dos** indique donc que je veux peut-être me sauver de quelque chose en le plaçant derrière moi, car c'est avec mon **dos** que j'enfouis les expériences qui m'ont causé confusion ou peine. J'y mets tout ce que je ne désire pas voir ou laisser voir aux autres, jouant ainsi à l'autruche. Je suis **profondément blessé**, incapable présentement d'exprimer ces émotions bloquées. Je refuse de voir ce qui ne fait pas mon affaire ! J'accepte ↓♥ de libérer maintenant les énergies retenues aux endroits qui font mal ! Un **dos** souple mais fort indique une certaine souplesse mentale et une grande ouverture d'esprit contrairement aux **raideurs dorsales** qui signifient orgueil, pouvoir et refus de céder. Assis bien confortablement, je peux avoir l'impression d'être protégé, en toute sécurité. Cependant, même si mon **dos** sert à y mettre ces choses indésirables et que je voudrais « jouer à l'autruche », j'accepte ↓♥ de voir ce qui me dérange et de l'exprimer. En agissant de la sorte, je me libère du fardeau que je portais. La **posture** adoptée donne des indications sur ce que je vis et sur ma façon de transiger avec les situations de ma vie : si je suis en réaction face à l'autorité, que je veux tenir mon bout face à quelqu'un ou devant quelque chose, je vais « raidir le **dos** » par orgueil. Si au contraire je vis de la soumission, que j'ai peur, que je me sens faible, je vais « courber le **dos** » et autant mes préoccupations sont grandes, autant « mon **dos** va me faire souffrir ». Certaines personnes intègrent davantage les difficultés de la vie dans l'écriture, le dialogue ou l'échange. Je choisis le moyen qui me convient le mieux et je laisse la vie couler en moi, afin d'apprendre à m'exprimer d'avantage et de m'affirmer quand j'en ai besoin. J'accepte ↓♥ que la vie me soutienne à chaque instant et je « relève les épaules », sachant que j'ai la force nécessaire pour réaliser tous mes projets.

DOS (maux de...) — HAUT DU DOS (7 vertèbres certicales)

Le **haut du dos** correspond à la région du cœur et au centre énergétique cardiaque. Les **maux de dos** ont trait aux premiers stades de la conception, aux besoins de base et à la structure la plus fondamentale de l'être. Les 7 vertèbres cervicales sont principalement concernées dans cette région. Les vertèbres cervicales ce rapportent à la communication et à mon degré d'ouverture face à la vie. Ma naïveté peut me rendre vulnérable à ce niveau. Si j'ai l'impression qu'on veut me juger, me critiquer ou me blesser, je pourrai être affecté sur ce plan et j'aurai tendance à me refermer comme une huître. Les

cervicales C1, C2 et C3 seront plus particulièrement atteintes si je me dévalorise au niveau de mes capacités intellectuelles tandis que les **cervicales basses** réagiront à de l'injustice que je peux avoir l'impression de vivre dans ma vie ou à celle que je vois autour de moi et qui me répugne. De plus, chaque vertèbre me donne des informations additionnelles sur la source de mon malaise :

C_1 = La **première vertèbre cervicale** qu'on nomme **ATLAS** et qui porte le numéro C_1, sert de support à la tête. Elle est un pilier qui garde la tête en équilibre. Si je m'en fais trop (« me casse la tête ») par rapport à une situation ou une personne, ma tête va s'alourdir jusqu'à me donner des maux de tête et C_1 pourra avoir de la difficulté à supporter la charge. Si je manifeste de l'étroitesse d'esprit, si je refuse de regarder toutes les facettes d'une situation, si je suis rigide dans ma façon de penser, C_1 réagira en cessant ses activités, n'étant plus capable de pivoter. Elle sera paralysée par ma peur, mon désespoir face à la vie, mon négativisme, ma difficulté à exprimer mes émotions. Un mauvais état de C_1 s'accompagne généralement de maux qui touchent la tête, le cerveau et le système nerveux, comme par exemple migraine, amnésie, vertiges, dépression nerveuse, etc. J'ai à apprendre à écouter mon intérieur, à garder mon esprit ouvert, à amener plus de calme dans ma vie afin de diminuer mon activité cérébrale, me permettant ainsi de voir la réalité sous un nouveau jour, avec plus de confiance.

C_2 = La **deuxième vertèbre cervicale** travaille en étroite collaboration avec C_1. On la nomme **AXIS**. C'est le pivot qui permet à C_1 de se mouvoir. C_2 est reliée aux principaux organes des sens, c'est-à-dire les yeux, le nez, les oreilles, la bouche (langue). C'est pourquoi ceux-ci seront touchés quand C_2 éprouve un malaise. Si je suis rigide dans ma façon de percevoir la vie, si je refuse de laisser aller mes vieilles idées afin de faire place à du nouveau, si je m'inquiète toujours pour le lendemain, C_2 risque fort de devenir aussi rigide. Souvent, mes larmes seront sèches puisque je refoule mes émotions et que mes chagrins, mes déceptions, mes regrets restent enfouis à l'intérieur de moi. Le « lubrifiant » (mes larmes de peine ou de joie) n'étant plus présent, C_1 ne pourra pas s'articuler sur C_2 aussi facilement. Il y aura irritation, échauffement, tout comme dans ma vie quotidienne. Ceci survient particulièrement dans les cas de dépression, d'émotivité excessive (si par exemple il y a un conflit familial), de colère, de révolte et tout ceci étant souvent causé par la peur d'aller de l'avant, de changer, de prendre ses responsabilités ; du jugement des autres et de soi-même, par de la non-estime de soi qui peut même mener à un désir de s'autodétruire (suicide). Je dois apprendre à prendre contact avec mes émotions et à les assumer, à prendre ma place en exprimant ce que je vis afin que le flot d'énergie recommence à circuler dans mon corps et que C_2

puisse recommencer à fonctionner en harmonie avec C_1 et que « tout baigne dans l'huile » !

C_3 = La **troisième vertèbre cervicale** C_3 est une éternelle solitaire. À cause de sa position, elle ne peut compter sur personne ou travailler en coopération avec d'autres vertèbres. Si ma C_3 ne se porte pas bien, je peux moi aussi avoir l'impression que je dois me débrouiller tout seul. Je peux aussi me replier sur moi-même, vivre « dans ma bulle » et éviter toute forme de communication (autant orale que sexuelle) avec mon entourage. « À quoi bon perdre mon temps ? De toute façon, on ne m'écoute jamais et on ne comprend jamais mes idées et mes états d'âme ! » Survient alors la révolte, le découragement, la détresse car ma sensibilité est touchée au plus profond de moi. Même l'angoisse peut s'emparer de moi. L'usure du temps fait son travail et mes rêves et mes désirs les plus chers s'évanouissent peu à peu. Je deviens irritable, amer devant une personne ou une situation que je n'arrive pas à digérer. La solitude peut tout autant être bénéfique pour me ressourcer, faire le point, voir clair dans ma vie, ou bien elle peut devenir un moyen de fuir mes émotions, la réalité envers laquelle je vis beaucoup d'incompréhension. Le choix me revient ! Je prends note qu'un malaise à C_3 peut entraîner des maux à mon visage (autant la peau, les os que les nerfs) ainsi qu'aux oreilles et aux dents.

C_4, C_5, C_6 = Les **quatrième, cinquième et sixième vertèbres cervicales** C_4, C_5, C_6 pour leur part sont localisées au niveau de la **thyroïde** et vont être en relation étroite avec celle-ci. Cette dernière joue un rôle majeur dans le langage, la voix (cordes vocales) et toute disharmonie en ce qui a trait à la communication — autant quand c'est moi qui m'exprime que par rapport à ce que d'autres personnes me communiquent — va entraîner C_4, C_5 et C_6 à réagir. Cela peut être que je me suis offusqué par rapport à ce que j'ai entendu, entraînant indignation et colère. C_4, C_5 et C_6 vont réagir encore plus fortement si en plus je n'exprime pas mes opinions, mes frustrations. Mon taux d'agressivité risque de monter de plus en plus, ce qui fermera les canaux de communication au niveau de ces 3 **vertèbres cervicales**. **J'avale de travers** ce qui se présente à moi. J'ai tendance à ruminer certains événements pour une longue période de temps. Il apparaît souvent aussi des malaises et des douleurs qui touchent tout mon système de communication verbale : bouche, langue, cordes vocales, pharynx, etc. et toutes les parties de mon corps se situant entre le niveau de ma bouche et des mes épaules peuvent être affectées. J'ai avantage à accepter ↓♥ que chaque expérience est une opportunité de grandir et qu'il y a une leçon à tirer de toute chose. Je dois laisser couler au lieu de m'entêter et d'en vouloir à la vie. Sinon, ma tête en vient à « bouillonner » et je me sens surchargé par toutes les tâches à accomplir et dont j'ai l'impression que je

ne pourrai en venir à bout. J'ai besoin de m'exprimer, soit par la parole, l'écriture, la musique, la peinture, ou toute autre forme d'expression qui va me permettre de me « reconnecter » à ma créativité, ma beauté intérieure. Tous mes sens seront alors stimulés, activés, ce qui activera ma thyroïde et permettra à C_4, C_5 et C_6 de fonctionner normalement. Les maux éprouvés dans cette région pourront ainsi se résorber.

C_7 = La **dernière vertèbre cervicale** C_7 est influencée grandement par tout mon côté moral, mes croyances et mon côté spirituel aussi. Si je vis en harmonie avec les lois de la nature, si j'écoute les messages que mon corps m'envoie et la vie en général, C_7 va fonctionner à son meilleur. Au contraire, si je vis de la colère, si je suis fermé aux opinions et aux façons de voir des personnes que je côtoie, si je m'élève et m'objecte face à d'autres idéologies que la mienne sans garder un esprit ouvert, C_7 réagira fortement et pourra affecter mes mains, mes coudes et mes bras qui pourront s'enflammer ou avoir de la difficulté à bouger. Le fonctionnement de ma glande thyroïde sera affecté. De même, des remords de conscience par rapport à une parole dite, un acte posé ou une pensée envoyée vers une personne va aussi affecter C_7. Si je vis des émotions intenses dans ma vie, que je suis déçu, que j'ai peur d'être rejeté, que je me cache sous ma carapace pour éviter d'être « encore » blessé, C_7 pourra être affectée. J'ai à apprendre à discerner ce qui est bon pour moi et ce qui ne l'est pas. J'ai à respecter les points de vue de chaque personne, même s'ils sont différents des miens. C'est en ouvrant mes bras aux autres que je vais apprendre le plus et que je serai plus à même de faire des choix qui m'amèneront à me sentir plus libre.

Aussi, les douleurs dans cette région du **dos** viennent d'émotions négatives **refoulées** que je traîne comme un boulet indésirable, que je refuse de voir en moi. J'ai de grandes **attentes** face aux autres mais j'ai de la difficulté à exprimer mes véritables émotions, si bien que la **colère**, la **peur de ne pas être aimé** ou le manque de **support** affectif apparaissent et j'ai l'impression d'avoir à penser à tout et d'avoir à tout faire. Je résiste beaucoup en croyant être incapable de me soutenir affectivement et j'ai la conviction que si mon entourage me témoignait plus d'amour et de soutien, tout irait beaucoup mieux. On peut retrouver ce genre d'attentes très élevées chez moi qui suis une mère ou un père de famille dévoué mais frustré par la lourde charge qui repose sur mes épaules. Je me sens alors **responsable du bonheur des autres** et cela devient **lourd à porter**. Le corps envoie donc des messages importants que je dois à présent écouter pour garder un bon équilibre émotionnel. À partir de maintenant, j'apprends à m'aimer davantage, je cesse de me juger et de me critiquer constamment ! Je redécouvre tout ce que j'avais caché et refoulé : mes ambitions, mes désirs, mes buts dans la vie et j'ai à accepter ↓♥ ma **capacité** à les accomplir. Ma confusion se dissipera et je n'aurai plus à « tourner le **dos** »

ou « faire **dos** » à une situation ou une personne car j'aurai acquis la **certitude** que je peux réaliser tout ce que je désire. J'accepte ↓♥ de libérer toutes ces énergies qui m'empêchent de m'épanouir pleinement. Il n'est pas surprenant que j'aie eu de la difficulté à m'aimer puisque je n'étais plus moi-même. Devenir moi-même m'ouvre toute grandes les portes de la vie et celles de mon cœur. Je cesse de critiquer et j'apprends à m'exprimer librement au lieu de refouler. J'accepte ↓♥ que je puisse avoir besoin de l'aide des autres et j'apprends de plus en plus à demander. Je respecte ainsi davantage la personne que je suis.

DOS (maux de...) — MILIEU DU DOS (12 vertèbres dorsales)

Le **milieu du dos** représente la grande région thoracique du corps comprise entre le cœur et les vertèbres lombaires. C'est une région de **culpabilité émotionnelle et affective**. Les **12 vertèbres dorsales**[47] se rapportent principalement à cette région :

D_1 = La **première vertèbre dorsale D_1** peut réagir fortement lorsque je me pousse à bout soit dans mon travail, soit dans le sport, bref dans toutes les situations où je vais au bout de mes forces mentales, physiques ou émotionnelles. Elle n'apprécie pas non plus un « boost », que ce soit sous forme d'alcool ou de drogue, quelle qu'elle soit. Sa sensibilité sera à ce moment à fleur de peau. Je me construis alors des moyens d'autoprotection afin de me protéger de mon entourage et d'éviter d'être blessé. Cela peut se manifester notamment dans mes gestes ou dans mes paroles : par exemple, je tends à éloigner les autres par ma froideur ou par des paroles blessantes. Cela peut même se manifester par une prise de poids importante, celui-ci étant ma protection naturelle et physique, car je veux inconsciemment « prendre plus de place » et en laisser moins aux autres. Cela peut aussi camoufler une timidité présente et avec laquelle j'ai de la difficulté à transiger. Elle sera encore plus mise en évidence si je crains de perdre l'amour des gens. Je dois être vigilant et éviter de me recroqueviller sur moi-même et de ressasser du noir constamment, étant toujours figé sur les mêmes idées et frustrations. Un mauvais état de D_1 peut amener des malaises à n'importe quelle partie de mon corps située entre mes coudes et le bout de mes doigts, ainsi que des difficultés respiratoires (toux, asthme, etc.).

D_2 = La **deuxième vertèbre dorsale D_2** va réagir facilement lorsque mon émotivité est touchée. Si j'accumule et j'étouffe mes émotions, D_2 va alors me donner un message et le « mal de **dos** » va apparaître. Si j'ai

---

47. **Vertèbres dorsales :** La façon d'identifier chacune d'elles est par la lettre **D** qui désigne *dorsale*, suivie du numéro séquentiel de la vertèbre. Une autre façon aussi est d'utiliser la lettre **T** pour désigner les vertèbres *thoraciques,* ce qui revient au même.

l'impression que je n'ai pas ma place dans la vie et dans la société, que la vie est « injuste » et que je me sens victime des événements, D_2 sera touchée. Je peux être particulièrement concerné par tout ce qui touche ma famille et je vis toute situation de conflit, de disharmonie d'une façon intense. Je peux avoir accumulé de vieilles rancunes. Je peux aussi remuer constamment des expériences passées, des souvenirs, en voulant figer ma réalité dans des événements passés au lieu de regarder vers l'avenir avec confiance et en vivant intensément le moment présent. Je peux appréhender une nouvelle situation qui m'amène une peur de l'inconnu. Est-ce que je vais avoir trop de responsabilités ? Est-ce que je vais être soutenu ou vais-je devoir me débrouiller tout seul ? Comment vont réagir les gens autour de moi ? Si je doute de moi, de mes capacités, je pourrai réagir en jouant les « dur à cuire », en devenant très autoritaire ; j'aurai ainsi l'**impression** de contrôler la situation, tout en sachant fort bien que je tremble de peur, allant même jusqu'à faire de l'angoisse. Je peux aussi devenir irritable par rapport à une personne ou un événement et je réagis par des sautes d'humeur. Une D_2 en mauvaise condition va souvent être accompagnée de malaises et de douleurs au cœur et aux organes qui s'y rattachent, ainsi qu'aux poumons. J'apprends à demander et à faire confiance en ma capacité de relever de nouveaux défis. Je laisse aller mon passé et je me tourne vers l'avenir en sachant que je suis maintenant capable de prendre ma place en harmonie avec mon entourage. Je peux aussi lire la section concernant le cœur afin d'avoir d'autres pistes.

D_3 = La **troisième vertèbre dorsale D_3** est principalement en relation avec les poumons et la poitrine. Je peux aller voir sous ces deux thèmes quelles sont les causes qui peuvent les affecter et j'aurai une piste afin de savoir pourquoi D_3 m'envoie aussi des messages. De plus, tout ce que je peux percevoir par mes sens et qui ne me convient pas tout à fait va faire réagir D_3. Puisque je suis très sensible à mon entourage, je me suis bâti un système où je sais ce qui est bien, ce qui est mal, ce qui est acceptable ↓♥ ou non. Je peux être figé et rigide dans ma façon de penser et de voir les choses. J'ai tendance à juger toute personne ou situation qui n'entre pas dans ma définition de « convenable ». Je peux réagir fortement devant ce que je considère être une « injustice ». Je peux même devenir colérique, voire même violent tant je ne suis pas d'accord avec ce que je vois, je perçois ou j'entends. Je peux aussi me construire un « scénario » dans ma tête, distortionnant la réalité, souvent à cause de ma peur de voir la réalité en face et aussi parce que ma réalité environnante me déprime. J'ai alors moins le goût de vivre, je n'ai plus le sentiment d'être en sécurité. La tristesse peut m'envahir, je n'ai plus le goût de lutter. La déprime prendra graduellement place en moi et je voudrai me couper de ce monde qui ne m'apporte que peine, frustration, anxiété. Je dois apprendre à voir la vie sous un nouveau jour. Accepter ↓♥ que je puisse ne pas vivre dans

un monde parfait mais que toute situation est parfaite parce que chacune d'elle me permet d'en tirer une leçon.

D_4 = La **quatrième vertèbre dorsale D_4** se rapporte aux plaisirs, aux désirs, aux tentations souvent inassouvis. Parfois, mes attentes sont démesurées, voir même presque irréalistes et je deviens irritable, colérique parce que « mes vœux » ne sont pas exaucés. J'en veux à la vie, à mon entourage. Au fond de moi, je sens un si grand vide, souvent affectif, que j'ai des tendances dépressives et la seule façon que je connaisse de contrecarrer cet état d'être et d'amener un peu de « piquant » dans ma vie sera d'y créer un état d'excitation, soit naturellement ou artificiellement. Je peux pratiquer des sports à émotions fortes (parachutisme, alpinisme, etc.), ou je peux prendre des drogues pour m'amener dans un état d'extase et de bien-être temporaire. Je me réfugie ainsi dans un monde imaginaire, à l'abri de tous. Cependant, je ne suis pas à l'abri des émotions que j'ai refoulées et que j'ai tenté de fuir. Je peux en apparence être très libre mais en réalité, je suis emprisonné dans ma colère, mes peines, mes frustrations, et par ma peur d'être asphyxié par l'amour des autres, car je n'ai jamais su le reconnaître et l'accepter ↓♥. J'ai alors tendance à rejeter les autres. Je m'oppose, je reste distant et je nourris ce fossé par ma mauvaise humeur, mon attitude dépressive. Il est important que je reconnaisse et que j'accepte ↓♥ mes émotions pour pouvoir les intégrer et me permettre de vivre pleinement ma vie. Quand **D_4** est affectée, il peut aussi s'ensuivre une difficulté à la vésicule biliaire.

D_5 = La **cinquième vertèbre dorsale D_5** est touchée lorsque je me retrouve dans une situation où j'ai l'impression de perdre le contrôle. Je me sens alors déstabilisé. Je peux même me retrouver en état de panique. Cela produit notamment sur le plan affectif par rapport à mon conjoint, un membre de la famille, un ami proche, etc. Ce contrôle se cache parfois sous une apparence de « vouloir aider quelqu'un », « le guider », « l'aider dans ses difficultés », mais au fond de moi, j'exerce un contrôle par rapport à cette personne en étant en position de « force », même inconsciemment. Si les choses ne se passent pas comme je le désire, je peux devenir frustré, critique, impatient et même colérique, et **D_5** réagira violemment. Je veux me donner une image de « dur à cuire » qui a le « dos large » et « qui est capable d'en prendre ». Mais, au fond de moi, je sais que j'en prends trop sur mes épaules, ce qui m'amène à être insécure, angoissé, révolté contre mon entourage que je rends responsable de mon mal-être. J'ai de grandes ambitions, ce qui me fait parfois m'éloigner de mes valeurs profondes et agir en contradiction avec celles-ci. Je me jette alors dans des relations artificielles avec les gens, vivant déception après déception, car l'amour vrai, simple n'est pas suffisamment présent. Il est important que je sois à l'écoute de mon intérieur, que je reprenne contact avec mon essence, avec

mes vraies valeurs afin que le calme revienne dans ma vie et que je voie clair dans les événements, m'épanouissant et étant capable de vivre l'amour vrai. Il est à noter que le mauvais état de **D5** est souvent accompagné de divers malaises affectant mon foie et ma circulation sanguine.

D6 = La **sixième vertèbre dorsale D6** va réagir lorsque je me critique et que je me juge sévèrement. Je peux avoir été élevé dans un environnement très strict où les valeurs et les lignes de conduite devaient être suivies à la lettre. Ayant grandi dans ce climat autoritaire et non permissif, je peux maintenant avoir des « cas de conscience » où je voudrais me faire plaisir, prendre du temps pour moi mais je juge cela « pas correct » et « je ne mérite pas ça ». Je me crée des soucis inutilement car je ne cesse d'analyser chacun de mes gestes, chacune de mes paroles, chacune de mes pensées, pour être certain que je « suis correct ». La culpabilité me ronge par-dedans. L'angoisse est très présente et je m'autopunis en me coupant du monde. J'ai de la difficulté à m'accepter ↓♥ tel que je suis. Je me sens victime de la vie, impuissant devant les événements. Je juge sévèrement ceux-ci, ne voulant pas accepter ↓♥ qu'ils sont là pour me faire grandir, mais les voyant plutôt comme des punitions, des injustices. Je vis alors dans la frustration et l'incompréhension, le ressentiment, envieux et jaloux des autres. C'est pourquoi à une **D6** en mauvais état s'accompagne souvent de malaises au niveau de l'estomac. J'ai avantage à être plus souple et permissif envers moi-même et j'apprends à voir du positif dans chaque événement, sachant que chaque expérience m'amène à me connaître davantage et à devenir meilleur.

D7 = La **septième vertèbre dorsale D7** est une travailleuse forcenée. Si dans ma vie, je me pousse à l'extrême dans les choses à faire, en n'écoutant pas mon corps lorsqu'il a besoin de se reposer et de relaxer, **D7** va lancer un cri d'alarme. Je peux vouloir ainsi oublier ou fuir quelqu'un ou une situation quelconque. Je peux vouloir oublier mes soucis financiers, affectifs, etc. En m'arrêtant, le découragement et l'insatisfaction par rapport à ma vie risquent de refaire surface, chose que je ne veux pas. J'accumule beaucoup de colère et d'agressivité ; tout gronde à l'intérieur de moi parce que « la vie n'a rien de bon à m'offrir ». Je m'entête, m'obstine et je suis même « boqué » sur certaines idées qui m'obsèdent. Je dois apprendre à apprécier ce que j'ai et ce que je suis et voir toute l'abondance qui est présente dans ma vie. J'ai le droit de prendre du temps pour moi, j'ai le droit de vivre des émotions au lieu de les laisser bouillir à l'intérieur de moi. Je me donne le droit de vivre ma peine, ma déception, mes peurs, car c'est ainsi que je pourrai les accepter ↓♥ et les changer en positif. Je peux faire mon ménage intérieur au fur et à mesure et permettre à **D7** de

fonctionner normalement. C'est ainsi que les maux qui accompagnent souvent une D_7 en mauvais état et qui touchent souvent le pancréas et le duodénum pourront aussi s'en aller.

D_8 et D_9 = Les **huitième** et **neuvième vertèbres dorsales** D_8 et D_9 que je retrouve à la hauteur du diaphragme et qui sont étroitement liées se ressemblent en tout point. C'est pourquoi elles sont traitées ensemble. Elles sont affectées principalement lorsque je vis de l'insécurité en raison d'une peur que j'ai de perdre le contrôle sur une situation ou une personne. Je me sens plus sûr de moi lorsque je dirige parfaitement tous les aspects de ma vie, que j'orchestre parfaitement toute situation afin de savoir exactement à quoi m'attendre. Je me cache dans ma bulle de verre, n'ayant pas à me poser de questions ni à faire d'efforts pour changer quoi que ce soit dans ma vie. Je vis toutes mes émotions « par-dedans ». Mais si ce « présumé équilibre » est troublé, D_8 et D_9 effrayées vont réagir fortement, se recroquevillant de peur. Le désespoir peut prendre place et j'ai le mal de vivre. J'ai de la difficulté à voir la lumière au bout du tunnel. Je peux avoir dédain de la vie et je me dirige vers un gouffre que je ne peux vaincre qu'en faisant confiance en la vie et en laissant aller le contrôle que j'exerce. Car c'est en laissant aller que je gagne la maîtrise de ma vie. Je prends note qu'une D_8 endommagée peut s'accompagner de maux au diaphragme et à la rate (incluant les troubles du sang) tandis que D_9 en mauvais état sera accompagnée d'allergie ou d'un mauvais fonctionnement des glandes surrénales ou de l'urticaire.

D_{10} = Lorsque la **dixième vertèbre dorsale** D_{10} est atteinte, cela reflète souvent une insécurité profonde vis-à-vis laquelle je me sens désarmé, sans ressource. Ma confiance est à son plus bas et j'ai besoin « d'un petit remontant » afin de m'aider à me donner du courage et à oublier mes soucis. Souvent, cela peut être une plus grande consommation d'alcool ou de drogue que d'habitude qui me donnera ce « p'tit coup d'pouce ». Cependant, quand je reviens dans mon état normal, les « bibites » sont encore là et ma vie s'assombrit car je ne vois que le côté négatif des choses. Je vois tout en noir, refusant la vie, m'apitoyant sur mon sort. Je m'en fais pour des riens et je me mets en colère sans toutefois être capable de la manifester, ce qui affecte ma sensibilité qui devient à fleur de peau et qui fait que je m'emporte pour des bagatelles. Une D_{10} en mauvais état s'accompagne souvent de malaises aux reins, reconnus comme le siège de la peur. J'apprends à me faire confiance et j'apprends à voir la beauté autour de moi et celle qui se trouve en moi. J'ai le courage de demander de l'aide.

D_{11} = Les anomalies à la **onzième vertèbre dorsale** D_{11} se retrouvent généralement quand mon système nerveux a de la difficulté à fonctionner.

Ma très grande sensibilité à tous les niveaux amène D_{11} à se déformer car je déforme aussi la réalité afin de moins souffrir. Je la change à mon gré pour qu'elle soit comme je le veux. Je me « coupe » volontairement de mon entourage. Mais ceci ne peut durer qu'un certain temps et je dois tôt ou tard faire face à la réalité. À ce moment-là, une tension intérieure aura pris place, et j'aurai de la difficulté à transiger avec elle. Cela peut devenir tellement insupportable que je peux même avoir des idées suicidaires puisque je vis dans l'incompréhension et que j'ai peur de l'avenir, car je me sens **impuissant** à changer des choses dans ma vie. Je me considère « victime », blessé dans mes sentiments. Je rumine le négatif et je fais peu d'efforts pour me tirer de cette situation. Je dois apprendre à bouger et à aller de l'avant au lieu de stagner dans un état d'être comateux et me morfondre dans la passivité. Des maux à D_{11} s'accompagnent souvent de malaises aux reins ainsi que de maladies de peau (eczéma, acné, etc.). Je commence à croire aussi qu'il est possible de changer des choses dans ma vie mais que je dois être prêt à y mettre des efforts et à demander de l'aide.

D_{12} = La **douzième vertèbre dorsale** D_{12} est affectée notamment lorsque je vis dans un vase clos. J'ai tendance à critiquer, juger, sauter facilement aux conclusions, non pas parce que j'ai vérifié mais seulement parce que mes observations peuvent me donner de fausses impressions et que je les interprète à ma façon. Cela m'amène à vivre beaucoup de colère qui me « gruge par-dedans ». Mon mental est très actif. Ma sensibilité est « à fleur de peau ». Je me construis des châteaux de sable en Espagne. Je m'invente toutes sortes de scénarios. Puisque j'ai de la difficulté à transiger avec mon entourage, je vis beaucoup d'insécurité. Je peux entretenir des idées morbides, n'étant plus capable d'absorber quoi que ce soit dans ce que je vois, dans ce que je sens ou dans ce que je perçois et enviant ce que les autres ont. Une affection au niveau de D_{12} s'accompagne souvent de malaises intestinaux, de douleurs aux articulations, d'une circulation lymphatique déficiente et aussi parfois d'affections aux trompes de Fallope. J'apprends à communiquer, à aller vérifier avec les personnes concernées afin d'enlever le doute et l'insécurité qui m'habitent. Je vois ainsi plus clair dans ma vie et le calme s'installe en moi.

Aussi, les malaises au **milieu du dos** sont le signe clair d'une relation difficile avec la vie et les situations de mon existence. Cette région du **dos** correspond également au mouvement d'extériorisation de l'énergie de vivre qui passe à travers moi. Cela signifie qu'en période de maturité intérieure (lorsque je prends de l'expérience), plusieurs qualités divines telles la confiance, l'amour, le détachement (c'est-à-dire le libre arbitre, surtout sur le plan affectif) sont mises à l'épreuve. Mes **maux de dos**, y inclus le **dos courbé**, peuvent signifier plusieurs choses : de la culpabilité dans des situations où **je n'ai pas** à me sentir coupable, de **l'amertume** ou une **faible confiance en moi** reliée à une vie

que je sens très lourde à porter. Je peux avoir l'impression « qu'on est toujours sur mon **dos** ». Si j'ai un **mal de dos**, cela dénote un grand sentiment **d'impuissance** face à une situation présente difficile à traiter et où j'aurais besoin d'aide. Le désespoir peut apparaître car **je ne me sens pas assez soutenu sur le plan affectif** et je souffre aussi d'insécurité. J'ai tendance à retenir mes émotions et je vis beaucoup dans le passé. J'y reste attaché. Je me sens instable et anxieux. Le but à atteindre réside dans une expression plus active de l'énergie divine. J'ai besoin d'être clair en tout, avec moi-même et les autres, sans véhiculer les sentiments d'un passé boiteux pour faire place à un **ici et maintenant** calme et serein. J'ai besoin d'aide et d'encouragement, de me brancher avec mon être intérieur qui veille sur moi sans cesse. Mon corps me donne des signaux importants. Demander de l'aide n'est pas honteux. Au contraire, c'est un signe d'intelligence puisque cette aide me permet d'aller de l'avant. Je vois l'importance de mon identité propre et je suis prudent avec mon ego et mes peurs. J'apprends à communiquer avec mon être intérieur par la méditation ou la contemplation ; j'y trouverai maintes solutions et réponses. Être en contact avec mon être intérieur, c'est choisir de mieux vivre les situations de la vie.

DOS (maux de...) — BAS DU DOS

Souvent confondue avec les reins et communément associée au **mal de reins** cette région est située de la ceinture au coccyx. C'est une partie du système de **soutien**. Des douleurs à cette région dénotent la présence d'**insécurités matérielles** (travail, argent, biens) **et affectives**. « J'ai peur de **manquer** de... ! », « Je n'y arriverai jamais ! », « Je ne pourrai jamais réaliser cela ! » expriment bien les sentiments intérieurs vécus. Je suis tellement **préoccupé** pas tout ce qui est matériel que je ressens de la tristesse car il y a un vide et ce vide me fait mal. Je peux même baser ma valeur personnelle sur le nombre de biens matériels que je possède. Je vis une très grande dualité, car je désire avoir autant la « qualité » que la « quantité », autant par rapport à mes relations interpersonnelles que par rapport à ce que je possède. J'ai tendance à en prendre trop sur mes épaules et j'ai tendance à éparpiller mes énergies. Je tente de tout faire pour être aimé et je m'attarde à ce que les autres pensent de moi. Il peut s'agir aussi d'inquiétude face à une ou d'autres personnes. Je m'en fais pour elles et j'ai peut-être tendance à « prendre les problèmes des autres sur mon dos » et vouloir les sauver. Mon **impuissance** face à certaines situations de ma vie me rend **amer** et je refuse de me soumettre, mais j'ai peur. Ce sentiment **d'impuissance** qui peut me mener jusqu'à la **révolte** pourra me mener à un « lombago » ou « tour de reins ». Je ne me sens pas soutenu dans mes besoins de base et mes besoins affectifs. J'ai de la difficulté à faire face aux changements et à la nouveauté qui se présentent à moi car j'aime me sentir en sécurité dans ma routine et mes vieilles habitudes. Cela dénote souvent que je suis **inflexible** et **rigide** et que je voudrais être soutenu à <u>ma</u> façon. Si j'accepte ↓♥ que les autres puissent m'aider à leur manière, je vais découvrir et

prendre conscience que j'ai tout le soutien dont j'ai besoin. Je deviens ainsi plus autonome et responsable. S'il s'agit de **pincement des disques lombaires**, je mets probablement trop de pression sur moi-même à faire des choses pour me faire aimer. Puisqu'une période de repos est nécessaire, j'en profite pour regarder ce qui se passe dans ma vie et redéfinir mes priorités. Comme **je ne me sens pas soutenu**, je deviens **rigide** (raide) envers les autres. Ai-je tendance à blâmer les autres pour mes difficultés ? Ai-je pris le temps d'exprimer mes besoins ? J'accepte ↓♥ que mon seul soutien vient de moi-même. En reprenant contact avec mon être intérieur, j'établis un équilibre dans mes besoins et je rejoins toutes les forces de l'univers qui sont en moi. Ces forces me donnent confiance en moi et en la vie car je sais qu'elles m'apportent tout ce dont j'ai besoin : physique, émotif ou spirituel. Je suis soutenu en tout temps ! Les **5 vertèbres lombaires** sont concernées dans cette région :

L_1 = La **première vertèbre lombaire** L_1 est atteinte lorsque je vis un sentiment d'impuissance face à quelqu'un ou quelque chose qui ne me convient pas et que j'ai l'impression que je ne peux changer, que je dois subir. Je deviens alors inerte, sans vie. Je dépense beaucoup d'énergie sur des choses souvent mineures mais que j'amplifie tellement qu'elles prennent alors des proportions catastrophiques, ce qui peut même faire apparaître un sentiment de désespoir. Je peux vivre de l'insécurité face à des aspects de ma vie mais qui n'a pas vraiment de raison d'être. Je veux tout contrôler mais cela n'est pas humainement possible. Je peux aussi vivre des conflits intérieurs entre ce que je veux faire mais que je ne me permets pas. Cela fait monter en moi frustration, agressivité et colère. Ces sentiments durcissent mon cœur si je ne m'en libère pas et me rendent amer de la vie. Une vertèbre L_1 en mauvais état peut amener des malaises en ce qui a trait aux fonctions de digestion (intestin et côlon) ou d'élimination (constipation, dysenterie, etc.). Je prends conscience du pouvoir que j'ai de changer le cours de ma vie, et la mienne seulement ! Je refais mes priorités afin de bien canaliser mes énergies.

L_2 = L'état de la **deuxième vertèbre lombaire** L_2 dépend beaucoup de ma flexibilité face à moi-même et aux autres. La solitude et l'amertume souvent causées par une timidité prononcée sont aussi des facteurs importants qui peuvent affecter L_2. Je suis prisonnier de mes émotions : ne sachant pas comment les vivre et les exprimer, celles-ci étant parfois vives et explosives, je mets des masques pour me protéger et éviter qu'on puisse voir ce qui se passe à l'intérieur de moi. Mon malaise peut devenir tellement grand que je veux « engourdir » mon mal avec de la boisson, des drogues, le travail, etc., et L_2 criera alors au secours. J'ai tendance à broyer du noir et à vivre dans un état dépressif que j'apprécie un tout petit peu car je suis dans un rôle de victime qui ne m'oblige pas à passer à l'action

et à changer des choses dans ma vie. Tout comme L_1, un sentiment d'impuissance et aussi beaucoup de tristesse vont affecter L_2. Je suis amer face à la vie parce que je serais supposé profiter des plaisirs de la vie mais que souvent, je ne me le permets pas, à cause de mes « obligations » ou par devoir, afin de montrer le bon exemple. Je dois apprendre que je n'ai pas à être parfait. Je peux parfois me sentir incapable ou impuissant face à une situation. Je n'ai pas à m'en vouloir ou à être en colère : je ne dois qu'être vrai avec moi-même et les autres et exprimer simplement mes peines, mes joies, mes doutes, mes incompréhensions, mes frustrations afin d'être plus ouvert face aux autres et que L_2 reprenne vie aussi. Il est à noter qu'une vertèbre L_2 en mauvaise condition peut m'amener des malaises à l'abdomen, l'appendice ou aux jambes, où je pourrais voir apparaître des varices.

L_3 = La **troisième vertèbre lombaire** L_3 est principalement affectée quand je vis des situations familiales tendues ou orageuses. Je me retiens de dire ou de faire des choses pour ne pas blesser et ne pas déranger les autres. Mais en faisant cela, c'est à moi-même que je fais du mal. Je joue les rôles de « bon garçon » ou de « bonne fille » en manifestant une très grande flexibilité. Mais je deviens « bonasse », ce qui m'amène de la frustration, surtout si j'ai à mettre mes désirs de côté. Et peut-être, aussi, que je me mets de côté, notamment à cause de ma culpabilité et de ma timidité qui m'amèneront à me rejeter moi-même. L_3 réagit aussi si j'évite de communiquer mes émotions, en raison de ma grande sensibilité, ne sachant trop comment ces émotions vont être reçues. Je deviens « paralysé », impuissant même, dans mes émotions, dans mon corps, dans mes pensées, ce qui empêche ma créativité de se manifester et tout ce qui y est rattaché, notamment la communication et la sexualité qui restent « rigides » et « frigides ». Pour surmonter le découragement, je dois tendre les bras vers les autres et oser exprimer mes émotions afin que mon plein potentiel créatif se réveille et se manifeste. La mauvaise condition de L_3 peut amener des malaises aux organes génitaux, à l'utérus (chez la femme), à la vessie ou aux genoux, tels que l'arthrite, l'inflammation ou des douleurs.

L_4 = Quand la **quatrième vertèbre lombaire** L_4 se rebelle, c'est souvent parce que j'ai de la difficulté à transiger avec la réalité de tous les jours. Je peux me complaire dans un monde imaginaire et cela peut m'amener à vivre dans la passivité, étant un peu las de voir ce qui se passe autour de moi. Un certain laisser-aller s'installe. « Pourquoi s'en faire de toute façon ? » Je subis les événements plus que je ne les crée, ce qui peut me laisser un goût amer. Tout comme L_4, j'ai parfois besoin de me protéger en me fermant car je peux facilement me laisser distraire ou influencer par ce qui m'entoure, notamment par ce que les gens peuvent

dire de moi, et ma sensibilité peut être grandement touchée. Je me casse aussi la tête exagérément et mon discernement est parfois biaisé ou défaillant car mon mental est très rigide, ce qui m'empêche d'avoir une vue d'ensemble d'une situation et, par le fait même, des solutions ou des avenues possibles face à elle. Je veux alors contrôler au lieu d'écouter ma voix intérieure. Je dois apprendre à écouter cette dernière afin de reprendre la maîtrise de ma vie. Je reprends mon pouvoir de créer ma vie comme je le veux et je retrouve le goût d'accomplir de grandes choses ! Il est à noter qu'une vertèbre L_4 en mauvais état peut entraîner des douleurs dans la région de mon nerf sciatique et de la prostate chez l'homme.

L_5 = Je peux me demander ce qui se passe dans ma vie lorsque la **cinquième vertèbre lombaire L_5** est atteinte. Aurais-je une attitude de mépris ou de nonchalance envers une personne ou une situation ? Je peux vivre un peu de jalousie, de mécontentement, de frustration, mais pourtant j'ai déjà beaucoup, la vie m'a choyé et j'ai de la difficulté à le reconnaître. Ma vie est teintée de luxure (à tous les niveaux) et j'ai à apprendre à apprécier ce que j'ai, et à cultiver mes relations interpersonnelles : j'ai de la difficulté surtout sur le plan affectif, à être vrai et à me sentir bien, car au fond de moi, je vis une grande insécurité et j'ai de la difficulté à exprimer ce que je vis. Donc, j'aurai tendance à être un peu dépressif, puisque je passerai souvent d'un conjoint à un autre sans trop savoir pourquoi cela m'arrive, me sentant « correct » dans ce que je vis. J'inventerai toutes sortes de scénarios et mon attention sera toujours centrée sur les petits détails anodins, ce qui m'empêchera d'avancer et de passer à autre chose. Une certaine amertume peut assombrir ma vie et m'empêcher de jouir de celle-ci. J'apprends à savourer chaque instant qui passe et à apprécier toute l'abondance qui fait partie de ma vie. Une mauvaise condition de L_5 peut m'occasionner des maux de jambes, des genoux aux orteils.

Le **bas du dos** fait aussi partie du système du centre du **mouvement**. Si j'ai de la difficulté à transiger avec la société, tant du point de vue des directions à prendre que du soutien que j'attends d'elle, je peux vivre de la **frustration** ou du **ressentiment**. Je ne veux pas « dealer » avec certaines personnes ou certaines situations. Mes **rapports personnels** avec mon entourage **en souffrent**. Je peux aussi avoir de la difficulté à accepter ↓♥ que j'avance en âge. « Je deviens vieux » et j'ai à apprivoiser lentement la notion de **mortalité**. Finalement, le **bas du dos** est relié très étroitement aux deux centres d'énergie inférieurs, le coccyx et le deuxième centre d'énergie qui est relié plus spécifiquement à la sexualité. Si je vis des conflits intérieurs ou extérieurs face à celle-ci, si j'ai **refoulé** mon énergie sexuelle, une douleur au **bas du dos** pourra apparaître. Les **4 vertèbres sacrées** et les **5 vertèbres coccygiennes** sont en rapport avec cette région. Lorsque les **vertèbres**

sacrées sont affectées, je peux avoir l'impression que je n'ai pas de « colonne » et que j'ai besoin de quelqu'un d'autre pour me soutenir. Je suis constamment « testé » par la vie afin de voir quel est mon niveau d'intégrité et d'honnêteté. J'ai un potentiel énorme mais est-ce que je suis prêt à faire les efforts nécessaires pour accomplir mes buts ? Les vertèbres du bas sont les suivantes :

S_1, S_2, S_3 = Puisque les 3 **premières vertèbres sacrées** sont soudées ensemble, elles seront traitées ensemble. Elles forment un tout. Elles réagissent à la rigidité que je manifeste, à mon étroitesse d'esprit par rapport à certaines situations ou à certaines personnes, à mon esprit fermé qui refuse d'entendre ce que les autres ont à dire. Je veux avoir le contrôle pour me sentir fort et en sécurité et, si je le perds, je vais rager, tempêter, et je peux avoir le goût de « botter le derrière » de quelqu'un tant je suis frustré et plein d'amertume. Tous ces sentiments ont bien souvent leur source dans mes relations affectives qui ne vont pas toujours comme je le désire. La communication, tant verbale que sexuelle, est déficiente, pour ne pas dire inexistante, et je suis constamment en remise en question. J'ai l'impression d'avoir à nager contre le courant et je me sens dans un « cul-de-sac ». J'ai avantage à prendre un moment d'arrêt et à voir clair dans ma vie, à réfléchir à ce que je veux et à édifier une base solide.

S_4, S_5 = Tous les désirs ont leur source dans les **quatrième et cinquième vertèbres sacrées**. Si je suis capable de bien les gérer, si je prends le temps de me reposer et de faire des choses que j'aime, S_4 et S_5 vont bien fonctionner. Cependant, si je vis de la culpabilité, me traitant de paresseux et me confrontant à mes devoirs et à ma moralité, jugeant ma conduite « pas correcte », S_4 et S_5 risquent de réagir fortement. J'ai le droit de faire des choses pour moi et m'évader parfois, mais je dois éviter que cela devienne un moyen de fuite m'évitant de faire face à mes responsabilités. C'est à ce moment que la paresse peut devenir non bénéfique : elle me garde dans un état passif de lassitude qui m'empêche d'aller de l'avant. C'est pourquoi, dans des cas extrêmes, mes pieds seront aussi atteints. La seule façon de guérir le **sacrum** fêlé ou cassé, c'est l'immobilité physique et le temps. Le **sacrum** est relié au deuxième centre d'énergie qui se situe au niveau de la première vertèbre lombaire. Un déséquilibre de ce centre énergétique peut transparaître dans les malaises physiques suivants : du coté des organes génitaux, il peut y avoir infertilité, frigidité ou herpès ; du coté des reins : cystite, calculs ; en ce qui a trait à la digestion et de l'élimination : incontinence, diarrhée, constipation, colite, etc. Les déviations de la colonne vertébrale (scoliose) naissent habituellement à ce niveau et entraînent avec elles des maux de dos. Le deuxième chakra, ou centre d'énergie, influence mes rapports avec mon entourage et un malfonctionnement de celui-ci, qui affecte mon **sacrum**, sera le signe de mon stress, de mes angoisses, de mes peurs et de ma tendance dépressive

que je dois apprendre à gérer. Quant au **coccyx**, il est relié au premier chakra, ou centre d'énergie, siège de la survie. Il représente le fondement de ma sexualité, l'accomplissement adéquat de mes **besoins de base** (sexualité, nourriture, protection, abri, amour[48], etc.). Le **coccyx** est formé de **cinq vertèbres coccygiennes** qui sont soudées ensemble. Il représente ma dépendance face à la vie ou à quelqu'un d'autre. Il y a de fortes chances que mon corps me dise que j'ai à m'arrêter lorsque j'ai mal au **coccyx**. C'est mon insécurité qui se manifeste par rapport à mes besoins de base, de survie, notamment le fait d'avoir un toit, de la nourriture, des vêtements, etc. La nourriture ici englobe les besoins physiques mais aussi émotionnels et sexuels. Toute personne a besoin d'amour dans sa vie. Elle a aussi besoin de communication par relations sexuelles avec un ou son partenaire. Ces besoins sont souvent niés et réprimés, notamment à cause de mes principes moraux et religieux , ce qui m'amène à être insatisfait. Je peux me sentir alors impuissant dans tous les sens du terme et la colère mijote à l'intérieur de moi. Je veux fuir toute situation qui fait mal à ma sensibilité et face à laquelle je peux vivre de la culpabilité. Je dois mettre mon orgueil de côté, c'est-à-dire mes peurs. Je dois faire confiance à la vie et surtout me faire confiance dans ma capacité à m'exprimer et à me prendre en mains. Lorsque j'éprouve des difficultés reliées à cet aspect de moi-même, je vérifie intérieurement jusqu'à quel point je suis (je veux être) dépendant d'une personne qui, consciemment ou non, satisfait certains besoins dans ma vie. Je suis capable d'accomplir mes propres actions, d'être autonome. Il est possible que les personnes auxquelles je **m'attache** soient beaucoup plus dépendantes affectivement que moi et qu'elles aient besoin de ce genre de relation. J'accepte ↓♥ de voir jusqu'à quel point je fais preuve d'indépendance et de vigueur dans ma vie. Je dois laisser aller tout sentiment **d'inquiétude** face à mes besoins de base et prendre conscience **maintenant** des forces qui m'habitent et affirmer que je suis la personne la mieux placée pour assurer ma propre survie. Puisque le **coccyx** est relié au premier chakra, un déséquilibre au niveau de ce centre d'énergie peut amener des troubles physiques, les plus courants touchant le rectum ou l'anus (hémorroïdes, démangeaisons), la vessie (troubles urinaires, incontinence), la prostate. On peut retrouver également des douleurs à la base de la colonne vertébrale, une prise ou une perte de poids considérable (obésité, anorexie) et une mauvaise circulation sanguine au niveau des jambes (phlébite), des mains et des pieds. Ces malaises me donnent une indication que j'ai besoin de rééquilibrer ce centre d'énergie.

---

48. **Amour :** L'amour dont il est question ici est comme **l'amour d'une mère pour son enfant.** Lorsque mon coccyx est affecté, il se peut que je vive la peur de perdre ou de ne pas avoir au moins un amour semblable à celui qu'un enfant est en droit d'attendre de sa mère. C'est de ce genre d'amour qu'il est question ici et non pas d'une relation amoureuse entre adultes.

DOS — FRACTURE DES VERTÈBRES (voir aussi : OS — FRACTURE)

La **fracture d'une vertèbre** est généralement le résultat d'une révolte intérieure, une réaction **d'inflexibilité** mentale reliée à l'autorité. Je vois la vie avec une étroitesse d'esprit telle que **je m'attire** cette **fracture**. Mes pensées sont trop **rigides**, je refuse de me plier à certaines idées nouvelles qui m'éloignent de l'amour et qui m'apportent de la douleur. Je suis intransigeant et souvent très orgueilleux et j'aurais avantage à développer plus **d'humilité**. Le **dos** est mon soutien et mon support ; le voir blessé est inconfortable. J'accepte ↓♥ mes attitudes présentes en sachant que je peux les modifier dès maintenant. La vie est belle à vivre avec son flot de changements et il est important de respecter cela. Je reste ouvert à la vie, car je sais qu'elle est bonne pour moi. Je me laisse porter par le courant de la vie.

DOULEUR

Quelle que soit la douleur, elle est reliée à un déséquilibre d'ordre émotionnel ou mental, **à un sentiment profond de culpabilité ou de peine.** C'est une forme d'angoisse intérieure et, parce que je me sens coupable d'avoir fait quelque chose, d'avoir parlé ou même d'avoir eu des pensées « malsaines » ou « négatives », je me **punis** en manifestant inconsciemment une douleur d'intensité variable. La question à me poser : Suis-je vraiment coupable ? Et de quoi ? La douleur vécue présentement ne fait que masquer la véritable cause : la culpabilité. Mes pensées sont très puissantes et je dois rester ouvert pour bien identifier ces culpabilités. Je n'ai pas à éviter celles-ci, mais à les affronter, car ce sont des peurs que j'aurai besoin d'intégrer tôt ou tard. La **douleur** aux os indique que la situation m'affecte au plus profond de mon être, tandis qu'aux muscles, c'est davantage une **douleur** d'ordre mental. La **douleur** me « branche » instantanément et **m'oblige** à sentir ce qui se passe dans mon corps. Dans un sens, elle est positive car elle me permet de me « connecter » à moi-même en tant qu'âme et de devenir conscient. Lorsque la **douleur** est « chronique », cela signifie simplement que, depuis l'apparition de la **douleur**, je n'ai pas affronté la cause réelle de cette **douleur**. Plus je tarde à en prendre conscience, plus la **douleur** revient régulièrement jusqu'à devenir « chronique ». Il est important que j'accepte ↓♥ de vérifier l'origine de ma **douleur** et que je demeure ouvert afin de régler la « vraie » cause de ma **douleur**. L'endroit où est localisée la **douleur** me donne des indications sur la cause réelle de celle-ci.

DOUTE

Le doute est directement relié au mental. C'est un état obsessionnel qui m'empêche de me « brancher » clairement dans le physique. Le **doute** peut résulter de questionnements tels que : l'ai-je fais ou pas ? Je me pose des questions très terre à terre ou au contraire sous forme métaphysique, portant sur la valeur de la vie, de la religion, du devoir, de la

vérité, etc. Je remets constamment mes décisions en question, je me demande si j'ai fait le bon choix face aux situations de ma vie. Le **doute** peut troubler et empoisonner mon existence. Le meilleur remède est de commencer à écouter ma voix intérieure et de faire davantage confiance à la vie. En rassurant mon moi intérieur, j'accepte ↓♥ de rester libre des attaches mentales qui freinent mon évolution spirituelle. Lorsqu'il s'agit de mes relations avec les personnes de mon entourage, plutôt que de m'empoisonner l'existence avec le **doute**, **j'apprends à vérifier** mes besoins, mes impressions, mes intuitions auprès de ces personnes.

DROGUE (voir aussi : DÉPENDANCE)

Véritable fléau de l'humanité, les **drogues** constituent l'une des pires **fuites** de l'être humain pour sa survie. Extraites de plantes ou de substances fabriquées synthétiquement, les **drogues** dites « douces » (marijuana, haschich, etc.) ou « dures » (PCP, cocaïne, héroïne, etc.) sont souvent utilisées pour un ou plusieurs des motifs suivants : désespoir, honte, fuite extrême, peur de l'inconnu et des responsabilités. La **drogue** est mon refuge, je me **protège contre moi-même**. Puisque je refuse de vivre et d'être responsable, mes faiblesses intérieures risquent de m'amener vers les **drogues**. J'ai peur de faire face à la réalité et d'avoir à faire des efforts. Ma volonté s'endort et j'ai de moins en moins tendance à prendre des décisions. Je me « laisse vivre »... Plusieurs **drogues** entraînent souvent de grandes dépendances qui ne font que refléter mes « propres dépendances » intérieures : délinquance, parent(s) absent(s), introversion, névrose, compulsivité émotionnelle ou sexuelle que je tente de refouler en dopant mon mental. L'impression d'être séparé, voire même « arraché » soit d'un être cher (parent, frère, sœur, animal etc.) ou d'un endroit ou d'une situation qui m'apportait beaucoup de bonheur peut m'amener à vivre un vide intérieur que je veux fuir par la **drogue**. Ces **drogues** qui sont des stimulants me permettent de « planer », d'atteindre certains sommets et de vivre une expérience qui me donne l'illusion d'être enfin « heureux » en m'évadant. Je ne peux plus m'en passer et ma dépendance s'accentue et s'aggrave avec le temps. Le premier pas est la prise de conscience, franche et sans masque : pourquoi ai-je recours à ces substances ? Je deviens conscient qu'il y a toujours une raison. Peu importe la nature de celle-ci, j'accepte ↓♥ de découvrir la vraie raison. Je m'accepte ↓♥ tel que je suis et j'apprends à exprimer mes besoins. Cesser de consommer me demande beaucoup de courage, mais la recherche de la paix intérieure est ma motivation. Parvenir à être moi-même en toute circonstance me permet d'atteindre et de vivre la vraie paix intérieure et de me sentir à ma place dans ce grand univers.

Haschich — Marijuana : à la recherche d'un monde sans problème, fuite.
Amphétamine, cocaïne : stimule la productivité : recherche du succès, de l'amour, de la reconnaissance.

LSD, mescaline, champignons magiques, héroïne : recherche de sensations et expansion de la conscience.

Opium : amène jouissance, paresse et donne une fausse apparence de paix intérieure.

DUODÉNUM (ulcère au...) (voir : ESTOMAC [maux d'...])

DURILLONS (voir : PIEDS — DURILLONS)

DYSENTERIE (voir : INTESTINS — DIARRHÉE)

DYSTROPHIE MUSCULAIRE
(voir : MUSCLES — DYSTROPHIE MUSCULAIRE)

ECCHYMOSE (voir : PEAU — BLEUS)

ÉCLAMPSIE (voir : GROSSESSE — ÉCLAMPSIE)

ECZÉMA (voir : PEAU — ECZÉMA)

ÉGOCENTRISME

Lorsque je suis **égocentrique**, j'ai tendance à rapporter tout ce qui m'entoure à moi. Je me considère alors comme le centre du monde. À la différence de la personne égoïste, je pourrai penser aux autres et les aider en autant que cela est conforme à mon propre intérêt. Si je vis de cette façon, c'est que j'ai besoin d'équilibrer mon insécurité intérieure pour m'empêcher de vivre de la soumission. J'ai à prendre conscience qu'au-delà de moi, il y a les autres. Tout en gardant la place qui me revient dans la vie, je peux considérer le point de vue des autres.

ÉJACULATION PRÉCOCE

L'**éjaculation précoce** ou éjaculation prématurée peut être reliée à mes premières expériences sexuelles. Lorsque je me masturbe, je me sens **coupable** parce que je le ressens comme étant « mal » ou « défendu ». Je me dépêche donc d'atteindre l'**éjaculation**. Le plaisir dans le défendu a toujours eu un attrait très fort et, même de façon inconsciente, je tente de le revivre. Je peux aussi m'imposer des **pressions** et de la **nervosité** dans mon **désir de performance**. Je veux me prouver à moi et à ma/mon partenaire « ce dont je suis capable », avec des résultats contrariants et souvent inattendus. J'ai à me détendre et à réapprendre le plaisir sexuel relié à la masturbation dans un

climat libre de contraintes et de culpabilité. Seul ou avec ma/mon partenaire, je redécouvre le plaisir de la masturbation en retardant de plus en plus le moment de l'**éjaculation**. Cela devient un jeu dans lequel je trouve beaucoup de plaisir. Je peux aussi entreprendre une psychothérapie qui m'aidera à atténuer cette culpabilité que j'ai pu vivre dans mon enfance ou qui fera diminuer mon anxiété à vouloir performer en développant davantage de confiance en moi.

EMBOLIE (voir : SANG — CIRCULATION SANGUINE)

EMBONPOINT (voir : POIDS [excès de...])

ÉMOTIVITÉ

L'**émotivité**, ou plutôt l'**hyperémotivité**, fait que toutes mes émotions sont à fleur de peau. Un rien me bouleverse. Lorsque je suis dans cet état, je me sens paralysé, ma vue se brouille et je peux même en perdre l'équilibre. Je vis **insécurité, peur et anxiété** et j'ai tendance à tout dramatiser. J'ai aussi tendance à moins être dans l'action, à moins accomplir des tâches, à réaliser très peu de projets car la peur me paralyse. Je deviens émotionnellement et physiquement fragile. J'ai alors le réflexe de m'isoler du monde pour me protéger. Les symptômes physiques reliés à l'**hyperémotivité** sont : accélération du rythme cardiaque, serrement de gorge, digestion difficile (allant même jusqu'à des ulcères d'estomac), constipation, diarrhée et raideurs musculaires. Ayant peur de l'inconnu, je vais donc prendre des habitudes afin de diminuer l'angoisse liée à cet inconnu. D'où vient cette agitation ? Elle peut être le résultat d'un traumatisme affectif, de conflits répétés, d'un climat habituel de vie à base d'insécurité (affective ou matérielle), etc. J'accepte ↓♥ de reprendre contact avec mon essence propre, de considérer mon **émotivité** comme un mode de communication avec les autres. La méditation, la relaxation ou toute technique qui m'amène à me calmer peut m'aider à reprendre contact avec mon être intérieur et à rééquilibrer mes émotions. De cette façon, je redécouvre mes vrais besoins et j'apprends à me faire confiance, car je sais que tout me vient de façon parfaite pour mon évolution.

EMPHÉTAMINE (consommation de...) (voir : DROGUE)

EMPHYSÈME PULMONAIRE
(voir : POUMONS — EMPHYSÈME PULMONAIRE)

EMPOISONNEMENT (..., ... par la nourriture)

L'**empoisonnement** ou l'**intoxication** survient quand une substance

toxique s'introduit dans mon corps : un ensemble de troubles physiques s'ensuit. Lorsqu'il y a **empoisonnement**, j'ai à regarder **qui ou quoi empoisonne mon existence**. Ce n'est pas tant la nourriture qui est en cause que le reflet de mes propres pensées. D'ailleurs, toutes les personnes qui ont pris la même nourriture ne vont pas toutes souffrir d'**empoisonnement**. Je prends conscience de la situation ou de la personne qui me dérange à ce point. Je cherche vers qui ou vers quoi je suis entraîné et quelles sont les **pensées empoisonnées** que j'entretiens face à cette personne ou à cette situation. Qu'est-ce qui empoisonne mon existence ? Qu'ai-je à comprendre de cette situation ? J'accepte ↓♥ de la ramener à sa plus simple expression et je la résume en un mot : peine, frustration, jalousie, etc. Puisque tout ce que je n'accepte ↓♥ pas revient dans ma vie et ce, de plus en plus fort jusqu'à ce que je l'accepte ↓♥, j'ai intérêt à **m'ouvrir ici et maintenant** et à accepter ↓♥ avec mon cœur cette situation. Dès lors, je réalise que cette personne ou cette situation est là pour m'aider à me dépasser et à avancer.

EMPYÈME (voir : ABCÈS)

ENCÉPHALITE (voir : CERVEAU — ENCÉPHALITE)

ENCÉPHALOMYÉLITE FIBROMYALGIQUE
(voir : FATIGUE CHRONIQUE [syndrome de...])

ENDOMÉTRIOSE

L'**endométriose** est la formation de fragments de muqueuses à l'extérieur de la paroi utérine. Elle est reliée au refus inconscient de la maternité. Mes aspirations et ma vie de couple me font-elles craindre qu'un enfant change tout dans ma vie ? Je doute de mes capacités d'être une bonne mère. Il peut aussi arriver que je n'accepte ↓♥ pas le monde dans lequel je vis. Si je n'accepte ↓♥ pas ce monde, comment puis-je y amener un autre être ? Pourtant, avant même de naître, j'ai choisi de venir en ce monde. Je prends conscience de la relation entre mes craintes, mes doutes, mon incertitude et la situation que je vis et j'accepte ↓♥ d'exprimer ouvertement ce que je ressens.

ENFANT BLEU

La venue de l'**enfant bleu** est liée à une malformation de son cœur au stade embryonnaire, qui a comme conséquence de remettre en circulation le sang pauvre en oxygène (sang bleu) dans la grande circulation artérielle, sans passer par les poumons pour y recevoir plus d'oxygène (sang rouge). Si je suis un **enfant bleu**, aussi appelé **bébé bleu**, j'ai pu capter, dans le sein de ma mère, une grande peur qu'elle avait en elle de s'ouvrir à l'amour du monde extérieur. Cela pouvait provenir d'une grande blessure et d'un « repli sur soi par

rapport à l'amour » causés par un événement qui lui aurait brisé le cœur. Je ne dois pas tenir ma mère responsable de mon état. Par la loi des affinités, je suis arrivé dans cette famille parce que j'avais des défis semblables à relever par rapport à l'amour. Je ne fais que manifester plus concrètement dans le physique la prise de conscience que j'ai à faire et, ma mère et moi, nous pourrons nous aider mutuellement en cela. Je prends dès à présent conscience que l'amour est la vie elle-même et que mon pouvoir grandissant d'amour formera un bouclier d'amour qui me protégera lors de mes échanges avec le monde extérieur.

ENFANT HYPERACTIF (voir : HYPERACTIVITÉ)

ENFLURE, BOURSOUFLURE

L'**enflure** et la **boursouflure** proviennent du fait que mes reins ne fonctionnent pas bien. **Limitation** est le mot clé. Je retiens tout ce que je veux pour moi parce que je me sens **bloqué, limité**. Même mon mécanisme de pensées est « figé ». Je prends tellement en considération les sentiments des autres que je fais abstraction des miens. J'ai peur d'exprimer ce que je ressens. Je me sens **impuissant** et je vis de la **mélancolie**, de la **tristesse** et une **grande lassitude**. Je crois que je suis voué à l'échec, ce qui m'empêche d'aller de l'avant. J'ai développé un complexe d'infériorité et j'ai très peur. Je peux avoir le sentiment que la vie est très injuste, vivant un grand vide intérieur et beaucoup de mélancolie. Je ne peux agir pour moi, je démontre donc beaucoup d'autorité envers les autres et je tente de prendre des décisions à leur place. Comme je cache à tout le monde ce qui me dérange, je prends conscience de l'urgence d'exprimer mes besoins. J'accepte ↓♥ d'apprendre à communiquer mes besoins et je réalise qu'il est possible de le faire sans que l'autre personne se sente attaquée. En me permettant d'être moi, je retrouve la joie de vivre et, du même coup, un regain d'énergie. Ma compréhension envers les autres devient plus grande parce que je m'exprime et que je me comprends mieux moi-même.

ENGELURES (voir : PEAU — ENGELURES)

ENGOURDISSEMENT — TORPEUR

L'**engourdissement** se caractérise par un membre qui est insensible, lourd, qui fourmille et qui souvent ne peut pas bouger. L'**engourdissement** physique est le reflet de mon **engourdissement** mental. Je souffre, je suis blessé. J'ai tellement mal que j'ai décidé de ne plus ressentir. J'**engourdis mes sentiments**. Je me « retire » parce qu'une partie de moi a été blessée et que je ne veux plus la sentir. Donc, je me rends moins sensible. Il s'agit d'une « mort » partielle afin de m'éviter de souffrir. Ces blessures sont souvent présentes

depuis l'enfance, elles se sont aggravées au fil des ans et je les porte comme un fardeau. Je n'ai pas appris à m'aimer et je me suis fermé à l'amour au lieu de partager cet amour et ma compassion. C'est une forme de fuite. Cela peut représenter pour moi une froideur intérieure, un désir de retenir l'amour, un manque de dynamisme. La partie de mon corps affectée ainsi que le côté (gauche ou droit) me permet d'identifier à quel niveau se situe ma blessure. Mon corps me dit qu'il est temps de retrouver ma spontanéité face à la vie, que je dois réveiller en moi plus d'amour, de dynamisme et d'enthousiasme sur l'aspect de ma vie qui est concerné. J'augmenterai ainsi ma qualité de vie en ce monde, ce à quoi j'ai droit. J'accepte ↓♥, ici et maintenant, d'apprendre à m'aimer davantage et de m'ouvrir réellement à l'amour, au lieu de **retenir** cet amour et ma compassion. Je lève la barrière que j'avais installée depuis si longtemps. Plus j'apprends à m'aimer, plus je réalise qu'il y a un retour : je reçois amour et amitié. Cette sérénité que je cherchais depuis toujours à l'extérieur jaillit maintenant de moi et je la communique aux autres.

ENNUI (voir aussi : DÉPRESSION, MÉLANCOLIE)

Dès que je dis **je m'ennuie** (je me nuis), c'est que je n'utilise pas ma force et mon potentiel. Pourquoi ai-je toujours besoin de la compagnie des autres comme stimulant ? L'**ennui** est de la mélancolie qui, à long terme, peut me mener à la **dépression nerveuse si je ne réagis pas**. La mélancolie est reliée à un manque, à un vide que je ressens dans ma vie. Je prends conscience de cet état. Je dois me laisser guider par mon moi supérieur puisque toutes les ressources sont en moi. J'accepte ↓♥ d'être à l'écoute de ma voix intérieure. La méditation et des traitements énergétiques peuvent m'aider. Il m'appartient de diriger ma vie car je suis entier et autonome dans mon univers.

ENROUEMENT (voir aussi : APHONIE)

Lorsque mon timbre de voix devient sourd, rauque ou éraillé, c'est alors que j'ai la voix enrouée. L'**enrouement** signifie que je souffre d'épuisement mental et physique. Quelque chose empêche mes « roues » de tourner sans anicroche. Je vis un blocage émotionnel, une émotion vive, et je retiens mon agressivité. Comme la gorge se rapporte au centre d'énergie de la vérité, de la communication et de l'expression de soi (chakra de la gorge), je peux me sentir pris par la vérité que j'ai de la difficulté à assimiler et par mes convictions personnelles. J'ai recours à certains palliatifs ou certains stimulants tels café, alcool, cigarettes, etc. Et, quand l'effet disparaît, l'**enrouement** réapparaît. La fatigue que je ressens amplifie les inquiétudes et les soucis auxquels je ne voulais pas faire face. Je prends conscience que j'ai besoin d'un temps d'arrêt et j'accepte ↓♥ de me donner le repos et le temps nécessaires pour me régénérer. En étant reposé, les situations et les événements reprennent leur proportion réelle, je suis beaucoup plus objectif et plus lucide pour prendre les décisions qui s'imposent.

ENTÉRITE (voir : GASTRO-ENTÉRITE)

ENTORSE (voir : ARTICULATIONS — ENTORSE)

ÉNURÉSIE (voir : INCONTINENCE)

ENVIE (voir : PEAU — TACHES DE VIN)

ÉPAULE(S) (en général)

Les **épaules** représentent ma capacité de porter une charge. Mes **épaules portent mes joies, mes peines, mes responsabilités et mes insécurités**. Comme toute autre personne, je ne suis pas exempt de porter un fardeau. Si je me rends responsable du bonheur et du bien-être des autres, j'augmente alors le poids que je porte et j'ai mal aux **épaules**. J'ai l'impression d'avoir « trop à faire » et de ne jamais être capable de tout accomplir. Je peux aussi avoir l'impression qu'on m'empêche d'agir, soit à cause d'opinions différentes ou qu'on ne veut tout simplement pas m'assister et m'appuyer dans mes projets. J'ai aussi mal aux **épaules** lorsque je vis de grandes insécurités affectives (**épaule** gauche) ou matérielles (**épaule** droite) ou que je me sens écrasé par le poids de mes responsabilités, tant affectives que matérielles. J'ai tellement peur de demain que j'en oublie de vivre aujourd'hui. Les difficultés auxquelles je me heurte, la responsabilité d'avoir à créer, à faire et à performer, tout cela peut « m'écraser ». Je peux vouloir me prouver que je peux quand même faire front aux situations en ayant les **épaules** projetées vers l'arrière, ma poitrine étant plus mise en évidence, mais la réalité est que mon dos est faible et distorsionné par la peur. Si la partie affectée de mon **épaule** concerne les os (fracture, cassure), cela aura davantage rapport à mes responsabilités fondamentales. Si la partie affectée de mon **épaule** concerne les muscles, cela aura davantage rapport à mes pensées et à mes émotions. J'apprends aussi à laisser circuler l'énergie de mon cœur jusqu'aux **épaules** et ensuite dans mes bras, ce qui évitera la rigidité et la douleur, car mes **épaules** représentent l'action et aussi le mouvement, de la conception jusqu'à la matière. C'est à travers elles que mes désirs intérieurs de m'exprimer, de créer et d'exécuter passent, car ils ont pris naissance au niveau de mon cœur. L'énergie émotionnelle doit se diriger jusque dans mes bras et mes mains pour réaliser lesdits désirs. Si je me retiens de dire ou de faire des choses, si je « m'encabane[49] » au lieu de plonger dans la vie, si je porte des masques afin de camoufler mes peurs et mes appréhensions, mes **épaules** seront tendues et plus rigides. Si l'os de mon **épaule** va jusqu'à fêler ou casser, il existe dans ma

---

49. **Je « m'encabane » :** Vient du mot « cabane » et qui veut dire *s'enfermer* dans un endroit. Au sens figuré, cela signifie *se replier sur soi*.

vie un conflit qui est très profond et qui touche l'essence de ce que je suis. La tension ou tout autre malaise que j'éprouve dans la région des **épaules** me donne une indication selon qu'il s'agit de l'**épaule** droite ou gauche. Si mon **épaule droite** est affectée, il s'agit de mon côté masculin actif : je peux vivre un conflit ou une tension par rapport à mon travail, à ma façon de réagir face à l'autorité. C'est le côté « raide et contrôleur » qui prend le dessus tandis que si mon **épaule gauche** est affectée, la tension que je peux vivre a trait à l'aspect féminin de ma vie, c'est-à-dire créatif et réceptif, à mon habileté à exprimer mes sentiments. Je prends conscience de ce qui m'écrase, j'accepte ↓♥ que je suis responsable de MOI et je laisse aux autres le soin de s'occuper de leur bonheur. J'apprends à déléguer. Une **épaule gelée** signifie qu'elle devient froide et douloureuse et qu'elle est gênée dans sa complète utilisation. Est-ce que je deviens froid et indifférent par rapport à ce que je fais (juste pour le faire ?) ou est-ce que je veux vraiment le faire ? Il existe une profonde tension qui indique que je veux vraiment faire quelque chose de différent de ce que je fais présentement. J'accepte ↓♥ aussi d'apprendre à vivre l'instant présent, ce qui me permet d'alléger le poids que je porte sur mes **épaules**. Je fais confiance à l'univers qui pourvoit à mes besoins quotidiens.

ÉPAULES VOÛTÉES

Les **épaules voûtées** donnent communément lieu à des expressions telles que **Bosse de Bison** ou **Bossu**. En plus de ce qui s'applique au mal d'**épaule**, les **épaules voûtées** symbolisent que je baisse pavillon devant la vie et son fardeau. Je n'en peux plus de porter seul tout ce poids et je crois que c'est sans espoir. En plus de porter tous mes nombreux problèmes, j'ai l'impression aussi d'avoir à porter le fardeau des gens qui m'entourent. « Leur sort est entre mes mains ! » Je traîne beaucoup de culpabilité par rapport à mon passé. Si mes **épaules** sont en plus **crispées**, il y a un état constant de tension à l'intérieur de moi. Je suis ainsi constamment aux aguets, prêt à parer toute situation imprévue, prenant ainsi la responsabilité du bonheur des autres. J'accepte ↓♥ qu'il est grand temps que je prenne soin de moi et que je laisse les autres s'occuper de leur bonheur. Cette forme de **déviation** prononcée de ma colonne vertébrale peut aussi me signaler une **obligation** à l'**humilité**. Peu importe la raison antérieure de mon état, je dois apprendre à développer l'humilité car ce blocage énergétique provient de grandes colères passées qui m'affectent encore aujourd'hui et qui sont accompagnées de beaucoup d'irritation face à certaines personnes ou à certaines situations. Comme je suis responsable à 100 % de ce qui m'arrive, j'accepte ↓♥ mon choix, consciemment ou non, et j'en suis responsable. C'est sans doute le plus grand défi de ma vie. Je suis à l'écoute de ma voix intérieure, elle me guide dans ce que je dois faire pour être plus heureux. Un massage ou un traitement énergétique peut m'aider à me centrer dans le temps présent et à prendre contact avec mon moi supérieur pour reconnaître mes propres besoins.

ÉPICONDYLITE (voir : COUDES — ÉPICONDYLITE)

ÉPIDÉMIE

Une **épidémie** est la propagation d'une maladie contagieuse. Le plus souvent, elle a trait à une maladie d'origine infectieuse. Il peut être facile pour moi de penser que si je contracte la maladie en même temps que plusieurs autres personnes, ce n'est pas à cause des émotions que je vis mais plutôt parce que « **l'épidémie** n'épargne personne ». En fait, la différence entre le fait que je contracte la maladie seul ou avec d'autres, c'est tout simplement que nous sommes plusieurs à vivre des situations semblables. De la même façon, je peux vivre de l'insécurité personnelle et collective concernant la politique, l'économie, l'environnement, comme je peux vivre de la colère personnelle en même temps que d'autres personnes. La nature de la maladie m'indiquera ce dont je dois prendre conscience dans ma vie. Je redonne ainsi l'amour à la partie de moi-même qui le réclame pour retrouver plus de paix et d'harmonie dans ma vie.

ÉPILEPSIE (voir : CERVEAU — ÉPILEPSIE)

ÉPISTAXIS (voir : NEZ [saignements de...])

ÉPUISEMENT (voir : BURNOUT)

ÉQUILIBRE (perte d'...) ou ÉTOURDISSEMENTS
(voir : CERVEAU — ÉQUILIBRE [perte d'...])

ÉRUCTATION ou ROTER (voir aussi : ESTOMAC)

L'**éructation** est l'émission bruyante par la bouche de gaz provenant de l'estomac. Bien que, dans nos coutumes, ce soit considéré comme très impoli, les orientaux y voient un signe d'appréciation et de remerciement pour un bon repas. L'**éructation** est reliée à ma volonté d'aller trop vite. De cette façon, j'évite aussi d'affronter mes peurs. La tension monte dans le fait d'avoir à digérer de nouvelles idées et je sens le besoin de me libérer de cette tension. J'apprends à ralentir et à prendre le temps nécessaire pour mes repas. Je prends conscience qu'en allant trop vite, je passe à côté de tant de belles choses qui rendent la vie agréable. J'accepte ↓♥ de prendre le temps de vivre, je me sens moins essoufflé par le rythme trépidant de la vie et je ne m'en porte que mieux.

ÉRUPTION (... de boutons) (voir : PEAU — ÉRUPTION [... de boutons])

ESTOMAC (en général)

L'**estomac** reçoit la nourriture et la digère pour combler les différents besoins de mon corps en vitamines, en protéines, etc. Je nourris mon cerveau de la même manière par les situations et les événements de ma vie. Chaque **estomac** a son fonctionnement propre. Même si la forme générale est la même, la digestion peut être différente d'une personne à l'autre. Ainsi, la forme de mon **estomac** est en rapport avec ma personnalité. Mon **estomac** reflète la façon dont j'absorbe et j'intègre ma réalité et **ma capacité à digérer les nouvelles idées ou les nouvelles situations.** Il peut être comparé à un baromètre indiquant mon degré d'ouverture et ma façon de réagir dans la vie. Les problèmes d'**estomac** surviennent lorsque ma réalité quotidienne est en conflit avec mes désirs et mes besoins. Ces conflits se retrouvent habituellement au niveau de mes relations familiales, amicales ou au niveau de mes relations de travail.

ESTOMAC (maux d'...)
(voir aussi : ESTOMAC — BRÛLEMENTS D'ESTOMAC)

Je connais le travail effectué par mon **estomac** et je sais qu'il représente ma **façon de digérer, d'absorber et d'intégrer les événements et les situations de ma vie.** Les **tiraillements** dans l'**estomac** sont souvent reliés à un besoin d'amour, de « nourriture émotionnelle » et d'aliments. La nourriture représente l'affection, la sécurité, la récompense et la survie. Si je vis un vide quelconque dans ma vie, je voudrai le combler avec de la nourriture, particulièrement dans les moments de séparation, de mort, de perte ou de pénurie d'argent. La nourriture peut aussi m'aider artificiellement à me « libérer » des tensions matérielles ou financières. J'éprouve comme un **manque** indispensable à ma survie. La **fermentation,** pour sa part, provient du fait que je ne veux pas faire face à certaines émotions que je vis par rapport à des personnes ou à des situations. Je mets ces émotions de côté, mais celles-ci sont toujours présentes, s'accumulent, « fermentent », sous l'effet de mon attitude « acide ». Je ressasse sans cesse certaines situations que j'ai vécues et que « je ne digère pas ». J'ai donc tendance à « ruminer » des situations passées et à vivre les mêmes attitudes et les mêmes émotions négatives. Celles-ci me restent donc sur l'**estomac**. Il est très difficile pour mon **estomac** de digérer des émotions non vécues. Comme ma réalité est en conflit avec mes rêves et mes besoins, cela m'amène à vivre diverses émotions. Je n'exprime pas mes contrariétés, je suis irrité. La **colère** et l'**agressivité** grondent en moi, mais je les refoule. Et vlan ! Voilà l'**ulcère** et les **brûlements d'estomac**. J'ai de grandes **peurs**, ma digestion devient laborieuse parce que mon **estomac** est nerveux et fragile. Quelle est la situation de ma vie « que je ne digère pas ? » Je vis beaucoup d'inquiétude, due notamment à ma faible confiance en moi, qui rend difficile l'acceptation ↓♥ de mes émotions. Les **maux d'estomac** vont survenir lorsque je vis une contrariété dans le domaine de mes finances

personnelles ou de ma vie professionnelle. Certaines situations sont tellement répugnantes et dégoûtantes que mon **estomac** refuse de les digérer. Je réagis face à ma réalité d'une façon négative et « acide » et je souffre d'indigestions et de nausées. La digestion est très lente si l'**estomac** est tendu et rigide, évitant que des changements prennent place dans ma vie. Je prends conscience que je dois montrer plus d'ouverture dans la vie et j'accepte ↓♥ que les situations et les événements sont là pour me faire grandir. L'acceptation ↓♥ fait en sorte de les transformer en expériences et la pression ou la tension disparaît.

ESTOMAC (cancer de l'...) (voir : CANCER DE L'ESTOMAC)

ESTOMAC — BRÛLEMENTS D'ESTOMAC

Comme son nom l'indique, un **brûlement d'estomac** est le signe que quelque chose, une situation, un événement, une personne me **brûle**, m'**acidifie**, me met en **colère**. Je trouve la situation irritante, injuste et je vis de l'impuissance intérieurement. Lorsqu'une telle situation m'arrive, je peux me demander : « Qu'est-ce qui me brûle ou me met en colère ? Qu'est-ce que je n'aime pas et que je n'arrive pas à digérer[50] » ? Il est fort possible également que je m'accroche à cette colère d'une manière inconsciente car j'ai peur de m'affirmer, de me laisser aller et d'exprimer mes besoins, mes désirs et mes intentions au niveau du cœur. Je suis unique en tout et les autres sont différents de moi en tout. Je dois donc rester ouvert et attentif à mes propres besoins et accepter ↓♥ la responsabilité entière de mes actes, même si les gens sont différents de moi. Le fait de ravaler, de refouler une émotion (de la colère, du chagrin, de la rage) augmente l'acidité des gaz gastriques et, du même coup, m'empêche d'avaler n'importe quoi d'autre (car les brûlements manifestent une forme de **pression intérieure** dans la région de l'**estomac**). Je dois voir les liens entre mes vrais sentiments et les **brûlements d'estomac**. Je reste calme et j'observe ma façon d'être, mes réactions par rapport aux situations que je vis ainsi que mon attitude face aux événements quotidiens. En centrant mon attention sur ma conviction que la vie est bonne et que mes besoins sont tous comblés au moment opportun, mon estime personnelle augmente et mes prochaines colères seront moins intenses. Je prends le temps d'apprécier chaque moment de ma vie et mon **estomac** s'en porte mieux !

---

50. « **Je n'arrive pas à digérer** » : Ici, l'expression doit être prise au sens figuré. Il pourrait s'agir d'une personne de qui je dis : « *Elle, je n'arrive pas à la digérer.* » Cela veut dire que je n'estime pas cette personne, je lui en veux pour quelque chose, etc.

ESTOMAC — GASTRITE (voir aussi : INFLAMMATION)

La **gastrite** est une inflammation aiguë ou chronique de la muqueuse de l'**estomac**, ce lieu où commence le processus de digestion. S'il y a inflammation, il y a irritation et colère par rapport à quelque chose ou à quelqu'un que je ne digère pas : certaines choses ne se passent pas comme je le voudrais, ou ce peut être une ou des personnes qui n'agissent pas comme je le désire. Je peux avoir le sentiment d'avoir été trompé et d'être pris dans une situation. Je suis irrité par quelque chose absorbé par mon système de digestion et la réalité « digérée » me dérange au plus haut point. J'apprends à accepter ↓♥ les situations et les autres tels qu'ils sont, sachant que le seul pouvoir que j'ai est le pouvoir sur moi-même.

ÉTAT VÉGÉTATIF CHRONIQUE
(voir : CERVEAU — ÉTAT VÉGÉTATIF CHRONIQUE)

ÉTERNUEMENTS

L'**éternuement** est causé par l'excitation ou le chatouillement des parois intérieures des narines qui provoque une expulsion d'air brusque et simultanée par le nez et par la bouche. **Éternuer** signifie que **quelque chose ou quelqu'un me dérange**. Je regarde ce que je suis en train de faire et qui est avec moi. Qu'est-ce qui m'indispose, la situation ou la personne ? Suis-je en train de **critiquer** quelqu'un ou de me **critiquer** moi-même ? Inconsciemment, je sens le besoin de m'extirper d'une certaine situation, de m'éloigner d'une personne. Qu'est-ce que je veux rejeter dans ma vie ? De qui ou de quoi est-ce que je veux me débarrasser ? J'identifie la cause et j'accepte ↓♥ de prendre la place qui me revient et d'agir de façon à rétablir l'harmonie, soit en m'expliquant avec la personne concernée ou en rectifiant la situation.

ÉTOUFFEMENTS (voir : RESPIRATION — ÉTOUFFEMENTS)

ÉTOURDISSEMENTS (voir : CERVEAU — ÉQUILIBRE [perte d'...])

EUTHANASIE (voir aussi : MORT [la...])

L'**euthanasie** n'est pas une maladie mais un acte par lequel nous voulons épargner des souffrances jugées intolérables à une personne incurable. Ainsi, cet acte permet une mort sans souffrance. Je peux vivre un malaise moral si je suis dans la position d'avoir à décider pour l'autre personne si l'on doit abréger ses jours. Il est important que je reste branché sur ma conviction que la vie existe même après ce qui est appelé la mort, si cela fait partie de mes croyances. Si tel n'est pas le cas, je peux me demander si la personne qui est devant moi

manifeste vraiment la vie. Je prends conscience que cela fait partie d'un choix individuel. Je peux informer mes proches verbalement ou par écrit de la décision qu'ils pourraient avoir à prendre pour moi au cas où je ne serais pas conscient pour pouvoir prendre une telle décision dans l'avenir.

ÉVANOUISSEMENT ou PERTE DE CONNAISSANCE
(voir aussi : CERVEAU — SYNCOPE, COMA)

L'**évanouissement** est une **perte de conscience** temporaire de durée variable, allant d'un court instant à une demi-heure. Si j'ai une **perte de connaissance** complète, brutale et de courte durée, on parle de **syncope**. Si la perte de connaissance dure une plus grande période de temps, il s'agit d'un **coma**. Quoi qu'il en soit, une **perte de connaissance** me permet de **fuir la réalité**. Je me désiste momentanément parce que je suis si fatigué que ma résistance est à plat. Je suis incapable de faire face aux situations de ma vie. J'alterne entre des états de **peur**, d'**angoisse**, de **découragement** et d'**impuissance**. J'ai souvent peur de perdre le pouvoir et de ne pas « être à la hauteur » de certaines personnes ou de certaines situations. Lorsque je m'accroche, je bloque toutes les énergies et les forces qui sont en moi. Je prends conscience que je dois cesser de m'accrocher au passé et à mes vieilles idées. Je laisse la vie suivre son cours. J'accepte ↓♥ de faire confiance à l'univers puisque tout est là pour mon évolution.

EWING (sarcome d'...)
(voir : OS [cancer des...] — SARCOME D'EWING)

EXCÈS D'APPÉTIT (voir : APPÉTIT [excès d'...])

EXCÈS DE POIDS (voir : POIDS [excès de...])

EXCROISSANCES (voir : POLYPES)

EXHIBITIONNISME

L'**exhibitionnisme** a trait à l'exhibition des organes génitaux. L'**exhibitionnisme** est relié directement à l'éducation que j'ai reçue et à la manière dont je vis ma **sexualité**. En effet, si on m'a appris que la sexualité était bestiale, sale et avilissante, j'ai sûrement tenté de la réprimer et, si je ne l'ai pas fait, j'agis en fonction de ce que j'ai appris. Ainsi, je sens le besoin de me libérer de cette contrainte que je vis par rapport à ma sexualité. Le fait de m'adonner à l'**exhibitionnisme** est pour moi une façon de repousser mes propres limites pour me faire accepter ↓♥. Je prends conscience que l'être humain a été créé avec des besoins sexuels. J'accepte ↓♥ que la sexualité est

quelque chose de beau et de sain par lequel je peux m'épanouir. La sexualité fait aussi partie de mon évolution sur le plan physique.

EXTINCTION DE VOIX (voir : APHONIE)

FACE (voir : VISAGE)

FATIGUE (en général)

La **fatigue** me donne l'impression d'être à plat. Intérieurement, je suis vidé. Où est passée ma motivation ? Mes inquiétudes, mes peurs, mes peines et mes blessures intérieures m'amènent à lutter et à résister. Plutôt que de centrer mon énergie pour trouver le point commun à mes difficultés, je l'éparpille dans trop de directions à la fois. Je désespère même de trouver une solution. Je vis une certaine lassitude face à la vie, une **fatigue** intérieure parce que j'ai à me débattre pour continuer à avancer. La dépression est même possible. J'éprouve un sentiment d'incompétence, de manque et d'absence d'intérêt. Cela indique une perte de direction et d'intention, un besoin de renouer avec la joie intérieure et l'amour de la vie. J'ai besoin d'un temps d'arrêt, de repos pour faire le point et le plein d'énergie. Je cesse de m'accrocher au passé et j'accepte ↓♥ de vivre l'instant présent car chaque instant m'apporte l'énergie dont j'ai besoin.

FATIGUE CHRONIQUE (syndrome de...) ou
ENCÉPHALOMYÉLITE FIBROMYALGIQUE (E.M.F.)
(voir aussi : CHRONIQUE [maladie...])

Le **syndrome de la fatigue chronique ou ENCÉPHALOMYÉLITE fibromyalgique** peut survenir à la suite d'une attaque virale et peut durer plusieurs années. Il se peut aussi que cela survienne parce que mon système de défense naturelle du corps, mon système immunologique, est affaibli. Il se peut aussi que mon psychique soit atteint, en raison d'une dépression, du stress, de la démotivation, du surmenage, etc. Mentalement, je suis épuisé et cela se reflète par mon instabilité émotive. Physiquement, je souffre de maux de tête et ma force musculaire s'amenuise petit à petit. Le moindre effort m'amène une **fatigue** intense. J'ai perdu le goût de vivre. Où sont passés mes rêves et mes ambitions ? J'ai aussi très peur de la vie et des responsabilités. Je me sens incapable de répondre à ce qu'on attend de moi. En fait, la maladie me permet de me retirer, elle est mon excuse pour ne pas agir et, peut-être, un moyen de recevoir plus d'attention. Je me sens ainsi plus en sécurité dans ma maladie que dans ma « confrontation » avec la vie. Qu'est-ce que je vivais au moment de l'attaque virale ? Avais-je décidé de quitter mon foyer ? Est-ce que je venais de vivre un décès, une rupture, un rejet ? Je prends conscience que tout cela est relié à l'amour, soit **l'amour que j'ai pour moi**. J'accepte ↓♥ d'apprendre à

m'aimer davantage. **Je suis la personne la plus importante dans ma vie**. En apprenant à m'aimer, je fais les choses pour moi et je profite de chaque instant. Je fais partie de l'univers où la réciprocité est loi. Je m'aime donc j'attire l'amour des autres en retour et je les aime aussi. Je fais confiance à l'univers qui m'aide à avancer chaque jour.

FAUSSE-COUCHE (voir : ACCOUCHEMENT — AVORTEMENT)

FÉMININ (principe...) (voir aussi : MASCULIN [principe...])

.. Que je sois homme ou femme, le cerveau droit et le côté gauche du corps représentent le **principe féminin** (le yin), siège de la **créativité**, des **dons artistiques**, de la **compassion**, de la **réceptivité**, des **émotions** et de **l'intuition**, il a trait à ma nature intérieure. Il se manifeste aussi par la tendresse, la sensibilité, la douceur, l'harmonie, la beauté, la pureté. Il me relie à ma nature féminine et à celle des autres. Les principales difficultés éprouvées sont reliées à l'expression des sentiments. Est-ce que je me sens bien lorsque je réconforte quelqu'un ? Suis-je capable de dire « *je t'aime* », « *j'ai de la peine* » ? Je ne me sens pas à l'aise quand je suis celle ou celui qui reçoit, en particulier lorsqu'il s'agit d'amour. Que je le veuille ou non, le **principe féminin** fait partie de moi. L'attitude que j'ai développée face à ma **nature féminine** a un lien direct avec les relations que j'ai entretenues avec les femmes de ma vie : mère, fille, amie, épouse, etc. La façon dont je vais exprimer ma féminité (soit la facilité ou la difficulté) dépendra en grande partie du modèle parental et de mon identification à l'un ou l'autre des parents.

FÉMININS (maux...)

Les **maux féminins** m'indiquent que j'éprouve des difficultés à accepter ↓♥ d'être femme. Je ne sais même pas comment exprimer ma féminité. Agir pour répondre aux attentes de ce qu'une femme doit être me fait peur. J'ai peur de me soumettre. Pourtant, j'ai grandi dans l'entourage de femmes qui devaient être « fortes », prendre des décisions, etc. ; en fait, elles portaient la culotte[51]. Ai-je vécu dans un milieu où les femmes étaient soumises et avaient abdiqué leur propre personnalité ? Je prends conscience qu'en raison de l'éducation que j'ai reçue, j'ai développé beaucoup plus mon côté masculin ou je me suis promis d'être le contraire de la soumission et d'être moi-même en assumant mon côté masculin au détriment de ma féminité. J'accepte ↓♥ d'être femme parce qu'en tant que femme, je suis entière et j'exprime mes sentiments. Je peux être forte et savoir donner douceur, amour,

---

51. **Porter la culotte :** Se dit de la personne qui dirige ou détient l'autorité, par exemple au foyer. Ainsi, lorsque c'est la femme qui *porte les culottes* au foyer cela signifie que c'est elle qui dirige et prend les principales décisions dans le foyer.

compréhension, etc. Chaque femme a sa façon bien à elle d'exprimer sa féminité, à moi de choisir la mienne. Je réaliserai à quel point je suis heureuse d'être femme.

FERMENTATION (voir : ESTOMAC [maux d'...])

FESSES

Les **fesses** sont la partie charnue du corps sur laquelle je m'assois, je prends place, **MA PLACE** (le pouvoir). Lorsque je serre les **fesses** ou que je marche les **fesses serrées**, je me sens menacé, j'ai peur de perdre le contrôle, je retiens. Je ne désire pas être remarqué car cela pourrait m'amener à changer, à accepter ↓♥ des choses, des événements ou des situations que je ne suis pas prêt à assumer. Même les **fesses serrées**, je peux prétendre que tout va bien et continuer à sourire. Par contre, si je marche les **fesses** très relâchées avec un balancement de hanches très prononcé, je prends la place, la mienne et celle des autres. J'aime le pouvoir parce qu'en dirigeant, je m'assure le contrôle. Je n'ai pas à changer : je tente de forcer les autres à changer ! Je prends conscience que je suis accroché à mon passé, à mes idées, à mes vieilles blessures, et que je peux même vivre de la rancune ou de la colère. J'accepte ↓♥ de lâcher prise et d'aller de l'avant et de m'ouvrir aux nouvelles expériences de la vie.

FEUX SAUVAGES (voir : HERPÈS [...buccal])

FIBRILLATION VENTRICULAIRE
(voir : CŒUR — ARYTHMIE CARDIAQUE)

FIBROMATOSE (voir : MUSCLES — FRIBROMATOSE)

FIBROMES et KYSTES FÉMININS (voir aussi : KYSTE)

Plus souvent qu'autrement, les **fibromes**[52] apparaissent à l'utérus, siège de la **maternité**, de ma **féminité** et de ma **sexualité**, donc de tout ce qui concerne mon foyer, ma famille et par rapport auxquels je peux avoir vécu un choc émotionnel (blessure ou abus passés). Peut-être me suis-je sentie blessée par mon partenaire et que je n'ai pas su m'exprimer pour rétablir l'harmonie ? Est-ce que des sentiments de **culpabilité**, de **honte** ou de **confusion intérieure** refoulés depuis très longtemps m'habitent et ont formé cette masse de tissus mous ? Cette dernière peut provenir d'un choc émotionnel lié à mes premières expériences sexuelles ou à un arrêt de grossesse qui m'aurait perturbé. Je suis consciente que les tissus mous représentent les « patterns »

---

52. **Fibrome :** Tumeur bénigne formée de tissus fibreux.

mentaux inconscients. Il y a donc accumulation de ces « patterns » mentaux et d'attitudes négatives qui ont maintenant pris une forme solide. Il est temps pour moi de communiquer avec mon conjoint ou avec tout autre membre de ma famille et d'exprimer ce que je ressens. Pour ce qui est de la honte, de la culpabilité et de la confusion, j'accepte ↓♥ d'avoir agi au meilleur de ma connaissance et de mon évolution à ce moment-là. Je me pardonne et je me libère de ce fardeau. Je me sens beaucoup plus légère et chaque jour qui passe me fait comprendre que je m'accepte ↓♥ et que je suis de plus en plus heureuse en tant que femme.

FIBROSE (voir : SCLÉROSE)

FIBROSE KYSTIQUE (voir : MUSCLES — FRIBROSE KYSTIQUE)

FIÈVRE (en général) (voir aussi : CHALEUR [coup de...])

Lorsque la température de mon corps s'élève à plus de 37°C, je fais de la **fièvre**. La **fièvre** est symptomatique **d'émotions qui me brûlent**. Ces émotions se transforment en **colère** contre moi et les autres, ou contre un événement. Elle envahit mon corps tout entier. Pourquoi ai-je besoin d'aller à cet extrême ? Est-ce ma façon de compenser pour prendre du repos et recevoir plus d'amour et d'attention ? Ai-je besoin de ce temps d'arrêt pour m'ajuster à une réalité qui change très rapidement ? Il s'agit généralement d'une émotion « brûlante » qui surgit ou de la vie qui devient « trop chaude » à traiter (« dealer ») , et qui prend la forme d'une colère intense, d'une indignation, d'un désappointement, d'inquiétudes. Si je suis un enfant, la **fièvre** soudaine peut se rattacher à des conflits intérieurs, à de la rage, ou à une blessure refoulée. Moi, comme enfant, je n'ai pas la capacité de comprendre mentalement mes émotions, je les exprime donc par mon corps. Quoiqu'il en soit, je dois identifier la cause de cette **fièvre** et j'y trouve une accumulation d'irritation et de colère, qui surgit souvent quand je « rumine » les malheurs passés. Je prends conscience de mes besoins et j'accepte ↓♥ d'apprendre à communiquer pour exprimer ce que je ressens. Désormais, je n'accumule plus : je sais que le dialogue est la solution.

FIÈVRE (boutons de...) (voir aussi : HERPÈS/ [... en général] / [... buccal])

La poussée de **boutons de fièvre** est en relation directe avec mes prises de conscience. Je me pose beaucoup de questions face à moi-même et à ma vie en général. Je suis en conflit entre mon identité propre et mes relations avec les autres. La seule façon que mon corps a trouvée pour extérioriser mon conflit émotionnel et m'en libérer, ce sont ces **boutons** accompagnés **de fièvre**. Qu'est-ce qui m'empêche d'être moi ? Ma crainte du rejet ! Lorsque cela arrive, je dois trouver la raison pour laquelle je ne suis pas en harmonie

avec moi-même. Je prends conscience de mon besoin d'être moi-même en toutes circonstances. J'accepte ↓♥ aussi de m'exprimer, car mon entourage ne peut deviner ce qui me préoccupe. Puisque j'accepte ↓♥ les autres tels qu'ils sont, je m'attire donc la compréhension. En redevenant moi-même, l'harmonie reprend sa place dans ma vie.

FIÈVRE DES FOINS (voir : ALLERGIE — FIÈVRE DES FOINS)

FIÈVRE DES MARAIS (voir : MALARIA)

FISSURES ANALES (voir : ANUS — FISSURES ANALES)

FISTULE

La **fistule** est la formation d'un canal reliant directement et anormalement deux viscères (fistule interne) ou un viscère avec la peau (fistule externe). Pour qu'un tel canal se forme, il faut qu'il y ait un blocage important à ce niveau qui perdure depuis un certain temps. Inconsciemment, j'étais tellement **anxieux**, je me suis **retenu et j'ai bloqué** la voie d'évacuation normale. Qu'est-ce qui se cache derrière mon anxiété ? J'ai peur d'être rejeté ou abandonné, d'être ridiculisé ou de me tromper. J'ai des réticences à me laisser aller. Je prends conscience que, derrière toute émotion, il y a l'orgueil et plus il y a d'orgueil, plus ma peur est grande. J'ai besoin de me recentrer dans le temps présent et d'être à l'écoute de mon intuition. La vie est une école où j'apprends. Si je bloque mon apprentissage, je bloque aussi mon évolution.

FISTULES ANALES (voir : ANUS — FISTULES ANALES)

FLATULENCE (voir : GAZ)

FOIE (maux de...) (voir aussi : CALCULS BILIAIRES, JAUNISSE)

Les **maux de foie** proviennent de ma propre attitude. Mes frustrations accumulées, mes haines, ma jalousie, mon agressivité contenue sont autant de facteurs déclencheurs de **problèmes du foie**. Ces sentiments camouflent une ou des peurs qui ne peuvent pas être exprimées autrement. J'ai tendance à **critiquer** et à **juger** les autres très facilement. Je me plains constamment. Je résiste à quelqu'un ou à quelque chose. Je vis beaucoup de mécontentement. J'accepte ↓♥ difficilement les autres tels qu'ils sont. La joie de vivre est souvent inexistante car j'envie les autres, ce qui me perturbe et me rend triste. Jusqu'à quel point cependant suis-je prêt à faire des efforts, tant sur le plan matériel que dans mon cheminement spirituel ? Je n'ai pas encore compris que **ce que je reproche à l'autre n'est que le reflet de moi-même.** Il n'est que mon

144

miroir. Je me plains tout le temps et je demande aux autres de changer. Où est ma bonne volonté ? Quel est l'effort de ma part ? Je manque aussi de joie de vivre, de simplicité. Je pourrai développer un **cancer du foie** si toutes les émotions qui me sont néfastes me « grugent » depuis un bon moment. Il arrive souvent qu'il résulte d'un conflit par rapport à la famille ou à l'argent, spécialement quand j'ai peur de manquer de quelque chose. Il est temps que je prenne conscience que je dois m'accepter ↓♥ tel que je suis et apprendre à m'aimer davantage. Être capable d'amour et de compréhension envers moi ouvre la voie à ma compréhension et à l'amour des autres. Je retrouve la joie de vivre.

FOIE (abcès du...)

Comme le **foie** est relié à la critique, un **abcès du foie** m'indique une grande insatisfaction dans ma vie, qui peut provenir du fait que les événements ne se déroulent pas comme je veux, que je m'en fais trop pour certaines situations ou que la joie et l'amour qui alimentent ma vie sont insuffisants. Cela est un message que la vie me donne pour développer ma flexibilité et mon ouverture et m'amener à aller chercher l'amour et la compréhension dont j'ai besoin pour découvrir davantage cet amour qui est en moi.

FOIE (crise de...) (voir aussi : INDIGESTION)

Le **foie** métabolise les aliments, élimine les excès de protéines, de gras et de sucre et purifie le sang de ses impuretés. Il est essentiel à la vie. Il est connu comme le « siège de la **colère** et de la **critique** ». Le **foie** est aussi relié à mon comportement et représente ma facilité d'adaptation aux événements et aux circonstances de la vie. Les émotions négatives que je ressens (peine, haine, jalousie, envie, agressivité) entravent le bon fonctionnement du **foie**. Mon **foie** a la capacité d'accumuler du stress et de la tension intérieure. C'est aussi dans mon **foie** que se déposent mes pensées et mes sentiments amers et irritants qui n'ont pas été exprimés ou résolus. C'est pourquoi, lorsque je nettoie mon **foie** par des moyens physiologiques (par la phytothérapie ou autrement) ou énergétiques, je me sens alors plus calme et plus en contact avec moi-même. Les désordres du **foie** peuvent même m'amener à vivre la dépression, celle-ci étant perçue comme de la déception face à moi-même. Je peux vivre à ce moment de la tristesse, de la lassitude, un laisser-aller général. Lorsque mon **foie** est engorgé, il affecte les niveaux spirituels et intérieurs de ma conscience. Je peux y perdre ma voie et la direction que je dois prendre. Le **foie** donne la vie autant qu'il peut entretenir ma peur de cette même vie. À moi d'agir pour qu'il me donne la vie.

FOIE — CIRRHOSE (... du foie)

La **cirrhose** est une maladie inflammatoire du **foie** causée, entre autres, par la consommation abusive d'alcool. La **CIRRHOSE** se retrouve chez celui

qui se sent poussé par la vie, par des événements ou par certaines situations qui le contraignent à avancer. Comme je me sens poussé contre mon gré, je résiste et je m'accroche à mes opinions. Je vis de la rancœur et de l'agressivité. Cette maladie est le reflet de ma colère, de mon ressentiment face à la vie et à ce qui m'arrive. Je suis plein d'une agressivité intérieure latente et je me culpabilise constamment parce que j'ai la conviction d'avoir « raté » ma vie. Je passe mon temps à me blâmer et à critiquer les autres. Je m'endurcis tellement que je n'arrive plus à voir la lumière au bout du tunnel. Afin de m'aider à renouer avec la vie, j'accepte ↓♥ de vivre l'instant présent et de voir ce qui m'arrive de bien « maintenant ». J'ouvre mon cœur et je porte mon attention sur chaque geste, sur chaque action ici et maintenant et j'apprends à ne pas être mon plus sévère juge. En étant plus tolérant envers moi-même, je le serai aussi envers les autres, ce qui amènera beaucoup plus d'harmonie et de bonheur dans ma vie. Je vérifie mes intentions véritables, je reste ouvert à l'amour et je me pardonne dans ce que je suis.

FOIE (congestion au...) (voir : CONGESTION)

FOIE — HÉPATITE
(voir aussi : ALCOOLISME, INFECTION, INFLAMMATION)

L'**hépatite** est une infection du **foie** causée soit par un virus, par des bactéries, par l'alcool ou par des médicaments et elle affecte entièrement le corps. Les symptômes sont la faiblesse, la jaunisse, la perte d'appétit, les nausées, la fièvre et le malaise abdominal. Le **foie** est le « donneur de vie », nettoyant le sang de ses poisons et excès, et gardant notre état émotionnel (le sang) dans un juste équilibre. Le **foie** est l'endroit où je peux accumuler des émotions empoisonnantes et de la haine excessive. Il est le **siège de la colère**. Les mots ou les maladies finissant par « ite », comme **hépatite**, indiquent de l'irritation, de la colère. L'**hépatite** peut être reliée à mes relations personnelles ou à une situation difficile. Ce rassemblement d'émotions négatives amène faiblesse et désespoir et cause colère, culpabilité et conflits de priorités. Lorsque je me fais du « mauvais sang » pour un rien, ça m'amène à vivre beaucoup de colère, de rancune, de rage et même de la haine qui peut conduire à la violence contre soi-même, ou contre les autres. L'**hépatite virale A** trouve sa source dans une rancœur que je peux avoir face à la nourriture elle-même ou face à un problème à connotation alimentaire. Nous pouvons prendre l'exemple d'un mari refusant de payer la pension alimentaire. L'**hépatite virale B** met en évidence une rancœur vécue par rapport à quelque chose ou à quelqu'un qui m'a été imposé. C'est comme si j'ai été « injecté » dans une situation que je refusais. Par exemple, on peut m'avoir obligé à participer à un concours de danse. L'**hépatite virale C** survient à la suite d'une grande rancœur par rapport à l'inconnu. Par exemple : Qui sont mes parents ?, Où suis-je né ? Je peux éprouver beaucoup de résistance face à de nouvelles situations dans ma vie qui m'amènent à apporter des

146

changements. Je peux vouloir m'accrocher à mes préjugés et à mes idées préconçues. Je profite du temps de repos que je dois prendre pour faire le point sur ma vie. Je me libère des préjugés, des colères que j'entretenais en moi.

FOIE (pierres au...) (voir : CALCULS BILIAIRES)

FOLIE (voir aussi : PSYCHOSE)

La **folie**, aussi appelée **aliénation mentale** ou **psychose**, survient lorsque je n'en peux plus et que **je rejette le monde dans lequel je vis.** Je me sens agressé et persécuté de toute part, surtout par ma propre famille. Pour moi, la vie n'est que souffrance. Je m'enferme dans mon propre univers où je me sens très bien. Rien ne peut m'atteindre. C'est ma façon de me couper définitivement de ma famille et du monde extérieur. C'est la fuite et l'évasion. Je peux me libérer de cette **folie** en recevant de l'amour et de la compréhension. Si je crois que la « folie me gagne », je dois me prendre en mains, accepter ↓♥ que tout ce qui m'arrive a une raison d'être et que cela me permet de devenir plus responsable, plus libre, plus maître de ma vie. Je peux ainsi transiger plus facilement avec les nouvelles situations qui s'offrent à moi.

FOULURE (voir : ARTICULATIONS — ENTORSE)

FOURMILLEMENT

Le **fourmillement** est une sensation de picotement à la surface du corps qui survient habituellement de façon spontanée après une compression mécanique d'un nerf ou d'un vaisseau sanguin. L'endroit où le **fourmillement** se produit sur mon corps m'indique la contrariété ou l'irritation temporaire que je peux vivre par rapport à un aspect de ma vie. J'en prends conscience et je laisse circuler l'énergie librement.

FRACTURE (voir : OS — FRACTURE [... osseuse])

FRIGIDITÉ (voir aussi : FÉMININ(S) [maux...])

La **frigidité** consiste en un insatisfaction sexuelle chez la femme pendant les rapports sexuels. Il y a généralement un traumatisme profond ou un conflit intérieur. La peur est au centre de cet état : peur de mes pulsions sexuelles et du plaisir qui pourraient me faire paraître « indécente », peur de m'abandonner et de perdre le contrôle. J'ai peur de « perdre quelque chose » en me « soumettant » à la sexualité. En réalité, il s'agit de la peur d'affronter ce que je cache à l'intérieur de moi. Lorsque cette peur est présente, je crois souvent que je suis laide et sans valeur. J'ai honte et je me culpabilise profondément. Cela résulte souvent d'un abus sexuel vécu dans l'enfance, ou du conditionnement

parental disant que « le sexe est mauvais » ou de la croyance que « l'amour et le sexe ne vont pas ensemble ». Ces perceptions étant enfouies dans l'inconscient, je désire me retirer de toute participation, rejeter la sexualité sans savoir pourquoi d'une manière consciente. L'éducation que j'ai reçue a un très grand impact sur ma **frigidité**. La sexualité était-elle considérée avilissante et représentative des plus bas instincts de l'être humain ? Ai-je entendu parler de résignation et de soumission face aux relations sexuelles, avec comme sous-entendu qu'il n'y avait là aucun plaisir ? Ai-je été abusée sexuellement dans mon enfance ? Si oui, je rejette inconsciemment ma sexualité et j'éprouve de la difficulté à me laisser toucher sans ressentir de la peur et du dégoût. Je prends conscience qu'il n'y a rien d'indécent dans la sexualité. Au contraire, lorsqu'elle est exprimée entre partenaires consentants qui vivent une relation d'acceptation ↓♥ et d'amour profond, **elle est belle et saine**. J'accepte ↓♥ de m'ouvrir à mon partenaire, de lui exprimer mes peurs, mes craintes. J'accepte ↓♥ aussi de lui faire connaître mes besoins. Je réalise que la sexualité fait partie de ma dimension physique et qu'elle est une source d'épanouissement pour mon évolution.

FRILOSITÉ

Je suis une personne **frileuse** si je crains le **froid** ou si j'ai une grande sensibilité au **froid**. Cette **frilosité** apparaît souvent à la suite d'un événement où j'ai vécu une séparation avec une personne, un animal ou même un objet (un toutou par exemple) à qui je tenais et que je sais que je ne reverrai jamais. Je vis un grand vide, un grand **froid** car j'ai perdu l'amour, l'attention, le contact physique avec l'objet de la séparation. Surtout lorsque je suis enfant, je crois ou on m'a enseigné que quand quelqu'un part (meurt), il s'en va au ciel. Mais il fait **froid** au ciel ! Et je me mets à être **frileux** car, si je suis en contact avec le **froid,** je le suis aussi avec la personne décédée ! Ainsi, je prends conscience que j'ai besoin de plus de « chaleur » dans ma vie, ou si l'on veut, de plus d'amour ou de me réconcillier avec ce qui m'a séparé de ce qui représentait pour moi l'amour. Il est important de prendre conscience de l'événement qui a « déclenché » la **frilosité** et de vraiment accepter ↓♥ (reconnaître) le départ de la personne (objet, animal) de laquelle j'ai été séparé pour faire la paix avec moi-même et avec la situation.

FROID (coup de...)

Le **coup de froid** survient lorsque mon mental se raidit. Je me sens mis en cause et menacé. Le **coup de froid** me fournit **l'excuse pour être seul.** Je prends conscience que je me raidis face aux événements de ma vie. Quelle est la raison pour laquelle je me sens menacé ? Je vérifie ce qui a causé cette tension (personne ou événement) et je réalise que ce sont mes peurs, mes craintes et mon besoin de plaire aux autres. J'ai besoin d'être aimé et apprécié. J'accepte ↓♥ de lâcher prise et de ne pas me juger. J'agis avec plus de souplesse

face à moi ; les autres ne sont que le reflet de moi-même. Dans la vie, tout ce qui m'arrive est là pour m'apprendre à me dépasser et me faire grandir.

FRONT

Le **front** est situé au niveau du cerveau et, puisqu'il fait partie de ma tête, il représente mon individualité et la façon dont je fais face à ma vie et aux événements, rationnellement plutôt qu'émotivement. Je peux dire que la forme de mon **front** et ses caractéristiques particulières m'indiquent la façon dont **j'affronte** mes responsabilités. Mon ouverture d'esprit est révélée par la largeur de mon **front** : plus celui-ci est étroit, plus je suis rigide et plus j'ai besoin de m'ouvrir à de nouvelles idées. Toute blessure à mon **front** révèle une peur ou une culpabilité par rapport à mes propres idées et mes propres opinions qui sont différentes de celles des autres et que j'ai de la difficulté à assumer pleinement, sachant que je risque de déranger mon entourage. Mon intégrité personnelle est très importante et il est primordial que je me respecte dans ce que je suis, en restant ouvert aux opinions des autres, et en sachant que j'ai le droit d'avoir une opinion différente.

FURONCLES (voir : PEAU — FURONCLES)

FURONCLES VAGINAUX (voir : PEAU — FURONCLES VAGINAUX)

GAI[53] (voir : HOMOSEXUALITÉ)

GALE ou GRATELLE (voir : PEAU — GALE ou GRATELLE)

GANGLION (... lymphatique)
(voir aussi : ADÉNITE, ADÉNOPATHIE, CANCER DES GANGLIONS
[... du système lymphatique])

Un **ganglion** est un petit corps arrondi situé sur le trajet d'un vaisseau lymphatique ou d'un nerf. Si j'ai de la difficulté à faire face à une situation et qu'au lieu d'en parler et de demander de l'aide, je garde tout pour moi, **je garde secret** mon découragement et mon désespoir, j'ai envie de tout laisser aller, la nostalgie face à ma vie va se manifester au bout d'un certain temps par un ou des **ganglions**. Mon estime de moi a diminué et ma peur de l'avenir me fera vivre de l'angoisse. Je vis sur la défensive. Il se peut que j'aie aussi des difficultés de communication avec les autres et que cela m'affecte émotionnellement ou me cause des peurs dans mes relations avec les autres. Il est important d'aller voir sur quelle partie du corps les **ganglions** apparaissent

53. **GAI :** De l'anglais GAY

car cela me donne une piste sur la raison de cette manifestation. Par exemple, si je me fais du souci par rapport à quelque chose que je veux exprimer mais que je garde à l'intérieur, il y a des chances qu'un ou des **ganglions** apparaissent dans la région de la gorge. S'il y a des choses que je ne veux pas entendre, alors les **ganglions** près de mes oreilles peuvent gêner mon audition. J'ai avantage à communiquer mes besoins à tous les niveaux afin que mon désespoir s'en aille et qu'il fasse place à l'espoir et à la joie de vivre.

GANGRÈNE (voir : SANG — GANGRÈNE)

GASTRITE (voir : ESTOMAC — GASTRITE)

GASTRO-ENTÉRITE (voir : INTESTINS — GASTRO-ENTÉRITE)

GAUCHER

Un **gaucher**, de façon générale, est nommé ainsi parce qu'il utilise plus sa main et son bras **gauches** que sa main et son bras droits, dans des activités telles qu'écrire, jouer de la musique, faire du sport, etc. Autrefois, dans notre éducation, on accordait une grande importance au fait d'être droitier, ce qui se traduisait par le fait qu'être droitier c'était « être correct » et être **gaucher** voulait dire « n'être pas correct ». Même que l'expression « *Hé que tu peux être gauche !* » voulait dire être **maladroit**. Nous passons présentement de l'ère du Poisson à celle du Verseau, i.e.[54] que nous passons du côté rationnel à notre côté davantage intuitif et créatif. Il est reconnu qu'empêcher un enfant d'être **gaucher**, si cela est une tendance naturelle, peut l'amener à développer des tics, des maladresses, des troubles affectifs, de la difficulté à parler ou à lire, lui faire développer un sentiment de culpabilité ou d'infériorité. Si j'ai vécu des sentiments semblables parce qu'on m'obligeait à être droitier, il serait souhaitable que je rétablisse la paix envers moi-même en me donnant de la compréhension et de l'acceptation ↓♥ dans ce que j'ai vécu. Puisque le **côté gauche** représente le côté affectif, intuitif, la sensibilité, bref le côté « féminin » de mon être, si je suis **gaucher**, que je sois un homme ou une femme, mon côté créatif est très développé, j'ai une facilité particulière à apprendre la musique, le chant, bref toute forme d'art. C'est inné en moi. Le **gaucher** peut aussi avoir une personnalité plus introvertie, réservée, tandis que le droitier a tendance à être plus extraverti et à aller vers les autres. Il ne me reste qu'à accepter mon potentiel créatif et à mettre à profit ma grande sensibilité pour que le tout se manifeste pleinement. Quel que soit le cas, je m'accepte ↓♥ tel que je suis, en sachant que j'ai des forces particulières qui font de moi une personne unique.

---

54. **i.e. :** C'est-à-dire

GAZ (douleurs causées par des...) ou FLATULENCE
(voir aussi : GONFLEMENT / [en général] / [... de l'abdomen])

Quand je m'accroche ou que je veux retenir une personne ou une situation, c'est comme si je garde des choses indésirables et non bénéfiques pour moi et qui se manifestent sous forme de **gaz. J'ai peur et je m'agrippe** car je suis anxieux et j'ai l'impression que je vais perdre quelque chose ou quelqu'un d'important, tant sur les plans affectif, intellectuel, matériel que spirituel. Je peux aussi m'efforcer à « avaler » (au sens figuré) une situation, une personne ou une émotion qui va à l'encontre de mes principes et de ma conscience. Conséquence de cela : je gonfle. J'apprends à faire confiance et à laisser aller en sachant que j'ai toujours ce dont j'ai besoin.

GÉLINEAU (syndrome de...) (voir : NARCOLEPSIE)

GENCIVES (maux de...)

Les **gencives** servent de support aux dents, à la solidité de ces dernières et leur état dépend grandement de l'état des **gencives**. Une douleur aux **gencives** peut être reliée soit à une décision que j'aurais dû prendre il y a déjà très longtemps et que je remets à plus tard, ayant peur des conséquences que cette décision peut avoir sur ma vie ; soit d'une décision que j'ai déjà prise mais que je n'exécute pas. Je suis dans un état passif de peur, d'insécurité, d'incertitude face à mon avenir. Si, de plus, mes **gencives** saignent, j'ai une perte de joie par rapport à ces décisions face auxquelles je me sens déchiré, tourmenté. Des **gencives** sensibles manifestent ma grande sensibilité émotionnelle et ma vulnérabilité, car j'ai besoin de beaucoup d'amour, que j'ai l'impression de ne pas recevoir ou que j'ai peur de perdre. J'ai besoin de m'affirmer et d'avoir davantage confiance en moi puisque les **gencives** supportent les dents et que ces dernières ont rapport aux décisions. J'apprends à me faire confiance dans les décisions que je prends et je fais aussi confiance à la vie qui m'apporte tout ce dont j'ai besoin. Je deviens ainsi davantage moi-même et j'apprends à m'affirmer librement.

GENCIVES — GINGIVITE AIGUË

Une infection aux **gencives** indique que je vis de la peur ; cela peut être envers moi-même par rapport à une décision que j'ai prise et que je regrette ou une décision prise que je remets en question ; ou cela peut être par rapport à mon indécision (à prendre une décision). Cette peur peut aussi viser une autre personne (par exemple, mon patron ou mon conjoint) dont les décisions peuvent me concerner directement et face auxquelles je n'ai aucun contrôle. Je vis frustration et mécontentement, cela pouvant mener à des confrontations qui ne sont peut-être pas nécessaires. J'apprends à canaliser cette peur, à l'exprimer afin d'éviter que mes **gencives** s'enflamment. La **gingivite**

implique habituellement un saignement à la **gencive** qui m'indique une tristesse ou une perte de joie face au fait de ne pas être capable de m'exprimer, soit qu'on ne me le permet pas ou que moi-même je m'empêche de dire certaines choses : je peux avoir l'impression que ce que je dis n'a pas d'importance et qu'on ne m'écoutera pas. Comme les **gencives** sont les fondations sur lesquelles mes dents reposent, je peux vivre aussi de la colère, de la tristesse, ayant l'impression que mes fondations s'effondrent et me laissent un sentiment d'impuissance face aux événements de la vie ou face à autrui. Je peux prendre un moment de silence avec moi-même pour refaire mes forces. Je prends conscience que chaque événement de ma vie est là pour me faire grandir et que tout changement important est nécessaire pour que je puisse atteindre les buts que je me suis fixés.

GENCIVES (saignements des...) (voir aussi : SANG — SAIGNEMENTS)

Les **gencives** qui saignent démontrent une insécurité, un doute face à une décision à prendre dans ma vie. Ai-je raison de douter, de regretter ? Je prends la responsabilité et j'accepte ↓♥ les changements qui surviennent dans ma vie en toute sérénité. Je me fais confiance car je sais que les choix que je fais sont là pour me faire grandir davantage, pour me permettre de poursuivre mon évolution.

GÉNITAUX (organes...) (en général)

Les **organes génitaux** différencient les hommes et les femmes. Ils sont reliés au **principe masculin**[55] et au **principe féminin**[56] en chacun de nous. Ils sont aussi reliés au siège de l'énergie sexuelle, des gonades et du chakra de base[57]. Si je vis des difficultés en ce qui a trait à ma sexualité, c'est habituellement mes **organes génitaux** qui seront touchés.

GÉNITAUX (maux des organes...)
(voir aussi : FRIGIDITÉ, IMPUISSANCE, VÉNÉRIENNES [maladies...])

Les difficultés que j'éprouve avec mes **organes génitaux** me manifestent soit une **peur**, une **culpabilité**, de la honte, de la méfiance, des regrets, de la **colère** par rapport à ma sexualité, ce qui risque de se traduire par des **maladies vénériennes,** de la **frigidité, de l'impuissance**, etc. Cette région est reliée à mes gonades (les testicules chez l'homme, les ovaires chez la femme) et l'énergie sexuelle reliée à la sexualité est très puissante puisqu'elle a pour but premier de perpétuer l'espèce. Cependant, il se peut que j'utilise cette énergie à mauvais escient. La notion de plaisir reliée à la sexualité me met en contact avec un de mes besoins fondamentaux, **le plaisir**, et me connecte à

---

55. **Principe masculin :** (voir : MASCULIN [principe...])
56. **Principe féminin :** (voir : FÉMININ [principe...])
57. **Chakra de base :** Relié au centre d'énergie au niveau du coccyx.

mon enfant intérieur blessé. Ainsi, ma sexualité peut m'amener à mettre en évidence ces peurs, ces blessures, ces rejets qui font partie de moi. Je peux ne pas m'accepter ↓♥ dans le corps (sexe) que je suis, je peux vivre un conflit intérieur entre mes désirs physiques et ceux d'ordre religieux ou spirituel ; si j'ai peur de dire non et que j'ai des relations sexuelles pour éviter d'être rejeté, de peur de perdre l'amour d'une personne, juste dans un but égoïste, etc., toutes ces situations peuvent m'amener à avoir des difficultés à ce niveau. Il existe une confusion ou un conflit intérieur, une difficulté dans la communication et le partage. Je ne me sens pas toujours respecté, considéré et j'ai de la difficulté à faire confiance aux gens. De plus, si mes parents désiraient une fille et que je suis un garçon ou vice versa, ou que moi-même, j'aurais voulu être de l'autre sexe, ceci peut m'amener à vivre des **problèmes génitaux** parce que je rejette une partie de ma sexualité et il se peut que je me sente coupable d'être qui je suis. Je dois enlever toute culpabilité afin que ma sexualité devienne l'expression de mes qualités aimantes et de l'attention que je porte aux autres. Il est important que l'amour soit présent dans mes expériences sexuelles et aussi à chaque fois que je me regarde dans un miroir, afin de m'accepter ↓♥ de plus en plus tel que je suis.

GENOUX (en général) (voir aussi : JAMBES)

Les **genoux** sont les articulations sur lesquelles je m'agenouille, je m'abandonne à la hiérarchie normale ou à ce qui est au-dessus de moi et aussi au mouvement et à la direction qui prennent place. Les **genoux** manifestent donc mon degré de flexibilité et servent à amortir les chocs quand la pression est trop forte. Ils seront affectés si je me dévalorise par rapport à mon physique ou mes performances sportives. Si j'ai de la difficulté à plier les **genoux**, je démontre par là une certaine rigidité. Cela peut venir de mon ego qui est très fort et qui est orgueilleux. Un **genou** qui plie facilement est un signe d'humilité et de flexibilité. Les **genoux** sont nécessaires pour maintenir ma position sociale et mon statut.

GENOUX (maux de...)

Si j'ai des **problèmes aux genoux**, je dois m'interroger à savoir si je suis entêté, rigide, orgueilleux. Si mes **genoux ne répondent plus**, est-ce qu'il se peut que je vive un conflit avec l'autorité (soit mon patron, mes parents, etc.) ? Ou ai-je peur de prendre une certaine action pour aller de l'avant ? Ai-je l'impression que je dois « plier » dans une certaine situation ou que je doive me « plier » devant quelqu'un ou quelque chose ? Si j'ai des **fluides** au niveau des **genoux**, est-ce que je me retiens émotionnellement contre le flot naturel des événements (résistance au mouvement) ? Si mes **genoux** sont **endommagés**, il peut s'agir d'arrogance, d'entêtement ou d'une résistance qui rend tout progrès ou avancement rigide et douloureux. Je peux aussi me dévaloriser, me diminuer face à mon physique ou mes performances sportives

et il y a alors de fortes chances que je me blesse aux **genoux**. L'**inflammation** ou la **douleur** peut indiquer une rigidité face à l'autorité ou par rapport au système de lois en vigueur. Je peux avoir souvent l'impression que je dois obéir (ex. : devant un parent, professeur, patron, même un conjoint, etc.) et « ça ne me tente pas du tout » ! Je peux vivre un conflit mental, une obstination égoïste à ne pas me laisser aller ou à me donner. Les dommages osseux ou des tissus mous sont reliés à un profond conflit intérieur et impliquent l'abandon, à un niveau plus profond, l'abandon de mon ego et de mon orgueil. C'est pourquoi, si je veux éliminer les malaises qui affectent mes **genoux**, je dois accepter ↓♥ de m'ouvrir au monde qui m'entoure et accepter ↓♥ que je puisse avoir à changer ma manière d'être sur certains aspects. Dans le cas de l'**hygroma** qui affecte plus particulièrement les religieuses, je dois me demander quel conflit est-ce que je vis par rapport à ma spiritualité et les implications qui en découlent dans ma vie. La douleur que je vis chaque fois que je me mets à genoux (pour prier par exemple) me rappelle mon conflit intérieur et le besoin de décider pour moi-même ce que je veux dans ma vie et de faire les changements appropriés. J'accepte de m'agenouiller devant quelqu'un ou devant une situation, ou peut-être tout simplement devant la vie en général, afin que je puisse recevoir de l'aide et que je m'ouvre à une nouvelle réalité que je ne pouvais voir avant puisque j'étais emprisonné dans mon propre univers. Et j'ai tout le potentiel nécessaire pour accepter ↓♥ de nouvelles responsabilités. Si je vis de la frustration et de la culpabilité parce que je me rends compte que je veux toujours avoir raison et que mon désir d'une puissance sociale supérieure est insatiable, je m'arrête et je me questionne sur mes vraies valeurs afin de revenir à l'essentiel et afin de me permettre de revenir dans mon cœur au lieu de laisser mon côté rationnel tout décider.

GERÇURE (voir : PEAU — GERÇURE)

GINGIVITE (voir : GENCIVES — GINGIVITE AIGUË)

GLANDES

Les **glandes** sont des organes sécréteurs dont le produit est excrété à l'extérieur par un canal. Par exemple, les **glandes** endocrines (thyroïde, surrénales, etc.) sécrètent leur produit dans le sang. Comme chacune de celles-ci est reliée à un centre d'énergie (chakra), un mauvais fonctionnement de mes **glandes** endocrines manifeste un déséquilibre ou une disharmonie de mes centres d'énergie. Les **glandes**, quelles qu'elles soient, injectent des produits dans mon corps qui s'apparentent à des carburants dont celui-ci a besoin pour fonctionner, pour mettre en action d'autres organes.

GLANDES (maux de...)

Un mauvais fonctionnement d'une ou des **glandes** m'indique que j'ai de la difficulté à trouver une motivation, un « carburant » pour démarrer un nouveau projet, ou à passer à l'action face à une situation (j'ai tendance à remettre à plus tard). Cela peut se situer aussi sur le plan rationnel, où je vis de la confusion et que j'ai de la difficulté à voir clair par rapport aux choses à faire. Cela dénote une certaine insécurité intérieure. J'apprends à me faire confiance car je possède toutes les qualités nécessaires pour aller de l'avant et passer à l'action.

GLANDES LACRIMALES (voir : PLEURER)

GLANDE PITUITAIRE ou HYPOPHYSE

La **glande pituitaire** est une glande endocrine logée sous le cerveau, au-dessous de **l'hypothalamus** et qui, sécrétant les stimulines qui agissent sur les autres **glandes endocrines,** joue un rôle majeur dans la régulation des sécrétions hormonales. Elle agit donc comme **glande maîtresse** par rapport aux autres glandes du corps. Elle joue le rôle de chef d'orchestre. Son bon fonctionnement aide à l'équilibre de mes côtés rationnel et intuitif. Si un déséquilibre se manifeste, soit que mon côté rationnel « surchauffe » et que je ne laisse pas de place à mes côtés intuitif, créatif et émotionnel, soit que mon côté intuitif, mes dons psychiques « surchauffent » à leur tour, car je veux aller trop vite, en prenant des cours, en lisant toutes sortes de livres, en essayant toutes sortes de techniques, etc., et je crée un déséquilibre car mon corps physique ne peut supporter tous les changements intérieurs qui prennent place. Puisque la **glande pituitaire** contrôle le bon fonctionnement de mon organisme, je m'assure que mon corps et mon esprit sont en équilibre en évitant les excès et je m'assure la maîtrise de mes pensées et de mes émotions. Si mon **hypophyse** est atteinte d'une **tumeur,** je peux vivre un sentiment profond d'**impuissance,** ayant l'impression de ne pas être capable d'atteindre les objectifs que je m'étais fixés. Au sens figuré, c'est comme si je m'allonge le bras le plus possible pour atteindre la pomme qui est dans l'arbre mais que je n'y arrive pas. L'obstacle peut être physique ou émotionnel. J'ai l'impression d'être « trop petit » (au sens propre et figuré) pour atteindre l'objectif et je peux avoir peur des moyens à utiliser pour parvenir à mes fins. Comment puis-je me hisser au sommet ? Je prends conscience que les objectifs que je me suis fixés sont peut-être trop élevés. J'apprends à être très compréhensif et patient envers moi-même, sachant que je fais toujours mon possible et que je veux ce qu'il y a de mieux pour moi et pour les autres. En étant vrai, je serai toujours fier de moi, quelles que soient mes réalisations.

GLANDES SALIVAIRES (voir aussi : OREILLONS, SALIVE)

Un mauvais fonctionnement de mes **glandes salivaires**, lesquelles produisent très peu ou trop de salive, m'indique que je vis une insécurité face au fait de trouver la nourriture nécessaire à ma survie. C'est peut-être que je n'ai pas l'argent pour m'acheter des aliments ou que j'en ai, mais que je ne sais pas comment l'employer. Donc, de la nourriture est disponible mais je ne peux pas l'acheter, je n'y ai pas accès. J'en aurai « l'eau à la bouche » et je vivrai un sentiment de manque. J'accepte ↓♥ cette situation en prenant conscience que moi aussi j'ai le droit de bien me nourrir et que la vie me procure tout ce dont j'ai besoin.

GLANDES SUBLINGUALES (voir : GLANDES SALIVAIRES)

GLANDES SURRÉNALES (voir : SURRÉNALES [maux de capsules])

GLAUCOME (voir : YEUX — GLAUCOME)

GLOBE OCULAIRE (voir : YEUX [en général])

GLOBULES SANGUINS (voir : SANG)

GOITRE (voir : THYROÏDE — GOITRE)

GONFLEMENT (en général)

Le **gonflement** apparaît généralement quand je vis une résistance émotionnelle et que je refoule mes émotions. J'accumule ces émotions parce que je vis de l'impuissance ou que je ne sais pas comment les exprimer pour éviter de blesser quelqu'un ou tout simplement de me faire blesser moi-même. Le **gonflement** peut être aussi un moyen de protection et je peux me demander : Pourquoi est-ce que je sens le besoin de me protéger ? et « face à qui ou à quoi » ? J'apprends à exprimer ce que je vis afin de me libérer et ainsi de faire disparaître ces **gonflements**.

GONFLEMENT (... de l'abdomen)

Le **gonflement de l'abdomen** m'amène à prendre conscience que je vis de la frustration par rapport à mon conjoint, à mes enfants ou à ma famille. Je me sens probablement limité sur le plan affectif ou dans l'expression de mes sentiments envers des personnes de mon entourage. Si je prends le temps, je m'aperçois qu'en changeant ma façon de voir les choses et en ayant une

attitude plus positive, je prends conscience de toute l'abondance qui est dans ma vie, tant sur les plans affectif, intellectuel, émotif, matériel, etc.

GORGE (en général)

La **gorge** contient les cordes vocales (le larynx) et le pharynx. Elle me permet d'exprimer qui je suis et me permet aussi d'échanger avec les personnes qui m'entourent. La **gorge** est reliée au centre d'énergie laryngé, aussi appelé chakra de la gorge (cinquième chakra), centre de la créativité, de la vérité et de l'affirmation. Il travaille aussi en étroite collaboration avec le centre d'énergie sacré ou deuxième chakra, le centre de l'énergie sexuelle, la sexualité étant une façon de communiquer avec une autre personne. Ce centre d'énergie est important pour l'affirmation de soi. Aussi, il est dit : « La pensée crée, le verbe manifeste. » Ainsi, par la parole, j'amène mes pensées à se matérialiser dans le monde physique. Alors, même si des pensées négatives peuvent avoir des répercussions sur ma santé, des paroles négatives pourront en avoir davantage. Ceci est vrai pour le côté positif aussi. J'ai donc avantage à parler de façon positive, respectant ainsi mon temple de chair qui abrite ma partie divine. Plus j'exprimerai la vérité par cette voie de communication, plus je pourrai échanger harmonieusement avec mon environnement.

GORGE (maux de...) (voir aussi : AMYGDALES, MUGUET)

C'est avec ma **gorge** que j'avale la réalité, là où je prends la vie par la respiration, l'eau et la nourriture. C'est aussi là que je libère mes sentiments, du cœur jusqu'à la voix. Elle est le pont à double sens entre la tête et le corps, l'esprit et le physique. Si ma **gorge** me **fait mal**, je peux me culpabiliser soit d'avoir dit certaines paroles, ou de penser que j'aurais dû exprimer quelque chose. C'est comme si je m'autopunis par la douleur. Il est peut-être temps que je dise ce que je vis afin de m'en libérer. Ma **gorge** peut aussi s'**enflammer** si je refoule de la rage et que cette émotion **me monte à la gorge**. Si je ne dis pas vraiment ce que je veux dire ou qu'il existe un conflit dans mon expression de soi, alors ma **gorge** sent ce refoulement. La **gorge** étant l'expression de l'affirmation de soi, si j'ai de la difficulté à m'affirmer, je peux vouloir compenser cela en devenant autoritaire envers moi-même ou envers les autres, ce qui limite mon énergie sur ce plan-là. L'**infection à la gorge** par la bactérie streptocoque est l'une des formes d'infection les plus fréquentes. Cela implique irritation et retenue d'énergie. La **gorge** représentant aussi la conception, l'acceptation ↓♥ de la vie, si j'ai des difficultés au niveau de la **gorge**, je peux vivre un profond conflit dans l'acceptation ↓♥ de mon existence. En ayant de la difficulté à avaler, je peux me demander quelle personne ou quelle situation ai-je de la difficulté à avaler, ou quelle réalité je me sens obligé d'avaler même si cela ne me convient pas (cela peut être par exemple quelque chose qui vient à l'encontre de mes principes). Je peux alors tenter de me couper de ma réalité physique, voulant peut-être fuir l'obligation

d'affirmer qui je suis, mes besoins, et par le fait même, celle d'apporter des changements dans ma vie. Le chakra de la **gorge** et le chakra sexuel sont reliés plus directement. Les deux ont rapport à la créativité : le chakra de la **gorge** concerne la créativité de mes pensées tandis que le chakra sexuel concerne la créativité dans la matière. Aussi, ces deux centres d'énergie ont rapport à la communication : par ma voix, je communique mes pensées et par ma sexualité, je communique physiquement mes sentiments. Ainsi, si j'ai des problèmes à la **gorge**, il est bon que je me pose des questions sur ce que j'ai à exprimer sur moi-même et je dois aller investiguer si je vis de la frustration quant à ma sexualité. Je dois apprendre que le bonheur et la liberté viennent de **ma capacité à m'exprimer dans la Vérité,** m'approchant ainsi de plus en plus de mon essence divine.

GORGE (chat dans la...)

Le **chat dans la gorge** manifeste bien malgré moi quelque chose que je désire exprimer mais que je garde à l'intérieur de moi. Ai-je peur qu'on rie de moi, qu'on me critique, qu'on me rejette, d'être incompris ? Cette peur a certainement rapport à « ma sensibilité » consciemment ou inconsciemment. J'ai à me faire confiance et à dire les choses telles qu'elles sont, en demeurant vrai avec moi-même ; j'acquerrai ainsi le respect des autres et de moi-même.

GORGE — LARYNGITE
(voir aussi : ANNEXE III, ENROUEMENT, INFLAMMATION)

La **laryngite** est une inflammation du larynx, accompagnée de toux et d'enrouement. Cette infection est causée par la difficulté à m'exprimer par crainte du ridicule, très souvent face à l'autorité. Cela peut être lié au fait de vivre du rejet de la part des autres, et si je m'affirme, d'être incompris d'eux. **Je refoule de la révolte, je me sens étouffé**. Lorsque je me tais au lieu de m'exprimer par honte, par crainte ou par culpabilité, ces sentiments que je cache par le silence causent un blocage d'énergie qui se traduit par une **laryngite.** Une grande résistance peut alors se manifester lorsque les émotions tentent plus tard de s'exprimer. Le larynx est enflammé et il y existe un haut niveau d'énergie émotionnelle reliée à la voix et à l'expression de soi. Ma créativité tente de trouver sa propre affirmation ; elle veut être libre de parler et « vocaliser » habilement ses émotions. Je dois apprendre à dire les choses, à exprimer mes sentiments, ce qui permettra à cette énergie de circuler librement. Si, dans ma personnalité présente, j'ai de la difficulté à m'exprimer en disant les choses, je peux alors m'exprimer en les écrivant. Comme le larynx est relié au centre d'énergie de la **gorge** qui est la communication, je peux communiquer mes sentiments en les écrivant, même si je garde ces écrits pour moi. Cela permettra une meilleure communication avec moi-même.

GORGE — LARYNX
(voir aussi : APHONIE, CANCER DU LARYNX, ENROUEMENT)

Le **larynx** est la partie des voies aériennes supérieures située entre la trachée et le pharynx. Une affection au niveau du **larynx** survient généralement à la suite d'un événement où j'ai eu « le souffle coupé ». J'ai eu tellement peur « qu'aucun son ne pouvait sortir de ma bouche ». J'ai été pris par surprise et bien souvent, je me sens en danger, au point où j'ai l'impression que ma vie est en péril. Il est important que je retrace cet événement qui s'est probablement passé juste avant que mon **larynx** ne soit touché par la maladie. Je pourrai ainsi enlever le traumatisme qui est resté « accroché » à mon **larynx** et lui permettre de guérir.

GORGE NOUÉE

J'ai la **gorge nouée** quand je vis de l'anxiété. Je me sens alors « pris à la **gorge** ». Je peux me sentir insécure mais je dois faire confiance à la vie. J'apprends à m'exprimer librement et à dépasser mes peurs.

GORGE — PHARYNGITE (voir aussi : ANNEXE III, RHUME)

La **pharyngite** est beaucoup plus connue sous l'expression **mal de gorge**. Toutes les émotions, les sentiments ou les énergies qui bloquent ma **gorge** se doivent d'entrer par le nez ou par la bouche. Ou encore, elles viennent des profondeurs de mon être intérieur et elles bloquent au niveau de la **gorge**. Ce sont souvent des émotions ou des situations que je ravale et que j'ai de la difficulté à accepter ↓♥. Donc, je sens (nez) que cela ne va pas, ou je n'absorbe pas (bouche) une ou des énergies qui se présentent à moi. Parfois, ce sont les mêmes émotions qui se sont amplifiées après un rhume. Ces émotions m'affectent plus profondément, plus près de mon intérieur qu'un simple rhume. Je me dois donc d'analyser ce sentiment qui accroche et bloque au niveau de la **gorge** pour pouvoir l'accepter ↓♥ et le laisser aller.

GOUTTE (voir aussi : ACIDOSE, CALCULS RÉNAUX)

La **goutte** est une maladie métabolique caractérisée par l'accumulation d'acide urique dans l'organisme, et qui se traduit par des atteintes articulaires, particulièrement du gros orteil et parfois par une lithiase rénale (calculs rénaux). Elle atteint aussi fréquemment les mains, les poignets, les doigts, les genoux, les chevilles et parfois, les coudes. L'accumulation d'acide urique signifie que je retiens des émotions négatives qui devraient normalement être relâchées dans l'urine. Ainsi, je me fige dans des attitudes et des « patterns » mentaux qui font de mon habileté à bouger un acte douloureux et maladroit. Mon corps devient rigide comme mes pensées et mon attitude face à moi-même et les autres. Je peux manifester beaucoup d'impatience quand les choses ne se passent pas comme je le veux. J'ai besoin de **dominer, de**

contrôler entièrement ma vie, ce qui peut être parfois très difficile. Donc, la **goutte** se présente chez quelqu'un de très ambitieux et rigide ou, au contraire, chez une personne qui n'a aucun but, aucun enthousiasme face à l'avenir. J'ai des ambitions très limitées et il ne faut pas m'en demander trop. Sinon, « c'est la **goutte** qui fait déborder le vase » ! Alors, le désespoir me gagne. Comme la **goutte** se présente souvent chez des hommes d'âge mûr, j'ai peut-être à apprendre à laisser les autres être, plutôt que de dominer ; de faire confiance à la vie plutôt que de contrôler ; d'être plus flexible envers moi-même ou les autres au lieu d'être rigide. Je n'ai plus à vivre de conflit intérieur entre les plaisirs de la vie et les devoirs : je me vois « obligé » d'être inactif et d'apprécier « un repos bien mérité » ! J'ai avantage à laisser davantage d'amour entrer en moi pour équilibrer et libérer les émotions négatives, douloureuses, blessantes et coléreuses, afin de retrouver mouvement, liberté, bien-être.

GRAISSE et EMBONPOINT (voir aussi : POIDS [excès de...])

Si je suis une personne ayant de **l'embonpoint**, je suis quelqu'un d'hypersensible et qui éprouve le besoin de se protéger. Ce besoin de me protéger se retrouve principalement au niveau du deuxième chakra[58], celui de la sexualité et du troisième chakra[59], celui des émotions. Les hommes semblent avoir besoin de se protéger davantage sur ce plan-là. J'apprends à avoir confiance en moi-même et en la vie, afin de permettre à cette **graisse** protectrice de s'en aller. J'exprime mes émotions librement et j'apprends à m'aimer tel que je suis.

GRAND MAL (voir : CERVEAU — ÉPILEPSIE)

GRATTELLE (voir : PEAU — GALE)

GRINCEMENT DE DENTS (voir : DENTS [grincement de...])

GRIPPE (voir aussi : CERVEAU — ENCÉPHALITE, COURBATURE, ÉTERNUEMENTS, FIÈVRE, MUSCLE, RESPIRATION [maux de...], TÊTE [maux de...])

Il s'agit d'un état lié à la présence d'un virus causant fièvre, frissons, maux de tête, douleurs musculaires, éternuements, problèmes respiratoires, etc. La **grippe** qui atteint mon corps plus violemment qu'un rhume peut me forcer à rester alité pour une certaine période de temps. Comme la **grippe** est une maladie infectieuse et que celle-ci est reliée à la colère, je peux me demander

---

58. **Deuxième chakra :** Situé entre le nombril et le pubis.
59. **Troisième chakra :** Situé au niveau du plexus solaire, à la base du sternum ou de la cage thoracique.

qui ou quoi « ai-je pris en **grippe** », expression voulant dire contre qui ou contre quoi suis-je en colère ? Les symptômes qui se manifestent plus particulièrement m'indiquent davantage ce que je vis présentement : la fièvre est reliée à la colère, les éternuements sont reliés à la critique, au fait de vouloir se débarrasser de quelqu'un ou d'une situation, etc. Il s'agit souvent d'une situation conflictuelle sur le plan familial : il s'est dit quelque chose ou une situation a été vécue que « je ne peux pas avaler » car des règles ou des limites ont été transgressées. Il y a donc eu une dispute où j'avais l'impression que mon espace vital était violé ou que je risquais de perdre quelque chose ou quelqu'un qui m'appartenait. Beaucoup de cas de **grippe** sont attribuables aux croyances enracinées dans la société, la peur aussi, comme par exemple : « J'ai eu tellement froid aujourd'hui, je suis certain que je vais attraper la **grippe** ! » Je dois me demander pourquoi j'ai la **grippe**. Est-ce que j'ai besoin de repos ? Est-ce que je m'oblige à être alité afin de ne pas faire face à mes responsabilités au travail ou dans la famille, etc. ? La **grippe** peut aussi naître à la suite d'une situation où j'ai vécu un grand désappointement, une grande déception ou une frustration qui m'amène à vouloir ne plus sentir ce qui se passe autour de moi (nez congestionné) et qui amène aussi une respiration plus difficile. J'ai avantage à exprimer mes émotions et à laisser couler mes larmes afin de décongestionner tout mon corps et que l'harmonie s'installe.

GRIPPE ESPAGNOLE (voir : CERVEAU — ENCÉPHALITE)

GROSSESSE (maux de...)
(voir aussi : ACCOUCHEMENT, SANG — DIABÈTE)

Même si la **grossesse** est d'ordinaire joyeuse et enrichissante, elle peut aussi être effrayante par ses soucis cachés, ses doutes, ses peurs et ses inquiétudes, spécialement quand c'est la première fois. Ces sentiments cachés trouveront une façon de sortir si, comme future mère, je ne suis pas capable de les exprimer verbalement. Parfois, je peux avoir l'impression que les défis à relever sont si grands par rapport à ce que je suis capable de prendre, que je peux inconsciemment rejeter l'enfant. Voici quelques exemples de malaises que je peux vivre pendant la grossesse : des **brûlures d'estomac** m'indiquent une difficulté à avaler la réalité de ce qui arrive ; la **constipation** met à jour ma peur de laisser aller, que j'essaie de retenir les choses comme elles sont maintenant tout en sachant que la venue d'un enfant amène des changements majeurs dans ma vie ; un **nerf sciatique douloureux** manifeste ma peur d'aller de l'avant, dans la nouvelle direction que la vie m'apporte ; un **diabète gestationnel** est la conséquence de la tristesse que je vis pendant cette période. Il se peut aussi que je vive du mécontentement, que j'aie peur de vivre du rejet à voir ainsi mon corps changer et que je veuille que le fait d'être « grosse cesse ». J'apprends à faire confiance et j'accepte ↓♥ que j'aie tous les outils nécessaires afin de m'amener à vivre cette expérience merveilleuse dans la joie et l'harmonie.

GROSSESSE[60] (... prolongée)

Lorsqu'une **grossesse se prolonge** au-delà de la période habituelle, comme mère, je peux désirer inconsciemment de continuer à porter cet enfant le plus longtemps possible, appréciant cet état où je sens mon enfant en sécurité et où le lien entre la mère et l'enfant est si fort. Je veux le garder à « l'abri des intempéries » de la vie de tous les jours. Je peux avoir peur de ces nouvelles responsabilités qui m'attendent avec ce nouvel enfant qui va naître. Vais-je être à la hauteur de la situation ? Cela va-t-il changer quelque chose dans mon couple ? Vais-je être une bonne mère ? Mes inquiétudes face à cette naissance peuvent me faire retarder la venue de l'enfant. Il se peut aussi que mon enfant se sente tellement bien dans cet environnement sécurisant qu'il veuille y rester le plus longtemps possible. Je peux entrer alors en contact avec son aspect divin, le réconforter, lui assurer que je ferai tout ce qu'il m'est possible de faire pour m'occuper de lui, que je continuerai de l'aimer et que j'ai hâte de pouvoir le tenir dans mes bras. J'ai à me détacher de mon enfant et à me convaincre qu'il a tous les outils nécessaires afin d'affronter les défis qu'il rencontrera. Tout ce dont il a besoin, c'est mon amour et mon affection.

GROSSESSE — ÉCLAMPSIE
(voir aussi : CERVEAU — ÉPILEPSIE,
TENSION ARTÉRIELLE — HYPERTENSION [trop élevée])

Il peut survenir en fin de **grossesse** une **éclampsie** qui est une affection grave caractérisée par des convulsions associées à une hypertension artérielle. Elle se produit généralement chez la femme qui en est à sa première **grossesse**. Elle est semblable à une crise d'épilepsie, se caractérisant par une perte de conscience, une raideur des membres suivie de convulsions. **L'éclampsie** m'atteint si je suis une femme qui, par insécurité ou culpabilité, va rejeter la **grossesse** ou tout ce que peut représenter la venue de l'enfant. Je peux aussi vivre de la rancune face à mon conjoint, car je le rends coupable et responsable de la **grossesse**. Dans d'autres cas, cela peut être moi comme mère qui, ayant de la difficulté à accepter ↓♥ la venue au monde imminente de mon enfant, vais me rejeter, me sentant incapable d'assumer mes nouvelles responsabilités. J'apprends à regarder la venue de mon enfant avec une attitude positive sachant que j'ai tout le bagage nécessaire pour l'aider dans son cheminement.

GROSSESSE ECTOPIQUE ou EXTRA-UTÉRINE (G.E.U.)

Une **grossesse ectopique** se développe en dehors de la cavité utérine. Dans ce cas, il se peut que comme mère, je vive une angoisse face à l'accouchement et que je me retienne d'enfanter. J'ai à apprendre à laisser aller

---

60. La **grossesse** dure environ 9 mois ou 273 jours à partir de la date de fécondation.

le processus normal de la vie et à laisser l'énergie circuler librement à l'intérieur de moi afin que les éléments de la vie prennent la place qui leur revient selon le plan divin.

GROSSESSE NERVEUSE

Je peux vivre dans mon corps physique les mêmes états qu'une personne enceinte même si je ne le suis pas, ceci étant appelé alors **grossesse nerveuse**. Une **grossesse nerveuse** manifeste une incertitude, une insécurité par rapport à mes responsabilités versus mes désirs. Je peux désirer avoir un enfant mais est-ce que je me sens à la hauteur, est-ce que j'ai l'impression d'être capable d'assumer et de remplir tous les besoins et les désirs de l'enfant ? Peut-être pas... Si la **grossesse nerveuse** se manifeste chez une femme célibataire, je dois aller voir aussi si je vis des difficultés en ce qui concerne ma sexualité. J'ai peut-être le goût d'avoir un enfant, mais je n'ai pas le goût d'avoir une relation affective avec une autre personne. Je peux aussi avoir peur de toutes les responsabilités que cela implique d'avoir un conjoint même si j'en désire un. Même si la **grossesse nerveuse** se manifeste surtout chez la femme, il peut arriver que ce phénomène se produise chez un homme. Je peux me demander comment cela peut se produire. Il est important que je me souvienne, que je sois homme ou femme, que je possède les deux côtés à l'intérieur de moi, le côté YIN (femme) et le côté YANG (homme). Même si je suis un homme, je peux développer mon instinct maternel et certaines peurs qui y sont associées et ainsi, développer les symptômes d'une **grossesse nerveuse** par empathie ou symbiose énergétique. Je vérifie alors quelles sont les insécurités que mon enfant intérieur vit présentement. Je pourrai ainsi le rassurer, lui prodiguer l'amour et l'attention dont il a besoin afin que tout rentre dans l'ordre.

HABITUDES (voir : DÉPENDANCE)

HAINE

Beaucoup de maladies ont pour cause la **haine**. Entretenir de la **haine** nous fait détester des personnes, rend méchant, nous pousse à lancer des paroles blessantes avec la rage au cœur. Quand je vis de la **haine**, de la rage, j'ai l'impression que quelque chose brûle en moi, en divers systèmes : digestif, pulmonaire et aussi en relation avec la vésicule biliaire et le foie. Dans l'évolution de ces signes que le corps manifeste, s'annoncent des « mal aises » de plus en plus graves. Je peux m'attirer jusqu'à un cancer. L'amour est la base de toute vie. J'apprends à me pardonner et à pardonner aux autres. J'accepte ↓♥ de comprendre les personnes, les situations autrement, avec amour.

HALEINE (mauvaise...) (voir : BOUCHE — HALEINE [mauvaise...])

HALITOSE (voir : BOUCHE — HALEINE [mauvaise...])

HALLUCINATIONS
(voir aussi : ALCOOLISME, DÉPENDANCE, DROGUE, TOXICOMANIE)

Lorsque je suis épuisé physiquement ou moralement, je peux me faire une montagne d'idées noires, souvent fausses. Ainsi, je peux perdre pied avec le réel sans en avoir conscience, je peux décrocher du réel. Confronté à une réalité que je ne veux pas voir, je m'en invente une même si elle peut être fausse. Alors, je peux me donner raison et prouver ma propre interprétation de cette réalité que je ne peux accepter↓♥. Ces interprétations, ces mondes imaginaires, créés de toute part par moi-même, peuvent aussi faire ressortir mes propres peurs. Je peux avoir des **hallucinations** quand je vis un niveau de stress très élevé. Si, par exemple, je suis en train de chercher un document dont j'ai absolument besoin et dont la perte représenterait des millions de dollars, mon cerveau pourra créer une image de ce document (hologramme) qui me semblera très réel et qui va, l'espace de quelques moments, faire tomber mon niveau de stress. Par la suite, m'apercevant que j'ai **halluciné**, je peux maintenant penser plus clairement et je pourrai soit demander qu'on m'aide à le chercher ou alors explorer d'autres endroits où le document va probablement se trouver. Sans cette **hallucination**, j'aurais continué à être « prisonnier » de mon état de stress. En ce qui a trait aux **drogues**, elles provoquent un état de conscience en expansion. Ainsi, la personne peut expérimenter des dimensions auxquelles elle n'a pas ordinairement accès. Pourquoi je prends de la **drogue** ? Est-ce une fuite de mes souffrances intérieures que je n'arrive pas, faute d'aide, à affronter ? Je peux devenir dépendant des **drogues**, quelles qu'elles soient. Elles peuvent me procurer un état de bien-être temporaire. Mais une fois « straight », c'est-à-dire revenu à la normale, ce n'est plus la même chanson. Alors, où chercher ? En soi. On n'y entre qu'avec l'amour et également par son cheminement personnel et spirituel. Une spiritualité qui me libère des chaînes du passé et qui me redonne ma liberté et mon autonomie. Il se peut aussi qu'à la suite d'un accident, d'un stress intense ou simplement de mon développement personnel et spirituel, mon troisième œil s'ouvre de plus en plus, ce qui m'amène à voir des couleurs autour des personnes, des courants d'énergie dans l'espace ou des présences translucides (non matérielles) dans mon entourage. Je peux avoir ainsi l'impression que j'**hallucine** surtout parce que ma sensibilité est habituellement plus grande quand j'ai ce genre de perception. Alors, je fais confiance et je me sens entouré de lumière blanche et dorée, sachant que je suis constamment guidé et protégé. J'aime de plus en plus découvrir et expérimenter ma vraie réalité, le « Je Suis ».

HANCHES (voir aussi : BASSIN)

Elles portent mon corps en parfait équilibre et sont situées entre le bassin et le fémur[61]. Mes **hanches** permettent à mes jambes de bouger afin de faire avancer mon corps vers l'avant. C'est elles qui <u>déterminent</u> si je vais de l'avant ou non. Elles représentent mes croyances de base face à ce que sont ou à ce que devraient être mes relations avec le monde. Comme le bassin et les **hanches** forment un ensemble, ils représentent **le fait de m'élancer dans la vie.** Donc, les **hanches** représenteront aussi mon niveau de détermination à avancer dans la vie. J'accepte ↓♥ d'avancer avec joie et confiance dans la vie, sachant que tout est expérience pour m'aider à découvrir mes richesses intérieures.

HANCHES (maux de...)

C'est à partir des **hanches** que s'amorce le mouvement des jambes, donc, la démarche. Les jambes servent à avancer librement. Je peux me retenir d'aller de l'avant. D'où l'indécision pour avancer dans la vie. Par les **problèmes de hanches**, mon corps m'indique une certaine raideur, une rigidité ; donc, je vis de l'inflexibilité face à une situation ou à une personne. Cela peut provenir d'une situation où je me suis senti trahi par quelqu'un ou abandonné et cela m'a tellement affecté que je remets en cause mes relations avec les autres. De plus, j'ai le goût d'établir de « nouvelles règles » pour me protéger et éviter d'être encore blessé. Je peux avoir une inquiétude face à l'avenir ; donc, j'angoisse lorsque j'ai à prendre une décision importante car je peux avoir l'impression que je ne m'en vais nulle part ou que je n'aboutirai jamais à rien. Quand mes **hanches** me font mal, mon corps me donne un message. Il m'aide à développer ma conscience afin que j'avance dans la vie avec confiance et sécurité et me montre à être plus flexible dans ma manière de prendre des décisions, m'assurant ainsi un meilleur avenir. Quand il y a une douleur, il y a une culpabilité quelconque. Aussi, une **douleur aux hanches,** ou des **hanches** qui ne veulent plus bouger, peut m'indiquer que je bloque mon plaisir sexuel par crainte ou culpabilité. Je peux même vivre de l'impuissance tant au niveau sexuel que dans ma capacité à m'accepter ↓♥ tel que je suis, avec mes goûts, mes désirs, mes plaisirs. Je serai troublé sexuellement et émotivement, empêchant ainsi mes **hanches** de fonctionner normalement. Cette impuissance peut aussi se vivre dans le fait que je ne me sens pas ou plus capable de prendre ma place et de m'opposer à quelqu'un ou quelque chose. Cette situation m'oblige à réfléchir sur les limites que je me donne. Je suis en équilibre et j'avance dans la vie avec confiance et sérénité. Je remercie la vie pour tout ce qu'elle me fait expérimenter à chaque instant. J'apprends à vivre en équilibre avec ces expériences.

---

61. **Fémur :** Os long que l'on retrouve le long de la cuisse et qui forme son squelette.

HASCHISCH (consommation de...) (voir : DROGUE)

HAUTE PRESSION (voir : TENSION ARTÉRIELLE — HYPERTENSION)

HÉMATOME (voir : SANG — HÉMATOME)

HÉMIPLÉGIE (voir : CERVEAU — HÉMIPLÉGIE)

HÉMORRAGIE (voir : SANG — HÉMORRAGIE)

HÉMORROÏDES (voir aussi : AMPOULES, ANUS, GROSSESSE, INFLAMMATION, INTESTINS — CONSTIPATION, SANG / SAIGNEMENTS / VARICES, TENSION ARTÉRIELLE — HYPERTENSION)

Les **hémorroïdes** sont des varices, des dilatations élargies des veines, une sorte d'ampoule. Elles sont situées dans la région de l'anus et du rectum. Étant donné que les **hémorroïdes** peuvent survenir dans les cas de **constipation,** de **haute pression,** de **grossesse**, je vais vérifier dans ces maladies si je vis une ou des situations qui s'y rattachent. Lorsqu'il y a de la **douleur**, c'est relié à du stress, lorsqu'il y a des **saignements**, c'est relié à une perte de joie. Les **hémorroïdes** m'indiquent une tension et un désir intérieur de forcer l'élimination, comme si j'essayais de faire sortir quelque chose très fortement ; en même temps, l'action de retenir se manifeste. Le conflit entre pousser et retenir crée un déséquilibre. Les veines laissent supposer une situation indiquant un conflit émotionnel entre l'action de rejeter et de repousser et l'action de vouloir retenir et de bloquer l'émotion à l'intérieur de soi. Par exemple, ce conflit peut surgir chez les enfants qui se sentent émotionnellement abusés par leurs parents (qui veulent les rejeter) et qui malgré tout les aiment et veulent qu'ils restent avec eux en les retenant. D'autres causes sont reliées aux **hémorroïdes** : un sentiment intense de culpabilité ou une vieille tension mal ou non exprimée, que je préfère souvent garder pour moi et que je vis face à une personne ou une situation qui « me fend le derrrière ».

Le corps me donne un signal d'alarme. Quelque chose dans ma vie a besoin d'être « éclairé ». Je vis sûrement du stress, une surcharge de pression par rapport à laquelle je me sens coupable. J'ai peut-être des échéances à respecter et j'ai beaucoup de difficulté à laisser aller, à faire confiance et je peux me sentir obligé de remplir mes obligations et mes responsabilités même si ce que je veux, c'est de parler et d'exprimer mes besoins afin de rectifier ou d'ajuster certaines situations. En plus, je porte ce fardeau seul car l'orgueil que je vis m'incitera à ne pas demander d'aide de qui que ce soit. Il se peut aussi que je vive un sentiment de soumission par rapport à une personne ou à une

situation où je me sens diminué, comme si j'étais un « trou d'cul ». Quand je trouve la cause métaphysique de mon malaise, j'en prends conscience et j'accepte ↓♥ cette situation temporaire qui m'aidera à trouver de l'aide pour m'en dégager. Mes pensées et mes actions sont soutenues par l'amour. Tout s'harmonise en moi et les **hémorroïdes** disparaissent.

HÉPATITE (voir : FOIE — HÉPATITE)

HERNIE

La **hernie** est un ballonnement de tissus mous ou un organe saillant à travers la paroi musculaire, là où existe un point faible permettant cette sortie. Il peut s'agir d'une tumeur formée par un viscère qui est sorti, à travers un orifice naturel ou accidentel, hors de la cavité qui le contient normalement. La **hernie** est provoquée par une pression du tissu mou au-dessous du muscle au moment où il est faible et sous-utilisé. Les **hernies** peuvent varier d'endroit. Elles sont plus fréquentes le long de la paroi abdominale (**hernie de la paroi abdominale**). Au diaphragme, elle est appelée **hernie diaphragmatique**. Le lieu indique sa nature et son message. Par exemple, celles des bébés sont habituellement liées à une mauvaise cicatrisation du cordon ombilical après sa coupure. Cette enflure peut exprimer mon refus comme bébé de quitter le nid douillet de ma mère ou mon refus de naître. Chez l'adulte, elle peut représenter un grand désir non exprimé de rompre avec une situation ou une personne qui m'est désagréable et avec laquelle je me sens engagé. Cela peut concerner une rupture de mon couple provoquée par moi ou mon conjoint et que j'ai de la difficulté à accepter ↓♥. Est-ce que je trouve la vie lourde à porter ? Elle peut aussi exprimer une autopunition parce que je m'en veux, me sentant impuissant ou incapable de réaliser certaines choses. Je vis ainsi beaucoup de frustration face à moi-même. Par le contrôle de ma contrainte, j'atteins un niveau où tout explose ou plutôt « implose » en moi. Étant donné que je n'ai pas libéré extérieurement ma détresse, elle doit trouver une façon de sortir. La paroi abdominale protège mes organes internes et les gardent en place. Par conséquent, la **hernie dans le muscle** peut être liée au désir de garder mon univers à sa place en ne permettant pas la libération de l'agressivité ou d'expressions plus fortes. Est-ce que je me permets de la libérer ? Je peux me sentir coupable d'être dans cet état et je me sens poussé et forcé à aller trop loin, ou j'essaie d'accomplir mon but d'une manière excessive. Il y a une « poussée mentale » (stress) qui essaie de jaillir. Je veux sortir d'un état ou d'une situation qui n'est pas agréable et dans lequel je me sens contraint de rester. Il s'agit d'une certaine forme d'autopunition. C'est le moment d'un nouveau départ. J'ai besoin d'exprimer ma créativité. Maintenant, je me permets d'être moi-même en m'extériorisant plus librement. Je vis plus d'amour pour moi-même et les autres car je sais qui « Je Suis ».

HERNIE DISCALE (voir aussi : DOS [maux de...])

Un disque est une structure ronde et plate située entre chaque paire de vertèbres de la colonne vertébrale et entourée d'une substance semblable à de la gelée (comme de la gélatine) qui sert d'amortisseur. Dans une **hernie discale**, la pression venant d'une ou de plusieurs vertèbres compresse cette masse gélatineuse à sortir, réduisant l'effet absorbant et créant de la douleur sur les nerfs avoisinants. Dans une **hernie discale**, en plus de ce qu'une **hernie** signifie, il y a un relâchement anormal des liquides, impliquant, d'un point de vue métaphysique, les émotions. Il y a aussi de la douleur aux nerfs, impliquant l'énergie mentale et la culpabilité. Tout cela indique un profond conflit affectant tous les aspects de mon être. Dans la situation de la **hernie discale**, le mot clé ici est **pression**. Je peux la sentir au niveau de mes responsabilités familiales, financières, à mon travail etc. C'est comme si j'exerçais une pression sur moi-même en dépassant mes limites, en me prenant pour quelqu'un d'autre. Cette pression peut venir de moi, des autres ou d'ailleurs. J'ai l'impression d'être seul dans la vie et de n'avoir aucun appui, hésitant à l'avouer aux autres et, surtout, à moi-même. Ce qui me donne un sentiment d'être prisonnier et indécis. Il est important que je me réfère à la partie affectée de l'épine dorsale pour comprendre davantage ce qui se passe en moi. Je me sens maintenant soutenu par la vie. Je me libère de toutes culpabilités et de toutes pressions. Je m'aime comme je suis. Je fais de mon mieux et je laisse le reste à Dieu.

HÉROÏNE (consommation d'...) (voir : DROGUE)

HERPÈS (... en général, ... buccal) (voir aussi : BOUCHE)

L'**herpès**, genre d'éruption cutanée groupée de vésicules inflammatoires, est communément appelé **feux sauvages**. Ce virus infecte une quantité innombrable de gens et en plus, il reste dans le corps pour la vie. Même après plusieurs années de « sommeil », il apparaît. Le virus *herpès simplex* (HSV) peut faire fondamentalement éruption sous la forme d'ulcères affectant surtout la bouche, les lèvres ou les parties génitales. Plusieurs causes sont reliées à l'**herpès** :

— Cela peut être de la frustration parce que je n'ai pu réaliser certains désirs et je me sens quelque peu « impuissant », « incapable ».

— Je veux éloigner quelqu'un pour ne pas me laisser embrasser ; soit que je le juge ou que je veux le punir.

— Je peux m'en vouloir d'avoir dit certaines paroles blessantes.

— Je peux porter un jugement sévère contre une personne du sexe opposé et en le généralisant à tout l'ensemble (Ex. : « Les hommes sont tous... »).

Autant de manières pour me garder à distance des autres, car les régions où l'**herpès** se développe sont habituellement les lèvres et les parties génitales,

lieux de base pour la communication personnelle, verbale ou affective avec les autres personnes. Les ulcères peuvent m'indiquer que je vis une peine émotionnelle et mentale (car le tissu mou et les fluides sont impliqués), que je vis un genre d'éruption ou une grande douleur intérieure. Puisque c'est avec les lèvres que j'embrasse les personnes aimées (conjoints, enfants, parents, etc.), l'**herpès buccal** m'indique que je peux vivre une situation dans laquelle je vis une séparation par rapport à une personne que j'avais l'habitude d'embrasser. Le contact au niveau de la peau des lèvres a été retiré pour quelque raison que ce soit et l'**herpès** apparaît. Sur le nez (plus rare), l'**herpès** m'indique que je peux vivre de la rage liée au fait qu'on pense, dans mon entourage, que j'ai « le nez fourré partout ». Les éruptions semblent étroitement reliées au stress et aux situations conflictuelles, spécialement lorsque je fais quelque chose à contrecœur ou lorsque je vais à l'inverse de mes sentiments intérieurs (ex. : lorsque j'ai une expérience sexuelle avec une personne avec laquelle je ne veux pas être). Aussi, l'**herpès** peut me donner le message que je vis un chagrin, une lassitude face à la vie, un manque d'amour-propre. Ce virus apporte sur la table toutes les questions de honte, de culpabilité, de compromis et de reniement de soi qui sont reliées à la sexualité (en observant la partie du corps affectée, je pourrai en trouver la cause.) Je cesse de me juger et de juger sévèrement les autres. J'apprends à m'ouvrir aux autres. Je me fais de plus en plus confiance dans mes relations intimes. Je m'aime davantage et le soleil revient dans ma vie. Je suis fier d'être qui je suis.

HERPÈS GÉNITAL ou HERPÈS VAGINAL
(voir aussi : PEAU — DÉMANGEAISONS, VAGIN — VAGINITE)

L'**herpès vaginal,** selon la croyance populaire, provient de la culpabilité sexuelle et du désir inconscient de s'autopunir. L'**herpès génital** peut apparaître s'il y a absence de contact sexuel. Je pouvais avoir un conjoint et l'on s'est séparé. Ou alors, nous pouvons être séparés physiquement, par exemple si l'un des deux est parti en voyage d'affaires pour une certaine période de temps. Le contact physique avec la peau de mes organes sexuels étant absent, et parce que je vis cette « séparation » très difficilement, je manifesterai mon malaise avec un **herpès vaginal**. Il se peut aussi que ma frustration soit vive en rapport avec mes relations sexuelles, soit qu'elles ne sont pas satisfaisantes ou au contraire, qu'elles soient pleinement satisfaisantes et qu'elles fassent remonter des souvenirs malheureux. Autrement dit, je peux me demander pourquoi j'ai été autant d'années à vivre de l'insatisfaction alors qu'aujourd'hui, cela va si bien, pourquoi n'ai-je pas connu cela avant ? Dans l'éducation religieuse populaire, on allait jusqu'à prétendre que c'était voulu par Dieu pour nous punir. Le sentiment de honte m'amène même à vouloir nier, à ne pas accepter ↓♥ mes organes génitaux. Les parties génitales ont été des boucs émissaires de bien des religions. J'aime mon corps et je me réjouis de ma sexualité. Dieu m'a créé à son image. Je m'émerveille de la beauté que je suis.

HIV (voir : SIDA)

HODGKIN (maladie de...) (voir aussi : CANCER DES GANGLIONS [... du système lymphatique], SANG — LEUCOPÉNIE)

La **maladie de Hodgkin** est une affection cancéreuse touchant essentiellement les ganglions lymphatiques ainsi que la rate et le foie. Elle se manifeste par une perte des forces causée par une diminution des globules blancs. Elle est fortement reliée à une **grande culpabilité** que je vis. Elle a d'autres causes tout aussi importantes :

— Je ne me trouve pas assez bon, l'estime de moi est à son plus bas, allant même jusqu'à refuser qu'on me dise des compliments.
— Je crains d'être désapprouvé.
— Je peux vivre un grand découragement, une perte du goût de vivre (le sang signifie la joie), une perte de mes défenses (globules blancs).
— Je me sens dans une course frénétique : je sens le besoin de démontrer aux autres ou à moi-même que je suis quelqu'un et que je peux accomplir de grandes choses.
— Je peux nourrir des sentiments de haine, de rancœur contre quelqu'un ou contre une situation.

Ma grande joie, c'est de m'aimer pour ce que je suis. Je me fais confiance et je vais à mon rythme. Mon corps se régénère puisque je me branche à **La Source** qui est en moi.

HOMICIDE

Je peux avoir le désir de tuer quelqu'un. Si je nourris ce désir avec du ressentiment et de la haine, je m'expose à l'égrégore[62] d'énergie négative concernant cette forme de pensée qui me poussera peut-être à passer à l'action. **Qu'est-ce que je veux tuer en moi ? Ma souffrance, ma hargne, ma haine... ?** Ma blessure intérieure me semble insupportable. La souffrance que je vis à l'intérieur me demande du courage. Le courage de demander de l'aide. Le courage de faire confiance à une personne qui pourra m'accueillir inconditionnellement. Une personne à qui je pourrai me confier.

HOMOSEXUALITÉ

Y a-t-il une exclusion à l'Amour ? L'**homosexualité** est-elle une maladie ? Certains essaient de prouver que l'**homosexualité** pourrait être inscrite dans notre bagage génétique. L'**homosexualité** est un langage d'amour qui est de

---

62. **Égrégore :** Il s'agit d'une énergie sous forme de conscience, formée par la pensée de plusieurs ou d'une multitude de personnes.

plus en plus accepté ↓♥ par notre société contemporaine. Elle peut être une étape dans la recherche de mon identité ou un choix de vie pour mon évolution ou pour faire évoluer la société. Combien de parents se sont surpassés dans leur amour pour y inclure leur enfant **gai** (nom donné à l'**homosexualité** masculine) ou **lesbienne** (nom donné à l'**homosexualité** féminine). Il y a deux côtés en moi. Le côté féminin (YIN ou intuitif) et le côté masculin (YANG ou rationnel). Il se peut que n'acceptant ↓♥ pas mon identité, je tente de retrouver chez une personne du même sexe le côté que j'ai rejeté. Il se peut aussi que je recherche un père, une mère. **Quel que soit mon choix d'orientation sexuelle, il est important que je le fasse en harmonie avec mon être.** Si je choisis l'**homosexualité** parce que je rejette les personnes de l'autre sexe pour une raison ou pour une autre, je me retrouverai à vivre des situations semblables à celles que j'aurais eu à vivre avec des personnes de l'autre sexe, parce que j'ai ces prises de conscience à faire. Lorsque mon choix d'orientation sexuelle est clair pour moi, que je sois **homosexuel** ou hétérosexuel, je ne devrais pas me sentir menacé par ceux qui ont une orientation différente de la mienne. Si je suis en réaction par rapport à ceux qui ont une orientation différente de la mienne, alors je dois me poser sérieusement la question à savoir de quoi ai-je peur par rapport à cette situation ? De quoi ai-je besoin de me protéger en étant contre ? Aurais-je peur d'avoir un côté de moi qui est **homosexuel** et de me l'avouer ? J'ai à prendre conscience que l'importance doit être mise sur l'amour que deux personnes ont entre elles et que cet amour doit être vrai peu importe leur orientation sexuelle. Je peux demander à mon guide intérieur de m'aider à comprendre au niveau du cœur, de m'accepter ↓♥ tel que je suis et d'accepter ↓♥ les autres, tels qu'ils sont.

HOQUET

Le **hoquet** est provoqué par des contractions spasmodiques subites et involontaires du diaphragme. Je peux vivre une révolte intérieure, une culpabilité, un autojugement. Cela perturbe mon organisme. Toujours le **hoquet** ? Il peut être fréquent et durable. C'est une expérience très incommodante et désagréable pour la personne qui l'a. Est-ce qu'il y a quelque chose d'incommodant et de désagréable dans ce que je vis ou dans ce que je voudrais vivre mais qui ne se manifeste pas, et qui me cause de la frustration ? Est-ce qu'il y a des bruits, des pensées que je ne peux arrêter ? Le **hoquet** est-il programmé « Ex. : chaque fois que je bois de la boisson gazeuse, j'ai le **hoquet** »? Je prends la vie plus calmement. J'apprends à goûter et à apprécier ma vie pleinement. J'accepte ↓♥ que tout est en place, dans le plan divin, que tout est « O.K. », et le **hoquet** disparaîtra.

HTA (HYPERTENSION ARTÉRIELLE)
(voir : TENSION ARTÉRIELLE — HYPERTENSION)

HYDROPHOBIE (voir : RAGE)

HYGROMA (voir : GENOUX [maux de...])

HYPERACTIVITÉ (voir aussi : AGITATION)

L'**hyperactivité** se retrouve plus fréquemment chez les enfants dont les activités sont intenses et constantes. Il est bien de faire la distinction entre un comportement dynamique et **hyperactif**. Si je suis un **enfant hyperactif**, j'ai un comportement turbulent et dérangeant, voire même étrange. C'est la façon habituelle que j'ai d'ignorer les situations et les circonstances autour de moi en devenant tellement impliqué dans ce que je fais que je n'ai pas à mettre l'attention sur « ma » réalité immédiate, peut-être parce que cette réalité n'est pas soutenante et réconfortante. C'est une façon de me rebeller contre les circonstances et les sentiments qui ne sont pas exprimés mais qui sont plus sentis (comme les peurs parentales et les inhibitions). Nous savons que l'**hyperactivité** est causée par les additifs artificiels : l'excès de sucre, les colorants et le *fast-food*. La nourriture de ce type est souvent le symbole du parent essayant de combler l'amour dont je peux manquer. Par exemple : Il me donne du chocolat alors que j'ai davantage besoin d'une « collade ». Lorsque je suis un **enfant hyperactif**, c'est souvent que j'ai besoin d'être centré davantage sur mon moi intérieur et mon cœur. Comme parent, avant de penser à mettre mon enfant sous médication, j'aurais grandement avantage à essayer des traitements qui agissent sur le plan énergétique, comme par exemple la détente, l'acupuncture, l'homéopathie, etc. Il se peut que l'**enfant** soit **hyperactif** parce qu'il est en résonance ou si l'on veut, en contact intérieur avec ce qu'on appelle notre enfant intérieur (l'enfant intérieur du parent) qui lui, vit une grande tension ou une grande insécurité. Si nous-mêmes comme parents ne sommes pas centrés énergétiquement, comment demander à notre enfant de l'être. J'aurais alors avantage à me prendre en mains pour moi-même, d'abord, ainsi que pour le bien-être de mon enfant.

HYPERÉMOTIVITÉ (voir : ÉMOTIVITÉ)

HYPERCHOLESTÉROLÉMIE (voir : SANG — CHOLESTÉROL)

HYPERGLYCÉMIE (voir : SANG — DIABÈTE)

HYPEROREXIE (voir : BOULIMIE)

HYPERTENSION (voir : TENSION ARTÉRIELLE — HYPERTENSION)

HYPERTHERMIE (voir : FIÈVRE)

HYPERTHYROÏDIE (voir : THYROÏDE — HYPERTHYROÏDIE)

HYPERVENTILATION (suroxygénation)
(voir aussi : ACIDOSE, ANXIÉTÉ, FIÈVRE)

L'**hyperventilation** consiste en une inspiration rapide et une expiration courte, amenant un excédent d'oxygène dans l'organisme. Les causes peuvent être l'acidose, l'anxiété, la fièvre, un exercice physique intense. Je souffre d'**hyperventilation** parce que je n'accepte ↓♥ pas le changement. En conséquence, j'éprouve un sentiment d'inquiétude face à la nouveauté et j'hésite à faire confiance à la situation actuelle ; je refuse de m'abandonner. Mon corps me donne un message et j'en prends conscience. Je respire normalement, je me laisse aller, je m'abandonne. Ma vie se transforme, je me réjouis. Je me libère de toutes mes craintes. Je respire avec joie dans la vie.

HYPOACOUSIE (voir : OREILLES — SURDITÉ)

HYPOCONDRIE (voir aussi : AGORAPHOBIE, ANXIÉTÉ, DÉPRESSION, HALLUCINATIONS)

Je suis **hypocondriaque** si je me préoccupe de façon excessive de ma santé. Cela peut devenir pour moi une obsession de penser que je pourrais être malade. Je vis une insécurité profonde face à cette perte de contrôle que pourrait représenter l'arrivée de la maladie. Je n'accepte ↓♥ pas de souffrir par la maladie parce que je sais au fond de moi que je souffre déjà dans mon être intérieur. Cette crainte peut devenir si grande que je peux décrocher de la réalité et avoir des hallucinations. J'ai besoin de reprendre contact avec moi-même. En utilisant une approche énergétique ou de psychothérapie, cela m'aidera à reprendre davantage confiance en moi et en ma capacité divine d'ouverture que je peux manifester face à la vie.

HYPOGLYCÉMIE (voir : SANG — HYPOGLYCÉMIE)

HYPOPHYSE (voir : GLANDE PITUITAIRE)

HYPOSALIVATION (voir : SALIVE — HYPOSALIVATION)

HYPOTENSION (voir : TENSION ARTÉRIELLE — HYPOTENSION)

HYPOTHYROÏDIE (voir : THYROÏDE — HYPOTHYROÏDIE)

HYSTÉRIE (voir aussi : ÉVANOUISSEMENT, NERFS [crise de...], NÉVROSE)

Je suis **hystérique** lorsque je vis une névrose et que j'exprime mon conflit psychique de façon corporelle, que ce soit sous la forme d'une crise de nerfs, de convulsions, de pertes de connaissance, etc. Lorsque je fais une crise d'**hystérie**, je décroche de la réalité, je me réfugie dans l'imaginaire et je peux avoir tendance à exprimer mon conflit intérieur en public. Je vis une profonde insatisfaction personnelle quant à ma sexualité, ce qui m'amène à jouer le jeu de la séduction, à maintenir les gens à distance ou encore à avoir une apparente froideur afin de me protéger de ma grande sensibilité. Lorsque je vis cet état, cela met en évidence la douleur et la peine intérieure que je peux ressentir. J'ai besoin de guérir ma blessure intérieure afin que je puisse retrouver un plus grand équilibre, une plus grande harmonie et une plus grande paix intérieure, afin de faire cesser ces tourments. Je demande à être guidé pour choisir l'approche thérapeutique qui me permettra d'atteindre cet état de mieux-être.

ICTÈRE (voir : JAUNISSE)

ILÉITE ou MALADIE DE CROHN
(voir : INTESTINS — CROHN [maladie de...])

IMPATIENCE (voir aussi : NERVOSITÉ, SANG — HYPOGLYCÉMIE)

L'**impatience** dénote un stress intérieur, une insécurité ou une tension qui m'ébranle et affecte mon système nerveux. Je deviens plus irritable, plus expéditif dans ce que j'ai à dire ou à faire. J'ai besoin de prendre quelques moments pour me détendre et pour trouver la source de mon irritation.

IMPUISSANCE (voir aussi : ANGOISSE, ANXIÉTÉ, PEUR)

En tant qu'homme, si je suis incapable d'obtenir ou de maintenir une érection lors d'une relation amoureuse, alors je souffre de l'**impuissance**. Cela m'amène certainement à vivre de l'insatisfaction dans mes rapports sexuels. Sur le plan médical, même si l'**impuissance** peut être **organique**, c'est-à-dire provenir d'une cause physique ou provenir d'un aspect **psychologique**, je dois considérer du point de vue métaphysique que la cause provient d'un facteur psychologique ou métaphysique (au-delà du physique), même inconscient. L'**impuissance** est souvent reliée à la peur de s'abandonner à une femme[63] et aussi de perdre le contrôle face à soi-même ou face à l'autre personne. Étant un homme, j'ai souvent beaucoup de responsabilités et je peux vivre beaucoup de pression et de stress au travail, et la société en général me demande de performer. Transposant cette demande dans ma sexualité, je

---

63. Ou à un homme si mes rapports sexuels se font avec un homme .

peux sentir une pression sexuelle me poussant à performer et qui crée une grande tension intérieure me « faisant perdre mes moyens ». N'osant pas en parler à mon ou ma partenaire, j'en viens à vivre beaucoup de culpabilité, de confusion jusqu'à avoir peur de perdre l'autre personne. Une grande angoisse éprouvée lors de mes rapports amoureux peut provoquer ce blocage qui me fait vivre de l'**impuissance.** Cette angoisse peut provenir du fait que, lors d'un rapport sexuel, je suis davantage en contact avec mon côté affectif. Comme homme, je ne suis pas habitué à manœuvrer avec mes émotions. Je suis en contact plus conscient avec mon enfant intérieur blessé qui peut vivre de l'insécurité, de la peur, du rejet, de l'incompréhension. Aussi, si dans mes relations amoureuses précédentes j'ai eu l'impression de vivre des échecs que j'ai trouvés dévalorisants, alors je pourrai ne pas me sentir « à la hauteur » de la situation lors d'un prochain rapport sexuel. Mon insécurité, mon sentiment d'incapacité et d'échec, de haine de moi, de culpabilité ou de négligence peut m'amener aussi à vivre de l'**impuissance.** Je peux vivre le départ de ma femme comme une séparation tant sur le plan émotionnel que physique. Comme le contact physique sexuel n'est plus possible, mes organes sexuels perdent leur sensibilité. L'**impuissance** peut aussi avoir sa source dans un événement passé qui m'a marqué : je peux avoir été abusé physiquement ou psychologiquement dans la tendre enfance ; je peux garder de la rancune face à une relation affective antérieure, ayant l'impression que j'ai été victime d'une trahison. **L'impuissance** est aussi une façon d'avoir du pouvoir sur l'autre en retenant sexuellement un(e) partenaire qui abuse ou en demande trop. Je peux avoir l'impression que mon territoire (mes possessions, mon environnement immédiat, ce à quoi je m'identifie) est en danger. Je peux avoir une perte d'intérêt pour les femmes en général, ce qui se transposera sur le plan physique si le désintéressement perdure. Finalement, si j'identifie ma partenaire à ma mère, si cette dernière occupe une place trop importante dans ma vie, en me soumettant à elle et en ayant peur de ne pas lui plaire, en me sentant **impuissant** à la rendre heureuse et à lui faire plaisir, ceci pourra se transformer en **impuissance** sexuelle. Le complexe d'Œdipe[64] n'a probablement pas bien été vécu. J'ai à redéfinir ma place, à prendre contact avec mes émotions et à laisser aller le contrôle afin que l'énergie circule librement dans tout mon corps, au lieu de rester dans ma tête, afin d'amener une relaxation physique et mentale.

INCIDENT (voir : ACCIDENT)

---

64. **Complexe d'Œdipe :**   Il est caractérisé dans le développement de l'enfant, généralement entre 3 et 6 ans, par un fort attachement affectif pour le parent du sexe opposé : le garçon vers sa mère, la fille vers son père.

INCONTINENCE (... fécale, ... urinaire)
(voir aussi : VESSIE [maux de...])

Que l'**incontinence** soit **fécale** — incapacité à retenir les selles — ou **urinaire** — pertes involontaires de l'urine — les deux situations ont rapport au contrôle. Il se peut que la vie veuille m'enseigner à être plus flexible et à laisser aller les gens et les situations. La perte de contrôle, soit de mes selles ou de mon urine, m'oblige à faire une prise de conscience en ce sens. Je dois laisser de côté mes pensées rigides qui ne sont qu'une protection que je m'impose pour me protéger de ma sensibilité là où je ne peux contrôler la situation. Dans le cas d'**incontinence fécale**, je peux me demander quelle est la personne ou la situation « qui me fait chier ». Il se peut que je sois <u>en très forte réaction par rapport à l'autorité</u> et le fait d'avoir à subir cette autorité m'amène à vivre cette situation d'**incontinence**. Pour moi, l'autorité peut être la vie elle-même qui m'amène à faire des changements que je ne veux pas faire. Je peux aller voir dans mon enfance qui représentait l'autorité pour moi et envers qui j'ai pu être en réaction. Dans le cas d'**incontinence urinaire**, cette libération incontrôlable et inconsciente d'émotions négatives que représente l'urine peut être un moyen d'avoir plus d'attention et d'affection. La cause sous-jacente à ceci peut être un sentiment de rejet, de n'avoir aucun mérite, d'insécurité ou d'avoir peur de l'avenir. L'urine représente des émotions négatives normalement relâchées lorsqu'elles ne sont plus nécessaires ou voulues. Cette libération souvent nocturne indique un conflit à un niveau plus profond et dont je n'ai même pas conscience. Étant incapable de « contrôler » la fuite d'urine ou de selles, je suis incapable de contrôler ce qui arrive dans ma vie, notamment mes émotions et cela peut faire peur. Il est important que ces peurs et insécurités intérieures s'expriment. Je peux aussi laisser aller trop facilement des choses ou des personnes qui me sont chères, sans avoir le courage ou la force d'aller chercher ce que je veux. Ayant beaucoup d'attentes face à la vie, je suis déçu et je me « laisse aller » ; cela peut être tant par rapport à mon corps qu'à mon esprit. Une grande peur ou nervosité peut aussi causer l'**incontinence**, surtout chez les enfants. Je prends conscience qu'il est impossible de tout contrôler ce qui se passe dans ma vie. J'apprends à faire confiance et j'apprends à aimer la nouveauté et l'inattendu.

INCONTINENCE POUR L'ENFANT (voir : « PIPI AU LIT »)

INDEX (voir : DOIGTS — INDEX)

INDIGESTION (voir aussi : EMPOISONNEMENT [..., ... par la nourriture], MAL DE VENTRE, NAUSÉES, SALMONELLOSE)

L'estomac est l'endroit par lequel mon corps physique assimile la nourriture. Si je fais une **indigestion**, mon corps rejette cette nourriture et

j'en suis affecté par des nausées, des vomissements ou des douleurs abdominales. Il en est de même avec la réalité, les pensées, les sentiments, les émotions que je vis et qui vont aussi causer une **indigestion** si j'ai de la difficulté à transiger avec celles-ci. Il y a un désordre, une disharmonie à l'intérieur de moi. Quelle est la situation ou la personne que j'ai de la difficulté à digérer ? Qu'est-ce qui se passe dans ma vie que je ne peux plus endurer, car cela en fait trop en même temps ? Je peux même en venir à être révolté contre cette situation ou contre cette personne que je critique sévèrement. Cela peut aussi être quelque chose que j'ai vu ou entendu qui m'était désagréable et qui « ne passe pas bien ». L'anxiété, l'insécurité me mettront « l'estomac à l'envers » et la digestion ne pouvant se faire normalement, je vais rejeter physiquement la nourriture comme je rejette des nouvelles idées ou des situations que je vis. J'apprends à mettre de l'amour dans la ou les situations, car j'ai une prise de conscience à faire. L'amour est l'ingrédient qui m'aidera à digérer et à faire passer les situations dans ma vie, en harmonie avec mon être.

INFARCTUS (en général)

De façon générale, un **infarctus** est la mort d'une partie des tissus d'un organe, aussi appelé **nécrose**, provenant de l'obstruction de l'artère qui amenait le sang à cette région. Même si des régions comme l'intestin, la rate, les os et les veines peuvent être atteintes, les régions les plus exposées sont le cerveau, les poumons et le myocarde, qui est une enveloppe du cœur. Comme la circulation sanguine est arrêtée brusquement par un caillot ou un dépôt de lipides (une sorte de gras) dans une artère, cela implique que la joie ne circule plus dans cette région, amenant même la mort des tissus. Selon la région affectée, je peux me demander ce qui a amené mon corps à me dire : « c'est assez, je n'en peux plus, une partie de moi se meurt ». J'ai à vérifier quels sont les besoins que j'ai pu mettre de côté et de quelle façon je pourrais remettre les choses en ordre dans ma vie pour m'aider à vivre pleinement des expériences remplies de joie et de satisfaction.

INFARCTUS (cérébral)
(voir : CERVEAU — ACCIDENTS CÉRÉBRO-VASCULAIRES [A.C.V.])

INFARCTUS (... du myocarde)
(voir : CŒUR — INFARCTUS [... du myocarde])

INFECTIONS (en général) (voir aussi : ANNEXE III, DOULEUR, FIÈVRE, INFLAMMATION, SYSTÈME IMMUNITAIRE)

L'**infection** se définit par le développement localisé ou généralisé d'un germe pathogène[65] dans l'organisme, que ce soit des bactéries, des virus, des

---

65. **Pathogène :** Qualifie ce qui entraîne la maladie.

champignons ou des parasites. Cette situation survient lorsque le système immunitaire ne parvient pas à combattre ce germe envahissant. Ce germe peut être relié dans ma vie à une situation ou à une personne avec qui je vis un conflit souvent intérieur et que je n'ai exprimé à personne. Puisqu'il n'a pas été résolu, celui-ci surgira sous forme d'**infection**. Le fait de vivre de l'irritation ou un dérangement affaiblit mon système immunitaire qui ne peut empêcher une invasion de se manifester. Je dois me poser la question : *qu'est-ce qui m'irrite ou m'affecte si profondément ?* Je peux vivre un désordre ou un traumatisme émotionnel, une crise familiale ou dans le milieu de travail ou lié au fait que je me stresse trop avec la vie. Je dois accepter ↓♥ les changements en cours, en laissant de côté la grande colère que je peux vivre. La signification de cette colère sera d'autant plus importante si l'**infection** est accompagnée de douleur ou de fièvre. Il est important d'aller voir quelle partie de mon corps est affectée. S'il s'agit par exemple d'une **infection** de mes organes sexuels, je vis une situation conflictuelle qui m'irrite et me fait vivre beaucoup de colère par rapport à ma sexualité ou à la façon dont je perçois celle-ci. L'**infection** va subsister aussi longtemps que je n'aurai pas réglé la situation, et je peux tarder à trouver une solution car j'ai peur des conséquences et des changements que cela va apporter dans ma vie. L'**infection** survient souvent à la suite d'un affaiblissement de mon système immunitaire, ce qui implique que c'est l'amour de moi-même qui est en jeu. Je dois me demander quelles sont les attitudes, les pensées que je dois changer ou les actions que je dois prendre pour amener plus d'amour dans ma vie. Comme je sais que les gens heureux ont un système immunitaire fort, je fais en sorte de prendre les moyens pour que l'amour grandisse en moi et qu'ainsi, l'amour devienne mon bouclier, ma protection.

INFECTIONS URINAIRES (voir : URINE [infections urinaires])

INFECTIONS VAGINALES (voir : VAGIN — VAGINITE)

INFIRMITÉS CONGÉNITALES

Une **infirmité** est une faiblesse, une absence, une altération ou la perte d'une fonction. La personne aux prises avec une **infirmité congénitale** aura de grands défis à relever dans sa vie. Il est important d'aller voir quelle partie du corps est affectée. Cela va être une indication du défi particulier que la personne s'est donné. Cette **infirmité** peut aussi résulter de situations conflictuelles non résolues que mes parents vivaient lorsque j'étais un fœtus ou avant, ou de mes grands-parents ou arrières grands-parents, et que je revis afin de les intégrer et d'apprendre la leçon de vie qui y est rattachée.

INFLAMMATION (voir aussi : ANNEXE III)

Une **inflammation** est une réaction locale de l'organisme contre un agent pathogène, caractérisée par la rougeur, la chaleur, la douleur et la tuméfaction (enflure, gonflement). Elle est l'expression corporelle d'une **inflammation** intérieure. Je suis **enflammé** et **enragé** par quelque chose ou quelqu'un, et cela s'exprime par mon corps. Je dois me demander quel aspect de ma vie me rend « rouge de colère », « bouillant », et qui m'amènera ultimement à vivre de la culpabilité, si celle-ci n'est déjà pas la cause de **l'inflammation.** Il est important de regarder quelle partie du corps est affectée afin d'avoir une information additionnelle sur la cause de **l'inflammation**. Il est important d'aller vérifier si une difficulté sexuelle a été vécue dans le passé, refoulée et non résolue, ou si j'ai vécu un sentiment de perte que je n'ai pas accepté ↓♥ et envers lequel je vis beaucoup d'irritabilité. Il me sera alors possible de prendre conscience de cette situation et d'avoir une compréhension nouvelle et positive de celle-ci.

INQUIÉTUDE

L'**inquiétude** se manifeste par de l'agitation, de l'angoisse, de l'appréhension. Elle résulte d'une insécurité intérieure que je vis et qui me rend très émotif. Mon **inquiétude** peut avoir sa source dans mon enfance, principalement si j'ai vécu de l'insécurité physique ou sociale, ou que j'ai eu l'impression de manquer de quelque chose sur le plan affectif, de mon éducation, ou que je me suis senti **abandonné** à un certain moment. Cette **inquiétude** peut réapparaître à l'âge adulte, lorsque je revis une situation semblable à celle que j'ai vécue dans mon enfance et qui « réactive » ce sentiment. J'ai à apprendre à faire confiance à la vie. J'ai aussi à apprendre à me faire confiance. Je dois être plus fort que mes angoisses afin de les contrôler, au lieu que ce soient elles qui me contrôlent et alimentent mon sentiment d'impuissance face à la vie.

INSOLATION (voir aussi : ACCIDENT, CHALEUR [coup de...], PEAU)

Si je m'expose trop longuement au soleil, je risque de faire une **insolation** qui se traduira par un coup de soleil (brûlure de la peau) et un coup de chaleur qui est une élévation de ma température dans mes centres nerveux. Que ce soit par accident (je me suis endormi au soleil) ou par un mauvais calcul du temps d'exposition, ou pour toute autre raison, je dois vivre de la culpabilité pour amener la vie à me « punir ainsi ». Si je suis en vacances, je peux me demander si je pense vraiment mériter ces vacances. La peau a un rapport avec ce que je vis intérieurement et ce que je vis extérieurement. Est-ce qu'il se peut que je vive de la frustration liée au fait de prendre conscience que ma vie, extérieurement, n'est pas toujours ce que je voudrais qu'elle soit intérieurement. L'intensité du coup de soleil ou du coup de chaleur m'indique l'importance d'une certaine

forme de désespoir qui m'habite. J'ai besoin d'augmenter mon estime de moi, de reconnaître qui je suis, de m'apprécier à ma juste valeur. Je demande à la vie de me montrer et de m'aider à apprécier les belles choses qu'elle me donne. Je rayonnerai ainsi davantage et je n'aurai plus besoin que « le soleil me tape dessus » pour me rappeler de prendre ma place dans la vie.

INSOMNIE

L'**incapacité à dormir** correspond à une profonde frayeur à s'abandonner et à se laisser aller. Je vis de l'insécurité et je veux avoir le contrôle sur tout ce qui se passe dans ma vie. Toutefois, quand je dors, mes « facultés mentales » dorment aussi et je suis plus vulnérable, car mes sens sont plus alertes et ouverts à l'inconnu. C'est pourquoi, en gardant mon mental occupé avec toutes sortes d'idées, toutes sortes de situations mêmes fictives et que je m'invente, j'empêche le sommeil de me gagner. Ma vie est teintée par la tension, l'anxiété, la culpabilité et parfois même, une certaine paranoïa. Cela peut résulter d'un sentiment que mon ego ou ma survivance a déjà été menacé d'une certaine façon, ce qui est compréhensible si j'ai expérimenté certains traumatismes profonds, tels un vol, un viol, etc. Il y a des chances que j'éprouve une nervosité extrême et que j'aie de la difficulté à me positionner et à prendre des décisions. C'est aussi comme si je mourrais chaque fois que je m'endors et cela réveille des craintes dont notamment l'inconnu de la nuit. L'**insomnie** peut être reliée fortement à de la **culpabilité** consciente ou inconsciente. Pour une raison ou pour une autre, je peux avoir l'impression que « je ne mérite pas de me reposer ». Ce peut être parce que je me sens coupable de ne pas réussir dans la vie, de ne pas faire tout ce qu'il faut pour mes enfants, etc. Je peux aussi m'avoir programmé en pensant que « dormir est une perte de temps ». La glande du thymus est étroitement reliée au sommeil et, du même coup, à l'énergie du cœur. L'**insomnie** peut donc être aussi reliée à mon aptitude à m'aimer moi-même, à faire confiance à l'amour et par le fait même, à la vie. J'apprends à relaxer et à relâcher le contrôle afin de permettre au sommeil de prendre place dans ma vie.

INTESTINS (maux aux...) (voir aussi : CANCER DU CÔLON / DE L'INTESTIN, INTESTINS / COLITE / CONSTIPATION / DIARRHÉE, INDIGESTION)

L'**intestin** est le centre d'absorption et d'intégration de la nourriture et des aliments aussi bien que celui des pensées, des sentiments et de ma réalité actuelle. Tout ce qui me cause de la tristesse, de la crainte, de la confusion, de la révolte, de la honte ou toute autre pensée ou sentiment discordant peut trouver une libération et créer des **problèmes intestinaux**. Puisque c'est à ce niveau que se fait la digestion, si je suis contrarié et que je me sens la victime d'un « coup bas », d'une « vacherie » ou que j'ai l'impression que quelqu'un m'a fait un « coup de cochon », j'aurai un malaise aux **intestins** car je ne le

digérerai tout simplement pas ! Je serai particulièrement touché s'il s'agit d'un membre de ma famille qui est le « salaud ». Ne pouvant pas digérer cette situation, elle va se manifester par un problème au niveau de mes **intestins.** Si c'est mon **intestin grêle** qui est touché, je peux avoir tendance à juger les situations qui se présentent à moi en ayant des opinions très tranchées par rapport à mes notions de « bien » et de « mal ». J'aurai aussi tendance à avoir l'impression de manquer de beaucoup de choses dans ma vie. Les **intestins** (particulièrement le **gros intestin**) sont aussi reliés à **mon habileté à me laisser aller**, à me sentir suffisamment en sécurité intérieurement pour être spontané. **Mes intestins symbolisent le fait de laisser circuler les événements dans ma vie**. Je peux avoir un besoin très fort de **retenir** et de **contrôler** ce qui m'arrive. Je m'accroche à certaines choses, à des personnes ou à des situations, souvent même jusqu'à vivre de la jalousie et de la possessivité et mes **intestins** sont congestionnés par tout ce que je retiens et qui n'est plus utile, pouvant causer, entre autres, la **constipation**. J'apprends à être autonome et à me dire que j'ai toutes les ressources nécessaires à l'intérieur de moi pour créer ce que je veux. La seule personne sur qui je peux avoir du contrôle, c'est moi-même !

INTESTIN (cancer de l'...) (voir : CANCER DE L'INTESTIN)

INTESTINS — COLIQUE (voir aussi : GAZ)

La **colique** est une ou des contractions résultant d'une **grande tension intérieure**, d'une situation qui m'**insécurise** et qui m'énerve tellement qu'apparaissent la congestion intestinale, les douleurs à l'estomac, aux canaux glandulaires et aux voies urinaires. Je doute de mes capacités, je manque de confiance en moi, j'ai peur de ne pas être à la hauteur, j'ignore comment m'y prendre pour résoudre un problème. Un exemple typique qui a trait aux **coliques du nourrisson,** est celui de moi en tant que mère qui a peur de ne pas prendre soin de mon bébé correctement, de ne pas en faire suffisamment. Le bébé ressent intérieurement mon anxiété et devient, à son tour, inquiet (l'enfant qui souffre de **colique** doit être entouré de calme, de patience et d'amour). J'accepte ↓♥ que dans la vie, tout arrive pour le mieux. Donc, je **lâche prise**, je fais tout mon possible avec amour. Ce que je voyais comme des problèmes et des insécurités devient tout simplement des expériences qui m'aident à poursuivre mon évolution et à grandir. Des exercices de respiration, de relaxation et de méditation peuvent m'aider à reprendre contact avec mon être intérieur, à réaliser toutes les forces qui sont en moi et à faire disparaître mon **impatience** face à une personne ou une situation qui m'**agace**.

INTESTINS — COLITE (mucosité du côlon)
(voir aussi : INFLAMMATION, INTESTINS)

La **colite** (ite = colère) est une inflammation parfois ulcéreuse du côlon, le

gros **intestin**. Le rôle du côlon peut être comparé à ma façon de me comporter, de traiter avec mon propre univers. Lorsque je suis incapable d'être moi-même face à l'autorité et face à mes relations personnelles (conjoint, parents, professeurs, patrons, etc.), je contrôle mes gestes et mes actions parce que je crains la réaction de la personne dont je veux avoir l'approbation et l'amour. Les **colites** se manifestent souvent chez les enfants qui craignent les réactions de leurs parents qui manifestent beaucoup de sévérité et qui sont très exigeants envers eux. J'ai **tellement besoin d'affection, d'amour et de valorisation** que je veux **plaire à tout prix** (même jusqu'à étouffer ma personnalité et mes besoins fondamentaux). Je ne suis pas moi-même et je n'ose pas exprimer mes émotions ; je les refoule. Je ravale à plusieurs reprises des choses que je trouve indigestes. Cette **dépendance affective** m'amène à vivre de la colère qui me ronge intérieurement, de la frustration et de l'humiliation. Si je vis ces sentiments à l'extrême, un **ulcère** surgira. Mes réactions émotionnelles m'ont averti que je devais changer mon attitude mais je n'ai pas compris. C'est maintenant le signal physique. Comment agir ? J'accepte ↓♥ que le bonheur vienne de ce que je ressens à l'intérieur. **J'apprends à m'aimer**, à être moi-même et je **prends ma place**. J'acquiers de l'indépendance et de l'autonomie et je réalise que je suis de plus en plus heureux parce que j'agis maintenant en conformité avec ma propre nature.

INTESTINS — CONSTIPATION (voir aussi : CANCER DU CÔLON)

La **constipation** prend place à l'intérieur de l'**intestin** lorsque les mouvements musculaires qui permettent l'élimination se font au ralenti, ce qui provoque un engorgement des déchets. Ces déchets ne sont que la manifestation physique de mes idées noires, de mes préoccupations, de ma colère, de la jalousie qui m'encombrent. La **constipation** est souvent associée à une diète pauvre en fibres alimentaires. Ceci est l'indication d'une grande volonté de **contrôler** les événements de ma vie et qui résulte d'une insécurité intérieure. Je suis une personne **très troublée qui a besoin de l'approbation des autres**. Par mon insécurité, je suis même porté à être mesquin. Les situations favorisant la **constipation** peuvent se produire lorsque j'expérimente une situation financière difficile, lorsque j'ai des relations conflictuelles ou lorsque je pars en voyage, car c'est là où je suis le plus susceptible de me sentir inquiet et « sans ancrage ». Je **m'accroche à mes vieilles idées et à mes biens personnels**. Ce que je connais déjà me permet un certain contrôle et me **donne une illusion de sécurité**. J'ai tellement peur d'être jugé que je refoule ma spontanéité, je m'empêche d'avancer. Je refoule aussi mes « problèmes » et mes émotions passés, de peur qu'ils ne refassent surface et que j'aie à y faire face. Quand me suis-je permis de prendre ma place et d'être moi-même ? Quelle est la dernière fois où je me suis senti libre et plein d'entrain ? Qu'est-ce qui me retient ? Je dois absolument **laisser aller** tout ce qui ne me convient plus, **lâcher prise**. J'accepte ↓♥, ici et maintenant, de me libérer du passé, d'aller de l'avant et de vivre une vie plus excitante. Je me sens beaucoup plus détendu car je fais confiance à la vie.

INTESTINS — CROHN (maladie de...)
(voir aussi : APPENDICITE, INTESTINS — DIARRHÉE)

L'**iléite** se définit comme une inflammation de la dernière partie de l'**intestin** grêle, l'iléon, caractérisée par de fortes douleurs. Dans le cas de maladies bactériennes ou virales, elle peut prendre l'apparence d'une crise d'appendicite. Les infections conséquentes au SIDA et à la tuberculose peuvent provoquer une inflammation de l'iléon mais les cas chroniques aigus se rapportent à la **maladie de Crohn**. Il peut s'agir d'une forme d'autopunition à la suite d'un sentiment de culpabilité intense. Cela touche mon estime personnelle : je ne me sens pas « à la hauteur », « pas correct », « bon à rien », « un moins que rien ». Je me déprécie tellement que j'en viens à penser que personne ne m'aime et qu'on veut me faire sentir inférieur. Ces sentiments s'ajouteront à une situation où je vis un manque, que se soit au niveau matériel ou affectif. J'ai l'impression que l'objet de ce manque m'a été usurpé d'une manière méprisable, répugnante. À cela peut s'ajouter la peur de mourir. La révolte alors gronde à l'intérieur de moi. Cela ne fait qu'augmenter ma crainte d'être rejeté par les autres. Comme j'ai l'impression de n'être rien, cette maladie peut m'aider à recevoir l'attention dont j'ai besoin et que je n'ai pas l'impression de recevoir. Mon estime personnelle est basse et je suis <u>trop ouvert, énergétiquement, au niveau de mon ventre, à recevoir n'importe quoi</u>, y compris ce qui est négatif dans mon entourage et qui peut m'affecter. Je me rejette à ce point que c'est comme si, énergétiquement, mon ventre devenait une poubelle et <u>que je permettais</u> aux gens de mon entourage de déverser leur énergie négative vers moi. Je me laisse rentrer dedans parce que je ne prends pas suffisamment ma place et que je rejette les situations, ce qui me fait vivre des diarrhées. Je suis en profonde recherche de mon identité personnelle ou spirituelle et la gravité de la maladie m'indique jusqu'à quel point cela touche à un aspect de ma vie qui est fondamental, voire essentiel. Les moyens que je pourrais prendre pour augmenter mon estime personnelle et permettre de trouver véritablement mon identité, <u>la place</u> que j'occupe dans ma famille ou dans la société, m'aideraient à retrouver plus de calme et d'harmonie dans ma vie. Le fait de trouver vraiment la place qui me revient me procurera une protection naturelle face à mon environnement. La vie est belle, j'ai moi aussi le droit de vivre !

INTESTINS — DIARRHÉE

La **diarrhée** se manifeste par un déplacement si rapide de la nourriture de l'estomac à l'**intestin** qu'elle n'a pas le temps d'être entièrement assimilée. **Cet état est souvent causé par la peur ou le désir d'éviter ou de fuir une situation ou une réalité tout à fait désagréable ou *nouvelle* pour moi.** Un flot d'idées nouvelles arrive et je n'ai pas le temps d'intégrer ceci. Je me sens pris au piège par quelque chose de nouveau pour moi et cela met ma sensibilité intérieure à l'envers ! Je me **rejette**, je m'en prends à moi-même et je suis

désespéré ! J'ai une image de moi très moche dans l'instant présent. Je me culpabilise. Je suis dépassé par ces événements. J'ai vraiment besoin de quelque chose de différent. Ce n'est pas la nourriture mais bien mes pensées **qui ne conviennent plus**. Si je véhicule constamment l'idée du rejet ou des sentiments de rejet (la peur de se sentir rejeté ou le désir de rejeter les autres) ou une situation où je me sens pris, il y a de grandes chances pour que j'aie la **diarrhée**. Si je n'écoute pas la vie et ses signaux (comme certaines personnes vivent), la **diarrhée** spontanée peut se manifester aussi. J'accepte ↓♥ de prendre le temps de voir, de sentir et d'écouter mon cœur pour voir ce qui se passe dans ma vie. Ainsi, j'intègre et j'assimile les situations de mon existence. Lorsque je ralentis vraiment, je réalise à quel point je passais tout droit (tout comme les aliments) et ne prenais pas le temps de voir les bontés et les beautés de la vie. Mon corps m'avertit que je dois faire confiance à la vie, que je suis supporté, que personne ne m'abandonne.

NOTE : Certains voyageurs en visite dans les pays pauvres du Tiers-Monde attrapent la **diarrhée**. La découverte d'une pauvreté immense et de la misère ouvre le cœur et dérange inconsciemment le mental autant que l'organisme physique. C'est souvent une réaction inconsciente.

INTESTINS — DIVERTICULITE

La **diverticulite** (ite = colère) est l'inflammation des petites cavités (**diverticules**) des parois du côlon (le gros intestin). Ce malaise est relié à de la **colère** retenue dans ma vie quotidienne. Je vis présentement une situation dans laquelle je me sens prisonnier et dont je n'arrive pas à voir l'issue ; cela me cause de la tension ou de la pression. Je me sens pris au piège. Cela me cause beaucoup de douleur et de peine. Le premier pas vers la solution est l'acceptation ↓♥. Comment puis-je régler une chose dont je refuse d'accepter ↓♥ l'existence ? J'accepte ↓♥ donc la situation comme étant une réalité et je reste ouvert au canal divin qui m'apporte l'amour nécessaire pour intégrer cette expérience. De par mon acceptation ↓♥ et mon ouverture, diverses solutions me sont offertes car je ne suis plus aveuglé par la colère.

INTESTINS — GASTRO-ENTÉRITE (voir aussi : ESTOMAC / [maux d'...] / GASTRITE, INTESTINS — DIARRHÉE, NAUSÉES)

La **gastro-entérite** est une inflammation aiguë des muqueuses **gastriques et intestinales** caractérisée par des vomissements et une diarrhée d'origine infectieuse. Il se peut qu'on puisse déterminer la « cause extérieure » et la relier à de l'ingestion d'eau ou d'aliments contaminés. Cependant, il faut aller voir la « cause intérieure » qui m'a fait vivre cet événement. Ici, l'irritant est beaucoup plus important que dans un cas de gastrite, car cela affecte non seulement le point où entrent les aliments mais aussi le point de départ du processus d'intégration, ce qui indique que je suis si irrité et si frustré par ce qui m'arrive que je ne peux absorber quoi que ce soit.

Je veux donc rejeter une situation ou une personne — quand ce n'est pas la vie elle-même — et je suis « rouge de colère », ce qui m'amène à vivre la diarrhée et le vomissement. J'ai de la difficulté à accepter ↓♥ les événements. Je peux retenir certains schèmes de pensée mentaux rendus maintenant inutiles. Une personne ou une situation m'est indigeste et se retourne contre moi en m'enflammant émotionnellement. Le désespoir me gagne et ma sensibilité est grandement perturbée. J'ai à m'ouvrir à une nouvelle réalité, à de nouvelles idées et à réapprendre à faire confiance aux autres et en la vie, en étant capable de manifester mon désappointement au lieu de le laisser gronder à l'intérieur et de me créer des maux de toutes sortes.

INTESTINS — RECTUM (voir aussi : ANUS)

Le **rectum** est le segment terminal du gros intestin qui fait suite au côlon sigmoïde et aboutit à l'orifice anal. Si quelqu'un ou quelque chose dans ma vie me contrarie et que je juge cela « mal famé » ou « salop », je voudrai expulser cette chose ou cette personne de mes pensées et de ma vie. Si je n'y arrive pas, des douleurs ou des saignements apparaîtront au **rectum**. La situation vécue implique très souvent un ou des membres de la famille. J'apprends à rester ouvert et à essayer de comprendre le pourquoi de la situation qui me dérange. Je vois que même si moi j'ai l'impression que quelqu'un a mal agi, cette personne avait probablement de bonnes raisons d'agir de la façon dont elle l'a fait et que ses motifs étaient bien fondés. Cette situation implique souvent que je me demande quelle est la place qui me revient, où je m'en vais dans la vie. Mon orientation sexuelle pourra notamment être remise en question. Il y a une grande remise en question pour savoir qui je suis, quelle direction je dois prendre. Je peux me sentir très seul et abandonné. J'apprends à reconnaître mes qualités et je crois que peu importe les décisions prises, ce qui en résultera sera toujours pour le meilleur.

INTESTINS — TÆNIA ou TÉNIA

Le **tænia** est un ver parasitaire que l'on retrouve dans l'intestin et qui peut avoir quelques milimètres ou plusieurs mètres de long. Aussi appelé **ver solitaire**, le **tænia** se développe chez une personne qui a l'impression qu'on lui impose des idées ou des façons de penser contraires aux siennes. Je me sens triste et incompris, abusé et sale. Je peux avoir l'impression que des « parasites » rôdent autour de moi. Puisque j'ai de la difficulté à m'affirmer et à dire non, je me laisse « gruger » mon énergie. Les préoccupations, les peines que j'ai de la difficulté à laisser aller vont aussi favoriser l'apparition du **tænia**. Ce goût amer rend ma digestion difficile, mes poumons laissent passer une énergie corrompue et les vers parasites s'installent, amenant irritation et nervosité. Pour guérir mon intérieur, je soigne mes idées, je fais place au plaisir et à la joie. Je prends la place qui me revient dans la vie.

INTOXICATION (voir : EMPOISONNEMENT [..., ... par la nourriture])

ITE (maladies en...) (voir : ANNEXE III)

I.V.G. (Interruption Volontaire de Grossesse)
(voir : ACCOUCHEMENT — AVORTEMENT)

IVRESSE (voir : ALCOOLISME)

JALOUSIE

Le dictionnaire définit la **jalousie** comme « un sentiment de dépit, mêlé d'envie » lié au fait qu'un autre obtient ou possède ce que j'aurais voulu obtenir ou posséder. Elle est le résultat d'une insécurité intérieure et d'une faible estime de soi et d'une faible confiance en moi qui m'amène à douter de ma capacité à créer des choses dans ma vie ou à avoir peur de perdre ce que j'ai (notamment mon conjoint). J'en viens à développer de l'agressivité et de la frustration. Je prends conscience que mes frayeurs m'amènent à exercer du contrôle sur une personne ou une situation. En fait, ce sont mes angoisses qui exercent un contrôle sur ma vie. J'apprends à faire confiance en la vie et je prends les moyens pour guérir ces blessures intérieures par la psychothérapie individuelle ou de groupe ou par une approche énergétique qui m'amènera à me connecter davantage sur mon propre pouvoir intérieur. Je me sentirai alors plus libre, plus confiant et je pourrai transposer cette liberté et cette confiance vers les autres afin de vivre plus d'harmonie avec moi-même et avec les gens qui m'entourent.

JAMBES (en général) (voir aussi : SYSTÈME LOCOMOTEUR)

Les **jambes** me transportent vers l'avant ou vers l'arrière, me donnent une direction propre, de la stabilité, de la solidité et une assise ferme. **Elles représentent donc ma capacité à avancer dans la vie, à aller de l'avant**. Mes **jambes** me permettent d'aller ou de ne pas aller à la rencontre des gens, de me rapprocher ou de m'éloigner de ceux-ci. Mes **jambes** reflètent donc tous les sentiments que je peux vivre par rapport au mouvement et à la direction à prendre et elles représentent aussi tout le domaine des **relations** avec mon entourage. Des **jambes** faibles m'indiquent qu'il y a peu d'énergie qui circule dans celles-ci, ce qui dénote chez moi un manque d'assurance, une incapacité à rester debout et à être fort devant une certaine situation ou une certaine personne. J'ai alors tendance à être dépendant des autres. Je cherche mon soutien et ma motivation chez les autres au lieu de les trouver à l'intérieur de moi. La grosseur de mes **jambes** me donne aussi des informations : si j'ai de **petites jambes,** j'ai plus de difficulté à être branché sur le monde

physique, matériel et j'aimerais mieux déléguer les responsabilités qui y sont liées que d'avoir à les assumer. Au contraire, si j'ai de **grosses jambes**, celles-ci supportent un trop gros poids : les responsabilités que j'ai décidé de prendre (surtout sur le plan matériel) et pas seulement les miennes, celles des autres parfois que j'ai acceptées ↓♥ par « obligation ».

JAMBES (maux aux...)

Lorsque j'ai de la difficulté avec mes **jambes**, je dois m'arrêter et me poser la question : *Quelle est la situation actuelle ou que je vois venir qui me fait avoir peur de l'avenir ?* Je résiste au changement, je me sens « paralysé » et je peux être tellement effrayé que j'ai le goût de prendre « mes **jambes** à mon cou » ; mais est-ce vraiment la solution ? Avec qui ai-je des difficultés rationnelles qui sont source de tension et de conflit ? J'avance et j'évolue à chaque jour, à chaque moment, et des **problèmes aux jambes** ne font que manifester qu'il existe présentement des obstacles que je dois enlever afin de continuer ma route vers un plus grand bonheur et une plus grande harmonie. Quelle que soit la nouvelle situation qui se présente à moi, je peux me faire confiance et aller au-delà de ma résistance au changement.

JAMBES — PARTIE INFÉRIEURE (mollet)

La **partie inférieure de mes jambes** se trouve au niveau du **mollet**, lequel est soutenu par les os du tibia et du péroné. Les **mollets** me permettent d'avancer. Ils représentent aussi une protection par rapport à mon passé alors que je vais de l'avant dans la vie. Si j'ai **mal** ou que j'ai des **crampes** aux **mollets**, je suis obligé de ralentir mon rythme. Est-ce que je veux arrêter certains événements qui m'attendent et me font peur ? Est-ce que j'ai l'impression que les événements se bousculent, que tout va trop vite ? Mon corps me dit que je peux faire confiance à l'avenir et que la vie s'occupe de moi.

JAMBES — PARTIE SUPÉRIEURE (cuisse)

La **partie supérieure de mes jambes**, à la hauteur de la **cuisse** qui est portée par l'os du fémur, reflète ma tendance à retenir des choses, plus souvent liées à mon passé. Si je revis constamment le passé ou si je vis de la culpabilité par rapport à certains événements, cela aura pour effet de s'emmagasiner dans mes **cuisses**, celles-ci devenant plus grosses. Je peux aussi avoir gardé de la rancune ou de l'amertume. C'est comme si mon passé me retenait vers l'arrière et m'empêchait d'aller de l'avant. Mes blessures et mes traumatismes me font « traîner la jambe ». De grosses jambes peuvent aussi être un signe que j'emmagasine trop (tant sur le plan matériel, émotionnel, qu'intellectuel), que je garde des choses « au cas où » ! par insécurité, par peur de manquer de quelque chose ou de quelqu'un. Tout comme les écureuils, je fais des réserves en prévision d'une disette possible mais souvent non fondée. Il est bon que je « fasse du ménage » afin de ne garder que ce qui est bénéfique pour moi.

JAMBES — VARICES (voir : SANG — VARICES)

JAUNISSE ou ICTÈRE (voir aussi : FOIE [maux de...],
SANG / [maux de...] / CIRCULATION SANGUINE)

La **jaunisse** est causée :
1) par un excès de bilirubine, sous-produit du foie décomposant les vieilles cellules sanguines rouges.
2) par l'excès de bile entrant dans le flot sanguin.

Le résultat est une coloration jaune de la peau et du « blanc de l'œil ». Comme c'est relié au nettoyage du système sanguin, j'ai donc de la difficulté à « nettoyer » mes émotions. J'éprouve des émotions amères très intenses d'envie, de désappointement, de frustration, au point où « je fais une **jaunisse** de telle situation » et je « tourne au jaune ». Je vis beaucoup de rancœur. Je deviens tellement tranchant et excessif dans mes idées et mes opinions que je m'y accroche, créant un déséquilibre à l'intérieur de moi. Je dois apprendre à m'ouvrir aux gens qui m'entourent car j'ai beaucoup à apprendre d'eux.

JOINTURE (voir : ARTICULATIONS)

KÉRATITE (voir : YEUX — KÉRATITE)

KÉRION (voir : CHEVEUX — TEIGNE)

KILLIAN (polype de...) (voir : NEZ — KILLIAN [polype de...])

KLEPTOMANIE (voir aussi : DÉPENDANCE, NÉVROSE)

Si, de façon compulsive, je suis porté à commettre des vols sans raisons utilitaires, alors je souffre de **kleptomanie**. Je vis une tension qui provient d'un vide intérieur allié à un sentiment de culpabilité. Alors, pour moi la fin justifie les moyens et c'est comme si je me lançais le défi de pouvoir m'approprier ce qui est défendu. J'en retire un soulagement, même si le remords peut se manifester à moi par la suite. Il se peut qu'inconsciemment, j'espère qu'on va me prendre « la main dans le sac » car c'est pour moi une façon d'attirer l'attention. Le fait de poser un geste défendu peut être pour moi une façon de démontrer ma révolte face à l'autorité et de « baver » celle-ci. Cette autorité que je n'ai pas acceptée ↓♥ étant jeune était soit celle de mon père, de ma mère ou de la personne qui avait la charge de mon éducation. Je peux me diriger en psychothérapie afin de pouvoir identifier ce vide intérieur ou cette révolte face à l'autorité et de pouvoir remettre de l'amour dans la situation. Je vivrai ainsi une plus grande paix intérieure et « les autres s'en porteront mieux aussi ».

KYSTE (voir aussi : OVAIRES [maux aux...], TUMEUR[S])

Un **kyste** se forme lorsque j'entretiens des remords face à une situation passée, lorsque je garde en moi de la peine, du chagrin, des souffrances ; ce peut être aussi des remords face à un projet, à un désir que je n'ai pu réaliser. Je me suis « gonflé », j'ai « accumulé » des informations, des données de toutes sortes pour un projet que je n'ai jamais pu rendre à terme : elles sont demeurées prisonnières de mon corps et de mon esprit. C'est un refus de pardonner. « Je me pardonne, je m'aime, je me tourne vers l'avenir, je suis donc en paix. » Le **kyste** peut correspondre aussi à la solidification d'attitudes et de « patterns mentaux » qui se sont accumulés inconsciemment durant une certaine période de temps. Ceux-ci peuvent me servir de barrière de protection, me gardant emprisonné dans un cadre bien délimité et m'évitant de faire face à certaines personnes ou à certaines situations. Cela a aussi pour résultat de me freiner ou de m'empêcher d'aller de l'avant car j'ai de la difficulté à m'ouvrir à d'autres opinions ou aux autres façons de penser. Mon ego peut être profondément blessé et ma rancœur se solidifie pour devenir un **kyste**. J'accepte ↓♥ de laisser circuler l'énergie librement à travers moi et j'ai confiance dans le fait de mettre de l'avant mes projets et je demande à voir les solutions pour que tout « coule » mieux dans ma vie.

LANGUE

La **langue** est un organe musculaire auquel est relié le goût. Si je veux exprimer une pensée verbalement, j'ai besoin de ma **langue**. Si je me « mords la **langue** » je dois me demander si je m'en veux pour ce que je viens de dire, si je vis de la culpabilité. J'ai la **langue engourdie ou enflée** quand je veux goûter davantage à la vie, ou que j'ai du « dégoût » face à une personne, une chose ou une situation. J'apprends à « goûter » toutes les joies qui s'offrent à moi.

LANGUE (cancer de la...) (voir : CANCER DE LA LANGUE)

LARMES (voir : PLEURER)

LARYNGITE (voir : GORGE — LARYNGITE)

LARYNX (voir : GORGE — LARYNX)

LARYNX (cancer du...) (voir : CANCER DU LARYNX)

LASSITUDE (voir aussi : FATIGUE [en général], SANG — HYPOGLYCÉMIE, TENSION ARTÉRIELLE — HYPOTENSION [trop basse])

Je ressens la **lassitude** quand mon corps est fatigué, j'ai le goût d'abandonner. L'ennui et le découragement gagnent mon cerveau. Souvent, mon sang s'appauvrit, la joie de vivre n'étant plus présente. Je peux reprendre goût à la vie en faisant des choses que j'aime, en me faisant plaisir. Cela m'aidera à me « remonter le moral ».

LÈPRE (voir aussi : CHRONIQUE [maladie...],
NERFS, PEAU / [en général] / [maux de...])

La **lèpre** est une maladie infectieuse chronique qui atteint la peau, les muqueuses, les nerfs. La personne qui en est atteinte se sent sale, impure, elle ne se sent pas à la hauteur. Elle s'autodétruit. Si j'ai la **lèpre**, j'ai l'impression que je n'ai pas tout ce qu'il faut pour assumer ma vie, mes responsabilités. De toute façon, est-ce que je mérite de vivre ? J'ai tendance à me poser souvent cette question et je vais me laisser aller[66], me sentant incapable de changer quoi que ce soit dans ma vie. J'accepte ↓♥ dorénavant de me nourrir de pensées d'amour et d'harmonie afin de me refaire une nouvelle peau qui reflétera davantage l'être divin que je suis.

LESBIENNE (voir : HOMOSEXUALITÉ)

LEUCÉMIE (voir : SANG — LEUCÉMIE)

LEUCOPÉNIE (voir : SANG — LEUCOPÉNIE)

LEUCORRHÉE
(voir aussi : CANDIDA, INFECTIONS, PEAU — DÉMANGEAISONS,
SALPINGITE)

La **leucorrhée** est aussi appelée **pertes blanches** ou **pertes vaginales**. C'est une infection vaginale qui démontre soit un refus d'avoir des relations sexuelles, soit de la culpabilité ou de l'agressivité envers mon partenaire, ou le fait de ne pas en avoir. Elle résulte souvent de mon impression que je suis impuissante face à mon conjoint, et comme j'ai l'impression de n'avoir aucun pouvoir sur lui, cette maladie devient comme un outil de manipulation qui me fera sentir en contrôle de la situation et donc, de mon conjoint, parce que c'est MOI qui décide si je peux avoir des relations sexuelles ou non. Je dois prendre ma place, reconnaître ma vraie valeur et me convaincre que je suis la seule personne qui peut avoir le contrôle sur moi et sur ma vie.

---

66. **Laisser aller :**Ici, on fait référence au fait de « démissionner » et non pas de « se détacher »

LÈVRES

Par les **lèvres**, je peux comprendre **l'ouverture ou la fermeture d'esprit**, ce que je veux ou ne veux pas dire. Je peux percevoir de la tension, des soucis, des chagrins ou des craintes par le fendillement ou l'assèchement des **lèvres**. Elles peuvent être charnues si j'ai de la joie, du plaisir, de l'amour dans le cœur, ou plutôt minces lorsque je suis plus retenu et même rigide face à mes désirs et aux plaisirs de la vie. Chez une femme, les **lèvres** du **vagin** subissent les mêmes répercussions causées par les mêmes troubles sauf qu'il y a plus de chance que tout malaise ou toute maladie relié à celles-ci se rapporte à l'expression de sa sexualité et de sa féminité. **La lèvre inférieure représente mon côté masculin, rationnel, la raison, et la lèvre supérieure représente mon côté féminin, réceptif, émotionnel.** Il est important que j'exprime mes sentiments, autant négatifs si je suis mécontent (sinon mes **lèvres** peuvent enfler), que positifs tels que des compliments, mon affection, mon appréciation etc. Car c'est avec mes **lèvres** que je peux donner un baiser et montrer mon amour aux gens que j'aime.

LÈVRES SÈCHES

J'ai les **lèvres sèches** quand je ressens une grande fatigue, quand je me sens seul ou quand j'ai des soucis. Ma joie de vivre s'en va et j'éprouve peu de plaisir dans mes échanges avec les autres. Cette perte de joie sera d'autant plus grande si, en plus, mes **lèvres** vont jusqu'à **saigner**. Je me permets d'augmenter ma communication avec les autres et « d'embrasser la vie » avec plus d'amour.

LÈVRES VAGINALES (voir : VULVE)

LITHIASE BILIAIRE (voir : CALCULS BILIAIRES)

LITHIASE URINAIRE (voir : CALCULS RÉNAUX)

LOCOMOTION (voir : SYSTÈME LOCOMOTEUR)

LOMBAGO (voir : DOS [maux de...] — BAS DU DOS)

LOMBALGIE (voir : DOS [maux de...] — BAS DU DOS)

LORDOSE (voir : COLONNE VERTÉBRALE [déviation de la...] — LORDOSE)

LOUCHER (voir : YEUX — STRABISME CONVERGENT)

LOUPE (voir : KYSTE, PEAU / [en général] / [maux de...])

LSD (consommation de...) (voir : DROGUE)

LUMBAGO (voir : DOS [maux de...] — BAS DU DOS)

LUPUS (voir : PEAU — LUPUS)

LUXATION (voir aussi : ACCIDENT, COLÈRE, DOULEUR)

La **luxation** concerne le déplacement de deux extrémités osseuses d'une articulation. Ce peut être l'épaule, le coude, les doigts, le genou, les vertèbres, la hanche. Souvent, une **luxation** survient à la suite d'un coup, d'un choc ou d'un mouvement forcé. Je connais l'expression qui dit : « Je me suis <u>déboîté</u> le genou » ou « Je me suis <u>déboîté</u> l'épaule. » Selon l'endroit où s'est effectuée la **luxation,** je dois me demander quelle peur ou quel choc émotionnel me donne l'impression d'être pris « comme si je me faisais mettre en boîte ». Mon corps a ainsi réagi à l'inverse en assumant le contrecoup émotionnel. Je prends conscience de la liberté que j'ai à l'intérieur de moi et je laisse entrer de la lumière intérieure sur toutes situations qui semblent me limiter, afin que je développe plus d'harmonie envers la vie.

LYMPHATISME

Le **lymphatisme** se caractérise par une pâleur anémique, une mollesse des tissus et une peau fine. En d'autres mots, ne pas se faire violence, ne rien faire, démontrer un laisser-aller, un manque d'audace et de vitalité, ne trouver aucune motivation dans la vie. C'est un signe que je dois me reprendre en mains, bouger, mettre des choses de l'avant afin de faire circuler l'énergie et de sortir de cette léthargie qui m'amène à en faire de moins en moins et à m'enfoncer de plus en plus dans le négativisme.

LYMPHE (maux lymphatiques)
(voir aussi : CANCER DES GANGLIONS [... du système lymphatique], GANGLION [... lymphatique], INFECTIONS, SYSTÈME IMMUNITAIRE)

La **lymphe** contient des globules blancs, des protéines et des lipides (des formes de gras). Elle lutte contre les infections et rejette ce qui est mauvais pour le corps. Les glandes enflées ou les nœuds lymphatiques bloqués peuvent impliquer un blocage émotionnel ou un reniement des émotions, me laissant ainsi sans protection et vulnérable à tous poisons envahisseurs ou néfastes de

certains sentiments. Elle me dit de faire attention à mes pensées, de bien gérer mes émotions et d'accepter ↓♥ que la joie circule librement en moi. Je dois revenir à l'essentiel et mettre mon attention sur les vraies valeurs de la vie plutôt que sur le matériel et les choses dont j'ai l'impression de manquer.

LYMPHOME (voir : HODGKIN [maladie de...])

MÂCHOIRES (maux de...)

Les **mâchoires** sont des os essentiels pour manger, pour commencer le processus de digestion et d'assimilation de ce que je prends, soit la nourriture ou la réalité qui m'entoure. Les **problèmes de mâchoire** peuvent survenir lorsque je serre les dents parce qu'il y a du refoulement et que je retiens toute l'énergie reliée à la colère, à l'obstination, à l'entêtement, et peut-être même à une envie inconsciente de me venger de quelqu'un ou de quelque chose. Lorsque je **grince des dents,** je vis de l'insécurité. Je peux voir aussi mes **mâchoires** se décalcifier et se ramollir. Elles me montrent comment moi aussi je peux être « mou » dans certaines situations, spécialement quand j'ai l'impression qu'on a ri de moi et qu'on ne prêtait pas attention à ce que je disais. Il s'en suit une très grande dévalorisation de moi-même. Je peux aussi me sentir dominé, étant impuissant à m'exprimer, soit à cause de ma timidité ou de mes peurs. On peut aussi m'avoir défendu de parler, ce que j'ai interprété comme : « Je ne dois pas avoir grand chose d'intéressant à dire !!! ». Lorsque mes **mâchoires bloquent**, je suis dans l'incapacité de m'exprimer, de contrôler ce qui m'entoure, je refoule mes émotions. Je dois me détendre, laisser l'énergie circuler librement.

MAIGREUR (voir aussi : ANOREXIE, POIDS [excès de...])

Une sous-alimentation ou une consommation excessive peut entraîner la **maigreur** ou se transformer en **obésité**. La nervosité, l'anxiété, la consommation de médicaments, les grandes peurs ou de très grandes joies sont des facteurs qui font qu'un individu engraisse et que l'autre maigrit. La personne **maigre** est souvent très émotive, avec une très grande sensibilité et ne sait pas toujours comment exprimer ses sentiments, car ayant déjà été blessée, elle veut se protéger pour ne plus avoir à souffrir. Cette même sensibilité se retrouve chez une personne ayant un **excès de poids**, celle-ci se créant une protection et une barrière par son physique plus imposant. Les gens qui sont **anorexiques** refusent de vivre, aime mieux mourir que d'accepter ↓♥ l'amour.

MAINS (en général)

Les **mains** représentent ma capacité de prendre, de donner ou de recevoir. Elles sont l'expression intime de moi-même dans l'Univers et la puissance du

toucher est tellement grande que je me sens impuissant quand mes **mains** sont endommagées. Elles ont un caractère unique : tout comme mes empreintes digitales, elles représentent mon passé, mon présent et mon avenir. J'ai entre les **mains** les situations de mon quotidien et l'état de mes **mains** me montre jusqu'à quel point je saisis ma réalité, comment j'exprime l'amour aussi bien que la haine (sous la forme du poing). Si j'ai les **mains froides**, je me retire émotionnellement d'une situation ou d'une relation dans laquelle je suis impliqué. Je peux aussi refuser de prendre soin de mes besoins de base et de me faire plaisir. Les **mains moites**, elles, m'indiquent un taux excessif d'anxiété et de nervosité. Je suis débordé par mes émotions, me sentant peut-être trop impliqué ou trop actif dans une certaine situation de ma vie quotidienne. Si j'ai de la **douleur** ou des **crampes**, c'est que je me refuse à être flexible face aux situations présentes. Je dois me demander ce qui me dérange ou ce que je ne veux pas réaliser. Je peux avoir un sentiment d'incapacité ou vivre une grande peur face à l'échec. Cela m'amène à vouloir tout « maîtriser » avec mes **mains**, à vouloir tout posséder au cas où quelque chose ou quelqu'un me « filerait entre les doigts ». Si, de plus, mes **mains saignent** (ex. : mains sèches, eczéma, etc.), il y a sûrement une situation dans ma vie, un rêve, un projet que j'ai l'impression de ne pas pouvoir réaliser et cela m'amène à vivre de la tristesse. Alors, la joie de vivre s'en va. Si mes **mains paralysent**, je peux me sentir « paralysé » en ce qui a trait aux moyens à prendre pour réaliser une certaine tâche ou une certaine action et je vis de l'impuissance par rapport à cela. Aussi, la paralysie des **mains** peut survenir à la suite d'une activité mentale très intense où je me sens surexcité, contrarié et où la pression bout à l'intérieur de moi. Peut-être même que j'ai le goût de « tordre le cou » à quelqu'un avec mes **mains**. Si je me **blesse les mains**, peut-être que je résiste au toucher, évitant une certaine intimité, soit le toucher que je peux donner ou recevoir d'une autre personne. Cette crainte d'entrer en contact peut être rattachée à un événement présent particulier qui me rappelle un abus vécu dans le passé. J'apprends à lâcher prise et à « tendre les **mains** vers le ciel », en prenant conscience que le seul pouvoir que j'ai est sur moi-même et non pas sur les autres.

MAINS (arthrose des...) (voir : ARTHRITE — ARTHROSE)

MAINS — DÉVIATION DE DUPUYTREN
(voir aussi : DOIGTS — / ANNULAIRE / AURICULAIRE)

La déviation de **Dupuytren** est une affection de la main caractérisée par une flexion de certains doigts vers la paume, principalement l'annulaire et l'auriculaire, et ce, de façon permanente. Cette maladie dénote une « crispation » dans mes attitudes, laissant transparaître une certaine fermeture face à mon conjoint ou à mes enfants. J'ai avantage à devenir plus flexible et ouvert en exprimant davantage mes états d'âme.

MAJEUR (voir : DOIGTS — MAJEUR)

MAL DE L'AIR (voir : MAL DE MER)

MAL D'ALTITUDE (voir : MAL DES MONTAGNES)

MAL AU CŒUR (voir : NAUSÉES)

MAL AU DOS (voir : DOS [en général...])

MAL DE GORGE (voir : GORGE — PHARYNGITE)

MAL DES MONTAGNES (voir aussi : APPÉTIT [perte d'...] BALLONNEMENTS, OREILLES — BOURDONNEMENTS D'OREILLES, NAUSÉES, TÊTE [maux de...], VERTIGES)

Lorsque je vais en altitude, il peut se produire un ensemble de troubles qui proviennent du fait que l'oxygène y est plus rare. Lorsque je monte ainsi, je change de niveau de conscience, ce qui peut provoquer un choc pour moi. Les troubles que je vis ne sont que le reflet de mes angoisses et de mes blessures intérieures conscientes ou inconscientes. Il est certain que plus j'aurai un corps physique en forme, plus il me sera facile de supporter, jusque dans le physique, ces changements de conscience intérieure. J'ai à apprendre à rester calme et confiant envers moi-même et envers la vie et à développer davantage ce sentiment de liberté qui m'habite.

MAL DE MER (voir aussi : MAL DES TRANSPORTS)

Le **mal de mer** est la sensation de ne pas avoir le contrôle de la situation, de se faire ballotter par les événements de la vie, l'impression de tout perdre. N'ayant pas « les deux pieds sur terre », je vis une certaine insécurité qui prend des proportions encore plus grandes quand j'ai des appréhensions face à l'avenir et face à tout ce qui est inconnu. Cela se manifeste par des nausées. Je dois me demander ce que je ne digère pas ou que j'ai envie de rejeter, que je n'ai pas accepté ↓♥ . Il arrive aussi très souvent que tout **mal des transports** (bateau, avion, auto, train etc.) soit relié à ma peur (consciente ou inconsciente) de la mort.

MAL DE TÊTE (voir : TÊTE [maux de...])

MAL DES TRANSPORTS
(voir aussi : ANXIÉTÉ, MAL DE MER, NAUSÉES, VERTIGES)

Je vis de l'insécurité, de l'inconfort. Cela dérange mes habitudes établies et je peux avoir l'impression de perdre le contrôle de ce qui se passe dans ma vie. L'inconnu m'effraie. Je dois avoir confiance dans l'avenir, je dois accepter ↓♥ de vivre de nouvelles expériences, en sachant que j'en sortirai grandi.

MAL DE VENTRE (voir aussi : INTESTINS, VENTRE)

Pour l'enfant comme pour l'adulte, le **mal de ventre** démontre un sentiment d'abandon, de solitude. C'est le refus de communiquer, la crainte de ne pas être écouté. Je peux faire en sorte de me parler pour me rassurer et me donner plus confiance en moi-même. J'accepte ↓♥ , de plus, de communiquer avec mon entourage en laissant circuler l'amour vers les autres.

MAL DE VOITURE (voir : MAL DE MER)

MAL DU VOYAGE (voir : MAL DES TRANSPORTS)

MALADIE(S)

Lorsque la santé d'un être vivant est affectée, il fait face à la **maladie**. Cependant, la **maladie** implique une cause, des symptômes, des signes cliniques, une évolution, un traitement. Elle est un signe que mon corps m'envoie pour m'informer d'un conflit ou d'un traumatisme que je vis par rapport à moi-même et/ou par rapport à mon environnement. Décoder le message m'aidera à retrouver la santé plus rapidement.

MALADIE D'ADDISON (voir : ADDISON [maladie d'...])

MALADIE D'ALZHEIMER (voir : ALZHEIMER [maladie d'...])

MALADIE DE BECHTEREWS (ANCYLOSING, STONDYLITIS)

La **maladie de Bechterews** est le résultat d'une rigidité et d'un manque de souplesse dans sa façon de penser. Je mets mon ego de côté, celui-ci prenant trop de place. Je dois accepter face à l'amour d'être plus flexible (envers moi-même), de faire confiance aux situations de la vie.

MALADIE DE BRIGHT (voir : BRIGHT [maladie de...])

MALADIE CHRONIQUE (voir : CHRONIQUE [maladie ...])

MALADIE DE CROHN (voir : INTESTINS — CROHN [maladie de...])

MALADIE DE DUPUYTREN
(voir : MAINS — DÉVIATION DE DUPUYTREN)

MALADIE chez L'ENFANT
(voir aussi : MALADIES DE L'ENFANCE)

De façon générale, on se réfère aux malaises ou **maladies** décrites dans ce dictionnaire. Aussi, si je suis cet enfant qui vit un malaise ou une **maladie**, il y a de forte chance que l'expression de la **maladie** manifeste le malaise intérieur de l'un ou l'autre de mes parents. Mes parents pourront ne pas développer de maladie mais ma grande sensibilité me connecte à la réalité intérieure de mes parents. Je suis alors en résonnance avec l'enfant intérieur de mes parents. La maladie que j'ai présentement ne met en évidence que la prise de concience que j'ai à faire **aussi**. Mes parents ne sont pas coupables de ce que je vis.

MALADIES DE L'ENFANCE
(voir aussi : MALADIE CHEZ L'ENFANT, OREILLONS)

La rubéole, la rougeole, la picote, la coqueluche, les oreillons, la scarlatine, la varicelle, bref, toutes les **maladies propres à l'enfance** coïncident habituellement avec des périodes d'évolution de l'enfant. Ces **maladies** arrivent souvent durant les difficultés scolaires ou lorsque l'enfant vit un conflit parental et lorsqu'il est anxieux face à une situation. Ce peut être un temps de repos que le corps exige. En donnant à l'enfant de la tendresse, de l'amour, de l'attention, cela lui permettra de se renforcer afin d'avancer dans la vie avec plus de confiance.

MALADIE DE FRIEDREICH (voir : ATAXIE DE FRIEDREICH)

MALADIE DE HANSEN (voir : LÈPRE)

MALADIES HÉRÉDITAIRES

Au sens médical du terme, les **maladies héréditaires** se transmettent par les gènes provenant des cellules reproductrices d'un ou des deux parents. En fait, si je veux parler d'**hérédité**, ce sont plutôt les pensées, les émotions ou les conflits intérieurs des parents ou des grands-parents qui n'ont pas été réglés. Par exemple, si je dis que le diabète est **héréditaire** dans ma famille parce que mon grand-père était diabétique, mon père était diabétique et que je

suis diabétique, c'est plutôt que mon grand-père vivait de la **tristesse profonde** (la tristesse profonde <u>est la cause</u> métaphysique du diabète), que mon père vivait de la tristesse profonde et que moi, je vis de la tristesse profonde. Alors, au lieu de penser que ma maladie est **héréditaire** et que je ne peux rien y changer, je pourrai alors commencer à chercher comment changer mes pensées, mes émotions ou régler le conflit intérieur qui m'a amené à vivre cette maladie. En gardant à l'esprit que la maladie doit favoriser une prise de conscience personnelle, je sais cependant que la raison métaphysique de ma maladie en ce qui concerne mes pensées et mes émotions se retrouve chez l'un ou l'autre de mes parents ou chez les deux, bien qu'eux n'aient pas forcément développé la maladie.

MALADIE DE HODGKIN (voir : HODGKIN [maladie de...])

MALADIE IMMUNITAIRE (voir : SYSTÈME IMMUNITAIRE)

MALADIES INCURABLES

Incurable veut dire « qui ne peut être guéri par aucune forme de médecine. » Je dois me demander si cela fait mon affaire d'avoir une **maladie** dite **incurable**. En quoi cela peut-il m'arranger ? Suis-je tenu d'être d'accord avec cette étiquette **d'incurable** qui signifie qu'il n'y a plus rien à faire pour y remédier ? Je dois m'intérioriser pour trouver la cause profonde de ce mal : la peur, la colère, la jalousie... peuvent en être la cause. Je dois accepter ↓♥ que l'amour circule librement en moi, parce qu'il n'y a que l'amour qui peut tout guérir.

MALADIES INFANTILES (voir : MALADIES DE L'ENFANCE)

MALADIES KARMIQUES

Je viens sur terre pour poursuivre une évolution. J'ai des expériences à faire et à vivre pour arriver à une transformation intérieure. Si j'arrive au monde avec une infirmité, c'est que des « choses » n'ont pas été réglées dans d'autres vies (pour ceux qui y croient). Prendre conscience et accepter ↓♥ de vivre l'expérience sont les premiers pas vers une guérison, tant physique qu'émotionnelle. À ce moment-là, tout est possible, car la transformation intérieure mène à la guérison physique.

MALADIE DE PARKINSON
(voir : CERVEAU — PARKINSON [maladie de...])

MALADIE PSYCHOSOMATIQUE

Le mot **psychosomatique** indique le rapport qu'il peut y avoir entre l'esprit (psycho) et le corps (soma). À l'origine, on croyait que l'esprit avait une influence sur le corps et, inversement, que le corps avait une influence sur l'esprit. Toutefois, cette influence que l'on attribue au corps sur l'esprit a été peu à peu remisée, de sorte que le terme **psychosomatique,** dans le langage médical, signifie surtout la relation de l'esprit au corps. Qui plus est, lorsque je me fais dire que ma **maladie** est **psychosomatique,** c'est un peu comme si j'avais une **maladie** imaginaire et que cela se passait seulement dans ma tête. Du point de vue métaphysique, toutes les **maladies** ont leur origine au-delà du physique et, donc, je pourrais dire qu'elles sont toutes **psychosomatiques**. Je dois traiter mon corps au meilleur de ma connaissance en utilisant le savoir des professionnels de la santé, tout en cherchant la cause réelle qui a amené le malaise ou la **maladie** à se manifester. Le subconscient a un pouvoir énorme de régénération des tissus ou la capacité de produire des effets physiques suivant l'interprétation qu'il fait. Voici quelques exemples. On retrouve une personne morte dans le wagon frigorifique d'un train, alors qu'elle s'y était enfermée accidentellement. L'autopsie a révélé que la personne était morte gelée, alors que le système de réfrigération ne fonctionnait pas, ce que la victime ne savait probablement pas. Les personnes marchent pieds nus sur des braises et ne développent ni brûlure aux pieds ni cloche d'eau, le subconscient n'ayant enregistré aucun danger par suggestion, etc. **TOUTES LES MALADIES APPARAISSENT À LA SUITE D'UN CONFLIT, D'UN CHOC ÉMOTIONNEL, D'UN TRAUMATISME CONSCIENT OU INCONSCIENT. Le cerveau déclenche alors un mécanisme de survie biologique en rapport avec le conflit ou avec le traumatisme vécu. Il s'agit par la suite de pouvoir décoder le message pour modifier le programme que le cerveau envoie pour rétablir la santé.** Sachant cela, je dois cependant continuer à prendre soin de mon corps physique pour ramener celui-ci à un état représentant plus la santé.

MALADIE DE RAYNAUD (voir : RAYNAUD [maladie de...])

MALADIE DU SOMMEIL (voir : NARCOLEPSIE)

MALADIES TRANSMISES SEXUELLEMENT (M.T.S.)
(voir : VÉNÉRIENNES [maladies...])

MALADIES VÉNÉRIENNES (voir : VÉNÉRIENNES [maladies...])

MALAISE

Un **malaise** n'est pas une maladie mais plutôt un inconfort que je ressens et dont l'intensité peut varier. La façon de décoder le **malaise** est la même que pour une maladie. Cependant, les symptômes cliniques sont plus vagues et peuvent aller de l'indisposition à l'évanouissement. Comme pour la maladie, le **malaise** provient d'un conflit ou d'un traumatisme conscient ou inconscient. Le **malaise** peut être passager mais il peut indiquer un conflit intérieur à régler avant que le message ne soit envoyé plus fortement sous forme de maladie.

MALARIA ou PALUDISME
(voir aussi : COMA, FIÈVRE, SANG [maux de...])

La **malaria** se manifeste par de fortes fièvres. C'est de la critique et du refoulement contre quelqu'un ou contre une situation, souvent par rapport à une situation où je me suis senti séparé de quelque chose ou de quelqu'un que j'aime. La rancœur et le ressentiment se sont emparés de moi et mon mental prend plaisir à « ruminer » ces sentiments néfastes pour moi. Pour me libérer de cette fièvre, je dois m'intérioriser pour laisser sortir cette tension, régler cette situation.

MALENTENDANT (voir : OREILLES — SURDITÉ)

MAMELLES (voir : SEIN)

MANIE (voir aussi : ANGOISSE, ANXIÉTÉ)

Les **manies** sont des habitudes qui cachent de l'angoisse et de l'anxiété. Cet état d'agitation amène une surexcitation dans les mouvements et une humeur exaltée. C'est une façon de rechercher la paix et le calme. Ce peut être une forme de fuite puisque je m'oblige à évoluer toujours dans le même cadre, m'empêchant ainsi d'explorer de nouvelles avenues, afin de toujours me sentir en sécurité et maître de la situation. Je dois déterminer quelle est la source de cette anxiété afin de retrouver plus de calme intérieur et plus d'harmonie. Je verrai ainsi la vie avec plus de paix et de sérénité. Mes gestes et mes attitudes seront plus en accord avec ma sagesse intérieure.

MARCHE IRRÉGULIÈRE (voir : CLAUDICATION)

MARIJUANA (consommation de...) (voir : DROGUE)

MASCULIN (principe...) (voir aussi : FÉMININ [principe...])

Le **principe masculin** est représenté par le côté droit du corps et le côté gauche du cerveau. Il est aussi appelé le côté YANG, en médecine chinoise, ou le côté rationnel en Occident. Les qualités dominantes sont le courage, la puissance, la logique. C'est le côté rationnel, autonome, matérialiste de l'être. Il représente aussi l'aspect intellectuel, le côté actif de ma personne qui prend les idées et les intuitions de mon côté féminin et qui les met à exécution. **Chaque être humain, tant homme que femme, possède un côté masculin (YANG) et un côté féminin (YIN).** Puisque j'ai développé mon **côté masculin** en analysant et en voulant « devenir comme mon père », il y a de fortes chances que nous ayons tous les deux des points très similaires par rapport aux qualités et aux caractéristiques nommées au début. Je dois me souvenir que c'est lorsque je peux équilibrer mon **côté masculin** et mon côté féminin que je peux atteindre ma pleine réalisation.

MASOCHISME (voir : SADOMASOCHISME)

MASTITE (voir : SEIN — MASTITE)

MASTOÏDITE (voir aussi : FIÈVRE, INFLAMMATION, OREILLES — OTITE)

La **mastoïdite** est l'inflammation qui se produit à la base de l'os temporal, appelé mastoïde, juste en arrière des oreilles. La **mastoïdite** peut se produire lorsque je refuse d'écouter. Je suis contrarié dans ce que je viens d'entendre, par rapport à quelqu'un ou à quelque chose qui me dérange. Je vis de la peine et, quand je suis enfant, je peux ne pas comprendre ce qui est dit, ce qui provoque de l'insécurité. Ma crainte me fait vouloir ne plus entendre ce qui se dit. « Je suis en paix. L'harmonie et la joie circulent en moi. MERCI ! »

MAUVAISE HALEINE (voir : BOUCHE — HALEINE [mauvaise...])

MAUX DIVERS

Lorsque je vis des **maux divers** plus ou moins définis, cela est souvent le signe d'un besoin d'amour. J'ai besoin d'être réconforté, serré dans des bras où je pourrai me sentir compris, accepté ↓♥ tel que je suis. Je fais confiance à la vie et je vais chercher cet amour dont j'ai besoin à travers les situations de la vie, les animaux et les personnes qui sont prêtes à me prodiguer cet amour.

MAUX DE TÊTE (voir : TÊTE [maux de...])

MÉCHANCETÉ (voir aussi : RAISON [j'ai...])

La **méchanceté** est un désir maladif, de la haine exprimée dans le but de faire mal, que ce soit en parole ou en action. Je veux ainsi me prouver que je suis « correct » et que « j'ai raison ». Cela peut provenir de grandes blessures, ce qui m'amène à retourner ma hargne et ma frustration vers les autres. Comme j'en veux à la vie ou à des personnes pour la souffrance que je vis, je veux me venger, pensant y trouver une quelconque satisfaction. C'est une façon pour moi de faire sortir mon agressivité pour aller chercher plus de paix intérieure. Lorsque je peux identifier un tel comportement chez moi, je peux demander de l'aide afin d'être mieux avec moi-même. Car même si j'exprime mon irritabilité par de la **méchanceté**, je me rends bien compte que cela n'apaise ma souffrance que temporairement. Je pourrai ainsi développer des attitudes d'ouverture et de bonté envers les gens qui m'entourent et vivre une plus grande paix intérieure.

MÉCONTENTEMENT

Je ne suis pas satisfait de ce qui se passe dans ma vie. Je pourrais pourtant l'être, mais il y a toujours un « mais... » Je suis peut-être trop perfectionniste. Je refoule de la pression, j'ai un désir de vengeance non exprimé verbalement. Le **mécontentement** se voit souvent dans l'expression du visage. Je dois chercher la cause de ce **mécontentement** pour ainsi me permettre d'apporter des changements positifs en prenant des moyens appropriés pour y parvenir. Je serai alors le premier à bénéficier de plus de joie dans ma vie, ce qui se reflétera dans mon entourage.

MÉDECINE

Le mot **médecine** vient de maladie. Ainsi, même s'il existe une **médecine** préventive et prédictive, la **médecine** s'occupe davantage des maladies, des traumatismes, des infirmités et des façons pour y remédier. Lorsqu'un médecin peut poser un diagnostic sur une maladie que j'ai, il lui est alors plus facile de choisir quel genre de traitement peut être appliqué. Ce siècle a permis à la **médecine** de faire des bonds gigantesques avec d'importantes découvertes en chimie et en biologie, à l'aide des nouvelles technologies. La **médecine**, dans bien des cas, s'est montrée très efficace là où on pouvait arriver à poser un diagnostic. Cependant, lorsque mon malaise ou ma maladie ne peut être identifié, il arrive que la **médecine** soit impuissante à m'aider. Je peux alors investiguer les causes de ce malaise ou de cette maladie à l'aide de l'iridologie, de la psycho-kinésiologie, des lectures énergétiques ou d'autres formes d'investigations en faisant appel à des personnes responsables ayant une éthique professionnelle reconnue.

MÉDIACALCOSE (voir : ARTÉRIOSCLÉROSE)

MÉLANCOLIE
(voir aussi : ANGOISSE, CHAGRIN, DÉPRESSION, PSYCHOSE, SUICIDE)

La **mélancolie** est un état de tristesse profonde. Je me sens fautif, je vis un état dépressif grave et j'ai de la difficulté à supporter cette douleur morale. Mes déplacements, même physiques, en sont affectés. Je fais face à une insatisfaction, à une contrariété, à un chagrin qui amènent un manque de joie. Cette tristesse m'amène à me sentir « mêlé dans mes émotions » qui deviennent de plus en plus sombres. J'ai l'impression de tourner en rond. « J'affirme que la joie habite tout mon être. » Je me fixe des buts réalisables qui m'aideront à retrouver davantage cette énergie de vie en moi, dissipera la tristesse et qui laissera place à plus de joie et de satisfaction.

MÉMOIRE (... défaillante)
(voir aussi : ALZHEIMER [maladie d'...], AMNÉSIE)

La **mémoire** a la faculté d'emmagasiner les idées, les émotions et de ramener au conscient ce dont l'on veut bien se rappeler. Je peux, après un choc émotionnel, occulter de ma **mémoire** des peurs, des craintes, du chagrin. C'est le subconscient qui refuse au conscient de se souvenir. C'est pour moi une façon, même inconsciente, de fuir une forme de réalité que je trouverais difficile à vivre. J'accepte ↓♥ de prendre pleinement la responsabilité de ma vie, prenant conscience que chaque situation est ici pour m'aider à mieux me connaître et à me sentir plus libre.

MÉNINGITE (voir : CERVEAU — MÉNINGITE)

MÉNOPAUSE (maux de...)

À l'automne de la vie, le corps de la femme change et je dois l'accepter ↓♥. C'est une période grandement émotionnelle qui atteint particulièrement mes sentiments reliés au fait d'être encore aimable et désirable, mais surtout aimée et désirée. Je fais le point sur ma vie et je peux avoir des regrets de ne pas avoir fait ceci ou cela, avoir l'impression de ne pas avoir profité pleinement de la vie. Dans la première moitié de ma vie, souvent appelée « la période active », je suis dans l'action, je « fais », je procrée, je bâtis. C'est mon côté rationnel, actif, organisateur, aussi connu comme mon côté masculin, ou « Yang », qui prédomine. Mais maintenant, je me sens diminuée et je peux vouloir continuer toutes mes « corvées » domestiques et mes tâches sociales au lieu de laisser surgir toute ma féminité, ma douceur, ma créativité qui sont mon côté féminin, Yin. Les **bouffées de chaleur** que j'expérimente à la **ménopause** manifestent un conflit intérieur et mon côté féminin se fait « étouffer » par ces symptômes que mon côté masculin provoque. La seule façon efficace de les faire disparaître consiste à retrouver la femme utile, expérimentée et pleine de sagesse car mon **entêtement** à ne pas suivre le courant de la vie pourra se

transformer en mal de tête ou en migraine. Même si je ne suis plus procréatrice, je dois trouver ma direction spirituelle. J'ai besoin de trouver la **Femme** en moi. C'est un peu comme à la retraite : j'ai maintenant le temps de travailler en toute liberté, d'échafauder d'autres plans, d'autres défis. Je découvre un nouveau sens aux mots « Liberté » et « Individualité », me permettant de **renaître** à une nouvelle vie. Mon attention est maintenant portée sur moi et sur mon conjoint au lieu d'être uniquement portée sur les enfants (dans bien des cas) et la famille. Je découvre une nouvelle raison de vivre. C'est un peu comme un recommencement, je peux faire des choses que j'aime et que j'ai choisies. La crainte de vieillir peut devenir plus présente et réelle. Je peux même inconsciemment faire réapparaître des menstruations pour m'aider à retourner dans le passé et à « m'accrocher » à une jeunesse physique qui a disparu. Il est donc important que j'accepte ↓♥ et que je fasse le deuil de ma jeunesse afin de vivre pleinement le moment présent. J'accepte ↓♥ les transformations qui surviennent, autant à mon corps qu'à ma vie intérieure, spirituelle ainsi qu'à ma vie sociale et familiale. Je vis dans la simplicité. Je savoure chaque moment et j'ai le pouvoir de créer ma vie, grâce à toutes les expériences que j'ai vécues jusqu'à maintenant et qui font que je possède une sagesse et un trésor extraordinaires.

MÉNORRAGIES (voir : MENSTRUATION — MÉNORRAGIES)

MENSTRUATION (maux de...)

Les **menstruations** sont l'écoulement, par le vagin, de sang provenant de la muqueuse utérine Elles surviennent périodiquement chez une femme non enceinte, entre la puberté et la ménopause. Les **douleurs menstruelles** peuvent être reliées à de la **culpabilité** et de la **colère**. Ces sentiments peuvent trouver leur source dans une expérience où j'ai été abusée sexuellement, plus particulièrement avant la puberté. Si j'ai l'impression aussi que mes parents sont déçus d'avoir mis au monde une fille, je pourrai tout faire pour avoir l'air d'un garçon et ainsi être aimée de mes parents. Je peux inconsciemment **retarder ou faire arrêter mes menstruations**. Je refuse ma féminité, et peut-être aussi ma sexualité, croyant que c'est sale ou péché. Il se peut que, même inconsciemment, je sois déçue de ne pas avoir été enceinte, car c'est la perte de sang (reliée à la perte de joie) qui indique généralement si je suis enceinte ou non. Cette déception de ne pas être enceinte provient de la mémoire incluse, celle de l'espèce, qui veut que je sois faite pour la procréation qui assure sa survie. Ainsi, les pertes de sang, reliées d'un point de vue métaphysique à une perte de joie, m'indiquent, dans une certaine mesure, ma peine, même inconsciente, de ne pas avoir été enceinte, liée à ma programmation génétique pour la préservation de l'espèce. Si mes pertes « sortent de ma normalité » c'est-à-dire qu'elles diminuent, pouvant même aller à l'arrêt des **menstruations**, ou si au contraire elles augmentent, je dois

alors vérifier un ou l'autre des aspects mentionnés plus haut que je peux vivre dans ma vie et qui expliquerait ce changement. Plus j'accepterai ↓♥ que c'est simplement une réponse de mon corps à une programmation, plus cette période se déroulera en harmonie. Je me dois d'accepter ↓♥ en tant que femme de vivre en harmonie avec ce corps qui fonctionne selon des cycles.

MENSTRUATION — AMÉNORRHÉE

L'**aménorrhée** est l'**absence ou la suppression des règles** chez la femme, communément appelées **menstruations**. L'**aménorrhée**, qui survient alors que la femme est en âge d'avoir ses règles, peut être reliée au rejet de la féminité ou aux **inconvénients** d'être une femme ; à de la culpabilité pouvant provenir des paroles ou des actions du partenaire sexuel ; aux sentiments vécus lors de certaines règles. La femme vit une certaine crainte, un malaise ou de la culpabilité. Pour remédier à cela, elle se programme mentalement et fait cesser ses règles, en refusant la vie, en décidant de cesser de procréer. Je refuse peut-être de vivre ce que ma mère a déjà vécu par rapport à mon père et je refuse de servir inconsciemment de **généticienne** (outil de reproduction) dans ma relation présente, car je me rappelle la douleur que je ressentais en voyant ma mère triste dans sa relation amoureuse. Je refuse de vivre cette expérience. La femme a grandement intérêt à accepter ↓♥ au niveau du cœur son partenaire et à lui faire confiance, surtout si l'homme est très ouvert à la femme qu'il aime.

MENSTRUATION — MÉNORRAGIES (voir aussi : FIBROMES)

Les **ménorragies** sont l'augmentation anormale de l'abondance et de la durée des règles pouvant provenir de la présence d'un fibrome utérin. Elle sont reliées à de la non-acceptation ↓♥ d'avoir des enfants ou à de grandes pertes de joie face au fait que je ne peux pas enfanter, que ce soit parce que je suis infertile ou parce que j'utilise un moyen de contraception afin d'éviter de devenir enceinte.

MENSTRUATION — SYNDROME PRÉMENSTRUEL (SPM)
(voir aussi : DOULEUR)

On observe le **syndrome prémenstruel** lors de la période qui précède les **menstruations.** Il se traduit par de la nervosité, des maux de dos, de tête et de ventre. Cela est dû à un déséquilibre hormonal. C'est le processus de rejet et de culpabilité qui commence à faire surface. La période menstruelle est pour la femme le rappel qu'elle vit dans un univers dominé par les hommes. Cela indique donc comment le **syndrome prémenstruel** amène des situations qui me font m'interroger sur ma perception en tant que femme dans ma relation avec ma féminité, surtout si je veux réussir une carrière professionnelle. Je peux être troublée, confuse et je me laisse influencer par les

stéréotypes imposés par la société. Je m'aime et je m'accepte ↓♥ comme je suis et je laisse place à l'évolution.

MESCALINE (consommation de...) (voir : DROGUE)

MIGRAINES (voir : TÊTE — MIGRAINES)

MILIEU DU DOS (voir : DOS — MILIEU DU DOS)

M.N.I. (Mononucléose infectieuse)
(voir : SANG — MONONUCLÉOSE)

MŒLLE ÉPINIÈRE (voir aussi : SCLÉROSE EN PLAQUES)

La **mœlle épinière** est la partie du système nerveux central contenue dans le canal rachidien, à l'intérieur de la colonne vertébrale. Elle fait suite au bulbe rachidien et se termine au niveau de la deuxième vertèbre lombaire. Puisqu'elle transmet les données du cerveau aux parties du corps concernées, un malaise à ce niveau m'indique que je peux avoir de la difficulté à mettre en pratique dans le monde physique mes pensées et toute ma créativité. J'ai tellement besoin de tout calculer et planifier à la perfection, sans jamais me tromper, que la spontanéité n'a pas sa place dans ma vie. Puisque la mœlle épinière travaille de cette façon, ma trop grande rigidité entraînera des malaises et des dysfonctionnements. J'apprends à m'écouter, à faire les choses par intuition en sachant que je fais toujours pour le mieux et que l'erreur n'existe pas : tout est expérience pour m'aider à grandir.

MONONUCLÉOSE (voir : SANG — MONONUCLÉOSE)

MORPIONS

J'attrape des **morpions,** ordinairement, par contact vénérien. Je me sens coupable, je me sens sale d'avoir eu des relations sexuelles en dehors des cadres permis dans notre société ou je peux avoir l'impression qu'elles n'ont pour but que de combler mes besoins personnels sans que je sois engagé avec l'autre personne. J'accepte ↓♥ que toute situation vécue est une expérience et j'apprends à reconnaître mes besoins et ce qui est bon pour moi.

MORT (la...) (voir aussi : AGORAPHOBIE, ANXIÉTÉ, EUTHANASIE)

La **mort** n'est pas une maladie mais un état. Elle arrive lorsque les fonctions vitales de mon corps telles que battements du cœur, respiration, activités cérébrales cessent : mon corps ne pourra plus reprendre ses fonctions,

à moins que l'on puisse utiliser des moyens mécaniques ou autres pour en réactiver certaines. Il arrive, dans le cas de maladies graves comme certains cancers, le SIDA, les maladies incurables, etc., que je guérisse juste avant le moment appelé **la mort**. En effet, alors que j'intègre dans mon cœur et dans l'amour la prise de conscience que j'ai à faire, il se peut que je sois libéré de toute souffrance physique et morale. Si je suis trop avancé dans la maladie, mon cerveau peut me débrancher après que la prise de conscience soit faite. C'est pourquoi il est si important que je comprenne dans mon cœur et que j'accepte ↓♥ la raison qui a fait que je vis cette maladie. Plus j'accepterai ↓♥ ce que la vie m'enseigne, plus je pourrai partir[67] en harmonie, dans la lumière et dans l'amour. Mes proches ont un grand rôle à jouer dans ce processus de guérison en acceptant ↓♥ au niveau du cœur mon départ afin que je puisse continuer ma route en toute liberté. Plus j'intégrerai de situations avant de quitter mon corps physique, plus j'aurai pris de l'avance sur le travail qu'il me reste à faire après mon départ. Puisque la vie continue (pour ceux qui y croient !), je préfère que l'on parle de moi en disant que je suis « parti », que j'ai « quitté mon corps physique », que je suis « passé dans les autres mondes ». Cela me semble plus réel d'utiliser ces expressions que de dire que je suis « mort ».

M.T.S. (Maladies Transmissibles Sexuellement)[68]
(voir : VÉNÉRIENNES [maladies...])

MUCOSITÉS AU CÔLON (voir : INTESTINS — COLITE)

MUGUET (voir aussi : BOUCHE / [en général] / [malaise de...], GORGE / [en général] / [maux de...], INFECTIONS [en général])

Le **muguet** est une maladie contagieuse due à une levure et caractérisée par la présence de plaques d'un blanc crémeux causée par les muqueuses buccales et pharyngiennes, c'est-à-dire dans la bouche et dans la gorge. Cette maladie est très fréquente chez les enfants. Elle apparaît à la suite des cris et des pleurs incessants de mon enfant qui désire avoir des caresses, des contacts physiques avec nous, ses parents. Si je me mets à la place de l'enfant, un bébé en particulier, je me rappelle que j'ai besoin du contact de ma mère ou de mon père pour me sentir en sécurité et hors de danger car je sais que je suis vulnérable. La seule façon que j'ai d'aller chercher l'attention de mes parents pour qu'ils me prennent dans leurs bras est de crier et de pleurer. C'est la seule façon qu'on me « gorge » (larynx !) de chaleur humaine. Puisque mes parents peuvent mal interpréter ces cris et penser que j'ai faim, soif, froid, etc., je

---

67. **Partir :** Ce terme est préféré à « mourir ».
68. **M.T.S. (maladies transmissibles sexuellement) :** En Europe, plus particulièrement en France, on va parler de M.S.T. (maladies sexuellement transmissibles)

n'obtiendrai pas ce dont j'ai besoin. Et mon **larynx,** organe essentiel de la phonation, n'étant pas capable de remplir mon besoin de contact physique, déclenchera le **muguet**. Il s'agit pour mes parents de me prendre dans leurs bras le plus souvent possible, de me caresser, de me sécuriser pour que le **muguet** s'en aille. Lorsque le **muguet** apparaît chez moi, l'adulte, il se peut que cela survienne à la suite d'une infection de mes poumons, de mes voies respiratoires. Mes besoins sont alors les mêmes que ceux de l'enfant mentionnés plus haut, à la différence que c'est mon enfant intérieur qui a besoin d'attention et d'être sécurisé. Ma partie adulte peut réconforter cet enfant qui est en moi et le rassurer. L'harmonie s'installera davantage, ce qui permettra à la santé de prendre sa place.

MUSCLE(S) (en général...)

Les **muscles** sont contrôlés par la force mentale; c'est la vie, la puissance et la force de nos os. C'est le reflet de ce que nous sommes, croyons et pensons devenir dans la vie. Les muscles représentent l'effort à déployer et le travail à accomplir pour aller de l'avant. Les **muscles,** correspondant à mon énergie mentale, sont nécessaires afin de bouger, de passer à l'action. Quand il y a des **maladies musculaires**, je dois me référer aux parties de mon corps atteintes pour déterminer la cause qui est exprimée. Je vais voir à quelles situations mentales, à quel « patterns » ou à quels comportements cette partie du corps se rapporte.

MUSCLES — DYSTROPHIE MUSCULAIRE

La **dystrophie musculaire** est une maladie où les **muscles** s'affaiblissent et dégénèrent parfois rapidement. Elle est reliée à un si **grand désir de contrôler les situations et les gens** que je perds tout contrôle. J'ai le sentiment que, pour moi, tout est perdu d'avance et mon corps est si fatigué par ce stress qu'il s'abandonne et s'autodétruit progressivement. Je ne suis pas assez bon, ou bien je ne me crois **pas capable d'être à la hauteur**. Ma vie est « moche », elle ne m'intéresse plus. J'ai vraiment peur de ne pas réussir ma vie et je ne fais plus d'efforts. Par conséquent, mes **muscles,** qui représentent l'action, deviennent malades et c'est maintenant ma propre peur qui prend le contrôle et je me laisse contrôler par la société. La **dystrophie musculaire** est une maladie grave et souvent incurable, mais son état peut se stabiliser si j'y mets les efforts nécessaires. J'accepte ↓♥ de lâcher prise, de **rester ouvert et d'affronter mes propres peurs ici et maintenant** ! Lorsque j'affronte mes craintes et que je les identifie, je n'ai plus besoin de tout diriger. J'accepte ↓♥ d'aller de l'avant, de me libérer du besoin de contrôler qui, en fait, n'est que la projection de mes peurs.

MUSCLES — FIBROMATOSE

La **fibromatose** provient de tumeurs fibreuses (fibromes) ou de l'augmentation des fibres dans un tissu (fibrose) qui amène de la raideur au niveau de mes muscles et de mes tissus fibreux, ce qui provoque une douleur intense. Les tissus mous ont trait à ma façon de penser. Les douleurs que je ressens m'avertissent que je vis beaucoup de stress et de tension, d'où une fatigue mentale intense. Elles me font réaliser que **je manque de souplesse**, que **je suis rigide et angoissé** particulièrement au regard de mes pensées et de mes attitudes. En raison de mes propres conflits intérieurs, j'empêche l'énergie de circuler librement dans mes muscles. Je prends conscience de ces tensions : d'où viennent-elles ? Est-ce une fatigue mentale reliée à ce que je fais, à ma façon d'être et de m'exprimer ? La partie de mon corps affectée m'aide à trouver la cause. Il se peut que je doive changer de direction. J'accepte ↓♥ d'être ouvert et je sentirai les nœuds de tension disparaître. Je suis ici pour évoluer. Le fait de me raidir me cause toutes ces douleurs. Je vis l'instant présent et j'apprends à faire confiance.

MUSCLES — FIBROSE KYSTIQUE

La **fibrose kystique** est la formation de masses de tissus mous sur mes muscles et mes tissus fibreux. Ma façon de penser rigide et mes « patterns » mentaux font que j'ai refusé d'avancer dans la vie. Je me suis accroché à tant de vieilles idées que je n'ai pas suivi le courant de la vie. Les douleurs que je ressens me paralysent. Je suis découragé, rien ne marche dans ma vie. Je peux avoir l'impression de toujours m'être retenu soit de faire ou de dire des choses, ayant peur des conséquences. C'est pourquoi mes jambes et mes bras sont souvent affectés puisque cela symbolise ma peur de prendre les situations de la vie (bras) et ma peur d'avancer dans la vie (jambes). Je me plains, je m'apitoie sur mon sort et je voudrais que les autres en fassent autant. J'accepte ↓♥ de m'ouvrir davantage à la vie et je laisse aller mes vieilles idées. De cette façon, je prends un nouvel essor dans la vie et la place qui me revient dans l'univers.

MUSCLES — MYASTHÉNIE

La **myasthénie** est une affection chronique neurologique caractérisée par une fatigabilité, c'est-à-dire un affaissement musculaire. Même s'il est rare que je vive une telle maladie, lorsque cela arrive, c'est que je vis du découragement, un manque de motivation et que je suis « fatigué de la vie ». J'ai l'impression que je ne pourrai jamais faire ce que je veux ou que je ne pourrai jamais réaliser mes rêves. Je prends conscience de ce qui me décourage au point de me laisser dépérir. Lorsque j'aurai trouvé, je pourrai plus facilement changer la situation. Si je ne trouve pas la cause exacte de mon conflit, je peux quand même chercher des sources de motivation qui m'amèneront éventuellement à trouver la solution à mon conflit.

MUSCLES — MYOPATHIE

Le terme général de **myopathie** concerne toutes affections qui touchent les fibres musculaires. Or les **muscles**, du point de vue métaphysique, sont étroitement reliés à mon mental, à ma façon de penser. Je me dévalorise constamment. Je veux empêcher une situation d'avancer, je veux arrêter tout mouvement par rapport à quelqu'un ou à quelque chose qui fait partie de ma vie en ce moment ; c'est pourquoi mes **muscles,** qui me permettent de faire des mouvements et de me déplacer, vont se détériorer. C'est en regardant la partie affectée de mon corps et ce que cela m'empêche de faire que j'aurai une bonne indication de la nature des pensées que je dois changer. Je reconnais cependant que cela arrive toujours pour m'aider à agrandir mon champ de conscience, pour me permettre de vivre plus d'amour, de liberté, de sagesse.

MUSCLES — MYOSITE

La **myosite** est une inflammation des **muscles** qui provoque une faiblesse et une rigidité musculaire, les **muscles** étant reliés à l'effort. Elle provient du stress face à des efforts que je dois fournir, que ce soit face à un travail physique, intellectuel ou émotionnel que je n'ai pas nécessairement le goût de faire, parce que cela me demande beaucoup d'énergie, mais face auquel je me sens « coincé ». Comme j'ai l'impression que je suis obligé de le faire et que je n'ai pas vraiment le goût de fournir l'effort, je ressens très peu de motivation. Je prends mon temps, je demande de l'aide ou je me donne plus de temps pour accomplir mes tâches afin de faire reposer mes **muscles** et de refaire mes énergies.

MUSCLES — TÉTANOS (voir aussi : MUSCLES — TRISMUS)

Une personne atteinte du **tétanos** verra en premier lieu les **muscles** de sa mâchoire se contracter de façon très douloureuse. Par la suite, ce sont les **muscles** respiratoires et cardiaques qui seront touchés. Cela démontre une grande irritation intérieure provoquée par des pensées nuisibles à mon bien-être. Au lieu de les exprimer, je les ravale et les étouffe en moi. J'accepte ↓♥ de laisser l'amour me purifier, je fais place à l'harmonisation.

MUSCLES — TRISMUS (voir aussi : MUSCLES — TÉTANOS)

Le **trismus** se caractérise par le resserrement involontaire des mâchoires, lequel est dû à la contraction des **muscles**. C'est souvent le premier signe m'indiquant que je suis atteint du tétanos. Cette situation peut se produire lorsque je ressens de l'agressivité. En refusant d'exprimer mes sentiments, j'ai l'impression de garder le contrôle. Je refuse de m'ouvrir par crainte d'être jugé, rejeté, incompris. En me refermant, je ferme aussi la porte à l'amour. J'ai intérêt à faire confiance, à exprimer clairement mes désirs et à faire place à l'amour.

MYASTHÉNIE (voir : MUSCLES — MYASTHÉNIE)

MYCOSE (... entre les orteils) ou PIED D'ATHLÈTE
(voir : PIEDS — MYCOSE)

MYCOSE (... du cuir chevelu, poils et ongles)
(voir : CHEVEUX — TEIGNE)

MYOME UTÉRIN (voir : FIBROMES et KYSTES FÉMININS)

MYOPATHIE (voir : MUSCLES — MYOPATHIE)

MYOPIE (voir : YEUX — MYOPIE)

MYOSITE (voir : MUSCLES — MYOSITE)

NAISSANCE (la façon dont s'est passée ma...)
(voir aussi : ACCOUCHEMENT)

Pendant les neuf mois de ma gestation, lorsque je n'étais qu'un fœtus, tous mes sens étaient déjà éveillés et j'ai eu connaissance de tout ce que ma mère, mon père et les gens autour de moi ont pu verbaliser. De même, je pouvais ressentir les émotions, les « états d'âme » de ceux-ci, plus particulièrement ma mère, avec laquelle j'entretenais des liens très étroits et intenses. La façon dont je peux avoir interprété ce que j'ai entendu ou ressenti pendant cette période va avoir une répercussion sur mes comportements dans l'avenir.

Par exemple, je peux avoir eu l'impression que « j'ai fait souffrir maman » lors de l'accouchement quand, bien souvent, elle a elle-même contribué à augmenter le niveau de douleur par son anxiété, ses peurs et aussi par le fait qu'elle revoit inconsciemment sa propre **naissance** qu'elle peut avoir trouvée très douloureuse. J'ai pu interpréter aussi que c'est à cause de moi que ma mère a failli mourir. Je traînerai alors toute ma vie ce sentiment de culpabilité « d'avoir fait mal à maman » que je revivrai face à d'autres personnes.

De plus, la façon dont s'est passée ma **naissance** ou les moyens utilisés pour faciliter celle-ci vont aussi influencer des comportements que je reproduis dans ma vie de tous les jours et qui font justement référence à **la façon dont ma naissance** s'est produite. Voici des exemples de situations les plus fréquemment rencontrées :

Si je suis né **prématurément,** je vais souvent manifester de l'impatience : je veux avoir fini une tâche avant même de l'avoir commencée. De plus, si j'ai été **placé en couveuse** pour une certaine période de temps, je revivrai souvent la même solitude profonde et une impression de vivre de l'impuissance face à certaines situations ou à certaines personnes, ce qui m'amène à m'isoler et à avoir un niveau d'énergie très bas. Je peux vivre un sentiment de rejet intense du fait que j'ai eu l'impression que ma mère m'a délaissé après ma naissance.

Au contraire, si je suis né **en retard**, je vais avoir de la difficulté à être ponctuel et à remettre des travaux à temps. Je prends mon temps et je me sens souvent bousculé dans les choses à faire. J'aime aussi que les choses soient faites à ma manière. Je pourrai démontrer de l'agressivité face aux personnes qui veulent me faire sentir coupable de mes retards, car j'aurai l'impression que c'est à cause des événements extérieurs si je suis en retard.

Une **naissance** qui doit être **provoquée** dénote souvent que je n'étais pas prêt à venir au monde ; je peux alors vivre beaucoup de frustrations qui m'accompagneront tout au long de ma vie. Je peux aussi développer une méfiance par rapport à mon entourage.

Si ma mère a eu besoin d'une **anesthésie** pour me mettre au monde, je peux avoir tendance à m'endormir à tout moment et j'« anesthésie » la réalité, je ne perçois pas clairement et j'interprète à ma façon les événements, selon les peurs que j'entretiens.

Si je me retrouve avec **le cordon ombilical enroulé autour du cou**, je me sens « étouffé » par les gens ou les situations. Je peux être plus fragile au niveau de la gorge, j'ai de la difficulté à m'exprimer, à communiquer simplement et affirmativement. J'ai tendance à me sentir « pris à la gorge ». Patrick Drouot a mentionné dans un de ses livres qu'un fort pourcentage (60 % +) de personnes nées avec le **cordon ombilical** autour du cou ont pris conscience lors de régressions dans une ou l'autre de leurs vies passées qu'elles avaient été pendues.

Si je suis né **par césarienne**, j'ai généralement de la difficulté à mener des projets à terme ; un effort prolongé et constant m'est difficile. Le découragement me gagne facilement. Je pourrai avoir l'impression aussi que la vie ou que les gens me traitent injustement ou, si l'on veut, que je n'ai pas le juste retour des efforts que je mets pour accomplir une tâche. « Rendez à *César* ce qui appartient à *César !* ».

Si je suis né **par le siège**, je vis souvent de la culpabilité, notamment parce que j'ai l'impression de faire souffrir les gens autour de moi. Je retiens beaucoup

et j'ai de la difficulté à laisser aller et à faire confiance. Je vis alors beaucoup de tension intérieure. Tout ce que je vis est difficile et semble durer une éternité. Je pourrai aussi avoir l'impression que je me sens limité dans mes actions et dans mes projets. C'est comme si les gens et les circonstances de la vie faisaient en sorte de vouloir me faire céder dans des nouvelles actions que je veux entreprendre.

Si l'utilisation de **forceps** a été rendue nécessaire, ceux-ci saisissant et protégeant ma tête afin de faciliter mon expulsion lors de ma **naissance**, je peux souffrir de maux de tête, de douleurs au crâne et j'ai l'impression de me heurter à beaucoup de difficultés dans ma vie, particulièrement au début d'un projet, ou d'une nouvelle relation. J'aurai l'impression que je devrai « tenir tête » aux circonstances qui se présentent pour mener à bien mon nouveau projet ou ma nouvelle relation.

Je peux demander à mes parents les détails de ma **naissance**. Le seul fait de prendre conscience des difficultés vécues à ce moment va m'aider à comprendre et à changer les comportements qui en découlent et qui peuvent me déplaire.

NAISSANCE PRÉMATURÉE (voir : ACCOUCHEMENT PRÉMATURÉ)

NARCOLEPSIE ou MALADIE DU SOMMEIL
(voir aussi : COMA, ÉVANOUISSEMENT, INSOMNIE, SOMNOLENCE)

La **narcolepsie** est une tendance irrésistible à s'endormir. Je m'endors soudainement et cela peut durer de quelques secondes à plus d'une heure. Si cela s'accompagne d'une diminution de mon tonus musculaire, aussi appelée **catalepsie**, on parle alors du **syndrome de Gélineau.** Le sommeil devient un échappatoire face à des peurs et à des résistances. Je dis non à l'évolution et je refuse d'accepter ↓♥ ce qui se passe dans ma vie. Je vais donc **fuir** parce que je n'ai plus le goût de voir ou de sentir certaines personnes ou certaines situations. Ne sachant pas comment résoudre cette situation, étant incapable de m'affirmer, je vais me retirer dans mon **sommeil**, cela étant la solution la plus facile. À ce moment-là, j'ai tendance à agir en victime, me sentant impuissant ou pensant ne pas avoir les outils nécessaires afin de faire face à ce qui me fait peur. J'ai donc avantage à me prendre en mains et à foncer, quitte à demander de l'aide à un ami ou à un parent, afin d'être dans l'action et de créer ma vie comme je le veux.

NAUPATHIE (voir : MAL DE MER)

NAUSÉES ou VOMISSEMENTS

La **nausée** se définit comme une envie de vomir et s'accompagne d'une impression de malaise général. Je ressens un sentiment de peine et j'éprouve de la douleur face à une réalité qui cause un dérèglement dans ma vie et que je voudrais pouvoir éviter. La **nausée** est un signe que j'éprouve du **dégoût** et que je **rejette** soit une chose, une personne, une idée, une situation, ou peut-être même, une émotion. Je vis soit de la révolte, de la colère, de la peur, du dégoût, de la frustration ou de l'incompréhension face à celle-ci. Lorsque ce rejet devient suffisamment important, l'effet de **vomissements** peut survenir car je tends à manifester physiquement ce rejet. J'ai à prendre conscience que j'ai absorbé quelque chose de ma réalité ou de mon être qui crée le désir de l'exprimer immédiatement. Et si ça ne se fait pas avec la parole, ce sera manifesté par des **nausées**. Un début de grossesse est souvent accompagné de **nausées** et, dans cette condition, je dois accepter ↓♥ les changements dans ma vie que l'arrivée du nouveau-né va apporter. Je demande la paix et j'accepte ↓♥ de digérer les émotions et les conflits que cet événement produit dans mon quotidien.

NÉPHRITE (voir : REINS — NÉPHRITE)

NÉPHRITE CHRONIQUE (voir : BRIGHT [maladie de...])

NERFS (en général)

Les **nerfs** sont des organes qui reçoivent et qui donnent des informations à tout le corps en provenance des sentiments, des pensées et des sens. Les activités conscientes sont contrôlées par les **nerfs** périphériques qui prennent leur source à l'épine qui est la demeure du système nerveux. Les activités inconscientes, par exemple les battements du cœur ou la respiration, sont contrôlées par le système nerveux automatique. Par la méditation ou par une profonde relaxation, je peux obtenir un contrôle conscient sur ce système. Je peux être affecté de plusieurs manières car le système nerveux couvre plusieurs activités fonctionnelles. Les **nerfs** sont comme le système électrique de mon corps. Si mes circuits sont surchargés parce qu'il y a trop « de tension », cela affecte le fonctionnement de mon organisme. Cette tension peut provenir du fait que j'ai des inquiétudes face à l'avenir et que j'ai peur aussi que les projets que je veux réaliser ne se rendent pas à terme. Les **nerfs** sont donc **à la base de la communication** et s'ils ne fonctionnent pas adéquatement, je peux me demander dans quelle sphère de ma vie j'aurais avantage à communiquer et à recevoir ce que les autres ont à dire. Si j'ai les **nerfs en boule** ou les **nerfs à fleur de peau**, cela me rappelle ma grande sensibilité et, bien que je puisse m'être senti blessé par le passé, je peux apprendre à faire confiance aux autres et à la vie.

NERFS (crise de...) (voir aussi : HYSTÉRIE, NÉVROSE)

La **crise de nerfs** est aussi appelée **nombrilisme**. Il s'agit d'une montée d'énergie, de vibration à l'intérieur de moi qui bloque soit au niveau de la parole par manque ou incapacité de communiquer son point de vue ou au niveau d'une activité, alors qu'il m'est impossible de réaliser, d'accomplir une action. Alors, le blocage devient si fort, si gros que je ne peux libérer l'énergie dans l'harmonie et **il y a explosion**. Cela m'amène à dire des paroles extrêmes ou à poser des gestes extrêmes. Il est bon lors de ces moments de tension de m'arrêter et d'en prendre conscience tout en prenant de grandes respirations et en relaxant profondément. Il faut que j'accepte ↓♥ la situation et que je prenne le temps de faire baisser la pression tout en rééquilibrant mes émotions.

NERFS — NÉVRALGIE (voir aussi : DOULEUR)

La **névralgie** peut être définie comme un mauvais contact sur le parcours d'un fil électrique. Les fils électriques représentent tous nos **nerfs**. C'est une douleur vive sur un **nerf** causée par une trop forte tension sur son parcours. Si le **nerf** est coupé, c'est que la communication, la libre circulation de l'énergie en moi est coupée. L'endroit où la douleur est située m'indique le genre d'émotion impliquée. Un sentiment de culpabilité et le désir d'être toujours dans les normes établies par la société seront souvent la source d'une **névralgie.** Si elle se situe dans un bras ou dans une main, cela m'indique qu'une pression (telle que l'engagement) ou une autre émotion (telle que l'impuissance) m'empêche de « prendre » une décision ou une direction harmonieuse dans ma vie. Si la **névralgie** est dans une jambe, dans un mollet ou dans un pied, c'est un pas de plus dans une nouvelle direction que l'émotion bloque et, par conséquent, la libre circulation des énergies dans ma vie. En prenant conscience de l'aspect de ma vie (par la partie du corps affectée) qui est affecté par l'anxiété ou par l'insécurité, je pourrai y remédier plus facilement et trouver les solutions et tout l'amour que la situation me demande.

NERF — NÉVRITE

Une **névrite** est l'inflammation d'un ou de plusieurs **nerfs**. La partie de mon corps qui est affectée par le ou les **nerfs** m'indique sur quel aspect de ma vie j'ai une prise de conscience à faire. Même si la **névrite** peut « sembler » trouver sa source dans une infection, l'alcoolisme, dans certaines maladies ou dans les effets secondaires de certains médicaments, il est souhaitable que je trouve ce qui m'amène à vivre de la colère dans la communication que j'ai à avoir avec moi-même. En rétablissant cette communication avec moi-même et en m'apportant la compréhension dont j'ai besoin, je retrouverai davantage de calme dans ma vie et dans mon corps.

NERF SCIATIQUE (le...) (voir aussi : DOULEUR, DOS / [maux de...] / BAS DU DOS, JAMBES / [en général] / [maux aux...])

Le **nerf sciatique** commence dans la partie lombaire (bas du dos) de la colonne vertébrale ; il traverse la fesse, la cuisse et la jambe et descend jusqu'au pied. La douleur ressentie me paralyse. Il se peut que la douleur se manifeste plus dans une jambe que dans l'autre. Je suis alors inquiet financièrement. Si ma jambe droite est en cause, c'est peut-être parce que j'ai peur de manquer d'argent et de ne pouvoir faire face à mes responsabilités dans ce qui s'en vient pour moi. Si la douleur se situe dans ma jambe gauche, mon manque d'argent peut intensifier mon sentiment de ne pouvoir tout donner, sur le plan matériel, aux gens que j'aime. Je crains que leur amour pour moi en soit affecté. Je m'illusionne, je me crois très spirituel et détaché des biens matériels (une sorte d'hypocrisie). Cependant, **la peur de manquer d'argent** me poursuit et me rend très **anxieux**. Je travaille très fort, j'ai de grandes responsabilités et, malgré tous mes efforts, j'éprouve quand même certains ennuis financiers. Mon corps se raidit : **je me sens coincé**. Je me remets sans cesse en question. Qu'est-ce que je ne fais pas ? Est-ce que je possède les connaissances et le talent nécessaires pour faire face à une nouvelle situation ? Mon **insécurité** m'amène à me **révolter**, j'en veux à la vie. J'en viens à développer un sentiment d'infériorité. Je peux me refuser de me « plier » à une personne ou une situation. Insidieusement, **l'agressivité** s'installe et ma communication avec les autres s'en ressent. J'ai intérêt à me **calmer les nerfs** car, en ce moment, j'ai l'impression d'avoir les **nerfs en boule**. Je prends conscience de ma **confusion intérieure** et de ma douleur (tant intérieures qu'extérieures) au regard de la ou des directions de ma vie, **ici et maintenant**. Cette douleur résulte souvent de mon entêtement à vouloir m'accrocher à mes vieilles idées au lieu de m'ouvrir au changement et à la nouveauté. Cette situation est fréquente chez la femme enceinte qui vit une confusion intérieure et une douleur concernant la direction maintenant prise dans sa vie : des doutes, des craintes et des inquiétudes peuvent faire surface... Je n'ai pas à me juger, mais à m'accepter ↓♥ tel que je suis. J'accepte ↓♥ que **la source de ma véritable sécurité est en moi** et non dans les biens que je possède. Je lâche prise et je fais confiance à l'univers, car il est abondance pour tous sur tous les plans : physique, mental et spirituel. En faisant confiance à l'univers, je fais confiance à la vie. Je choisis d'accepter ↓♥ la souplesse, je découvre la vraie richesse, celle que j'ai à l'intérieur de moi. La vraie valeur d'un être se mesure à sa grandeur d'âme. J'accepte ↓♥ mes limites, je prends conscience de mes craintes, je les intègre. Je décide d'avancer dans la vie, je me laisse guider en toute sécurité pour mon plus grand bien.

NERVOSITÉ

La **nervosité** est un signe indiquant que je manque de confiance en moi, en mon entourage et en l'avenir. Le fait de vouloir faire trop vite ou de parler

très rapidement trahira ma **nervosité**. Cela me montre que je dois faire confiance en la vie de façon à savoir qu'il n'est pas nécessaire de tout contrôler à la perfection pour que la vie soit belle et aimante. Je prends conscience que ma **nervosité** dissimule l'instabilité, la crainte d'un événement que je redoute. Je dois donc m'en libérer en faisant confiance à mon être intérieur tout en relaxant régulièrement.

NEURASTHÉNIE
(voir aussi : BURNOUT, DÉPRESSION, FATIGUE [en général])

La **neurasthénie** est un état de fatigabilité physique et psychique extrême. Ses symptômes se traduisent par la difficulté à prendre des décisions et par la confusion. Bien que je ne présente aucun trouble organique, je peux avoir des difficultés à digérer, des douleurs physiques, une émotivité extrême et être très faible. La **neurasthénie** ressemble en plusieurs points à une **dépression.** J'aurai alors tendance à me retirer dans la solitude et à broyer du noir. C'est mon attitude négative qui produit cette maladie. Au lieu de mettre mon attention sur « tout ce qui ne va pas dans ma vie », j'ai avantage à dire *Merci* pour ce que j'ai. J'ai à me prendre en mains, à faire des projets et à accepter ↓♥ que j'ai tout le potentiel pour atteindre tous les buts que je me fixe. La joie et le bonheur pourront alors prendre encore beaucoup de place dans ma vie.

NÉVRALGIE (voir : NERFS — NÉVRALGIE)

NÉVRITE (voir : NERF — NÉVRITE)

NÉVROSE (voir aussi : ANGOISSE, HYSTÉRIE, OBSESSION)

Comme la dépression et la psychose, la **névrose** est causée par des émotions non maîtrisées ou par la recherche d'une identité qui remplacerait celle que je refuse. Même si je garde contact avec la réalité et que je peux continuer de vivre en société, je peux vivre un sentiment d'angoisse, mon jugement peut être altéré et ma vie sexuelle peut s'en ressentir sous forme d'impuissance ou de frigidité. Je cherche à reprendre la place qui me revient et j'ai besoin qu'on me donne de l'attention afin de me valoriser. J'ai aussi besoin de trouver un sens à ma vie qui me permettra de me libérer des tensions que je vis. Je serai libre car je porterai mon attention sur le but fixé, source de bonheur et de satisfaction. Je me dois donc d'accepter ↓♥ ma nature profonde qui est d'aimer les autres et de m'aimer moi-même sans nécessairement être obligé de comprendre toute la vie de A à Z pour m'accepter ↓♥ tel que je suis.

NEZ (voir aussi : ODEUR CORPORELLE)

Le **nez** est l'organe par lequel l'air (la vie) passe pour atteindre mes poumons. L'air est très important. En plus de recourir à nos deux narines pour

respirer, on peut le faire par la bouche. Une difficulté de respiration peut me renseigner sur les difficultés que j'ai dans ma vie. Si je refuse de vivre ou si j'ai de la difficulté à transiger avec mon entourage parce que ce que je sens ou ce que je ressens ne me convient pas, ma capacité de respirer par le **nez** sera diminuée. C'est comme si je voulais chasser une situation conflictuelle par mon **nez.** Si la **narine gauche** me pose un problème, c'est du côté émotionnel ou affectif que je dois chercher le message, alors que la **narine droite** m'informe d'une difficulté rationnelle. Quel que soit le cas, je peux même avoir à remonter au moment de ma naissance pour découvrir la source de mon malaise au **nez.** Si j'ai dû être opéré au **nez** pour me permettre de mieux respirer, c'est comme si je disais oui à mon intuition, à mon senti, à la vie. Si j'adopte cette attitude d'ouverture et de confiance en moi, je pourrai guérir tout malaise touchant mon **nez.**

NEZ (maux au...)

Le **nez** est l'organe de l'odorat. C'est le sens qui me permet de vivre, d'être en contact avec l'atmosphère, avec l'extérieur. L'odorat est un des sens les plus puissants que j'ai et il est relié à mon premier centre d'énergie (chakra) situé au niveau du coccyx. Le **nez** est la double ouverture sur la vie ! Les narines droite et gauche sont les canaux de l'intérieur et de l'extérieur. Si mon corps met une barrière dans le canal de la respiration, c'est pour m'indiquer que je m'isole de quelqu'un de mon entourage ou de quelque situation qui m'affecte, qui me dérange ou que je n'accepte ↓♥ pas, de là l'expression populaire: « *celle-là, je ne peux plus la sentir !* » Je désire me « couper » de quelque chose pouvant toucher mon côté secret et intime, tant au regard de mes pensées qu'au plan physique ou émotionnel. C'est une personne ou une situation que je critique, que je juge comme « sentant mauvais » et vis-à-vis laquelle je peux avoir de la rancœur et même du dégoût. Ce peut même être aussi une odeur que je n'aime pas, peut-être parce qu'elle me rappelle un événement que je voudrais oublier, et que je qualifie de puant. Mon odorat est étroitement relié à ma mémoire holographique (en trois dimensions) des événements. Par mon odorat, il peut être très facile de me souvenir d'événements agréables comme d'événements désagréables. Il est important que je prenne conscience de cet état de restriction dans ma respiration pour libérer les autres de leurs décisions que je n'ai pas à juger, à critiquer. Je cesse donc de juger les gens, les situations, leurs choix et leurs décisions comme je me libère moi-même de mes choix et de mes décisions. Ceci permet à la vie de circuler librement en moi et à l'amour de grandir.

NEZ (congestion) (voir : CONGESTION)

NEZ (éternuements) (voir : ÉTERNUEMENTS)

NEZ (ronflements) (voir : RONFLEMENTS)

NEZ (saignements de...)

Le **nez** étant l'organe par lequel l'air circule pour aller à mes poumons et le sang étant le transporteur de l'air, de l'oxygène dans tout mon organisme, le **saignement de nez** me montre que je laisse partir de la joie, de l'amour de la vie hors de mon corps, hors de mon être. **J'ai donc une perte de joie par rapport à quelque chose que je ressens.** Cela indique sûrement une grande déception dans ma vie. J'éprouve un sentiment qui me dit que je ne suis pas reconnu ou aimé à ma juste valeur. Je dois donc apprendre à me reconnaître moi-même, à m'aimer moi-même, donc à comprendre que je dois mon bonheur seulement à ce que je pense de moi-même. Une ancienne croyance provenant de la nuit des temps me dit qu'une mauvaise émotion ou une mauvaise situation s'en va en dehors de ma vie.

NEZ — KILLIAN (polype de...) (voir aussi : TUMEUR[S])

Le **polype de Killian** est une tumeur bénigne qui se développe dans un sinus ou dans la fosse nasale correspondante et qui a pour effet d'obstruer plus ou moins complètement le côté affecté. Comme pour les tumeurs en général, j'ai subi un choc émotionnel par rapport à ce que j'ai « ressenti ». La douleur me fait me refermer et m'amène à ressentir à nouveau des situations qui pourraient m'affecter. Je situe le **polype**, cette « boule de chair », et je pourrai trouver ce qui a pu me perturber soit du côté gauche, l'aspect affectif, émotionnel, ou du côté droit, l'aspect rationnel ou lié aux responsabilités. Si je dois me faire enlever le **polype**, je dis merci à mon corps pour l'information qu'il m'a donnée et j'accepte ↓♥ dans mon cœur la prise de conscience que j'avais à faire.

NEZ QUI COULE DANS LA GORGE

Tout liquide dans mon corps représente un aspect de mes émotions. Si mon **nez coule dans ma gorge** au lieu que le liquide sorte à l'extérieur de mon corps, cela indique que je « ravale » mes émotions ou mes larmes. J'ai tendance à me recroqueviller sur moi-même et à « pleurer sur mon sort ». Il est important que je me reprenne en mains, que je fasse des choses pour moi, afin de reprendre goût à la vie et d'accomplir ma mission.

NEZ — SINUSITE

Lorsque je suis affecté d'une **sinusite,** je vis un blocage au **nez** et ce sont les **sinus** de la face qui sont concernés ici. Cette infection des **sinus** est reliée à l'impuissance face à une personne ou à une situation : **Je ne peux pas la sentir** ou **la moutarde me monte au nez**. J'imagine la sensation d'avoir de la moutarde forte dans le **nez,** ça m'étouffe, ça me brûle... Je peux aussi

pressentir un danger ou une menace qui fait surgir une peur à l'intérieur de moi. Le danger peut être réel ou imaginaire ; le résultat sera le même. Je peux avoir l'impression que « quelque chose ne sent pas bon », « qu'il y a quelque chose de louche ». Le message que je dois comprendre est de sentir l'amour autour de moi et de l'inspirer au plus profond de moi.

NODULES

Un **nodule** est une lésion cutanée ou muqueuse qui est bien délimitée, presque sphérique et palpable et qui peut se loger à différentes profondeurs de la peau (derme, épiderme ou hypoderme). Il se retrouve communément sur les cordes vocales ou dans l'oreille. Ce **nodule** m'aide à prendre conscience que je vis de la déception, de la rancœur face à un projet que je n'ai pu réaliser parce que **j'ai frappé un nœud** qui m'a fait m'éloigner de mon but ou ne m'a pas permis de l'atteindre. Ce peut être tant sur le plan professionnel qu'affectif. Ma communication (cordes vocales) peut être en cause ; j'aurais voulu dire des choses que je n'ai pas osé dire ou j'ai l'impression d'avoir trop parlé et de m'être « mis les pieds dans les plats ». Ce peut être aussi quelque chose que j'ai entendu (**nodule** au niveau de l'oreille) et qui m'a dérangé au point « d'arrêter le chantier qui était en construction ». L'important, c'est de décider que tout arrive au bon moment. Le **nodule** apparaît habituellement à l'endroit de mon corps où je ne veux pas me faire toucher car le fait de me faire toucher par quelqu'un (même par quelqu'un que j'aime ou en qui j'ai confiance, comme par exemple un médecin) me rappelle mon premier choc, un événement douloureux. Je prends conscience de ce qui a freiné mon élan afin de pouvoir le dépasser. L'important, c'est d'atteindre le but fixé, quels que soient les embûches et les retards qui se trouvent sur mon chemin. Je n'en serai que plus fier et content de moi !

NOMBRIL (voir : OMBILIC)

NOSTALGIE (voir aussi : MÉLANCOLIE)

La **nostalgie** est une mélancolie causée par un regret. Habituellement, lorsque je suis **nostalgique**, cela implique que je regarde à travers un nuage embrouillé d'émotions, hors du temps présent, avec le sentiment qu'il me manque quelque chose. C'est une forme de rêverie. Il ne faut pas cependant que ce « rêve » devienne une fuite régulière du moment présent. Cette **nostalgie** peut ne pas me nuire, à condition que je n'en fasse l'expérience qu'à l'occasion et sans exagération. Je dois apprendre à savourer pleinement le moment présent afin que chaque seconde qui passe soit vécue comme une expérience unique et riche d'enseignement.

NUQUE (... raide) (voir aussi : COLONNE VERTÉBRALE, COU)

La **nuque** est la région de mon corps par où toutes les énergies (ondes) doivent passer pour aller se répartir dans tout mon corps. La **nuque** est au sommet de ma colonne vertébrale. Ma colonne est le soutien, la structure de mon corps. Ma **nuque** est donc le pivot de ma tête. Une **nuque raide** est une démonstration d'un refus ou d'un engorgement d'énergie. La tête ne peut plus tourner dans différentes directions. Je peux avoir l'impression de manquer de soutien et j'ai tendance à être entêté et rigide dans ma façon de penser. Ceci m'amène à être passif, évitant de mettre des choses de l'avant et d'être dans l'action. Je me dois de laisser circuler ces pensées diverses qui bloquent ma tête et qui ne demandent qu'à être exécutées par mon corps physique. J'ai l'impression de ne pas avoir toutes les qualités nécessaires à la réalisation de mes désirs et de mes idées qui risquent de rester à l'état de « projet » ou de « rêve irréalisable ». Donc, cette raideur me dit que je me dois d'être plus souple dans mes pensées et dans mes émotions. Je me dois d'accepter ↓♥ les différentes sensations qui viennent à moi et de les laisser circuler librement. La **nuque** permet à ma tête de regarder différentes options de la vie ou différents paysages qui s'offrent à moi. Je me dois de regarder avec amour ces différents paysages, sans critique ni jugement, en toute liberté, comme un fleuve permet à l'eau d'y circuler dans un va-et-vient perpétuel, sans contrainte ni restriction. Maintenant que j'accepte ↓♥ toutes les richesses que j'ai à l'intérieur de moi, je n'ai plus à me préoccuper de ce que les autres pensent de moi car je suis maintenant pleinement conscient de tout le potentiel qui m'habite.

OBÉSITÉ (voir : POIDS [excès de...])

OBSESSION

L'**obsession** est une maladie de la pensée. Lorsque je suis **obsédé** par quelque chose ou par quelqu'un, toute mon attention, toute mon énergie est dirigée vers celui-ci ou celle-ci. Ces idées me viennent de façon répétitive et menaçante. Je demeure cependant conscient du caractère irrationnel que sont ces idées. Il n'y a rien d'autre qui compte. Si j'ai une personnalité **obsessionnelle**, il y a de fortes chances que je sois une personne remplie de doutes, ayant beaucoup de difficulté à prendre des décisions, et que je vive de l'ambiguïté amour-haine, face à moi-même et face aux autres. Les **obsessions** peuvent revêtir des formes très diverses : cela peut être une phobie face à quelque chose ou à quelqu'un, cela peut être des « ruminations mentales » sur « ce qui pourrait se produire si... », la folie du doute, ou une compulsion à commettre certains actes qui peuvent être sans conséquence, ou qui peuvent aussi être criminels, mêmes suicidaires, mais qui ne sont pratiquement jamais suivis de passage à l'acte. La plupart du temps, j'ai une crainte angoissante face à « quelque chose qui pourrait arriver » par négligence ou par faute personnelle et qu'il faut éviter. Ma priorité, c'est d'entretenir mon **obsession**, même

inconsciemment. Mon système de pensée est paralysé. Je suis nourri par l'objet de mon **obsession**. Je comble ainsi un vide intérieur et une grande insécurité. Pour que je vive de l'**obsession,** il faut que je vive une sorte de tension intérieure, d'inquiétude ; alors, il serait temps pour moi de trouver un point d'intérêt dans ma vie qui m'apporte plus de calme et plus de paix intérieurs. Je pourrai ainsi profiter davantage de ce que la vie m'apporte.

ODEUR CORPORELLE (voir aussi : NEZ)

En général, tous les liquides contenus dans le corps humain représentent mes émotions. Dans ce cas-ci, une **odeur corporelle** désagréable est le signe que des émotions néfastes débordent et que je dois exprimer celles-ci au lieu de tout retenir à l'intérieur de moi. Cela peut être de l'irritabilité, du mécontentement, de la haine, de la frustration, de la rancune, du dégoût face à une personne ou une situation, etc. Cela peut être aussi le signe d'un relâchement d'une émotion intense et qui est reliée à la partie du corps où la transpiration arrive. Une personne qui a une bonne **odeur corporelle** aura généralement de belles pensées et sera en harmonie avec son entourage. Il arrive que je suis une personne qui a reçu une vie avec une mission spirituelle élevée, que je meure « en **odeur** de sainteté ». On peut alors réellement sentir comme un parfum de fleur qui se dégage du corps. Aussi, si je lis des textes spirituels, que je suis en état de méditation ou de contemplation, ou que je me sente dans un état où je suis très heureux, alors je peux dégager une senteur comme l'œillet, la rose, le bois de santal et divers autres parfums. Les personnes pourront sentir ou non le parfum que je dégage. Même si cela est rare, je peux être une personne qui est capable de sentir les maladies et même les sentiments chez une autre personne. Ainsi, chaque maladie a une **odeur** particulière, au même titre que les maladies ont une couleur particulière dans le champ magnétique que l'on appele l'aura. Si la **transpiration est abondante**, c'est le signe que je vis beaucoup de nervosité intérieure, d'insécurité ou que j'ai de grandes angoisses. Je laisse sortir par les pores de ma peau tout ce que je refoule et qui reste emprisonné à l'intérieur de moi. Je dois apprendre à m'affirmer et à exprimer mes sentiments tant positifs que négatifs afin de me dégager, de faire place à du neuf et que de belles pensées d'amour me nourrissent.

ODORAT (voir : NEZ)

ŒDÈME

L'**œdème** est un renflement causé par une rétention d'eau. Il cause une boursouflure et est très fréquent dans les chevilles et les pieds. Il peut se retrouver aussi dans les autres articulations ou les tissus conjonctifs. Les liquides dans le corps représentant mes émotions, il se peut que je retienne ou refoule mes sentiments intérieurs. Je peux aussi nier mes impulsions ou **sentir des limitations et des barrières par rapport aux choses que je désire**,

amenant découragement et désappointement. Je peux aussi <u>vouloir retenir quelqu'un ou quelque chose</u>, soit de mon passé ou soit dans le présent et m'y accrocher comme à une bouée de sauvetage. Sinon, je vais me noyer dans ma peine, dans ma déception, dans mon amertume face aux événements. La fonction de la partie du corps affectée par **l'œdème** ajoute d'autres informations. Au niveau des jambes et des pieds, je peux vivre un très grand désir d'aller dans une direction différente, mais je me sens émotionnellement pris dans la direction dans laquelle je vais, me sentant incapable de m'affirmer et de m'en libérer. Lorsque **l'œdème** se forme à la suite d'un coup, d'une blessure ou qu'une partie de mon corps cherche à se reconstituer, cela est appelé l'**œdème de guérison**. Dans certains cas, mon corps amène alors ce liquide comme pour diminuer la friction, et aider l'environnement immédiat de la partie affectée à se reconstituer. **L'œdème** amène le besoin de reconnaître et de découvrir l'expression de mes émotions **embouteillées** et **renfermées**. J'apprends aussi à lâcher prise afin de me permettre d'avancer et d'effectuer des changements positifs dans ma vie.

ŒIL (voir : YEUX [en général])

ŒSOPHAGE (l'...)

L'**œsophage** est le passage pour les aliments afin que ceux-ci soient digérés. Si j'ai des émotions ou des idées qui « passent de travers », **l'œsophage** se crispe et le passage est plus difficile, pouvant même provoquer de l'irritation, celle-ci manifestant mon irritation intérieure face à quelque chose ou face à quelqu'un que j'ai de la difficulté à tolérer. Mes appréhensions, mon angoisse, ma peine amèneront mon **œsophage** à se contracter, pouvant même aller jusqu'à obstruer complètement le passage. Comme **l'œsophage** est le passage entre ma bouche qui représente l'entrée de nouvelles idées et mon estomac, les idées que j'ai à digérer, si j'éprouve une forte colère ou de la haine face à quelque chose dans ma vie « qui ne passe pas », je pourrai développer un cancer de **l'œsophage**. Je dois laisser aller toute amertume et voir chaque expérience de ma vie comme une occasion de grandir afin que les joies de la vie me nourrissent.

OIGNON (voir : ORTEILS — OIGNON)

OLFACTION (voir : NEZ)

OMBILIC

L'**ombilic** est l'ouverture de la paroi abdominale du fœtus par laquelle passe le cordon ombilical. Peu de temps après la naissance, il devient une cicatrice, et il est communément appelé **nombril**. Une douleur à ce niveau

implique que je dois m'ouvrir davantage aux autres au lieu de rester centré sur moi. Il se peut que je sois en train de « **couper le cordon ombilical** », c'est-à-dire ma dépendance envers ma mère, mon milieu familial. C'est par le **nombril** que lorsque j'étais fœtus, j'ai reçu toute la nourriture essentielle à ma croissance et à ma survie. Une anomalie ou un malaise à ce niveau peut donc aussi me donner une indication de quelque chose dont j'ai un besoin vital dans ma vie et que je ne reçois pas ou au contraire quelque chose que je voudrais rejeter, évacuer car consommé ou reçu en trop grande quantité et qui n'est peut-être plus bénéfique pour moi. Le **nombril** est aussi considéré par certaines personnes comme un centre d'énergie important pour l'ouverture puisqu'il existe même un groupe que l'on appelle « les adorateurs du **nombril** » qui font des exercices de méditation sur cette partie du corps qui représente l'ouverture du passage de la vie alors que j'étais un fœtus dans le ventre de ma mère. J'apprends à reconnaître mes qualités avec humilité, évitant ainsi de « me prendre pour le **nombril** du monde » et me permettant de voir toute la beauté qui existe en chaque être et en chaque chose.

OMBILICALE (hernie...) (voir aussi : HERNIE)

La **hernie ombilicale** peut être une manifestation de mon désappointement ou de mon regret d'avoir dû me détacher de l'environnement douillet et sécuritaire qu'était le ventre de ma mère. Maintenant, j'ai l'impression que je dois me débrouiller seul et j'ai des efforts à faire pour atteindre les buts que je me suis fixés et qui deviennent tout à coup beaucoup moins excitants. J'accepte ↓♥ que j'ai tout le potentiel nécessaire pour atteindre mes objectifs et que la vie me supporte entièrement.

OMOPLATE

L'**omoplate** est un os plat, large et mince faisant partie du squelette. Avec la clavicule, l'**omoplate** sert à unir le bras au tronc. De la douleur à cet endroit peut indiquer une révolte face à l'autorité, car je me sens coincé ou écrasé par celle-ci. Les difficultés (fracture ou autres) au niveau de l'**omoplate** peuvent provenir d'une contrariété entre ce que je suis, représenté par le tronc, et ce que je veux exprimer, représenté par mes bras qui sont le prolongement de l'énergie du cœur. J'accepte ↓♥ de considérer ce que je suis dans mon entier pour que je manifeste de l'harmonie dans ma vie, dans les actions que je pose.

ONGLES (en général)

Les **ongles** représentent le tissu dur et mon énergie la plus profonde et spirituelle. Ils se manifestent sur mon corps aux endroits les plus « prolongés ». Ils peuvent être affectés lorsque mon activité (ou ma dextérité), ma direction tendent à changer et que j'ai de la difficulté à faire face à ces changements. Les **ongles** représentent ainsi le sentiment de **protection** que j'ai par rapport à tout ce qui se passe autour de moi. J'ai le choix d'utiliser mes **ongles**

négativement (pour agresser, pour me défendre et pour faire mal, comme chez les animaux), soit positivement en les utilisant pour ma dextérité et ma créativité. Quelle que soit l'énergie utilisée, je peux découvrir l'état de celle-ci en définissant l'état de mes **ongles**.

ONGLES (se ronger les...)

Si je me **ronge les ongles**, cela indique une nervosité intérieure très grande. Cela peut être aussi une insécurité profonde de ne pas être capable d'être ou de faire ce que l'on attend de moi. S'il s'agit d'un enfant, cela peut manifester la présence de rancune ou de frustration face à un parent, cette situation pouvant aussi survenir lorsque je suis devenu adulte. Je peux me sentir incapable de me prendre en mains et de m'autosuffire et je veux que les autres s'occupent de moi. Je peux aussi **ronger mon frein** en refoulant mon agressivité; en **mettant de l'eau dans mon vin**, je peux laisser entrevoir un débordement imminent d'émotions non exprimées. J'ai donc avantage à exprimer toutes mes émotions et à aller chercher ma sécurité et ma confiance à l'intérieur de moi.

ONGLE INCARNÉ

Un **ongle incarné** indique de la culpabilité ou de la nervosité face à une nouvelle situation. Il peut aussi représenter un conflit entre mes désirs mentaux et spirituels. S'il s'agit de l'**ongle d'un doigt**, il s'agit d'une situation de mon quotidien et, plus fréquemment, s'il s'agit de l'**ongle d'un orteil**, il s'agit d'une situation ou d'une décision face à l'avenir. Dans le cas du **gros orteil**, l'**ongle incarné** peut représenter mon inquiétude face à la pression que je crois devoir affronter dans l'avenir et face à laquelle je me sens déjà coupable car j'appréhende de ne pouvoir vivre cet avenir avec harmonie et succès. Il est important de voir quel doigt ou quel orteil est touché afin d'avoir des informations supplémentaires sur la facette de ma vie par rapport à laquelle j'ai à m'ajuster tout en éliminant ma culpabilité.

ONGLES JAUNES (syndrome des...)

Le syndrome des **ongles jaunes** se manifeste lorsque les **ongles** de mes doigts ou de mes orteils ont une couleur jaune verdâtre, qu'ils sont épais et recourbés. Médicalement parlant, cela se produit lorsque la circulation de mon système lymphatique est inadéquat, lui-même provenant de trouble respiratoire chronique. Alors que mes **ongles** sont une protection pour mes doigts et mes orteils, mon corps me manifeste que je dois augmenter mes protections car je me sens fragile et je ne fais pas face aux événements de la vie (poumons = vie) dans les petits détails qui se présentent à moi aujourd'hui ou demain. Je trouve ma vie terne. Je cherche en moi ce qui peut amener plus de passion dans ma vie. J'augmente en moi l'énergie vitale pour qu'elle se manifeste jusqu'au bout de mes doigts.

ONGLES MOUS et CASSANTS

Les **ongles** représentent ma vitalité, l'état de mon énergie vitale. Des **ongles cassants** expriment un déséquilibre quant au niveau de mon énergie et quant à l'utilisation que je fais de celle-ci. Des **ongles mous** expriment la lassitude que je vis, l'indifférence qui m'habite. Ma vie est aussi terne que mes ongles. C'est à moi d'y mettre du piquant et de voir à bien utiliser mon énergie.

OPIUM (consommation d'...) (voir : DROGUE)

OPPRESSION

Lorsque je me sens **oppressé**, j'ai la sensation d'un poids sur la poitrine, donc au niveau des poumons. Je peux aussi avoir l'impression d'étouffer. Cela peut être mes émotions qui m'accablent, mes soucis qui pèsent lourd, ma révolte qui gronde. Je peux me sentir accablé par l'autorité, et « le pouvoir » par qui j'ai l'impression d'être abusé. Je peux sentir de la **pression** face à une personne ou une situation provenant d'une insécurité intérieure profonde qui fait que je voudrais voir se régler la situation le plus rapidement possible. Je reprends le pouvoir qui m'appartient. Je prends conscience de la liberté que je possède. Je libère mes sentiments négatifs afin de faire place au calme et à l'amour.

OPPRESSION PULMONAIRE

Un tel état démontre qu'il y a un déséquilibre entre la pression de mon intérieur et celle de l'extérieur. **C'est un sentiment très fort qui bloque la libre circulation de la vie en moi.** Je dois donc en prendre conscience et me demander si cette forte pression vient de mon intérieur et ce qui, dans ce sentiment probablement très fondamental, m'empêche de respirer régulièrement et profondément. J'inspire donc la lumière qui éclaire et l'amour qui purifie ces émotions, lesquelles seront ainsi équilibrées.

OREILLES (en général) (voir aussi : OREILLES — SURDITÉ)

La vue et l'ouïe me permettent de me situer dans l'environnement. Je peux voir des choses sans qu'il n'y ait de son, je peux entendre des sons sans nécessairement voir d'où provient ce son. À eux seuls, ces deux sens forment une sorte de « trois dimensions » de mon environnement. Ainsi, les **oreilles** me permettent d'entendre tous les sons qui m'entourent, autant ceux qui sont harmonieux que disharmonieux. La **surdité** totale ou partielle peut survenir lorsque je ne peux traiter ou accepter ↓♥ ce que j'entends. Si je suis sourd, c'est qu'il s'est installé un processus sélectif d'informations et que je veux entendre seulement ce qui fait mon affaire et que je me coupe de tout ce qui se dit et de ce qui ne me convient pas. Ce processus sélectif est très efficace car il permettra de « reconnaître », par exemple, la voix de mon enfant que je cherche dans une

foule. De la même façon, ce processus agira à l'inverse pour ce que je ne veux pas entendre. D'une façon indirecte, les **oreilles** permettent un maintien de l'équilibre corps-esprit évoluant dans l'Univers. Cet équilibre me tient debout, en alerte, me permettant d'être centré et de suivre ma voie.

OREILLES (maux d'...) (voir aussi : OREILLES / ACOUPHÈNE / BOURDONNEMENTS D'OREILLES / OTITE)

Des **maux d'oreilles** surviennent quand je vis de la peine, que je suis irrité ou que je me sens blessé par des choses que j'ai entendues. Je peux aussi avoir l'impression que personne n'écoute ce que j'ai à dire ou je suis déçu par rapport à ce que j'aimerais me faire dire et que l'on ne me dit jamais (compliments, remerciements, etc.). C'est comme si je voulais me renfermer et ne plus être en contact avec ce qui m'entoure. Le **mal d'oreilles,** lui, survient à la suite d'une critique qui est **venue à mes oreilles** et qui m'était destinée ou destinée à une autre personne. Ce que j'entends m'angoisse et me fait mal, tant physiquement qu'émotionnellement. S'il s'agit d'une **infection à l'oreille**, j'ai probablement entendu des paroles qui me causent de l'irritation, un bouleversement émotionnel, un conflit ou de la disharmonie. S'il s'agit d'une **otite**, je vis beaucoup d'impuissance face à ce que j'ai entendu. Si un enfant vit un malaise à ses **oreilles**, cela peut exprimer un conflit relié à l'environnement familial ou à l'école. Les **maux d'oreilles** sont fréquents chez les enfants qui entendent tout ce que les grandes personnes disent, les disputes de leurs parents, sans pouvoir donner leur point de vue. J'apprends à garder mes **oreilles** « ouvertes » en tout temps, tout en développant ma capacité à me détacher de ce que j'entends. Mon cœur peut ainsi rester ouvert en tout temps.

OREILLES — ACOUPHÈNE
(voir aussi : OREILLES — BOURDONNEMENT D'OREILLES)

L'**acouphène** est le phénomène qui fait que j'entends des sons tels que sifflements, bourdonnements, des grésillements sans que cela ait un rapport avec mon environnement. Cela peut être passager ou permanent et peut se produire avec des intensités sonores différentes. Lorsque cela m'arrive, je dois prendre le temps de me questionner si j'ai été à l'écoute de ma voix intérieure. C'est comme si je n'étais pas parfaitement syntonisé sur « mon poste de radio intérieur ». Lorsque je syntonise un poste de radio qui est en ondes et qui n'émet pas de musique ou de parole, je peux « entendre le silence ». Par contre, si je déplace le récepteur sur une fréquence où il n'y a pas de poste qui émette, j'entends grésillement ou du sifflement, comme si j'utilisais un poste à onde courte. Y a-t-il des émotions que j'aurais refoulées de crainte de troubler mon équilibre intérieur ? Ainsi, la vie me rappelle d'être à l'écoute de ma voix intérieure, de mes besoins et de mes désirs. Je dois me prendre en mains afin de diminuer le « niveau de bruit ou les interférences » qui peuvent exister dans

mes pensées et dans mes émotions. Car le fait d'entendre ces sifflements ou ces bourdonnements m'indique peut-être aussi qu'il y a quelque chose que je ne veux plus entendre et que ces sons vont « étouffer » pour éviter que cela parvienne à mes **oreilles**. J'accepte ↓♥ d'ouvrir davantage mes **oreilles** intérieures (situées à 8 à 10 cm en arrière de mes **oreilles** physiques) pour être plus en mesure de capter ma voix intérieure. Je peux demander aussi à entendre plus consciemment les sons de la nature et les mélodies célestes afin de bénéficier de plus de paix et de repos en moi-même. Toute approche holistique telle que yoga, détentes dirigées, acupuncture, ostéopathie, vitaminothérapie, énergie, etc., peut aider à diminuer le niveau de stress et à ramener la tranquilité intérieure. Il se peut que j'entende aussi comme le son d'un ruisseau, d'un torrent, le tintement des cloches (petites, moyennes ou grosses), de la cornemuse, du vent dans les arbres, du bourdonnement des abeilles, des milliers de violons. Ces sons correspondent à des sons que je peux entendre sur différents plans de réalités intérieures et peuvent me permettre de déterminer sur quel plan je me syntonise. Cela signifie alors que mon **oreille** intérieure est ouverte à entendre davantage la réalité de ces mondes.

OREILLES — BOURDONNEMENT D'OREILLES
(voir aussi : OREILLES — ACOUPHÈNE)

Les **bourdonnements** sont reliés au **refus d'écouter** sa voix intérieure, les signes intérieurs qui guident sa vie. Je « fais à ma tête », je refuse d'entendre certaines paroles que je trouve déplaisantes. Je peux même être entêté. Je résiste car j'ai peur de **savoir la vérité**, d'être au courant d'une situation ou même de prendre éventuellement une décision. Cela peut même me mettre en disharmonie et je déclencherai un **bourdonnement d'oreilles** pour ne pas entendre... J'ai l'impression qu'une personne pense à moi alors qu'en réalité **c'est** souvent le contraire. Je peux être tendu à cause des idées qui me « trottent » dans la tête. En acceptant ↓♥ de rester ouvert au niveau du cœur, je peux entendre les paroles avec plus de détachement. Je ne suis plus obligé de faire la **sourde oreille**.

OREILLES — OTITE

L'**otite** est une inflammation à une ou aux deux **oreilles**, et qui a son origine dans l'inconfort que je peux vivre face à quelque chose que j'entends ou que j'ai entendu dernièrement. L'**otite** est fréquente lorsque je suis enfant, notamment par rapport à ce que mes parents peuvent se dire entre eux ou par rapport à ce que je peux me faire dire, n'étant souvent pas capable d'exprimer mon mécontentement ou ma frustration. Que je sois adulte ou enfant, même si cette peine peut provenir de ce que j'entends, elle peut provenir aussi de ce que je n'entends pas comme par exemple : « Je t'aime », « Félicitations pour ce que tu viens de faire », etc. En général, quand j'ai une **otite**, il y a du liquide qui apparaît derrière le tympan. Ce que j'entends doit alors passer à travers

cette eau avant d'être entendu. Cette situation est la même que lorsque j'étais bébé dans le ventre de ma mère. Donc, je recherche, même inconsciemment, par une **otite**, à retrouver cet environnement privilégié. Je préfère peut-être faire « **la sourde oreille** », me « **boucher les oreilles** » pour ne plus avoir à entendre. Je me replie sur moi-même, n'ayant que tristesse, lassitude, incompréhension comme compagnons. C'est un signal pour mes parents que moi, l'enfant qui a une **otite,** je vis un conflit intérieur et qu'il est important qu'ils m'amènent à exprimer ce que je vis afin d'amener une guérison rapide. Comme adulte, l'**otite** me permet de me questionner par rapport à ma voix intérieure et de voir : « *Est-ce que j'écoute celle-ci ?* », « *Est-ce que je reçois des messages qui me dérangent et qui me mettent en colère par rapport à ce que j'ai à faire ou par rapport à ce que l'on me demande de faire ?* » C'est par l'écoute, tant intérieure qu'extérieure, que je peux avancer dans la vie, celle-ci me permettant d'être centré et d'éviter des obstacles inutiles.

OREILLES — SURDITÉ

« *Mieux vaut être sourd que d'entendre cela !* » Je choisis de ne plus entendre, je décide de m'isoler des autres. Me sentant facilement rejeté, je me « bouche les **oreilles** » car je ne veux plus être ennuyé. Ne sachant parfois quoi répondre, je fais la **sourde oreille**. J'ai peur d'être manipulé et je n'accepte ↓♥ pas la critique, je ne veux pas « entendre » raison ; donc, en créant cette barrière, je m'isole de plus en plus, je m'entête à ne pas entendre. Pourtant, que je le veuille ou non, le temps fait en sorte que les problèmes non réglés dans ma vie reviennent tous un jour et que je devrai y faire face. J'aurais intérêt à « tendre l'**oreille** » et écouter ma voix intérieure qui est la meilleure conseillère dans ma vie. Le plus bel acte d'amour que je puisse faire est d'ouvrir mon cœur. J'accepte ↓♥ d'entendre les messages et je m'ouvre aux autres.

OREILLONS (voir aussi : GLANDES SALIVAIRES, INFECTIONS [en général], MALADIES DE L'ENFANCE)

Les **oreillons** sont une infection virale contagieuse qui se manifeste le plus souvent par l'inflammation de certaines glandes, notamment les glandes salivaires. Il y a quelque chose ou quelqu'un dans ma vie par rapport auquel je vis de l'irritabilité. J'aurais le goût de « cracher » dessus tant j'en ai le dédain. À moins que ce ne soit quelqu'un d'autre qui voudrait en faire autant par rapport à moi ! Les **oreillons** affectent généralement plus les enfants que les adultes, ceux-ci ayant beaucoup de difficulté à exprimer leur colère et leur frustration. Au lieu de dédaigner une personne (ou une situation), je devrais plutôt regarder ce que j'ai à apprendre de celle-ci.

ORGANES GÉNITAUX (voir : GÉNITAUX [organes...])

ORGELETS (voir aussi : FURONCLES)

L'**orgelet** est un petit furoncle rouge et douloureux situé au bord de la paupière, à la base d'un cil. Il se manifeste quand je vis de la tristesse, du ressentiment face à quelque chose ou quelqu'un que je vois et qui ne me convient pas. Il se peut qu'une personne ait une opinion différente de la mienne, qu'elle fasse les choses différemment et que cela soit perçu comme « une souillure » à mes yeux. La différence entre la conjonctivite et **l'orgelet** est que dans ce dernier, je trouve de la « laideur » dans la situation. Au lieu de refouler mes émotions, j'ai avantage à les exprimer, car elles pourraient apparaître sous forme **d'orgelets.**

ORTEILS

Les **orteils** représentent les détails de l'avenir. Si je vis de l'insécurité face à cela, des **crampes** surgissent, et si je vis de la culpabilité, je peux me **cogner l'orteil**, me **couper** (s'il y a perte de joie) ou me **blesser** plus sévèrement (orteil cassé, fêlé). Si j'ai un **oignon,** qui est une déformation du **gros orteil**, il y a un conflit à un niveau très profond. Cette partie du pied correspond à la période des quelques semaines suivant la conception et indique une faiblesse dans l'engagement à être vraiment ici (en vie). **L'oignon** apparaît généralement au moment de vivre une relation avec un(e) partenaire ou un parent que je trouve très dominant. Comme je laisse l'autre prendre les décisions, je fuis ma responsabilité devant mes propres décisions. L'expression « mêle-toi de tes **oignons** » exprime bien le fait que je trouve que des personnes de mon entourage s'occupent de mes affaires et que cela ne les regarde pas, à moins que se soit moi qui me fasse des reproches de m'occuper indirectement des affaires des autres. **L'oignon** peut disparaître si je me prends en mains, j'assume mes responsabilités, me permettant ainsi de vivre pleinement ma vie. Comme les **orteils** sont la partie de mon corps qui va en premier de l'avant, des **orteils vers le bas** peuvent indiquer une insécurité à aller de l'avant, un désir de « s'agripper au sol » pour éviter d'avancer. J'ai donc tendance à rester sur place. Je m'empêche « d'entrer dans la vie ». Les **orteils vers le haut**, eux, indiquent la tentative de m'échapper de la vie, de m'élever vers les réalités plus abstraites que terrestres. Les **orteils crochus** m'indiquent une grande confusion dans la direction à prendre et une absence de liberté et de clarté intérieures, ce qui m'amène à vouloir fuir. **L'orteil en marteau** m'indique un stress et une répugnance à aller de l'avant. Cela peut être aussi la peur d'une façon d'être abstraite ou peu structurée. Pour connaître la signification métaphysique de chacune de mes **orteils,** je peux me référer à la signification de chacun de mes doigts en commençant par le pouce, pour le **gros orteil,** pour finir par le petit doigt, l'auriculaire, pour le **petit orteil**. Il suffit simplement de transposer la signification des doigts, qui sont les détails du quotidien, vers celle des **orteils** qui sont les détails de l'avenir.

OS (en général)

Les **os** sont la charpente solide du corps, les piliers. À l'intérieur même de l'**os** existe la mœlle, le plus profond noyau de mon être, là où naissent les cellules immunes possédant l'habileté de me protéger. Les **os** concernent ma structure, la charpente fondamentale sur laquelle mon être entier est construit. Donc, ils se rapportent aussi à la structure des lois et principes fondamentaux avec lesquels j'ai à transiger chaque jour et qui sont appliqués par l'autorité (police, instituteurs, parents, etc.) pour me permettre d'avoir un certain soutien et pour que le bon ordre règne.

OS (maux aux...)

Des malaises ou des maladies aux **os** reflètent, y compris le **cancer des os**, une rébellion face à cette autorité à laquelle je résiste et vis-à-vis laquelle je peux même aller jusqu'à me révolter, me sentant incapable ou impuissant à agir face à une certaine situation dictée, soumise à certaines lois ou principes existants. Je peux me demander si je me sens profondément bouleversé ou perturbé par rapport à mes croyances de base, à mes convictions intimes. Si un malaise ou une maladie affecte mes **os**, je dois me demander face à quelle facette ou quel aspect de ma personne **je me dévalorise**. Si je regarde et analyse quelle partie du squelette est affectée, j'aurai une bonne indication quant à l'aspect de mon existence qui est touché.

OS (cancer des...) (voir aussi : CANCER [en général])

Si j'ai un **cancer des os**, je vis un conflit très profond où j'ai l'impression que je ne vaux rien, que je ne suis qu'un moins que rien. J'ai l'impression de n'avoir aucune valeur et je suis tellement rempli d'émotions que je garde à l'intérieur de moi celles qui **me trempent jusqu'aux os**. Je peux vivre une situation où mes structures et mes principes sont fondamentalement ébranlés, remis en question. Cette situation peut m'avoir pris par surprise et je me sens **fait à l'os**. J'ai à apprendre à reconnaître mes qualités. C'est en devenant plus ouvert et flexible que je pourrai plus facilement transiger avec l'inattendu et le « non-conventionnel ». C'est en apprenant à exprimer ce que je vis, mes émotions que j'éprouve souvent très intensément, que je pourrai guérir et que mes **os** pourront se régénérer.

OS (cancer des...) — SARCOME D'EWING
(voir aussi : CANCER [en général])

C'est une forme de **cancer des os** qui est plus susceptible de m'arriver entre l'âge de 10 et 15 ans, même s'il est rare. Comme ce **cancer** atteint les **os** de mes jambes, cela signifie une grande peur d'avancer dans la vie. Je crains de ne pas avoir tout ce qu'il faut pour « affronter » l'avenir. Mon corps crie de douleur devant l'insécurité qui m'habite. Je crois ne pas être en mesure de

m'insérer dans le monde adulte. J'apprends à faire confiance en la vie sachant que celle-ci m'apportera les occasions dont j'ai besoin pour vivre en société.

OS — ACROMÉGALIE

L'**acromégalie** se caractérise par une croissance exagérée des **os** des extrémités et de la face. L'hormone de croissance sera donc secrétée en beaucoup plus grande quantité que la normale. Si je suis dans cette situation, je me demande quelle est la situation ou je me suis senti trop petit pour atteindre ou réaliser un projet. Ou est-ce que je me suis senti trop petit, trop menu et trop faible pour pouvoir prendre ma place et me faire respecter ? La réponse de mon corps a été de grandir démesurément afin de m'aider à prendre plus facilement ma place. Je lui dis merci !

OS — FRACTURE (... osseuse)
(voir aussi : DOS — FRACTURE DES VERTÈBRES)

Les os représentent la structure des lois et des principes du monde dans lequel je vis. Lorsqu'il y a **fracture**, celle-ci est l'indication que je vis présentement **un conflit intérieur profond.** Il peut être en relation avec de la **révolte** ou des **réactions face à l'autorité** (dont je veux me couper). Cette **fracture** me signale que je ne peux continuer ainsi et qu'un changement s'impose. La localisation de la **fracture** m'informe quant à la nature de ce conflit. Si la **fracture** a eu lieu lors d'un accident, il faut voir quelle culpabilité je vis par rapport à cette situation. Les **os** représentent aussi le soutien, la stabilité et une **fracture** peut être un avertissement que j'ai à me séparer de mon passé, à le laisser aller avec flexibilité afin d'éviter un stress inutile et afin de passer à une autre étape de mon évolution. Mes standards envers moi-même ou la société font-ils que j'exige une certaine perfection au point d'être rigide ? Ai-je mis davantage d'attention sur les activités physiques au détriment des aspects spirituels de ma vie ? Pour retrouver cette liberté intérieure, je prends conscience de ce qui me dérange. J'accepte ↓♥ de m'aimer suffisamment pour exprimer ce que je ressens. En retrouvant ma liberté intérieure, je retrouve la liberté de mes mouvements.

OS — DIFFORMITÉ

Les **os** peuvent se déformer à cause de la pression que je me mets ou que j'ai l'impression d'avoir à supporter. Je suis plus rigide mentalement. J'ai à apprendre à être plus flexible par rapport à mes principes de vie. Mon ouverture d'esprit me permettra d'apprécier différentes facettes de la vie et de découvrir que l'amour est présent sous différents aspects.

OS — DISLOCATION

Le mot **dislocation** (dis-location) signifie une « perte de location »,

comme si j'étais hors circuit ou dans une voie tout à fait contraire à ce qui se passe. Une **dislocation** est reliée à un profond sentiment de **déséquilibre**. Au niveau de l'articulation, l'**os** se déplace et « sort » complètement du siège de celle-ci. La **dislocation** me montre jusqu'à quel point je ne suis pas ou je ne me sens pas dans la bonne direction. Comme l'**os** est relié au noyau de mon être, à l'énergie fondamentale, la **dislocation** indique un profond changement dans l'énergie la plus profonde de mon être. Ai-je encore ma place dans l'univers ? Qu'est-ce qui me dérange au point où je me sens si confus ? Je vérifie et j'accepte ↓♥ de faire la ou les prises de conscience qui s'imposent, ce qui me permettra de me dépasser et de voir du nouveau dans ma vie. La **dislocation** est suffisamment douloureuse pour que je prenne conscience que je dois changer afin de ne pas la revivre.

OS — OSTÉOMYÉLITE

L'**ostéomyélite** est une infection de l'**os** et de la mœlle de l'**os** qui affecte habituellement une partie située près d'une articulation et survient plus souvent chez les enfants ou les adolescents. L'**ostéomyélite** se retrouve surtout sur les **os** longs tels que tibia, fémur, humérus. Les articulations donnent mouvement et expression à l'énergie contenue dans mes **os**. Une infection implique une irritation qui crée une faiblesse intérieure. Je vis colère et frustration face à l'autorité et face à la façon dont la vie est structurée et « régimentée ». Je peux aussi avoir l'impression de ne pas être assez soutenu et **supporté**. Mais, j'ai à apprendre à faire confiance, à lâcher prise et à accepter ↓♥ que l'Univers me supporte. L'infection ne veut que mettre en lumière certains conflits que je vis présentement. Si l'**ostéomyélite** vient d'une blessure antérieure, il est possible que les causes originelles de cette blessure n'aient pas encore été traitées.

OS — OSTÉOPOROSE

L'**ostéoporose** implique une perte de la trame protéique des **os** qui deviennent poreux. Elle implique une perte dans l'intention du désir « d'être », une perte d'intérêt et de motivation à être « ici » au plus profond niveau de soi. Je vis du découragement. Je suis las de toujours avoir à me battre contre l'autorité ou contre les lois de l'être humain. L'**ostéoporose** apparaît habituellement chez la femme après la ménopause. Puisque ce sont les **os** qui sont touchés, c'est-à-dire mes structures et croyances de base, je peux me demander quelles sont les croyances auxquelles je m'accroche et que je devrais peut-être changer puisque maintenant, je ne peux plus avoir d'enfants. Je peux encore être autant « utile » et « productive », non pas en ce qui a trait à la procréation mais à d'autres niveaux, tant personnel, social ou professionnel et que cela est tout autant valorisant et enrichissant. Je dois donc surmonter **cette tendance à me dévaloriser**, me pensant inutile, « bon à rien ». J'ai à faire confiance à la vie et à me trouver de nouvelles sources de motivation.

OTITE (voir : OREILLES — OTITE)

OUBLI (perte des choses) (voir aussi : ACCIDENT)

L'**oubli** se manifeste par une défaillance momentanée ou permanente de la mémoire. Cela peut être un signe que je m'accroche à certains événements ou à des personnes, souvent de mon passé, et face auxquels je dois me détacher, car je vis dans le passé au lieu de jouir du moment présent. Je peux aussi être préoccupé par une ou des situations dans ma vie et cela m'empêche d'être complètement présent. Si j'**oublie** ou je perds mes **clefs**, mon **portefeuille**, ou ma **bourse,** alors il se peut très bien que je sois **à la recherche de mon identité.** Je peux me sentir coupable de prendre du repos, de m'offrir des douceurs, de vouloir de l'attention (parce que ce n'est pas raisonnable) et ainsi, je me punis en perdant mes choses. J'apprends à laisser aller les choses et les personnes, je laisse le passé en paix et je m'ouvre à toutes les beautés de la vie qui sont ici et maintenant.

OVAIRES (en général) (voir aussi : FÉMININS [maux...])

Les **ovaires** représentent mon désir d'enfanter et aussi ma créativité, mon habileté à créer, ma féminité, du fait d'être une femme et d'être comblée ou satisfaite comme femme.

OVAIRES (maux aux...)

Les **problèmes ovariens** indiquent un profond conflit quant au fait d'être femme, à l'expression de ma féminité, ou au fait d'être mère. Je peux aussi avoir mis de côté le côté créatif qui est présent en moi. C'est comme si je me « coupe » d'une partie de moi-même, car les **ovaires** sont le commencement de la création de la vie et ils se situent dans le pelvis, qui est la région où je peux donner naissance à un enfant, mais aussi à de nouveaux aspects de moi-même, là où je peux me redécouvrir. Il peut donc y avoir un conflit intérieur face à la création et à la découverte de ma propre voie. Un **kyste ovarien,** lui, indique l'accumulation d'énergie émotionnelle ou des sentiments conflictuels reliés à l'énergie ovarienne. Quant au **cancer des ovaires,** celui-ci peut se développer à la suite d'un événement où j'ai vécu la **PERTE** d'une personne chère. Le correspondant du **cancer des ovaires** chez l'homme est le **cancer des testicules.** Il arrive très souvent que ce soit un de mes enfants mort dans un accident, à la suite d'une maladie ou d'un avortement. Cela peut être une personne avec qui je n'ai pas de lien de sang mais que « j'aime autant que s'il (elle) était mon enfant ». Le **sentiment de perte** peut être vécu face à un élément abstrait, comme par exemple : « *Depuis qu'il a ce nouveau travail, mon mari n'est plus à la maison, il rentre tard, nous ne nous parlons presque plus, il a toujours son travail en tête. J'ai perdu mon mari ! Si ça continue comme ça, le travail va avoir raison de notre mariage...* » Donc, « j'ai

perdu » l'homme que je connaissais avant et avec qui j'étais heureuse, ce qui n'est plus le cas aujourd'hui. Cela peut être **la perte** d'un projet qui me tenait à cœur et qui a avorté. D'ailleurs, si j'étais l'instigateur de ce projet, j'en parlais aux autres comme étant « mon bébé ». Quelle que soit la situation, il est important que j'accepte ↓♥ tous les sentiments qui m'habitent, que je les exprime afin que ma blessure intérieure puisse guérir et que je puisse me tourner vers l'avenir avec un regard plus positif et rempli de projets à réaliser.

PALAIS (voir : BOUCHE — PALAIS)

PALUDISME (voir : MALARIA)

PANARIS

Le **panaris** est l'inflammation aiguë d'un doigt ou plus rarement d'un orteil. Si les **doigts** sont affectés, j'ai de la difficulté à mettre des choses de l'avant par rapport aux détails du quotidien, tandis que les **orteils** concernent plutôt les détails de l'avenir. Je suis passif, indifférent et mon énergie d'action qui a besoin d'être extériorisée sort par mes doigts ou mes orteils. J'ai besoin de sortir de moi toutes ces émotions et toutes ces pensées néfastes refoulées.

PANCRÉAS (voir aussi : SANG / DIABÈTE / HYPOGLYCÉMIE)

C'est dans le **pancréas** qu'est maintenu le taux d'insuline qui aide à la stabilisation du taux de sucre dans le sang. S'il est en déséquilibre, survient alors le **diabète** ou l'**hypoglycémie** (reportez-vous à ces maladies pour plus de détails). Le **pancréas** représente ma capacité à exprimer et à intégrer l'amour à l'intérieur de moi et ma capacité de transiger avec les sentiments opposés (exemple : la colère) sans créer de la douleur. Il s'agira souvent d'une situation qui met en cause un autre membre de la famille et dont l'enjeu consiste à acquérir plus de pouvoir ou d'argent (par exemple dans le cas d'un héritage). Si je vis une situation que j'ai une très grande difficulté à avaler et que **je trouve ignoble**, je pourrai aller jusqu'à développer un **cancer du pancréas**. Il est relié à ma joie de vivre et au centre d'énergie (chakra) du plexus solaire qui est situé à la base de mon sternum, à quelques centimètres au-dessus de mon nombril. J'ai à prendre conscience de mes besoins et à mettre les choses de l'avant afin d'aller chercher ce que je veux. Je n'ai pas besoin d'aller chercher de stimulants artificiels pour me « nourrir » (drogues, nourriture, sexualité, etc.), je n'ai qu'à apprendre à m'aimer tel que je suis. J'ai besoin de m'offrir « de petites douceurs ».

PANCRÉAS — PANCRÉATITE (voir aussi : ANNEXE III)

Je vis beaucoup de rage face à la vie car elle ne m'offre plus de « douceurs ». Je veux la rejeter. Au lieu d'attendre que les « douceurs » viennent à moi, c'est à moi de m'en offrir, sachant que je les mérite.

PARALYSIE (en général)

La **paralysie** est une impossibilité d'agir, un arrêt du fonctionnement de l'activité d'un ou de plusieurs muscles. Elle peut affecter un organe, un système d'organe ou tout le corps. **Cette maladie est reliée à la fuite** : est-ce que j'essaie d'éviter ou de résister à une situation ou à une personne ? **C'est souvent la peur qui me paralyse.** Ce que je vis peut me sembler tellement insoutenable et insurmontable que je désire me « couper », me rendre insensible, ayant l'impression qu'il n'y a pas de solution envisageable, n'étant pas capable d'assumer pleinement mes responsabilités. Je peux aussi vivre ou avoir vécu un traumatisme profond qui me demande « d'arrêter de vivre » car cela en fait trop. Il est possible aussi qu'une intense haine ou un manque de confiance face à moi-même soit telle que la seule sécurité contre la mauvaise action soit l'inaction totale ! Je peux aussi être très rigide quant à ma façon de penser, et si tout ne se dessine pas comme prévu, ma réaction est de me retirer, de m'évader. Il est important que je prenne conscience de la pression qui me hante, par rapport à ce qui arrive ou à ce qui va arriver, afin de la maîtriser et de permettre à la partie **paralysée** de « recommencer à vivre ». Je peux me sentir « **paralysé** » dans une situation où je ne peux pas bouger ou qui ne m'offre aucune latitude face aux choix ou aux actions à prendre. La partie du corps affectée me donne des indications supplémentaires quant à la source de mon malaise et de ma peur. Si par exemple ma jambe droite est **paralysée**, cela peut être la peur face à ce qui s'en vient pour moi dans mon futur travail, dans mes responsabilités familiales ou dans mes responsabilités comme citoyen.

PARALYSIE CÉRÉBRALE (voir : CERVEAU — PARALYSIE CÉRÉBRALE)

PARALYSIE INFANTILE (voir : POLIOMYÉLITE)

PARANOÏA (voir : PSYCHOSE — PARANOÏA)

PARESSE

La **paresse** est une tendance à éviter toute activité, à refuser tout effort. Elle est reliée à de la lassitude par rapport à ma vie en général, un laisser-aller, car je n'ai pas le goût de faire des efforts ou de me forcer à faire quoi que ce soit. Je commence à agir, à faire des choses afin de me redonner énergie, entrain, joie de vivre.

PARKINSON (maladie de...)

(voir : CERVEAU — PARKINSON [maladie de...])

PAROLES (voir aussi : APHONIE)

Les **paroles** que je prononce aujourd'hui créent mon avenir. On dit que la pensée crée, que le verbe (la **parole**) manifeste. Ainsi, lorsque je parle, j'amène déjà mes pensées à se concrétiser sur le plan physique, comme si la **parole** était matérielle. De la qualité de mes paroles, du choix de mes mots dépend l'harmonie ou la disharmonie dans laquelle je SUIS ou je m'en vais. Si le chant est mélodieux, si je parle avec mon cœur, si la gaieté, le positivisme, les encouragements sortent de ma bouche, j'attire le soleil. Si mes **paroles** ne sont que médisance, négativisme, colère, destruction, j'attire alors nuages gris, orages et intempéries. **Le choix est mien !**

PAUPIÈRES (en général)

Les **paupières** recouvrent et protègent mes yeux. Des **paupières** gonflées, irritées sont le signe que je vis de la tristesse qui s'exprime par des larmes, mais je veux me retenir, garder en-dedans de moi ma douleur. Je dois fermer les yeux quand je veux me reposer ou dormir, ce mouvement étant fait volontairement. Mais si mes **paupières** sont mi-fermées en permanence, il y a quelque chose ou quelqu'un dans ma vie que je veux fuir ou que je n'ai pas le courage de regarder en face. Si, en plus, je vis une grande tension, mes **paupières** ont tendance à cligner plus rapidement. Je me ferme les yeux pour mieux me centrer, m'intérioriser mais il est aussi important que je les ouvre tout grand pour voir toutes les beautés de l'Univers et voir toutes les possibilités qui se présentent à moi.

PAUPIÈRES (clignement des...)

Mes **paupières** ont tendance à cligner plus vite quand je vis un stress ou une tension plus grande que d'habitude. Je suis « survolté » par rapport à ce que je vois. J'amène dans ma vie des moments de calme et de détente et j'apprends à « voir » le côté positif de toute chose.

PEAU (en général)

La **peau** recouvre tout mon corps et elle délimite ce qui est « à l'intérieur » et ce qui est « à l'extérieur », c'est-à-dire mon individualité. Par sa superficie, ma **peau** est l'organe le plus important de mon corps. C'est une couche protectrice qui cerne avec précision mon espace vital et qui laisse transparaître fidèlement et inconsciemment mon état intérieur. Si je suis une personne douce, telle sera ma **peau**. Si ma sensibilité est très grande, ma **peau** sera aussi très sensible. Au contraire, si je suis plutôt dur avec moi-même ou avec les autres, ma **peau** sera elle aussi dure et épaisse. Si ma **peau** est irritée, il y a

quelque chose ou quelqu'un dans ma vie qui m'irrite. Une grande insécurité rend ma **peau moite** tandis qu'une **peau** qui transpire beaucoup évacue les émotions que je retiens et que j'ai besoin d'évacuer. La qualité de mes relations avec le monde extérieur sera donc représentée par l'état de ma **peau.**

PEAU (maux de...)

La **peau** est comme l'écorce d'un arbre. Elle nous montre qu'il y a des problèmes extérieurs ou intérieurs. Elle isole les cellules de mon corps, mes composantes face à mon environnement extérieur. Si ma **peau** a des **anomalies**, il y a de fortes chances que je sois une personne qui donne beaucoup d'importance à l'opinion des autres et à ce qu'ils peuvent dire à mon sujet. Étant peu sûr de moi et ayant peur d'être rejeté ou de me faire blesser, je vais me créer une maladie de **peau** qui deviendra une « barrière naturelle » qui permettra de garder une certaine distance avec mon entourage. La **peau** étant un tissu mou qui est relié à l'énergie mentale, elle exprime mes insécurités, mes incertitudes et mes soucis profonds. La **peau** reflète donc constamment mes sentiments intérieurs, d'où l'expression « être rouge de colère ». Ma **peau** peut changer de couleur lorsque je suis gêné ou alors je peux éprouver de la honte. C'est donc la ligne de démarcation physique, mon masque entre mon intérieur et mon extérieur. Si ma **peau est sèche**, c'est qu'elle manque d'eau. L'eau est le deuxième élément (après l'air) nécessaire à la vie. Mes relations avec la vie sont donc sèches, arides. Je me bloque intérieurement dans mes relations avec mon entourage. Je peux avoir l'impression de « sécher sur place ». Je dois rechercher la joie dans ma communication avec autrui. La **peau morte** floconnée indique que je me laise aller à de vieux schèmes mentaux. Si des **boutons** marquent la surface de ma **peau**, c'est que j'exprime extérieurement des problèmes de relations, de communication avec mon entourage, concernant des points précis. Si ma **peau** montre des signes d'**inflammation**, je me dois alors d'être moins irrité face à certaines situations de conflit intérieur ou extérieur. Si ma **peau est grasse**, c'est que je retiens, que je garde trop d'émotions pour moi. Je peux vouloir fuir une situation ou une personne comme si on essayait de m'attraper, comme le petit cochonnet huilé que l'on veut attraper et qui nous glisse entre les doigts. Je dois laisser circuler l'énergie afin que mes pensées négatives puissent disparaître. Je dois regarder calmement, froidement les frustrations que je nourris afin que ma **peau** soit plus claire et moins épaisse. Plus je deviens transparent et vrai avec les autres, plus ma **peau** va être transparente. Une **démangeaison** me montre qu'il y a une ou des pensées irritantes qui montent à la surface de ma **peau** et que je me dois de les regarder en face pour qu'elles cessent d'attirer mon attention et de me déranger. Plus je suis capable d'apprécier mes qualités et de m'offrir de petites douceurs, plus ma **peau** va « transpirer » ce bien-être par sa douceur et sa clarté. Plus je suis capable de communiquer librement mes émotions, plus ma **peau** se détend et resplendit.

PEAU — ACNÉ (voir aussi : PEAU / BOUTONS / POINTS NOIRS, VISAGE)

Au visage, l'**acné** est reliée à l'**individualité** (tête = individualité) et a rapport à l'harmonie que je vis intérieurement et à ce qui se passe extérieurement. Le **visage** est cette partie de moi qui fait face aux autres en premier, celle qui me permet d'être accepté ↓♥ ou rejeté. L'**acné** peut survenir lorsque je suis émotionnellement et mentalement en conflit avec ma propre réalité. Ce conflit est relié à l'expression de soi et à ma propre nature intérieure. **Ainsi, l'acné est une expression visible d'irritation, de ressentiment, de rejet, de peur, de honte ou d'insécurité face à moi ou aux autres et témoigne d'une non-acceptation ↓♥ de moi-même. Je me trouve moche et parfois même dégoûtant** ! Ces expressions sont toutes liées à l'affirmation de mon identité, à l'amour et à mon acceptation ↓♥ inconditionnelle de moi-même. L'**acné** se manifeste physiquement par des lésions cutanées (de la **peau**) situées sur l'épiderme. Je sais que le *fast-food* (la restauration rapide) peut favoriser l'apparition de l'**acné** et affecter le fonctionnement du foie, siège de la colère. En tant qu'adolescent, l'**acné** est souvent reliée aux changements intérieurs que je vis, au moment où je dois choisir entre la peur de m'ouvrir à moi-même et aux autres (résistances, choix, décisions) et ainsi rompre (d'une façon souvent inconsciente) tout contact avec autrui, ou bien, **faire face** aux changements dans ma vie, aux ajustements par rapport à mon monde intérieur et à ma vision du monde extérieur. N'étant plus enfant et pas tout à fait adulte, je peux me sentir dans une position inconfortable en rapport avec **ma propre image**. Il se peut même que j'aie peur de **perdre la face** par rapport à ce que l'entourage peut penser de moi ou des jugements qu'il porte sur moi. Autrement dit, l'**acné** se manifeste par une peur inconsciente de ma sexualité, par une tentative d'extériorisation de ce que je suis vraiment. Comme adolescent, mon comportement est d'entrer en contact avec les autres, même si je veux ardemment faire le contraire. Je m'enlaidis pour filtrer les gens que je ne désire pas dans mon champ magnétique ou dans mon environnement ; j'établis des frontières et je n'y laisse entrer que les gens avec qui je suis vraiment bien ; je veux rester en paix sans être dérangé par les autres que j'éloigne inconsciemment ; je me replie sur moi et je veux rester ainsi ; je n'arrive pas à m'aimer suffisamment, alors les autres ne peuvent pas m'aimer et je sais que quelque chose me harcèle et crée de la négativité sous ma **peau** ; je me compare aux autres et je me trouve toutes sortes de défauts (trop gros, trop grand, etc.) ; je me sens limité dans mon espace vital et je me rejette ; je me sens contrôlé et dirigé par mes parents d'une manière excessive ; je m'identifie à l'un de mes parents pour faire plaisir à l'autre, plutôt que de garder ma propre identité. En acceptant ↓♥ au niveau du cœur les changements en moi, je resterai à l'écoute de mes besoins fondamentaux (sexuels ou autres) d'une manière saine et naturelle. Je découvrirai un jour la personne qui correspondra à mes attentes. L'**acné** peut se situer sur différentes parties du corps. **Au**

niveau du dos, elle représente mon passé, mes habitudes, mes peurs antérieures et mes angoisses. C'est une façon de me rejeter. Ou bien, je peux diriger le rejet vers les personnes à qui je reproche leur manque de soutien et d'appui à mon égard. Quand elle se situe sur le **haut du dos**, elle représente la colère refoulée ou de l'irritation qui essaie de trouver un soulagement. **Sur la poitrine,** elle représente l'avenir et ce qui est prévu pour moi. L'**acné** signifie la **recherche de mon espace vital** et du **respect des autres** face à celui-ci. J'ai à prendre ma place avec le cœur et même, si nécessaire, à exprimer aux autres quel est mon espace et la place qu'ils peuvent prendre en rapport à mon espace vital. Je m'accepte ↓♥ et m'aime tel que je suis et je cesse de vouloir plaire aux autres à tout prix !

PEAU — ACRODERMATITE

L'**acrodermatite** est une maladie de la **peau** qui affecte essentiellement la paume des mains et la plante des pieds, là où se situent quatre des vingt et un centres d'énergie (chakras) mineurs du corps. Cela m'indique un besoin de donner davantage d'amour avec mes mains puisque le centre d'énergie situé dans la paume de chaque main est une extension du centre d'énergie du cœur qui représente l'amour. Je peux apprendre une technique de guérison par imposition des mains, ce qui m'aidera à laisser circuler cette énergie d'amour que je bloque pour moi-même. Je peux aussi faire des travaux manuels de créativité, de la peinture ou du dessin, afin de permettre à cette énergie de passer plus librement à travers mes mains. Pour ce qui est des pieds, je dois me considérer comme marchant sur un terrain sacré et laisser l'énergie qui m'habite circuler librement vers la terre, sachant que je reçois constamment en laissant cette énergie circuler.

PEAU — ACROKÉRATOSE (voir aussi : PEAU — ACRODERMATITE)

Comme pour l'acrodermatite, l'**acrokératose** affecte la plante des pieds et la paume des mains par un épaississement de l'épiderme. J'utilise mon énergie mentale pour me protéger d'avoir à donner par mes mains et de me sentir davantage en harmonie avec la terre. Je libère mon mental de ces angoisses et je peux tenir compte des suggestions faites pour l'**acrodermatite** pour faire circuler l'énergie.

PEAU — AMPOULES

L'**ampoule** est une accumulation d'eau qui se forme entre deux parties de la **peau**, soit le derme et l'épiderme, à la suite d'une friction répétée au même endroit. L'accumulation d'eau ainsi formée agit à titre de protection naturelle du corps. Elle met donc en évidence mon manque de protection, notamment au niveau émotionnel, ou mon manque de résistance. L'**ampoule** est le rappel d'une **faiblesse émotionnelle** et l'endroit où elle se situe donne une indication du niveau de la faiblesse. Une **ampoule** aux **pieds** est reliée à ma notion de sécurité, le sol sur lequel je marche, la direction que je prends. Si elle

est à l'arrière du **talon**, elle est liée à ma mère, à mes propres qualités maternelles. Une **ampoule** aux **mains** m'amène à voir l'irritation et la frustration dans ce que je fais ou dans la manière dont je mène ma vie. Ainsi, en regardant où se situe l'**ampoule**, je peux me demander ce qui **m'agace** dans ma vie, ce qui me cause une friction et provoque chez moi de la peine (l'eau) même inconsciente. L'**ampoule** est là pour m'apporter plus de « lumière » sur ce que je vis.

PEAU — ANTHRAX (voir aussi : FURONCLES)

L'**anthrax** est une infection de la **peau**, constituée par la réunion de plusieurs furoncles et qui s'étend au tissu conjonctif sous-cutané. Je vis alors de l'agressivité malfaisante provenant du fait que j'ai le sentiment que l'on a **entravé** ma liberté personnelle de façon **injuste et inacceptable**. Je prends conscience que j'ai à apprendre comment trouver la place qui me revient et que j'ai le pouvoir de changer toute situation dans ma vie. Je n'ai qu'à le décider.

PEAU — BLEUS

Les **bleus** portent aussi le nom de **contusions**. Il s'agit d'une meurtrissure de couleur rouge, bleuâtre ou noire, qui survient lorsque je me frappe sur un objet dur qui écrase la **peau**. Cette contusion est reliée à une **expression refoulée**, une douleur mentale ou une angoisse profonde que je ne verbalise pas. Elles peuvent survenir dans les moments de grande fatigue lorsque je suis décentré. Je me sens **coupable** pour quelque raison que ce soit, je veux **me punir**, j'adopte l'attitude d'une victime, je manque de résistance face aux événements de la vie (prédisposition aux **contusions**). La vie m'avertit donc instantanément qu'en frappant cet objet, je ne me dirige pas dans la bonne direction (peu importe celle-ci). Habituellement, l'objet est immobile, si bien que **je le frappe en allant vers lui au lieu du contraire**. Donc, je m'autopunis. Est-ce que je regarde où je vais ? Est-ce que je me meus avec douceur dans la vie ou ai-je tendance à agir brusquement ? Suis-je assez attentif pour continuer ou trop faible et fatigué par mes meurtrissures et mes blessures intérieures qui se manifestent maintenant sur mon physique ? Suis-je assez calme intérieurement ? Je dois peut-être réviser mes positions pour être en mesure d'éviter les obstacles qui se présentent sur mon chemin. J'ai à prendre le contrôle de ma vie. Il est très important que je choisisse et que j'assume des décisions qui sont en harmonie avec moi-même et mon évolution.

PEAU — BOUTONS
(voir aussi : HERPÈS / [... en général, ... buccal], PEAU — ACNÉ)

Les **boutons** sont souvent reliés à l'acné. Alors que l'acné est habituellement localisée sur certaines parties du corps (visage, dos, etc.), les **boutons** peuvent se retrouver sur l'ensemble du corps. Ce sont de petites

bosses rougeâtres qui peuvent contenir du pus, selon l'infection en cause. J'ai des **boutons** parce que j'exprime de **l'impatience**, je veux aller au-devant des choses et vite ! Si le pus se manifeste, je suis en **colère**, je **bous à l'intérieur**. Je me sens contrarié et soucieux, je vis peut-être une petite tristesse intérieure et, dans le cas de **boutons** sur l'**ensemble** du corps, un découragement généralisé. Les **boutons** au visage sont reliés à l'individualité. C'est la même signification que l'acné faciale. Je me rejette, je filtre les personnes qui passent mes « barrières », je veux la paix sans être approché. Je cherche quelqu'un ouvert à l'amour qui sera prêt à m'écouter. Je prends le temps avant de dire ou faire quelque chose, en me souvenant que je suis pleinement guidé !

PEAU — CALLOSITÉS (voir aussi : PIEDS — DURILLONS)

La **callosité** est un épaississement et un durcissement de la **peau**, liés à des frottements répétés, donc à des attitudes et à certains schèmes de pensées **rigides** que je véhicule actuellement. Plusieurs régions du corps peuvent être affectées. La **peau** est reliée à l'énergie mentale et lorsque celle-ci s'accumule ou se cristallise, en réaction de peur par rapport à une situation quelconque, survient alors une immobilité ou une inertie empêchant le déplacement de cette énergie, sans flexibilité dans mes pensées. Je reste ouvert **même si j'ai peur**. Cette peur m'amène à fermer et à rétrécir ma vision objective de la vie. Je découvre la cause de ma peur et alors, l'énergie bloquée et accumulée sur l'épiderme commencera à se diffuser en harmonie avec moi. Ma **peau** reviendra souple et jeune. La région où se manifeste la **callosité** peut m'apporter des informations supplémentaires : par exemple, au niveau de l'épaule, je **durcis** mes idées et mes attitudes par rapport aux responsabilités de ma vie et ainsi de suite...

PEAU — DÉMANGEAISONS
(voir aussi : PEAU — ÉRUPTION [... de boutons])

La **démangeaison** est reliée à la **peau**, l'organe sensoriel le plus étendu du corps humain. La **démangeaison** est une irritation, quelque chose qui « se glisse » sous la **peau** et qui m'affecte à un endroit particulier ou qui m'**irrite** intérieurement. Je me **sens contrarié** par des désirs insatisfaits et une certaine **impatience** s'installe et fait que je me gratte, gratte, gratte... Ces grattements m'indiquent que les situations de ma vie ne vont pas selon mes désirs. Les choses n'avancent pas assez rapidement pour moi. La vie me pousse à faire des changements rapides. Je vis de l'**insécurité** et des **remords** en conséquence de tout cela. Que dois-je faire pour changer cet état ? **J'identifie la « cause » de l'irritation.** Est-ce reliée à mon père, à ma mère ou à quelqu'un que j'aime ? Est-ce une situation que je veux intérieurement changer ? Si l'irritation est généralisée à l'ensemble du corps, elle affecte donc tout mon être d'une manière très intense. Si elle est à un endroit particulier, je trouve la réponse selon la partie du corps affectée. Qu'importe la réponse, je l'accepte ↓♥ car je

sais qu'elle est bénéfique pour moi. Je n'ai plus besoin de fuir ou de quitter ce que je vis pour que les **démangeaisons** disparaissent. Par contre, s'il s'agit d'allergies, je regarde à quoi ou à qui je suis allergique. Je n'aurai plus besoin de me sentir mal au point de me gratter sans cesse. En mon for intérieur, je sais que l'ouverture du cœur guérit beaucoup de maux !

PEAU — DÉMANGEAISONS À L'ANUS
(voir : ANUS — DÉMANGEAISON ANALE)

PEAU — DERMATITE

La **dermatite** est l'inflammation de ma **peau**. C'est la partie de mon être qui prend contact en premier avec l'univers et conséquemment, reflète plusieurs de mes peurs et de mes insécurités intérieures. Une inflammation est une irritation refoulée essayant de s'exprimer. Cette colère peut être autant envers moi-même qu'envers les autres. La **dermatite** est une façon de réagir si quelqu'un « se glisse » sous ma **peau**, me bouleverse, me dérange ou si une situation me cause de la frustration. Elle met en évidence un besoin de contact physique (habituellement par le toucher) qui demande à être comblé ou le besoin d'éviter un contact qui m'est imposé et que je rejette. Ayant de la difficulté ou n'osant pas dire à l'autre personne d'arrêter, ma **peau** « **bout** » **de colère,** ou au contraire, je peux avoir de la difficulté à manifester mon besoin de contact humain, de caresse, etc. L'important est de respecter mes besoins, de faire part de ceux-ci aux personnes concernées, et la **dermatite** pourra se résorber naturellement.

PEAU — ECZÉMA

L'**eczéma** est une affection de la **peau** surmontée par des zones rouges pouvant apparaître autant chez l'adulte que chez l'enfant. Je suis une personne hypersensible. **Je n'ai pas appris à m'aimer** et, comme je crains d'être blessé, je vis beaucoup en fonction de ce que les autres attendent de moi. J'ai peur d'être abandonné. Si j'ai de l'**eczéma**, j'ai déjà vécu une situation de séparation très intense. Celle-ci peut même remonter au moment où j'étais dans le ventre de ma mère. Dans ma vie, j'aurai tendance à recréer des situations où je me sentirai séparé, particulièrement des gens que j'aime. L'**eczéma** « touchant » la **peau**, ce qui me manque, même inconsciemment, c'est le contact, le toucher de la personne avant la séparation, que j'ai maintenant perdu ou que je n'ai plus que rarement. C'est donc ma **peau** qui faisait contact avec l'autre et ce contact m'ayant été **retiré**, ma **peau** exprime son besoin d'être touchée sous forme d'**eczéma.** Cela m'amène à m'isoler, à me retirer et à me déprécier. **Je m'oublie constamment au détriment des autres.** J'accorde beaucoup d'importance à ce que les gens peuvent penser de moi ou à la façon dont ils me perçoivent. L'image que je projette est très importante. J'éprouve de la difficulté à être moi. Ne pas savoir où me mène

mon destin me crée beaucoup d'inquiétude et alors, l'anxiété me gagne. Je passe du désespoir à la révolte ou à la colère. Ce désespoir qui « mijote » va « faire irruption » par vagues. Tous ces facteurs réunis m'amènent à vivre de la **frustration** et de l'**irritation**. Alors même que je cherche à plaire à tout le monde, j'omets de prendre en considération mes propres besoins ; tout cela afin de me faire aimer des autres. J'agis en fonction des attentes des autres au lieu de faire ce qui me plaît. **Je rejette qui je suis.** Je ne m'aime pas comme je suis donc, le fait que la **peau**, qui est apparente et que tous les gens peuvent voir soit en mauvais état, voire même « laide », va confirmer dans le physique comment je me perçois intérieurement. Plus je me rejette et plus j'attire des gens autour de moi par qui je vais avoir l'impression d'être rejeté ; ma peur du rejet va se manifester ! Cela m'amène à « battre en retraite » et à me couper de la réalité extérieure quand au fond de moi, ce que je veux, c'est de me rapprocher des gens. Je peux aussi être « irrité » émotionnellement sans que j'en sois conscient. Je vais avec l'**eczéma** ériger une **barrière** physique entre moi et les autres afin de me **protéger** et d'éviter de me sentir menacé ou blessé. Toutefois, dans le cas d'un bébé, je vais développer une **croûte de lait** parce que j'ai besoin davantage de chaleur humaine et de contact physique avec les gens que j'aime. Me sentant « isolé », je vais manifester de l'**eczéma** afin de me rapprocher des autres. J'ai besoin d'amour et d'attention. Dans le cas d'un enfant, mon besoin d'être touché se manifeste avec celui d'avoir un contact **peau sur peau** (au sens propre du terme) avec une personne qui m'aime et non pas un contact où il y aurait une couverture ou des vêtements qui empêcheraient ce **contact physique**. Que je sois un adulte ou un enfant, cette croûte représente ce que je dois laisser aller pour enfin devenir moi, ce moi caché depuis si longtemps. J'ai à laisser aller certaines attitudes, certains schèmes mentaux afin de me détacher de mon passé et de me concentrer sur les actions à prendre afin de réaliser mon potentiel. J'ai à m'accepter ↓♥ tel que je suis et à m'aimer. **CE QUE JE NE ME DONNE PAS MOI-MÊME NE PEUT M'ÊTRE DONNÉ, TELLE EST LA LOI DE LA RÉCIPROCITÉ.** J'identifie donc mes besoins réels et j'agis en fonction de ceux-ci. J'apprends à vivre pleinement l'instant présent, sachant que chaque geste que je pose aujourd'hui forme mon demain. J'avance dans la vie avec confiance.

PEAU — ENGELURES (voir aussi : FROID [coup de...])

Les **engelures** sont des rougeurs causées par le froid que l'on retrouve aux extrémités comme les oreilles, le nez, les mains, les pieds. Ces rougeurs violacées sont épaisses, froides et parfois très douloureuses. Les **engelures** forment parfois de petites cloques d'eau sur la surface de la **peau**. La vie me brûle et j'ai **gelé** mes réactions. Lorsque l'**engelure** se retrouve aux mains et aux talons, cela me permet de bouger plus lentement. Je m'empêche de ressentir. D'un autre côté, je m'accroche à ces situations et je ne vois rien d'autre. Physiquement, je donne l'impression d'être un fonceur alors qu'intérieurement, je me sens vidé, épuisé. Je n'ai plus le goût d'avancer et mon goût de vivre s'arrête, s'immobilise.

Je me demande même pourquoi je vis. Plutôt que de voir seulement les aspects négatifs de mes expériences, **j'accepte ↓♥ de lâcher prise sur le passé et de m'ouvrir à la vie**. Lorsque je m'ouvre à la vie, je suis à nouveau en mesure de voir tout l'amour dont je suis entouré et de vivre en harmonie avec ce que je suis et avec mon entourage.

PEAU — ÉPIDERMITE
(voir aussi : ANNEXE III, HERPÈS, PEAU — ZONA)

L'**épidermite** est une atteinte inflammatoire de l'**épiderme**, cette partie extérieure de la **peau**. Il existe certainement une tension entre ce que je vis intérieurement et ce qui se passe dans ma vie extérieurement. En étudiant ce à quoi est reliée la **peau** et les problèmes de **peau** sur le plan métaphysique, j'arriverai à mieux saisir ce que je vis afin d'y remédier.

PEAU — ÉRUPTION (... de boutons)
(voir aussi : PEAU — DÉMANGEAISONS)

Une **éruption de boutons** est l'apparition de petites rougeurs accompagnées de petites excroissances à la surface de la **peau**. Ma **peau** est la première partie de moi qui entre en contact avec l'univers. La rougeur est reliée à mes émotions et la **démangeaison,** le signe de ma contrariété. Je suis irrité face à des retards et frustré par une situation ou par quelqu'un. Cette **éruption** peut aussi être reliée à la honte et à la culpabilité que je ressens. La plupart du temps, il y a eu un état de stress intense par rapport à mes émotions et c'est ce qui fait apparaître les **boutons**. Comme la terre manifeste des **éruptions** volcaniques parce qu'il s'accumule une trop forte pression sous la surface de la croûte terrestre, la **peau** manifeste des **éruptions** causées par des tensions intérieures qui veulent se libérer. Si je me retrouve dans une situation semblable dans l'avenir, mon corps s'en souviendra et une nouvelle **éruption** surgira. Je me sens contrarié intérieurement, je peux me sentir menacé, je peux même me rejeter en tant que personne. Mon insécurité m'amène à me « retirer », avec l'espoir peut-être de ne pas être approché par personne. Inconsciemment, je peux même utiliser ce moyen pour attirer l'attention. La région du corps affectée m'indique à quel niveau se situe ma contrariété. Je prends conscience de la cause et j'accepte ↓♥ d'exprimer ce que je ressens. Cela me libère et ma **peau** s'éclaircit à nouveau.

PEAU — FURONCLES (voir aussi : INFLAMMATION)

Un **furoncle** se définit comme étant une inflammation de la **peau** causée par une bactérie, caractérisée par une masse blanchâtre de tissu mort. J'ai l'impression que quelqu'un ou quelque chose **empoisonne** mon existence et comme je refoule à l'intérieur toute ma colère, mes angoisses, j'en aurai « par-dessus la tête » et le trop plein se manifestera par un ou des **furoncles**. Puisque les **furoncles** touchent la **peau**, la colère vécue est souvent la résultante d'une

situation où j'ai été **séparé** de quelqu'un ou de quelque chose qui m'était cher et avec qui je ne peux plus avoir de contact physique (par le toucher). L'endroit de mon corps où le **furoncle** se manifeste me donne une indication par rapport à l'aspect de ma vie qui suscite chez moi tant de colère et sur la raison pour laquelle « cela » bout à l'intérieur de moi. Par exemple, un **furoncle** sur mon épaule gauche m'indique de la frustration par rapport à mes responsabilités familiales et à celles de mon couple. Je peux avoir l'impression d'en avoir trop et que mon conjoint n'en fait pas assez. J'ai avantage à exprimer la colère que je vis et à demander de l'aide, s'il y a lieu, pour éviter que je ne m'empoisonne de la sorte par des **furoncles.**

PEAU — FURONCLES VAGINAUX

Tout **furoncle** indique de la frustration non verbalisée. S'il se manifeste au niveau de mes organes sexuels, se peut-il que je vive de la colère par rapport à mon conjoint (ou partenaire sexuel) et à la façon dont la sexualité est vécue (par exemple : je peux être frustré par rapport à la durée, à la fréquence, à l'intensité de nos relations sexuelles) ? Et si je n'ai pas de partenaire au moment où les **furoncles** apparaissent, je peux vivre de la colère face au fait que je ne vis pas ma sexualité comme je le veux, faute de conjoint. Quelle que soit ma situation, si j'ai un conjoint, il est important que je communique mes besoins, ma frustration, pour qu'à deux nous apportions les changements nécessaires à une sexualité plus épanouie. Si je n'ai pas de partenaire, j'accepte ↓♥ ma situation présente comme étant la meilleure pour le moment. En ayant une attitude positive, j'augmente mes chances de rencontrer une personne avec qui je pourrai développer une belle relation et qui saura me satisfaire à tous les niveaux.

PEAU — GALE ou GRATTELLE

La **gale** est une maladie cutanée causée par des parasites, caractérisée par des démangeaisons. Qu'est-ce qui me démange au point de susciter tant d'impatience et d'agacement ? Est-ce qu'il y a une situation dans ma vie que je désire voir changer depuis un certain temps sans que rien ne se passe ? C'est peut-être que les choses ne se passent pas comme je le désire et à la vitesse que moi je veux. Je me laisse déranger, infester, par une personne, une chose ou une situation et j'ai avantage à lâcher prise et à ne pas vouloir tout contrôler dans ma vie. Je regarde où la **gale** se situe, sur quelle partie de mon corps, afin de découvrir la source de mon malaise. J'ai à laisser aller le cours de la vie et à me dire qu'il y a un moment pour chaque chose. J'ai confiance que tout est en place et en harmonie.

PEAU — GERÇURE

Les **gerçures** sont des crevasses douloureuses que l'on rencontre le plus fréquemment aux mains et aux pieds. Je vis probablement de l'irritation prononcée par rapport à quelqu'un, à quelque chose ou par rapport à une situation. Comme les **gerçures** se rencontrent très souvent l'hiver, celles-ci

étant causées par le froid, je peux avoir l'impression de m'être fait **brûler vif** par une personne ou par une situation, car le froid intense peut brûler autant que le feu. S'il s'agit de **gerçures** aux mains, cela affecte plus mon quotidien, tandis qu'aux pieds, je peux appréhender ce qui s'en vient pour moi dans le futur.

PEAU — KÉRATOSE

(voir aussi : PEAU — ACROKÉRATOSE, PIEDS / DURILLONS / VERRUES)

La **kératose** se caractérise par un épaississement de la couche superficielle de la **peau**. Sur la **peau**, cela peut se présenter comme des surfaces rougeâtres, rugueuses, pouvant former une croûte. Comme la **peau** est la jonction entre le monde extérieur et le monde intérieur, je peux avoir de telles peurs que dans mon environnement, je sens le besoin de me protéger en formant « une barrière plus épaisse ». La couleur rougeâtre m'indique de la frustration refoulée par rapport à ce que je vis. L'endroit où se forme la **kératose**, que ce soit sur les bras, les cuisses, le visage ou les mains, m'indique sur quel aspect de ma vie je sens le besoin de me protéger. Je peux envoyer des pensées d'amour à mon corps à l'endroit où se forme la **kératose** afin d'intégrer la prise de conscience que j'ai à faire. La confiance face à la vie augmentera en moi et je pourrai retrouver la souplesse naturelle de ma **peau**.

PEAU — LUPUS

Il existe différentes sortes de **lupus**. Cependant, le **lupus** en général est une maladie inflammatoire qui peut toucher un grand nombre d'organes. On attribue son origine au système auto-immunitaire. Je développe un **lupus** quand je vis un profond découragement, de la haine ou de la honte envers moi-même, ce qui fait que mon système de défense s'affaiblit. Mon mal-être a bien souvent sa source dans une culpabilité émotionnelle profonde qui me ronge de l'intérieur. Je préfère me punir plutôt que de m'affirmer. Je baisse les bras, je capitule car j'ai l'impression qu'il n'y a aucune issue possible, aucune solution, et je peux vivre de la frustration face à mon impuissance. La mort est une échappatoire et je refuse d'accepter ↓♥ l'amour et le pardon envers moi-même ou envers les autres. Réapprendre à m'aimer moi-même constitue une étape importante, voire essentielle, à ma guérison. Je peux demander de l'aide intérieurement ou demander à des personnes compétentes de m'aider afin d'amorcer ce processus de guérison intérieure.

PEAU — MÉLANOME MALIN

Le **mélanome malin** est aussi appelé le **cancer du grain de beauté**. Il s'agit d'une tumeur, le plus souvent maligne, au niveau de la **peau,** et qui provient des cellules qui sont chargées de pigmenter cette dernière (mélanocytes). Le **mélanome** apparaît à l'endroit de mon corps que je peux relier à un événement où **je me suis senti souillé**, taché. Je remets en question mon intégrité physique. Je peux aussi avoir vécu un événement où je

me suis senti **arraché** de quelqu'un ou de quelque chose qui m'était cher (les maladies de **peau** étant souvent reliées à une séparation). J'apprends à remettre de l'amour dans la situation qui est la source de ce **mélanome**. Bien que cela ait pu être difficile au moment où j'ai vécu cela, j'accepte ↓♥ de voir quel élément positif ou quelle sagesse en a résulté.

PEAU — POINTS NOIRS (voir aussi : VISAGE)

Les **points noirs** ou **comédons** sont de petites saillies à la surface de la **peau**, noirâtres au sommet et causées par une hypersécrétion de sébum[69]. Ils sont l'expression extérieure de mon sentiment intérieur d'être sale, « pas propre » et de « ne pas valoir grand-chose », et indique que je me mésestime. J'apprends à m'aimer tel que je suis et à être fier de moi et alors, le teint de mon visage (où l'on retrouve généralement les **comédons**) deviendra éclatant.

PEAU — PSORIASIS

Le **psoriasis** consiste en une surproduction de cellules cutanées, créant un entassement des cellules mortes, un épaississement de la **peau**, des plaques rouges épaisses ou en gouttes et qui sont recouvertes de fragments de substances cornées blanchâtres. Si j'ai du **psoriasis**, je suis parmi les 2 % de la population du globe qui ont cette maladie. Aussi, je suis généralement hypersensible et j'ai un très grand besoin d'amour et d'affection qui n'est pas comblé, me rappelant peut-être une autre période difficile de ma vie. À ce moment-là, j'ai probablement eu un très grand sentiment d'abandon ou d'être séparé de quelqu'un ou de quelque chose qui m'était cher. Car le **psoriasis** implique qu'il y a eu une double séparation[70], c'est-à-dire le plus souvent face à deux personnes différentes. Cela pourrait être qu'on m'a séparé de mes deux parents lorsque j'étais enfant. C'est la **peau** qui est « touchée » car, pour moi, étant un enfant, ce dont j'ai le plus besoin, c'est du contact physique avec mes parents ou avec toute autre personne que j'aime et avec qui je me sens proche. La double séparation peut être celle avec ma mère et un de mes frères ou une de mes sœurs, ou avec mon conjoint et un projet de travail (« mon bébé »), ou n'importe quelle autre combinaison qui implique une séparation avec deux personnes ou de deux situations que j'aime et qui me tiennent à cœur. Le fait d'être ou de me sentir séparé m'empêche d'avoir ce contact, surtout par rapport au toucher, donc de ma **peau**, avec ces personnes que j'aime. Il y aura donc apparition du **psoriasis**. Maintenant, j'ai tellement peur d'être blessé que je veux garder une certaine distance entre moi et les autres. Le **psoriasis** est une belle façon qu'a mon corps de se protéger contre trop de rapprochement physique et de se protéger contre ma vulnérabilité. Je vis donc

---

69. **Sébum :** Une forme de gras, en partie des triglycérides qui se forment surtout à la surface de l'épiderme.
70. **Double séparation :** Dans le cas de l'eczéma, il s'agit d'une simple séparation, avec une seule personne ou situation.

un conflit intérieur entre mes besoins de rapprochement et ma peur qui me fait garder mes distances. Je dois donc me libérer de certains « patterns » mentaux et attitudes qui se sont accumulés et qui, maintenant, n'ont plus raison d'être, étant éteints et morts. J'accepte ↓♥ maintenant ma sensibilité ; j'apprends à faire des choses pour moi et non pas seulement en fonction de ce que les autres attendent de moi. Et bien que le **psoriasis** soit probablement survenu à la suite d'un événement douloureux ou d'un choc émotionnel, j'accepte ↓♥ que cela fasse partie du processus naturel de la vie et de ma croissance et que je devienne plus fort et plus solide intérieurement.

PEAU — SCLÉRODERMIE (voir aussi : SYSTÈME IMMUNITAIRE)

La **sclérodermie** se caractérise par le durcissement de la **peau**, la perte de sa mobilité et de sa souplesse. Étant une personne souffrant de cette maladie, je suis souvent très dur envers moi-même et je me suis souvent senti blessé. Vivant une grande insécurité, je crois devoir constamment me protéger des gens qui m'entourent. Pour y arriver, je m'endurcis tellement que je deviens un bloc de glace. La guérison se trouve dans l'ouverture aux autres. Ainsi, j'accepte ↓♥ d'ouvrir mon cœur à l'amour, de sentir la chaleur et le bien-être qui se trouvent autour de moi, cette chaleur qui descend au plus profond de moi et fait fondre ce bloc qui me glace.

PEAU — TACHES DE VIN

Ces **taches de vin**[71] aussi appelées « envies », sont des malformations très fréquentes des petits vaisseaux sanguins, aussi appelées capillaires, localisées sur la partie superficielle de la **peau**. Si à ma naissance, j'avais une **tache de vin**, je peux commencer par examiner sur quelle partie de mon corps la **tache** se situe. Cela correspond habituellement à une émotion forte, souvent de colère ou de peine, vécue par ma mère lorsqu'elle me portait et dont j'ai été affecté « aussi ». Puisque la chirurgie ou le traitement au laser permet de faire disparaître en tout ou en partie ces **taches**, je vais prendre conscience de la relation que cela a avec moi pour l'intégrer et m'amener à être davantage moi-même.

PEAU — URTICAIRE

L'**urticaire** se caractérise par l'apparition de plaques rouges sur différentes parties du corps. Celles-ci, légèrement bombées, provoquent de vives démangeaisons. **L'urticaire** provient, selon le cas, d'une intoxication alimentaire, liée à la prise de certains médicaments ou autres substances, mais cet état peut s'aggraver avec le stress et les tensions. Si je souffre **d'urticaire**, je suis très probablement une personne vivant beaucoup de rejet. Je n'aime pas

---

71. Sur le plan médical, cela est appelé **angiomes matures** ou **angiomes plans**.

l'être que je suis et ma crainte d'être blessé est si forte que, pour être aimé, je fais les choses en fonction de ce que les gens attendent de moi. Ma peur d'être rejeté se concrétise puisque je me rejette moi-même. Ma **peau** abîmée par ces plaques rouges me fait sentir laid et indésirable. Je suis comme une bête **marquée au fer rouge** ; je suis dépendant de mon propriétaire. Puisque je vis en fonction des autres, je m'empêche de faire des choses pour moi ; je n'ose pas accomplir de nouveaux projets, ce qui augmente mon sentiment d'impuissance. Je choisis d'être le maître de ma vie, je deviens la personne la plus importante pour moi. J'avance et je me fais confiance.

PEAU — VERRUES (en général) (voir aussi : TUMEUR[S])

Les **verrues sont une infection virale de la peau** qui cause un excès dans la production de cellules, créant une masse dure et indolore (tumeur bénigne). Cette masse est l'accumulation de barrières que je dresse sur ma route. Des barrières de peine, de rancœurs, liées à certains côtés de moi que je juge laids et détestables, provoquant un sentiment de culpabilité. Si j'ai par exemple des **verrues** sur le dos de mes mains, je me juge très sévèrement par rapport à mon écriture et à celle des autres. L'apparition de **verrues** vient combler un vide affectif. Je considère que je ne mérite pas mieux que cette chose laide. Si je crois être laid, mon corps deviendra laid ; c'est simplement le reflet de mes attitudes intérieures. Si j'ai honte de ce que je fais ou bien que je souhaite quelque chose mais que je crois ne pas le mériter, il est possible que des **verrues** apparaissent. Il est important d'aller voir sur quelle partie de mon corps la **verrue** est apparue, afin de connaître quel aspect de mon corps ou de ma vie est affecté. En acceptant ↓♥ ce que je suis, un être digne d'amour, je n'aurai plus besoin de **verrues** pour me le rappeler et elles disparaîtront.

PEAU — VERRUES PLANTAIRES
(voir : PIEDS — VERRUES PLANTAIRES)

PEAU — VITILIGO

Le **vitiligo** est une dépigmentation de la **peau,** laquelle est considérée comme étant la plus fréquente. Ainsi, ma **peau** devient blanche en certains endroits de mon corps et par plaques. Cela peut se produire sur n'importe quelle partie du corps, y compris le visage et les mains. Je peux en être affecté si je ne me sens pas concerné par les choses ou par les personnes qui m'entourent. J'ai l'impression de ne plus avoir d'identité. Je n'ai pas de sentiment d'appartenance face à ma famille, à ma communauté, à mes collègues de travail ou à mon peuple. Comme j'aurai l'impression d'avoir été taché, ce qui peut représenter un sentiment d'impureté, je voudrai que cette tache « disparaisse » et au lieu d'une tache foncée, je me retrouverai avec une tache blanche. Cela peut être relié à un sentiment de vouloir « disparaître » ou de devenir « transparent » afin de passer inaperçu. Je peux avoir vécu une ou des expériences sexuelles où ce sentiment

de souillure ressortira. Aussi je peux avoir l'impression qu'on m'a **séparé** d'un ou de plusieurs êtres chers et je trouve cela moche. Je peux avoir eu l'impression d'avoir été incapable d'arrêter ou d'empêcher cette séparation. Je vais donc me culpabiliser et me dévaloriser, me sentant souillé, sale par rapport à cette situation. L'endroit particulier du corps qui est affecté m'indique quel aspect de moi-même est concerné. Je prends conscience de l'importance de ma vie.

PEAU — ZONA

Le **zona** se reconnaît à l'éruption qu'il entraîne sur la **peau**, laquelle se manifeste unilatéralement et en bande, suivant le trajet d'un nerf. Les nerfs étant nos moyens de communication intérieure, la douleur que provoque cette éruption indique une brisure de communication dans la région affectée. Je me suis senti agressé et je vis une profonde amertume. Une situation ou une personne m'a blessé, provoquant de **la tension** alors que mon corps désire de **l'attention**. Je pourrai de plus avoir l'impression d'avoir été souillé, taché. Mon premier réflexe est de me retirer, de me fermer, croyant ainsi éviter d'autres blessures. J'ai ce comportement parce que la situation me fait vivre **une grande insécurité intérieure**. En agissant de cette façon, je retourne vers moi cette agression dont je crois avoir été la victime ; je donne raison à mes agresseurs. L'éruption boursouflante a pour but de me faire prendre conscience que je vis une réaction ou une irritation émotionnelle intense face à quelqu'un ou à quelque chose qui m'occasionne un stress excessif et qui rend mes prises de décisions difficiles. Mon corps me dit de faire confiance au courant de vie qui est en moi. J'accepte ↓♥ ma sensibilité puisqu'elle fait partie de moi.

PÉDICULOSE (voir : MORPIONS)

PELADE (voir : CHEVEUX — PELADE)

PELLICULES (voir aussi : CHEVEUX [maladie des...])

Les **pellicules** sont la couche calleuse et sèche de la peau ayant l'aspect de flocons blancs et qui se retrouvent la plupart du temps sur le cuir chevelu. Puisqu'il y a accumulation de peau morte, il y a aussi accumulation d'attitudes et de « patterns morts » dont je n'ai plus besoin. Mon cuir chevelu est relié au mental, à l'abstrait ; ce sont ces schémas de pensées mentaux que je dois laisser aller afin de faire place à plus d'ouverture et plus de flexibilité. Que je sois très actif ou au contraire très inactif intellectuellement (par exemple, si je laisse les autres penser à ma place), les deux peuvent produire des **pellicules**, puisqu'il existe dans les deux cas un déséquilibre par rapport à mon fonctionnement rationnel et mental. Je m'ouvre de plus en plus aux nouvelles façons de fonctionner dans la vie et je me sens de plus en plus flexible, me laissant conduire par le courant de la vie.

PELVIS (voir aussi : BASSIN, HANCHES)

Le **pelvis** est l'ouverture de la région pelvienne charpentée par les hanches et la colonne. Les douleurs à cette région sont souvent perçues comme des élancements. Le mot est très approprié car c'est cette région pelvienne, supportée par les hanches, qui m'aide à avancer, à être en mouvement, et donc **à « m'élancer » dans la vie ou dans un nouveau projet**. Ce projet peut être de donner naissance à quelqu'un, mais aussi à moi-même, surtout en ce qui concerne de nouvelles attitudes ou de nouveaux comportements. Cela implique une communication soit sur le plan sexuel, soit interpersonnel. Il est important que je me fasse confiance dans les décisions à prendre face aux nouvelles directions à choisir, que je mette des choses de l'avant afin de découvrir toute la richesse de mon monde intérieur et toutes les possibilités qui s'offrent à moi.

PÉRICARDITE (voir : CŒUR — PÉRICARDITE)

PERTE D'APPÉTIT (voir : APPÉTIT [perte de...])

PERTE DE CONNAISSANCE (voir : ÉVANOUISSEMENT)

PERTES BLANCHES (voir : LEUCORRHÉE)

PERTES VAGINALES (voir : LEUCORRHÉE)

PEUR (voir aussi : REINS [problèmes rénaux])

La **peur** est une crainte ou une appréhension que j'éprouve face à un danger **réel ou imaginaire**. Lorsque j'ai **peur**, mon cœur bat la chamaille, je deviens tendu. La **peur** prend place à l'intérieur de moi lorsque je me sens inquiet, peu sûr de **moi,** découragé, que je suis très émotif, etc. L'objet de ma **peur** peut être soit la peur de l'échec, de l'abandon, du rejet, la peur d'être blessé, etc. ; elle devient tellement réelle à mes yeux que tout mon corps va réagir à celle-ci et particulièrement mes **reins**. Ma **peur** ne fait qu'augmenter les chances que tout ce que j'appréhende arrive. **La peur de la maladie elle-même peut être un facteur déterminant pour l'apparition de celle-ci.** Il est important que je prenne conscience ici que ce sont mes peurs qui contrôlent ma vie et non pas les gens ou les situations. Parmi les six peurs fondamentales, il y a : (1) la peur de mourir, (2) la peur de la maladie, (3) la peur de la pauvreté, (4) la peur de perdre l'amour d'un être cher, (5) la peur de la vieillesse, (6) la peur de la critique. Je décide donc dès à présent de remplacer la **peur** par la confiance. Je demande toujours d'être guidé et protégé dans les actions que j'ai à prendre ou dans les paroles que j'ai à dire, pour le bien-être de tous.

PHARYNGITE (voir : GORGE — PHARYNGITE)

PHLÉBITE (voir : SANG — PHLÉBITE)

PICOTE (voir : MALADIES DE L'ENFANCE)

PIEDS (en général)

Les **pieds** représentent mon contact avec la terre d'énergie nourricière. Ils sont en rapport avec les relations que je vis avec ma **mère** ainsi qu'avec les conflits face à celle-ci, lesquels peuvent remonter aussi loin que ma conception. Mes **pieds** me donnent de la stabilité dans mes déplacements vers un but, un désir ou une direction. Ils m'aident à me sentir en sécurité dans ma relation avec l'univers. Ils représentent la position que je prends face aux situations qui se présentent à moi. Le fait d'avoir un **pied gauche** plus fort que le **pied droit** (ou vice-versa) peut me renseigner sur les différentes tendances que je dois privilégier dans mes déplacements ou contacts avec le sol, tant physiques que mentals ou spirituels. De plus, si je marche les **pieds** tournés vers l'extérieur, je peux vivre de la confusion face à la direction prise ou avoir une dispersion de mes énergies dans différents projets, tandis que si mes **pieds** sont tournés vers l'intérieur, je vis une fermeture ou une résistance face aux directions à prendre dans ma vie.

PIEDS (maux de...)

C'est par mes **pieds** que je me déplace sur le chemin de la vie. Mon cerveau est le poste de commande de mes **pieds**. La science de la réflexologie nous enseigne que tout notre corps est réparti sur toute la surface de nos **pieds**. Donc, tous les problèmes que je peux relier à mes **pieds** me permettent de savoir quel endroit de mon corps me parle. Un problème relié à mes **pieds** m'indique un conflit entre la direction et le mouvement que je prends, et témoigne de mon besoin de plus de stabilité et de sécurité dans ma vie. L'avenir et tous ses imprévus me font peur. Quand j'ai mal aux **pieds**, je dois ralentir le pas. Est-ce par ennui ou par découragement face à toutes mes responsabilités et face à toutes les choses que j'ai à faire et qui me semblent impossibles à réaliser ? Ou au contraire, ne vais-je pas à 300 kilomètres à l'heure et mon corps me dit de ralentir avant de « faire un accident » ? Une crampe au **pied** gauche ou au **pied** droit m'indique à quel niveau se situe l'hésitation ou le refus d'avancer ou quelle est la direction que j'ai peur de prendre. Le blocage est-il à l'intérieur ou à l'extérieur de moi ? J'ai à prendre position dans une situation donnée et je peux avoir peur de « **perdre pied** » et « **je ne sais plus sur quel pied danser** ». Un **pied plat** m'indique une colonne vertébrale très droite, très rigide, et donc, que j'ai une structure moins souple. Puisqu'il n'y a aucun espace entre mon **pied** en entier et la terre sur laquelle je marche, cela dénote

que mes frontières personnelles sont mal délimitées. Je me sens donc vulnérable et, pour me protéger, je « survolerai » la surface des choses au lieu de créer un contact plus en profondeur et de bien « prendre racine », que ce soit dans une relation affective, dans un travail ou dans tout autre domaine. Cela a aussi comme conséquence que je vais entremêler mon travail et ma vie privée, les deux se chevauchant très souvent, peu importe ce qui arrive, et au détriment du reste de mes relations. À l'opposé, si j'ai l'**arche du pied haute**, cela me renseigne sur un déplacement plus lourd comme une colonne vertébrale très chargée. Cela dénote aussi que j'ai clairement séparé ma vie publique et ma vie privée. Cela m'amène à être à l'écart et silencieux, ayant de la difficulté à amorcer une communication et à aller au-devant des autres. Une retenue de mes émotions face à la direction à prendre dans ma vie se traduira par des **pieds enflés** et l'excès de ces émotions qui se libèrent se traduira par de la **transpiration**. Des **pieds froids** m'amènent à me questionner par rapport à mes relations avec ma mère et à voir ce qui peut m'amener à avoir des **pieds froids**, voire glacés. Il peut s'agir tout simplement de mes rapports avec elle que je trouve distants et « froids ». Je dois donc aimer mes **pieds** car ce sont eux qui transportent tout mon être sur le chemin de la vie. Plus je les aime et les accepte ↓♥, plus sera facile le travail qu'ils accomplissent.

PIED D'ATHLÈTE (voir : PIEDS — MYCOSE)

PIEDS — DURILLONS ou CORS AUX PIEDS
(voir aussi : PEAU — CALLOSITÉS)

Je vais de l'avant avec mes **pieds** mais quelque chose me dit que cela accroche un peu... C'est le **durillon**, cette petite boursouflure qui m'indique une attitude d'appréhension dans ma vie présente. C'est la crainte d'avancer vers l'inconnu avec confiance car je n'arrive pas à rester « naturel », à faire les choses simplement. Aller de l'avant est difficile pour moi. Je m'élance vers l'avenir mais j'hésite et je pousse trop ou peut-être pas assez. Je cherche la cause en premier. Qu'est-ce qui me fait vivre ceci ? La tristesse et le chagrin, la crainte de ne pas réussir ? Bien sûr, je peux réduire la grosseur de mes **cors** mais c'est insuffisant car je ne travaille pas avec la vraie cause. J'accepte ↓♥ de voir ce qui me dérange à ce point et qui m'empêche d'aller de l'avant. Je serai ainsi plus en « accord » avec la vie. Ma confiance en l'avenir n'en sera que plus grande.

PIEDS — MYCOSE (... entre les orteils) ou PIED D'ATHLÈTE
(voir aussi : PEAU / [en général] / [maux de...], SYSTÈME IMMUNITAIRE)

La **mycose** apparaît sous forme de démangeaison. Une peau croûtée et fendue qui indique que mon mental est irrité ou contrarié, que je me sens limité ou incapable d'avancer de la façon que je voudrais et par rapport à ce qui m'attend dans l'avenir. J'ai de la difficulté à m'accepter ↓♥ tel que je suis et je voudrais avoir l'acceptation ↓♥ et l'adoration des gens qui m'entourent, tout

comme l'« athlète » qui a réussi et qui est adoré. Cela produit un stress et de la douleur interne. L'irritation des orteils est reliée aux détails et aux directions de ma vie future, à l'abstrait et aux concepts énergétiques. Ce sont des peurs et un manque de compréhension. Je peux me visualiser sur une route où il est agréable d'avancer et où je me sens pleinement confiant. Cela m'aidera à laisser aller les peurs et m'apportera plus d'harmonie dans la vie.

PIEDS — VERRUES PLANTAIRES (voir aussi : PIEDS — DURILLONS)

Une **verrue plantaire** se remarque habituellement par l'apparition d'une petite particule translucide sous le **pied,** autour de laquelle se forme une callosité, provoquant de la douleur lorsque sous pression. Une **verrue au pied** m'indique que je vis des craintes face à mon avenir et face à mes responsabilités. La douleur qu'elle provoque veut me faire comprendre que je ressens de la colère dans ma manière de concevoir la vie. Il est probable que je me laisse facilement arrêter par les petites embûches qui se posent devant moi. Il se peut aussi que je vive une dévalorisation par rapport à mes capacités ou habiletés physiques dans les sports. Je peux être un très bon sportif au-dessus de la moyenne et vivre de la dévalorisation parce que je m'oblige à toujours être le meilleur ou à toujours être aussi performant en toutes circonstances. Je peux avoir l'impression que « mes **pieds** ne font pas aussi bien que les pieds des autres ». J'ai aussi l'impression « de jouer au hockey comme un **pied** », ce qui veut dire que je me compare aux autres et que je me sens très inférieur par rapport à leur capacité physique. Mon corps me dit qu'il est inutile de me faire autant de mal et que je peux avancer dans la vie en toute confiance. Je dois accepter ↓♥ autant mes forces que mes faiblesses et en persévérant, je pourrai moi aussi réussir.

PIERRES AU FOIE (voir : CALCULS BILIAIRES)

PIERRES AUX REINS (voir : CALCULS RÉNAUX)

« PIPI AU LIT » (voir aussi : INCONTINENCE [... fécale, ... urinaire])

Le fait de se laisser aller durant le sommeil me renseigne sur certaines émotions de crainte ou de peur que vit mon enfant **face à l'autorité** parentale ou scolaire. Si je suis cet enfant qui vit de l'**incontinence**, il peut s'agir pour moi d'une façon de libérer les émotions (que l'urine représente) que je retiens pendant la journée, souvent parce que j'ai peur qu'on me punisse ou par peur de déplaire aux autres et de ne plus être aimé. Tout comme les animaux vont marquer leur territoire avec leur urine, de même moi, comme enfant, je peux sentir inconsciemment le même besoin d'en faire autant, comme pour définir mon « petit territoire d'enfant » que j'ai peur qu'on m'enlève ou qu'on transgresse, vivant ainsi beaucoup d'insécurité. Mon

insécurité sera aussi ravivée si on me force à dormir dans la noirceur. Comme enfant, je peux vivre un sentiment de séparation intense face à quelqu'un ou à quelque chose que j'aime, et c'est comme si, pendant la nuit, j'appelle « à l'aide » car j'ai besoin de « chaleur ». Je me dois donc, en tant que parent ou éducateur, de prendre conscience de la sensibilité de l'enfant face à l'autorité, de l'aider à se libérer de ma trop grande autorité par des paroles d'amour qui se transforment chez lui en une confiance accrue.

PLEURER

Les larmes sont un écoulement des yeux, une libération d'émotions. Que ce soit lié à la joie, l'amour, la peur, la déception, le fait de **pleurer** me libère d'un trop plein de sentiments, de pensées très fortes. Ce peut être aussi que mes yeux ont été fasciné à la vue d'une scène qui était insupportable, horrifiante, mais que j'étais poussé à regarder, comme pour attraper chaque détail. Je peux **pleurer** aussi parce que je me sens incapable de communiquer ce que je ressens. Mes **pleurs** sont une évacuation de tristesse, de déception. J'ai donc une réaction qui fait baisser la pression. Je peux aussi utiliser mes larmes pour attirer l'attention, la sympathie afin que l'on s'occupe de moi. Les **conduits lacrymaux** bloqués m'indiquent qu'il y a une résistance quant à ma libre expression, liée peut-être à cette croyance que **pleurer**, « c'est seulement pour les bébés ». Mes larmes, en sortant de mes yeux, amènent avec elles des choses me privant de voir, peut-être par peur de ne pas pouvoir les **voir** se réaliser. Je me dois de les laisser aller librement, ce qui me libère d'émotions bouleversantes, entraînant la guérison et le ressourcement.

PLEURÉSIE (voir : POUMONS — PNEUMONIE)

PNEUMONIE (voir : POUMONS — PNEUMONIE)

POIDS (excès de...) (voir aussi : GRAISSE)

L'**excès de graisse** que mon corps emmagasine entre mon être intérieur et le milieu extérieur m'indique qu'inconsciemment je cherche, je veux m'isoler, soit dans ma communication avec l'extérieur ou encore, qu'il existe une émotion ou un sentiment prisonnier, « isolé » à l'intérieur de moi, et que je ne veux plus voir. Par mon **obésité**, je cherche **une forme de protection** que j'accumule continuellement dans mes pensées intérieures. Il y a un fossé entre moi et le monde extérieur. Je camoufle ainsi mon insécurité d'être exposé, d'être vulnérable et ainsi, je veux éviter d'être blessé soit par des remarques, par des critiques ou par des situations dans lesquelles je serais inconfortable, notamment face à ma sexualité. Je peux aussi interpréter mon **excès de poids** comme étant le fait que je veux tout posséder. J'entretiens donc des émotions comme l'égoïsme et des sentiments que je me refuse de

laisser aller. Cela peut aussi être un déséquilibre, une révolte face à l'entourage, une réaction à des gestes, à des situations que je ne veux plus voir ou dont je ne veux plus me souvenir. La nourriture terrestre représente aussi une nourriture émotionnelle. Donc, je vais manger excessivement pour **combler un vide intérieur** ou pour compenser le succès qui me laisse « émotionnellement » isolé. Je peux vivre une grande insécurité tant au niveau affectif que matériel et j'ai inconsciemment besoin d'emmagasiner afin d'éviter toute « pénurie » ou « manque » qui pourrait survenir. Ce manque peut avoir été vécu dans l'enfance et souvent par rapport à la mère, elle qui était mon lien direct avec la nourriture et la survie (tétée). L'**obésité** arrive souvent après un grand choc émotionnel ou une perte importante, et le vide vécu devient très difficile à supporter. **Je vis un grand sentiment d'abandon, un vide intérieur.** Je me sens souvent coupable du départ ou de la perte d'un être cher. Je cherche un but à ma vie, je cherche à accomplir « quelque chose de bien ». J'ai de la difficulté à prendre ma place avec mes paroles et mes gestes. Je le fais donc en prenant plus de place avec mon corps physique. De plus, **je me dévalorise par rapport à mon apparence physique :** une légère « imperfection » ou quelques livres gagnées vont prendre à mes yeux des proportions gigantesques et je ne peux plus voir et apprécier mes qualités et mes attraits physiques. Mettant toute mon attention sur « ce qui est disgracieux », mon corps se mettra à réagir à cela en ajoutant encore et davantage de **poids** pour me faire réaliser combien je suis dur envers moi-même et combien je me détruis, même seulement par mes pensées négatives. Le fait d'effectuer des exercices et d'être sur une diète ne sera pas suffisant pour maigrir car je dois prendre conscience de la vraie source de mon **excès de poids** qui résulte d'une situation d'abandon. Que je sois un enfant ou un adulte, je prends conscience que je me rejette moi-même. Je peux avoir **l'impression de me sentir limité** par rapport à différents aspects de ma vie ou à ce que je veux réaliser. Ce sentiment de limitation fera que mon corps prendra de l'expansion, et absorbera un surplus de **poids**. Aussi, si je suis une personne **qui accumule des pensées, des émotions ou des choses**, mon corps « accumulera » lui aussi mais sous forme de graisse. J'apprends à exprimer mes émotions, à reconnaître ma valeur et toutes mes possibilités. Je sais maintenant que tout vide que j'ai l'impression de vivre dans ma vie peut être rempli par de l'amour et des sentiments positifs envers moi-même. Par mon acceptation ↓♥ de moi-même et des autres, avec l'amour dont je m'entoure, je me libère donc de cette peine et de ce besoin de protection.

POIGNET (voir aussi : ARTICULATIONS)

Les **poignets** sont les articulations, les pivots qui permettent la mobilité et la flexibilité de mes mains et qui me relient à mes avants-bras. Une rigidité dans les **poignets** m'empêche donc de prendre avec harmonie ou de choisir tout ce que la vie me présente. Il y a donc une obstruction, un blocage ou un refus face aux actions que je devrais poser. Les activités qui demandaient de l'adresse en sont affectées. La **douleur** aux **poignets** peut représenter de

l'énergie refoulée concernant quelque chose qui doit être fait mais que je retiens et ne fais pas. La **fracture** ou l'**entorse** m'indique un profond conflit d'expression face à la vie et comment celle-ci se sert de moi pour faire son œuvre. Je dois m'immobiliser et ne plus bouger les mains. Je me dois donc de réfléchir sur ces douleurs de manière à prendre conscience du fait qu'il me faut libérer ces énergies avec amour et confiance, car leur libre circulation me permettra d'agir de façon constructive à travers ces actions.

POINTS NOIRS (voir : PEAU — POINTS NOIRS)

POITRINE

La **poitrine** est reliée à mon sens de l'identité et à la partie intérieure de mon être. C'est à ce niveau que repose mon cœur et mes poumons, organes essentiels au fonctionnement d'une vie autonome. Si j'ai un malaise ou une douleur à ce niveau, je peux me demander : « Est-ce que ma sensibilité face à mes relations familiales a été touchée ou affectée dernièrement ? », « Est-ce que j'ai peur de m'engager face à une personne ou une situation, ce qui m'amène à éviter les occasions de donner et de m'impliquer ? » Je prends conscience qu'il m'est très bénéfique de montrer mes vrais sentiments et ma vulnérabilité : je suis toujours gagnant quand je suis vrai !

POITRINE (angine de...) (voir : ANGINE DE POITRINE)

POLIOMYÉLITE

La **poliomyélite** est une maladie contagieuse produite par un virus qui se fixe sur les centres nerveux, en particulier sur la mœlle épinière, provoquant des paralysies qui peuvent être mortelles lorsqu'elles atteignent les muscles respiratoires. La **poliomyélite** antérieure aiguë est communément appelée **poliomyélite**. Comme c'est une maladie que l'on retrouve surtout chez les enfants, on l'appelle aussi la **paralysie infantile**. Si je suis atteint de cette maladie, le virus qui me paralyse est la **jalousie** et l'**impuissance**. J'envie ce qu'un autre ou ce que les autres sont capables d'accomplir. Je voudrais les freiner mais c'est moi-même que je freine et que je paralyse. Cette maladie veut me dire que je n'ai pas à envier les autres : je suis une personne extraordinaire avec des capacités immenses. J'ai autant de qualités et de forces que les autres et je dois accepter ↓♥ celles-ci. Au lieu de **fuir** et de mettre mon attention à **brimer** les autres, je reprends ici et maintenant le plein pouvoir sur ma vie et j'accepte ↓♥ que l'abondance fait partie intégrante de ma vie.

POLYARTHRITE (voir : ARTHRITE — POLYARTHRITE)

POLYOREXIE (voir : BOULIMIE)

POLYPES

Le **polype** est une tumeur bénigne qui se développe d'une muqueuse, par exemple les muqueuses buccales, nasales, intestinales et utérines. L'excroissance qui en résulte est un signe physique pour me montrer qu'il y a une personne ou une situation dans ma vie qui me dérange et que j'ai le goût d'éviter, de fuir, mais ce n'est pas possible. Au contraire, je me sens pris, coincé et **je ne peux pas m'y soustraire**. J'ai des émotions qui se solidifient en moi. Il serait avantageux pour moi d'accepter ↓♥ que quelque chose ou quelqu'un me dérange et de me demander qu'est-ce que j'ai à apprendre de tout cela ? De quelle façon pourrais-je me sentir plus libre ? En faisant face à mes responsabilités, le ou les **polypes** disparaîtront.

POUCE (voir : DOIGTS — POUCE)

POUMONS (en général) (voir aussi : BRONCHES)

C'est par l'action de mes deux **poumons** que la vie circule en moi. Ils sont donc les filtres de l'air dans tout mon corps. J'inhale la vie et je la retourne à l'Univers. Un bon fonctionnement de mes **poumons** permet d'aérer chacune de mes cellules. C'est par mes **poumons** que je prends conscience que « JE » existe. Un mal d'exister peut donc être reconnu par eux et cela me permet d'aérer ces sentiments négatifs qu'il me faut purifier par l'amour que j'inhale.

POUMONS (maux aux...)
(voir aussi : ASTHME, BRONCHES — BRONCHITE, SCLÉROSE)

Les affections du **poumon** telles que **pneumonie, bronchite, asthme, fibrose**, etc., sont le signe que j'ai une peur très profonde d'étouffer ou de mourir. Je me sens tellement anxieux que je me restreins à vivre dans un territoire très délimité qui lui aussi me semble incertain. Je peux avoir l'impression que j'ai perdu mon territoire[72] ou que je suis en train de le perdre. Si je le perds, c'est comme si je mourais, je ne serais plus rien ! J'éprouve donc une certaine difficulté à trouver ma place et à gérer mes relations avec le monde qui m'entoure. Les **poumons** servant à ma respiration, un mauvais fonctionnement de ceux-ci amène une difficulté en ce qui a trait au transfert de l'oxygène de l'air vers le sang, fonction vitale pour ma survie. Ce mauvais fonctionnement ne fait que mettre en évidence cette mort qui m'effraie et que j'ai avantage à apprivoiser. Si j'ai une douleur ou une difficulté respiratoire, je dois me demander si j'ai l'impression de me sentir étouffé ou oppressé dans ma

---

72. **Mon territoire :** Mon conjoint, ma famille, mes amis, mon travail, ma maison, mes idées, etc.

vie. Est-ce que j'ai l'impression de « manquer d'air », particulièrement par rapport à mes relations avec les membres de ma famille ? Est-ce que je me sens limité ou ai-je l'impression de ne pas mériter d'être heureux ? Je me sens triste et déprimé et je dois apprendre à reconnaître ma valeur personnelle et à faire les choses qui me font plaisir. Au lieu de « prendre plaisir » à entretenir de vieux souvenirs qui me rendent mélancolique et qui peuvent amplifier mon sentiment d'être seul et isolé, j'ai avantage à regarder tout ce que j'ai et toute l'abondance qui est présente dans ma vie. Je prends conscience que je suis constamment protégé et guidé. J'ai le droit d'avoir un territoire, une place bien à moi qui m'est personnelle et qui n'appartient à personne d'autre, tout comme les autres ont chacun leur propre territoire. C'est ainsi que peut exister l'harmonie et que je peux m'épanouir pleinement. Je reprends le pouvoir qui m'appartient et je respire la vie « à pleins poumons » !

POUMONS (cancer des...) (voir : CANCER DES POUMONS)

POUMONS — CONGESTION (voir : CONGESTION)

POUMONS — EMPHYSÈME PULMONAIRE

Quand je suis encore fœtus et que mes **poumons** se forment, cela marque mon engagement à être ici, mon accord à dire **oui** à la vie, ceci se faisant grâce à ma respiration. Si j'ai peur de la vie ou si je veux que quelqu'un d'autre prenne soin de ma propre vie, mes **poumons** pourront connaître certaines difficultés. En respirant superficiellement, je me protège contre le fait d'avoir à traiter avec la réalité. Je vis de l'anxiété et j'ai peur car je me sens menacé. Comme mes **poumons** se dilatent et se contractent, cela correspond à ma capacité d'élargir, de partager et d'entrer dans la vie ou à me contracter, m'isoler et me retirer de la vie. Être atteint d'**emphysème pulmonaire** signifie que j'ai de la difficulté à respirer et que je me sens oppressé par l'effort. Par la respiration, j'aspire la vie en moi. Pourquoi ai-je de la difficulté à prendre la vie ? Est-ce ma façon de **fuir** la vie ? La vie ne m'intéresse plus, je n'ai aucun intérêt. J'ai de grandes peurs et l'une d'elles, c'est de m'affirmer et de prendre ma place. Pourquoi la vie a-t-elle perdu tout son sens pour moi ? Je me sens coincé. Je n'ai pas appris à être moi-même et à prendre la place qui me revient ; je vis en fonction des autres. Mes frustrations et mon mécontentement m'étouffent. J'ai l'impression que je ne mérite pas de vivre. Je prends conscience que chacun a sa place et que je dois prendre la mienne. **J'accepte ↓♥ de m'aimer davantage**, de m'affirmer et d'exprimer mes besoins, en un mot, d'être MOI. L'oppression que je ressentais est remplacée par l'apport d'air et de vie dans mes poumons. Je vois à nouveau toutes les possibilités que la vie m'offre. Je reprends le goût au bonheur.

POUMONS — PNEUMONIE et PLEURÉSIE

La **pneumonie** est l'infection du poumon provoquée par une bactérie ou par un virus, tandis que la **pleurésie** est l'inflammation aiguë ou chronique de la plèvre, membrane enveloppant les **poumons**. Les **poumons** étant l'organe de la respiration où se fait, où se produit la transformation de « mon » air pour tout « mon » corps, je vis donc un conflit intérieur qui m'affaiblit gravement. Je me dois donc de trouver l'émotion ou le sentiment qui irrite et limite le fonctionnement de ma relation avec l'air de ma vie intérieure, car ce ou ces blocages empêchent mon être de vivre pleinement. Ces sentiments profondément ancrés à l'intérieur de mon être, représentés par l'inflammation, peuvent me signaler que je suis profondément « choqué », « irrité ». Mon habileté à respirer devient très affectée par mes émotions, ma peur d'être seul ou d'être accablé, par ma révolte face à la vie. J'ai l'impression d'être « emmêlé » dans mes relations personnelles. Je peux me sentir étouffé par toutes mes responsabilités et je ne sais pas comment m'en sortir. Le découragement et le désespoir me gagnent, me demandant même quel est le sens à ma vie et si elle vaut vraiment l'effort d'être vécue. J'ai besoin de prendre du temps pour moi et de faire « le ménage » dans ma vie. Je ne garde que les responsabilités qui me reviennent et je remets à qui de droit celles que j'ai pris sur mes épaules et qui ne m'appartiennent pas. La vie sera ainsi plus facile et plus belle.

POUX (voir : MORPIONS)

PRESBYTIE (voir : YEUX — PRESBYTIE)

PRESSION ARTÉRIELLE ou SANGUINE
(voir : TENSION ARTÉRIELLE)

PROBLÈMES CARDIAQUES
(voir : CŒUR — PROBLÈMES CARDIAQUES)

PROBLÈMES DE PALPITATIONS
(voir : CŒUR — ARYTHMIE CARDIAQUE)

PROLAPSUS (descente de matrice, d'organe)

Le **prolapsus** indique un déplacement pathologique d'un organe vers le bas, lié au relâchement des éléments qui le maintenaient en place. Il est fréquent au niveau de la prostate, de l'utérus, du vagin, du rectum, de l'urètre ou de la vessie. Je vis alors un grand **laisser-aller,** un **abandon,** un **manque de contrôle**. Les muscles s'affaissent car mon niveau d'énergie est tellement

bas qu'il ne peut pas maintenir l'élasticité de l'organe. Je suis las, je vis un **désespoir intérieur** immense, celui-ci étant relié plus particulièrement à l'aspect de ma vie qui est représenté par l'organe atteint. Il est important que je trouve des moyens de reprendre ma vie en mains et que je sois actif. Je peux chercher ce que j'aime vraiment, que ce soit l'art, le sport, un passe-temps, afin de me redonner de la vitalité et le goût de vivre.

PROSTATE (en général)

La **prostate** est une glande de l'appareil génital masculin située sous la vessie et qui sécrète un liquide constituant l'un des éléments du sperme. Elle représente donc le principe et la puissance masculine.

PROSTATE (maux de...)

La **prostate** est reliée à mon sentiment de puissance et de capacité sexuelle. Puisque ce sont souvent les hommes plus âgés qui ont des troubles de **prostate**, je dois me demander : Est-ce que je me sens satisfait et à l'aise dans ma sexualité ? Est-ce que je vis de la frustration, de l'impuissance ou peut-être même de la confusion par rapport à ma sexualité et aussi face à ma recherche d'un(e) partenaire peut-être plus jeune ? Vaudrait-il mieux tout abandonner ? Je me sens peut-être maintenant inutile, inefficace, incapable d'être un « vrai homme ». Je vis la peur intense de ne pas être dans les normes sexuelles que la société a implantées. Je dois apprendre à me déculpabiliser et à cesser de me mettre de la pression par rapport à la « performance » que la société veut que j'atteigne. Je dois prendre conscience de ma valeur non pas selon mes « prouesses sexuelles » mais en regardant toutes les belles qualités humaines que je possède. Si j'ai une difficulté à la **prostate**, je dois me demander si je vis de la difficulté et de la culpabilité face à mes petits-enfants ou face à mes propres enfants qui, même devenus adultes, sont pour moi encore comme « tout petits » et « fragiles ». J'ai peur que ceux-ci soient en danger, soit moralement ou physiquement, et plus particulièrement face à toute situation qui peut être reliée à la sexualité et qui apparaît à mes yeux comme sale ou qui sort des normes habituelles et établies par la société. Si je n'ai pas d'enfant ou de petit-enfant, la difficulté peut être vécue avec un neveu ou un enfant du quartier que je considère « comme faisant partie de la famille ». J'ai à apprendre à faire confiance et le fait d'avoir peur qu'il arrive quelque chose de « grave » ou de « mal » aux gens que j'aime ne fait qu'attirer davantage l'objet de ma crainte. J'ai confiance que nous sommes tous guidés et protégés intérieurement, y compris ceux pour qui je me fais du souci. J'éviterai ainsi le développement du **cancer de la prostate**.

PROSTATE (descente de...) (voir aussi : PROLAPSUS)

Quand la **prostate** descend, elle met une grande pression sur la vessie. Elle indique que j'ai de la difficulté à relâcher les sentiments d'inutilité que je

me suis construits intérieurement, l'urine représentant la libération de mes émotions négatives. Je reconnais de plus en plus ma valeur et je sais que ma contribution à la société est inestimable.

PROSTATE — PROSTATITE
(voir aussi : ANNEXE III, INFECTION, INFLAMMATION)

La **prostatite** est l'inflammation de la **prostate**. Je peux vivre de la déception ou de la frustration, soit face à ce que mon ou ma partenaire attend de mes prouesses sexuelles, soit face à moi-même, car je m'en veux de ne pas être plus « viril », plus « performant ». Je me juge vieux, « bon à rien », « fini ». Il est donc important que j'accepte ↓♥ que ma sexualité puisse avoir changé et évolué avec le temps, mais qu'elle puisse être tout aussi excitante et entière.

PRURIT (voir : PEAU — DÉMANGEAISONS)

PSORIASIS (voir : PEAU — PSORIASIS)

PSYCHOSE (en général)

La **psychose** est une maladie mentale majeure, troublant gravement l'existence psychique de la personne dans ses rapports avec elle-même et avec le monde extérieur, comportant l'altération de la conscience de soi, d'autrui et du monde extérieur, de l'affectivité, de l'intelligence, du jugement, de la personnalité, ce qui va se traduire par un trouble marqué du comportement extérieur, le sujet vivant comme s'il était étranger à ce monde. La **paranoïa** et la **schizophrénie** sont des **psychoses**. Si je souffre de cette maladie, je veux fuir qui je suis et m'évader de ce corps que je n'accepte ↓♥ pas. Je me sens tellement mal à l'aise que j'ai l'impression de ne plus avoir d'identité, m'étant laissé envahir par les gens qui m'entourent. J'ai une faible estime de moi-même et je cherche par tous les moyens à me faire aimer et à recevoir de l'attention. La **psychose** peut résulter aussi d'un événement où j'ai vécu un choc émotionnel tellement grand que j'ai voulu me couper de la réalité, mon mental ne comprenant pas « pourquoi cela pouvait m'arriver à moi » ! Et j'ai caché des événements, des émotions dans mon subconscient mais ils y sont encore et je vais devoir tôt ou tard y faire face afin de les intégrer et d'apprendre la leçon de vie qui y est rattachée. C'est en libérant de leur prison mentale ces événements qui me contrôlent inconsciemment et qui me font agir de façon impulsive que je vais pouvoir reprendre le plein contrôle sur ma vie et que je vais vivre en paix avec moi-même. La **psychose infantile,** pour sa part, peut résulter d'une relation perturbée entre l'enfant et ses parents. Comme enfant, je peux vivre du rejet lié à la révolte inconsciente de ma mère ou parce que je suis soumis à des révélations sexuelles trop précoces pour être intégrables, etc. Moi comme enfant, je m'enferme dans un état d'indifférence, d'inertie et de

stagnation quant à mon développement mental, ou je m'enferme dans un monde à part qui cesse d'être communicable et qui sert de moyen de protection. C'est comme si je ne suis pas capable de trouver ma place et de me prendre en charge. Je me replie dans une « séparation protectrice », ayant vécu un profond rejet ou une « sécheresse affective », et ayant l'impression de ne pas pouvoir être ce que mes parents veulent que je sois, ces derniers étant contrôlés par leurs peurs, leurs désirs, leurs craintes, leurs fantasmes à l'égard de moi, leur enfant.

PSYCHOSE — PARANOÏA

Le comportement **paranoïaque** peut être considéré comme un syndrome qui naît d'un sentiment d'infériorité ayant la valeur d'une protestation, d'une compensation, d'une revanche ou d'une punition. La **paranoïa** se définit comme une **psychose** caractérisée par la surestimation de soi, la méfiance, la susceptibilité, la rigidité psychique, l'agressivité et qui engendre un délire de persécution. Cependant, si je suis **paranoïaque,** je continue de garder mes capacités intellectuelles. La personne atteinte de **paranoïa** a des obsessions, des idées fixes, sur lesquelles toute son attention se porte. Si je suis atteint de **paranoïa**, je me sens victime de tout ce qui m'arrive et je suis constamment sur mes gardes. Mes blessures émotionnelles, ma grande sensibilité, les peurs qui m'habitent et mes regrets aussi, notamment face à mes expériences que je juge comme des échecs, n'ayant pas reçu tout le succès que j'avais escompté, tout cela m'amène à fuir et à me couper d'une réalité avec laquelle j'ai de la difficulté à transiger. Je dois prendre conscience que mes pensées négatives obsessionnelles sont néfastes pour moi et que j'ai avantage à prendre de plus en plus mes responsabilités face à ma vie, étant capable de créer celle-ci comme je le désire.

PSYCHOSE — SCHIZOPHRÉNIE

La **schizophrénie** est une façon de me cacher et de cacher aux autres ma vraie identité. Souvent, le **schizophrène** a grandi dans un cadre familial très rigide dans lequel il a perdu sa vraie identité. Ne sachant plus qui je suis, je décide alors de devenir quelqu'un d'autre. C'est un refus total[73] de mon **JE SUIS**. Ce que je vis est tellement intense que mon état **schizophrénique** devient une solution de détresse à un stress trop grand ; **j'ai l'impression qu'il n'y a pas de solution à ma situation, donc ma seule chance de survie est de fuir.** Comme personne souffrant de **schizophrénie,** je possède souvent un intellect très fort et j'ai besoin de comprendre ce qui m'arrive plutôt que de simplement l'accepter↓♥. Comme **schizophrène,** je vis habituellement dans un climat de menace et, me sentant menacé, je déforme la réalité, à défaut de quoi je panique et la peur s'empare de moi. Parfois, il arrive

---

73. Il y a différents degrés d'intensité de la maladie.

aussi qu'ayant de grands dons psychiques, je les développe de manière exagérée. Nous vivons tous de la **schizophrénie** à un pourcentage plus ou moins élevé. En effet, lorsque j'ai enregistré une blessure intérieure dans mon enfance (surtout entre 0 et 12 ans) sous forme de rejet, de soumission, de colère, d'incompréhension, d'abandon, etc., j'aurai tendance à déformer la réalité lorsque dans ma vie d'adulte, un événement aura réactivé cette blessure. C'est comme si je développais des mécanismes, parfois inconscients, pour m'empêcher de revivre la douleur ou le souvenir de cette douleur que j'ai pu vivre antérieurement. Parmi ces mécanismes de défense, notons le fait de changer de sujet automatiquement lorsqu'on vient pour aborder une situation où je me suis senti blessé ; je peux avoir un comportement incohérent lorsqu'on touche à un sujet comme par exemple aller chercher le sel dans le réfrigérateur et qui passera pour « une distraction », etc. J'aurais avantage à redécouvrir l'être merveilleux que je suis et à accepter ↓♥ la responsabilité de ma vie.

PSYCHOSOMATIQUE (maladie...)
(voir : MALADIE PSYCHOSOMATIQUE)

PUBIENNE (toison...)

La **toison pubienne** cache en partie les organes génitaux et le pubis. Si elle est **fournie**, cela dénote une peur par rapport à ma sexualité, quelque chose que je veux dissimuler. Au contraire, une **toison clairsemée** ou **absente** dénote une vulnérabilité par rapport à ma vie sexuelle ou face à mes rapports avec mon conjoint. Je m'épanouis dans ma sexualité en exprimant mes peurs et en faisant de plus en plus confiance.

PUBIS (os du...)
(voir aussi : ACCIDENT, OS — FRACTURES [... osseuses], TENDONS)

Le **pubis** est une pièce osseuse formant la partie antérieure de l'os iliaque, l'os large et plat qui forme le bassin. Il sert à protéger naturellement les organes génitaux. Comme plusieurs muscles de l'abdomen et de la cuisse s'insèrent à cet endroit, il peut parfois se produire une **tendinite** qui représente du désappointement relié à ma sexualité, et entre ce que je veux et ce que je vis. Une **fracture** à ce niveau implique une plus grande peur ou culpabilité dans les actions que je pose ou que je ne pose pas au regard de ma sexualité. Je peux avoir l'impression que ma « performance » laisse à désirer. J'accepte ↓♥ d'apprendre à reconnaître mes vrais besoins sexuels afin de me permettre de m'épanouir davantage dans ce que je suis.

PYORRHÉE (gingivite expulsive) (voir : GENCIVES [maux de...])

PYREXIE (voir : FIÈVRE)

RACHITISME

Le **rachitisme** est une maladie de la croissance affectant le squelette et occasionnée par un défaut de minéralisation osseuse (trouble du métabolisme du phosphore et du calcium) par carence en vitamine D. Si je suis atteint de cette maladie, la malnutrition que je vis sur le plan physique met en lumière celle que j'ai l'impression de vivre d'un point de vue personnel et affectif. Je vis un vide ou un manque de tendresse, d'amour. Je peux avoir l'impression que je suis seul au monde et que personne ne me comprend. Je n'ai donc pas le soutien dont j'ai besoin et je me sens vulnérable. Cette maladie m'affecte surtout comme enfant. Je dois me rappeler que je suis constamment protégé et que l'amour universel est présent partout. Je me dois d'accepter ↓♥ cet amour et de le laisser me nourrir afin de faire partir la maladie qui n'aura plus alors de raison d'être, car j'aurai compris que je dois tout d'abord me donner de l'amour avant de pouvoir en donner aux autres.

RAGE

La **rage** est une maladie épidémique qui affecte certains mammifères (renard, chat, chien, etc.), lesquels la transmettent à l'être humain, généralement par morsure. La crainte morbide de l'eau ou **hydrophobie** est l'un des premiers signes de la **rage,** de même que la peur des mouvements de l'air qui est **l'aérophobie.** Si j'ai la **rage,** il y a de fortes chances que je sois « plein de **rage** » et de colère, celles-ci étant dirigées face à moi-même ou face à une personne ou une situation. Je prends conscience qu'il n'y a pas qu'avec la force et la violence que je peux régler mes différends et mes désaccords. J'apprends à communiquer calmement mes besoins, mes opinions, mes sentiments, tout en me respectant et en respectant l'autre personne.

RAGE DE DENTS (voir : DENTS [maux de...])

RAIDEUR (... articulaire, ... musculaire)

La **raideur musculaire** causée par l'accumulation d'acide lactique implique une accumulation d'énergie mentale rigide et bloquée. Je manifeste ainsi des schèmes de pensée rigides et de l'entêtement, ainsi qu'un refus ou une incapacité de « me rendre ». Je résiste au mouvement. Cela peut être aussi face à l'autorité. Je dois vérifier mes attitudes mentales en relation avec la partie du corps qui connaît la **raideur.** Si ce sont les **articulations** qui sont **raides,** soit au niveau de mes membres ou soit au niveau de ma colonne vertébrale, il y a une résistance profonde manifestée par l'os, démontrant une rigidité profonde et un refus d'aller de l'avant. J'ai alors avantage à devenir plus ouvert et flexible face aux nouvelles directions qui se présentent à moi. Au lieu de résister, je laisse couler et je vis au rythme de la vie et des saisons.

RAISON (J'AI...)

Si je manifeste une attitude de **j'ai raison** en permanence, je dois me demander : « Pourquoi est-ce que je suis fermé à l'opinion des autres ? De quoi est-ce que je veux me protéger ? » Je dois prendre conscience que les gens de mon entourage peuvent rester calmes vis-à-vis de moi, garder leur distance, faire attention à ne pas me heurter et aller même jusqu'à penser que **JE SUIS MALADE.** Je prends conscience qu'en écoutant les autres, qu'en me donnant la chance de changer d'avis, qu'en acceptant ↓♥ que les autres puissent aussi avoir des opinions valables, j'augmente mon degré d'amour, d'ouverture, de liberté dans le respect mutuel et le partage.

RANCUNE

Si je vis de la **rancune** face à une personne ou face à une situation, j'éprouve un profond ressentiment et j'ai le goût de me venger. Je vais même cultiver ces sentiments négatifs, me percevant comme la personne qui a été brimée, blessée et qui est une victime. J'ai avantage à accepter ↓♥ avec mon cœur les événements et à me tourner vers l'avenir au lieu de ruminer le passé sans cesse : sinon, mon cœur va se durcir et mon corps va réagir par un malaise ou une maladie.

RATE

La **rate** est un organe qui aide à la production et au maintien des cellules immunes du sang. Elle est liée directement à l'hypothalamus et au thymus, ainsi qu'au pancréas pour la production de l'insuline[74]. Si ma **rate** ne fonctionne pas bien, il se peut fort bien que moi aussi j'aie de la difficulté à bien fonctionner, la raison majeure étant que je reste fixé sur des idées noires et négatives. Cela baisse mon niveau d'énergie et je n'ai plus le goût de rien faire. Ce négativisme est souvent relié à ma façon de me voir : laid, « pas correct », pas bon, etc. J'ai plutôt le goût de dormir et d'être passif. Je me nourris de colère et il n'y a rien de bien gai dans ma vie. Quelqu'un ou quelque chose « me tombe sur la **rate** ». Les difficultés au niveau de la **rate** me donnent une indication sur les peurs que je peux vivre face au **sang**, comme par exemple celle de manquer de sang, de trop en perdre (comme au moment des menstruations). Je peux penser que mon sang n'est « pas bon » ou tellement rare que je doute qu'on pourrait me sauver la vie en cas d'accident majeur où j'aurais besoin d'une transfusion sanguine. **La peur de la mort est donc souvent présente en arrière-plan.** La **rate** veillant à la qualité des globules rouges du sang, un mauvais fonctionnement de celle-ci peut m'indiquer une grande blessure intérieure qui reste à guérir. C'est comme une plaie qui saigne. Le sang représentant la joie de vivre, je peux avoir

---

74. **Insuline :** Hormone sécrétée par le pancréas et aidant à le régulariser en diminuant le taux de sucre sanguin (glucose).

l'impression que la vie est un combat tellement dur que je devrais peut-être baisser pavillon et battre en retraite. Au lieu d'être toujours obsédé par des idées négatives que j'ai tendance à exagérer, je devrais plutôt me changer les idées en trouvant des moyens de me « dilater la **rate** ». Je dédramatise ma vie et j'apprends à rire de moi-même et de certaines situations. J'apprends à communiquer au fur et à mesure mes émotions afin de garder mon équilibre et l'harmonie dans tout mon corps.

RAYNAUD (maladie de...)

La **maladie de Raynaud** est caractérisée par une circulation constrictive, brutale et douloureuse des petites artères des mains, des pieds, des oreilles, du nez et des pieds mais surtout des doigts, créant de la pâleur, des membres engourdis qui peuvent devenir bleus ou pourpres. Le sang ne circule donc pas bien dans les extrémités. Les émotions qui devraient circuler dans le sang sont stagnantes. Lorsqu'un ou plusieurs de mes doigts est affecté, je peux aller chercher la signification du ou des doigts en question, ce qui m'éclairera davantage sur l'aspect de ma vie qui est concerné. Les membres affectés se sentent abandonnés et « vivent » un sentiment de perte. Je dois alors me poser ces questions : « Est-ce que moi, dans ma vie, je vis du rejet ? Est-ce que j'ai peur de m'exprimer et de prendre ma place ? Est-ce que j'ai terminé une relation amoureuse à laquelle je m'accroche ? » À un certain degré, je me suis coupé de l'Univers qui m'entoure et j'ai besoin de trouver ma place et j'ai besoin de réintégrer cet Univers dans lequel je joue un rôle important. Si je vais à sa rencontre, mes extrémités seront à nouveau nourries d'amour et de compréhension.

RECTUM (voir : INTESTINS — RECTUM)

RÈGLES (maux de...) (voir : MENSTRUATION [maux de...])

REGRETS

Si je me nourris de **regrets**, je nourris mon corps de peine, de chagrin, de mécontentement face à ce que j'aurais dû faire ou non, dire ou penser. Mes **regrets** me rongent à l'intérieur et abaissent mon niveau d'énergie. Ils créent un terrain propice à la maladie. J'apprends à avoir une attitude positive en sachant que je fais toujours au mieux de mes connaissances. J'apprends de mon passé et cela me permet de m'améliorer, de prendre de l'expérience, de devenir plus sage.

REINS (problèmes rénaux)
(voir aussi : CALCULS [en général] / RÉNAUX, PEUR)

Les **reins** maintiennent l'équilibre du milieu intérieur en épurant le sang des substances toxiques et en compensant les « entrées » dans le milieu

intérieur par des « sorties » (sécrétions d'urine). Ils participent aussi au contrôle de la pression artérielle. Au sens figuré, puisque les **reins** débarrassent le corps des déchets, c'est comme s'ils nettoient mon corps des idées négatives qui l'habitent. Un mauvais fonctionnement de mes **reins** dénote une rétention de mes vieux patterns émotifs ou bien une retenue de certaines émotions négatives qui ne demandent qu'à être libérées. Elles se manifestent le plus souvent par des **pierres aux reins**, aussi appelés **calculs rénaux**. Je fais sans cesse des « calculs » (rénaux !) pour savoir ce qui m'appartient ou ce que je risque de perdre. Je veux imposer mes limites et mes frontières afin de ne pas en « perdre » un centimètre ! Les **reins** sont aussi connus comme le « siège de la peur ». Lorsqu'ils s'affaiblissent ou qu'ils sont endommagés, il peut y avoir une peur que je ne veux pas exprimer ou que peut-être je ne veux même pas m'avouer à moi-même. Mon discernement est ainsi touché. J'aurai donc tendance à vivre des extrêmes, soit que je devienne très autoritaire, avec une tendance prononcée pour la critique, ou au contraire, que je devienne soumis, indécis, me sentant impuissant et vivant déceptions après déceptions. La vie pour moi est « injuste ». J'aurai de la difficulté à prendre des décisions. Si mes **reins** arrêtent de filtrer le sang, c'est comme si mon corps voulait garder le plus possible de ce liquide afin de ne pas le perdre ou de peur d'en manquer. Je dois donc me questionner et me demander quelle situation aurait pu engendrer une peur associée à un liquide (par exemple, si j'ai déjà eu peur de me noyer, le liquide serait ici l'eau). Cela peut être aussi le fait d'avoir failli ingurgiter un liquide toxique. Les **tubes collecteurs des reins** seront eux touchés si j'ai l'impression d'avoir à lutter pour mon existence. Je me sens dépossédé, abattu à la suite d'un événement marquant de ma vie. Les **problèmes aux reins** surviennent souvent à la suite d'un accident ou d'une situation traumatisante où j'ai eu peur de mourir. J'ai l'impression de n'être devant « rien » (**rein**), d'être devant le néant. J'ai l'impression d'avoir tout perdu, que tout mon monde s'écroule. J'ai peur d'être incapable d'affronter la vie. Les **reins** symbolisent aussi la collaboration (puisqu'il y en a deux et qu'ils doivent travailler en étroite collaboration). Je dois me demander comment est ma relation avec mon partenaire présentement. Est-ce que je le rends responsable de tous mes maux ? Est-ce que j'ai tendance à « déverser mes déchets » sur les autres et leur empoisonner la vie avec mes « problèmes » ? Si c'est le cas, mes **reins** auront de la difficulté à fonctionner et je pourrai même avoir une **insuffisance rénale**. J'ai alors à « collaborer », sans que j'en aie le choix, à une machine, le générateur d'hémodialyse, qui va m'aider à épurer mon sang. Je dois repenser tout mon système de relation avec mon entourage. Il est grand temps que je me prenne en mains, que j'apprenne à découvrir mes vrais besoins. Je prends la responsabilité de ma vie et je cesse de blâmer les autres. Je suis capable d'assumer mes choix. Mon discernement sera sûr et précis. Je collaborerai à 100 % avec la vie et j'aurai alors « des **reins** solides ».

REINS — ANURIE (voir aussi : REINS [problèmes rénaux])

L'**anurie** est l'arrêt de la production d'urine par les **reins**. Si je souffre d'**anurie,** je peux me sentir « nu » (à nu) et sans protection face à la vie ; mon risque d'avoir peur augmente plus que d'habitude (**rein** = siège de la peur) et j'ai tendance à m'accrocher à mes vieilles croyances. De plus, l'urine représente de vieilles émotions à éliminer du corps. Si je m'accroche à mes vieilles possessions, à mes croyances, à mes craintes, à mes doutes ou à mes manies (très puissantes sur le plan métaphysique), je manifeste l'**anurie,** c'est-à-dire la suppression de la sécrétion urinaire (on dit communément : les **reins** sont bloqués). L'angoisse peut être tellement grande que c'est comme si je devais « me retenir », de crainte de laisser aller mes émotions de peine qui sont souvent représentées par le *liquide* à laisser circuler. L'intensité de cet arrêt (un arrêt complet signifie la mort) me donnera une bonne indication sur ce que je dois laisser aller de vieux afin de m'ouvrir à de nouvelles pensées. Je fais du ménage et je me départis de toute émotion, relation ou bien qui ne m'est pas bénéfique et je les remplace par du nouveau, du positif. J'ai confiance en la vie qui s'occupe de me procurer tout ce dont j'ai besoin.

REINS — NÉPHRITE (voir aussi : COLÈRE, INFLAMMATION, PEUR)

Le terme **néphrite** désigne de façon générale l'ensemble des maladies des **reins**. Cependant, on utilise également ce terme pour désigner une inflammation des **reins**. Cela correspond à de la frayeur et à de grandes angoisses face à la vie. Ce sont des frustrations ou des déceptions qui n'ont pas été canalisées mais refoulées au fond de moi. Je deviens exagérément en réaction ou surexcité face à quelque chose qui me contrarie et face auquel je peux me sentir impuissant, sans savoir quelle leçon de vie j'ai à en tirer. Je dois faire confiance à la vie.

REINS — PIERRES AUX REINS (voir : CALCULS RÉNAUX)

REINS (tour de...) (lumbago) (voir : DOS [maux de...] — BAS DU DOS)

RENVOIS (voir : ÉRUCTATION)

REPLI SUR SOI

Le **repli sur soi** peut être une merveilleuse façon de m'arrêter, de prendre du temps pour moi, de découvrir mes besoins. Cela peut aussi s'appeler de l'introspection. Cependant, si cette période se prolonge et qu'au lieu d'être un moment de croissance et de connaissance de soi elle devient une occasion de me fermer au monde, de « brasser » des idées négatives, de m'apitoyer sur mon sort et de jouer à la victime, je risque alors de vivre un malaise profond, autant

psychologique que physique. Je reste ouvert face à l'Univers tout en me respectant dans mes besoins afin de vivre dans la joie et l'harmonie.

RESPIRATION (en général)

La **respiration** est une fonction qui préside aux échanges gazeux entre moi comme être vivant et le milieu extérieur. Il s'agit donc d'une voie d'accès pour la vie afin qu'elle pénètre à l'intérieur de moi. Si je peux respirer profondément, cela représente mon habileté à donner vie et force à mes émotions. Une **respiration** superficielle m'indique une peur ou une résistance par rapport à la vie, particulièrement dans des moments de détresse ou de panique, et m'indique que j'ai tendance à refouler mes émotions. Je vis ma vie de la façon dont je respire, cela peut être d'une façon superficielle, dénudée de sens, ou bien que je peux vivre au rythme des saisons. Le rythme entre « prendre » (inspirer) et « donner » (expirer) se fera en harmonie ; les voies de communication entre moi et le monde extérieur seront ouvertes et libres.

RESPIRATION (maux de...)
(voir aussi : ASTHME, GORGE [maux de...], POUMONS [maux de...])

Mes difficultés sur le plan respiratoire dénotent un conflit entre la place que j'occupe dans la vie et celle que j'aimerais occuper. Cela peut être aussi un conflit entre mes désirs matériels et spirituels ou alors un conflit entre mon désir de vivre et celui de « tout lâcher ». Je peux me sentir étouffé par les choses que je m'oblige à faire ou par les personnes que je me sens obligé de rencontrer. De plus, si mes **difficultés respiratoires** sont cycliques, je dois me demander quel événement ou quelle personne se trouve à être l'élément déclencheur de celles-ci ; qu'est-ce qui me « coupe le souffle » ou bien est-ce qu'il se peut que je veuille « qu'on me laisse respirer » ? Je peux devenir tellement exaspéré que mes **problèmes respiratoires** pourront devenir, souvent inconsciemment, une façon de manipuler mon entourage pour avoir ce que je désire. Je peux me sentir limité. J'aurai aussi de la difficulté à respirer si j'hésite à donner, à partager soit des choses ou des sentiments. J'ai peur de prendre, d'absorber ou de fusionner en moi de nouvelles choses ou peut-être la vie elle-même avec toutes les joies qu'elle peut apporter. Je dois apprendre à laisser aller les résistances, à laisser couler et à m'abandonner en faisant confiance à la vie. Je serai alors plus en mesure de trouver la place qui me revient dans l'Univers.

RESPIRATION — ASPHYXIE
(voir aussi : ASTHME, RESPIRATION [maux de...])

L'**asphyxie** est un trouble respiratoire manifesté par l'arrêt de la **respiration** ou l'obstruction (consciente ou non) des voies amenant l'oxygène aux poumons et permettant la **respiration**. Cet état très spontané

est relié à une méfiance face à la vie, à son déroulement et face à certaines peurs profondes manifestées durant l'enfance. Cet état peut provenir de l'insécurité à rester coincé ou « fixé », comme si je me sentais « fixe » (**as- « fixe » -ie**) dans une situation où j'étouffe et que j'étais incapable de bouger. Il est même possible que l'**asphyxie** soit reliée à une « fixation mentale » par rapport à la sexualité, car en état d'**asphyxie**, c'est souvent la gorge qui manifeste le blocage ; elle est reliée à l'expression de soi, à la créativité et à la sexualité. Je suis maintenant prêt à voir autre chose, à bouger, à me **défixer** et à faire confiance à la vie ! Je dois prendre mes responsabilités et cesser de mettre une attention **fixe** sur les frustrations de l'enfance. Elles sont présentes et je fais ce qu'il faut pour les intégrer.

RESPIRATION — ÉTOUFFEMENTS

L'**étouffement** indique que je me sens coincé, que je manque d'air et d'espace. La **gorge** correspond au centre d'énergie relié à la vérité, à l'expression de soi, à la créativité et indirectement, à la sexualité. Je peux me sentir « pris à la gorge » ; une idée a passé « de travers » ; je me sens hautement critiqué. J'ai tellement refoulé mes émotions qu'il y a un trop plein. Malgré tout, je tente encore de les réprimer. Ces émotions sont pourtant très présentes dans ma vie quotidienne et, inconsciemment, je les alimente jusqu'à ce qu'elles m'**étouffent**. Il est possible que certaines situations soient tellement difficiles à avaler qu'elles m'**étouffent** aussi. Pourquoi ai-je si peur d'être moi et de m'exprimer ? Serait-ce par peur du rejet parce que je crois que je ne peux être aimé en étant moi ? Je dois absolument lâcher prise et accepter ↓♥ de laisser monter en moi tout ce qui y est enfoui. La solution est d'apprendre à communiquer et d'exprimer mes besoins. Quel soulagement je ressens déjà ! Et je réalise que les autres ne sont pas des devins et que nos besoins respectifs peuvent toujours être satisfaits dans le respect de l'autre et dans l'harmonie.

RESPIRATION — TRACHÉITE

Aussi connue sous le nom de **« bronchite aiguë »**, **la trachéite** est une inflammation de la trachée, ce conduit où passe l'air du larynx, des bronches et des bronchioles. Mes voies respiratoires ainsi touchées, cela démontre que je me sens étouffé. L'air étant la vie, je ressens une grande tristesse et souvent de la colère. Je me sens incompris par mon entourage, ce qui m'amène progressivement dans un état dépressif. Mon corps me dit de respirer librement et de laisser place à l'amour.

RÉTENTION D'EAU (voir aussi : ENFLURE, ŒDÈME)

La **rétention d'eau** est souvent causée par un mauvais fonctionnement des reins. Mon corps « fait des réserves » et cela met en lumière le fait que je puisse emmagasiner des choses ou des émotions parce que j'ai horreur de perdre quelque chose ou quelqu'un. J'ai aussi tendance à me critiquer, ou à

critiquer les autres. Cela découle soit de ma difficulté à m'affirmer ou, au contraire, de mon égo qui est un peu trop grand et qui me fait prendre ma place ainsi que celle des autres. Je camoufle ainsi mes angoisses. Ma relation face à l'autorité sera aussi très chaotique, car je me sens souvent victime d'injustice. Je dois prendre la responsabilité de ma vie et apprendre davantage le respect et l'humilité. J'apprends à prendre la place qui me revient par droit divin, sachant avec confiance que tout est disponible, en autant que j'en fasse la demande.

RÉTINITE PIGMENTAIRE (voir : YEUX — RÉTINITE PIGMENTAIRE)

RÉTINOPATHIE PIGMENTAIRE
(voir : YEUX — RÉTINITE PIGMENTAIRE)

RHINO-PHARYNGITE (voir : GORGE — PHARYNGITE)

RHUMATISME
(voir aussi : ARTHRITE RHUMATISMALE, ARTICULATIONS, INFLAMMATION)

Le **rhumatisme** se définit par une affection douloureuse aiguë et le plus souvent chronique, qui gêne le bon fonctionnement de l'appareil locomoteur. J'aurai de la raideur dans mes articulations, ceci rendant les mouvements plus difficiles. Cela manifeste ma rigidité, mon inflexibilité et mon entêtement face à certaines personnes ou certaines situations. Je crains de me faire blesser, je vais donc montrer une image comme quoi je suis « au-dessus de tout », que « tout va bien » même si au fond de moi, ce n'est pas le cas. Dans mon monde à moi, je vais me considérer comme la victime des injustices qui m'arrivent. Je ressasserai sans cesse « mes petits malheurs », ceci conduisant à de la **critique,** que ce soit envers moi-même ou envers les autres. Je ne me donne aucune chance ; je suis exigeant et je trouve que la vie que je goûte a une saveur aigre. Je dois me demander si je suis tourmenté par rapport à une situation où je vis de l'ambiguïté : « *Est-ce que je le fais ou non ?* », « *Est-ce que je le frappe ou pas ?* », etc. Je vis un conflit de séparation à l'intérieur de moi où, par exemple, face à mon enfant, je veux être proche de lui mais je ne le peux pas. Si j'ai frappé mon enfant et que je le regrette par la suite, il y a de fortes chances que la main qui a effectué le geste sera touchée par le **rhumatisme**. Mon estime de moi est donc à son plus bas car je me dévalorise sans cesse. Je m'en fais pour les autres, surtout lorsqu'il s'agit de mes enfants. Je m'appuie sur eux car ils sont souvent ma raison de vivre et la raison qui me fait avancer. Si ceux-ci sont blessés, qu'ils trébuchent, j'ai peur qu'ils ne soient pas capables de se relever et je me demande : « Qu'est-ce que j'aurais dû faire de plus ou autrement ? » La culpabilité et la responsabilité sont grandes et la dévalorisation aussi. Je prends conscience de mon grand besoin d'amour. J'apprends à prendre soin de moi-même et à assumer mes émotions, car elles sont toutes positives et elles me

permettent de me connaître davantage. Je me mets au volant de ma vie et, de victime que j'étais, je deviens créateur de ma vie. Je sais que tout est possible. Il ne suffit que d'être patient et d'accepter ↓♥ d'avancer à mon propre rythme en évitant de me mettre de la pression.

RHUME

Le **rhume** est une affection qui entraîne une toux et un écoulement nasal. Elle entraîne aussi des courbatures, de la fatigue ; le nez devient obstrué. Elle est très répandue et contagieuse. Puisqu'un germe ou un virus affecte mon corps, cela indique une défaillance de mon système immunitaire. Cela peut provenir de **la confusion de mes pensées,** du fait que je ne « sais plus où donner de la tête ». Je me demande alors par où je dois commencer. Le **rhume** m'amène alors un temps de répit où je peux me « protéger » des gens pendant un certain temps et « garder mes distances ». Puisqu'il y a libération de sécrétions, je vis probablement une situation émotionnelle particulière qui m'affecte et face à laquelle je vis plein d'émotions qui ne demandent qu'à être libérées. Y a-t-il une chose sur laquelle je veux vraiment pleurer sans l'admettre ? Puisque mon nez est obstrué, y a-t-il une personne ou une situation qui « me pue au nez » et que je veux éviter de sentir ? Comme le **rhume** peut affecter autant la poitrine (le corps) que la tête (l'esprit), il peut y avoir déséquilibre en mettant toute mon attention sur l'un et en ignorant l'autre. J'ai besoin d'un temps d'arrêt pour me permettre de voir clair dans ma vie. J'ai besoin de reprendre des forces. J'adopte de nouvelles attitudes et de nouveaux comportements. Je fais le ménage dans ma vie et je cesse de laisser les croyances populaires m'affecter (« le **rhume** frappe fort cet hiver ! » ou bien « j'ai toujours le **rhume** quand vient le mois de décembre »). L'harmonie peut ainsi s'installer et je deviens maître de ma vie.

RHUME DES FOINS (voir : ALLERGIE — FIÈVRE DES FOINS)

RIDES

Les **rides** sont des crevasses cutanées. Elles peuvent être d'expression ou de vieillesse. Il y a **rupture** des fibres élastiques du derme et il y a atteinte du reste du tissu conjonctif. Les **rides** apparaissent lorsque je vis un choc émotionnel, un chambardement intérieur. Je peux vivre aussi une **rupture** ou un événement où je dois me détacher d'une personne, d'une situation ou d'un bien matériel. Cela m'amène à vivre du chagrin, du désespoir, de l'incompréhension et de la douleur intérieure. Si j'apprends à accepter ↓♥ que tout événement de ma vie est là pour m'aider à grandir et que c'est par le détachement que je manifeste l'amour inconditionnel, mes **rides** n'auront plus de raison d'être et celles-ci pourront disparaître. La sagesse apporte la vraie jeunesse du cœur.

RONFLEMENT

Le bruit que j'émets en respirant pendant mon sommeil et qui provient d'un obstacle entre mes voies nasales et le larynx s'appelle **ronflement**. Si je **ronfle**, je dois me poser les questions : Est-ce que je m'accroche à mes vieilles idées, attitudes, biens matériels ? Est-ce que je m'entête à rester dans une relation ou dans une certaine situation qui n'est pas bénéfique pour moi ? Est-ce que je suis fatigué ? Est-ce que mes sinus sont engorgés ? Quelle est la chose que je respire difficilement et qui me suit même pendant la nuit (ex. : odeur de mon conjoint, d'un parfum. etc.) ? Ou peut-être que je veux « attraper » mon conjoint qui couche près de moi et ôter la distance qui nous sépare (autant physiquement qu'émotionnellement). Je cherche donc à me rapprocher de celui-ci. Je dois apprendre à laisser aller et à faire de la place pour du nouveau. Je fais en sorte que mes communications soient claires et libres de tout sous-entendu ou de toute ambiguïté.

RONGER LES ONGLES (voir : ONGLES [se ronger les...])

ROTER, ÉRUCTER (voir : ÉRUCTATION)

ROTULE

La **rotule** est un os de forme triangulaire qui permet les mouvements de flexion-extension de l'articulation du genou. L'expression « être sur les **rotules** » signifie que je suis épuisé. Si j'ai de la douleur ou que ma **rotule** est déformée, je peux vivre de la colère, de la déception et de l'irritation par rapport à mes rêves qui me semblent hors d'atteinte ou irréalisables. Je fléchis les genoux ; je me sens battu. Le moment est venu de prendre du temps pour moi, que je me lève (debout) et que je prenne des initiatives afin de réaliser mes rêves les plus chers. C'est en y croyant qu'ils pourront prendre forme.

ROUGEOLE (voir : MALADIES DE L'ENFANCE)

RUBÉOLE (voir : MALADIES DE L'ENFANCE)

RYTHME CARDIAQUE (trouble du...)
(voir : CŒUR — ARYTHMIE CARDIAQUE)

SADOMASOCHISME

Le **sadomasochisme** implique une relation où l'un des partenaires exprime sa **domination (sadisme)** et l'autre exprime sa **soumission (masochisme)**. Il arrive que des personnes consentantes y trouvent un

certain équilibre dans leurs relations. Cependant, si je sens le besoin de pratiquer cette forme de relation, je veux certainement me libérer d'un certain stress intérieur, soit en pouvant contrôler ou en me soumettant. Je me libère ainsi de certaines angoisses que je peux avoir. Je dois prendre conscience que je peux développer, dans mon subconscient, ce programme : je suis libre lorsque je contrôle et je me sens mieux après ou, dans l'autre cas, je me sens libre lorsque je me soumets « volontairement » et je me sens mieux après. Ce programme risque de ressurgir dans ma vie au moment où je m'y attends le moins. Ainsi, dans des conditions de stress important, je pourrai identifier que contrôler ou me soumettre sera la solution. Je dois être attentif au fait que **je deviens ce sur quoi je porte mon attention.** Ainsi, ce comportement qui peut paraître négatif risque d'amplifier ces attitudes négatives en moi. Je prends conscience de mon désir de me libérer de mes peurs et de mes limitations et du fait que j'ai à développer davantage l'humilité que la soumission, le fait d'être guidé que de contrôler. Je pourrai ainsi aller chercher une satisfaction pour mon plus grand épanouissement personnel.

SAIGNEMENTS (voir : SANG — SAIGNEMENTS)

SAIGNEMENTS DE NEZ (voir : NEZ [saignements de...])

SAIGNEMENTS DES GENCIVES (voir : GENCIVES [saignements des...])

SALIVE (en général) (voir aussi : GLANDES SALIVAIRES, OREILLONS)

Avoir l'eau à la bouche, **baver d'envie** pour quelque chose ou pour quelqu'un. L'inflammation des glandes salivaires est ce qu'on appelle **les oreillons**. Si je suis atteint de cette maladie, je vis souvent de la frustration et j'ai le sentiment que l'on me crache dessus, sur mes idées. Je me sens dénigré et j'ai parfois envie de cracher à mon tour au visage des gens. Si je souffre de dépression, je suis souvent porté à manger rapidement, à avaler mes aliments tout rond, ce qui provoque un manque de **salive** et la sensation d'étouffer. La **salive** a le pouvoir d'éliminer le développement des microbes. Elle permet aussi, par son pouvoir humectant, de facilité les sons au niveau de la gorge, de mieux avaler les aliments. Elle favorise la première étape de digestion en transformant les amidons. Trop de **salive** ou pas assez la rend inefficace, inutile. En me faisant confiance dans mes décisions, en décidant de laisser entrer la joie à la place des regrets, en avançant avec confiance, je redonne tout son pouvoir à ma **salive.**

SALIVE — HYPOSALIVATION (voir aussi : BOUCHE)

L'**hyposalivation** est un manque de **salive**. La **salive** est l'humeur aqueuse et un peu visqueuse qui humecte la bouche et les aliments. Les glandes

salivaires sécrètent la **salive** qui aide la digestion. Je peux respirer par la bouche, au lieu de par le nez. Cela entraîne un assèchement de la bouche et des voies respiratoires. Comme la bouche représente mon ouverture à la vie, je peux me demander en quoi mes désirs ou mes appétits sont présentement « à sec » et pourquoi ils ne se manifestent pas comme je le voudrais dans ma vie. Je peux trouver que les événements de la vie ne me nourrissent pas suffisamment et que je perds de l'intérêt dans ma vie. Je prends conscience du don de la vie. La vie me donne tout ce dont j'ai besoin pour bien intégrer les situations que je vis.

SALMONELLOSE (voir aussi : EMPOISONNEMENT
[..., ... par la nourriture], INDIGESTION, INFECTIONS [en général], INTESTINS — DIARRHÉE, NAUSÉES)

La **salmonellose** est une infection provenant d'une bactérie qui se loge dans le tube digestif. Cette bactérie est habituellement transportée par la nourriture. Comme les symptômes de la maladie sont divers : vomissements, diarrhée, infections, je peux me demander ce qui m'amène à vivre autant d'irritabilité. Même s'il serait facile pour moi de penser que je ne suis pas responsable de ce qui m'arrive puisque c'était la nourriture qui était infectée, donc une cause extérieure, je dois me rappeler que le hasard n'existe pas et que les éléments extérieurs ne sont ici que pour m'aider à déclencher le malaise que je vis présentement dans ma vie par rapport à une situation « que je ne digère pas et qui me met en colère ». Plus vite je remettrai de l'harmonie dans cette situation que j'ai pu identifier, plus vite ma santé s'en trouvera améliorée. Je serai plus riche d'une expérience qui m'aide à développer plus de sagesse.

SALPINGITE (voir aussi : CHRONIQUE [maladie...],
FÉMININ(S) [maux...], INFECTIONS [en général])

La **salpingite** est une infection aiguë ou chronique des trompes. Cette maladie est souvent reliée à de l'impuissance face à un partenaire sexuel. Ai-je l'impression ou ai-je peur que mon conjoint sexuel me « trompe » ? Ai-je moi-même l'impression qu'une personne qui m'est proche comme mon conjoint, mon père, un de mes frères, ami, etc. m'a **trompé**, par ses attitudes ou par ses gestes et que cela a fait monter tant de colère en moi ? Quelle que soit la situation, très souvent celle-ci impliquera un aspect de la sexualité que j'ai trouvé **moche** ou **dégradant**. J'accepte ↓♥ de mettre de l'amour dans la situation afin de pouvoir percevoir la vérité dans l'expérience que la vie m'apporte. Je me retrouverai ainsi plus heureuse avec plus de joie de vivre et de sérénité.

SANG (en général)

Pour assurer le bon fonctionnement de son véhicule, on doit lui procurer une bonne essence. <u>L'essence</u> du corps est le **sang** qui, pour être efficace, doit

circuler librement dans tout mon corps. Si l'essence contient des saletés, elle risque d'endommager le moteur qui est le cœur. **Le sang représente la joie de vivre** et les impuretés qui s'y trouvent provoquent des malaises dans tout mon corps. Suivant ce dont je me nourris, l'estomac produira une énergie qui fortifiera mon **sang** ou le rendra anémique ; tout comme pour mon véhicule, je dois choisir la bonne essence. Le **sang** représente l'énergie qui circule en moi. Il est le centre même du cœur. Une mauvaise circulation m'indique que l'amour est bloqué ; je n'arrive plus à exprimer mes sentiments, je suis en conflit avec l'amour. Le message de mon corps est : je laisse **couler** le **sang** dans mes veines, je laisse l'amour arriver jusqu'à mon cœur, j'accepte ↓♥ de recevoir et je retrouve la joie de vivre. Je fais place aux idées nouvelles.

SANG (maux de...) (voir aussi : SANG / ANÉMIE / LEUCÉMIE, etc.)

Une mauvaise circulation du **sang** indique un manque de joie de vivre dans ma vie. Je me sens engourdi, mes idées s'embrouillent. Pour retrouver la joie, j'accepte ↓♥ les nouvelles idées, je reconnais les beautés qui m'entourent, je souris à la vie.

SANG — ANÉMIE
(voir aussi : SANG / CIRCULATION SANGUINE / LEUCÉMIE)

Le **sang** représente la **joie de vivre**, **l'amour** et les **émotions**. Lorsque les globules rouges du **sang** sont insuffisants ou que le nombre de cellules sanguines est faible, il s'ensuit souvent un manque de fer dans le **sang** puisque le fer est au centre de la molécule qui forme les globules rouges. Cet état est relié à un manque de joie, de force et de profondeur dans l'amour que j'ai pour moi et les autres ; à mes croyances dans ma capacité d'aimer vraiment avec force et détermination ; **à un découragement et au refus de vivre** ; ou à l'impression d'être sans valeur et d'avoir des résistances face à l'amour, d'où cette dévalorisation de ma personne. On peut même vivre du désespoir et de la résignation. Je peux aussi manifester beaucoup de rigidité face aux événements de la vie. En résumé, tous ces symptômes sont le résultat d'une grande faiblesse au niveau sanguin. En anglais, le « Fer » s'appelle « Iron » et on peut faire un jeu de mot en changeant « Iron » (fer) par « I run » qui veut dire en français « je cours ». De même, on peut remplacer le mot « fer » par son homonyme « faire ». Ainsi, la personne **anémique** ne sent plus suffisamment de joie et de motivation à accomplir tout ce qu'il y a à **faire** (il y a un manque de « faire », ou un manque « à faire ») et ne se sent plus en mesure de **courir** pour obtenir ce qu'elle veut. Mais pour quelle(s) raison(s) je refuse d'utiliser l'énergie de l'univers qui est disponible pour moi ? De quoi ai-je peur ? Qu'est-ce qui me fait me « ronger les **sangs** » ? Je n'ai qu'à dire **oui** à cette belle énergie prête à servir ma vie avec amour. À partir de maintenant, je regarde, j'observe et je découvre la joie autour de moi. Elle est partout : famille, travail et amis. Ces êtres de lumière sont là eux aussi pour m'aider à grandir.

SANG — ARTÈRES

Les **artères** sont les « vaisseaux qui conduisent le **sang** du cœur aux organes ». Ces mêmes vaisseaux sanguins (ainsi que tous les autres conduits sanguins, veines, capillaires, etc.) sont le moyen pour l'amour de manifester les qualités divines. Ils logent partout dans le corps et communiquent avec chaque partie de celui-ci. Les **artères** sont reliées aussi à tout ce qui s'appelle la « vie ». Elles font circuler la **joie de vivre** et elles me permettent de **communiquer, d'exprimer mes émotions**, de garder le contact avec l'univers. Si la tension nerveuse monte davantage, elle entraîne un déséquilibre émotionnel qui peut résulter d'un conflit intérieur entre mon « monde physique » et « mon monde spirituel ». Lorsque j'ai de la difficulté ou que je cesse d'exprimer mes émotions, je me **ferme** (bloque) et il peut en résulter différentes maladies liées au cœur telles l'artériosclérose, la thrombose, l'angine de poitrine, les varices. La joie de vivre cesse de circuler en moi. Je peux me dévaloriser face aux actions que j'accomplis. Afin que l'énergie circule plus régulièrement et empêche le développement de certaines **scléroses**, représentant des blocages énergétiques, je dois faire preuve d'une ouverture plus constante à la joie et à la circulation de cette joie en restant ouvert au niveau du cœur, en acceptant ↓♥ de changer d'attitude et de m'ouvrir à l'amour, afin que cet amour soit acheminé dans tout mon corps.

SANG — CHOLESTÉROL[75]
(voir aussi : SANG / [en général] / CIRCULATION SANGUINE)

Le **cholestérol** est relié au **sang**, symbole de la **joie de vivre**. Le **cholestérol** provient des aliments. Notre organisme le synthétise à partir du foie. Il lubrifie mes vaisseaux sanguins, il alimente le système nerveux et le maintient équilibré. Sa fonction normale est d'empêcher l'usure prématurée des vaisseaux sanguins par le passage du **sang**, mais s'il est présent en surplus dans le corps, il se dépose et réduit progressivement le diamètre des vaisseaux sanguins. Pourquoi ? **Parce que je n'ai plus la joie de vivre !** En mon for intérieur, je crois que je ne mérite pas d'être heureux, d'être joyeux et **cette joie circule mal !** Je peux avoir une montée de **cholestérol** après certains événements comme, par exemple, après avoir pris ma retraite, parce que je n'ai plus la joie de vivre que j'avais avec mes compagnons de travail ou les gens que je rencontrais au travail. Cette montée peut aussi se produire lors du départ de quelqu'un que j'aimais et qui m'apportait de la joie dans ma vie. Ici, au lieu de développer un diabète qui est de la tristesse profonde, mon corps interprétera

---

75. **Cholestérol :** Il y a deux types de cholestérol : l'un que l'on nomme **LDL** (provenant du terme anglais **L**ow **D**ensity **L**ipoproteins *[lipoprotéines de basse densité]*), aussi appelé « mauvais » cholestérol et il y a le **HDL** (du terme anglais **H**igh **D**ensity **L**ipoproteins *[lipoprotéines de haute densité]*), aussi appelé « bon » cholestérol.

l'événement plutôt comme un manque de joie de vivre et fera monter le taux de **cholestérol**. Il peut aussi en être de même lors de la perte de mon animal de compagnie et enfin, lors de toute situation qui peut faire que consciemment ou inconsciemment, ma joie de vivre a diminué dans ma vie. Ce peut être aussi dans le cas ou **je veux réaliser un projet**, construire ou ériger quelque chose qui me tient à cœur mais je ne peux avoir d'aide de personne. **Je ne peux donc compter que sur moi-même et celà m'affecte grandement**. Si je laisse cet état s'aggraver, je risque de vivre un jour une **attaque cardiaque**. En effet, si je ne règle pas la situation qui me fait vivre ce manque de joie, cela touchera l'aspect de ma vie qui est l'amour. Quand ma joie diminue, c'est comme si je sentais moins l'amour en moi, c'est pourquoi le manque de joie aura pour effet d'affecter mon cœur. La plupart du **cholestérol** animal (provenant des viandes et des produits laitiers) fait partie de la diète trop riche des Occidentaux. Les aliments contenant beaucoup de **cholestérol** représentent une certaine satisfaction égoïste de mes appétits. Je me sens bien, sans penser un instant que ce surplus risque de changer et même de détruire ma santé ! C'est une illusion de croire que je fais plaisir à mon corps. Je vérifie si je m'aime d'une manière un peu trop « égoïste ou égocentrique ». En absorbant des aliments contenant trop de **cholestérol**, je renie les joies de la vie. Un jour, j'aurai à payer pour ça. Est-ce que je désire ce malaise ? J'accepte ↓♥ de changer immédiatement en laissant circuler la joie en moi, tout comme l'enfant émerveillé devant les beautés de la vie ! Je neutralise ma peur de vivre dans la joie et j'accepte ↓♥ que celle-ci fasse partie de ma vie.

SANG — CIRCULATION SANGUINE (voir aussi : CŒUR)

La **circulation sanguine** est reliée au cœur et au **sang**, symbole de vie. Le **sang** passe par tous les canaux du corps : artères, artérioles, veines, veinules, capillaires. Ces canaux sont nécessaires à la distribution de l'amour, de la joie et de la vie à travers le corps entier. Mon cœur (centre d'amour) accepte ↓♥ de donner le **sang** (énergie) à chaque partie de mon être, quelle que soit son importance, sans discrimination. Le **sang** représente ma vigueur, mon plaisir de vivre et ce que je suis actuellement dans cet univers. Toutes les difficultés circulatoires sont reliées au **sang** et à la totalité de mon être. Si je vis une situation difficile sur le plan émotionnel ou mental, l'énergie qui anime mon être s'affaiblit. Cette faiblesse du **sang** et de la **circulation sanguine** signifie que je me retire émotionnellement d'une situation qui m'affecte pour l'instant car je n'ai pas assez « d'énergie » pour aller de l'avant. Je me protège de mes émotions trop énergétiques car c'est douloureux de les sentir présentes à ce point. Je ne laisse pas circuler suffisamment l'amour dans ma vie. Je m'autocritique sévèrement, je suis en peine, je vis beaucoup de tristesse intérieure. Ma joie de vivre et ma bonne humeur baissent, mes idées deviennent confuses, j'ai une vie sociale peu excitante, morne et plate. J'ai besoin de faire « circuler » beaucoup de projets, d'idées, de sensations. Sinon, tout va « figer », à cause de mes tracas, de mes peines, de ma fatigue, de ma

colère ; une surexcitation ou une obsession qui déséquilibre la **circulation sanguine** aura le même effet. Le manque de joie m'amène donc à fuir mes responsabilités. J'ai des blocages qui me font éviter certaines situations. C'est une manière de dire **non** à la vie. Ainsi, plusieurs « patterns » risquent de remonter à la surface (le contrôle, le laisser-aller, l'indifférence face à la vie, le besoin exagéré d'attention, le désir de vouloir mourir...). Les troubles de la **circulation sanguine** se manifestent d'abord aux mains et aux jambes, aux parties les plus externes et actives de mon corps, celles qui me dirigent dans l'univers. Une mauvaise **circulation** affectant mes **jambes** est liée à ma direction émotionnelle, aux émotions sur lesquelles je peux compter et auxquelles je tiens. Quand mes **mains** sont affectées, c'est l'expression de mes émotions et un désir de cesser ce que je suis en train de faire. Dans les deux cas, il s'agit d'un retrait sur le plan intérieur, le retrait de la pleine participation émotionnelle à mon univers. Les différentes afflictions sanguines sont l'athérosclérose, l'artériosclérose, l'élévation du taux de cholestérol, la thrombose, etc. J'accepte ↓♥ de **me regarder en face et surtout j'observe mon attitude face à la vie !** La vie n'est-elle pas assez extraordinaire au point d'en profiter pleinement ? J'ouvre mon cœur à l'amour, je me prends en charge et je me laisse guider par la vie. Il arrivera toujours ce qu'il y a de mieux pour moi.

SANG COAGULÉ (... dans les veines ou dans les artères)

Le **sang** représente la joie qui circule dans mon corps. Lorsqu'il **coagule**, c'est comme si je décidais de mettre un bouchon qui a pour effet de couper toute circulation. Je décide de laisser circuler la joie en moi, je m'éveille à une nouvelle vie.

SANG — DIABÈTE
(voir aussi : MALADIES HÉRÉDITAIRES, SANG — HYPOGLYCÉMIE)

Le **diabète**, aussi appelé **diabète sucré,** se manifeste par une sécrétion insuffisante d'insuline par le pancréas qui résulte en une incapacité de celui-ci à maintenir un taux de sucre raisonnable dans le **sang.** Un excès de sucre sanguin survient alors et le **sang** est incapable d'utiliser adéquatement les sucres dans le flot sanguin. Ces sucres en excès causent un taux trop élevé de sucre dans l'urine qui devient sucrée. **Comme le sucre est relié à l'amour, à la tendresse et à l'affection, le diabète reflète divers sentiments de tristesse intérieure.** C'est le mal d'amour, un manque d'amour certain car j'ai besoin, à cause de mes blessures antérieures, de contrôler l'environnement et les gens qui m'entourent. Eh oui ! **Si j'ai le diabète, je vis habituellement des tristesses à répétition, des émotions refoulées empreintes de tristesse inconsciente et absentes de douceur.** La douceur a disparu au profit d'une douleur continue. Je commence alors à manger du sucre sous toutes les formes possibles : pâtes

alimentaires, pain, friandises, etc., pour compenser. Le plan affectif, social ou financier peut en prendre un coup. Je cherche à compenser par tous les moyens possibles. Je me limite dans beaucoup de domaines. Je deviens « amer » (amertume) face à la vie, c'est la raison pour laquelle je trouve ma vie « amère » et je compense par un état plus « sucré ». Comme j'ai de la difficulté à recevoir de l'amour, je me sens étouffé et surchargé, coincé dans une situation incontrôlable et excessive. Le **trop plein** est éliminé dans l'urine. J'ai donc un grand besoin d'amour et d'affection, mais je ne sais pas agir et réagir quand je pourrais en recevoir. J'ai de la difficulté à recevoir l'amour des autres et la vie est sans plaisir pour moi. C'est difficile de me laisser aller et d'exprimer l'amour véritable. Mes attentes sont souvent démesurées (je veux que les gens réalisent mes désirs) et elles m'attirent des frustrations, de la colère face à la vie et le repli sur soi. **Je vis beaucoup de résistance face à un événement que je veux éviter mais que je me sens obligé de subir.** Par exemple, ce peut être une séparation, un déménagement, un examen, etc. **S'ajoutera à cette résistance un sentiment de dégoût, de répugnance, de dédain face à cet événement.** L'**hyperglycémie** va donc apparaître à ce moment. J'ai besoin de me prendre en main dès maintenant. J'ai besoin de changer les situations qui m'affectent en commençant à voir de l'amour et de la joie dans toutes choses. Le **diabète** (ou **hyperglycémie**, trop de sucre dans le sang) et l'**hypoglycémie** (pas assez de sucre dans le sang) (toutes deux reliées au manque de joie) sont reliées directement à l'amour que je suis capable d'exprimer pour moi-même et pour les autres. Dans le cas du **diabète gestationnel,** qui survient habituellement après la seconde moitié de la grossesse, je dois me poser les mêmes questions que celles que se pose la personne qui souffre du **diabète.** Il se peut que de la tristesse profonde, de la répugnance ou de la résistance se révèle à ma conscience. Cette grossesse peut activer et amplifier en moi le souvenir plus ou moins conscient de ces sentiments que j'ai pu vivre dans mon enfance et la conséquence sera le **diabète.** Après l'accouchement, le retour de mon état normal m'indique que ces sentiments ont disparu ou que leur importance a grandement diminué, ce qui amène un rétablissement du taux de sucre sanguin (glucose). Il y a tellement d'amour disponible ; suis-je vraiment conscient de l'amour que les gens ont pour moi ? Les gens m'aiment et je dois le voir à partir de maintenant. J'accepte ↓♥ le passé d'une manière détachée, pour ce qu'il est. C'est en ouvrant mon cœur que les miracles se produisent !

SANG — GANGRÈNE (voir aussi : AMPUTATION, INFECTIONS)

La **gangrène** est le résultat d'un ralentissement et finalement, de l'arrêt du flot sanguin dans une ou des parties du corps, ce qui amène la mort des tissus. Le flot sanguin est relié à l'expression ou au retrait de mon amour à l'Univers, et aussi à ma joie de vivre. Donc si, par exemple, la **gangrène** affecte mes jambes, c'est que le retrait, ou la coupure d'amour à l'intérieur de

moi est si profond qu'il arrête complètement tout mouvement vers l'avant. Habituellement, dans ce cas-ci, la peur de l'avenir et l'insécurité face à ce qui s'en vient pour moi sont très présentes. Je m'intoxique par ma culpabilité enracinée, par la honte ou par le chagrin et une partie de moi est en train de mourir. La vie s'en va, la joie n'y est plus. Dans le cas de la **gangrène sèche,** le **sang** n'irrigue plus les tissus. J'ai donc à reprendre contact avec moi et avec la joie qui doit m'habiter sur cet aspect de ma vie qui concerne la partie de mon corps affectée. Dans le cas de la **gangrène humide**, qui résulte en plus d'une infection, je fais face à des pensées empoisonnantes, à des pensées de mort envers moi-même ou envers la vie. La **gangrène gazeuse** (plus rare) que l'on rencontre surtout chez les diabétiques est favorisée par une collection de **sang** dans un tissu ou par un corps étranger. Des gaz nauséabonds provenant de la prolifération de germes infectieux se forment sous la peau. Non seulement les idées de mort d'une partie de moi-même sont-elles présentes, mais aussi un profond rejet de cette même partie m'amène à vivre cette situation. J'ai besoin de faire réintégrer le **sang**, l'amour dans l'expression de qui je suis, dans ma vie. J'apprends à m'accepter ↓♥ tel que je suis et à redécouvrir les joie de la vie.

SANG — HÉMATOME
(voir aussi : ACCIDENT, SANG / [en général] / CIRCULATION SANGUINE)

Un **hématome** fait suite à une hémorragie où une certaine quantité de **sang** s'accumule dans un tissu ou un organe. Comme un **hématome** survient presque toujours à la suite d'un traumatisme, je dois me demander quelle peur ou quelle culpabilité m'empêche de laisser circuler librement la joie dans ma vie. L'accumulation du **sang** m'indique que je dois mettre plus de joie dans ma vie et la partie affectée me renseigne sur quel aspect de ma vie j'aurais avantage à manifester cette joie.

SANG — HÉMATURIE (voir aussi : ADÉNOME,
VESSIE / [maux de...] / CYSTITE, URINE [infections urinaires])

L'**hématurie** est la présence du **sang** dans l'urine de façon microscopique[76] ou macroscopique[77]. Comme l'urine représente mes vieilles émotions que je laisse aller et comme une perte de **sang** m'indique une perte de joie, alors l'**hématurie** symbolise une tristesse plus ou moins vive face à mes émotions passées qui me déchirent intérieurement. Je dois chercher quels sont ces événements qui m'ont déchiré émotionnellement pour que je puisse m'apporter douceur et compréhension et que s'installe la guérison.

---

76. **De façon microscopique :** Qui n'est pas visible à l'œil nu dans l'urine : qui est détecté au microscope seulement.
77. **De façon macroscopique :** Qui peut être détecté à l'œil nu dans l'urine, soit par sa teinte rougâtre ou les traces de sang qui peuvent y paraître.

SANG — HÉMOPHILIE (voir aussi : MALADIES HÉRÉDITAIRES, SANG / [en général] / [maux de...] / CIRCULATION SANGUINE / DIABÈTE)

L'**hémophilie** est une maladie héréditaire liée à un trouble de la coagulation du **sang**. Puisque mon **sang** a de la difficulté à coaguler, une coupure, une blessure peuvent entraîner des pertes de **sang** qu'il est difficile d'arrêter, ce qui peut mettre ma vie en danger. Même si cette maladie est héréditaire, il n'en demeure pas moins que je vis cette situation parce qu'il me faut effectuer une prise de conscience par rapport à la joie. Au moindre accident ou incident, ma vie risque d'être mise en danger si je n'interviens pas rapidement. J'ai besoin de prendre conscience dans ma vie de ce qui peut me porter à vivre du désespoir au point où je pourrais « mourir au bout de mon **sang** ». Je peux regarder en quoi le **diabète**, sous certains aspects, peut ressembler à ce que je vis. Même si la découverte de la cause ne change pas en moi le fait d'être **hémophile**, il n'en demeure pas moins que je pourrai avoir l'impression que les inconvénients de cette maladie diminuent grandement, tout en restant vigilant, et que j'ai de plus en plus le sentiment de vivre une vie normale avec plus de joie dans mon cœur.

SANG — HÉMORRAGIE

Une **hémorragie** est caractérisée par une perte de **sang** violente et soudaine. Cette effusion incontrôlée de **sang** est souvent associée à un bouleversement ou à un traumatisme émotionnel. Ce sont mes émotions trop longtemps retenues, telles la hargne et l'angoisse, qui deviennent incontrôlables intérieurement, et qui jaillissent soudainement. Je peux vivre des événements qui ne se passent pas selon mes attentes ou selon mes désirs. À bout de résistance, épuisé moralement, je lâche prise et une grande part de joie de vivre quitte soudainement mon corps. Étant à l'écoute de mon corps, je peux reconnaître un message qui m'aidera à mieux vivre en harmonie. J'apprends à lâcher prise et à exprimer mes émotions plus librement. Me sentant plus libéré, je porte mon attention sur la joie qu'il y a en moi et autour de moi.

SANG — HYPOGLYCÉMIE (voir aussi : ALLERGIES [en général], CERVEAU — ÉQUILIBRE [perte de...], SANG — DIABÈTE)

L'**hypoglycémie** se caractérise par une diminution anormale de glucose dans le **sang**. La partie du pancréas secrétant l'insuline est suractivée. En conséquence, les cellules et les muscles sont privés du glucose énergétique. Cette situation est à l'opposé de ce que l'on rencontre chez les diabétiques. Elle est causée par un excès d'insuline ou d'exercice. Le sucre représente une forme de **récompense, d'affection, de douceur et de tendresse**. Il est la manifestation de l'amour, selon la métaphysique. Présentement, suis-je à la recherche de cet amour ? Est-ce que je l'attends de l'extérieur ? Est-ce que je mange du sucre pour combler ce manque ? Plusieurs manifestations sont liées à l'**hypoglycémie** :

— Elle peut se manifester parce que <u>je donne tellement aux autres que je n'ai plus rien à me donner</u>. Cela me montre le besoin de commencer par m'aimer, par me respecter dans mes besoins. En me donnant plus, je peux ensuite donner davantage et aimer les autres . Je ne peux donner aux autres ce que je ne me donne pas à moi-même ;

— Elle peut surgir également lorsque <u>je vis une tension ou une pression intérieure excessive</u> sur laquelle je crois que je n'ai pas le contrôle ;

— Elle provient <u>de mes fortes émotions, d'une tristesse profonde</u> me causant de l'angoisse et même de l'hostilité face aux autres. Est-ce que j'ai des attentes auxquelles on ne répond pas (qui ne sont pas satisfaites) ?

— Je peux aussi vivre une peur intense face à quelque chose ou à quelqu'un qui me **dégoûte** et que je préfère éviter. Je dois **résister** de toutes mes forces pour essayer d'éviter cette chose qui me répugne. Elle peut être autant un objet, un geste ou qu'une parole dite et qui m'a « levé le cœur ».

— Une allergie alimentaire peut aussi être la cause « physique » de cette baisse de sucre sanguin. Je dois donc faire les vérifications physiques qui s'imposent et trouver à qui ou à quoi je suis allergique.

J'accepte ↓♥ ce qui m'arrive. Je décide de rendre ma vie plus joyeuse. Je réponds à mes attentes. Mon corps est un sage, un ami fidèle auquel je suis réceptif.

SANG — LEUCÉMIE
(voir aussi : SANG / ANÉMIE / CIRCULATION SANGUINE)

Lorsque mes globules blancs prolifèrent de façon incontrôlée, j'ai ce que j'appelle le **cancer du sang** ou la **leucémie**. Le **cancer du sang,** c'est la joie qui ne circule pas librement dans ma vie. J'ai de la haine enfouie profondément en moi. Je m'autodétruis, je refuse de me battre. Si je suis un enfant atteint de **leucémie**, c'est que j'éprouve un refus de renaître, je suis profondément déçu de ce que je vois sur terre. Je veux repartir, quitter ce corps. La **leucémie** apparaît souvent après la perte d'un être aimé (ce peut même être un animal que j'affectionnais particulièrement). Cette forme de **cancer** est reliée directement à l'expression d'amour à l'intérieur de soi. Elle peut aussi apparaître après un événement marquant pour moi qui m'a amené à me dévaloriser. Cette dévalorisation touchera mon être en entier et je la vivrai d'une façon très intense et profonde. Prenons l'exemple d'un jeune garçon qui se fait refuser une place au sein de l'équipe de hockey du village ou de son quartier. C'est le drame ! C'est comme si la vie n'avait plus aucun sens et qu'elle ne vallait pas « la peine » d'être vécue. Je peux avoir l'impression que je dois me surprotéger constamment pour obtenir ce que je veux. Je peux avoir vécu une frustration intense et avoir violemment étouffé mes émotions. Si mon amour ou mon désir de vivre a été d'une façon ou d'une autre blessé, mon attitude à aimer peut

devenir méfiante, confuse et aliénée. Je veux donc m'isoler de tous sentiments. J'ai à apprendre à aller avec la vie plutôt que contre elle. Je prends les moyens appropriés pour changer en moi la survie par la vie. Je serai ainsi plus en paix avec moi-même et je ne sentirai plus le besoin de me défendre outre mesure.

SANG — LEUCOPÉNIE

La **leucopénie**, c'est la baisse des globules blancs, le déséquilibre du **sang**. Les globules blancs deviennent alors des petits soldats qui baissent les armes. Je n'ai plus le goût de lutter. Ce peut être une forme de fuite puisque je m'oblige à évoluer dans le même ordre, m'empêchant ainsi d'expérimenter de nouvelles choses, afin de me sentir toujours en sécurité et maître de la situation. J'ai besoin de prendre soin de moi afin de refaire mes forces intérieures et, ainsi, de reprendre davantage goût à la vie avec tout ce que cela comporte d'excitant.

SANG — MONONUCLÉOSE
(voir aussi : ANGINE, FATIGUE, RATE, TÊTE [maux de...])

La **mononucléose** est une infection caractérisée par l'augmentation des lymphocytes qui font partie des leucocytes ou globules blancs du **sang**. Cette maladie se retrouve surtout chez les adolescents ou chez les jeunes adultes. Elle est aussi appelée **la maladie du baiser** puisqu'elle peut se transmettre par la salive. Si je suis un adulte et que j'ai cette maladie, je cherche à voir ce qui a pu m'affecter, comme si j'étais un adolescent, ou ce que cela me rappelle lorsque j'étais adolescent. Je veux vivre pleinement, je sens un changement à l'intérieur de moi et **j'ai l'impression d'avoir à me battre constamment pour obtenir ce que je veux.** Mon système de défense se développe pour compenser les attaques et les limitations que j'ai l'impression de recevoir de la vie. Je me sens seul face aux obstacles qui se présentent devant moi. Je développe une **mononucléose** quand je me sens coupable face à une situation ou quand je veux plus de permission, lorsque je critique les gens ou la vie en général. La **mononucléose** a un lien avec les problèmes de la **rate**, car il y a une augmentation du volume de celle-ci. Je me dois de faire le ménage dans ma vie et d'y mettre plus d'amour envers moi et envers les autres. Je reprends courage et confiance en moi et, alors, je retrouverai l'énergie et la joie de vivre qui me permettront d'expérimenter plus d'amour.

SANG — PHLÉBITE

La **phlébite** est définie par le blocage du **sang** dans les veines, principalement au niveau des membres inférieurs. Elle est causée par un caillot provenant d'une infection ou d'une blessure. Le **sang** représente la libre circulation de la vie dans les veines de mes membres inférieurs. Mon moyen de locomotion est donc limité, irrité et défectueux, car ce blocage du **sang** m'indique une perte de joie liée aux jambes, lesquelles me transportent vers

différentes destinations de ma vie. Selon que dans la jambe gauche (mon intérieur) ou droite (mon extérieur) ou aux deux jambes, la perte de joie pourra m'identifier à quel niveau ou dans quel sens j'ai une hésitation ou un refus d'avancer, d'accepter ↓♥ une nouvelle destination. Je me fais du **mauvais sang** face à certaines situations que la vie me présente. Je vis donc un arrêt, un ralentissement en raison d'une émotion, d'un sentiment qui limite ma joie, mon bonheur de vivre. J'ai tendance à blâmer les autres, je les rends responsables des manques que je peux vivre et m'enlèvent ma joie de vivre pour aller de l'avant. Il est important que je laisse aller la peine, le mécontentement, la frustration que je vis et que je me responsabilise par rapport à ce qui arrive dans ma vie. J'accepte ↓♥ que j'ai le pouvoir de créer ma vie comme je le veux ; je dois cependant accepter ↓♥ que j'ai droit au bonheur et que je mérite que la joie et la paix illuminent ma route.

SANG — SAIGNEMENTS

Les **saignements** peuvent être comparés à des larmes, à une perte de joie. Lorsque je souffre, les larmes coulent, ma peine est si intense que c'est comme si je pleurais du **sang**. Où s'en va ma joie de vivre ? Pourquoi cette peine, cette agressivité qui me fait voir rouge ? Je prends conscience de la chance que j'ai de vivre et je retrouve la joie. Je me libère de toute ma tristesse et j'accepte ↓♥ de recevoir ce que la vie me donne.

SANG — SEPTICÉMIE

La **septicémie** est une infection grave (empoisonnement généralisé) du **sang**. C'est ce qu'on appelle **se faire du mauvais sang** ou **s'empoisonner la vie**. J'aurais avantage à me demander « par qui ou par quoi je me laisse empoisonner l'existence ». Je décide d'accepter ↓♥ que j'ai l'entière responsabilité de mes choix et je prends conscience des joies de la vie.

SANG — THROMBOSE
(voir aussi : SANG — CIRCULATION SANGUINE)

Le **sang** circulant dans mes veines représente la joie de vivre. Une **thrombose**, qui se définit par une formation de caillots de **sang** dans une veine ou dans une artère, provoque un blocage empêchant le **sang** de circuler librement. Cet état démontre qu'il existe également un blocage dans la libération et dans la circulation de l'amour. Me sentant seul, je suis peiné et j'ai l'impression que les difficultés auxquelles je me heurte sont trop lourdes à supporter et que je ne suis pas capable de les surmonter. Je perds ma joie de vivre. Ma vie me semble stagnante, je me sens négligé, abandonné et incompris. J'ai l'impression de ne plus avoir d'amour en moi, je deviens inflexible ; je suis de plus en plus ferme dans ma façon d'agir et de penser, ce qui provoque le durcissement de mes artères. Cette manifestation atteint mon corps tout entier. Quand elle apparaît sur mes jambes, elle m'indique une

crainte d'aller de l'avant, une tendance à demeurer « figé », en perte de mouvement. Cela peut aussi signifier l'insécurité que j'éprouve à voir s'éloigner un amour ou à me voir m'éloigner de cet amour. En tentant ainsi de le retenir, j'augmente les chances de le voir mourir. Je m'ouvre de plus en plus à la vie et j'accepte ↓♥ les changements comme des signes de mon évolution.

SANG — VARICES

Les **varices** se situent habituellement aux jambes. Elles sont le résultat de veines hypertrophiées. Mes jambes me permettent d'avancer dans la vie, de me déplacer d'un endroit à l'autre. Des **varices aux jambes** démontrent une mauvaise circulation. Ainsi, je peux en conclure que l'endroit où je suis ne me convient plus ou que je n'aime pas ce que j'accomplis présentement. Je n'y trouve plus la joie. Il peut s'agir d'une relation affective ou encore d'un travail qui m'est devenu monotone. Le **sang** représente la joie de vivre et la circulation de l'amour dans mon Univers et mes veines en sont le moyen de locomotion. Le **sang** dans mes veines est sur le chemin du retour, vers mon cœur, rapportant avec lui tout l'amour qu'il a reçu de l'Univers. La **varicosité** peut indiquer qu'un profond conflit émotionnel est directement relié à la capacité de m'aimer et de recevoir tout cet amour. La direction que je prends ou le sol sur lequel je me tiens ne me donne pas ce à quoi je m'attends, émotionnellement parlant. Cela bloque et embrouille mon « mouvement émotionnel ». J'ai l'impression de traîner un poids énorme, comme le prisonnier qui doit traîner son boulet constamment. Il s'agira souvent d'un poids financier, l'argent me causant bien des maux de têtes et **l'avarice** me guettant. En général, j'ai plus l'impression de subir des situations que de les créer. Des **varices aux jambes** apparaissent souvent lors d'une grossesse, ce qui démontre que certaines craintes sont rattachées à cet état ; comme femme enceinte, j'ai peur de partager cet amour avec une autre personne, de perdre mon individualité dans mon nouveau rôle de mère. Je me sens débordé et j'ai peur de ne pas tout accomplir, car j'ai tendance à amplifier les petits détails. C'est alors que le découragement peut survenir. Pour rétablir cette situation, il est important que j'apprenne à aimer ce que je fais. Je suis libre de choisir et de circuler librement.

SARCOME D'EWING (voir : OS [cancer des...] — SARCOME D'EWING)

SCARLATINE (voir : MALADIES DE L'ENFANCE)

SCHIZOPHRÉNIE (voir : PSYCHOSE — SCHIZOPHRÉNIE)

SCIATIQUE (le nerf...) (voir : NERF SCIATIQUE [le...])

SCLÉRODERMIE (voir : PEAU — SCLÉRODERMIE)

SCLÉROSE (voir aussi : INFLAMMATION, SYSTÈME IMMUNITAIRE)

La **sclérose** est une inflammation qui vient durcir le tissu conjonctif, lequel est nécessaire et présent dans le corps tout entier. Une personne atteinte de **sclérose** voit son système immunitaire attaqué, car il y a détérioration du tissu conjonctif. Il est important de prendre conscience que si je suis touché par cette maladie, c'est moi-même que j'attaque, ce qui peut amener la **sclérose** à s'étendre à la grande majorité de mes organes. Cette inflammation provoque une sorte d'énergie brûlante qui fait ressurgir de la rage longtemps refoulée. Les tissus se durcissant, cela suggère le durcissement de mes pensées, de mes attitudes, créant ainsi un déséquilibre sur le plan énergétique. Mon corps entier ou n'importe laquelle de ses parties peut être affectée par la **sclérose**. Il est donc important de prendre conscience de ce que je vis intérieurement. En me fermant à l'amour, cela peut indiquer que je me sens indigne de cet amour, que je me sens coupable et que j'ai honte de vivre. J'accepte ↓♥ de m'ouvrir à l'amour, je reconnais ma valeur divine, je suis tout, je peux tout.

SCLÉROSE EN PLAQUES

La **sclérose en plaques** se définit comme une inflammation des enveloppes qui entourent les voies nerveuses du cerveau et de la moelle épinière. Le corps tout entier en est affecté et cet état peut survenir à différents moments de la vie. C'est comme si mon corps était **piégé,** placé dans une cage et de plus en plus limité dans l'enchaînement de ses mouvements. Si je suis atteint de **sclérose en plaques,** je suis généralement affecté par de grandes souffrances me faisant voir la vie avec découragement. Une profonde révolte anime tout mon être. Je me sens obligé de devoir tout faire moi-même ; étant très perfectionniste, je refuse de me tromper et j'accepte difficilement de l'aide. La pensée de l'échec me terrorise. Je crains d'être laissé pour compte, d'être **plaqué** là. **J'ai très peur qu'on me « laisse tomber ».** Je peux aussi avoir peur de tomber, autant au sens propre qu'au sens figuré, et craindre que cette chute entraîne la mort. Toutes ces peurs qui impliquent un déplacement vertical et qui peuvent m'amener à croire que ma vie est en danger peuvent déclencher la **sclérose en plaques**. Ce peut être la chute d'une échelle, le risque de tomber dans un précipice, la perte abrupte d'altitude dans un avion, quelque chose qui me tombe sur la tête, etc. Très souvent, je me juge ou je peux juger les autres très sévèrement, ce qui entraîne **un grand sentiment de dépréciation, de dévalorisation et de diminution de ma personne.** Lorsque je me sens diminué, j'ai l'impression que la vie m'écrase. Ainsi, c'est d'abord par mes jambes que la maladie manifestera ses premiers signes et que je pourrai avoir l'impression d'écraser. Ma défense à toutes ces peurs qui

m'habitent sera de **vouloir tout contrôler,** de vouloir que tout se passe comme je le veux. La **critique**, qui est souvent dirigée vers moi-même, emprisonne ma vie. Je crois que la souffrance fait partie de mon lot de tous les jours et que je ne mérite pas le repos. Mes efforts pour me dépasser sont constants et, malgré tout, toujours insuffisants. Mon corps fatigué refuse ainsi de poursuivre cette lutte du plus fort et veut me faire comprendre que je peux aussi avoir besoin des autres et que j'ai à apprendre à faire confiance. L'inflammation implique une rage **brûlante** et très émotionnelle, pouvant affecter toute mon existence. Je peux me questionner : « Est-ce que je souhaite vraiment être libre ? » Je peux inconsciemment, de cette façon, me venger de quelqu'un ne m'ayant pas manifesté suffisamment d'amour ! Cette forme de cage, dans laquelle mon corps se retrouve, me protège peut-être de devoir admettre mes vrais sentiments ! La répression émotionnelle peut me conduire à une incapacité d'aller de l'avant dans mes émotions, entrainant ainsi une confusion musculaire et mentale. Mon corps me dit de lâcher prise, de me libérer de mes chaînes. La clé se trouve à l'intérieur de moi. J'accepte ↓♥ de faire confiance à mon guide intérieur et je reconnais en chacun la présence de ce guide, qui amène chaque personne à agir au meilleur de sa connaissance. Je manifesterai alors plus de flexibilité et de compréhension.

SCOLIOSE (voir : COLONNE VERTÉBRALE [déviation de...] — SCOLIOSE)

SCRUPULE

Le **scrupule** se retrouve chez une personne qui vit de l'inquiétude face à sa conscience. Avoir **mal à l'âme** ou se **ronger** le sang. Je choisis de vivre en harmonie, j'accepte ↓♥ de digérer les nouvelles idées, je retrouve mon entrain.

SEIN (en général)

Une personne ayant de gros **seins** (qu'elle soit homme ou femme) a souvent commencé dès son plus jeune âge à se sentir obligée de materner les autres pour se sentir aimée. Même si je possède cette habileté à prendre soin des autres, je réalise que, souvent, j'agis ainsi parce que j'ai peur du rejet et que, me sentant admiré pour ce côté de moi, je m'attire ainsi la reconnaissance de ceux qui m'entourent. À l'opposé, si j'ai de petits **seins**, il se peut que je doute de mes capacités de mère et que j'éprouve constamment le besoin de prouver que je peux l'être. Le **sein gauche** représente l'aspect plus émotionnel, plus affectif de mon côté maternel, tandis que le **sein droit** est associé au rôle et aux responsabilités de la femme dans la famille ou dans la société. Si mes **seins** sont **mous** et **pendants**, j'ai intérêt à apprendre à devenir plus ferme dans ma façon de parler et d'agir. Les **seins** représentent aussi la féminité chez la femme. Ils sont souvent exagérément admirés. L'apparition des **seins** équivaut à devenir femme. Ils provoquent bien des réactions pour la femme. Je peux avoir peur de devenir un *sex symbol*, d'être ridiculisée. Je peux vivre de la honte,

de l'embarras, me sentir rabaissée. Je peux ne pas vouloir d'enfant(s) parce qu'il me rappelle, consciemment ou non, un « choc » passé. Il est possible que je vive certaines craintes d'être à la fois femme et mère. Je choisis d'accepter ↓♥ de recevoir autant que je donne, j'accepte ↓♥ ma féminité.

SEINS (maux aux...) (DOULEURS, KYSTE)
(voir aussi : CANCER DU SEIN, SEIN — MASTITE)

Lorsque j'éprouve des **maux aux seins**, je dois m'interroger à savoir si j'adopte une attitude surprotectrice ou dominatrice envers mes enfants ou envers mon conjoint. Un **kyste** peut survenir si je me sens coupable face à une maternité ou si j'ai subi un choc émotionnel. À trop vouloir protéger les gens que j'aime, je les empêche de vivre, je prends les décisions à leur place, je deviens **mère poule**. J'ai avantage à laisser ceux que j'aime devenir autonomes afin qu'eux aussi deviennent des personnes responsables.

SEIN (cancer du...) (voir : CANCER DU SEIN)

SEIN — MASTITE

La **mastite,** qui est l'inflammation du **sein**, rend celui-ci très douloureux et peut survenir lors de l'allaitement, qu'il faut alors interrompre. Toujours en relation avec la maternité, je provoque un malaise qui m'obligera à cesser d'allaiter sans vivre de la culpabilité. Ce peut aussi être moi qui ai l'impression d'être trop maternée, soit par mon conjoint ou par quelqu'un de mon entourage. Ces douleurs aux **seins** peuvent aussi démontrer que je suis trop dure envers moi-même. Ainsi, j'accepte ↓♥ de laisser les autres libres de leurs choix, j'apprends à m'aimer. Je reconnais que chacun de nous grandit avec ses expériences.

SÉNESCENCE (voir : VIEILLISSEMENT [maux de...])

SÉNILITÉ

Lorsque les facultés physiques et psychiques sont atteintes alors que je suis une personne âgée, on va parler de **sénilité**. La **sénilité** est une maladie que l'on peut relier à la fuite. En retournant dans l'enfance, je retourne vers la sécurité qu'elle m'apporte. Je choisis ainsi de laisser les autres s'occuper de moi, je veux qu'ils me prennent en charge. Si je suis atteint de **sénilité**, je dois prendre conscience qu'il n'est pas nécessaire de fuir. Si je veux récolter cette attention tant désirée, je dois moi-même la semer. Je bénéficie de la protection divine, je vis en paix et en toute sécurité. À chaque moment de ma vie, je prends conscience de la force de l'Univers.

SEXUELLES (déviations et perversions en général)

Lorsqu'en tant qu'individu, je suis aux prises avec une **déviation sexuelle**, c'est que je souhaite rejeter et refouler une grande partie de mon être, je vis constamment une lutte intérieure. Par ce fait, mon corps me dit d'accepter ↓♥ chaque aspect de moi que j'associe à un défaut. Chaque être possède un côté masculin et un côté féminin. Quand je suis un homme, j'accepte ↓♥ ma féminité, ou ma masculinité quand je suis une femme. Je deviens humble, je décide de m'affirmer. Je choisis d'unifier tout mon être car chaque facette de moi demande à s'exprimer.

SEXUELLES (frustrations...) (voir aussi : ÉJACULATION PRÉCOCE)

Souvent reliées à une éducation très stricte envers tout ce qui a trait à la sexualité, je crois sincèrement que les organes génitaux sont immoraux et sales, je vis de la culpabilité. Il est préférable que j'accepte ↓♥ de vivre ma sexualité sainement puisqu'elle fait partie de ma qualité de vie.

SEXUEL (harcèlement...)

Si je vis du **harcèlement sexuel**, c'est que je vis des grandes peurs, parfois inconscientes, de me faire manipuler par de la tendresse et par une forme d'amour. Il est certain que j'ai à me faire respecter comme personne mais je dois d'abord identifier les sources qui sont en cause afin de pouvoir reprendre le pouvoir qui est le mien et continuer à vivre « plus normalement ».

SIDA (s̲yndrome d'i̲mmunod̲éficience a̲cquise)

Si je porte le virus du **sida** (V.I.H. : v̲irus d'i̲mmunodéficience h̲umaine) et que je suis en santé, on dira simplement que je suis **séropositif** et il se peut que je ne développe jamais la maladie. Si mon système immunitaire faiblit comme conséquence du virus V.I.H., alors je pourrai dire que j'ai le **sida** qui est la maladie. Si je suis une personne atteinte du **sida**, je vois mon système immunitaire devenir déficient en cellules-T (lymphocytes ou variétés de globules blancs du **sang** et de la lymphe) et ainsi, il devient incapable de me protéger contre certaines infections comme la pneumonie et le cancer. Le **virus du sida** est transmis par le sang (sang contaminé lors d'une transfusion sanguine, seringue infectée, blessure en contact avec du sang infecté, etc.) ou le liquide sexuel. La glande du thymus (située devant la trachée), étant là où se forment les cellules en T, est ainsi affectée et, par le fait même, l'énergie du cœur l'est également. Le système liquide du corps, étant le siège du transfert viral, correspond à l'énergie émotionnelle, soit le sang. Le sang relié au cœur symbolise l'amour et les peines, la créativité. Ainsi, je peux dire que mon système émotionnel est en déséquilibre et incapable de s'exprimer librement.

Je vis une grande culpabilité face à l'amour, j'ai l'impression de ne pas être à la hauteur. Mon système devient faible et de plus en plus vulnérable à toutes formes d'invasion. J'aurais intérêt à prendre conscience que je refoule des émotions comme la peur et la colère, que je renie l'être que je suis au point de souhaiter ma destruction complète. **De mon incapacité à m'aimer et à m'accepter ↓♥ tel que je suis, il résulte que je n'arrive plus à me protéger.** Ma force intérieure qui, normalement, est appuyée par l'amour, l'acceptation ↓♥ et un désir intense de vivre, s'affaiblit et se mine lentement. **Même inconsciemment, la mort peut m'apparaître comme la solution à mon désespoir.** Vivre une expérience sexuelle peut s'avérer très révélateur émotionnellement. Même spirituellement, cela peut m'amener à vivre des événements bénéfiques dès que l'énergie sexuelle surgit depuis le chakra de base[78] qui est la source de mon élan spirituel. Par contre, si cette énergie est mal utilisée, soit uniquement comme autogratification et complaisance, elle peut se retourner contre moi. Sans une sincère manifestation de pureté, elle pourra se transformer en énergie maladive ou gênante. J'apprends donc à reconnaître les énergies qui sont en moi et je les utilise pour le meilleur de mon évolution. J'accepte ↓♥ qui je suis, un être divin et magnifique.

SINUS PILONIDAL (voir aussi : DOS / [maux de...] / BAS DU DOS, INFECTIONS [en général])

Le **sinus pilonidal** est une infection de mon système pileux au niveau du muscle près du coccyx, à la base de la colonne vertébrale. Je vis de la frustration, de l'irritation ou de la révolte par rapport à une situation dans laquelle je vois mes besoins de base en danger, ceux-ci ne pouvant plus être comblés comme je le désire. Cet état de « manque » peut me rappeler une situation de ma jeune enfance, pouvant même remonter jusqu'au moment où j'étais fœtus, et où, là aussi, j'ai eu l'impression que je manquais de quelque chose ou de quelqu'un qui m'était, à ce moment-là, vital. Il peut s'agir d'un élément physique, comme par exemple un endroit chaud où demeurer, des vêtements confortables ; cela peut être aussi lié au plan affectif, comme par exemple, l'amour et la tendresse de mes parents. Quelle que soit la situation, il est important que je demande à l'Univers de m'aider à ce que tous mes besoins de base soient comblés et que je fasse entièrement confiance à celui-ci. Il faut que j'accepte ↓♥ aussi d'avoir vécu une situation de manque lorsque j'étais plus jeune mais qu'elle était là pour m'apprendre à développer ma foi et pour m'aider à apprécier maintenant tout ce que je possédais et que je possède aujourd'hui et dont je devais prendre conscience.

---

78. **Chakra de base :** L'un des sept principaux centres énergétiques du corps situé au coccyx, à la base de la colonne vertébrale.

SINUSITE (voir : NEZ — SINUSITE)

SOIF
(voir aussi : INSOLATION, REINS [problèmes rénaux], SANG — DIABÈTE)

La **soif** est un phénomène naturel qui m'amène à rétablir l'équilibre de substances comme le sel, le sucre, entre autres, dans mon système sanguin. Lorsque ma **soif** est exagérée, mes pensées sont troubles, mon cœur bat « la chamade », je n'arrive plus à voir clair, ma gorge s'assèche et j'ai **soif**. Quelque chose manque à mon bonheur. Boire ! Pendant un court instant, ma **soif** diminue, mais elle revient très vite car elle relève de mon mental. Je dois donc en découvrir la cause : qu'est-ce qui m'ennuie dans ma vie ? Mon travail me semble-t-il ennuyeux ? Quelle pensée ou quelle peur assèche ma bouche ou mon esprit ? Lorsque j'aurai trouvé, cette **soif**, en apparence intarissable, sera contrôlée. Les épices fortes sont reconnues pour accentuer le désir sexuel. Utilisé adéquatement, cet excitant peut permettre d'éliminer la **soif**. Par contre, une relation sexuelle insatisfaisante aura pour effet d'augmenter la **soif**, d'ajouter au sentiment de manque... Pour combler ce manque, ce désir de boire représente mon besoin de vie, puisque l'eau représente la vie. Je m'ouvre davantage à la vie et à l'amour pour trouver enfin la situation qui « apaisera ma **soif** ».

SOLEIL (coup de...) (voir : INSOLATION)

SOMMEIL (maladie du...) (voir : NARCOLEPSIE)

SOMMEIL (trouble du...) (voir : INSOMNIE)

SOMNAMBULISME (SOMNAMBULE)

Lorsque je suis **somnambule**, c'est que je vis une grande tension intérieure parfois inconsciente. Je peux chercher à fuir une situation qui me préoccupe trop. Je « m'exprime » de cette façon pour laisser échapper cette tension. J'expérimente souvent le fait d'être (même inconsciemment) « en dehors de mon corps ». Lorsque cet événement se produit, mon « corps astral » dirige mon corps physique à partir de cette position « hors du corps ». C'est pourquoi, comme **somnambule**, je peux marcher les yeux fermés et « voir » quand même les obstacles car je les vois avec la vision de mon corps astral. Pour diminuer ce **somnambulisme** dans ma vie, il serait préférable que je communique davantage ce que je vis avec mon conjoint, avec mes parents, avec un ami, ou simplement que je l'écrive. Je pourrai retrouver plus de calme intérieur et normaliser mes heures de sommeil.

SOMNOLENCE

Il peut m'arriver de **somnoler** après avoir dégusté un bon repas. C'est une façon agréable de prolonger ce moment. Je n'ai plus à penser, je me laisse vivre. Il est aussi naturel de voir un vieillard qui s'endort durant la journée puisqu'il arrive à la fin de sa vie. Il reste là, fatigué, attendant la mort. Mais, si je suis une personne d'âge adulte et qu'il m'arrive régulièrement de **somnoler** dans la journée, inconsciemment, je refuse de vivre, je me cache, je fuis pour ne plus avoir à choisir, à décider, à agir. Mon corps me dit de reprendre contact avec la vie.

SOURD-MUET (voir aussi : OREILLES — SURDITÉ)

Si je suis **sourd** pour une raison congénitale ou que j'ai perdu l'ouïe dans ma petite enfance et que je n'ai pu apprendre à parler, alors on dira de moi que je suis un **sourd-muet**[79]. Mon degré d'audition peut varier cependant de 0 % à 30 %. Dans mon expérience de vie, il est certain qu'il y a des choses que je ne voulais pas entendre, ce qui m'amène à vivre cette situation. Afin de clarifier ce que je ne voulais pas entendre, je peux investiguer du côté de mes parents et plus spécialement du côté de ma mère pour trouver ce qu'elle ne voulait pas entendre. Ce peut être une situation où elle se serait dit : « Je ne veux plus en entendre parler », alors qu'elle me portait. Je suis responsable de ce qui m'arrive et, si cela m'a affecté, c'est que, moi aussi, j'avais quelque chose à comprendre. Je prends conscience de cette situation et je développe de plus en plus l'écoute intérieure qui me permettra de profiter des joies de la vie et qui me permettra de m'épanouir avec les gens qui m'entourent.

SPASMES

Un ou plusieurs **muscles** se contractent de façon involontaire et non rythmée : j'ai alors un **spasme**. Les **spasmes** forment comme un nœud. Je me crispe, je veux retenir l'amour, j'ai peur de perdre cette personne que j'aime tant. Ces **spasmes** créent en moi un sentiment d'inquiétude, d'impuissance. Ce nœud de souffrance que je n'arrive pas à contrôler provient d'une multitude de désagréments ou d'irritants qui donnent un goût amer à ma vie. Il fait vivre en moi des émotions, de la culpabilité reliée à ma sexualité. Je reconnais que les nœuds étouffent et que, pour conserver l'amour autour de moi, j'accepte ↓♥ de me détacher.

---

79. **Sourd-muet :** En Amérique du Nord surtout, on va préférer le terme « **sourd** » à « **sourd-muet** » car, bien que la personne n'entende pas, elle est néanmoins capable d'émettre des sons ou même des mots grâce à l'orthophonie.

SPM (syndrome prémenstruel)

(voir : MENSTRUATION — SYNDROME PRÉMENSTRUEL)

SQUELETTE (voir : OS)

STÉRILITÉ

La **stérilité** est définie comme l'inaptitude à se reproduire. La **stérilité** peut indiquer un rejet, une résistance inconsciente à l'idée d'avoir un enfant. Il se peut aussi que je désire un enfant uniquement pour combler les attentes des personnes qui m'entourent mais, qu'au fond de moi, je ne le souhaite pas vraiment. Je peux aussi croire qu'ainsi j'arriverai à retenir mon conjoint. Ayant peur d'accoucher ou d'être incapable de tenir mon rôle comme parent (peur de la responsabilité, des problèmes financiers...) ou ne souhaitant pas faire vivre à mon enfant les souffrances que j'ai vécues, je provoque la **stérilité**. Je peux aussi éprouver la crainte de revivre par ma grossesse les souvenirs des moments où ma mère me portait et qui ont pu m'affecter. Je dois comprendre que le désir d'avoir un enfant peut être très grand mais la peur aussi, qu'elle soit consciente ou non; c'est la différence qui peut peser dans la balance pour que le processus de grossesse s'enclenche ou non. J'aurais avantage à vérifier si j'ai pu vivre des expériences dans le passé, que je sois l'homme ou la femme, qui ont pu m'amener à vivre certains blocages sexuels. Un travail en psychothérapie ou énergétique peut être très approprié dans ce cas. Il peut aussi arriver que je n'aie pas à vivre cette expérience d'être parent. Il est donc très important que je me questionne sur la nature de mon désir d'avoir un enfant et que je fasse confiance à mon moi intérieur dans ma décision de donner la vie ou non.

STRABISME (voir : YEUX — STRABISME)

STRESS

Toute situation qui crée une demande plus grande à mon organisme m'amène à vivre du **stress**. Le **stress** peut être psychologique (la pression de mon entourage), physique (une forte demande pour mon corps liée au travail, au sport, à la chaleur, au froid, etc.), chimique ou biochimique (prise de médicaments, chimiothérapie, changement hormonal). Le **stress** lui-même est en somme moins important que ma réaction face à celui-ci. Il peut être tout aussi positif, stimulant et créatif que menaçant pour mon corps. Selon ma réaction face aux situations, événements, sentiments et aux difficultés, l'effet stressant sera bénéfique ou nocif pour moi. Il est important de constater que même un événement heureux peut m'amener à vivre un **stress** important. Ainsi, je peux gagner un million de dollars à la loterie, ce qui peut avoir comme conséquence de me faire vivre une dépression parce que j'aurai l'impression d'avoir tellement de choses à changer dans ma vie que j'aurai peur de ne pas

pouvoir y arriver. Vais-je garder mon emploi avec les gens que j'estime ? Mes amis resteront-ils les mêmes avec moi ? Vais-je devoir déménager ? Serai-je capable de m'adapter à tous ces changements ? J'ai besoin de regarder à l'intérieur de moi et de questionner mes réactions, mes motifs et mes attitudes plutôt que de jeter le blâme sur les situations extérieures. J'apprends à relaxer et à considérer les bienfaits du **stress**.

SUBLINGUALE (glande...) (voir : GLANDES SALIVAIRES)

SUBLUXATION (voir : LUXATION)

SUCER SON POUCE

En **suçant mon pouce**, je souhaite ainsi recréer la sensation de bien-être que je ressentais lorsque j'étais dans le ventre de ma mère. Il arrive aussi que le pouce soit remplacé par le médius (majeur), lequel représente la sensibilité. La chaleur et l'humidité de ma bouche me procurent la sécurité, l'impression d'être à l'abri du monde extérieur. J'ai à renforcer mon sentiment de sécurité intérieure, tout en prenant soin de moi et en me faisant plaisir.

SUICIDE (voir aussi : ANGOISSE, ANXIÉTÉ, MÉLANCOLIE)

Si je pense au **suicide**, je prends la décision de m'autodétruire. Je me sens vide d'énergie, cette idée hante ma pensée sans arrêt. Je deviens mélancolique, solitaire, plein d'amertume. Je n'arrive plus à créer le contact avec l'extérieur. Ma souffrance est telle que je ne vois plus la lumière. **Le suicide est relié à la fuite**. Alors, je peux me demander ce que je cherche à fuir : ma douleur intérieure, mes responsabilités, mon vide intérieur, mon manque d'amour, etc. Si je consomme de la drogue, de l'alcool et que mon alimention est pauvre en certains nutriments essentiels à l'équilibre de mon système nerveux, alors je peux être plus sujet à avoir des idées suicidaires. Je décide de faire confiance, je ferme les yeux : la lumière est dans mon cœur. **J'en parle à quelqu'un ou j'écris sur un papier la détresse que je vis en demandant de l'aide.**

SURDIMUTITÉ (voir : SOURD-MUET)

SURDITÉ (voir : OREILLES — SURDITÉ)

SUROXYGÉNATION (voir : HYPERVENTILATION)

SURRÉNALES (maux de capsules)
(voir aussi : CUSHING [syndrome de...], PEUR, STRESS)

La fonction première des **glandes surrénales** est de produire une hormone que l'on appelle adrénaline. Elles sont reliées au premier CHAKRA (centre d'énergie) que l'on appelle **centre coccygien**. Ces **glandes** ont pour fonction de régulariser le pouls et la pression sanguine et permettent au corps de ressentir les situations dangereuses. Lorsque je me sens en danger, ou si je suis réellement en danger, ma perception peut être différente, mais mon corps répondra aussitôt à toute situation de stress et de tension qu'il sent comme menaçante, que cette situation se manifeste ou pas. Ainsi, on peut constater que le corps répond sérieusement aux avertissements qu'un stress peut provoquer. Je peux relier ce danger à une situation dans ma vie où j'ai peur de perdre soit du temps, de l'argent, une récompense, un conjoint, etc. parce que **j'ai pris une « mauvaise décision » ou une « mauvaise direction » dans ma vie**. Je veux donc aller très vite et très loin dans un ou des domaines de ma vie mais cela implique une grande détermination, des choix judicieux et je ne me donne pas droit à l'erreur, qui n'est en fait qu'une expérience de vie. D'où un niveau de stress intense. Les **surrénales** se retrouvent au-dessus des reins qui sont considérés comme le siège de la peur et de la peine. L'adrénaline qui se libère lorsque je suis en état d'excitation aura pour effet de me stimuler et me rendra créatif ou, à l'opposé, pourra me causer des dommages, voire même me détruire. Une trop grande accumulation de stress entraîne un épuisement total. Le syndrome du « ça passe ou ça casse » peut alors se manifester de façon régulière. J'ai intérêt à me défaire de mon attitude défaitiste et je décide de me fixer un but dans la vie. J'adopte un style de vie simple et je m'ouvre davantage, je retrouve mon équilibre.

SYNCOPE (voir : CERVEAU — SYNCOPE)

SYNDROME[80] DE BURNETT
(voir : BUVEURS DE LAIT [syndrome des...])

SYNDROME DES BUVEURS DE LAIT
(voir : BUVEURS DE LAIT [syndrome des...])

SYNDROME DE CUSHING (voir : CUSHING [syndrome de...])

---

80. **Syndrome :** Un syndrome n'est pas une maladie proprement dite mais bien un ensemble de symptômes dont on ne connaît pas la cause précise.

SYNDROME DE FATIGUE CHRONIQUE
(voir : FATIGUE CHRONIQUE [syndrome de...])

SYNDROME DE GÉLINEAU (voir : NARCOLEPSIE)

SYNDROME DES ONGLES JAUNES
(voir : ONGLES JAUNES [syndrome des...])

SYNDROME DE SURUTILISATION
(voir aussi : DOS [maux de...], INFLAMMATION, TENDONS)

Le **syndrome de surutilisation** est une maladie rencontrée principalement chez les musiciens. Elle se caractérise par une inflammation des tendons des doigts, du poignet, des coudes ou parfois des épaules ou du cou. Cela peut produire des douleurs au dos. Il est dit que les « positions contraignantes » peuvent amener jusqu'à 53 % des musiciens d'orchestres symphoniques à souffrir de maux de dos. Comme musicien, je suis souvent confiné dans des espaces restreints, jouissant d'un confort peu adapté à l'emploi. Il se peut que les heures longues de pratique m'amènent à trouver le travail lourd à supporter lorsque ce sont mes épaules qui sont affectées. L'insécurité d'emploi et la compétition féroce dans ce milieu me font vivre de grandes peurs et je ne me sens pas suffisamment soutenu ; voilà d'où viennent mes maux d'épaules. J'ai à rester flexible et à harmoniser mon énergie mentale et spirituelle lorsque mes tendons sont affectés. Chaque partie du corps m'envoie un message approprié sur ce que je vis. Même si cela « peut sembler » être en rapport avec ma profession de musicien, il n'y a pas de hasard. J'identifie la partie concernée pour faire la prise de conscience qui m'aidera à me sentir mieux dans ce que je fais.

SYNDROME D'IMMUNODÉFICIENCE ACQUISE (voir : SIDA)

SYNDROME DU CANAL CARPIEN (voir : CRAMPE DE L'ÉCRIVAIN)

SYNDROME PRÉMENSTRUEL
(voir : MENSTRUATION — SYNDROME PRÉMENSTRUEL)

SYPHILIS (voir : VÉNÉRIENNES [maladies...])

SYSTÈME IMMUNITAIRE (voir aussi : SIDA)

La défense de mon organisme est assurée par un **système d'autoprotection,** lequel est essentiel pour me protéger des agressions

venant du monde extérieur comme les bactéries, les virus, les champignons microscopiques et tous les autres problèmes potentiels. Sans le fonctionnement total et complet de ce système, c'est la mort. Il est en relation directe avec mes états émotionnels et une profonde douleur dans mon existence peut réduire de façon dramatique sa force. Les cellules immunes se développent au départ dans la mœlle osseuse et celles qui deviendront des cellules-T sont transportées, à leur maturité, jusqu'à la glande du thymus située près du cœur. Sa localisation par rapport au cœur me fait prendre davantage conscience de la relation « corps-esprit » qui existe. Le **système immunitaire** répond aux sentiments et à l'ensemble de mes pensées, qu'elles soient positives ou négatives. Ainsi, toutes pensées de colère, d'amertume, de haine et de ressentiment auront tendance à affaiblir mon **système immunitaire**. Par ailleurs, toutes pensées d'amour, d'harmonie, de beauté et de paix intérieure auront tendance à renforcer mon **système immunitaire**. Le thymus est la glande endocrine qui est associée au chakra (centre d'énergie) du cœur. Donc, quand mon **système immunitaire** est atteint, mon besoin d'amour est lui aussi très grand. Mon cerveau est lui aussi très lié à mon **système immunitaire** et certains états d'esprit auront un effet puissant pouvant affecter le fonctionnement de mon système.

SYSTÈME LOCOMOTEUR (voir aussi : OS)

Le **système locomoteur** est relié à ma mobilité et à ma flexibilité, de même qu'à mon ouverture intérieure et à mon ouverture extérieure. Il rassemble les os, les muscles, les tendons et les ligaments. La charpente soutenant tout mon corps est constituée des os. **Ce sont eux qui représentent mes principes moraux, ma structure, mon honnêteté, ma droiture, ma stabilité**. Lorsque je deviens trop rigide dans mes pensées, mes os aussi le deviennent et risquent de casser plus facilement. **Les extrémités de mon corps et mes muscles, quant à eux, symbolisent l'action et le mouvement**. Grâce à mes mains, je peux « saisir » les choses, m'y retenir. **Mes jambes me permettent d'avancer dans la vie**. Une difficulté à me mouvoir m'indique que j'ai peur de progresser. Un manque d'humilité ou un refus de « plier » ou d'admettre mes erreurs aura pour effet que j'aurai du mal à plier les genoux. Mes pieds représentent la stabilité. Je garde ainsi contact avec la terre ferme, j'ai « les deux pieds sur terre ». Chaque partie de mon corps m'aide à prendre conscience de ma souplesse ou de ma rigidité. Je choisis d'être à l'écoute de mon corps car il est le guide de mon état intérieur.

SYSTÈME LYMPHATIQUE (voir aussi : GANGLION [lymphatique])

Le **système lymphatique** est composé de ganglions et des vaisseaux qui transportent la lymphe jusqu'au courant sanguin. Il joue un rôle important dans le fonctionnement du système immunitaire. Le **système lymphatique**

est, d'une certaine façon, en parallèle avec le système sanguin. Il est lié plus directement au côté émotionnel, affectif de moi-même. Si mon système nerveux est relié plus directement à mes pensées avec mon corps énergétique ou astral, mon **système lymphatique** est relié plus directement au côté affectif de mon corps énergétique ou astral. L'amour est certainement le meilleur moyen de garder le **système lymphatique** en santé et efficace.

SYSTÈME NERVEUX (voir aussi : NERFS [en général])

Mon **système nerveux** est composé des nerfs et des centres nerveux qui servent à la coordination et à la commande de différentes parties de mon corps, ainsi qu'à la réception d'informations sensorielles, psychiques et intellectuelles. En fait, mon **système nerveux** est relié plus directement à mes pensées en rapport avec la partie de mon corps énergétique ou mental. C'est le système de connexion électrique sur le plan physique qui permet à mes pensées de prendre action dans ce monde.

TABAGISME (voir : CIGARETTE)

TACHES DE VIN (voir : PEAU — TACHES DE VIN)

TACHYCARDIE (voir : CŒUR — ARYTHMIE CARDIAQUE)

TÆNIA ou TÉNIA (voir : INTESTINS — TÆNIA)

TALON

Souffrir d'un **mal au talon** m'indique que je vis de l'angoisse, que je me sens incompris et **non appuyé dans les choses à faire**. Le **talon** étant le point d'appui de mon corps, une douleur à cet endroit démontre que je vis de l'incertitude face à mon avenir. Je me sens hésitant et insatisfait de moi ou de ma vie et il me semble que je perds la maîtrise de mon corps. Comme c'est sur mes **talons** que repose tout mon corps, je peux sentir le besoin d'avoir un appui solide dans la vie pour pouvoir continuer d'avancer en toute sécurité. Mon corps me dit que je peux me faire confiance et avancer en toute sécurité.

TARTRE (voir : DENTS [maux de...])

TEIGNE (voir : CHEVEUX — TEIGNE)

TENDINITE (voir : TENDON [en général])

TENDON (en général)

Le **tendon** est le trait d'union entre le muscle et l'os sur lequel il s'insère. Il est constitué de tissu conjonctif. Ce tissu de consistance molle, donc constitué d'énergie mentale qui s'unit à l'énergie spirituelle, a pour effet d'unifier l'expression et le mouvement complet. Cela crée un lien direct avec mon « corps-esprit ». La rigidité de mes **tendons** reflète des tendances rigides. Si mon énergie mentale est raide, rigide, je deviens inflexible. Ainsi, mon tissu mou ressentira cet état, provoquant de cette façon sa rigidité. Lorsque je vis un conflit entre ce que je pense devoir faire et ma voix intérieure qui me dit vraiment ce que je veux faire, je ressens alors une douleur dans les **tendons**. J'aurai tendance à me dévaloriser. Mon énergie mentale **(tendon)** décide d'une direction alors que mon énergie fondamentale, profonde et spirituelle **(os),** souhaite aller dans une direction opposée. Je peux regarder quel **tendon** est touché et j'aurai une indication quant à l'aspect de ma vie que je dévalorise. Par exemple, si je fais une **tendinite** au poignet, je dois me demander : « Dans quelle activité, où j'ai besoin de mes poignets et de mes mains, ai-je l'impression que je ne suis pas assez bon ou que je pourrais faire mieux ? » Je reconnais l'importance d'équilibrer mes énergies et j'avance dans la vie.

TENDON D'ACHILLE

Le **tendon d'Achille** relie le muscle du mollet à l'os du talon. C'est le **tendon** le plus puissant du corps : il peut supporter jusqu'à 400 kilos (880 livres). Il permet à mes pensées et à mes désirs, tant physiques que spirituels, de se réaliser. Il sert aussi à exprimer tout blocage au mouvement de la cheville. Par exemple, je peux avoir un grand désir de stabilité mais cela est difficile à réaliser à cause d'une situation financière précaire. Je continue à mettre des choses de l'avant pour réaliser mes rêves et pour atteindre les buts que je me suis fixés.

TÉNIA (voir : INTESTINS — TÆNIA)

TENNIS ELBOW (voir : COUDES — ÉPICONDYLITE)

TENSION ARTÉRIELLE — HYPERTENSION (trop élevée)

L'image représentant une personne souffrant **d'hypertension** est le **presto**[81]. Je suis cette personne qui accumule, durant de longues périodes, des pensées et des émotions qui ne sont pas exprimées ; je suis souvent hypersensible et je me contrôle mal. Mes colères et mes contrariétés sont ravalées, faisant ainsi bouillir mon intérieur. Je peux aussi avoir tendance à la

---

81. **Presto :** Chaudron fermant hermétiquement, avec un contrôle de vapeur, et servant à faire cuire les aliments sous pression.

procrastination ou à remettre à plus tard les choses que j'ai à dire ou à faire par peur ou manque de confiance en moi, et j'en viens à vivre une tension nerveuse intense, car je vois tout cela comme une montagne et je ne sais pas si je serai capable d'accomplir tous mes projets. Je peux aussi fabuler, amplifier mes problèmes, et ma culpabilité aura tôt fait d'augmenter la « pression ». Mon désir de tout contrôler et de solutionner les situations de ma vie augmente ma pression qui peut devenir insoutenable. Vivant une peur profonde d'être rejeté, je me sens en danger et je reste sur mes gardes. **L'hypertension** que je vis peut aussi trouver sa source dans ma peur de la mort, celle-ci étant consciente ou non, et dans mon désir de tirer partie au maximum de ma vie, car je veux réaliser les multiples buts que je me suis fixés. J'ai intérêt à apprendre à laisser sortir la vapeur tout doucement. J'évite l'accumulation qui provoque l'explosion. J'apprends à me faire confiance.

TENSION ARTÉRIELLE — HYPOTENSION (trop basse)

Contrairement à l'hypertension, **l'hypotension** se retrouve chez une personne dont la pression est trop basse (à noter qu'une personne peut avoir une pression sous la normale et se sentir en pleine forme. Sa pression est donc adéquate pour elle étant donné que sa qualité de vie n'en est pas affectée). Si je suis une personne qui fait de la **basse pression**, cela peut indiquer que mon désir de vivre est manquant. J'ai l'impression que rien ne va, qu'il m'est inutile de faire des efforts car, de toute façon, j'ai le sentiment que ça ne marchera pas. Je me sens vidé de mon énergie et je n'arrive plus à porter le poids des événements. Je me laisse aller au découragement. Le cœur n'y est plus. Je vis en victime et j'ai l'impression que ma vie ressemble à un cul-de-sac. **L'hypotension** peut mener à une perte de conscience. Elle est le signe que je veux fuir mes responsabilités, certaines situations ou certaines personnes, car le fait d'y faire face va m'amener à me positionner et à faire des actions que je n'ai peut-être pas le goût de faire. Le message que mon corps me donne est de me faire confiance et de foncer. Je choisis de me laisser guider par ma force intérieure.

TESTICULES (en général)

Les **glandes sexuelles mâles** représentent l'aspect masculin. Un problème aux **testicules** est souvent relié aux peurs, à l'insécurité, aux doutes concernant le fait d'être un homme. Il peut indiquer un manque d'acceptation ↓♥ de sa sexualité, de sa préférence sexuelle. La peur d'être jugé selon ma performance peut conduire jusqu'à l'impuissance. Lorsque je vis une situation tendue, il m'arrive d'avoir l'impression d'être **tenu par les couilles,** principalement si mon partenaire est une personne de pouvoir. J'ai intérêt à m'interroger sur mes sentiments face à ma virilité et à revoir ma conception du principe masculin.

TESTICULES (cancer des...) (voir : CANCER DES TESTICULES)

TÉTANIE

La **tétanie** se caractérise par des crises qui font se contracter mes muscles et mes nerfs, principalement aux extrémités. Je sens mes mains, mes pieds, tous mes muscles se crisper. Cet état provient d'une hyperexcitabilité et se produit lors de contrariétés. Dans certains cas, lors de crises importantes, mes doigts se resserrent et mon pouce vient se cacher sous mes doigts en se repliant à l'intérieur de ma main, comme s'il voulait s'isoler du monde extérieur. Peut-être que moi aussi, je veux m'isoler, me « couper » du monde, ayant peut-être même le désir inconscient de mourir, car je n'ai plus le goût de vivre, je n'ai plus de joie de vivre. J'ai à apprendre le contrôle de soi. J'élimine les pensées négatives et je minimise l'effet de contrariété.

TÉTANOS (voir : MUSCLES — TÉTANOS)

TÊTE (en général)

La **tête** est mon centre de communication, **elle est reliée à mon individualité**. Elle est souvent appelée le « centre de contrôle ». C'est par elle que passent toutes mes émotions et toutes mes communications, par l'entremise de mes cinq sens. Si je vis des difficultés ou des malaises à la **tête**, je dois me demander si je vis un conflit touchant mes pensées et ma vie spirituelle ou ma croissance personnelle. Cela s'explique par le fait que la **tête** est constituée d'os, qui sont faits d'un tissu dur et qui symbolisent mon énergie spirituelle, et que ces os entourent le tissu mou et les fluides, qui symbolisent mes énergies mentales et émotionnelles. Si les deux aspects sont en harmonie, il y aura fusion de mon corps et de mon esprit. Toutefois, si le sang qui est dans ma **tête** ne circule pas bien ou qu'il exerce une pression, cela m'indique que j'ai de la difficulté à exprimer ou à recevoir l'amour et tout sentiment qui m'habite (car le sang transporte mes sentiments dans tout mon corps). Ma **tête** recevant et exprimant les différents aspects de ma communication, de même que les sensations et les impressions du corps qui les manifeste extérieurement, j'apprends à rester ouvert face à mon entourage, à accepter ↓♥ les messages qui parviennent à mes sens et à travers tout mon corps pour apprendre les leçons de la vie qui m'apporteront un plus grand éveil spirituel.

TÊTE (maux de...)

Il y a plusieurs causes aux **maux de tête**. Par exemple : le stress et la tension, quand je m'efforce tant bien que mal « d'être » d'une certaine façon ou de « faire » telle chose. Le **mal de tête** apparaît souvent quand j'essaie trop fort mentalement d'accomplir quelque chose ou quand je suis obsédé par ce

qui s'en vient et que je suis inquiet de ce qui m'attend dans l'avenir. Je vis à ce moment beaucoup d'anxiété et de préoccupation. Je peux aussi réagir à de fortes pressions exercées par des situations ou des événements qui m'entourent. Je peux vivre un sentiment intense d'échec, de doute, de haine de soi qui donne vie à la critique et, surtout, à l'autocritique. Je suis pris, « emboîté » dans ma **tête,** n'aimant pas ce que je vois, et me jugeant sévèrement, me donnant moi-même « des coups de **tête** ». Le **mal de tête** peut aussi provenir de la négation et de la suppression de mes pensées et de mes sentiments que je crois inacceptables ou inappropriés. Soit que je n'ai pas le courage de les exprimer, ou tout simplement que je ne les écoute pas, car je rationalise, j'intellectualise tout ce que je vis. « C'est bien ou c'est mal ! » Je veux peut-être trop comprendre, aller trop vite, vouloir savoir ou avoir réponse à mes questions tout de suite. Mais le temps n'est peut-être pas venu et j'ai à développer ma patience et ma confiance que tout arrive au bon moment. Le **mal de tête** exprime aussi souvent des émotions négatives qui sont « prises au piège » dans ma **tête**, telles que l'insécurité, le tourment, les ambitions excessives, l'obsession à être parfait, etc. qui causent une dilatation sanguine. Finalement, si j'ai peur de faire face à une certaine réalité, je pourrai me trouver un autre endroit où mettre mon attention et fuir, cela étant le **mal de tête.** Un **mal de tête** au niveau du **front** aura plus trait à une situation dans mon travail ou liée à mon rôle social tandis que s'il se situe sur le **côté de la tête** (près des tempes), c'est plutôt mon côté émotionnel (famille, couple) qui est impliqué. Quelle qu'en soit la cause, le **mal de tête** est directement relié à mon individualité et j'ai à apprendre à être plus patient et plus flexible envers moi-même et envers les autres. « Mes idées sont de plus en plus claires », et j'apprends à redonner la place qui revient autant à mon intellect qu'à mes émotions, afin d'atteindre l'équilibre. Je serai alors plus en harmonie avec moi-même, je me sentirai la tête plus dégagée et plus légère.

TÊTE — MIGRAINES

Les **migraines** sont souvent associées à des troubles de vision et de digestion : je ne veux plus voir et je ne veux plus digérer ce qui se passe dans ma vie. Ce sont des angoisses, de la frustration face à une situation où je suis incapable de prendre une décision. Je peux avoir le sentiment de quelque chose qui doit être fait ou accompli ou qui m'est demandé. La **migraine** expose ma résistance reliée à mon incapacité d'accomplir ce qui m'est demandé. Ma **tête** « surchauffe » et me fait mal juste à l'idée du but à atteindre qui me semble inaccessible. Ma **tête** ressemble à un « presto »[82], la pression étant tellement forte que je ne sais pas toujours quelle solution ou quelle attitude adopter. Il y a conflit entre mes pensées, mon intellect qui est surchargé, mes besoins et désirs personnels. Est-ce que je me sens à la hauteur

---

82. **Presto :** Chaudron fermant hermétiquement, avec un contrôle de vapeur, et servant à faire cuire les aliments sous pression.

ou ai-je l'impression d'être incompétent, surtout sur le plan intellectuel ? Je dois prendre conscience que je suis en train de fuir ce qui me dérange ou que je sens de l'incompréhension et un manque d'amour de la part de quelqu'un. **Les migraines** peuvent aussi être reliées à des problèmes sexuels, tels que le refoulement depuis l'enfance, et qui refont surface. C'est comme un combat à l'intérieur de moi qui se déroule entre mes pensées et ma sexualité, cela me monte à la **tête**. Je peux avoir l'impression que c'est comme si ma **tête** allait éclater. Je dois comprendre que, lorsque j'ai une **migraine**, j'ai une prise de conscience à faire, j'ai des choses à changer et je dois être capable de les changer, c'est-à-dire de passer à l'action. La **migraine** me donnant un temps d'arrêt, cela peut aussi être une façon d'obtenir davantage d'amour et d'attention. Je laisse les événements circuler librement dans ma vie et je reçois en retour joie, paix, harmonie.

THALAMUS

Le **thalamus** est un couple de volumineux noyaux de substance grise situés de chaque coté du troisième ventricule du cerveau antérieur, et qui servent de relais pour les voies sensitives. Une dysfonction de celui-ci m'indique de grandes remises en question face à moi-même, à ce que je suis et à comment on me perçoit. Je peux être enclin à être désespéré. J'ai peur du jugement des autres, peur qu'on me sous-estime. Je suis à la recherche de ma vraie identité. J'apprends à m'accepter ↓♥ tel que je suis et je réalise qu'en étant vrai avec les gens qui m'entourent, je manifeste ainsi beaucoup plus d'amour et j'entretiendrai des relations saines et durables.

THROMBOSE (voir : SANG — THROMBOSE)

THROMBOSE CORONARIENNE
(voir : CŒUR — THROMBOSE CORONARIENNE)

THYMUS (voir aussi : SIDA, SYSTÈME IMMUNITAIRE)

Le **thymus** est une petite glande logée dans le thorax et qui produit un type de globules blancs (lymphocytes T) jouant un rôle essentiel dans la réponse immunitaire de l'organisme. Le **thymus** est la glande endocrine qui est reliée directement au centre d'énergie du cœur, aussi appelé chakra du cœur. Son activité diminue avec l'âge. Une difficulté au **thymus** m'indique que j'ai l'impression qu'on est venu me soutirer quelque chose qui m'appartenait. Ce peut être un travail, un conjoint, un objet matériel, etc. On m'a « enlevé le pain de la bouche » ! Je me suis donc senti l'espace d'un moment « sans défense », ne sachant pas comment réagir. Je réalise combien je suis protégé dans ma vie de tous les jours. J'apprécie ce que j'ai dans le moment présent, car la vie n'est que mouvement et ce que j'aurai demain peut

être différent d'aujourd'hui. Plus je me détache du monde matériel, plus grand est mon sentiment de liberté !

THYROÏDE (en général)

La **glande thyroïde** se retrouve à la base du cou. Elle est reliée directement au centre d'énergie de la gorge, aussi appelé chakra de la gorge. Le rôle de cette glande est de sécréter deux hormones très importantes, soit la thyroxine et la triothyronine qui ont comme particularité de contenir de l'iode, reconnu pour être un antiseptique puissant et nécessaire au bon fonctionnement du corps tout entier. Sans elles, je ne pourrais vivre. Un cas d'hyper ou d'hypofonctionnement **thyroïdien** pourra se présenter si j'ai le sentiment de toujours ravaler des injures ou que la vie est injuste avec moi. Me complaisant dans ce rôle, j'en arrive même à provoquer autour de moi des situations problématiques afin d'être de plus en plus une pauvre victime. Le cou, reliant ma tête à mon corps, fait de cette région le lien entre le corps et l'esprit. Si mon orgueil est très fort et qu'il ferme mon cœur, je passe à côté de mes vrais besoins. Le centre d'énergie de la gorge représente ma créativité. J'apprends donc à m'exprimer librement et j'utilise tous mes moyens. Je développe mon esprit créateur.

THYROÏDE — GOITRE

Généralement, le **goitre** indique que ma glande **thyroïde** est suractive. Cela résulte d'une accélération de plusieurs processus corporels et mentaux. Cette glande est responsable, entre autres, de la régulation du processus respiratoire. Elle est étroitement reliée à mon désir de vivre, à mon engagement à entrer dans la vie. L'**hyperthyroïdie** est une réponse stressante qui dénote mon angoisse, mon chagrin, bref des émotions intenses non exprimées qui font gonfler ma glande **thyroïde** (gorge). **J'ai l'impression que tout va trop vite !** Cela peut aussi résulter du sentiment d'être étouffé par la vie. Ma glande **thyroïde** se questionne à savoir : « Est-ce que je dois continuer à maintenir la vie ou non ? » J'ai avantage à exprimer mes besoins, mes désirs, mes émotions au lieu de les refouler afin de permettre à ma glande **thyroïde** de fonctionner normalement. Dans le cas où le **goitre** résulte de l'**hypothyroïdie**, c'est-à-dire que la glande **thyroïde** travaille insuffisamment durant une longue période de temps, comme si elle s'évanouissait, cette manifestation laisse voir ma personnalité défaitiste et ma tendance au désespoir, car j'ai peu le goût d'accomplir des choses et j'adopte une attitude de « victime » face à ce qui m'arrive. Je vis ainsi beaucoup de contrariété et d'amertume et j'ai l'impression que le monde entier m'en veut. J'ai à développer une attitude plus positive et à me prendre en mains afin de pouvoir atteindre mes objectifs.

THYROÏDE — HYPERTHYROÏDIE

Elle indique une hyperactivité, une trop grande activité, de la glande **thyroïde**. Mon métabolisme augmente, j'ai donc des chaleurs et je transpire. Je vis une grande déception de ne pouvoir accomplir ce que je veux réellement ou exprimer ce que j'ai à dire, parce que je réponds aux attentes des autres plutôt qu'aux miennes. Par conséquent, je vis de la rancune, de la frustration et de la haine envers tout ce qui ne correspond pas réellement à mes attentes. Je peux aussi toujours écouter les conseils des autres sans m'écouter intérieurement. De plus, je me donne des échéances dans les choses à faire très courtes, ce qui me demande de toujours me dépêcher afin de terminer à temps les projets en cours. **Il faut toujours faire plus vite !** Quand ma **thyroïde** est hyperactive, j'ai souvent de la difficulté avec le temps et avec le fait d'être en retard. Alors, mon corps me donne un message. Je prends conscience de mon pouvoir. Ainsi, je prends mes décisions et je crée mes actions selon mon discernement intérieur. Je suis cocréateur de ma vie.

THYROÏDE — HYPOTHYROÏDIE

L'**hypothyroïde** est un sous-fonctionnement de la glande **thyroïde**, une insuffisance thyroïdienne. Elle peut provoquer une proéminence des yeux. Les causes physiques sont : un dérèglement du système immunitaire, une destruction de la **thyroïde** par une thyroïdite formant des anticorps qui attaquent la glande, et une carence en iode qui entraîne : une hausse du taux de cholestérol, de la fatigue, des douleurs musculaires, un fourmillement et une froideur des extrémités, de la constipation et une baisse des réflexes. Le **découragement peut même apparaître**, me rendant morose, défaitiste et suscitant le sentiment d'être incompris. Mon corps me transmet un S.O.S. Les causes métaphysiques sont aussi importantes. Le chakra de la gorge est relié à ma communication et à ma créativité. Comment est ma communication avec moi-même, mes proches et les autres ? Comment est-ce que j'exerce ma créativité dans ce que je fais ? L'**hypothyroïdie** peut aussi provenir de mon incapacité d'affronter une situation qui réapparaît à plusieurs reprises dans ma vie et face à laquelle je ne sais pas comment réagir. Je suis créateur de ma vie. Je communique l'harmonie partout autour de moi. Confiant, je vois la vie avec un nouveau regard.

TICS (voir : CERVEAU — TICS)

TIMIDITÉ

La **timidité** me fait passer à côté de choses merveilleuses. J'évite les gens que je ne connais pas. Craignant d'être jugé, je renonce aux choses nouvelles prétextant qu'elles ne sont pas pour moi. Je baisse les bras, je refuse de me battre. J'ai tendance à me sécuriser dans la routine. Je m'aime peu et ma faible

estime de moi et mon peu de confiance en moi m'incitent à rester dans un cadre bien établi, où je ne me sens ni blessé, ni rejeté, ni incompris. Cette forme de fuite de ma **timidité** m'amène à rester en retrait. À quelque part, il est bien possible que cela fasse mon affaire car je me protège aussi de situations ou de personnes qui pourraient me blesser. Je prends l'habitude d'agir avec calme et je me donne la chance de découvrir, chaque jour, de nouvelles choses et de nouvelles personnes.

TISSU CONJONCTIF (fragilité du...)

Un tissu est un groupe de cellules ayant une même forme ou accomplissant une même fonction. Le rôle du **tissu conjonctif** en est un de soutien aux autres tissus du corps, assurant la nutrition des tissus musculaires, nerveux et de l'épithélium[83], de même que le remplissage des interstices (des fentes) qui se trouvent entre ces tissus. Je dois me demander : « De quoi ai-je besoin, moi, pour me nourrir, tant émotionellement, physiquement que spirituellement ? » Est-ce que je me sens assez soutenu ou ai-je l'impression d'avoir à tout faire moi-même, incluant le fait d'avoir à « remplir les trous » au travail ou à la maison, par exemple ? Puisque je me dévalorise facilement, je dois me rendre utile et important. Je me sens souvent brimé dans ma liberté et j'ai tendance à remettre aux autres la responsabilité de mes maux. Je suis porté à être rancunier et je pardonne difficilement. J'ai avantage à communiquer mes états d'être, mes besoins : ceci m'aidera à me découvrir, à prendre ma vie en main et à aller chercher l'aide dont j'ai besoin et à laquelle j'ai droit.

TORPEUR (voir : ENGOURDISSEMENT)

TORTICOLIS (voir : COU — TORTICOLIS)

TOUR DE REIN (lumbago) (voir : DOS [maux de...] — BAS DU DOS)

TOUX (voir aussi : GORGE / [en général] / [maux de...])

La **toux** est un état souvent minimisé, voire même nié. Pourtant, elle démontre une irritation ; que ce soit au niveau de la gorge ou des poumons, je vis une tension nerveuse qui m'irrite et dont je veux me libérer. Je peux me sentir étouffé par une situation, par une personne. Je vis de la frustration, j'aurais envie de crier, de « cracher » ma peine, mais mon éducation m'en empêche. En toussant, je parviens à me libérer de mes émotions. Ce peut être autant la solitude, l'amertume, la tristesse, l'incompréhension, la frustration, l'ennui, etc. En acceptant ↓♥ de reconnaître ce qui m'irrite, ma **toux** s'en ira.

---

83. **Épithélium :** Un tissu qui recouvre les surfaces de l'organisme de l'extérieur ou de l'intérieur.

Ce peut très bien être un aspect de moi-même que j'ai de la difficulté à accepter ↓♥. Si elle persiste, c'est que je n'arrive pas à me libérer. Il serait bon que je prenne un temps d'arrêt pour découvrir les causes de mon irritabilité pour enfin arriver à corriger les situations qui sont irritantes et pour me sentir bien avec celles que j'ai à accepter ↓♥.

TOXICOMANIE (voir aussi : ALCOOLISME, CIGARETTE, COMPULSION NERVEUSE, DÉPENDANCE, DROGUE, POUMONS [en général])

La **toxicomanie** se caractérise par la consommation abusive de différents produits toxiques, régis par la loi ou non, parmi lesquels se retrouvent le tabac, les médicaments, l'alcool et les drogues sous toutes ses formes. Je développe ainsi une dépendance psychique ou physique. **Ce besoin irrésistible de consommer démontre une grande frayeur de me voir tel que je suis. Je préfère la fuite, l'inconscience. Ne sachant comment m'aimer, je ne peux concevoir que les gens qui m'entourent m'aiment et m'apprécient.** Je me cache dans un monde « fantastique » où je crois que rien ne pourra m'atteindre, jamais. Je m'endors tout doucement en refoulant mes blessures au plus profond de moi. J'ai mal et même moi, je ne le vois plus. En me donnant la chance d'être moi-même, je peux découvrir l'être merveilleux que je suis et m'ouvrir à l'amour.

TRACHÉITE (voir : RESPIRATION — TRACHÉITE)

TRAITS TOMBANTS, MOUS

Mes **traits** sont **tombants, mous** quand j'ai le sentiment que tout et que tous les gens me laissent « tomber ». Ma peau devient flasque, sans vie. Mes paupières descendantes font voir la tristesse dans mes yeux. Je me laisse aller. J'en veux à la vie. Je manque de « fermeté » dans mes décisions. J'ai besoin de me « remonter le moral », de reprendre goût à la vie. Je me donne la permission de profiter de chaque instant de ma vie, je fais place à l'enfant qui est en moi.

TRANSPIRATION (voir : ODEUR CORPORELLE)

TREMBLEMENTS (voir aussi : PARKINSON [maladie de...])

Les **tremblements** touchent plus particulièrement les membres supérieurs du corps et principalement les mains. Ce sont des mouvements irréguliers qui surviennent souvent après une colère excessive ou après une frayeur ou une faiblesse physique. Me sentant pris, mes **muscles** se tendent et se mettent à trembler. Je suis comme un volcan en éruption, la hargne gronde en moi. Il se peut aussi que ce **tremblement** survienne à la suite d'une nouvelle ou d'une information dont je refuse de voir les conséquences consciemment. Il y a alors un conflit entre ma partie consciente et mon

subconscient. Cette tension qui existe entre les deux provoque un **tremblement** involontaire de l'une ou l'autre des parties de mon corps (bras, visage, jambes, tronc). Ce peut être à la suite d'une question que je me posais depuis tant d'années et dont j'ai la réponse, mais dont je doute de la véracité. L'énergie que j'avais accumulée dans mon inconscient à force de désirer ma réponse se libère sous forme de **tremblements.** J'apprends à prendre ma place, je me détends et je vis un jour à la fois.

TRISMUS (voir : MUSCLES — TRISMUS)

TRISTESSE (voir aussi : CHAGRIN, MÉLANCOLIE, SANG / CHOLESTÉROL / DIABÈTE / HYPOGLYCÉMIE)

La **tristesse** se définit comme « un état naturel ou accidentel de chagrin, de mélancolie ». Une **tristesse** profonde peut m'amener à devenir **diabétique**. C'est mon corps tout entier qui refuse la joie de vivre. J'ai l'impression que rien ne me sourit, je sens la peine qui coule en moi, mon cœur qui se déchire ; ce vide immense semble vouloir s'agrandir au fond de moi pour faire de la place à cette boule de peine. Je veux qu'elle éclate, j'ai besoin de « piquant » dans ma vie, de chaleur qui mettra en ébullition toutes les larmes qui sont en moi et qui quitteront ainsi mon corps, comme la vapeur qui rejoint le ciel. Je pourrai ainsi combler ce vide de douceur et de tendresse. Et les idées noires se dissiperont ; je retrouverai mon dynamisme et ma joie de vivre.

TROMPE (infection d'une...) (voir : SALPINGITE)

TUBERCULOSE (voir aussi : POUMONS [maux aux...])

La **tuberculose** est une infection par le bacille de Koch qui se loge souvent à l'intérieur des poumons mais qui peut aussi atteindre par voie sanguine les reins, le système urinaire, etc. Les principaux symptômes sont, entre autres, des bronchites répétitives, une fatigue anormale, de la fièvre prolongée, du crachement de sang. Chacun d'eux me montre que je ressens de la colère et que ma vie est sans joie. J'ai l'impression d'être délaissé, abandonné, de perdre mes moyens. Je souhaiterais garder pour moi seul les gens que j'aime. Mon égoïsme m'amène à être jaloux de ce que les autres possèdent et je me sens « victime », en en voulant au reste du monde et en cherchant à me venger de lui. Puisque ce sont les poumons qui sont touchés, **la tuberculose met aussi en évidence ma peur de la mort qui est très présente et qui envahit mes pensées.** C'est la raison pour laquelle après les guerres, il y a une recrudescence de la **tuberculose** car, dans bien des cas, j'ai pu me retrouver dans des situations où des bombes sont tombées près d'où je me trouvais, que l'ennemi pouvait « me descendre » (me tuer). En fait, j'ai

vécu plusieurs situations où j'aurais pu mourir. Il est très important que je prenne conscience de l'objet de cette peur et que je sache que je suis protégé en tout temps. J'ai à dépasser cette peur de la mort et à vivre le moment présent, en savourant chaque instant.

TUMEUR(S) (voir aussi : KYSTE)

Une **tumeur** est comparable à un amas de tissus informe, pouvant se retrouver dans différents endroits du corps. Elle survient généralement à la suite d'un choc émotionnel. En gardant en moi de vieilles blessures, des pensées négatives face à mon passé, celles-ci s'accumulent et forment une masse qui finit par devenir solide. J'ai intérêt à prendre conscience que cette masse bloque le passage d'une partie de mon énergie qui demande à circuler librement. Il est important que je puisse exprimer cette détresse qui est en moi ; je dois prendre au sérieux ce message que mon corps me donne. Je fais place au présent, j'exprime mes sentiments. Si je m'y refuse, j'aurai l'impression qu'une petite voix à l'intérieur de moi me dit : **Tu meurs**[84] à petit feu.

TUMEUR AU CERVEAU (voir : CERVEAU [tumeur au...])

TYMPANISME

Le **tympanisme** est l'augmentation de la sonorité du thorax ou de l'abdomen. On peut le déceler en frappant une zone du corps avec les doigts : cela « résonne » comme sur un tambour. Cet état peut être le signe que je suis une personne d'une très grande sensibilité et que je garde en moi mes émotions au lieu de les laisser aller librement. Pour me protéger de ma sensibilité, je « raisonne » mes émotions pour avoir l'impression, avec mon intellect, de garder le contrôle sur elles. J'accepte ↓♥ de vivre pleinement mes émotions, car elles sont une richesse pour découvrir différentes facettes de moi-même.

ULCÈRE(S) (en général)

Un **ulcère** peut se retrouver sur la peau à l'extérieur du corps (bras, jambes, cornée de l'œil, etc.), ou sur la paroi d'un organe interne (estomac, intestin, foie, bouche, etc.). Un **ulcère** m'amènera à prendre conscience que je vis de grandes frayeurs et de l'insécurité. Il m'indique qu'un stress intense m'habite et que **je me sens rongé, dérangé, dévoré.** Selon l'endroit du corps où se développe mon **ulcère**, il m'est possible de découvrir ce qui provoque cet état. Par exemple, s'il se retrouve dans ma bouche, je peux me demander ce que j'ai à dire. Des **ulcères d'estomac** démontrent qu'il y a

---

84. **Tu meurs:** Du verbe *mourir*

quelque chose que je digère mal. Règle générale, un **ulcère** m'indique que je laisse les choses ou les gens m'irriter. J'apprends à laisser couler, à me calmer.

ULCÈRE BUCCAL (HERPÈS) ou CHANCRE
(voir : BOUCHE [malaise de...])

ULCÈRE PEPTIQUE ou GASTRIQUE (duodénum ou estomac)

Des **ulcères à l'estomac** peuvent se produire si j'ai une faible estime de moi. Je veux tellement faire plaisir aux autres que je suis prêt à avaler n'importe quoi. En agissant ainsi, je refoule mes émotions et mes propres désirs ; je ne me respecte pas et je finis par reprocher aux autres de ne pas me respecter. Je me sens grugé en dedans de moi et j'en arrive à dramatiser chaque événement de ma vie. J'ai de plus en plus de difficulté à **digérer** toutes ces contrariétés, ces inquiétudes. C'est comme un trop plein d'irritants qui se transforme en **ulcère**. Cet irritant peut être une personne ou une situation que je veux éviter de voir ou d'affronter mais cela est impossible et « cela » me reste sur l'**estomac** ! Je voudrais « expulser » cet irritant de mon espace vital, de mon « territoire ». J'ai tendance à me critiquer sévèrement et je peux même en venir à m'autodétruire. Mon corps m'indique qu'il est grand temps que je découvre les qualités qui sont en moi, que je m'apprécie à ma juste valeur et que j'accepte ↓♥ mon besoin d'amour.

URÉMIE (voir aussi : REINS [problèmes rénaux])

L'**urémie** est un taux d'urée anormalement élevé ou anormalement bas dans le sang. L'**urée** est la composante principale de l'**urine**. Cela provient habituellement d'une insuffisance rénale dans le cas d'un taux élevé ou d'une insuffisance hépatite (du foie) grave dans le cas d'un taux anormalement bas. L'**urine** est reliée à mes vieilles émotions qui demandent à être éliminées.

URÉTRITE (voir aussi : ANNEXE III)

L'**urétrite** est une inflammation du canal conduisant l'urine du col de la vessie à l'orifice de l'urètre. Cet état m'indique que j'accepte difficilement de céder le passage à une situation nouvelle et que je fais place à de l'agressivité. J'ai intérêt à laisser circuler plus librement les nouvelles idées et à garder l'esprit ouvert face à mes opinions qui peuvent changer, sachant que je suis constamment en évolution et en changement.

URINE (infections urinaires) ou CYSTITE
(voir aussi : INCONTINENCE [... urinaire], INFECTIONS [en général], LEUCORRHÉE, VAGIN — VAGINITE)

L'**urine** représente mes vieilles émotions dont je n'ai plus besoin et que j'élimine de mon système. Une inflammation de la vessie ou du conduit

urinaire (**cystite**) occasionne de la douleur lorsque **j'urine** (même en petite quantité), ainsi qu'un désir constant **d'uriner**. Cela est plus fréquent chez les jeunes femmes, les diabétiques, les femmes enceintes. Comme c'est une infection, cela implique que ce malaise est très souvent relié à de la colère que j'ai accumulée. Ce peut être aussi du ressentiment, de l'irritation ou tout autre sentiment **brûlant** qui touche de nouveaux aspects de moi-même ou de mes relations personnelles. Comme dans le cas d'une **vaginite** (ou **leucorrhée**), je peux vivre un sentiment de frustration par rapport à mes relations sexuelles. Puisque mon système urinaire et mon système reproducteur (vagin) sont en communication, l'un peut affecter l'autre. Il se peut que mes relations sexuelles aillent admirablement bien et que je ne comprenne pas pourquoi je vivrais de la frustration. Justement parce que tout va très bien, je peux me demander : « Pourquoi a-t-il fallu que j'attende autant d'années pour réussir à avoir des relations sexuelles satisfaisantes ? » De là peuvent venir ma frustration et ma colère non exprimées. Aussi, par exemple, une **cystite** peut survenir à la suite d'une séparation. N'ayant pas été capable d'exprimer mes émotions négatives, des peurs font surface ainsi que des conflits intérieurs par rapport à ce qui s'en vient pour moi. Ayant de grandes attentes non comblées, je blâme les gens qui m'entourent pour ce vide et, la plupart du temps, mon conjoint en écope. Je vais de frustration en frustration puisque je laisse aux autres la responsabilité de mon bien-être. Il est donc temps que je me prenne en mains, que j'accepte ↓♥ la responsabilité de ma vie. Je prends la décision d'aller de l'avant, je renais à moi-même, indépendamment des relations présentes et antérieures.

URTICAIRE (voir : PEAU — URTICAIRE)

UTÉRUS (en général)
(voir aussi : CANCER DU COL UTÉRIN, FÉMININ [maux...])

L'utérus symbolise mon état de femme, <u>**c'est le foyer de ma**</u> <u>**créativité**</u>. C'est dans ce sanctuaire chaleureux et sécurisant que se fait la nidation. Des problèmes **d'ovaires ou d'utérus** m'indiquent qu'il est temps que je développe ma créativité qui me redonnera le pouvoir de gérer ma vie. J'ai intérêt à me questionner à savoir : « Comment je me sens en tant que femme ? Est-ce que je me sens coupable, honteuse ou trahie dans le fait d'avoir eu ou non des enfants ? Est-ce que je trouve difficile d'être femme, épouse, mère, femme d'affaires, amante ? » Peut-être ai-je l'impression de régresser ! À cette région du pelvis, il m'est possible de redonner naissance, de faire renaître de nouveaux aspects de mon être ; je peux aller de l'avant dans ma recherche de moi. Si une maladie se développe dans mon **utérus**, comme une tumeur par exemple, je peux me demander comment je perçois la sexualité des autres, et particulièrement celle de mes enfants et de mes petits-enfants. Est-ce que j'ai l'impression qu'elle n'est « pas correcte », « qu'elle sort de l'ordinaire », « que

ça ne se fait pas » ? Est-ce que je les sens en danger moral ou physique ? Risquent-ils de se faire blesser ? Y a-t-il quelque chose que je trouve « moche » par rapport à mes enfants et à leur vie de couple ? Suis-je dérangé par rapport au rôle ou par la place que chaque membre de la famille prend ? Toutes ces interrogations peuvent concerner soit mes enfants ou mes petits-enfants réels ou un neveu, un voisin ou un élève que je considère comme tel. Quelle que soit la situation, je prends conscience que je n'ai aucun pouvoir sur la vie des autres et que chacun vit sa vie à sa façon. J'ai donné la meilleure éducation à mes enfants de la meilleure façon possible et je peux en être fière !

UTÉRUS (cancer du col de l'...) (voir : CANCER DU COL UTÉRIN)

VAGIN (en général)

Le **vagin** est cette membrane musculaire qui est située entre la vulve et l'utérus chez la femme. Les maladies qui sont reliées au **vagin** vont souvent avoir leur source dans ma frustration à ne pas pouvoir accomplir l'acte d'union charnelle, soit parce que je ne me le permets pas moralement ou parce que je n'ai pas cet homme avec qui je pourrais vivre de nouvelles expériences. J'accepte ↓♥ de m'ouvrir à l'amour sous toutes ses formes afin de m'épanouir pleinement.

VAGIN — DÉMANGEAISONS VAGINALES
(voir : DÉMANGEAISONS VAGINALES)

VAGINAL — HERPÈS (voir : HERPÈS VAGINAL)

VAGINALES (pertes...) (voir : LEUCORRHÉE)

VAGINAUX (spasmes...) (voir : SPASMES)

VAGINITE (voir aussi : CANDIDA, LEUCORRHÉE, URINE [infections urinaires])

La **vaginite** est une infection du **vagin** (semblable à la candida ou champignons) avec, en plus, des odeurs nauséabondes. Dans la majorité des cas, elle démontre que j'entretiens de la frustration envers mon partenaire sexuel ou encore que je vis de la culpabilité. Si j'utilise le sexe afin d'exercer un pouvoir ou un contrôle sur mon conjoint, il est possible que je connaisse régulièrement des **problèmes de vaginite**. Ce peut être l'excuse idéale pour ne pas faire l'amour et ainsi, punir mon conjoint en le privant de sexe. L'intimité qu'engendre une relation sexuelle peut déclencher plusieurs sentiments reliés à la mémoire ou à la peur : peur de me sentir incomprise ou blessée à nouveau. De plus, l'émission d'odeurs désagréables permet de libérer

des émotions négatives, des peines et des angoisses accumulées, lesquelles sont profondément enfouies dans le tissu vaginal lui-même. Le **vagin** est l'endroit d'où émergent tous mes sentiments concernant la sexualité : si ceux-ci sont positifs, je vivrai du plaisir sexuel. Au contraire, une infection apparaît si je vis de la culpabilité, des peurs, de la honte, des conflits, de la confusion, ainsi que mes souvenirs d'expériences abusives, ou si je veux m'autopunir. Je reste ouverte à vivre une sexualité harmonieuse. Cela fait partie de la vie et du bonheur auquel j'ai droit.

VARICELLE (voir : MALADIES DE L'ENFANCE)

VARICES (voir : SANG — VARICES)

VÉGÉTATIF CHRONIQUE (état...)
(voir : ÉTAT VÉGÉTATIF CHRONIQUE)

VÉGÉTATIONS ADÉNOÏDES
(voir aussi : AMYGDALES)

La maladie des **végétations adénoïdes**, communément appelées **végétations**, est une infection touchant plus particulièrement les enfants. Cela se traduit par l'hypertrophie des amygdales pharyngées situées en arrière des fosses nasales provoquant une obstruction au niveau du nez, qui oblige ainsi l'enfant à respirer par la bouche. Étant d'une très grande sensibilité et doté d'une intuition très développée, je bloque mon nez afin d'éviter de sentir les choses qui me blessent. Ce peut être un détail tout à fait banal et anodin auquel je donnerai des proportions et une ampleur éléphantesques. Il m'arrive parfois de sentir que je n'ai pas ma place dans cette famille ; je vis de la colère et je me sens rejeté. Des tensions ou des conflits familiaux sont propices à l'apparition des végétations. J'accepte ↓♥ de prendre la place qui me revient dans l'harmonie, je fais part de mes sentiments et je reconnais les bienfaits de l'intuition.

VEINES (maux aux...) (voir aussi : SANG — CIRCULATION SANGUINE)

Une **veine** est un vaisseau sanguin qui ramène le sang des organes vers le cœur. Lorsque les **veines** reviennent des poumons vers le cœur, elles rapportent le sang « rouge » purifié, chargé d'oxygène. Lorsque les **veines** reviennent des autres organes vers le cœur, elles rapportent le sang « bleu » dépourvu d'oxygène et chargé d'oxyde de carbone CO_2. Dans la vie, je n'ai jamais eu de **veine** ! C'est comme dire que je n'ai jamais pu trouver la joie de vivre. Le sang circule dans mes **veines** ; le sang, c'est la vie, la joie de vivre. Je suis constamment en contradiction avec ma voix intérieure et ce que je réalise dans ma vie. Je me sens déçu, dépassé. Je vis dans un état d'inertie, je ne vois

même plus les belles choses qui m'arrivent. Je manque d'énergie, je me sens vide. Je ne me sens pas soutenu par la vie ou par mon entourage et je vois tout en noir. Mes **veines coronaires** seront particulièrement touchées si j'ai peur de perdre quelqu'un ou quelqu'un chose que « je possède » et que je résiste à laisser aller. Je le vis comme un danger qui guette mon territoire, c'est-à-dire soit <u>mon</u> conjoint, <u>ma</u> maison, <u>ma</u> famille, <u>mon</u> travail, <u>mes</u> idées, etc. J'accepte ↓♥ de laisser circuler la joie en moi. Je reconnais les bons moments, j'apprends à me détendre et je retrouve la paix intérieure.

VEINES — VARICES (voir : SANG — VARICES)

VÉNÉRIENNES (maladies...)

Une **maladie vénérienne** peut suggérer qu'un sentiment de culpabilité subsiste face à ma sexualité. Souvent, l'éducation religieuse m'a montré la sexualité comme quelque chose de sale et d'impur. Me sentant honteux, je crois devoir me punir en rejetant mes parties génitales. Je m'autopunis en m'autodétruisant. L'énergie sexuelle est extrêmement importante et puissante, elle fait partie intégrante de mon programme génétique pour la survie de l'espèce. Par conséquent, une **maladie vénérienne** implique une affection ou une infection liée à cette énergie. Si je la mésestime, elle aura tendance à se retourner contre moi, à devenir « malade », me donnant ainsi l'occasion de découvrir que ce que je fais est en disharmonie avec le flot naturel et l'équilibre de cette énergie. Il est important que j'accepte ↓♥ que la sexualité est une façon d'exprimer mon amour et mon désir de m'unir à l'autre.

VENTRE
(voir aussi : GONFLEMENT [... de l'abdomen], INTESTINS [maux aux...])

Le **ventre** ou **abdomen** est la partie inférieure et antérieure du tronc humain, renfermant principalement les intestins. Tout comme dans ma vie de tous les jours, si je me gave trop vite de nourriture, j'ai le « **ventre** plein », j'ai le goût de dormir et je vis un certain inconfort. Je dois apprendre à prendre mon temps, à ingérer chaque situation nouvelle une à une, afin de me laisser le temps de m'adapter aux changements qui ont lieu dans ma vie, m'évitant ainsi de vivre de l'impatience et de la frustration. Puisque c'est dans l'**abdomen** que l'enfant croît et qu'il se prépare à se déplacer de l'état solitaire à un état plus social, l'**abdomen** est donc la région des **relations**. Toutes difficultés dans cette région sont reliées aux conflits ou aux blocages entre moi-même et l'univers dans lequel je suis, ceux-ci étant exprimés à travers les relations personnelles qui font ma réalité. J'ai donc avantage à apprendre à reconnaître mes pensées, mes sentiments à travers les autres et dans l'univers qui m'entoure. Puisque c'est dans l'**abdomen** que résident ma plus profonde intention et mon sentiment de ce qui est bon ou mal, des malaises à ce niveau me donnent une bonne indication de ce qui se passe dans ma vie intérieure et au niveau de mes émotions.

VENTRE (mal de...) (voir : MAL DE VENTRE)

VERRUES (en général) (voir : PEAU — VERRUES [en général])

VERRUES PLANTAIRES (voir : PIEDS — VERRUES PLANTAIRES)

VER SOLITAIRE (voir : INTESTINS — TÆNIA)

VERS, PARASITES
(voir : CHEVEUX — TEIGNE, INTESTINS — TÆNIA, PIEDS — MYCOSE)

VERTÈBRES (fractures des...)
(voir : DOS — FRACTURE DES VERTÈBRES)

VERTIGE, ÉTOURDISSEMENTS
(voir aussi : SANG — HYPOGLYCÉMIE)

Avoir des **vertiges ou des étourdissements** est **une façon de fuir** un événement ou une personne que je refuse de voir ou d'entendre. Je peux avoir l'impression qu'une situation évolue trop vite pour moi et j'ai peur des changements qu'elle apportera dans ma vie. C'est comme si je n'avais pas de repère pour me diriger et donc je peux avoir l'impression que « mon père », ou celui qui représente l'autorité, est absent ou qu'il devrait m'aider davantage par rapport aux directions à prendre. Je préfère me fermer, je fuis. Je voudrais tout contrôler, autant ce qui se passe à l'intérieur qu'à l'extérieur de moi mais, cela étant impossible, je deviens instable et anxieux. Dans la plupart des cas, si je souffre de **vertiges et d'étourdissements**, je peux souffrir d'hypoglycémie. Il est important que je découvre la joie de vivre, que je m'offre de petites douceurs et que je fasse confiance à l'avenir.

VÉSICULE BILIAIRE (voir aussi : CALCULS BILIAIRES, FOIE [maux de...])

La **vésicule biliaire** est un réservoir membraneux situé sous le foie et où s'accumule la bile que celui-ci sécrète. Les difficultés à ce niveau sont reliées à des « patterns » émotionnels et mentaux qui sont remplis d'amertume et d'irritation, face à ma vie ou face aux autres. Si ceux-ci se figent et durcissent, ils se transformeront en **calculs biliaires**. Si ma **vésicule biliaire** ne fonctionne pas bien, il se peut que cela découle de mon insécurité ou de mes inquiétudes face à quelqu'un que j'aime et qui m'est cher. Le fait de vivre de l'attachement face à cette personne peut m'amener à vivre des émotions que j'ai de la difficulté à gérer et à assumer. Je peux aussi avoir l'impression d'avoir toujours à justifier mes actes et de souvent percevoir les situations de ma vie comme « injustes », ce qui

m'amène à vivre beaucoup de colère. J'ai donc avantage à me libérer de ces sentiments amers irritants. Je dois plutôt considérer chaque expérience que je vis comme une occasion de mieux me connaître et d'utiliser ma sensibilité de façon positive et créatrice, au lieu de contrôler ou de manipuler les autres.

VESSIE (maux de...) (voir aussi : URINE [infections urinaires])

La **vessie** est le réservoir où l'urine est en « attente » d'être libérée. Elle représente aussi les « attentes » que je nourris face à la vie. Des **problèmes de vessie** m'indiquent que je peux avoir tendance à m'accrocher à mes vieilles idées, que je refuse de lâcher prise. Je résiste au changement à cause de mon insécurité. Les malaises démontrent que je vis de l'anxiété depuis très longtemps et qu'il est temps pour moi de laisser aller librement mes émotions négatives indésirables. Ainsi, ma **vessie** m'empêchera de me **noyer** dans ma propre négativité. Des **infections urinaires** sont l'indication que je vis beaucoup de frustrations, de la peine et de l'insécurité non exprimées. Je peux me questionner pour connaître ce que je retiens dans ma vie et que j'ai intérêt à libérer. Ces sentiments peuvent être vécus dans une situation où ce qui m'appartient et ce que je considère comme faisant partie de mon territoire sont mis en cause. Ce peut être, par exemple, une situation où j'ai « la nausée » chaque fois où j'arrive à la maison et qu'elle est toute sale et en désordre. La **vessie** représente aussi le domaine des relations personnelles. Il arrive donc souvent que ces infections se déclarent dans la période entourant la lune de miel, lors d'une relation dérangeante ou conflictuelle, ou encore, à l'occasion d'une rupture. La lune de miel ou une première expérience sexuelle peut m'amener à vivre divers problèmes, voire même des déceptions pouvant déclencher de la colère ou du ressentiment face à mon partenaire, comme s'il était responsable de mon insatisfaction. Une relation en rupture est généralement l'aboutissement de « non-dits », d'émotions refoulées dans mon intérieur. C'est comme si j'enfouissais au plus profond de moi mes problèmes psychologiques, provoquant une pression constante. J'ai à comprendre qu'en me libérant de cette pression, j'éprouverai inévitablement un soulagement. Je me libère de mes vieilles croyances et je fais place à la nouveauté dans ma vie.

VESSIE — CYSTITE (voir aussi : ANNEXE III)

La **cystite** est une inflammation de la **vessie**. Certains événements ou certaines situations m'amènent à retenir mon **irritation** et mes **frustrations**. Je suis tellement contrarié <u>dans mes attentes</u> que ma vessie **s'enflamme**. Je vis un état de grande pression. Je prends conscience qu'il est essentiel de lâcher prise pour m'en libérer car, <u>en me retenant</u>, je bloque mon énergie, seulement parce que j'ai peur. Le mécontentement face aux événements, qui produit une tension nerveuse, va enflammer ma **vessie**. J'accepte ↓♥ de vivre l'instant présent au maximum et je réalise qu'en étant ouvert, je me permets de goûter à de merveilleuses expériences.

VIEILLISSEMENT (maux de...)

En **vieillissant**, il arrive que mon corps perde de sa flexibilité. J'avance plus difficilement, ma dextérité se détériore. Que veut me dire mon corps ? Il est probable que je regrette des éléments de mon passé, que je crois que je n'ai plus ma place dans ce monde, qu'il est temps pour moi de **m'arrêter.** Je crois aussi que la vie était meilleure avant. Je refuse de voir les belles choses d'aujourd'hui. Mes pensées sont tournées vers hier et je critique le présent. Cette rigidité dans ma façon de penser est transmise à tout mon être. J'accepte ↓♥ de m'ouvrir aux changements et je crois que j'ai encore à apprendre et à donner. Ainsi, mon état s'améliore de jour en jour.

VIEILLISSEMENT PATHOLOGIQUE (voir : SÉNILITÉ)

V.I.H. (Virus d'Immunodéficience Humaine) (voir : SIDA)

VIOL (voir aussi : ACCIDENT, PEUR)

Le **viol** est relié à une grande culpabilité par rapport à sa sexualité, surtout en pensée, par « peur de ce qui pourrait arriver ! » Donc, le **viol** dont il est question ici est relié à la sexualité, c'est-à-dire à un rapport sexuel imposé sans le consentement de la personne. Même si je n'ai pas eu à vivre une telle expérience sur le plan sexuel, il se peut néanmoins que j'aie pu la vivre sous d'autres aspects. En effet, si je me suis déjà fait voler chez-moi, en entrant, je peux vivre un sentiment intense comme si on m'avait **violé**. La façon dont je laisse les gens me traiter en ce qui a trait à mes goûts personnels, mes idées, mes valeurs peut être perçue comme un **viol**. Je peux vivre un **viol** à l'intérieur du mariage aussi. Si j'ai eu à vivre un **viol**, ou un abus sexuel, je peux regarder si mon ignorance de la sexualité, même inconsciente, était à ce point grande que j'ai pu « attirer » (énergétiquement parlant) cette situation comme pour me libérer de ma peur. **Consciemment, je n'ai pas voulu cette situation**, mais je dois comprendre le fonctionnement du subconscient pour me rendre compte qu'il peut programmer un événement pour me libérer de ma peur. Je dois être vigilant et ne pas penser que je suis coupable de ce qui m'est arrivé, mais plutôt chercher à voir pourquoi cela m'est arrivé, pour m'aider à guérir la blessure laissée en moi. Si je crois, pour moi-même ou parce qu'on me l'a dit, que je serai marqué le restant de mes jours par une telle situation, alors je ferais bien de commencer à considérer sérieusement que **C'EST FAUX. Il existe des moyens de guérir complètement d'une telle situation**. Il ne restera que le souvenir de l'événement, historiquement parlant, mais il n'y aura plus de peine, de tristesse, de colère, d'amertume, ni de haine de quelque sorte, parce que tout aura été guéri, parce que **la prise de conscience au niveau du cœur aura été faite avec la compréhension qui y est associée**. Je fais confiance dans les possibilités infinies que la vie m'apporte et

j'apprends à prendre la place qui me revient, à prendre ma place ! Ainsi, je serai en mesure d'être pleinement maître des événements de ma vie.

VISAGE (voir aussi : PEAU / ACNÉ / BOUTONS / POINTS NOIRS)

Mon **visage** est la première partie de mon être qui aborde ou qui accueille l'univers. Habituellement, un seul coup d'œil me donne des impressions sur quelqu'un, selon que son **visage** est radieux, lumineux, souriant ou, au contraire, sombre, irrité, triste. Le **visage** se rapporte donc à mon image, à mon identité, à mon ego. Si je veux cacher un aspect de ma personnalité ou si je me cache quelque chose à moi-même, mon **visage** porte ce masque aussi en devenant tendu et grimaçant. De même, si je me dévalorise, si je critique, si je me sens incompétent, si j'ai l'impression que personne ne m'aime, mon mal-être intérieur s'exprime par l'apparence de la peau de mon **visage** qui devient boutonneuse ou qui s'assèche. Une irritation mentale rend ma peau imparfaite. Pour que les traits et la peau de mon **visage** s'éclaircissent, s'adoucissent et se nettoient d'eux-mêmes, il est important que je nettoie tout d'abord mon intérieur et que je me débarrasse des sentiments et des pensées négatifs que j'entretiens et que je fasse place à plus d'amour, à plus de compréhension, plus d'acceptation ↓♥ et à plus d'ouverture. Mon **visage** s'illuminera encore davantage et je n'aurai plus besoin de porter de masque.

VITILIGO (voir : PEAU — VITILIGO)

VOIX (extinction de...) (voir : APHONIE)

VOIX — ENROUEMENT

Lorsque mon timbre de **voix** devient sourd, rauque ou éraillé, c'est alors que j'ai la **voix enrouée**. L'**enrouement** signifie que je souffre d'épuisement mental et physique. Quelque chose empêche mes « roues » de tourner sans anicroche. Je vis un blocage émotionnel, une émotion vive et je retiens mon agressivité. Comme la gorge se rapporte au centre d'énergie de la vérité, de la communication et de l'expression de soi (chakra de la gorge), je peux me sentir pris par la vérité que j'ai de la difficulté à assimiler et par mes convictions personnelles. J'ai recours à certains palliatifs ou à des stimulants tels café, alcool, cigarettes, etc., et, quand l'effet disparaît, l'**enrouement** apparaît. La fatigue que je ressens amplifie les inquiétudes et les soucis que je ne voulais pas regarder. Je prends conscience que j'ai besoin d'un temps d'arrêt et j'accepte ↓♥ de me donner le repos et le temps nécessaires pour me régénérer. En étant reposé, les situations et les événements reprennent leur proportion réelle, je suis beaucoup plus objectif et lucide pour prendre les décisions qui s'imposent.

VOMISSEMENTS (voir : NAUSÉES)

VULVE (voir aussi : LÈVRES)

De la même façon que les lèvres du visage sont considérées comme les portes de la bouche, les **lèvres vaginales** représentent celles de l'appareil génital. Un sentiment de vide, d'épuisement, de lassitude peut provoquer une inflammation ou d'autres troubles à la **vulve**. Je me sens « vulnérable », impuissante, je rejette tous contacts physiques, je me sens sans joie à l'intérieur de moi. L'origine des **maladies de la vulve** est normalement d'ordre psychique. L'angoisse et les craintes viennent enflammer une **vulve** souvent après qu'on ait eu à prendre de nombreuses décisions. Je suis fatiguée d'avoir à décider, et c'est une façon de manifester mon impuissance, mon impression d'être diminuée devant les événements. Je choisis de me sentir valorisée et j'accepte ↓♥ la responsabilité de mes choix.

YEUX (en général)

Mes **yeux** sont le miroir de l'âme. Ils me permettent de voir à l'extérieur et, par eux, je peux exprimer toutes les émotions et tous les sentiments que je vis intérieurement. Selon leur profondeur, il est possible de découvrir mes rapports avec le monde extérieur. Le fonctionnement de **mes yeux** reflète la façon dont je vois la vie et ma relation avec celle-ci. Chaque **œil** représente un aspect particulier de mon être. L'**œil gauche** représente l'aspect intérieur, émotionnel et intuitif. Il me sert de vigie, en me permettant de rester aux aguets devant tout ce qui peut constituer un danger et de réagir promptement. L'**œil droit**, quant à lui, traite rationnellement l'univers et les situations extérieures. C'est l'**œil** de la reconnaissance qui me permet de façonner mon identité. **Des problèmes aux yeux** sont l'indication qu'il existe des choses que je refuse de voir et qui remettent souvent en question mes principes fondamentaux et mes notions de justice. En tournant au fond de moi mon regard avant de le fixer vers le monde, j'y trouverai ainsi une nouvelle vue d'ensemble et un regard neuf sur la route de mon existence. Mon regard est vrai et sans jugement.

YEUX (maux d'...)

Des **maux d'yeux**, entre autres la cécité, sont une façon de me fermer à ce que je vois. Je choisis d'ignorer ce qui se passe autour de moi, je renonce aux impressions visuelles qui me remettent en question. Plutôt que d'accepter ↓♥ une réalité qui pourrait être douloureuse, répugnante ou confuse, je préfère **fermer les yeux**. La **cécité** peut être causée par le diabète (voir cette maladie) ou encore, par l'accumulation de choses que je refuse d'accepter ↓♥, m'apportant confusion et un sentiment de ne plus savoir où aller. Souvent blessée par un choc, par un traumatisme ou par une grande peur intérieure, ma vue se retire et l'énergie des

organes visuels aussi. Il peut notamment s'agir de la crainte de perdre quelqu'un ou quelque chose qui m'est cher. Pourtant, la noirceur extérieure semble généralement apporter une ouverture intérieure, un univers privé, secret et coloré. Je m'ouvre donc davantage à mon esprit intérieur. Une **déformation de l'œil** (astigmatisme, myopie, presbitie) indique que je cherche de façon démesurée à trouver des réponses à l'extérieur, plutôt qu'à l'intérieur de moi. Plus je cherche à l'extérieur de moi-même, plus je m'éloigne de mon noyau intérieur. Une **vision voilée** (cataracte, glaucome) dénote que ma version de la réalité est contraire à celle que je vois. Cela m'indique que je mets difficilement mon attention sur l'essentiel, que je refuse ce que je vois. Je prends conscience de la beauté qui m'entoure et je me donne du temps pour regarder.

YEUX (maux chez les enfants)

Un **problème aux yeux** chez un **jeune enfant** laisse présager un stress par rapport à sa famille, un refus de voir ce qui s'y passe. Lorsqu'il se développe à l'école, cela démontre que je vis de l'anxiété face à l'inconnu. Un **problème aux yeux** qui survient à l'adolescence dénote une peur de la sexualité. Il est important que moi, comme parent, j'amène mon enfant à communiquer ses peurs afin de le rassurer et de l'aider à dépasser celles-ci.

YEUX — ALEXIE CONGÉNITALE

L'**alexie congénitale** est aussi appelée **aveuglement des mots** ou **cécité verbale**. C'est une incapacité pathologique[85] à lire. Soit que je puisse lire les lettres sans les mots, ou lire les mots sans lire les lettres ou que je ne lise pas tous les mots d'une phrase, ce qui m'empêche d'en comprendre le sens. Si je suis affecté par cette maladie, je peux vivre une grande **préoccupation** ou une attention exagérée concernant les pensées que je véhicule. Plus je mets l'attention (de façon exagérée) sur des aspects de ma vie qui en ont peu besoin, plus je risque de souffrir en restant fermé à des pensées qui freinent mon évolution. J'ai besoin de m'ouvrir intérieurement à mon intuition et à mon imagination, deux facultés merveilleuses que l'âme[86] que je suis possède pour s'exprimer. Si je veux régler cette maladie, je n'ai qu'à regarder ce en quoi ma vie est dérangée, ce que la maladie m'empêche ou m'évite de faire, de dire ou de voir. En ouvrant mon cœur, je règle cette situation d'une manière **consciente**. Il est plus facile pour moi en tant qu'enfant de manifester l'écoute intérieure, car je suis plus « branché » que les adultes, **je lis plus facilement les messages d'amour de mon cœur !** Alors je m'ouvre à mon intuition et je manifeste davantage ma créativité.

---

85. **Pathologique :** Une maladie, scientifiquement parlant.
86. **L'âme :** L'étincelle divine que je suis, ma conscience.

YEUX — ASTIGMATISME

L'**astigmatisme** est un défaut de sphéricité[87] de la cornée ou du cristallin. La courbure verticale de la cornée est plus importante que la courbure horizontale ou inversement. Cette malformation dénote généralement une peur de me regarder en face, tel que je suis. Une **mauvaise coordination des yeux** peut signifier que ma façon d'agir et mes pensées sont en désaccord avec mon entourage, causant ainsi des conflits intérieurs. Je peux vouloir me créer une réalité différente et tenter de me dégager de l'influence de mes parents ou de toutes autres personnes que je considère abusives. Souvent confrontés à de la rage, à de la colère ou à des peurs durant ma jeunesse, **mes yeux** ont gardé cette expression de frayeur et les muscles entourant l'**œil** sont demeurés en constant état de choc. Mes **yeux** pourront devenir irrités si ce que je vois extérieurement ou intérieurement m'irrite. L'**astigmatisme** peut aussi être le résultat d'une grande curiosité. Mon besoin insatiable de tout voir a « usé » **mes yeux**. De cette façon, mon corps me dit de prendre le temps qu'il faut pour apprécier les choses. Cela peut aussi vouloir dire que j'ai intérêt à reconnaître ma propre beauté, l'être magnifique que je suis.

YEUX — AVEUGLE

Je suis considéré comme **aveugle** si j'ai 10 % de vision ou moins. Si je vis cette situation, je peux me demander ce que je ne veux pas voir ou ce que j'ai peur de voir dans ma vie, une personne ou une situation. Si cela m'est arrivé à la suite d'un accident ou d'une maladie, je peux chercher la cause qui pourrait être liée à cette perte de vision. Je peux alors travailler à intégrer cette cause pour la prise de conscience que j'ai à faire et accepter ↓♥ à nouveau de « voir » en permettant à ma vision intérieure de se développer de plus en plus dans l'amour et dans la compréhension.

YEUX — AVEUGLEMENT

En refusant **d'ouvrir les yeux**, de voir le monde extérieur, je n'ai d'autres choix que de regarder en moi et de prendre conscience de mon Univers intérieur. J'accepte ↓♥ de voir la richesse qui m'habite, la lumière qui est en moi.

YEUX — CATARACTE

La **cataracte** est une maladie où le cristallin (lentille biconvexe de l'**œil**) devient graduellement opaque au point où la vision se voile et se distorsionne, ce qui entraîne la cécité[88] à plus ou moins longue échéance. Cette forme d'incapacité physique arrive dans ma vie au moment où je ne désire plus voir

---

87. **Sphéricité :** Qui a rapport à la courbure.
88. **Cécité :** Synonyme d'aveugle ou de perte de la vue.

intérieurement ce qui se passe devant moi, ce qui s'en vient ou ce qui risque d'influencer ma vie et les décisions que j'aurais à prendre. Ce que j'ai vu ou que je vois pour le futur m'amène à me dire : « Je n'en crois pas mes **yeux** ! ». Ma vision baisse car l'énergie ne va plus à cet endroit. Elle se ternit et s'assombrit, je vois l'avenir d'un **œil** obscur et voilé, sans joie ni gaieté de cœur. Il est possible que j'aie une attitude égocentrique et que je veuille voir la vie seulement à ma façon sans tenir compte de la réalité d'autrui. C'est une attitude égoïste qui peut même me faire croire que je suis supérieur aux autres. Cette **cataracte** m'éloigne du présent, me retire de l'univers qui m'entoure. Ça me déplaît à certains niveaux et je dois prendre conscience des aspects extérieur et intérieur des choses. La **cataracte** apparaît normalement vers la fin de la vie, au moment où la peur de vieillir et de devenir impotent ou impuissant s'installe. « Je ne veux pas voir la future image de moi-même si elle n'est pas encore là, de peur qu'elle me déplaise trop. » Je perds ma souplesse d'esprit et d'action, je deviens moins tolérant et j'oublie souvent les événements qui viennent de m'arriver. Je n'ai donc pas intérêt à voir le futur qui peut me paraître très sombre (les **cataractes** sont fréquentes dans les pays en voie de développement). Cependant, je peux lever ce voile qui m'empêche de voir ma vraie réalité en plaçant mon attention sur ma lumière intérieure. J'accepte ↓♥ de faire l'effort de regarder à l'intérieur de moi et j'y verrai toute la lumière et la beauté qui m'entourent.

YEUX — CERNES

Généralement, des **yeux fortement marqués par des cernes** sont le signe de fatigue, souvent causée par une allergie, laquelle est le résultat d'une dépendance envers un produit. Mon corps m'indique ainsi que j'ai à être plus indépendant et que mon bonheur doit dépendre de moi seul. L'approbation des autres devient alors un plus et non une condition à mon bien-être.

YEUX — COMMOTION DE LA RÉTINE
(voir aussi : CERVEAU — COMMOTION)

Sur le plan physique, la **commotion** survient à la suite d'un choc violent (direct ou indirect) à une partie de mon organisme qui entraîne des lésions cachées, nécessitant un examen plus approfondi. Dans le cas d'une **commotion de la rétine**, je refuse de voir ce qui me saute aux **yeux** parce que j'ai de la difficulté à changer ma vision des choses. J'accepte ↓♥ de lâcher prise, de laisser tomber mes anciennes pensées ou mes anciennes façons de voir et je fais place aux nouvelles pensées qui sont déjà là. À compter de maintenant, je suis à l'écoute et je me laisse guider par mon intuition et par mes sentiments. Je me sens beaucoup plus libre et serein.

YEUX — CONJONCTIVITE

La **conjonctivite** est l'inflammation de la membrane transparente recouvrant l'intérieur de la paupière et le globe oculaire. Il existe un rapport direct entre la **conjonctivite** et ce que je vois. Inconsciemment, je **refuse de voir une situation ou un événement** avec lequel je suis en désaccord ou qui me blesse. Cela m'amène à vivre de la frustration, de l'irritation et de la révolte. « Je ne peux pas supporter ce que je vois ! ; Ça me brûle de voir une telle chose ! » C'est comme si mes **yeux** veulent laver sans cesse la **saleté** que je vois dans la situation qui me met en **colère**. Le résultat entraîne un gonflement et un engourdissement mental aussi bien qu'un débordement émotionnel similaire à l'action de pleurer. Je préfère être temporairement aveugle car ce que je vois me fait souffrir. Je prends le temps de m'arrêter et j'**accepte ↓♥ de voir cette situation qui me dérange et je me demande pourquoi il en est ainsi**. Je demeure ouvert et réceptif : ainsi je m'évite de revivre une **conjonctivite**.

YEUX — DALTONISME (non-perception des couleurs)

Être **daltonien**, c'est voir le monde sans ses couleurs, grisâtre et indifférencié. Il peut arriver que se soient des couleurs précises que je ne puisse pas voir. Je dois donc me demander dans quelle situation de ma vie ai-je connu un stress immense et qui faisait référence à cette ou ces couleurs que je ne peux pas distinguer. Par exemple, si je ne peux voir le rouge, peut-être ai-je frôler la mort quand j'étais jeune parce qu'un train rouge se dirigeait sur moi. Le rouge étant maintenant associé à un haut niveau de stress et symbolisant la mort qui me guette, je ne voudrai plus, inconsciemment, voir cette couleur. S'il s'agit de toutes les couleurs que je ne peux pas distinguer, le même principe peut s'appliquer. Je peux aussi avoir décidé un jour de ne plus « rêver en couleurs » afin d'éviter d'être déçu. Puisque nos rêves d'aujourd'hui créent la réalité de demain, je vais cesser de voir les couleurs dans ma vie quotidienne. Je peux dès maintenant décider des couleurs, faire place à mon imagination. J'imagine le rose, le vert ou le bleu. Comme un artiste, je décide du mélange des couleurs. Je m'imprègne de cette unité que m'offre le monde. Je laisse libre cours à ma fantaisie, j'exprime ma joie de vivre de mille et une façons.

YEUX — DÉCOLLEMENT DE LA RÉTINE

Le **décollement de la rétine** est une affection de l'**œil** causée par la séparation de la rétine et du feuillet sous-jacent sous l'effet du passage du liquide vitréen sous la rétine. Le **décollement de la rétine** découle d'une situation où j'ai vu quelque chose se passer devant moi et a provoqué un stress immense. J'ai l'impression que cette image d'un événement que je trouve horrible va **rester imprégnée dans ma mémoire toute ma vie !** Il est important que je fasse face à cette image au lieu de vouloir la cacher au fond d'un coffre ou de la nier. Je peux demander l'aide d'un thérapeute qui m'aidera

à trouver pourquoi j'ai dû voir cet événement troublant et à identifier la leçon de vie que je dois en tirer. Ce processus étant fait, je vais m'éviter d'autres situations où je pourrais développer un autre **décollement de la rétine**.

YEUX — GLAUCOME

Le **glaucome** implique un blocage du canal d'écoulement de l'**œil**, empêchant ainsi les liquides de se libérer. Ces liquides représentent toutes les larmes qui auraient dû couler tout au long de ma vie et qui, s'étant accumulées, occasionnent une pression sur la rétine, causant ainsi la détérioration de la vue. Il atteint plus fréquemment les gens de plus de soixante ans, qui ont souvent le sentiment **d'en avoir assez vu.** Il peut être le signe de vieilles rancunes et d'un refus de pardonner. Je peux avoir l'impression d'être dépassé, j'ai peur de l'avenir. Me sentant facilement fatigué, la vie devient différente et plus difficile à accepter ↓♥ émotionnellement. Je refuse de me voir vieillir ; les images du futur ne peuvent être vues et cela me convient parfaitement. Je choisis d'ôter le voile, j'accepte ↓♥ de voir avec amour et tendresse. Puisqu'un **œil** atteint de **glaucome** réagit comme une loupe, il y a quelque chose ou quelqu'un dans ma vie dont je voudrais me rapprocher le plus rapidement possible. Je peux avoir l'impression d'être passé à côté de certaines choses dans ma vie et j'éprouve du ressentiment envers elles. C'est comme si des occasions me filaient entre les doigts juste quand je suis sur le point d'obtenir ou d'accomplir quelque chose.

YEUX — HYPERMÉTROPIE et PRESBYTIE

La **presbytie** est un état qui m'empêche de voir les objets de près. Elle dénote une peur du présent. Qu'y a-t-il dans ma vie, près de moi, que je refuse de voir ? Il peut s'agir de mon incapacité à « mettre au point » et à voir clairement ce qui m'est accessible et près de moi. Je me laisse davantage intéresser par les autres, par mes relations personnelles et par les événements extérieurs, plutôt que de regarder en moi et de développer de plus en plus mon moi intérieur. Cet état peut avoir été causé par un choc ou par un traumatisme m'ayant fait croire que ce présent n'était pas pour moi. En devenant extraverti et en regardant au loin, je choisis d'ignorer ce qui se passe près de moi, mes rêves sont tournés vers l'avenir. Mes **yeux** deviennent comme une vigie qui guette continuellement au loin ce qui se passe. Je vis de l'inquiétude car ce que je vois présentement me rend inquiet : je vieillis, les enfants quittent la maison, je deviens plus triste. Ainsi, ma vision se transforme en fonction de ce que je veux et de ce que je ne veux pas voir. Dans le cas où seulement un des deux **yeux** est concerné, il est important que je considère les situations reliées au côté du corps affecté (gauche : intuitif, droit : rationnel). J'accepte ↓♥ de voir la vie aujourd'hui, avec toutes ses beautés et je sais que je suis en sécurité, ICI ET MAINTENANT.

YEUX — KÉRATITE (voir aussi : INFLAMMATION, ULCÈRE)

La **kératite** est une inflammation de la cornée, accompagnée de douleurs importantes pouvant se présenter sous forme d'ulcères. Elle survient lorsque je vis de la peine par rapport à quelque chose ou à quelqu'un que je vois et qui me met en colère. Cela me met dans des états tels que j'irais jusqu'à frapper une personne physiquement ou, au sens figuré, je pourrais vouloir que le « malheur frappe les personnes ou les situations concernées » afin de me donner une certaine satisfaction. Ce peut être aussi moi qui veux me cacher de quelque chose ou de quelqu'un afin de ne pas être vu. La **cornée** étant la « vitre » de l'**œil**, je devrai opacifier celle-ci pour qu'elle soit remplacée par un « mur » qui me protège. Mon corps me dit simplement que **j'ai à apprendre à regarder la vie avec d'autres yeux, avec une nouvelle attitude d'ouverture et de compréhension.** Je peux voir des choses qui ne font pas mon affaire, qui ne me conviennent pas et j'ai à me détacher de ce que je vois. J'ai à apprendre à laisser aller le contrôle que je veux exercer sur les choses, sur les personnes ou sur les situations qui m'entourent et sur lesquelles je n'ai aucun pouvoir.

YEUX — MYOPIE

La **myopie** rend difficile ma vision au loin. Mon insécurité face à l'avenir me fait voir les événements plus gros et plus inquiétants qu'ils ne le sont en réalité. Il semble que je ne sois pas prêt à les affronter. Je peux voir ce qui est près de moi alors que ma vision éloignée est embrouillée, en raison des muscles oculaires contractés et tendus. En somme, je suis en mesure de traiter avec ma réalité immédiate et ma vie « au jour le jour » avec une grande facilité. Par contre, il m'est difficile de créer ma propre vision de l'avenir et de voir les possibilités devant moi, ayant à surmonter la peur de ce qui s'en vient. Si je suis **myope**, je peux avoir tendance à être gêné et introverti, ce qui peut résulter d'expériences de mon enfance que j'ai vécues comme effrayantes ou abusives (comme le regard hostile ou enragé d'un parent). Par exemple, si un professeur ou un oncle me battait, je suis devenu **myope** parce que j'avais peur de lui et que je ne voulais pas le voir car, seulement à sa vue, je devenais nerveux, inquiet, sachant ce qui m'attendait. Habituellement, à moins d'avoir vécu un autre conflit, ma vision de près va être meilleure que la moyenne, car je sais, même inconsciemment, qu'il est important que je vois bien ce qui se passe près de moi pour pouvoir me défendre ou pour poser les bons gestes quand cette menace sera près de moi et pour ne pas qu'elle me blesse. La **myopie** indique généralement une subjectivité excessive. L'expression « ne pas voir plus loin que le bout de son nez » décrit bien cet état d'être. Ne pas vouloir voir au loin par lassitude ou paresse ou, encore, à force de déceptions de la vie. « Je n'en crois pas mes **yeux** » illustre bien comment je me sens. M'apitoyer sur moi-même est parfois plus facile que d'agir. En acceptant ↓♥ de voir le monde extérieur, cela me permet d'apprendre sur moi. Ma vision s'élargira en

développant mon espace intérieur. Je choisis de nouvelles routes, je me fais confiance.

YEUX — NYSTAGMUS

Le **nystagmus** est une suite de mouvements saccadés et rapides des globes oculaires, indépendants de la volonté, souvent symptomatiques d'une affection du centre nerveux. Si mes **yeux** souffrent de **nystagmus**, c'est que ceux-ci sont constamment en mouvement de balayage. Je dois me demander quand est apparu le **nystagmus** dans ma vie. Cela va habituellement concorder avec une période où je vivais une situation dans laquelle un danger existait et que j'ai cherché, sans arrêt, j'ai « balayé » toutes les possibilités qui s'offraient à moi pour pouvoir m'en sortir. Il est important que je retrace cet événement pour prendre conscience de la source de cette maladie et ainsi pouvoir la guérir. Je prends conscience que le danger pouvait être réel pour moi dans le passé mais que, maintenant, celui-ci n'existe plus et que je suis constamment guidé et protégé.

YEUX — RÉTINITE PIGMENTAIRE ou RÉTINOPATHIE PIGMENTAIRE

La **rétinite pigmentaire**, appelée aussi **rétinopathie pigmentaire**, est considérée comme une maladie héréditaire qui fait que les cellules visuelles réceptrices de la lumière dégénèrent. Elle touche habituellement les enfants. L'**œil** ne peut s'adapter à l'obscurité et le champ visuel diminue avec le temps. Je ne vois donc plus la lumière. Cette maladie se développera si j'ai honte de ma personne, de qui je suis, autant sur le plan physique qu'intellectuel. Je voudrais que les autres dirigent leur regard ailleurs que sur moi. Il se peut que je sois un perfectionniste et que le fait « d'en voir grand » devant moi me cause un grand stress. Je peux avoir peur de ne pas venir à bout de tout ce qui m'attend dans la vie. Mon corps répond à ce stress en diminuant mon champ de vision, espérant ainsi diminuer mon stress. J'ai à apprendre à m'accepter ↓♥ tel que je suis et à porter un regard positif par rapport à qui je suis, étant une personne unique et exceptionnelle.

YEUX — STRABISME (en général)

Le **strabisme** dénote des contradictions et des incertitudes face à mes relations avec mon entourage, un perpétuel combat entre un besoin de solitude et celui d'être admiré, un désir d'indépendance confronté à la peur d'être seul. La douceur du silence est constamment en contradiction avec ce besoin de questionner. J'apprends à cerner mes vrais besoins et à me sentir bien dans quelque situation que ce soit.

YEUX — STRABISME CONVERGENT

Le **strabisme convergent (ou loucherie)** est une déviation des **yeux** vers le nez. Il implique généralement que je refuse de voir les choses telles qu'elles sont réellement, souvent à cause de l'insécurité qu'elles représentent pour moi. Il se peut que, de cette façon, je souhaite échapper à des personnes que je considère menaçantes pour moi. Selon l'**œil** qui louche, je peux découvrir certains aspects de ma personnalité. S'il s'agit de **mon œil gauche qui louche vers l'intérieur**, je suis une personne craintive souffrant d'un fort complexe d'infériorité. Si, au contraire, **c'est mon œil droit**, je suis probablement très susceptible et rancunier. C'est une façon de centrer toute mon attention et mon intelligence sur moi-même ou sur une chose ou sur une personne que je me dois de surveiller constamment. **L'œil gauche louchant à l'extrême vers le haut** dénote que je suis rêveur, irrationnel et dépourvu de la notion du temps. Si c'est **mon œil droit**, je suis une personne indisciplinée et dotée d'une intelligence irrationnelle. Le **strabisme** a également pour effet de me faire voir les choses seulement en deux dimensions. Afin d'unifier ma perception, j'ai intérêt à observer les choses sous tous les angles et à en accepter ↓♥ la réalité. Je deviens attentif à tous les messages que mon corps me transmet et je découvre les plaisirs d'une vision de la vie dans sa globalité.

YEUX — STRABISME DIVERGENT

Comme pour le **strabisme** convergent, le **strabisme divergent** est aussi une **déviation des yeux** mais, cette fois-ci, **vers l'extérieur**. Il dénote également une peur de regarder le présent en face. Lorsque c'est **l'œil droit** qui est atteint, cela démontre qu'un effort intellectuel est mis en branle afin de faciliter la relation entre l'intelligence et la situation. J'ai l'impression que mon intelligence tourne en rond, ce qui peut faire de moi un candidat potentiel à la dépression. S'il s'agit plutôt de **mon œil gauche**, je suis une personne d'une grande sensibilité. Les actions que je poserai le seront en fonction de cette sensibilité. J'accepte ↓♥ de vivre le moment présent et de regarder chaque situation en face. Ma sensibilité me permet désormais de prendre des décisions éclairées, en sachant que je suis constamment guidé et protégé.

ZONA (voir : PEAU — ZONA)

ANNEXE I

CORPS (en général) (voir aussi : les parties correspondantes...)

Voici les parties du corps et la signification métaphysique générale rattachée à chacune d'elles.

Les cheveux	Ma force.
Le cuir chevelu	Ma foi en mon côté divin.
La tête	Mon individualité.
Les yeux	Ma capacité de voir.
Les oreilles	Ma capacité d'entendre.
Le nez	Ma capacité de sentir ou de ressentir les personnes ou les situations.
Les lèvres	Ma lèvre supérieure est reliée au côté féminin[89] et la lèvre inférieure, au côté masculin[90].
Les dents	Mes décisions, reliées au côté féminin en haut, reliées au côté masculin, en bas.
Le cou	Ma flexibilité, ma capacité de voir plusieurs côtés des situations de la vie.
La gorge	L'expression de mon langage verbal et non verbal, ma créativité.
Les épaules	Ma capacité de porter une charge, des responsabilités.
Les bras	Ma capacité de prendre les personnes ou les situations de la vie. Ils sont le prolongement du cœur. Ils servent à exécuter les ordres. Ils sont reliés à ce que je fais dans ma vie, par exemple mon travail.
Les coudes	Ma flexibilité dans les changements de directions dans ma vie.
Les doigts	Les petits détails du quotidien.
Le pouce	Relié aux soucis ou à mon intellect ou à mon audition.
L'index	Relié à des peurs ou à ma personnalité (ego) ou à mon odorat.
Le majeur	Relié à de la colère ou à ma sexualité ou à ma vision.

---

89. **Côté féminin : voir :** FÉMININ (principe...)
90. **Côté masculin : voir :** MASCULIN (principe...)

L'annulaire	Relié à du chagrin ou à mon union ou à mon toucher.
L'auriculaire	Relié à de la prétention ou à ma famille ou au goût.
Le cœur	Mon amour.
Le sang	La joie qui circule dans ma vie.
Les seins	Mon côté maternel.
Les poumons	Mon besoin d'espace, d'autonomie. Reliés à mon sentiment de vivre.
L'estomac	Ma capacité de digérer de nouvelles idées.
Le dos	Mon support, mon soutien.
Les articulations	Ma flexibilité, ma capacité de me plier aux différentes situations de ma vie.
La peau	Ma liaison entre mon intérieur et mon extérieur (équilibre).
Les os	La structure des lois et des principes du monde dans lequel je vis.
L'utérus	Mon foyer.
Les intestins	(Surtout le gros, le côlon) : ma capacité de relâcher, de laisser aller ce qui m'est inutile ou de laisser circuler les événements dans ma vie.
Les reins	Le siège de la peur.
Le pancréas	La joie qui est en moi.
Le foie	Le siège de la critique.
Les jambes	Ma capacité d'avancer dans la vie, d'aller vers le changement, vers les nouvelles expériences.
Les genoux	Ma flexibilité, ma fierté, mon orgueil, mon entêtement.
Les chevilles	Ma flexibilité dans les nouvelles directions de l'avenir.
Les pieds	Ma direction (piétiner sur place). Ma compréhension de moi-même et de la vie (passé, présent, futur).
Les orteils	Les détails de mon avenir.

ANNEXE II

Liste des principaux malaises et des principales maladies et de leur signification probable abrégée.

Abcès	Souvent relié à une difficulté à exprimer quelque chose qui m'irrite ou qui me contrarie. Cette difficulté se manifestera alors sous forme d'abcès.
Accident	Souvent relié à de la peur ou à de la culpabilité.
Acné	Souvent reliée à un manque d'estime de soi, au désir de tenir les gens loin de soi, de peur d'être blessé.
Acouphène	Souvent relié au besoin d'être à l'écoute de ses besoins intérieurs, de ses valeurs.
Alcoolisme	Souvent relié au désir de fuir ses responsabilités physiques ou affectives de peur d'être blessé « à nouveau ».
Allergies	Souvent reliées à de la colère ou à de la frustration face à une personne ou à un événement associé au produit allergène. À qui ou à quoi suis-je allergique lorsque cette situation s'est présentée ?
Alzheimer	Maladie souvent reliée au désir de fuir les réalités de ce monde et de ne plus vouloir prendre de responsabilités.
Amputation	Souvent reliée à une grande culpabilité.
Angoisse	Souvent reliée au sentiment de me croire limité, restreint avec une impression très marquée d'étouffer dans une situation.
Anorexie	Souvent reliée à une très basse estime de soi et au désir inconscient de vouloir « disparaître ».
Appendicite	Souvent reliée à la colère parce que je me sens dans un « cul-de-sac ».
Arthrite	Souvent reliée à de la critique envers soi ou envers les autres.
Articulations	Souvent reliées à un manque de flexibilité face aux situations de la vie.
Autisme	Souvent relié à de la fuite car j'ai de la difficulté à transiger avec le monde qui m'entoure.
Basse pression	Souvent reliée à une forme de découragement.
Boulimie	Souvent reliée au besoin de vouloir combler un vide intérieur affectif.
Brûlure, brûlement, fièvre	Souvent reliés à de la colère qui bout à l'intérieur de moi ou envers une personne ou un événement.
Burnout	Souvent relié à la fuite d'une émotion intense vécue au travail ou dans des occupations diverses.
Cancer	Souvent relié à une grande peur ou à une grande culpabilité, au point de ne plus vouloir vivre, même inconsciemment.
Cellulite	Souvent reliée à la peur de m'engager et à ma tendance à retenir des émotions du passé.
Cholestérol	Souvent relié à ma joie de vivre qui circule difficilement.
Cigarette	Souvent reliée à un vide intérieur que je veux combler.

Cœur	Souvent, toutes les maladies reliées au cœur ont rapport à un manque d'amour de moi, de mes proches ou de mon environnement.
Constipation	Souvent reliée au fait de vouloir retenir les personnes ou les événements de ma vie.
Crampe	Souvent reliée à de la tension dans l'action prise ou à prendre.
Démangeaisons, irritations	Souvent reliées à de l'impatience, de l'insécurité, ou à de la contrariété contre moi-même.
Dépression	Souvent reliée au fait de vouloir m'enlever de la pression dans ma vie. Alors, je fais une « dé-pression ».
Diabète	Souvent relié à de la tristesse profonde qui survient à la suite d'un événement où j'en ai voulu à la vie.
Diarrhée	Souvent reliée au fait de vouloir rejeter les solutions ou les situations qui s'offrent à moi pour avancer dans la vie.
Douleur	Souvent une forme d'autopunition face à un sentiment de culpabilité. Elle peut être parfois reliée à un besoin d'attention, à de la peur ou à de la colère.
Eczéma	Souvent relié au fait de ne plus avoir de contact avec un être aimé.
Empoisonnement	Je dois me demander : qui ou quoi m'empoisonne l'existence ?
Enflure (œdème)	Souvent reliée au fait de me sentir limité ou d'avoir peur d'être limité ou arrêté dans ce que je désire faire.
Engourdissement	Souvent relié à un désir de se rendre moins sensible à une personne ou à une situation.
Entorse	Souvent reliée à une situation où je résiste, me sentant inquiet et ayant besoin d'augmenter mon ouverture et ma flexibilité.
Étouffement, essoufflement	Souvent reliés au fait de me sentir anormalement critiqué, pris à la gorge, en manque d'espace vital et d'avoir de la difficulté à vivre ce que je veux vivre.
Étourdissement, perte de connaissance, coma	Souvent reliés à un désir de fuir une situation ou une personne lorsque j'ai l'impression que cela évolue trop vite.
Fatigue	Souvent reliée au fait que j'éparpille mes énergies et que je me laisse facilement contrôler par mes peurs, par mes insécurités, par mes inquiétudes.
Gangrène	Souvent reliée à de la rancune ou à de la haine face à une situation en rapport avec l'aspect de ma vie qui est représenté par la partie affectée.
Gaz	Souvent relié à quelque chose ou à quelqu'un auquel je m'agrippe et qui n'est plus bénéfique pour moi.
Grippe	Souvent reliée à de la colère car j'ai « en grippe » quelqu'un ou quelque chose.
Haute pression	Souvent reliée à des soucis et à des tracas de longue date.
Hypoglycémie	Souvent reliée à de la tristesse issue de la résistance face aux événements de la vie.
Incontinence	Souvent reliée au désir de vouloir tout contrôler dans ma vie.
Infarctus	Souvent relié à l'amour que je dois davantage accepter ↓♥ de recevoir.
Infections	Souvent reliées à de la frustration face à différents aspects de ma vie.

Insomnie	Souvent reliée au fait de rester « accroché » à une forme de culpabilité.
Leucémie	Souvent reliée au fait de ne plus vouloir me battre pour obtenir ce qui représente l'amour dans ma vie.
Malaise	Souvent relié au fait de vouloir extérioriser une tension intérieure.
Mononucléose	Souvent reliée à une grande peur d'avoir à affronter une situation qui m'amènerait à m'engager sur le plan affectif.
Nausée	Souvent reliée à un aspect de ma vie que je veux rejeter parce qu'il me dégoûte.
Nerf sciatique	Souvent relié à une grande insécurité en rapport avec mes besoins de base : logement, nourriture, argent.
Paralysie	Souvent reliée à de la fuite car une peur me paralyse.
Peau	Souvent, les maladies de la peau ont rapport avec le sentiment de ne pas avoir le « contact » physique ou autre pour me procurer l'amour dont j'ai besoin.
Poids (excès de...)	Souvent relié au fait d'accumuler des choses, des idées, des émotions, de vouloir se protéger, de se sentir limité, de vivre un vide intérieur.
Poumons	Souvent les maladies reliées aux poumons ont rapport au fait de pouvoir prendre l'espace vital, « l'air » dont j'ai besoin pour me sentir libre et pour pouvoir vivre.
Raideur (articulation)	Souvent reliée à un manque de flexibilité, à de l'entêtement, à de la résistance ou à de la rigidité, surtout face à une figure d'autorité.
Rhumatisme	Souvent relié à de la critique, soit envers moi-même ou envers les autres.
Ronflement	Souvent relié à de vieilles idées, à des attitudes ou à des biens matériels auxquels je m'accroche et que j'ai avantage à laisser aller.
Saignements	Souvent reliés à une perte de joie (sang = joie).
Sclérose en plaques	Souvent reliée au fait d'avoir des pensées rigides envers moi, envers les autres et envers les situations de la vie.
Scoliose	Souvent reliée au fait que j'ai l'impression de porter tellement de responsabilités sur mes épaules que je veux les fuir.
Sida	Souvent relié à une grande déception et à une grande culpabilité face à l'amour et à la sexualité.
Tics	Souvent reliés à une tension intérieure très grande. Les tics apparaissent habituellement au moment où je vis de la pression face à l'autorité.
Torticolis	Souvent relié à un ou à des côtés (aspects) d'une situation que j'évite de voir ou que je veux fuir.
Tumeur, kyste	Souvent reliés à un choc émotionnel qui se solidifie.
Zona	Souvent relié à une grande insécurité face à la perte de l'amour de quelqu'un ou d'une situation (ex. : le milieu de travail) qui me procure cet amour.

ANNEXE III

ITE (maladies en...)

Toutes les maladies en « **ite** » sont habituellement reliées à de la colère ou à de la frustration puisqu'elles sont reliées à des inflammations. En voici quelques exemples :

amygda**lite**
appendi**cite**
arth**rite**
bronch**ite**
burs**ite**
co**lite**
conjonctiv**ite**
cyst**ite**
divertic**ulite**
épicondy**lite**
épiderm**ite**
gastro-enté**rite**
gingiv**ite**
hépat**ite**
il**éite**
kérat**ite**
laryng**ite**
mast**ite**
néph**rite**
ostéomyé**lite**
ot**ite**
ova**rite**
pharyng**ite**
phlé**bite**
poliomyé**lite**
prostat**ite**
salping**ite**
tendin**ite**
urét**rite**
vagin**ite**

COURS OFFERTS PAR JACQUES MARTEL ET SON ÉQUIPE

Retrouver l'enfant en soi   **Durée : 40h.**

L'atelier **"Retrouver l'enfant en soi"** est le fruit de plusieurs années d'expérience basées sur le travail avec l'enfant intérieur. Ce travail a mis en évidence les résultats éloquents qu'on a vus se produire pendant les consultations privées ou les cours en groupe. Les animateurs d'**ATMA inc.** utilisent des exercices déjà éprouvés et y intègrent leurs propres techniques d'intégration du cœur afin d'obtenir des résultats encore plus efficaces.

Comment peut-on obtenir des résultats si probants ? Quel est le mécanisme mis en branle et utilisé pour réussir à guérir des blessures qui datent d'aussi loin que la conception ?

Il s'agit d'un mélange ou plutôt d'une chimie presque magique qui transforme les blessures passées qui sont source entre autres de colère, de tristesse, de fuite, d'agressivité etc., et qui sont conscientisées et transmutées par l'**Amour** afin d'emmener des guérisons immédiates et permanentes. Le climat de confiance qui s'installe dans le groupe, l'ouverture qui se fait graduellement face à l'animateur et face aux autres participants permet à l'**Amour** d'atteindre les couches les plus profondes de notre être.

Lorsque j'étais enfant, j'ai vécu des situations où j'ai eu de la peine, de la colère, etc. et je n'ai pas pu exprimer mes émotions. Ou alors, je peux avoir exprimé ces émotions, ces états d'être mais la réponse ou le « feed-back » que j'ai reçu de mon entourage et plus spécifiquement des gens qui m'entouraient et que j'aimais, soit mes parents, mes frères et soeurs, mon professeur etc. a été jugé « négatif ».

Je me suis alors replié sur moi-même, et j'ai « ravalé » mes émotions. La blessure formée à ce moment s'est imprégnée au niveau de l'**Amour**. Cette blessure s'imprègne dans ma mémoire émotive et à chaque fois que je revis une situation semblable, cette blessure est stimulée et réouverte inconsciemment, ce qui a pour effet de me faire réagir parfois d'une façon impulsive, avec des comportements incompréhensibles. Des comportements où la logique n'a pas sa place: c'est ma mémoire émotive qui se défend afin d'éviter de revivre le traumatisme que j'ai vécu étant enfant.

Le mental (mon côté rationnel) et même mon corps physique se sont inventés des façons de se protéger afin d'éviter

de revivre ces émotions pénibles de l'enfance. Plus j'avance en âge et plus mon coeur risque de se durcir. J'enfouis de plus en plus profondément mes vieilles blessures et la couche devient de plus en plus épaisse.

Puisque je suis venu sur cette Terre pour expérimenter l'**Amour** sous toutes ces formes, et qu'étant jeune j'ai jugé des situations ou des personnes où j'ai perçu une absence d'**Amour**, je vais m'attirer des situations semblables dans ma vie afin de me donner des opportunités de changer ma perception et mon interprétation des événements qui se sont passés et ainsi remettre de l'**Amour** dans toutes ces situations. En faisant ainsi, je brise les maillons qui me retiennent à mon passé. Je défais ou plutôt je neutralise les « patterns » qui sont propres à mon chemin de vie. La tristesse est remplacée par la joie, le vide fait place à un sentiment de plénitude, la solitude que je vivais devient soudainement une amie qui m'est indispensable afin de me retrouver et de découvrir qui je suis.

Pour parvenir à ce processus de transformation des événements passés, je dois accepter de prendre contact avec mon enfant intérieur. De prendre contact tout d'abord avec les émotions qui sont à la surface et d'ensuite plonger plus profondément dans les dédales de mon intérieur.

Je vais tout au long de cet atelier apprivoiser petit à petit l'enfant qui est en moi: je vais lui parler, l'amener à me communiquer ce qu'il vit, ces états d'âme afin de l'aider à extérioriser les émotions qu'il a refoulées pendant toutes ces années. Il est important de le laisser aller à son propre rythme. **Tout se passe en harmonie et dans le respect de qui il est.** Je vais prendre conscience de faits qui se sont passés et que ma mémoire a complètement occultés, simplement afin de se protéger et d'éviter de revivre cette souffrance encrée à l'intérieur de moi.

Même si je m'en vais à l'autre bout du monde, mon enfant intérieur blessé, lui, me suit partout. Même si je veux nier qu'il existe, il continue de frapper à la porte de mon coeur pour que je l'écoute et que je l'aide et le supporte. C'est à moi de lui tendre la main. C'est à moi à l'accueillir dans ce qu'il vit. C'est à moi à l'aider à s'ouvrir car c'est comme cela que je vais découvrir qui je suis vraiment et je pourrai ainsi développer mon plein potentiel. J'aurai repris tout le pouvoir qui m'appartient et qui m'est essentiel afin d'avoir la maîtrise de ma Vie.

L'important, c'est de me donner du temps, d'être compréhensif et aimant. Je ne peux pas changer toute ma vie en quelques jours mais je peux guérir des blessures vieilles de cent ans, qui vont me permettre d'être mieux avec moi-même, d'être plus en paix, plus en harmonie avec

mon entourage ; je vais être plus conscient de ce qui se passe dans ma vie et je vais avoir des outils pour changer des choses dans ma vie. Je ne dois pour se faire qu'être prêt à accueillir l'**Amour** dans ma vie.

Il se peut que je trouve parfois difficile de découvrir des étapes de mon passé, des situations que j'avais toujours niées ; mais ce qui est merveilleux maintenant, c'est que **j'ai le pouvoir de changer tout ce que j'ai perçu de négatif comme des opportunités de grandir**. Et que c'est la somme de toutes mes expériences qui font l'être merveilleux que je suis aujourd'hui.

Je me dois d'être vrai avec moi-même. Je me dois de risquer au maximum. Je me dois de foncer. Car aussi grand est l'effort, aussi grande est la récompense.

Je prends le temps ici de souligner un point très important: moi, étant enfant, j'ai pu avoir interprété que l'un ou l'autre de mes parents, ou même les deux, ne m'aimaient pas. Je ne mets nullement en doute leur **Amour** et les efforts constants qu'ils ont faits afin de me donner le maximum. Mais que mes parents portent eux aussi un enfant blessé et que leur propre état les rend incapables de combler les manques de leur progéniture.

Le résultat final est que <u>**je vais devenir mon propre parent**</u> et qu'enfin je n'aurai pas à chercher à l'extérieur de moi pour trouver l'**Amour**.

Car qui mieux que moi peut connaître les besoins de mon enfant intérieur ? ?

Cet atelier peut aider grandement à résoudre les conflits programmants et déclenchants qui sont la cause de l'apparition des malaises et des maladies.

CONSCIENCE DE SOI

Durée : 21 h.

L'atelier Conscience de Soi propose au participant de revivre en douceur ses émotions d'enfant qui freinent son épanouissement personnel et professionnel. A l'aide d'une méthode propre à cet atelier, il peut refaire le film de sa vie. Ce sont les choix conscients et inconscients que j'ai faits lorsque j'étais enfant qui déterminent le contexte dans lequel je vis ici et maintenant. J'ai beau changer le téléviseur ou la vidéo, ce sont toujours les mêmes images qui, dans ma vie, défilent... à mon grand désespoir ! J'apprends à décoder mes malaises et mes maladies, à identifier mes peurs afin de les dépasser pour mieux gérer les situations quotidiennes. Pour vivre en harmonie, il faut que j'identifie les blocages. Revivre en douceur mes émotions d'enfant pour qu'enfin l'adulte que je suis puisse se prendre en charge dans l'amour et la compréhension. En finir avec la culpabilité, la tristesse, la colère... Vivre en harmonie avec soi et les autres, contribue à améliorer les conditions de vie au travail, à la maison, etc...

S'AFFIRMER

Durée : 16 h.

S'affirmer veut dire prendre sa place, sans soumission, sans agressivité. Cet atelier permet d'accroître la communication dans les relations personnelles, familiales et professionnelles. Le participant apprend à être vrai envers lui-même et envers les autres, à se faire confiance, à prendre la place qui lui revient : "la première place".Dans des exercices de mises en situation, le participant apprendra à dire "non", à dire « oui » , à se faire dire "non", à se faire dire "oui". Il apprend la différence entre la soumission, l'agressivité et l'affirmation afin d'être plus à l'aise dans ce qu'il a à communiquer. Le participant pourra ainsi utiliser les techniques apprises afin de mieux gérer son quotidien. Cet atelier est particulièrement bénéfique pour toute personne qui, dans son travail, est en relation avec le public ou se trouve dans le secteur de la vente.

COMMUNICATION SPIRITUELLE

Durée : 21 h.

Il est possible pour chaque personne de communiquer avec un guide spirituel de haut niveau ou avec son propre moi supérieur. En prenant contact davantage avec toutes les ressources de joie, de paix, de sagesse et de lumière qui se trouvent à l'intérieur de lui, le participant a accès à un nouveau niveau de conscience lui permettant de vivre encore plus intensément le fait d'être un canal ouvert d'amour et de lumière.

S'OUVRIR À SA DIMENSION INTÉRIEURE   Durée : 18 h.

Cet atelier se compose essentiellement de détentes guidées ainsi que d'exercices pratiques suivis de partages; ceci permet aux participants de s'ouvrir davantage à leur dimension intérieure et à l'Amour, laissant ainsi cette énergie apporter les guérisons ou les prises de conscience les plus appropriées dans l'instant présent. Ainsi, chaque participant pourra expérimenter l'assertion suivante : « Plus je m'ouvre, plus je me découvre ». Cet atelier se veut accessible à tous, tant pour les personnes qui débutent leur démarche de croissance personnelle que pour celles qui ont déjà cheminé.

RELATION D'AIDE   Durée : 18 h.

L'atelier Relation d'Aide apporte des réponses aux questions suivantes, souvent posées, lorsque l'on désire aider une personne, tant au niveau personnel que professionnel : Quelle approche dois-je utiliser ? Comment aider sans me faire blesser ? Est-ce profitable ou nuisible ? Quelle est ma responsabilité face à cette aide que je souhaite apporter ? À l'aide de différents exercices de mises en situation, de techniques particulières, le participant sera en mesure d'expérimenter différents aspects de la relation d'aide. Il pourra, par la suite, aider de façon harmonieuse son prochain, en tenant compte de ses propres limites. Une meilleure ouverture permettra aussi d'obtenir une vision plus objective pour régler les situations conflictuelles qui peuvent survenir dans le quotidien, que ce soit au travail, à la maison, etc...

LE POUVOIR DE L'ENGAGEMENT   Durée : 18 h.

Cet atelier se veut une explication par rapport à l'engagement et les bénéfices que je peux en retirer. En effet, il peut m'être arrivé à plusieurs reprises de me demander si je dois m'engager ou non par rapport à certaines situations que je vis dans ma vie personnelle ou professionnelle. Comme participant, je serai à même de me rendre compte quels sont les avantages que je peux en retirer sous différents aspects de ma vie. Ainsi pour moi, il deviendra plus facile de pouvoir prendre les décisions les plus appropriées dans les événements qui se présentent à moi. S'engager veut dire aussi « prendre part à la vie »; la question est : Suis-je prêt à vivre davantage ?

ATELIER SUR LA SEXUALITÉ   Durée : 21 h.

Sa place dans ma vie ; mon côté féminin (Yin) et mon côté masculin (Yang) ; l'âme sœur ; la place de la sexualité dans mon cheminement personnel et spirituel ; le désir de l'âme ; la sexualité comme outil de survie biologique de l'espèce ; l'amour et la sexualité ; le rejet, l'abandon dans mes rapports sexuels. La différence entre les hommes et les femmes par rapport à la sexualité. Les différentes orientations sexuelles. Dans cet atelier, chacun pourra s'ouvrir davantage à cet aspect de lui-même pour vivre un plein épanouissement. Je peux vivre cet atelier seul même si je vis en couple, puisque le seul vrai pouvoir que j'ai, c'est sur moi-même, pour qu'ainsi l'amour soit plus présent dans ma vie.

Pré-requis :
1. une grande ouverture d'esprit
2. avoir 18 ans ou être accompagné d'un des deux parents
3. avoir suivi l'atelier Retrouver l'Enfant en Soi avec un animateur accrédité par ATMA inc. Présence du conjoint souhaitée mais non obligatoire.

REIKI - Niveaux : 1, 2, 3 et Maîtrise

Le REIKI renforce et accélère le processus naturel de guérison. Il vitalise le corps et l'esprit. Le REIKI est un cadeau à se faire, un cadeau pour la vie. Si vous désirez pratiquer le REIKI sur vous-même ou sur les autres, vous devez être initié au REIKI. L'enseignant de REIKI transmet, au cours de journées d'initiation, des symboles sacrés et secrets qui rendront les participants aptes à améliorer leur santé et celle de leurs proches...!

- **Niveau 1 & 2 - Durée : 16 h.**
- **Niveau 3 - Durée : 6 h.**
- **Maîtrise - Durée : 6 h.**

ATELIER DE THÉRAPEUTE

Durée : 32 h.

Atelier de 4 jours pour thérapeutes et personnes désirant se perfectionner en technique d'auto-guérison. Jacques Martel enseignera sa technique d'intégration au niveau du cœur, technique qu'il a perfectionnée depuis bientôt dix ans. Cette méthode permet et aide à intégrer différentes situations de vie interprétées comme négatives avec un taux de réussite, dans la majorité des cas, de 80 à 100 %. Le participant acquiert ainsi la connaissance d'un savoir-faire qu'il peut utiliser comme outil de travail. Des pré-requis sont nécessaires, puisque cela demande que le thérapeute « s'implique » dans le processus de guérison, ces pré-requis contiennent des éléments à l'application de la méthode.

LES ATELIERS PRÉ-REQUIS ET LEUR IMPORTANCE POUR L'ATELIER DE THÉRAPEUTE SONT :

1 - Retrouver l'Enfant en Soi : Afin d'être plus conscient de l'importance de ce qui est vécu entre la conception et l'âge de 12 ans, et de pouvoir le guérir dans l'amour.

2 - S'Affirmer : Afin d'être plus conscient de la place que j'ai dans ma vie, d'acquérir plus en profondeur des notions de responsabilité.

3 - Relation d'Aide : Afin de développer plus de facilités à partager ses expériences de vie, et les apprentissages à faire circuler la lumière dans un but thérapeutique et d'intégration.

4 - Conscience de Soi : Afin d'être plus conscient des règles de décodage des malaises et des maladies, et de la capacité que nous avons de changer notre passé en changeant le film de vie. Seront reconnus seulement les ateliers pré-requis par un animateur accrédité par ATMA Inc.

POUR INFORMATION : **ATMA INC.**
C.P. 8818
STE-FOY, (QUÉBEC), CANADA
GIV 4N7
℃ (418) 990-0808
FAX : (418) 990-1115
Courriel : info@atma.ca

AU SUJET DE L'AUTEUR

Né à Montréal en septembre 1950, monsieur Martel a terminé en 1977 sa formation comme ingénieur électricien à l'université Laval de Québec et est devenu membre de l'ordre des ingénieurs du Québec ('77 à '87). Il a suivi en 1987 une formation au Collège des Annonceurs en radio et Télévision du Québec (CART). Il a été le président fondateur du **Centre de Croissance ATMA** (janvier '90) qui est devenu **ATMA inc. en juillet '96 et dont il assume la présidence**. Il a été membre de la Corporation des Praticiens en Médecine Douce du Québec (CPDMQ) de 1996 à 2002. De '94 à '98, il occupe la présidence de l'Association Canadienne et Québécoise des Maîtres REIKI (ACQMR).

À la fin des années '70, monsieur Martel a agi à titre de professeur en électricité et électronique à l'intérieur de formations données aux adultes par le centre de main-d'œuvre du Canada (CMC) et il a enseigné aussi dans l'entreprise privée pour aider à former des techniciens en électricité. De 1978 à 1988, il se spécialise en vitaminothérapie, aussi appelée approche ortho-moléculaire. Il a une formation autodidacte dans le domaine se basant sur les recherches de psychiatres, chimistes et autres chercheurs de réputation mondiale. Il a été membre de l'association canadienne pour la santé mentale en '85 et '86. De '76 à '88, à titre bénévole, il est un membre actif au sein d'un mouvement voué à la connaissance de soi. De '78 à '88, il agit à titre de conférencier pour ce mouvement et il occupe aussi lesfonctions de responsable des relations publiques, organisateur de séminaires, etc. De '86 à '88 il participe comme animateur et recherchiste à plus d'une centaine d'émissions télévisées sur la santé et le bien-être qui sont diffusées dans la grande région de Québec et plusieurs séries seront diffusées à travers la province de Québec à la télévision communautaire. C'est en 1988 qu'il amorce une formation en croissance personnelle avec madame Claudia Rainville. Il devient animateur d'ateliers de croissance personnelle et en janvier 1990 il travaille à temps plein comme psychothérapeute et animateur d'ateliers de croissance personnelle.

Depuis 1990, monsieur Martel poursuit sa formation personnelle et professionnelle et il a acquis au cours des années une solide réputation dans ce domaine. Son expérience l'amène à agir à titre de consultant auprès de thérapeutes et autres professionnels de la santé. C'est en 1993 qu'il devient Maître REIKI. En '96, il termine sa formation comme rebirthteur professionnel à l'Institut Héléna Marcoux.

C'est en 1991 que naît le projet d'un ouvrage qui **s'intitulera "LE GRAND DICTIONNAIRE DES MALAISES ET DES MALADIES "**. De par sa formation d'ingénieur électricien, il allie un côté pratique qui s'ajoute à son intuition. Ainsi, les nombreux ateliers et conférences que monsieur Martel a donnés confirment le lien étroit qui existe entre, d'une part, les malaises et les maladies et d'autre part les pensées, les sentiments et les émotions comme source de conflits dans le déclenchement des maladies. Sa formation en '97 avec M. Claude Sabbah confirme sa théorie et va dans le sens du dictionnaire déjà commencé.

Monsieur Martel anime des ateliers au Québec et en Europe. L'intérêt suscité depuis plusieurs années par le public et les thérapeutes pour le livre « Le grand dictionnaire des malaises et des maladies » démontre la pertinence d'un tel ouvrage. Les CDs de détente guidée « ATMA, Guide de relaxation et d'harmonisation» et «ATMA, le corps de Cristal, le corps de Lumière » sont un complément apprécié au livre dans une perspective de guérison et de mieux-être.

Le livre « Entre l'Esprit et le Cœur » avec le CD audio du livre permettent une plus grande ouverture de conscience. Monsieur Martel aide à former des thérapeutes avec la technique de guérison émotionnelle qu'il a développée au cours des années; celle-ci est enseignée dans l'atelier Thérapeutes.

Références		
Liste des personnes que Jacques Martel a consultées ou avec lesquelles il travaille en collaboration		
nom/adresse	**téléphone**	**domaine d'activités**
Lucie Bernier	(418) 573-6075	Psychothérapeute, Maître REIKI (formation et traitement énergétique), conférencière, ateliers de croissance personnelle.
George Wright 350, Gingras, app. 502 Sainte-Foy (Québec) GIX 4C4	(418) 990-0958 Email : george.wright@videotron.ca	Psychothérapeute, conférencier, animateur d'ateliers de croissance personnelle pour les individus et les entreprises.
Frances Boyte 101, rue Saint-Paul, # 4 Québec GIK 3V8	(418) 650-3256 Fax : (418) 694-0184 Email : francesboyte@hotmail.com	Diététiste-Nutritionniste. Consultations individuelles en diéto-thérapie, nutrition clinique et nutrition sportive. Ateliers de planification de menus auprès de groupes. Formation en alimentation auprès du personnel d'entreprises.
Nicole Gagné Centre énergétique Gagné 55, R.R. 5, ch. De la rivière, Magog JIX 3W5	(819) 843-1521	Massothérapie, relation d'aide, balancement énergérique, REIKI, voyance, ateliers de croissance personnelle.
Marie-Claude Nadeau 1400, Jean-Devin, # 2 Ancienne-Lorette G2E 5J3	(418) 871-4251	Astrologue Animatrice d'ateliers de croissance personnelle.
Sylvie Desaulniers 4614, Caroline-Valin Cap-Rouge GIY 3RI	(418) 658-3838	Acupunctrice
Nicole Cloutier 74, Verret, #6 Loretteville G2B IG8	(418) 847-4572	Massage, relation d'aide, régression, REIKI, homéopathie, fleurs de Bach, ateliers de crois- sance personnelle.
Héléna Marcoux 1238, rue de l'Espérance Ancienne-Lorette (Québec) G2E IT6	(418) 877-4410 Fax : (418) 864-7714 Email : heletal.intl@videotron.ca	Formatrice en massothé- rapie et en respiration consciente (rebirth), relation d'aide, ateliers de croissance personnelle.
Denise Laliberté 1474, avenue Saint-Joseph Plessisville G6L 2H6	(819) 621-0580	Psychothérapeute, Maître REIKI (formation et traitement), ateliers de croissance personnelle.

Références		
Liste des personnes que Jacques Martel a consultées ou avec lesquelles il travaille en collaboration		
nom/adresse	**téléphone**	**domaine d'activités**
La Giroflée 3320, chemin Sainte-Foy Sainte-Foy GIX IS3	(418) 658-7780	Magasins d'aliments naturels et produits de santé..
Alain Rossette Rue de la Bastidonne 13678 Aubagne Cedex France	(33) 04 42 18 90 94	Thérapeute, hormonisation morphogénétique et hologrammique.

La liste ne comprend pas de médecin puisque
chacun a habituellement son médecin traitant.

BIBLIOGRAPHIE

Louise Hay, **Transformer votre vie**, éditions Soleil, 1990

Louise Hay, **L'amour sans condition**, éditions Vivez Soleil, 1992

Claudia Rainville, **Participez à l'Univers, Sain de Corps et d'Esprit**, éditions FRJ, 1989

Claudia Rainville, **Métamédecine, la guérison à votre portée**, éditions FRJ, 1995

Debbie Shapiro, **The body mind workbook**, Element Books limited, 1990

Lise Bourbeau, **Qui es-tu?**, éditions Écoute ton Corps, 1988

Shalila Sharamon & Bodo J. Baginski, **REIKI Guérir, Rééquilibrer grâce à la Force de Vie Universelle**, Guy Trédaniel, 1991

Brigitte Müller et Hordt H. Günther, **REIKI, Guéris toi-même**, Le courrier du Livre, 1994

Marguerite De Surany, **Pour une Médecine de l'Ame**, éditions Guy Trédaniel, 1987

Marguerite De Surany et Jean-Claude Jourdan, **Les deux inséparables Crâne-Colonne, union de l'âme et de l'esprit**, éditions Guy Trédaniel, 1992

Lavon J. Dunne, **NUTRITION ALMANAC (Third Edition)**, McGRAW-HILL, 1990

James F. Balch, M.D., Phyllis A. Balch, C.N.C., **Prescription for Nutritional Healing**, Avery publishing group inc., 1990

Encyclopédie de décodage biologique en corrélation psycho-cérébro-organique, Holoconcept

Claude Sabbah, **La biologie des êtres vivants décrite sous forme d'histoire naturelle**, notes de cours, séminaires 1, 2, 3, Holoconcept, 1997

Bertrand Duhaime, **L'humanité métaphysique**, A.U.M. Les ateliers universels de motivation

Michel Odoul, Rémy Portrait, **Cheveux, parle moi de moi. Le cheveu, fil de l'âme**, Édition Dervy, 1997

Claude-Gérard Sarrazin, **Le Symbolisme du corps Humain**, édition Sélect, 1981

Jean-Pierre Guiliani, **L'alphabet du corps humain**, Verlaque, 1997

Lise Benoît, Michel Thomas, **Techniques de guérison (le dictionnaire)**, L'art de s'apprivoiser, 1997

Serge Michalski et Louise Paradis, **L'effet choc des mots**, Louise Courteau, 1994

Serge Castonguay, **Ton corps te parle, écoute-le**, de Mortagne, 1988

George Howe Colt, **The healing revolution**, Life, september 1996

Réal Fournier, **Comment faire pour réapprendre à aimer être au monde**, Les immobilisations Saplu inc., 1992

Les chakras et l'énergie subtile de l'être, L'aumisme Kshetram

Barbara Ann Brennan, **Hands of light**, Bantam books, 1987

Hilarion, **Body signs**, Marcus books

Hilarion, **Answer**, Marcus books

Hilarion, **Symbols**, Marcus books

Hilarion, **Threshold**, Marcus books

COMMENTAIRES

Vous pouvez faire parvenir vos commentaires, vos suggestions, *vos expériences personnelles suite à l'utilisation de la technique d'intégration* décrite dans ce livre, à l'adresse suivante :

Par écrit :   **Les éditions ATMA internationales**
                      C.P. 8818
                      Québec (Québec) Canada
                      G1V 4N7

Par Fax :   **Fax : (418) 990-1115**

Par Internet : **Courrier électronique : info@atma.ca**

Les commentaires reçus deviennent la propriété de la maison d'édition. Cependant, la maison d'édition s'engage à ne divulguer que les initiales de l'auteur des commentaires, afin d'assurer la confidentialité dans le cas ou ceux-ci pourraient être utilisés pour faciliter la compréhension des principes décrits dans cet ouvrage ou dans des ouvrages futurs.

Adresse du site Internet : www.atma.ca

Courrier électronique : info@atma.ca

Pour recevoir une information sur les activités de Jacques Martel pour la Communauté Européenne, veuillez remplir et retourner le bulletin ci-dessous, à l'adresse suivante :

Holoconcept
Rue de la Bastidonne
13678 Aubagne Cedex – France

www.holoconcept.net

DEMANDE D'INFORMATION POUR LA C.E.E. CONCERNANT LES STAGES DE JACQUES MARTEL

Je souhaite recevoir une information pour les conférences et les stages de Jacques Martel qui auront lieu dans la Communauté Européenne.

Nom :.. Prénom :..

Adresse :..

....

Code Postal :.............................. Ville :..

Téléphone :.............................. Courriel :..

Profession :..

Holoconcept : Formation Continue no 9319746013   *Siret : 409 969 151 00029*

352

ATMA
Guide de relaxation et d'harmonisation

Disque Compact (CD) de détente guidée pour la guérison intérieure et l'ouverture de la conscience

LA MUSIQUE :

ATMA
Guide de relaxation
et d'harmonisation

Par Jacques Martel

Une détente en profondeur de toutes les parties du corps
plus une harmonisation des centres d'énergie
qui aide à être en contact avec son Être intérieur.

La musique originale a été composée spécialement pour ce moment de détente par **Claude Demers** , du Studio SÉLECSON, de Saint-Nicolas, dans la banlieue de Québec (Québec), Canada. **Elle a pour but de créer une ambiance de bien-être et d'ouverture**. Ainsi, des sons particuliers sont utilisés, tels que le son du vent, des cloches, de la flûte, des vagues, des violons, du roulement des tambours, etc. Toutes ces sonorités constituent des environnements acoustiques reconnus dans les mondes intérieurs et qui correspondent plus spécifiquement à des sons représentatifs du niveau de conscience dans lequel on se trouve.

De plus, **les arrangements musicaux aident la personne à s'ouvrir à partir de ses énergies de base et à les amener à des niveaux de réalité supérieurs**. La musique favorise aussi un rappel de la période qui a précédé notre venue en ce monde, créant ainsi un lien avec nos vies antérieures. En outre, certains arrangements permettent **d'harmoniser en douceur les deux hémisphères du cerveau** pour assurer de façon plus consciente l'intégration des énergies de guérison.

TEXTE DE DÉTENTE :
(42 min. 36 sec.)

DANS LA PREMIÈRE PARTIE, le texte de détente est **inspiré de l'approche méthaphysique du corps, utilisant la symbolique de**

chacune des parties du corps pour obtenir une détente plus en profondeur. Par exemple, les reins représentent nos peurs. Ainsi, « je laisse aller mes peurs... » et « j'accepte de faire confiance en moi-même et dans la vie... » permettent de faire le lien entre la partie de mon corps qui est conncernée et la partie qui lui est correspondante sur le plan des émotions ou des pensées. L'expression **« J'ACCEPTE »** utilisée dans le texte de détente réfère à l'intégration, au niveau du coeur, d'une situation donnée. Ici, **« J'ACCEPTE »** veut dire j'ouvre mon coeur à la transformation de mon être dans l'amour pour une plus grande ouverture de ma conscience.

DANS LA DEUXIÈME PARTIE, la lumière se manifestant dans les centres d'énergie (chakras) **permet une plus grande harmonisation de l'être avec son environnement physique et spirituel, un plus grand équilibre de l'énergie circulant dans le corps physique et dans les corps subtils.** C'est aussi une autre façon d'ouvrir la conscience à des changements harmonieux. Les suggestions qui sont faites permettent également d'ouvrir davantage les canaux énergétiques naturels en référant à l'essence de chaque centre d'énergie par la couleur appropriée, soit le blanc (de haut en bas) et les couleurs correspondantes (du bas vers le haut). Les cloches permettent d'amplifier la portée de la suggestion et de produire un point d'ancrage plus significatif dans le physique.

OBJECTIF DE LA DÉTENTE :

Afin de nous ouvrir davantage à la vie, la détente favorise une diminution du niveau de tension générale du corps que le rythme de la vie moderne nous impose. La détente permet une conscientisation des différentes parties du corps en relation avec les pensées et les émotions. Il est ainsi possible que le corps réponde plus rapidement à un changement intérieur, permettant à la personne de faire les ajustement appropriés afin que ses pensées ou ses émotions soient davantage en harmonie avec son évolution. Un meilleur contact avec le moi supérieur ou un guide spirituel de haut niveau peut s'accomplir afin d'amener les énergies de guérison, les énergies de l'amour universel et inconditionnel, à se manifester.

Les prises de conscience intérieures ou l'ouverture de la conscience de l'intérieur peuvent mener à une **intégration de ses pensées ou de ses émotions,** conduisant à une guérison intérieure qui peut être suivie d'une guérison extérieure. La déten,te peut être utilisée par des personnes en santé pour leur permettre d'atteindre un niveau d'harmonie plus élévé. Les personnes vivant une situation de maladie, pour leur part,

profiteront grandement de cette détente. L'écoute de ce message de détente procurera aux personnes atteintes de maladies dites « chroniques » certains bienfaits, comme elle aidera les personnes en phase terminale à quitter ce monde avec plus de douceur, de calme et de paix intérieure. De plus, par la détente, les enfants, nouveau-nés ou autres, peuvent être amenés à accepter davantage leur corps physique dans ce monde.

PARTIE MUSICALE
(19 min. 10 sec.)

Sur la partie musicale du CD, on retrouve la musique qui a servi à la détente. Après plusieurs écoutes du message de détente, l'utilisateur peut, en n'écoutant que la partie musicale, parvenir à une détente complète du corps sans les paroles. Les adeptes de musique de détente ou nouvel âge apprécieront la partie musicale du CD. Au total (partie détente et musicale), on crée ainsi une ambiance de détente de plus de 61 minutes idéale, pour se reposer ou dormir.

Rêver plus efficacement, est-ce possible ? OUI !

Je peux écouter le CD en me couchant le soir et en l'écoutant pendant 21 jours et ainsi créer une ambiance intérieure propice à travailler avec le **Maître du Rêve** afin que je puisse vivre les situations les meilleures pour mon évolution.

La détente aide à neutraliser certains effets négatifs qui se sont produits dans la journée et **me permet de dormir dans un sommeil plus réparateur**. Ainsi, je détends tout mon corps et je m'ouvre aux énergies d'amour pour que s'effectuent en moi les transformations les plus appropriées selon mon évolution, en douceur et en profondeur. Même si je m'endors pendant l'écoute, le travail se fait pareil.

La détente peut être jouée dans la chambre de jeunes enfants (même de quelques mois) pour leur bénéfice et leur apporter la compréhension nécessaire au niveau du coeur à leur intégration graduelle en ce monde.

Pour aider à harmoniser ses chakras à tous les jours

En effet, le CD permet dans un premier temps de **détendre toutes les parties du corps** en utilisant la signification métaphysique au niveau des pensées ou des émotions de chacune des parties du corps. Chaque partie du corps est reliée directement ou indirectement à l'un ou l'autre des chakras et prépare ceux-ci à une plus grande ouverture.

La deuxième partie aide à **harmoniser les chakras**, utilisant la lumière blanche de haut en bas et jusqu'à la terre ; aussi, la lumière blanche provenant de la terre mère illumine les sept chakras du bas vers le haut de leur couleur correspondante, pour ainsi tendre vers un équilibre parfait.

Ceci permet d'atteindre un état de bien-être et de sérénité pour m'amener à vivre davantage de bonheur dans ma vie.

ATMA
Le corps de Cristal, le corps de Lumière

Une détente qui favorise l'harmonie et la guérison dans tout le corps et m'ouvre à la dimension de mon corps de Lumière.

DANS LA PREMIÈRE PARTIE de la détente, un liquide orangé qui entre dans mon enveloppe de cristal aide à réparer et régénérer tous les tissus de mon corps. De plus, mes molécules d'ADN qui contrôlent le développement de mes cellules sont harmonisées avec les énergies de l'univers afin d'aider chacune de mes cellules à atteindre une santé parfaite.

DANS LA DEUXIÈME PARTIE de la détente une lumière blanche se manifeste à l'intérieur de mon corps de cristal afin de me permettre de découvrir toute la dimension de mon corps de lumière avec l'ouverture de conscience correspondante.

OBJECTIF DE LA DÉTENTE : permettre à mon corps de garder une santé optimale ou d'aider à la rétablir en purifiant le corps physique et énergétique et, ensuite, d'ouvrir la conscience pour permettre de garder l'amour ou ramener cet amour dans la situation qui a engendré la non-harmonie, cause de la maladie.

Un complément idéal au CD : « **ATMA, Guide de relaxation et d'harmonisation** », ainsi qu'au livre : « Le **grand dictionnaire des malaises et des maladies** » par le même auteur Jacques Martel, psychothérapeute.

Disponible dans les librairies du Québec et distribué par Québec-Livres.

NOUVEAU CD

« ATMA, la musique des Sphères »

ATMA, la musique des Sphères

Cette musique permet l'ouverture de conscience et peut être utilisée lors de séances de méditation, de traitement énergétique, de relaxation, de REIKI, de massage, etc.

La musique me permet de vivre un état de bien-être. Elle aide à élever la conscience et à la maintenir en harmonie avec l'être intérieur. Elle m'emmène vers des sphères plus élevées afin que j'accepte ⬇❤ de plus en plus la **lumière** en moi. Cette musique permet l'ouverture de conscience et peut être utilisée lors de séances de méditation, de traitement énergétique, de relaxation, de REIKI, de massage, etc.

Titre des pièces :

1. Retour à la Source
Extrait musical de « ATMA, le corps de Cristal, le corps de Lumière » © 2000

2. Sprirale Cosmique
Extrait musical de « ATMA, Guide de relaxation et d'harmonisation » © 2000

3. Conscience
Extrait de l'album « Terre de Vie » © 1992

Musique originale composée par Claude Demers et Studio Sélecson, Lévis (Québec) Canada

Disponible dans les librairies du Québec et distribué par Québec-Livres.

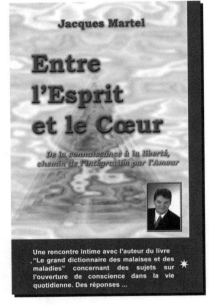

359

À PARAÎTRE À L'AUTOMNE 2003

ATMA,
Le chant
de l'Univers, HU

Un mantra universel qui ouvre la conscience, apporte la protection et aide à retrouver le chemin du retour à la Source.

TABLE DES MATIÈRES

Certaines maladies ont été regroupées afin qu'elles soient plus près de leurs compléments d'information. C'est ainsi que ce qui se rapporte directement au **SANG** a été regroupé en utilisant les renvois appropriés tels que :

ANÉMIE (voir : SANG — ANÉMIE)
DIABÈTE (voir : SANG — DIABÈTE)
HYPOGLYCÉMIE (voir : SANG — HYPOGLYCÉMIE)
LEUCÉMIE (voir : SANG — LEUCÉMIE)

Ainsi, pour avoir le plus d'information possible sur l'**ANÉMIE,** je devrai lire les articles suivants :

SANG (en général)
SANG (maux de...)
SANG — ANÉMIE

Dans le cas où je me retrouve dans une sous-section, par exemple si je veux de l'information sur l'**ANÉMIE,** je la retrouve sous **SANG — ANÉMIE**. Même si ce n'est pas inscrit dans **voir aussi,** cela suppose que <u>je devrai lire</u> la partie **SANG (en général)** et **SANG (maux de...)**.

De la même façon, lorsque je me retrouve dans une autre sous-section, comme pour **ECZÉMA** que je retrouve dans **PEAU — ECZÉMA,** je devrai lire aussi l'information sur **PEAU (en général)** et **PEAU (maux de...)**. Il en sera de même pour les autres sections lorsque les mentions **(en général)** et **(maux de...)** apparaîtront.

Parmi les malaises, maladies ou parties du corps qui regroupent plusieurs malaises ou maladies, mentionnons :

ALLERGIES	DOIGTS	OREILLES
ANUS	DOS	OS
ARTHRITE	ESTOMAC	PEAU
BOUCHE	FOIE	PIEDS
BRONCHES	GLANDES	POUMONS
CANCER	GORGE	REINS
CERVEAU	INTESTINS	RESPIRATION
CHEVEUX	JAMBES	SANG
CŒUR	MUSCLES	SEINS
COLONNE VERTÉBRALE	NEZ	VAGIN
DENTS	ONGLES	YEUX

Comment les malaises et les maladies sont-ils classés ?

De façon générale, ils sont inscrits dans la table des matières, par ordre alphabétique du malaise ou de la maladie comme, par exemple :

ACIDOSE 5

Cette maladie est dans les « A » à la page 5.

Lorsqu'on retrouve la mention suivante :

ADDISON (maladie d'...) 7

On remplace les « **...** » par le titre qui précède la parenthèse, c'est-à-dire : **maladie d'ADDISON.**

Lorsque, après le nom de la maladie, on a la mention « voir » entre parenthèses ( ), comme dans l'exemple suivant :

EMBONPOINT (voir : POIDS [excès de...])

nous devons nous reporter à **POIDS (excès de...)** et retrouver dans les « P » le titre de cette maladie pour avoir l'information sur la maladie elle-même en rapport avec EMBONPOINT.

On peut aller chercher un complément d'information sur la maladie elle-même ou sur des aspects qui s'y rattachent en consultant d'autres maladies. Ainsi la mention **« voir aussi »** nous conduit à un complément d'information sur la maladie qui est présenté comme suit :

AGORAPHOBIE (voir aussi : ANGOISSE, MORT, PEUR)

Si, par exemple, je me retrouve dans la partie **« voir aussi »** qui suit la maladie, indiquée ici avec la barre oblique /, comme l'exemple qui suit :

CHEVEUX — TEIGNE
    (voir aussi : CHEVEUX / CALVITIE / PELADE / [perte de...])

cela devra se lire :   (voir aussi : CHEVEUX — CALVITIE,
                      CHEVEUX — PELADE,
                      CHEVEUX [perte de...])

Afin que l'exercice de prononciation soit plus efficace, je m'imagine que mes paroles sortent de moi au niveau du cœur comme si ma bouche se trouvait au niveau de mon cœur. Il s'ensuit que je puis ressentir au cœur de l'exercice soit des picotements dans différentes parties de mon corps, des courants de chaleur qui peuvent se promener dans différentes parties de mon corps, aussi de la peine, de la tristesse ou toute autre sorte d'émotions qui peuvent monter. Il suffit de rester calme si des émotions fortes de peine ou de tristesse se manifestent car les choses sont habituellement sous contrôle et c'est comme si mon corps savait ce qu'il est capable de prendre.

Si pour une raison ou pour une autre, j'avais des craintes de vivre trop d'émotions, je peux faire l'exercice en ayant une personne qui peut me soutenir dans ce que je vis, une personne responsable ou un thérapeute.

Je peux faire cet exercice, si je le désire, après une méditation ou après l'écoute d'une musique de détente ou d'une détente dirigée. Je peux faire l'exercice, aussi, en prenant le texte de la préface ou le texte d'introduction.

Les informations qui suivent visent à donner davantage d'explications sur l'utilisation de cette technique d'intégration. D'abord, précisons que, pour moi, le terme "intégration" réfère au fait de devenir conscient dans son être ; cela veut aussi dire, dans une certaine mesure, "guérison" au sens que le malaise où la maladie ne sont qu'un message que le corps m'envoie pour me permettre de faire une prise de conscience sur ce que je vis présentement.

J'ai d'abord utilisé cette technique dans les ateliers "Retrouver l'Enfant en Soi" que je donne depuis mars '93. Elle est utilisée dans le cas où l'adulte écrit une lettre à son enfant intérieur et lorsque l'enfant intérieur répond à l'adulte.

Que se passe-t-il lors de l'application cette technique qui consiste à lire syllabe par syllabe le texte en prenant au moins une seconde pour chaque syllabe. Ce qu'il faut comprendre d'abord, c'est que plus vite je lis et plus ma lecture se situe au niveau de mon mental, dans ma tête. Plus je lis lentement, plus la lecture est en contact avec le centre d'énergie du cœur aussi appelé chakra du cœur. Tous les malaises et les maladies sont des interprétations, conscientes ou inconscientes, que j'ai faites par rapport à une situation ou une personne d'un manque d'amour. Alors, c'est comme si ce message, ou même cette blessure, pourrions-nous dire, a été enregistré au niveau de l'amour qui correspond, pour l'être humain, au centre d'énergie du cœur.

Mes blessures par rapport à un manque d'amour sont enregistrées dans mon cœur sous forme de rejet, d'abandon, de colère, d'incompréhension, de tristesse, de déception etc. . Pour pouvoir faire le changement de ce message enregistré à l'intérieur de moi-même, je dois activer l'information au point de départ, c'est-à-dire je dois être en contact avec le dossier qui fait que cette blessure a enregistré une information qui s'active lorsqu'une situation semblable se produit dans ma vie. C'est comme si la situation permettait d'activer l'émotion parce qu'elle est mise en résonance par l'événement qui se produit.

Ainsi, lorsque j'active la situation dans mon cœur qui m'a causé de la peine, de la tristesse, de la colère, etc., j'ouvre ainsi le centre d'énergie du cœur à laisser entrer l'énergie d'amour pour apporter la guérison et, par le fait même, la prise de conscience qui l'accompagne ou vice-versa.

© Technique d'intégration par prononciation monosyllabique rythmique et séquentielle

Je peux me servir des informations contenues dans le livre pour effectuer des changements au niveau de mes émotions. En procédant à l'exercice qui suit, je peux activer ma mémoire émotive et permettre que, de ma tête vers mon cœur ↓♥, une partie des émotions soit guérie dans l'amour.

Il s'agit que je prenne le texte d'un malaise ou d'une maladie et que je le lise syllabe par syllabe, en prenant au moins une seconde par syllabe. Par exemple, prenons la maladie suivante : l'**arthrite**. Le texte qui suit :

ARTHRITE (en général)

L'**arthrite** est définie comme étant l'inflammation d'une articulation. Elle peut affecter chacune des parties du système locomoteur humain : que ce soit les os, les ligaments, les tendons ou les muscles. Elle se caractérise par de l'inflammation, de la raideur musculaire et de la douleur qui **correspondent** sur le plan métaphysique à de la **fermeture,** de la **critique,** du **chagrin,** de la **tristesse** ou de la **colère.**

<u>devient</u> :

AR-THRI-TE (en-gé-né-ral)

L'**ar-thri-te**-est-dé-fi-nie-com-me-é-tant-l'in-flam-ma-tion-d'u-ne-ar-ti-cu-la-tion.-El-le-peut-af-fec-ter-cha-cu-ne-des-par-ties-du-sys-tè-me-lo-co-mo-teur-hu-main,-que-ce-soit-les-os,-les-li-ga-ments,-les-ten-dons-ou-les-mus-cles.El-le-se-ca-rac-té-ri-se-par-de-l'in-flam-ma-tion,-de-la-rai-deur-mus-cu-lai-re-et-de-la-dou-leur-qui-**cor-res-pon-dent**-sur-le-plan-mé-ta-phy-si-que-à-de-la-**fer-me-tu-re**,-de-la-**cri-ti-que**,-du-**cha-grin**,-de-la-**tris-tes-se**-ou-de-la-**co-lè-re**...

<u>Et je continue la lecture avec le texte au complet</u> que je lis dans le livre. **Il est très important d'aller très lentement,** <u>au plus une syllabe par seconde ou plus lentement encore</u>. Il n'est pas important que je me demande si mon intellect comprend ou non les mots ou les phrases que je prononce. Il se peut qu'il y ait des émotions de peine ou de tristesse qui se manifestent pendant l'exercice ; il s'agit de mettre de l'amour dans la situation. Je peux prendre le texte d'une maladie que j'ai présentement ou d'une maladie que j'ai déjà eu ou d'une maladie que je pourrais avoir peur de contracter. Si je vis des émotions pendant l'exercice, je peux le reprendre plus tard dans la journée ou une autre journée, jusqu'à ce que je ne vive plus d'émotions et que je me sente à l'aise avec le texte.

Groundé : vient du terme anglais " ground" signifiant la terre. Ici, cela se rapporte au fait de se sentir connecté à la terre ou au monde matériel. Cela peut vouloir dire quelqu'un qui est "réaliste" en opposition à une autre personne que l'on pourrait dire qu'elle est dans les "nuages" au sens figuré.

Intégrer : fait référence au fait d'assimiler une situation ou une idée à l'intérieur de moi. Lorsque cela fait référence à une blessure émotionnelle et que je dis que j'ai intégré la situation, cela veut dire que j'ai complètement guéri la blessure intérieure qui était rattachée à cette situation et que j'ai fait la prise de conscience qui allait avec cette expérience.

Ma bulle : expression utilisée pour faire référence à l'espace qui m'entoure et qui m'appartient, mon espace vital au niveau énergétique.

Mon Moi supérieur : cela fait référence à la partie supérieure de moi-même qu'on appelle conscience, âme, etc.

Mon guide intérieur : comme pour l'explication du " moi supérieur ", cela fait référence à cette partie qui est à l'intérieur de moi et qui peut me guider, si cela fait partie de ma croyance.

Occultation : le fait d'effacer de ma mémoire consciente ou de ma sensibilité.

Pattern : provient du terme anglais "pattern" qui signifie ici *un schéma de pens*ée qui fait se répéter des événements dans ma vie.

Psychique : qui se situe au niveau de mes pensées, au niveau mental.

Réincarnation : c'est un aspect qui est de plus en plus abordé dans les nouvelles approches thérapeutiques et c'est pourquoi l'auteur y fait référence à l'occasion. Cependant, l'auteur veut que le lecteur se sente tout à fait libre d'adhérer ou non à cette idée sachant que les mentions faites au sujet de la réincarnation le sont qu'à titre d'information seulement.

Yin et Yang : le Yin est le nom que l'on donne en médecine chinoise pour l'énergie de polarité négative, féminine ou intuitive; le Yang est celui que l'on donne à l'énergie de polarité positive, masculine ou rationnelle. On rencontre ces termes, Yin et Yang, en acupuncture entre autre. Lorsque les termes Yin et Yang sont utilisées dans le texte, ils réfèrent à la polarité énergétique ou à l'aspect intuitif ou rationnel en nous plutôt qu'à l'acupuncture.

Cependant, la personne qui utilise ce livre pour son information le fait pour elle-même, et c'est son droit le plus strict. L'auteur et l'éditeur déclinent toute responsabilité pour les actes qui pourraient être posés à la suite de la lecture de ce livre et qui pourraient amener le lecteur à poser des gestes ou à prendre des décisions pouvant aller à l'encontre de son bien-être.

Le masculin est employé dans le texte dans le but de simplifier et d'alléger l'écriture et, sauf dans les cas de certaines maladies propres aux hommes ou aux femmes, le texte, rédigé au masculin, s'adresse autant aux femmes qu'aux hommes.

Ma faculté mentale fonctionne parfois avec les homonynes, des mots qui ont le même son lorsqu'on les prononce comme par exemple: les mots, les maux. Les exemples mentionnés dans ce livre font référence à l'expérience de l'auteur de son milieu québécois où la langue parlée est ce qu'on appelle le canadien français. D'autres références suivant d'autres milieux francophones pourront être trouvées éventuellement et pourront être ajoutées. Il n'en tient qu'à vous, aussi, de trouver les associations de mots qui pourraient être faites et qui permettraient d'expliquer davantage les sentiments, les pensées ou les émotions qui pourraient être reliés à une maladie.

↓♥ : Ce symbole que l'on retrouve dans le texte représente l'énergie associée à l'image mentale ou associée à une émotion liée à une situation que je fais passer de ma tête vers mon cœur ! Il s'y produit alors soit une guérison dans l'amour, soit le renforcement d'une attitude positive.

La plupart des termes ou expressions qui suivent ont été expliqué en " bas de page " lorsqu'ils se présentaient pour la première fois. Cependant comme on ne lit habituellement pas un dictionnaire comme un roman, l'auteur a voulu reprendre les explications sur des termes ou expressions que l'on peut retrouver çà et là dans le texte pour clarifier le sens qu'il a voulu lui donner pour certains termes, entre autre, qui sont parfois utilisés dans le langage québécois et non pas nécessairement dans un langage de français international.

Dealer : provient du terme anglais " deal " qui veut dire une bonne affaire. Ici, cela signifie souvent relever un défi ou bien composer avec les événements ou les situations de la vie qui se présentent.

Être correct : expression voulant dire être en accord avec mes valeurs personnelles, quelles soient en harmonie ou non avec celles de la société, ou avec celles de la société dans laquelle je vis et auxquelles je m'identifie.

GÉNÉRALITÉS

Ce livre constitue un document de recherche sur « l'aspect » métaphysique (pensées, sentiments, émotions) des malaises et des maladies. Des mises à jour sont à prévoir dans le futur et elles seront faites sur le réseau Internet[3]. Aussi l'auteur s'excuse à l'avance pour toute erreur qui aurait pu se glisser et invite le lecteur à lui faire part de telles erreurs directement sur le site Internet ou par écrit.

L'auteur de ce livre ne prétend pas donner de conseil médical directement ou indirectement. Il ne prétend pas non plus poser de diagnostic directement ou indirectement. Les idées contenues dans ce livre le sont à titre d'information, comme possibilité d'investigation d'un malaise ou d'une maladie afin d'aider la personne elle-même, le médecin traitant ou le thérapeute à mieux comprendre l'origine du malaise ou de la maladie.

Les affirmations contenues dans ce livre ne le sont qu'à titre d'information. L'auteur est conscient du fait que les malaises et les maladies traités dans ce livre sont abordés à partir d'une approche métaphysique du malaise ou de la maladie et que plusieurs autres aspects relatifs à la santé peuvent être en cause. L'auteur est conscient du fait que les maladies peuvent être beaucoup plus complexes que ce qui est expliqué.

L'approche simplifiée de certaines maladies comme le cancer, le diabète, etc., a pour but de permettre au lecteur d'ouvrir une porte à la recherche de la cause métaphysique du malaise ou de la maladie avec un professionnel de la santé. L'idée de ce dictionnaire est d'abord de partir d'un point de vue simple du malaise ou de la maladie afin de rendre l'information le plus accessible possible à la compréhension d'un plus grand nombre de personnes. **Cette approche se veut complémentaire à toute approche allopathique[4] et holistique[5].**

Toute personne voulant apporter des changements à un traitement existant devrait en parler avec son médecin traitant ou son thérapeute professionnel. Les personnes vivant des situations de maladies telles que le diabète (insulino dépendant), les maladies cardiaques (nécessitant des comprimés journellement), etc., devront avoir un avis médical avant d'apporter des changements à leur médication, même si elles « croient » avoir trouvé la cause de leur maladie, et même si elles « croient » que tout est maintenant réglé et sous contrôle.

---

3. **Adresse Internet :** www.atma.ca

4. **Allopathique :** qui utilise un traitement médical dans le but de combattre la maladie. Ce terme sert habituellement à désigner la médecine conventionnelle.

5. **Holistique :** qui tient compte de l'aspect global de la personne, c'est-à-dire l'aspect physique, mental et émotionnel et même parfois, l'aspect spirituel.

Ce dictionnaire se veut un outil d'ouverture de conscience et de recherche pour soi-même. Lorsqu'il m'arrive quelque chose par rapport à ma santé, je vais relire ce qui est écrit dans ce dictionnaire afin d'être encore plus conscient de ce qui se passe. En effet, l'être humain a facilement tendance à occulter, c'est-à-dire à faire disparaître de sa mémoire consciente ce qui le dérange. Ainsi, lorsque je lis le dictionnaire, je le fais avec les yeux de quelqu'un qui veut apprendre et être davantage conscient de ce qui lui arrive. Mon côté mental et intellectuel prennent conscience de l'information avec laquelle je vais avoir à travailler. **Car le seul vrai pouvoir que j'ai, c'est le pouvoir sur moi-même; je suis créateur de ma vie. Plus j'en suis conscient, plus je peux faire les changements appropriés.**

Depuis un siècle, et plus particulièrement depuis les cinquante dernières années, nous avons fait un bond extraordinaire au point de vue technologique, ce qui a permis, dans bien des cas, d'améliorer nos conditions de vie. Malgré tout ce progrès, on ne se rend pas bien compte que la science n'a pas la réponse à tout et qu'il existe, sur cette planète, beaucoup d'hommes et de femmes qui souffrent de maladies. Que l'on vive dans des pays industrialisés ou en voie de développement, on doit prendre soin de soi et faire face aux questions suivantes : Qui suis-je ? Où vais-je ? Quel est mon but dans la vie ?

Il est important que je me serve de ce livre comme d'un outil de compréhension, d'investigation et de transformation. S'il me vient des idées nouvelles en lisant les textes, je dois me sentir à l'aise de les compléter avec mes propres mots. **Cet outil doit devenir un instrument vivant auquel chacun d'entre nous peut apporter sa contribution.** C'est ainsi que certains passages du livre ont été rédigés à la demande de personnes qui savaient que je travaillais à cet ouvrage. Ainsi, lorqu'on m'a demandé : « *Est-ce que tu as traité dans ton livre des allergies au beurre d'arachide ?* », la réponse a été : « *Non, mais je vais le faire.* » Il en a été de même pour plusieurs maladies qu'on m'a demandé d'inclure. C'est une des raisons pour lesquelles le livre est accessible sur Internet[2], non seulement pour la consultation, mais aussi pour y faire les mises à jour, y ajouter les commentaires des lecteurs, etc. Ceci permet une diffusion à la grandeur de la planète.

Je vous dis donc « bonne lecture » !

Jacques Martel
Psychothérapeute

---

2. **Adresse Internet :** www.atma.ca

à vivre des situations de malaises ou de maladies. Je dois donc prendre conscience de mon cheminement personnel ou, au sens large du terme, de mon cheminement spirituel. Là où j'ai découvert qu'il n'y avait pas ou peu d'amour, je dois redécouvrir que l'amour était présent quand même. Pas évident, me direz-vous ! Mais c'est comme ça. Si je me jette du haut d'un balcon et que je me casse une jambe, vais-je dire que Dieu m'a puni ? En fait, il existe une loi que l'on appelle la loi de la gravité qui tend à me ramener au sol. Cette loi n'est ni bonne, ni mauvaise, c'est la loi de la gravité. J'aurai beau argumenter et en vouloir à cette loi parce qu'à cause d'elle je me suis cassé une jambe ; cela ne changera rien à la loi car **LA LOI, C'EST LA LOI.** Ainsi, on explique toutes les maladies par un manque d'amour. On dit que **l'amour est le seul guérisseur.** Alors, si cela est vrai, ne suffirait-il pas simplement de donner de l'amour pour voir la guérison se manifester ? Cela est vrai, dans certains cas. En fait, c'est comme si l'amour devait entrer par certaines portes pour que la guérison se fasse, par ces portes qui ont été fermées à l'amour lors de mes blessures antérieures. Voilà tout un champ de découverte et de prise de conscience !

Ce livre ne vise pas directement à apporter des solutions aux malaises et aux maladies mais bien plus à m'aider à prendre conscience que ce que j'éprouve comme malaise ou comme maladie provient de mes pensées et de mes émotions et, qu'à partir de cela, je peux prendre les moyens que je juge à propos pour apporter des changements dans ma vie. Cependant, le seul fait de savoir d'où provient mon malaise ou ma maladie peut suffire à amener des changements dans mon corps physique. Dans certains cas, le changement positif peut être de 50 % et pouvant même aller jusqu'à 100 %, soit la guérison complète.

Pour ma part, lorsque j'ai connu les cours de croissance personnelle en 1988 et que j'ai pu prendre conscience des changements qui se passaient en moi, j'ai eu le sentiment que je commençais à renaître et j'ai vu poindre à l'horizon l'espoir de jours meilleurs. J'avais enfin trouvé un moyen de faire des changements importants dans ma vie et d'en voir les résultats. Il me fallait agir car j'étais en réaction par rapport à l'autorité, je vivais énormément de rejet, d'abandon et d'incompréhension. **Je savais tout cela mais encore fallait-il que je trouve le moyen de changer, de guérir mes blessures intérieures.** C'est pourquoi je me suis engagé dans ce domaine d'activité qu'est la croissance personnelle. Mon travail me permettait de travailler sur moi-même tout en travaillant avec les autres à les aider à ouvrir leur conscience. **Je crois sincèrement que chacun d'entre nous peut se prendre en main de façon de plus en plus autonome et que chacun d'entre nous peut accéder à un degré de sagesse, d'amour et de liberté supérieur ! Nous le méritons tous.**

douces. Il traite donc à la fois de l'approche allopathique, plus médicale, et de l'approche holistique qui comprend davantage l'aspect physique, mental, émotionnel et spirituel de mon être. Je souhaite ardemment que tous les professionnels de la santé, à quelque niveau qu'ils soient, se servent de ce dictionnaire comme complément à leur pratique, **comme outil de travail et d'investigation**, pour aider leurs patients dans leur processus de guérison. Pour ma part, j'ai expérimenté les opérations, la médecine traditionnelle, les médicaments, l'acupuncture, les traitements énergétiques, la radiesthésie, la naturopathie, les massages, la thérapie par les couleurs, la diététique, la vitaminothérapie, les essences florales du Dr Bach, la chiropratique, l'orthothérapie, l'iridologie, la psychothérapie, le rebirth (respiration consciente), l'homéopathie, etc. Je sais que si une technique était valable pour tout le monde, ce serait la seule qui existerait. Mais ce n'est pas le cas, car l'être humain est l'animal sur cette planète ayant le plus de possibilités mais aussi la plus grande complexité.

C'est la raison pour laquelle je dois essayer de comprendre par moi-même ce que je vis en me faisant aider par d'autres, au besoin, dans le domaine respectif de leur compétence. Le même auteur que je mentionnais plus haut écrivait un jour : « *ON DOIT APPRENDRE DE CEUX QUI SAVENT.* » C'est ainsi que je dois rechercher le meilleur de ce qui existe dans chacune des professions. Lorsque je me retrouve devant un médecin, je me dis qu'il en sait plus que moi sur la médecine et que je dois être attentif à ce qu'il me dit et à ce qu'il me propose, me laissant le libre choix de décider par la suite de mon orientation. De même, lorsque je me retrouve devant un acupuncteur, je suis attentif à ce qu'il me dit ou à ce qu'il me propose comme traitement parce qu'il connaît plus que moi le fonctionnement de l'équilibre énergétique de mon corps en fonction de mes méridiens. Il en va de même pour toutes les autres professions.

L'autre jour, une dame me disait qu'elle ne croyait pas à toutes ces histoires de pensées et d'émotions par rapport aux maladies. Je lui ai répondu que ce n'était pas nécessaire d'y croire. Après qu'on lui ait lu quelques textes qui se rapportaient à des malaises et à des maladies qu'elle avait déjà eus ou qu'elle avait encore, on a pu remarquer que son attitude avait changé et qu'elle était plus réceptive à cette approche. En fait, il y a une partie à l'intérieur de moi qui sait ce qui se passe et que ce qui est dit à mon sujet correspond à ce que je vis et que cela n'est pas dû au hasard. Il faut ici être prudent : je ne dois pas me sentir coupable de ce qui m'arrive et croire qu'on me dit que c'est ma faute si je suis malade. Je suis responsable de ce qui m'arrive mais, dans la plupart des cas, ce n'est pas ma faute. **C'est la méconnaissance des lois qui régissent les pensées et les émotions sur le corps physique qui m'amène**

ce que je sois suffisamment satisfait des résultats pour publier cet ouvrage. » Si je mentionne ceci, c'est aussi que cela demande beaucoup de travail, d'énergie et de volonté de faire des changements sur soi. Un auteur américain a écrit un jour : **« *Seuls les courageux et les aventureux auront l'expérience personnelle de Dieu.* »** Ce que je comprends de ce passage, c'est que ma détermination à relever les défis et le courage d'expérimenter des avenues nouvelles pour moi me procureront un certain état de réalisation et de bien-être. Cet état de bien-être correspond à la santé physique, mentale et émotionnelle.

De 1978 à 1988, j'ai travaillé dans le domaine de la supplémentation alimentaire que l'on peut appeler **l'approche orthomoléculaire,** qui veut dire « fournir à l'organisme les nutriments nécessaires, comme les vitamines, les minéraux et autres nutriments, sous forme de nourriture ou de suppléments alimentaires, pour aider à rétablir ou à maintenir **une santé optimale** ». Je me basais alors sur les travaux de psychiatres et autres médecins, biochimistes et divers chercheurs canadiens et américains (surtout) qui, par leur expérimentation, ont démontré qu'en donnant les nutriments nécessaires, on pouvait en arriver à améliorer, voire guérir dans certains cas la santé physique, mentale et émotionnelle. En fait, il existe plusieurs approches afin d'obtenir **une santé optimale** qui toutes ont leur importance, chacune d'elles agissant d'une façon ou d'une autre sur tous les aspects de notre être. En 1996, j'ai vu un reportage[1] à la télévision sur un hôpital, le Columbia-Presbyterian Hospital dans la ville de New York, où il était question d'un patient, monsieur Joseph Randazzo, qui allait être opéré pour trois pontages coronariens. Ce patient a bénéficié de séances de visualisation, de traitements énergétiques, de réflexologie avant son opération. Pendant l'opération, il bénéficiait de traitements énergétiques. Après son opération, ce même patient a participé à nouveau à des séances de visualisation, a reçu des traitements énergétiques et de réflexologie pour lui permettre de récupérer plus rapidement. Ces interventions ont porté fruit car le patient a récupéré beaucoup plus rapidement après cette opération majeure que ne l'aurait fait un autre patient dans des conditions habituelles. Le médecin pratiquant, Mehmet Oz, mentionnait qu'il faisait une telle expérimentation sur 300 de ses patients pour analyser les résultats de l'ajout de ces thérapies alternatives au traitement médical conventionnel.

Ainsi, le présent livre se veut un complément à toute approche, qu'elle soit médicale ou en lien avec les médecines

---

1. Aussi rapporté dans la revue *LIFE* de septembre 1996 sous le thème général « The **HEALING** revolution ».

de maladies. C'est pourquoi l'un des buts de ce livre est de démontrer qu'à quelque chose de non visible comme les pensées et les émotions, il y a une réaction qui, elle, est physique et mesurable, très souvent sous forme de malaises ou de maladies. Puis-je mesurer la colère ? Non, mais je peux prendre la mesure de ma fièvre lorsque j'en fais. Puis-je mesurer le fait que j'ai souvent l'impression d'avoir à me battre dans la vie pour obtenir ce que je veux ? Non, mais je peux mesurer le nombre de globules rouges sanguins qui ont diminué lorsque je fais de l'anémie. Puis-je mesurer le fait que la joie ne circule pas suffisamment dans ma vie ? Non, mais je peux mesurer mon taux de cholestérol sanguin trop élevé, et ainsi de suite. Alors, si je prends conscience des pensées et des émotions qui ont amené le malaise ou la maladie à prendre place, se peut-il qu'en changeant mes pensées ou mes émotions, je puisse ramener la santé ? J'ose affirmer que oui.

Cependant, cela peut être plus complexe ou plus profond que la partie où je peux en être conscient. C'est pourquoi je peux avoir besoin de faire appel à des personnes travaillant dans le domaine médical ou à d'autres personnes utilisant d'autres approches professionnelles pour m'aider à effectuer des changements dans ma vie. Si je dois me faire opérer et que je comprends ce qui m'a amené à vivre une telle situation, il est bien possible que je me remette beaucoup plus rapidement de mon opération qu'une autre personne qui n'a pas voulu savoir ce qui se passait dans sa vie ou qui l'ignorait tout simplement. De plus, si je n'ai pas compris le message de ma maladie, l'opération ou le traitement semblera faire disparaître cette maladie, mais cette dernière pourra se répercuter sur un autre aspect de mon corps, sous une autre forme, plus tard.

Il est à espérer qu'il y aura de plus en plus d'entreprises qui deviendront conscientes du bien-fondé d'aider leurs employés dans leur cheminement personnel, au plan émotionnel. Cela permettra de diminuer davantage les accidents dans l'entreprise et le taux d'absentéisme, et augmentera l'efficacité individuelle. Si ma vie personnelle, familiale ou professionnelle fait que je ne suis pas bien avec moi-même, j'aurai plus de chance de « m'attirer », même inconsciemment, une maladie ou un accident pour pouvoir prendre congé ou pour que l'on s'occupe de moi.

C'est en 1990 que m'est venue l'idée de rédiger un dictionnaire traitant des causes métaphysiques des malaises et des maladies, et en 1991 que je me suis mis à la tâche. À ce moment, je ne me doutais pas de la somme de travail qui m'attendait. Heureusement, car si je l'avais su, je crois que je n'aurais jamais mis en branle ce projet. Mais je m'étais dit « *Une chose à la fois ! Je vais y arriver ; je vais travailler jusqu'à*

faisait part ont été décodés assez rapidement et avec justesse, à mon grand plaisir. Quelque temps plus tard, une amie qui était dans l'assistance lors de cet atelier me dit : « *Jacques, tu devrais faire attention quand tu réponds aux gens et que tu donnes la réponse directement et rapidement. Les personnes qui étaient à mes côtés ont eu l'impression que l'atelier était arrangé pour que ça fonctionne.* » Il n'en était rien, bien entendu. Ce qu'il faut comprendre ici, c'est que premièrement, la personne qui est concernée par le malaise ou par la maladie sait que ce qui est énoncé est vrai pour elle mais ce n'est peut-être pas aussi évident pour les autres qui ne sont pas touchés personnellement. Deuxièmement, ce qui est nouveau et dévoilé à notre conscience peut nous sembler irréel. Nier cette réalité peut aussi être une façon de se protéger pour ne pas se sentir responsable de ce qui nous arrive.

Voici une anecdote illustrant ce constat. Le célèbre inventeur Thomas Edison rencontra les membres du Congrès américain pour leur présenter sa nouvelle invention, le phonographe, une machine parlante. Il est rapporté que lorsqu'il fit fonctionner son invention, certains membres du Congrès le traitèrent d'imposteur, disant qu'il devait y avoir une manigance quelconque puisque, pour eux, il était impossible que la voix humaine puisse sortir d'une boîte.

Les temps ont bien changé. C'est pourquoi il est important de rester ouvert aux nouvelles idées qui pourraient nous apporter des réponses innovatrices à bien des problèmes. Bien des personnes aux États-Unis et en Europe ont développé cette approche du lien qui existe entre les conflits des émotions et des pensées et la maladie, cela aide à faire connaître tout ce champ d'investigation non seulement au Québec (Canada) mais aussi ailleurs dans le monde.

Je dis souvent, au cours de mes conférences, que j'ai un mental qui est très fort mais que j'ai aussi une intuition très forte et que le plus grand défi de ma vie a été, et est encore aujourd'hui, de concilier les deux. Ma formation académique comme ingénieur électricien m'a amené à concrétiser l'aspect logique et rationnel des choses. La physique m'a enseigné qu'à une cause est lié un effet bien réel. C'est cette loi de cause à effet que, plus tard, j'ai pu appliquer au domaine des émotions et des pensées, quoi qu'il soit moins tangible que la physique elle-même. Mais est-ce bien vrai? Même dans un domaine qui relève de la physique comme l'électricité, on travaille avec quelque chose que l'être humain n'a jamais vu : l'électricité. Car en fait <u>on travaille avec les effets</u> comme la lumière, la chaleur, l'induction électromagnétique, etc. De la même façon, les pensées et les émotions ne sont pas nécessairement physiques au sens propre du terme mais peuvent avoir des répercussions physiques sous formes de malaises et

Je vois encore ces gens qui me regardent avec un air étonné et interrogateur, se demandant si je suis un voyant ou un extraterrestre pour savoir ainsi des choses sur leur vie personnelle sans qu'ils ne m'en aient parlé. En fait, la réponse est simple. Lorsqu'on sait décoder les malaises et les maladies et que l'on sait à quelles émotions ou à quelles pensées ils sont reliés, il est alors facile de dire à la personne ce qu'elle vit. Alors, je dis aux gens que c'est simplement la connaissance du fonctionnement de l'être humain et la connaissance des liens avec les pensées, les émotions et les maladies qui me permettent de donner cette information. Dans un sens, je leur explique que l'on pourrait entrer le plus de données possible dans un ordinateur et que quelqu'un pourrait donner les symptômes de son malaise ou de sa maladie, ou simplement de nommer celle-ci, et l'information pourrait sortir sur ce que le personne vit dans sa vie personnelle, qu'elle en soit consciente ou non. Alors, **ce n'est pas une question de voyance mais bien une question de connaissance.**

Aujourd'hui, avec l'expérience et les connaissances que j'ai, je puis affirmer qu'il est impossible qu'une personne souffre du diabète sans vivre de la tristesse profonde ou de la répugnance face à une situation qu'elle a vécue. Pour moi, il est impossible qu'une personne souffre de l'arthrite sans vivre de la critique envers elle-même ou quelqu'un d'autre ou envers des situations de sa vie. Pour moi, il est impossible qu'une personne vive des problèmes au foie sans vivre de la colère, de la frustration envers elle-même ou envers les autres, et ainsi de suite. On m'a parfois fait la réflexion suivante : « *Lorsque tu décodes les malaises et les maladies, " tu t'arranges " pour que cela fonctionne* ». On me dit alors que tout le monde vit de la colère, de la frustration, de la peine, du rejet, etc. À cela, je réponds que tout le monde ne réagit pas de la même façon. Prenons par exemple le fait que j'ai grandi dans une famille de douze enfants et dont le père était alcoolique et la mère, dépressive. Mes frères et mes sœurs auront eu les mêmes parents que moi mais chaque enfant, y compris moi-même, sera ou non affecté et le sera d'une façon différente en raison de son interprétation du vécu avec ses parents. Pourquoi? Parce que nous sommes tous différents et que nous avons à faire des prises de conscience différentes dans notre cheminement personnel. Ainsi, le phénomène de rejet pourra déclencher une maladie chez l'un et pas chez l'autre. **Cela dépend de la façon dont je me suis senti affecté, consciemment ou inconsciemment.** Si mon stress psychologique est suffisamment grand, il sera transposé dans un stress biologique sous forme de maladie.

Lors d'un atelier que je donnais sur l'approche métaphysique des malaises et des maladies, à l'occasion d'un salon sur la santé naturelle et les thérapies alternatives, les malaises et les maladies dont on me

INTRODUCTION

La santé a toujours été pour moi un sujet préoccupant. En effet, dès mon jeune âge, j'ai commencé à éprouver des problèmes de santé sans connaître exactement la cause de ceux-ci. Ma mère a été confrontée à des situations difficiles qui, pendant de nombreuses années, ont demandé des soins tels que des opérations, des traitements et qui ont occasionné des années d'hospitalisation.

En ce qui me concerne, comme on n'arrivait pas à trouver exactement ce que j'avais, c'est comme si un doute planait constamment : je croyais que ces maux pouvaient être psychologiques. Je me suis dit alors : soit que c'est « dans ma tête », soit qu'il y a une raison à ce qui se passe. J'ai décidé d'opter pour le deuxième choix et c'est alors que j'ai commencé à chercher ce qui m'amenait à vivre tous ces inconvénients.

En 1978, j'ai commencé à travailler dans le domaine de la santé, dans la supplémentation alimentaire. C'est alors que j'ai commencé à me rendre compte par moi-même, au cours des consultations individuelles que je faisais et par mon observation, qu'il pouvait exister un lien entre les émotions, les pensées et les maladies. J'avais commencé intuitivement à découvrir le lien qui existait entre certaines émotions et certaines maladies. C'est en 1988, alors que je me suis inscrit à des cours de croissance personnelle, que j'ai été mis en contact avec ce que l'on appelle aujourd'hui **l'approche métaphysique des malaises et des maladies.** Je nous revois, moi et d'autres, consultant la compilation des malaises et des maladies que Louise Hay avait faite dans son livre. Aussi, j'observais les gens qui commençaient leur investigation sur eux-mêmes ou sur les autres afin de vérifier le bien-fondé de ce qu'elle avançait, tout passionnés qu'ils étaient de découvrir des nouvelles avenues de recherche pour leur permettre de mieux comprendre ce qu'ils vivaient.

À partir de ce moment, mon intérêt pour cette approche n'a cessé d'augmenter, d'autant plus que je me réorientais dans le domaine plus spécifique de la croissance personnelle. Depuis ce jour, je n'ai cessé de vérifier, à travers mes consultations individuelles, les cours ou les ateliers que j'anime, la pertinence de ces données sur les malaises et les maladies. Aujourd'hui encore, je me vois, soit à l'épicerie ou lorsque je vais faire des photocopies, poser des questions à des personnes sur ce qu'elles vivent en rapport avec leurs malaises ou leurs maladies.

C'est ce que ce livre, que je considère comme un outil de transformation exceptionnel, se propose d'être. C'est une fenêtre ouverte sur ce monde encore très inconnu des émotions. Il est un instrument qui me donne la possibilité de m'ouvrir à la graine qui a permis que ce microbe, ce virus, cette tumeur ou toute autre affection physique germe dans mon corps et fasse irruption au grand jour. En me permettant de m'aimer et de m'accepter ↓♥ à travers toutes ces émotions mal ou non vécues, je ferai un pas vers plus d'harmonie, plus de paix, plus d'amour.

En apprenant à **déchiffrer** ce **nouveau dictionnaire des émotions,** je vais maintenant pouvoir investir sur mon **capital santé**, étant maintenant capable de prévenir et d'éviter bien des malaises qui me guettaient.

Au cours de ces dernières années où j'ai collaboré avec Jacques à la naissance de ce livre, j'ai été surprise de voir la somme de temps (des milliers d'heures) qu'il a fallu y investir, sans compter toute l'énergie et l'ouverture requises pour canaliser toutes ces informations qui étaient mal gérées et qui, bien souvent, touchaient soit une période de ma vie personnelle ou une situation vécue par une personne que je connaissais.

Nous avons tous été au moins une fois « malades » dans notre vie et le fait de « décortiquer » la cause d'un mal qui nous affecte ou affecte une personne proche nous amène à nous détacher (dans le sens de voir une maladie d'une façon positive et de nous défaire de l'emprise négative que nous lui laissons avoir sur nous) et à devenir un témoin et non plus une victime de tous ces maux.

C'est ce que je nous souhaite à tous, par l'entremise de cet outil. Que chacun d'entre nous devienne de plus en plus autonome, de plus en plus capable de reconnaître d'où proviennent les malaises et les maladies qui l'affectent ou pourraient l'affecter. Cette reconnaissance servira de prévention et apportera les changements nécessaires dans notre vie afin de regagner la santé. Il s'agit d'un complément extraordinaire qui s'ajoute à la multitude de techniques qui existent déjà, autant au niveau de la médecine traditionnelle que nouvelle, et qui s'avère essentiel non seulement pour une guérison au niveau physique, mais aussi au niveau du cœur (de l'amour) ↓♥, là où a lieu la vraie guérison...

À votre santé !

Lucie Bernier
Psychothérapeute,
Coordonnatrice des travaux

PRÉFACE

J'accepte ↓♥ ma guérison

Prendre conscience de qui je suis et de ce que je suis en train de devenir est toujours très excitant quand ce que je découvre par rapport à moi-même et face aux autres est beau et positif. Qu'en est-il lorsque les découvertes qui résultent d'un cheminement personnel, quel qu'il soit, m'amènent à voir des facettes cachées de ma personne et qu'elles impliquent que je devienne consciente des malaises et des maladies qui me sont arrivés ou qui auraient probablement pris place à l'intérieur de mon corps ?

Eh bien, c'est ce qui s'est passé tout au long de ces deux dernières années lorsque j'ai réalisé que les maladies s'étaient subtilement installées à cause d'émotions mal gérées et, qu'en apprenant à réharmoniser ce tourbillon d'émotions de toutes sortes qui m'habitaient, je pouvais avoir le pouvoir de guérison sur n'importe quel malaise ou n'importe quelle maladie que j'avais laissé s'installer en roi et maître dans mon **Temple de Chair.**

Bien sûr, la responsabilité que j'ai acceptée ↓♥ de reprendre face à ma santé a été un long processus d'introspection et de remise en question de mes valeurs et surtout, m'a apporté **la certitude que j'ai le pouvoir de me guérir.** Pour ce faire, j'ai eu le privilège, depuis maintenant neuf ans (1988), de connaître et de côtoyer Jacques et de pouvoir acquérir des connaissances lors des multiples conférences et ateliers qu'il a donnés. Par sa facilité à rendre simple et accessible un sujet qui pour plusieurs peut sembler très complexe, par son amour inconditionnel et son désir d'aider les gens à atteindre un plus grand bien-être autant physique, émotionnel que spirituel, il a été et est toujours un pilier, un guide qui sait m'aider à faire fuir ma culpabilité et à la remplacer par une prise en charge de ma vie, afin que je me sente de plus en plus libre, bien dans ma peau, maître de ma vie. Jacques m'a aidée à accepter ↓♥ la maladie, quelle qu'elle soit, comme une expérience positive, car elle est pour moi une occasion de m'arrêter, de m'interroger sur ce qui se passe dans ma vie. Pour bien des gens comme moi, la maladie m'a donné l'occasion de demander de l'aide, chose que je veux bien souvent éviter. Je dois me souvenir que **tomber, c'est humain ; mais se relever, c'est divin** et que, pour amorcer un processus de guérison, il est essentiel de s'ouvrir aux autres, de s'ouvrir à soi-même et, en tout premier lieu, de s'ouvrir à l'**Amour**, car tout malaise ou toute maladie peut guérir si je suis prête à accepter ↓♥ de laisser tomber mes œillères et à jeter un regard nouveau et positif sur toute situation que je peux vivre, aussi difficile puisse-t-elle être, car je sais que, lorsque j'aurai compris dans mon cœur la venue de cette expérience dans ma vie, elle pourra continuer sa route et je recouvrerai une santé parfaite.

REMERCIEMENTS

Je tiens à remercier d'une façon particulière **madame Lucie Bernier**, non seulement pour son travail de coordination des travaux du livre mais aussi pour son aide précieuse comme **collaboratrice** durant les deux dernières années de la production du livre. Son expérience de vie personnelle, de psychothérapeute, sa formation dans l'approche métaphysique des malaises et des maladies, son esprit de synthèse et son intuition ont permis de faire progresser les travaux de ce livre de façon significative.

Un merci spécial à **M. Claude Sabbah** qui, par ses recherches depuis plus de 30 ans, son expertise exceptionnelle, sa grande expérience et son enseignement de la biologie totale des êtres vivants sous forme d'histoire naturelle m'a permis d'aller encore plus loin dans les recherches et les constatations que j'avais faites à ce jour. Son esprit ouvert et son amour pour l'être humain sont pour moi un exemple à perpétuer, sachant que l'amour est le seul guérisseur dans le travail que nous accomplissons pour résoudre les conflits ayant amené la maladie à se manifester.

Je veux remercier aussi **monsieur George Wright**, psychothérapeute et ami personnel, pour son support constant et son encouragement face au travail que je trouvais parfois long et laborieux au cours des sept années de la production du livre.

Merci aussi à **madame Claudia Rainville** qui m'a permis de travailler à ses côtés (1988-89), avec qui j'ai pu approfondir et bénéficier de ses connaissances dans le domaine de la métaphysique des malaises et des maladies. Son dynamisme et ses convictions personnelles, alliés à son expérience, ont été pour moi une source de motivation dans la poursuite de mon orientation professionnelle axée davantage dans le domaine de la croissance personnelle.

Je tiens aussi à remercier les personnes suivantes pour leur participation à la réalisation de ce livre :

Mme Nicole Gagné	M. Jean Dumas
Mme Ginette Plante	Mme Ginette Caron
Mme Denise Quintal	Mme Danielle East
M. Simon Alarie	Mme Louise Drouin
M. Paul-Émile Drouin	M. Laurent Chiasson
Mme Denise Boucher	M. Bob Lenghan
M. Pierre Couture	Mme Fleurette Couture

Mon père : Noé Martel

Ce livre est dédié à tous les chercheurs de Vérité.

Infographie :

Pur Design communication visuelle inc. ☎ (418) 871-5883
3075, boulevard Hamel, bureau 232   Fax : (418) 877-4830
Québec (Québec)   www.pur-design.com
Canada G1P 4C6   info@pur-design.com

Distributeur pour le Canada :

Québec-Livres
2185, Autoroute des Laurentides   ☎ (450) 687-1210
Laval (Québec)   Fax : (450) 687-1331
Canada H7S 1Z6

Distributeur pour la Suisse :

Diffusion Transat SA   ☎ ++41(0)22/342.77.40
Route des Jeunes   Fax : ++41(0)22/343.46.46
Case Postale 1210
1211 Genève 26
Suisse

Pour l'Amérique :
Les Éditions ATMA internationales
Dépôt légal : Bibliothèque nationale du Québec
Dépôt légal : Bibliothèque nationale du Canada
ISBN 2-9805800-0-7

Pour l'Europe :
Les Éditions Quintessence
Dépôt légal : Bibliothèque nationale de France
ISBN 2-913281-00-1
Troisième trimestre 1998

Les Éditions ATMA Internationales
C .P. 8818
Sainte-Foy (Québec)
Canada G1V 4N7

☎ (418) 990-0808
Fax : (418) 990-1115
Adresse Internet :
www.atma.ca
Courrier électronique :
info@atma.ca

Éditeur pour l'Europe :

Les Éditions Quintessence
Rue de la Bastidonne
13678 Aubagne Cedex
France

☎ ++33(0)442 18 90 94
Fax : ++33(0)442 18 90 99
Adresse Internet :
www.holoconcept.net
Courrier électronique :
info@holoconcept.net

Le grand dictionnaire des malaises et des maladies

Déjà 35 000 exemplaires vendus au CANADA et en EUROPE

artel

Les éditions ATMA internationales

Adresse Internet : www.atma.ca

Silver Hair

CHAPTER ONE

THE GLORIES OF BEING SILVER:

Silver/gray/snow-white
hair is here to stay.

Take one look around your office, gym, school, supermarket, subway, mall, etc., and you'll see that silver is the new black. And blonde. And brown.

Many celebrities have proudly sported silver hair for years, such as Jamie Lee Curtis, Emmylou Harris, Bonnie Raitt, and Helen Mirren. But what's new is that it's *not* just the over-forty crowd who craves this hair color. There are young women who went silver early and have decided to ditch the dye and accept the gift nature gave them. One gorgeous example is the fashion features director of British *Vogue*, Sarah Harris, whose lovely silver locks are as chic as she is. Then you've got the young A-listers who have dyed their hair silver to look glam. Gwen Stefani,

Miley Cyrus, Lady Gaga, Rihanna, Kelly Osbourne, Kylie Jenner, Nicole Richie, Pink, and Rita Ora, among others, have strolled the red carpet and appeared in magazines with silver, slate, and snow-white locks. And their twenty- and thirtysomething fans are following suit. Yes, they're actually *dyeing to be silver*! Just think. Women are spending time and money to get the gorgeous color you may have right there on top of your head, even if it's currently undercover. I mean under *color*.

I attribute some of this silver hair envy to the animated Disney film

Sarah Harris, British *Vogue*

inspiration because of the white-haired character Daenerys Targaryen.

There are online tutorials on *Frozen*-inspired hair color, Twitter hashtags (like #grannyhair), and articles proclaiming that "gray has gone glam." I couldn't agree more. Think about it: *Silver* is a precious metal. It's a treasure, just like your natural hair color!

Despite its recent popularity, silver/gray/snow-white hair is not just a trend. It's here to stay. The silver hair movement is very similar to the curly hair movement. For years, ringlets, corkscrews, and waves were considered the ugly ducklings of the hair world, viewed as aberrations to be tamed and flattened within an inch of their natural lives rather than a beautiful part

Frozen and the gorgeous frosty locks belonging to Elsa, one of the main characters. The princess of Arendelle is a powerful woman who reveals a modern image of what it's like to go silver, and people of all ages have taken note: Silver can be unique and beautiful. Other young women I've talked to cite *Game of Thrones* as their *mane*

Kylie Jenner

Gwen Stefani

Rita Ora

Emilia Clarke, *Game of Thrones*

Emmylou Harris

of nature. Any curly girl who went to the salon got the "obviously you don't want those curls" attitude from the stylist, who assumed that she longed for a "blow-fry" to straighten her locks. For years I went through that as well, and when I finally saw how damaging it

was—both to my hair and my psyche—I was inspired to write *Curly Girl: The Handbook*. Today, more and more women not only embrace their curls but revel in them, because their curls are part of their unique selves. Women with silver hair, no matter how many or how few strands they have, experience something similar when their hair care consultants, as well as friends and family, assume the appearance of silver means it's time to color up. But embracing your natural hair is about *you*—no one else. It's about loving what Mother Nature intended for you, the *real* you. Or, I should say, the real *hue*!

In more than three decades as a hairstylist, I've talked to countless women who *want* to grow out their dyed hair and who talk longingly about getting out of the coloring cycle. Then something stops them. Many color their hair by default, because there's a stigma surrounding being naturally silver. We have been conditioned to believe that silver strands mean that you're old. But your hair is not the problem. And your hair is *not* what ages you. The first issue is mind over (gray) matter. I truly believe that *old* is just a word and that a great attitude is ageless. If you're active, energetic, and still engaged in life's wonders, then you naturally project a more youthful aura, regardless of your hair color. The same is true if you dive inside and get to know yourself a bit more. My grandma used to say, "If you don't go within, you go without." You can have the most beautiful things in the world, have your hair tinted a gorgeous shade, and perhaps get a nip or a tuck. But grasping for outside things to make you happy won't last for long. Doing the inside work and being comfortable and confident in your own skin gives you an ageless light that shines outward. In essence, everyone around you benefits from *you* being happy and feeling empowered. Your glorious silver hair is and can be a part of that!

Margaret Page, Silver Model

The Essential Difference Between "Letting Yourself Go" and "Letting Go"

Some women worry that going silver tells the world that you're throwing in the towel and not taking care of yourself. But there's a difference between "letting yourself go" and "letting go." The former means you aren't taking care of yourself, inside or out. The latter means you're not living by someone else's ideas of what they think you should look like. In fact, many women who've embraced their silver strands say they're actually reevaluating life's essentials and taking better care of themselves by staying fit, getting the right amount of rest, eating healthy, clearing clutter that doesn't serve them, and better managing stress.

> There are many approaches to going silver. Some are dramatic; some ease you into it.

Learn to Tone Out the Critics

Then there are the women who long to go silver but fear negative reactions from others. One woman told me *she* wanted to stop coloring her hair, but her husband strongly protested. "He's afraid of aging," she told me. Or the yoga teacher I know who has been dyeing her hair for decades. Because this conflicts with her practice, though, she longs to uncover her natural hair color. But her husband won't have it. "When we met, I signed up for a blonde," he says. (And she signed up for a guy *with* hair and *without* a belly!) Some women worry that ditching the dye and going silver will age them or will look unprofessional in the workplace. People also used to ask me if curly hair looked unprofessional. What *does* look unprofessional is any hair that is unkempt and uncared-for. When strands are given the TLC they need to be healthy, hydrated, and radiant, they look professional no matter their color or texture. In this book, I'll show you all the ways to care for those beautiful silver strands. For example, silver hair typically needs a great deal of the *right* kind of conditioning to look gorgeous—and professional. Silver hair is naturally lighter and brighter and actually suits most people, especially if you take care of your hair and of yourself!

I've come to realize that many women who feel like slaves to the hair coloring cycle are looking for an escape route—or a way to escape their roots. Some women have never considered the possibility of going silver, but when presented with it, the floodgates open. They respond so strongly to the conversation about going silver in hopes they'll get a little encouragement to try it. If this sounds like you, and if you want to the see the light of your silvery moon, grant yourself that permission. Only *you* can do this! It's *your* hair; you are its ultimate custodian. If you try going silver and don't like it, you are just one box of hair color or one salon appointment away from dyeing it back again. But you're not going to know what it's like to see the silver lining unless you give it a try.

Thinking Outside the Color Box

There are many ways to embrace your naturally changing shade. Obviously, you can just quit coloring altogether and completely grow out your dyed hair, and we have suggestions on how to do that with style. But there's no denying it—that approach can take a long time and requires patience and self-compassion. Fortunately, there are many other approaches. Some methods are dramatic; others gradually ease you into your new hue. As you will see later in the book, some women try several methods, resulting in a back-and-forth scenario that guides them either *to* the

Andrea Fishkin, Silver Model

silver promised land or *away* from it. Regardless, your silver hair will always be waiting in the wings. You just have to find the option that works for you and integrate it (or inte*gray*t it) into your lifestyle, starting with what already exists atop your head.

I consulted many color pros for this book to make sure I included the most reliable and logical information for your journey to silver. These experts, who provided information and helped guide the transitions of the real women you'll see throughout these pages, include Kristy Wilson, owner of the salon Uptown Curl, and Veronica Tapia of Jersey Curl Salon. Together, we'll show you how to make *your* silver hair gorgeous.

Not only will this book offer suggestions, solutions, and techniques for going silver, but it will encourage a conversation about authenticity, and about how we make our choices about our appearance—and why. Going for your silver means going more than root deep. One thing I hear constantly from women who've embraced this natural hue is that they wish they had done it sooner, especially those who've been coloring their hair for more than twenty years. In writing this book, I've discovered many women who started covering their silver strands as early as age twelve, and now, years or even decades later, they have no idea what might be shining beneath the surface. They lament the time and money spent in the salon and the stress of worrying about their quickly reappearing roots, and they resent having their lives revolve around hair dyeing.

One of the goals of this book is to help younger women embrace their silver from the very first strand. I think of it sort of like a vaccine. I want to help them see that silver is just another gorgeous hair color, delivered to their heads compliments of nature. As a result, I hope women won't feel societal pressure to color up the first time they spot a silver strand.

When I was a first-time vendor at the International Beauty Show in New York City, where my colleagues and I were selling *Curly Girl: The Handbook* and our new products, people stopped by our booth throughout the day, asking us which curling iron we had used to achieve our perfect curls. What we sadly realized was that the world was so accustomed to erasing what nature gave us that we had forgotten what real curls even looked like. Today, natural curls, waves, and coils are on display wherever you look. Gone is the knee-jerk tendency to hide our hair's inherent texture. This is a huge change, especially since at least 65 to 75 percent of people have naturally wavy or curly hair. Behind every straightening implement and blowout bar, there is a beautiful curly girl waiting to happen.

It's just a matter of time. My hope is that the same thing will happen with silver hair, and that the decision to keep your natural hue, color-complement it, or completely cover it up will feel like a *personal choice*, not a default reaction to society's insistence that we look a certain way. Just imagine all the time and energy you'll have for exploring a healthier and lighter, more playful sense of self, which will inevitably lead to a happier you!

My Gray Pride

I'm not suggesting that only *you* embrace your silver. I grew out my existing color, too. At the age of sixteen, I worked in a salon in Leicester, England. I started out as a colorist's guinea pig, experimenting with color on my naturally rusty-auburn strands. First, deep burgundy, purples, and reds were painted onto my hair. Later, at eighteen, living and working as a stylist

Lorraine's hair of many colors

in Hong Kong, I was talked into having a few random peroxide-blonde tips for a hair event. I lived in Tokyo in my early twenties, and while I was there I added a few more highlights. I hadn't planned on going totally blonde, yet highlighting quickly became my automatic reaction to the slightest hint of dark roots. Around the time that I moved to New York City, in my late twenties, I was getting blonder by the month, and then in my thirties I began to see a few silver strands. Yet I never even considered revealing them, as if doing so would be shameful. So what started as a few innocent highlights became a few more, and then a few more. (Blonde wasn't built in a day.) Before long, my blonde ambition became more like a blonde addiction. Eventually, despite my colorist's advice to ease up, I overdosed with peroxide and my whole head of hair became one-dimensional blonde, which made my spherical curls look like they had no definition. In certain lights, the color looked yellow and made my skin tone appear washed-out, something I was completely unaware of at the time. In fact, I thought it looked good! As a faux blonde, I did have a lot of

fun—until the next color application, and those became more and more frequent as the years went by.

There were many times during my overly blonde era (error) that my loving colorist would suggest I needed a few lowlights in order to give the blonde and my curls a bit more definition and dimension. I tried lowlights. Once. For approximately twelve hours! But I couldn't bear the darker lowlights against the blonde. To me, it looked like the light had gone off and a dull brown shade had been cast over the shocking yellow blonde, a hue I had become so accustomed to that anything remotely different was too dark for me. The next morning, a Sunday, at 7 a.m., I called my colorist, begging him to

Incoming silver

re-highlight my strands. Despite the fact that it was his *only* day off, he came into the salon that afternoon and gave me my fully blonde hair fix. In retrospect, my reaction was a bit extreme, but I was too deep into my delusion to see the light. And it went on this way for years.

While I was encouraging others to embrace their silver, it didn't even occur to me to practice what I was preaching. But over the course of writing this book, I decided it was time to walk the silver talk. One reason was an uncoloring epiphany I had at an uptown New York City hair salon in a high-end department store. As I waited to meet a friend there, I kept seeing women emerge from the salon. It was like a conveyer belt of women, who all seemed to be around the same age, leaving with the same bleached-blonde highlights and blow-fried, straight hairstyle. *Why do they all want to look alike in both texture and color?* I wondered. *Are they even aware that they look like clones?* The truth is, I shouldn't have been surprised. The blonde/yellow color application is a worldwide fauxnomenon. In fact, there is more bleached-blonde hair on this planet than any other hue. *Natural*

A great cut is everything.

blonde is so rare it's like spotting a snow leopard.

That day in New York was part of my motivation to commit to my uncoloring journey. What the heck was my real color, anyway? What had I been hiding all these years? Because we have a natural desire to avoid being uncomfortable in social situations, and because we compare ourselves to others, we tend to defend our false images of ourselves—and that is where the conflict lies. So I decided it was time to learn to find comfort in being uncomfortable and to begin to grow out my faux blonde so I would be true to everything I wrote in this book. But like most things that we care about, this project became about much more than changing my hair color. Embracing my silver hair has helped me on my journey to do a bit more soul-searching, what I call my own gut renovations.

Then there was the practical side of trying to embrace my natural hair color. I was tired of relying on and begging my very busy colorist to paint me every four weeks—sometimes even more often, because if the *teeniest, tiniest* speck of gray appeared, I'd be back in his chair. (I'm a hairstylist, but I'm not a practitioner of hair coloring.) Typically, the only time hairstylists tend to their own locks is at the end of a long, busy workday. So I would coyly ask my colorist if he could stay late to color my hair. He'd kindly oblige, and most of the time I would end up driving home with bleach in my hair, my head encased in plastic wrap, hoping there would be no traffic and that I wouldn't get stopped for speeding, as I had only a brief window before I needed to rinse out the bleach at home. Inevitably, as time went on, my silver lining would emerge sooner than it had before, because the artificial color gradually stopped adhering to the silver as well as it used to.

Also, what I didn't want to admit was that the continual bleach applications were wearing out my hair fibers,

> *The phrase I hear most often from women who have embraced their silver is "I wish I'd done it sooner."*

causing them to break and thus preventing my hair from growing past a certain point. I call this a "chemical haircut" or "chem cut," a phenomenon that doesn't pertain only to bleached or color-treated hair. It can be caused by chronic blow-frying, chemical straightening, over-shampooing and excessive use of silicone-based products that laminate the hair, because overprocessed hair fibers naturally weaken. This is why so many people resort to hair extensions and weaves. The bottom line is that I had more than enough reasons to try embracing my silver. Perspective opens up only when you are ready to see it, and finally I saw that my blonde hair was making my skin tone look washed-out, I was becoming frustrated with my coloring cycle, and my hair was getting increasingly damaged. It was similar to watching reruns of a movie you don't even like. I wanted to be done with it.

As I said, going silver started out as an excuse for me to be part of this book, but it has become a chance to set myself free from my constant color bind. One woman who embraced her natural hair color years ago told me, "My aunt colored her hair until she died, at the age of ninety-nine. I didn't want to be a prisoner like that. I wanted liberation." Amen. "Women want their time back," Kristy Wilson says of her many clients who have transitioned to silver. It's true. Life is too short not to love the hair you're in.

We must also become more conscious of the seemingly innocent products containing chemicals that go on and into our bodies. Think about it: If you can apply patches to the skin that help prevent cravings (like smoking cessation patches) or control estrogen levels (like the birth control patch), clearly the body can absorb chemicals. I often hear women claim their hair dye is "totally organic." But unless it's a temporary color rinse that lasts for just a day or two, there's no such thing as "natural" hair dye. Yes, some products

may be milder, and some replace ammonia with a coloring agent called ethanolamine that doesn't lift the hair cuticle as much. But if you're changing the hair's surface color in a short period of time with the intent for it to last for much longer, you need chemicals. For example, ammonia lifts the cuticle to let color molecules bond to the hair cortex, and peroxide (bleach) oxidizes color proteins to remove color. Without these chemicals, hair color would wash out with detergent shampoo.

At the start of my transition from blonde to silver, I was pleasantly surprised to see that the contrast between my colored blonde hair (a warm tone) and natural silver hair (a cool tone) wasn't so drastic. A lot of unnatural blondes with quick-growing silver experience this phenomenon, too. It's sort of like wearing a curly wig over curly hair, only to realize that your real curls, if you patiently allowed them to grow, might one day be as gloriously curly as the wig. I enjoyed my blonde ambition tour, but my transition was rewarding because I felt freer.

Positive OverTones

The reaction to my new hue from strangers and friends was also surprising. I had a few naysayers, but I realized that these negative responses were often more of a mirror into that person's own self-image. I received many more compliments than criticisms and created dozens of silver converts in the process. As soon as she saw my new hue, my friend Linda said, "You're just how you're supposed to look!" Years ago, when I finally embraced my curls, I allowed my hair to be exactly what

Katelyn Triola, Silver Model

it wanted to be. I had taken something that had once been the bane of my existence and celebrated it, along with billions of others. Exploring my silver has had the same impact as embracing my curls did. When it's growing out, the silver can look like a shining light peeking through the dyed hair: It really is *your* light shining through, both literally and figuratively.

A year and a half into this project, my hair was not as completely silver as I had thought it would be, especially once I cut out the remaining blonde on the top canopy, exposing the darker side underneath. Like going into an attic and blowing the dust off an heirloom, I was surprised to see remnants of my totally forgotten, long-time-no-see, rusty-auburn hair with strands of silver tinsel sporadically intertwined. What did appear to have a strong front-row presence was a *Bride of Frankenstein* silver streak around my face, which I love and which many people think I've colored on purpose. I like saying, "It's *all* me."

A Word to Colorists

If you're a hairdresser or colorist, you are a
beauty maker, and beauty comes in many
forms. Please don't be offended by this
book or see it as a threat to your business.
When prompted, the right thing to do is
to help clients see their natural silver light.
Most of us have built loyal clienteles, so
the benefits of encouraging a few longtime
clients to embrace their natural hair color
or integrate it into a new look will come
back to us a hundredfold. The hair industry
is at an all-time creative high right now.
We are seeing the most exquisite natural

multi-textured hair that was once hidden under straitjackets on women of all ages
in all professions. It is incredibly exciting to see many shades of silver, both natural
and imposed, become part of this innovative hair fest. By using this trend as an
opportunity to call upon creative ways to transition and transform our beautiful, loyal
color clients, we ensure they will stay with us well after the first lights of silver have
emerged. I see silver transitions becoming an added, specialized service, because
clients often opt for a color-supported transition, which can take a year or more of
appointments and treatments. Then again, some women will choose to embrace their
silver with highlights and other options that will still require our assistance in the
long term. Be a cheerleader who creatively helps clients toward their goal. You are a
beauty influencer. You are their guiding light.

Silver Lining Story

Ashley Briggs, 30

I discovered my first gray hair at just fourteen, and I began to color it. But after six years, I was tired of coloring every other week so I decided to just let the gray grow naturally. Not dyeing my hair has been an exciting, life-changing process that led me to find my true identity. I hear people fret about finding gray hair, but my silver makes me feel full and happy. It's like an uninhibited version of myself and demonstrates a level of confidence, because I don't need to color my hair to hide behind it. I never received compliments on my hair when I dyed it, but now I get them all the time. The other day, I was sitting in a restaurant and a waitress who wasn't in my section came over and said, "I don't want to be weird, but I love your hair." Because it grows in a cool pattern, my silver looks intentional, and I've actually had people argue with me that I get highlights! Life is easier because I don't have to color my hair all the time, and I feel better about the environment because I'm not using harsh chemicals that end up down the drain. A few people have said that I look too young to have silver hair already. My response? Going silver doesn't have an age requirement!

Escape Roots

How do you know if you're ready to transition from fully coloring your strands to embracing more of your natural pigment? Ask yourself these questions:

1. Are you coloring by default? In other words, are you doing it just because you've always done it?

2. Does it feel like you spend as much time with your colorist as your spouse/boyfriend/girlfriend/partner?

3. Over the course of a year, do you spend about one month's rent or mortgage payment on coloring your hair?

4. Has the time between colorings gotten shorter? For example, if you used to color every six to eight weeks, is it now every three to four?

5. Do you get cranky when it's time to color? One of my clients told me she feels a version of PMS when it's "her time."

6. Does the single-process color you've been getting for years fade within the first week?

7. Do you occasionally think you're going bald, because your white roots contrast with your colored hair, making it appear to float above your scalp?

8. Does it feel like your life revolves around coloring your hair and that you make plans or accept invitations based on when you'll be able to cover up those roots?

9. A week or two after coloring, do you find yourself touching up your roots with mascara, a color wax stick, spray-on color, or liquid eye shadow?

10. Do you actually dislike the hair color you are applying?

If you answered "yes" to one or more of these questions, it's probably time to give your natural hair color a chance to appear and see what you think. Even though several of the techniques in this book *do* include integrating color into your changing strands, you'll need to do this a lot less often—and not forever.

Silver Questions and Concerns

When I talk to women about going silver, I've noticed several common concerns.

"My silver strands aren't a nice color/texture."

When I was encouraging women to embrace their curls and waves after years of blow-frying and chemical straightening, they often told me, "I don't have curls; I just have frizz" or "Your curls are beautiful, but mine are ugly." But when each woman learned the right way to care for her strands, she realized that the gorgeous curls she never thought she could have were right there on top of her head; all they needed was the right treatment to be abundantly healthy. I hear the same thing now regarding silver hair. Some women say, "Your silver is pretty but mine is dull" or "My best friend looks great with silver hair, but I won't." But again, all you need is the right guidance for integrating the growing-out phase and caring for your natural hair color. And don't worry, this doesn't mean more work for you. It's just a new hair care routine to replace your old one.

For example, hair can become drier and coarser as it turns silver, so if you're not conditioning more often than you were when your strands were colored, of course they're not going to look radiant and healthy. They simply need more hydration. (See chapter 7 for silver hair care tips.) Also, seeing just an inch or two of your natural silver roots against hair that is dyed darker or much lighter can make your shade of silver seem more unappealing. This is why some women who start to embrace their silver give up and go back to dyeing. At first I was not thrilled with the look of my silver against the dyed blonde, but then I took a deep breath and thought about my big picture and long-term goal. The process of undyeing without chemical assistance doesn't happen overnight, so you do need patience, a few stylish hats to hide the roots, and some creative updos while you push through those first months, until your natural color reaches about the midsection of the crown. By then, it almost looks like a reverse ombré effect, and this is when it seems like a whole new hue has appeared. I promise! Getting a stylish haircut with shape, or just keeping the ends freshly trimmed and in optimum condition, is also important for gorgeous silver hair.

"Silver hair won't go with my skin/glasses/wardrobe."

Many of us have been wearing the same type of makeup, glasses, and clothes for years—decades, even—so uncovering a style that works with your new silver strands (and also your skin tone, which often lightens as we age) can be one way to further shake up your look. And you don't have to go at it alone. In chapter 8, I share makeup and wardrobe insights I received from experts like Stacy London, host of TLC's *What Not to Wear* and author of *The Truth About Style*; makeup gurus Julio Sandino, founder of Julio Sandino Makeup Studio in New York City; and Sonia Kashuk, founder of Sonia Kashuk Beauty. These tips will make you feel gorgeous sporting your naturally lighter crown of glory!

"I can't make up my mind: Should I go silver or not?"

If you're not ready to commit or don't even know how much silver hair you actually have, Kristy Wilson of Uptown Curl says, "I suggest that you let your natural color grow out for at least two months." This is when you can see the density of the silver and how different it is from front to back. Then you can decide if you want to embrace your natural hair color and which of the various techniques to use. *Yes*, you have to be patient during that time, but if your roots are driving you nuts, you can cover them up with a temporary root touch-up pen, powder, mist, or marker. Also, after eight weeks of natural growth, your colorist can better match your natural silver if you're going to use a color grow-out technique like highlights or a silver streak.

"My colorist said I don't have enough silver to stop dyeing my hair."

"Your colorist may be saying this because he/she doesn't know how to help you go natural or doesn't want to. Any amount of silver is enough," says Kristy. I wholeheartedly agree. You just need to give your hair those estimated two to three months to grow out and see what naturally exists. Then you and your colorist can decide which technique to work with. In fact, if you don't have a lot of silver, it's actually an easier transition, because it's not such an abrupt change.

"I've been seeing my colorist—and confiding in him/her—for years. I can't imagine giving up those appointments!"

There are few connections like that between a client and his or her colorist or stylist. It can be an intimate relationship that goes beyond your locks, and often your colorist has been in your life for years, perhaps longer than your partner or spouse. Also, in this go-go-go world, how often do you sit still, connect, and chat with someone for thirty minutes or more? But many techniques in this book actually do require some color, so although your appointments may not be as frequent, you don't have to completely end the relationship. And even if you choose to transition without coloring, you will still need haircuts, conditioning treatments, and advice on your emerging new hue. If the affection is mutual, take your colorist out for coffee or a drink!

"I'm worried I won't feel good about myself as a silver-haired woman."

Because silver is a bright hue, it can change your appearance, and you may need some moral support to maintain your inner and outer radiance. In fact, there were a few times when I felt like my inner radiance was temporarily challenged by going au naturel, as did some of the other women in this book. However, once you get over the transitional hump of the grow-out and find that you are still *you* and very much intact, you can decide to keep going toward all silver, go back to dyeing, or at least make what you have started work for you with integrated highlights or one of the other suggestions in this book. Women who have made the transition to full silver often say their confidence skyrocketed. Fashion designers are choosing naturally silver goddesses of all ages to model during their runway shows, allowing some to start new careers at the age of fifty! It also helps to stay healthy, both in body and mind, to look in your closet and think of wearing clothes and colors that will flatter your changing hue, and to find the right makeup for your skin tone. All of this will only add to that beautiful radiance.

The Reality Check (book)

There are so many perks to going silver, besides the fact that it will look beautiful once it is in full bloom.

YOU'LL SAVE CASH. I call this "silvernomics," and the savings can be staggering! Many women who color their hair find themselves at the salon at least every six weeks, or 8.6 times a year, so I'll use that figure to estimate the cost of coloring. Imagine that you color your hair for forty years, from age twenty-five to sixty-five, although it's often even longer than that. The average cost for color across the United States is $100. Using this number, getting your hair colored every six weeks would cost $860 per year. If you do this for forty years, that's $34,400! At a high-end Manhattan salon, hair coloring starts at around $150, which equals $1,290 a year, and $51,600 over the course of forty years! At Kristy's salon in Minneapolis, the average price for single-process (all-over) color is $122, which adds up to $1,049.20 per year. After forty years, you've set yourself back $41,968. The starting price for highlights at several Los Angeles salons is around $200, which is $1,720 a year. Forty years of these highlights is $68,800! Take into account that as years pass and hair gets grayer, color doesn't adhere to it as well, so you may find yourself coloring it even more often—sometimes every three to four weeks—so all these numbers go up exponentially!

YOU'LL SAVE THE TIME AND EFFORT IT TAKES TO GO TO SALON APPOINTMENTS.

A salon color appointment can take 2 to 3 hours. Do this every six weeks, and you'll spend between 17 and 26 hours a year at the salon—and that doesn't include travel time. Over forty years, that's between 680 and 1,040 hours, or 28 to 43 days of your life spent sitting in a salon chair.

IT'S HEALTHIER FOR YOUR HAIR AND BODY. Although most hair dye is safe, you're still applying chemicals to your hair and scalp on a regular basis. Many studies show that most products applied to your head and body seep into your skin and/or get very close to your eyes, ears, and nose. We are, after all, a walking ecosystem. As I mentioned earlier, even hair dyes that claim to be "natural" or "organic" have some chemicals in them, because these ingredients are the only way to actually change the surface of the hair for a long period of time. Embracing your natural hue means forgoing chemicals altogether, or at least using fewer of them. That's healthier not only for you but also for your carbon footprint, because these chemicals end up in our waters when we rinse them down the drain.

THE COMPLIMENTS WILL COME POURING IN. This is something I hear from so many silver sirens who surrender to their DNA. One woman told me that on the day she cut off the final few inches of colored hair and

Jennifer Ho-Dougatz, Silver Model

became totally silver, someone approached her on the subway about modeling. She started a new career and has been posing for the camera ever since! Other women say they get more compliments from both women and men than they did when they were overbleached blondes, brunettes, or redheads. Of course, what *you* think about yourself is most important, and many women say their silver makes them feel sexier, more open, and beautiful.

YOU WILL LOOK GREAT—AND, MORE IMPORTANT, YOU WILL LOOK LIKE YOU! As one woman told me, when she embraced her natural hue she finally felt like she wasn't "faking it" anymore. Many women are also motivated to eat well, get enough sleep, and exercise, so they naturally look and feel better all over.

YOUR LIFE WILL BE LESS STRESSFUL. If you're like most women whose silver roots grow quickly, you've accepted social invitations based on the rate of your root growth and the date of your next hair color appointment. You've skipped special occasions, plans with friends, time with your kids, working out, and other priorities in order to fit in coloring. But when your social calendar no longer revolves around hiding your roots—life begins to feel so much easier and freer.

Many women say their silver hair makes them feel sexier, more open, and beautiful.

DYE STAINS WILL BE A THING OF THE PAST. If you have dyed dark hair, one thing I'm sure you will not miss are dye splotches on your clothes, in your bathroom, and on your pillowcases, towels, and collar, as well as dripping down your face when it rains.

YOU'LL FEEL LIBERATED. Yes, you will be freeing your hair from chemicals and dye. But this kind of release goes deeper than it appears to. There's something so liberating about embracing the hair Mother Nature gave you, because it is yours and yours alone. I experienced this freedom years ago when I stopped fighting my curls. As I allowed them be what nature intended, my curls and I became friends. I felt the same way as I started to let my natural hair color emerge. Many of the women I spoke to for this book said that over time, discovering their hair's natural color helped them feel more fully present in their own lives. It all comes down to having the confidence to be yourself. When you begin to love yourself as you are, amazing things happen!

A Silver-Haired Fashion Icon

If you've ever wanted inspiration to go silver, all you have to do is take a look at the beautiful Sarah Harris, the fashion features director of British *Vogue*—and my silver crush! She didn't set out to create an iconic look when she embraced her silver hair in her teens, and yet she has. I give her a lot of credit for going against the grain, especially because she works in the image-driven world of fashion. By being true to herself, she has made naturally silver hair a major attraction in the fashion world. Her graceful demeanor is effortless, and many people covet her look. Here's more of Sarah's story:

Sarah Harris, *Fashion Features Director of British* Vogue

....

I was sixteen years old and sitting in the passenger seat of my mum's car, using the pull-down mirror to apply mascara. All of a sudden, I saw these silvery strands flickering in the sunlight. At first, I was horrified! And worried. After all, I was just a teenager! I pulled those silver hairs out, but that didn't help. More came in shortly after that. I decided they looked a bit like highlights, so I didn't let it bother me.

"No one believes it's natural except for colorists who know you can't get this color from a bottle."

I probably should have expected to go silver at an early age because my mum was completely silver when she was young. When I six or seven, my mother dyed her hair all the time. I remember her going to the salon every four weeks to have her roots colored brown, and even as a young girl I remember thinking I would not want to have to do that once a month. I guess my mum got tired of it, too, because by the time I was nine or ten she went completely silver. I wondered why she had to have gray hair and wished she was a blonde or brunette like everyone else's mothers. But then I started to notice the number of people who came up to her and complimented her hair, no matter where she was—the grocery store, shoe store, etc. Slowly, I began to appreciate the fact that her hair was unique. It also made her easy to spot at the school gates, because you could see her silver hair for a mile off. It was a rare sight.

I wasn't completely silver until I was twenty-eight or twenty-nine years old, and I never thought of dyeing it. It came in quite evenly all over my head—rather than in a patch or streak—so it looked deliberate. The color seems to change a bit throughout the year. In winter, it looks more ice-white; in summer, it looks more silver. That said, silver is not the easiest color to wear when you're tired or in the winter, because you can look washed-out. It's best to do a bit more with the rest of your appearance. A light suntan helps, as does foundation and mascara.

The only time I dyed my hair was for a story I was writing for American *Vogue*. I had to wear extensions for two weeks, and the hairdresser said that it would be hard to find those that matched my silver in the time period we had available. He convinced me to do a vegetable dye and promised it would wash right out when we were done with the story. But it wasn't that easy. I kept washing and washing, but it didn't come out completely, and my hair turned sort of bluish with this dark band across it. That really turned me off to the idea of dyeing.

Several times a week, I get comments on my hair from total strangers. It could be a young girl asking who my hairdresser is or what dye I use or a cab driver wondering if my hair is natural. No one believes it's natural except for colorists who know you can't get this color out of a bottle.

The Young and the Silver

I am so happy about the number of young women embracing their silver. May Lindstrom, the thirty-three-year-old founder of May Lindstrom Skin, had been coloring her hair for years. But she stopped when she became pregnant at age twenty-nine, and she has inspired other women to do the same.

"Hair dye can be damaging to hair, and it's applied to the scalp, one of the most absorbent parts of our body," May says. When she decided to grow out her dye, May was excited to embrace her sprinkling of silver, but every time she went to get a haircut or have her hair styled, she felt increasing pressure to defend her silver hair. More than that, "I didn't like realizing that I was so self-conscious about my appearance. It was a reality check for me," she recalls. Now Lindstrom is helping other women embrace their silver. "With the success of my company, I have a fairly public image. This has led to a conversation around my choice not to color but to embrace my silver hair at thirty-three years old. Women of all ages tell me that I've inspired them to return to their natural color, whatever that might have been or will be, which makes me feel incredible," May explains. "It feels good to make a change that supports all women. We are perfect exactly as we are. There's nothing more gorgeous than embracing your own beauty—silver and all. Not only will you feel more empowered and inspire this freedom in other women, but you'll attract like never before. There is something incredibly captivating about reveling in the comfort of your own skin and all the way through each strand of hair. I'm really proud to know that I can share this confidence with my daughter, and I'll never have to explain to her why I'm covering up such a natural part of myself."

Silver Lining Story

Wendy Lee, 48

I discovered my first silver strand when I was in my twenties. I dyed my hair, but decided to stop after three times because it drastically changed its texture. Also, no dye matched my original color, so I felt artificial. I didn't enjoy spending over three hundred dollars every six weeks or so, and going to the salon was an awful chore for me. I'm Asian, and Asians, in my opinion, particularly don't like gray hair, so at first I was encouraged—and in some cases begged—to dye my hair. My mother was one of the most vocal about this. However, now she thinks it's beautiful! My gray is mostly on the sides and top, so a lot of people think I highlight it, and I get lots of compliments. A guy in my office building asked if he could take a picture of my hair to show to his wife and encourage her to stop dyeing, too.

The Science of Silver Strands

So why does hair go silver in the first place? And how come some people lose their natural pigment early—in their teens or twenties—while others can sail into their sixties without a strand of silver? Your hair color is determined by cells in your hair follicles called melanocytes, which produce melanin, the same pigment that gives your skin and eyes their color. How much melanin you produce determines if you'll be a redhead, brunette, blonde, or somewhere in between. "Hair turns gray because the pigment granules that give it its color cease to form," explains renowned trichologist Philip Kingsley, founder of the eponymous hair care brand and of clinics in London and New York. There is still a bit of mystery surrounding our snowy locks, but scientists are researching the use of drugs to regulate the melanin in individual follicles, something I would never recommend for the purpose of changing your hair color!

Many people start to go silver in their thirties. The silver usually starts growing at the temples and eventually spreads to the crown. However, these beautiful strands can crop up at any age—even in the tween years—and the age of onset is often hereditary and has nothing to do with aging. In other words, if your mom or dad was sporting silver in high school, chances are you will, too. (Andrea's and Ivanna's stories, on pages 30 and 125, respectively, are great examples of women whose hair turned silver early in life.)

Silver Lining Story

Rebecca Purcell, 53, *Artist*

started going silver when I was eighteen years old with just a few strands coming through. I bleached or dyed my hair throughout my early twenties and colored it red in my late twenties and early thirties. Then one day I noticed that my hair was predominantly silver and decided to grow it out. However, when I told my colorist this, she was against it, telling me that silver hair was very unattractive. But I had my mind set, so I didn't go back to her for several months and in that time I grew out my natural color, pulling my hair back and wearing hats to cover the roots. Finally, when it had grown out a couple of inches, I knew it was mostly silver so I went back to my colorist and told her I was committed to this color transition. I had her put in blond streaks to break up the line of demarcation. Yes, it was a little crazy-looking with bleach streaks and red, but I embraced it. About six to nine months later, I was able to cut off the bleach and red parts and went fully silver after that. Once it was really grown out and it got white, I loved it. It was also incredibly refreshing and liberating to not have to keep going and coloring my hair.

The response I got—and still get—was incredible and continuous, with people commenting on my hair in a way that I had never experienced. They'd ask me if it was my real color and were amazed when I said yes. They were always excited by it and would say things like "I want my hair to look like that" or "I can't wait for my hair to get like that." I really enjoy getting those compliments and the feeling that I am empowering other women to stop dying. Today, I feel so identified with my white hair that I can't imagine it being any other color.

Silver Girl

Many adults cringe when they spot those first strands of silver. But imagine seeing them when you're a tween or a teen, a time when you're *already* concerned about your looks and morphing body. This is what happened to Andrea Fishkin, 35, a fashion adviser for Chanel in New York City:

My first silver hair peeked through when I was only twelve years old. I'll never forget the moment: I was on Main Street in East Hampton, New York, in front of the movie theater with my dearest family friends. Pam, the mom, looked at me and said, "Andrea, let me see your head for a second." Next thing I knew, I felt a quick pluck and saw her dangling a silver hair before my eyes. More came in quickly after that. My curly hair had always been a nuisance, and now I had to deal with silver! I was mortified. What would other kids think and say? I was so self-conscious that if I

Andrea Fishkin,
Silver Model

was in the stairwell at school, I worried that classmates on the stairs above me would see my silver hair when they looked down. I wanted to dye my hair, but my mom didn't want me to put chemicals on my head, so I started with vegetable dyes. Eventually, I moved on to regular hair dye. However, that didn't solve all my problems. I worried about who I would see when my roots grew in. Also, hair coloring was expensive, and I had to have it done every four to six weeks. Were my parents always going to pay for it? And the grow-out was annoying, especially if I had to wait a little longer because I wanted it superfresh for a party. How would I hide the silver in the meantime?

Then, after twelve years of dyeing, I was fed up with the whole process—mentally and physically. My life revolved around my hair color appointments. I also hated sitting at the salon waiting for the dye to seep in. Eventually, it just became clear to me that it was more important to accept who I am and live my life than to put so much energy into my hair. My mother, who is pure white now, also had silver at a young age but never, ever dyed it. She was happy with my decision, but even more important, I love it and embrace it more and more every year that goes by. I find it ironic that today many women are actually dyeing their hair silver. I love when someone compliments me and I can say that it's all mine!

Silver Hair Myths

Myth #1: Pluck one silver hair and two will grow in its place.

Because you can't remove the hair follicle by plucking, all you'll get is another silver hair. One silver hair. However, when it grows in, that hair will be shorter than the others, making it more obvious than if you'd just left it alone. The bottom line? Step away from the tweezers.

Myth #2: You can go silver overnight.

Rumor has it that in 1793, Marie Antoinette's hair transformed from brown to silver the night before she was to have her head chopped off. Many say this was caused by the stress of going to the guillotine, but unless you're playing with toxic radiation or chemicals, your hair color is determined months before it appears. Marie Antoinette's hair color that was seen for the first time publicly on that day was probably her own hair color, which had been hidden under the ornate wigs and hair powders she was known for using.

Myth #3: Not eating enough protein can cause gray hair.

Melanin, which gives hair its color, is not affected by protein. However, since hair is 97 percent protein, you *do* need this nutrient to keep your strands shiny and healthy. Two to three ounces of protein three times a day is enough for the average person; six ounces three times a day is better if you're very physically active, says nutritionist and author Esther Blum. Other important nutrients for your hair include healthy fats like those found in avocados, salmon, walnuts, coconut oil, flax, sardines, egg yolks, olive oil, and pasteurized butter, which keep your scalp hydrated and your hair glossy. Zinc, magnesium, and selenium—minerals found in almonds, walnuts, cashews, pumpkin seeds, brown rice, oats, and beans—and iron, found in beef, turkey, eggs, and beans—are believed to help alleviate thinning hair. Vitamins B_6—found in whole grains, lean meat, poultry, and beans—and folic acid, found in dark green veggies and lentils—are also important for healthy hair.

A Brief History of Dyeing

People have been experimenting with hair color for thousands of years. The Romans tried to cover their silver with ashes, coal, tar, charred eggs, boiled walnut shells, leeks, leeches, and earthworms. Even urine and bird poop were used to color hair. (Yes, you read that correctly!) The wealthy wore wigs made from the hair of conquered, fair-haired Germanic or Northern European people, and would sprinkle in actual gold dust to create a blonde look. It is believed that prostitutes in ancient Rome colored their hair yellow to signal their profession, and many did so with crushed marigold petals, pollen, and bleaching agents. It's also believed that some of our ancestors used hair color to indicate their rank on the battlefield. Queen Elizabeth's natural hair color made ginger red a popular hue, and women and men of nobility went to great lengths to try to emulate their queen using mixtures of cumin seed, saffron, celandine, and oil, and also wore wigs to match. Before Queen Elizabeth, red-and-ginger-colored hair had been associated with barbarians and witches.

CHAPTER TWO

ENLIGHTENED:

Letting Nature Lead the Way

One of the goals of this book is to help younger women embrace their silver from the very first strand.

So you've decided to embrace your natural hue. Congrats! The most obvious method is just to stop coloring and allow the silver to edge its way out. Doing this requires a dye-free vision of yourself, a big dose of determination, and a lot of patience. If this is your path, the only way out is through! There are some immediate benefits: This all-natural method means that you aren't coloring at all, so you save time, money, and effort while immediately enhancing the health of your hair. This is the method I chose, and it's been two and a half years so far. But it *was* an adjustment.

Before I started allowing my silver to appear, my motto as a hair care professional was "If I don't have great-looking hair, how are my clients supposed to take me seriously?" But in the early stages of my grow-out, that motto went out the window. This was the point when I had a one-and-a-half-inch line of silver hovering over my usual dyed blonde, and it looked like smoke coming out of yellow cinders.

Then, over a period of three to four months, that frosty cool tone spread down over my crown. It actually began to look deliberate, so much so that I named the color "graybré": Think reverse ombré with lighter, silver hues on top and darker hair at the ends. Still, it looked strange, and I understood why many women may give up on embracing their silver at this stage and hit the tube of hair dye again.

Growing into
my silver, slowly

During the first few months, my hair grew in as what appeared to be salt-and-pepper. Then the unexpected happened. When my new hair was at about ear-level, my natural color began to show itself as a tawny, blondish silver with a shock of white around the front, which looked like it had been highlighted. In preparation for this book, I had stopped coloring the hair underneath a year before I stopped coloring the roots.

I realized that, like any type of self-exploration, I had to face the process head-on. Instead of being doubtful, I became more and more curious. I wanted to follow the "white rabbit." I tried to be positive and think of it as unearthing buried treasure. *Celebrate it*, I'd tell myself. After all, what was the alternative? I knew that if I wasn't happy, I could always adapt or dye it again. But at this point my natural hue was intriguing to me, and I was determined to see it through.

In the Beginning ...

When these photos were taken, I had been growing the blonde canopy out for six months, but had been growing out the color underneath for one year. Curly hair seems to grow slower than straight hair because rather than growing down, its trajectory coils and springs back. Many curly girls get frustrated and complain that their hair is not growing, yet their roots are a constant reminder that it is, indeed. That said, one of the many benefits of having curls is that

their natural volume can help hide the line of demarcation between new hair and old color. I started using just a little less styling gel, which allowed my curls to expand to their natural fullness to soften the contrast between my natural silver and the blonde.

Lorraine at One Year, Three Months

Taking the long, natural route to my silver allowed me to gradually embrace my true hue.

Lorraine at One Year, Six Months

In the picture of my hair sectioned from the back, you can see a faint trace of my rusty-auburn past lingering in the midsection to the ends. Seeing my true hue felt like finally meeting a Facebook friend in person for the first time.

Lorraine at One Year, Nine Months

Lorraine at About Two Years

The road to silver has been enlightening and freeing.

Positively Silver

Be positive about your decision to go all silver. Keep your vision of your future hair as you let go of the hue that may not be serving you anymore. Of course, some days are better than others, and small adjustments can help, like a bit more pop on your eyes with eyeliner and mascara, some blush, and a stylish hat. During my grow-out, I imagined this journey like a road map, because a map has a beginning, middle, and end and takes you somewhere. The beginning has passed for me, I'm currently in the middle, and the end is what I am heading toward. Today, I intend to keep the promise to myself to see this through! During those moments when you think you might want to throw in the towel, try this: Wait just one more day before deciding to dye it back. You may feel differently tomorrow—and then you are already another day closer to uncovering the hair that wants to be discovered: your glorious new color.

Silver Lining Story

Janine Zeccardi, 44

had been coloring my hair since my early twenties, but with a two-year-old and a four-year-old, I had no time for myself and decided to stop. However, I was determined not to "let myself go" and continued to work out and take care of my skin. I felt that if I looked and felt good, I could make the gray hair cool. I wasn't thrilled about how my hair looked during the two and a half years it took to grow out, but now I don't even remember it being such a big deal. I get stopped on the street *a lot* by people asking questions about my hair and wanting to take pictures. I was even asked to audition for a Dove hair care ad.

I didn't grow out my gray to make a statement, but clearly I am! If you're considering going natural, go into it knowing you are going to have some bad-hair days and that some people are going to give their (unasked-for) opinions along the way! But in the end, it's worth it.

What to Expect When Expecting Silver

A Line of Demarcation

If you're going cold turkey, yes, you will have a landing-strip line between your dyed hair and your natural, gorgeous silver. Darker shades of dye are not as forgiving as lighter ones, because the contrast with your silver can be like a neon sign telling the world to look at your roots. A determined perspective is key. This line of demarcation is not always pretty, but think of it this way: The more silver you see, the closer you are to your goal. Also, each time you color your hair, although the goal is to apply the dye just to the roots, it tends to spread a bit beyond the new hair, overlapping with the already-dyed hair. Often, the color is pulled through to the ends of the hair, which results in overprocessed strands. After months and years of this, the ends get darker and darker. So during your grow-out, since layers of dye are no longer building up on your once-colored hair, it begins to naturally lighten up, and the contrast from root growth to ends will soften over time. If you are growing out darker tones and are truly uncomfortable with the line of demarcation, a few integrated highlights may help. (See suggestions in chapter 3.)

What to Do:

Distract Attention from the Landing Strip

- Avoid creating a strong part line. Soften it by allowing the hair to fall in its natural position after cleansing and conditioning. Rub your styling product evenly in your hands, then place your fingertips at the roots and splay them around your head at the scalp and shuffle them gently to get some natural lift. This splayed root-lift motion is also great for curly hair because it prevents the weight of your wet hair from pulling the hair flat at the scalp, which overly exposes the scalp and roots.

- If you have straight or fine hair, try crisscrossing your part. Starting with a straight part, move small sections of hair from one side to the other along your part. Using a bit of gel adds some height and makes the color change less noticeable.

- Create height at your part. You can do this by applying a bit of silicone-free, alcohol-free gel to bobby pins that are at least two inches long and close to the color of your hair. Then weave the pins through your roots, taking strands of hair from each side of your part, sort of like you're sewing a seam together. This works on wet or dry hair. Although you can remove the bobby pins after your hair dries, I actually leave mine in for added volume, which hides the roots even better. If your hair is thick or curly, you can't see the bobby pins when your hair is dry. This is a great technique for second- or third-day unwashed hair or to add lift and volume.

Pinning up the roots

- Root cover-ups, which come in a variety of forms, such as mascaras, sprays, powders, pens, and markers, are nonpermanent options that can help you get through the initial grow-out phase and that work well for touch-ups for special occasions. They wash out of the hair and are usually inexpensive and easy to apply. You can also try Manic Panic temporary colors or even some glitter gel to make roots less noticeable.

WHAT TO EXPECT:
A Change in the Texture of Your Hair

Natural hair often has a different texture from hair that is artificially colored. Silver strands tend to be drier and more wiry, which is why some women don't believe their silver will be pretty. Not true. We all have gorgeous silver potential hiding under our colored layer. It just needs some TLC.

What to Do:
Tweak Your Hair Care

New silver strands need extra hydration, the removal of dead ends, and a great shape to look their best. Conditioner is key—both for the existing colored hair and for the new virgin growth. The two contrasting colors will be equally thirsty, so hydrate them both often. Try deep conditioners or mix a teaspoon of coconut oil in half a cup of hot water, let it cool until it's warm, then pour it over the hair. (The warmth is important, so cool it only until it's a temperature you can tolerate.) Leave it on for one hour or, even better, overnight with a cap, and cleanse the next morning. (See more recipes in chapter 7.) Use only 100 percent sulfate-free shampoo so you don't strip your hair of its natural oils. If your hair is curly and multi-textured, rinse it with cool water to enhance its shine.

WHAT TO EXPECT:
Feelings of Ambivalence

At some point, usually in the first three months, you may get frustrated and feel like backing out. Doubting your decision to go silver is very common, especially if you have a big event or party coming up. Two of our models, Marie and Tricia, struggled with this. (See their stories in chapter 3.)

What to Do:
Keep Your Eyes on the Prize

Realize that every time you dye your hair it's like hitting the rewind button. In other words, you're just prolonging the process. Instead, imagine how much closer you'll be to your goal in a couple of weeks. Keep your expectations realistic and have patience. I'm not going to sugarcoat it: When you're growing in your natural color, you will need to download your mental GPS (Grow-out Patience Sustainability) to keep your sights set on where you are heading. Otherwise, you may get lost. So buckle up your determination and keep a clear vision until you reach your destination. As more than one beautiful silver-haired woman told me, "It's worth it! I'm so glad I stuck it out." And as I said earlier, you can always go back to dyeing, but you might just be surprised how much you like that light shining beneath when you give it a chance! Visualize your whole head free of color and don't get

stuck in the trap of "would have, should have, could have." Yes, the transition can be difficult, but once you reach your goal, you'll forget this difficult time and the rewards will be beauty and freedom. It can help to talk to silver friends or to go online and check out the millions of women confidently posting their silver selfies. These truly inspired me and reminded me that if they could do it, I could, too. It's sort of like looking at images of healthy, fit women when you're trying to shed a few pounds or get in better shape. It keeps your goal front and center.

Not Everyone Will Embrace Your Decision

You may be ready for this transition, but those around you may not be. Their intentions may be innocent, but anyone from a child at the grocery store to a saleslady to your own friends and family may comment on your new hair color.

Remember Whose Hair—and Decision—This Is

Being prepared for negative comments can help soften their blow and keep you steadily on your journey. Remember that *you're* the one who has to live with your hair and care for it, and you are doing it for yourself. You can't please all the people all the time, so just make sure you please yourself, knowing that you'll feel happier and more liberated once you achieve your goal. Still, you may have moments when someone else's comment makes you doubt your decision, so keep this in mind: There's a psychological theory that most people's critical remarks have more to do with their own insecurities—perhaps in some cases their own resistance to going silver. So take a deep breath, smile, and remind yourself what inspired this journey in the first place. And maybe try one of these comebacks, depending on your mood and the intention of the person offering advice: "I value the opinion that you keep to yourself," "We're all works in progress," and "Thanks. And what have *you* been up to?" Attitude will help you get through!

Your Hair Colorist May Fight You

It's not surprising that many hairdressers and colorists try to talk their clients out of transitioning to silver. After all, embracing this natural shade isn't something we hairdressers learn about in beauty school. In fact, colorists, when learning about the science of color, are taught that silver hair is a mistake because it is the absence of color. Whether some colorists truly believe natural silver doesn't look good, or they're worried about losing a client, they may not be supportive at first, or ever. But if they love you, they will set you free. If they're talented, they have many clients, and transitioning one is not going to hurt their livelihood. In fact, it can actually enhance it. From firsthand experience, I know that when you have an encouraging hairstylist who really listens and considers his or her clients' best interests, good word gets around.

Marie Williams, Silver Model

What to Do:
Hug It Out or Say Goodbye

Transitioning to natural silver hair, just like any journey, requires support and guidance from those around you—including your colorist. So if he or she isn't on board, it may be time to say: ciao, adios, au revoir, auf Wiedersehen. If you don't have a supportive hairdresser, find one. Healthy hair is important while transitioning. Consult good friends for recommendations or, if you see a silver-haired woman whose strands look gorgeous, ask her who styles her hair. Chances are she'll be flattered, and you may get some valuable information.

Regret That You Didn't Embrace Your Silver Sooner

Not everyone feels this way, but it *is* something I heard *over and over* from dozens of women, and I feel this way myself. In fact, I rarely heard any silver belle say she wanted to go back to dyeing. Even women who had been hesitant to start their journey to silver told me they wished they'd kicked their coloring habit when they were younger. Others said if they could go back in time, they never would have dyed their hair at all.

What to Do:

Nothing!

Just rejoice in the fact that you appreciate your silver strands *now*, and give them all the TLC they need.

Jennifer Ho-Dougatz, Silver Model

Color Erasers

I f you want your dyed hair to have a less noticeable line of demarcation as your silver grows in, a color remover, also called a color eraser, can help fade some of the artificial pigment, especially if your dyed hair is really dark. However, Kristy Wilson cautions that "results vary and you won't know exactly what color you'll be left with until you actually use one of these products." It depends on several factors, including your hair's chemical makeup, color history, and the artificial color used.

- At home, you can try a non-bleach-based color remover, like Color Oops, available at beauty supply stores. Test it first on a few strands of pigmented hair in a concealed area. This strand test may feel like an extra step, but it's really worth knowing what color you'll end up with before committing.

- A stylist will likely give you a more even all-over color than you can if you do it yourself. Hairstylists know that "color erasers go into the sulfite bonds of the hair's cuticle and shrink the artificial color molecules, so they can squeeze through the cuticle and get washed away," Kristy explains. "You can't see the molecules with the naked eye, but your hair will look less pigmented when you're done." Just make sure they do a strand test first.

- If you use a color remover at home and then go to a colorist, be sure to tell the colorist what you've done. There can be unusual color surprises if chemicals get mixed.

Feeling "More Me"

Patti Page, 64, *Professional Baker and Owner of Baked Ideas*

My hair color has always been my identity. I was constantly referred to as the "petite redhead." So I was afraid to stop coloring it, although I'd thought about it for years. When I'd leave the salon after having my hair colored, I could never relax, because I knew that every minute my hair was going from good to bad: i.e., my roots were coming in. I hated that! I'd also think, *OK, I have four weeks until I'll need to color again, but I have a wedding in three weeks. What am I going to do?* When I was considering going silver, I was concerned because I'm pale with light eyes. Would I look really washed-out? Almost all of my friends cautioned against going silver. But after talking to Lorraine (for months!), I was finally ready to give it a try.

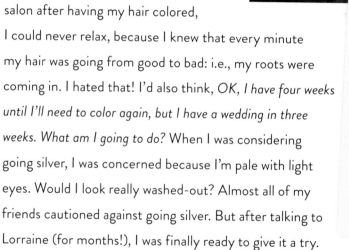

The first few months, I texted Lorraine in distress when I received any negative comments from friends or, even worse, no comments. "OK. So let's dye it back," Lorraine would say, trying to use reverse psychology on me. Of course, it worked. I didn't want to hit the reset button and find myself back in the coloring cycle and then have to go through this grow-out again.

For the first few months of growing my color out, I was tortured about it. I couldn't get my hair to look good. The silver roots at the crown against the red made it looked like I had a bald spot, something really noticeable because I'm short and most people are looking down on me. Another worry was that I feared people thought I was a lazy person who didn't color her hair. During that time, I had a wedding and a holiday party, so I used a root cover-up spray. They're not hard to apply and they wash out easily, too.

But after about four months, when more silver had come in, I actually started to like it. *Really* like it! My shade of silver was nice and actually looked good with the red, which had faded to more of a brown. Now I'm totally into it and realize I don't care what other people think. And I *love* not having to make time to have my hair dyed, something that didn't feel natural but that I'd done for almost twenty years. Now when I look at "before" pictures of myself, the red looks so fake, and I see that the natural silver better suits my style and personality. It's more me.

Patti's First Three Months

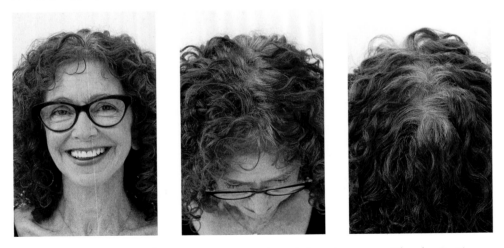

When Patti commented on my gray-bré and I told her I was growing out my hair color, I proposed the idea of her doing the same. Clearly, Patti was really ready to stop coloring, but was just looking for the opportunity. I'm not saying it was easy for her. For Patti—and most women—this early stage of growing out cold turkey is the hardest. Between her three-month and six-month photo shoots and the next, Patti texted me saying she was "kinda freaking out! I look a little crazy." But she stuck with it.

Patti at Six Months

Often people with red or dark hair worry that the line of demarcation will be really obvious. However, because you're not applying color from the roots to the ends anymore, the once-colored hair naturally starts to lighten up. This means the line of demarcation isn't such an eyesore. While we all know the term *salt-and-pepper* for hair that is both dark and silver, I love the term *cinnamon-and-sugar* for hair that is silver and red.

Patti at Nine Months

Patti is what I call a "quick silver," meaning that within weeks of starting her grow-out, her hair was noticeably silver. The benefit of being a quick silver is that you can quickly see how you'll look with your natural hair color. At this point, Patti had enough silver to start to accept it, and she began to like how it looked. For this photo shoot, I gave her a trim to remove some of the colored hair so her natural red hue would stand out more. I think she looks better with shorter hair, too. When it's longer, it looks like her hair is wearing her. Then colorist Kristy Wilson formulated a toner that matched her natural silver and used it on the dyed red ends. This broke up the band of color, softened it, and helped it better blend with her natural hue.

Silver Inspiration

Mindy Greenstein, 53,
Clinical Psychologist and Author

When my roots would show, it was like the real me showing through, and I colored it because I felt like the real me wasn't good enough for the world to see. One day I thought, *Why should the real me make me feel bad? What's wrong with letting my hair's natural color and texture come through?* First, I stopped straightening my hair so I could get comfortable with my natural wave. After experimenting with tips from *Curly Girl: The Handbook* and different products, I found an easy, wavy style I liked. This made me comfortable enough to start going silver. Also, the year before, I'd published a book, *Lighter as We Go*, about the positive aspects of aging, but here I was, covering up.

Find books, Facebook groups, blogs, Pinterest pages, etc., where you can get information, inspiration, and support for your choice. Avoid people who lack the imagination to recognize how good you might look in the end. When I knew my colorist wouldn't listen to me, I found someone who would.

I knew that my colorist wouldn't be willing to help with the transition, so I went to a different one. She did highlights and lowlights that camouflaged the line of demarcation. It looked good and I got only positive feedback. Then I thought about why people enjoy life more when they're older and realized it's because they don't care what others think. It's not that I'm letting myself go or don't care about my appearance. It's that I'm actually finding the "me" that I'm most comfortable with, that works with my lifestyle, and that I want to present to the world.

Six months after getting highlights, I decided to just go cold turkey. I was nervous at first, but excited to see my natural color. My mantra became "No more shit in my hair," and I haven't looked back since! Nine months later, my hair had grown in enough that I really started to like the color, and I got so many compliments. One person even said that I looked "so badass!" I can assure you that no one had ever used that word to describe me before.

Since I've embraced my natural texture and color, my hair is so much healthier. Without blow-drying and dye, it's softer and shinier. But more than that, I'm no longer a slave to my roots or my hairdresser and I feel more like myself. This is who I am and this is good enough. *I* am good enough. It's a real sense of freedom. I know that silver can be linked to getting old, but I'm a two-time cancer survivor. To me, getting old is a good thing! Now my hair is an expression of who *I* am, not the artistic talents of a colorist.

A lot of women have complimented my hair and said things like "If my silver was as nice as yours, I'd go natural." Yet the truth is, you don't know *what* kind of silver you're going to have. You have to let it grow in a little bit, and even then it changes. My silver looked different when I had just a small amount of blonde left on the ends and then when Lorraine cut it all off. You have to have faith. I did, and now I like my hair more than I ever have and feel more like myself than I ever have, too!

The day of my final photo shoot for this book was also the last day of my mother's life. She'd died early that morning, at the age of eighty-one. She was a force of nature, having survived the Holocaust as a child. She always thought I took life too seriously, that I should try to have more fun. That's why she loved hearing about my participation in this project. Her own hair was white, though that description doesn't do justice to the variety of silky whites, silvers, and even a touch of pewter that framed her face. I initially canceled the shoot, but, as I started absorbing my loss and thinking about the eulogy I'd give the next day, I could hear Mom's voice in my head: "So what if you're sad about me? Why should you miss out on the last chance to have your fancy photo taken?!" As soon as I walked onto the set, I knew I'd made the right choice. Everyone was so lovely, hugging me and—Ma would particularly appreciate this part—feeding me. Even though I was choking back tears, my smile for the camera was genuine. As I turned this way and that while the photographer clicked away, her eulogy started forming in my head.

People often ask me where I get my naturally silver hair done. No one ever asked me when I was blonde!

Mindy as a Faux-Blonde

Mindy's hair is far too yellow for her skin tone. You know there's a lot of gray underneath because the blonde is so yellow.

Mindy at Six Months

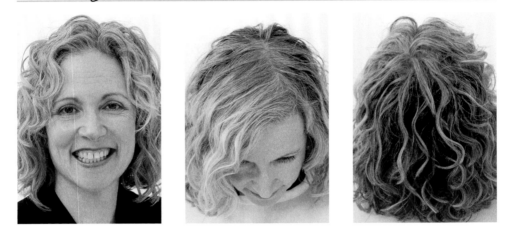

At Mindy's first photo shoot, all I did was cut her hair. Typically, blondes have an easier time transitioning, because there's not as much contrast between their natural icy ash color and the dyed blonde. Because of this, Mindy opted for the cold turkey technique.

Mindy at Nine Months

Often women who have fine hair like Mindy's choose to color even if they don't need to, because color gives the hair more body. Mindy's hair has little to no frizz and waves that are easily weighed down at the scalp, making the ends appear a bit stringy and the roots more obvious. Frequent conditioning is not right for everyone, especially those with fine hair. If you've got fine hair that tends to get wilted and weighed-down, try this:

- Use either cleanser or conditioner but not both, and make sure to thoroughly rinse all the conditioner out of your hair.

- After showering, bend over at the waist, flip your head upside down and, using a towel, scrunch and squeeze your hair upward the way you would scr unch up a piece of paper. This will remove excess water, which can weigh hair down, while preserving its natural movement. Next, lift your head upright, tilt it to the side, and scrunch the hair upward. Then, starting with the hair on one side of your face, take about a three-inch section, scrunch it up, and clip it in place at the roots. This prevents the weight of your wet hair from weighing down your locks as they dry, leaving them limp. Repeat this around your entire head. Wait at least ten to fifteen minutes or, if your hair is very fine, allow it to dry fully clipped up like this. Remove the clips and then apply a small amount of your favorite styling product, if you wish. This process will make your hair appear much fuller.

- Don't put any product in your hair while it's wet. Allowing the hair cuticles to open to their natural expansion gives the hair more body once it dries. Putting gel and creams on wet hair tends to weigh it down and often makes it look wet and wilted even after it has dried.

- To give hair a midday boost, bend over at the waist, let your hair hang down, and place your fingertips at the roots by splaying your fingers around your head at the scalp. Then lightly shuffle the roots. This will aerate your hair, boost volume, and increase circulation to your scalp—which feels great and can help alleviate headaches. You can also use a pick, being careful to lift the hair just at the root and not pulling the pick all the way through or the hair will frizz.

Mindy at Twelve Months

At this point, Mindy had only a tiny bit of dyed color left, so I cut her hair to remove most of it and give her hair some shape. Then she styled it with the scrunch method described above. Kristy suggested that once a month Mindy use a sulfate-free, purple cleansing wash or conditioner made for silver hair. The violet neutralizes the yellow, reducing any brassiness on the dyed hair. (For a recipe for a do-it-yourself blue/purple conditioning toner, see chapter 7.)

Riding the Silver Wave

Katelyn Triola, 28,
Floral and Event Designer

....

I was thirteen when I saw my first silver hair. It was so embarrassing, but my mom wouldn't let me dye it. She said it wasn't good for my hair. Instead, I would pluck the silver strands out with a tweezer. That was until my aunt told me that for every hair you pluck, you get eight more in its place, something I've since learned is a myth. By the time I was eighteen, my silver was much more noticeable. Once I was old enough, I began dyeing my hair. Nine years later, I spoke to my colorist about growing out the dye. She suggested continuing to color everything except a strip of silver around my face, so I could get used to it. I really liked the way it looked, so when I went back to my colorist seven months

Give it a try and ride the wave. The process of growing out your silver can be very frustrating. There are awkward phases—they made me upset at times. But I learned a lot about myself from the process. I looked within rather than judging myself based on my appearance. My hair doesn't define who I am—in any color—but I love not having to maintain a look or identity that my body wasn't naturally allowing. Now that I have fully grown out my silver, I can say that this experience has given me a greater sense of confidence. So give it a try, don't be afraid, learn from yourself, and love yourself, because true beauty comes from within.

later, she dyed even less of it and left most of the silver. Then I decided not to dye at all. Initially, my parents told me that I looked old with silver hair. "If money is the issue, I'll pay for you to get your hair done," my dad said. But I kept the silver. And now they like it and admire my decision.

A few years later, I decided to cut my hair to shoulder-length. The previous year had been an emotional roller coaster for me in terms of loss, change, and health scares, and very few things were in my control. It was December, so with a new year approaching, and hoping it would be a better one, I saw my haircut as an opportunity to let go of the remnants of the old year, a decision I was in control of. I know that it is just hair, but taking off about twelve inches and giving myself a new look became a cathartic experience for me. At first there was a bit of a shock factor after my haircut, because I realized just how fully silver I was! But it's nice to see my hair look more uniform than when it was long, because sometimes I felt the silver on top and dark brown on the bottom was a bit messy looking.

Within the past year, my silver hair has been received in such a positive way compared with when I first started growing it out. I constantly have people—women *and* men—coming up to me and asking if it's my natural hair color, giving me kudos for growing it out, and saying how cool it is. Recently someone asked me how I got it this color, and she couldn't believe it was natural. It's also amazing to see how many people struggle with the thought of growing out their dyed hair. Some people don't have confidence that it will look good, because they can't bear the awkward phase of growing out; some people feel their significant others won't like it or that they will just look old. It's been a great feeling to speak with these people, relate to how they feel, and hopefully encourage them to be themselves, not to be afraid, and to learn from the process, as I have.

Katelyn at Seven Months

When I first met Katelyn, her silver was really noticeable because of her dark hair, but her youthful energy made it look deliberate. In fact, many people stopped her on the street and asked her about it because they thought she did it on purpose. She was really focused on her goal of fully transitioning and was determined.

Katelyn at Nine Months

Here, Katelyn's hair is way beyond roots or a landing strip; it's graybré. It also looks even more deliberate and stylish, which really inspired people around her.

Katelyn at Twelve Months

Katelyn came to this photo shoot with her hair totally silver and it looked amazing.
We cut and pin curled it.

The Right Choice

Dianne Velez, 39,
Financial Industry

Going silver early runs in my family, so I wasn't surprised when I saw my first silver hairs at the age of seventeen. By the time I was nineteen, I had this patch in the front that looked like a skunk stripe, which I dyed. But eventually it became more and more prominent and, as a result, more and more difficult to cover. I had to go to the salon every three weeks. Finally, on my thirty-seventh birthday, I decided to embrace my silver.

One reason I didn't want to stop coloring was because I really looked forward to going to the salon. As a married, working mom of two kids, it was the only time that was totally *mine*, and I didn't want to lose that. I also *loved* my hair colorist. We even had a tradition where I'd have an appointment the day after Thanksgiving and she'd bring leftovers and wine. I called it "Thanks for Giving Color." But when I told her I wanted to embrace my silver, she did the research to help me transition. I work for a conservative financial institution and I didn't want to look unprofessional in my office with a big line of demarcation. Instead, we tried lightening my hair and applying toners. But my hair wouldn't hold the color, and the toners turned it a funky orange. I also played around with tinted dry shampoo, which wasn't great either. I was on vacation in Florida with my family when one day a crazy rainstorm came out of nowhere. My husband turned to me and said, "Why is your face all black?" I realized that the tinted dry shampoo was dripping down my face! At that moment, I knew I couldn't do it anymore. I needed to stop trying to fake it. So I cut my hair as short as possible and let it grow in on its own. In the end, I realized my natural color is nicer than anything I ever applied.

At first everyone around me hated it—especially my mother and mother-in-law. They're old-school Spanish and kept asking me why I was making myself look old. But now everyone accepts it and some people refuse to believe it's natural. And I absolutely love it, which is more important than anything.

Dianne's Hair with Five Months' Grow-out

Even though Dianne likes her hair a bit longer, she let me cut off the remaining color.

Dianne After We Shaped Her Hair and Cut Most of the Remaining Color

I love Dianne's hair in this photo—all of it. Because she preferred more closed curls, she was a bit nervous about the scrunch method I suggested to give her curls freer rein. (Personally, I want to go up to every "closed-caption curly girl" and fluff her out to see her curls open up!) She's her full silver-siren self here.

Depending on how Dianne parts her hair she can change how prominent her white streak is or whether it's there at all.

Finally Feeling Put-Together

Margaret Page, 57,
Fashion Stylist/Interior Designer

Yes, you have to be a little brave in the beginning, but it's worth it.

I dyed my hair for twenty years. But the color grew out so quickly and I thought it was really aging to see gray roots sticking out and framing my face. What's interesting is that I didn't even *like* the way the dye looked, so I was paying money to have hair that was flat and never shiny. I thought about it for about a year before I decided to embrace my silver. I colored it one last time before Thanksgiving and after that I went cold turkey. It was easier to start the grow-out process during the winter, when I could cover my roots with a beret and other hats. My hair was really long at the time, so over the year and a half that I was growing it out, I kept cutting it until it was shoulder-length, which also helped the transition, because the balance between dyed hair and silver hair changed.

Once it grew out and my hair was all natural silver, I loved it. It looks more youthful than having roots and a lot healthier, too. So many of us are struggling and fighting against what nature gave us, and Lorraine taught me how to love my hair, both the texture and the color. Now I honestly don't even think about my hair color anymore. It's so freeing!

A lot of women say, "I love your hair, but I could never do it." Yes, you have to be a little brave and just push through the beginning, but it's worth it. Once you get a good few inches going, it starts to look deliberate and people stop looking at you like "Why aren't you coloring your hair?" Although, to be honest, I never cared what people thought, because it's my hair!

With my natural silver color, I feel more like my true self. I'm no longer trying to fit a square peg into a round hole. When I was dyeing my hair and had gray roots, I never felt put-together, no matter what I did. Now, with my silver hair, I feel happier than ever. In fact, in the years that I've had my hair all silver, I've had a couple of nightmares that I colored my hair. I can't tell you how relieved I was when I woke up and it wasn't true!

Rainbow Hues

Giving your hair a temporary pop of color is as easy as a trip to your local art supply store. There, you can pick up a box of oil pastels and literally draw color onto your hair. You can choose an exposed piece on top, a lock underneath the rest of your hair, or a few pieces all over. Have fun, knowing it's risk-free. It will fade quickly and wash out with good sulfate-free hair cleanser.

We All Have a Light and a Dark Side.
Mine Is My Twin Sister!

Debbie Lyman and Naomi Rosenblum are identical twin sisters, but no one has trouble telling them apart: Debbie colors her hair while Naomi embraces her natural silver strands.

DEBBIE

I may be eight minutes older, but my identical-twin sister, Naomi, is the smarter one, because I'm a slave to coloring and she is not. For some time, I kept the salt-and-pepper look. It was beautiful and grew in so evenly that people thought I did it at a salon. But once it became more salt than pepper, I started lowlighting it to even it out. Then I got divorced, and, at the same time, my hair became salt, pepper, mustard, and ketchup from the lowlighting. In other words, it was oxidizing. I decided that in order to snag a new guy, I needed to look young, so I started coloring it. Now I also have highlights, which I did so the roots might not be as obvious. It didn't work.

I hate going to the salon every two weeks and that I'm a slave to my hair and neurotic about it. I work with a lovely young lady in her early forties, and some silver has appeared in her hair over the last few years. I made her promise me she'd never touch it. As director of operations at my organization, I joked to her that she would not get a raise if she even *thought* about using that money to color her hair. So far she has listened and it looks great! Now I'd give anything to stop coloring, but I worry that it would take forever to grow out. I'm extremely jealous of Naomi!

NAOMI

I was also in my mid-twenties when I discovered my first silver hair, and for a short period of time I got lowlights. But I did not enjoy being a slave to the lowlighting process and got really tired of worrying about the roots, so I stopped coloring, which was extremely liberating. When Debbie mentions that she's going to the colorist, I feel so relieved that there's one less thing in my life for me to deal with. I get so many compliments on my hair and am often asked if it's my natural color.

People have told me I'm their inspiration to stop dyeing their hair, which of course makes me feel proud, and others say if they knew their hair would be the same color as mine, they, too, would let it grow out. I always tell them they should definitely try it or they won't know for sure. Also, the younger you are when you decide to stop coloring your hair, the easier it is to grow out the roots. Because you don't have as much silver to cover up, there's less of a line of demarcation.

Why Would You Put Yourself Through This?

"I secretly wish that I had to go on *Survivor* so I would be forced to stop coloring my hair. I'd be on a desert island with no access to color, so I'd finally see what my natural hair color really looks like, something I haven't seen in more than fifteen years."

—Jill

"For me, 'that time of the month' isn't my period; it's when I have to go to the salon for my hair color appointment. I get in a bad mood because I dread going to the colorist every four weeks, the same way you dread getting your period."

—Beth

"It's not being gray that bothers me; it's the journey getting there."

—Jenny

"I chose my colorist because of the salon's proximity to my house, not because of her skill. In fact, she doesn't even do a good job, it's expensive, and I can't stand her voice. But even an overpriced, bad dye job by someone I don't like seems better than having roots."

—Jodi

"I know that my dyed hair is too dark for my face."

—Sheila

"My hair grows so fast that there is only one day a month that I *don't* have roots: the day I get my hair colored."

—Cindy

"I was a star swimmer all through high school and college and love being in the water. But now I don't swim at all because of the way the chlorine can affect my hair color. Yes, my life revolves around hair dye."

—Samantha

"Every six weeks, before I color my hair, I smear antihistamine cream over my forehead, ears, and neck. Otherwise, I get an itchy, blistery rash from the dye and it lasts for weeks."

—Sara

"This is crazy to admit, but the only way I think I could give myself permission to go silver is if I got cancer and lost my hair."

—Miriam

CHAPTER THREE

THE HIGHS AND LOWS
OF TRANSITIONING:

Highlights, Lowlights, Blending & Toning

ighlights and lowlights can make the grow-out a little easier, offering a smoother tone transition by blurring the line of demarcation. Although you will still be coloring your hair, chances are you'll do it less often than when you were covering up all of your silver—perhaps every six to eight weeks instead of two to four. Depending on their hair length, some women use these techniques for a short time to begin their transition to hair that is completely dye-free and natural in hue.

For example, you might start with highlights placed just below your natural roots. Once your natural color is close to being grown in, you can gradually stop the highlights and any coloring altogether. Other women use highlights and lowlights to embrace just a little of their natural hue. For example, if you are starting out with a solid, darker dyed color, choosing to highlight some of the hair from the roots down not only softens the overall base color and gives it some dimension, but it also helps to begin to integrate the tone of your natural silver at the roots, blurring the line of contrast. At first you may feel like you are replacing one color application with another, but all these color-weaning suggestions are hopefully baby steps to ease you toward loving your natural silver strands. In the weeks before you get highlights, lowlights, or any color, it's important to deep-condition regularly so your hair is in the best shape possible to receive the color. Also, your locks are fragile after coloring, especially if bleach is used, so deep-condition afterward as well.

Highlights

Highlights are sections of hair that are dyed lighter than your base color. "Going lighter can blend the silver while it's growing out," explains Edward Joseph Farley, a master colorist and curly hair specialist in New York City. When the highlights are strategically placed throughout your hair, they can also make your roots less obvious and camouflage some of your silver. Highlights are great if you have long hair or straight hair, or if you're transitioning from red or a darker base color, because they bring a lighter color through the length of the hair, helping you gradually adjust to your lighter, natural silver. Blonde or white highlights with toners can create a twilight-silver or platinum hue. They can also be designed to match the natural silver tone at the root line.

Silver highlights and lowlights

These suggestions and techniques will require some professional color advice, however. "I don't recommend that anyone attempt highlights at home, especially if your hair is really dark," cautions Veronica Tapia of Jersey Curl Salon. "In achieving silver highlights, first you have to bleach the hair and *then* put the silver toner over that. This isn't an easy process, so it's worth finding someone who knows what they're doing and investing in a salon appointment or two."

If you have been dyeing at home and your goal is to stop coloring altogether, some of these suggestions may initially require more time and money than you've been spending. But sometimes you have to take a few steps backward to go forward in this fast, *I-want-it-now* world. Tricia Regan (see page 95), who started out with very long, dark dyed hair, is a perfect example of someone who colored at home every three weeks but needed color assistance to transition to her natural hue. Tricia is now getting only the remaining colored hair professionally highlighted and is not touching her silver root growth. This does require time and money, but she goes to the salon much less often than she did before. For effective hair coloring, it is essential to follow the specific directions for each product and use the right developer formulation with the correct color formulation. That is why having the initial transition done at a salon is something to seriously consider. Most likely, your colorist will also apply a toner and suggest you use a semi- or demi-permanent (ammonia-free) color toner at home; both are available at beauty supply stores and online.

Elena Sisto, Silver Model and artist

What Is Toner?

A toner, also referred to as a gloss, is a translucent form of semipermanent dye that contains a small amount of ammonia. It can be used on either virgin or artificially colored hair in order to neutralize or manipulate an unwanted or uneven shade. The difference between hair color and toner is that while hair color is like solid paint, toner is like a shellac stain on wood. If you opt for highlights, most often you'll need a toner as well, because the highlights may not entirely erase or lift the color already on your hair, or they may do so in some areas more readily than others, making your color appear uneven and patchy in tone. Toners are mainly used on bleached and lightened hair. Like a topcoat of nail polish, a toner seals the cuticle and allows the color to last longer, often giving richness and shine in the process. Quick-fix toners can also be found in some sulfate-free shampoos, silicone-free conditioners, and styling products.

Toners for Brassy, Yellow, or Blo-range Hair

Have you seen that shade of blonde that's so yellow it looks like the color of a banana? Chances are, these people did not use a toner after they colored. When hair is lightened, bleach lifts up the hair's cuticle and exposes new pigment molecules to the air. Depending on the porosity of the hair and its prior shade, this can cause the hair to oxidize, giving it a blonde-orange (which I call "blo-range") or yellow cast, often referred to as "brassy." A toner can be applied after the bleaching process to neutralize and soften unwanted hues by changing the chemical makeup of the pigment in the hair shaft. This is known as a double-process color application. The toner is the magic formula that grabs onto these shades, creating a warm blonde, silver, platinum, or dusty pastel tone. It can also help blend in strands that may not have lightened evenly in the color process.

Toners for Warm Hair Shades

If you're growing out dyed blonde hair, a silver toner can even out the surface color to soften its yellow appearance. Just look at Jackie's hair which started out as what Kristy Wilson calls a "warm blonde." Kristy used a semipermanent cool ash toner to turn Jackie's yellow-blonde into a silver shade that is very similar to her natural hair color. By using a cooler ash toner as a transitional step while her dyed hair grows out, there will be no line of demarcation and Jackie can slowly get used to her natural hue. Because the toner is semipermanent, it will fade quickly, so Jackie may have to tone her hair several times as it grows out. However, since her hair is short and she has

Jackie's hair went from warm to cool with a simple toner application.

a fabulous naturally white streak around the front, this should be a painless and brief process. We suggest that she use a demi-permanent toner now and also when her dye is completely grown out. This will complement and add vibrancy to her natural hue well after she has grown out the dye.

Toners for Naturally Silver Strands

Because they don't contain any ammonia, demi-permanent toners can help reduce the yellowing that can occur on naturally silver strands and can be used to give hair fun pastel tones like purple, violet, and pink champagne, which is very flattering for all skin tones. The silver hair of one of our models, Antonia, tended to get a bit yellow because she rides her bike to work, and the sweat under her helmet yellows the silver, similar to how the armpit area on your favorite white shirt turns yellowish after a while. Antonia used a violet toner to turn her yellow-tinged hair a gorgeous iridescent silver. She may want to continue to use a toner as part of her hair care routine and would do well using a brightening sulfate-free shampoo that has a purple or violet tone, too.

How long you leave the toner in your hair depends on how light your hair is. "Women who have naturally white hair might also want to use non-sulfate clarifying treatments, because air pollution and mineral buildup from water can turn hair yellow," Kristy says. She suggests a salon treatment or Malibu C Hard Water Wellness Treatment, which you can buy online or at a beauty supply store. Another option is to make a paste from water and baking soda or powdered vitamin C to work into dry hair, focusing on the yellow tones. Leave it on for five to ten minutes, rinse well, and cleanse and condition, preferably with products that have blue, violet, or purple tones.

Various factors can determine how long a toner will last. It will fade faster if you wash your hair often with a sulfate shampoo, if you have hard water, if you use heated styling tools like flat irons and blow-dryers, and if you get a lot of unprotected sun exposure. Toners are not one-size-fits-all, and it's crucial to use the right one for your hair color, which can be tricky to determine. "I suggest you get a toner at a salon *first* and ask your hair care specialist to help you customize and choose what to use at home, such as a color foam," says Kristy. Toners are not as expensive as hair color, but for certain colors and hair textures, they may need to be applied more often. The amount of time you leave it in for may depend on the undertone and the desired effect.

When shopping for the right toner, we suggest gentle formulas like color foam toners. Don't choose your toner color based on the hair swatch that appears on the box on the shelf. Like stain on wood, the color your hair is now and the chemicals that have been used on it will affect the toned color. Most colorists will send you home with a care package that includes a toner and specific instructions, or will recommend what to buy at a beauty supply store. Write down these suggestions, or call your color practitioner if you're at the store and unsure what to buy.

Lowlights

Whereas highlights add color that's lighter than the base color, lowlights color sections of hair darker than the existing base color. There are a variety of lowlight applications and many colors that can be considered lowlights. They are often used to tone down and temper over-highlighted hair created either by balayage (a form of painting on color) or foiling selected strands and coloring them. Lowlights can be used to mimic the natural darker gray tones you may have at the roots to help them blend into the existing color as you start to allow it to grow out. Some people may use a mix of highlights and lowlights in the weaning-off process until the hair is totally natural, while others may continue using lowlights intertwined through their silver strands until they are ready to embrace them completely. As the silver becomes more prominent, the hair may reject the lowlight color and it may fade rather quickly.

We applied lowlights to Marie's hair to soften the transition to her glorious silver.

Jen's Zen Journey

Jen Hallowell, 53, *Personal Trainer and Yoga Instructor*

....

I was going to the salon every six weeks to get my hair colored—although I could have gone every four. While I was there, I'd also get my hair cut, so each salon visit was expensive and time-consuming. I was getting tired of it and had been thinking about growing out my colored hair for a while, but my hairdresser said it was too soon and that I didn't have enough silver to do it. "You need a much bigger patch," she told me. It turns out this wasn't correct, because when I met Lorraine and Kristy, they said how much silver you have doesn't matter. It just has to grow in so you can see it. I thought highlights were a great idea. My skin coloring seems to be getting lighter as I mature, so why not let my hair go lighter, too?

> Start as soon as you want to. If I'd started when I wanted to (not when my hairdresser told me to), I'd have been happily silver much sooner.

It's such a relief to not be going to the salon, because the second I left, I felt like the clock was ticking until I'd be back again. The hardest part of going silver was the line of demarcation. I work out a lot, and when I pulled my hair back into a ponytail, you could really see it. At first, my husband wasn't thrilled with the idea of me going silver, but now he sees how happy I am and loves it, too. Even though at times I felt self-conscious about the different colors in my hair, once I started, I never wanted to turn back. Part of this has to do with the fact that I've been focusing on yoga, which has opened my mind and heart to new possibilities and to loving my true self.

Jen, Two Months Color-Free

TECHNIQUE:
Silver Blended Highlights

Jen was like many women who think they're alone in considering embracing their natural hair color: She just needed a little support. At this photo shoot, it had been eight weeks since she'd last colored her hair. The silver was growing mostly in the back and underneath and seemed to be a dark silver-granite hue that was competing with her dye. Because Jen had a lot of brunette hair as a base, Kristy distributed silver highlights that matched her natural darker gray color. She placed them just below the roots but not *on* them, so Jen's natural hair could start its grow-out journey free of artificial color. This looked great and helped blend with her silver, giving it a cayenne-peppery transition. Kristy also toned the highlights with a silver toner.

Jen at Six Months

Jen at Nine Months

At this final shoot, Jen's dyed hair was totally grown out, so we didn't need to do anything to her gorgeous, natural hue but give her a playful haircut to match her playful and open spirit.

Time and Patience

Don't expect too much from your emerging hue at first. Your new color may appear to be dark steel, charcoal-toned, or whiter than snow-covered mountains. Often, the hair at the nape of the neck tends to be darker than the overlaying canopy hair. Also, you may think your whole head is going to be silver if you let the color grow out, but sometimes it comes in as sporadic streaks or tinsel patches, like mine and Jen's did. The bottom line is that you don't know what you'll get until you allow it to grow. Still, my bet is that you'll be pleasantly surprised!

A Question-hair

To find a colorist who can help you transition using highlights or lowlights and customize take-home toners, ask these questions of a salon or prospective stylist:

Is there a color correction specialist I can consult with before making an appointment?

The answer should be "Absolutely!"

Does the colorist have before-and-after photos of color transitions?

Many colorists post these on Facebook, Instagram, and other forms of social media.

How long have you been a colorist?

In this case, experience does matter.

What is the approximate cost and how much time is required?

The answer will vary depending on your hair's processing history, type, length, and porosity.

Marie's Game of Tones

Marie Williams, 45, *Hairdresser*

I was twenty-five years old when I noticed my first silver hair. I began coloring my hair right away and did so for about twenty years. But it required a lot of maintenance—especially more recently, because I was coloring about every two weeks and then seeing silver just a few days later. I'm a hairdresser, so I did my own color and was getting tired of sectioning my hair, going over the same white area in the front, the feel of chemicals on my scalp, and the dye stains on my walls, shower curtain, and towels. Then I saw this gorgeous, young, silver-haired woman on Facebook. *If my hair can look like that, I'm in*, I thought. I decided to give it a try. To ease into it, I stopped my all-over color and applied silver highlights and some lowlights. I loved it because it seemed sexy, urban, and modern.

During my transition, a few people said, "Are you ever going to cover those roots?" and my three older sisters worried that the baby of the family going silver would make *them* look bad. My eighty-year-old mother was shocked because she still colors her hair every four weeks. And they weren't the only ones. As a hairstylist, I was concerned about how I'd look to my clients. *How will I explain* not *covering my* own *silver when a big part of my business is color?* But to my surprise, the response was great. A lot of people thought I'd actually dyed my roots silver! The first few weeks were the most difficult, because my initial reaction to any hint of my natural color was to hurry and cover it up. Letting go of that habit and opening my mind to something new was the hardest part. It took a bit of trial and error. But over time it became easier and easier to see myself in a different light. I started to get excited about what my hair could eventually look like, and it was so liberating to not be a slave to my roots anymore. Embracing my hair's natural color makes me feel like I did when I embraced my curls. Instead of covering up, I'm authentically me! A lot of my clients have chosen to go silver because of me. It's amazing how many enlightening, wonderful questions and compliments people give me and the conversations people now want to have about my natural hair, a part of me I once dreaded acknowledging. This hasn't just been a hair transformation of mine; it's been an overall life improvement.

Marie's Silver Start at Three Months

When Marie arrived, her roots were an obvious contrast to her dyed brown hair. Kristy put silver highlights and pepper-brown lowlights throughout Marie's hair to help blend her roots so she didn't have such an obvious line of demarcation. Doing this also helps you get used to having lighter hair, especially if you're transitioning from a darker base color.

TECHNIQUE: Highlights and Warm Brown Lowlights

Marie at Six Months

For Marie, herself a hairdresser who says she can't keep her hands off her own hair, going silver has involved experimentation and a lot of trial and error. In her first session, Kristy gave her a tube of toner to take home after the highlights and lowlights were applied. But when Marie arrived at the next photo shoot, about nine weeks later, it seemed she'd used too much of the toner, because her hair was darker

than it had been. Lightening the hair with silver highlights means using bleach, which increases the porosity of the hair. When the hair is more porous, it can absorb too much toner, which is what had happened. Here, Kristy applied a purple-based toner to try to re-highlight Marie's hair and make her line of demarcation less noticeable. We didn't want to use bleach, as her hair was fragile from the various processes.

Marie at Various Points Along the Way

"After the last photo shoot, I didn't like the contrast of dark dyed color and silver," Marie said. So before this photo shoot, she applied two bleach caps—a mix of bleach, peroxide, and soap that is applied all over the head—to lift the previously deposited demi-color that had made her hair look too dark. Marie also added highlights and then toned them with a silver demi-permanent toner. Since Marie had done so much to her hair on her own and it was already so bleached out, Kristy didn't do anything to Marie's hair at this photo shoot, as she didn't want to risk damage or breakage.

Marie experimented—a lot—as she journeyed to silver. I believe that if she

hadn't done anything to her hair on her own, her silver would have been down to her jaw by this photo shoot. Kristy and I have both had clients who have stopped and started this process a few times until they decided to really go for it. This is totally normal. It's like any major life change—it's right only when you are truly ready.

This hasn't
just been a hair
transformation
of mine; it's been
an overall life
improvement.

With a Little Help from Her Friends

Tricia Regan, 53, *Filmmaker*

I spotted my first silver hair when I was thirteen. By the time I was thirty, more than half my head was silver—which wasn't good, since I was working in the very youth-oriented film industry. So I started using at-home semipermanent and then permanent color every two weeks. It was only about twenty dollars a month, compared to one hundred dollars or more at a salon, but I reached a point where it felt like I was being false by coloring my hair. I felt like I was lying to everyone, mostly myself. That's when I decided to gradually go silver.

If you're growing out a color and don't want to go "cold turkey," find a professional colorist who is willing to take on this process and who has a plan for you. I had been to several people, and they each had a different idea about how to go about it. I looked around until I found someone I trusted and who listened to my concerns.

Because I didn't want to quit coloring cold turkey, I started by going blonde with a lot of highlights. This helped me—and my colleagues—get used to the idea of silver. Then I got a few silver highlights to help my natural gray blend in better. I was a little freaked-out that I was actually *adding* silver. But I really liked it—until I noticed a greenish-blue cast on the silver highlights, which I was told happens because of uneven pigment absorption. My colorist told me about a rinse called Roux Fanci-Full Rinse, which has been around since the 1940s. You just put it on towel-dried hair and leave it in. This made the color perfect! You could still see the silver highlights, but they were toned down. About six weeks after that, I could really see my natural color coming in, and it's actually white, not silver. At first it looked like a white cap on top of my head. But the rinse helped tone it so it blended better and brought out the colors in the rest of my hair. After that, I was using it every day.

I was really nervous about what other people would say, so I was surprised by the positive response. One friend I've been close to for twenty years said the silver actually made me look younger. The hardest part is the first two months. The roots are noticeable, but you can't see enough of your silver to decide if you like it. Still it's worth sticking it out a bit longer in order to make an informed decision.

Colorist Tip

Evan Minney, *Evan Joseph Curls, Columbus, Ohio*

I've never had a client go silver and then turn back to color. Although it will take time and the process is challenging, once you achieve the end result, it's so satisfying both inside and out. Silver hair has nothing to do with age and everything to do with being confident and loving yourself just the way you are intended to be! I'm a big advocate in encouraging my clients to embrace what nature intended. It's more interesting and personalized. I don't need to worry about my business. I love what I do and I love the women who want to color their hair, too. There's enough room for all of us.

Tricia Before Her Transformation

Tricia was coloring her thick hair every two weeks with a shade that was far too dark for her features. She was ready to stop the madness and be more true to herself.

Tricia's Prep for Grow-Out

This photo shoot was about four to six weeks after Veronica Tapia of Jersey Curl Salon did the initial all-over lightening on Tricia's hair in order to make the transition to silver more gradual. Here, Tricia's hair was significantly lighter but still had so much color that Kristy didn't want to risk doing anything for fear of breakage or damage, so we just cut and styled Tricia's hair and begged her not to touch it until the next shoot!

This time, Tricia's roots were visible, so Kristy added silver highlights that matched her natural root color. She did this in a zigzag pattern to help blur the landing strip of white against the darker dyed hair. "The goal is to gradually get her hair lighter every time I see her, so she can get used to her lighter hair," Kristy said. It took a while for her to adjust to her lighter shade, which is very common when your color has been dark.

Tricia After Another Three Months

Kristy continued to add highlights to lighten the look of Tricia's hair overall.

Many Colors on the Journey

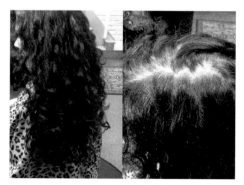

From brunette to auburn to blonde to silver.

Nine Months After Starting Her Journey

The ends of Tricia's hair were bothering her because they still seemed dark in contrast. Kristy used bleach to gently lift out some of the pigment. Then she used a toner to cool down the warm hue on the ends and match Tricia's natural silver. Throughout her transformation process, Tricia was diligent about keeping her strands hyper-conditioned.

Tricia is lightening up every day.

I was really nervous about what other people would say, so I was surprised by the positive response.

Ready, Willing, and Able

Victoria Flynn, 58,
Makeup Artist

....

Four years ago, I stopped coloring my hair, but I got so much flak from family members, coworkers, and even strangers that I got discouraged and went back to dyeing it blonde. Then I decided to try it again. This time, I didn't care what anyone said. I was tired of hiding what was natural, spending $160 every four weeks, and seeing the hair dye go down the shower drain the day after my salon appointment. Although *I* was positive that I wanted to make the transition, my colorist was resistant. "Why let your hair go silver when you can be a hot mama?" he asked. "I can be a hot mama *with* silver hair," I told him. I left and I never saw him again.

The process of growing out my unnatural blonde reminded me of watching a prize candle burn. You can't wait to see the prize inside your candle, but you can't make it burn any faster. I was so excited to discover what natural colors would emerge, and it was hard to be patient, but I couldn't make the hair dye grow out more quickly.

After six months, I got a silver toner to reduce the brassiness of the blonde hair and enhance my natural color. Then I cut more of my hair to get rid of the remaining blonde. I should have done this in the first place, but you don't always know what you're ready for until you try it!

My silver hair shows that I have self-confidence and know who I am.

Going silver has been very liberating, because coloring my hair ran my life. I don't have to worry about going swimming or if my color appointment will coincide with events like weddings or parties. Silver hair is beautiful, and my only regret is that I didn't embrace it earlier. I hope this will make my twenty-seven-year-old daughter comfortable with her natural color when her hair turns silver. I get a lot of double takes and compliments. Recently, I passed a couple on the stairs at Penn Station. The husband looked at my hair and then turned to his wife and said, "You should let your hair go silver, too." I also get more looks from men than I did before.

What's surprising is that my natural hair isn't just one color; it's got these beautiful highlights that are various shades of white and gray. I don't just *like* my natural color; I *love* it. Plus, my hair looks and feels so much healthier because I'm no longer applying chemicals. Silver shows that I have self-confidence and know who I am. I also think the lighter color softens the appearance of wrinkles. It's the covering up that makes you look older. I feel like I'm a better, happier version of myself. Today, when I see women with silver hair or it seems like they are transitioning, I tell them how gorgeous their natural hair is. How can it *not* be? It's part of you!

Victoria at Six Months

TECHNIQUE:
Demi-Permanent
Silver Toner

This is what Victoria looked like when she arrived for our first photo shoot. She hadn't colored her hair in six months, and her blonde ends really stood out against her natural silver.

I gave Victoria a trim to remove some of the dyed blonde ends. Then Kristy used a semipermanent toner to neutralize the brassy dyed color that was left and make it more of an ash tone that would blend with her natural hue. This is something you can do at a salon in one visit.

Victoria at Nine Months

I just cut and styled Victoria's beautiful silver bob.

By this photo shoot, Victoria's dyed blonde was pretty much grown out. All I had to do was give her a trim and she was totally silver! When I look at Victoria's "before" photo from the first shoot, I see someone *trying* to look younger. Once she embraced her authentic hue, she looked more youthful without the effort.

A Gradual and Comfortable Grow-out

Dian Griesel, 57, *Model*

From my twenties until my midforties, I had colored my hair every color from black to platinum blonde. When I decided to transition to silver at forty-five, my dyed hair color was light ash brown to dark ash blonde. I could see by the roots that I had a good amount of natural silver that was waiting to shine. To avoid a line of demarcation and transition to silver myself, not go to a salon, I tried this at-home technique: I started using Clairol Natural Instincts, a twenty-eight-day semipermanent hair color product from the drugstore, in the shade that most closely matched my dark ash-blonde dyed hair. I used this wash-out product for a few months. After twenty-eight days, that color gently faded as it rinsed out, because semipermanent color doesn't go as deep into the cuticle and cortex of the hair as permanent dye does. Next, I chose a color that was one shade lighter than that. When this washed out in about twenty-eight days, I went another shade lighter, and I kept repeating this process until I was ultimately using Clairol's "platinum" wash-out and my silver had basically grown in and my hair was totally natural. Sometimes I had a couple of twenty-eight-day periods with the same color. Throughout the process, my natural silver strands, underneath the wash-out coloring, looked like very fine, expensive highlights. This process leaves no lines at all; however, it took me four years to transition. Still, it was worth it for me to do it this slowly, because there was no line of demarcation or awkward grow-out period.

Finding Peace in Silver

Suzanne Stolzberg, 56,
Yoga Instructor and Acupuncturist

....

I never thought I'd let my hair go silver, but I got sick of having to waste one day of my weekend coloring it every three weeks. I dreaded the roots coming in and worrying about traveling and how long I could be away before I'd need to do a toxic dye job. I also hated my super-dried-out scalp and the dye stains on my beautiful bath towels and white bathroom tiles. (I constantly had to bleach the floor, which added even more toxins to my life!)

Still, although I wanted to do it, embracing my natural color wasn't easy. I fought it at first. Twice I had highlights woven in to help the blending process. The first time was great, but the second time the colorist damaged my hair and it started to fall out. After that, I decided never to process my hair again. I conditioned my hair a lot and found a colorist who puts a very light gloss in it to blend the silver that is coming in.

Take a deep look at why you need to control the outside. Is it the false belief that this will make us feel better on the inside? Will it hide time and cover up age? Why is age not exalted and rewarded? Our society is to blame, but we can change it for ourselves. Maybe the first step is letting go of all the cover-up.

After I truly let go, I loved the journey, which isn't just about hair but is one of self-acceptance and self-love. It helped me let go of the image I had about my hair, my appearance, and myself. When I see other women who are letting the silver come in, it looks like they are taking the stress out of their lives. In the end, not only am I healthier but so are my hair and my scalp! My curls are not as dry anymore, something that was always a problem when I was coloring my hair, no matter how much I conditioned.

Suzanne at Three Months

TECHNIQUE: Highlights and Toner

Sometimes all it takes is changing the tone from warm to cool to get comfortable with your natural silver. It looked great, but after this photo shoot Suzanne went to see another colorist, who did some bleaching and added highlights. Suzanne had been coloring for so long that it seemed strange to her *not* to color once a certain amount of time had passed. A lot of women experience this because they've been coloring their hair for decades. Unfortunately, these treatments were so harsh they made Suzanne's hair break off and fall out. She texted Kristy and me in a panic. We told her to hyper-condition and step away from the color.

Suzanne at Six Months

Suzanne definitely learned her lesson about not touching her hair and decided to go cold turkey at this point, a good idea because her hair grows quickly.

She had been maintaining the tone at home with a lavender conditioner, so we didn't do any coloring just toning. I just gave her a trim.

Suzanne at Nine Months

Suzanne's hair needed no help at this point. We gave her a trim and glossed up her glorious silver curls.

CHAPTER FOUR

SILVER STREAKS:

Face Framing in Silver Moonlight

Growing out just a streak of silver gives you a sneak peek at what silver will look like next to your face.

fter working with clients for decades, I've learned that sometimes it's not "What should I do?" but rather what you *shouldn't* do that allows exciting things to unfold. Releasing yourself from the coloring process, which has become second nature for many of us, is often a matter of time. Ironically, your "first nature" may have been overlooked and blanketed with color all these years. Many of the approaches in this chapter are about what *not* to do. These methods can be used to ease into the possibilities of being silver or as ways to embrace your first phase (the grow-out), or, as I like to call it, the "light of the new moon phase," when just a sliver of silver is illuminated.

By the Light of the Silvery Moon

Growing out a streak of silver is great if you want a fresh, fun look and/or a sneak peek at what silver looks like next to your face. However, it does require some patience, as it can take a while. First, decide where you want the streak. If you are planning to try growing in a streak while continuing to color the rest of your hair, see if you have an area at your roots that is a stronger silver than the rest. Perhaps you have a few icy patches throughout your hair's landscape. Or pick a section around your face for a more dramatic look. One streak or one on each side can look lovely. Wherever you choose, I suggest a section that's about three inches wide. You can also choose the entire underlayer at the nape.

If you want to continue to color the rest of your hair, ask your colorist to section off the potential streak area, cover it with a dollop of conditioner, and wrap it in foil or plastic wrap to protect it from the dye while the rest of your hair is dyed. It's also important to keep this streak wrapped and lifted up and away from your head while the dye is rinsed out. Once you've done this the first time, you are officially growing out a streak! Each time you color, it's crucial to protect the growing streak so its pure silver can shine through.

A variation is to color a lighter streak on one or both sides of your face and then let it grow in silver. The lighter color softens the roots. This requires bleaching the hair as light as possible—like pale blonde or white. You can leave this color or add a silver toner on top of it. The colorists I spoke to suggest asking a professional to do this rather than trying it at home.

When this naturally silver section begins to grow in, it illuminates your face and can actually make your tinted hair more interesting, a statement piece that says, "Even though I'm coloring my hair, I'm not *hiding* the fact that I'm silver either! I'm just keeping it interesting." And who knows? It might even become your signature look.

Rogue Streak

Jennifer Goldstein, 38, *Executive Beauty and Health Editor,* Marie Claire, *and Cohost of the* Fat Mascara *Beauty Podcast*

TECHNIQUE:
Allow one gray streak to emerge by coloring around it.

I've been graying since I was about sixteen, but I decided to stop dyeing my hair when I was thirty-four. My decision was two-part. First, I work in the beauty and fashion industry with all these cool, stylish men and women, and many of them have distinctive looks. But at 5'4", with brown hair, brown eyes, and a preference for wearing black, I look like a lot of other women, and at work and professional events, no one seemed to remember me! Often, I would see people whom I had met before and they would reintroduce themselves as if we'd never met. So I wanted to do something distinctive with my look, but I was too lazy to commit to, say, red lipstick every single day.

I began thinking about growing out the silver, and the same week that I was contemplating this, I met a makeup artist whose hair was half-white and half-black. I didn't even know if her white was natural or not, but it didn't matter. Her hair was inspiration enough, and I started to let my silver grow in. Only my temples and the streak are totally white at this point, and the hair around the streak is salt-and-pepper (dark brown that's about 50 percent gray). I'm dyeing the hair around the streak until I'm more fully white, and then I may grow out my whole head. Now I get so many "I love your hair" comments, whereas before I was just some lady with long brown hair. And everyone remembers me now! Sometimes they even say they remember my hair and know they've met me; they just can't remember my name. That's totally fine! People often stop me on the street to say they like it, and guys are always calling out *X-Men* names when they pass by me. I've gotten Storm and Rogue. I'd say it's definitely more of a Rogue situation.

Test-Drive a Streak

You can give a silver streak a test drive by looking for silver clip-in hair extensions at a beauty supply store or wig store. You may need to cut the length of the clip-in to blend with your style. Pick several silver hues and try them on for a few days, clipped in various spots on your head, such as the area framing the face or hidden underneath. The streak pictured here is clipped in to Jen's hair.

Some people's hair doesn't naturally grow in silver all over; instead, they get a hint of silver in the form of a streak. That's what happened to fashion expert Stacy London, whose gorgeous silver streak showed up when she was only in sixth grade.

Natural Streak of Light

Stacy London, 47,
Host of What Not to Wear,
author of The Truth About Style

've had my streak since I was twelve years old. I was battling my worst bout of psoriasis, a chronic skin condition. We tried everything to heal it, from slathering my skin with steroids to doing light treatments to taking tar baths. I also did a treatment where we put tar gel on my scalp and scrubbed it out with boric acid. I'm not sure if the streak was caused by the stress of this experience or the harsh treatments, but it started growing exactly at that time. I always thought it was great; a stylish, unique part of me. Although I got teased by other kids for my bad skin, they never made fun of my streak. In my twenties and thirties, it was a symbol of cool. It was only when I turned forty that people thought it signified age. Every day on social media, people tell me to dye my hair or that it makes me look old. But I've earned every strand of this silver. It's my signature and has nothing to do with age. It's simply a part of who I am and I embrace it and love it. I can't imagine *not* having it. In fact, when I worked with the hair care company Pantene, my contract said they could do anything to my hair except touch my silver streak. It's as much a badge of honor for me as any of the scars I have from my battle with psoriasis. It's proof that I got through it!

Streak of Color

Another streaky technique that can be fun for women who have already attained the coveted full head of silver is to use semipermanent or temporary dye on a section of hair around the front, framing the face, or at the temples or underneath the top layer on both sides of the neck. Woven into your silver, this contrast can be as subtle or as dramatic as you like. If you're going to try this method, why not be daring and try bold, rich colors, such as lavender, deep mermaid blue, purple, magenta, or even black? When the bold color fades, you can try something new—equally bold or more natural.

Lightening Up Her Life

When I first met Aida, I could see a tiny patch of silver roots and its stunning potential peeking out from under the black hair dye. She seemed interested, but not yet convinced, that allowing her silver buried treasure to shine would change her life. Well, she did it, and, as a result, I've seen a remarkable difference in her confidence. I know that not a day goes by that Aida doesn't get compliments on her hair from strangers.

Aida Cortez, 47, *Fitness Center Manager*

....

I'd been thinking about growing out my color for a while, but I was insecure about it. My best friend was totally against silver hair, and every time she saw me she'd say, "Time to dye it." Then there was my husband at the time, who told me that the silver made me look old. Comments like these were embarrassing, so I continued to dye my hair. The problem is that it grows so fast that I had to dye it every week at home. I hated the smell and how the color would get into my ears and drip down my neck into my shirt and onto the rug. My towels and pillowcases were black all the time because of the dye.

TECHNIQUE: Growing out a natural gray streak

Then my marriage ended. My life was in transition in terms of getting rid of a relationship that wasn't good for me, and trying to find out who I really was in all areas of my life. Coincidentally, at this time Lorraine came into the gym where I work and asked me about this silver tuft of hair that was peeking out from my roots. She said she thought it was beautiful, but I said, "Oh, I'm just late with my color." Lorraine encouraged me to grow out the dye, regardless of what other people were saying. I think she missed most of her exercise class because we were talking for so long!

Letting the silver be visible for everyone to see was a way of revealing the *real* me and embracing it. People notice me more, and their reactions are positive and priceless. Girls come up to me and ask me if I colored the front gray on purpose. I love that I can say, "No! It's all me." One woman said she liked my streak so much that she was going to let her white hair come out and stop coloring. It's taken a while to get used to this type of attention, but now I realize that the silver enhances my personality, and my whole life has changed as a result. For instance, after twenty years, I reunited with my estranged sister, who loves my streak of light!

Embrace who you really are and you'll be happier not only with your hair but with your life.

Colorist Tip

Estelle Baumhauer, *Color Director at eSalon, an At-Home Custom Hair Color Company*

The ultimate key to going silver is removing the previously dyed color. Haircuts, even small ones done often, are a must during this time. For clients who don't initially want to go without hair color, temporary color is a fantastic transitional option. Temporary color lasts around five washes but allows for a less-stark grow-out process. Brunettes or redheads will still need to do their roots around every two weeks until the hair has grown out. Blonde roots are less visible, so they can wait up to a month before a root touch-up with temporary color.

Romancing the Tone

This technique lets you ease into the growth of your natural hue by coloring only the roots exposed at the part of your hair—i.e., the silver lining that peeps through sometimes within days of coloring—while letting the under-layer grow natural. If your hair is longer and naturally straight, you can dye just the canopy, i.e., the visible hair on top. This allows the under-layer to start to grow out unprocessed and somewhat unnoticed.

TECHNIQUE:
The Eclipse

Lynn Demetrakis, 56,
Middle School Teacher

My twin brother's silver hair makes him look distinguished. But I thought mine made me look old, so I dyed it for sixteen years. Sometimes I'd color it myself, which made a mess of my bathroom, towels, and shirt; other times I'd have it professionally done every five to six weeks, which was time-consuming and expensive. Every time my roots grew in, I felt as if I was aging right before my own eyes. However, I never thought about *not* dyeing it, until Lorraine approached me in yoga class after spotting my roots showing in downward dog. She asked if I was growing out my color, but I wasn't. I was just delaying the visit to my colorist. For some reason, I didn't know I was so unhappy with this habit until it was brought to light (pun intended!). Lorraine suggested I go silver and I decided to give it a try. I knew I could always go back.

I got only positive reactions while growing it out. My twenty-two- and twenty-seven-year-old daughters thought it was cool, as did some of the seventh-grade students I teach. My husband never understood why I was coloring it in the first place, so he was fine with it. Friends, coworkers, and even strangers have asked about my hair. Recently I was out to dinner and the waitress came up to me and said, "I wish I could touch your hair. The color is amazing!" Embracing my gray has been really eye-opening—and "I" opening. My whole mind-set has shifted from thinking it made me look old to thinking it's really cool. In fact, I feel younger than ever! As Lorraine has aptly said, it's like doing yoga on your head, and the transition process allows our true light

to shine through. She's right. Going silver has inspired me to take better care of myself: I've lost weight, have been doing yoga more regularly, and feel the best I ever have about myself.

Being silver is a lot easier, too. All I need to do is wash with a blue hue conditioning toner when I cleanse.

Change your mind-set! Lorraine told me to think of the silver I had been covering as hiding my light. I had never looked at my silver hair as empowering or representing a rite of passage. Now I think, The best is yet to come.

Lynn at Three Months

Lynn hadn't colored her hair in three months when she arrived at our first photo shoot.

Kristy touched up just one inch of the roots at Lynn's part line and left everything underneath au naturel. This allows the silver to grow in subtly beneath the blanket of colored hair. This out-of-sight, out-of-mind approach is one of my favorite color transitioning techniques because it's the easiest and quickest. You're slowly introducing yourself to the idea of your own silver, you get this really nice distribution of highlights and lowlights as the silver grows in underneath, and it's a small amount of color compared to coloring your whole head. Kristy also highlighted and toned a section of hair on one side of Lynn's face to create a streak (left).

Lynn at Six Months

The original plan was to continue to color just the top layer of Lynn's roots, but she changed her mind and decided to just let her natural color grow in. This is a very common occurrence in the color transitioning process: Often you plan to go in one direction but along the way find yourself changing course. Early in the grow-out, in the midst of what is often the hardest part, Lynn got many compliments, and other women told her she'd inspired them to consider going silver themselves. At this point the only thing Kristy did was touch up her silver streak with toner to maintain the color.

Lynn at Nine Months

By now all Lynn's dyed color had grown out and she was totally natural silver. I think she actually looks younger all silver than she did when she arrived at our first photo shoot.

Silver Lining Story

Ivanna Soto, 20, *Student*

I was four years old when my first strand of silver hair was discovered. Shortly after that, I was diagnosed with vitiligo, a permanent skin condition that kills pigmentation cells in the skin and hair. Within a year and a half, my once-black hair was salt-and-pepper and my caramel-colored skin was completely pale. At school, the other children were extremely judgmental about it, and everywhere I went people would stare at me and make comments, because it was shocking that a four-year-old would have silver hair. Luckily, I have a supportive family and group of friends who helped me embrace my unique hair at a very young age. My mom would always tell me how beautiful my hair was and would never let me dye it. This gave me the strength to love my hair and block out any negativity. I slowly accepted my differences and didn't let people's stares or comments get to me. Embracing my silver hair has made me an extremely positive person, allowed me to become extremely confident, and helped me develop a radiant personality. Some people ask me if my hair is dyed, and others have told me that seeing my long, pretty silver hair made them want to grow out and embrace their natural hair color. This is an amazing feeling because I am taking this gift that God gave me and using it to inspire others.

CHAPTER FIVE

PIXIE MAGIC:

A Shortcut
to Great Style

Worn with the right attitude, a pixie can look great on anyone.

The pixie is bold, modern, both strong and sweet, and one of my favorite styles to cut. And, most appealingly for women giving up artificial color, it offers the simplest and most stylish "shortcut" to unearthing your silver treasure.

The most radical and freeing option for going silver is cutting the hair very short into a strong, modern pixie. By removing most or all of the previously colored hair, you're ready to start fresh with your natural hair. The most well-known pixie queen is my favorite actress and author, Jamie Lee Curtis, whose gorgeous gamine style has become her trademark and gives her a forever fresh, youthful yet sophisticated air. This hairstyle has also been made famous by classic stars like Mia Farrow

Ginnifer Goodwin

Jamie Lee Curtis

and more recently by younger actresses, such as Michelle Williams and Ginnifer Goodwin. Pixie cuts can make your cheekbones pop and lengthen the look of your neck. Worn with the right attitude, a pixie can look great on anyone.

Of course, there are lots of short cuts that look great and speed up your silver uncovering that are not pixies, and we'll show them here, too. Any cut that you feel great in is a good cut.

Dana Guerrero, 51,
Therapist and Yoga Teacher

....

I've had short hair for ten years and I love it because I'm a bit of a minimalist. I look put-together without having to do much. I met my husband when I had short hair and he has always loved it and my silver. When I color it, he gets disappointed, and I have to remind him and myself that my silver hair is just a cut or two away.

....

Dana's hair was dyed a dark brown, a color that seemed too harsh in contrast with her delicate skin tone. Her hair was also relatively short to start with, but the shape was rather blocky, with straight, even layers, so it looked like her hair was wearing her. Once Dana decided to allow her silver strands to emerge, I cut off the artificial color with one swoop of the scissors. Now her natural, multifaceted silvery shades give her tresses dimension and better complement her complexion. I think the cut softens all her beautiful features. I adore this look for Dana; it is in harmony with her lifestyle as a mother, yogi, and therapist.

Mara Riekstins, 60

'd been dyeing my hair brown since I saw the first silver strands, at the age of twenty-six. Then at fifty-six, I found out I had uterine cancer. I had a hysterectomy and six rounds of chemo. The people doing the chemo suggested I get a buzz cut so that losing my hair would be an easier transition. Once it started growing in, I was surprised because it was so white, but I had heard that's what happens before the pigment comes back. I got so many compliments on the color that I decided not to dye it. As it got longer I thought maybe I looked like Billy Idol and then Richard Simmons. Once I got a pixie cut, the style and color came together and I love it. I'm not sure if I'll dye it again or not, but right now I love *not* watching for and worrying about roots all the time!

I've seen a lot of women who have lost their hair from chemotherapy, and I've noticed that when they finish their treatments, if their hair grows back silver, many of them stop dyeing it. They surrender to the color and accept their hair's natural hue. Several beautiful cancer survivors have told me that after what they've been through, they actually welcome *any* hair and don't want to put any more chemicals on themselves. "People see *me* now, not my hair," a friend who once had long, dyed hair told me. Many women say they never realized how beautiful their natural color could be. They're not just *settling* for silver, they are *savoring* it!

An Extraordinary Makeover

Melissa Malebranche, 44, *Prospect and Stewardship Manager at the School of Professional Studies at New York University*

I struggled with my weight my whole life, so three years ago, at three hundred pounds, I had weight-loss surgery. I've lost almost one hundred and fifty pounds since and have had reconstructive surgery on areas like my arms and stomach. Part of this rebuilding of myself was letting my hair go natural both in color and texture. I know for a fact that if I had stayed three hundred pounds, I wouldn't have been comfortable with silver hair. But once I felt good in my own skin, I felt better about embracing my natural hair. The first step was the transition from relaxed hair to natural curly; embracing my silver was the second, especially because my constant hair color appointments were like a ball and chain. Then one day it hit me that trying to fight my silver hair was a losing battle. The color wasn't adhering the way it used to, and I was tired of it.

My mom and aunts color their hair every week. My mother will go to her grave with a bottle of hair dye in one hand and a bottle of relaxer in the other. I don't

Melissa at 300 pounds with dyed hair.

want to be that person. Since my hair was dark, I worried that the line of demarcation would look skunky. To make the grow-out more subtle, I dyed my hair blonde and stopped coloring it from there. Around the same time, I cut my shoulder-length hair really short, so it was a much easier and faster transition to silver.

I'm surprised by how many people stop me on the street or at work and tell me how much they love it. It's also amazing how many women approach me, compliment my hair, and then say, "You're so brave! I wish I could do the same thing." I understand where they're coming from because that was me a year

At this point, Melissa had lost more than 100 pounds and dyed her hair blonde to make transitioning to silver easier.

ago. But I had nothing to lose by embracing my hair color, and now I'd never dye it again. I used to think I'd feel ugly with silver hair, but not only do I love it, I realized the time when I felt the most unattractive was when I had to get my roots done. Roots look like a mistake and tell everyone that you let something slip by.

But the naturalness of your silver hair means you're owning it and you're confident and there's definitely something really sexy about that.

Mary MacDonald, *Gossips Hairstylists Inc., Toronto*

- Change your language and change your attitude! When growing in silver over a dark, ashy color, you are sugared licorice. When you have white coming into your golden-brown hair, you are salted caramel. You can also have vanilla ribbons cascading throughout your espresso or cappuccino hair. Your red-and-silver hair makes you a sugared strawberry.

- As hair loses its pigment, it also loses its warm tones. If you were a naturally golden brunette and have colored your hair for many years, you may not have the gold tones you remember, and your darker hair may be more ashy. If you had naturally red hair, your non-silver hair may grow in more golden blonde than red.

- Fine hair that is color-treated may feel thicker, because the dye opens up the cuticle and swells the hair shaft. So if your natural hair seems finer, it's really just not being "puffed-up" by chemicals.

Antonia's naturally silver-white hair is lovely, but it tends to get a bit yellow. She was ready for a change in tint and length. I gave her my "With or Without Hue" toner to apply. She left it on a bit longer to get the silver you see here. I trimmed it to a stylish pixie, and now she can ride around New York City on her bicycle and feel the breeze on her lovely neck.

CHAPTER SIX

DYEING TO BE SILVER:

When You Don't Want to Wait Another Day

Dyeing your hair silver is not something you should do at home, at least initially.

Naturally silver women and men aren't the only ones sporting this hue with pride. Born-this-way blondes, brunettes, and redheads who don't have a strand of silver in sight are actually dyeing their hair silver because they simply love the way it looks. As I mentioned earlier, this includes young celebrities like Gwen Stefani, Jennifer Lawrence, Miley Cyrus, Lady Gaga, Rihanna, Katy Perry, Kelly Osbourne, Kylie Jenner, Nicole Richie, Pink, and Michelle Williams, among others.

"Dyeing to be silver" is a fun way to change your appearance, and when it's done right, it can look gorgeous on almost everyone, regardless of age! Not only can you be silver—either in one streak, with highlights, or all over—but you can add other colors like lavender, pink, or mermaid blue for a totally different look. Also, the array of silver tones to choose from is seemingly endless—from ash, platinum, and pewter to stainless steel, silky white, and more. Whether you dye your hair silver in order to grow in your own silver or just for the beauty and fun of it, it is a big commitment, as we will explain. Whatever you choose, wear it with pride!

Lady Gaga

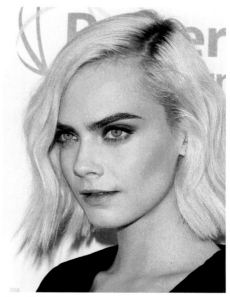

Cara Delevingne

Hilary Duff

Pink

Changing Her Attitude

Sam O'Brien, 31, *Assistant Editor*

....

When it comes to my hair, I was pretty conservative and hadn't changed my color or style, which hovered around a bob, in more than ten years. So I was ready for a totally different look and didn't want something subtle, like a lighter or darker shade of brown. I wanted something major. When I told my wife I was going silver, she was excited, but my mom didn't understand why I'd choose this color—probably because she's been covering her gray for years, and my sister was worried because she was getting married and wanted my hair to look good for her wedding.

When I first dyed it silver, a lot of people didn't even recognize me. Someone in my office introduced herself—although I'd known her for a while—and I got a lot of double takes. My wife really liked it and so did my sister (though she still wanted me to dye it back to brown for her wedding). What was interesting was how much the color changed every few days. One day it had a tint of blue; the next day it was purple. Then it turned more blonde than silver. Initially, I was using a shampoo that contained sulfates, which caused the silver to fade, so I switched to a sulfate-free product and began using a toner. Eventually it turned more blonde, which I liked, especially when the roots came in and there was that contrast. One thing I noticed: I was more approachable with silver-lavender hair. More people asked me for directions on the street and came up to me more than they ever did when my hair was dark. In the end, I went back to dark hair because I'm just not into the upkeep. But I enjoyed the adventure!

First, Kristy bleached Sam's dark brown hair to the lightest blonde the hair could take. Once Kristy had evaluated the tone of the bleached hair, she chose the appropriate shade of gray, then added a lavender toner over it. We followed up with Sam the next day and applied more toner, as it had already vaporized. I love the way this looks on Sam with the juxtaposition of her young, serene face and the lavender hue that was once equated with grannies and is now the exact opposite!

Sam's lavender-silver color turned blonde within weeks, so we applied more toner.

At the gentle urging of her bride-to-be sister, Sam went back to brown but kept her fresh new haircut.

Faux-Silver Hair Care

It's important to prepare your hair before you go silver. At least a month prior to the day, don't do any other coloring and apply deep-conditioning treatments for a couple of weeks. Dyeing your hair silver is not something you should do at home, at least initially, because it requires you to first remove the pigment from your hair with bleach, regardless of whether your hair is dyed or natural. Silver tones won't show up on dark hair; they will reflect only on lightened hair. After being bleached, your locks can be stained and toned silver. This two-step process is complicated and can take a lot of time—between three and six hours, depending on your hair length, color history, and the condition of your strands. For example, if you've been coloring, there can be several layers of pigment to lift, which takes longer than if you're removing your natural hue. It's crucial that you allow enough time to do this properly, because if the bleaching is patchy or if the silver dye isn't left on long enough, your silver can oxidize rapidly, turning anything from yellow to blue to purple.

It can look like a mood ring! In fact, even after spending hours at the salon, you may need to return within a day or two because silver oxidizes so quickly. Toning applications during your first week should be part of the package offered by the salon. At the very least they should give you detailed home-care instructions.

Silver tones can fade more quickly than other colors, so you will need frequent touch-ups. Your faux silver will need a lot of at-home TLC, more than your natural or previously tinted strands. It's important to use a 100 percent sulfate-free shampoo. Sulfates are actually detergents that strip the hair and fade color quickly, as well as rob the hair and scalp of any natural oils, leaving them parched. A conditioning toner is also a must to keep the silver from looking yellow. You can buy one or make one from chapter 7 yourself.

Look for blue toners made for either silver or blonde hair. Make sure you apply the toner to dry hair, because the open cuticle will absorb it, providing better coverage. Let it sit for about ten minutes, but keep checking in: You may need to leave it on longer or shorter depending on the oxidation and tone you prefer. (If you are nervous about the color or want a better sense of how long to leave it on, do a test on a small, hidden section of hair before applying the toner all over.) After the toner has been on for about ten minutes, wet your hair sparingly. The best way to do this is in the shower, but don't stand directly under the running water. Instead, stand to the side, cup water in your hands, and splash it over your hair. Evenly massage in the toner for a minute or two. Then rinse normally and well, and condition. Condition your dyed hair often since the bleach from this process is hard on it.

Dyeing to Be Gray

Colorist Tip

Veronica Tapia, *Jersey Curl Salon, Cliffside Park, New Jersey*

In hair school, if hair turned an ashy tone after highlighting, it was considered a mistake; now this same color is considered a fashion statement! I strongly suggest finding a colorist willing to go on the journey with you. It's a commitment and entails a lot of time, especially on the first visit. You also must be specific about the products you've used on your hair in the past few years. Some chemicals remain on the hair, some don't interact well with each other, and you can end up with a shade of "hue" knows what.

Olivia Pasquarelli, 22

My natural hair color is a very dark brown, and I don't have any natural gray or silver yet. But recently I dyed my whole head a silver pastel because I think the color is both eerie and magical. I love unnatural, different hair colors that stand out, so this is the perfect hue for me, especially because I wear mostly black clothes. A lot of people stop me in public to ask about my hair. Although one coworker said I should wait until I get old and my hair turns gray naturally, my dyed gray went over well in the corporate setting I work in.

However, it's a lot of time and energy. The lighter you can get your hair first, the

The day after the initial process

better. The best way to achieve a true pastel color is to start with completely white hair. I first wanted to dye my virgin dark brown hair all the way to an ultralight ash blonde by myself, but this could have badly damaged my hair or made it fall out, so I got it done at a salon. It was very expensive and took nearly seven hours! They had to bleach my entire head of hair twice and do the roots separately. They also had to condition between each bleaching and then tone my hair to get all the yellow out. After that, they cut off the dead ends and applied the silver dye. It was a long and expensive process for the initial dye, but after that I applied the toners more frequently at home to eventually get the look I wanted. Now it's getting quicker and easier to maintain.

Colorist Tip

Vickie Vela-Cambruzzi, *of Curls on Top in Laguna Beach, California, and creator of Invisi-Clips*

- Don't ask family and friends—especially those who color their hair—for their approval. They tend to project their own fears and insecurities about revealing their natural hair color.

- Take your time to consider this change. You want to be strong and firm in your decision. Embracing your silver hair makes a statement about being beautiful and empowered. It tells the world you are comfortable with being your authentic self down to the roots.

- For my curly clients, the transition tends to be easier with a longer style. It allows the hair to be worn up to hide the line of demarcation. Also, curls framing the face soften the features.

- The topic of growing out your natural silver hair is a daily conversation in my salon. I pride myself on being a stylist who encourages authenticity.

Be Totally Honest with Your Colorist

- Have you ever used a color eraser on your hair?

- Have you ever chemically straightened your hair?

- Did you have to dye or bleach your hair a few times before getting the shade you desired?

- Did you use at-home hair color? Which brand and which color?

- Do you use "clarifying" or regular shampoos on your processed color?

- Do your conditioners and styling products contain silicone?

- Do you use spray-in or wax touch-up sticks on your roots in between color treatments?

- Have you changed colorists several times in the past five years?

Along my transition route, the remnants of my rust hue hung on, unwelcome. Since I was not willing to cut my hair short, I decided to cut the color process short instead. I lifted the color on a few sections to make them white, then applied toner to turn them an icy gray, mimicking my natural silver hue. I followed up with "With or Without Hue," a blue conditioning toner, each time I cleansed my hair.

CHAPTER SEVEN

GLORIOUSLY GRAY TO STAY:

TLC & Homemade Recipes

You are the most active ingredient in your own hair care routine.

On my journey to going silver, I met many women who were intrigued by the idea of trying it themselves but who said, "I'd love to do it, but my silver's not pretty," or "I don't have nice silver," or some variation of this sentiment. The difference between silver hair that looks radiant and silver hair that doesn't is in how you care for it. If you don't give your precious strands enough tender loving care and hydration, then they're probably not going to look their healthy best. The bottom line: Yes, you do have a beautiful silver. Yes, you! Nature does not lie; it's just waiting to be uncovered (or uncolored)!

Say No to Shampoo with Sulfates

If you know anything about my advice on hair care, you know that I caution my clients to steer clear of shampoos that contain sulfates. These foaming agents give shampoo their frothy lather but are a major no-no because they are harsh detergents that strip your hair and scalp of their natural oils and protective antibodies. This isn't good for any hair color or texture, but it's even worse for silver (and curls) because these hair types tend to be a little more dry and coarse. Examples of sulfates include sodium lauryl sulfate, ammonium laureth sulfate, and sodium laureth sulfate. These are the same ingredients that are used in dishwashing soap and laundry detergent. You wouldn't want to cleanse your face with these products, and the scalp is an extension of your facial skin. You probably wouldn't wash a beloved cashmere sweater with them either, and your hair is a precious, delicate fiber. As its custodian, you're required to give it a lot of love. The bottom line is that hydration is crucial for gorgeous, luminous silver and these chemicals can dehydrate your

Treat your hair as you do your skin—delicately.

hair and scalp, making your color look lackluster.

Also, these ingredients don't rinse out of your hair easily. (Evidence of this is how dishwashing detergent clings to a damp kitchen sponge.) As you may know, sodium is salt. We season meat with salt to draw the meat's natural, flavor-rich oils to the surface. Similarly, the salts in sulfates draw the hair's natural sebum (oil) to the surface of the scalp. As the salt settles on the skin, it dries and turns into flakes that resemble dandruff. When this happens, your instinct is to shampoo *again* to get rid of the flakes. But you're just repeating the cycle. Depending on your hair type, this can cause severe dehydration of the scalp and hair—or the opposite: an excessively oily scalp and greasy hair. A conditioner can soften and hydrate your hair, but even the best product can't make up for the damage of sulfates.

Sulfates dry, open, and ruffle the outermost layer of the hair shaft, called the cuticle. This can cause several problems. First, an open cuticle on colored hair exposes the pigment molecules to the atmosphere, a process called oxidizing. When this happens to silver hair,

Gentle motion and friction are key to good cleansing.

it can turn yellow. Second, when the cuticle is open on hair that is not well hydrated, the hair reaches out and tries to steal water molecules from the atmosphere. This causes the topmost layer of hair to lift off the head, resulting in the dreaded *f* word: *frizz*. When the cuticle is frayed, your strands can get caught on one another like Velcro, causing knots, snarls, and tangles. Radiant, shiny strands have a closed cuticle that lies flat. This can be achieved only by conditioning.

I proudly started the "no shampoo movement" twenty years ago. Back then, every shampoo was sulfate-full,

hence the term "no shampoo." Now many varieties of sulfate-free shampoo are available, thank goodness. Although I'm still convinced many people damage their hair with the wrong products, I am adamant that you *must* clean the surface of your scalp and hair in order to avoid dryness, flakiness, and odor, and to remove buildup of dirt, sebum, and hair products, which can all cause clogged pores. You just want to cleanse gently. What really does the cleaning is your fingertips as they massage the cleanser into your scalp, creating friction that loosens and lifts away dirt, and then the rinsing. Together, the friction and the rinsing leave your scalp and hair clean.

Pinecones resemble hair cuticles—they open when devoid of moisture. Hydrate to keep cuticles closed and frizz-free.

In other words, you are the most active ingredient in your own hair care routine.

Unfortunately, a product may falsely say "sulfate-free" on the front of the package, because there are no regulations on what manufacturers can put on this part of a product label. So you must check the ingredient list or download an app (Think Dirty is a good one) that can help you decipher confusing hidden ingredients to make sure sodium lauryl sulfate (SLS), ammonium laureth sulfate, and sodium laureth sulfate aren't included.

Also, always look for cleansers and conditioners with a low pH, which measures how acidic or alkaline a substance is on a scale from 0 to 14. In case you don't remember from high school science class, anything between 0 and 6.9 is acidic, 7 is neutral, and anything between 7.1 and 14 is alkaline. Our hair and scalp have a pH between 4.5 and 5.5, a natural acidity that keeps fungi and bacteria at bay, keeps the cuticle closed, and is the best pH for gorgeous, healthy hair. Products that are too alkaline will cause frizz because they open the cuticle; those that are acidic can cause the cuticle to close, which is what we want. If a product states the pH on its bottle, which is rare, then you know you have a brand that is transparent. However, you can buy pH test strips online or at a pool maintenance store to test the pH of your products and your water.

The trickle-down effect is another reason to avoid sulfates, which have been shown to damage our waterways. Studies have also shown that sulfates penetrate the skin and enter the heart, lungs, and even the brain.

There are some other ingredients to avoid in hair care products:

- FRAGRANCES may contain up to four thousand synthetic ingredients of their own. They can cause skin irritation and rashes, vomiting, and irritability, and can affect the central nervous system.
- SILICONE is the active ingredient in 99 percent of shine products. Silicone is very inexpensive to produce and is often used in rubber, plastics, and polishes. Silicone-based products sit on the hair's surface, encasing each strand almost like plastic tubing. Silicone isn't absorbed by the hair, and it doesn't dissipate

into the atmosphere. There's a residue of silicone that stays on the hair because it is resistant to oxygen and moisture. Over time, the silicone builds up, distorting your hair's true form, dulling the color, and stealing its natural radiance. The strands eventually suffocate, the fragile skin on the scalp can become irritated, and the pores can become clogged. The best way to see if a product contains silicone is to test it on your hands. If it's slick and does not dissolve into the skin, it probably contains silicone.

- ISOPROPYL ALCOHOL is petroleum-derived and, in addition to being used in hair and skin products, it is used in antifreeze and shellac. Just like alcoholic beverages dehydrate the body, isopropyl alcohol does the same when applied to the hair. This dehydration can cause frizz, dryness, itchiness, and flakiness.

- PARABENS are widely used as preservatives in cosmetics as well as to ward off the growth of bacteria in foods and drugs. Those typically found on the ingredient list include methylparaben, propylparaben, and butylparaben. In recent years, experts have questioned whether they're safe; some say they may be linked to cancer and reproductive problems.

- COCAMIDE DEA OR MEA AND LAURAMIDE DEA, found in bubble baths and shampoos, are hormone-disrupting chemicals and potential carcinogens. **They're not healthy for anyone but are especially risky for children.**

- IMIDAZOLIDINYL UREA AND DMDM HYDANTOIN are two preservatives that release formaldehyde, which some people believe can cause respiratory and other health issues. They're found in hair care and skin care products as well as nail polish.

- MINERAL OIL is colorless and odorless. It is a by-product of the distillation of petroleum to produce gasoline. It's long been used as an ingredient in hair products, skin lotions, and cosmetics because it traps moisture inside. It forms a layer over your skin or hair to do so. It does not add any benefit and may contain toxins. You don't need it.

- Three additional ones to avoid as they give you nothing you need and may be harmful: diazolidinyl urea, behentrimonium chloride, propylene glycol.

Condition, Condition, and Condition Some More

The best way to enhance the health and radiance of your silver hair is to give it a continual foundation of hydration. It's not only the color of your hair that makes it beautiful; it's the *quality*, too. The chemicals in hair dye can leave hair dull and parched, changing the tone and color dramatically, but a lifelong conditioning routine can help hydrate, repair, and prevent frizz as well as further damage. Vibrant, healthy hair can erase at least ten years from your appearance. Once your hair looks and feels healthier, you'll like your silver more, which can make it a bit easier to wean yourself from your coloring habit. When I don't condition my curly hair for a couple of days, the silver can appear dull. Luckily, all it takes is cleansing and conditioning to bring it back to its brighter hue. A lot of people like to use hair oils as a conditioning treatment and then use a detergent shampoo to rinse them out. But this is counterproductive: It means you're stripping away all that conditioning goodness with detergent. Instead, for maximum hydration, rinse and remove the oil treatment with a conditioning cleanser.

Besides ensuring it's not silicone-based, here are some things to look for when choosing a conditioner for silver hair:

- A VIOLET HUE, which can help neutralize the yellow in your hair and protect the silver from deoxidizing. You can also add violet or blue food coloring to your conditioner.
- NATURAL OILS, such as avocado, olive, jojoba, pomegranate seed, rosemary, coconut, almond, aloe vera, and ghee (clarified butter). If you don't see these on your conditioner's ingredient list, you can buy them at your local health food store or online and mix them into your favorite conditioner.

- EMOLLIENTS, which soften hair and reduce frizz by smoothing the cuticle. Good emollients for silver strands include shea butter, wheat germ, and vegetable, olive, and walnut oils.
- PROTEINS coat the hair shaft and protect it. Look for plant proteins, such as wheat, wheat germ, and soy protein.
- HUMECTANTS, which absorb water from the atmosphere and hang on to it. They're absolutely crucial in a conditioner for silver hair. Good ones include panthenol, vegetable glycerin, and sorbitol.
- AMINO ACIDS AND ALOE VERA, which are moisturizers and add softness and control to silver strands.

Do You Know Your Hair's Porosity?

Knowing your hair's porosity can help you choose the best hair care routine for your strands. Low-porosity hair may not easily take in and absorb moisture from water and conditioners. This is a problem, because our hair needs hydration to be its healthiest. There are many reasons why this can happen, but hair can be rehabilitated simply by removing fake-shine products, silicones, and inorganic oils from your hair care routine, because these create a barrier that prevents moisture from getting in. Ironically, many people with low-porosity hair regularly apply more and more of these products in hopes of getting some hydration and shine, and the cycle continues. High-porosity hair is porous and readily takes in water and moisture from conditioners. To determine your hair's porosity, try this test: Pluck out a couple of strands and place them in a bowl of water. Low-porosity hair floats and high-porosity hair sinks. Both hair types benefit from sulfate-free cleansers, silicone-free conditioners, and a lot of respect and love.

Clear or Cream-Based Styling Products

For the same reasons that you don't want them in your cleanser or conditioner, make sure your silver hair styling products don't contain silicones, parabens, or alcohols. Quality ingredients are especially important in your styling products, because they may stay on your hair for days at a time, depending on your cleansing routine. Those that are drying, like alcohol, suck moisture from your strands, which can make them look wet, petrified, or crispy.

Clear styling products—and I mean those that are as clear as water—give shine to your silver mane as well as provide hold and shape. The only way to tell if a product is truly clear is if you can test it before buying or if the packaging is see-through. Watch out for clear glycerin products that promise a superficial shine. Often they contain silicone emollients that make strands look stringy and over time can dull the hair or, even worse, cause the silver to turn yellow.

Some people prefer cream-based styling products. They keep the hair well hydrated while allowing it to keep its natural movement and feel. If you like cream-based styling products but find they give your hair a matte finish, try diluting them slightly with spring water. This helps evenly distribute the product during styling.

Get a Clean Cut

You don't need to give your hair a major cut to keep it fresh. But you *do* need to trim it, which I call "oxygenating your hair." Similar to pruning a plant, trimming aids in a healthy growth cycle because it refreshes and aerates the ends by exposing the hair shaft, allowing it to take in oxygen and moisture from the atmosphere. This makes hair look better, especially when it's silver. Long, unkempt strands can look straggly, but if your tresses are oxygenated and well hydrated, your silver hair can look fabulously luminous and healthy. Think of it this way: If you have hair that goes past your bra line, the ends were probably at your scalp five years ago or more. Imagine wearing the same dress for five years without taking it off! People tend to treat their clothes better than they treat their hair, so rethink what you can do for your precious locks.

"Oxygenate" the ends by trimming or cutting "Curl by Curl™."

Skip the Heat Styling

If you've ever accidently left your iron on one area of cloth too long, you probably found that it left that spot singed. The same thing can happen when you overheat your hair with high-intensity turbo blow-dryers, flat irons, and curling implements. Too much heat styling can make any hair type look dry and lackluster, because high temperatures singe and weaken the hair and can cause frayed ends and dryness. This isn't good for any hair type or color, but

it's particularly a no-no for silver hair, which is already coarser. Silver hair also tends to have trouble absorbing

moisture, making it more susceptible to damage. Also, tugging at your hair while styling it can cause breakage, and the heat can make strands turn yellow. It can also put strain on your roots and widen the part, sort of like pulling on the seam of a delicate dress, making your hair look like it's thinning at the scalp.

Heat styling is a particularly bad idea if you're growing out color. When textured or curly hair is blow-fried to be straight and flat, it's like a neon sign highlighting the very thing you don't want to see: the silver strip at the roots. It also exposes the skin on the scalp, which tends to be lighter. This combined with the silver roots makes the colored hair appear as if it is floating on top of your crown. Unfortunately, this can look like a bald spot even when you have plenty of hair. Several women and men have told me that this actually made them think they *were* going bald.

Keep Your Hands Off Your Silver

I had a beautiful, longtime shampoo-free client who couldn't figure out why the naturally snow-white silver hair on the right side of her head was yellow. But as I watched her body language as we chatted, I noticed that she constantly used her right hand to push her hair out of her face. Her hair was reacting to the sweat and oil that naturally accumulate on the hands, similar to the way the armpit area of a white shirt turns yellow over time because of its exposure to sweat. Try to be conscious of how much you are

touching your hair, especially on hot, sticky days.

Be Conscious of Environmental Elements

Sun exposure, medications, tobacco smoke, detergent shampoo, mineral deposits in hard water, and even overhead or low-hanging lights can cause silver hair to turn yellow over time. Hard water contains a large amount of calcium, magnesium, and other minerals that can make it taste metallic, cause white, crusty faucets, leave spots on your drinking glasses, cause your skin and hair to feel dry, and also give silver hair a yellow cast. Installing a water softener or filter on your showerhead and tap can help. Distilled white vinegar can clean mineral deposits on faucets, and apple cider vinegar can help remove buildup and yellowing in the hair. If you suspect low-hanging overhead incandescent lights may be yellowing your hair at your desk or wherever you spend a lot of time, try switching to LED lights. They lack the heat of incandescent bulbs, which can cause hair to yellow.

Gently Tie Your Hair Up at Bedtime

Most of us move around in our sleep. When this happens, your hair rubs against your pillow, getting flattened, twisted, and tangled. This can lead to frizz, split ends, and broken strands. If you have long hair, putting it up and securing it in one position at night

allows the hair to rest and preserves the health and integrity of its fibers. Plus, this method often leads to great second- and third-day hair. Simply refresh your strands by spritzing them with the "Spray It with Love" conditioning spray on page 177.

Protect Hair While Swimming

Chlorinated swimming pool water and salt water can leave hair parched and dull and cause color—whether it's natural or not—to oxidize. But you don't have to avoid the pool or the beach. Just be sure to protect your hair. Fill an oil spray mister (found at most housewares stores) with liquid coconut or jojoba oil and spritz it onto your hair and into the lining of your swimming cap before you go into the pool or ocean. Since water and oil don't mix, this helps repel water, including that which contains high levels of chlorine or salt.

Protect Your Hair from the Sun

Your skin isn't the only body part that needs protection from the sun. "All hair, including silver hair, is susceptible to damage from the sun, which can lead to hair breakage and color fading, so using a hat or a protective product is vital," explains trichologist Philip Kingsley. Look for products called some version of "hair sunscreen" and that specifically

state that they have UV protection. And, as Philip says, a hat also works. Just make sure it covers all of your hair.

Use a Blue or Purple Rinse or Cleanser

Grandma was onto something when she used a blue or purple rinse or toner on her silver strands. It can reduce the yellowing that typically happens to silver hair. Remember the color wheel many of us learned about in school? Colors that are across from each other on the wheel neutralize or cancel each other out. So, since yellow is complementary to purple and is across the color wheel from blue and purple, a blue or purple rinse or toner can help neutralize your hair's yellow cast. It also brightens the hair and gives it an icy-cool appearance.

Colorist Tip

Shai Amiel, *Capella Salon, Studio City, California*

I love silver hair, both natural and dyed, but I am not a big fan of using a lot of bleach on darker hair in order to lift all the underlying yellow. However, if the yellow is not sufficiently lifted, it seeps through and the silver color fades within days. I prefer to let the silver grow out naturally. If you are already blonde, it is much easier to apply a silver toner to get the process started.

Silver Lining Story

Sandra Gering, 74, *Gallerist*

At the age of sixty-one, I was diagnosed with breast cancer. During six months of chemo and radiation, I lost my dyed platinum blonde hair and wore a wig. After that, I was happy to remove the wig and allow my curly silver hair to grow in. It wasn't that I was afraid to go back to coloring my hair after breast cancer; it was just that my natural silver looked amazing against my skin tone and, in my mind, made me look more beautiful, so I happily stuck with it. That was over thirteen years ago, and I've never looked back. Now my wash-and-wear hair is so easy to handle and has a beautiful, natural wave and simple, standout silver color.

And I'm not the only one who thinks so; I get compliments all the time. Also, it's important to me to use my time for the many projects I want to manifest in our world. Not spending hours artificially coloring my hair frees me up to accomplish my work. The best compliment I've gotten from other women is that they want to embrace their own natural color after seeing mine.

Try Some Homemade Recipes

Throughout my years in the world of hair care, I've created lots of easy, do-it-yourself recipes for cleansers, conditioners, and color toners that clean the scalp, ward off dandruff and dryness, minimize yellowing, prevent hair from oxidizing, and hydrate hair so that your silver—or any color—looks radiant. Creating homemade recipes is one of my favorite things to do, because it allows me to know exactly what I'm putting into and on myself. After all, at an estimated twenty square feet, your skin is your largest organ, and your pores absorb whatever you apply to them. Knowing the impact of topically applied chemicals is important, especially since women put an average of 168 of them on their bodies each day, according to a recent study. (And I'm sure most of that happens before 9 a.m.!)

I believe that if a plant, fruit, or vegetable ingredient is edible, it's probably got some topical benefits, too. For example, fresh strawberries contain enzymes and antioxidants to reduce skin inflammation and tone the complexion. Olive oil hydrates the body inside and out, softens the skin, and conditions the hair, and the pulp from an aloe vera plant is bursting with phytochemicals that rebalance the skin's pH and soothe skin ailments, from sunburn to chapped lips. This is why most of the recipes in this chapter use ingredients that you probably have on hand already, in your own kitchen or garden, or that you can easily purchase at your local health food store, plant nursery, or online. A few of these recipes are also ayurvedic and can help enhance the beauty of all hair types—even fine, thinning, and damaged hair.

Clear the Hair Herbal Cleanser

Makes one use

This cleanser is antimicrobial and antibacterial and gently removes surface debris from the body and hair without the abrasiveness of detergent shampoos or body washes. The soap nut (available at health food stores and online) emits its own foam, which contains botanical fruit acids that nourish and restore the hair's natural pH. When soap nut is used with ingredients such as fenugreek seeds and green gram, it acts as a synergistic conditioning agent and is great for eliminating dandruff. Fenugreek is rich in vitamins and minerals, is high in protein, and was even used by the ancient Egyptians. Gram is also protein-rich and lemon and orange peels are bursting with vitamin C oil. This hair and scalp cleanser stimulates blood circulation, which helps promote healthy hair and has been known to prevent thinning hair loss and excess oil if used consistently. The earthy smell is balanced with a few drops of essential oil. Make sure all ingredients are fresh or dried and sealed for preservation.

INGREDIENTS

3 tablespoons soap nut powder

2 tablespoons fenugreek seeds

2 tablespoons green gram

1 grated lemon or orange peel (grate first, then leave to dry for a day or two before use)

3 to 4 drops of your favorite essential oil (neroli, clary sage, sandalwood, bergamot, lavender, and geranium are all good choices)

YOU'LL NEED

A coffee grinder

A shatterproof container

1. Finely grind the first four ingredients in a coffee grinder, transfer to a shatterproof container, add the essential oil, and shake to mix.

2. In the shower, shake the container and apply the cleanser directly to the scalp with the fingertips and massage well into wet hair.

3. Leave the cleanser on for a few minutes or more while you wash your body.

4. Rinse well and use your favorite silicone-free conditioner.

STORAGE: Store in an airtight jar and refrigerate. Use within 30 days.

Three Healthy Scalp Masks

These masks help clarify the scalp—removing dirt, buildup, and debris—and can also be used on the face.

- Massage your scalp with coconut milk an hour before cleansing or conditioning.
- Take a few drops of safflower oil and massage it into your scalp for five minutes to replace fatty acids.
- Beat an egg yolk and work it into your scalp for five minutes.

"Berry" Effective Hair Tonic

Makes one use for long hair, two for short hair

This ayurvedic recipe uses amla, or Indian gooseberry, a fruit harvested from a tree that's considered sacred in India and that is known to strengthen hair follicles. It also contains powerful antioxidants that promote hair growth and are great for dry scalp and dandruff. You can use the berry tonic twice weekly or apply it every night to the scalp to help promote hair growth. Add an egg for protein enrichment.

INGREDIENTS

1½ cups Indian gooseberry (amla) juice

3 tablespoons lemon juice

OPTIONAL: 1 egg

YOU'LL NEED

A 2-cup or larger container

1. Combine gooseberry juice and lemon juice (and egg, if you like) in a container and mix well.

2. Apply tonic directly to your scalp and gently massage. Let it sit for at least 30 minutes.

3. Rinse well and then cleanse and condition your hair as usual.

STORAGE: Refrigerate leftovers; use within one week.

Silver Lining Story

Marion Beckenstein, 58, *Professional Singer*

M y style is pretty natural, and I resisted doing much in terms of makeup or hair color until my forties, when I started covering the silver with blonde. Some of this was professional pressure. I'm a singer, and for the purposes of the stage, almost no female singers go undyed. I also remember being told that the conductor wanted the silver-haired women to color their hair. At one point, I had some very blonde highlights, which I liked a lot. But then I realized they were quite close to my natural silver that I'd see coming in every few weeks. Lorraine and my friends encouraged me to let my silver grow in. They said it was beautiful and unusual. Since it was never really "me" to color my hair, and since I prefer not to use chemicals on my head, I stopped coloring.

Many people say that my face is very young looking so my hair color doesn't make me look old. This is nice, but kind of beside the point, as it's not really my desire to look as young as possible. It would be great for people to start moving away from that narrative; I'm hoping my small efforts might help. In general, most people have responded positively to the silver color. In fact, one hairstylist I consulted refused to even consider coloring my hair when I suggested it during a moment of weakness.

Namas-tea All-Purpose Aloe Elixir

Makes about one use

Known by the Egyptians as "the plant of mortality" and by the Russians as "the elixir of longevity," aloe vera has undeniable health benefits and is used in many skin and hair products. The gel can soothe sunburn, moisturize skin, remedy acne, promote hair growth, alleviate an itchy scalp, and give hair vitality and elasticity. Hair is primarily made of keratin, a protein that contains amino acids, oxygen, and tiny amounts of hydrogen, carbon, sulphur, and nitrogen. This is very similar to the chemical structure of aloe, making it a perfectly matched organic ingredient. Use this recipe any time your hair needs a nourishing boost. I suggest getting an aloe plant from a local nursery for its purest form.

To use this elixir as a hair mask, spray or pour the mixture over your entire head and leave it on for ten to fifteen minutes. It can also be used as a second-day refreshing mist on face and hair. You can also drink this elixir to help bolster your immune system and relieve indigestion—just add honey.

INGREDIENTS

4 or 5 tea bags green, lavender, chamomile, or black tea or 3 teaspoons loose tea

2 cups boiling water

2 large aloe leaves

YOU'LL NEED

A blender

A spray bottle

1. Steep the tea in the boiling water.

2. While the tea is steeping, slice the aloe vera leaves in cross sections and pop out the pulp.

3. Put the tea and the aloe vera pulp into a blender and blend just until mixed well. Don't over-blend.

4. Wait for the mixture to cool and then pour it into a spray bottle.

5. Wet your hair and spray the mixture directly onto the scalp.

6. Massage well with the pads of your fingers (not your nails).

7. Let it sit for at least 5 minutes.

8. Rinse, and follow with your favorite sulfate-free cleanser or silicone-free conditioner.

STORAGE: Refrigerate leftovers; use within one week.

Lavender and Verbena Herbal Hair Tonic

This delightful tonic contains many beneficial healing properties in addition to being naturally medicinal and antimicrobial. Organic apple cider vinegar helps neutralize a yellow cast on silver hair. Verbena has a therapeutic, calming effect and is known to diminish skin irritations, acne, and puffiness. Spritz it over the canopy of your hair or use as a spot-cleanser on yellowing patches. Use it every two weeks or whenever the yellow creeps in. It can also be used as a final clarifying rinse in the shower.

INGREDIENTS

2 cups water

5 teaspoons organic apple cider vinegar

A generous bunch of dried lavender sprigs or 5 drops lavender oil

A hearty stash of dried verbena leaves or 5 drops verbena oil

YOU'LL NEED

A 16-ounce glass canning jar

A strainer

A spray bottle

OPTIONAL: a small crystal, stone, or marble to place in the bottle to disperse the mixture when shaken

1. Boil the water and pour it into the canning jar.

2. Add the vinegar, lavender, and verbena; stir and cover.

3. Let the mixture steep and cool.

4. Strain the liquid and transfer it to a spray bottle.

5. Shake the mixture. Before cleansing your entire head of hair, spot-cleanse by spraying the tonic on any yellowing area. Let it soak in for 3 to 4 minutes.

6. If using as a clarifying rinse, simply pour a cup over your hair and then rinse with water.

STORAGE: Store in the refrigerator; keeps for about a month.

Toned-Up Conditioner

Makes one use

This recipe is great for silver sirens who want to ward off yellow, as well as for bleached blondes whose hair turns brassy as the color oxidizes. It can be used as often as you like, either to get rid of existing yellow or to prevent it. It's important to apply it to dry hair, as the cuticles are more open and can better absorb the toner. Dilute the recipe or use it less often if your hair gets too much of a blue hue—unless you like the blue. A good store-bought version of this conditioner is Clairol Shimmer Lights in Blonde & Silver.

INGREDIENTS

1 to 5 drops blue or purple food coloring (or more if needed) (For a deeper cast, try using blue Manic Panic hair dye.)

Your favorite sulfate-free and silicone-free cleanser or conditioner

1. Add 2 drops of the food coloring or dye to a palm full of cleanser or conditioner (for thick hair) or 1 drop to half a palm full (for shorter or naturally straight hair).

2. Mix with your finger until the ingredients appear well blended.

3. Apply the mixture directly onto the yellow area while hair is dry.

4. If this is your first time using this recipe, leave the mixture on the hair for 2 minutes. If you don't notice any improvement in the yellow, add more food coloring and leave it on longer.

5. If you want the blue hue to be more noticeable, leave the mixture on your hair for 10 to 20 minutes and then rinse. Another option is to not rinse at all. The first time I made this, I put it in my hair planning to rinse it out. But after 20 minutes, I liked the way it looked with a hint of blue and how it had settled in my hair. I left it in and skipped the rinse.

Love Is in the Hair

Makes one generous drenching use or weeks of spritzing

Pouring an herbal infusion over your hair and scalp after cleansing and conditioning not only provides naturally medicinal and antimicrobial benefits, but it also feels refreshing. Lavender is a flowering plant in the mint family that can be a pleasantly aromatic cleansing disinfectant and antiseptic. Rosemary is an herb of love and, like lavender, has an uplifting aroma. Thyme has been known for thousands of years as a superstar herb with antibacterial and medicinal properties and is burned in temples and homes to purify them. The clary in clary sage means "clear."

This elixir acts as a natural deodorizer and tonic for the skin on your scalp, face, hair, and body. The herbs suggested here are the best ones to use on all hair types and colors, including silver. If herbs are not available, try using essential oils to replace the herbs or add to this recipe. This infusion can be used as a refreshing mist for hotel rooms, your car, linens, yoga mats, or kitchen and is lovely sprayed on pillowcases to create a soothing sleep environment. A soft washcloth soaked in the elixir and placed on your forehead can relieve a headache. I love putting it in burlap-wrapped bottles as a unique gift for friends and family.

INGREDIENTS

12 ounces water

3 tablespoons of a combination of dried lavender, rosemary, clary sage, or thyme and/or essential oils (verbena optional)

YOU'LL NEED

A metal pan

A strainer

A spray bottle or plastic pitcher (depending on your preferred way to apply it to the hair)

OPTIONAL: a small crystal, stone, or marble to place in the bottle to disperse the mixture when shaken

1. Boil the water in a metal pan and then add the dried herbs.

2. Turn off the heat, cover, and let the mixture steep and cool for 15 minutes or more, depending on how strong you like it.

3. Strain the mixture to remove the dried herbs.

4. Transfer the liquid to a spray bottle or pitcher and add the optional small crystal, stone, or marble.

5. Spritz on hair for freshening and conditioning, or pour about a cup over your locks as a final rinse in the shower.

STORAGE: Refrigerate and use within a month.

Does She or Doesn't She?

In 1962, an ad campaign for Clairol read, "Does she . . . or doesn't she? Hair color so natural only her hairdresser knows for sure!" The goal was to destigmatize hair coloring, which at the time was considered taboo, and convince women that they could achieve natural-looking results in the comfort of their own bathrooms. Clairol promised that its product would "keep gray from ever showing." Although some people credit these ads for bringing coloring out of the closet, they also contributed to the idea that silver strands were a no-no and that they made you look old. Around the same time, people were starting to think in living color, as color TVs became increasingly common in American homes. I believe this brought even more attention to the perception of "right" and "wrong" hair colors.

Enriching Rice Water Conditioner

Makes one use

You're supposed to rinse rice before cooking it because the starch on its surface can make it sticky once it's cooked. The milky rice water that results from the rinsing offers amazing beauty benefits. It can improve the health of your scalp and your hair's elasticity. Additionally, rice water contains inositol, a carbohydrate that can be used to help repair hair as well as offer long-lasting protection from further damage. Rice water can also be used as a refreshing skin tonic or makeup remover.

Rice water's benefits can be further enhanced if it is left to ferment for one to two days unrefrigerated. At this point, it turns sour and becomes rich in antioxidants, minerals, and vitamins B and E, and has traces of pitera, a substance that has been used in Asia for centuries. Pitera has become popular among naturalists as an antiaging elixir due to its alleged ability to promote cell regeneration and help skin stay youthful and healthy.

INGREDIENTS

1 cup jasmine, white, or brown rice

3 cups spring water or filtered water

OPTIONAL: a few drops of your favorite essential oil

YOU'LL NEED

A bowl

A strainer

A plastic jug

1. If you think your rice may have been chemically treated, rinse it first in a strainer to remove any possible impurities before soaking it. Then pour the rinsed rice into a bowl and soak for 15 to 25 minutes.

2. Strain the nutrient-rich water from the rice into a plastic jug.

3. After cleansing hair with a sulfate-free product, pour the rice water over your head.

4. Massage it in and allow it to soak into your hair for at least 5 minutes.

5. Rinse well and follow with a silicone-free conditioner.

Silver Lining Story

Gennith Johnson, 34, *Speech-language Pathologist*

I saw my first silver hair when I was just ten years old, premature gray that I inherited from my father and paternal grandmother. I started experimenting with coloring it when I was in the tenth grade and colored my hair every few weeks for years. At one point, I developed an allergic reaction to the hair dye, which resulted in a dry and itchy scalp. But this didn't stop me! Sometimes my silver would take on various unwanted hues of green and purple when I dyed it. I realized that these added colors were caused by my relaxer, which became the impetus to accept my natural texture and to stop relaxing my hair. Still, I continued to color. Then one day about two years ago, I had my hair colored and styled at a salon in Washington, DC, and was stunned when the bill was almost five hundred dollars! That was my turning point. I promised myself I would never pay that much to have my hair done ever again. I realized that I wanted to invest my money and, most importantly, my time in other ways and enjoy my life without worrying about the maintenance of my hair color.

Ever since I embraced my silver and my natural self, I've really blossomed into a happier, more confident, and self-assured person. For years, all I wanted to do was fit in, but now I stand out. I'm unique, and my personality really shines through. Often I think of my dad and grandmother, who are now deceased, and appreciate our unique connection. People often ask me, "How did you get your hair like that?" or tell me that they think it's beautiful! One word that describes how I felt after embracing my silver is "free." Free of chemicals, free from being tied to a strict hair maintenance schedule, and free of society's standards of beauty.

Blue Dew Toning Hair Bath

Makes two uses

In this recipe, Mother Nature can help eliminate unwanted brassy tones in silver and blonde strands using the natural pigment from plants and fruits to create blue, purple, and violet water infusions. You can use any combination. Dried flowers are available online and in many plant nurseries and garden stores. The darker your hair, the darker you can go with pigment. It will give your hair a hue that will last at least until the next cleansing.

INGREDIENTS

1 cup of up to four of these pigmented flowers: betony (a blue/purple flower), hollyhocks (blue purple), indigo leaves (blue), woad leaves (blue), purple iris (blue), cornflower (blue), elderberry (lavender), blackberry (purple)

2 cups water (enough to cover the flowers)

YOU'LL NEED

A saucepan

A strainer

A glass or Pyrex container (mixture will stain plastic)

1. Chop the plants and place them in a saucepan. Add enough water to cover the plant material.

2. Bring it to a boil and simmer for about 10 minutes, until the plant blossoms have faded and the water is pigmented.

3. Let the mixture steep and cool for an hour. If the color is too strong, dilute the mixture with spring water.

4. Strain the plant infusion into the container. Set it aside or cool it in the refrigerator. The cool temperature adds shine.

5. After cleansing and conditioning, pour about a cup of the mixture over your hair. Use a paper towel to scrunch out excess water.

6. On really humid days, this is a fantastic frizz-fighting tonic. You can also add ½ to 1 cup fresh aloe vera pulp (the amount depends on the length of your hair and if you plan to save some of the recipe to use later) to create a leave-in gel with a hue.

STORAGE: Store in the refrigerator; use within two weeks. You can also pour some into ice cube trays and freeze, then thaw to remove yellow spots on days when you do not want to cleanse all of your hair.

Ginger and Tonic

Makes one use

Ginger, one of the most healing ancient roots, is naturally medicinal, with anti-inflammatory and antioxidant properties. This power plant, which is loaded with vitamins, minerals, and fatty acids, is known to help stimulate blood flow, prevent respiratory viruses, alleviate arthritis, and relieve digestive problems and joint pain, thanks to its warming thermogenic properties. When this ginger tonic is massaged into the scalp, it boosts blood flow, encouraging new growth by nourishing and stimulating hair follicles. You can use this tonic at least twice a week. With a tablespoon of brown sugar added, it becomes a fabulous exfoliant for the scalp, face, elbows, and heels.

INGREDIENTS

A 3-inch piece of ginger

2 tablespoons jojoba, sesame, or olive oil

OPTIONAL: 1 tablespoon brown sugar

YOU'LL NEED

A vegetable peeler

A grater

A bowl

1. Peel the ginger and freeze for eight hours or overnight. This makes grating and blending into the oil easier and prevents chunks.

2. Grate the frozen ginger over a bowl, into the oil. As you're grating it, the ginger will melt into the oil, making the texture smooth and easy to apply. If you'd like, add brown sugar to make this into a scrub.

3. Apply the mixture directly to the scalp, using the pads of your fingers to massage it in a circular motion.

4. Let it sit for 15 to 30 minutes.

5. Rinse well, massaging as you rinse.

6. Follow up with your favorite sulfate-free wash or cleanser or a silicone-free conditioner.

Spray It with Love

Makes four pre-conditioning uses or weeks of spritzing

This hydrating spray is just diluted conditioner, but it's great for refreshing and reviving your hair on days when you don't cleanse. Simply spritz it all over your hair and gently scrunch or spot-spray on areas that are frizzy, frayed, or wilted. It can be used as a pre-cleansing softening agent on dry hair to help it better absorb hydration. It also saves water by more thoroughly hydrating hair that tends to be water-resistant. The secret to using this spray solution as a pre-cleanse is to warm it up first by popping it in the microwave for a few seconds. The heat allows it to sink into those thirsty strands rather than simply coating the surface. When used as a daily hair refresher, however, it doesn't need to be warmed.

INGREDIENTS

½ cup silicone-free conditioner

2 cups spring water

YOU'LL NEED

A small crystal, stone, or marble to place in the bottle to disperse the mixture when shaken

A spray bottle

1. Combine the ingredients in the spray bottle. Add the crystal, stone, or marble. Shake well.

2. Spritz onto the hair as needed.

3. If using as a conditioning pre-cleanse, warm about ½ cup and slowly pour over dry hair while massaging it in. Follow with your usual cleansing routine.

STORAGE: Keep where you'll use it the most. In the summer months or on high-humidity days, you can put it in the fridge; used cold, it helps seal and close the cuticles. If it appears too thick to spray, simply water it down.

CHAPTER EIGHT

SILVER WEAR:

The Right Clothes, Makeup & Accessories

Loving Hue Is Easy Because You're Beautiful

As the color of your hair changes from blonde to silver or from dark to light, chances are you'll want to make a few tweaks to the rest of your appearance. To me, this is one of the really fun parts of going silver. Many of us have been wearing the same makeup, clothing styles, and colors for decades. Freshening up your look will not only make your silver look its best but also will give you a new, fabulous style.

Just a Touch of Pastel

"Wearing a lot of pastel doesn't look great on most people who go silver," says fashion consultant Stacy London, who is the author of *The Truth About Style* and hosted TLC's *What Not to Wear.* If you love pastels, choose just one small accessory in these hues. A lavender scarf with a dark blue top is a great combination. A pale blue silk top with a slim, bright red scarf is another good option. When possible, keep stronger, brighter colors around your face for maximum presence.

Change the Way You Think About Neutrals

Wearing gray and black fabrics near the face typically works best for darker to olive skin tones. "Dark neutrals like navy and rich chocolate browns are great alternatives to black. They still look sophisticated when you pair them with other colors, but they go better with all kinds of skin tones and all shades of silver hair," London explains. For example, navy and pink look sophisticated with all shades of silver hair. A midrange purple with navy is also a great, modern look.

Skip Khaki and Tan

Certain colors, when worn near the face, make most skin tones look washed out. Rather than tan, go for cream. It has a softness that complements silver hair, and it's not as stark as white.

Silver Lining Story

Roberta Spring, 62, *Associate Director, NBC News*

I was fourteen years old when I got my first silver in my chestnut-brown hair. John Travolta (yes, *that* John Travolta) sat behind me in my freshman homeroom in high school and would sweetly tease me about it. But I never considered coloring my hair, because I grew up with great examples of what I was going to look like as my hair continued to get more silver. My mother went silver in her thirties and my grandmother was always silver. I see my gray hair as a badge of honor and natural beauty.

Color Up with Jewel Tones

"Some women think they have to wear neutral colors when they go silver so their clothes aren't competing with their hair. They think their hair will somehow stand out too much or look weird with brightly colored clothing," says London, "but it doesn't work that way. Sometimes primary colors can appear too bright and harsh, but jewel tones, such as deep aquamarine, amethyst, emerald, and ruby, have a blue undertone that complements silver hair and warms up most skin tones without creating a harsh effect. I'm a huge believer in jewel tones with silver hair. The way the colors blend, complement, dance off each other—it's like looking at a symphony."

Select Your Gray-Toned Clothes Carefully

Some women also believe they have to give up wearing gray or silver clothes when their strands are turning these same frosty hues. But that's not necessarily true. "Just don't match your hair color," says London. "Either go for a lighter silver or gray or a darker silver." That way you don't appear as a monochromatic being from head to toe; you want your hair to pop.

Linda Wolff of CPW, a clothing boutique in New York City, adds, "Most colors look great on silver beauties when worn right. Black, charcoal, and navy all work. Red and baby pink can be tricky. It really depends on the person: their eye color, skin tone, and fashion sense. There is no single recipe just because you're silver."

Accessorize

Brightly colored scarves can immediately and stylishly boost any complexion. Oversize eyeglass frames in bold colors look great with silver hair—even if you don't need prescription lenses.

Makeup

- Add a little pop with cooler, brighter makeup shades. Go for a free makeup consultation and choose at least one item you love that's a little bolder than you used before, such as brighter blush or eye shadow.

- Your lips become more of a focal point when your hair is lighter—and especially when it's silver. Try a new pink, violet, or red lipstick. "You don't necessarily have to go bright; just make sure to get some noticeable contrast between skin and lip," explains makeup artist Sonia Kashuk.

- For a quick and lively boost, apply a rose stain to your lips, eyelids, and cheeks that works with all skin tones. We like Benetint Cheek Stain from Benefit Cosmetics, or Tarte Cheek Stain. These give you an immediate natural glow, like you have been running outside on a cool, crisp morning, as well as working triple duty as cheek, eyelid, and lip color.

- Stay away from silicone-based lip balms and glosses. They dry out your lips, making you feel like you constantly need to reapply them, but without any true moisture relief.

- "When it comes to eyes, try shadows on the matte or satin side rather than shimmers or sparkles, which may highlight the hooding that can happen with age," explains makeup artist Julio Sandino. "Cool tones tend to work best with silver hair that is brighter and whiter, while warmer tones are the way to go if the silver is on the muted side."

- Silver and light gray eye shadow can become your new neutrals, and they work well for any eye color. Brown tends to look too heavy on most women.

- Try mixing your face moisturizer with a skin foundation. This gives your complexion a natural, dewy look.

- "Foundation should complement your natural skin tone; however, a little added warmth might be beneficial if going silver makes you feel a bit dull or sallow," says Sandino. Blush is a great way to achieve a warm, healthy, and youthful complexion. Avoid bronzer or brown-toned shades, which can look muddy. "If you're fair-skinned,

try peach and soft pink tones. If your complexion is darker, you can use brighter pink and raspberry tones," says Sandino.

- Highlighter can also help keep your skin looking radiant. Place it on the tops of your cheekbones, your orbital bone (below your outer brow), and on the bridge of your nose.

- Steer clear of matte lipstick. As we get older, our lips tend to recede and lose their plumpness, and little lines may form around the mouth. A matte lipstick can accentuate all these changes, so use a shinier lip color.

- Silver-colored eyebrows can blend into the complexion. Enhance them with color and create some definition. "Choose a pencil, brow gel, or eye shadow a shade lighter than what your brow color once was, or try one to complement your own current natural brow color," says Sandino.

- A little eyeliner can make a big difference. A softly smudged dark navy or charcoal eyeliner can make your eye color pop. This is especially effective for lighter hair. When you apply eyeliner so it looks like literal lines around your eyes, it can make your eyes appear smaller and closer together. Be sure to apply it right into the root where the lashes grow, then softly smudge it with a cotton swab, small brush, or your fingertip.

- "Too much powder can make skin look dry, lessening its luminosity," says Sandino. Apply powder only to the T-zone area—forehead, nose, and chin—so your face does not appear overly matte.

Skin

- Silver hair requires paying extra attention to your skin. "Stylist and skin care specialist Linda Rodin always looks dewy fresh thanks to good-quality skin oil, which counteracts ashiness," explains London, referring to the skin care founder known for her gorgeous silver mane. Products to try include Jordan Samuel étOILe Facial Oil and The Blue Cocoon by May Lindstrom.

- "Massaging your fingers over your face every time you apply face products will encourage healthy blood circulation, muscle tone, and the penetration of your cleansers, lotions, and potions," says Jordan Samuel Pacitti, creator of Jordan Samuel Skin.

- Water is important—especially drinking eight glasses a day. "Drinking lemon water daily will help to hydrate the skin, balance alkaline, and make you glow from within," explains Pacitti.

- "Never underestimate the benefits of a great night's sleep and staying out of the sun," says Pacitti. When all else fails, sleep for ten hours and you'll look better the next day, with a new and improved glow!

- Drinking one tablespoon of apple cider vinegar in a cup of water as part of your wake-up call will offer endless health benefits: It alleviates heartburn and acid reflux, promotes healthy cholesterol, has anti-glycemic properties, is a natural antioxidant, and aids in nutrient absorption.

- If your teeth are a little bit yellow, try one of the many brands of whitening strips. This will make your smile and skin look brighter, which can take years off your appearance. Ask your dentist before applying. Whitening toothpaste and whitening gel pens can help but are not as effective.

Colorist Tip

Veronica Tapia, *Jersey Curl Salon, Cliffside Park, New Jersey*

If you really want to use color to go from non-silver hair to fully silver hair, do it in stages using Olaplex (a hair repair treatment used by professionals), especially if you are coming from a darker color, either natural or unnatural. Olaplex will help keep hair healthy as you lift out as much color as you can in the first phase. Wait a week and condition, condition, condition, letting the hair settle before doing one more round. This is what I did with Lorraine's hair. She was completely color-free when we decided we wanted to lighten only her darker rusty-auburn strands underneath so we could better mimic her natural silver hair splayed over the crown. We matched it perfectly, so natural and tinted hair can harmoniously grow out together.

Silver Lining Story

Deborah Wingert Arkin, 50

I lost my dad six years ago and then my mom two years later. Losing my parents at such an early age really made me think, *What am I spending my time on?* I have one daughter and time is so precious. Spending several hours at a salon once a month seemed like a waste—especially for someone who likes to get dressed and out of the house in ten minutes.

My hairstylist was amazing and encouraged me to go gray. He also gave me a really good cut, so that as the color grew out, it looked interesting and fun. This made the process much easier.

I started going gray at nineteen and tried everything from red to dark brown to black in order to create different personas, so I shouldn't be so surprised that I feel more like myself now that my hair is silver! To me, gray doesn't mean old; it's a lifestyle choice. Having my natural hair color has allowed me to simplify the rest of my life, too—and also respect myself and use my time well. For example, I will make the time to cook a really nice meal and eat it mindfully rather than eating fast food on the run. Instead of stressing in a chair while someone is coloring my hair, I'm focusing on being more present generally, and that makes me feel like I actually have more time. It's really empowering. You shouldn't feel bad if you want to dye your hair, but no woman should feel like she has to.

CONCLUSION:

Heads & Tales

lthough we are at the end of this book, many of you may just be starting your journey toward your own silver. Stay in the light! It's not always easy, and it requires patience and a determined vision. But remember: it is *transition*. There is a reason you're doing this—a final result you're shooting for. And what you will uncover as you un*color* will be enlightening in more ways than just what you see on your head.

When I decided to uncover my own silver, I did so partly so that I could better understand and experience what I had been urging some of my beloved clients to do for years, and also as part of writing this book. My first book, *Curly Girl: The Handbook*, was about embracing the curl. This idea naturally merged into embracing one's own naturally silver hue and appreciating and enjoying life after dyeing.

During the last few months, I had to talk myself off the ledge a couple of times by doing a few silver highlights to bridge the gap between the rusty color and my roots. But I was inspired by the many silver sirens I met along the way and the amazing women who took the journey to silver with me. Like I did, some women got negative reactions from those around them during the in-between phase, but what emerged as each strand of silver grew in was their own voice saying, "This is my hair. This is my authentic self. And if I love it, that's all that matters." The large majority of the silver foxes I have had the pleasure of meeting said they wished they had gone silver sooner and loved not being on the hair coloring time clock.

I hope this book will help you and people everywhere to see silver hair as another beautiful color in the stunning, rainbow world we live in and to honor the beauty of being as authentically true to yourself as you can be. This book goes out to all those who embrace the decision to go natural and who will learn to uncover and cherish the magnificence of their own beauty along the way.

Lorraine

Acknowledgments

To all the beautiful women who took part in this book, our silver models, thank you for trusting us with your gorgeous hair and letting us share the journey with you. We know you'll inspire so many women to embrace who they really are.

We graciously thank the silver locks stars on this dream team, Anne Kerman, Becky Terhune, Vaughn Andrews, Selina Meere, Rebecca Carlisle, and the quiet shepherds Carolan Workman, Jenny Mandel, David Schiller, Mark Stafford, and my first teacher, Loraine Peace.

We are thankful for Mary Ellen O'Neill, our lighthouse whose hue glowed and guided us and kept us on course. Thank you for all your time and effort in helping to shape this book; your insight made it better than we could have ever imagined! We also appreciate you, Anne and Becky, for coordinating the photo shoots and not having a heart attack each time we added "just one more silver siren" at the last minute.

A special thanks to Kristy Wilson for her dedication to this project while applying complicated color applications in a non-salon, makeshift setting. Thanks also to Kristy's assistant Justyne Forsgren.

Also, many thanks to Veronica Tapia, Larry Bianco, and all the experts who gave us great, color-full advice. A big thank-you to makeup artists Julio Sandino, Christie Puccio, and Catalina Ceballos, and our beauty and fashion influencers Linda Wolff, Mary Barone, Maria Cornejo, and Ruth Resnick.

Many thanks to Jeremy Saladyga for your beautiful photos, hard work, and endless patience during our photo shoots.

Lorraine's Acknowledgments

There are not enough thank-yous that I can give to Michele Bender for her unDyeing love and support from the roots right to the end.

I would like to express thanks to Carol and Mort Blum for generously opening their light-filled home to use as our studio space many times over.

I am eternally thankful for The Lights of my life, Kaih, Shey, Dylan, Veronica, Venaih, Silas, and my sister, Susan.

Michele's Acknowledgments

Lorraine, once again working with you was an incredible experience that was more than hair deep. I loved all our laughs, writing sessions, and photo shoots and am grateful for all the priceless life advice you shared along the way. You're a real inspiration, not only in terms of how you embrace your natural hair but how you embrace life.

Mom and Mort, thank you for contributing your beautiful loft for our photo shoots, but most of all, thank you for your never-ending support, love, and encouragement. I'm so lucky to have you both! Todd, thank you for being the most overprotective brother and friend. Not sure what I'd do without you and Vivien, my wonderful sister-in-law.

Jon, thank you for being an amazing source of advice, love, and friendship, and for patiently listening to all my work stories through the process of writing this book. I'm so grateful.

Zoe, Melissa, and Judy, thank you for the decades of friendship through good times and bad. Most people are lucky to have one great girlfriend; I'm beyond blessed with three! Linda Konner, thank you for our years working together.

Lily and Jonathan, you add joy to my life every day, more than I ever thought imaginable, and I am so grateful to be your mother. Thank you for putting up with the crazy time commitments, travel, and chaos that come with my work. I may be a writer, but I can't put into words how special you both are to me!

Photo Credits

PHOTOGRAPHY BY JEREMY SALADYGA

PHOTO RESEARCH BY KENNETH YU

ADDITIONAL PHOTO CREDITS:

ADOBE STOCK: Bogdan p. 152 (bottom center); MayArt (Mayabee) p. 161; MicroOne p. v; Stas111 p. vi; Vadim p. 152 (bottom left); Vitalily_73 p. 152 (bottom right). **MICHELLE D'AMICO:** p. 89. **ELENA DRAGOI:** p. 26. **GETTY IMAGES:** Vera Anderson/WireImage p. 129; Paul Archuleta/FilmMagic p. 139; Peter Augustin/Taxi p. 181 (top); Bryan Bedder/Getty Images Entertainment p. 3; Gabriel Bouys/AFP p. 136; Compassionate Eye Foundation/Stone p. 184 (top right); Markus Cuff/Getty Images Entertainment p. 4; Timur Emek/Getty Images Entertainment p. 24, p. 34; Epsilon/Getty Images Entertainment p. 126; Andreas Keuhn/The Image Bank p. 185 (bottom); Jon Kopaloff/FilmMagic p. 3; Andreas Kuehn/DigitalVision p. 11, p. 185 (top); Andreas Kuehn/Iconica p. 28; Andreas Kuehn/Stone p. ii, p. 183; Chelsea Lauren/WireImage p. 128; Ari Pearlstein/Getty Images Entertainment p. 3; Philip Ramey Photography LLC/Corbis Entertainment p. 139; Richlegg/E+ p. 152 (top); Kristin Sinclair/Getty Images Entertainment p. 3, p. 184 (top left); Frank Trapper/Corbis Entertainment p. 139; Noel Vasquez/Getty Images Entertainment p. 139. **HBO:** Macall B. Polay/Courtesy of HBO p. 4. **PETER HURLEY:** p. 106. **JEFFREY JENKINS:** p. 29. **ROBERTO LIGRESTI:** p. 43, p. 193. **AARON RICHTER:** p. 114. **COURTESY OF LORRAINE MASSEY:** p. 9, p. 16, p. 27, p. 44, p. 59, p. 72 (top), p. 73, p. 100, p. 132, p. 133, p. 134 (bottom), p. 145, p. 147, p. 160, p. 163, p. 174, p. 182, p. 184 (bottom), p. 189. **SPECIAL THANKS TO CHARLIE AT FUNNYFACE TODAY.**